habibi

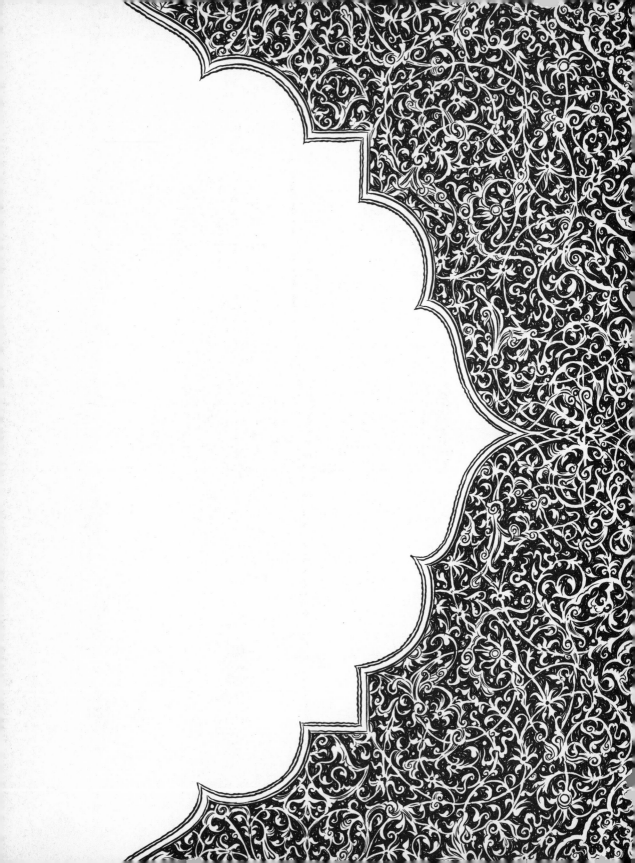

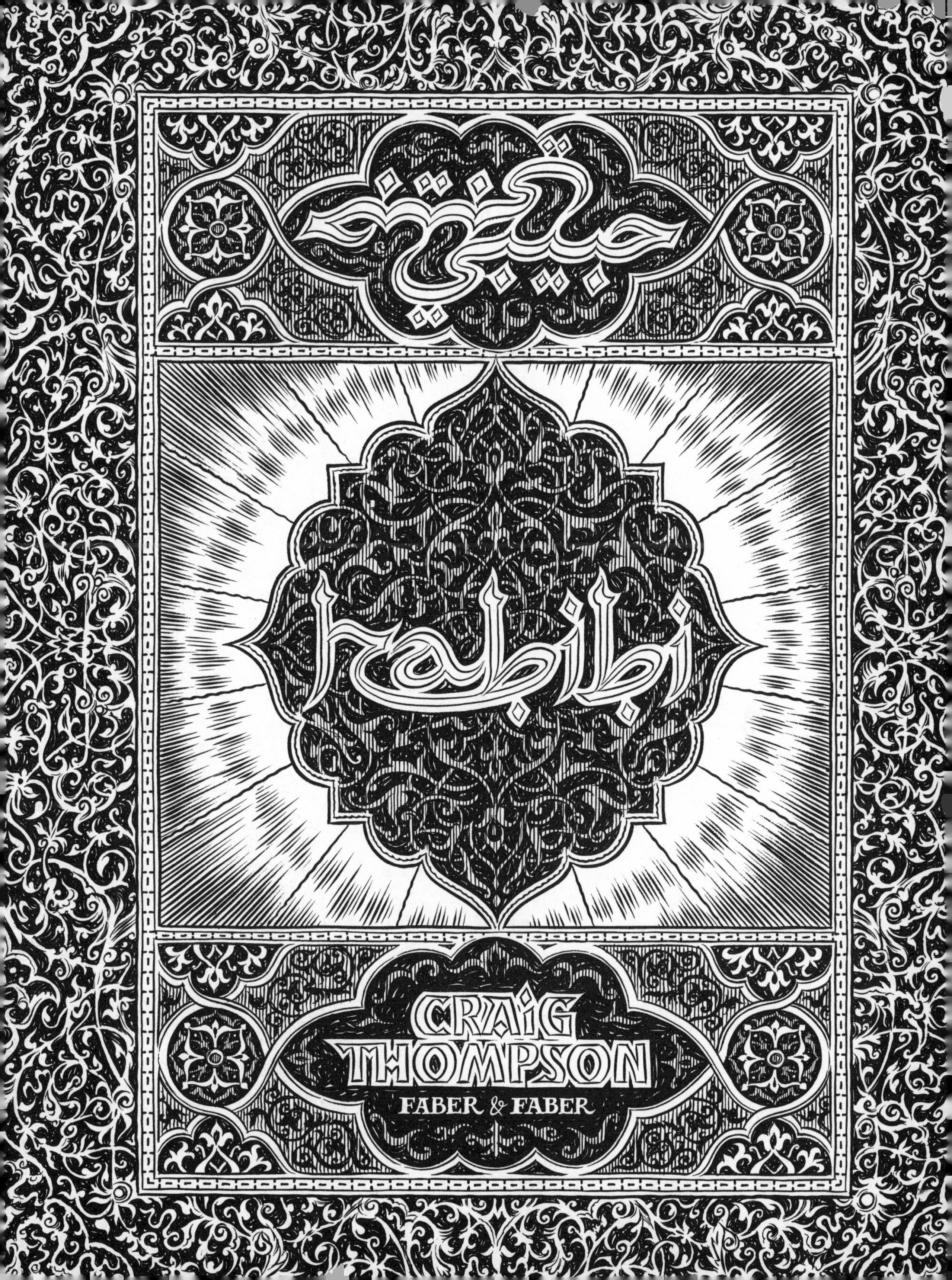
حبيبي
CRAIG THOMPSON
FABER & FABER

COPYRIGHT © 2011 by Craig Thompson

All rights reserved. Published in the United States by Pantheon Books, a division of Random House, Inc., New York. First published in the UK by Faber and Faber, Ltd. Bloomsbury House 74-77 Great Russell St. London WC1B 3DA

The right of Craig Thompson to be identified as author of this work has been asserted in accordance with Section 77 of the Copyright, Designs and Patents Act 1988.

A CIP record for this book is available from the British Library.

ISBN 978-0-571-24132-3

www.faber.co.uk

Book design by the author

9 8 7 6 5

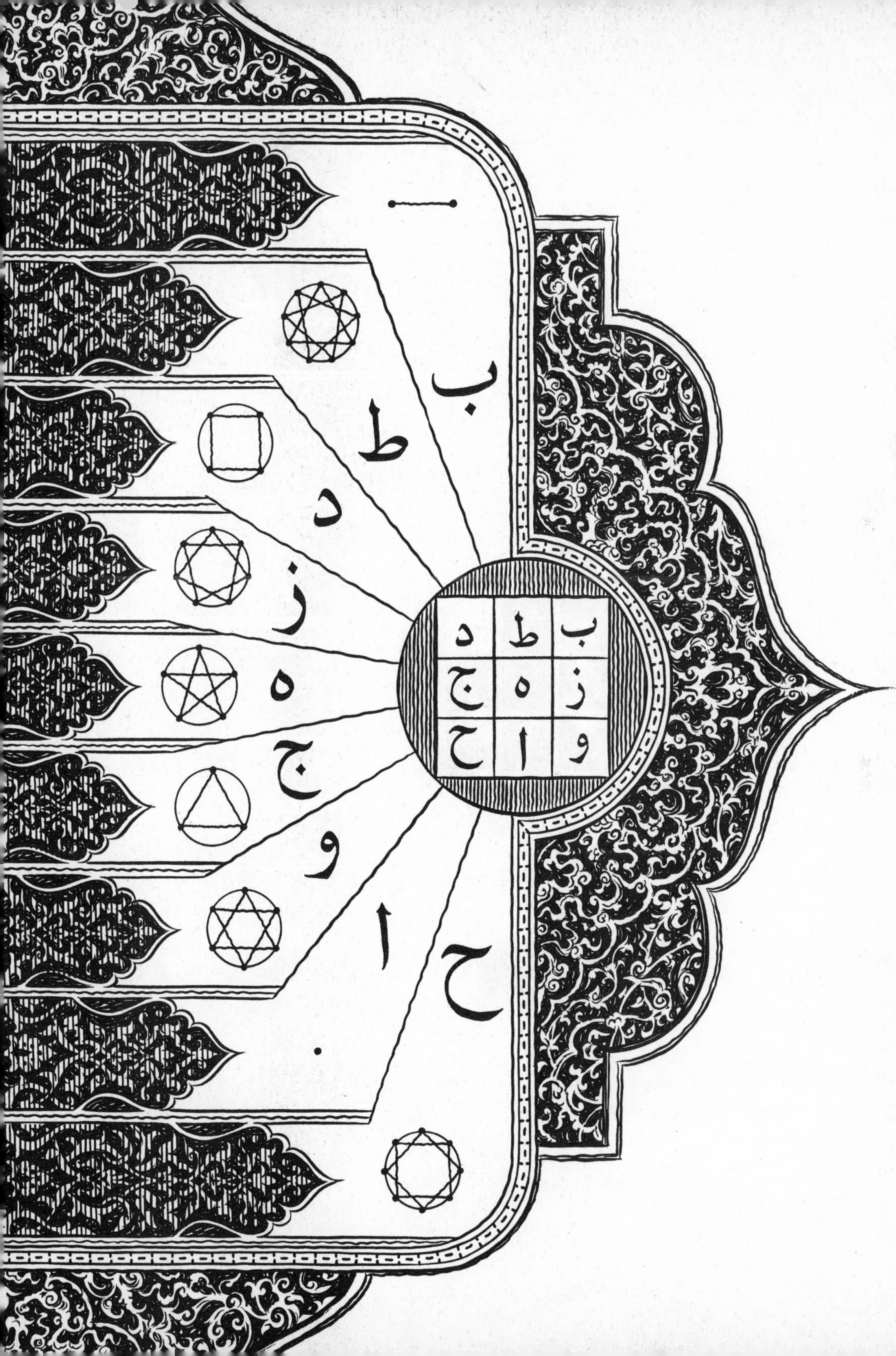

ب
ط
د
ز
ه
ج
و
ا
ح
ب ط د
ز ه ج
و ا ح

ب ط د
ز ه ج
و ا ح

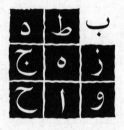

RIVER MAP

خريطة نهر

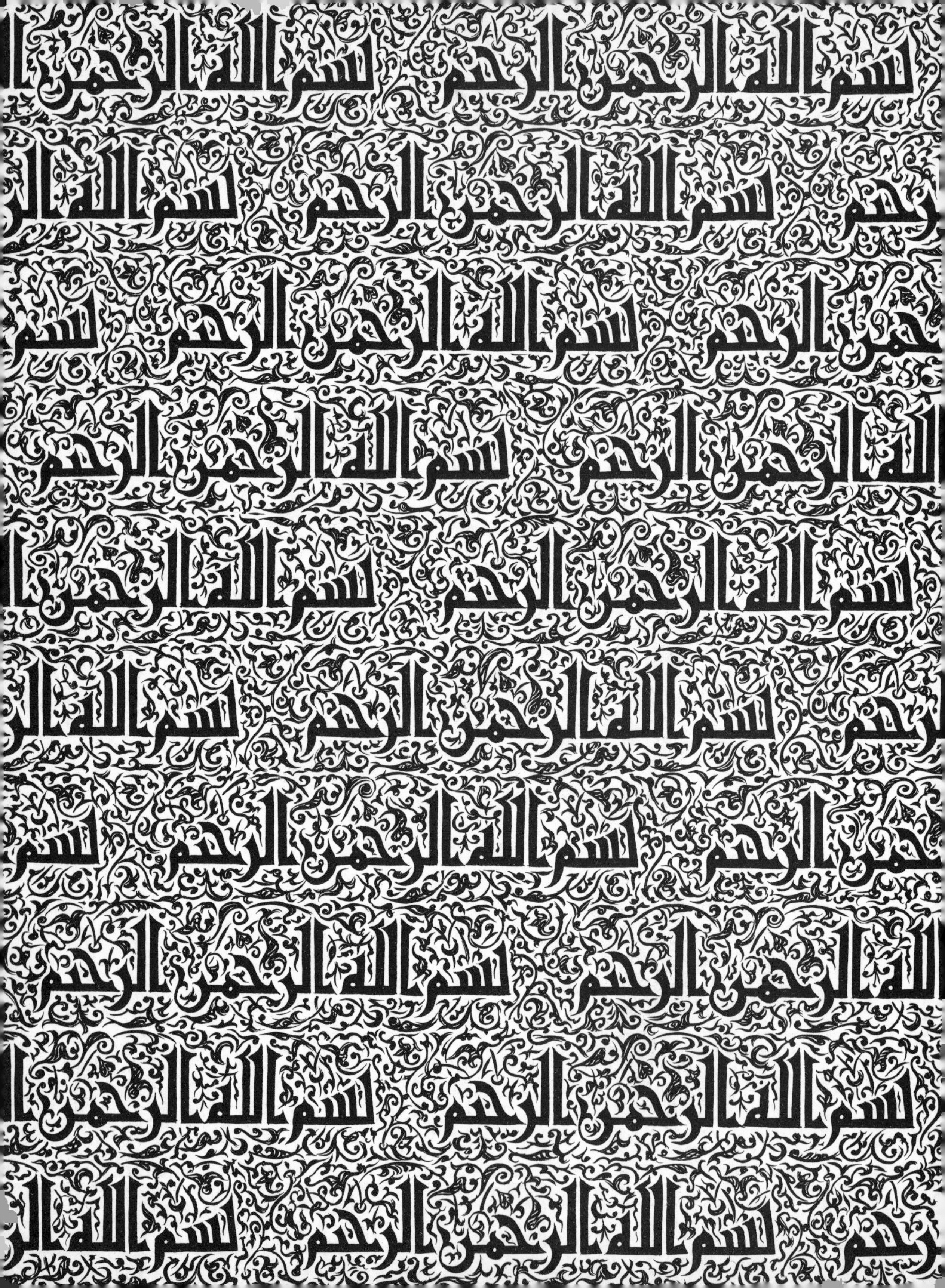
بسم الله الرحمن الرحيم

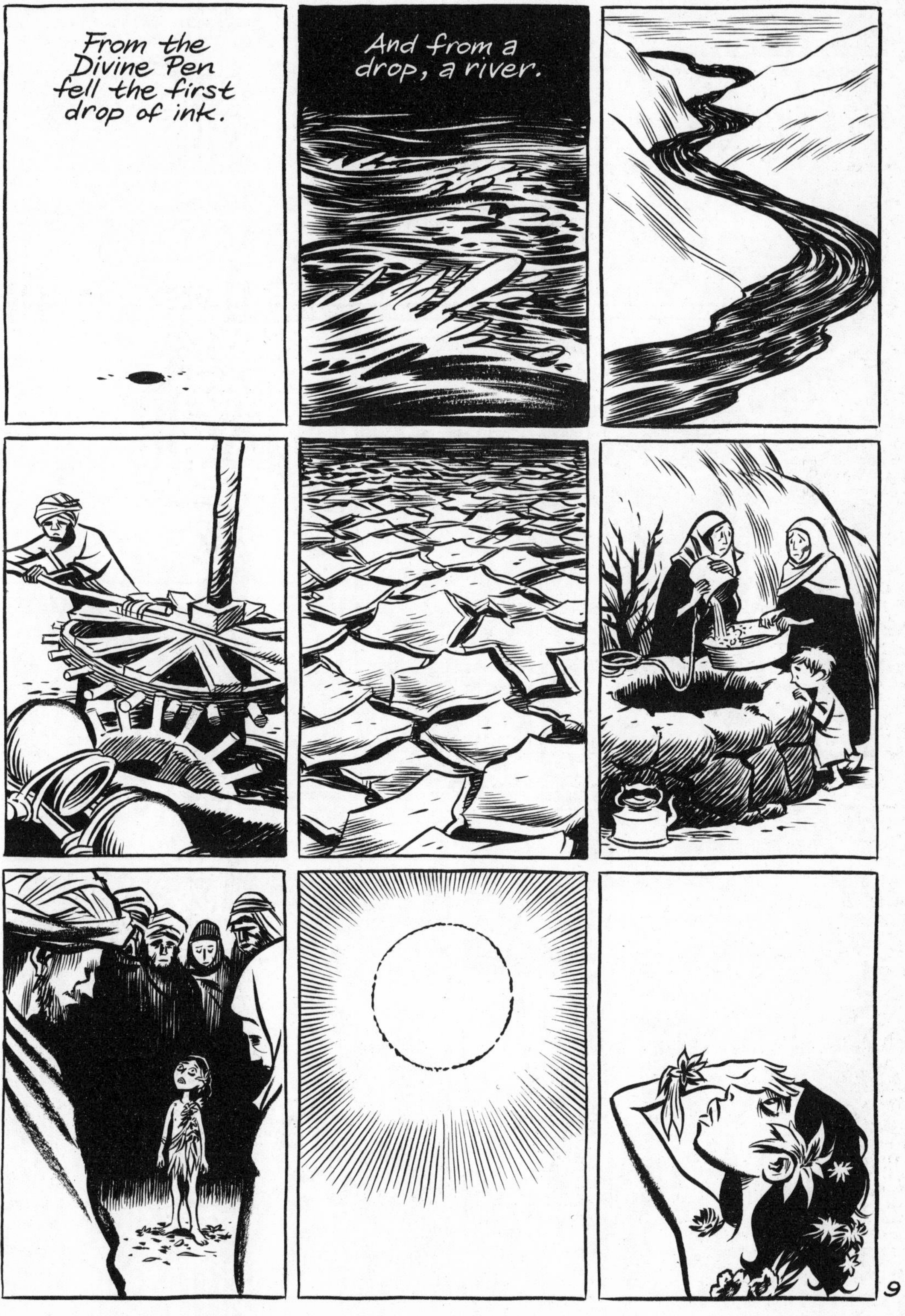
From the Divine Pen fell the first drop of ink.
And from a drop, a river.

When the land dried up with drought, my parents sold me into marriage.

Nine...

She is old enough?

She is old enough to be married.

She is old enough for . . .

Yes.

eh?

Yes. This is enough.

My husband was a scribe.

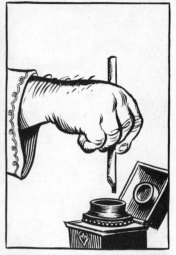

There.

That makes it official.

My father was illiterate.

VROON

This water...

... is like none you've ever tasted in this region.

This water is from the unspoiled country.

So clean,

So--

So pure.

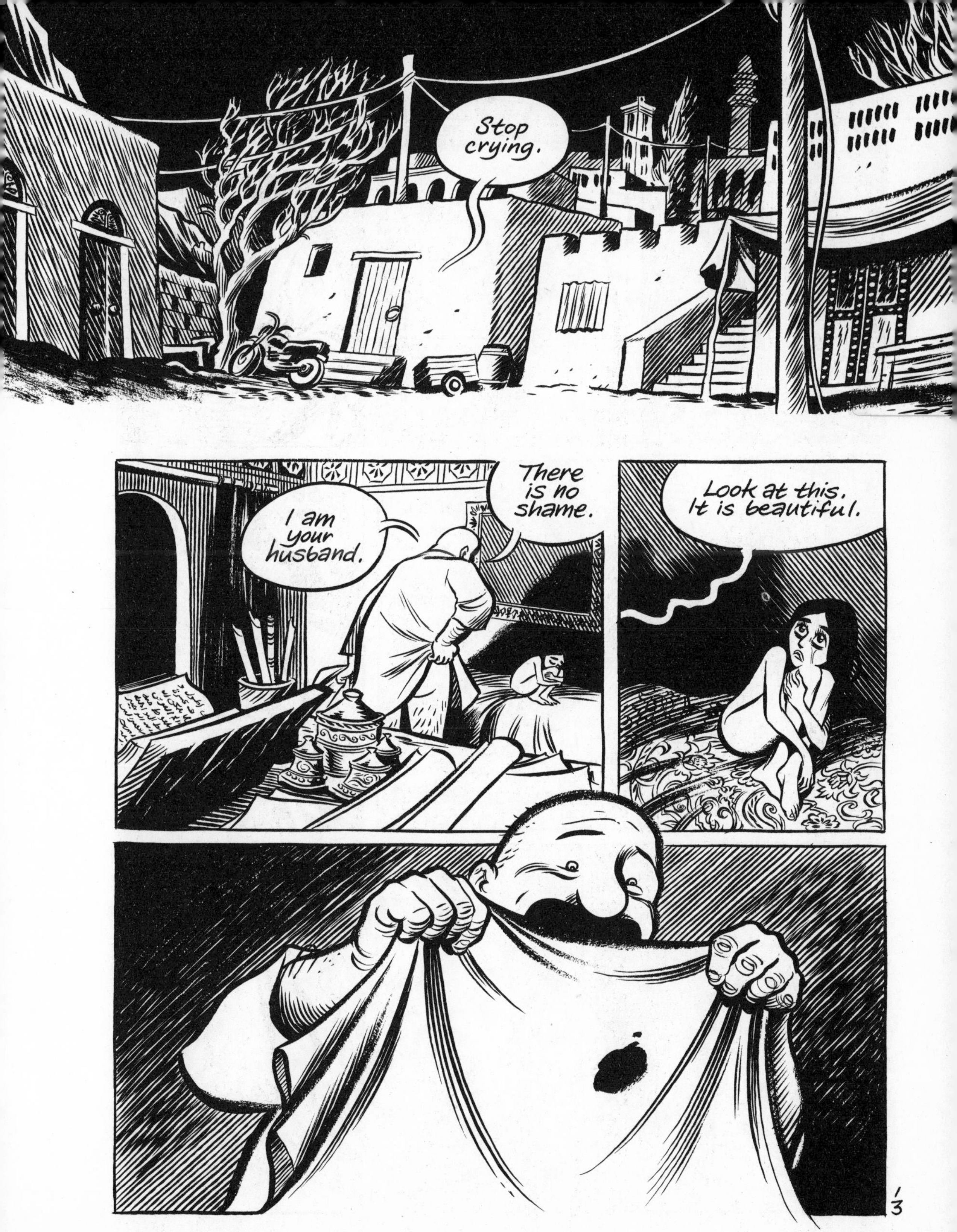
Stop crying.
I am your husband.
There is no shame.
Look at this. It is beautiful.

Tonight is cold.
Wrap yourself.
That's right. Wear it.
You should be proud of this mark.
It proves that you were pure.

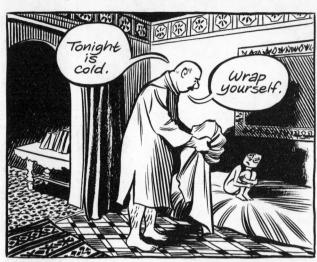

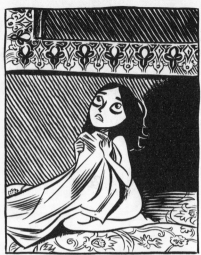

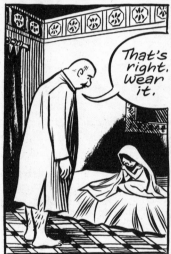

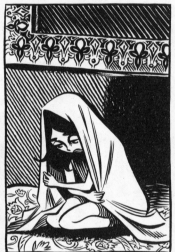

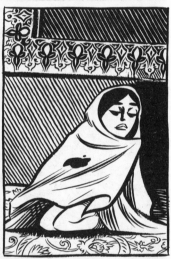

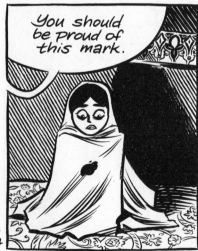

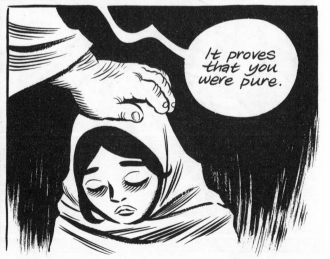

This line is the veil...

...and this point is the divine essence.

Who can lift the veil?

My husband copied manuscripts for a living.

The Sacred QUR'AN and the hadiths, One Thousand and One Nights, and the works of the great poets.

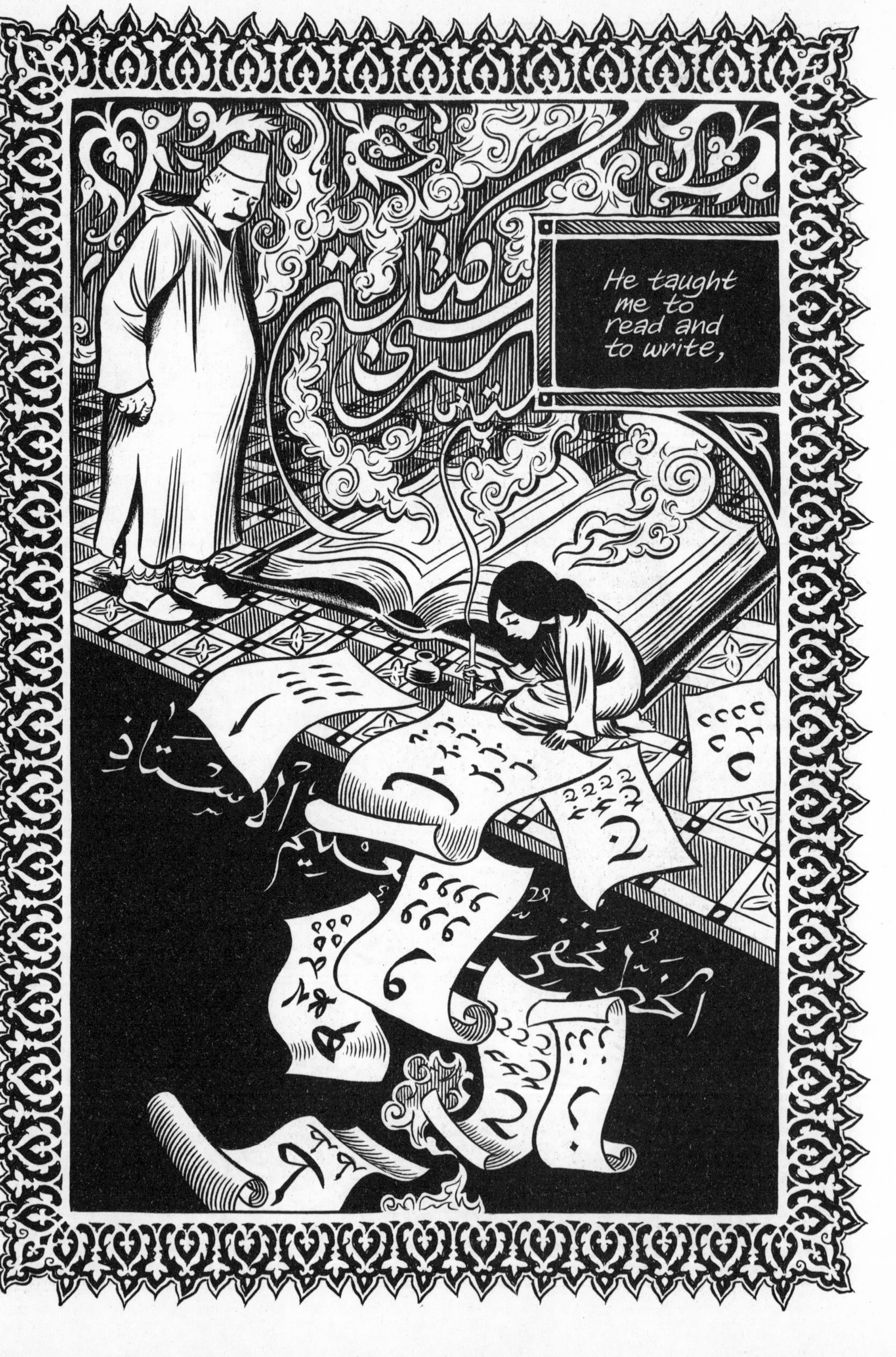
He taught me to read and to write,

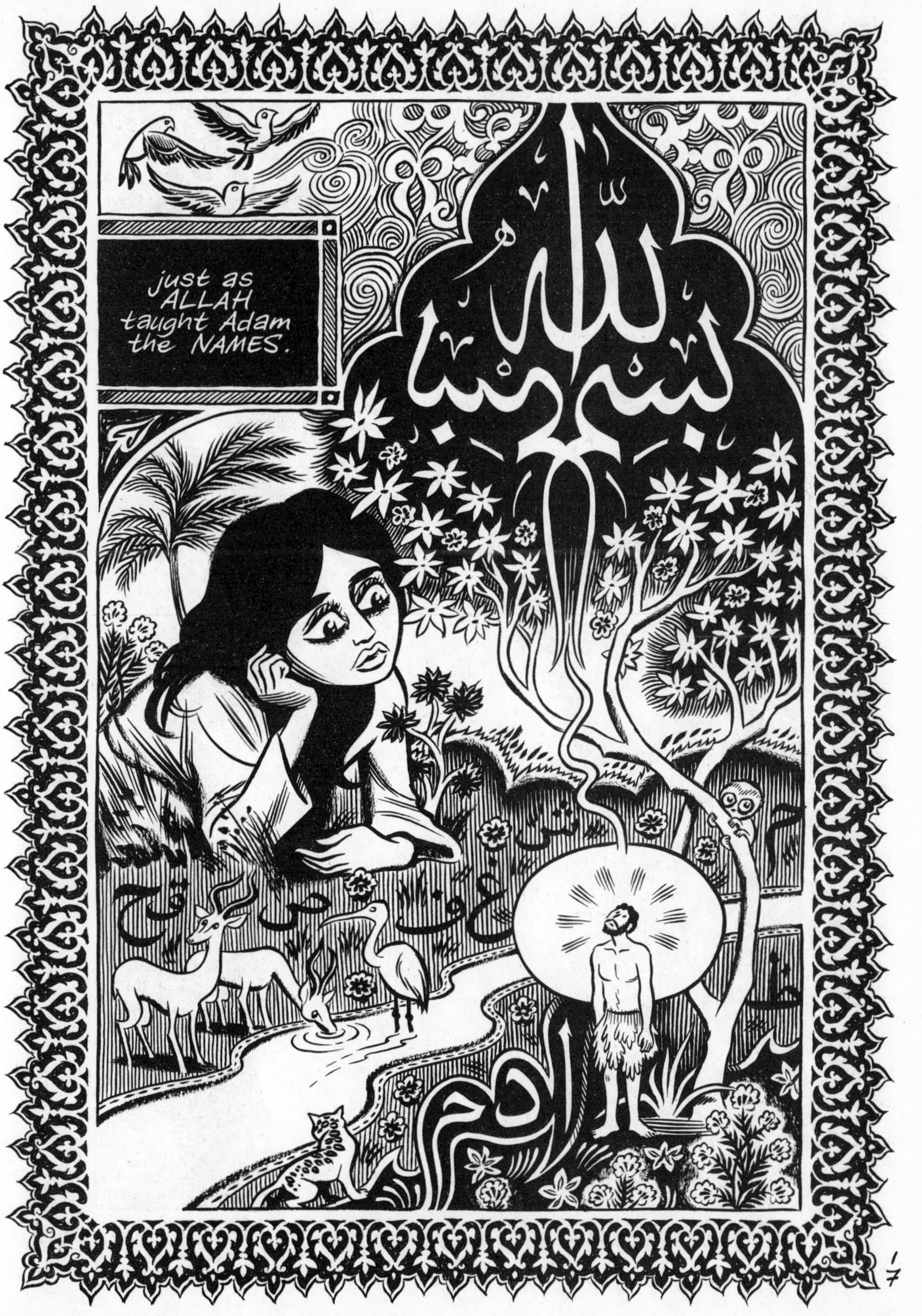
just as ALLAH taught Adam the NAMES.

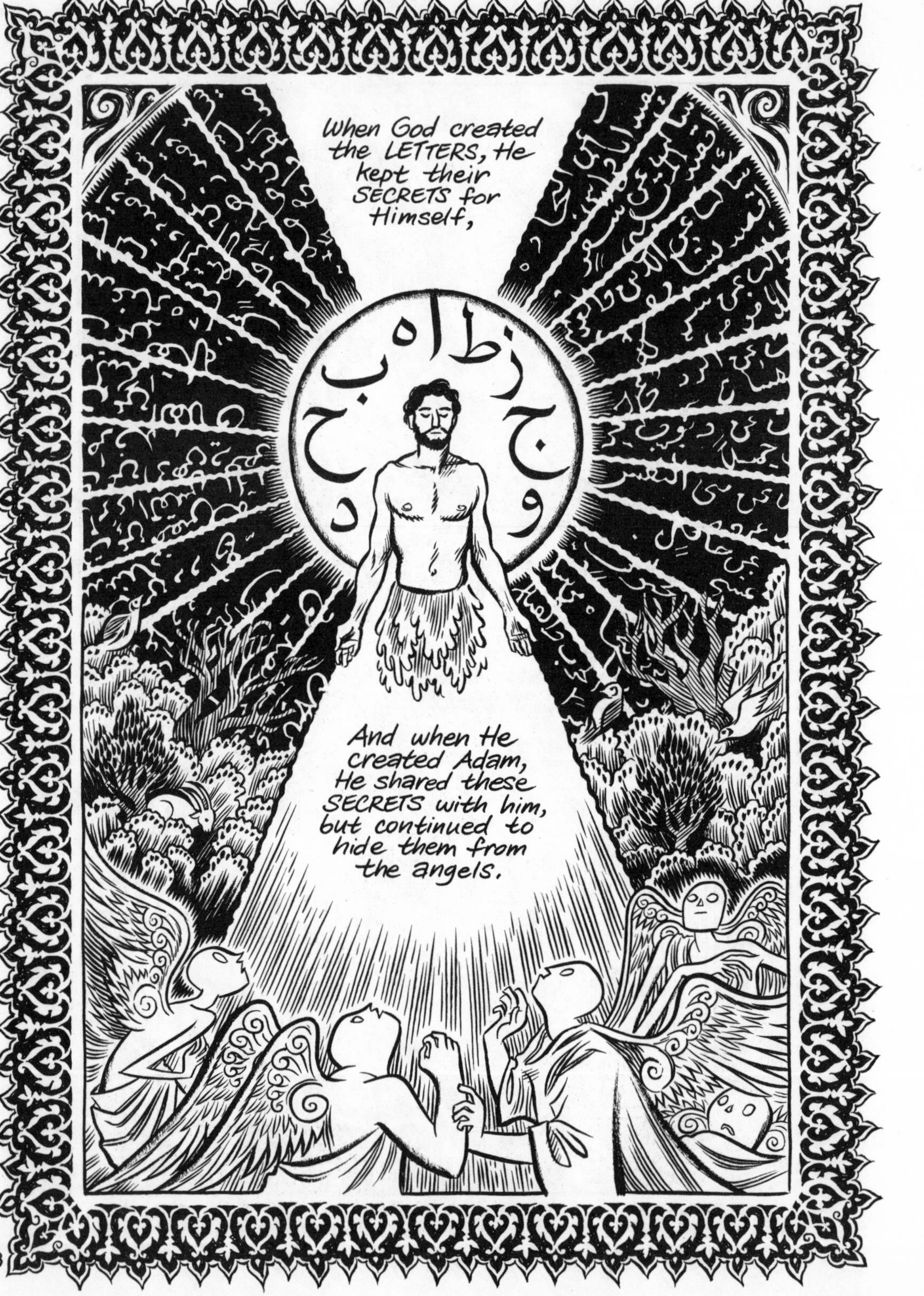
When God created the LETTERS, He kept their SECRETS for Himself,
And when He created Adam, He shared these SECRETS with him, but continued to hide them from the angels.

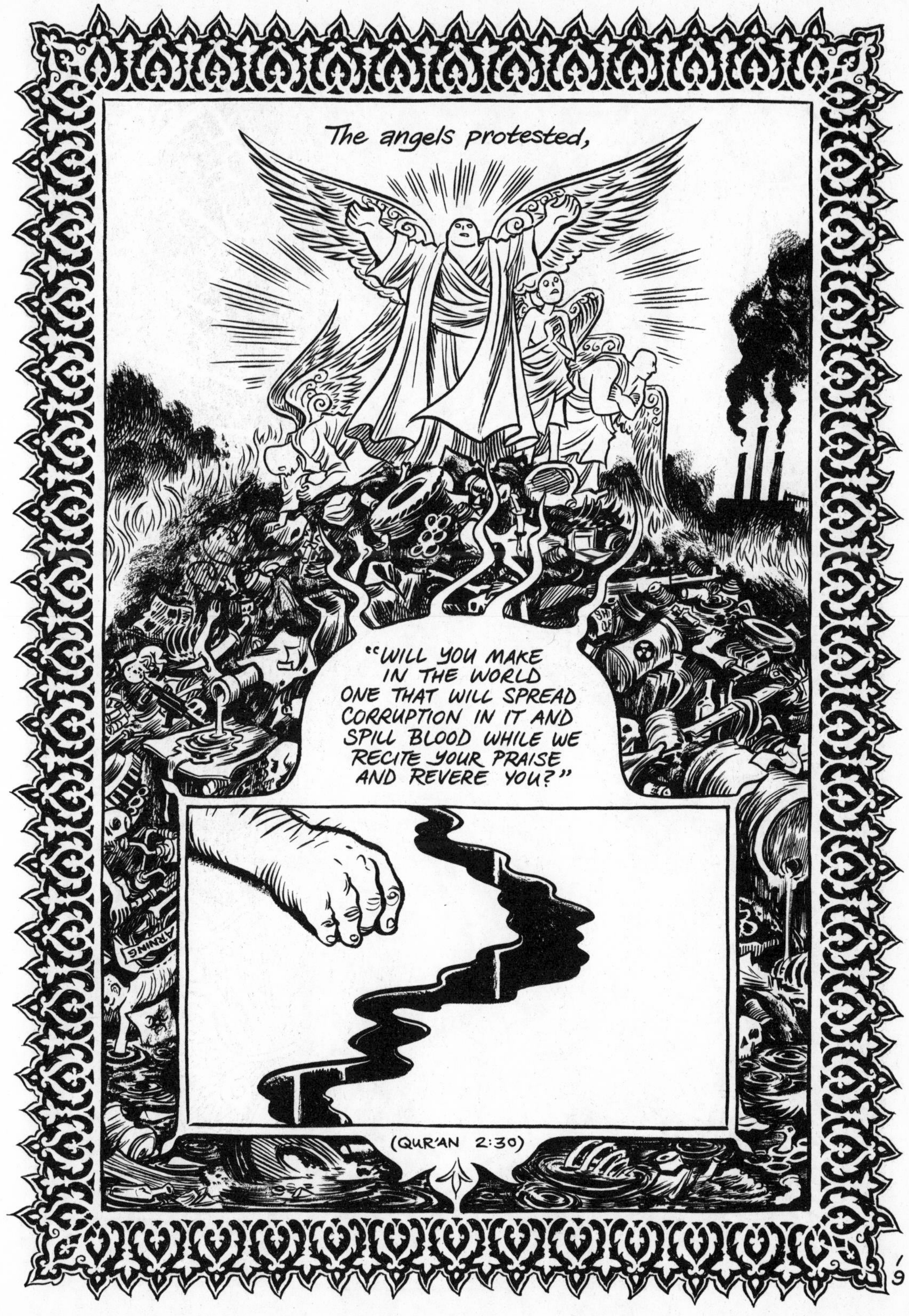
The angels protested,
"WILL YOU MAKE IN THE WORLD ONE THAT WILL SPREAD CORRUPTION IN IT AND SPILL BLOOD WHILE WE RECITE YOUR PRAISE AND REVERE YOU?"
(QUR'AN 2:30)

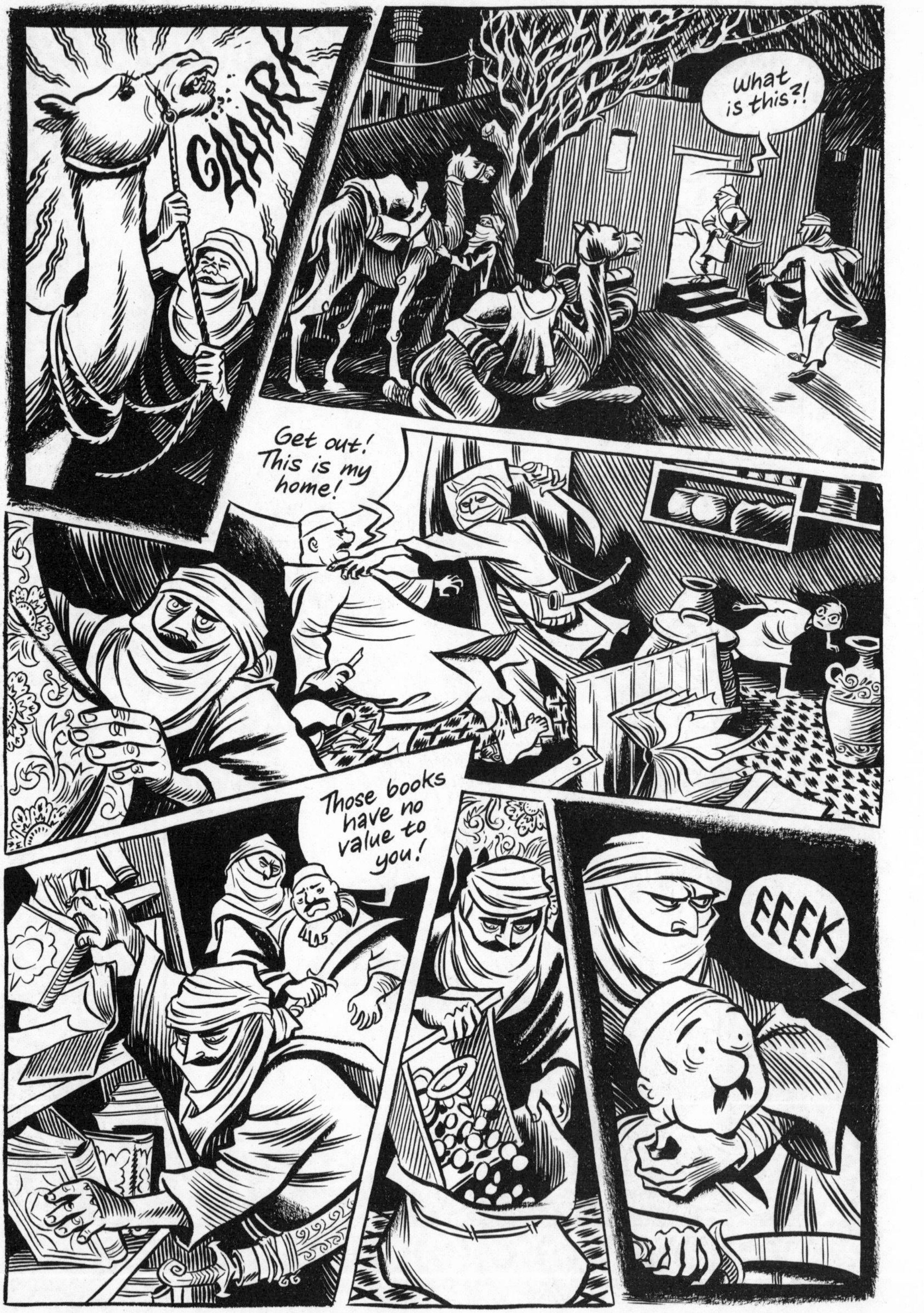
GAARK
What is this?!
Get out! This is my home!
Those books have no value to you!
EEEK

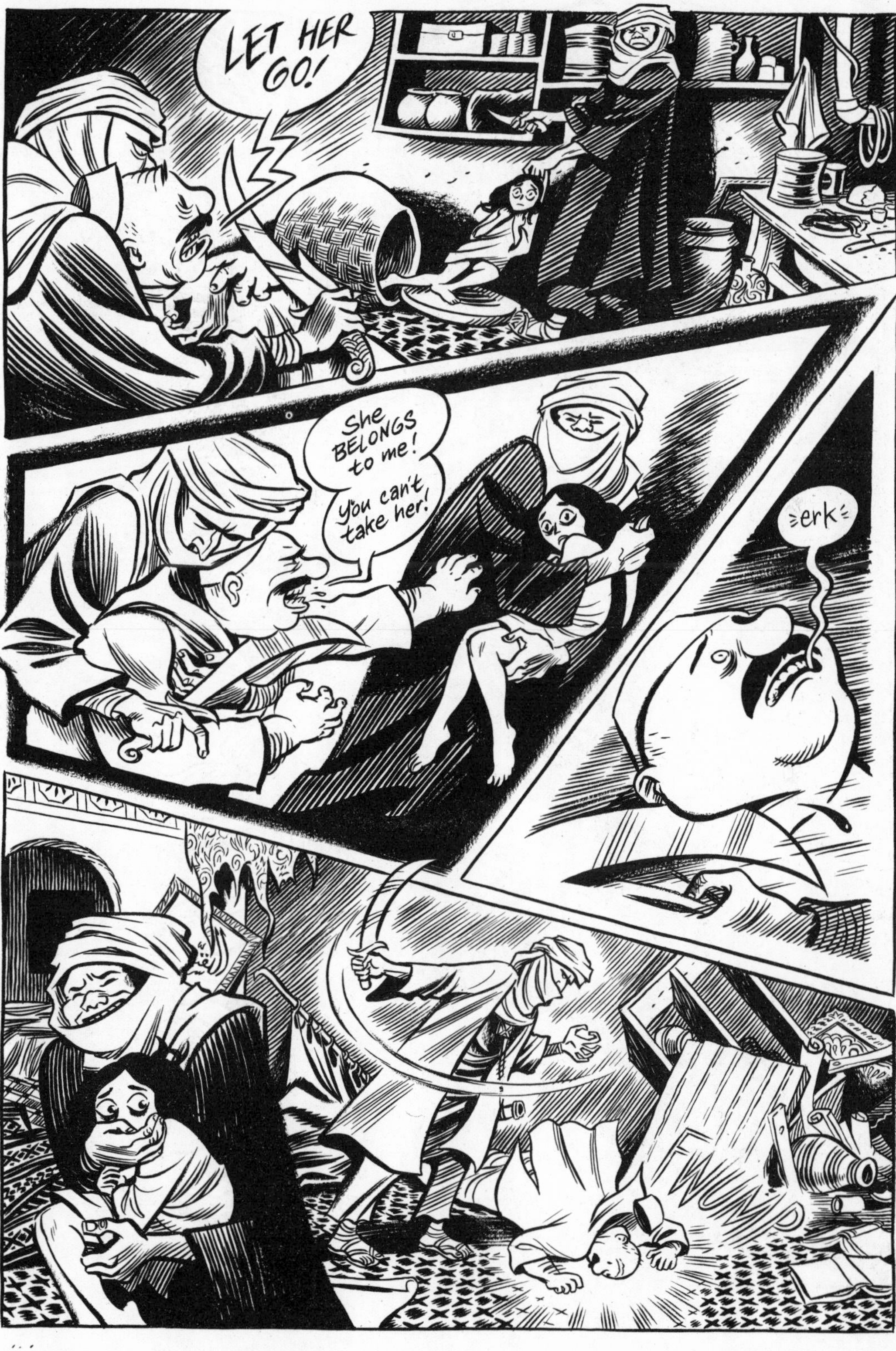
LET HER GO!
She BELONGS to me!
You can't take her!
erk

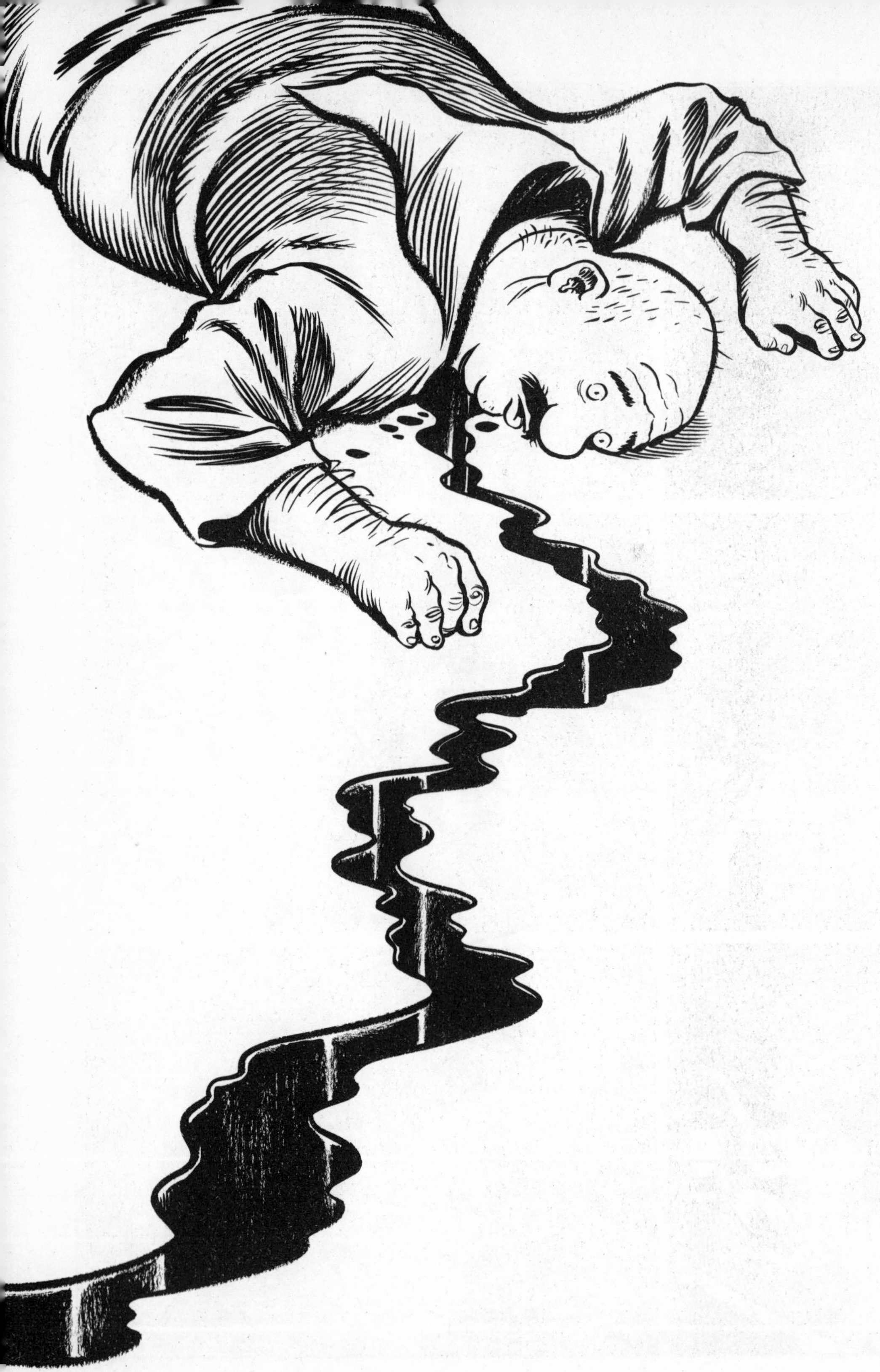

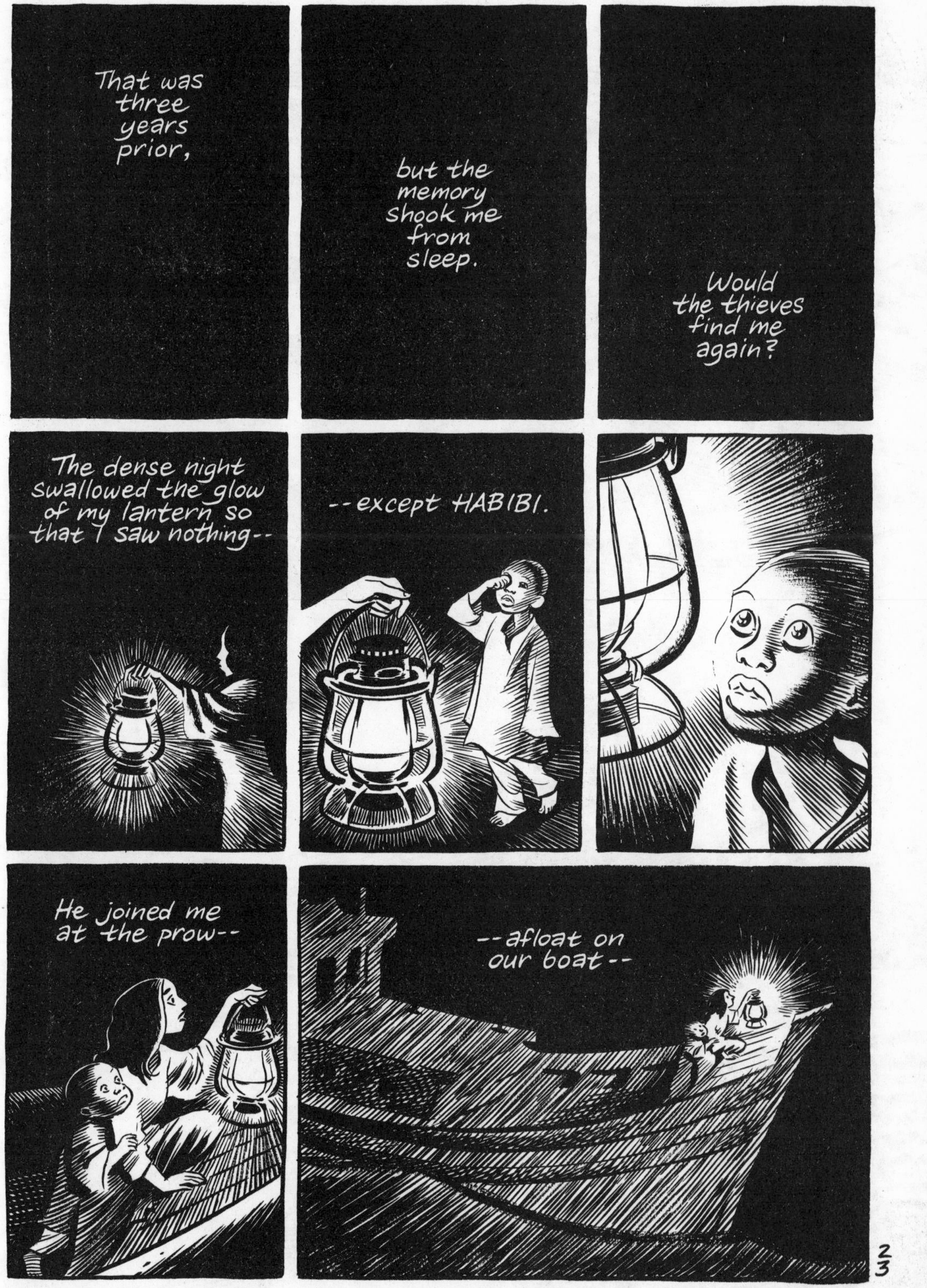
That was three years prior,
but the memory shook me from sleep.
Would the thieves find me again?
The dense night swallowed the glow of my lantern so that I saw nothing--
--except HABIBI.
He joined me at the prow--
--afloat on our boat--

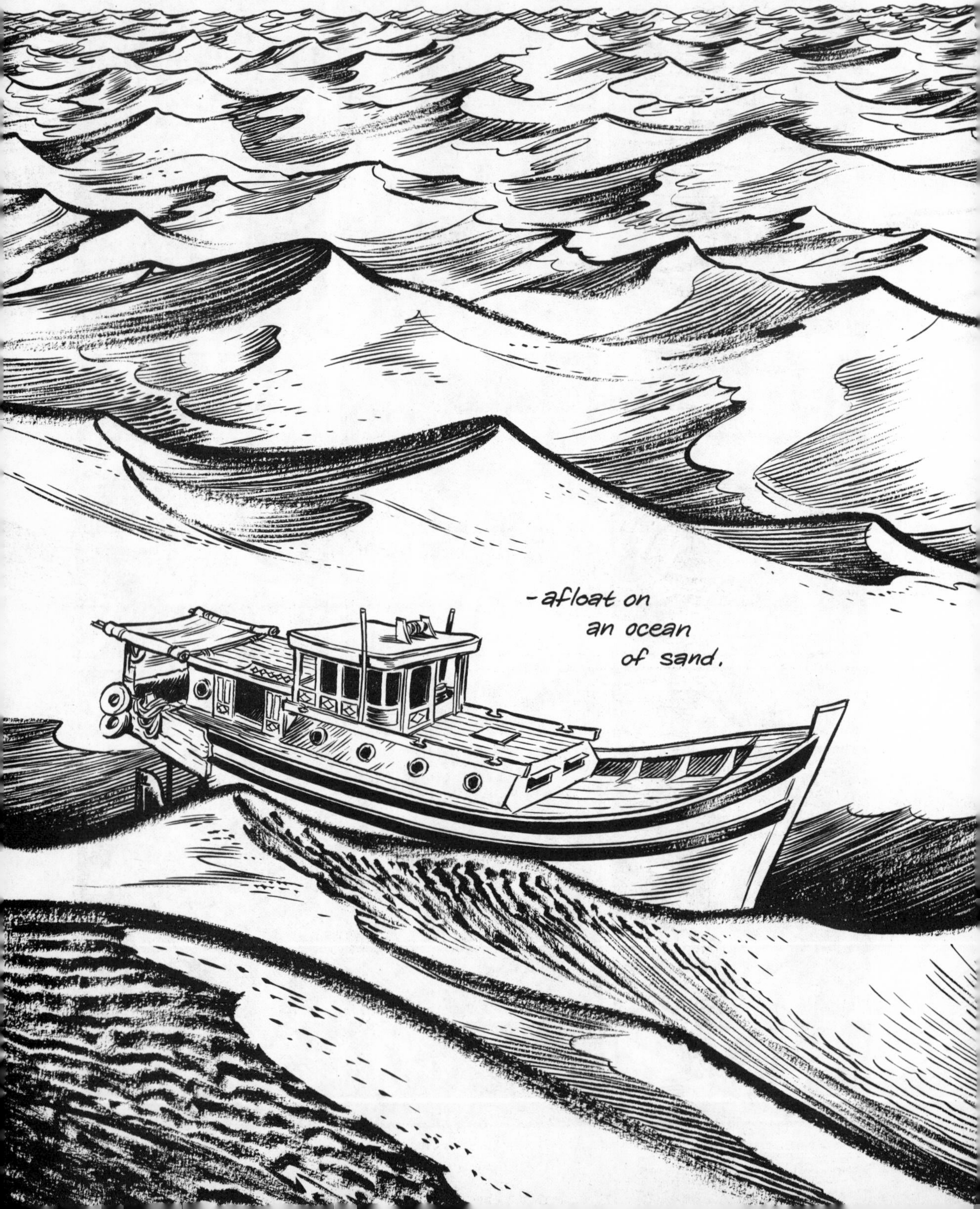
-afloat on an ocean of sand.

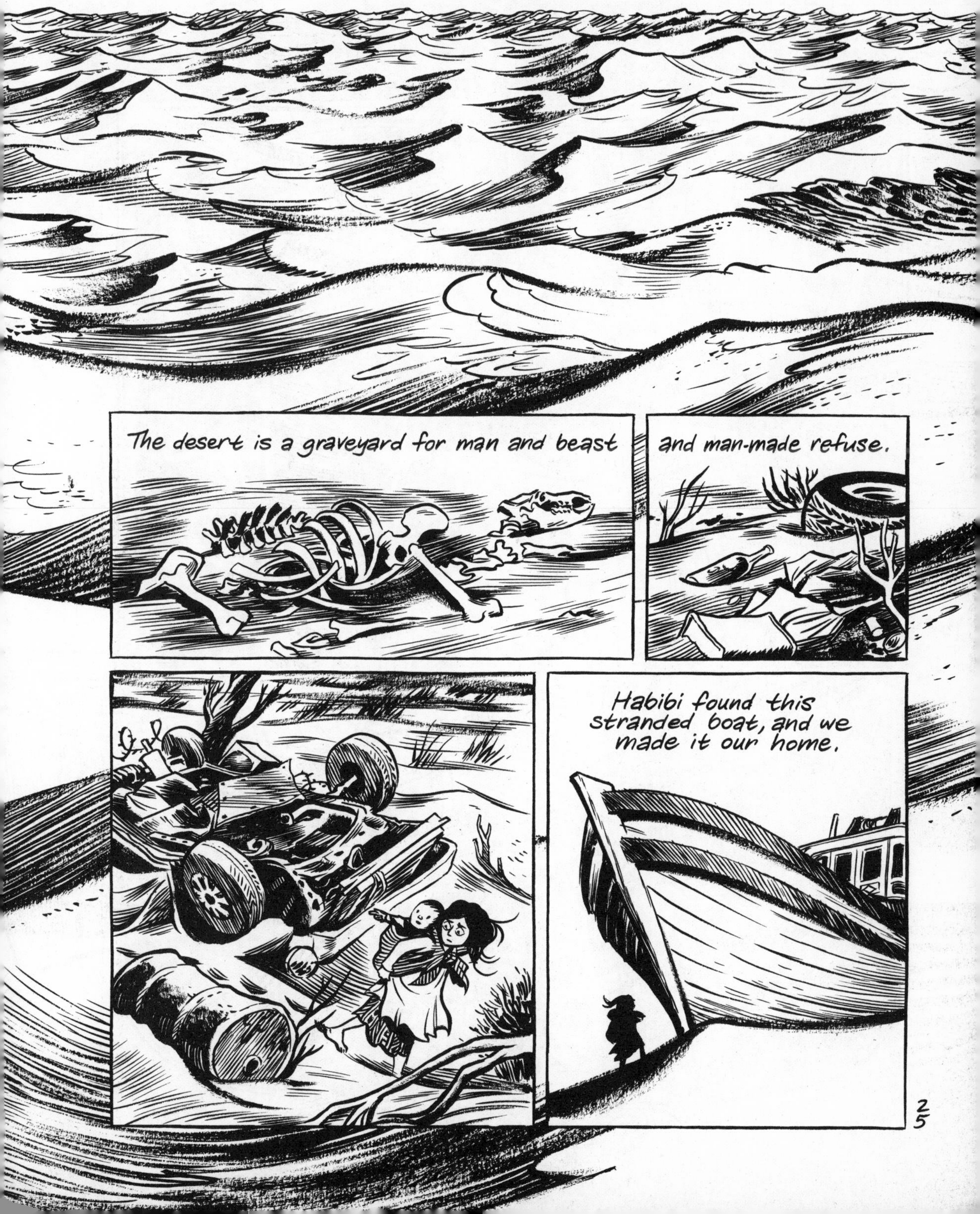
The desert is a graveyard for man and beast
and man-made refuse.
Habibi found this stranded boat, and we made it our home.

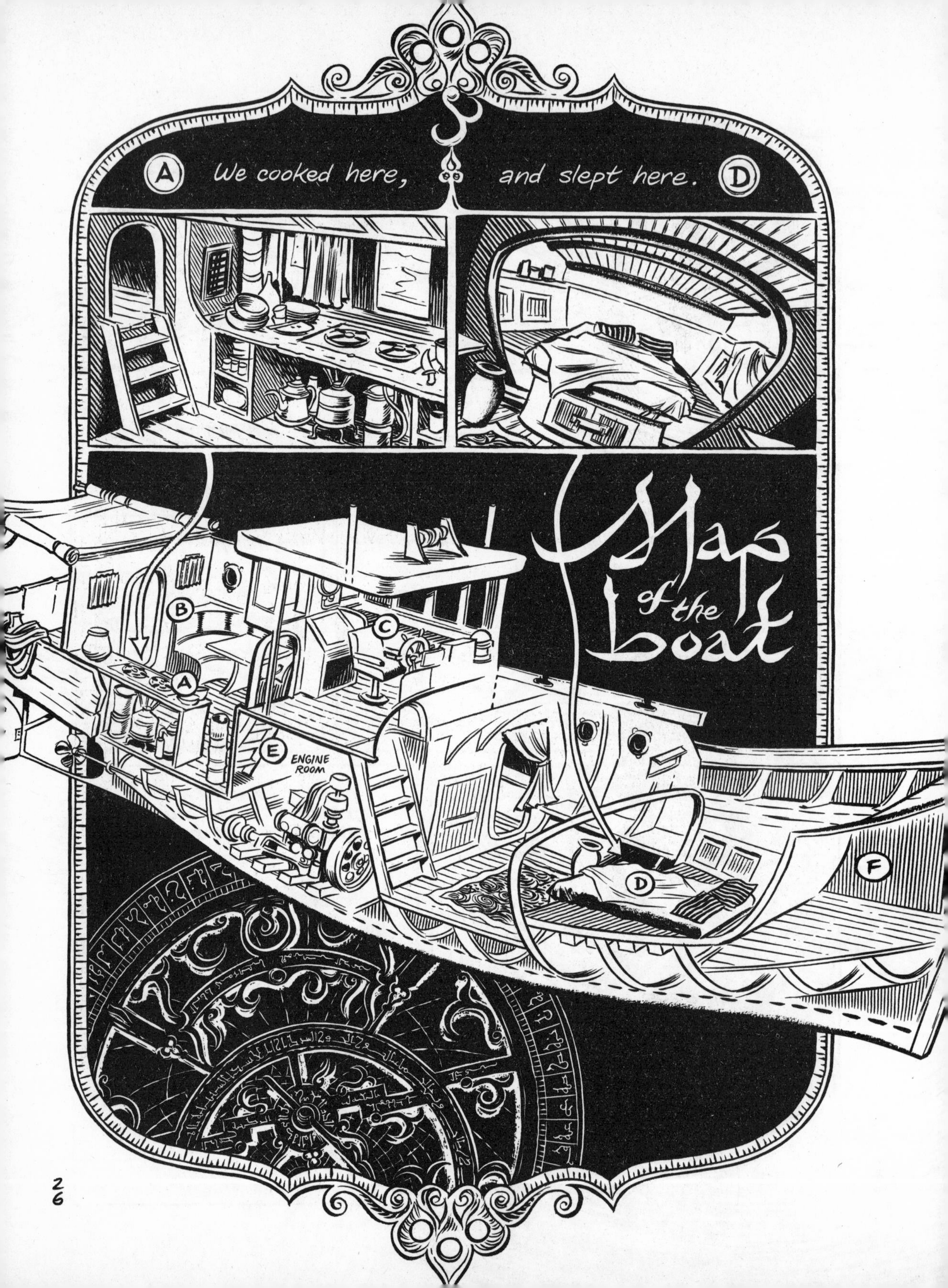
A We cooked here,
and slept here. D
Map of the boat
B
C
A
E
ENGINE ROOM
D
F

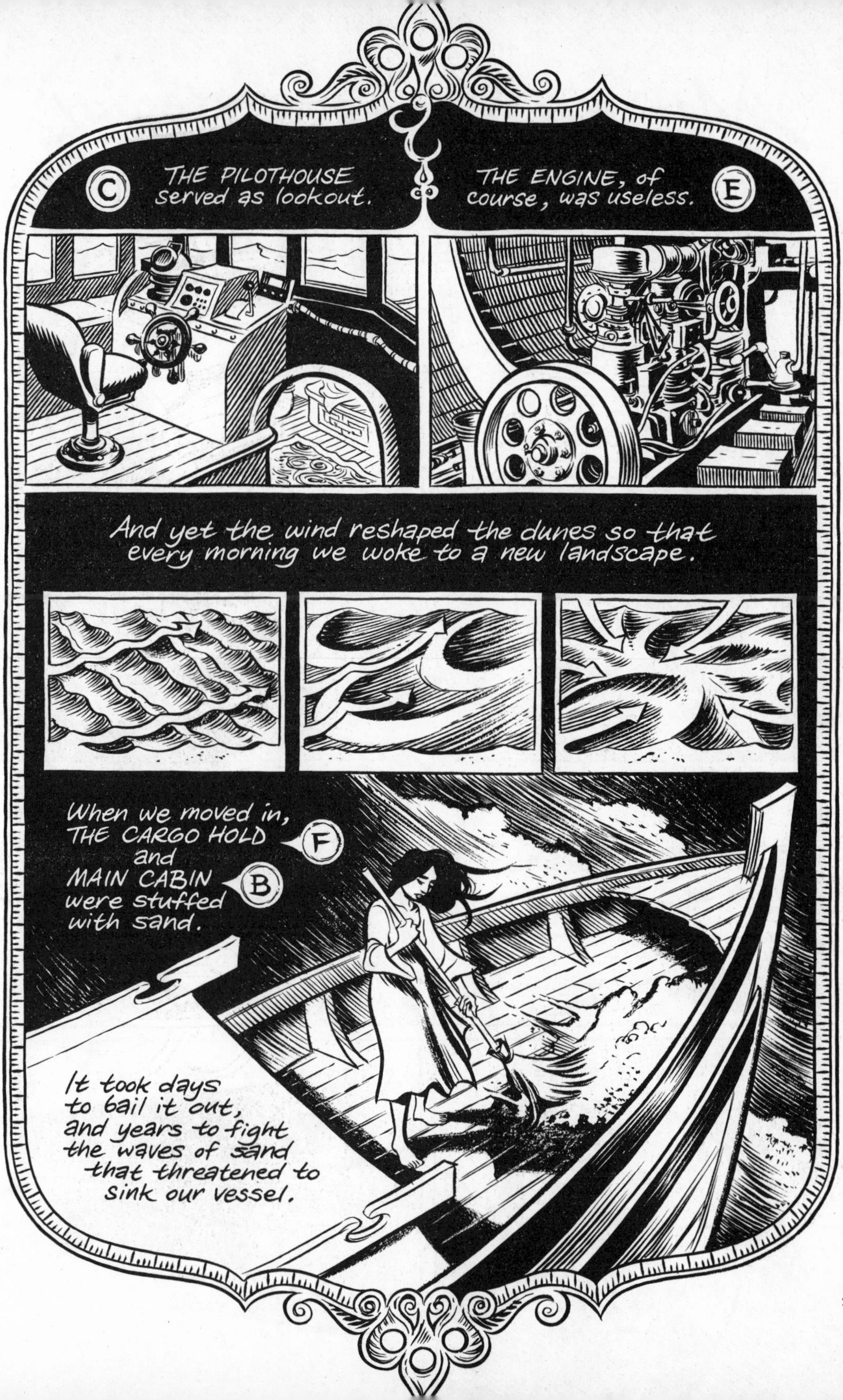
C
THE PILOTHOUSE served as lookout.
THE ENGINE, of course, was useless.
E
And yet the wind reshaped the dunes so that every morning we woke to a new landscape.
When we moved in, THE CARGO HOLD
F
and MAIN CABIN
B
were stuffed with sand.
It took days to bail it out, and years to fight the waves of sand that threatened to sink our vessel.

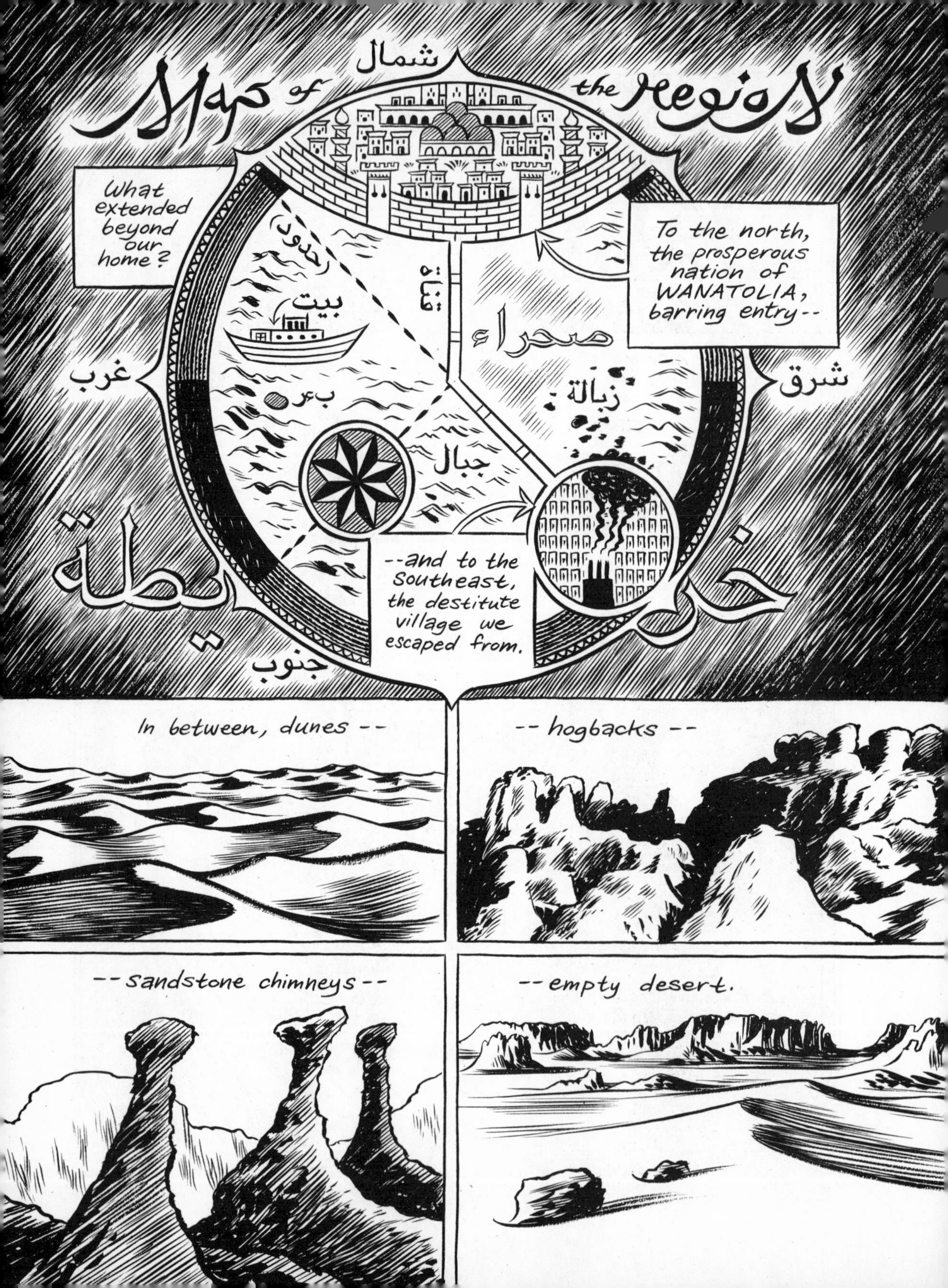

Map of the Region
شمال
What extended beyond our home?
To the north, the prosperous nation of WANATOLIA, barring entry--
حدود
قناة
بيت
صحراء
غرب
شرق
زبالة
جبال
--and to the Southeast, the destitute village we escaped from.
جنوب
In between, dunes --
-- hogbacks --
-- sandstone chimneys --
-- empty desert.

We were mostly alone--

--except for roaming nomads and thieves, exiled criminals, and merchant caravans.

Time for us to get inside.

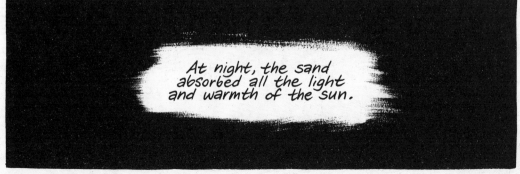

At night, the sand absorbed all the light and warmth of the sun.

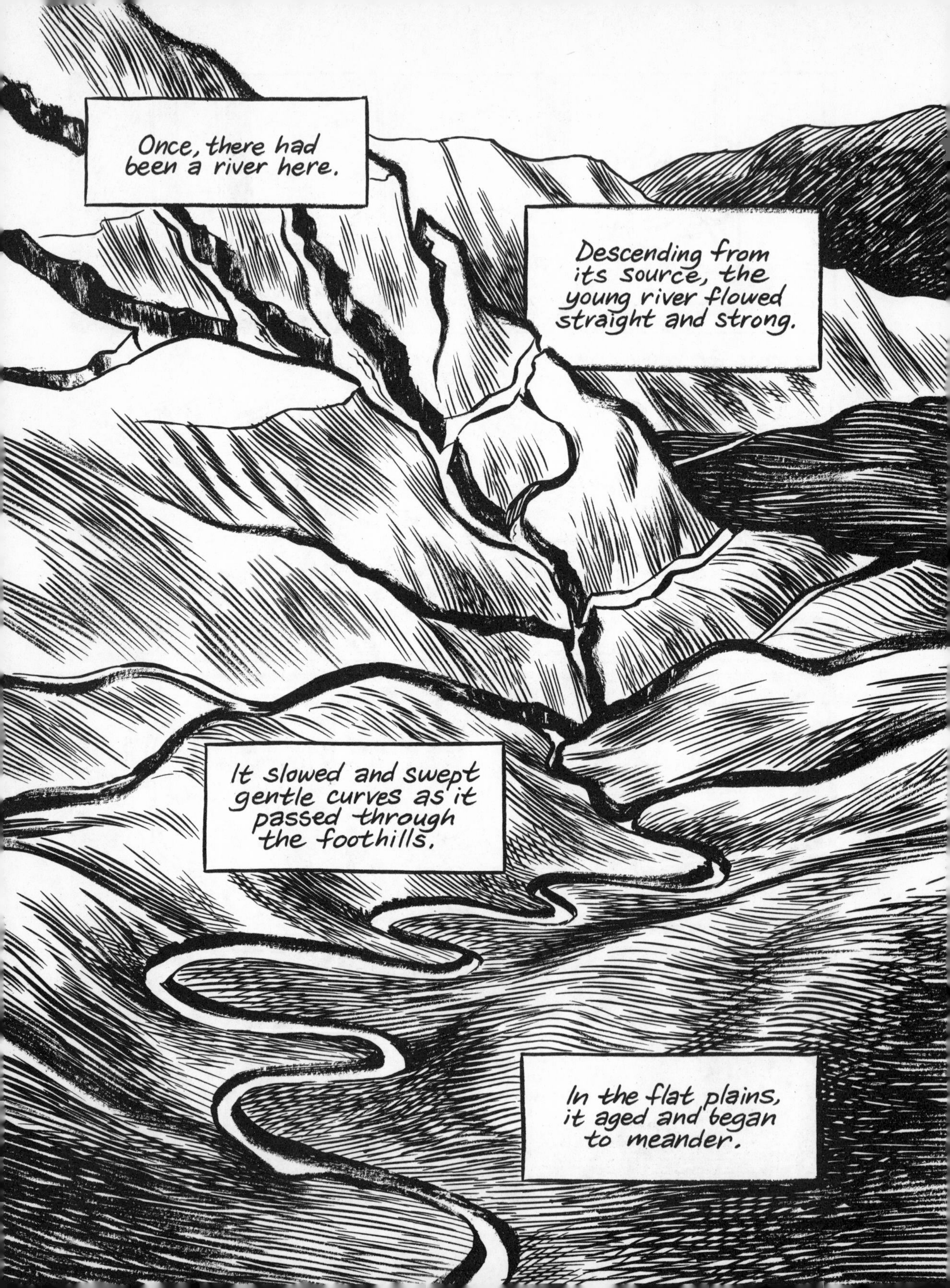
Once, there had been a river here.
Descending from its source, the young river flowed straight and strong.
It slowed and swept gentle curves as it passed through the foothills.
In the flat plains, it aged and began to meander.

meandering...

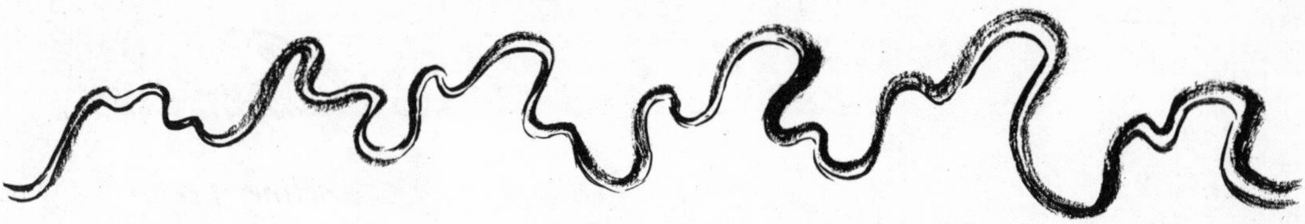

looping like letters,

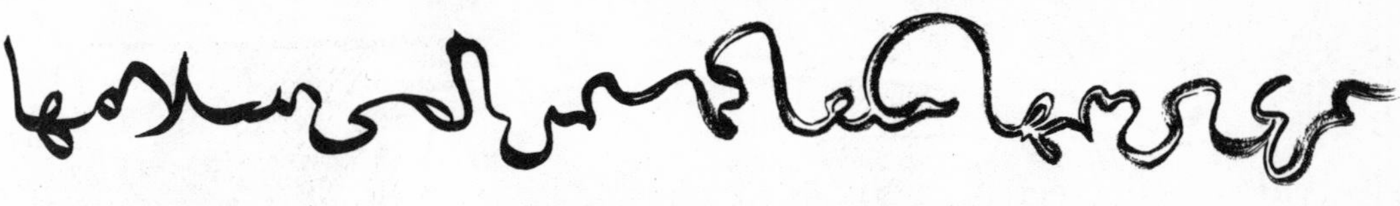

letters extending into stories,

وجلا السيول عن الطلول كأنها زُبُرٌ تُجِدُّ متونَها أقلامُها

until suddenly it stopped

جَزْأً فطالَ صِيامُهُ وصِيامُها . . .

-dried up-

. . .

a muted voice.

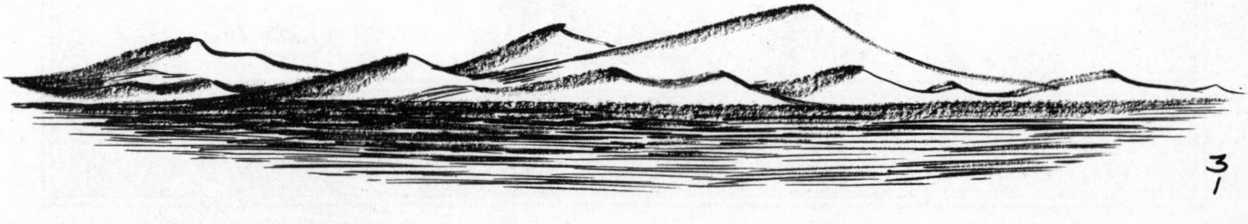

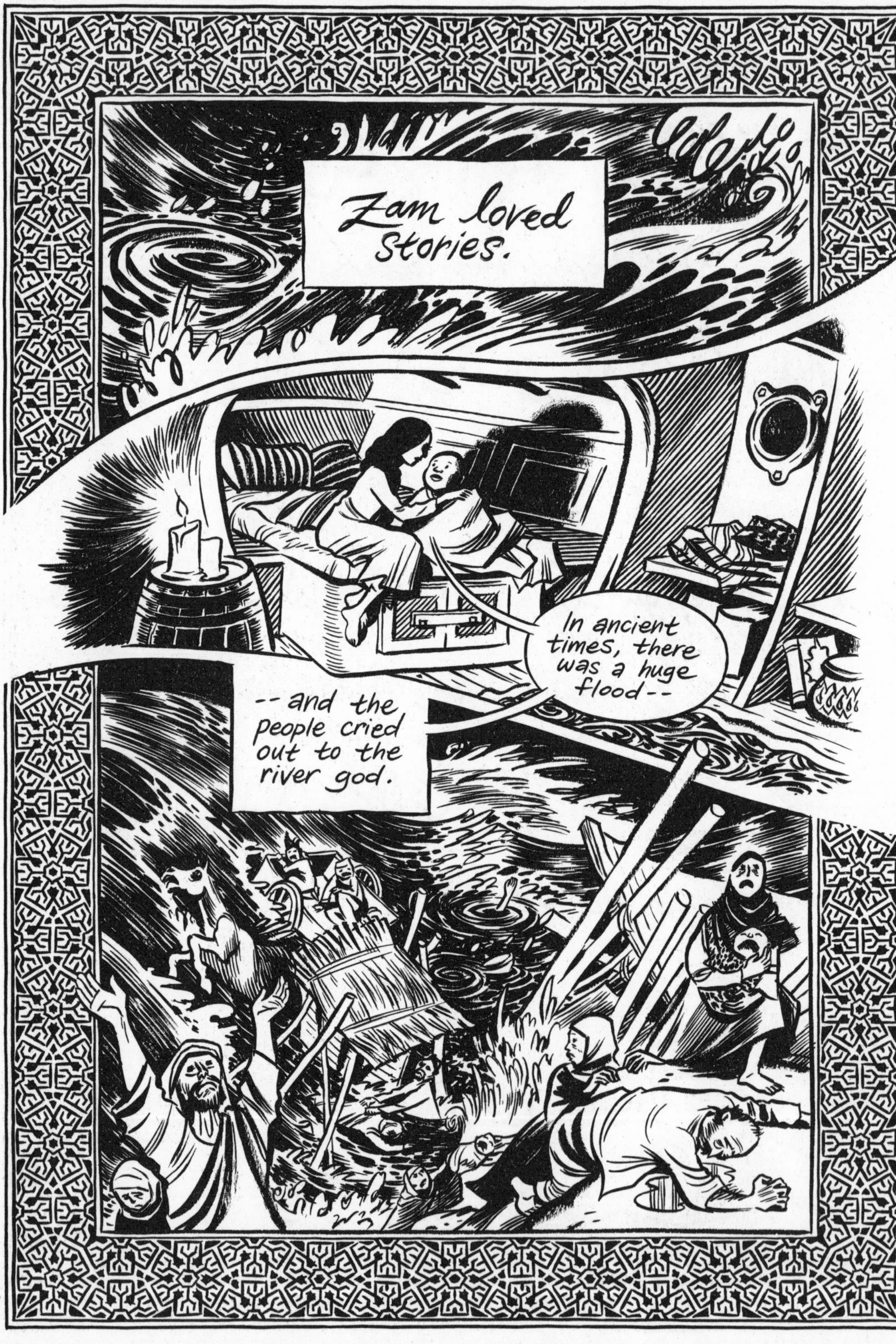
Zam loved stories.
In ancient times, there was a huge flood--
--and the people cried out to the river god.

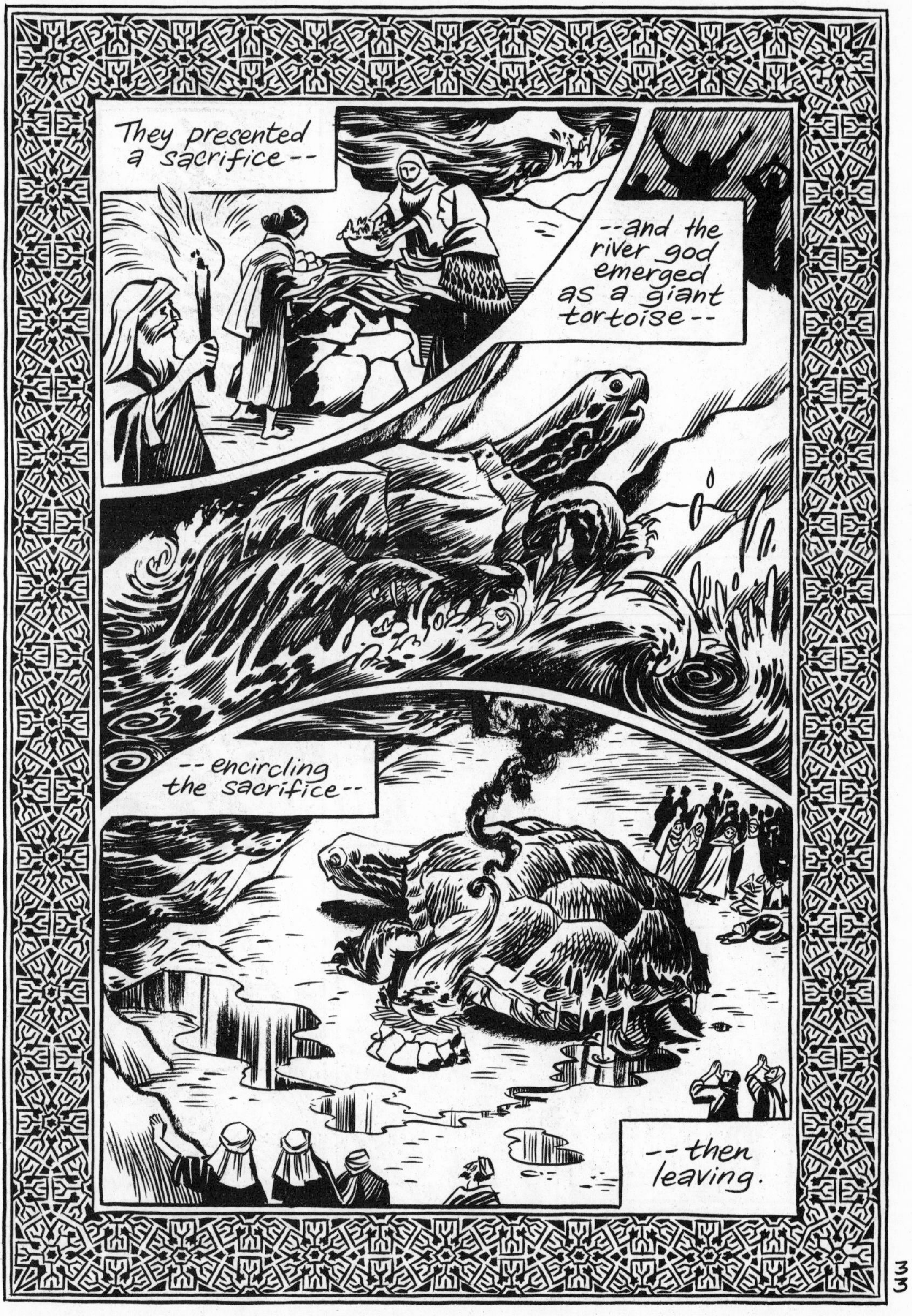
They presented a sacrifice--
--and the river god emerged as a giant tortoise--
--encircling the sacrifice--
--then leaving.

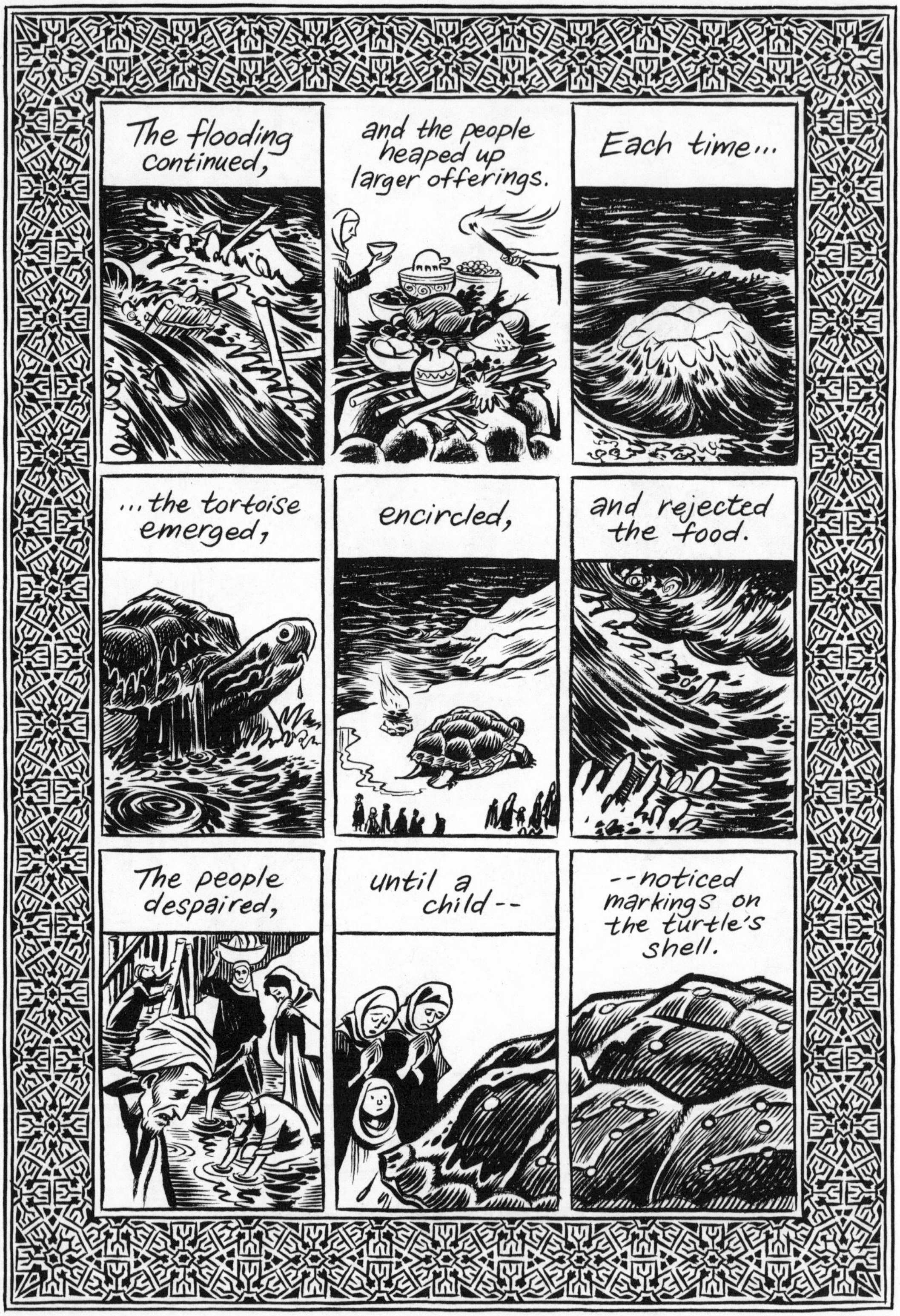
The flooding continued,
and the people heaped up larger offerings.
Each time...
...the tortoise emerged,
encircled,
and rejected the food.
The people despaired,
until a child--
--noticed markings on the turtle's shell.

They named it LUOSHU,
meaning RIVER MAP.

Nine squares ← Each square containing a number →

and every column in every direction added up to the same number –

With the presentation of fifteen sacrifices, the flooding stopped.

Each square had a numerical value → and a corresponding letter

4 9 2
3 5 7
8 1 6

15

Each square had a numerical value and a corresponding letter

ب ط د
ز ه ج
و ا ح

3/6

And the first letter in the first square ...

... is B.

B is for Bismillah.

The first words of the QUR'AN

The QUR'AN is not gathered in the order it was revealed to the Prophet,

but by approximate length of each sura (chapter) — longest to shortest.

The first sura revealed, in fact, is the 96th in the book's arrangement (9+6 = 15).

But every sura of the QUR'AN (except the ninth) opens with Bismillah.

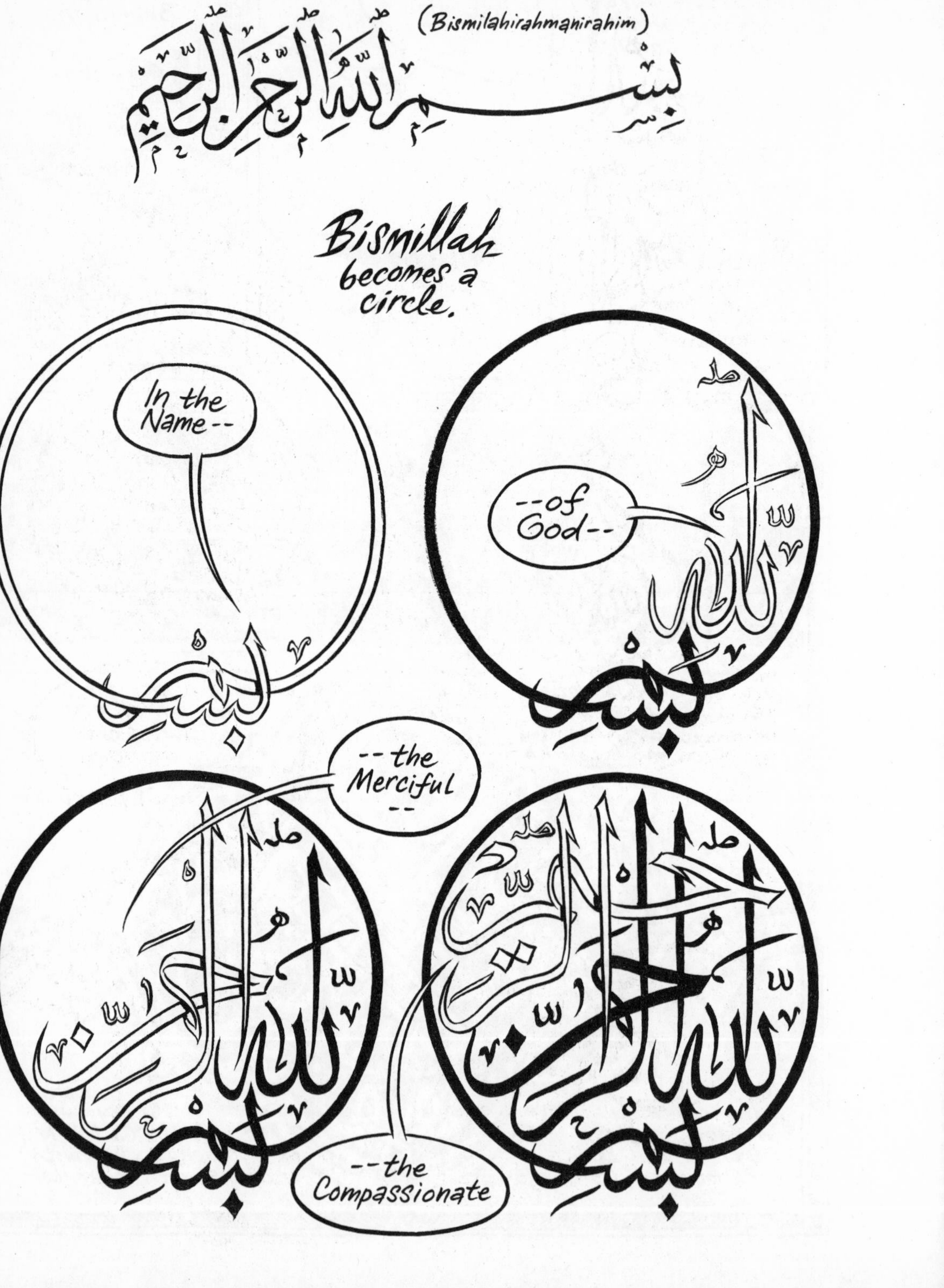
(Bismilahirahmanirahim)
بسم الله الرحمن الرحيم
Bismillah becomes a circle.
In the Name --
--of God--
-- the Merciful --
--the Compassionate

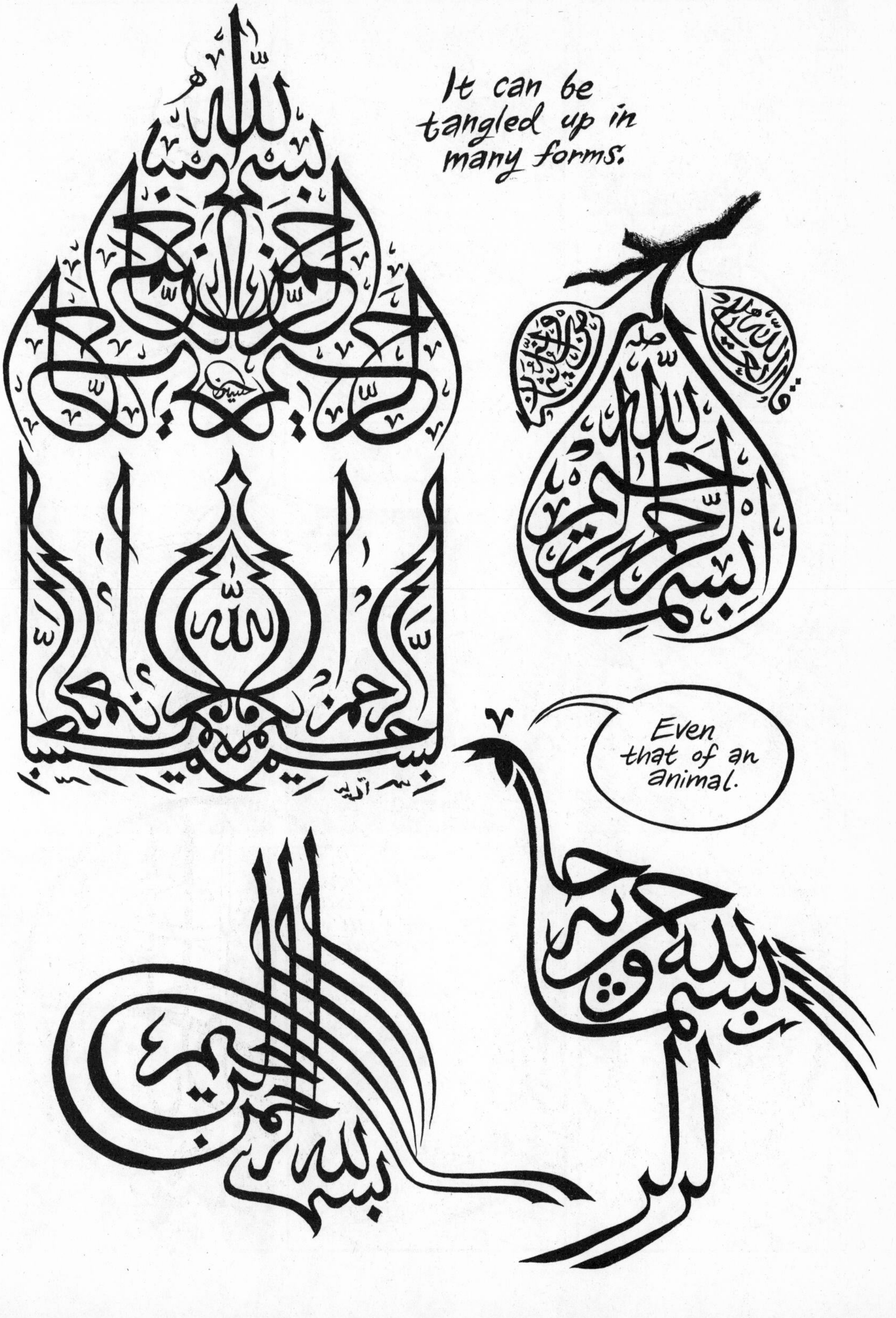
It can be tangled up in many forms.
Even that of an animal.

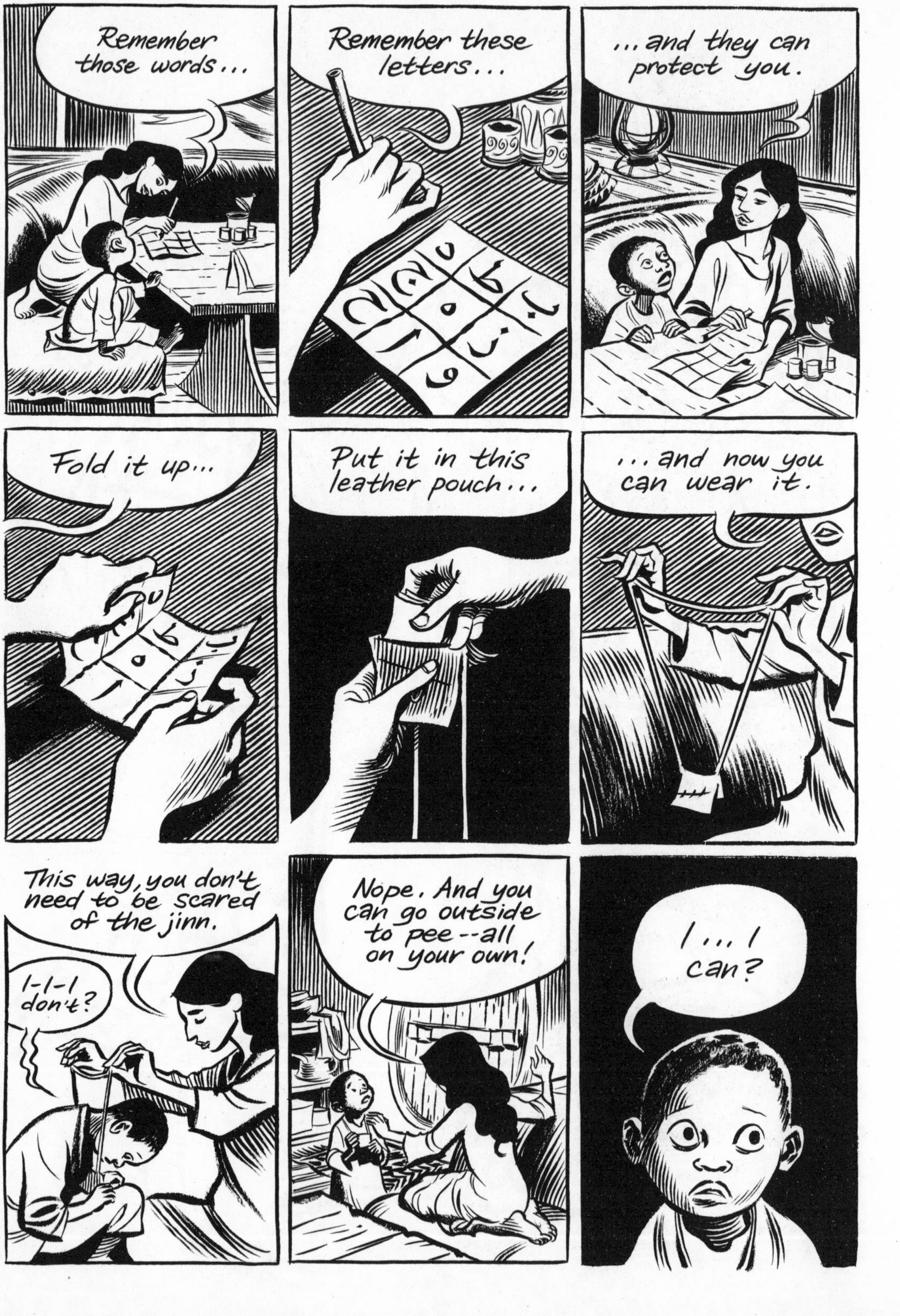

Remember those words...
Remember these letters...
...and they can protect you.
Fold it up...
Put it in this leather pouch...
...and now you can wear it.
This way, you don't need to be scared of the jinn.
I-I-I don't?
Nope. And you can go outside to pee--all on your own!
I... I can?

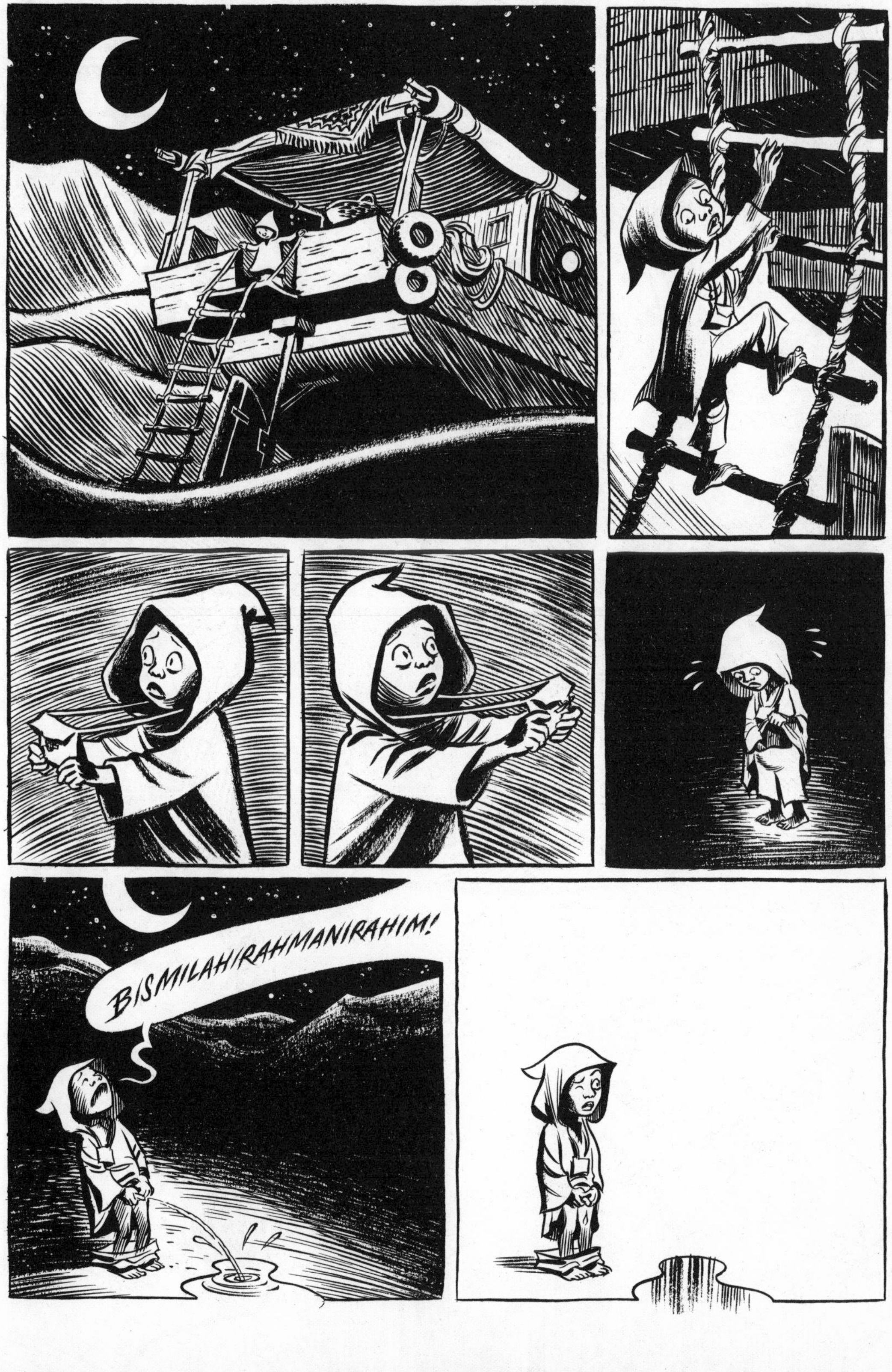
BISMILAHIRAHMANIRAHIM!

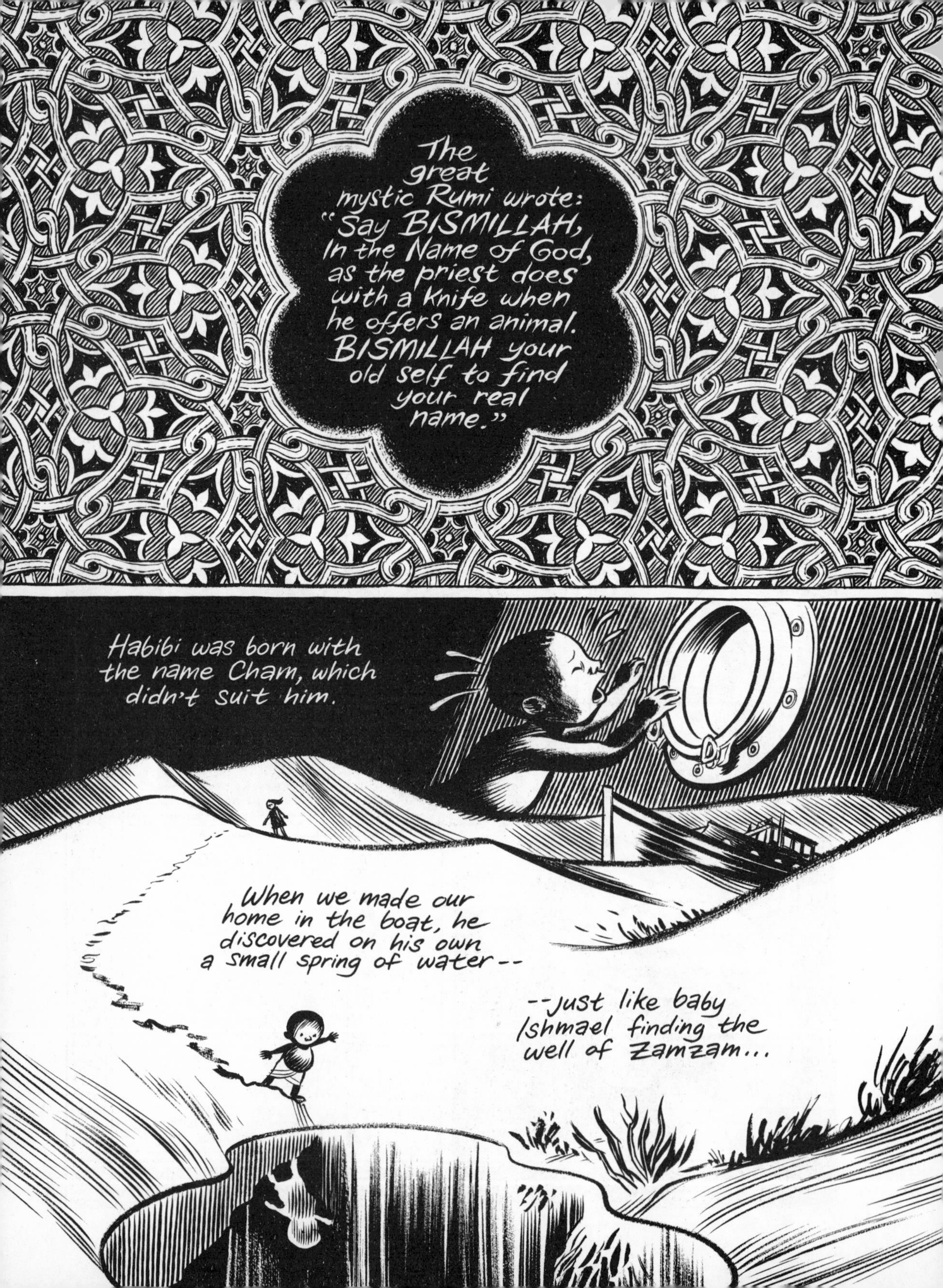

The great mystic Rumi wrote: "Say BISMILLAH, In the Name of God, as the priest does with a knife when he offers an animal. BISMILLAH your old self to find your real name."
Habibi was born with the name Cham, which didn't suit him.
When we made our home in the boat, he discovered on his own a small spring of water--
--just like baby Ishmael finding the well of Zamzam...

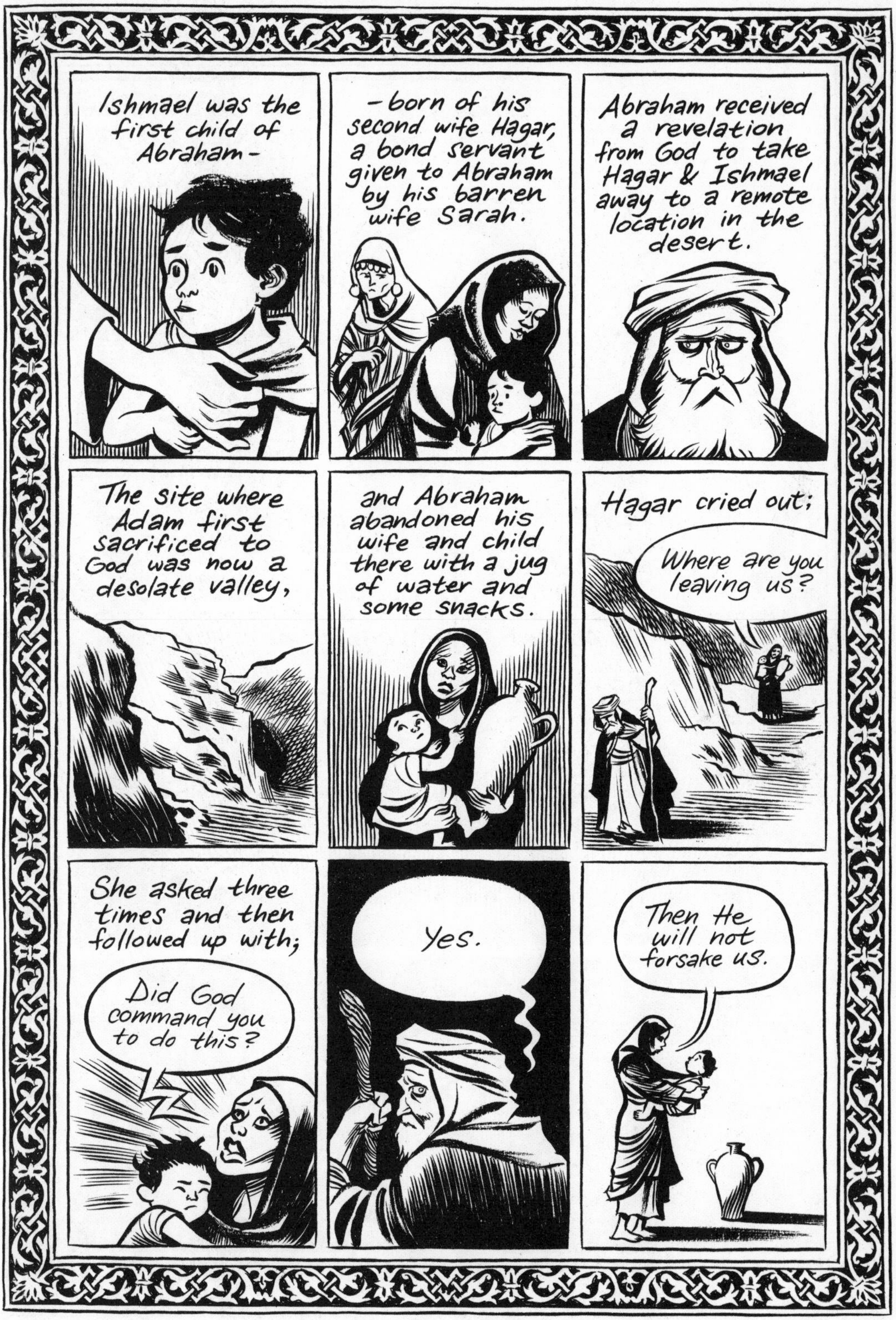
Ishmael was the first child of Abraham-
-born of his second wife Hagar, a bond servant given to Abraham by his barren wife Sarah.
Abraham received a revelation from God to take Hagar & Ishmael away to a remote location in the desert.
The site where Adam first sacrificed to God was now a desolate valley,
and Abraham abandoned his wife and child there with a jug of water and some snacks.
Hagar cried out;
Where are you leaving us?
She asked three times and then followed up with;
Did God command you to do this?
Yes.
Then He will not forsake us.

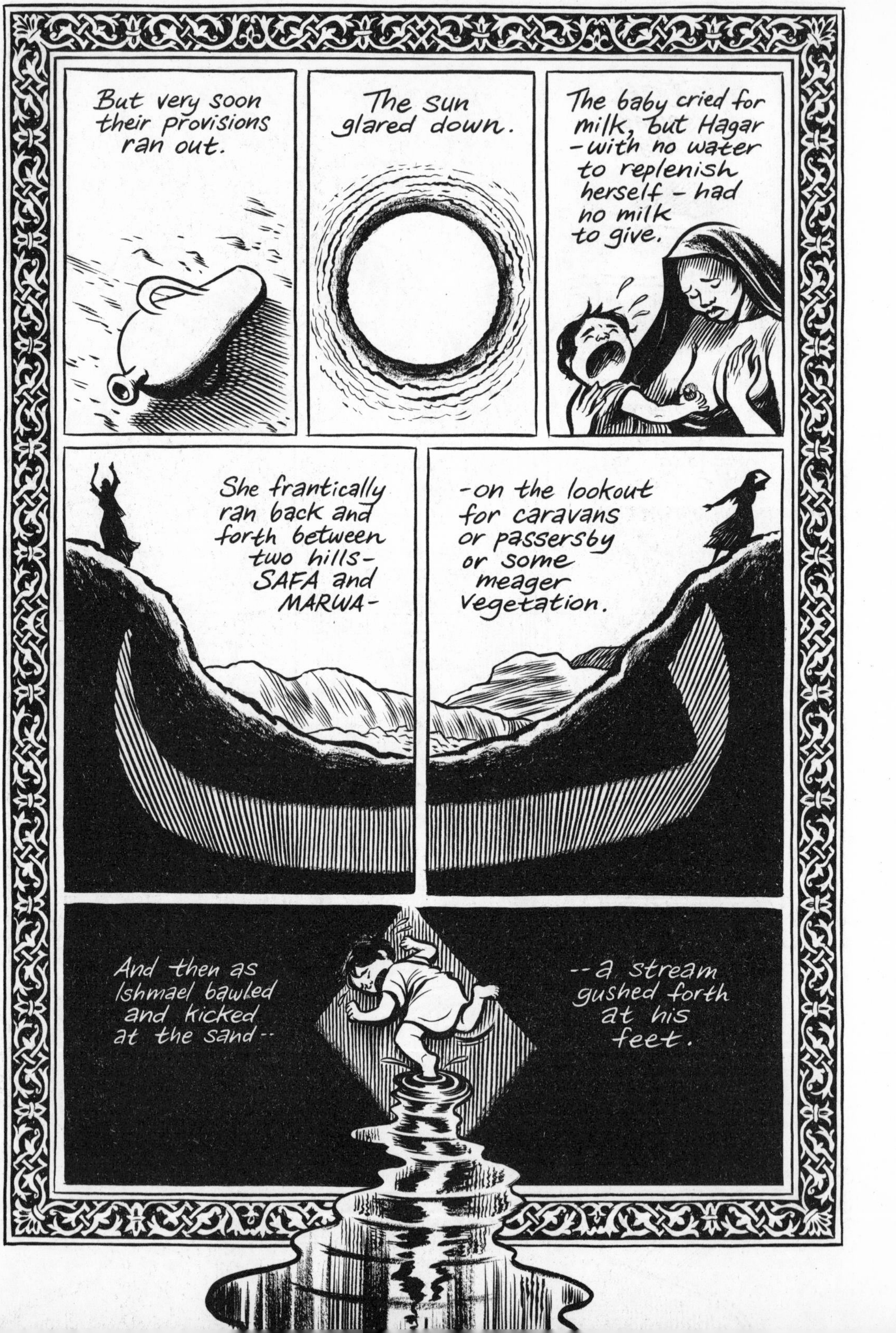
But very soon their provisions ran out.
The sun glared down.
The baby cried for milk, but Hagar -with no water to replenish herself - had no milk to give.
She frantically ran back and forth between two hills- SAFA and MARWA-
-on the lookout for caravans or passersby or some meager vegetation.
And then as Ishmael bawled and kicked at the sand--
--a stream gushed forth at his feet.

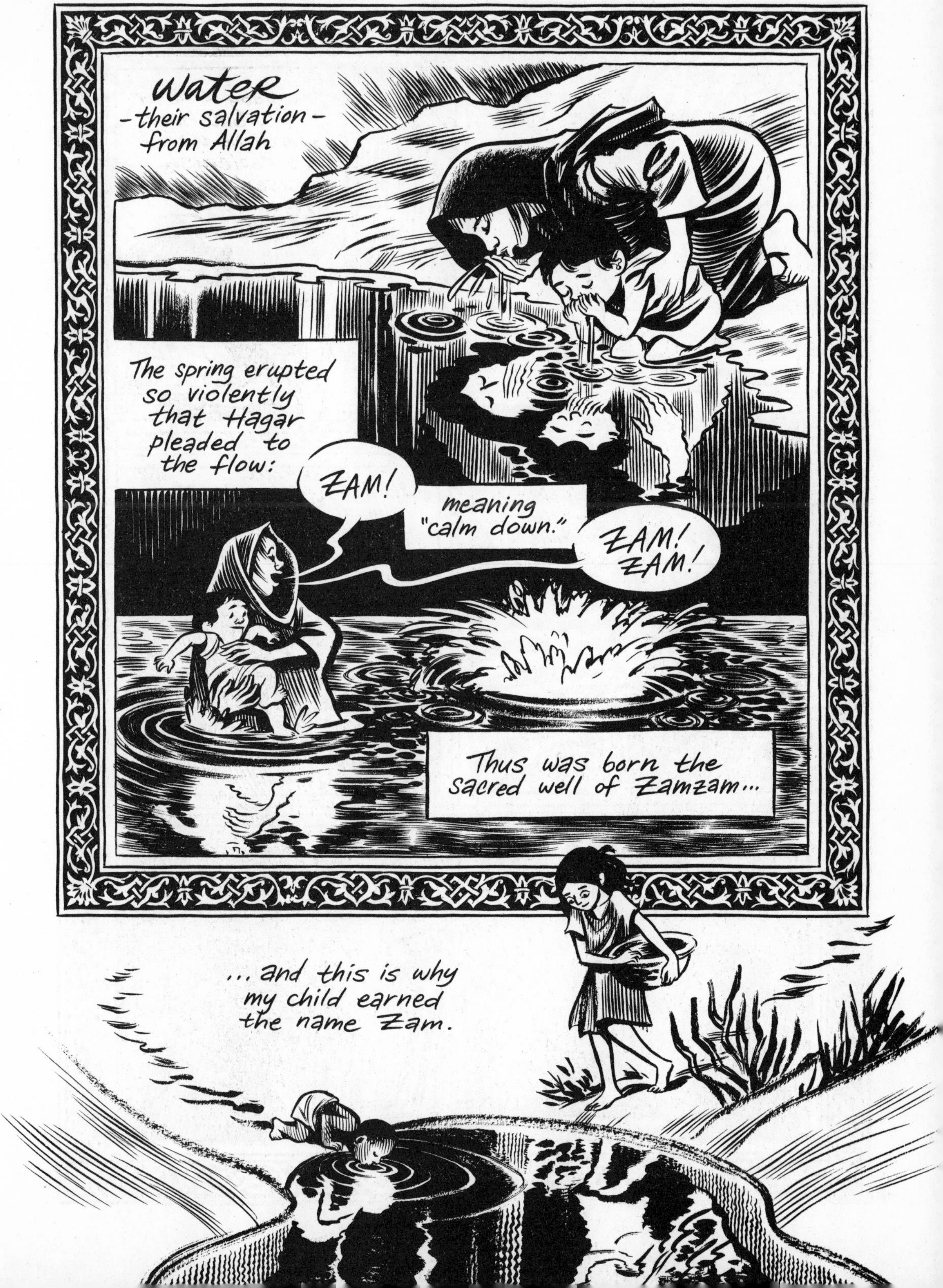
WATER
-their salvation-
from Allah
The spring erupted so violently that Hagar pleaded to the flow:
ZAM!
meaning "calm down."
ZAM! ZAM!
Thus was born the sacred well of Zamzam...
...and this is why my child earned the name Zam.

I, for my part, foraged for food to little avail.

How would we provide for ourselves?

Around the sacred well of Zamzam, a community and town slowly grew;

and so did Ishmael.

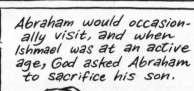

Abraham would occasionally visit, and when Ishmael was at an active age, God asked Abraham to sacrifice his son.

Some say Ishmael didn't count as a son, because he was born of a bond servant (essentially a slave)-

-and they claim it was Isaac, born of Sarah thirteen years later, who was offered for sacrifice.

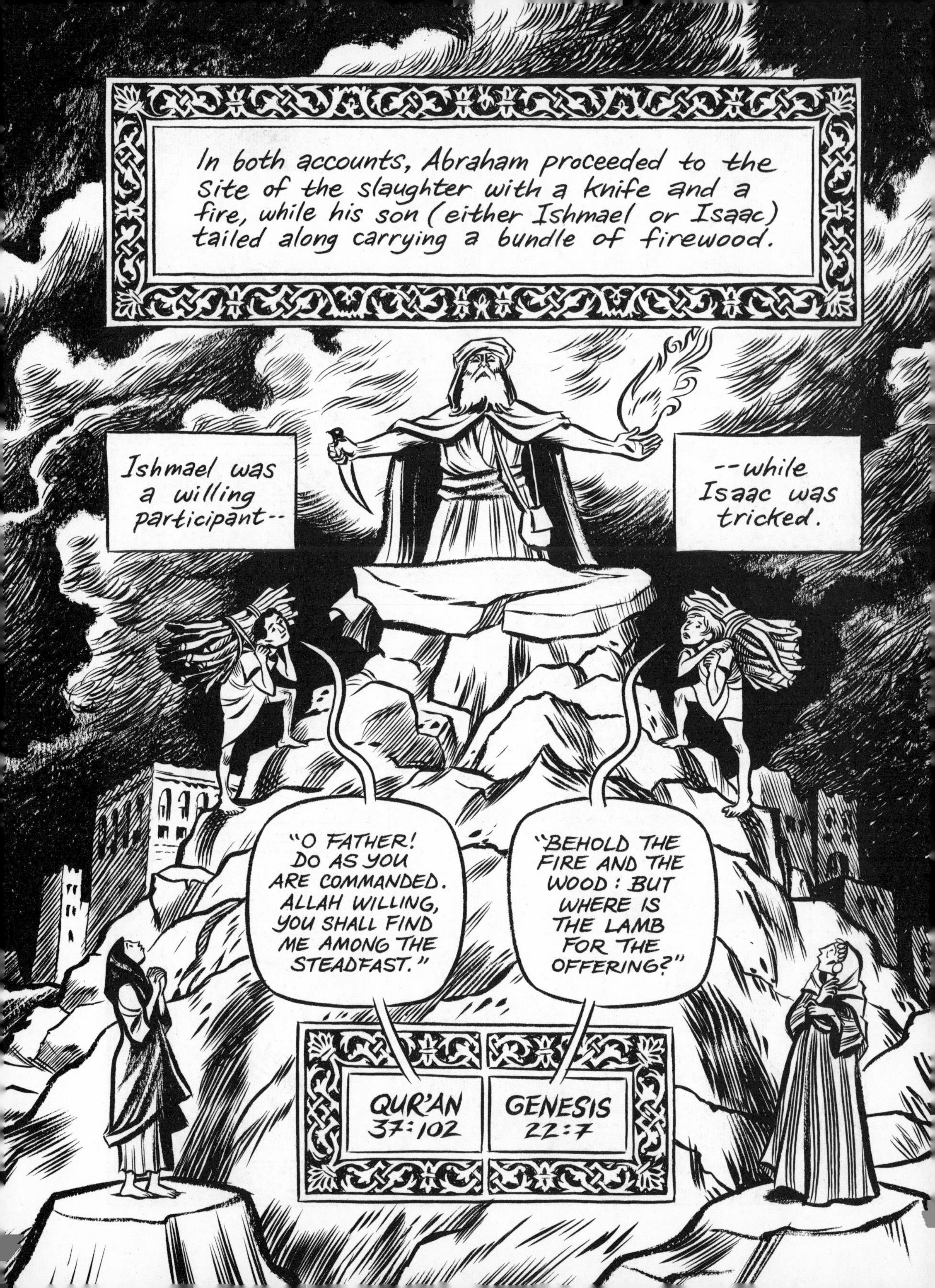
In both accounts, Abraham proceeded to the site of the slaughter with a knife and a fire, while his son (either Ishmael or Isaac) tailed along carrying a bundle of firewood.
Ishmael was a willing participant--
--while Isaac was tricked.
"O FATHER! DO AS YOU ARE COMMANDED. ALLAH WILLING, YOU SHALL FIND ME AMONG THE STEADFAST."
"BEHOLD THE FIRE AND THE WOOD: BUT WHERE IS THE LAMB FOR THE OFFERING?"
QUR'AN 37:102
GENESIS 22:7

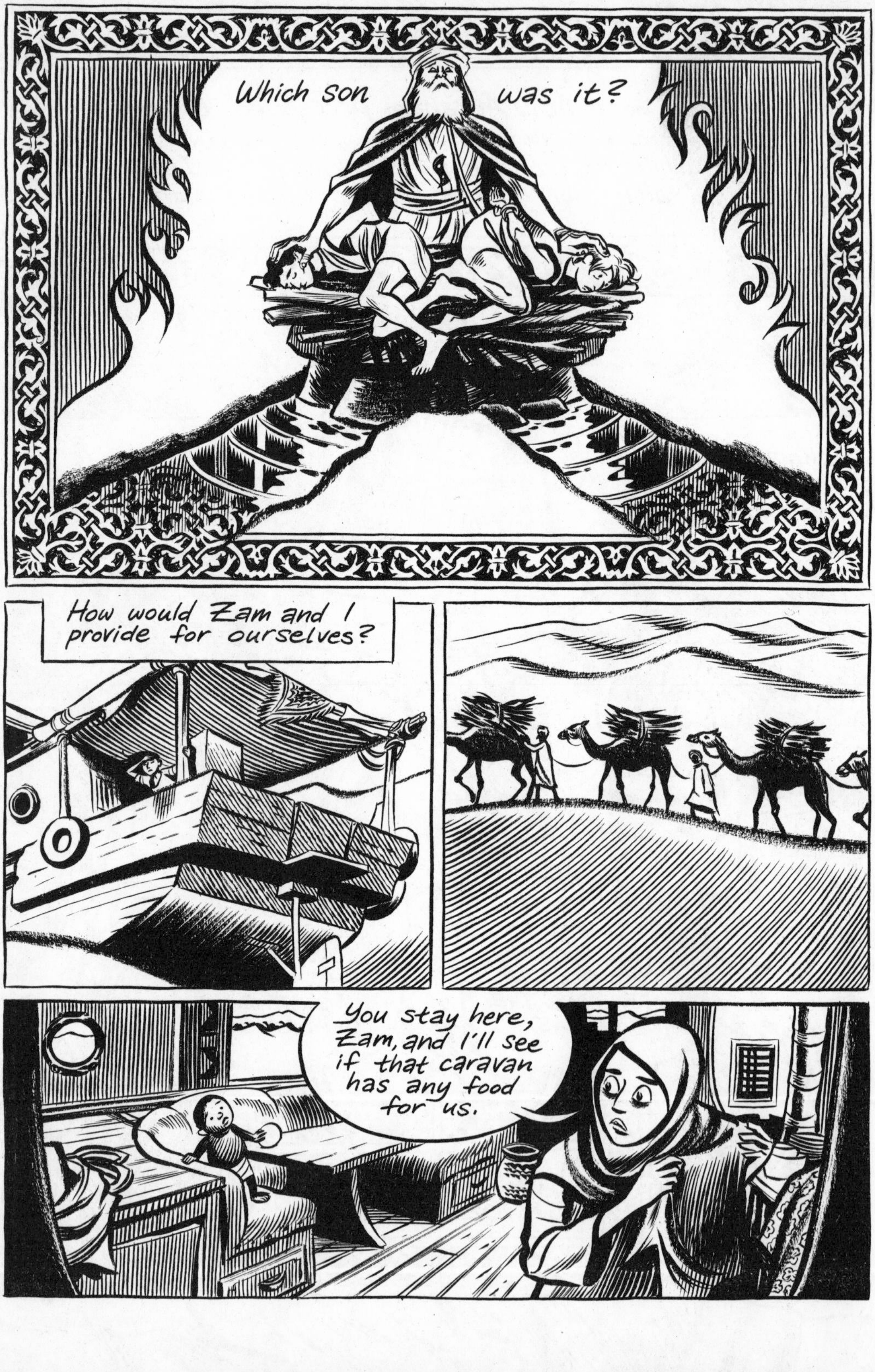
Which son was it?
How would Zam and I provide for ourselves?
You stay here, Zam, and I'll see if that caravan has any food for us.

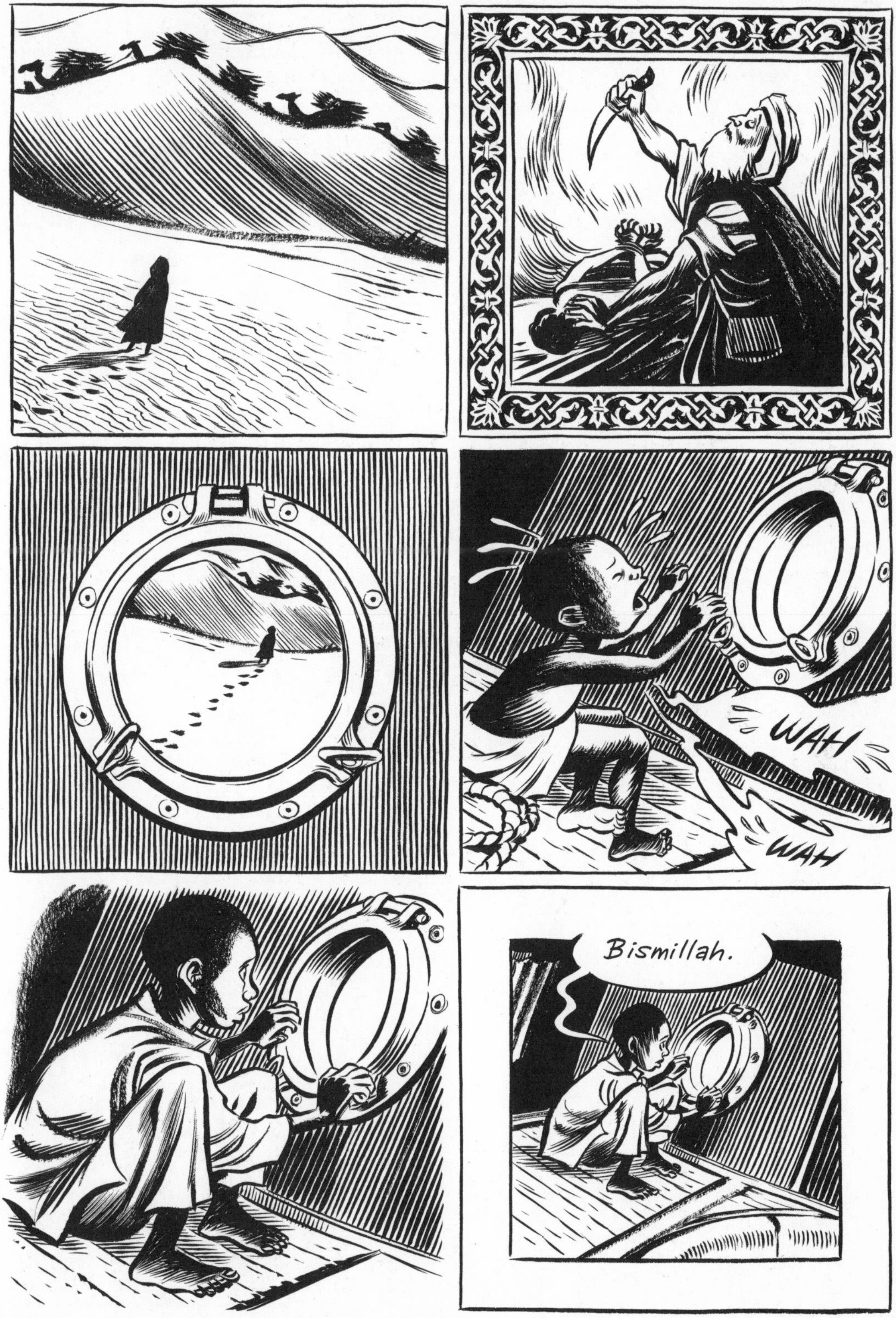
WAH
WAH
Bismillah.

د	ط	ب
ج	ه	ز
ح	ا	و

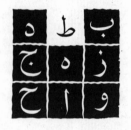

VEILS of DARKNESS

ظلمات ثلاث

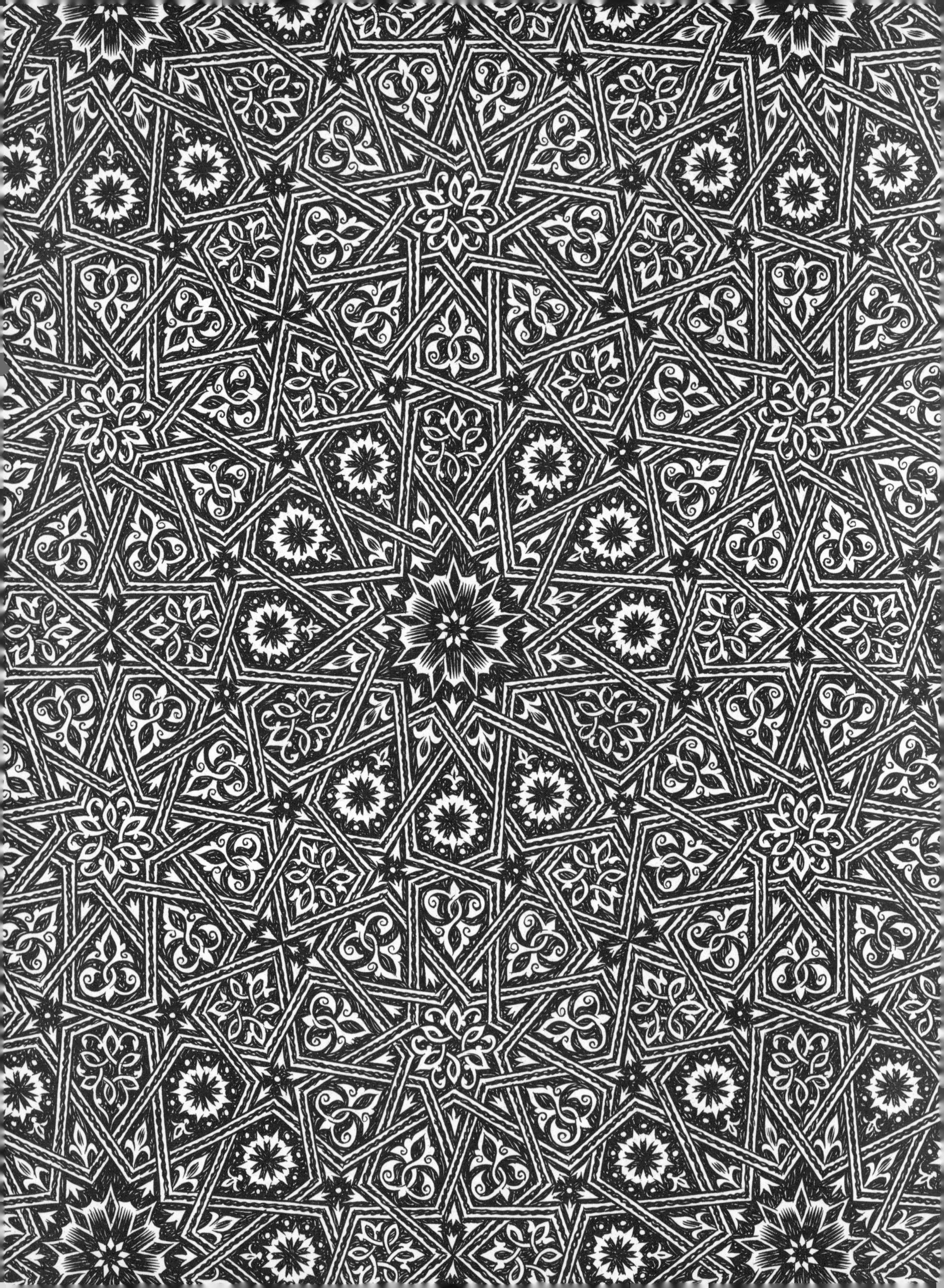

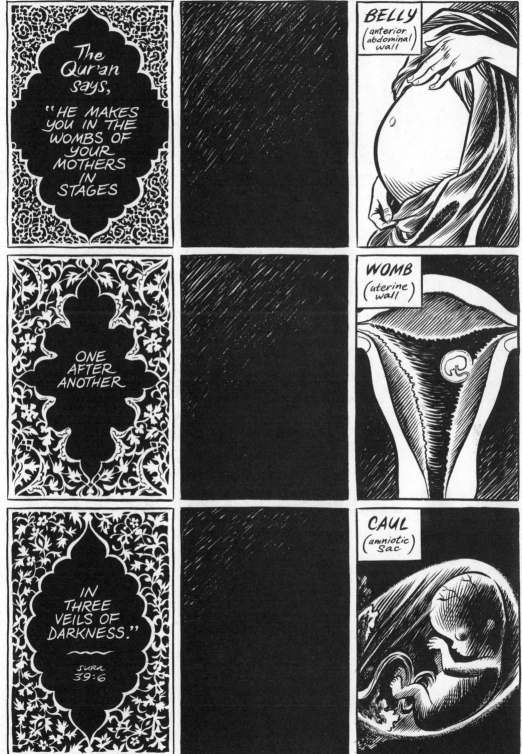

The Qur'an says,

"HE MAKES YOU IN THE WOMBS OF YOUR MOTHERS IN STAGES

ONE AFTER ANOTHER

IN THREE VEILS OF DARKNESS."

SURA 39:6

BELLY (anterior abdominal) wall

WOMB (uterine wall)

CAUL (amniotic) sac

53

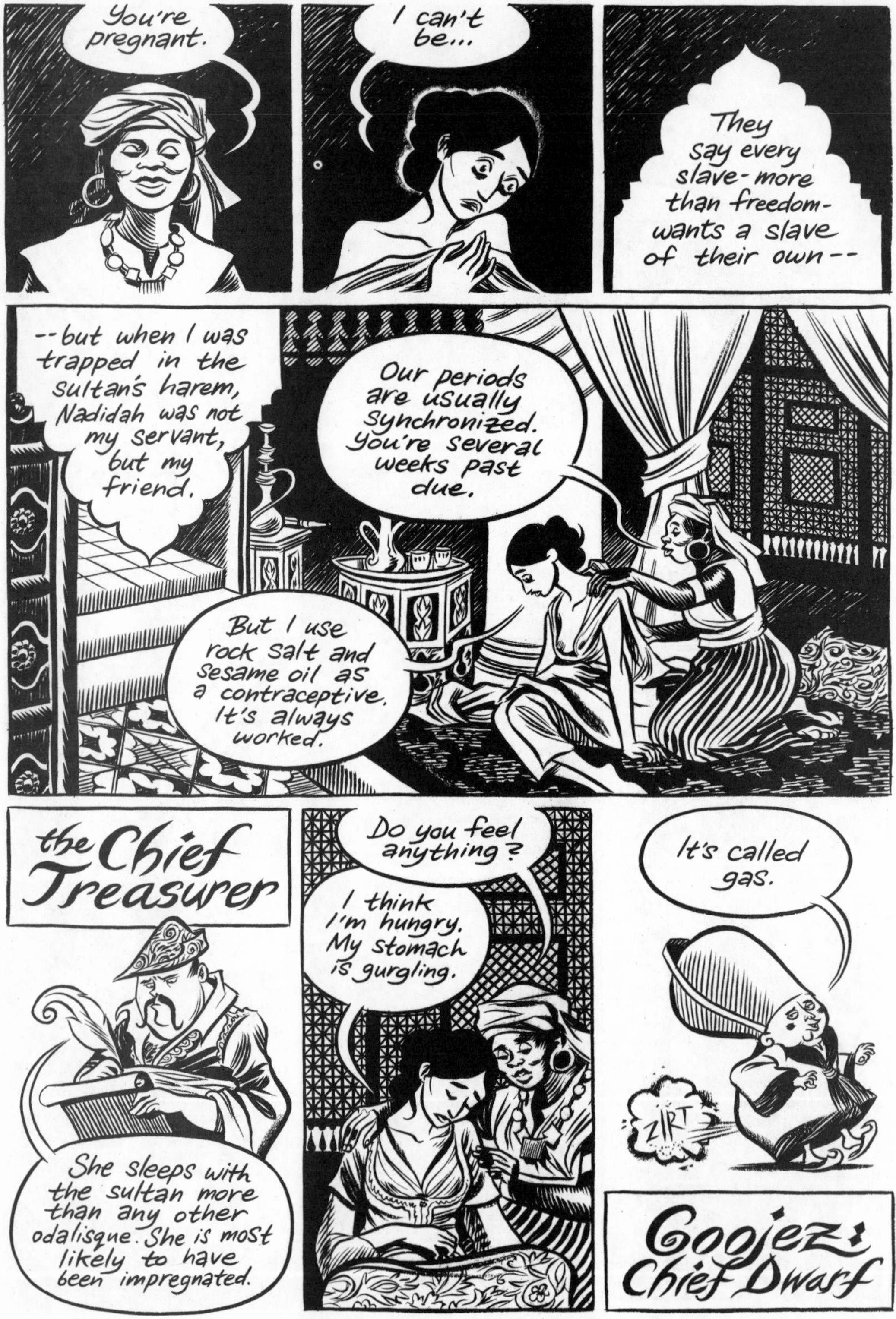
You're pregnant.
I can't be...
They say every slave- more than freedom- wants a slave of their own--
--but when I was trapped in the sultan's harem, Nadidah was not my servant, but my friend.
Our periods are usually synchronized. You're several weeks past due.
But I use rock salt and sesame oil as a contraceptive. It's always worked.
the Chief Treasurer
She sleeps with the sultan more than any other odalisque. She is most likely to have been impregnated.
Do you feel anything?
I think I'm hungry. My stomach is gurgling.
It's called gas.
ZIRT
Goojez: Chief Dwarf

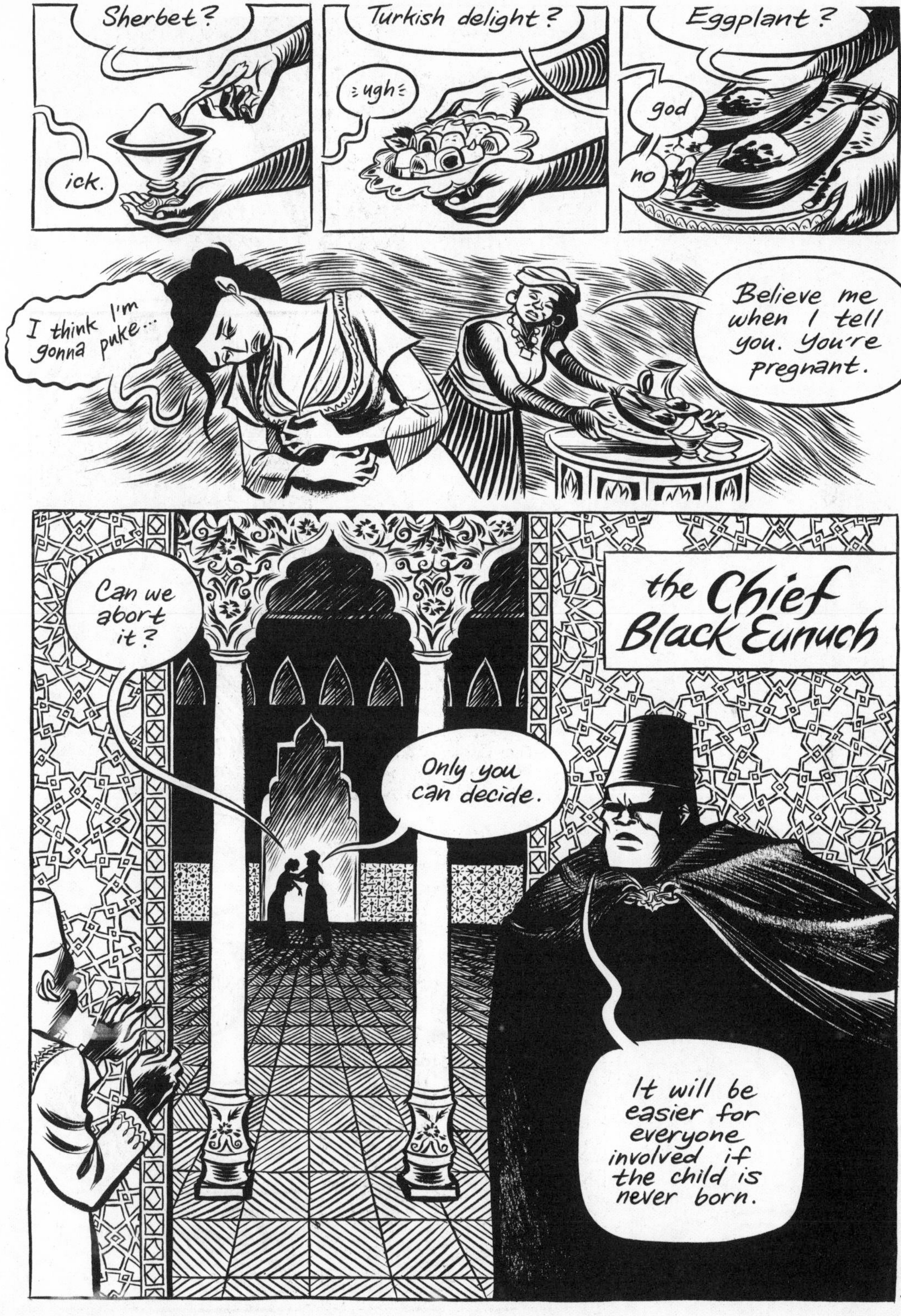
Sherbet?
ick.
Turkish delight?
ugh
Eggplant?
god
no
I think I'm gonna puke...
Believe me when I tell you. You're pregnant.
the Chief Black Eunuch
Can we abort it?
Only you can decide.
It will be easier for everyone involved if the child is never born.

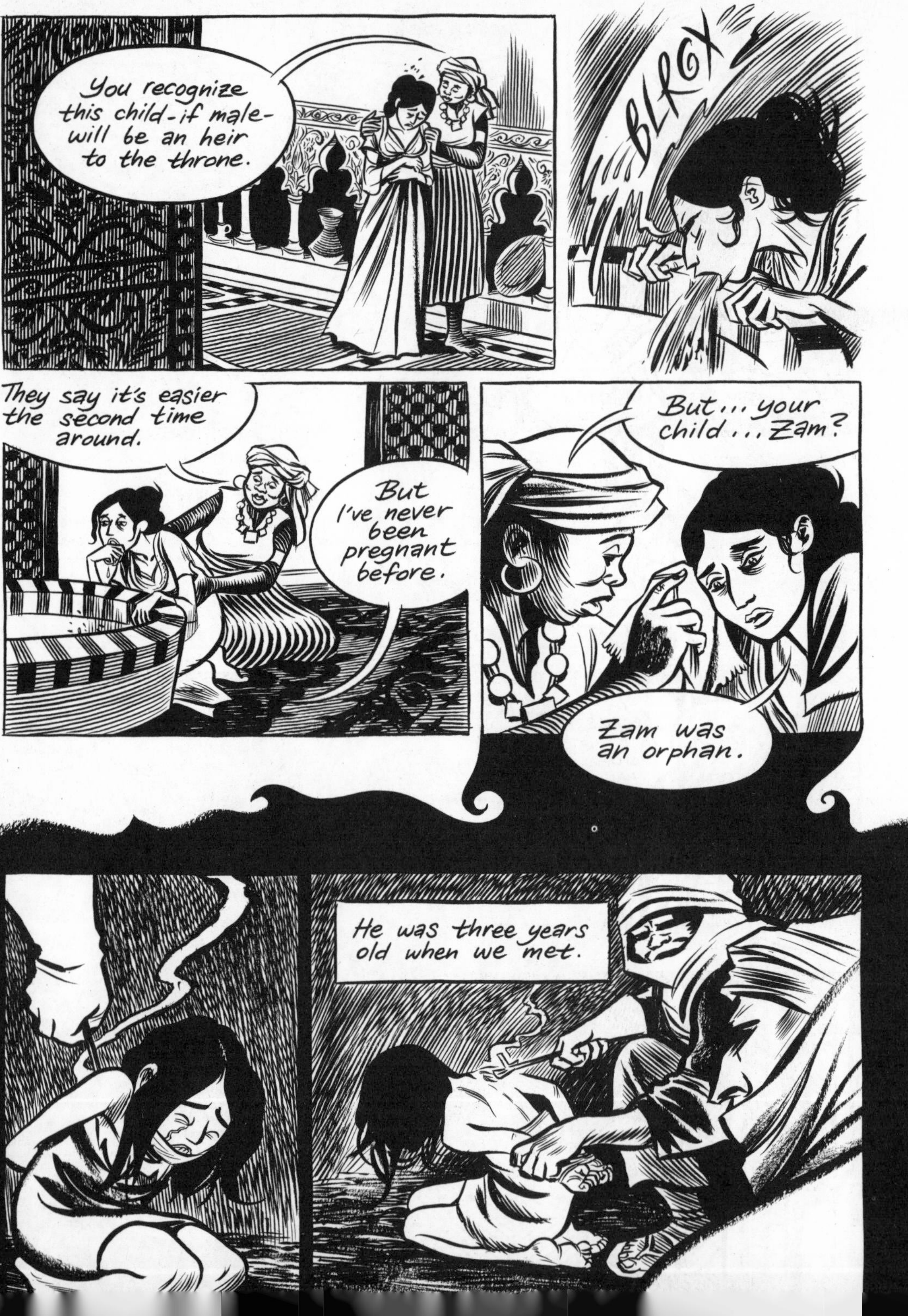
You recognize this child-if male-will be an heir to the throne.
BLRGX
They say it's easier the second time around.
But I've never been pregnant before.
But... your child... Zam?
Zam was an orphan.
He was three years old when we met.

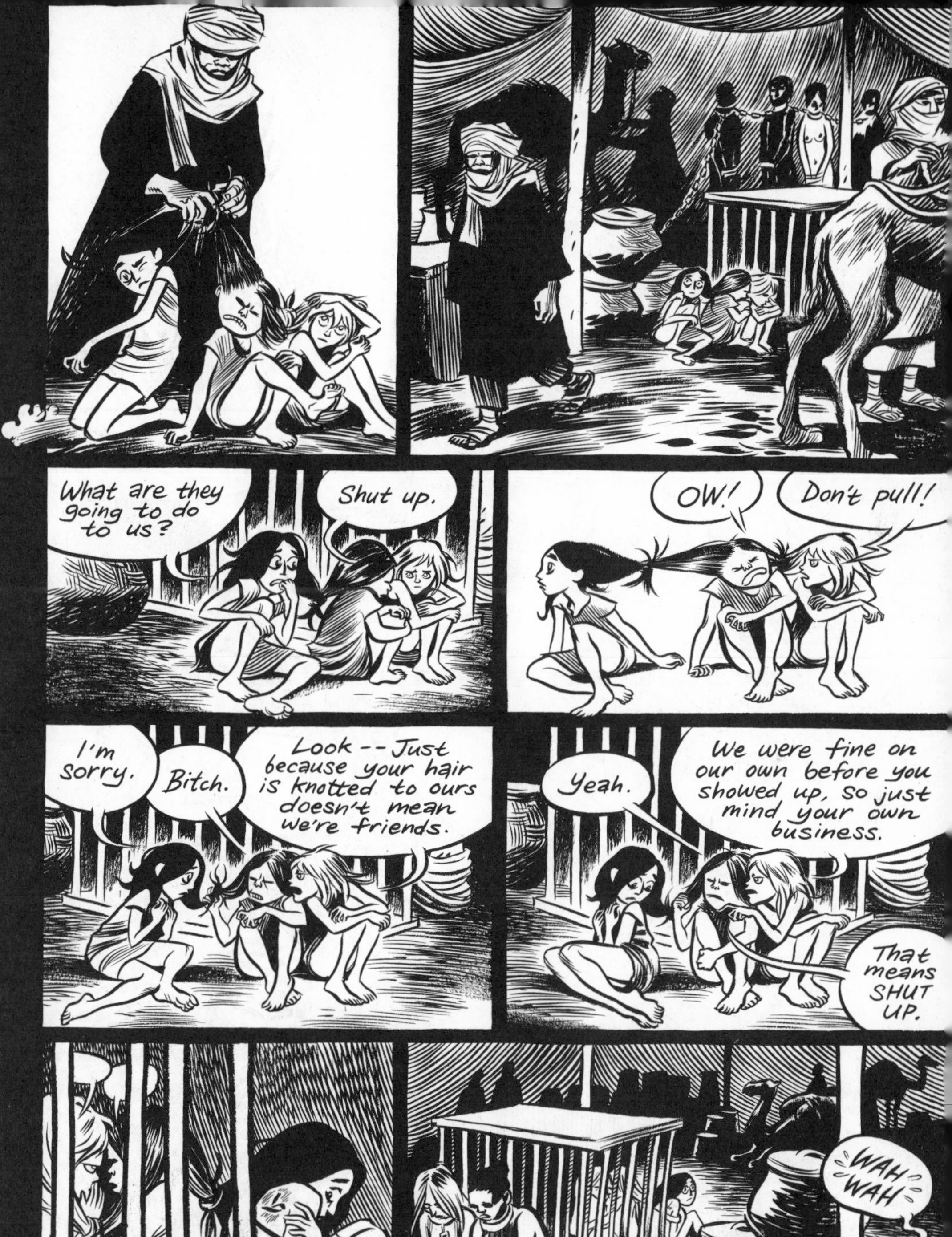
What are they going to do to us?
Shut up.
OW!
Don't pull!
I'm sorry.
Bitch.
Look -- Just because your hair is knotted to ours doesn't mean we're friends.
Yeah.
We were fine on our own before you showed up, so just mind your own business.
That means SHUT UP.
WAH WAH

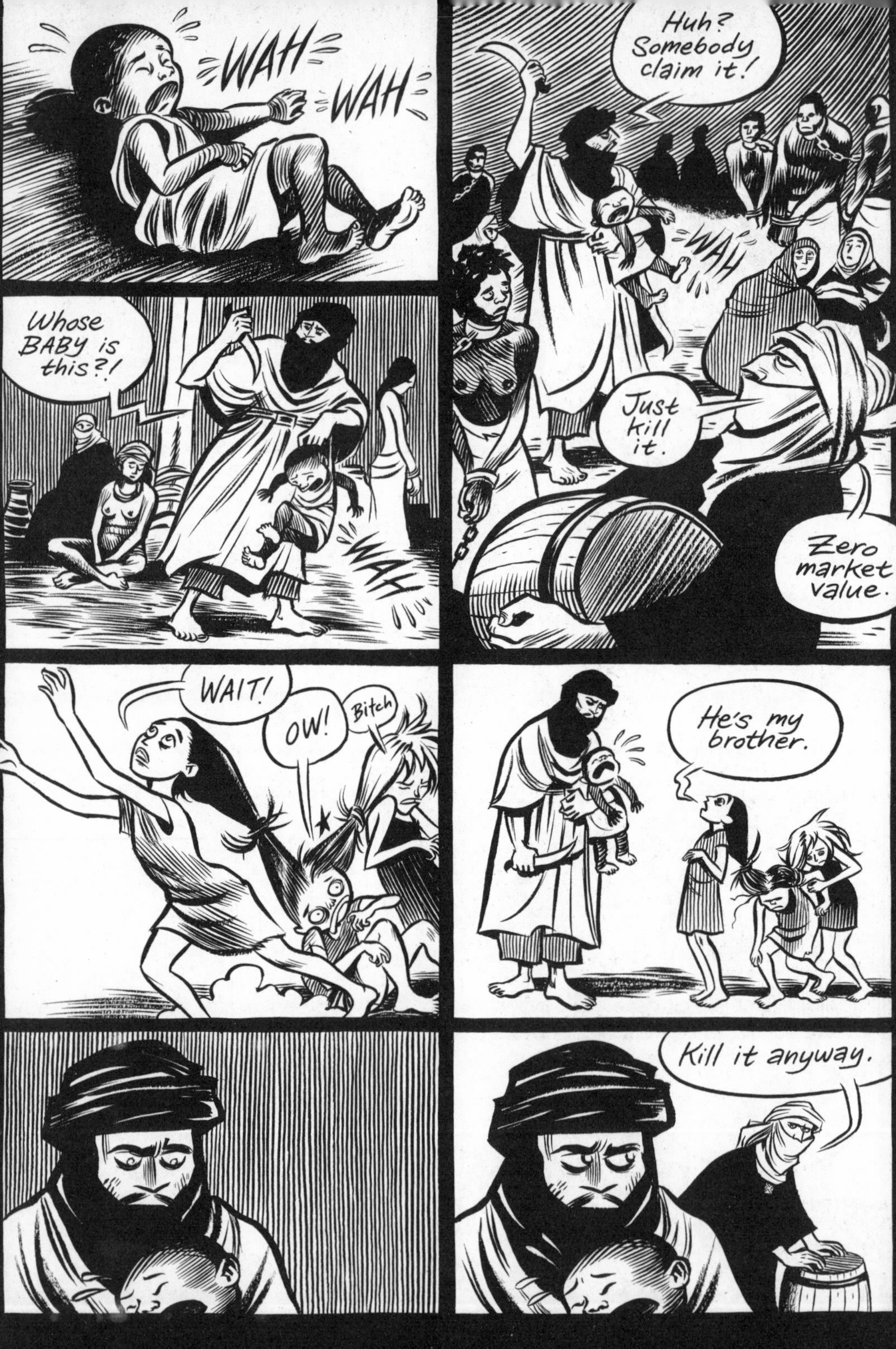
WAH
WAH
Whose BABY is this?!
WAH
Huh? Somebody claim it!
WAH
Just kill it.
Zero market value.
WAIT!
OW!
Bitch
He's my brother.
Kill it anyway.

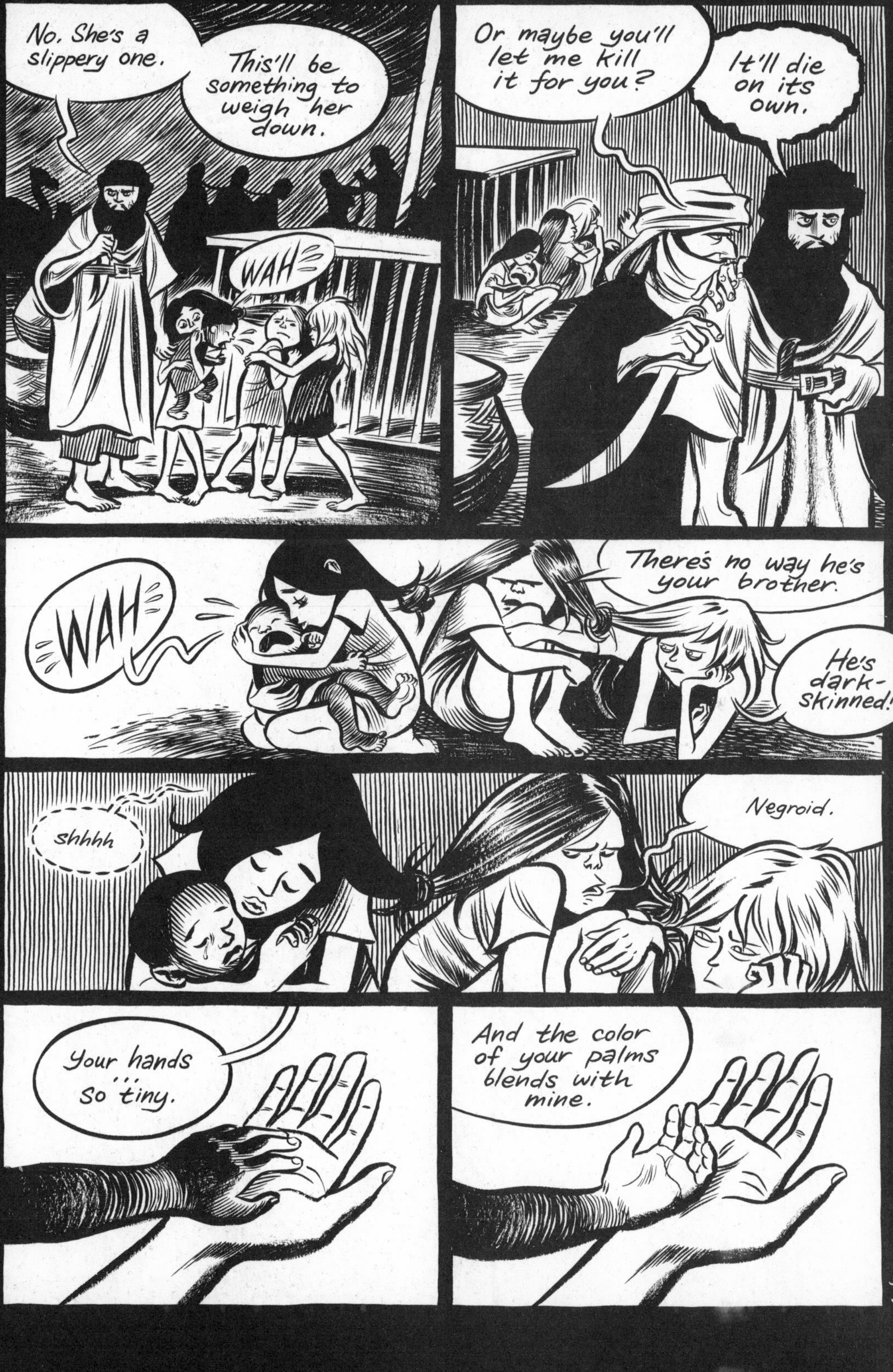

No. She's a slippery one.
This'll be something to weigh her down.
WAH
Or maybe you'll let me kill it for you?
It'll die on its own.
WAH
There's no way he's your brother.
He's dark-skinned!
shhhh
Negroid.
Your hands ... so tiny.
And the color of your palms blends with mine.

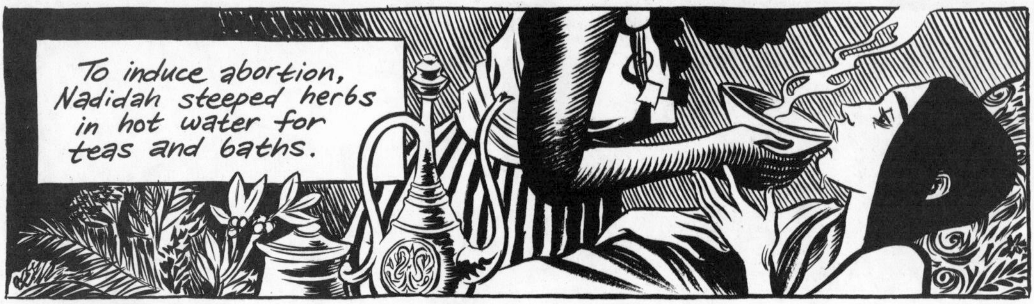
To induce abortion, Nadidah steeped herbs in hot water for teas and baths.

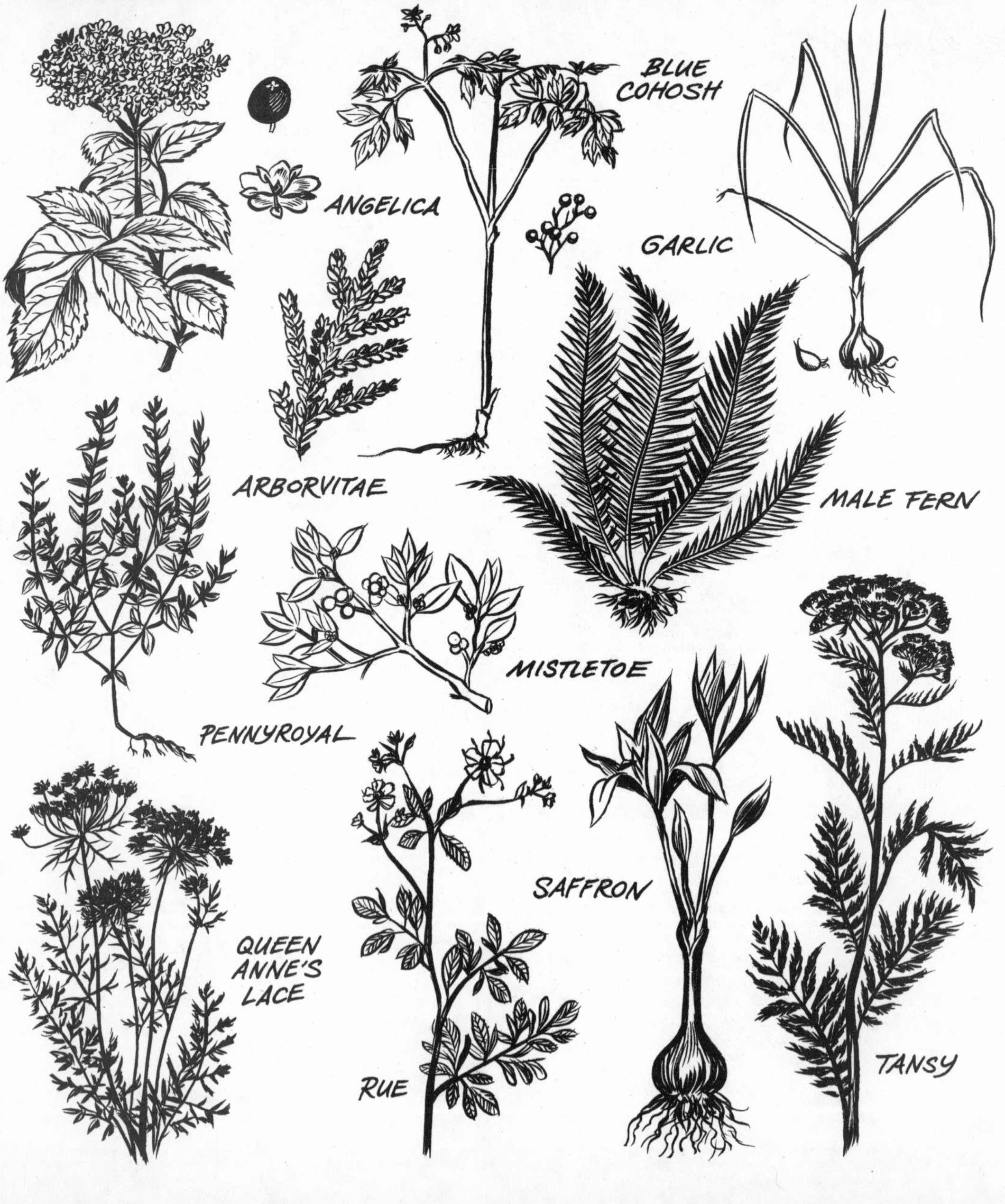
BLUE COHOSH
ANGELICA
GARLIC
ARBORVITAE
MALE FERN
MISTLETOE
PENNYROYAL
SAFFRON
QUEEN ANNE'S LACE
TANSY
RUE

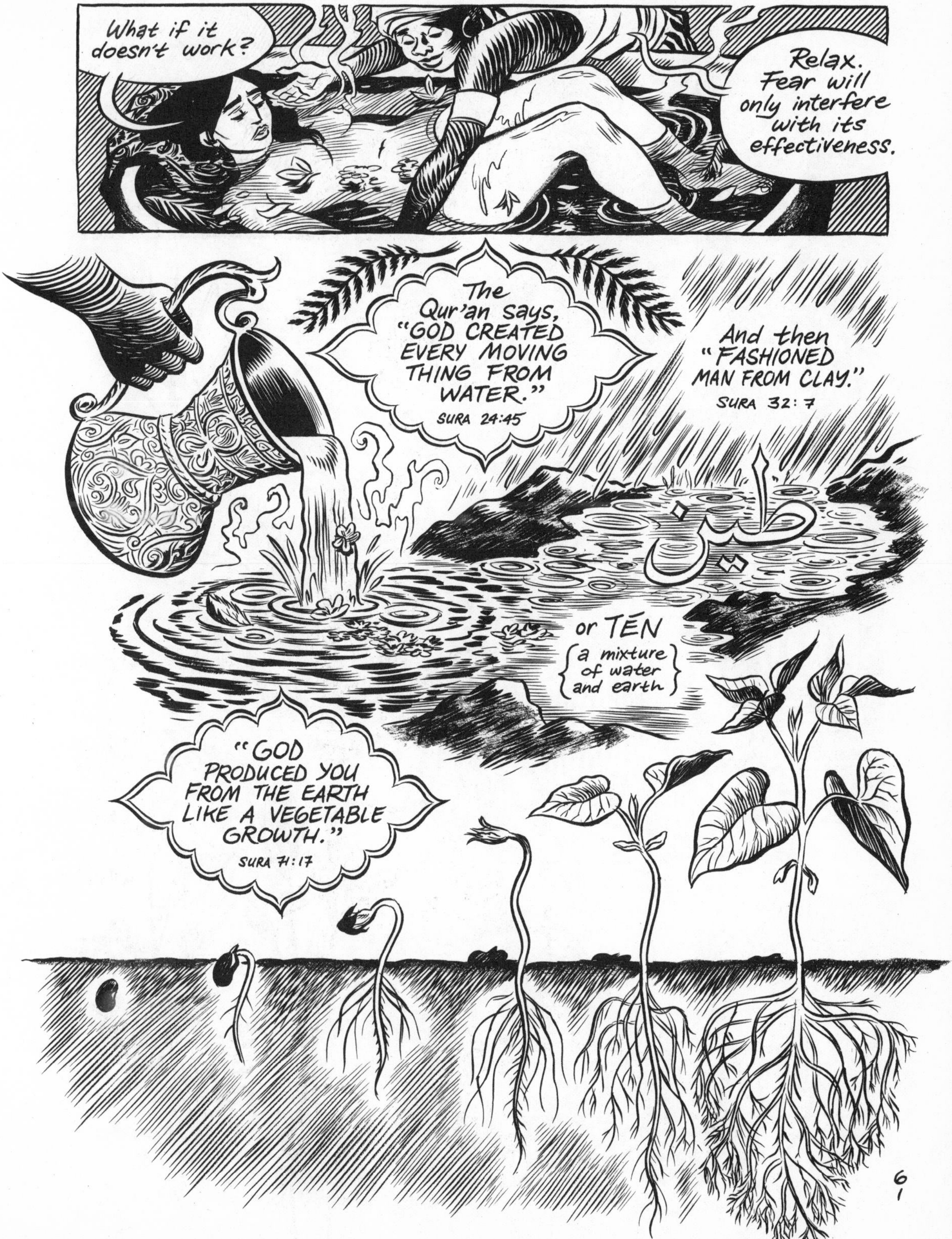
What if it doesn't work?
Relax. Fear will only interfere with its effectiveness.
The Qur'an says, "GOD CREATED EVERY MOVING THING FROM WATER." SURA 24:45
And then "FASHIONED MAN FROM CLAY." SURA 32: 7
طين
or TÉN {a mixture of water and earth}
"GOD PRODUCED YOU FROM THE EARTH LIKE A VEGETABLE GROWTH." SURA 71:17

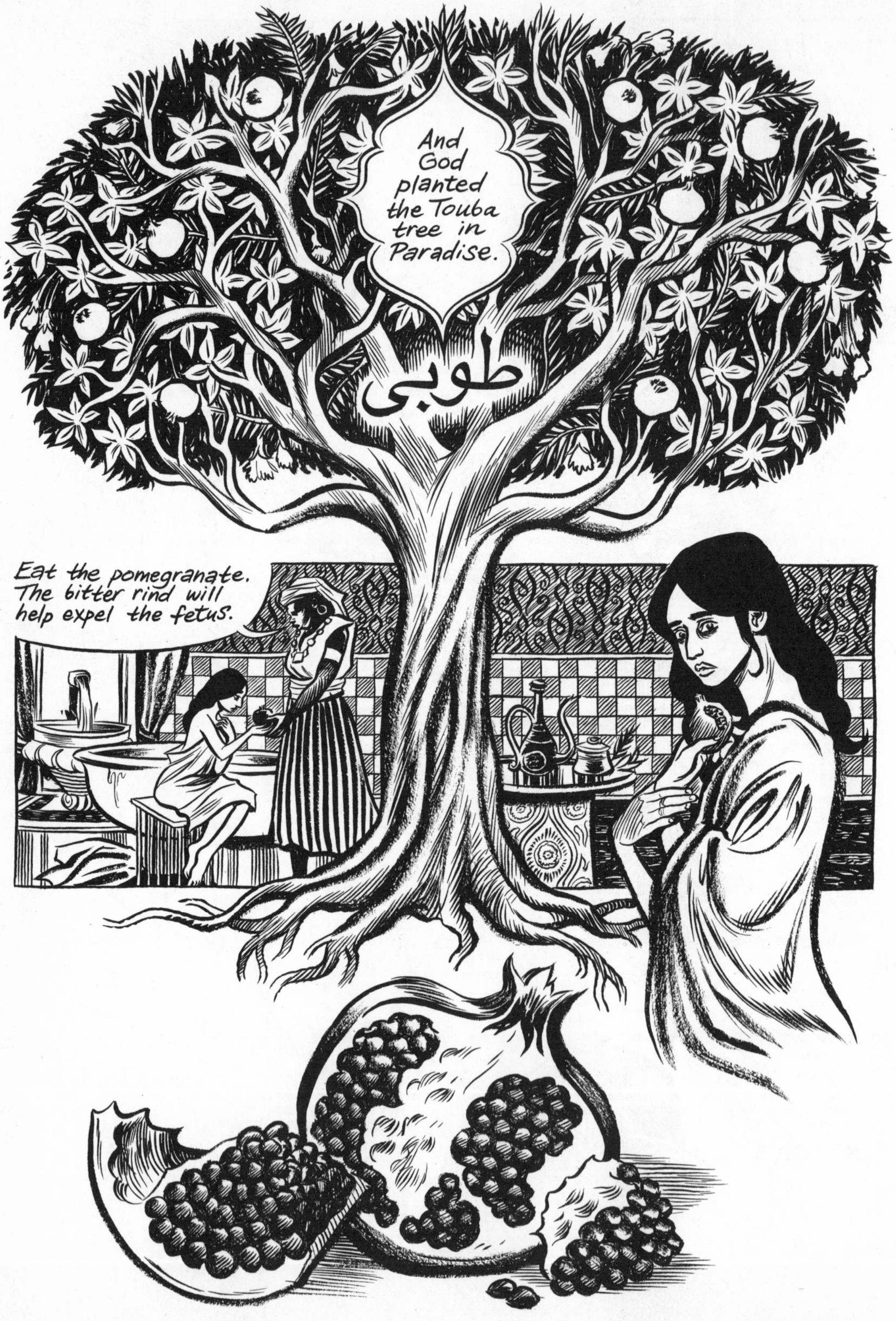
And God planted the Touba tree in Paradise.
طوبى
Eat the pomegranate. The bitter rind will help expel the fetus.

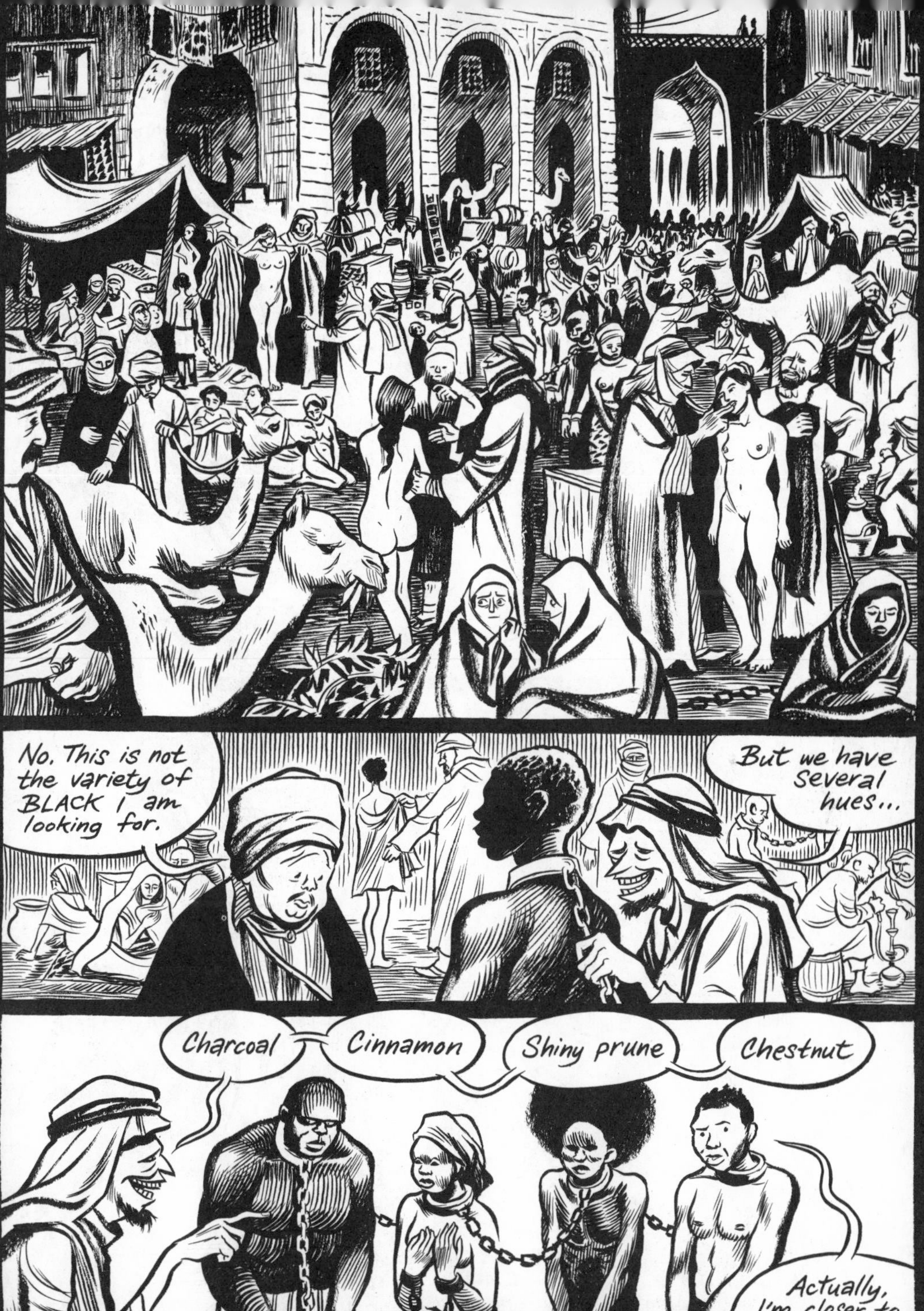
No. This is not the variety of BLACK I am looking for.
But we have several hues...
Charcoal
Cinnamon
Shiny prune
Chestnut
Actually, I'm closer to walnut.

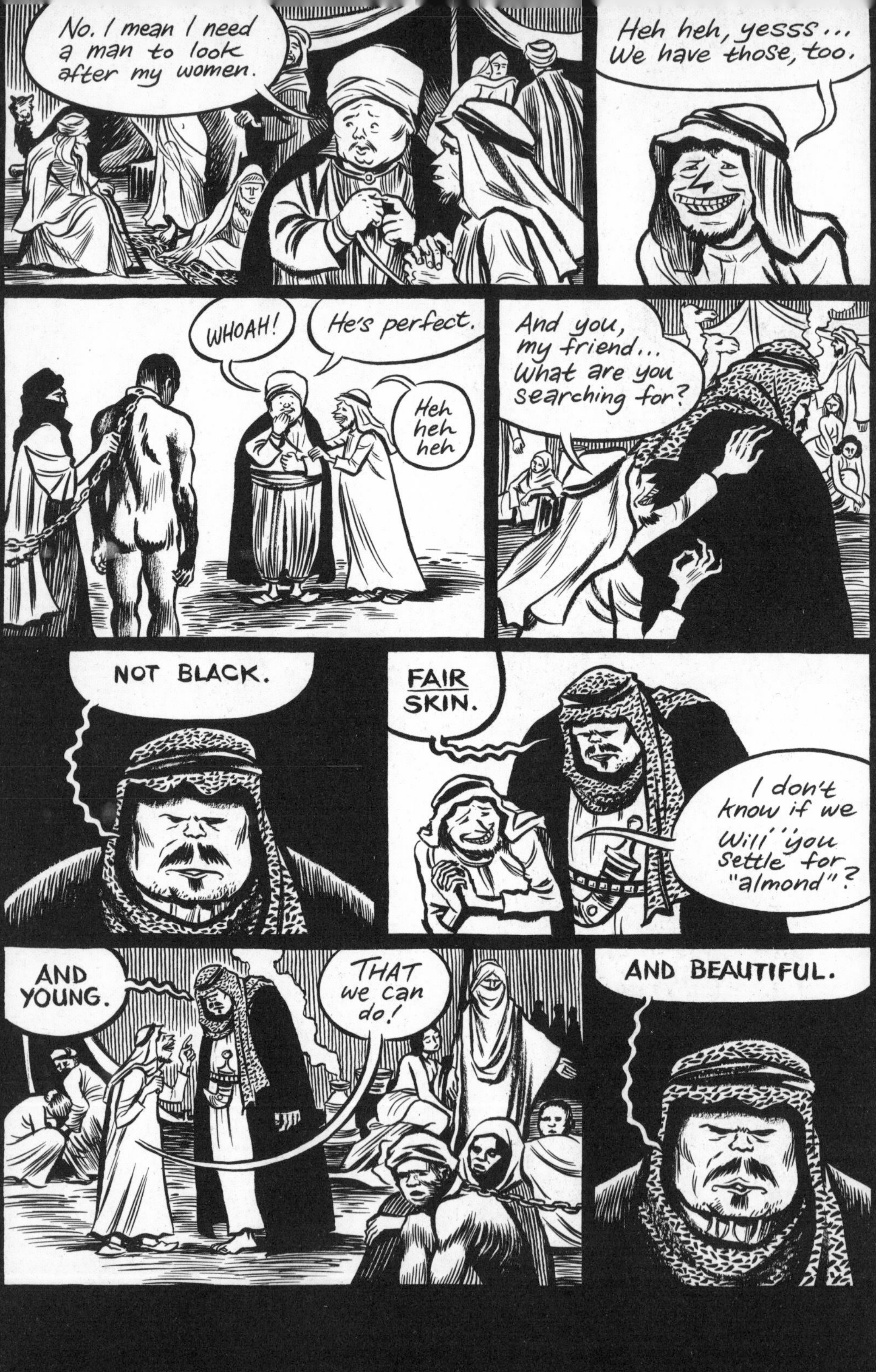
No. I mean I need a man to look after my women.
Heh heh, yesss... We have those, too.
WHOAH!
He's perfect.
Heh heh heh
And you, my friend... What are you searching for?
NOT BLACK.
FAIR SKIN.
I don't know if we
Will you settle for "almond"?
AND YOUNG.
THAT we can do!
AND BEAUTIFUL.

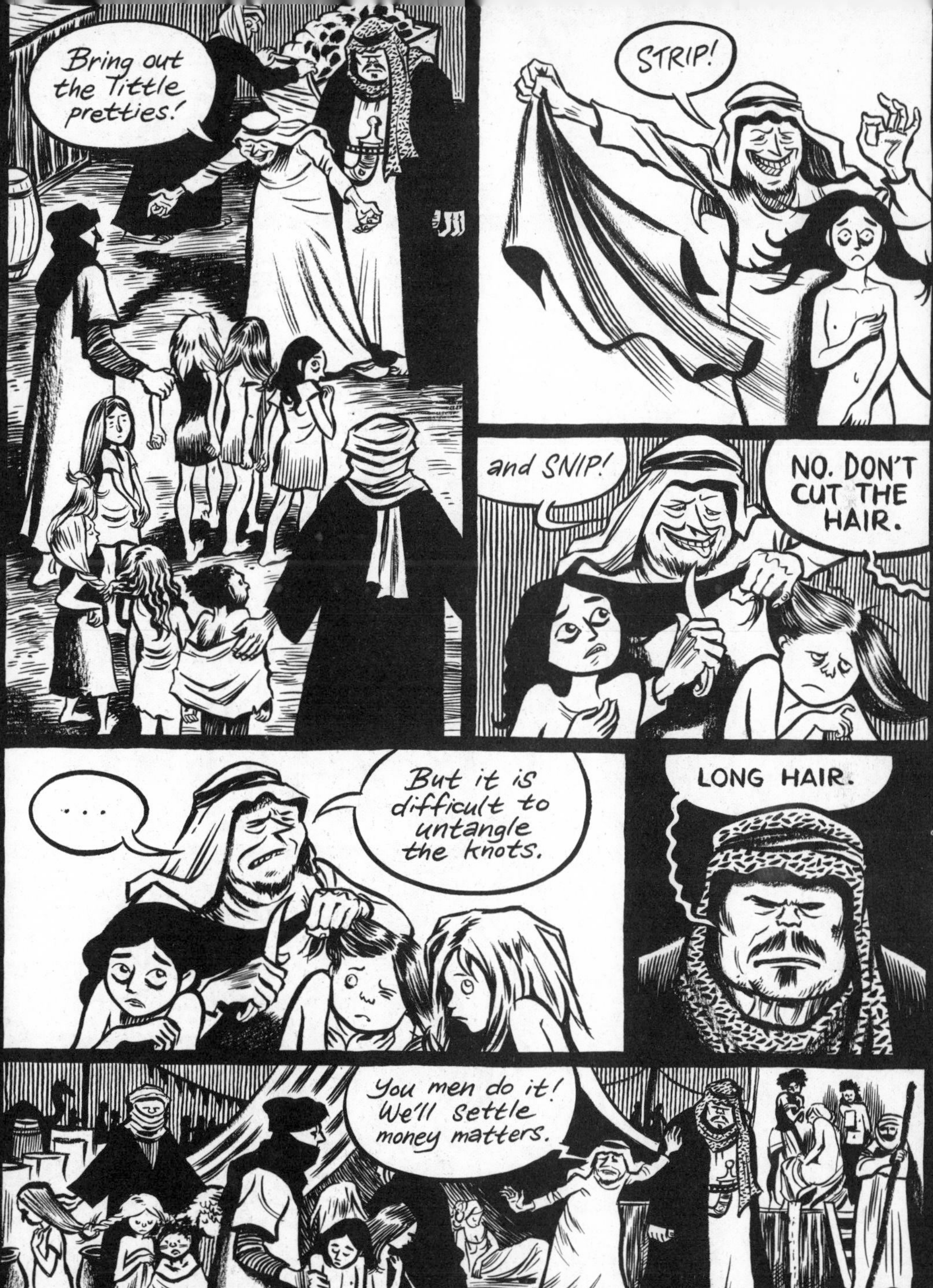
Bring out the little pretties!
STRIP!
and SNIP!
NO. DON'T CUT THE HAIR.
...
But it is difficult to untangle the knots.
LONG HAIR.
You men do it! We'll settle money matters.

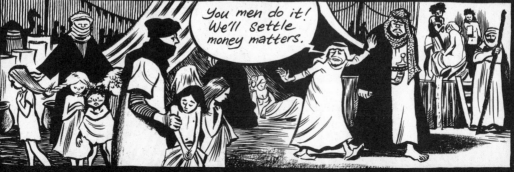

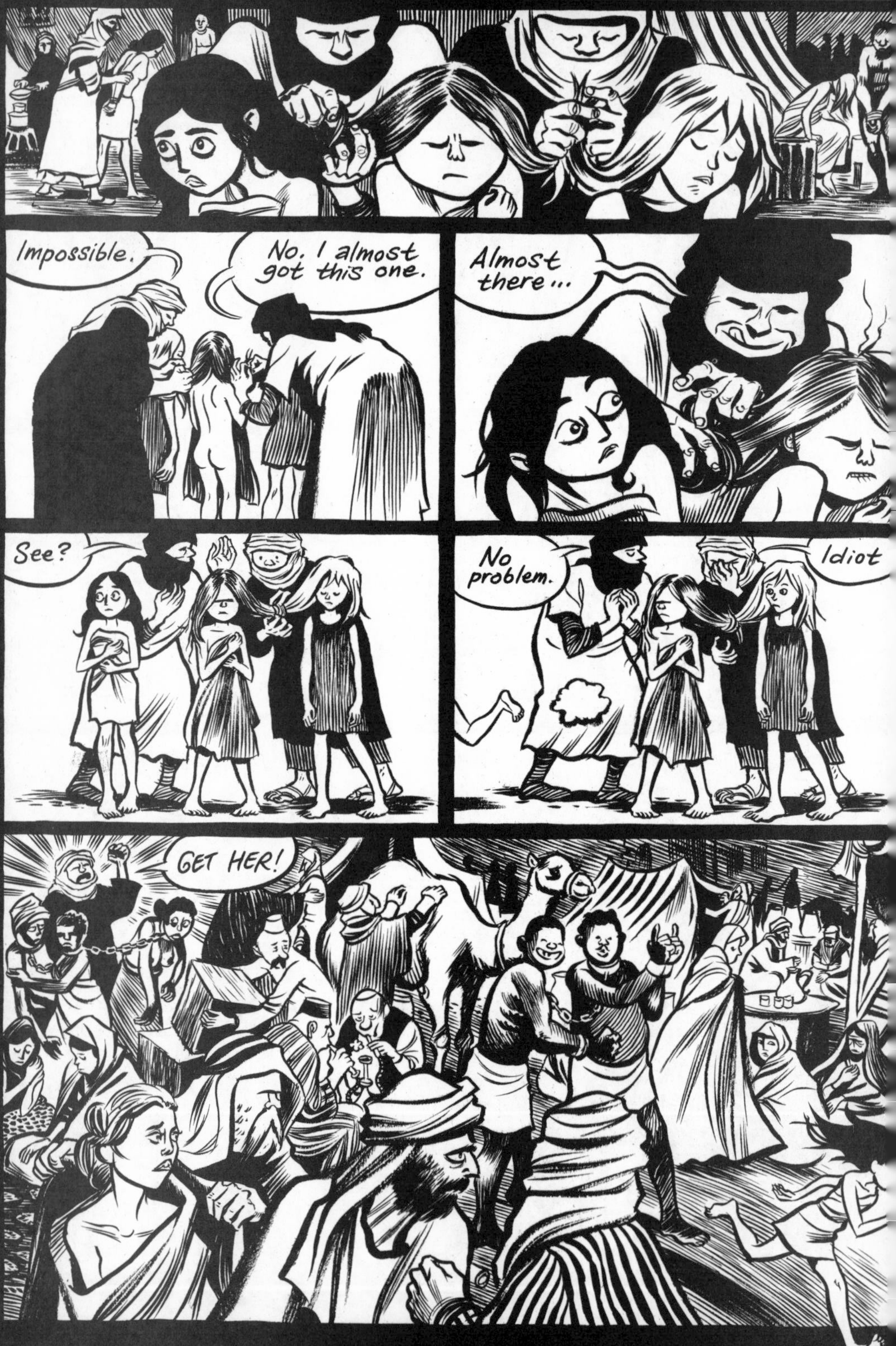

Impossible.
No. I almost got this one.
Almost there...
See?
No problem.
Idiot
GET HER!

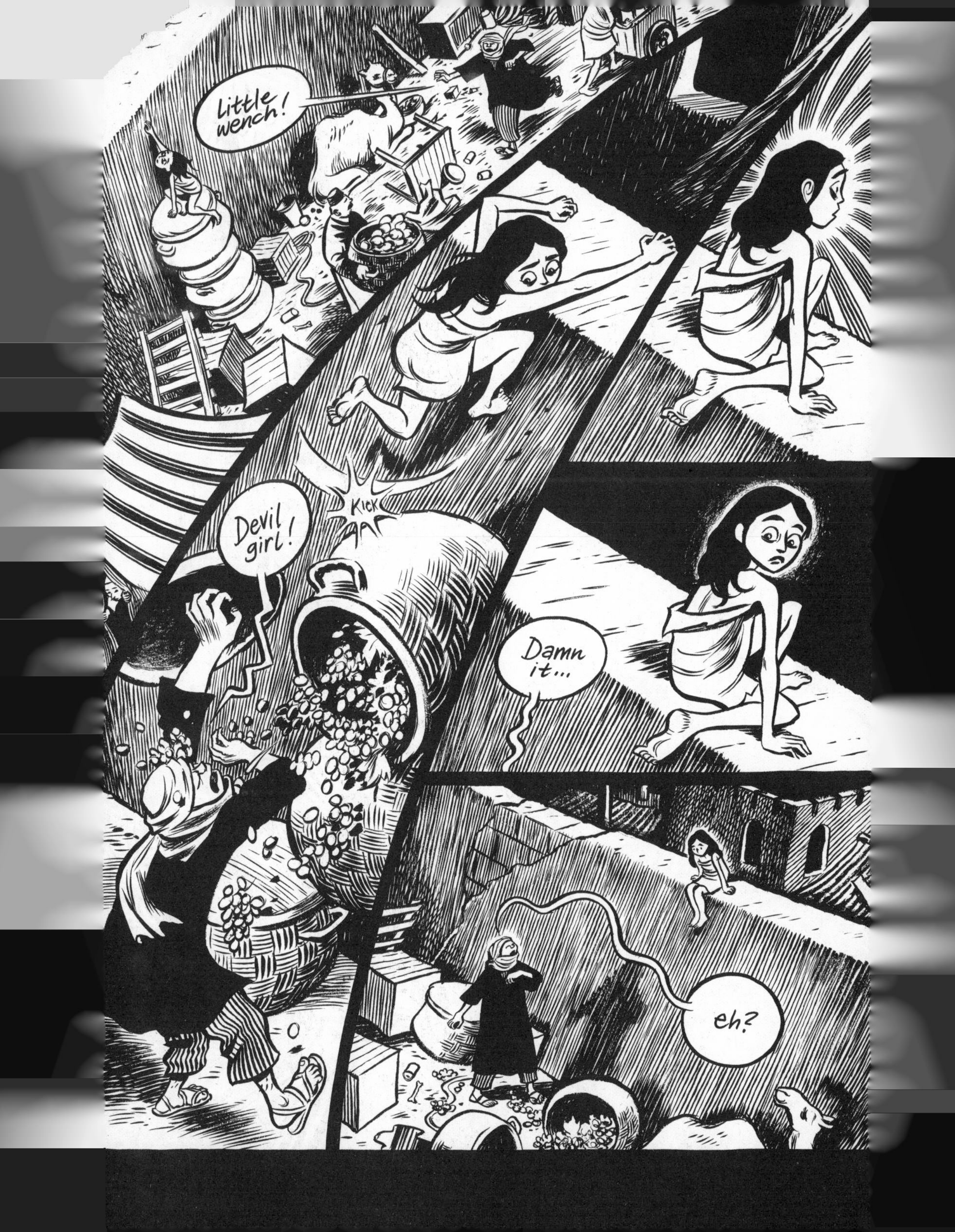
Little wench!
Devil girl!
KICK
Damn it...
eh?

So you are giving up?
Very wise choice ...
KRAK
The DEVIL is in you!
Catch that runt!

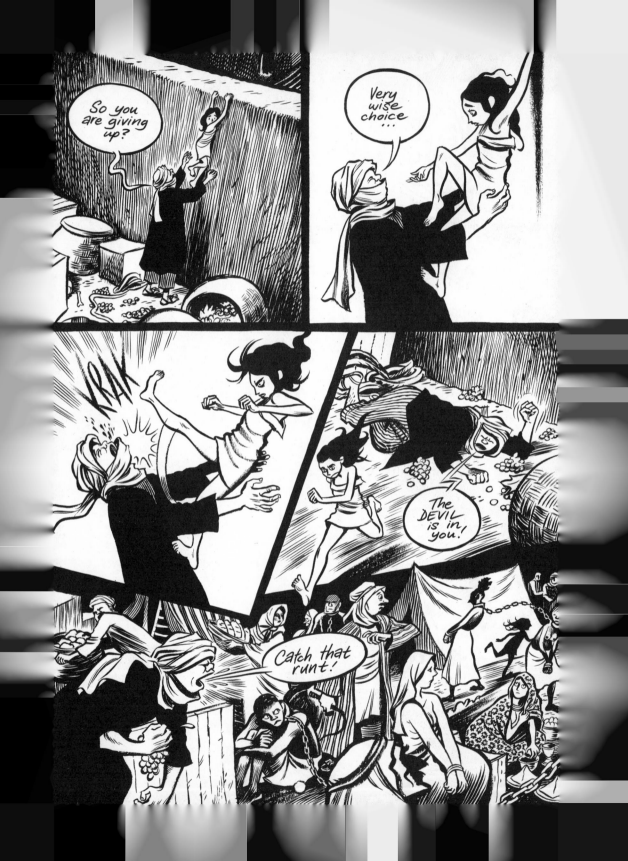

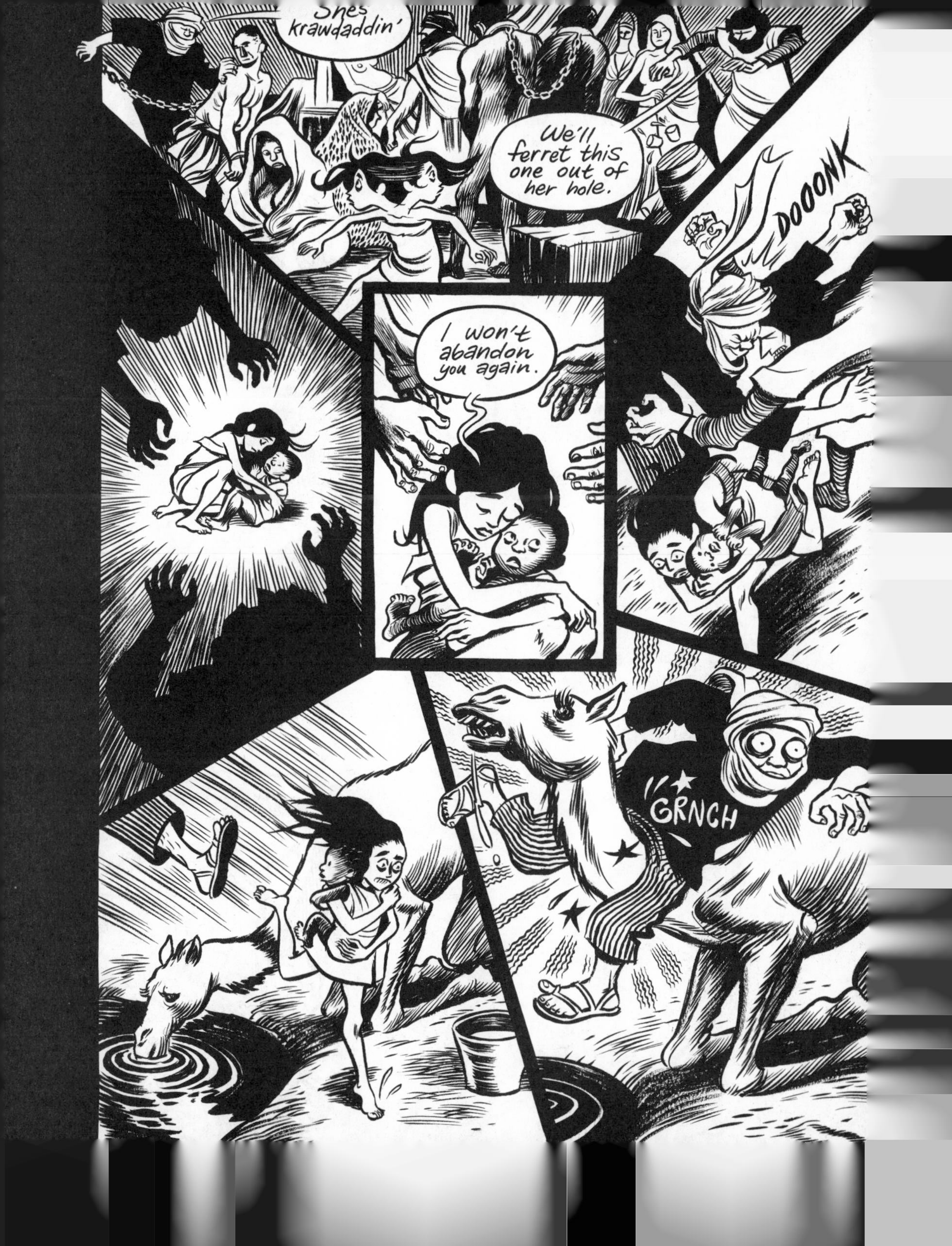
She's krawdaddin'
We'll ferret this one out of her hole.
DOOONK
I won't abandon you again.
GRNCH

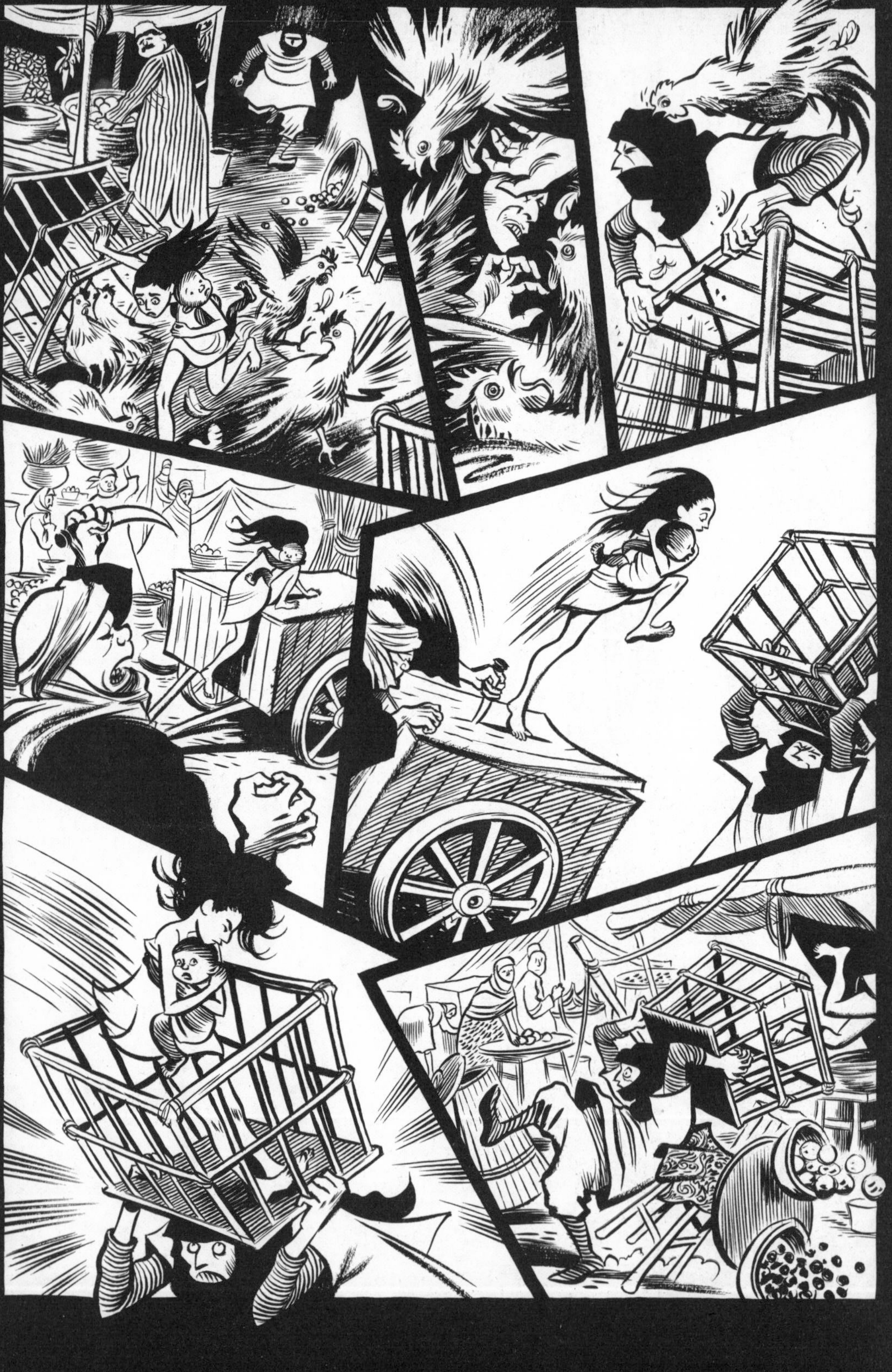

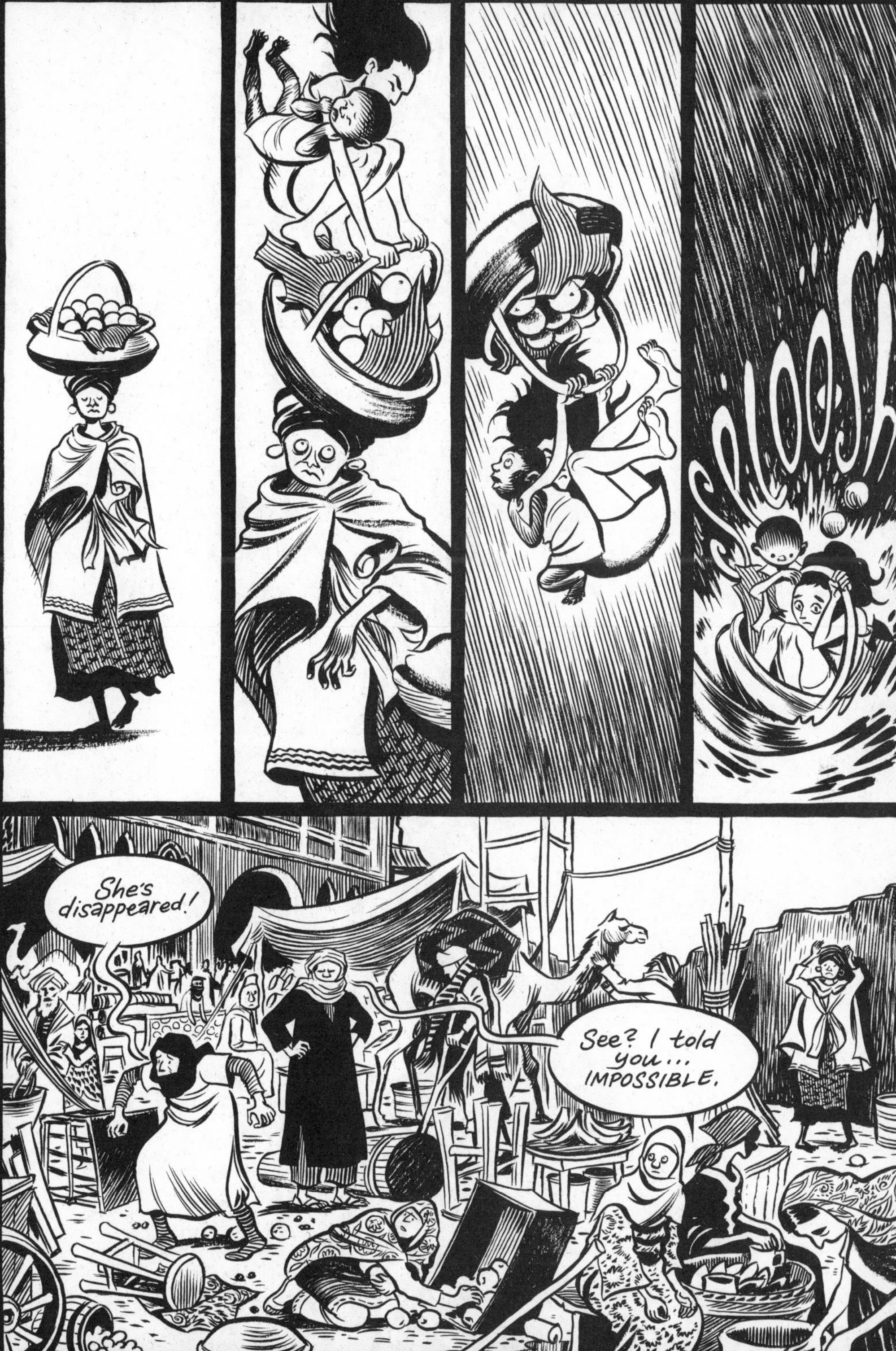
SPLOOSH!
She's disappeared!
See? I told you... IMPOSSIBLE.

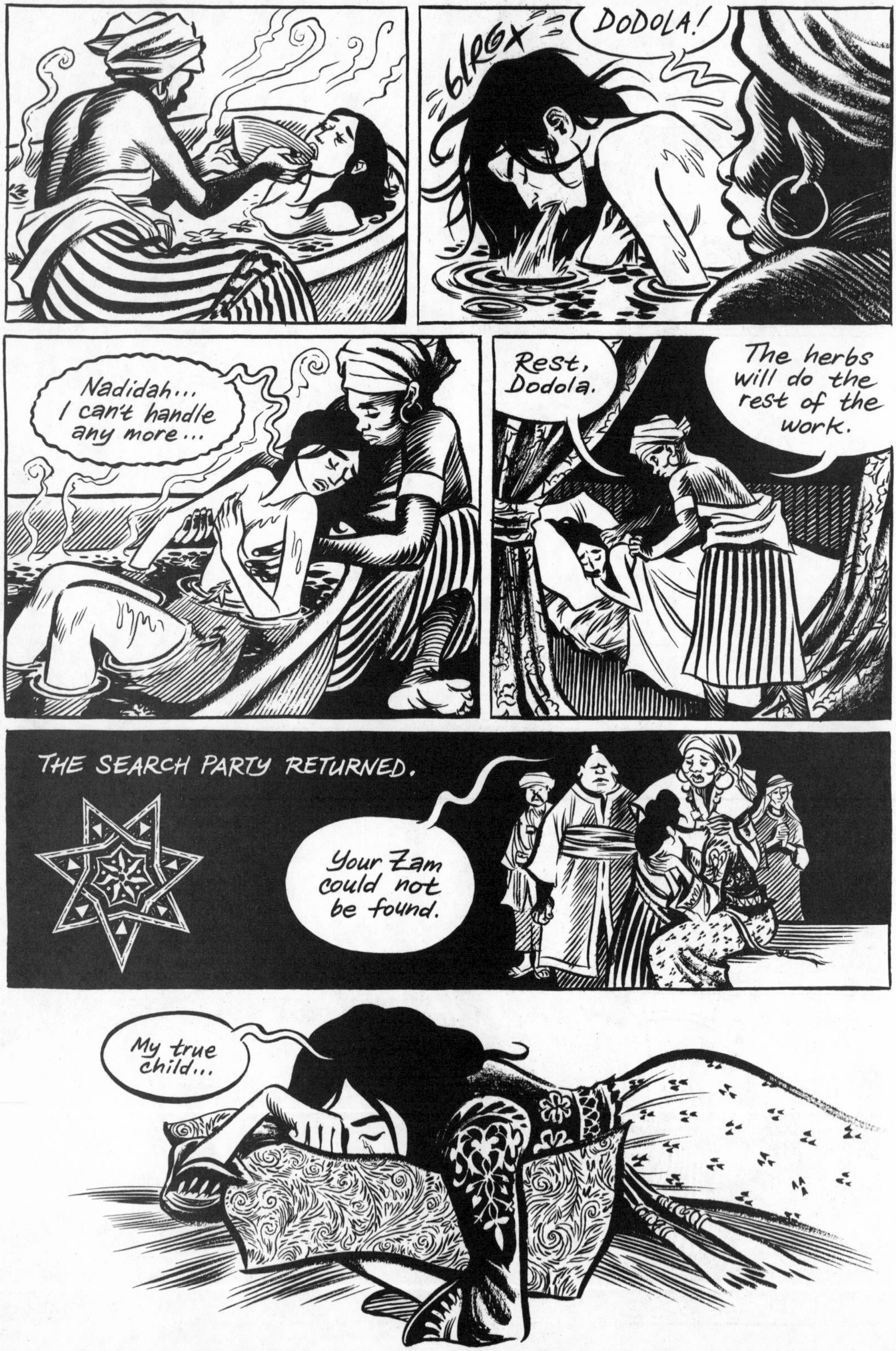

BLRGX
DODOLA!
Nadidah... I can't handle any more...
Rest, Dodola.
The herbs will do the rest of the work.
THE SEARCH PARTY RETURNED.
Your Zam could not be found.
My true child...

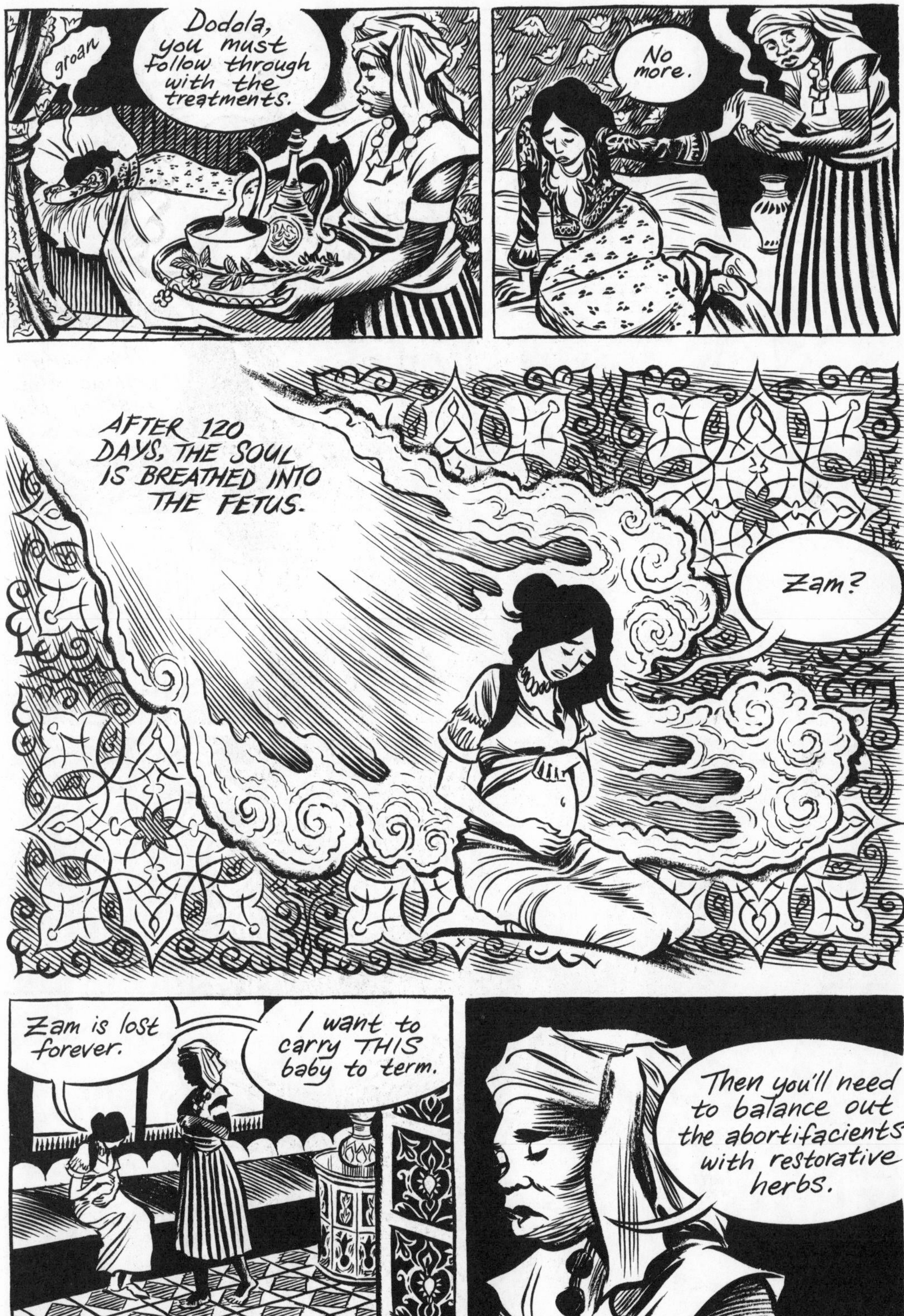
groan
Dodola, you must follow through with the treatments.
No more.
AFTER 120 DAYS, THE SOUL IS BREATHED INTO THE FETUS.
Zam?
Zam is lost forever.
I want to carry THIS baby to term.
Then you'll need to balance out the abortifacients with restorative herbs.

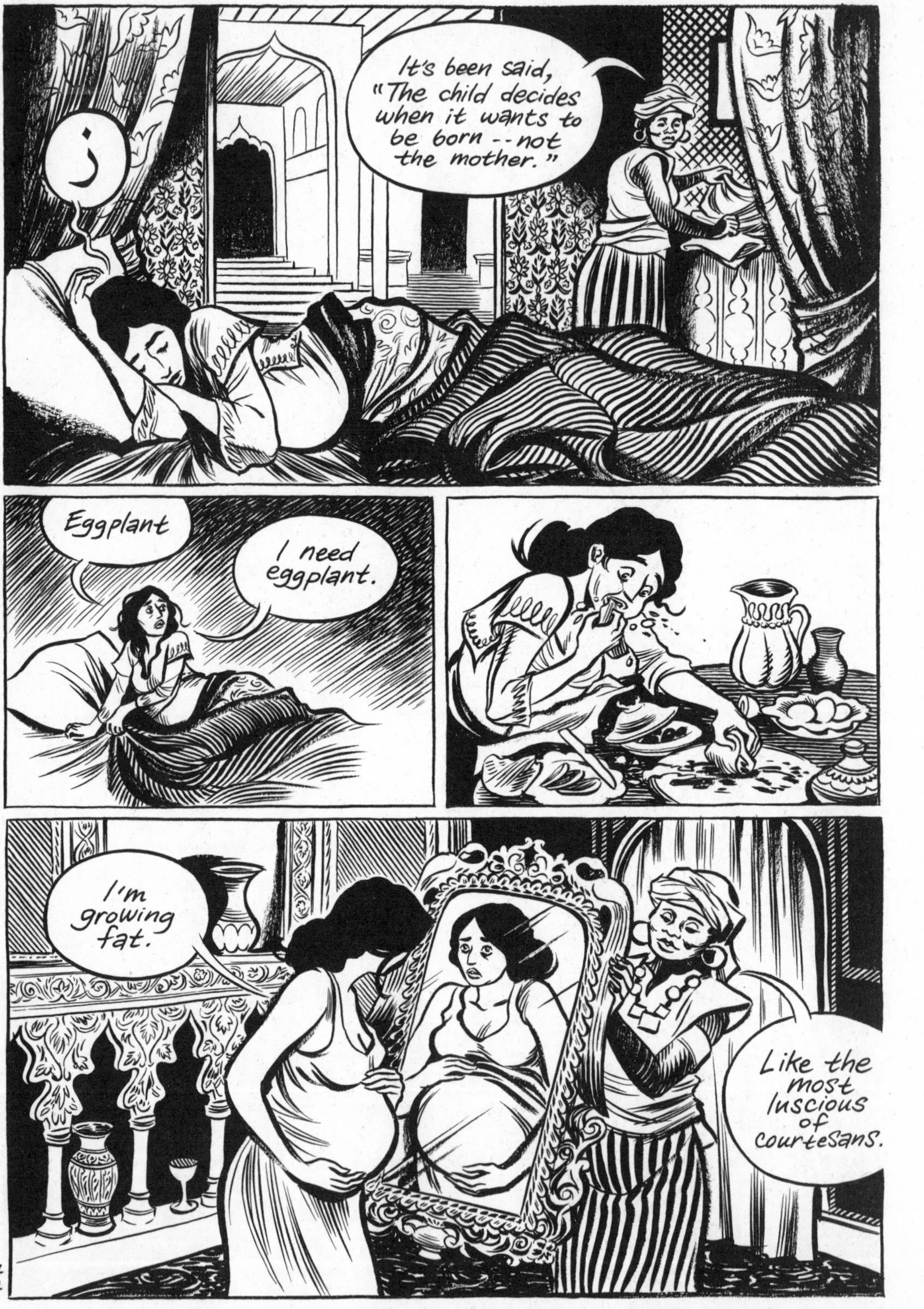
ز
It's been said, "The child decides when it wants to be born --not the mother."
Eggplant
I need eggplant.
I'm growing fat.
Like the most luscious of courtesans.

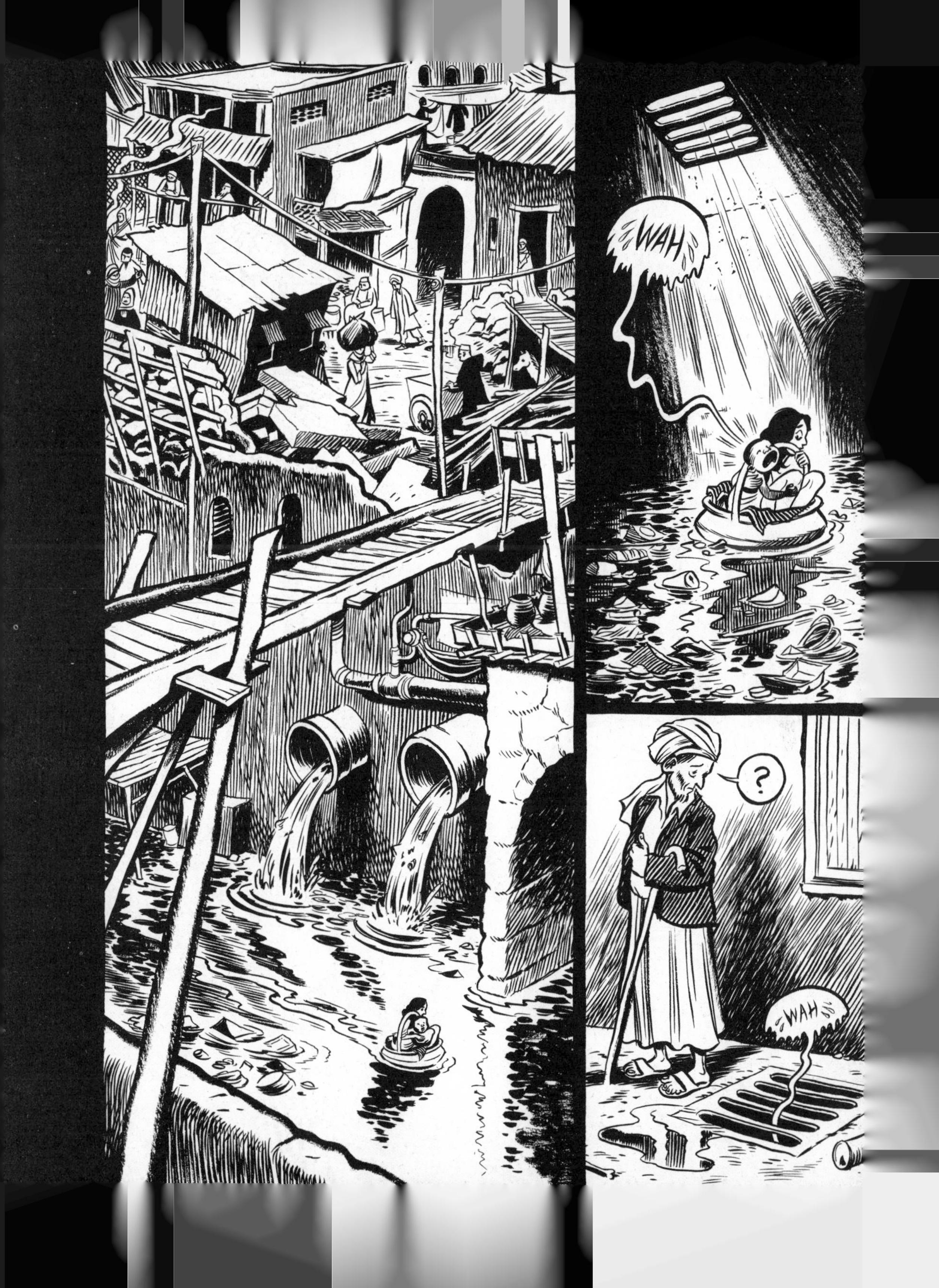
WAH
?
WAH

WAH
shhh... keep quiet.
Here. You're probably hungry.
WAH
GOMF
bLeh
WAH
WAH
MMMf
We don't want to be heard, little one.

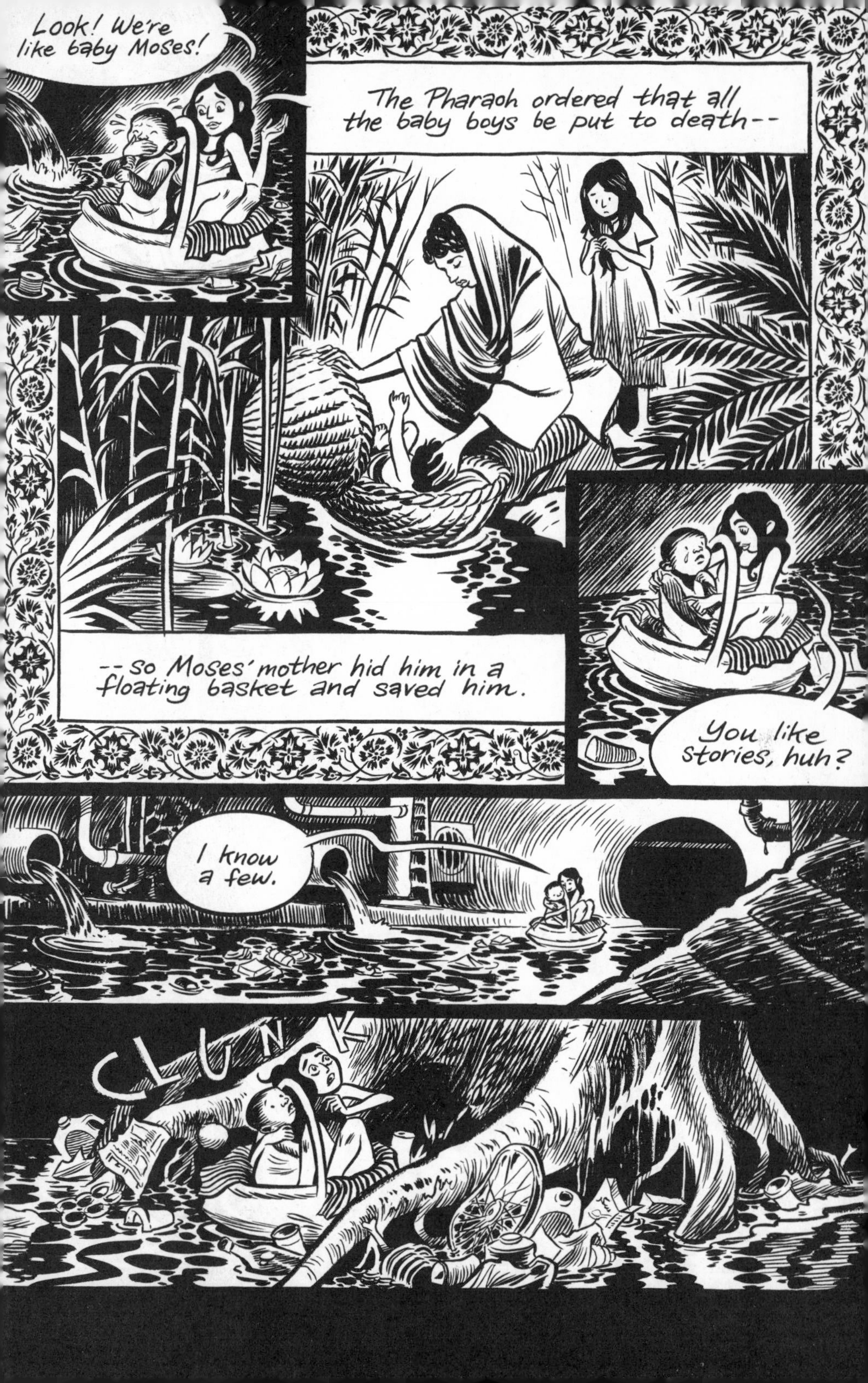

Look! We're like baby Moses!
The Pharaoh ordered that all the baby boys be put to death--
--so Moses' mother hid him in a floating basket and saved him.
You like stories, huh?
I know a few.
CLUNK

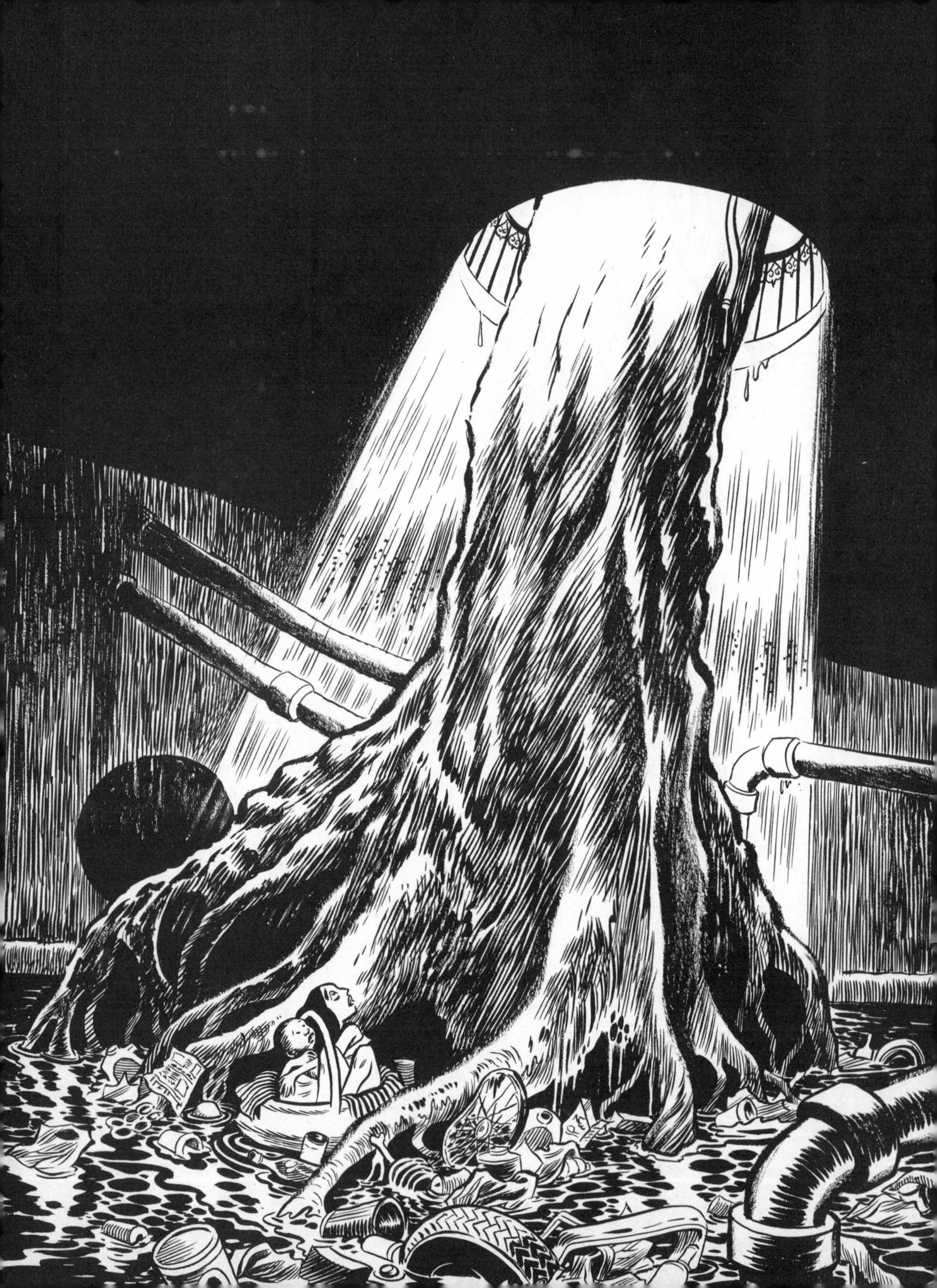

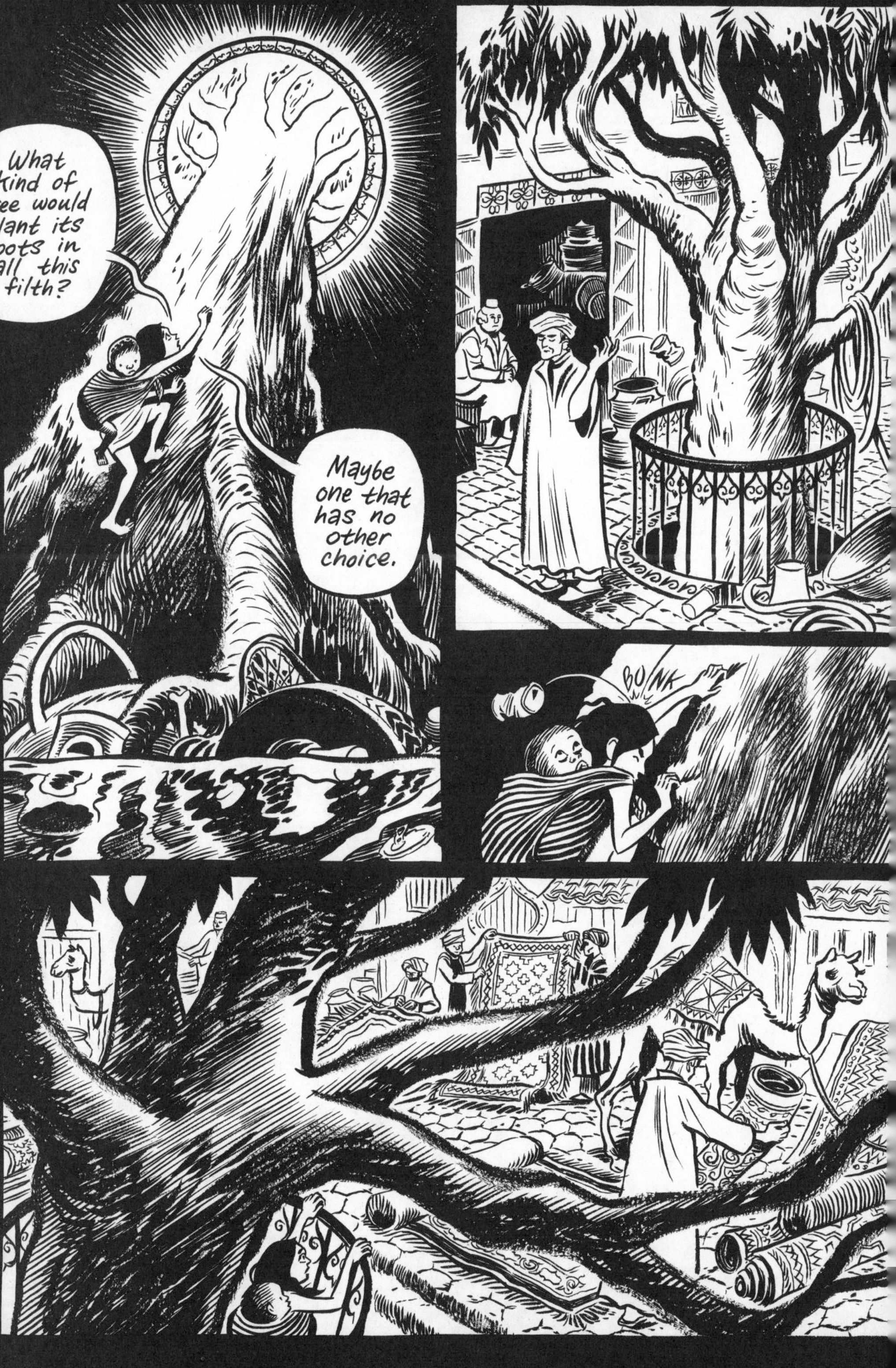
What kind of tree would plant its roots in all this filth?
Maybe one that has no other choice.
BONK

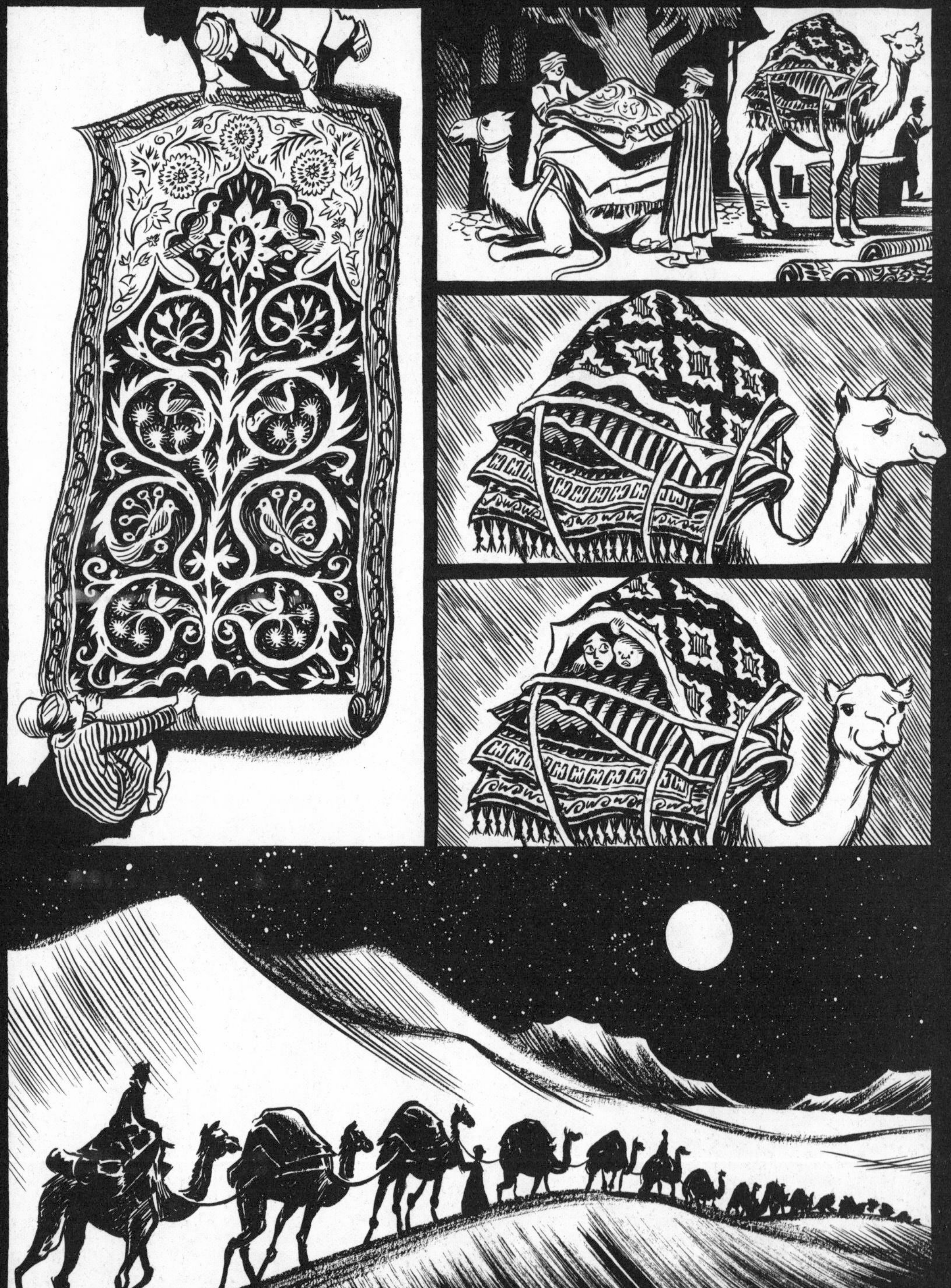

Like a plumb bob, a dark line fell from my navel.

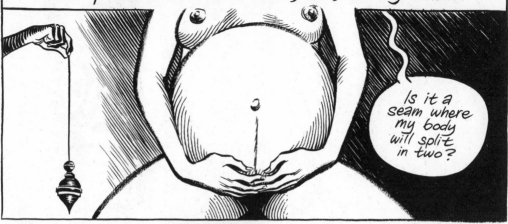

Is it a seam where my body will split in two?

This hair must go.

My little veil...

In the harem, it was a sin to have hair on one's privates.

Nadidah scraped it away with depilatory and a mussel shell.

What if she'd kept removing layers to find what was buried beneath?

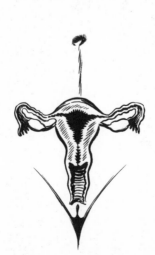

81

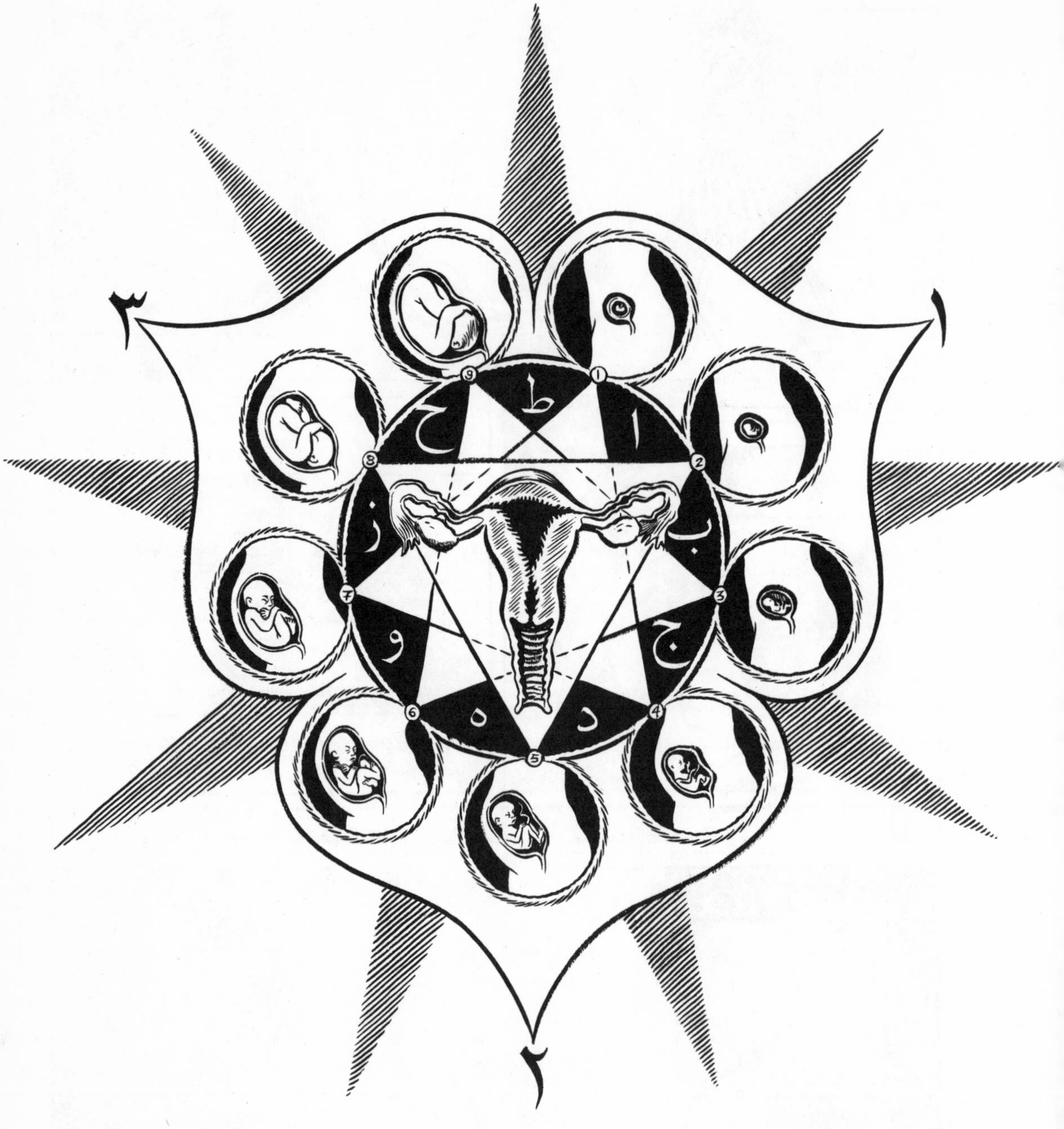
١
٢
٣
ا
ب
ج
د
ه
و
ز
ح
ط
1
2
3
4
5
6
7
8
9

What exactly IS this line?

It's your belly stripe.

My face is darker, too.

It's the mask of pregnancy.

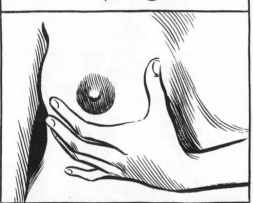

And my areolas flushed with deeper pigment.

They'd been tender and raw, and now excreted a viscous milk.

Like Moses striking water from a rock ...

What have I gotten myself into?

83

It's moving.

kicking

It's rearranging all my ribs.

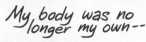
My body was no longer my own--

--but a container reshaped by its contents.

And now I'm never alone,

yet I've never felt so lonely.

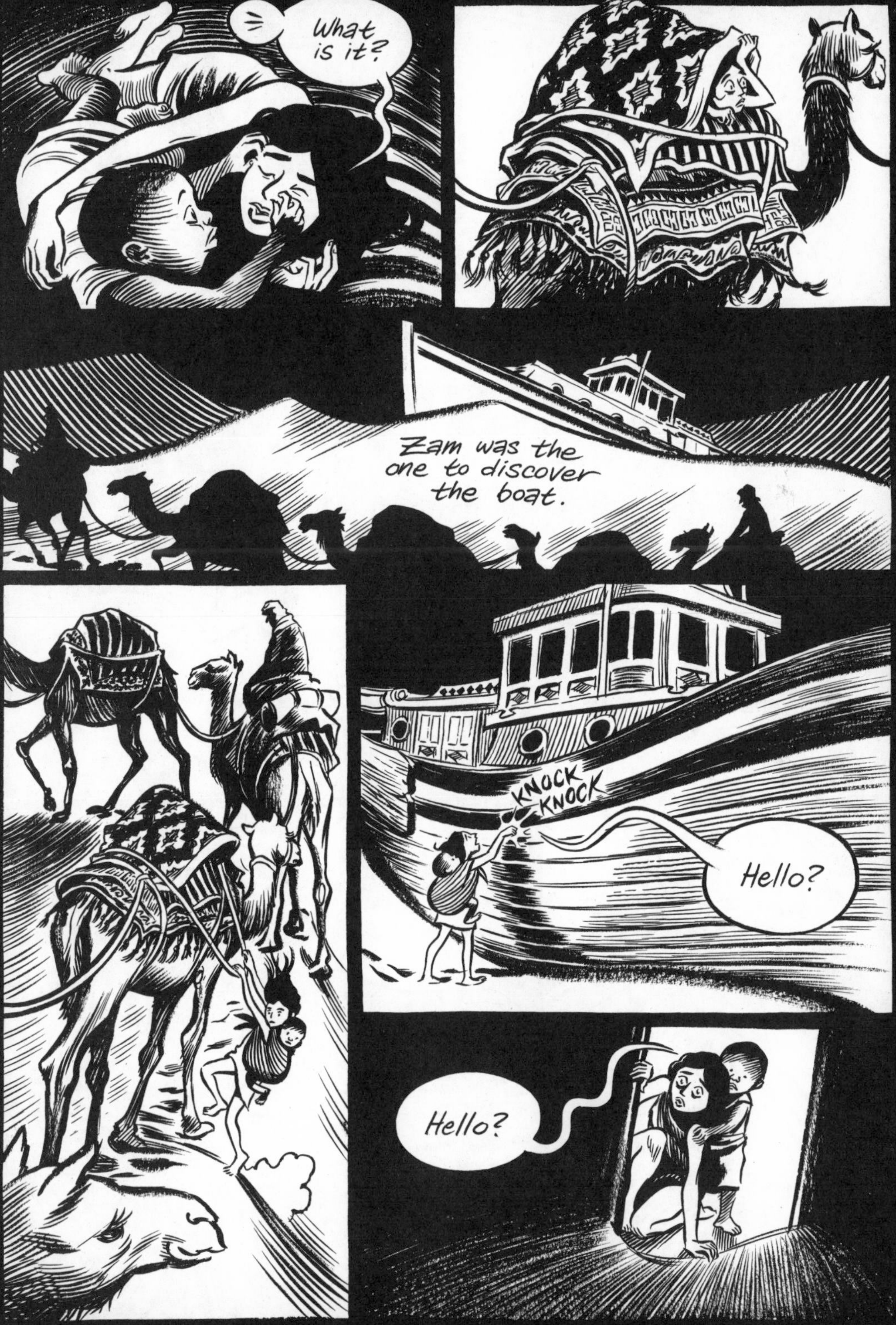
What is it?
Zam was the one to discover the boat.
KNOCK KNOCK
Hello?
Hello?

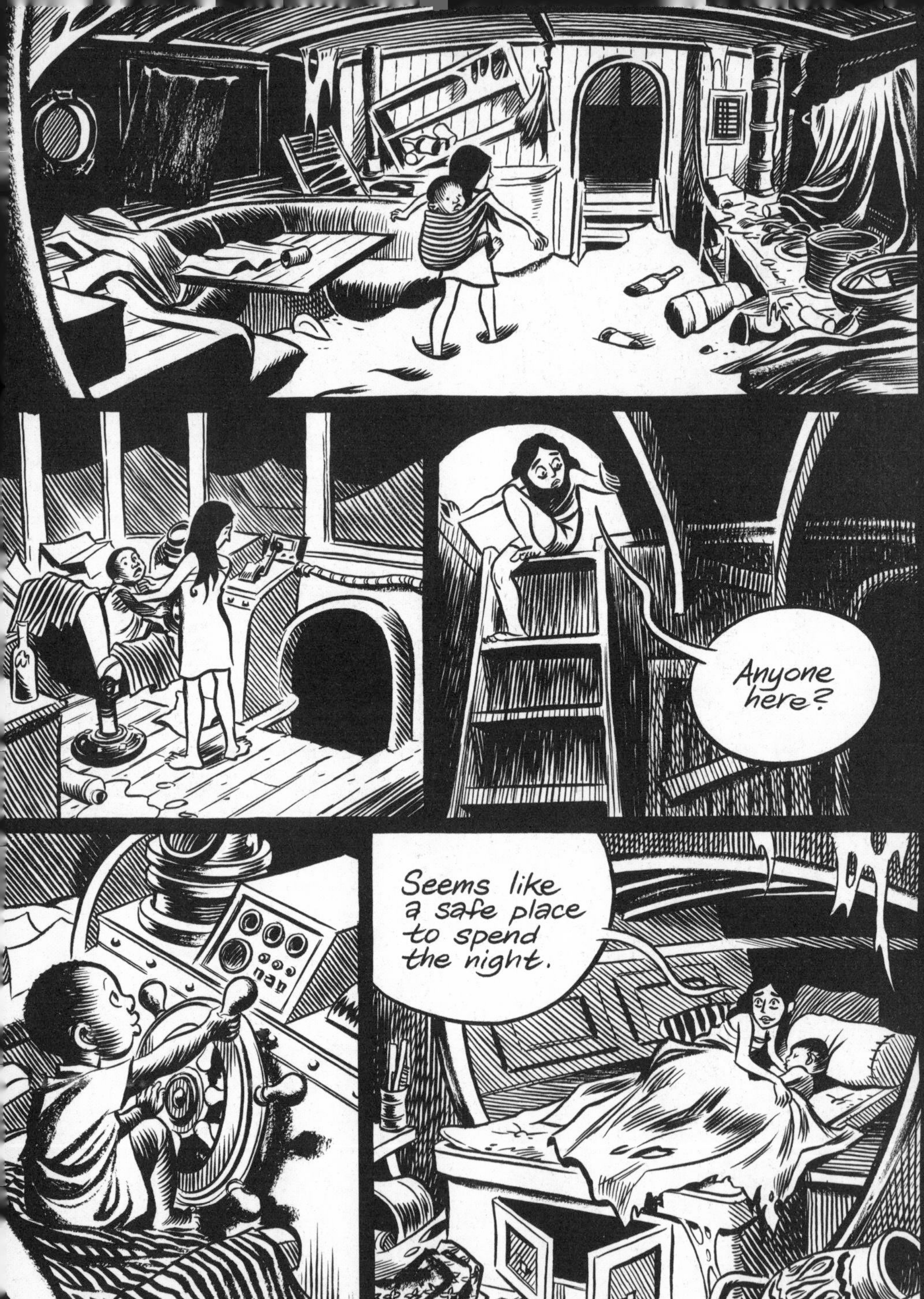
Anyone here?
Seems like a safe place to spend the night.

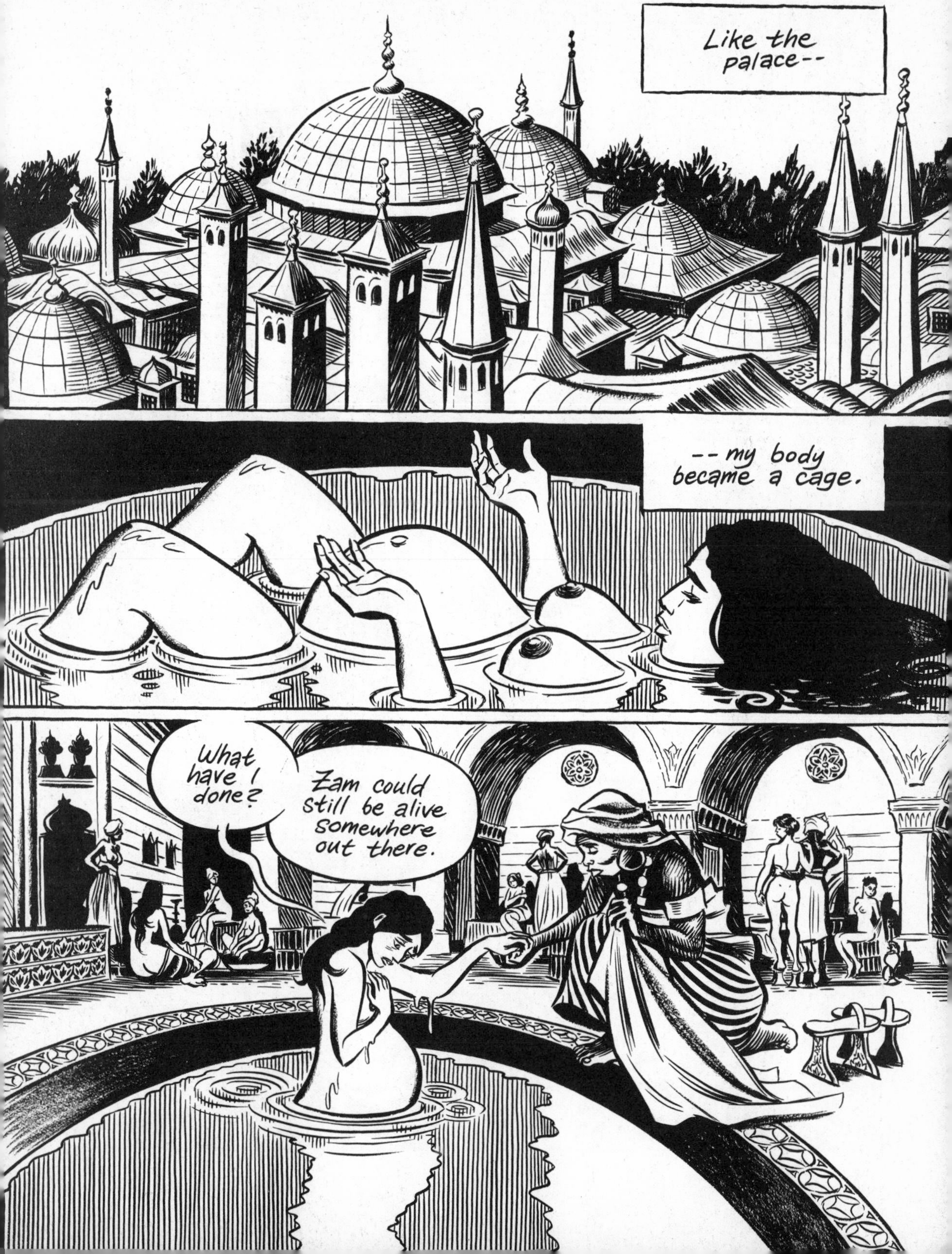
Like the palace--
--my body became a cage.
What have I done?
Zam could still be alive somewhere out there.

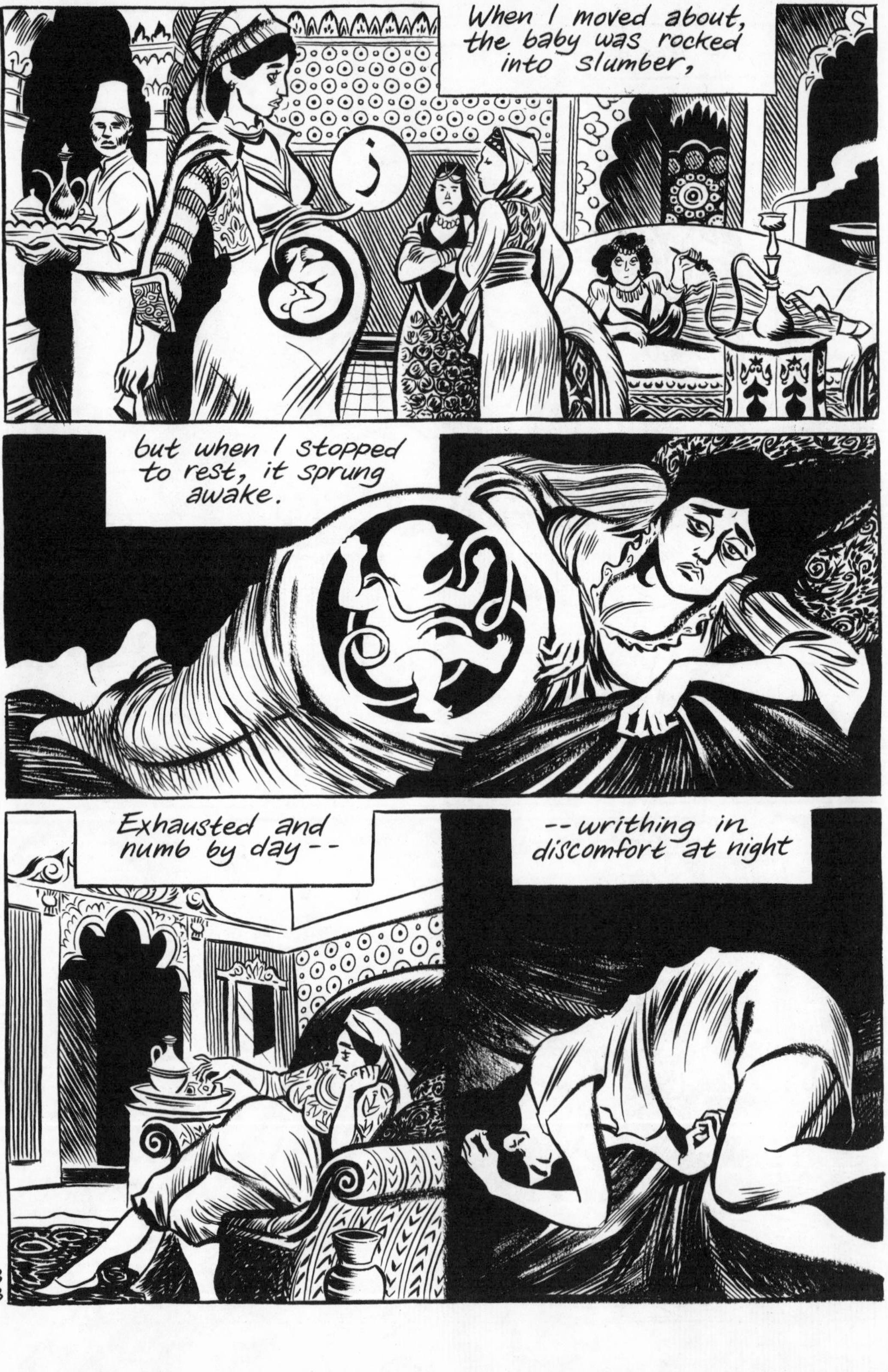
When I moved about, the baby was rocked into slumber,
ز
but when I stopped to rest, it sprung awake.
Exhausted and numb by day--
--writing in discomfort at night

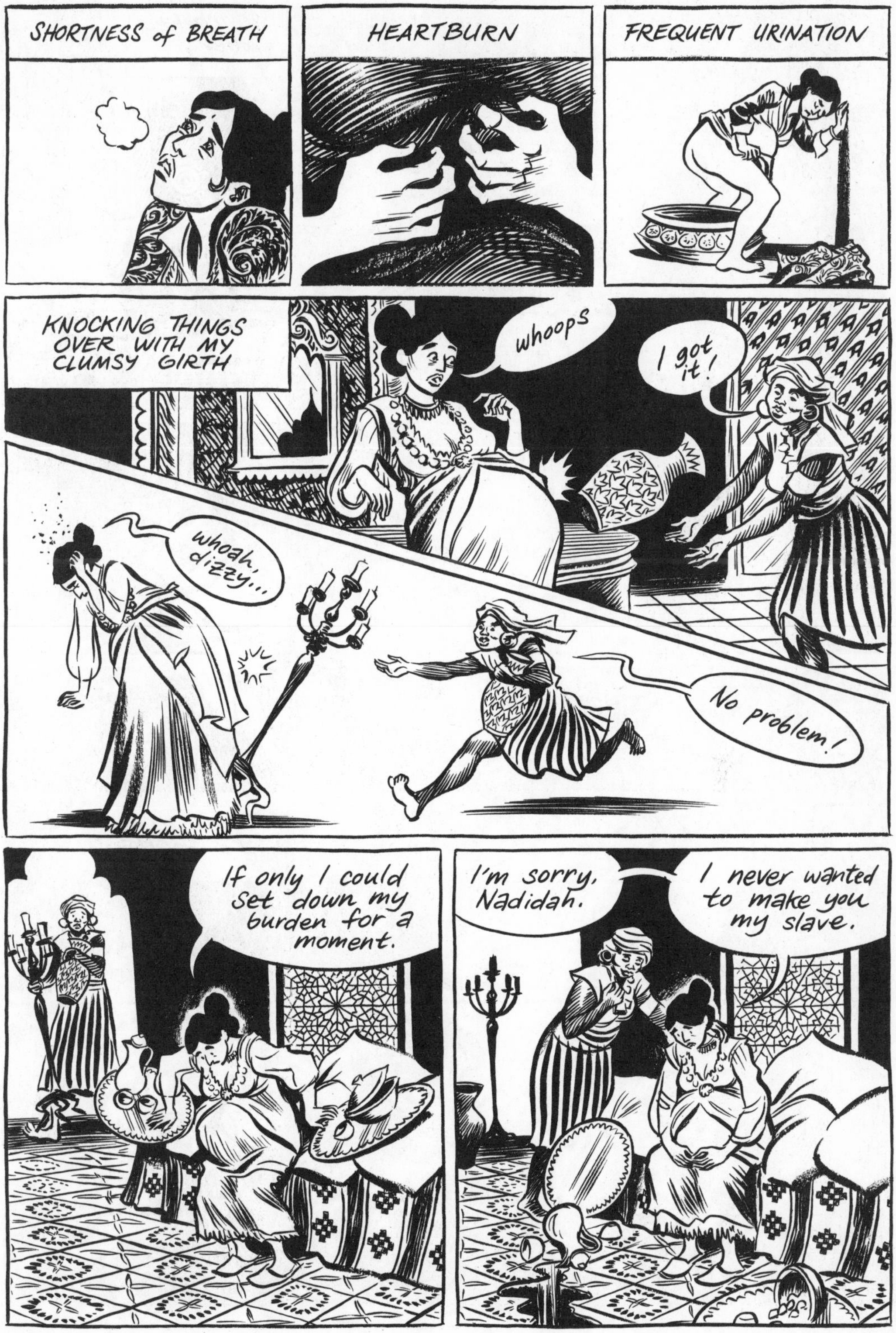

SHORTNESS of BREATH
HEARTBURN
FREQUENT URINATION
KNOCKING THINGS OVER WITH MY CLUMSY GIRTH
whoops
I got it!
whoah, dizzy...
No problem!
If only I could set down my burden for a moment.
I'm sorry, Nadidah.
I never wanted to make you my slave.

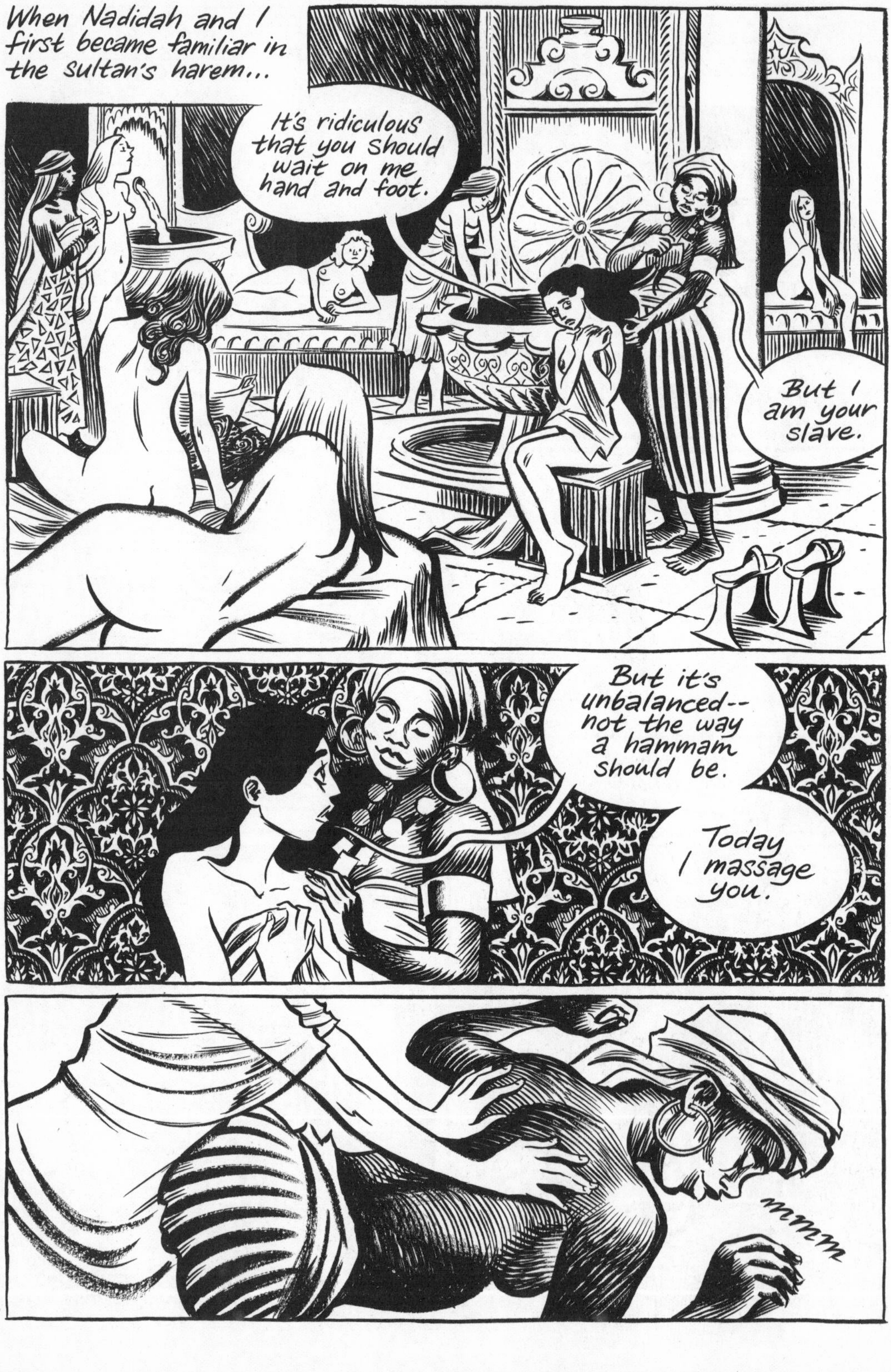
When Nadidah and I first became familiar in the sultan's harem...
It's ridiculous that you should wait on me hand and foot.
But I am your slave.
But it's unbalanced-- not the way a hammam should be.
Today I massage you.
mmm

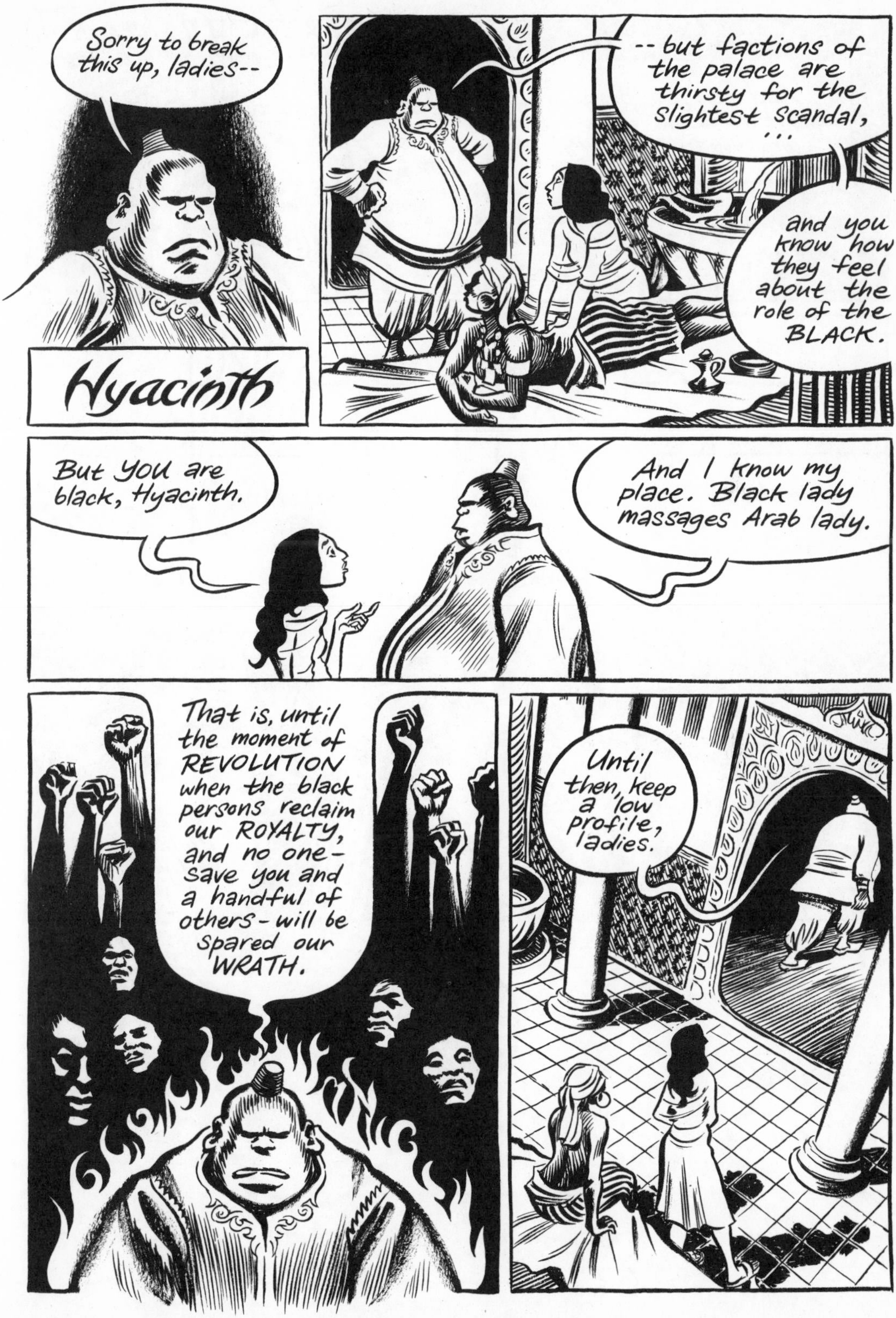
Sorry to break this up, ladies--
Hyacinth
--but factions of the palace are thirsty for the slightest scandal, ...
and you know how they feel about the role of the BLACK.
But YOU are black, Hyacinth.
And I know my place. Black lady massages Arab lady.
That is, until the moment of REVOLUTION when the black persons reclaim our ROYALTY, and no one - save you and a handful of others - will be spared our WRATH.
Until then, keep a low profile, ladies.

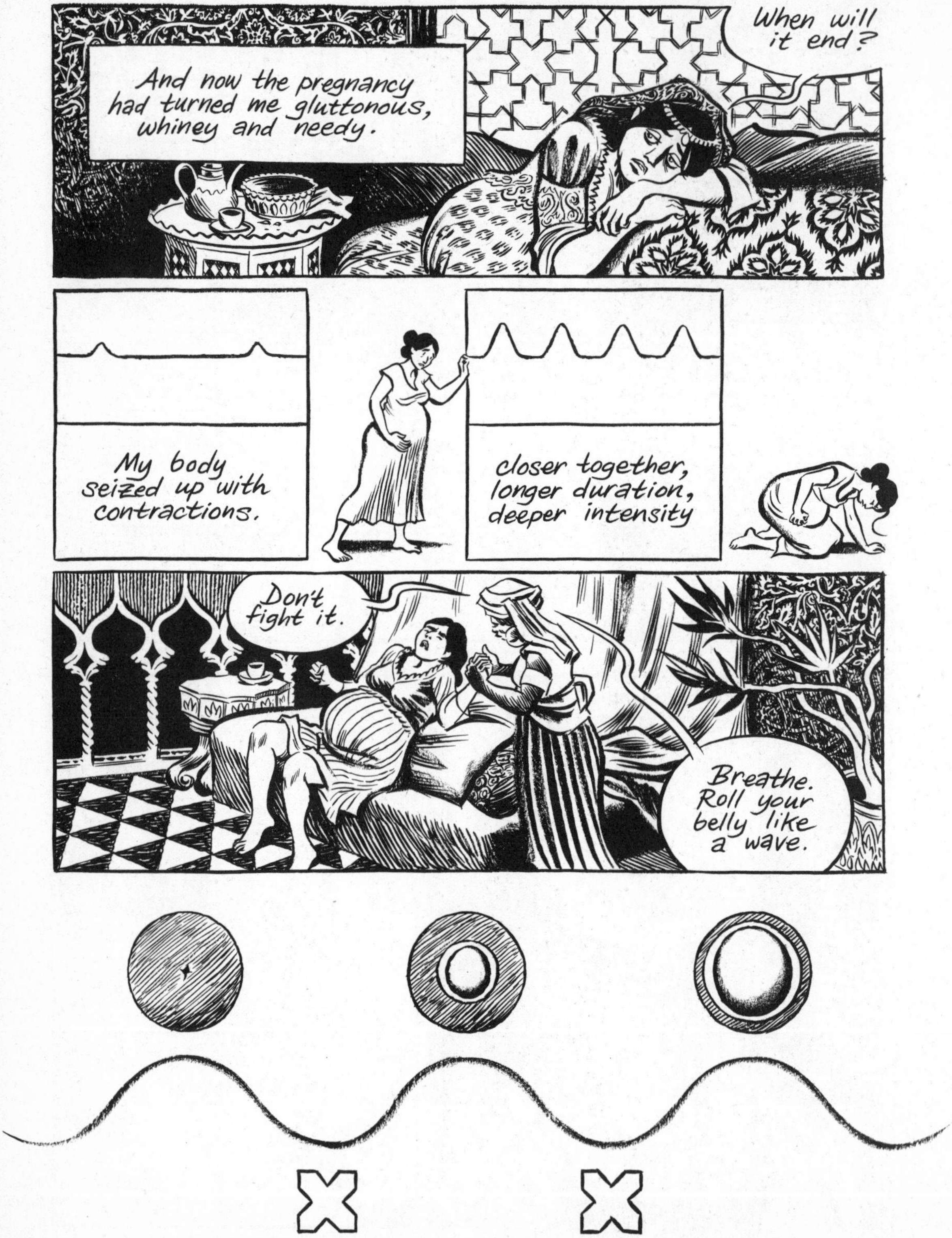
And now the pregnancy had turned me gluttonous, whiney and needy.
When will it end?
My body seized up with contractions.
closer together, longer duration, deeper intensity
Don't fight it.
Breathe. Roll your belly like a wave.

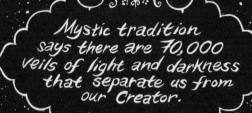

Mystic tradition says there are 70,000 veils of light and darkness that separate us from our Creator.

Every baby is born weeping for the soul knows its separation from ALLAH.

= WAH =

And when a child cries in its sleep, it is the soul remembering some piece of what has been LOST.

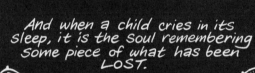

= WAH =

WAH

There, there, little Zam...

9
3

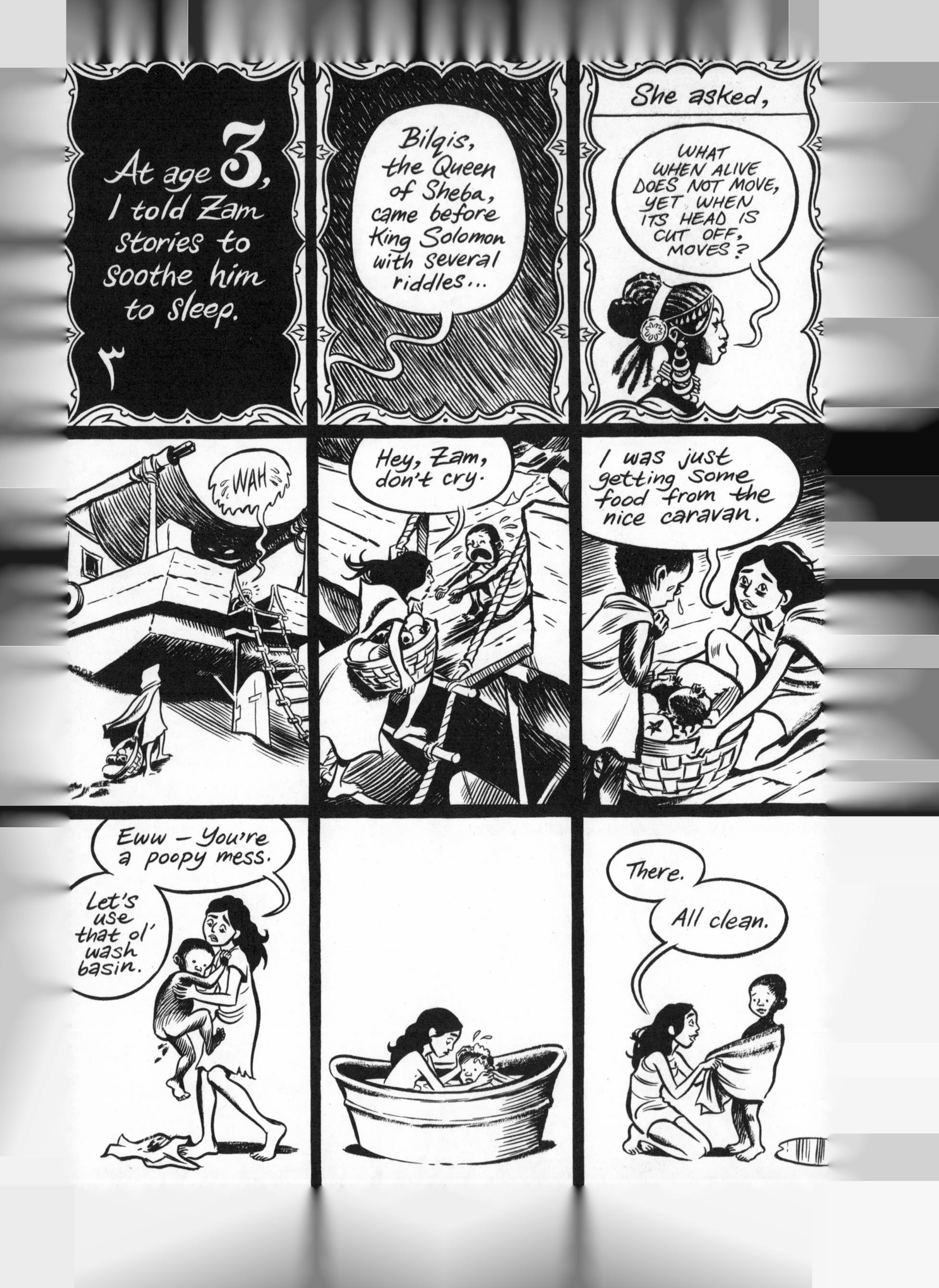
At age 3, I told Zam stories to soothe him to sleep.
٣
Bilqis, the Queen of Sheba, came before King Solomon with several riddles...
She asked,
WHAT WHEN ALIVE DOES NOT MOVE, YET WHEN ITS HEAD IS CUT OFF, MOVES?
WAH
Hey, Zam, don't cry.
I was just getting some food from the nice caravan.
Eww – You're a poopy mess.
Let's use that ol' wash basin.
There.
All clean.

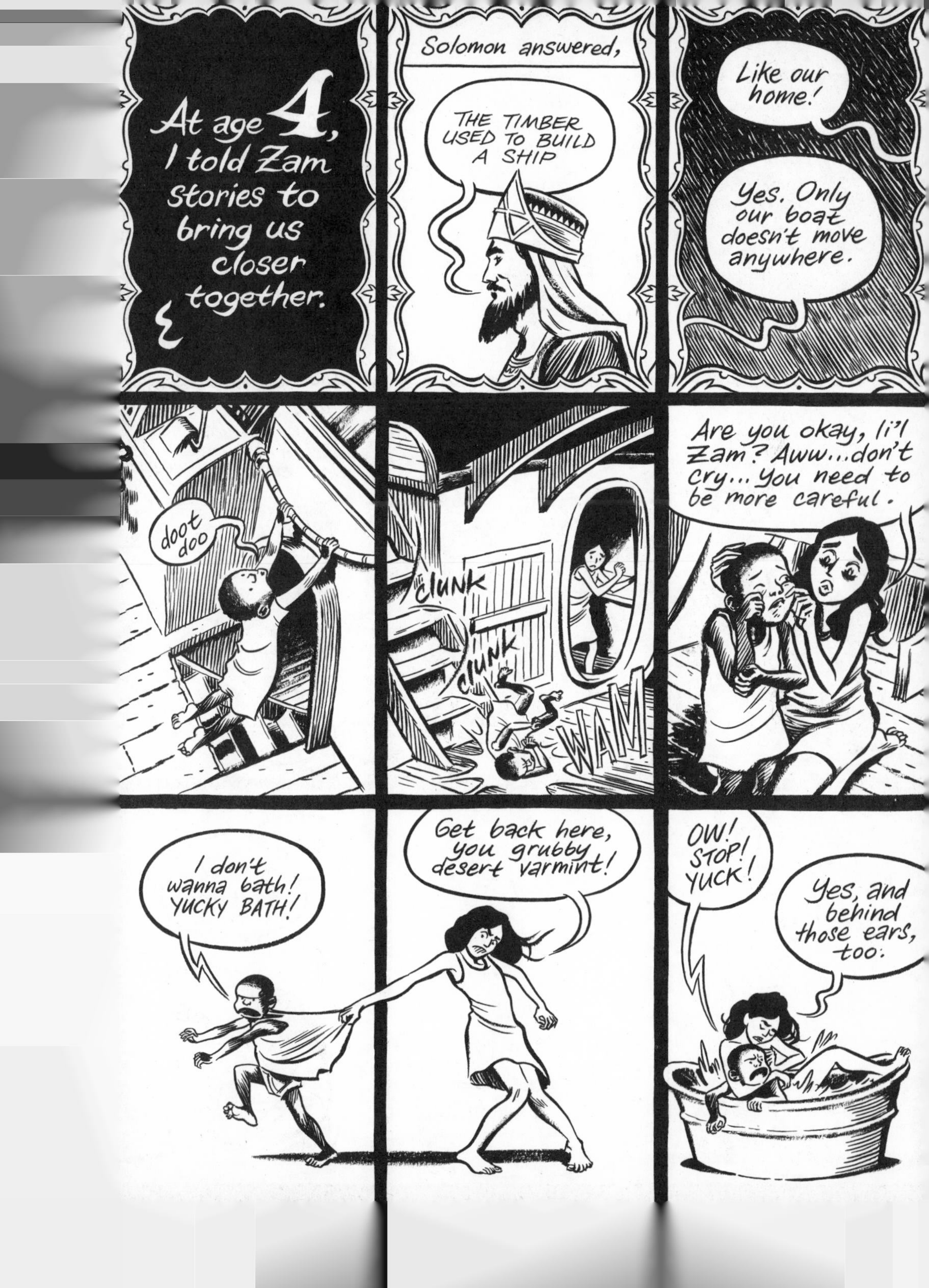
At age 4, I told Zam stories to bring us closer together.
Solomon answered,
THE TIMBER USED TO BUILD A SHIP
Like our home!
Yes. Only our boat doesn't move anywhere.
doot doo
CLUNK
CLUNK
CLUNK
WAM
Are you okay, li'l Zam? Aww...don't cry... You need to be more careful.
I don't wanna bath! YUCKY BATH!
Get back here, you grubby desert varmint!
OW! STOP! YUCK!
Yes, and behind those ears, too.

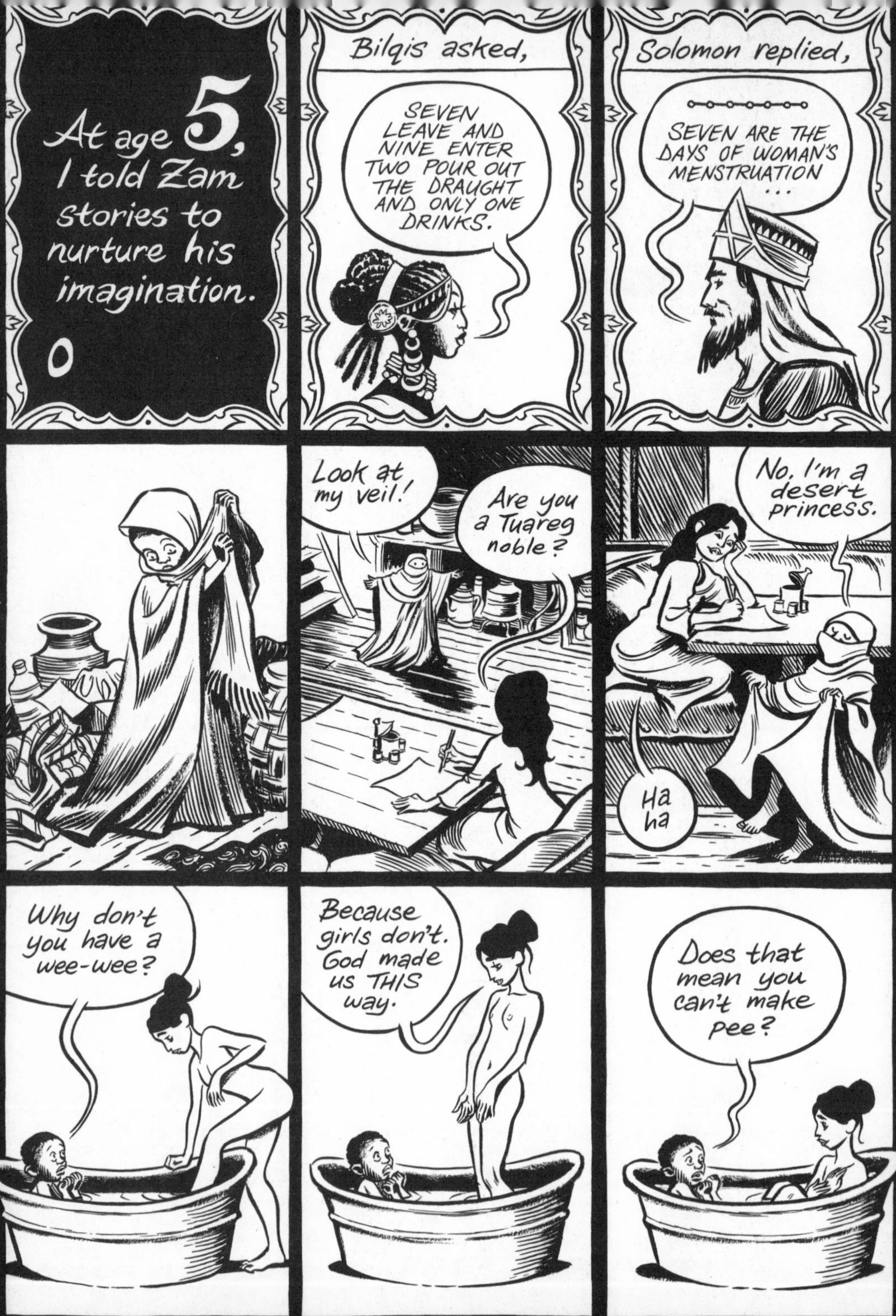
At age 5, I told Zam stories to nurture his imagination.
O
Bilqis asked,
SEVEN LEAVE AND NINE ENTER TWO POUR OUT THE DRAUGHT AND ONLY ONE DRINKS.
Solomon replied,
SEVEN ARE THE DAYS OF WOMAN'S MENSTRUATION . . .
Look at my veil!
Are you a Tuareg noble?
No. I'm a desert princess.
Ha ha
Why don't you have a wee-wee?
Because girls don't. God made us THIS way.
Does that mean you can't make pee?

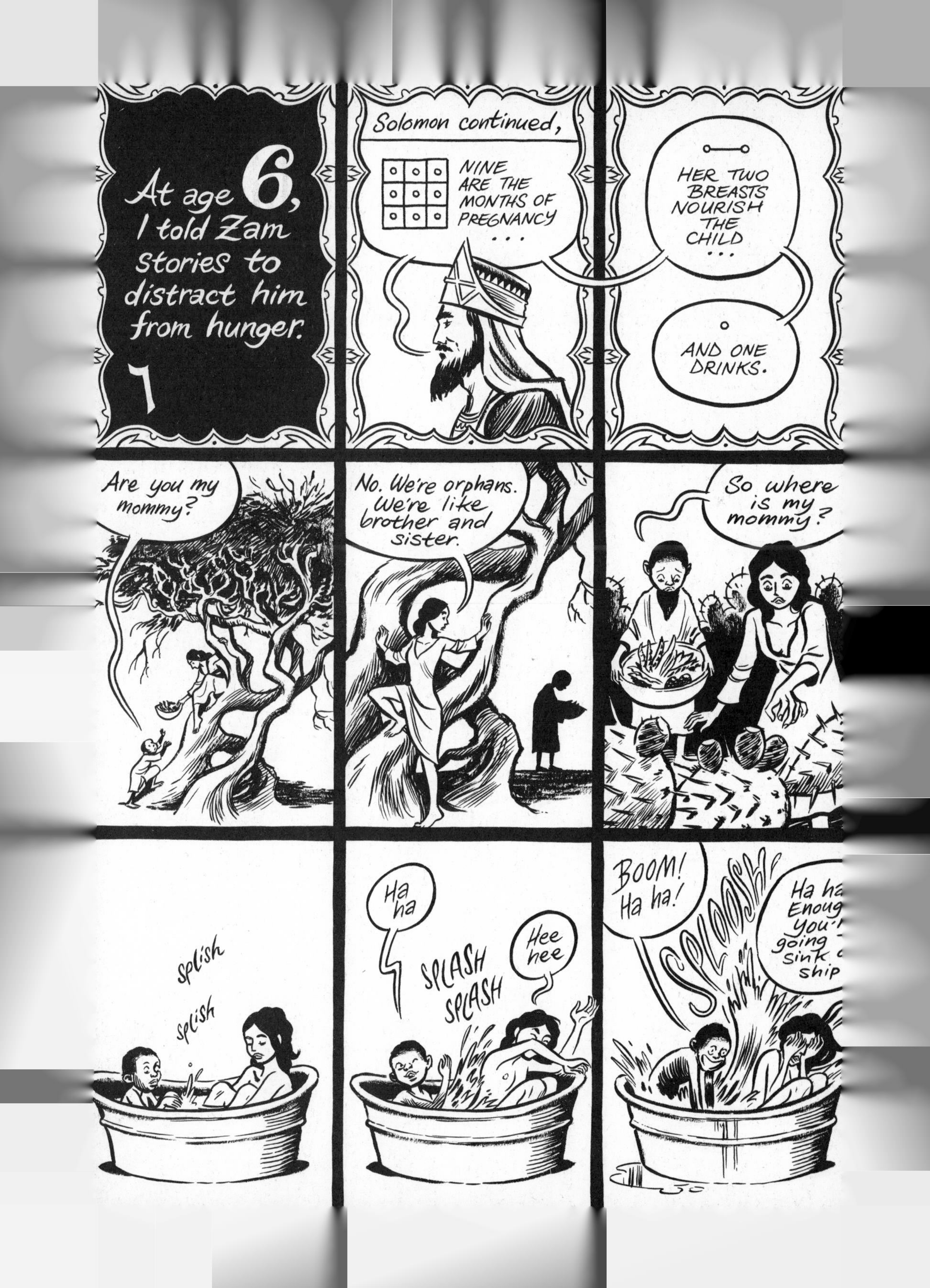

At age 6, I told Zam stories to distract him from hunger.
Solomon continued,
NINE ARE THE MONTHS OF PREGNANCY . . .
HER TWO BREASTS NOURISH THE CHILD . . .
AND ONE DRINKS.
Are you my mommy?
No. We're orphans. We're like brother and sister.
So where is my mommy?
splish
splish
Ha ha
SPLASH SPLASH
Hee hee
BOOM! Ha ha!
SPLOOSH!

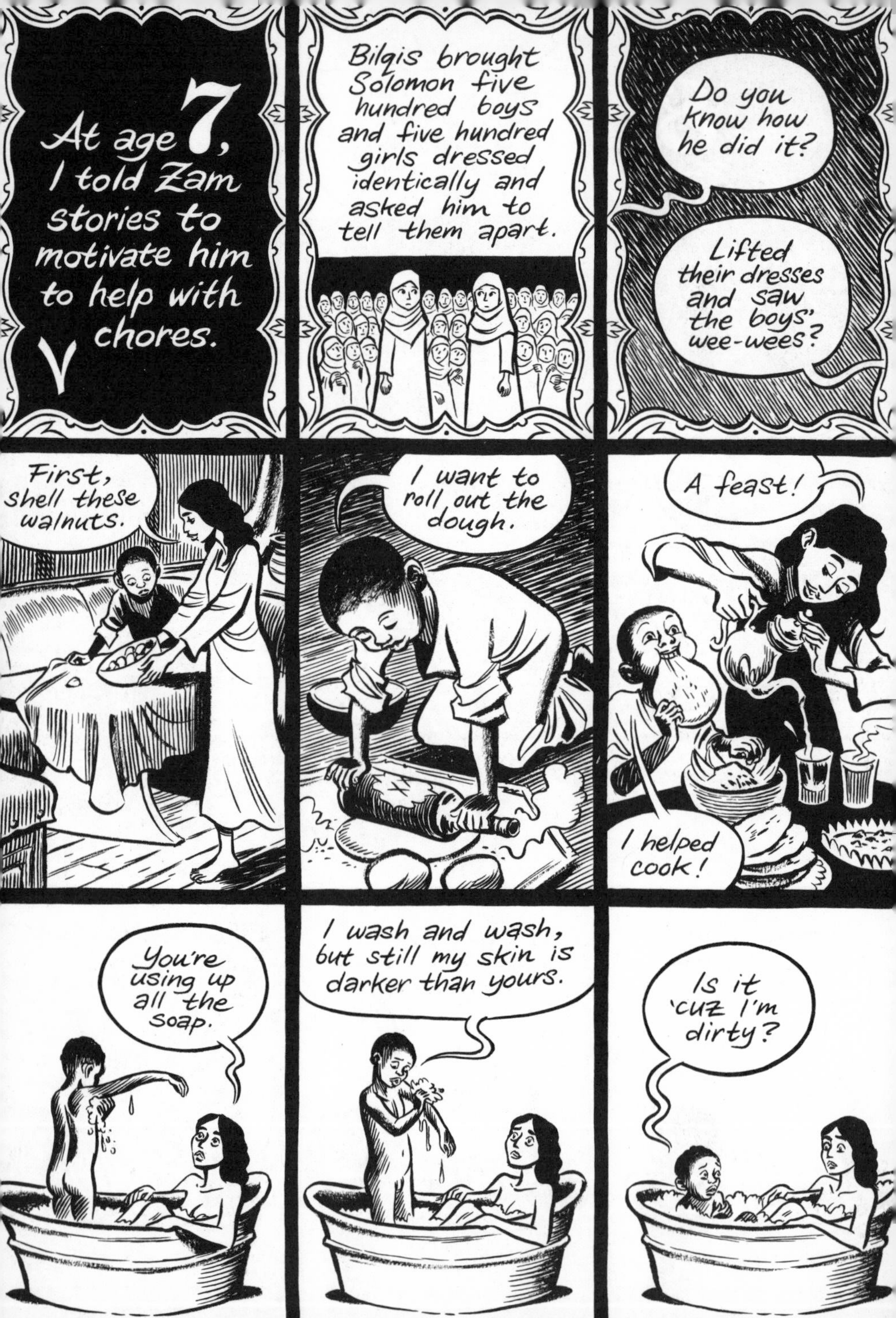
At age 7, I told Zam stories to motivate him to help with chores.
Bilqis brought Solomon five hundred boys and five hundred girls dressed identically and asked him to tell them apart.
Do you know how he did it?
Lifted their dresses and saw the boys' wee-wees?
First, shell these walnuts.
I want to roll out the dough.
A feast!
I helped cook!
You're using up all the soap.
I wash and wash, but still my skin is darker than yours.
Is it 'cuz I'm dirty?

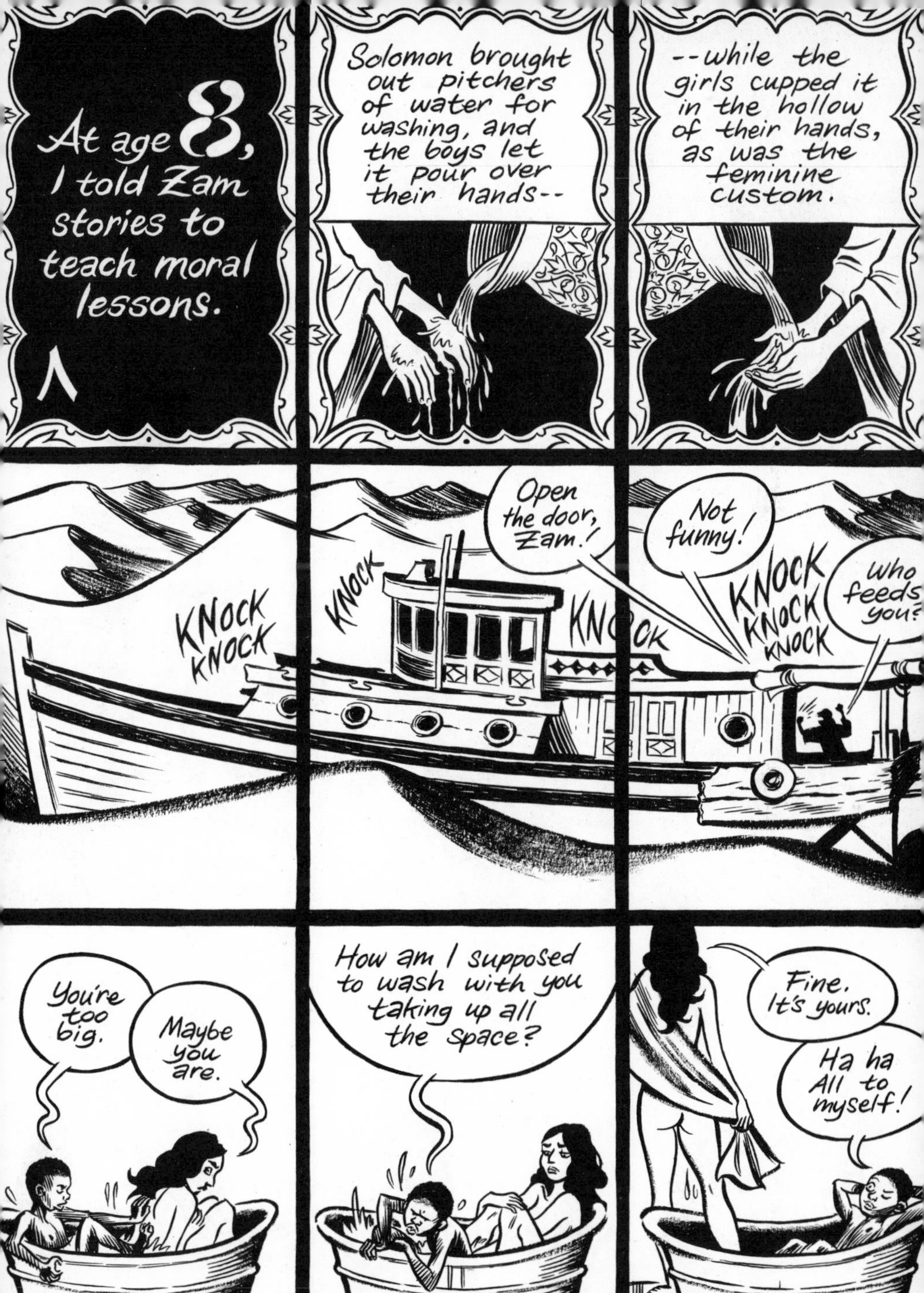
At age 8, I told Zam stories to teach moral lessons.
٨
Solomon brought out pitchers of water for washing, and the boys let it pour over their hands--
--while the girls cupped it in the hollow of their hands, as was the feminine custom.
KNOCK KNOCK
KNOCK
Open the door, Zam!
KNOCK
Not funny!
KNOCK KNOCK KNOCK
Who feeds you?
You're too big.
Maybe you are.
How am I supposed to wash with you taking up all the space?
Fine. It's yours.
Ha ha All to myself!

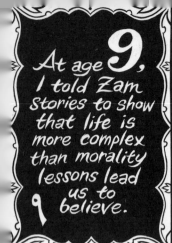

At age **9**, I told Zam stories to show that life is more complex than morality lessons lead us to believe.

Bilqis brought Solomon a log of cedar, and asked him to determine which end had been the branches and which the root.

Again Solomon summoned for water, and had the log placed in it.

Your husband was killed?

Are you sad?

I'm happy you and I are together.

When I grow up, I'll marry you!

Ha ha Thanks, Zam!

I help and wash you, too!

uh heh... tickles...

uh, okay.

You can stop, Zam.

I'm clean.

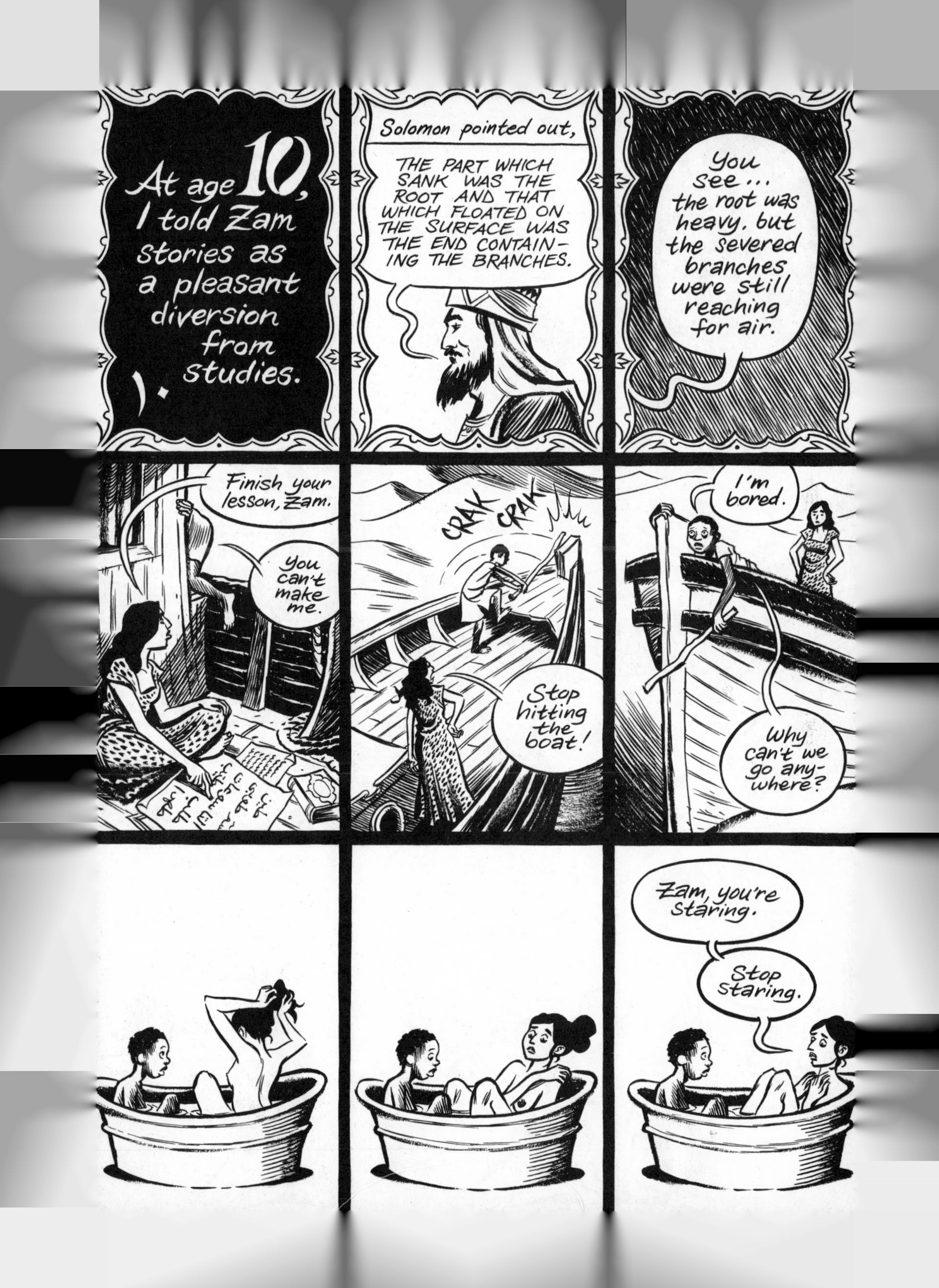
At age 10, I told Zam stories as a pleasant diversion from studies.
Solomon pointed out,
THE PART WHICH SANK WAS THE ROOT AND THAT WHICH FLOATED ON THE SURFACE WAS THE END CONTAINING THE BRANCHES.
You see... the root was heavy, but the severed branches were still reaching for air.
Finish your lesson, Zam.
You can't make me.
CRAK
CRAK
Stop hitting the boat!
I'm bored.
Why can't we go anywhere?
Zam, you're staring.
Stop staring.

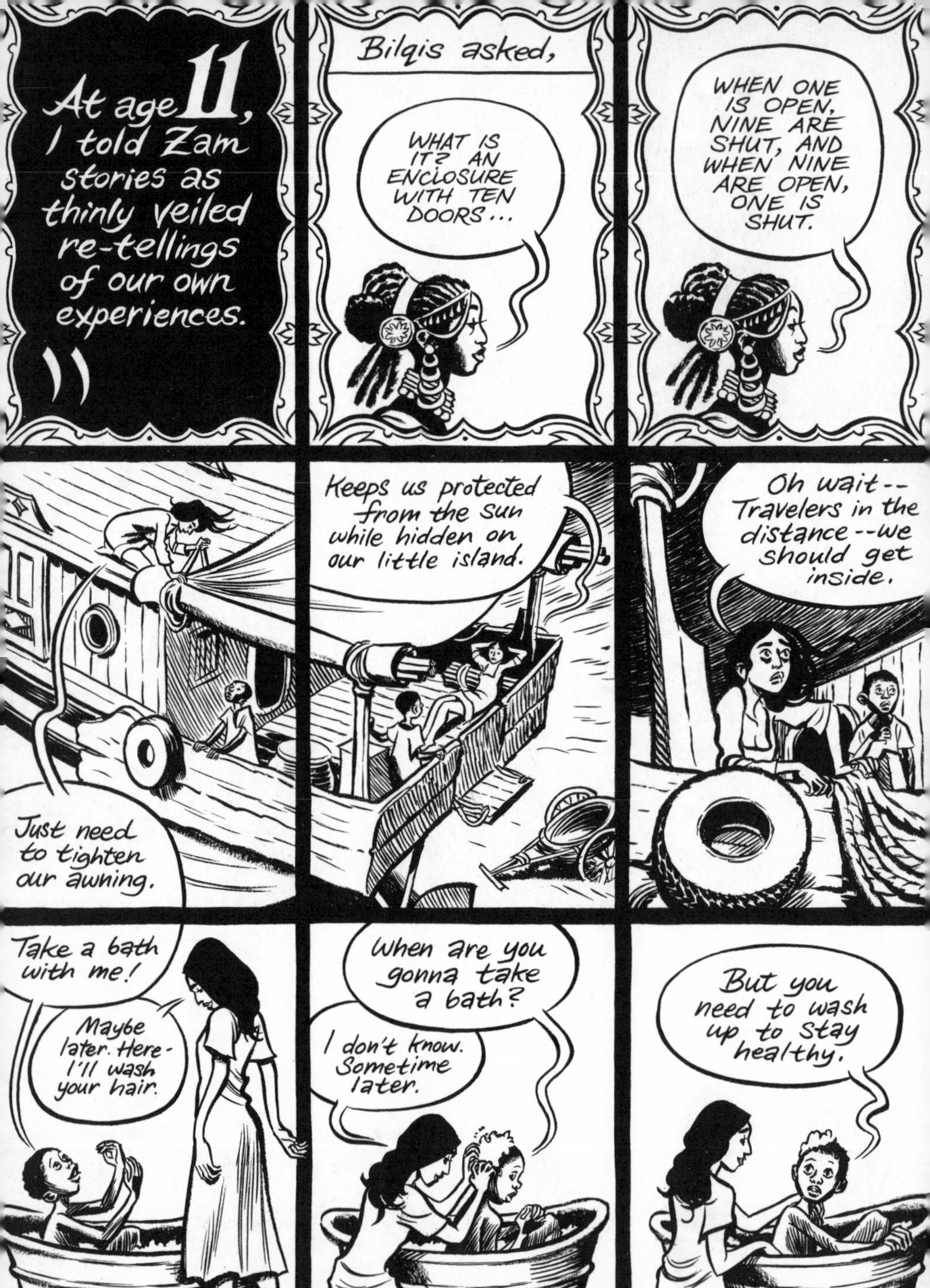
At age 11, I told Zam stories as thinly veiled re-tellings of our own experiences.
Bilqis asked,
WHAT IS IT? AN ENCLOSURE WITH TEN DOORS...
WHEN ONE IS OPEN, NINE ARE SHUT, AND WHEN NINE ARE OPEN, ONE IS SHUT.
Just need to tighten our awning.
Keeps us protected from the sun while hidden on our little island.
Oh wait-- Travelers in the distance--we should get inside.
Take a bath with me!
Maybe later. Here- I'll wash your hair.
When are you gonna take a bath?
I don't know. Sometime later.
But you need to wash up to stay healthy.

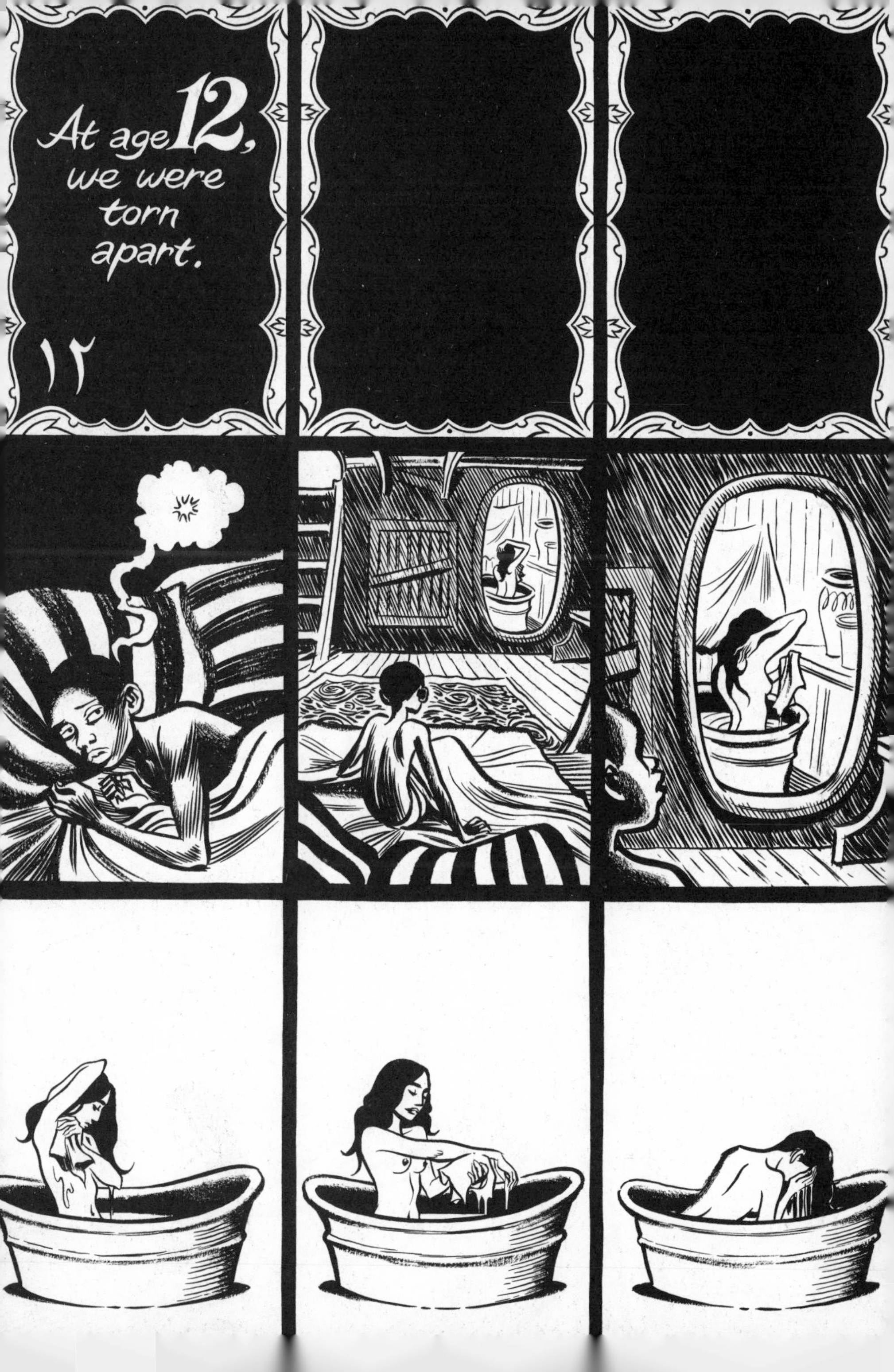
At age 12, we were torn apart.
١٢

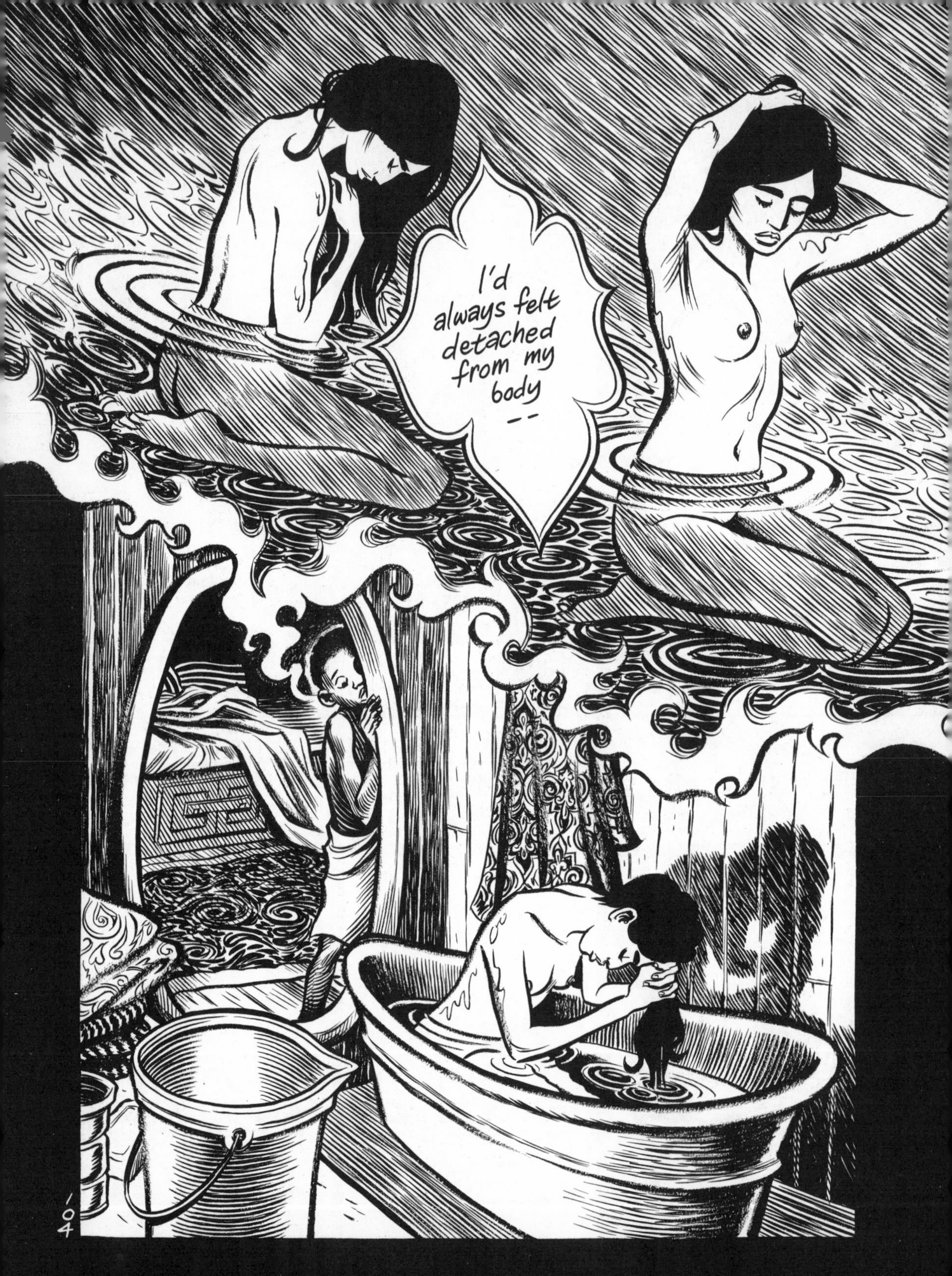
I'd always felt detached from my body --

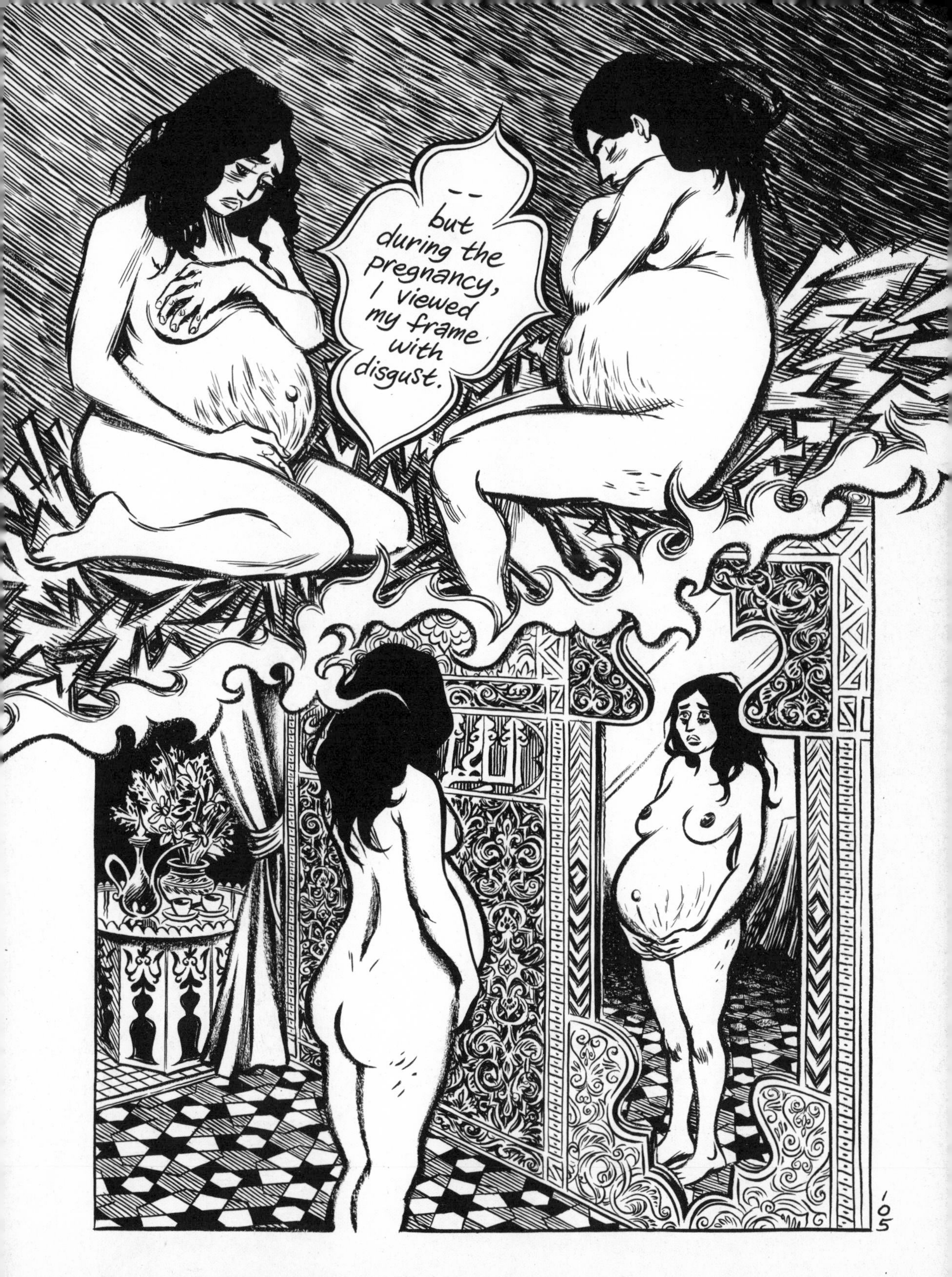
-- but during the pregnancy, I viewed my frame with disgust.

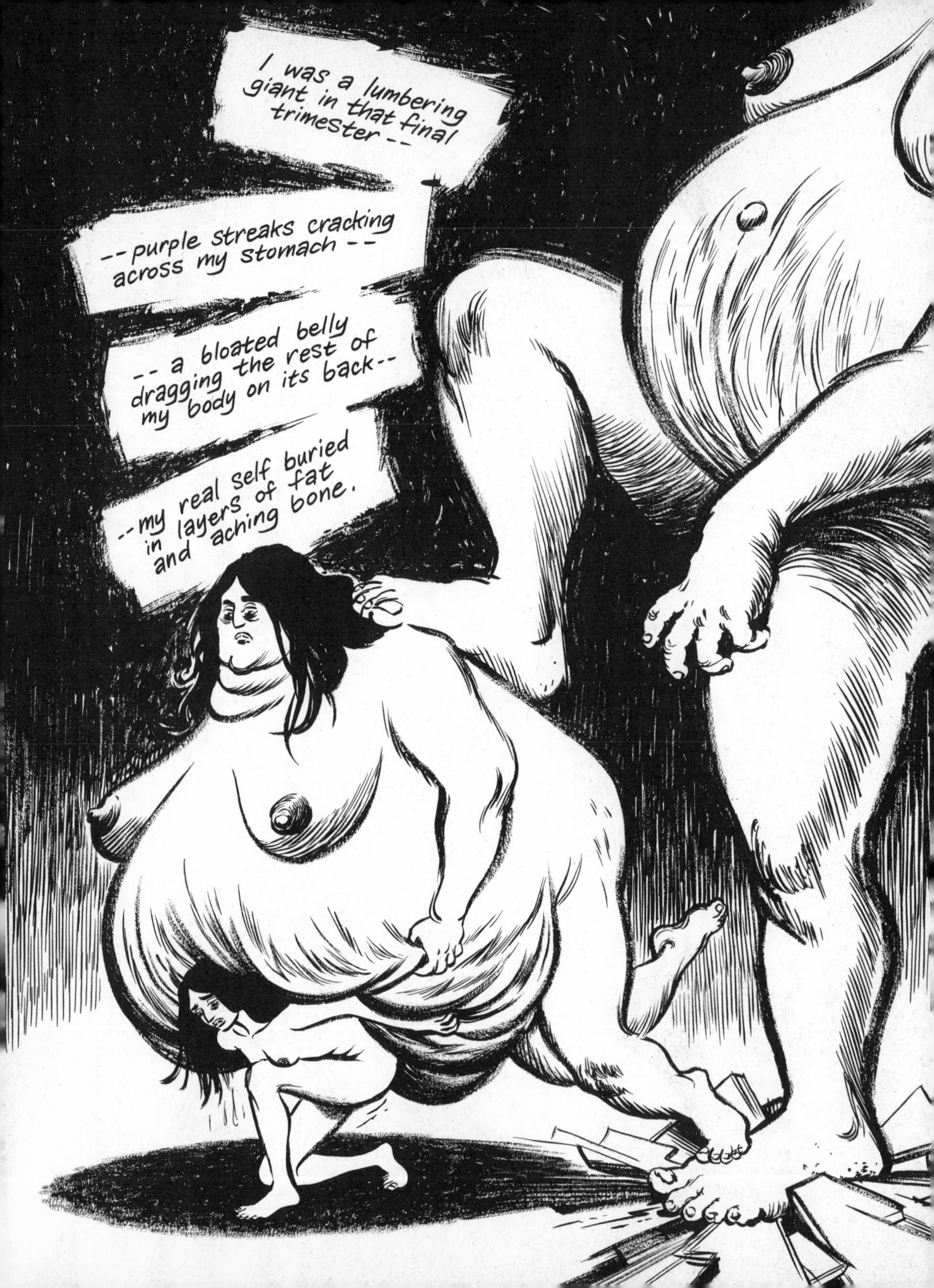
I was a lumbering giant in that final trimester --
-- purple streaks cracking across my stomach --
-- a bloated belly dragging the rest of my body on its back --
-- my real self buried in layers of fat and aching bone.

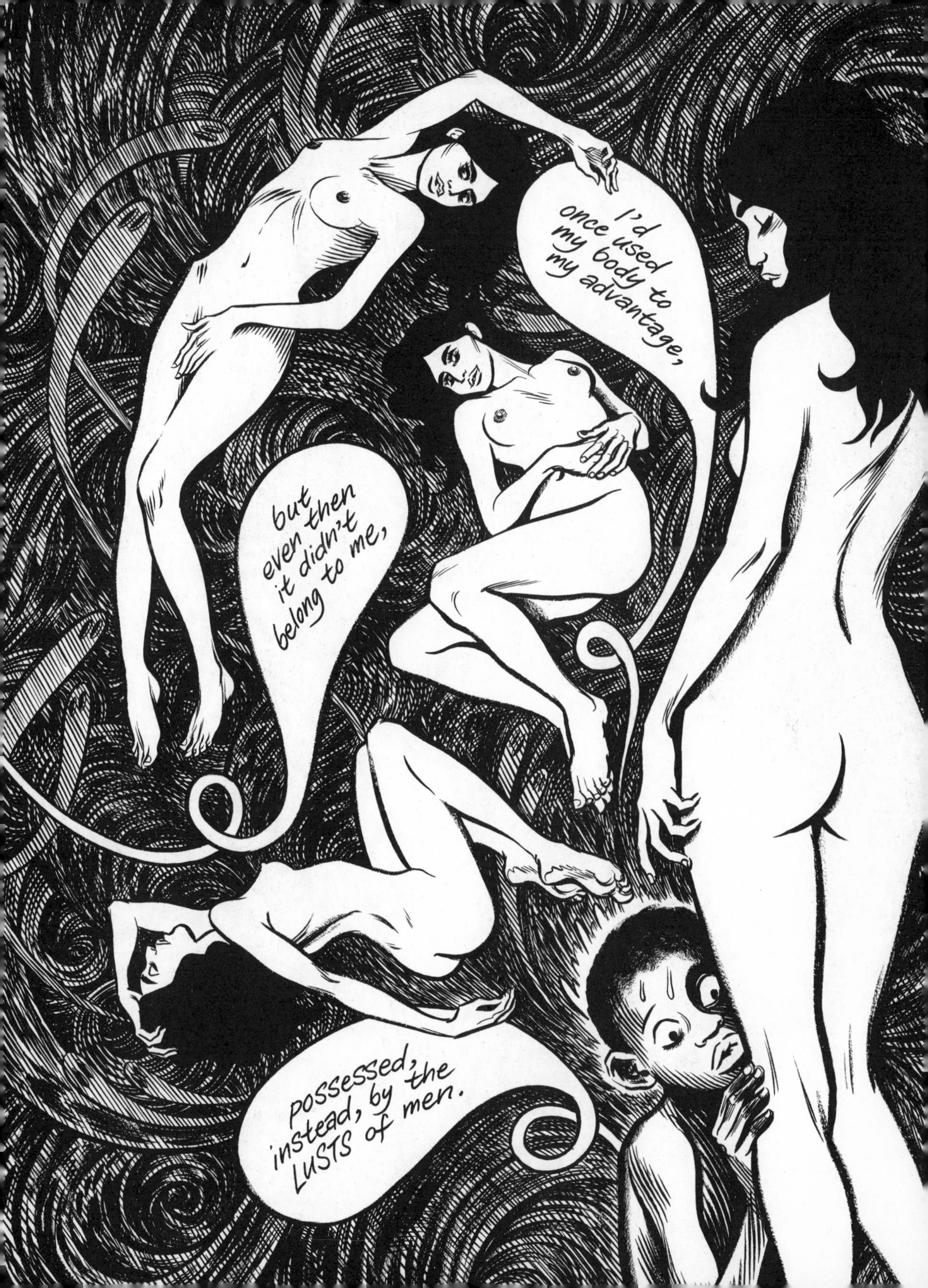
I'd once used my body to my advantage,
but even then it didn't belong to me,
possessed, instead, by the LUSTS of men.

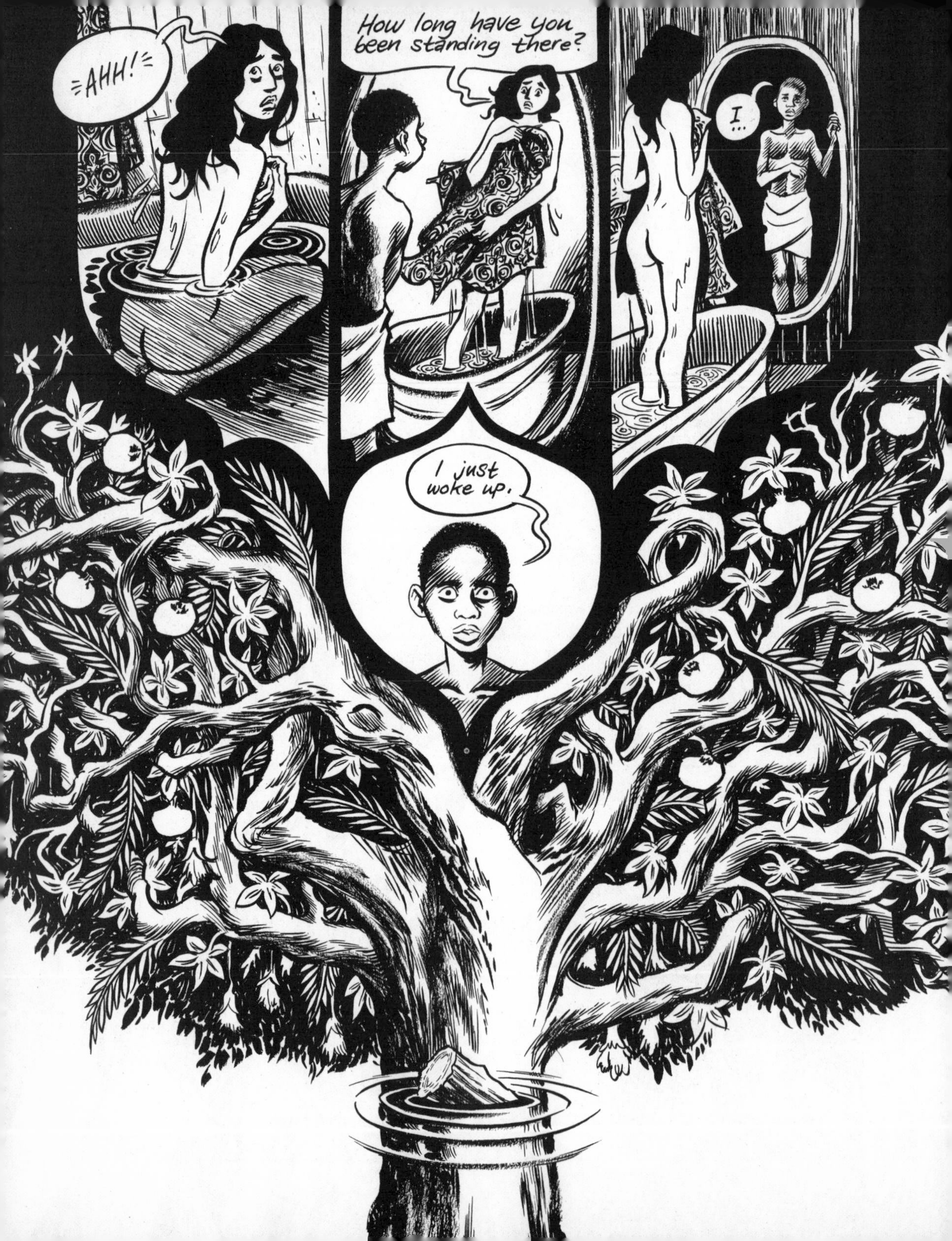
AHH!
How long have you been standing there?
I...
I just woke up.

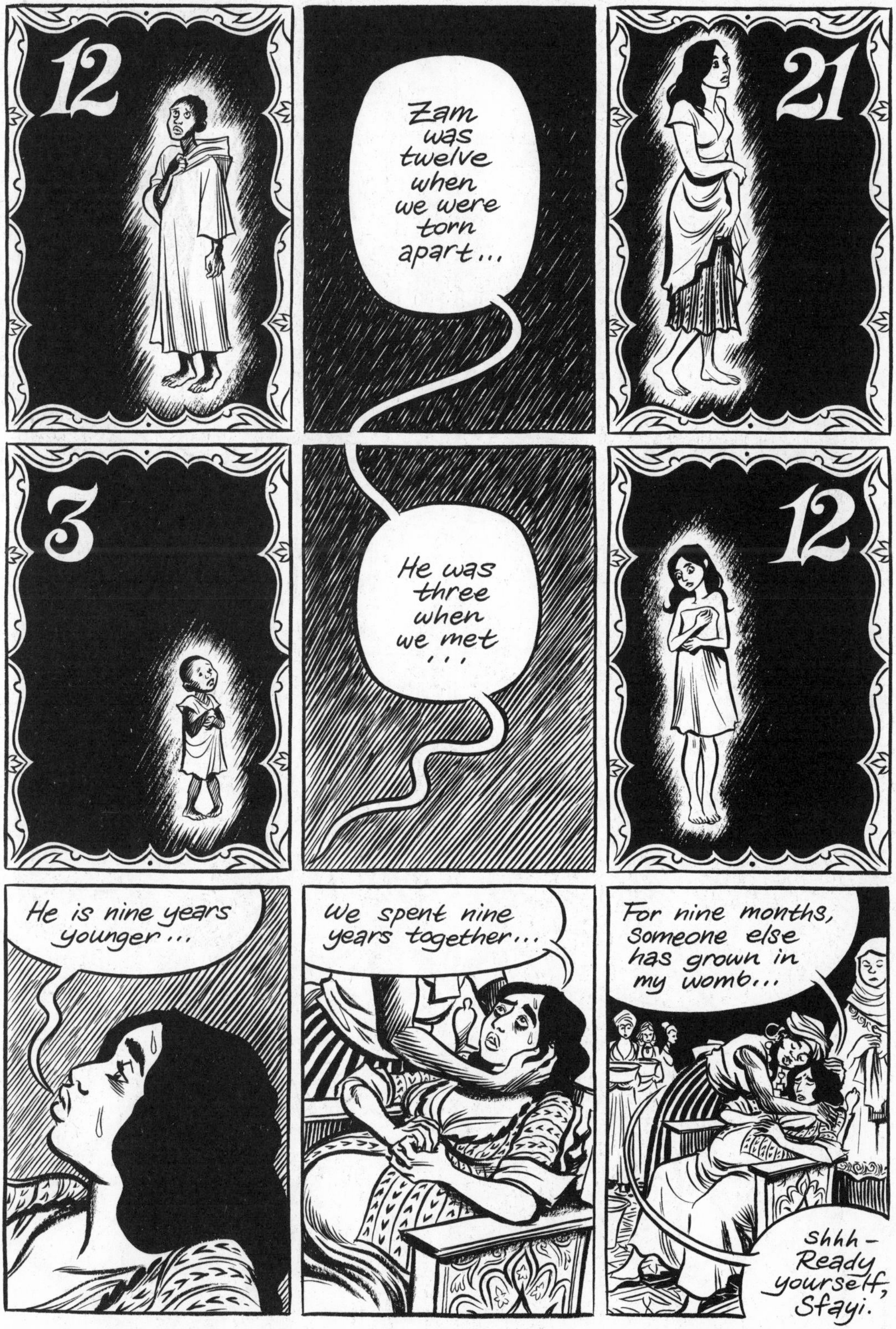
12
Zam was twelve when we were torn apart...
21
3
He was three when we met...
12
He is nine years younger...
We spent nine years together...
For nine months, someone else has grown in my womb...
Shhh- Ready yourself, Sfayi.

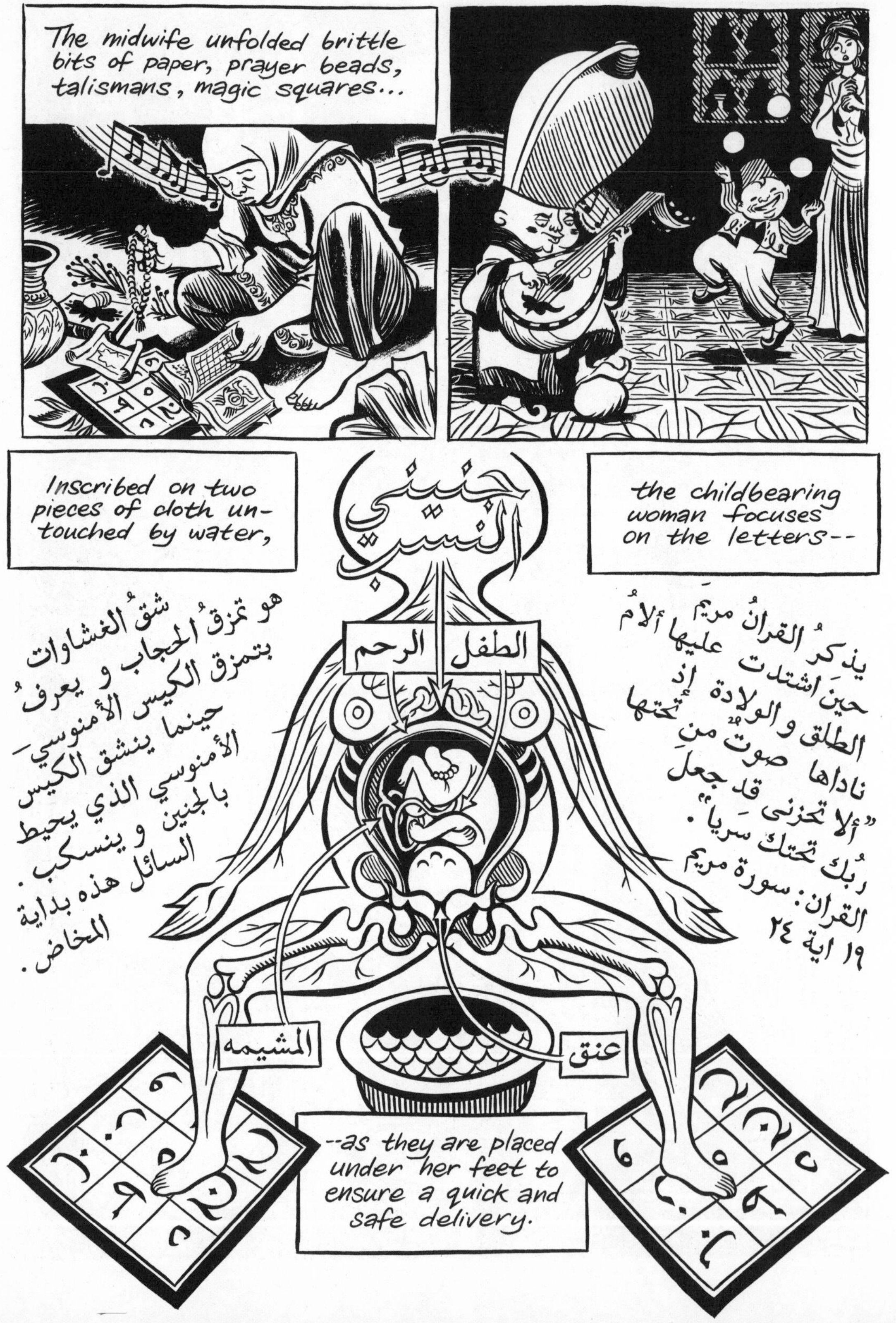
The midwife unfolded brittle bits of paper, prayer beads, talismans, magic squares...
Inscribed on two pieces of cloth untouched by water,
جنبني النشب
the childbearing woman focuses on the letters--
شقُ الغشاوات
هو تمزقُ الحجاب و يعرفُ
بتمزق الكيس الأمنوسي-
حينما ينشق الكيس
الأمنوسي الذي يحيط
بالجنين و ينسكب
السائل هذه بداية
المخاض.
الطفل
الرحم
يذكرُ القرانُ مريمَ
حينَ اشتدت عليها ألامُ
الطلق و الولادة إذ
ناداها صوتٌ منِ تحتها
”ألا تحزنى قد جعلَ
ربُك تحتك سَريا“.
القران: سورة مريم
١٩ اية ٢٤
المشيمه
عنق
--as they are placed under her feet to ensure a quick and safe delivery.

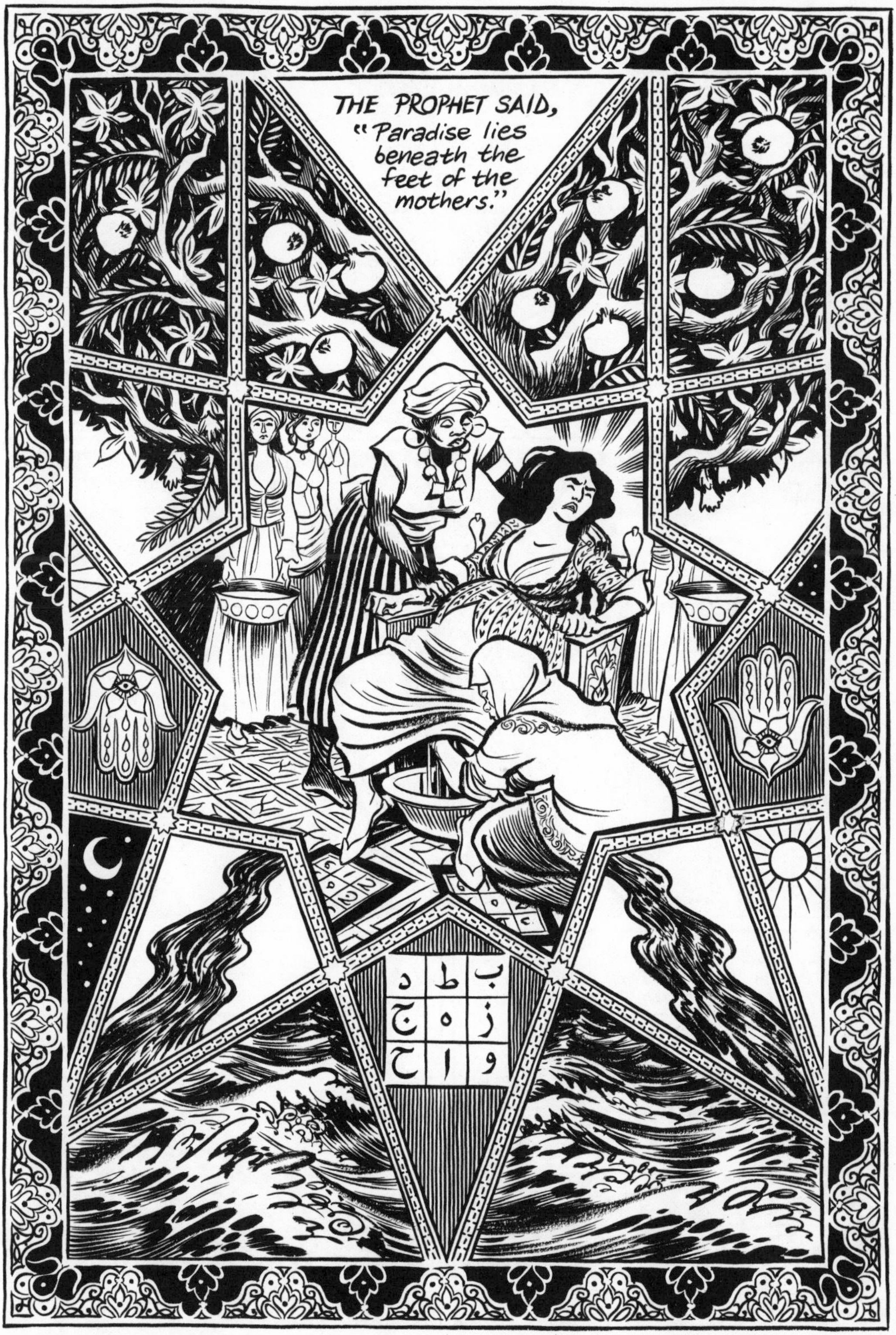
THE PROPHET SAID,
"Paradise lies beneath the feet of the mothers."
ب ط د
ز ه ج
و ا ح

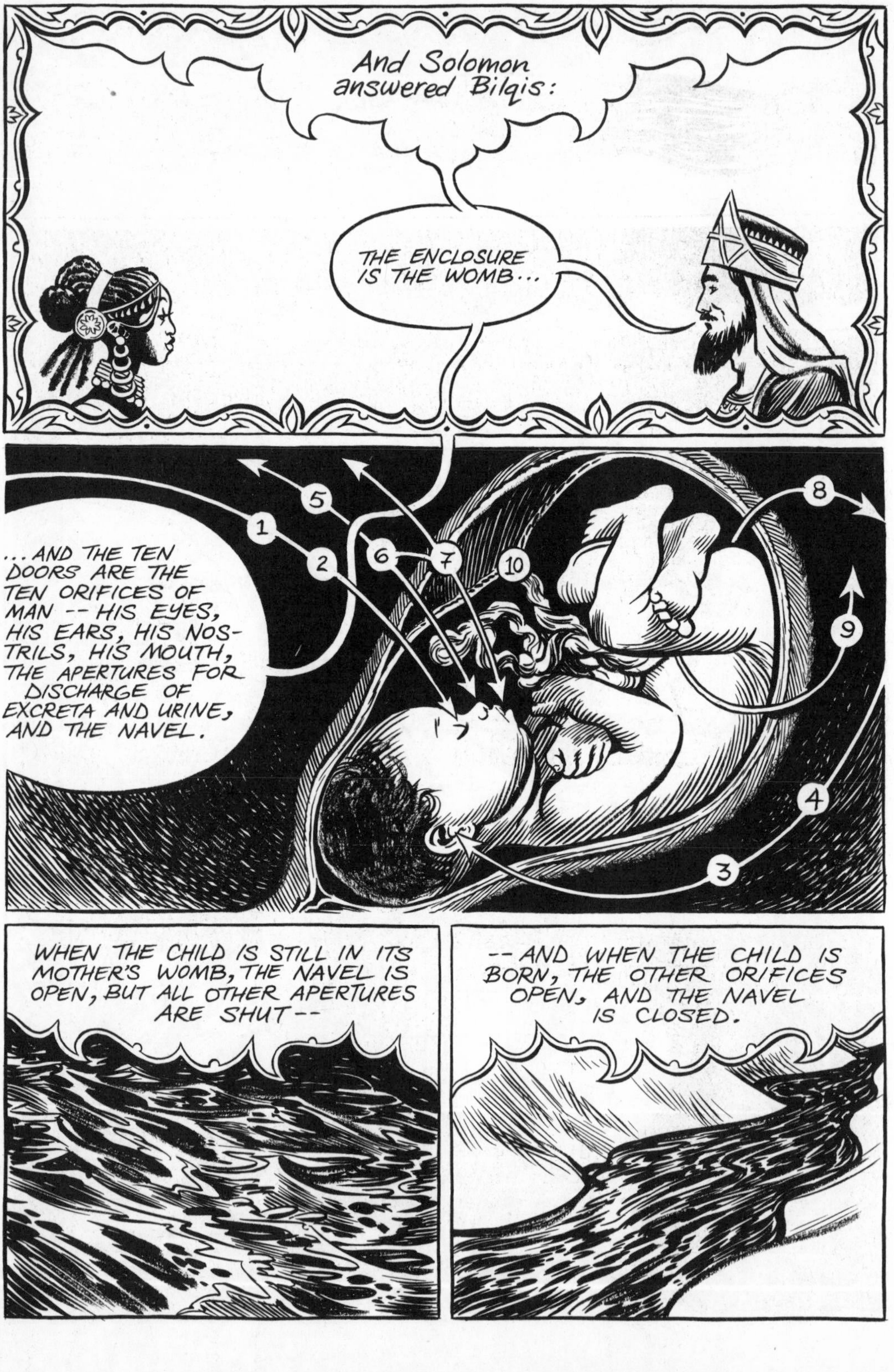
And Solomon answered Bilqis:
THE ENCLOSURE IS THE WOMB...
...AND THE TEN DOORS ARE THE TEN ORIFICES OF MAN -- HIS EYES, HIS EARS, HIS NOS-TRILS, HIS MOUTH, THE APERTURES FOR DISCHARGE OF EXCRETA AND URINE, AND THE NAVEL.
WHEN THE CHILD IS STILL IN ITS MOTHER'S WOMB, THE NAVEL IS OPEN, BUT ALL OTHER APERTURES ARE SHUT--
--AND WHEN THE CHILD IS BORN, THE OTHER ORIFICES OPEN, AND THE NAVEL IS CLOSED.

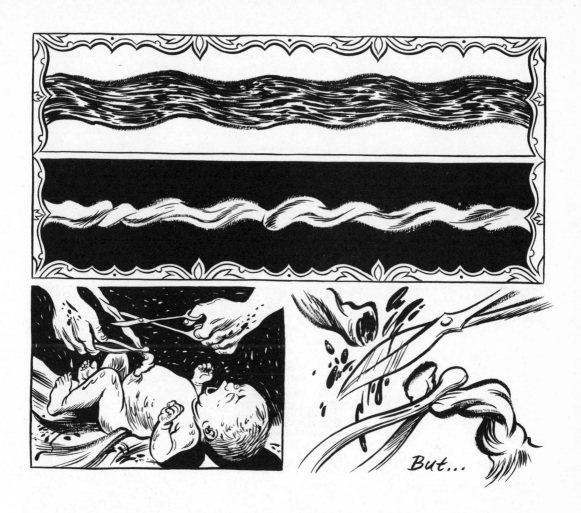

But...

This is not my baby.

د	ط	ب
ج	ه	ز
ح	ا	و

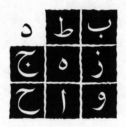

سبي
عدن

RAPING
EDEN

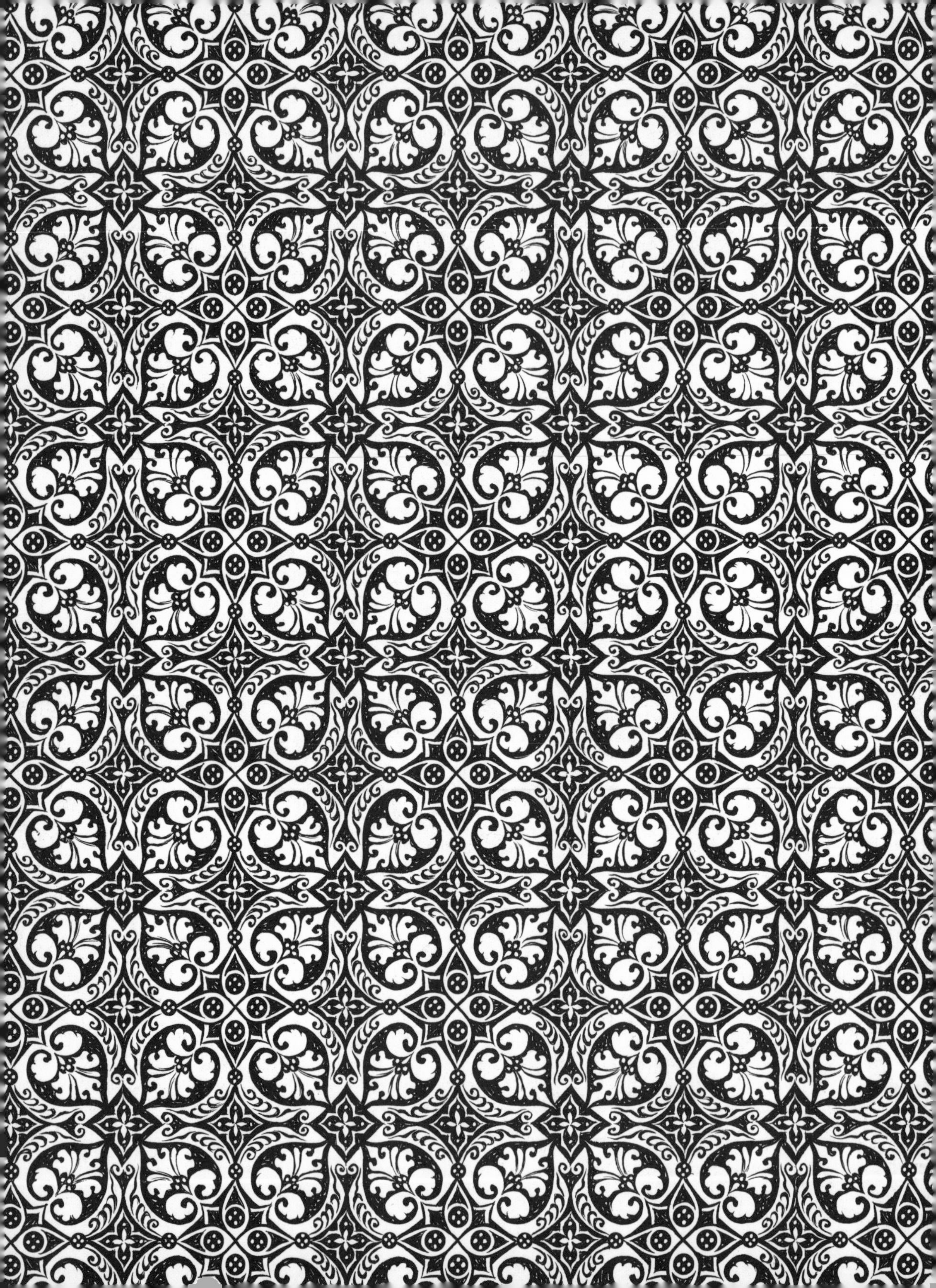

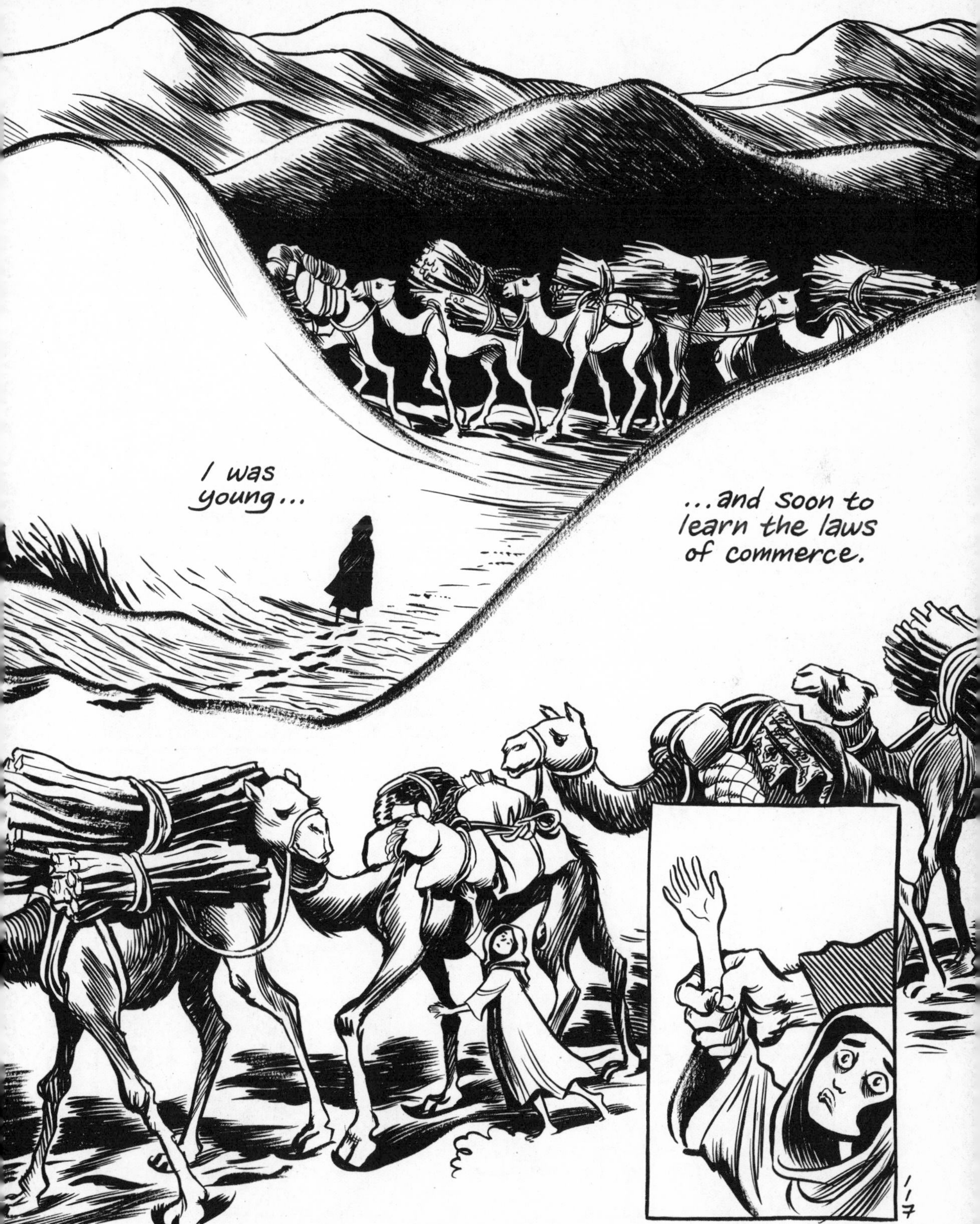
I was young...
...and soon to learn the laws of commerce.
117

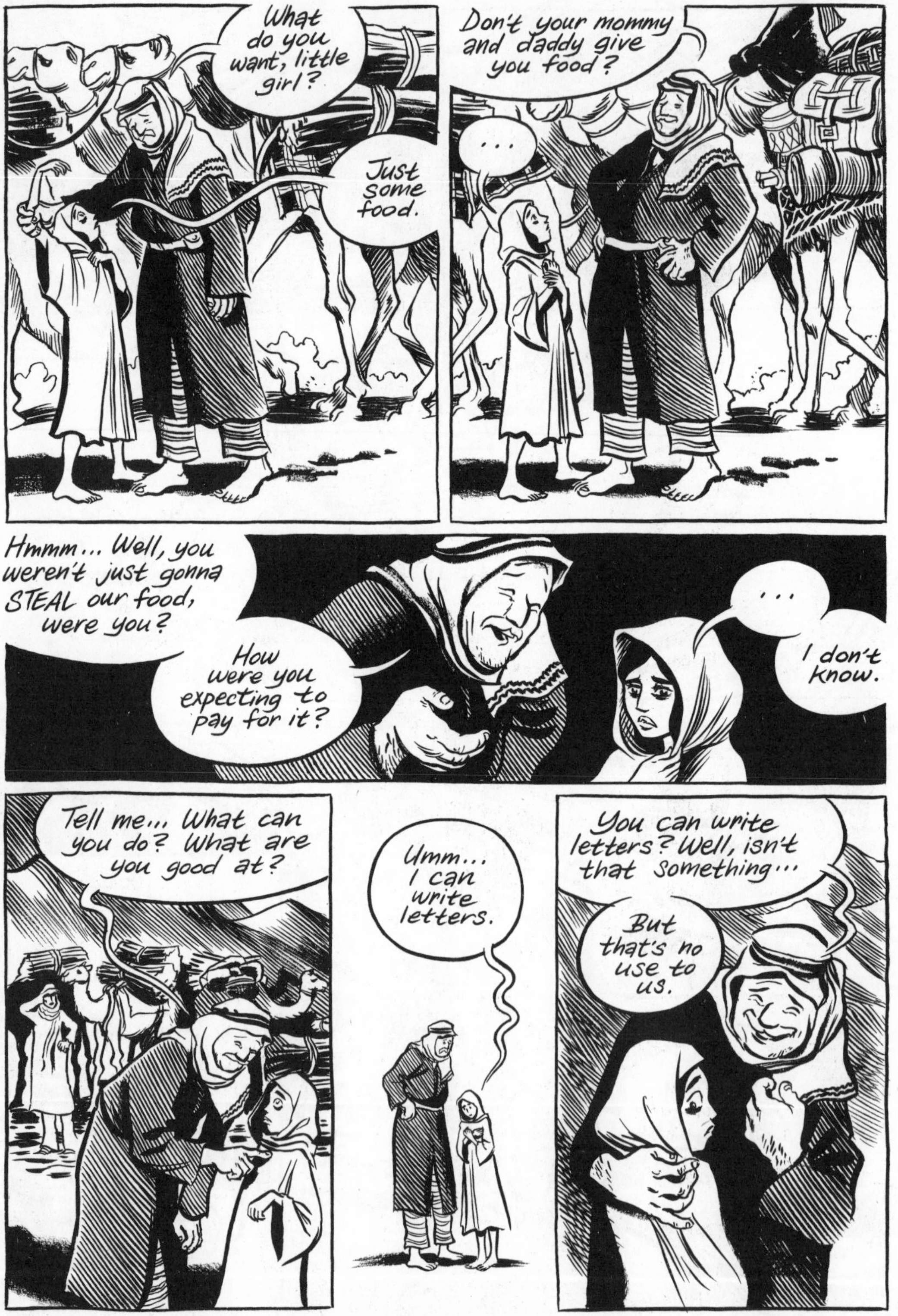
What do you want, little girl?
Just some food.
Don't your mommy and daddy give you food?
...
Hmmm... Well, you weren't just gonna STEAL our food, were you?
How were you expecting to pay for it?
...
I don't know.
Tell me... What can you do? What are you good at?
Umm... I can write letters.
You can write letters? Well, isn't that something...
But that's no use to us.

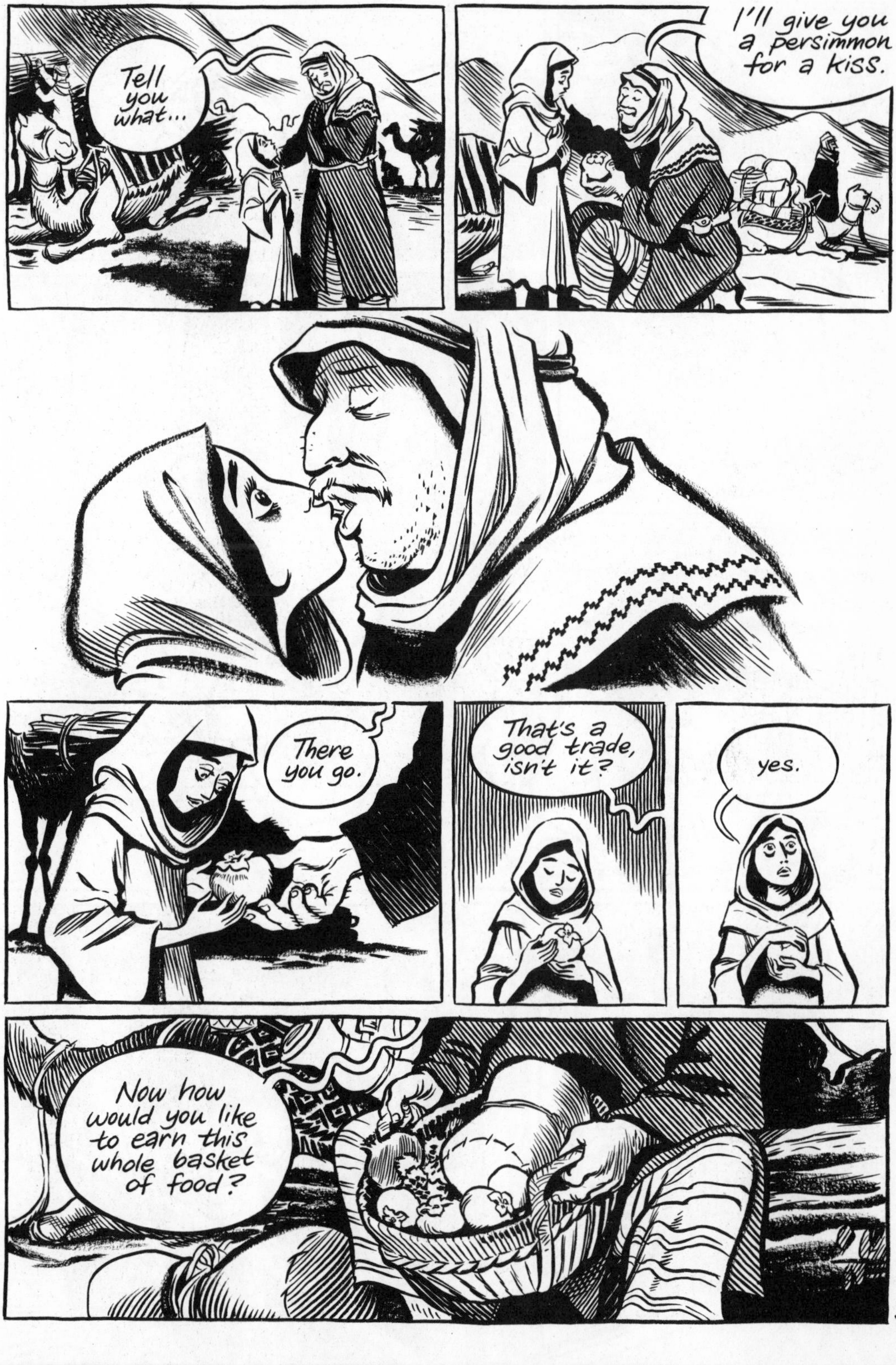
Tell you what...
I'll give you a persimmon for a kiss.
There you go.
That's a good trade, isn't it?
yes.
Now how would you like to earn this whole basket of food?

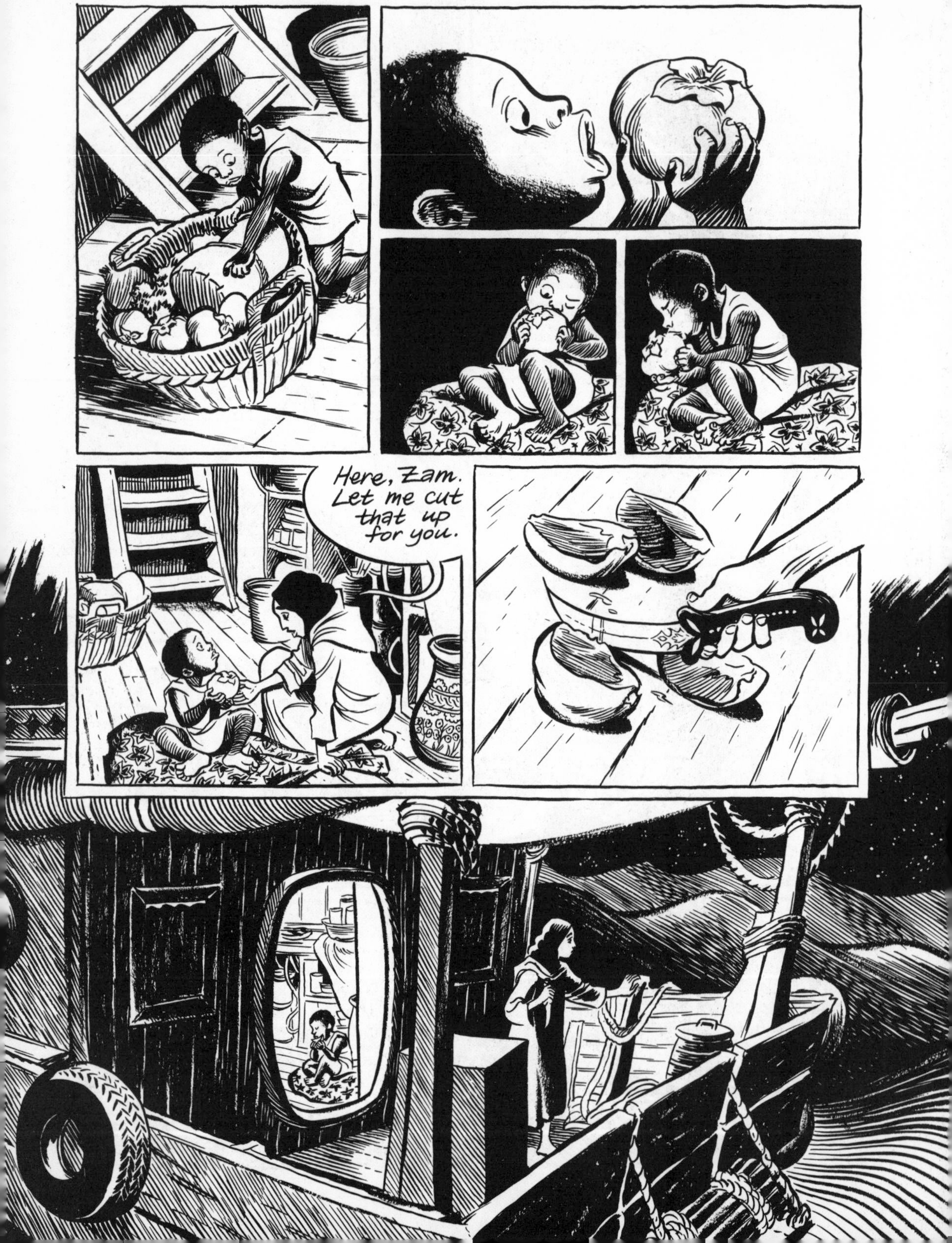
Here, Zam. Let me cut that up for you.

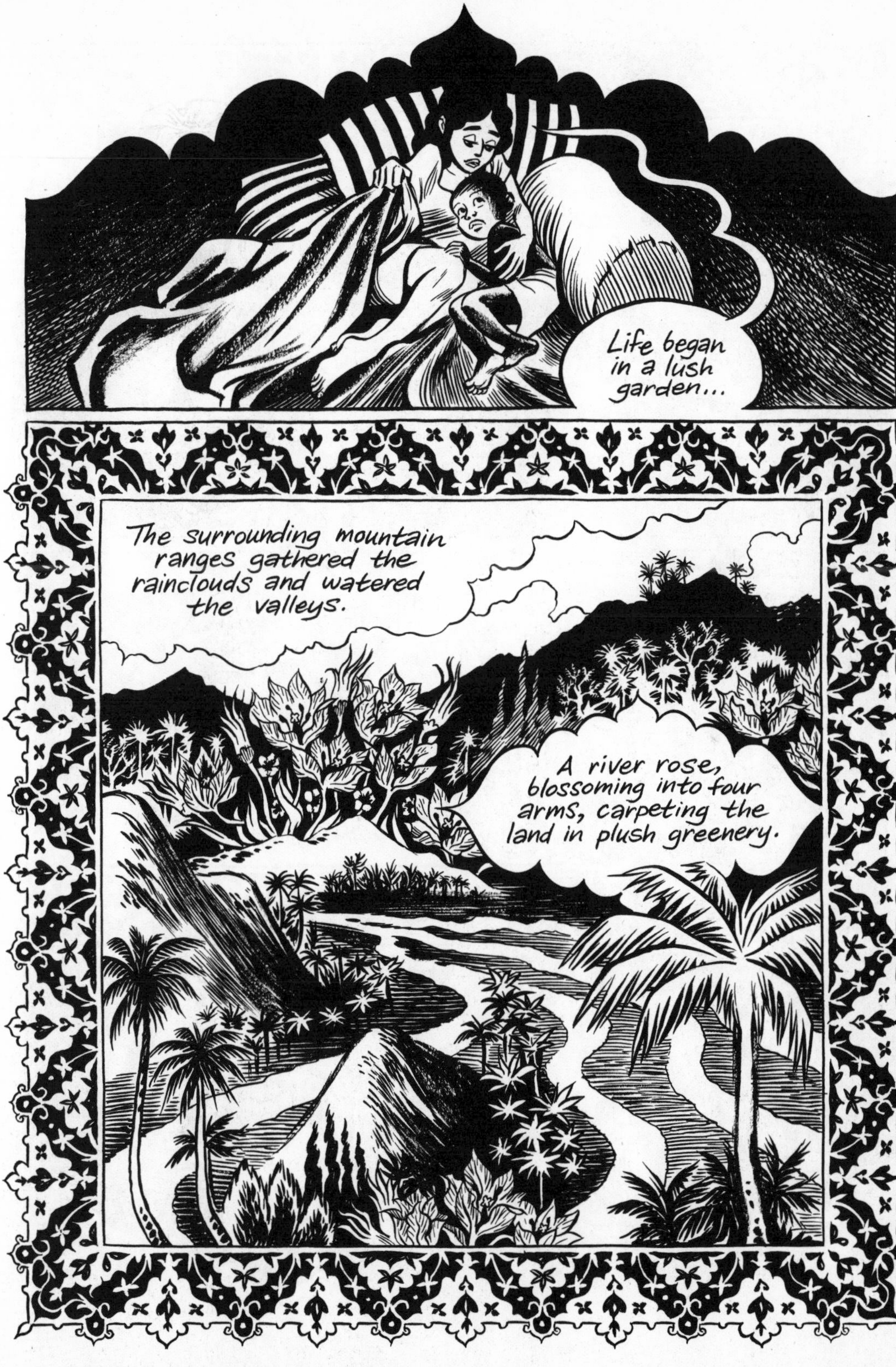
Life began in a lush garden...
The surrounding mountain ranges gathered the rainclouds and watered the valleys.
A river rose, blossoming into four arms, carpeting the land in plush greenery.

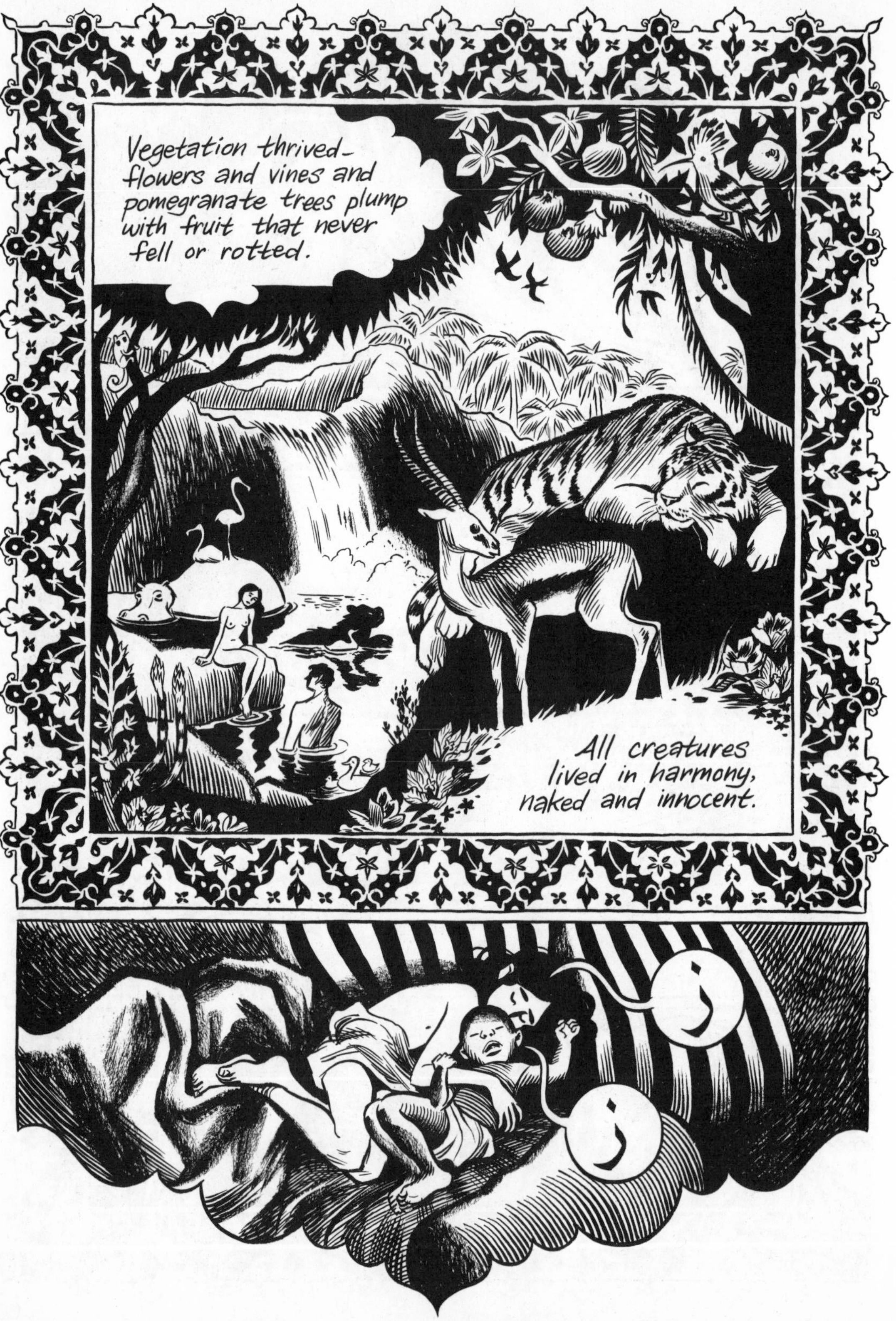
Vegetation thrived-flowers and vines and pomegranate trees plump with fruit that never fell or rotted.
All creatures lived in harmony, naked and innocent.
ز
ز

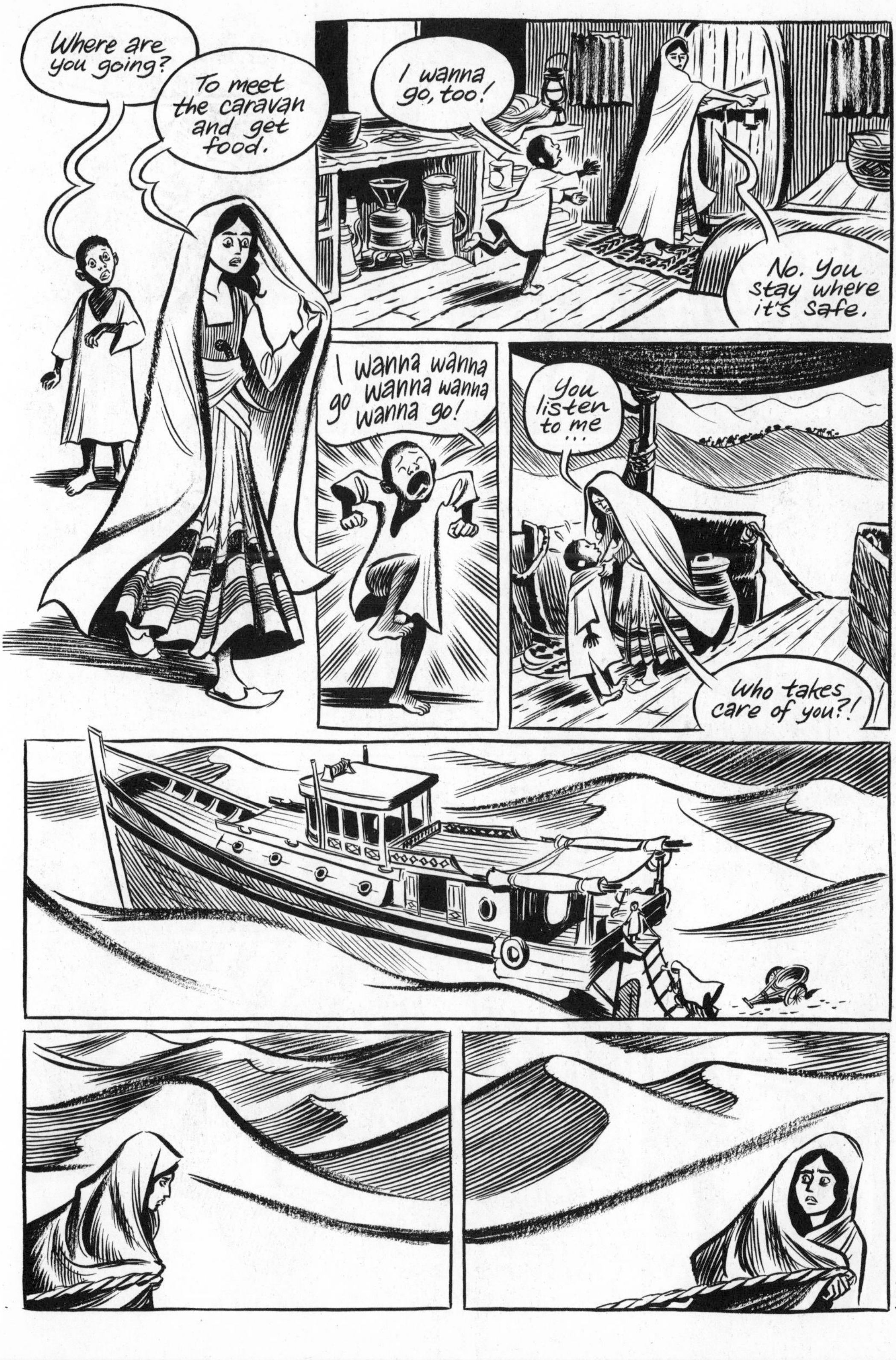
Where are you going?
To meet the caravan and get food.
I wanna go, too!
No. You stay where it's safe.
I wanna wanna go wanna wanna wanna go!
You listen to me ...
Who takes care of you?!

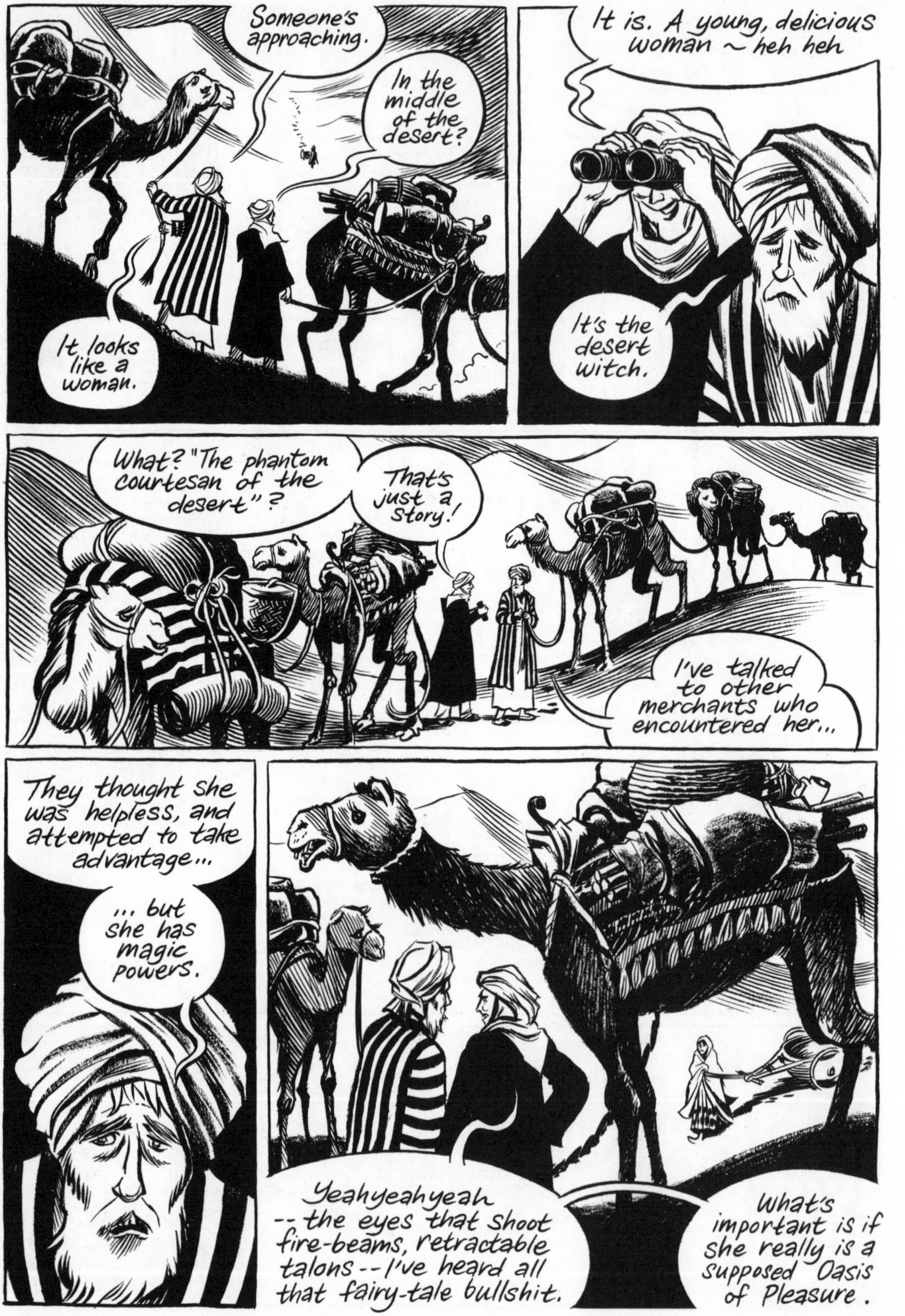
Someone's approaching.
In the middle of the desert?
It looks like a woman.
It is. A young, delicious woman ~ heh heh
It's the desert witch.
What? "The phantom courtesan of the desert"?
That's just a story!
I've talked to other merchants who encountered her...
They thought she was helpless, and attempted to take advantage...
... but she has magic powers.
Yeahyeahyeah -- the eyes that shoot fire-beams, retractable talons -- I've heard all that fairy-tale bullshit.
What's important is if she really is a supposed Oasis of Pleasure.

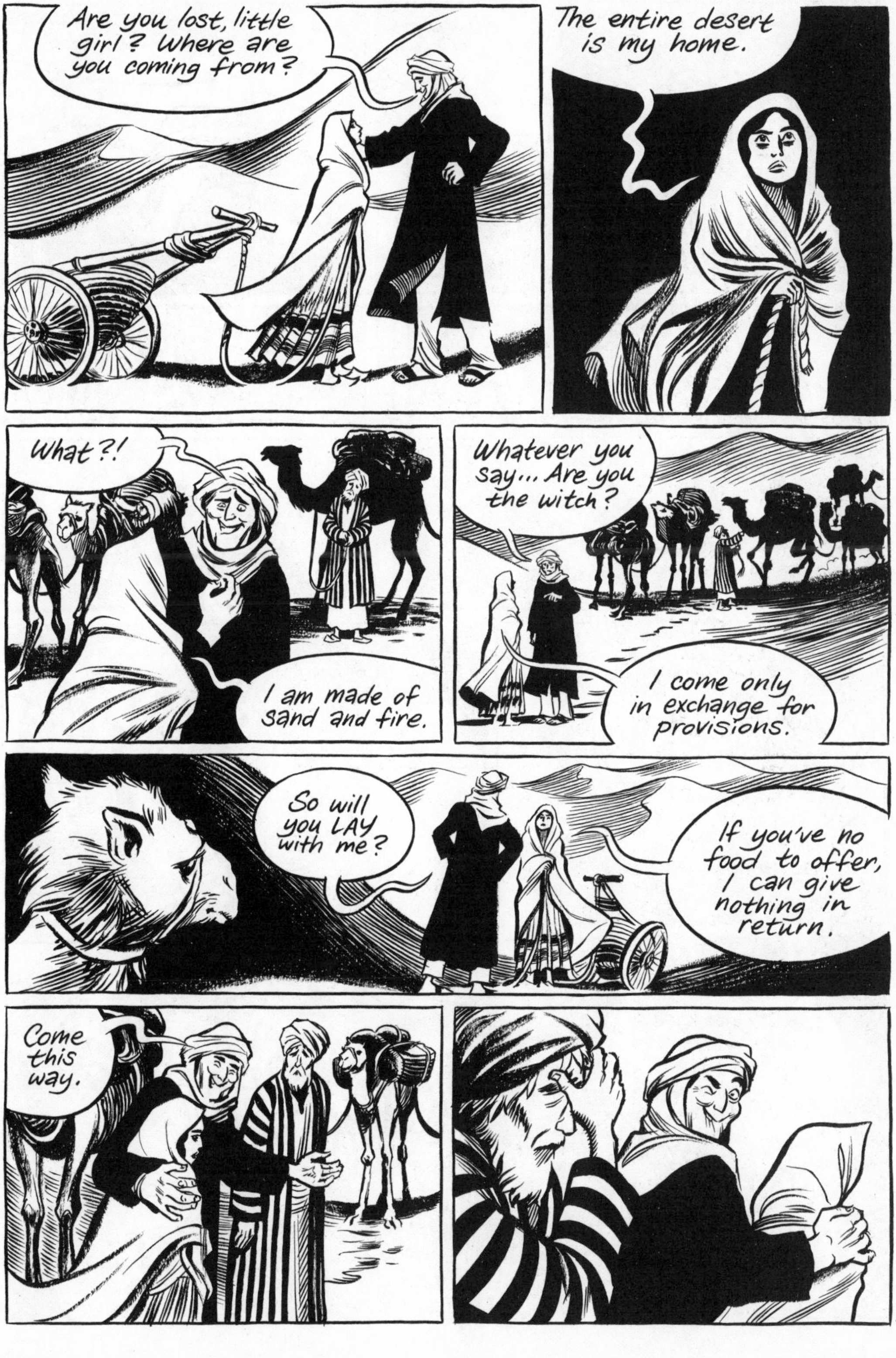
Are you lost, little girl? Where are you coming from?
The entire desert is my home.
What?!
I am made of sand and fire.
Whatever you say... Are you the witch?
I come only in exchange for provisions.
So will you LAY with me?
If you've no food to offer, I can give nothing in return.
Come this way.

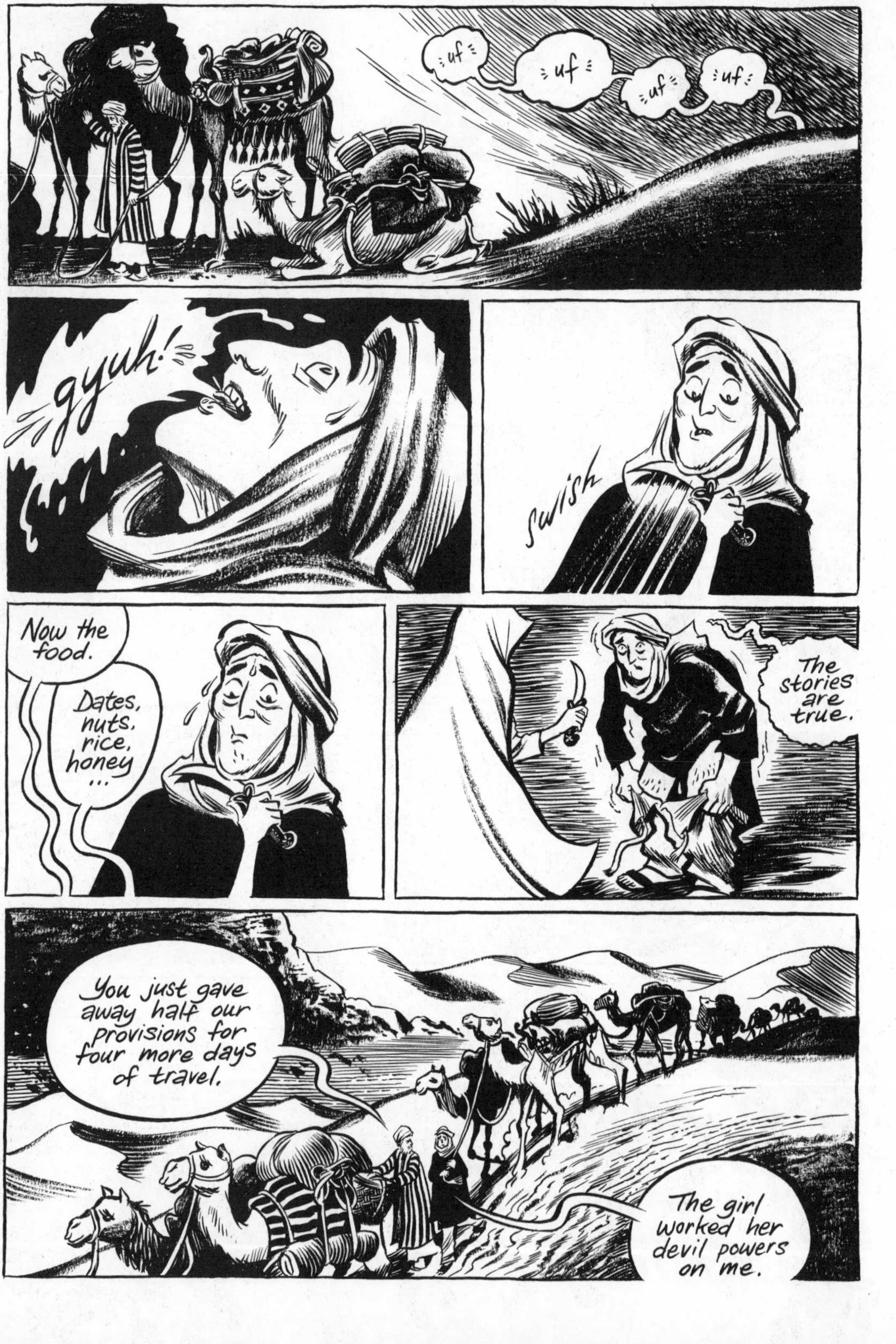

uf
uf
uf
uf
gyuh!
swish
Now the food.
Dates, nuts, rice, honey ...
The stories are true.
You just gave away half our provisions for four more days of travel.
The girl worked her devil powers on me.

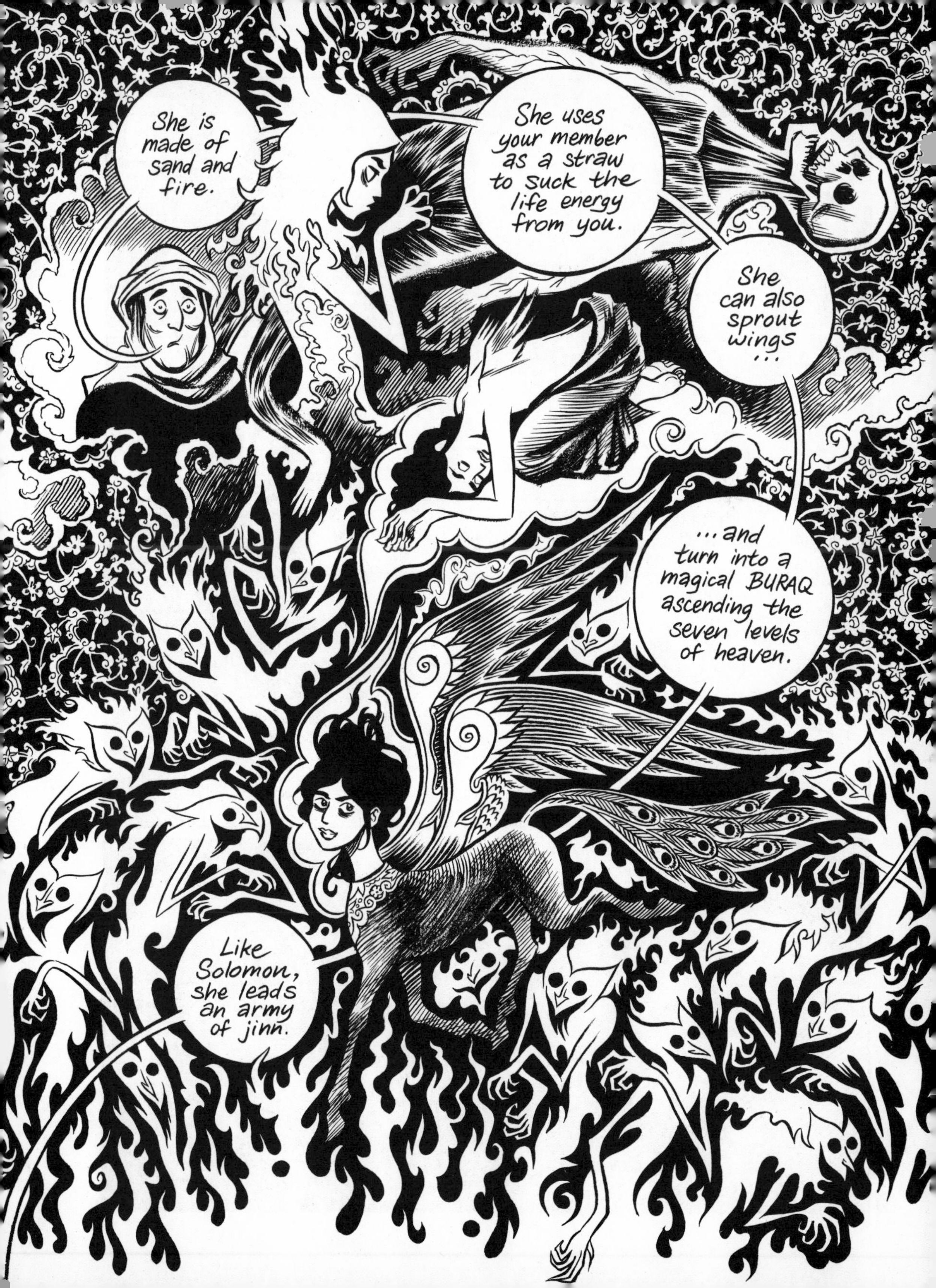
She is made of sand and fire.
She uses your member as a straw to suck the life energy from you.
She can also sprout wings ...
...and turn into a magical BURAQ ascending the seven levels of heaven.
Like Solomon, she leads an army of jinn.

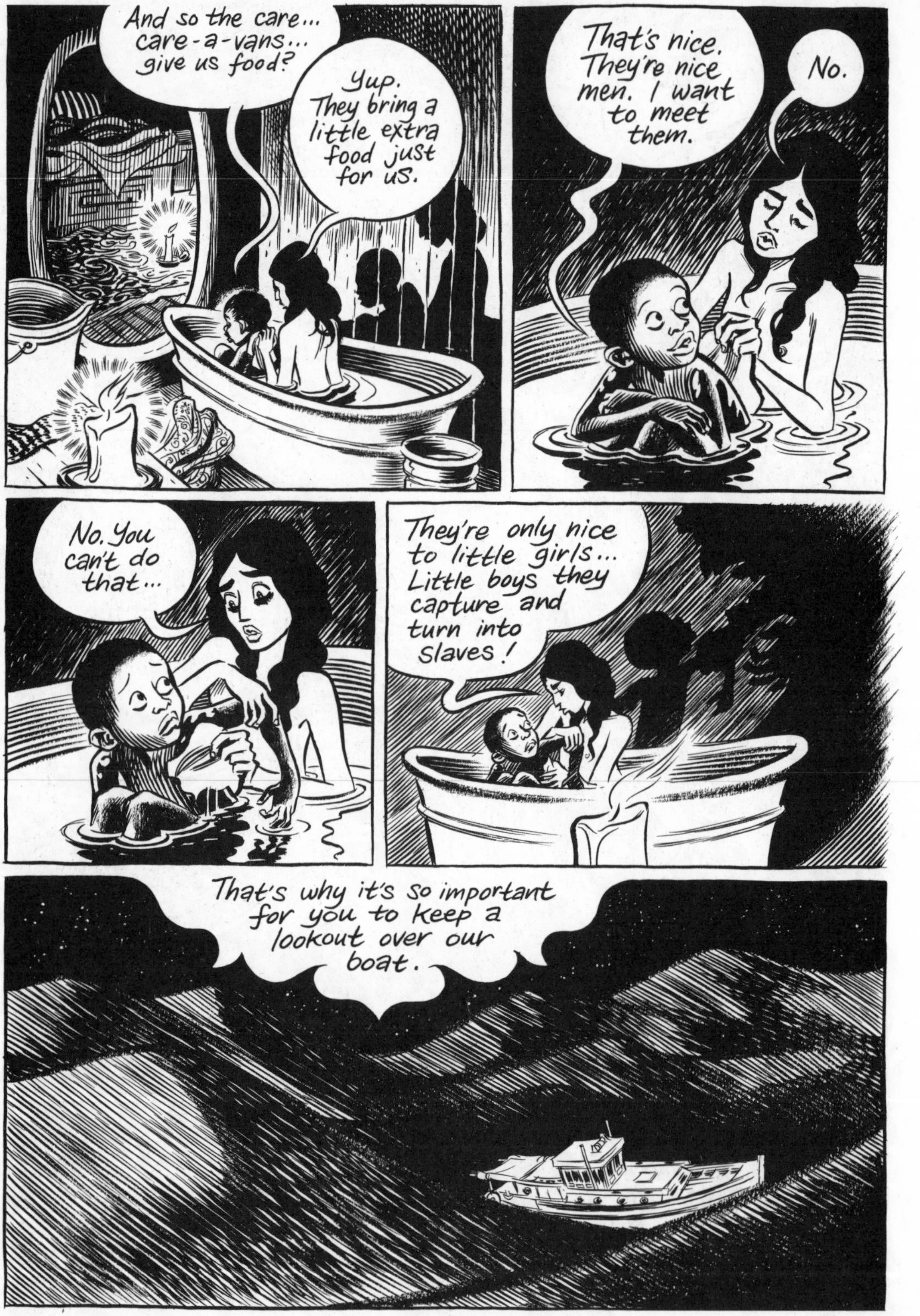
And so the care... care-a-vans... give us food?
Yup. They bring a little extra food just for us.
That's nice. They're nice men. I want to meet them.
No.
No. You can't do that...
They're only nice to little girls... Little boys they capture and turn into slaves!
That's why it's so important for you to keep a lookout over our boat.

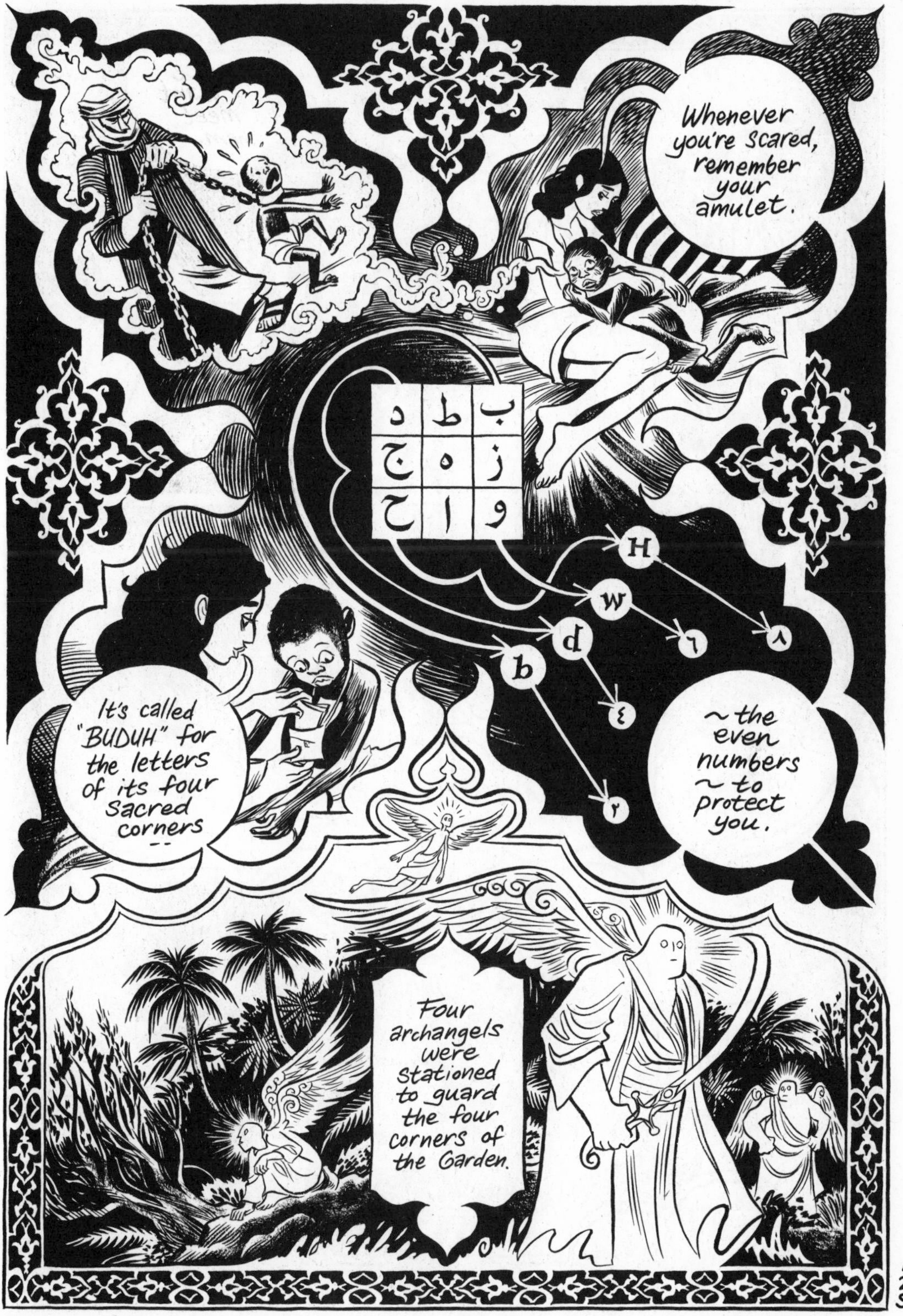
Whenever you're scared, remember your amulet.
ب ط د
ز ه ج
و ا ح
H
W
d
b
٨
٦
٤
٢
It's called "BUDUH" for the letters of its four sacred corners --
~the even numbers ~to protect you.
Four archangels were stationed to guard the four corners of the Garden.

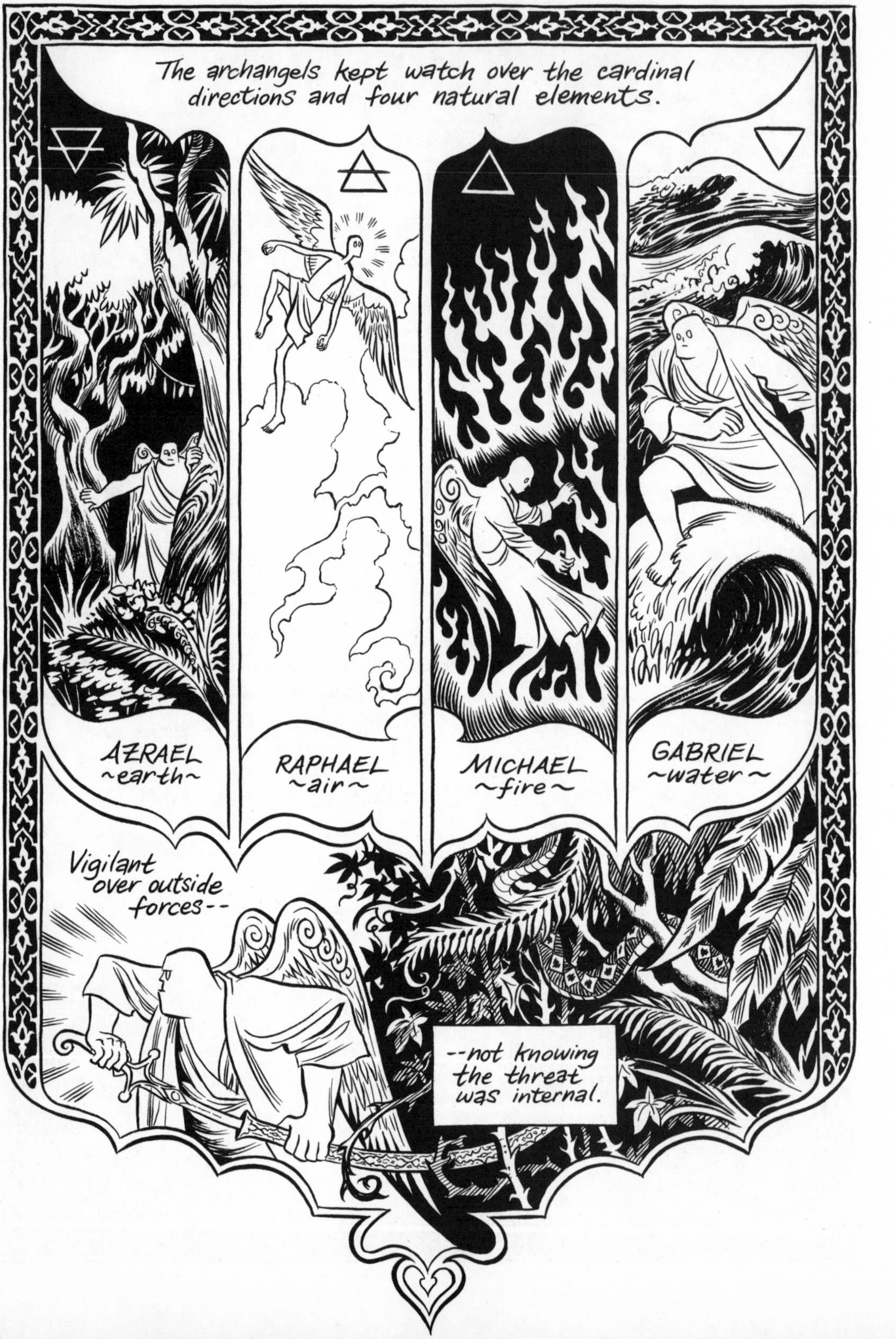
The archangels kept watch over the cardinal directions and four natural elements.
AZRAEL ~earth~
RAPHAEL ~air~
MICHAEL ~fire~
GABRIEL ~water~
Vigilant over outside forces--
--not knowing the threat was internal.

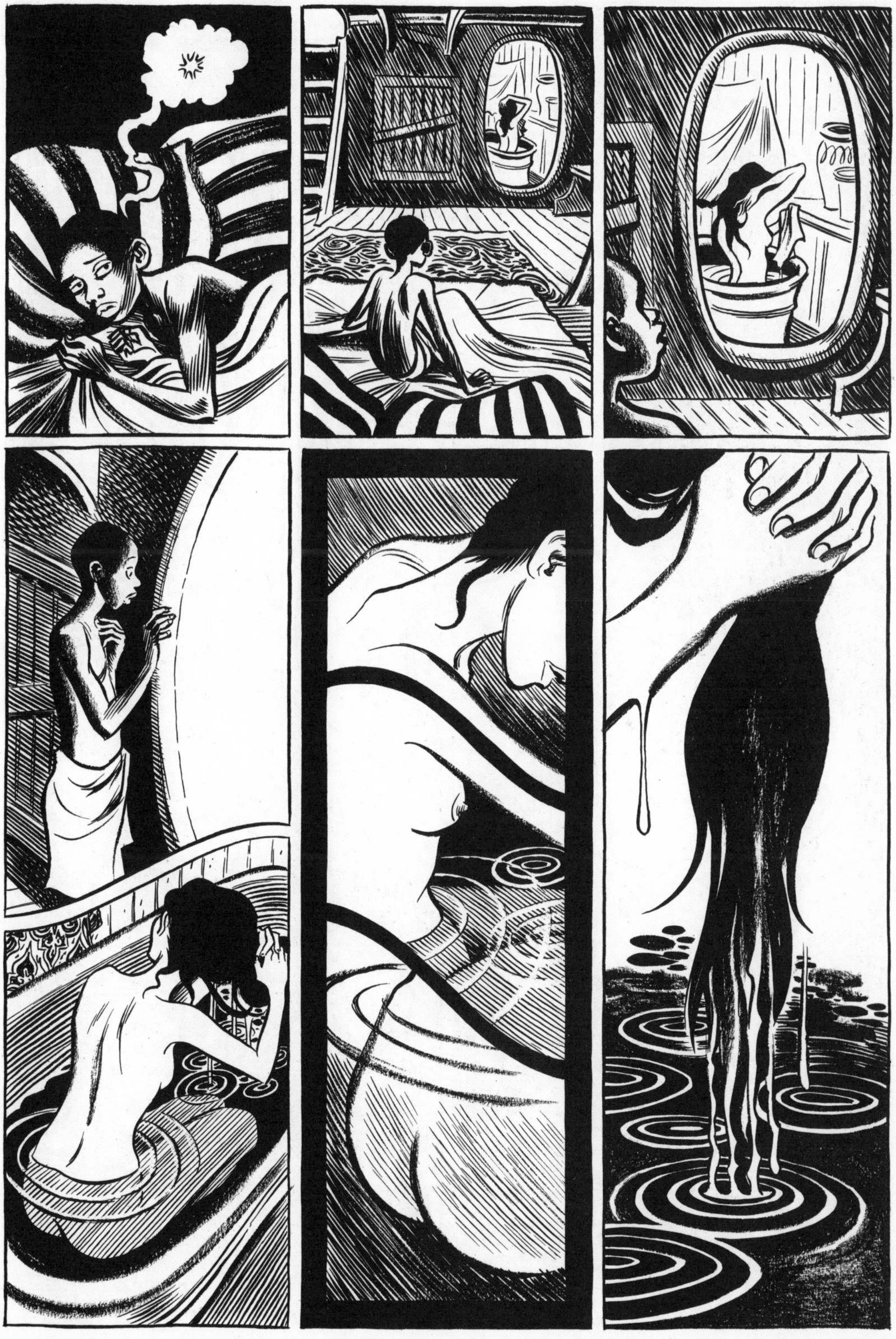

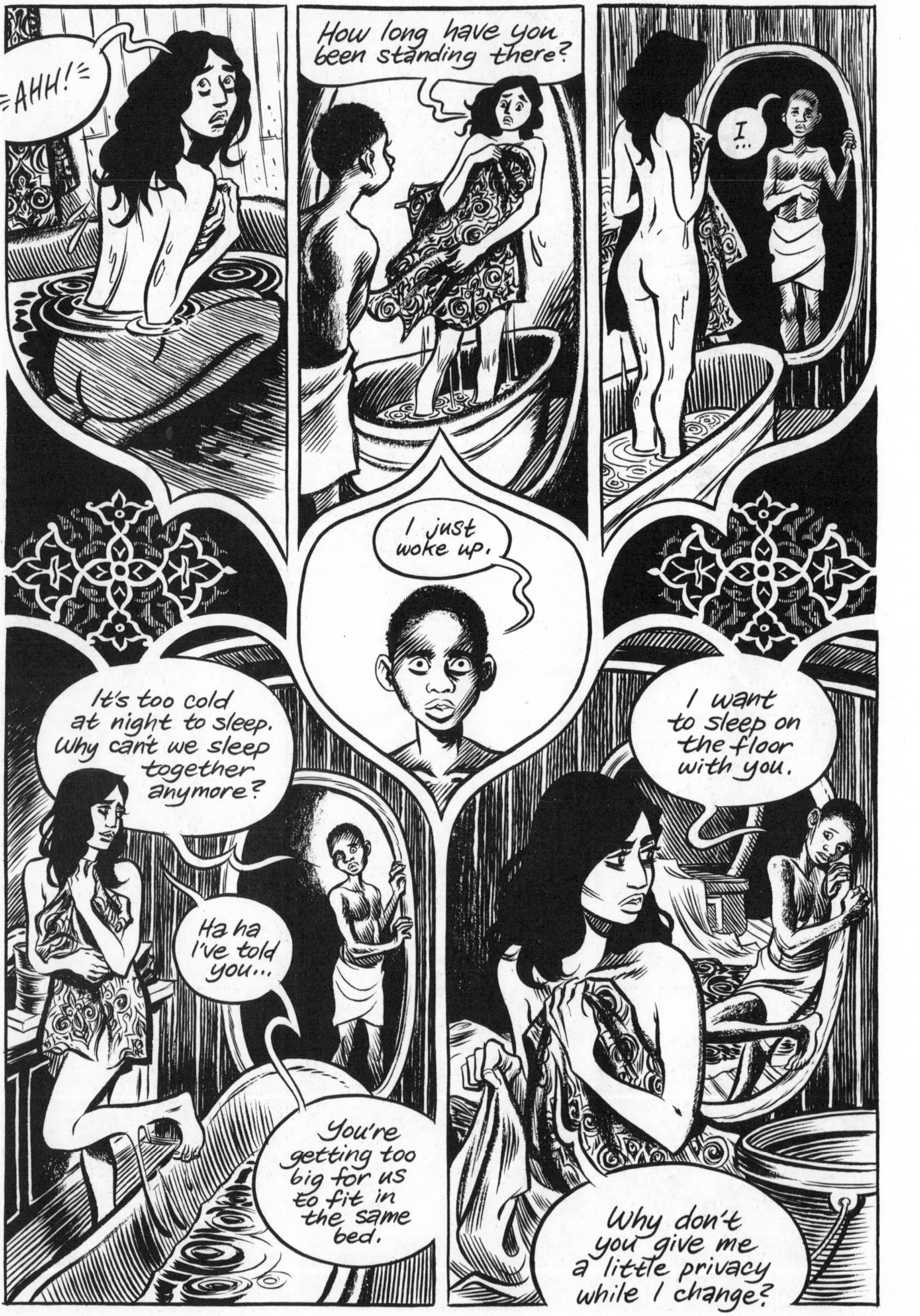
AHH!
How long have you been standing there?
I...
I just woke up.
It's too cold at night to sleep. Why can't we sleep together anymore?
Ha ha I've told you...
You're getting too big for us to fit in the same bed.
I want to sleep on the floor with you.
Why don't you give me a little privacy while I change?

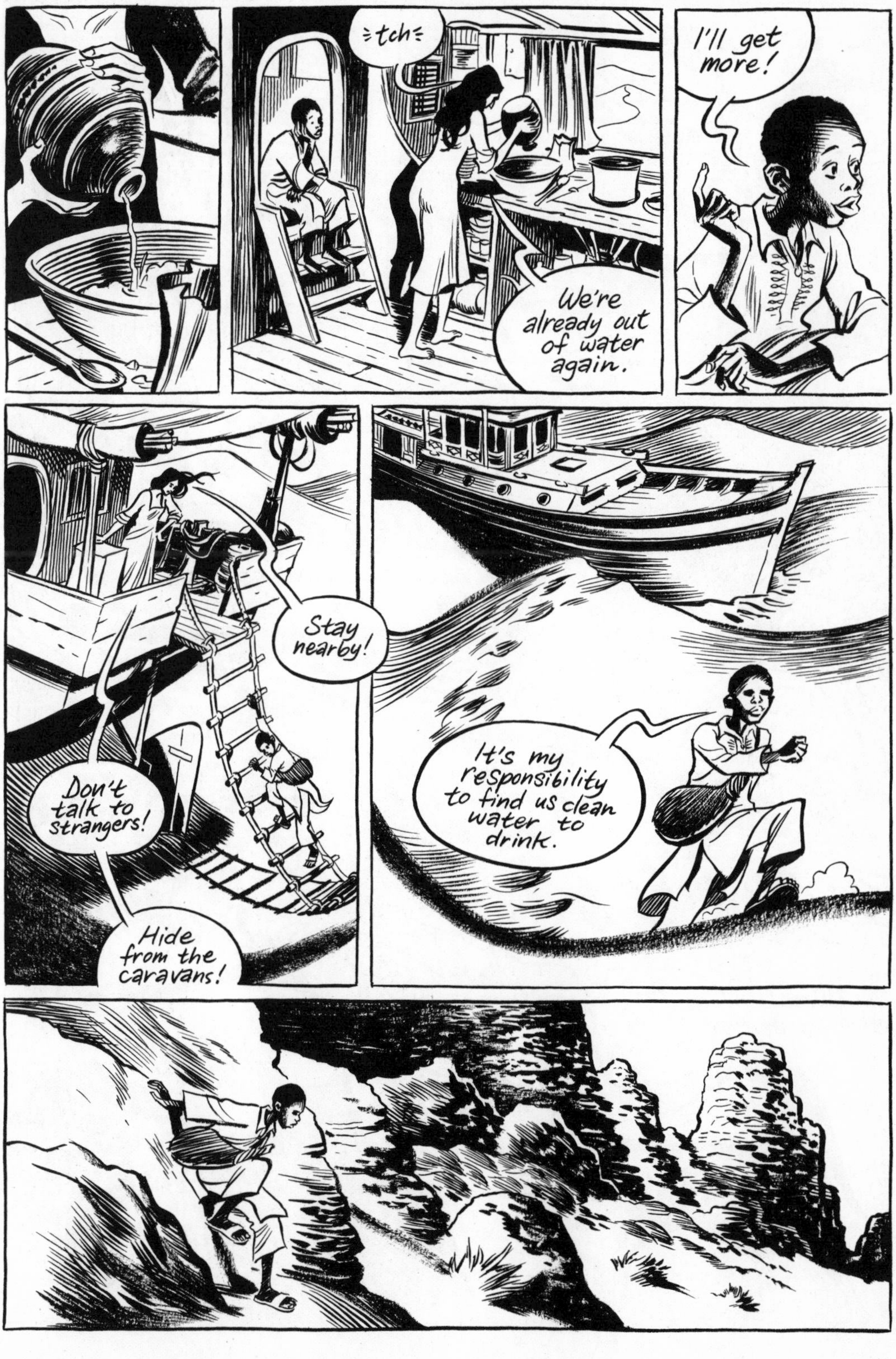
tch
We're already out of water again.
I'll get more!
Stay nearby!
Don't talk to strangers!
Hide from the caravans!
It's my responsibility to find us clean water to drink.

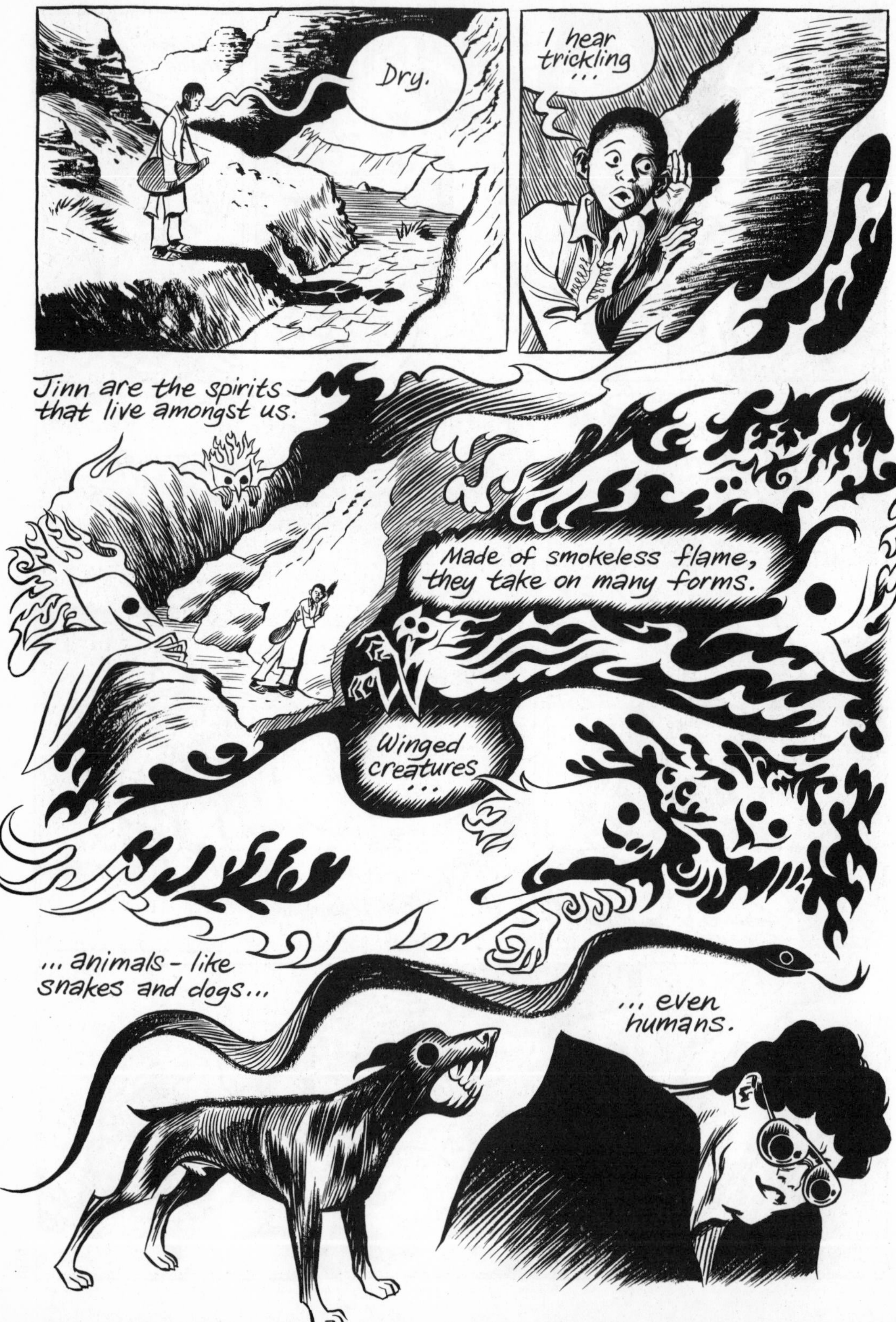
Dry.
I hear trickling ...
Jinn are the spirits that live amongst us.
Made of smokeless flame, they take on many forms.
Winged creatures ...
... animals - like snakes and dogs...
... even humans.

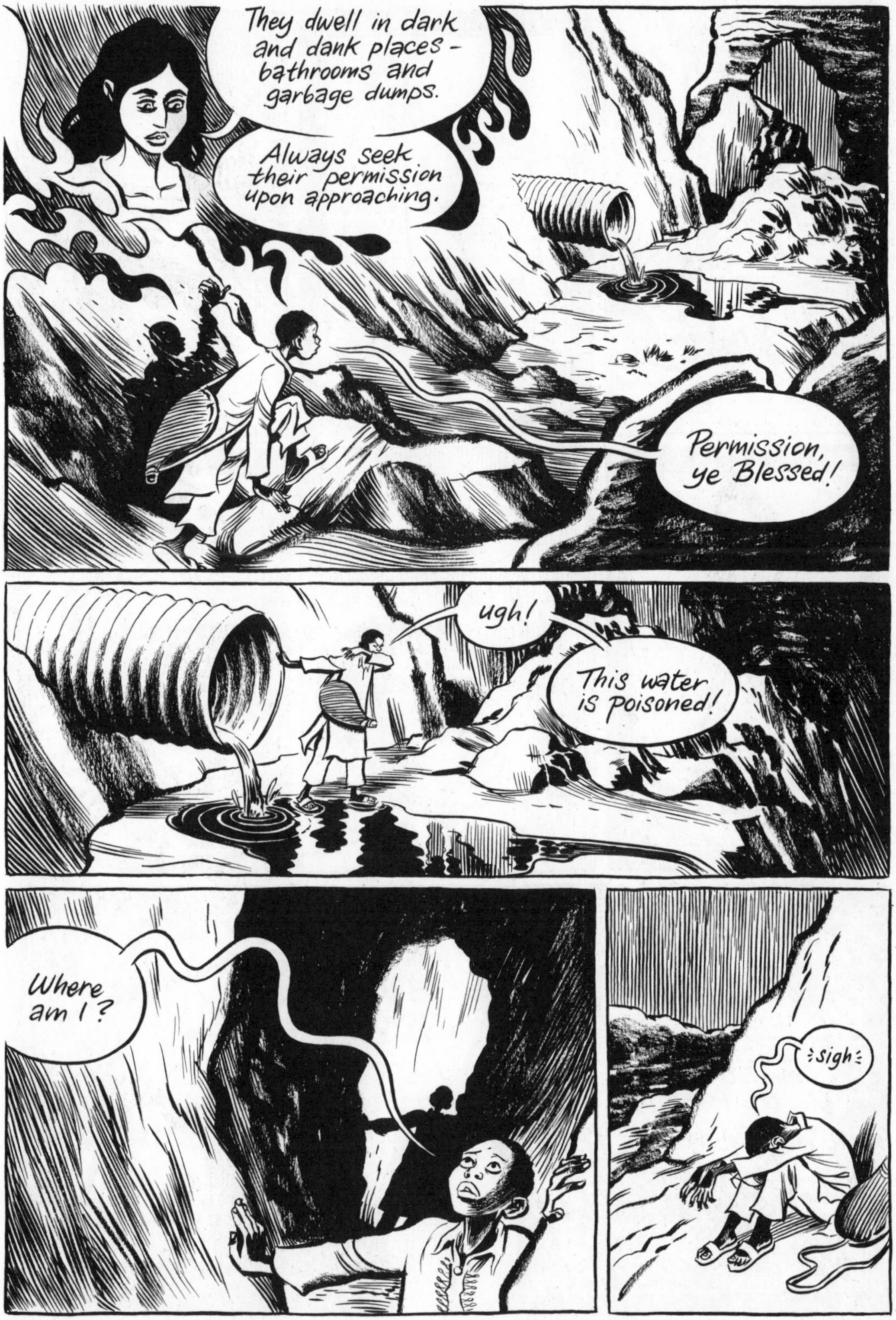
They dwell in dark and dank places - bathrooms and garbage dumps.
Always seek their permission upon approaching.
Permission, ye Blessed!
ugh!
This water is poisoned!
Where am I?
sigh

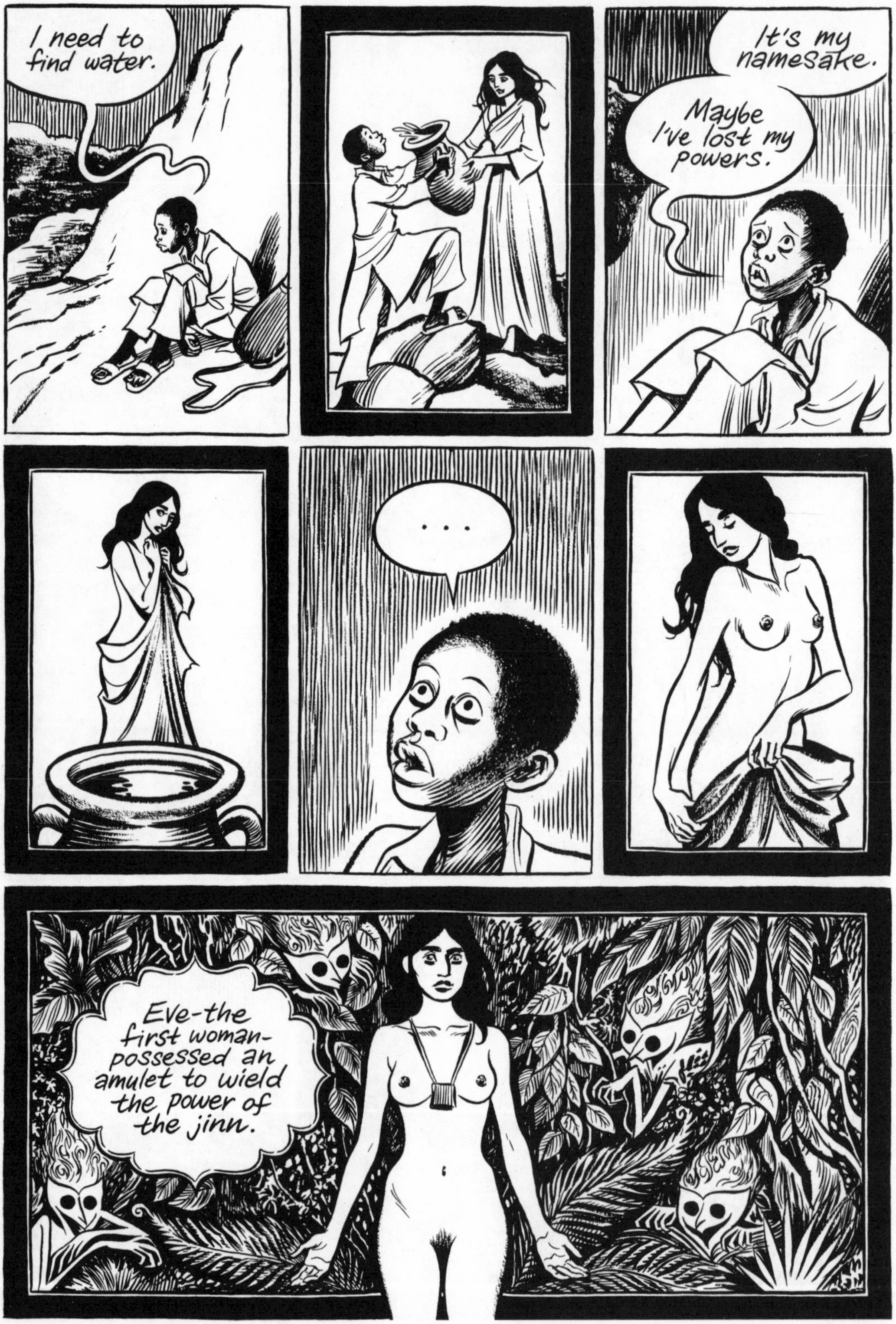
I need to find water.
It's my namesake.
Maybe I've lost my powers.
. . .
Eve-the first woman-possessed an amulet to wield the power of the jinn.

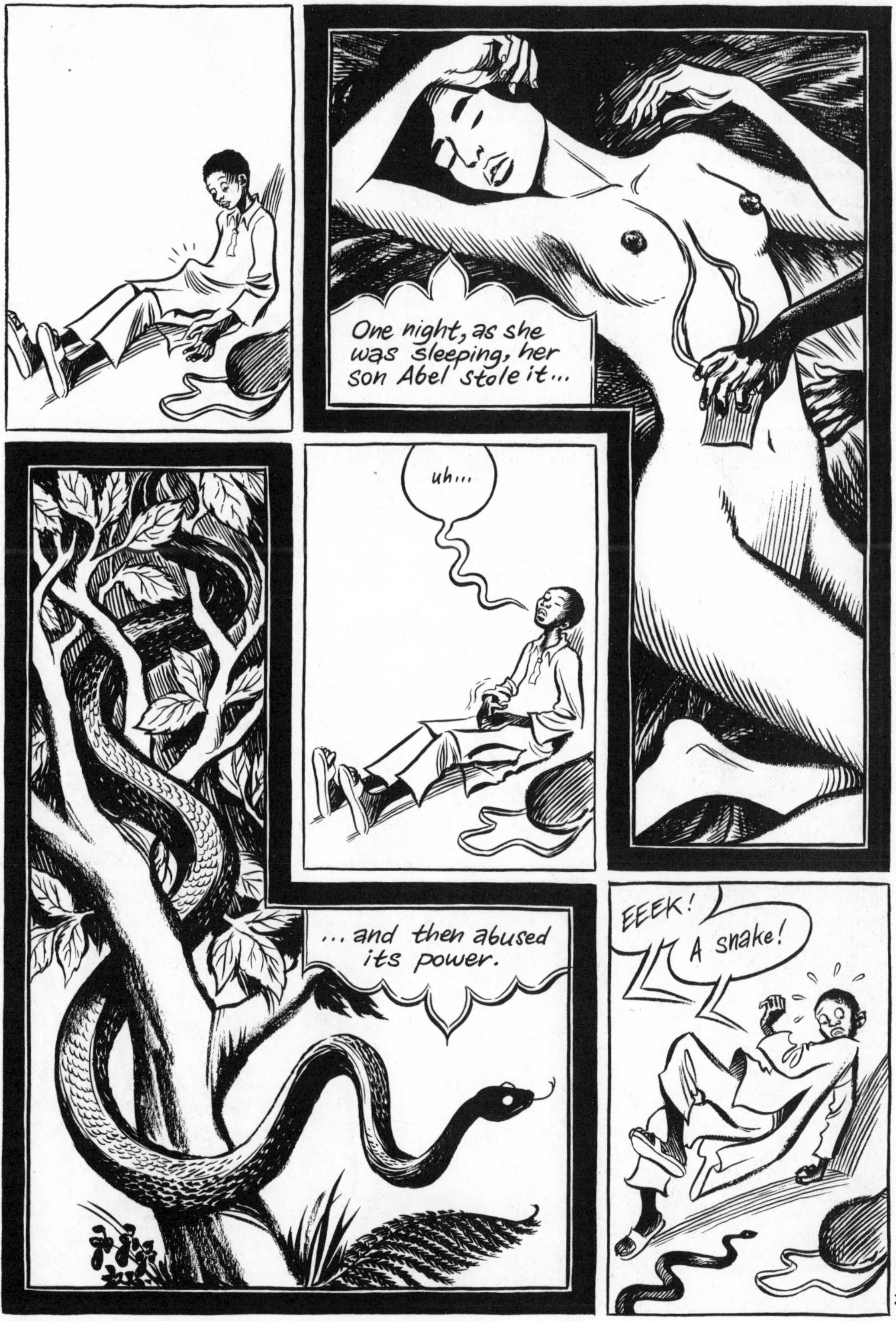

One night, as she was sleeping, her son Abel stole it...
uh...
...and then abused its power.
EEEK!
A snake!

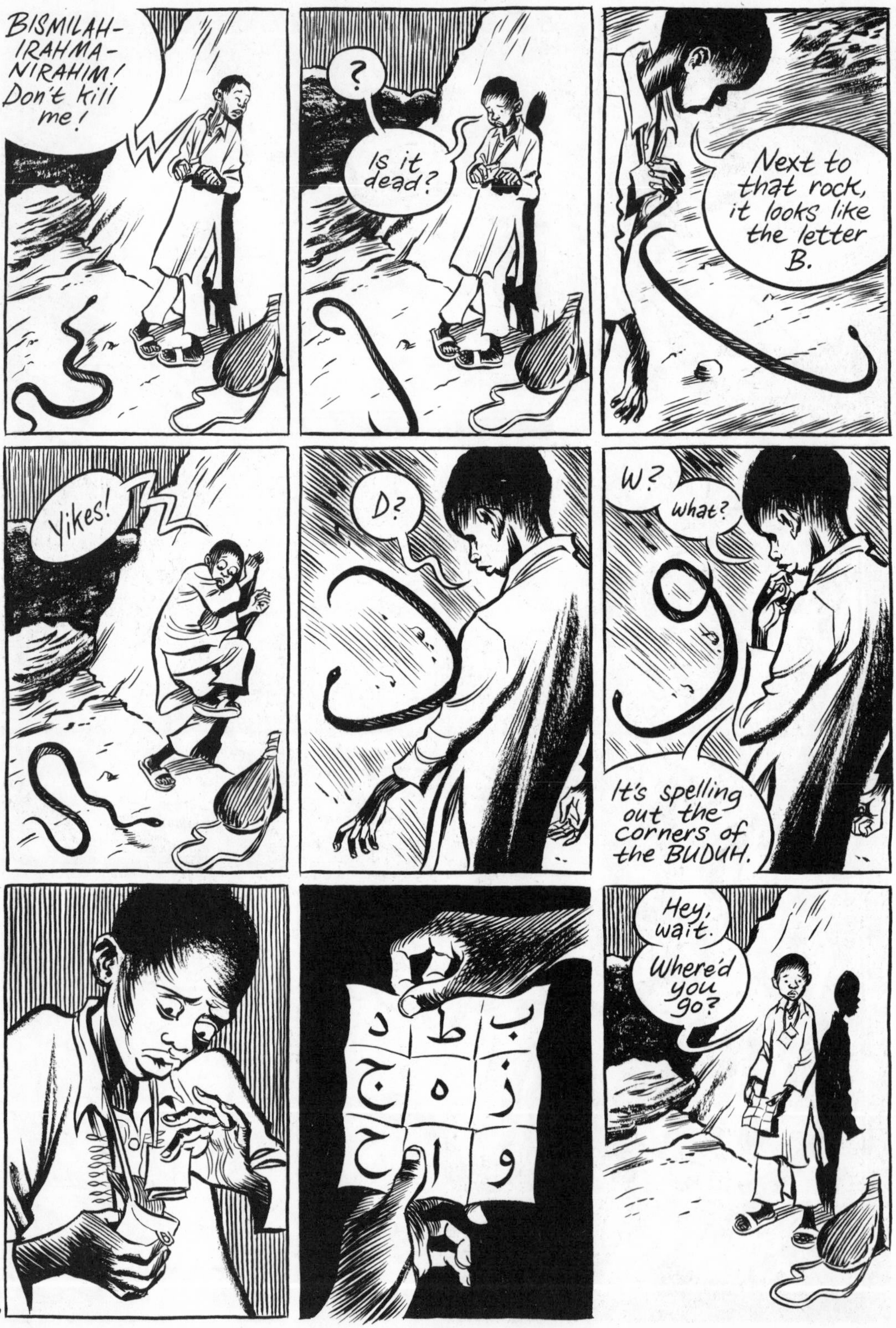
BISMILAH-IRAHMA-NIRAHIM! Don't kill me!
?
Is it dead?
Next to that rock, it looks like the letter B.
Yikes!
D?
W?
what?
It's spelling out the corners of the BUDUH.
ب ط د
ز ه ج
و ا ح
Hey, wait.
Where'd you go?

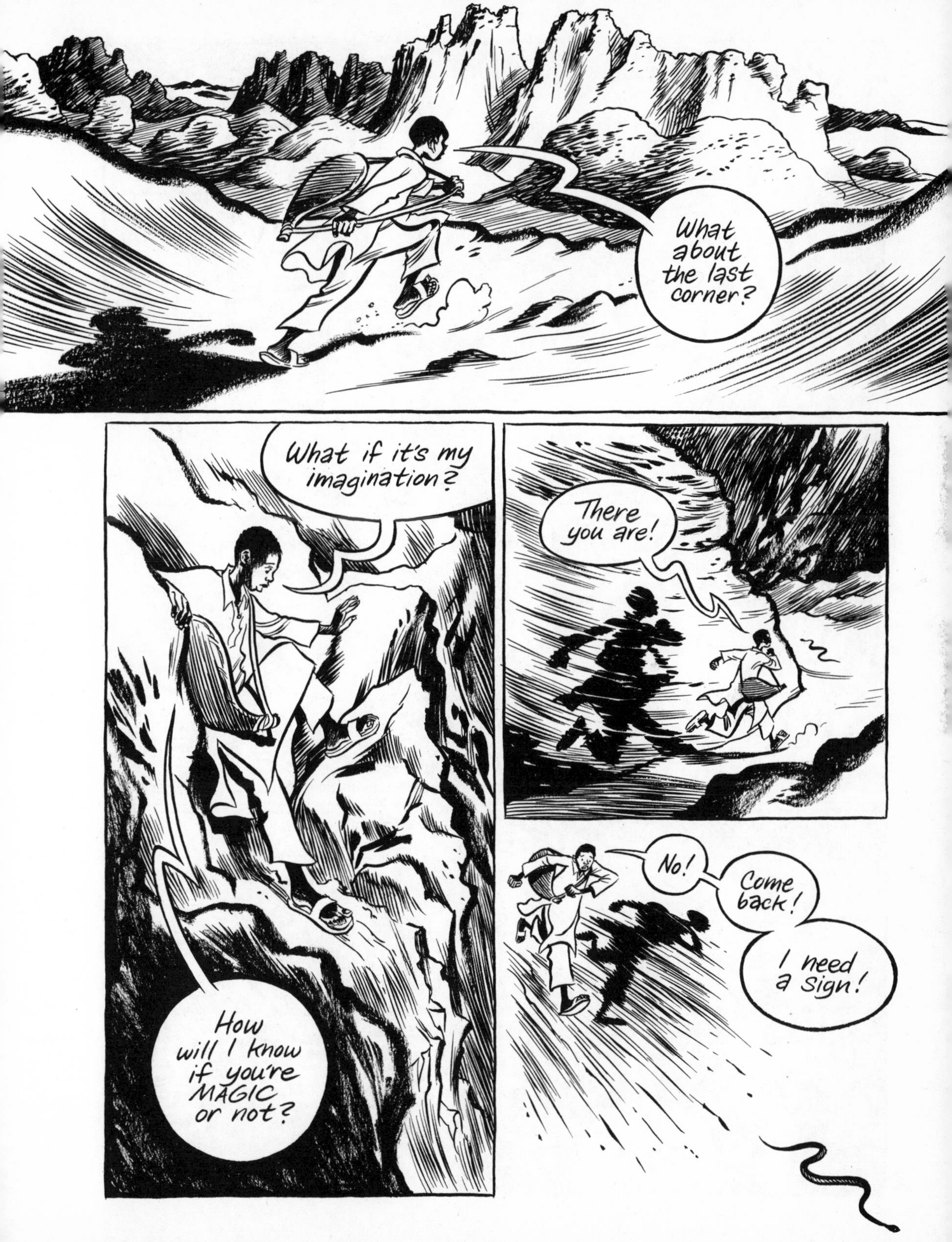
What about the last corner?
What if it's my imagination?
How will I know if you're MAGIC or not?
There you are!
No!
Come back!
I need a Sign!

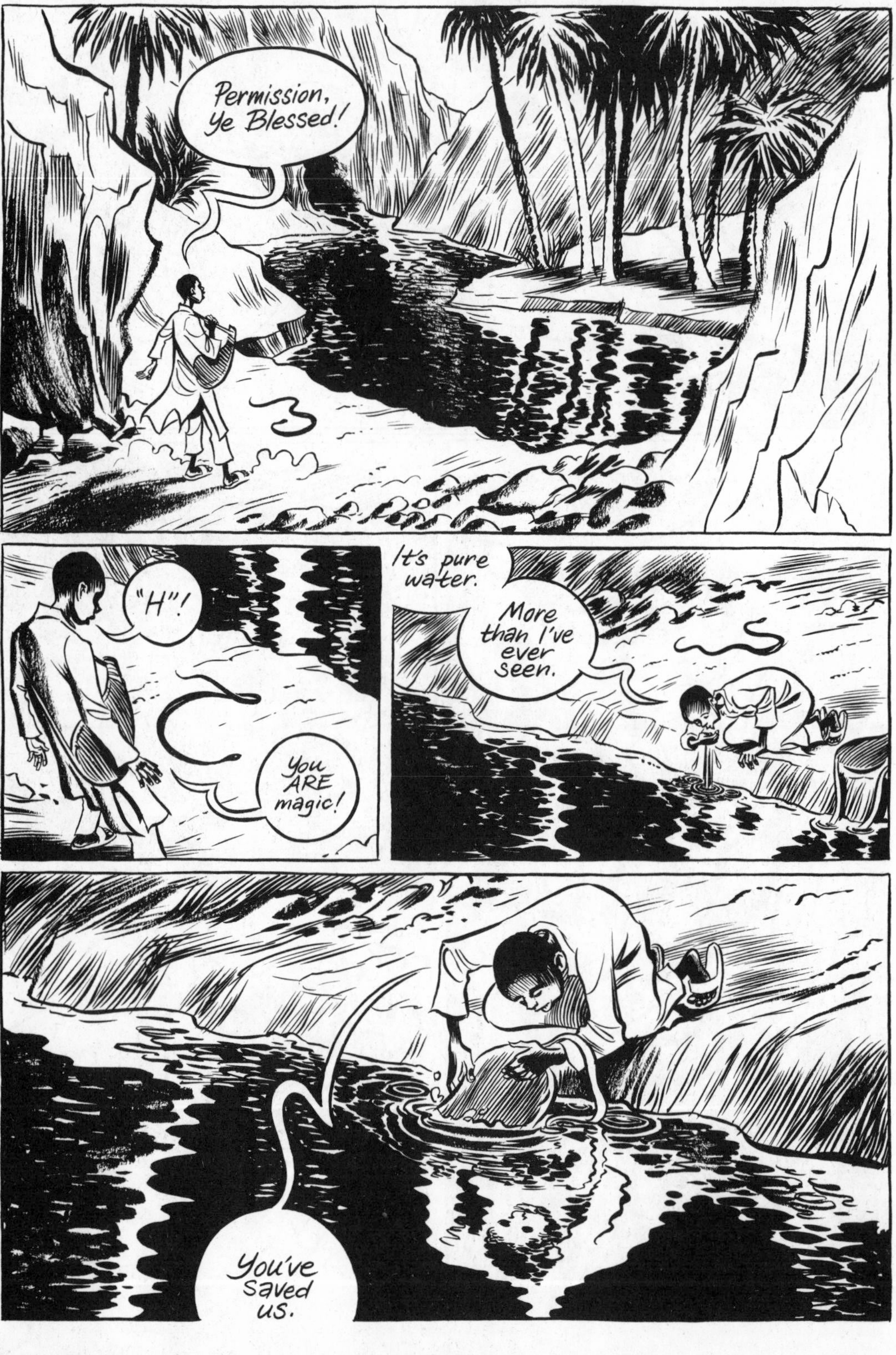
Permission, Ye Blessed!
"H"!
You ARE magic!
It's pure water.
More than I've ever seen.
You've saved us.

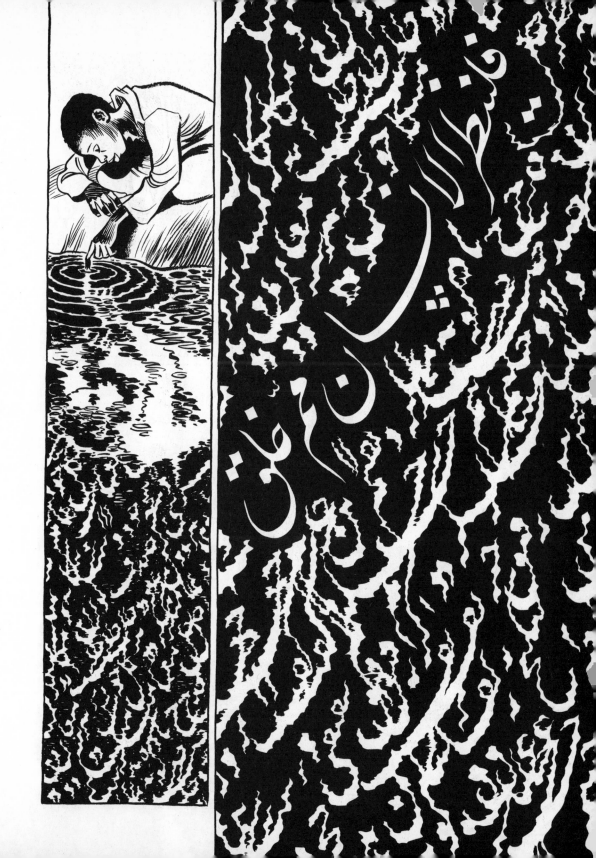

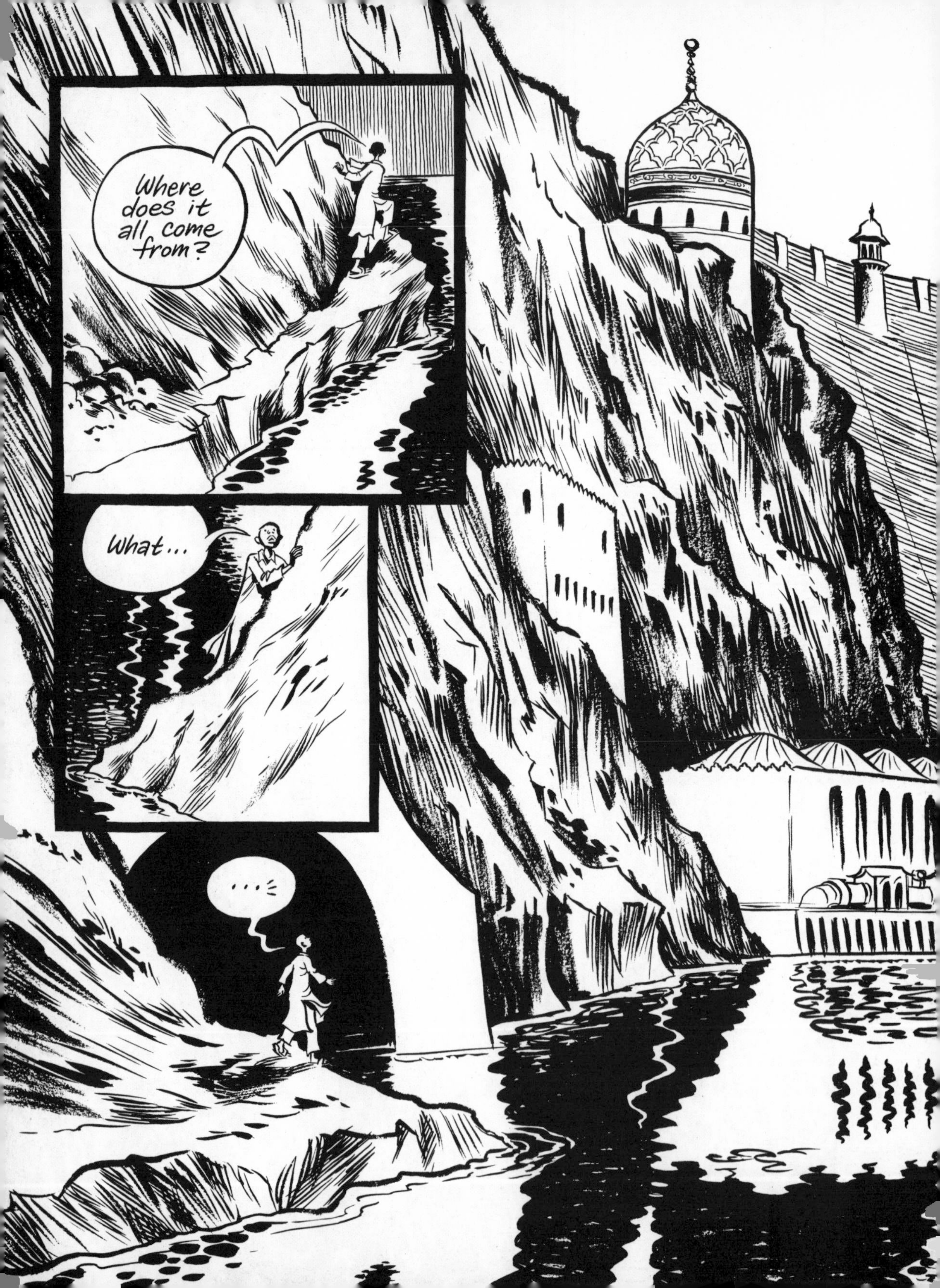
Where does it all come from?
What...
...

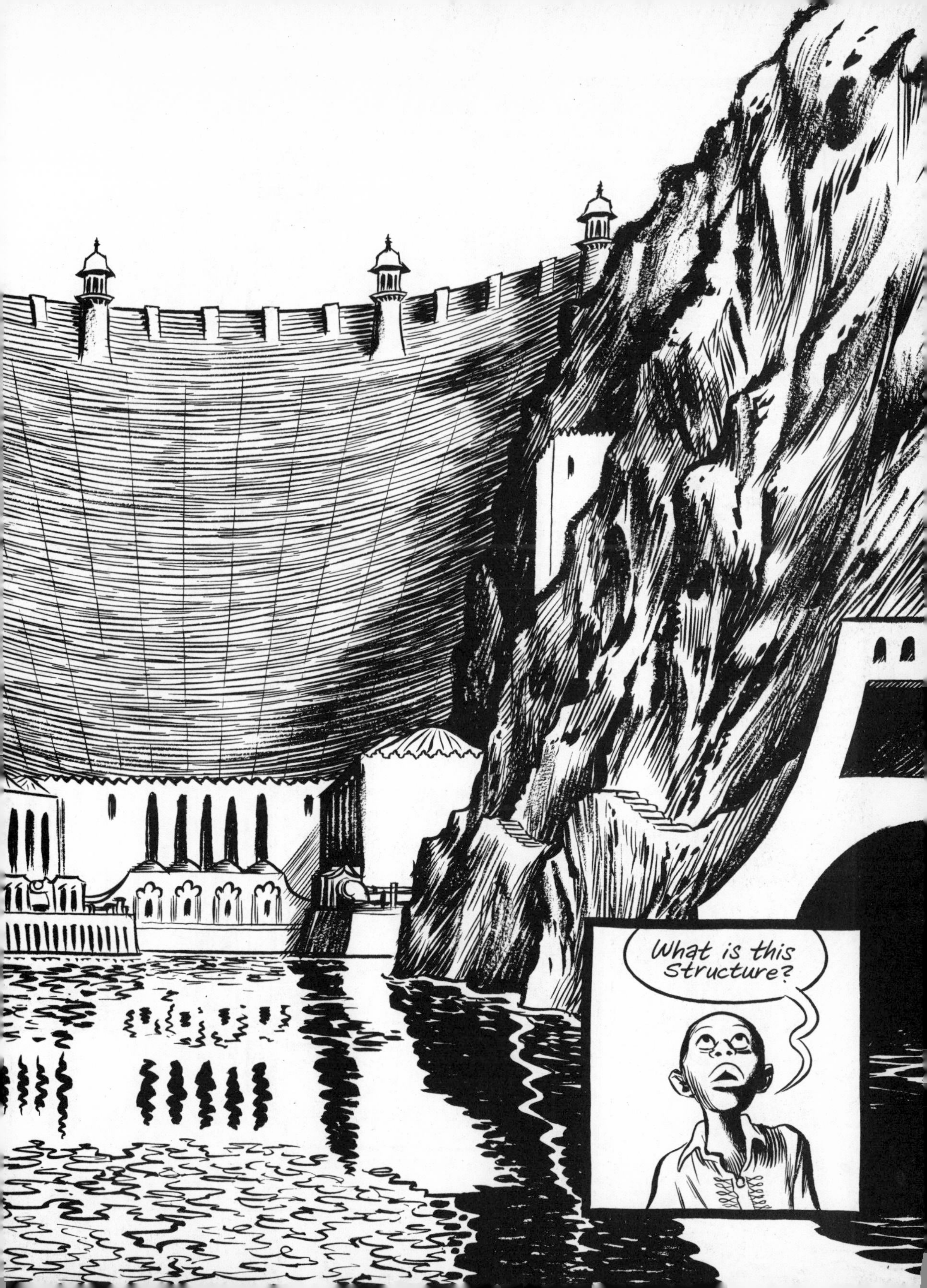
What is this Structure?

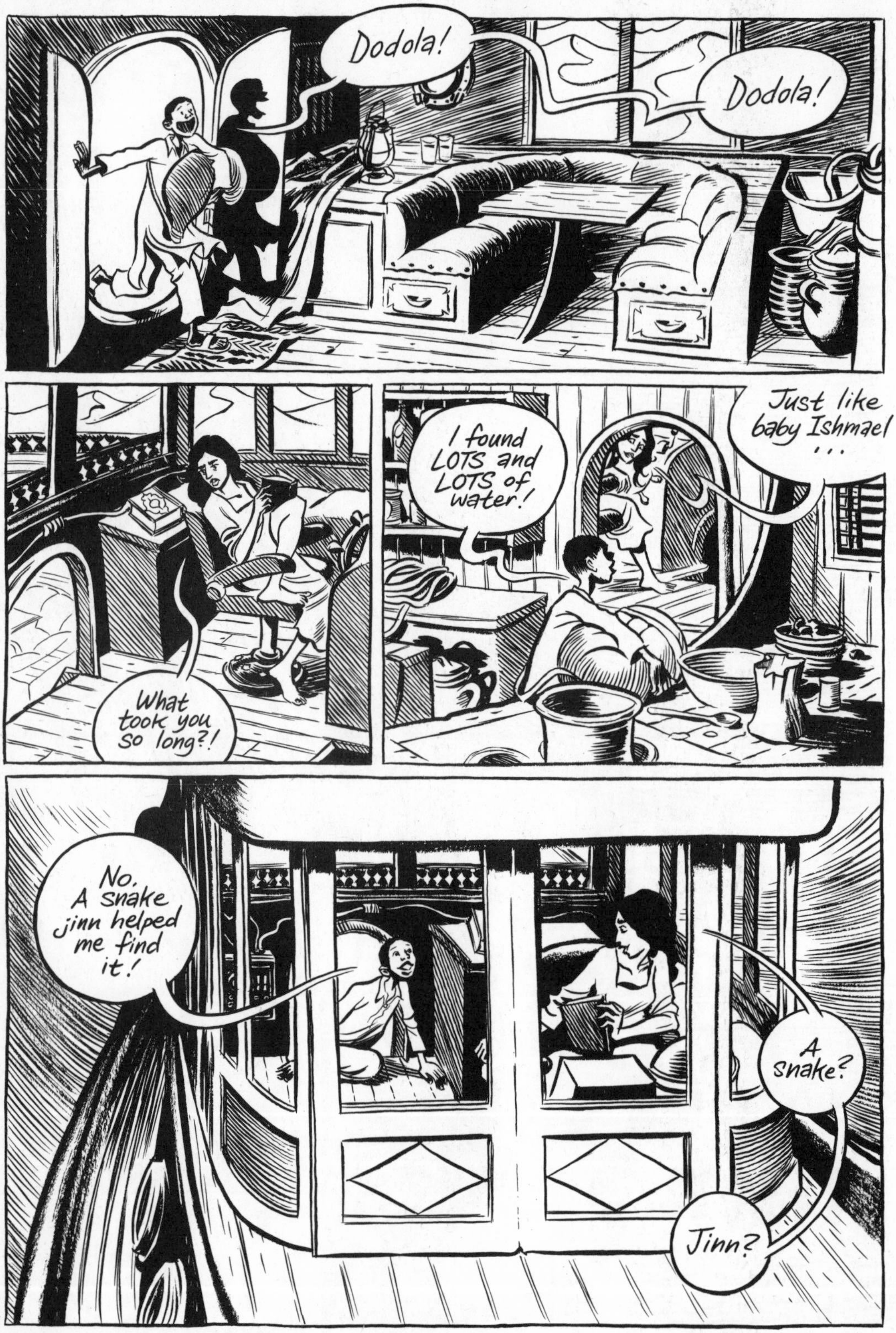
Dodola!
Dodola!
What took you so long?!
I found LOTS and LOTS of water!
Just like baby Ishmael . . .
No. A snake jinn helped me find it!
A snake?
Jinn?

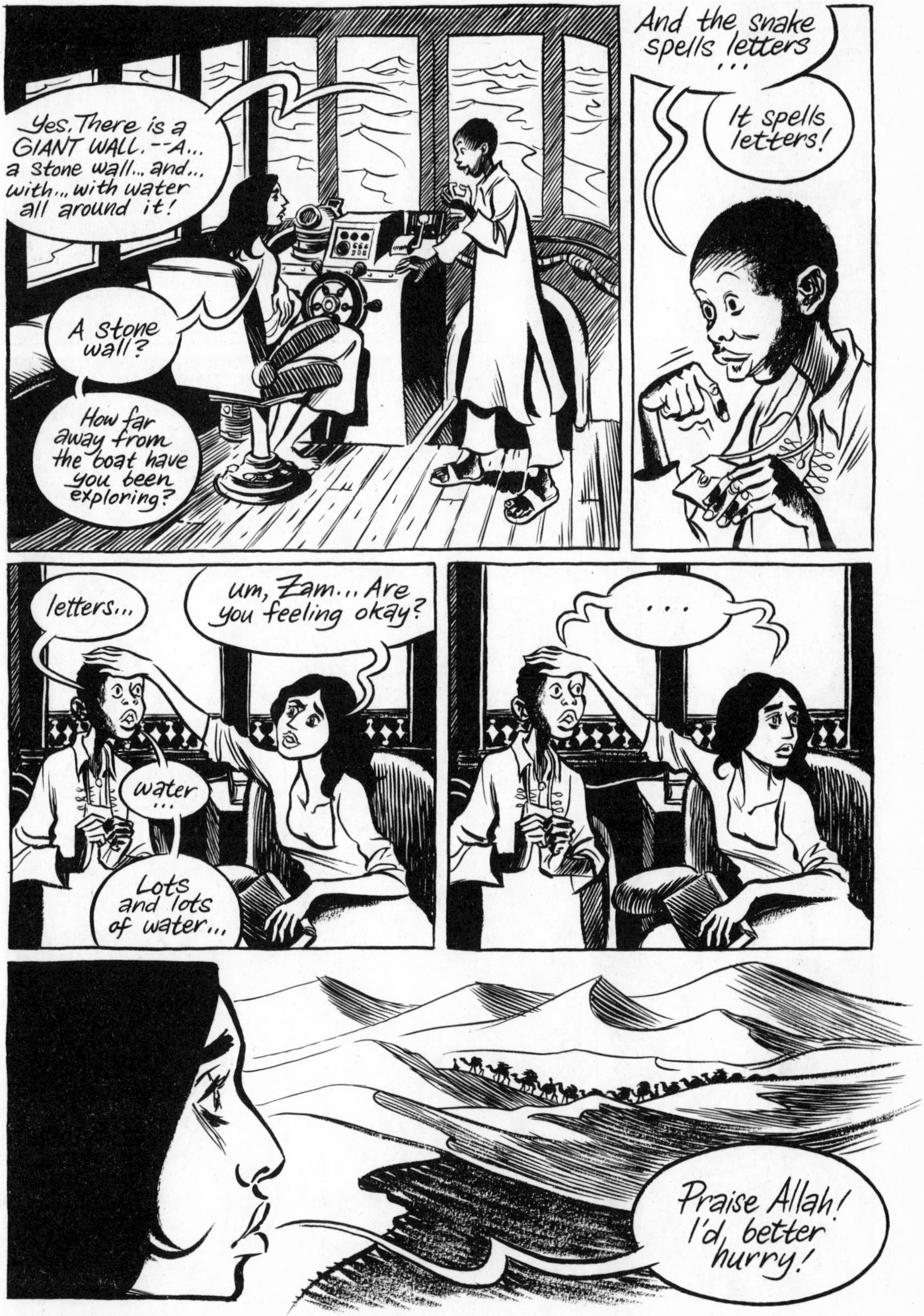
Yes. There is a GIANT WALL. --A... a stone wall... and... with... with water all around it!
A stone wall?
How far away from the boat have you been exploring?
And the snake spells letters ...
It spells letters!
letters...
um, Zam... Are you feeling okay?
water ...
Lots and lots of water...
...
Praise Allah! I'd better hurry!

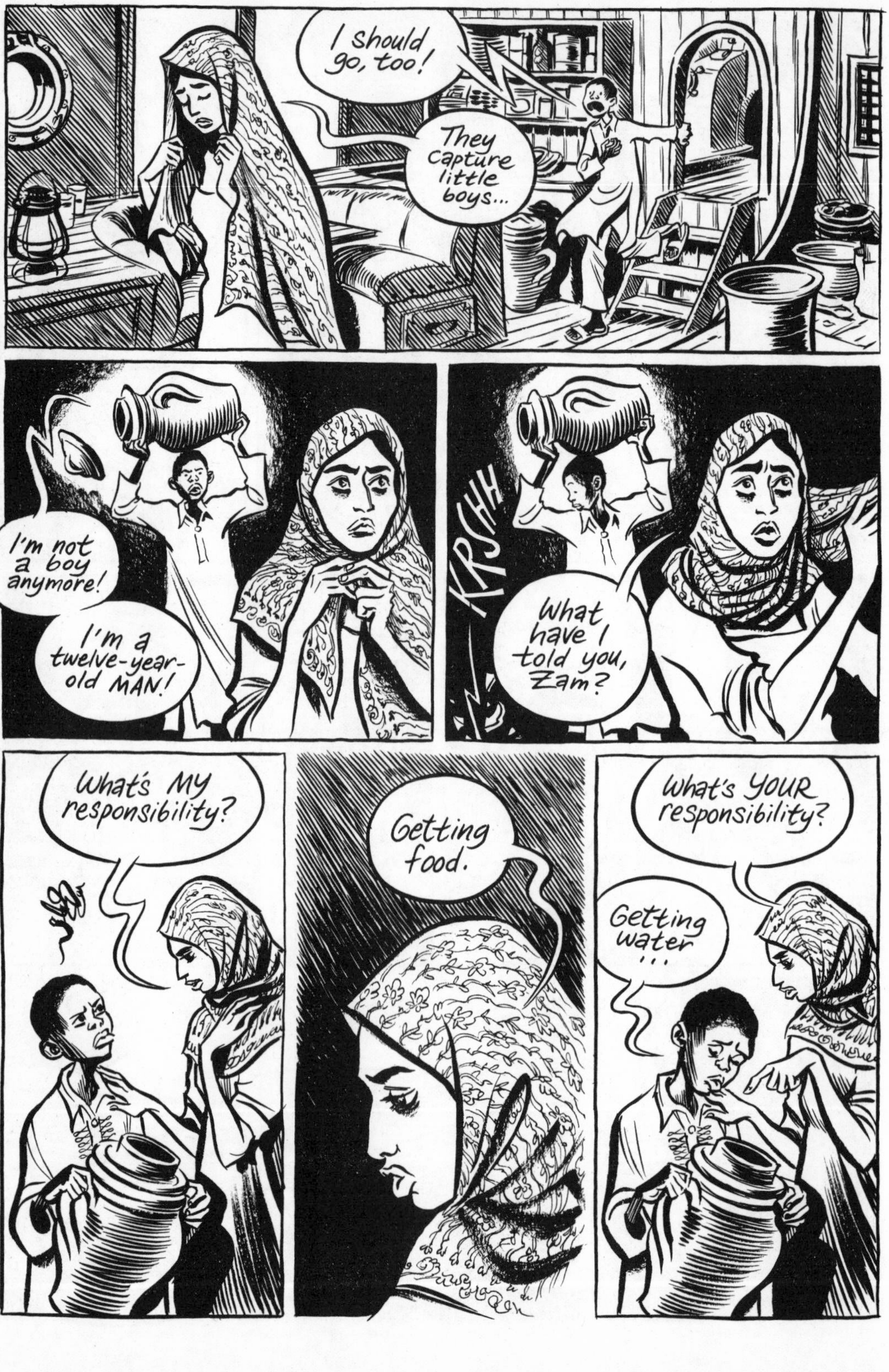

I should go, too!
They capture little boys...
I'm not a boy anymore!
I'm a twelve-year-old MAN!
KRSHH
What have I told you, Zam?
What's MY responsibility?
Getting food.
What's YOUR responsibility?
Getting water...

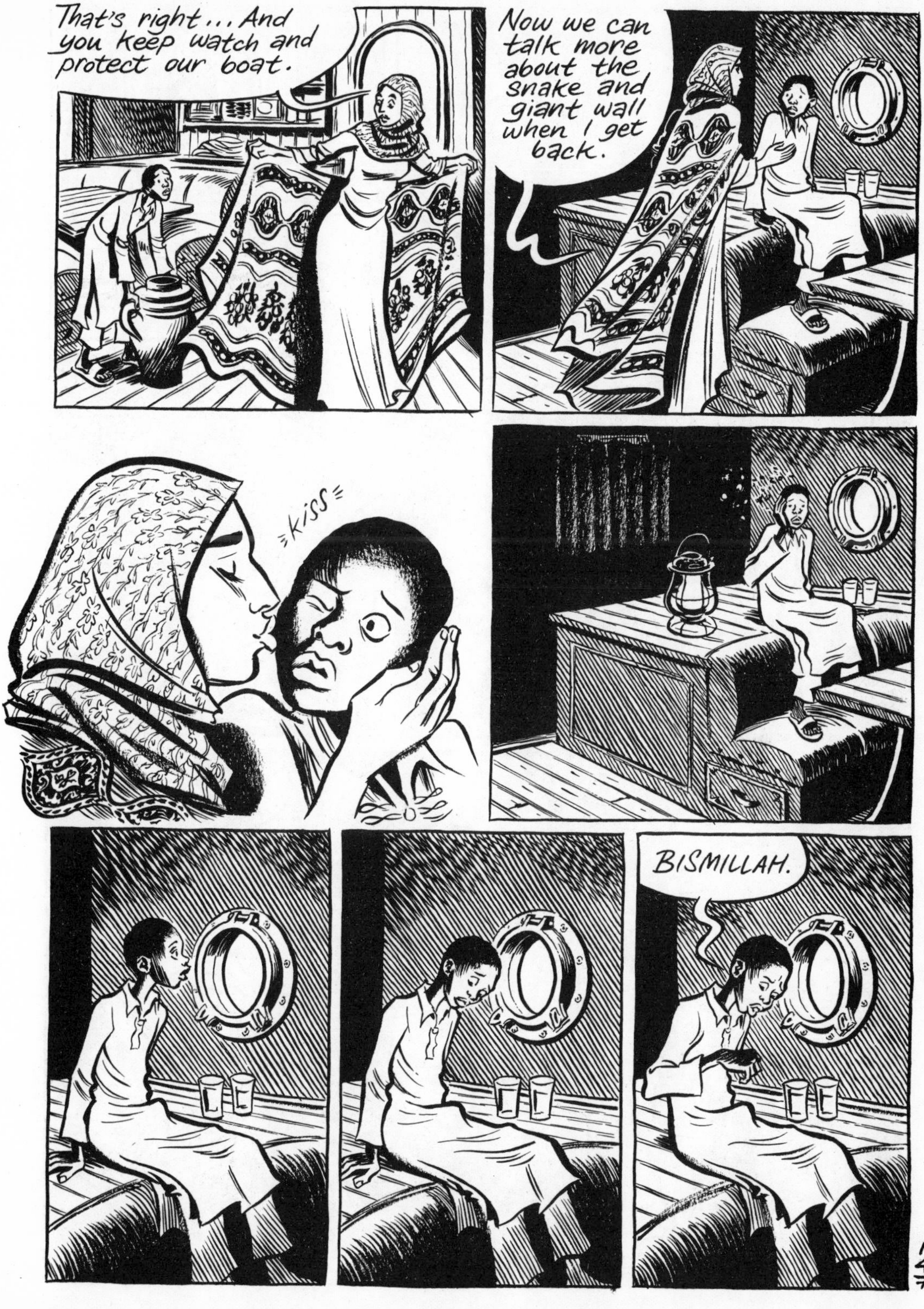
That's right... And you keep watch and protect our boat.
Now we can talk more about the snake and giant wall when I get back.
KISS
BISMILLAH.

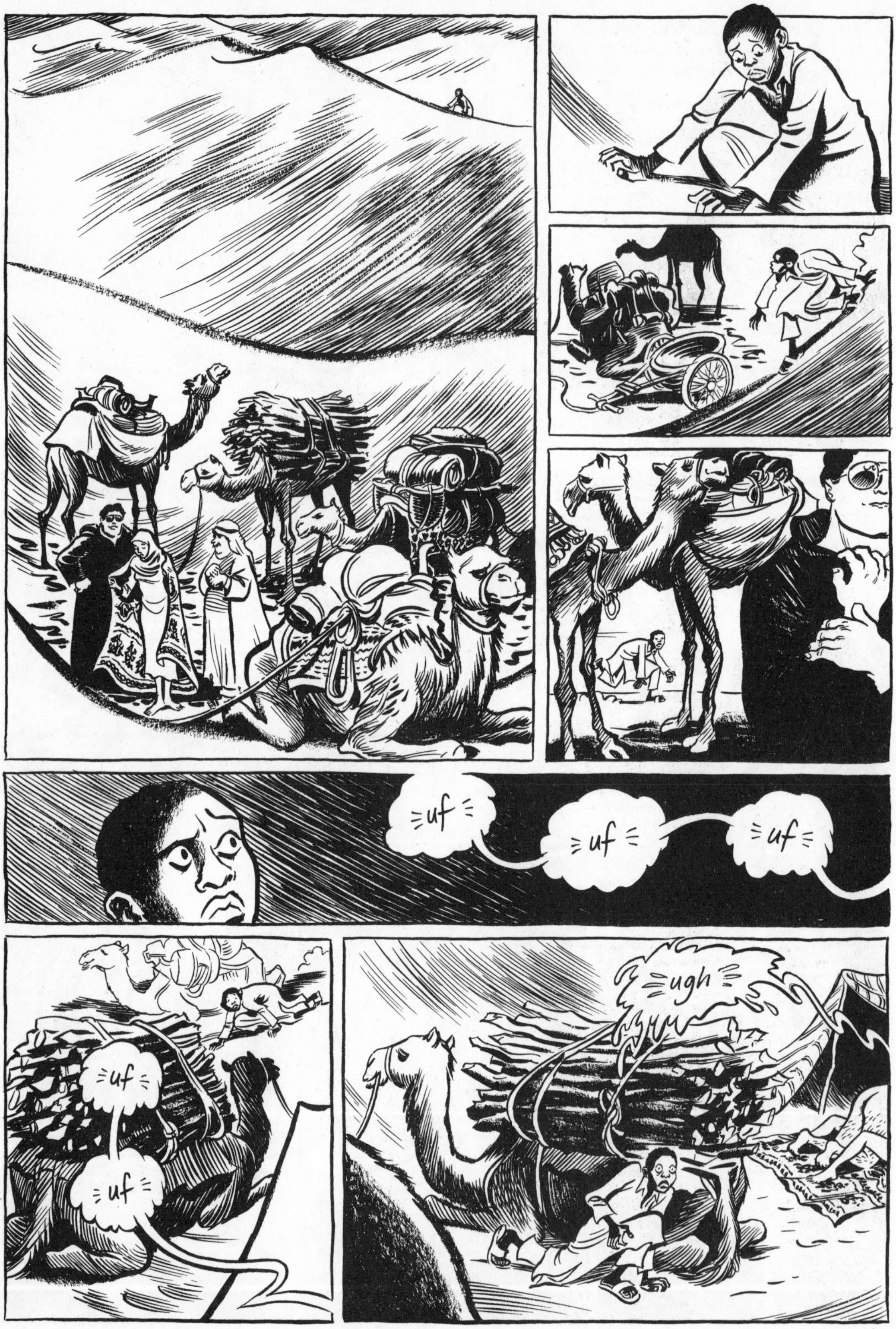
uf
uf
uf
uf
uf
ugh

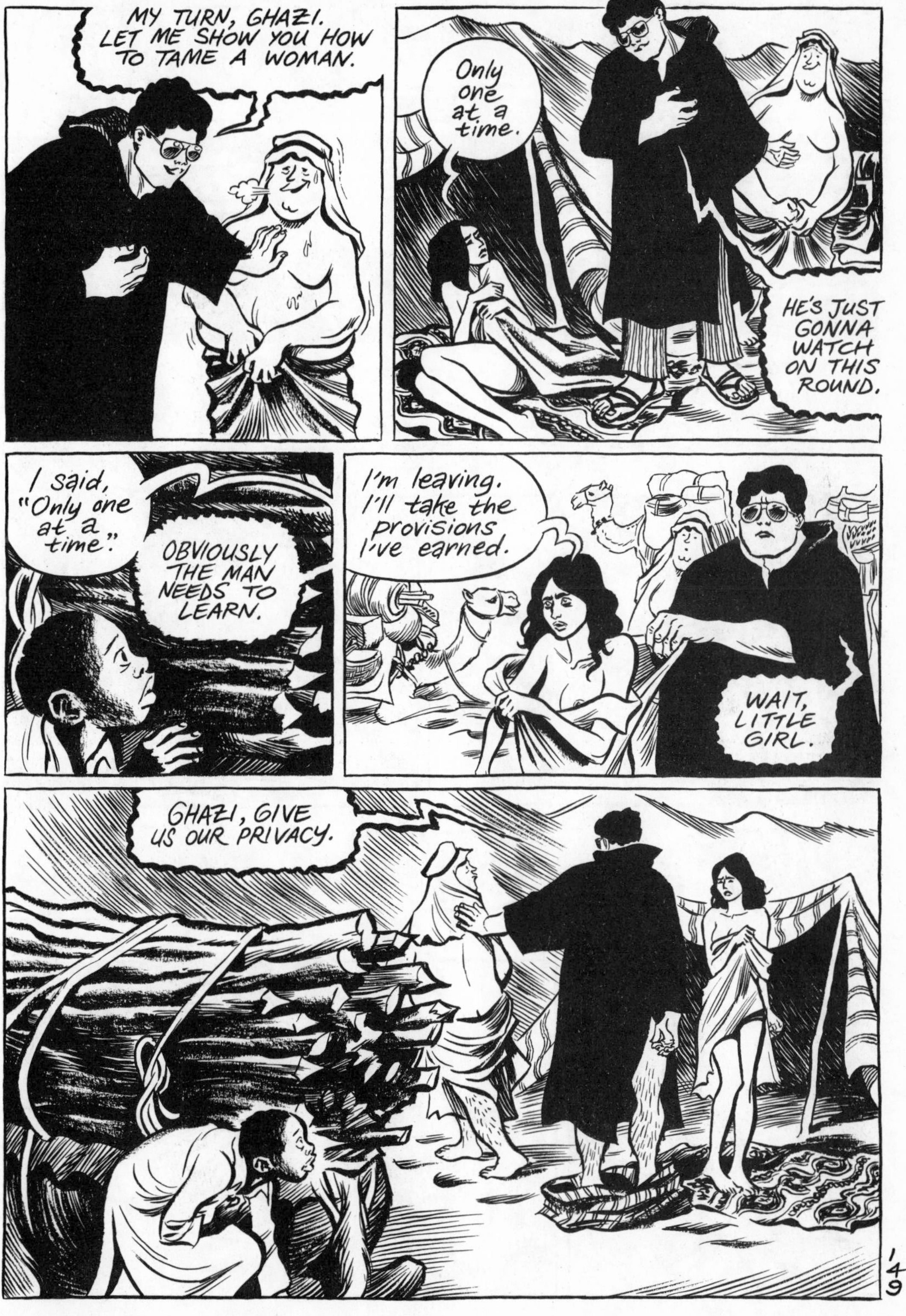
MY TURN, GHAZI. LET ME SHOW YOU HOW TO TAME A WOMAN.
Only one at a time.
HE'S JUST GONNA WATCH ON THIS ROUND.
I said, "Only one at a time".
OBVIOUSLY THE MAN NEEDS TO LEARN.
I'm leaving. I'll take the provisions I've earned.
WAIT, LITTLE GIRL.
GHAZI, GIVE US OUR PRIVACY.

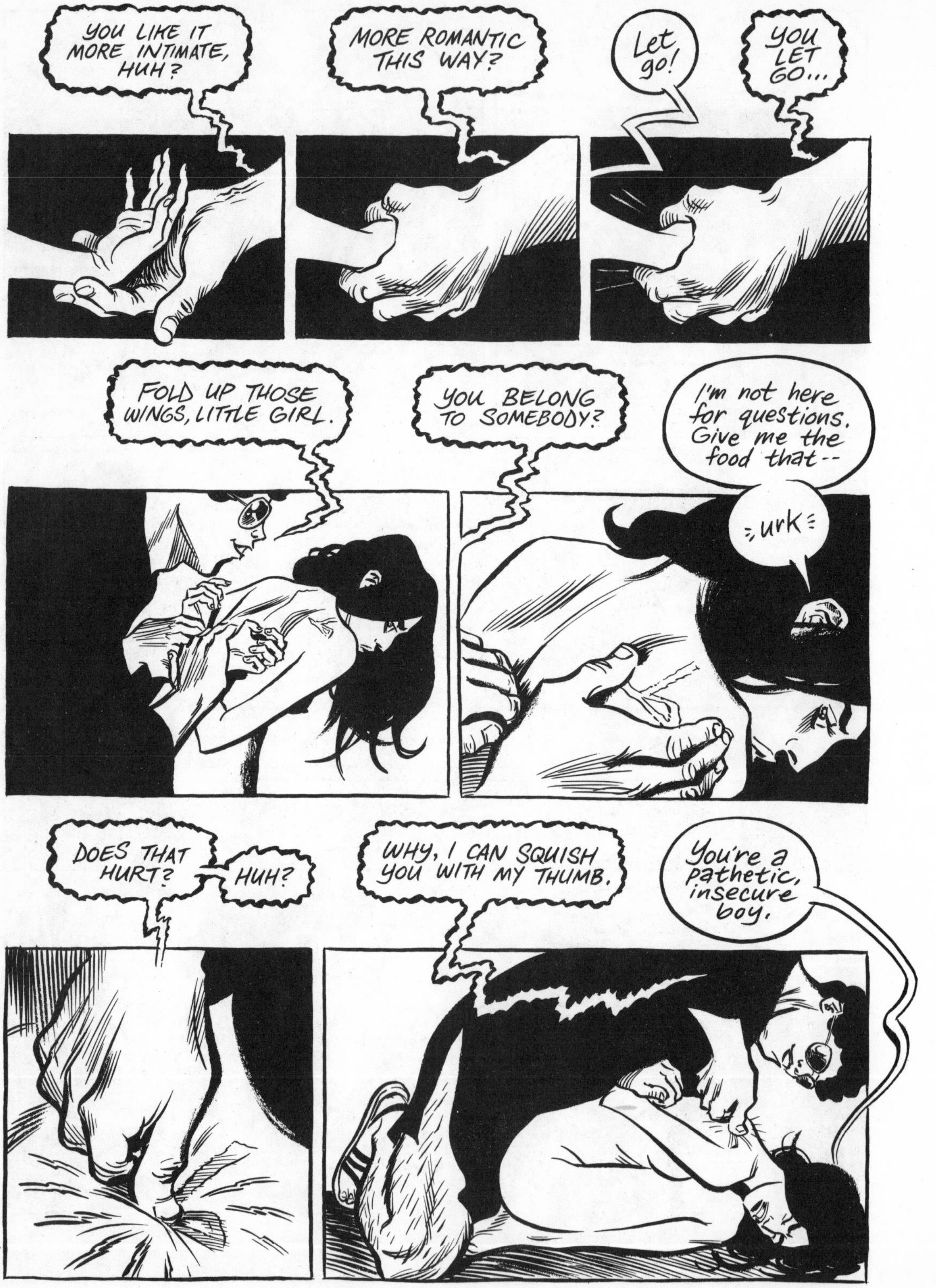

YOU LIKE IT MORE INTIMATE, HUH?
MORE ROMANTIC THIS WAY?
Let go!
YOU LET GO...
FOLD UP THOSE WINGS, LITTLE GIRL.
YOU BELONG TO SOMEBODY?
I'm not here for questions. Give me the food that--
urk
DOES THAT HURT?
HUH?
WHY, I CAN SQUISH YOU WITH MY THUMB.
You're a pathetic, insecure boy.

BOY?!
DOES THIS LOOK LIKE IT BELONGS TO A BOY?!
Yes!
I'M OLD ENOUGH TO BE YOUR FATHER!
You're too ugly for us to be related.
DOES DADDY NEED TO TAKE AWAY YOUR TOYS?

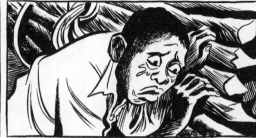

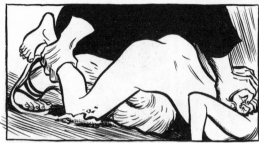

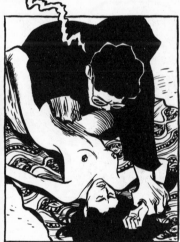

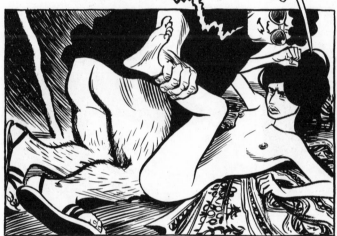

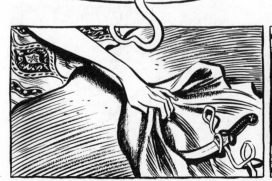

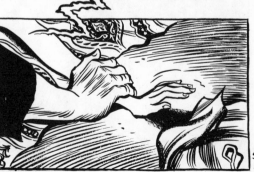

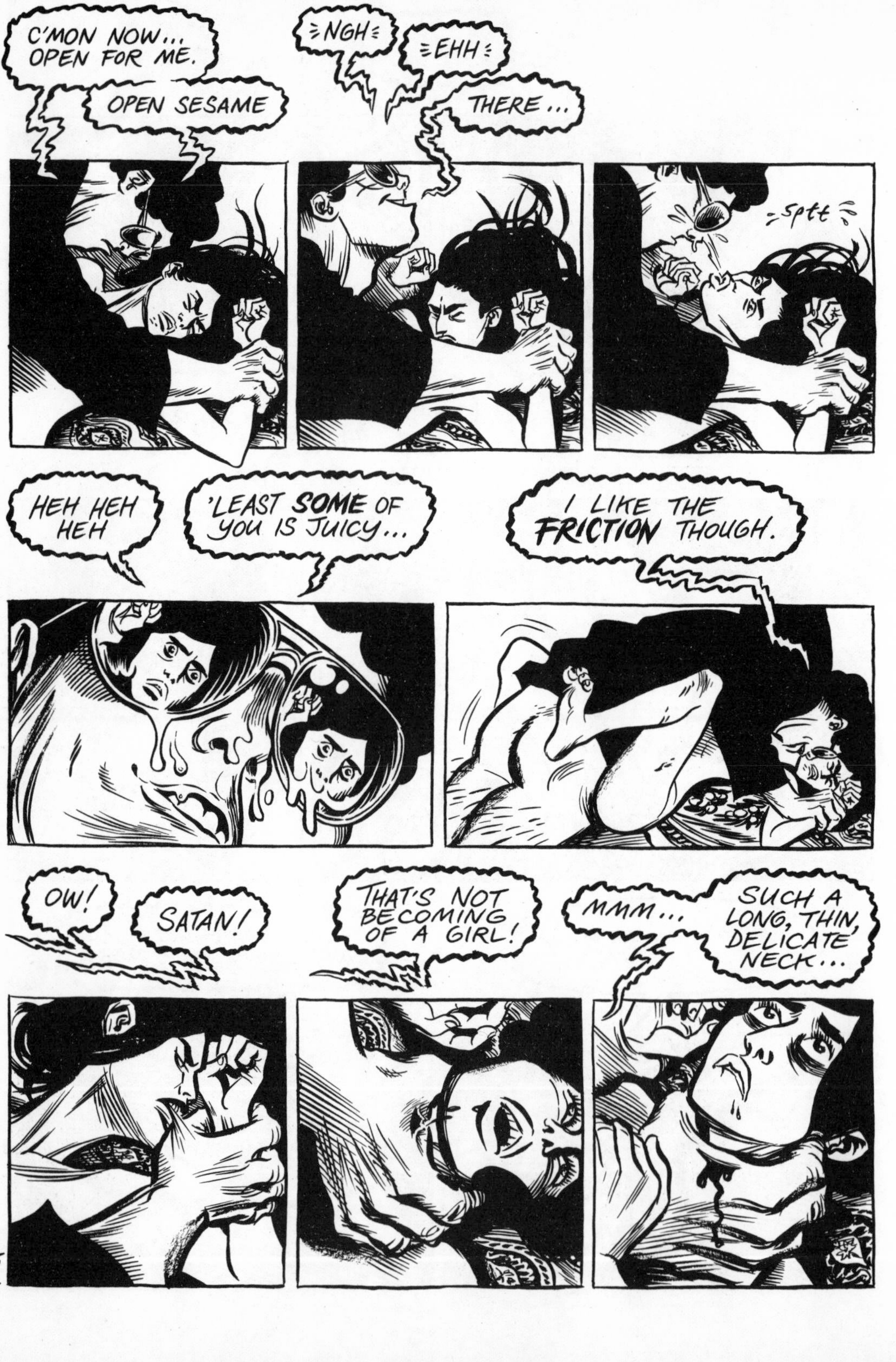
C'MON NOW... OPEN FOR ME.
OPEN SESAME
NGH
EHH
THERE...
sptt
HEH HEH HEH
'LEAST SOME OF YOU IS JUICY...
I LIKE THE FRICTION THOUGH.
OW!
SATAN!
THAT'S NOT BECOMING OF A GIRL!
MMM...
SUCH A LONG, THIN, DELICATE NECK...

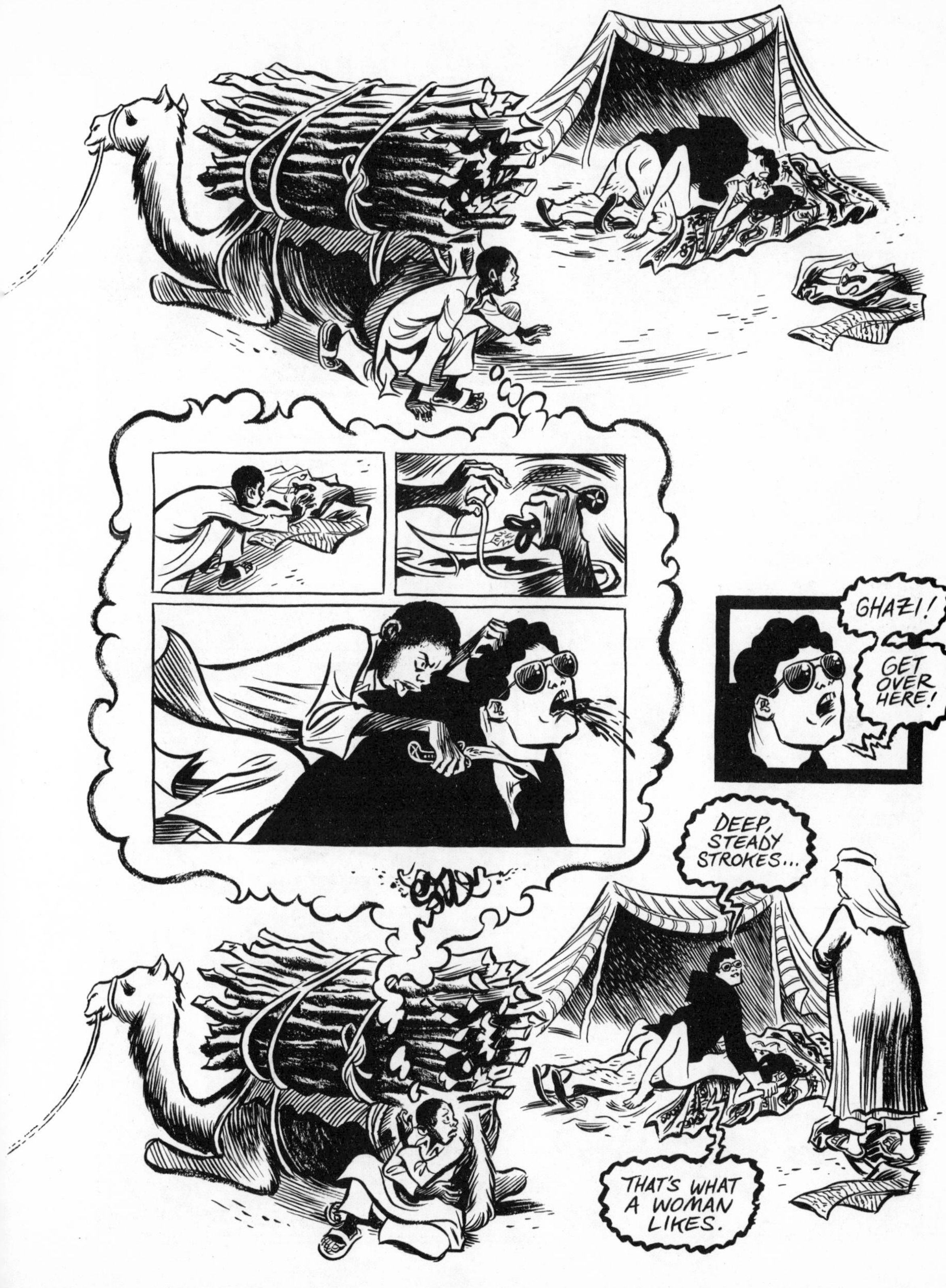
GHAZI!
GET OVER HERE!
DEEP, STEADY STROKES...
THAT'S WHAT A WOMAN LIKES.

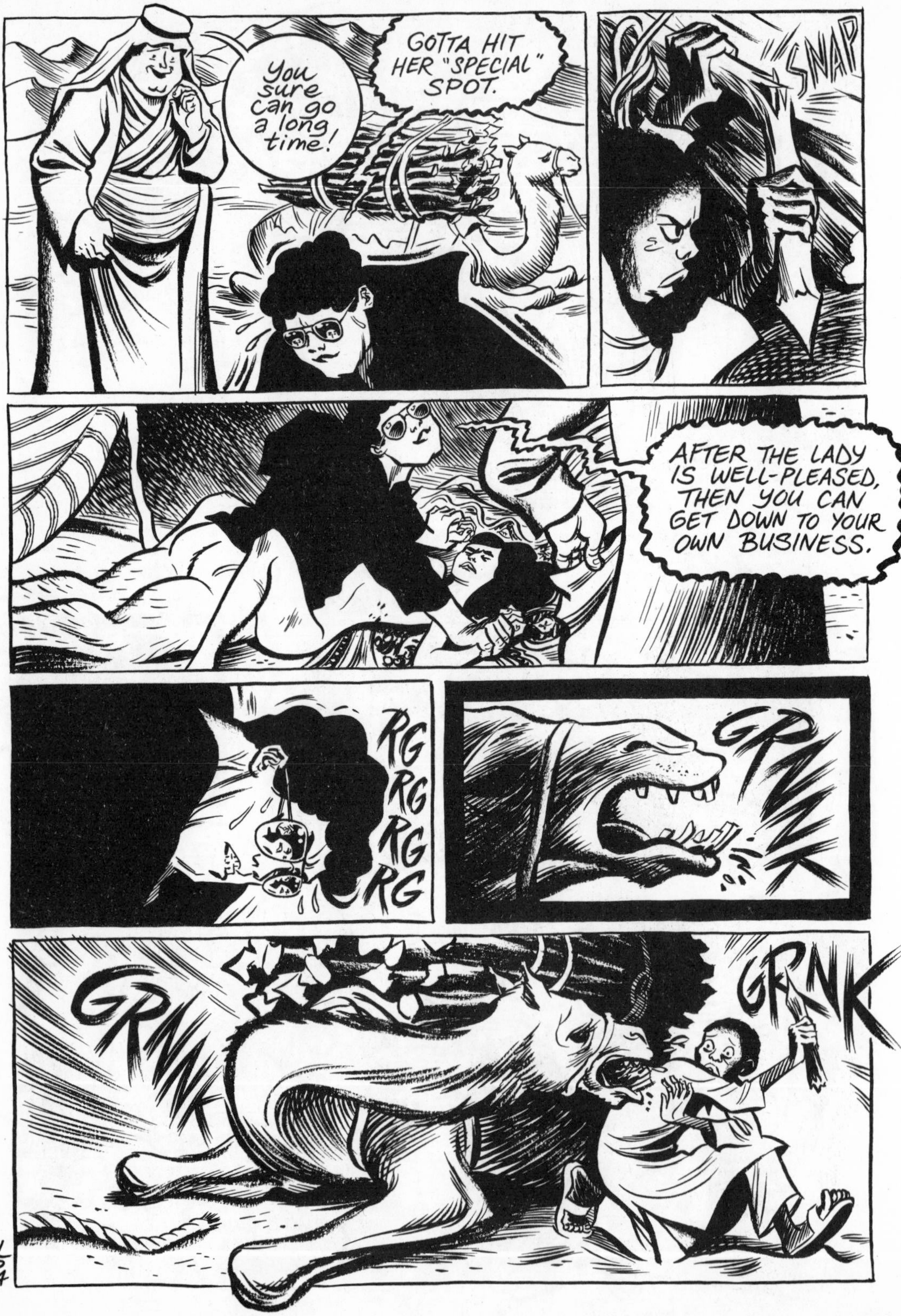

You sure can go a long time!
GOTTA HIT HER "SPECIAL" SPOT.
SNAP
AFTER THE LADY IS WELL-PLEASED, THEN YOU CAN GET DOWN TO YOUR OWN BUSINESS.
RG RG RG RG RG
GRNNK
GRNNK
GRNK

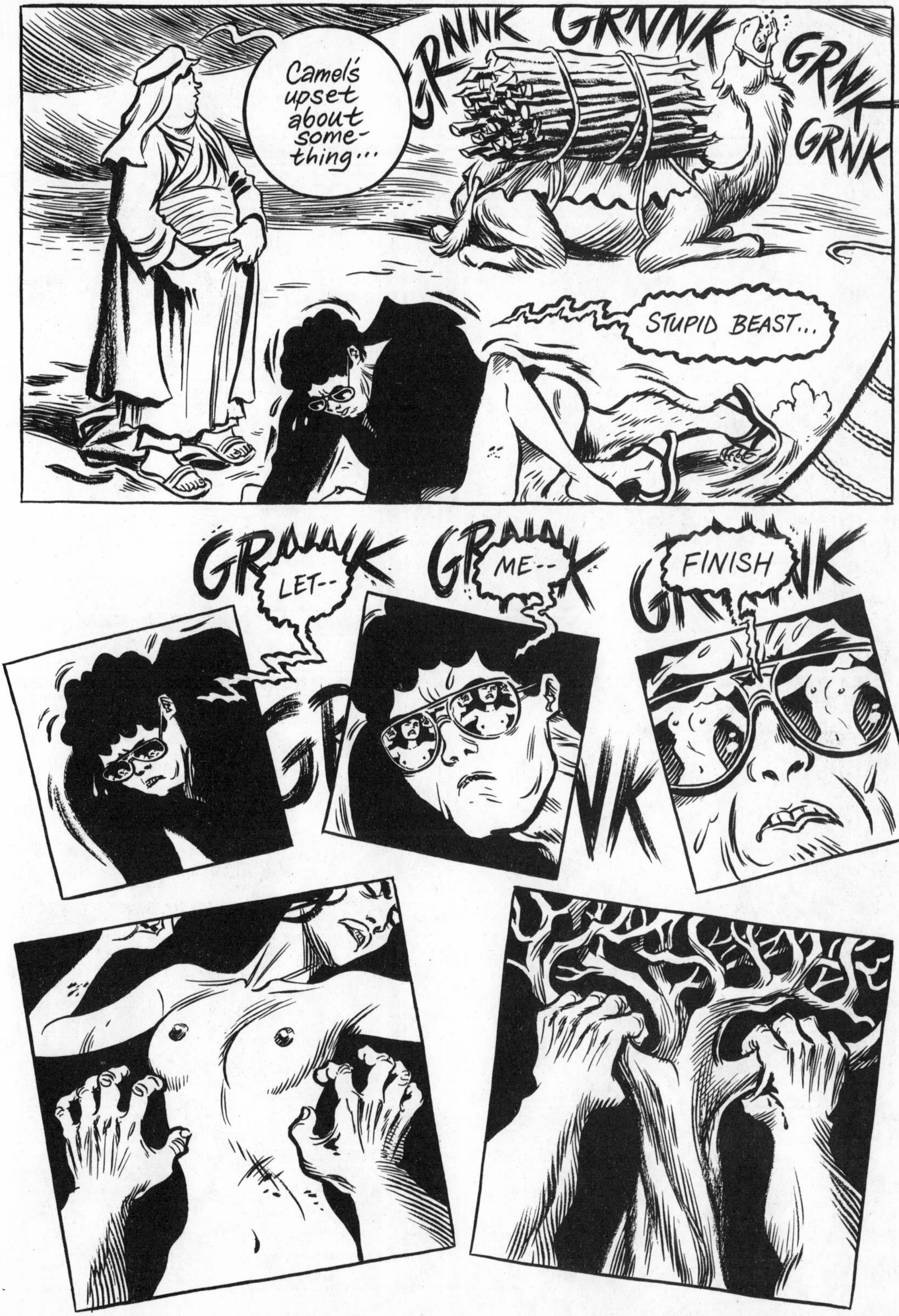
Camel's upset about some-thing...
GRNK GRNNK GRNK GRNK
STUPID BEAST...
LET--
ME--
FINISH

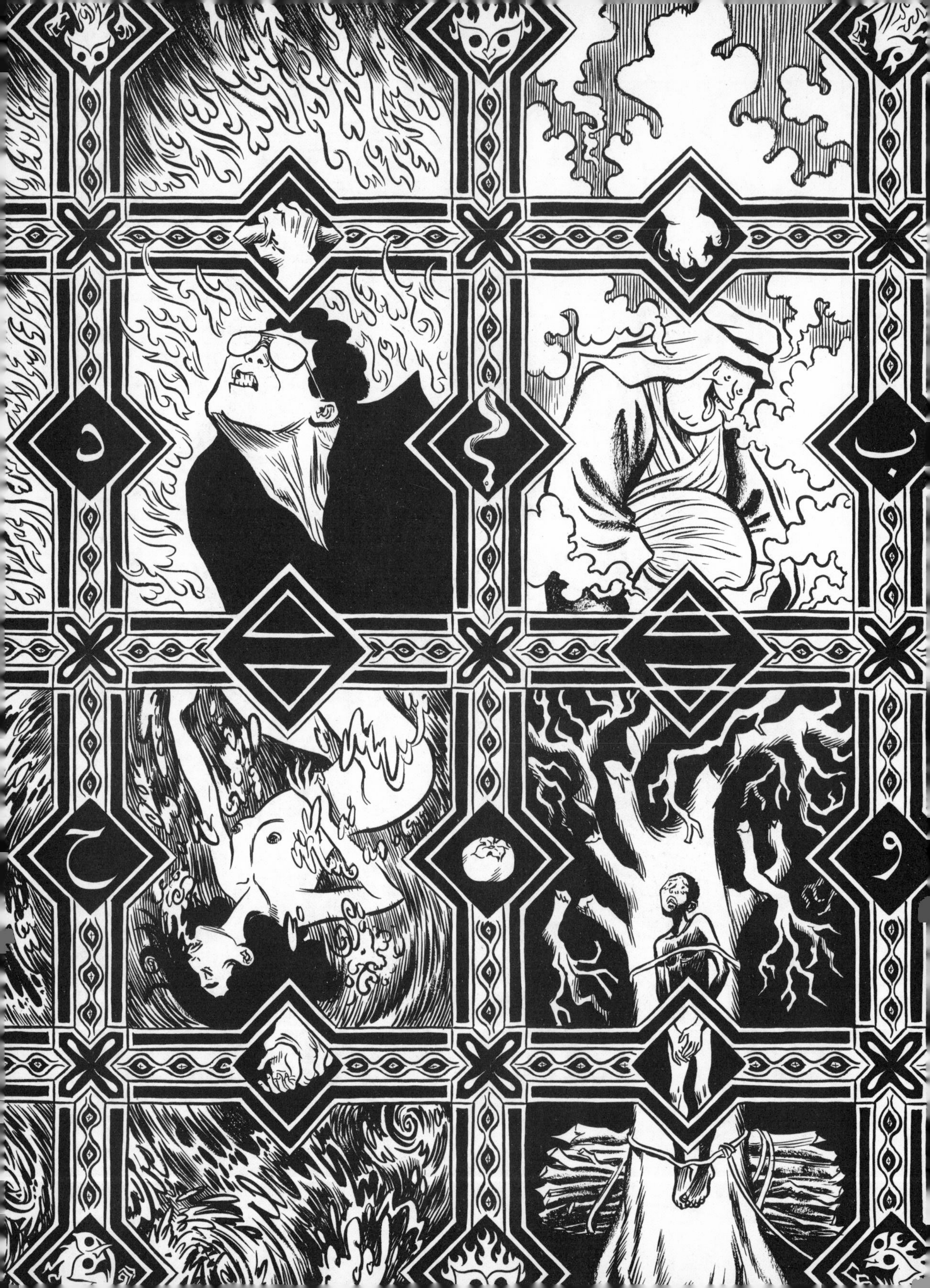
ب
د
و
ح

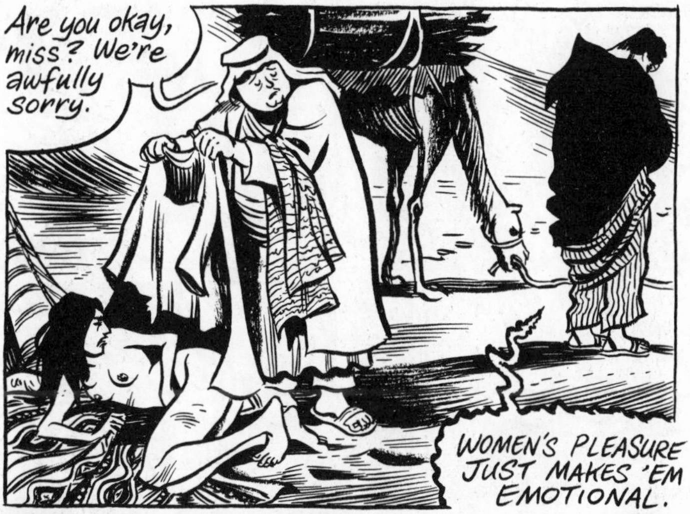
Are you okay, miss? We're awfully sorry.
WOMEN'S PLEASURE JUST MAKES 'EM EMOTIONAL.

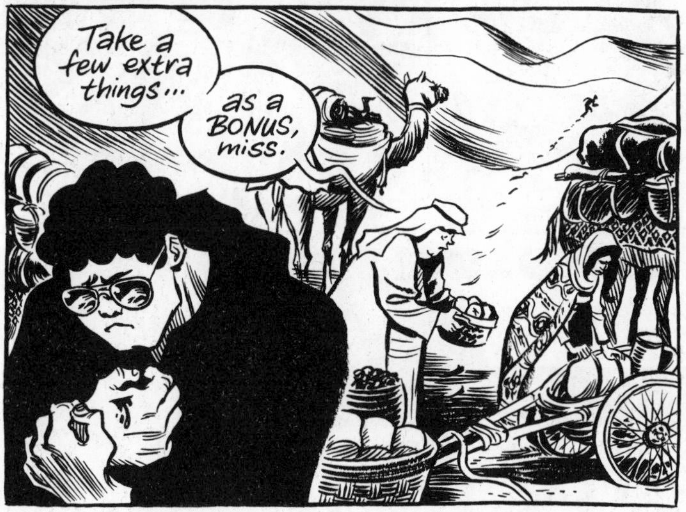
Take a few extra things...
as a BONUS, miss.

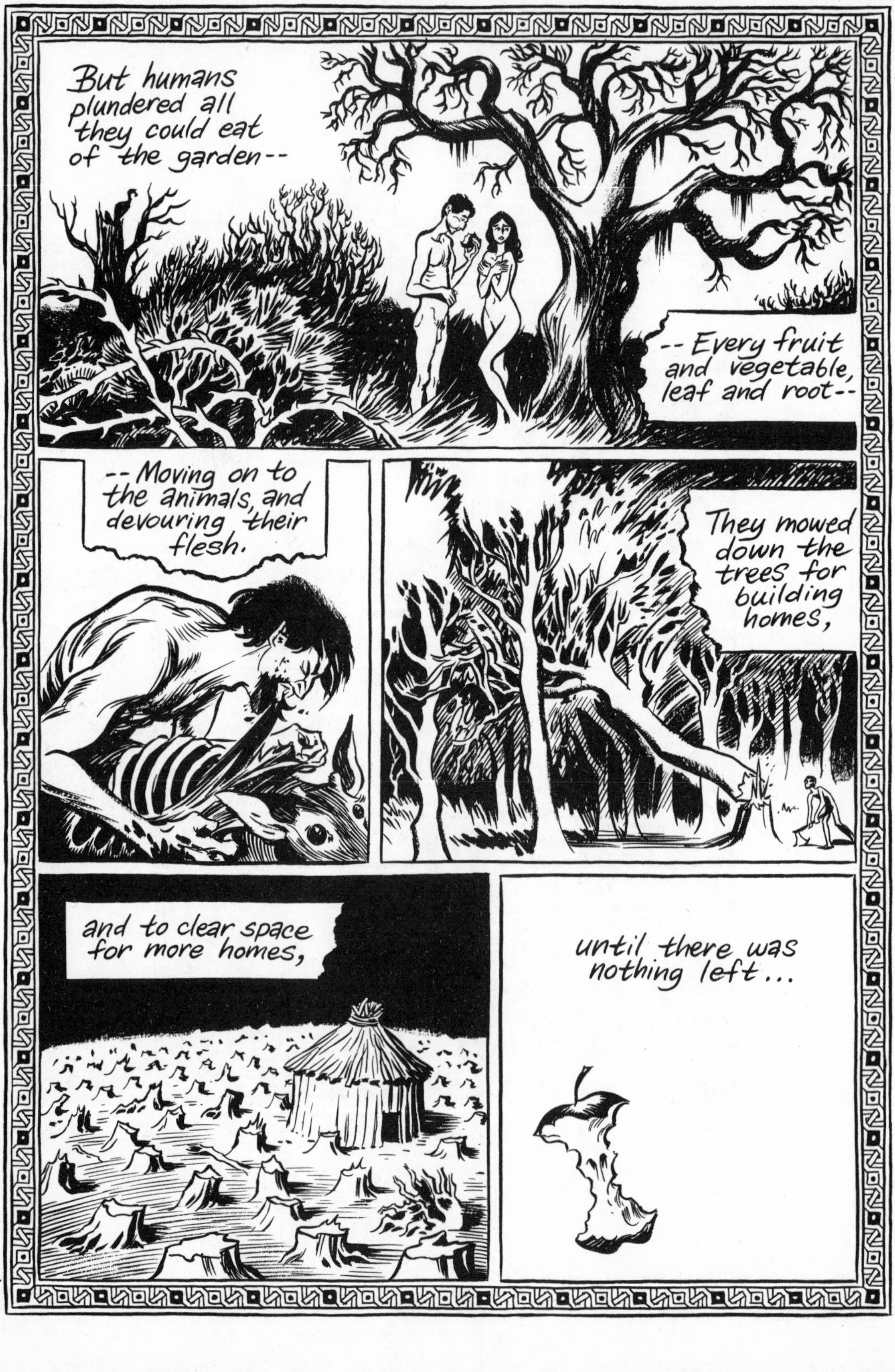
But humans plundered all they could eat of the garden--
--Every fruit and vegetable, leaf and root--
--Moving on to the animals, and devouring their flesh.
They mowed down the trees for building homes,
and to clear space for more homes,
until there was nothing left...

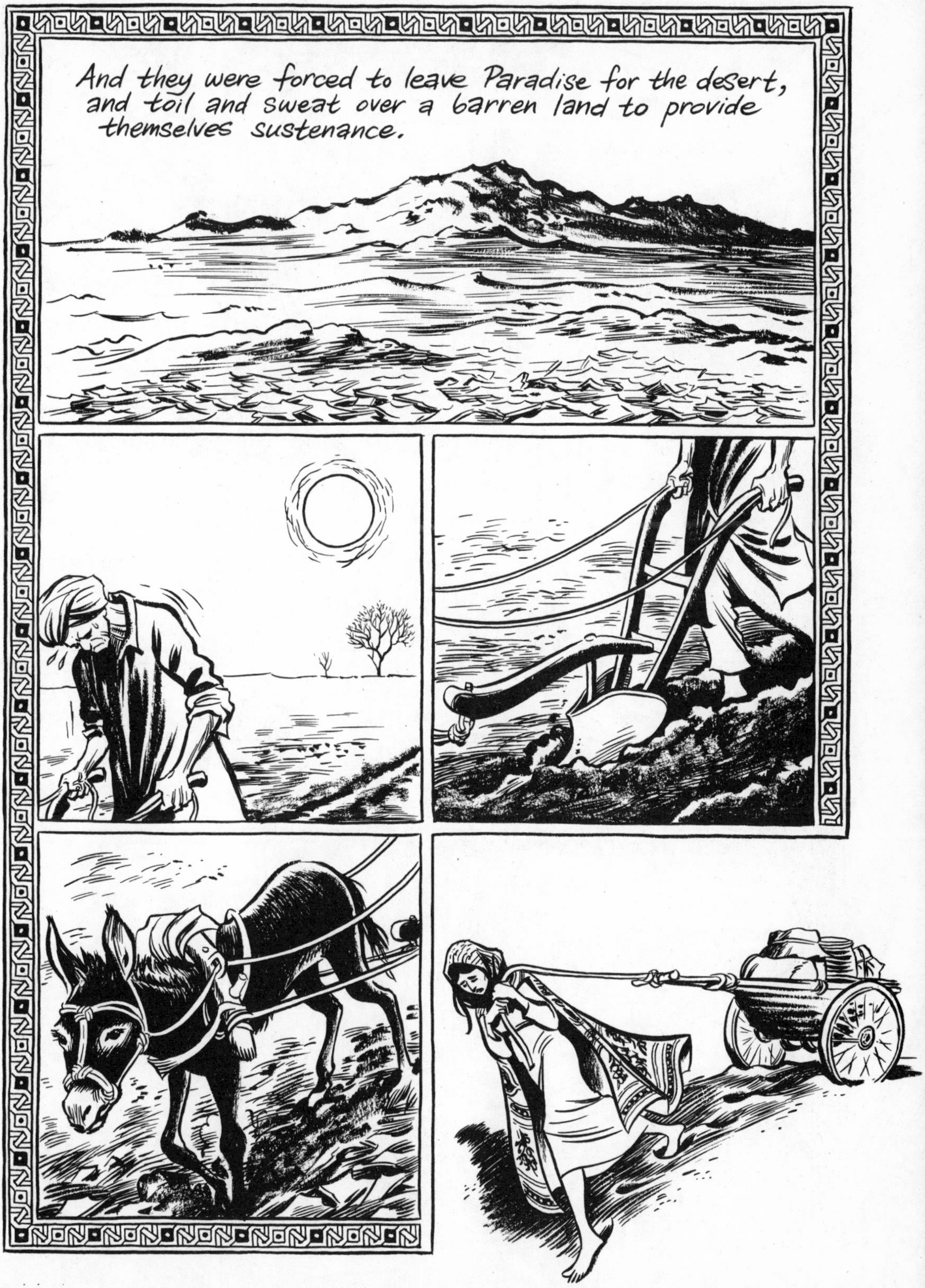
And they were forced to leave Paradise for the desert, and toil and sweat over a barren land to provide themselves sustenance.

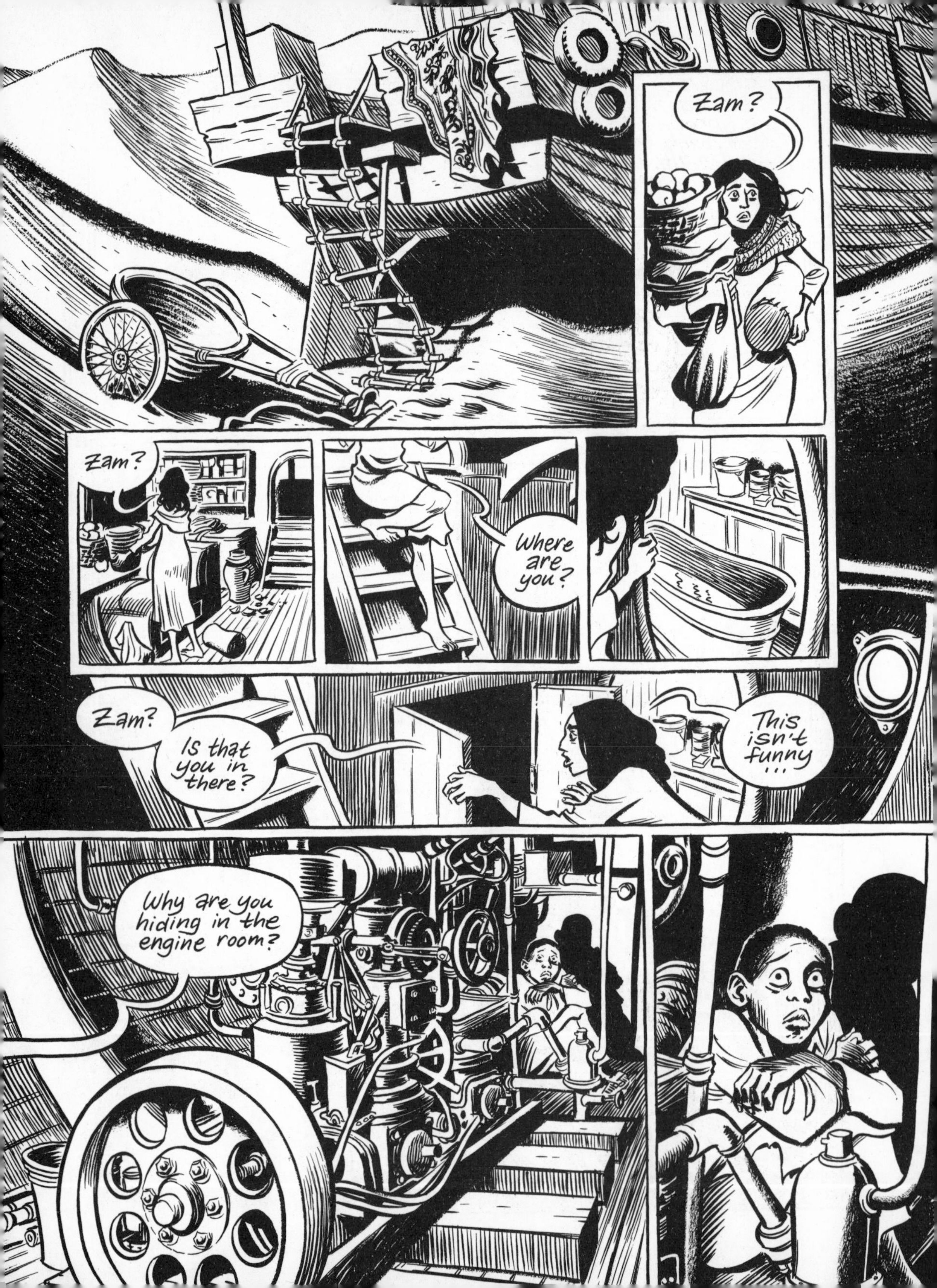
Zam?
Zam?
Where are you?
Zam?
Is that you in there?
This isn't funny ...
Why are you hiding in the engine room?

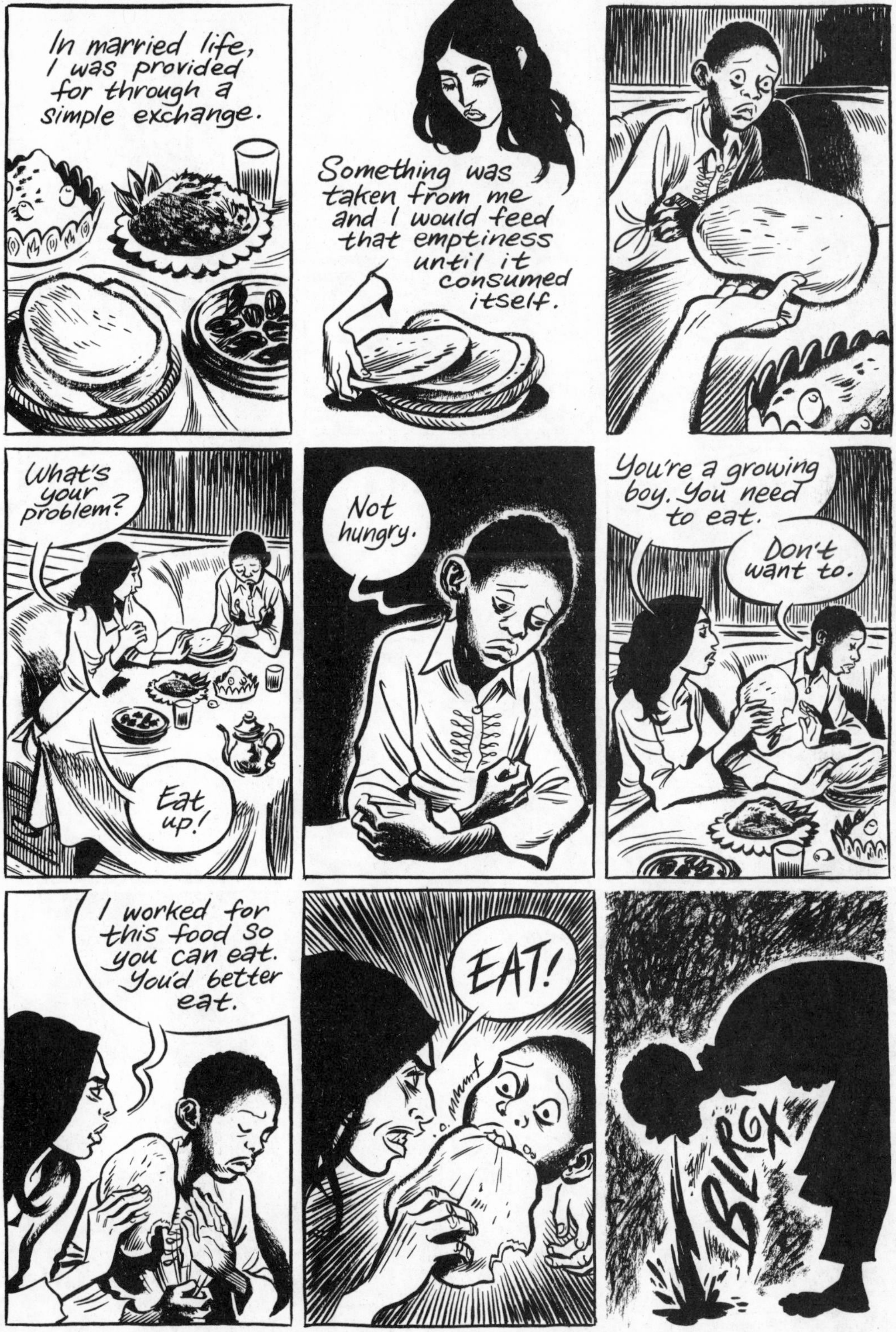
In married life, I was provided for through a simple exchange.
Something was taken from me and I would feed that emptiness until it consumed itself.
What's your problem?
Eat up!
Not hungry.
You're a growing boy. You need to eat.
Don't want to.
I worked for this food so you can eat. You'd better eat.
EAT!
BLRGX

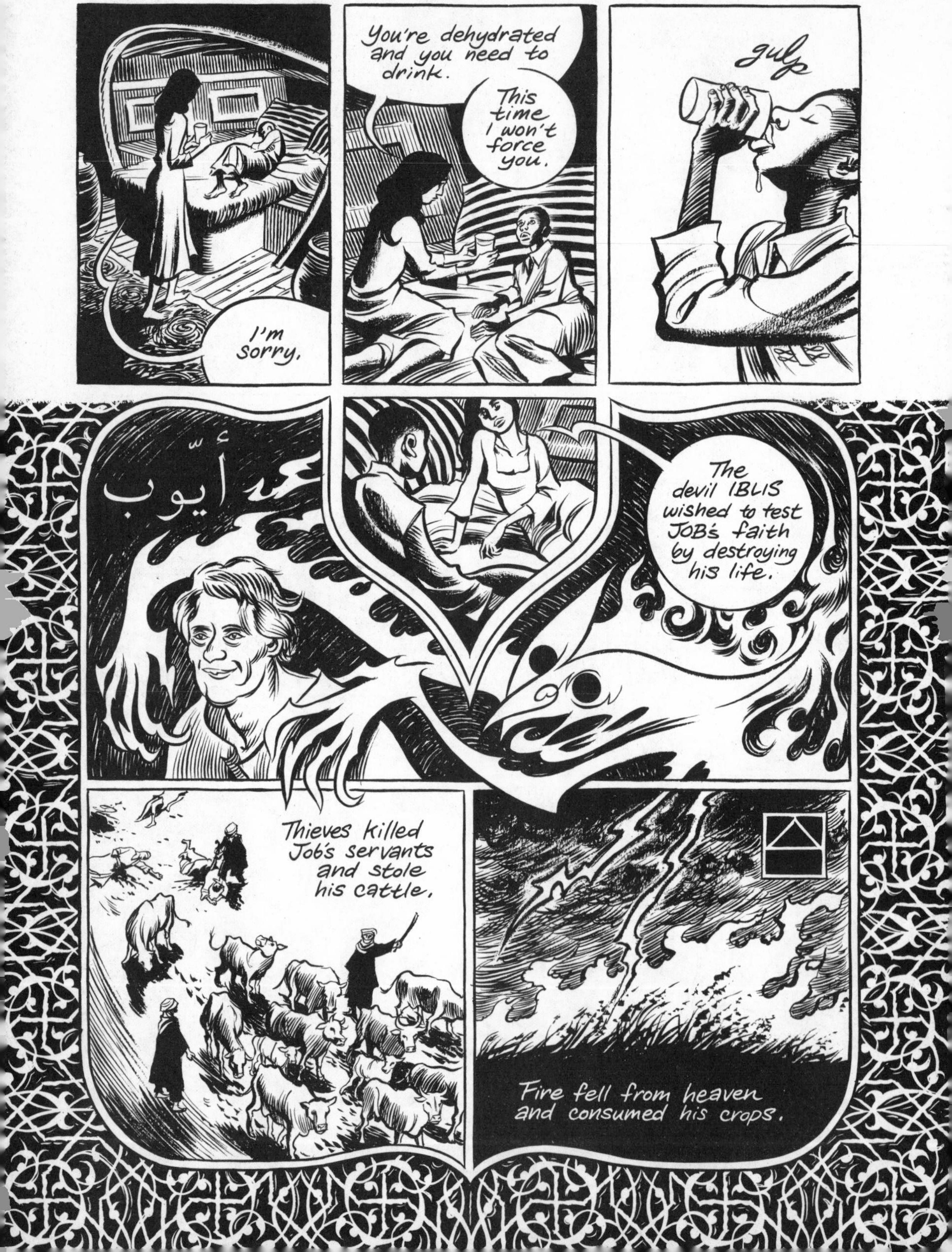
I'm sorry.
You're dehydrated and you need to drink.
This time I won't force you.
gulp
أيّوب
The devil IBLIS wished to test JOB's faith by destroying his life.
Thieves killed Job's servants and stole his cattle.
Fire fell from heaven and consumed his crops.

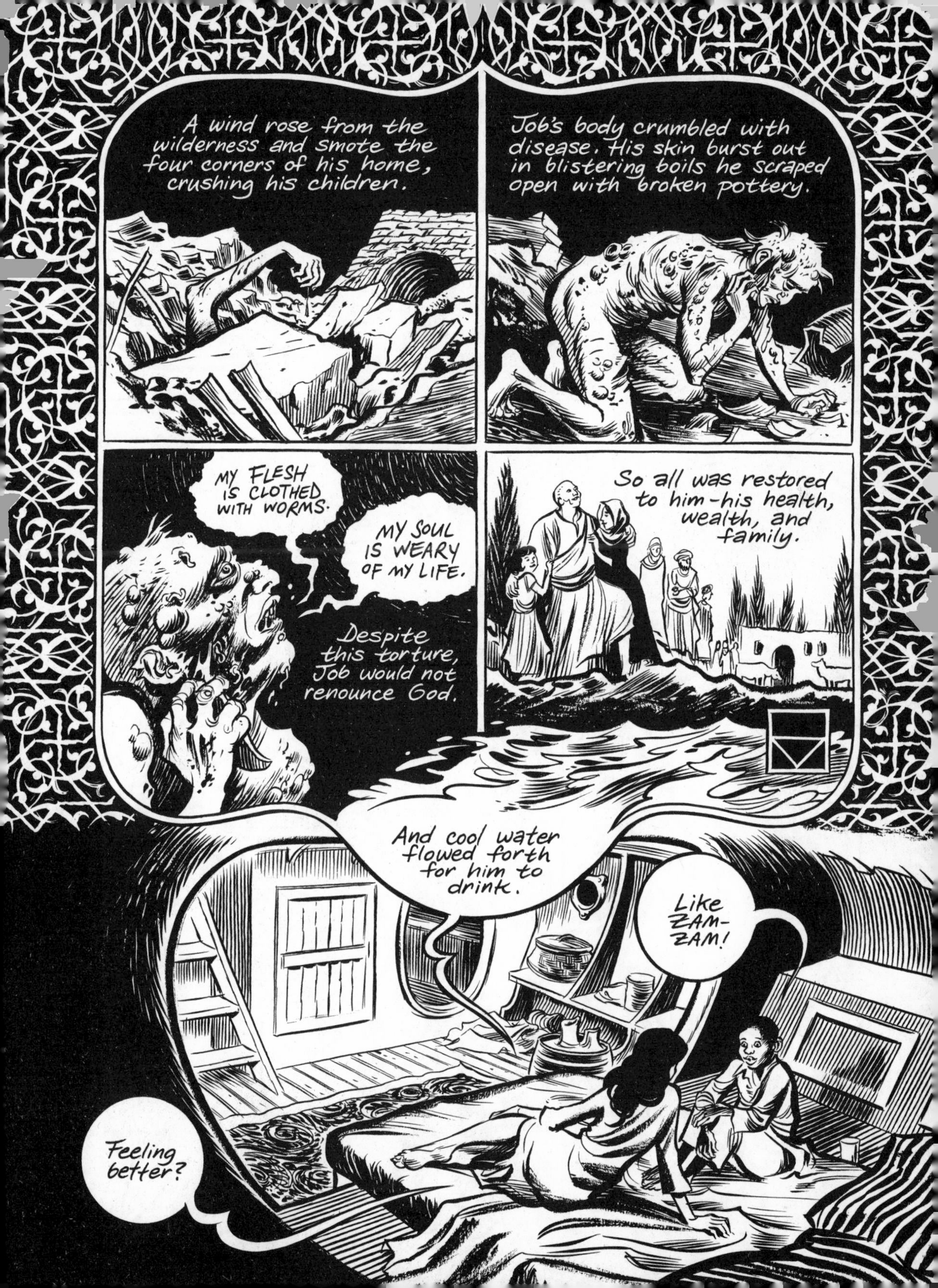
A wind rose from the wilderness and smote the four corners of his home, crushing his children.
Job's body crumbled with disease. His skin burst out in blistering boils he scraped open with broken pottery.
MY FLESH IS CLOTHED WITH WORMS.
MY SOUL IS WEARY OF MY LIFE.
Despite this torture, Job would not renounce God.
So all was restored to him-his health, wealth, and family.
And cool water flowed forth for him to drink.
Like ZAM-ZAM!
Feeling better?

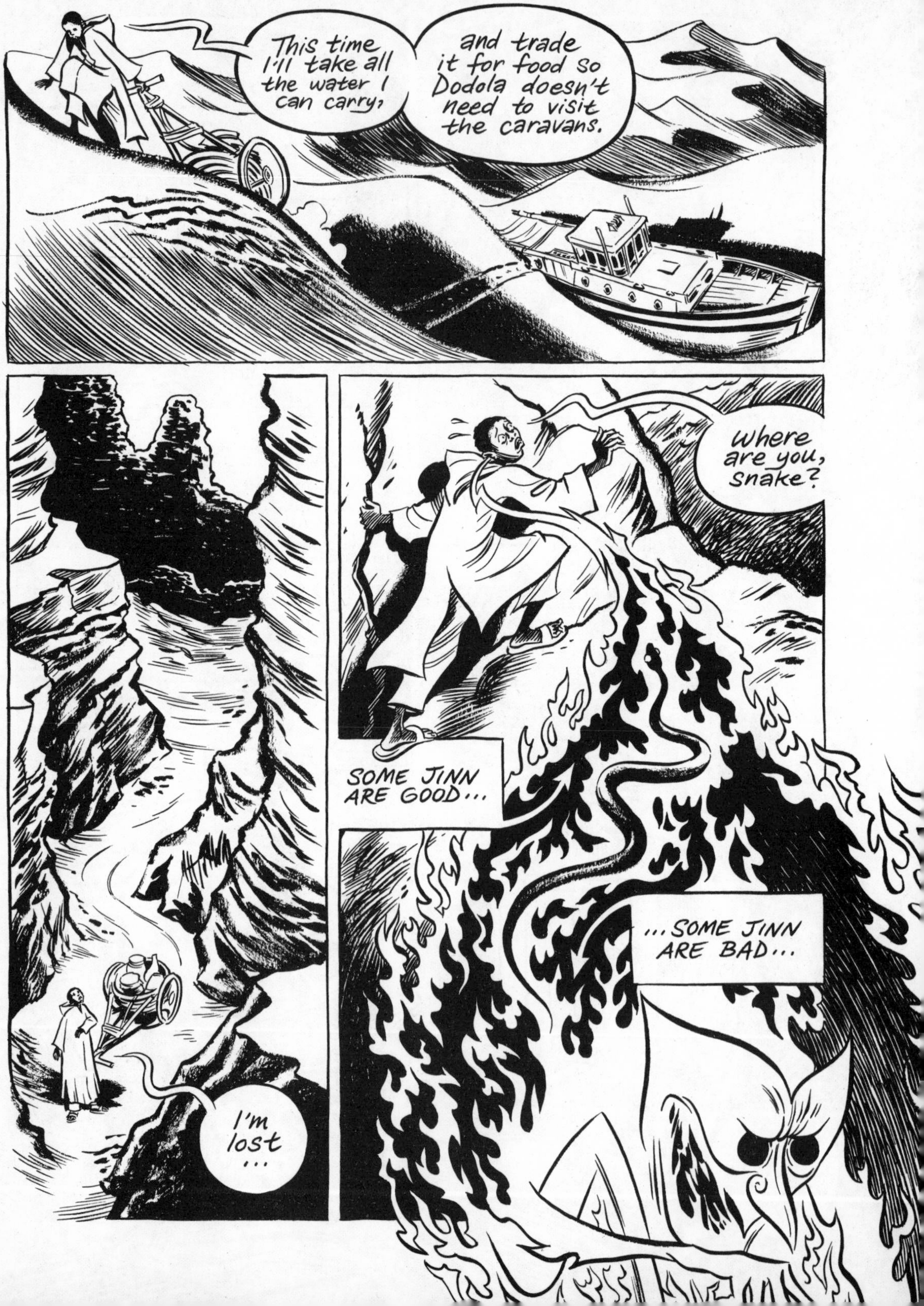
This time I'll take all the water I can carry,
and trade it for food so Dodola doesn't need to visit the caravans.
I'm lost ...
Where are you, snake?
SOME JINN ARE GOOD...
...SOME JINN ARE BAD...

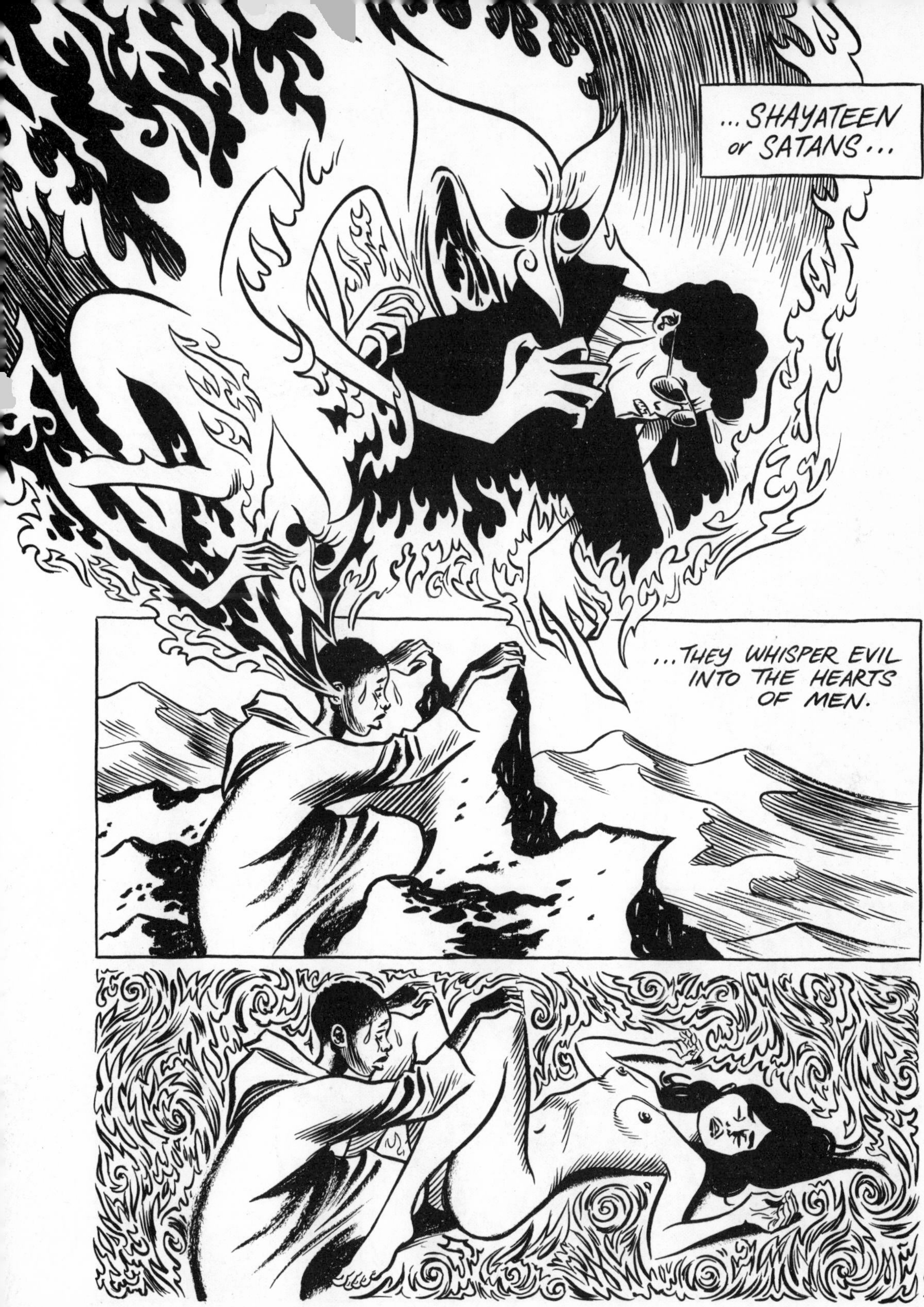
...SHAYATEEN or SATANS...
...THEY WHISPER EVIL INTO THE HEARTS OF MEN.

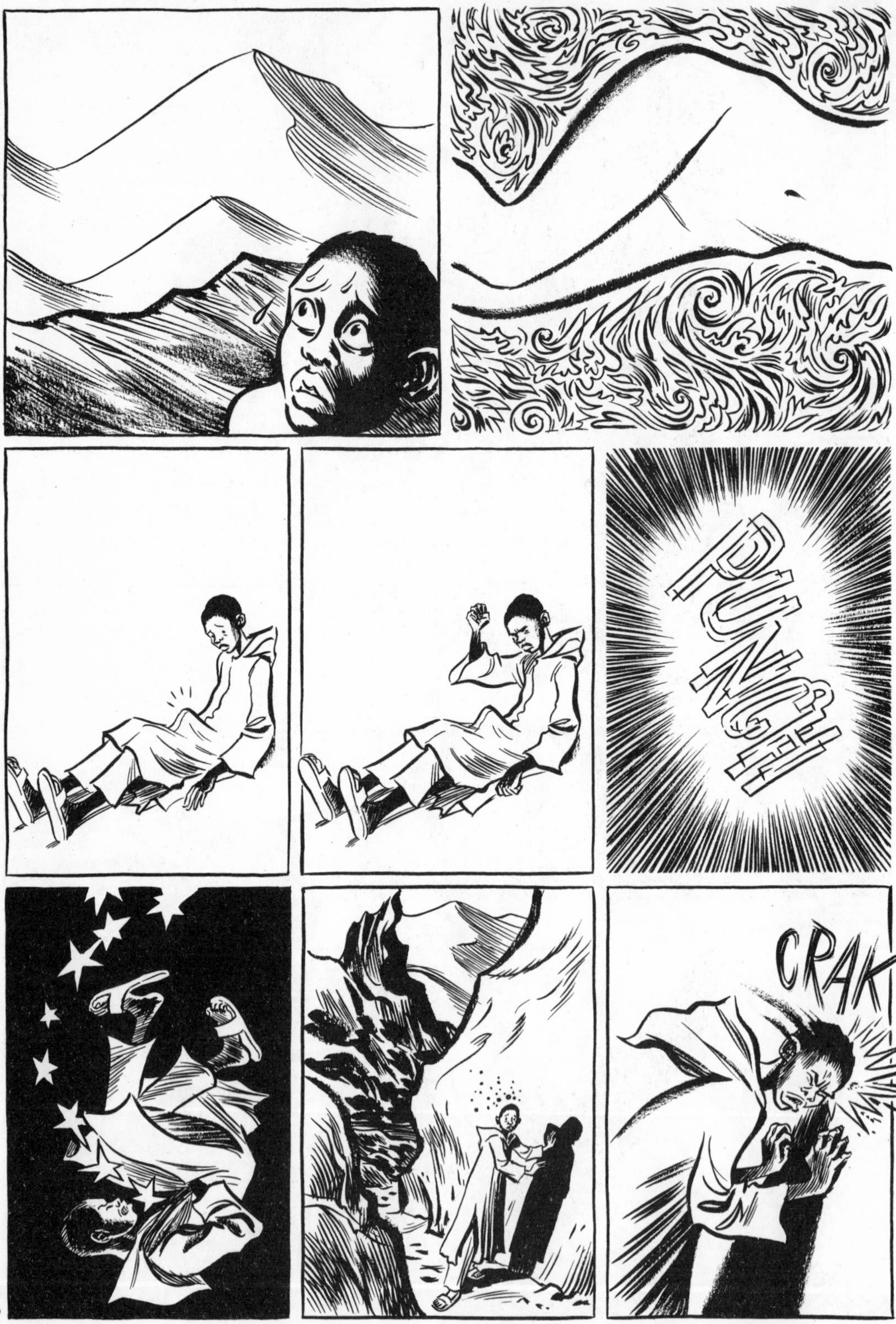
PUNCH
CRAK

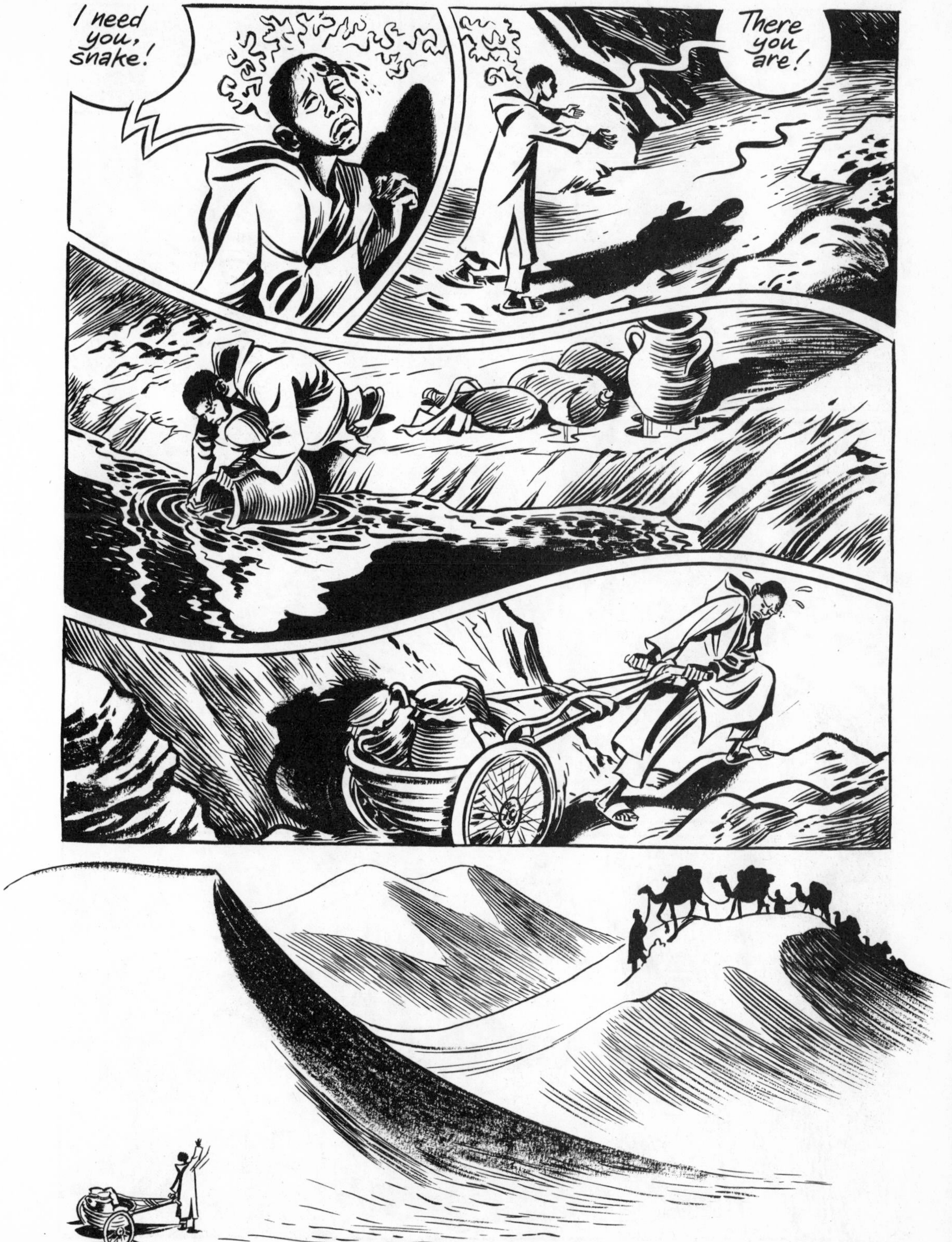
I need you, snake!
There you are!

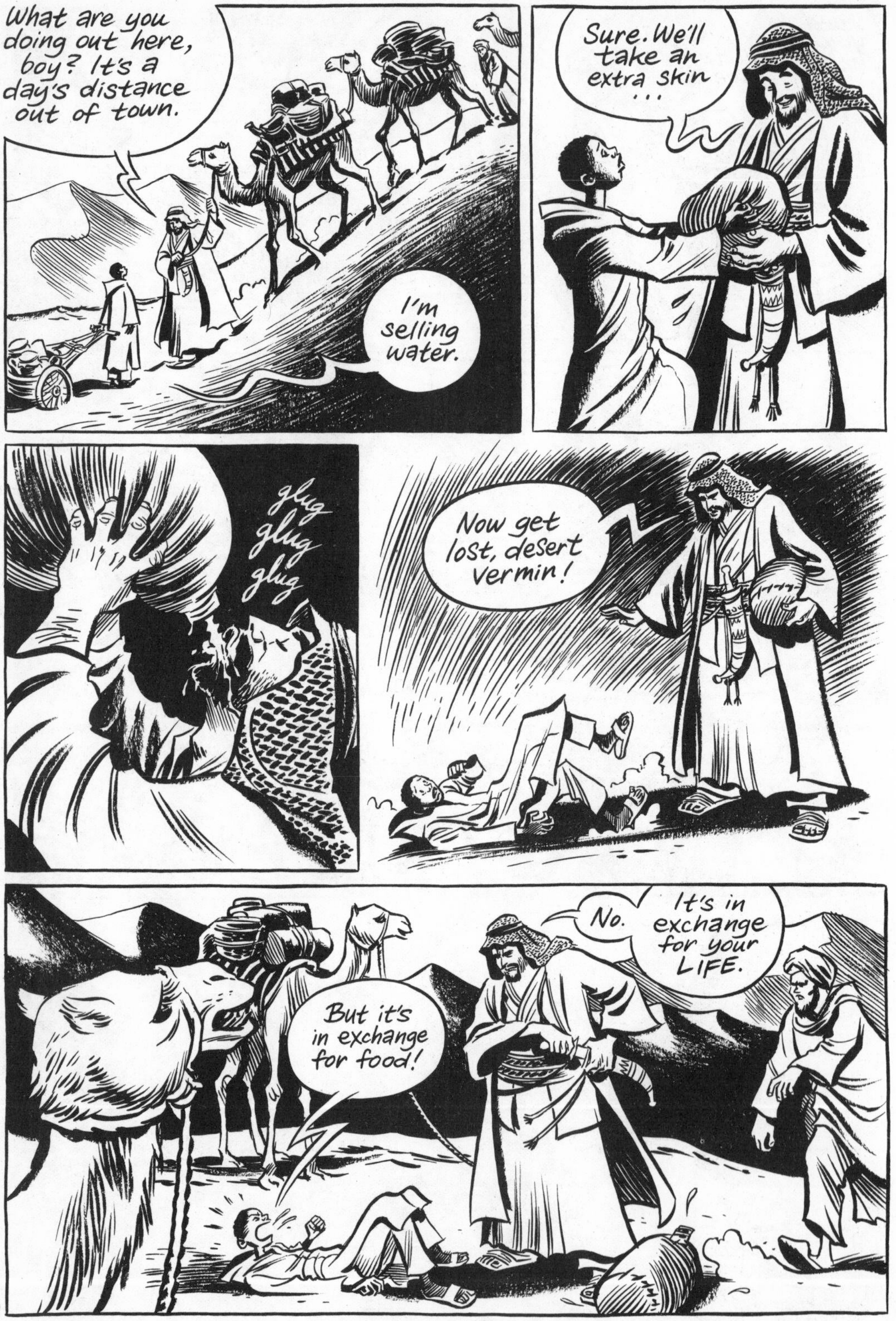
What are you doing out here, boy? It's a day's distance out of town.
I'm selling water.
Sure. We'll take an extra skin . . .
glug glug glug
Now get lost, desert vermin!
But it's in exchange for food!
No.
It's in exchange for your LIFE.

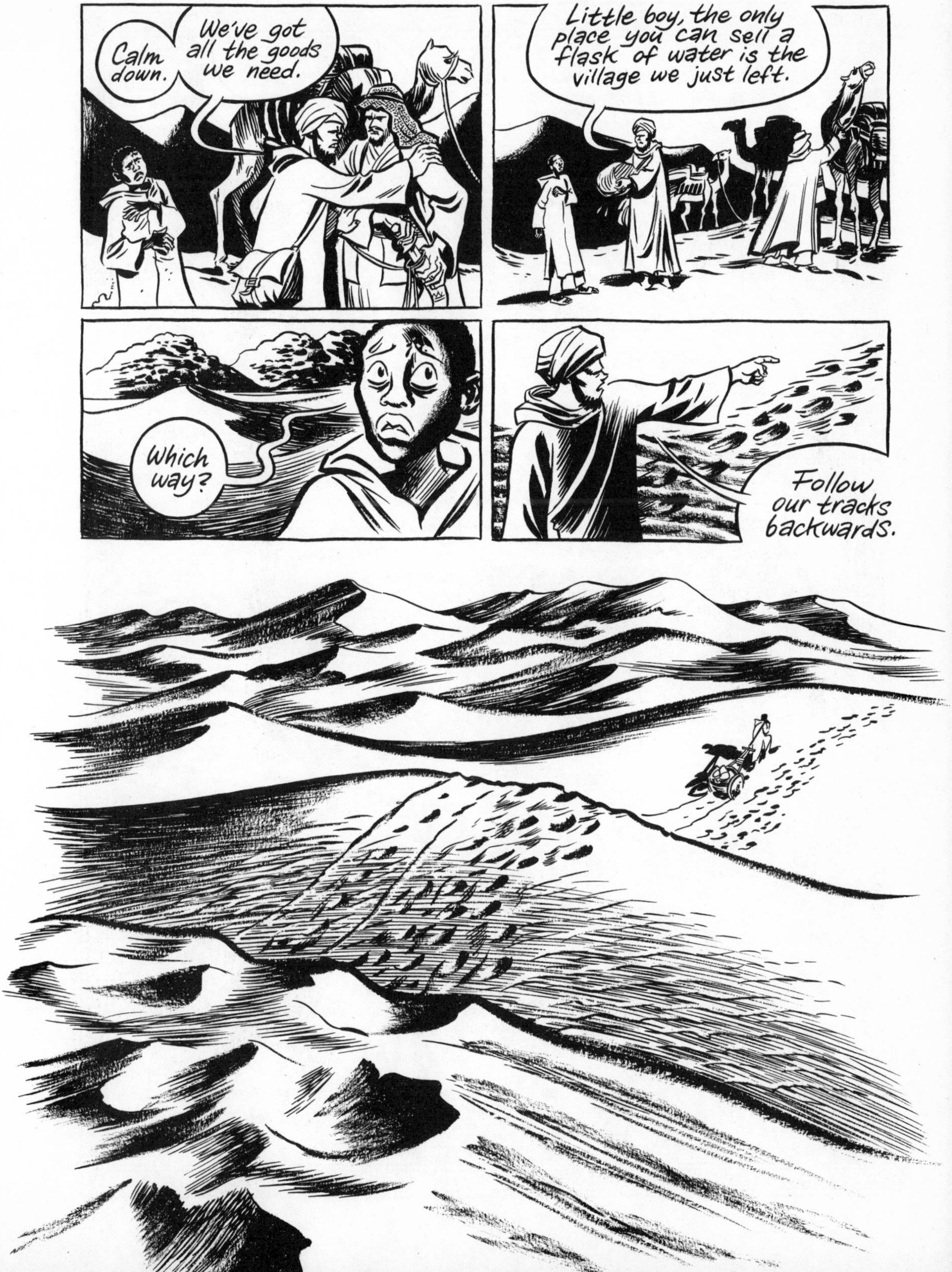
Calm down.
We've got all the goods we need.
Little boy, the only place you can sell a flask of water is the village we just left.
Which way?
Follow our tracks backwards.

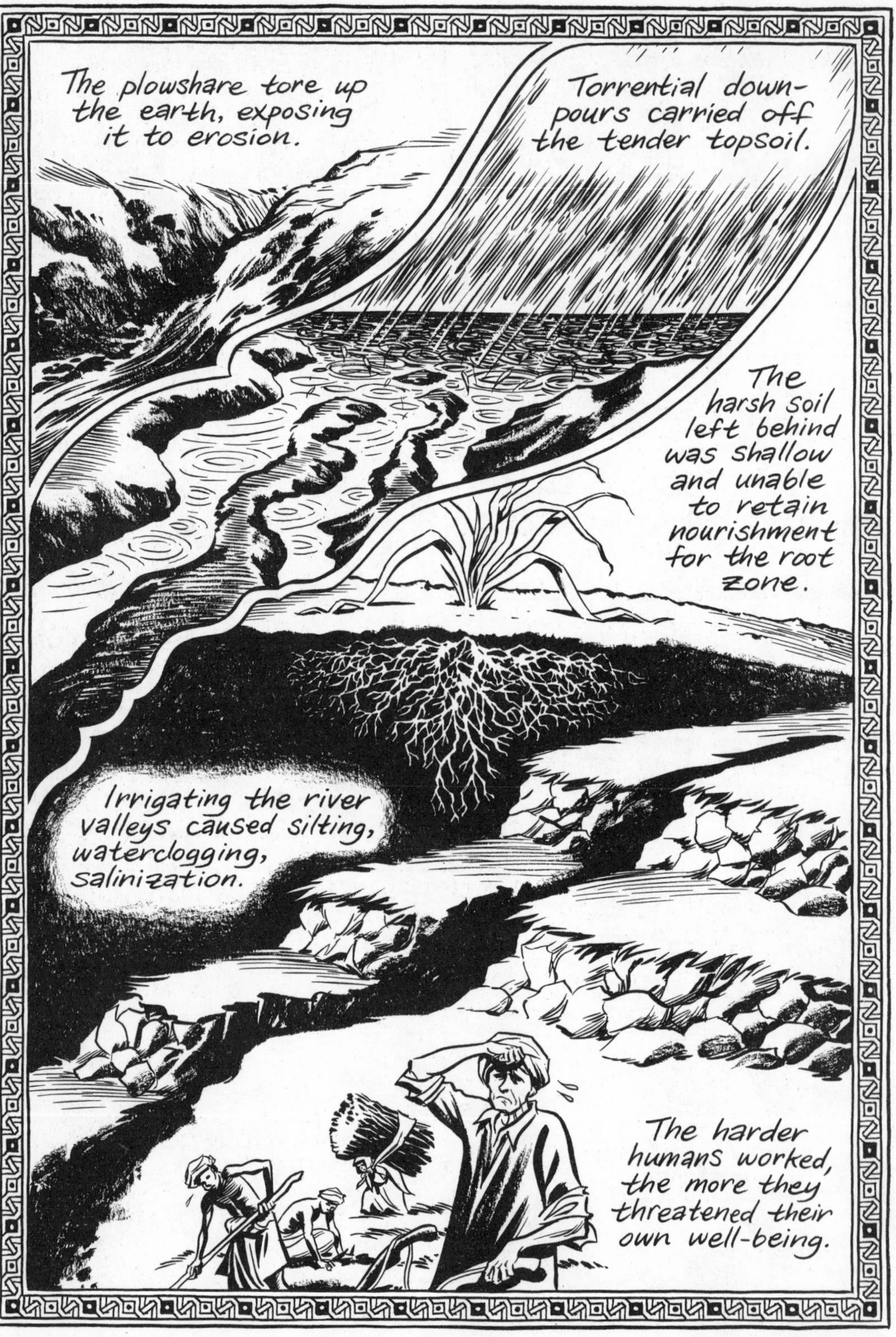
The plowshare tore up the earth, exposing it to erosion.
Torrential down-pours carried off the tender topsoil.
The harsh soil left behind was shallow and unable to retain nourishment for the root zone.
Irrigating the river valleys caused silting, waterclogging, salinization.
The harder humans worked, the more they threatened their own well-being.

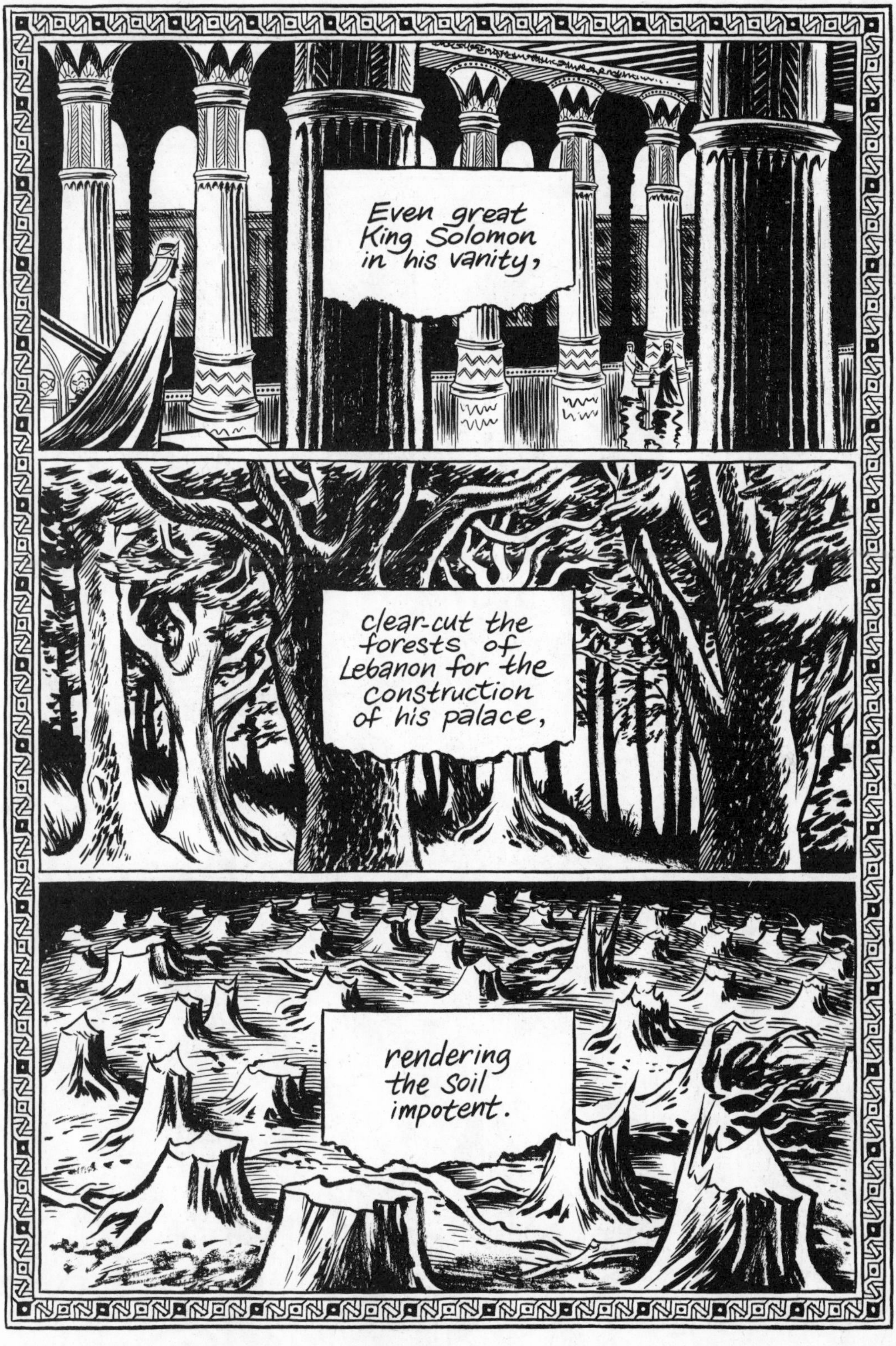
Even great King Solomon in his vanity,
clear-cut the forests of Lebanon for the construction of his palace,
rendering the soil impotent.

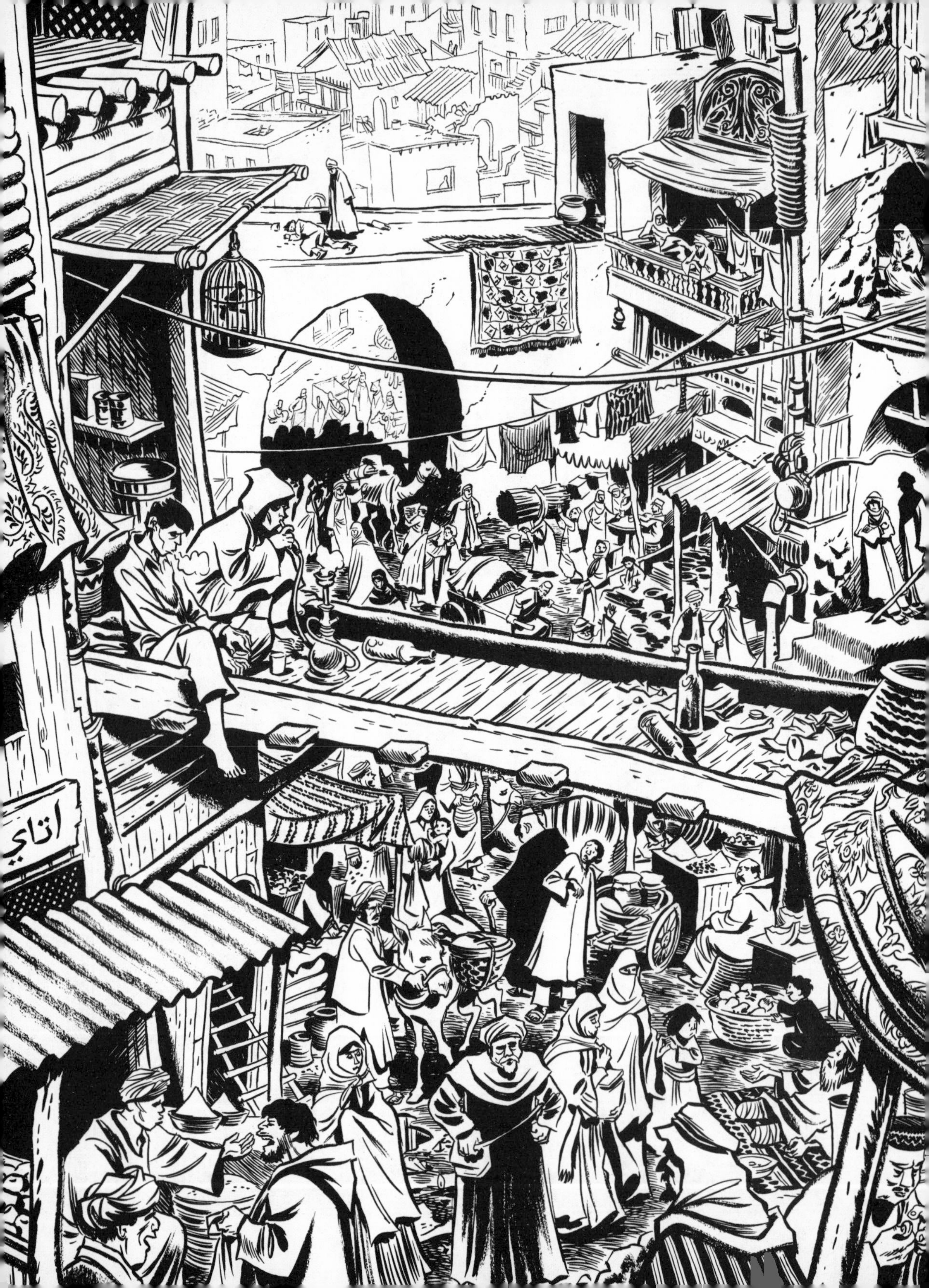
اتاي

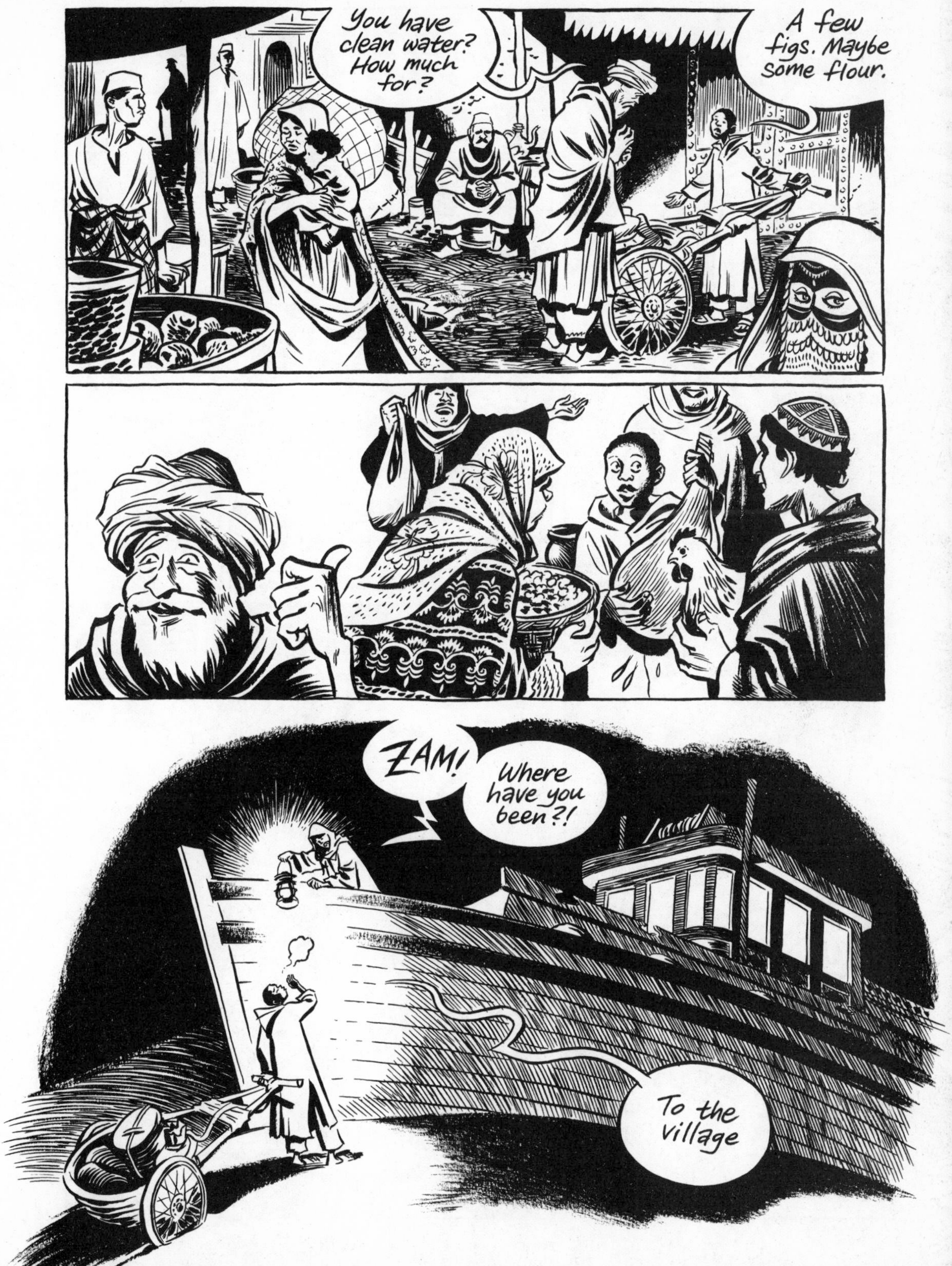
You have clean water? How much for?
A few figs. Maybe some flour.
ZAM!
Where have you been?!
To the village

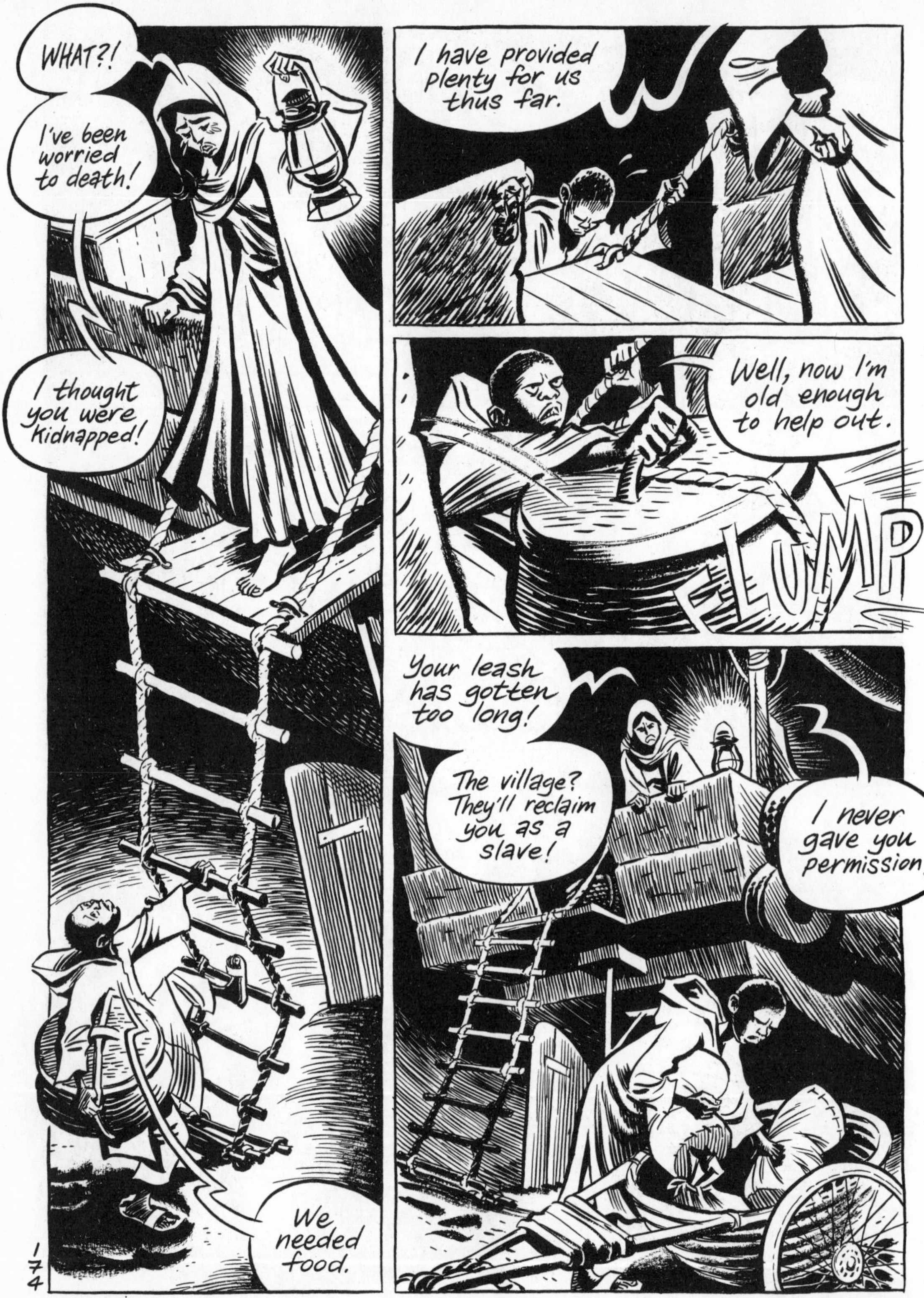
WHAT?!
I've been worried to death!
I thought you were kidnapped!
We needed food.
I have provided plenty for us thus far.
Well, now I'm old enough to help out.
FLUMP
Your leash has gotten too long!
The village? They'll reclaim you as a slave!
I never gave you permission!

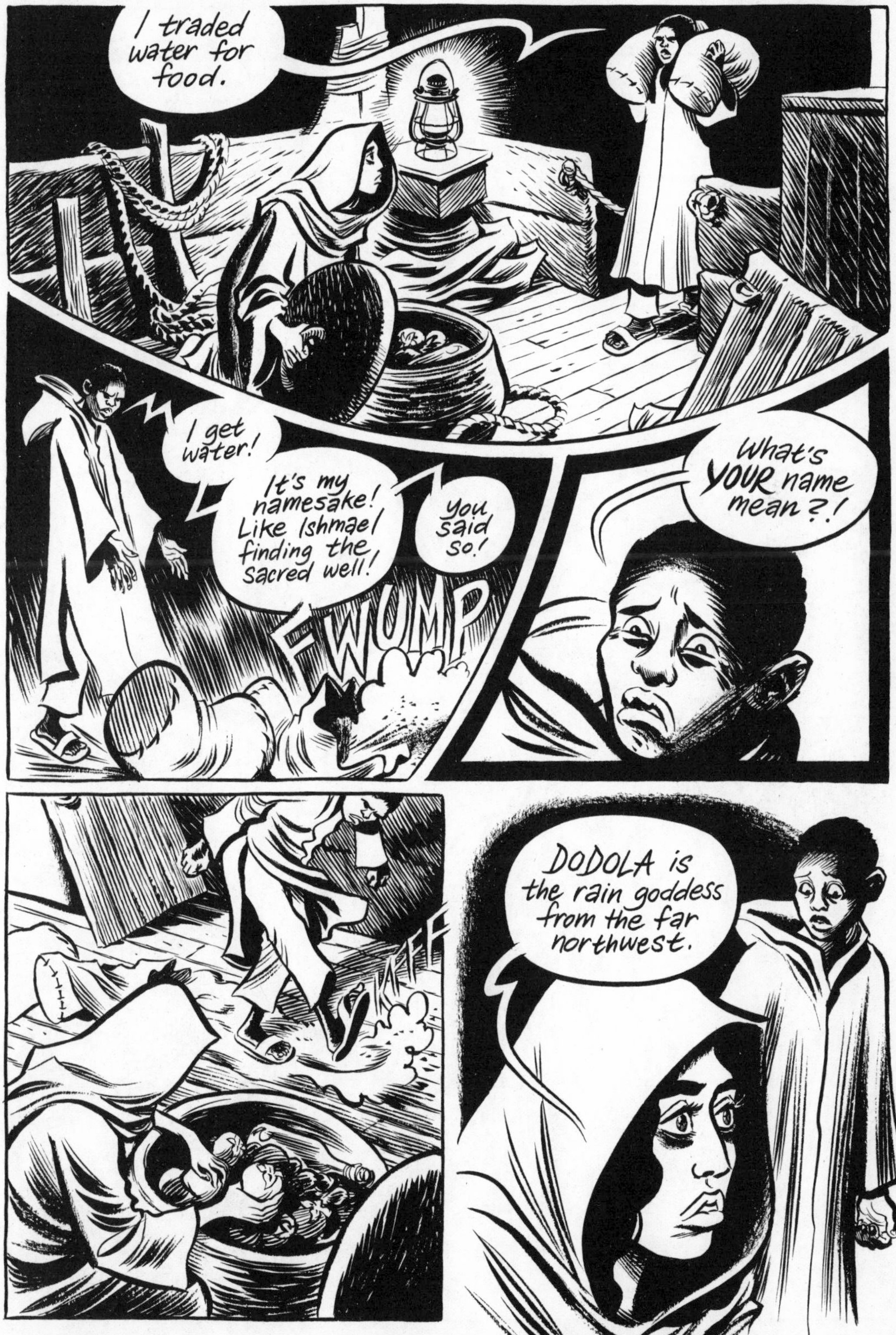
I traded water for food.
I get water!
It's my namesake! Like Ishmael finding the sacred well!
You said so!
FWUMP
What's YOUR name mean?!
KAFF
DODOLA is the rain goddess from the far northwest.

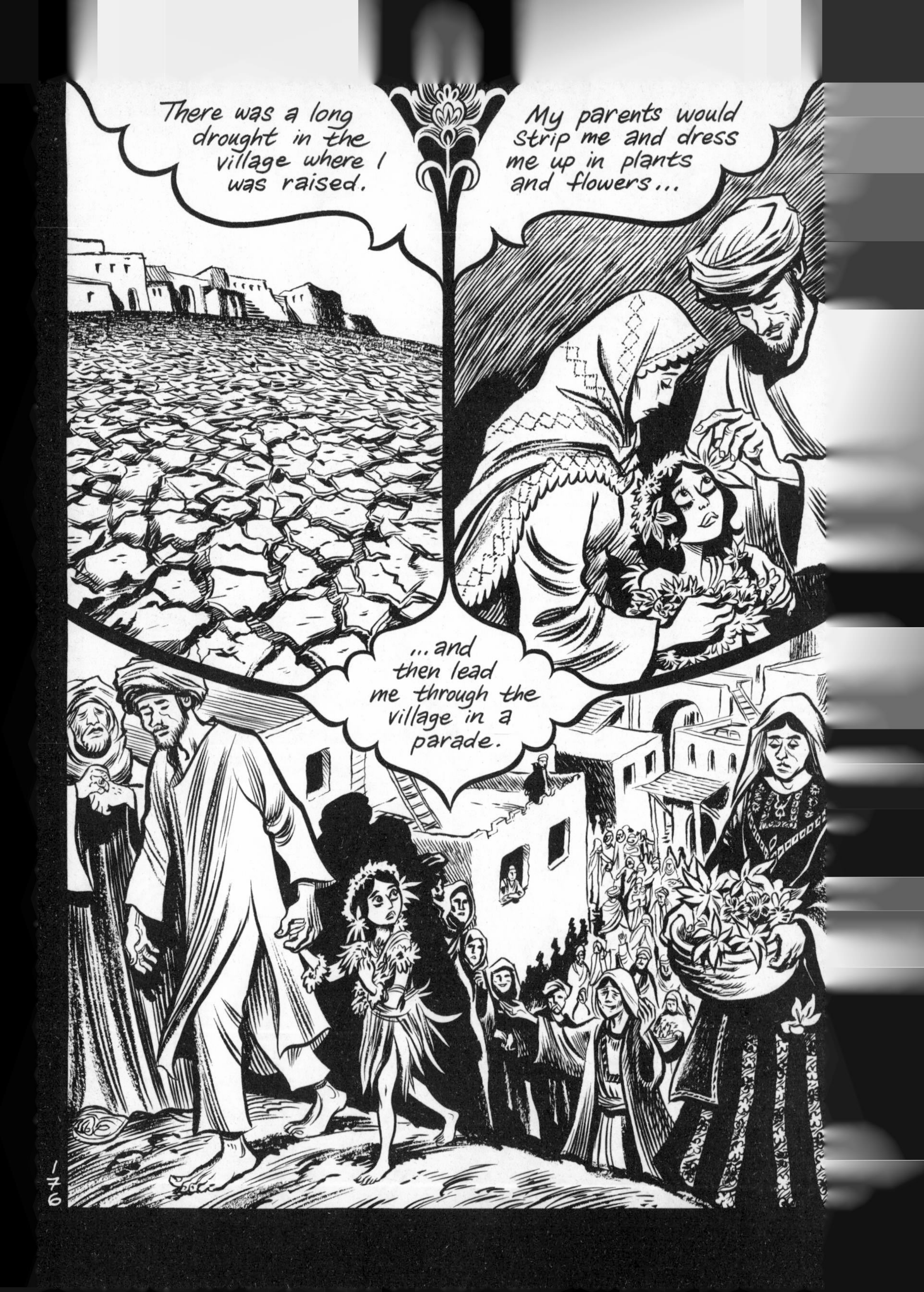
There was a long drought in the village where I was raised.
My parents would strip me and dress me up in plants and flowers...
...and then lead me through the village in a parade.

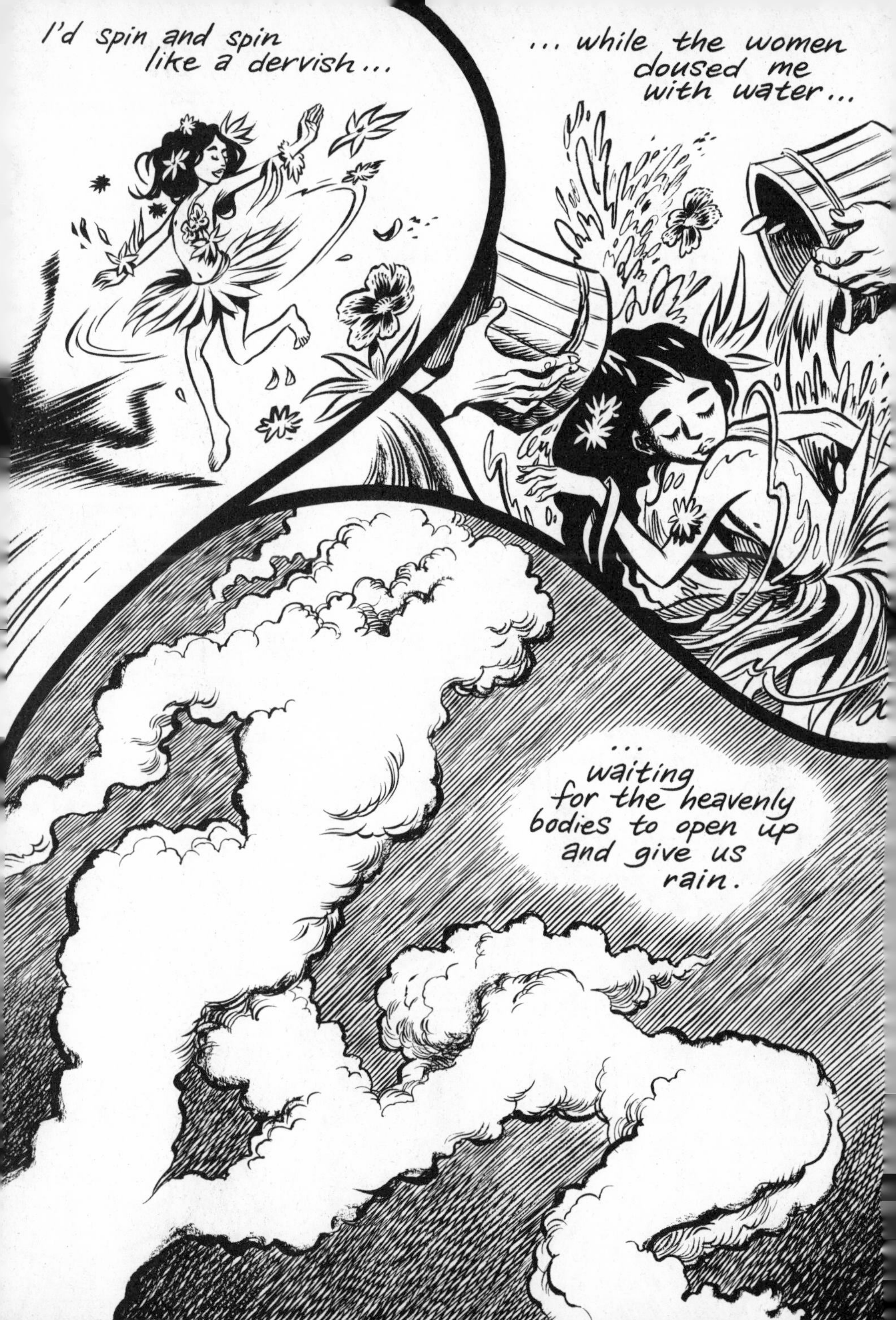
I'd spin and spin like a dervish...
... while the women doused me with water...
... waiting for the heavenly bodies to open up and give us rain.

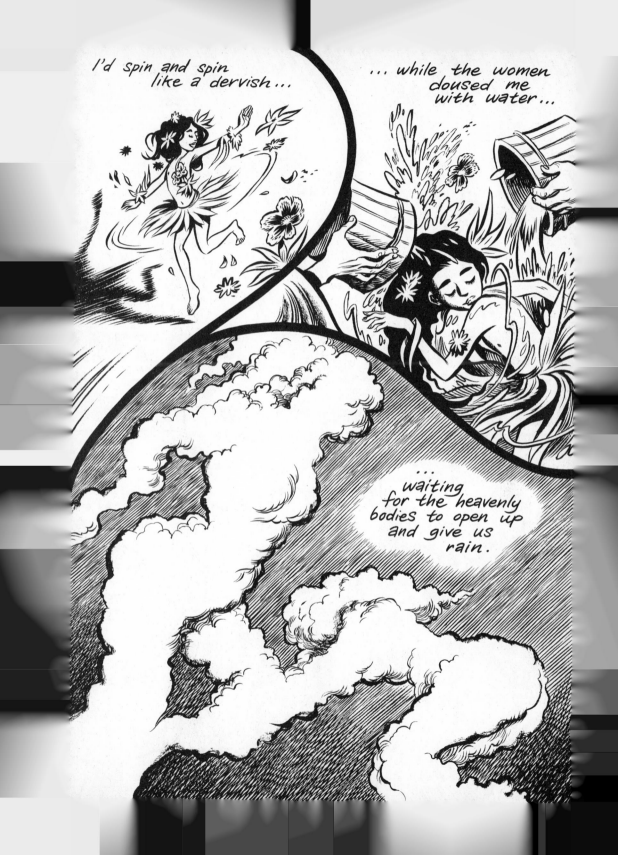

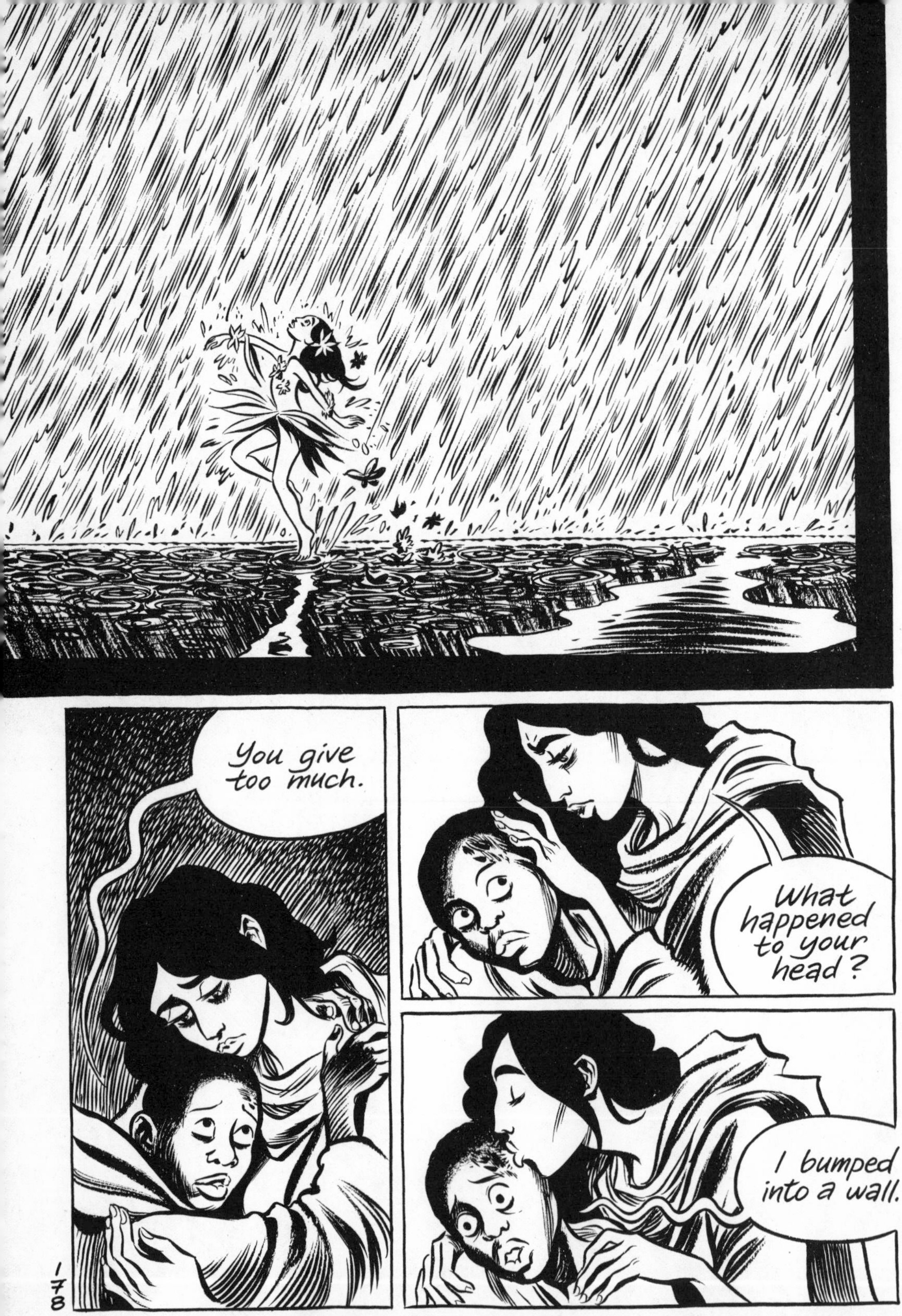
You give too much.
What happened to your head?
I bumped into a wall.

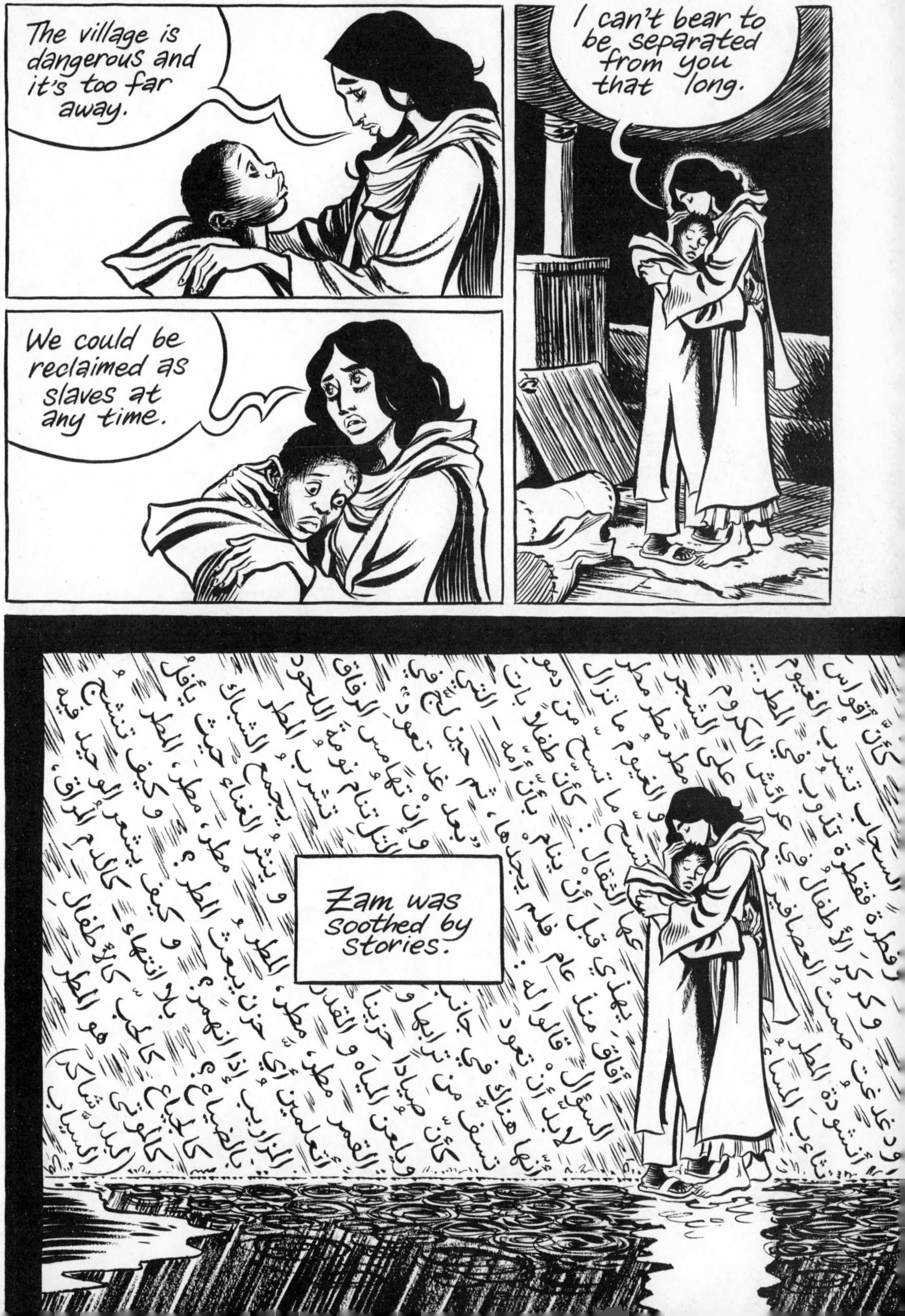
The village is dangerous and it's too far away.
I can't bear to be separated from you that long.
We could be reclaimed as slaves at any time.
Zam was soothed by stories.

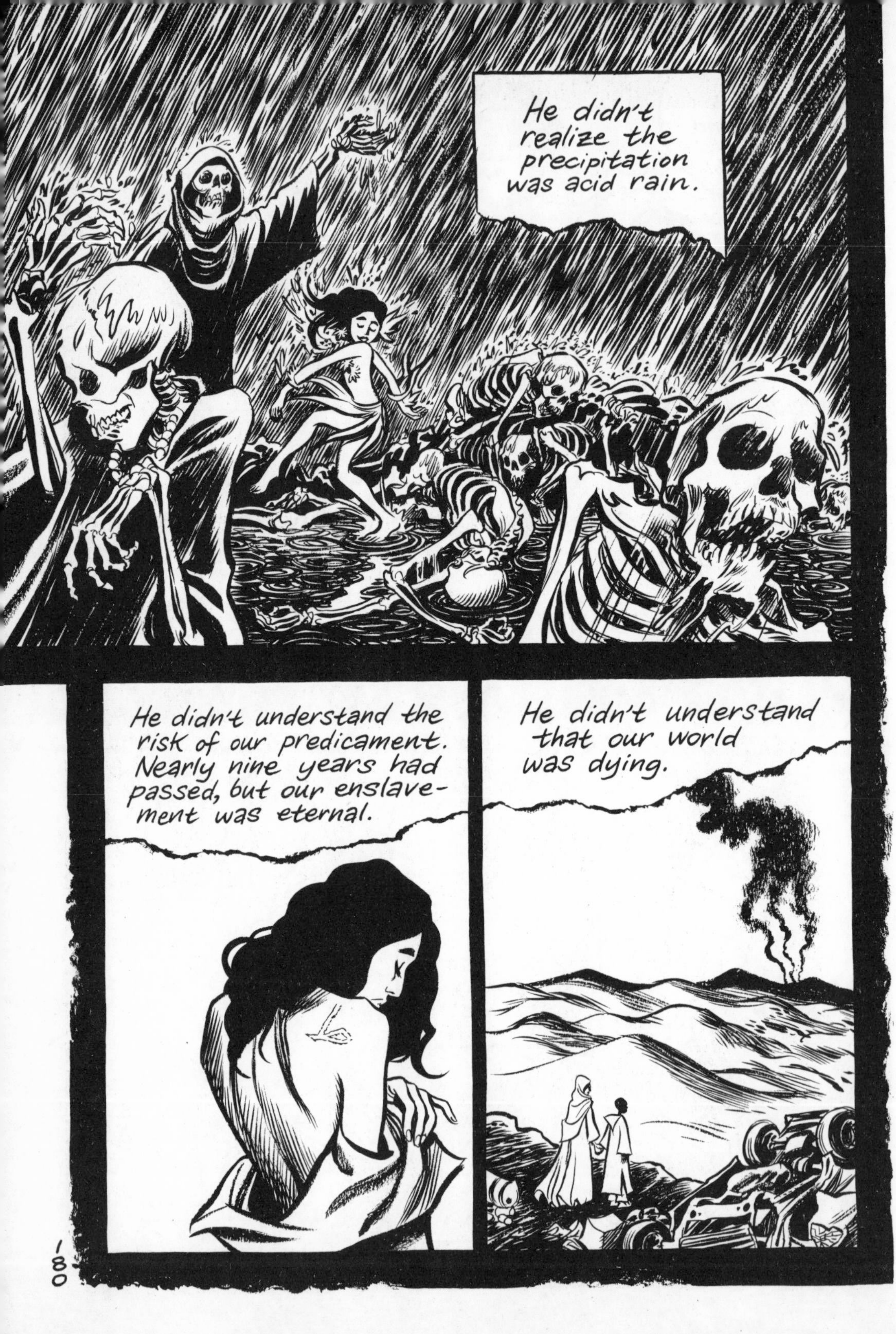
He didn't realize the precipitation was acid rain.
He didn't understand the risk of our predicament. Nearly nine years had passed, but our enslavement was eternal.
He didn't understand that our world was dying.

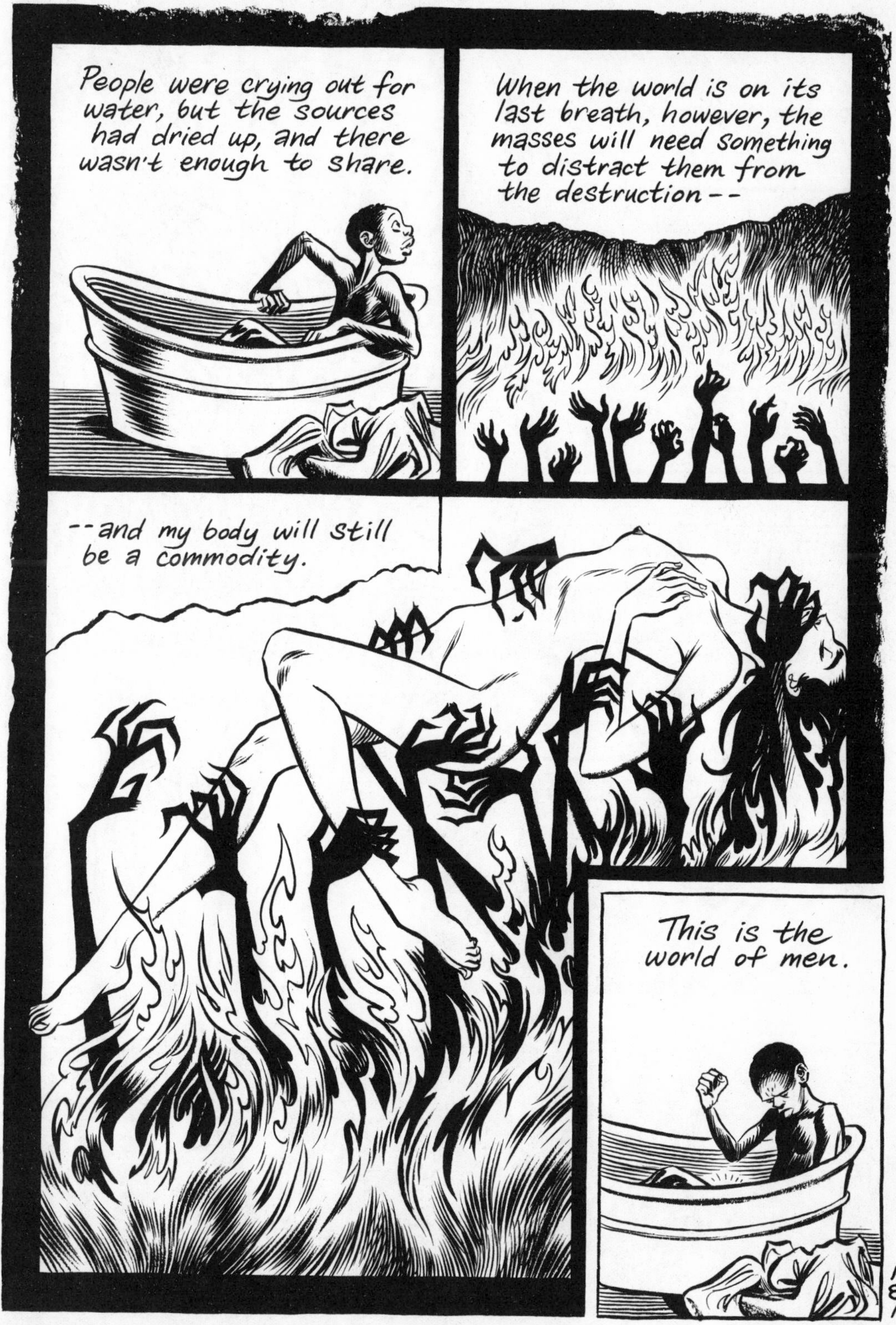
People were crying out for water, but the sources had dried up, and there wasn't enough to share.
When the world is on its last breath, however, the masses will need something to distract them from the destruction--
--and my body will still be a commodity.
This is the world of men.

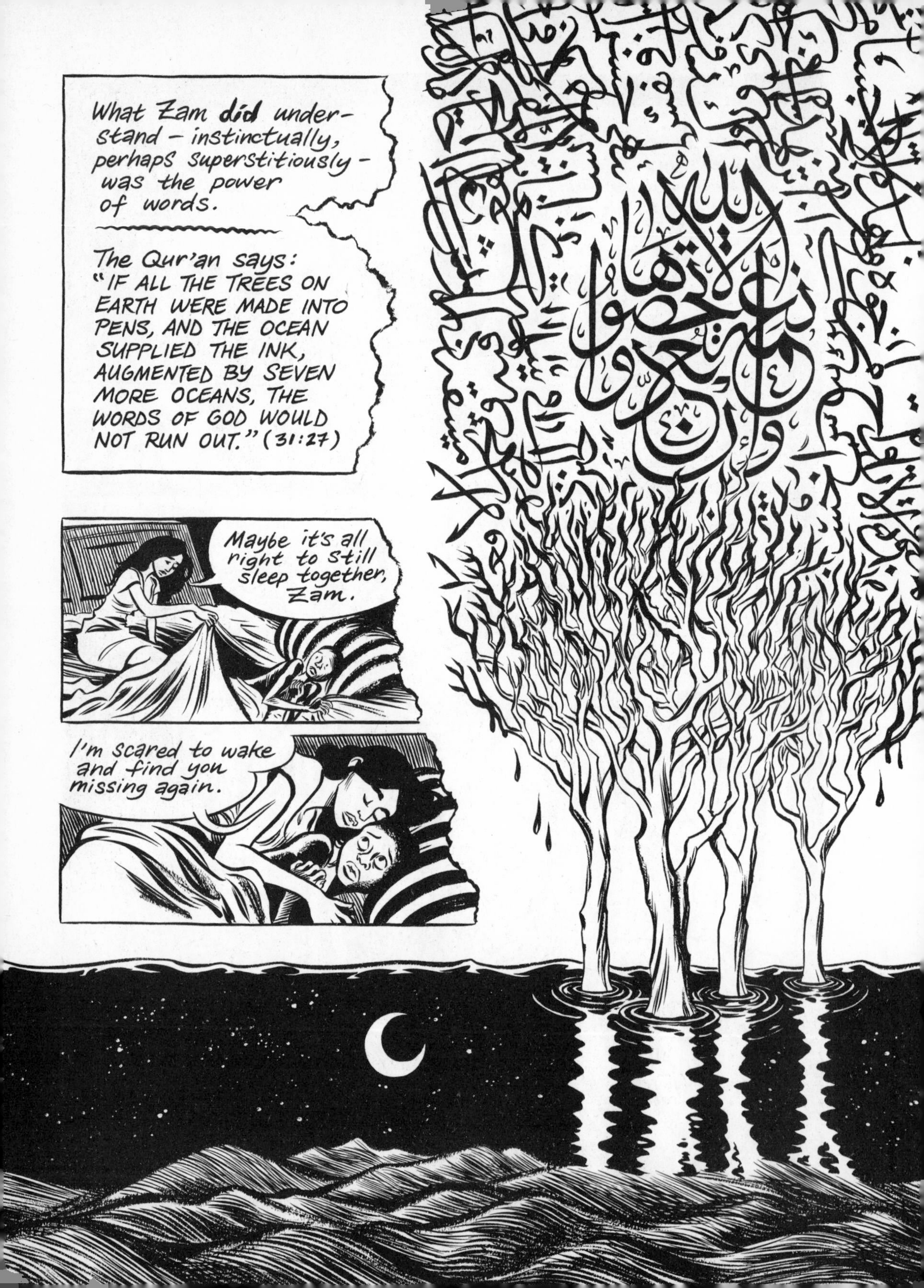
What Zam **did** understand – instinctually, perhaps superstitiously – was the power of words.
The Qur'an says: "IF ALL THE TREES ON EARTH WERE MADE INTO PENS, AND THE OCEAN SUPPLIED THE INK, AUGMENTED BY SEVEN MORE OCEANS, THE WORDS OF GOD WOULD NOT RUN OUT." (31:27)
Maybe it's all right to still sleep together, Zam.
I'm scared to wake and find you missing again.

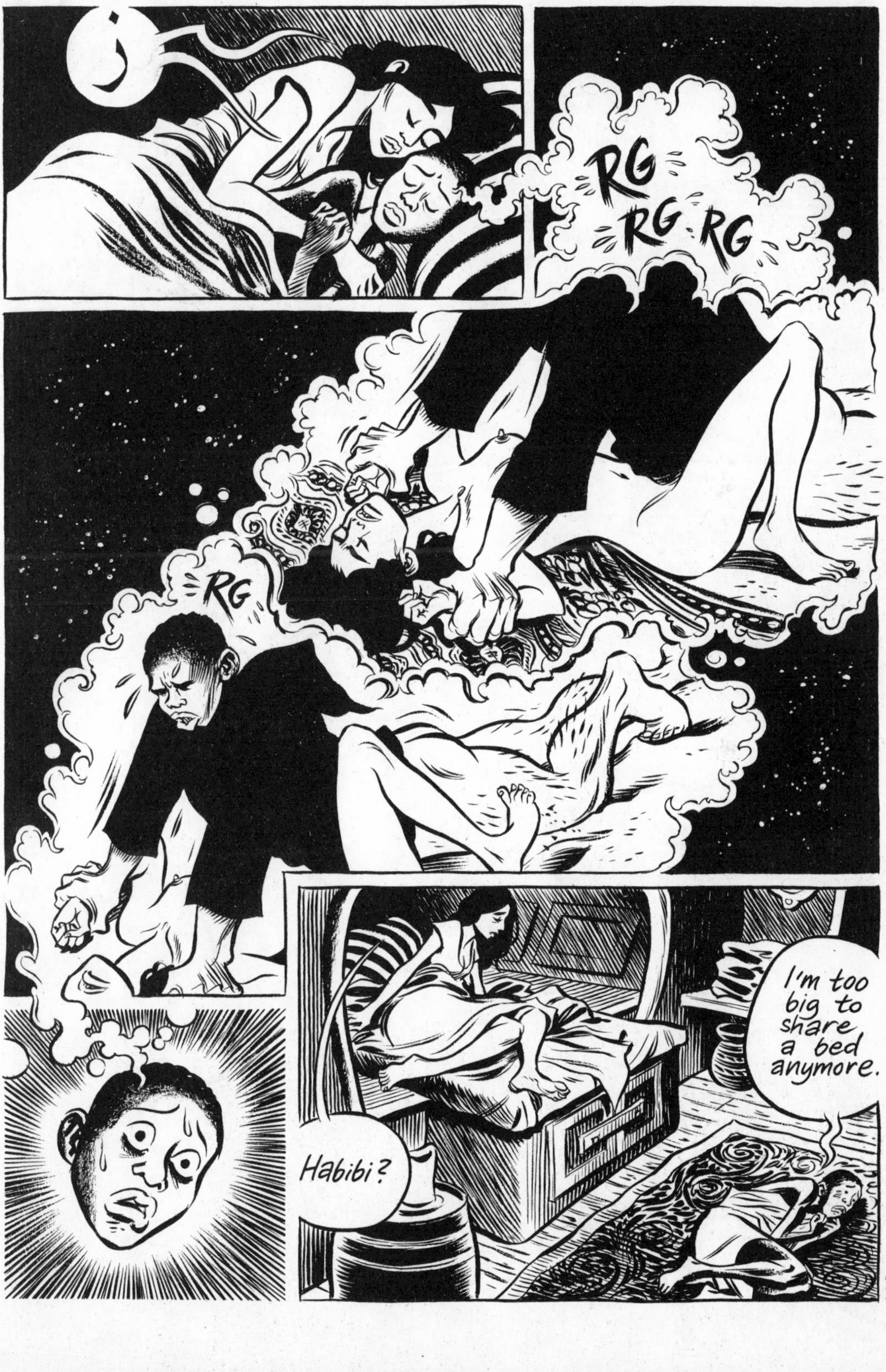
RG
RG RG
RG
Habibi?
I'm too big to share a bed anymore.

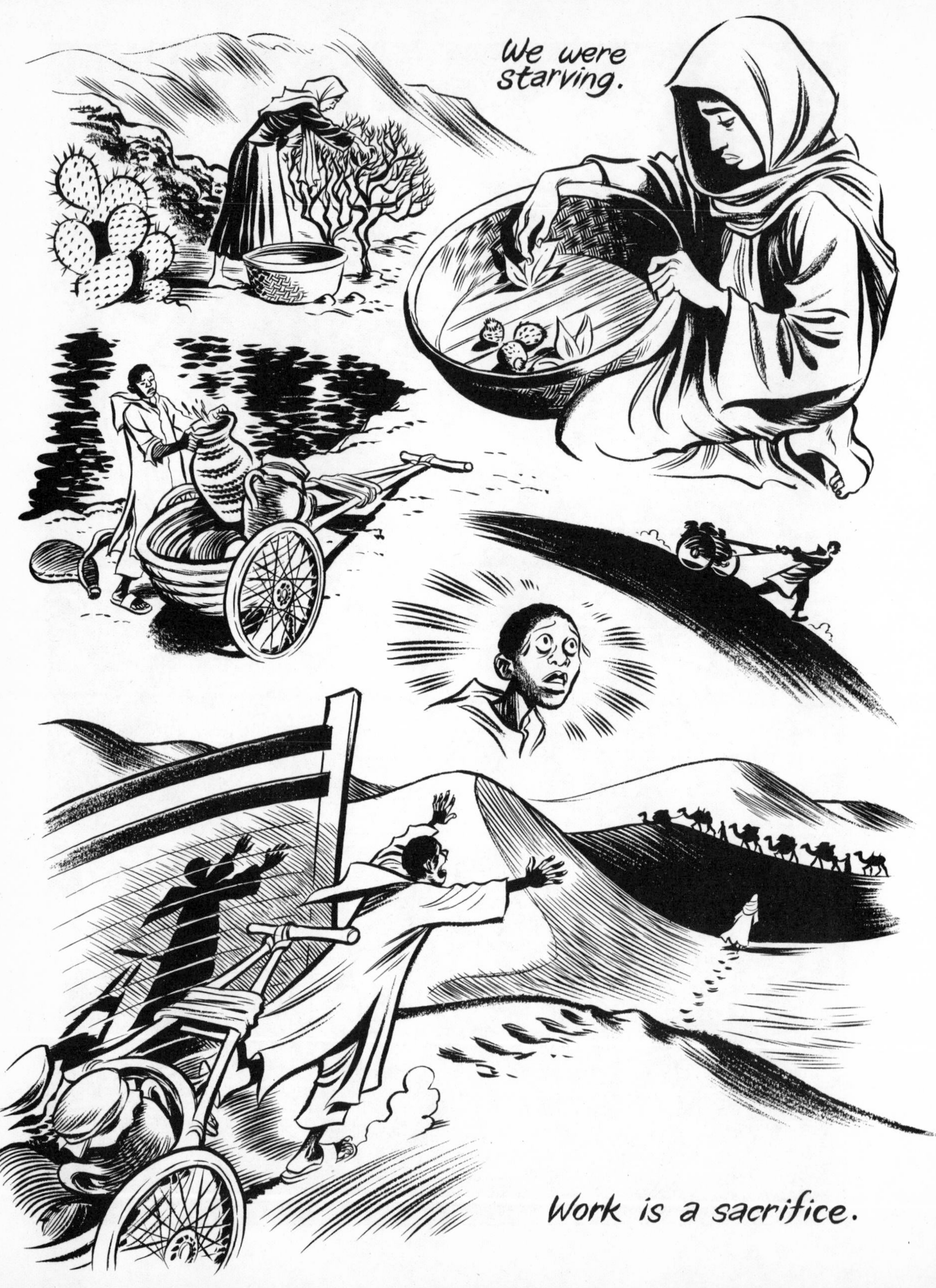
We were starving.
Work is a sacrifice.

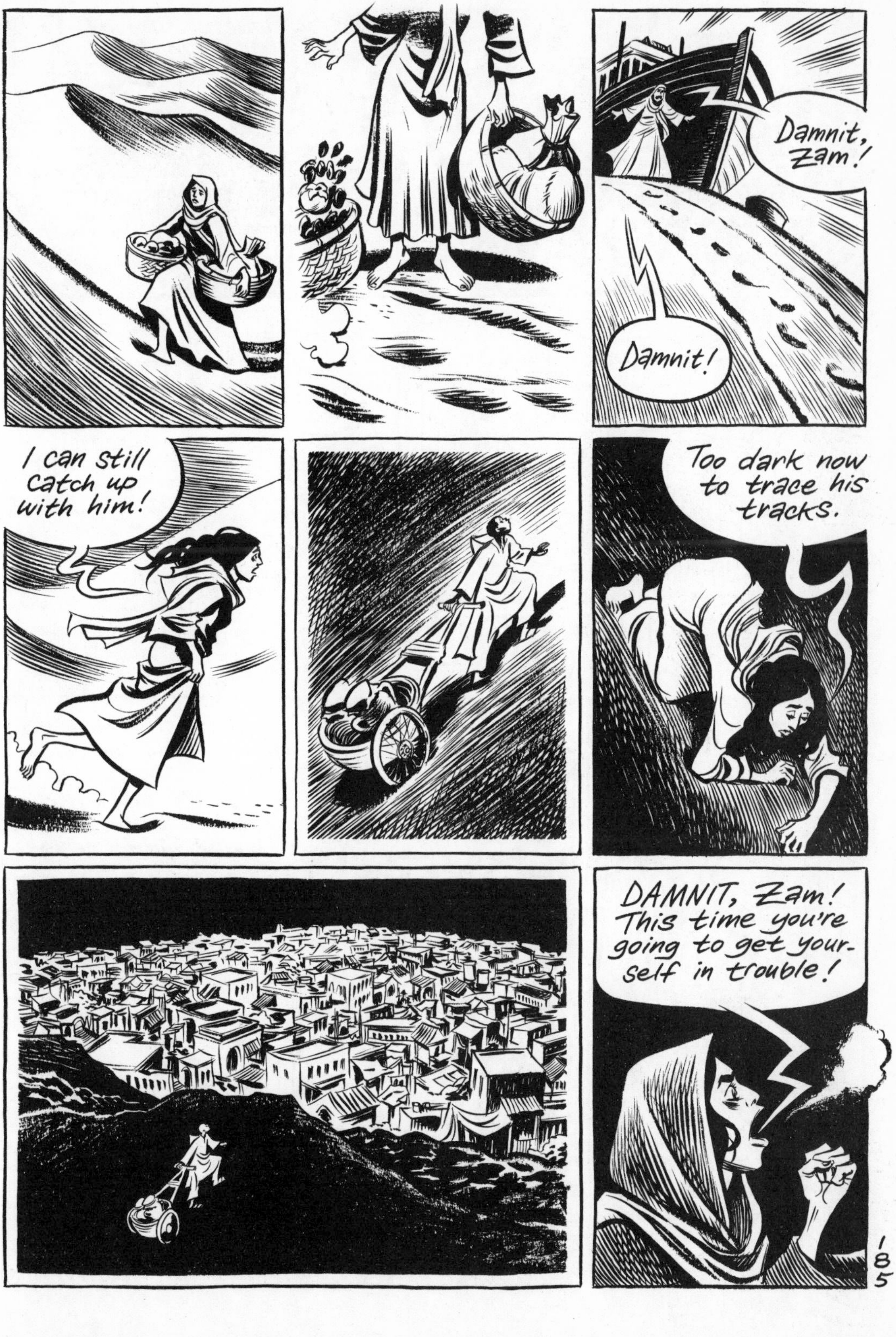
Damnit, Zam!
Damnit!
I can still catch up with him!
Too dark now to trace his tracks.
DAMNIT, Zam! This time you're going to get yourself in trouble!

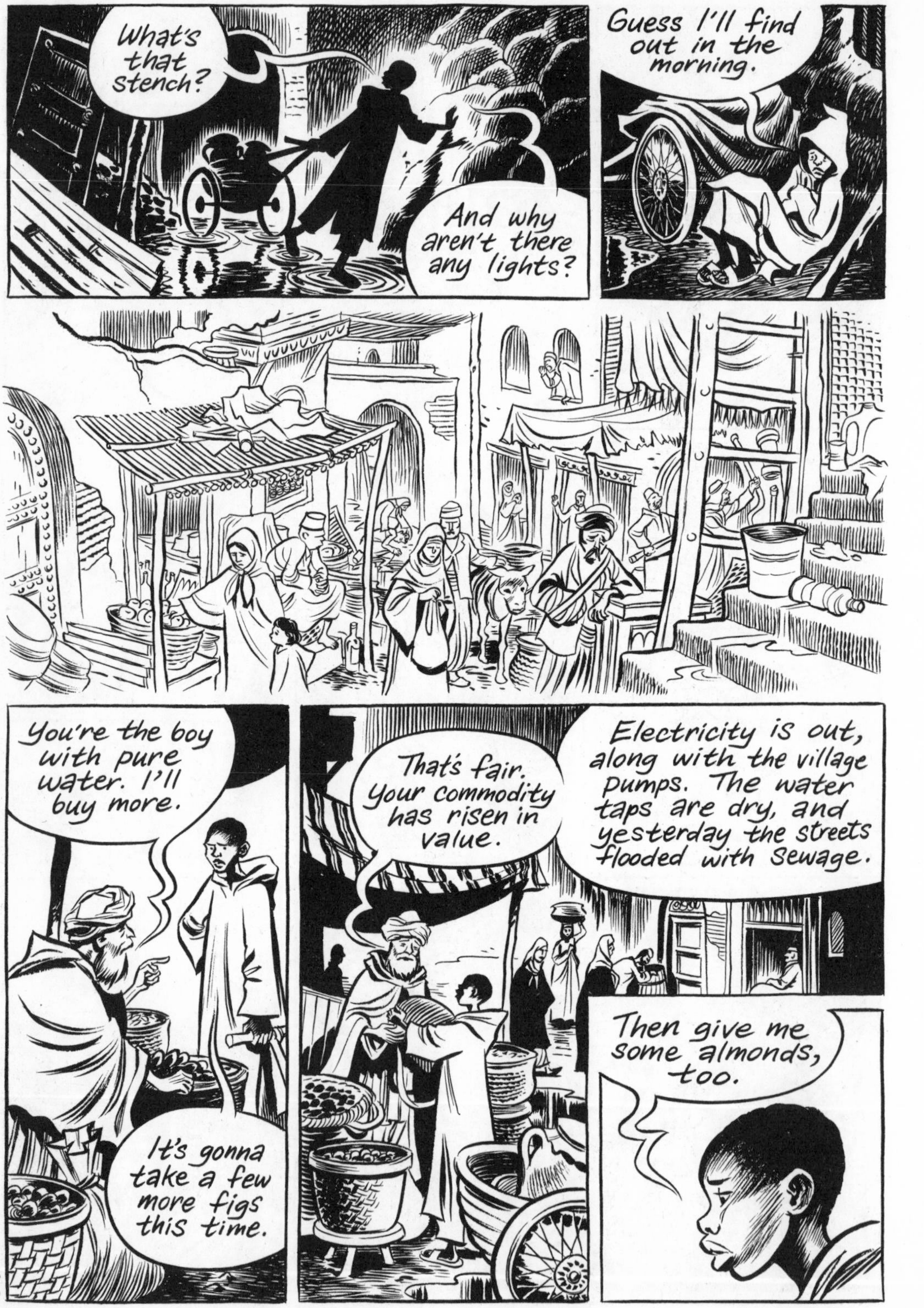
What's that stench?
And why aren't there any lights?
Guess I'll find out in the morning.
You're the boy with pure water. I'll buy more.
It's gonna take a few more figs this time.
That's fair. Your commodity has risen in value.
Electricity is out, along with the village pumps. The water taps are dry, and yesterday the streets flooded with sewage.
Then give me some almonds, too.

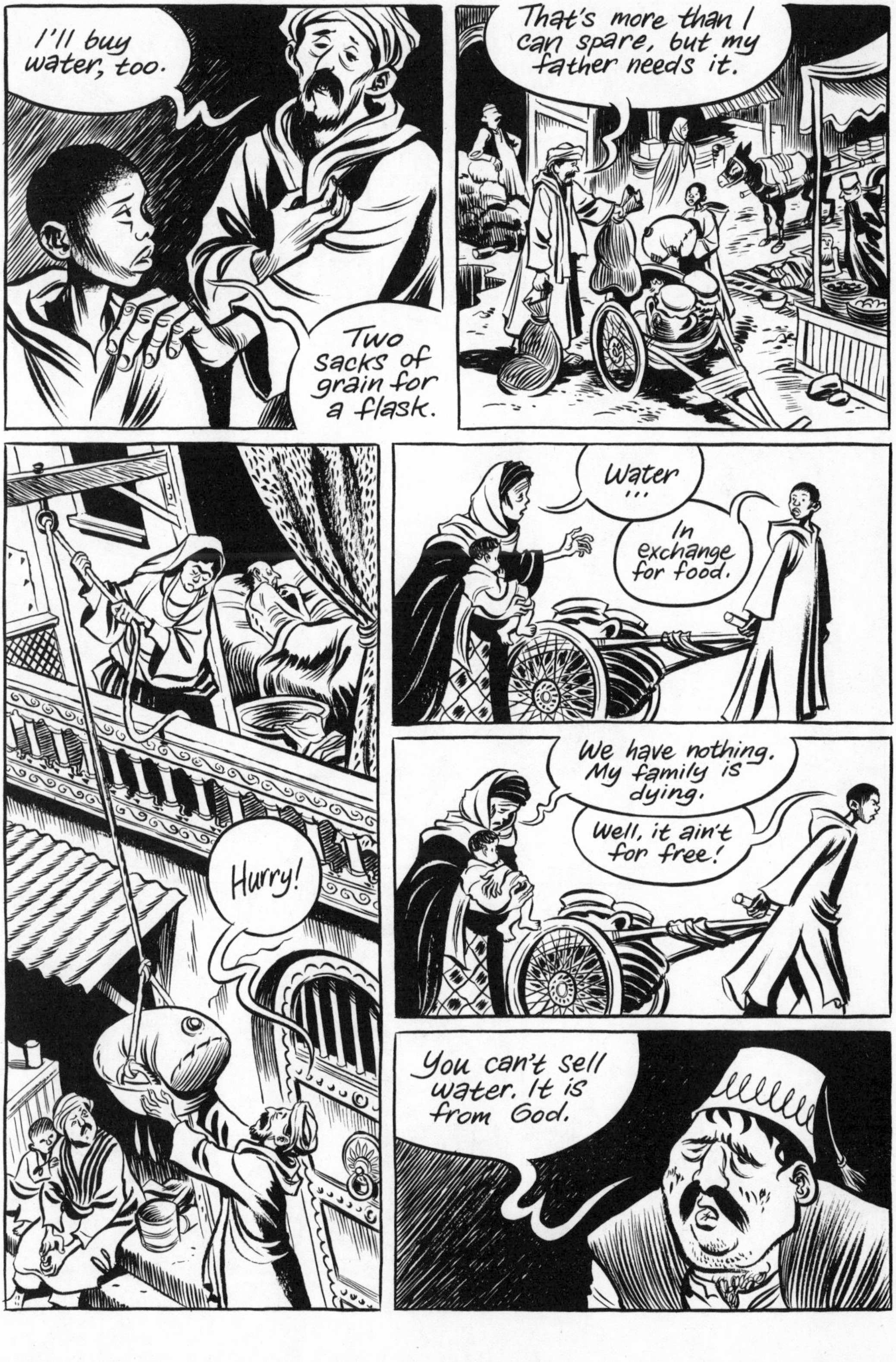
I'll buy water, too.
Two sacks of grain for a flask.
That's more than I can spare, but my father needs it.
Hurry!
Water ...
In exchange for food.
We have nothing. My family is dying.
Well, it ain't for free!
You can't sell water. It is from God.

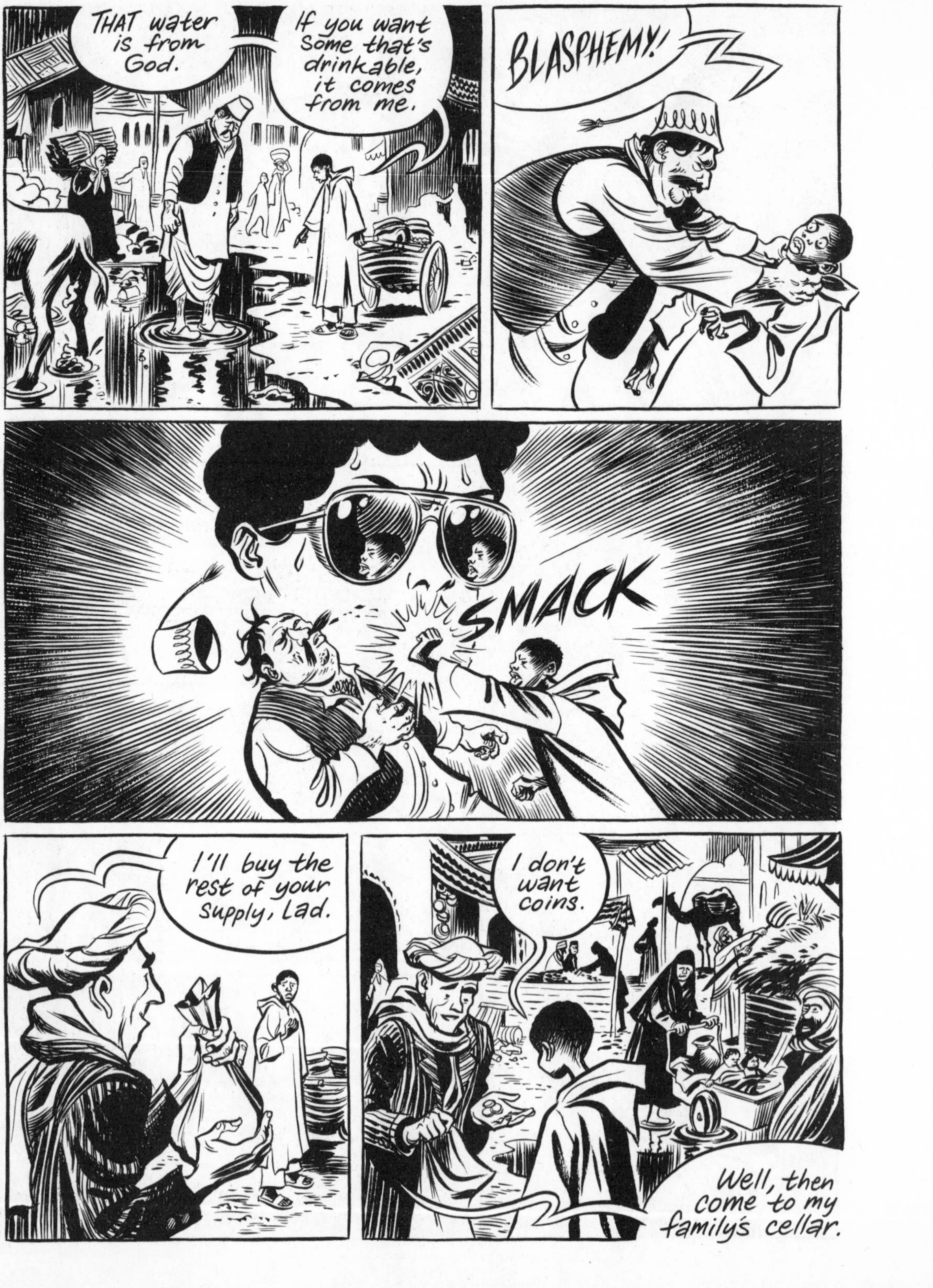
THAT water is from God.
If you want some that's drinkable, it comes from me.
BLASPHEMY!
SMACK
I'll buy the rest of your supply, lad.
I don't want coins.
Well, then come to my family's cellar.

Fully stocked.
We are prepared for the END.
We'll die like everyone else, but at least we'll last a couple more weeks; and as a new father, that gives me a certain assurance.
CLANG BOM
CHKCHK
CLANG CLANG
What's that racket?
CLANG
CHK BOM
It's the HIJRAS.

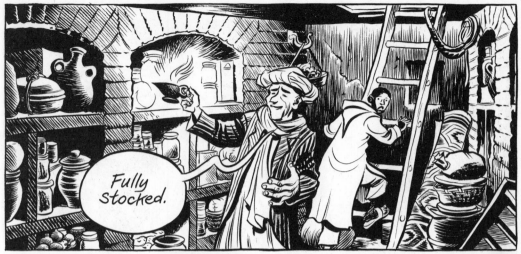

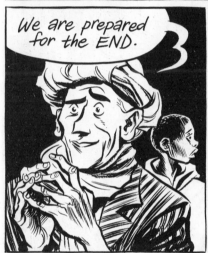

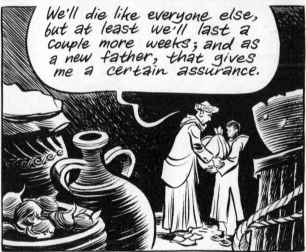

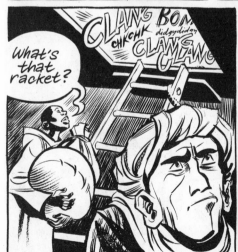

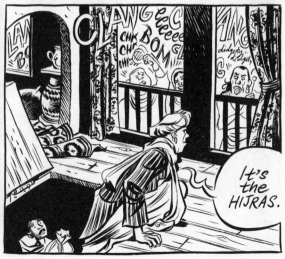

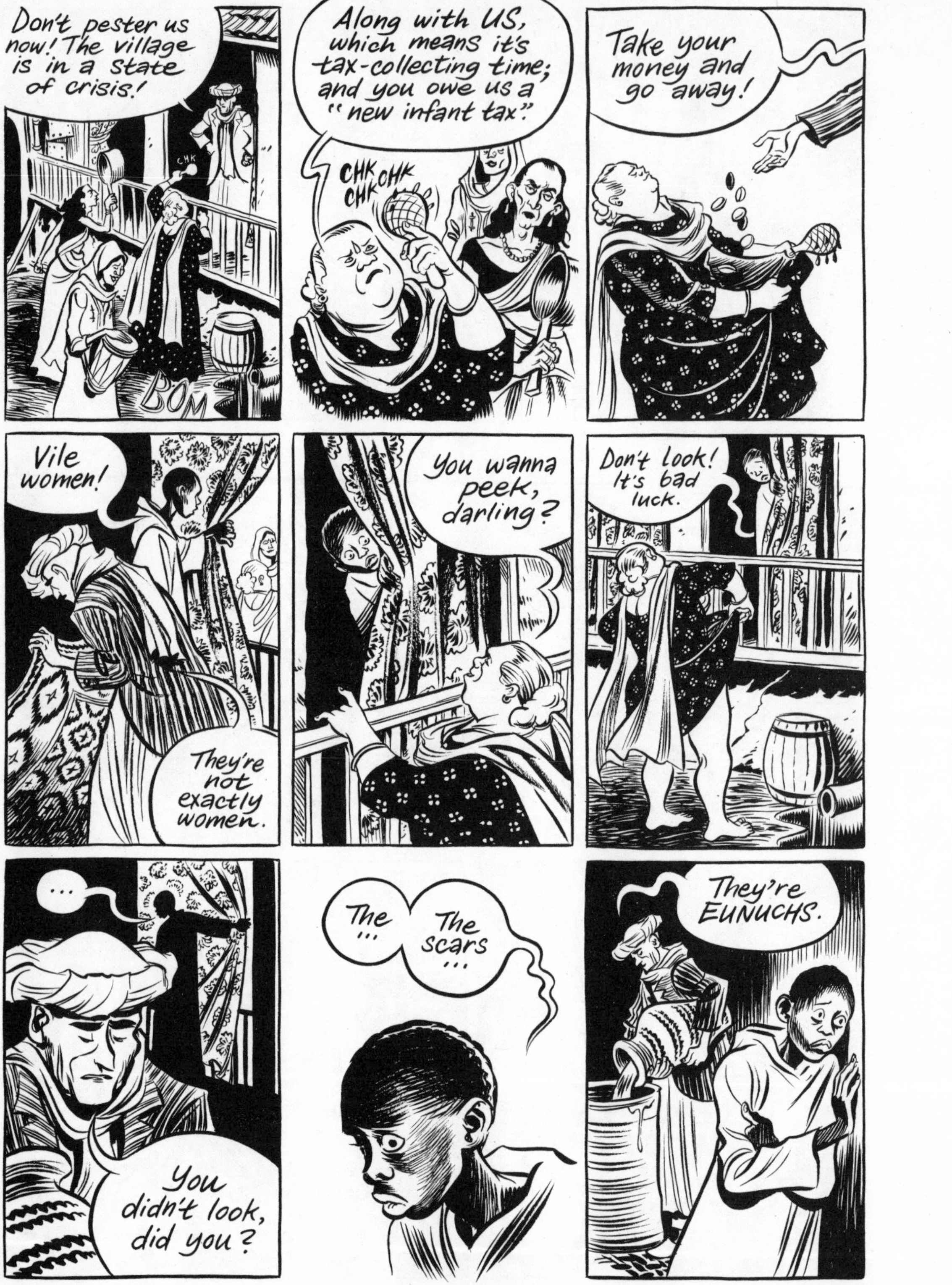
Don't pester us now! The village is in a state of crisis!
CHK
BOM
Along with US, which means it's tax-collecting time; and you owe us a "new infant tax."
CHK CHK CHK
Take your money and go away!
Vile women!
They're not exactly women.
You wanna peek, darling?
Don't look! It's bad luck.
...
You didn't look, did you?
The ...
The scars ...
They're EUNUCHS.

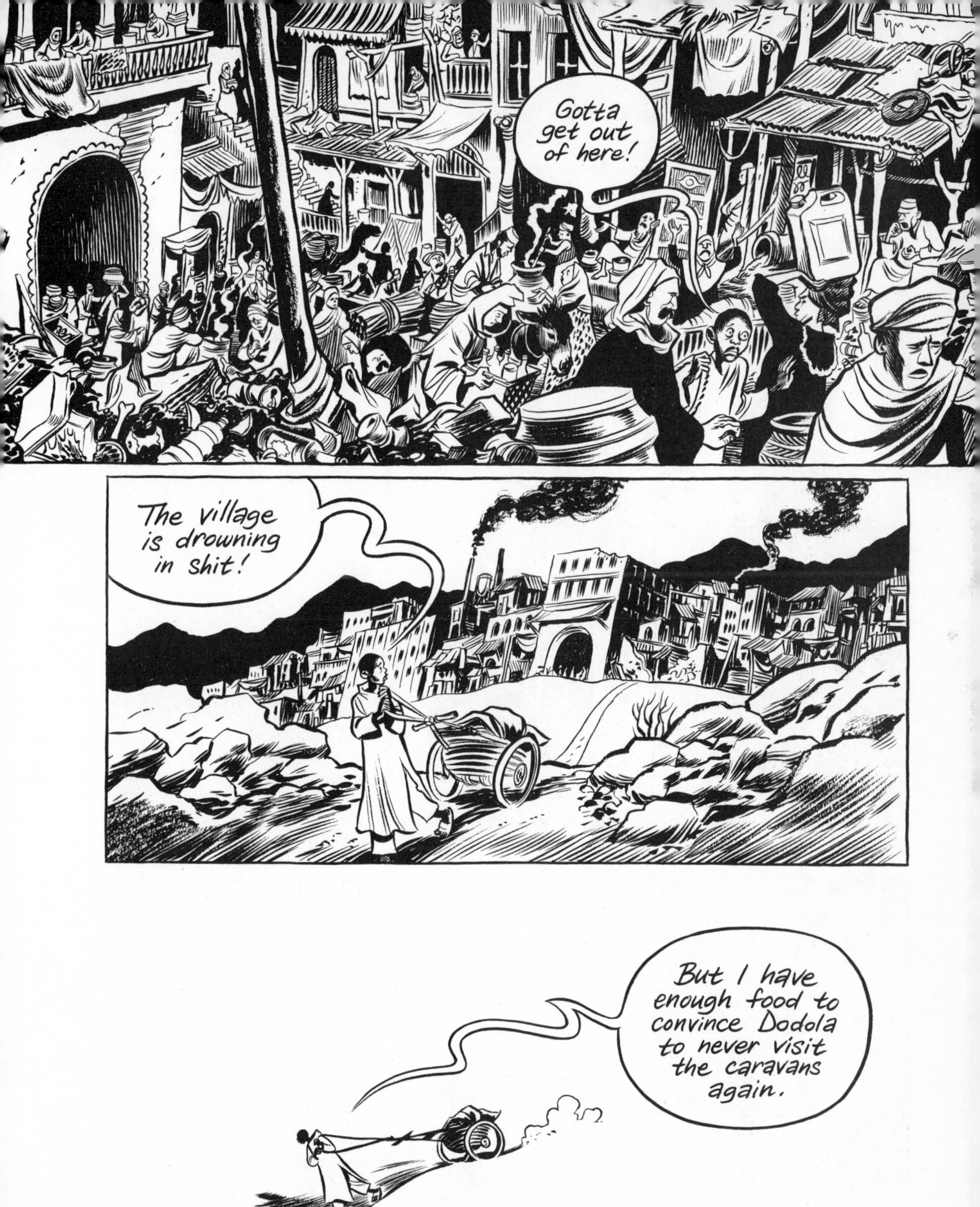
Gotta get out of here!
The village is drowning in shit!
But I have enough food to convince Dodola to never visit the caravans again.

د	ط	ب
ج	ه	ز
ح	ا	و

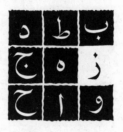

سراب

MiRAGE

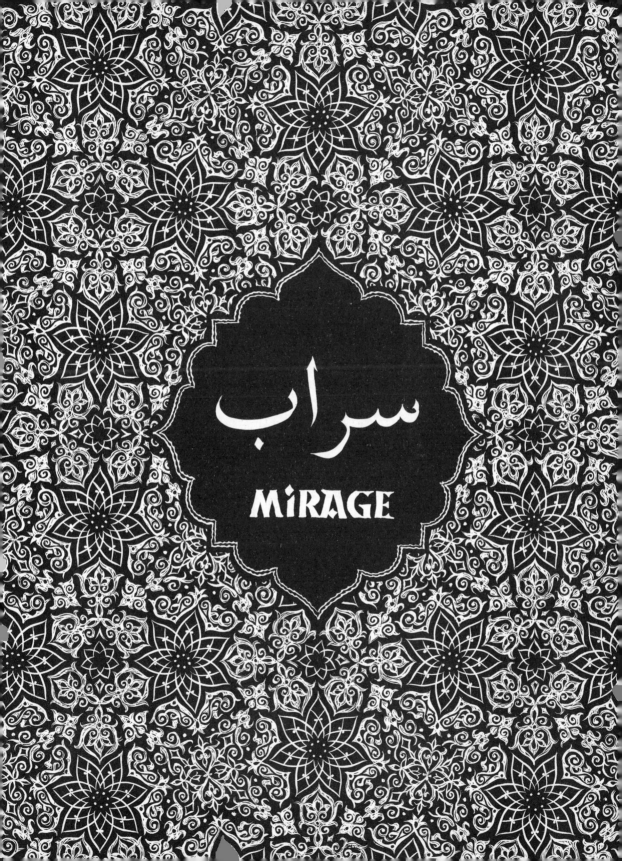

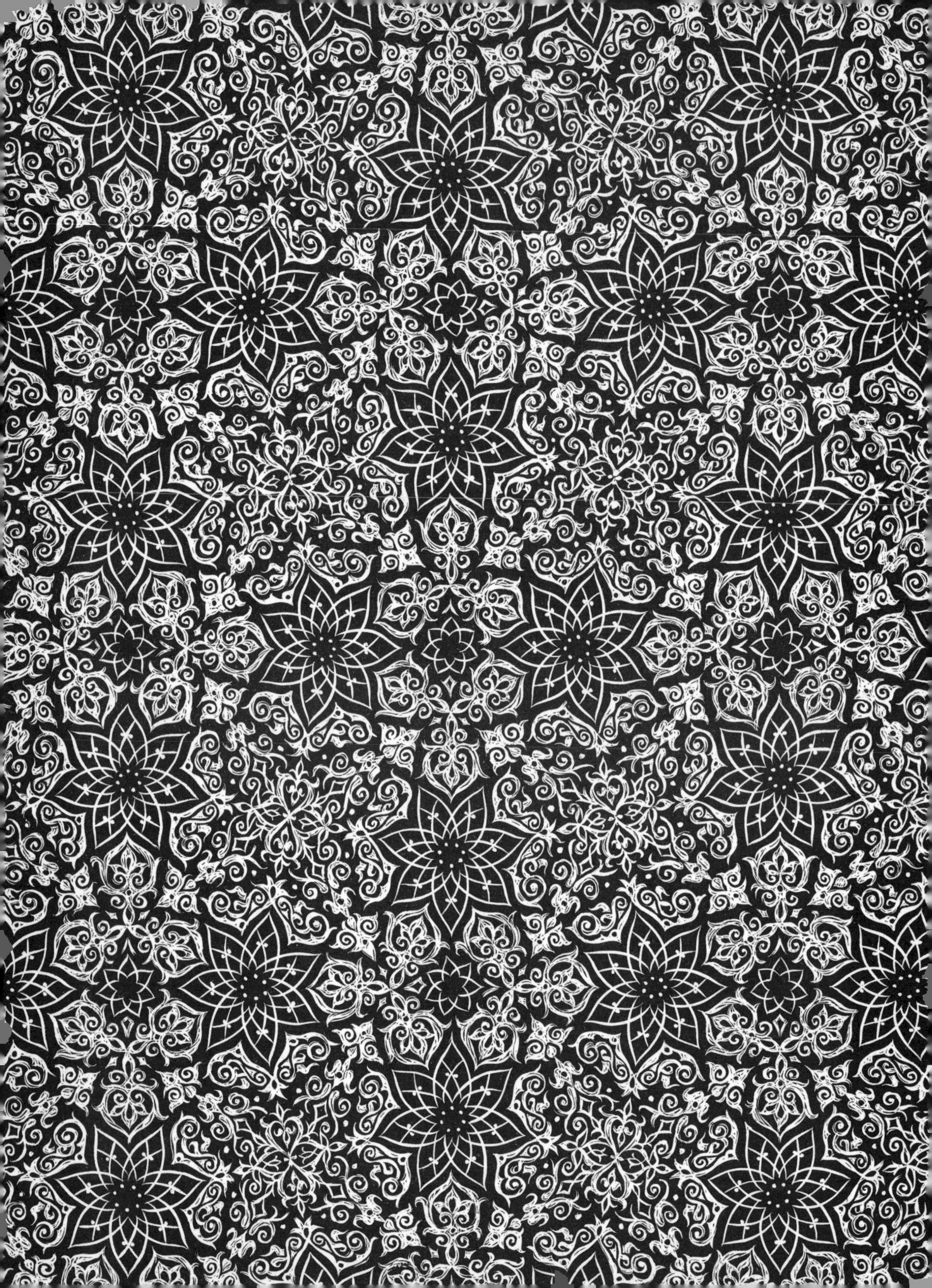

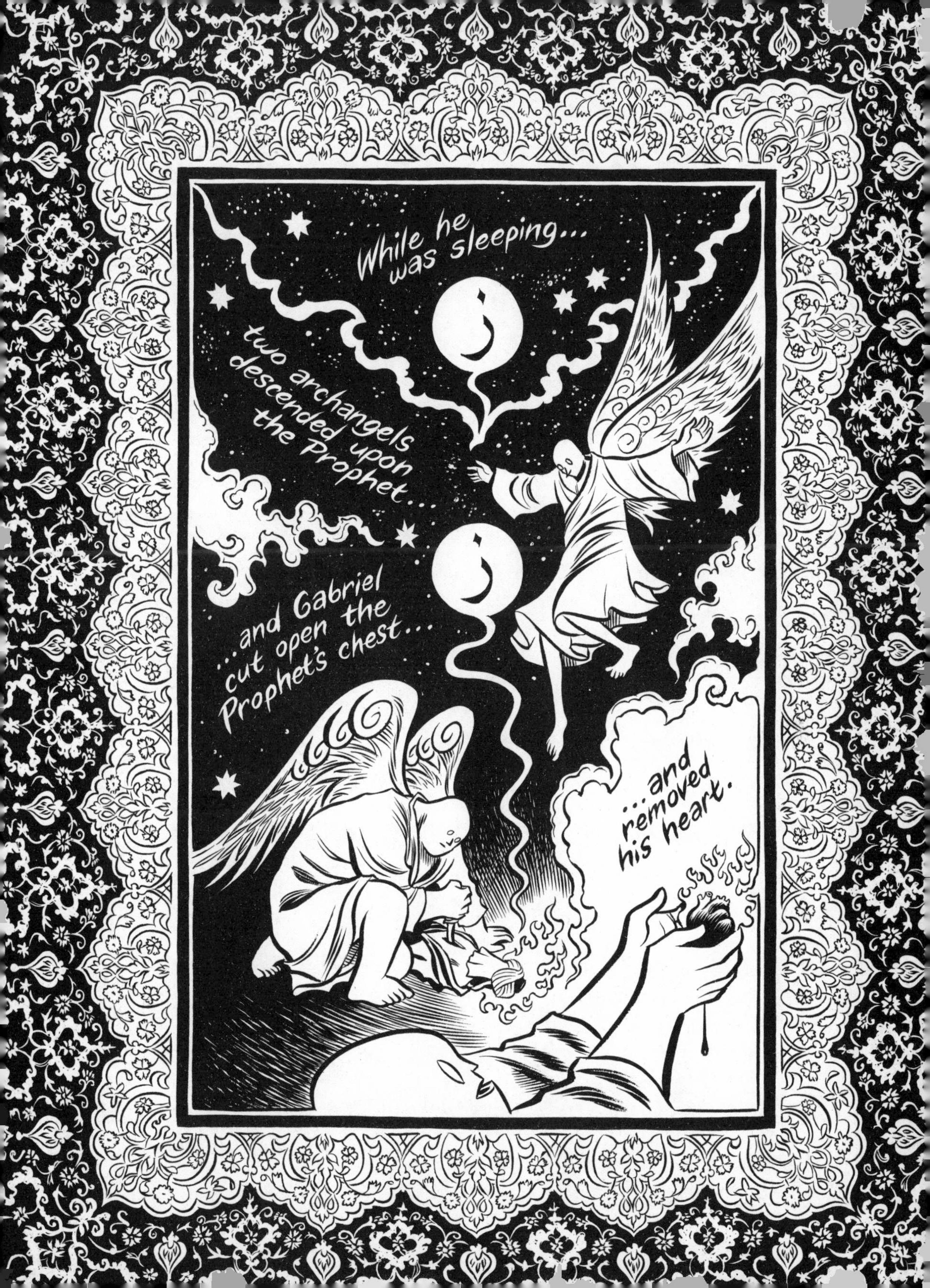

While he was sleeping...
two archangels descended upon the Prophet...
...and Gabriel cut open the Prophet's chest...
...and removed his heart.

The hadiths say that sleep is a likeness of death.

The soul wanders from the body.

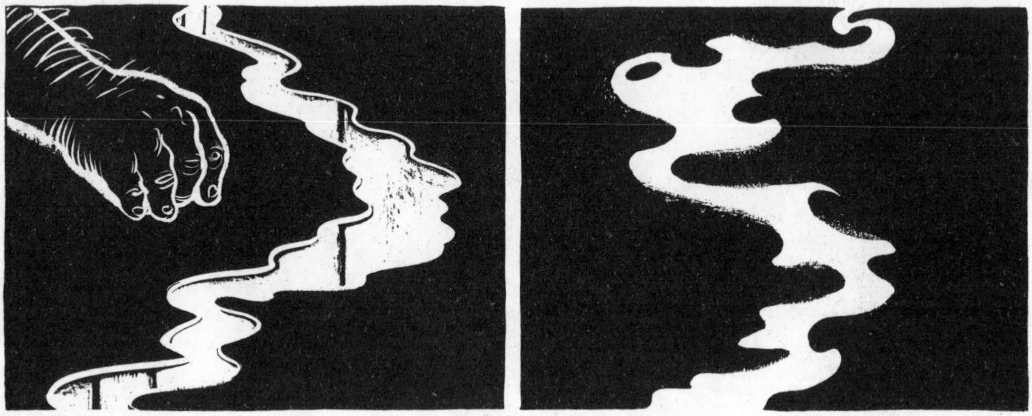

I tried to grasp it,

then wondered~

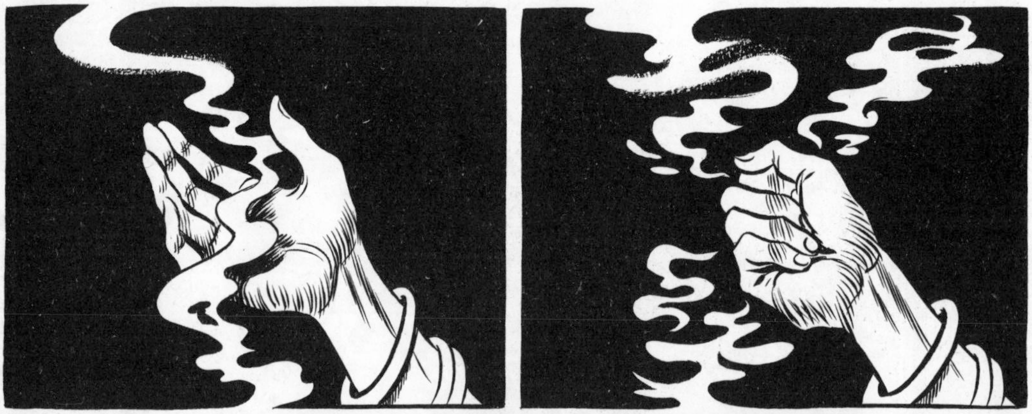

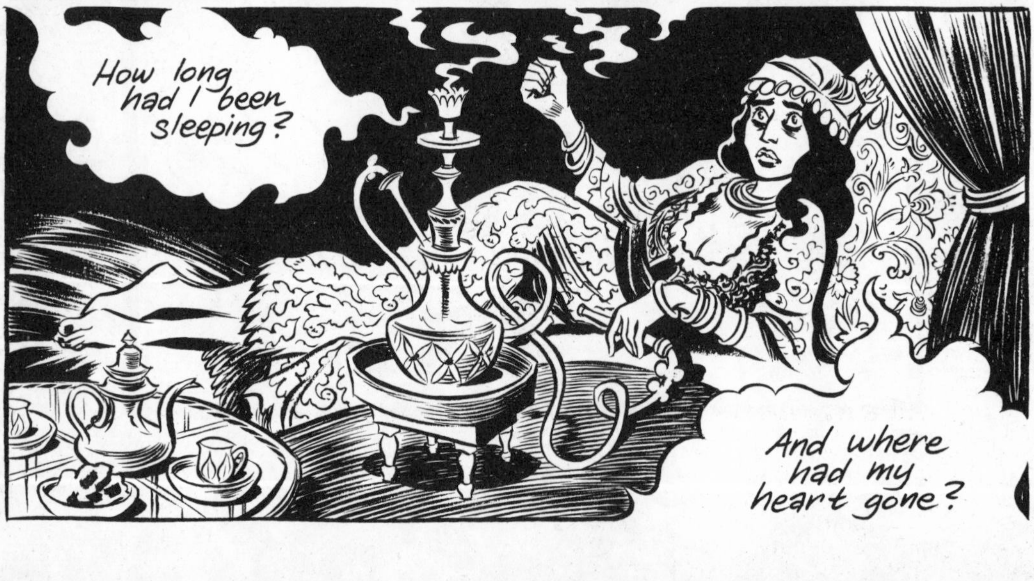
How long had I been sleeping?
And where had my heart gone?

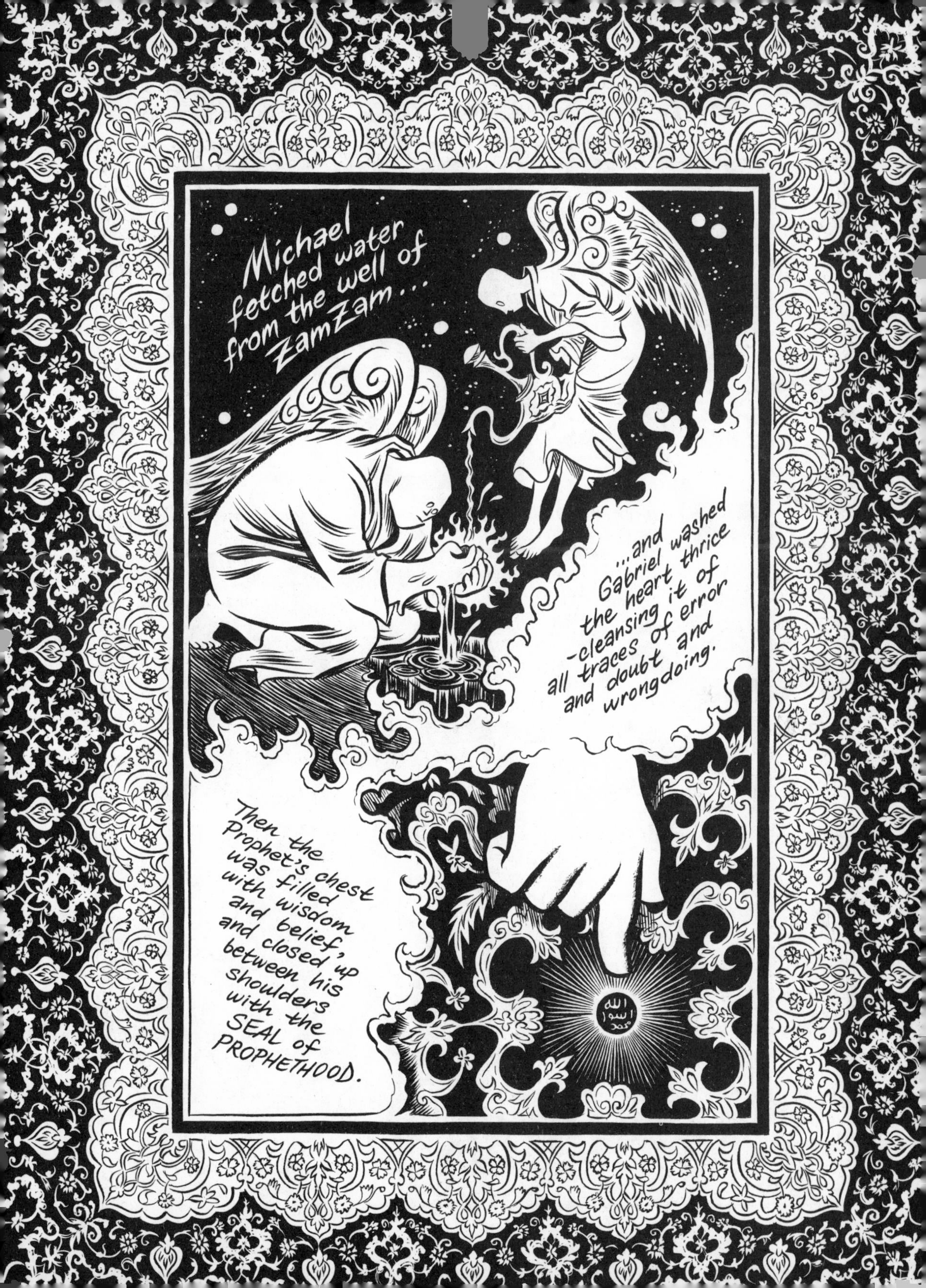
Michael fetched water from the well of ZamZam...
...and Gabriel washed the heart thrice -cleansing it of all traces of error and doubt and wrongdoing.
Then the Prophet's chest was filled with wisdom and belief, and closed up between his shoulders with the SEAL of PROPHETHOOD.

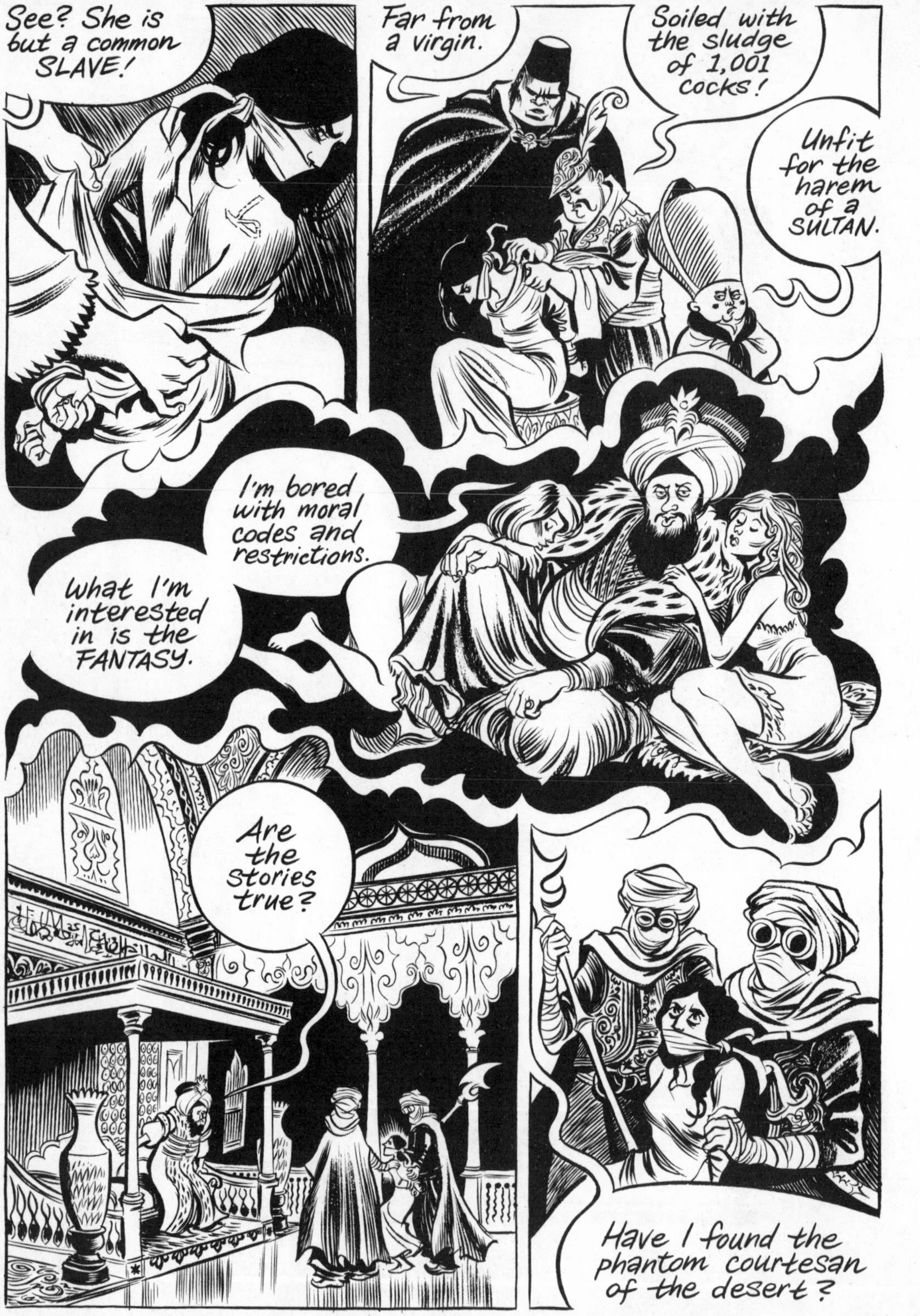

See? She is but a common SLAVE!
Far from a virgin.
Soiled with the sludge of 1,001 cocks!
Unfit for the harem of a SULTAN.
I'm bored with moral codes and restrictions.
What I'm interested in is the FANTASY.
Are the stories true?
Have I found the phantom courtesan of the desert?

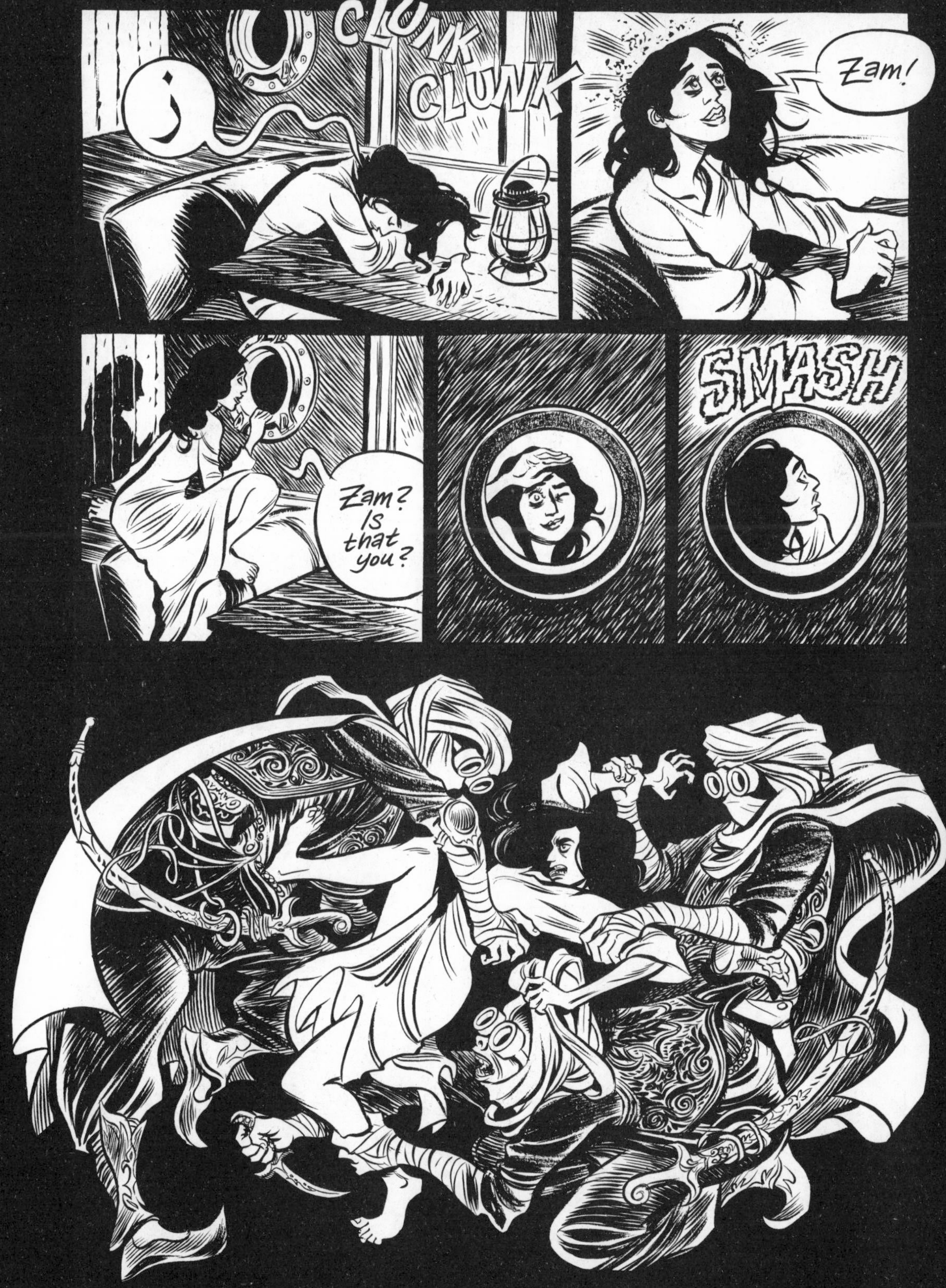
ز
CLUNK CLUNK
Zam!
Zam? Is that you?
SMASH

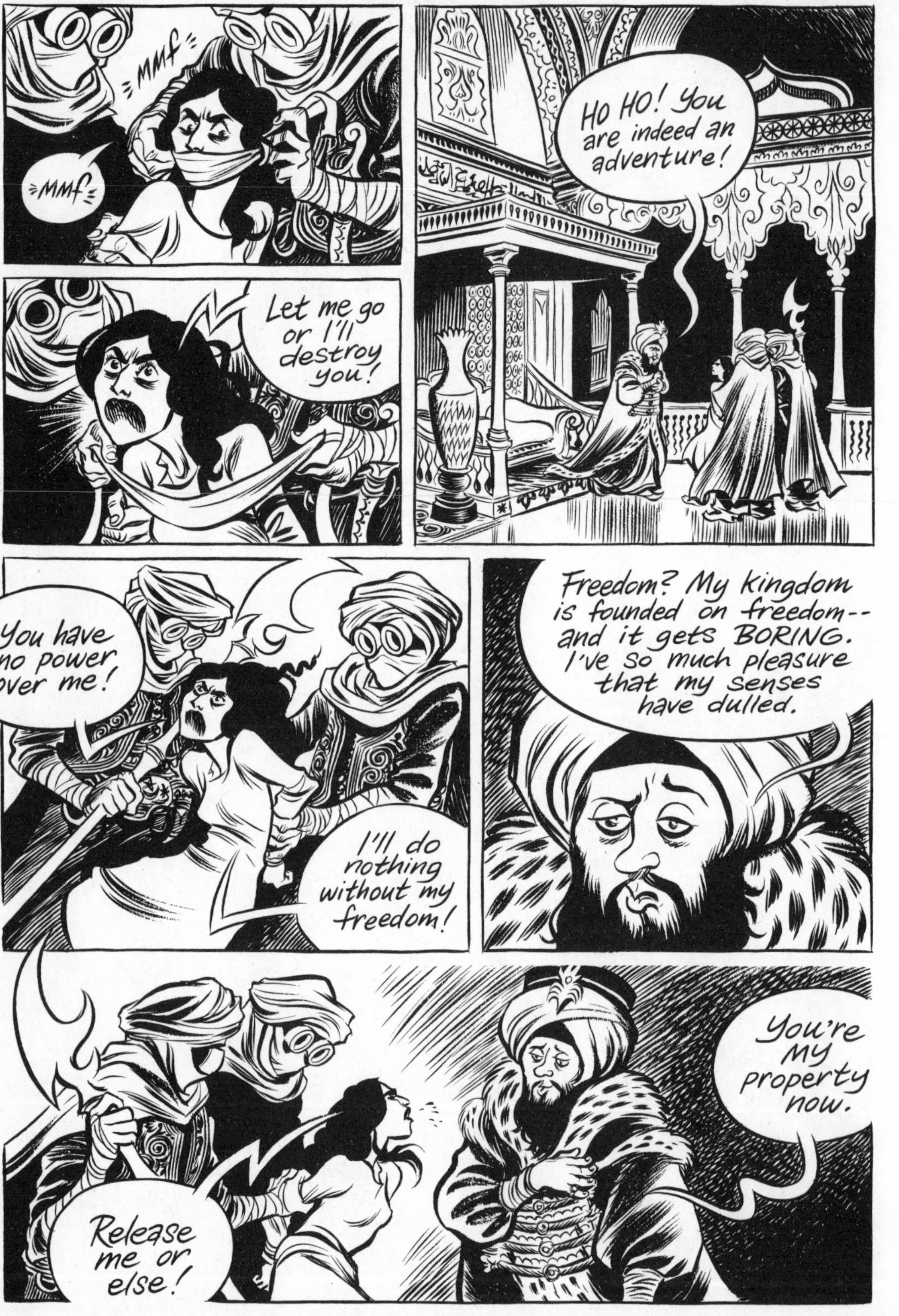

MMf
MMf
HO HO! You are indeed an adventure!
Let me go or I'll destroy you!
You have no power over me!
I'll do nothing without my freedom!
Freedom? My kingdom is founded on freedom-- and it gets BORING. I've so much pleasure that my senses have dulled.
Release me or else!
You're MY property now.

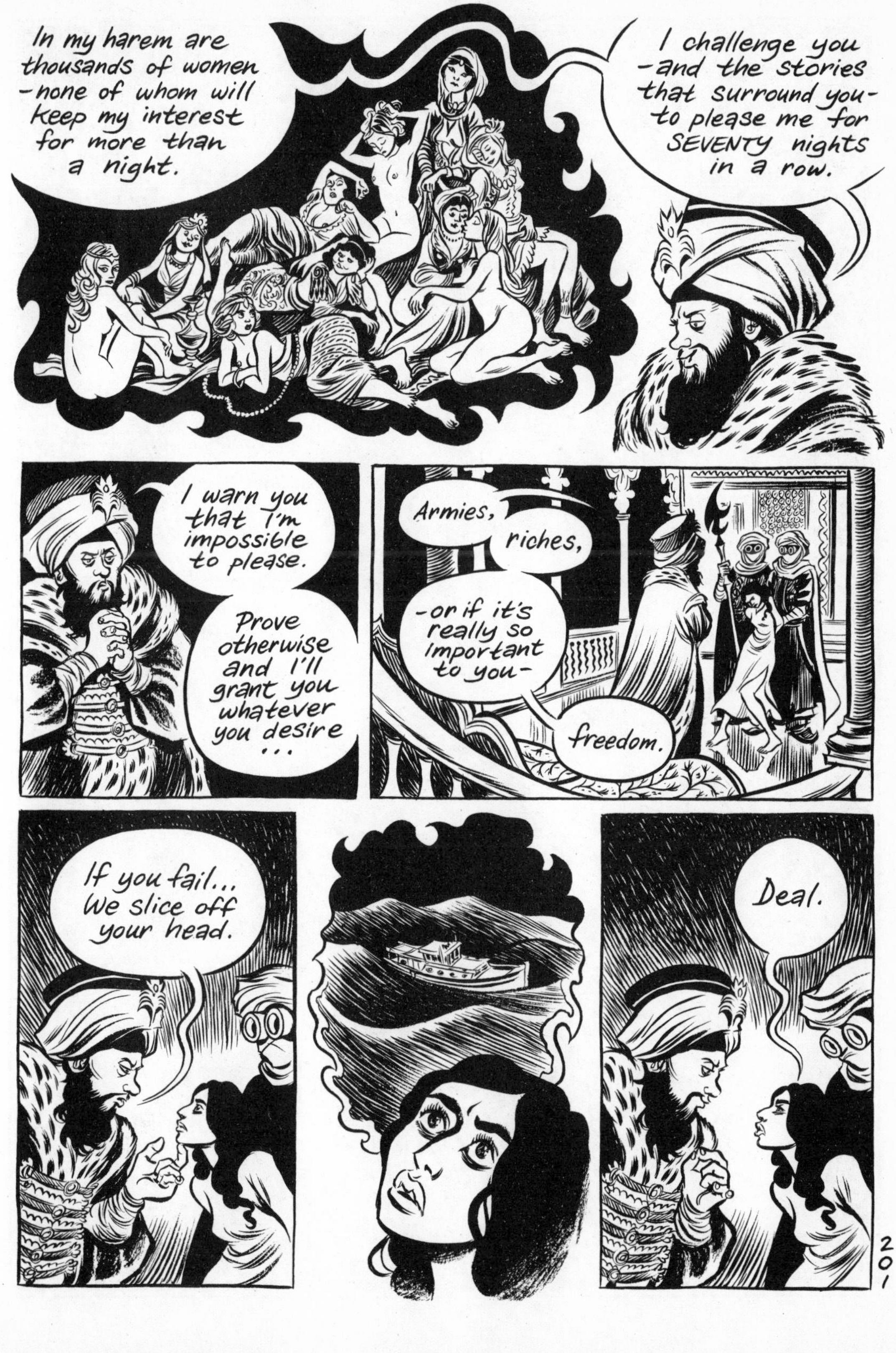

In my harem are thousands of women -none of whom will keep my interest for more than a night.
I challenge you -and the stories that surround you- to please me for SEVENTY nights in a row.
I warn you that I'm impossible to please.
Prove otherwise and I'll grant you whatever you desire ...
Armies,
riches,
-or if it's really so important to you-
freedom.
If you fail... We slice off your head.
Deal.

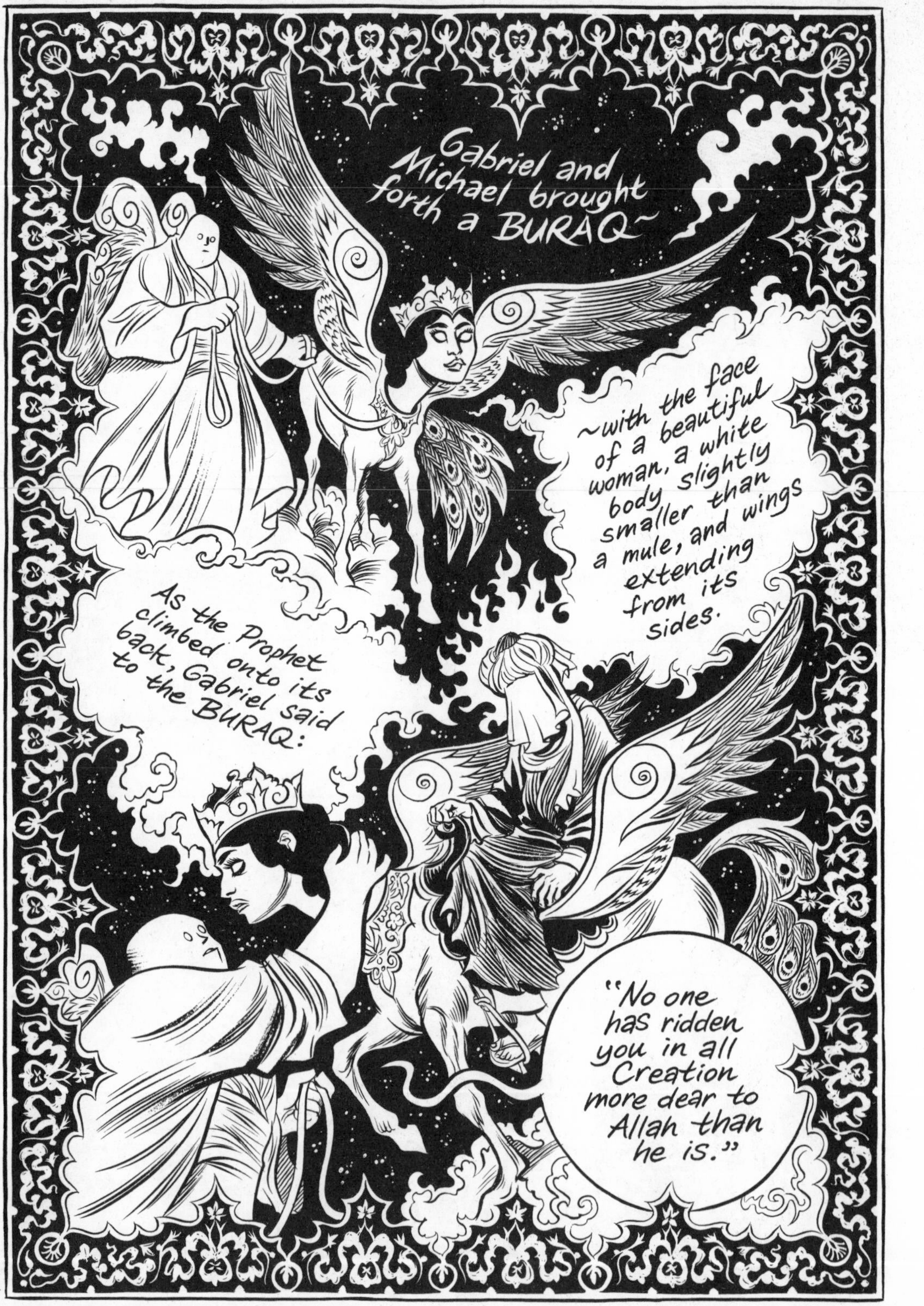
Gabriel and Michael brought forth a BURAQ~
~with the face of a beautiful woman, a white body slightly smaller than a mule, and wings extending from its sides.
As the Prophet climbed onto its back, Gabriel said to the BURAQ:
"No one has ridden you in all Creation more dear to Allah than he is."

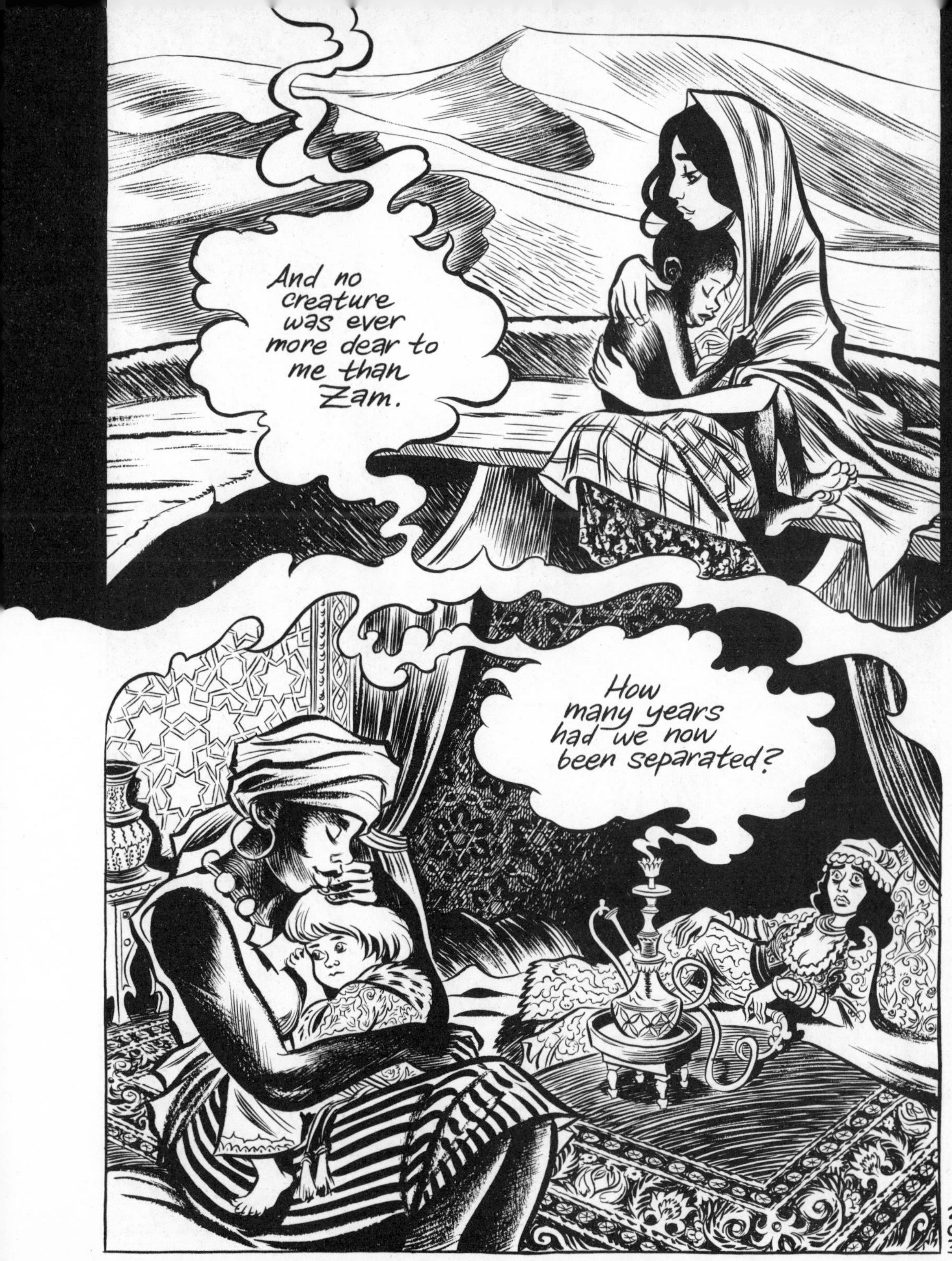
And no creature was ever more dear to me than Zam.
How many years had we now been separated?

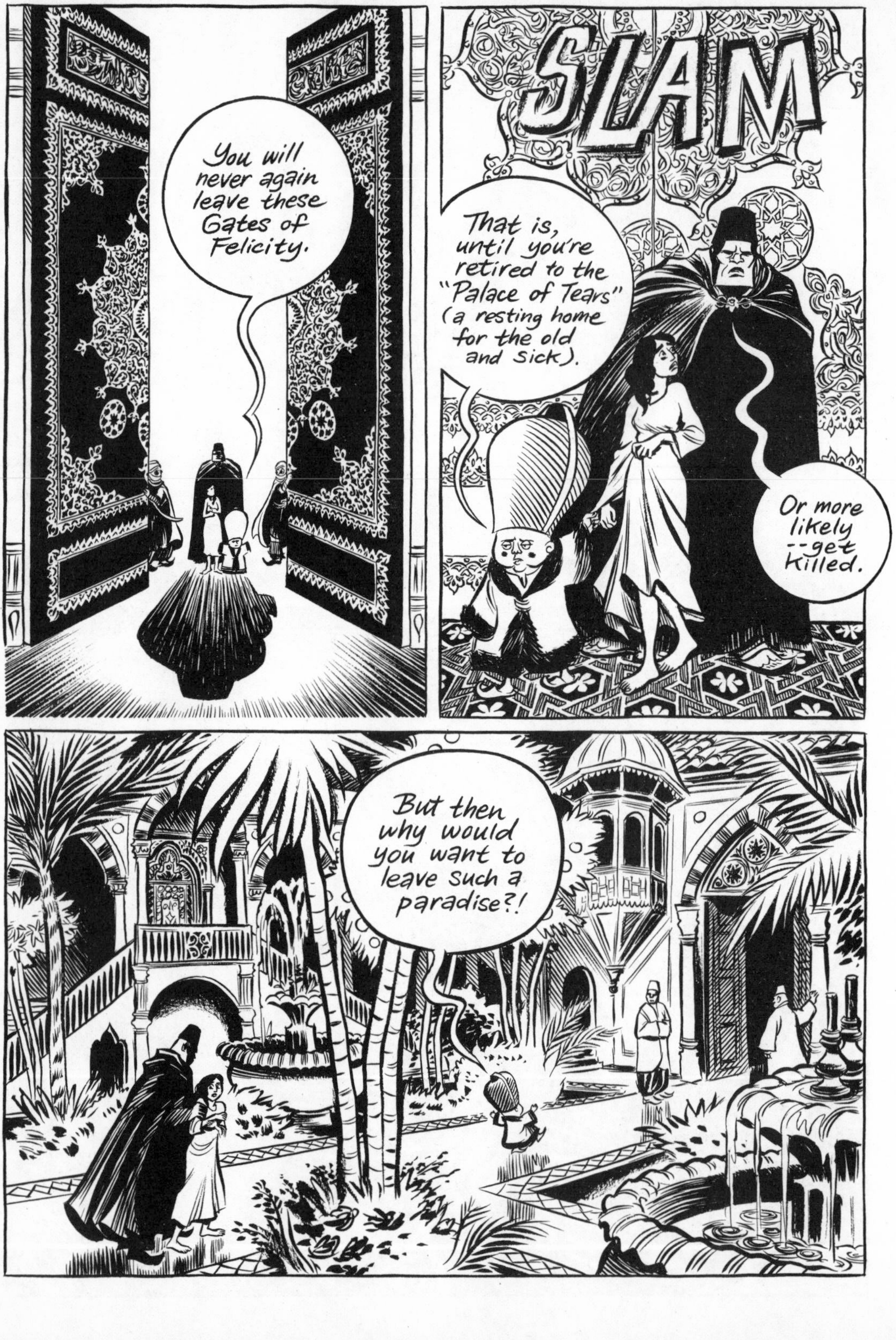
You will never again leave these Gates of Felicity.
SLAM
That is, until you're retired to the "Palace of Tears" (a resting home for the old and sick).
Or more likely --get killed.
But then why would you want to leave such a paradise?!

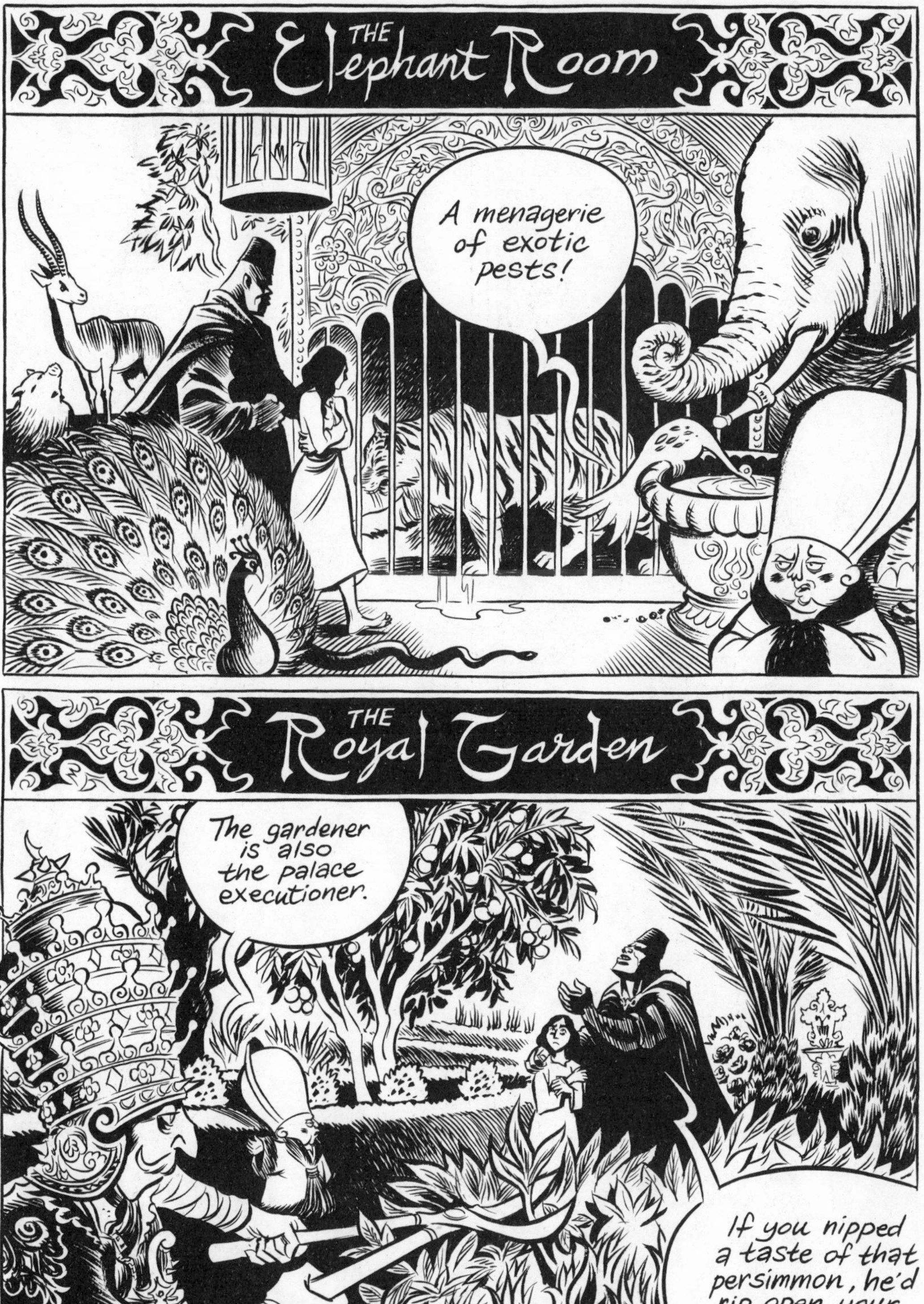
THE Elephant Room
A menagerie of exotic pests!
THE Royal Garden
The gardener is also the palace executioner.
If you nipped a taste of that persimmon, he'd rip open your stomach to retrieve it.

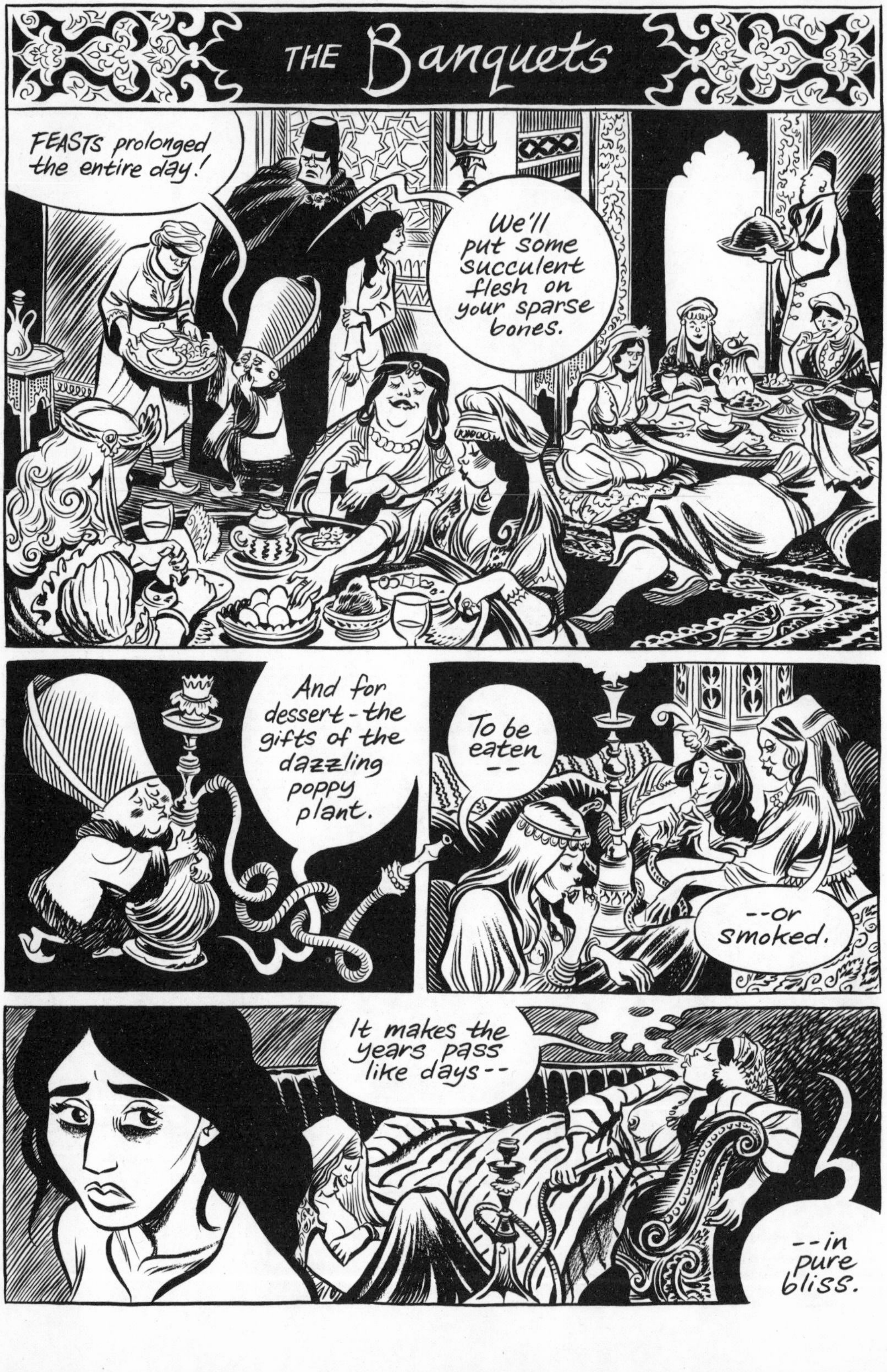
THE Banquets
FEASTS prolonged the entire day!
We'll put some succulent flesh on your sparse bones.
And for dessert - the gifts of the dazzling poppy plant.
To be eaten --
--or smoked.
It makes the years pass like days--
--in pure bliss.

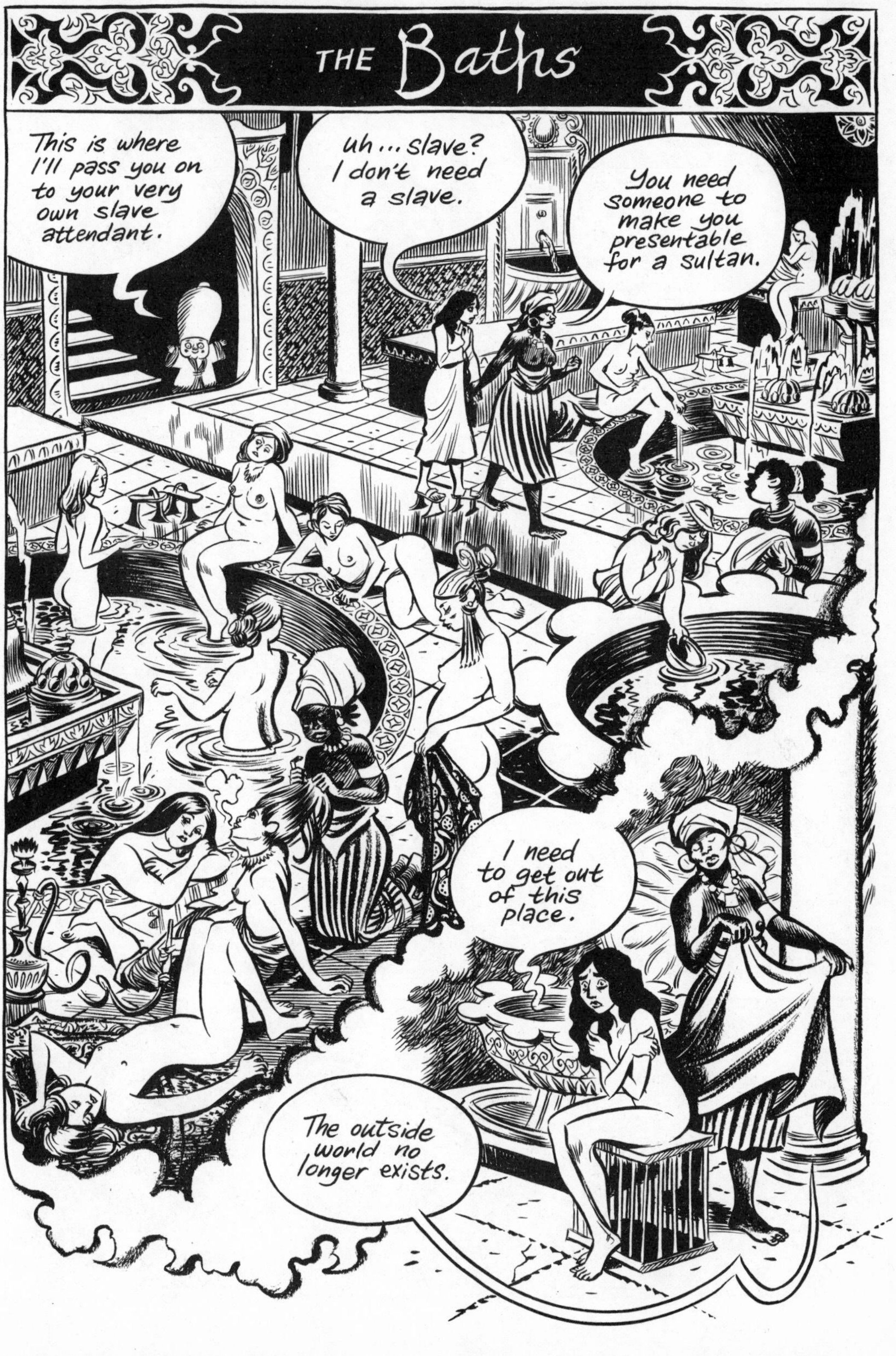
THE Baths
This is where I'll pass you on to your very own slave attendant.
uh ... slave? I don't need a slave.
You need someone to make you presentable for a sultan.
I need to get out of this place.
The outside world no longer exists.

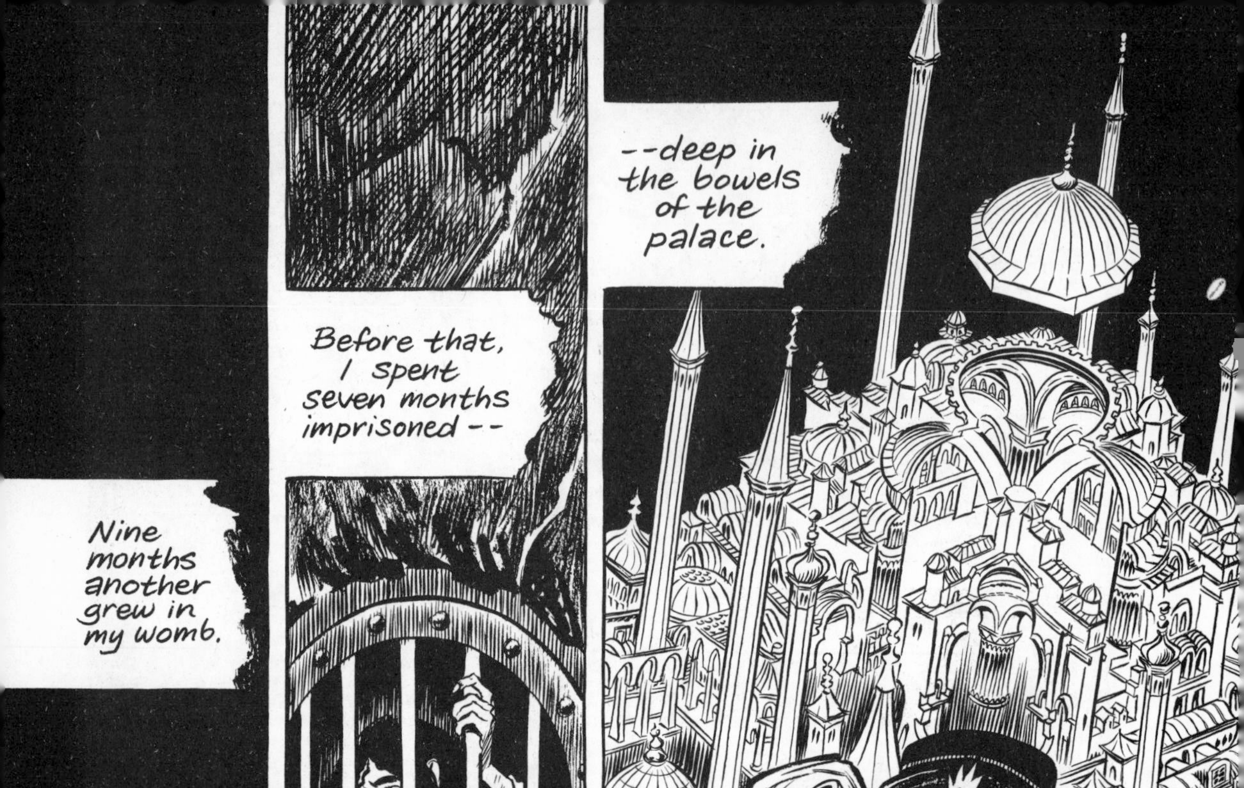
--deep in the bowels of the palace.
Before that, I spent seven months imprisoned --
Nine months another grew in my womb.

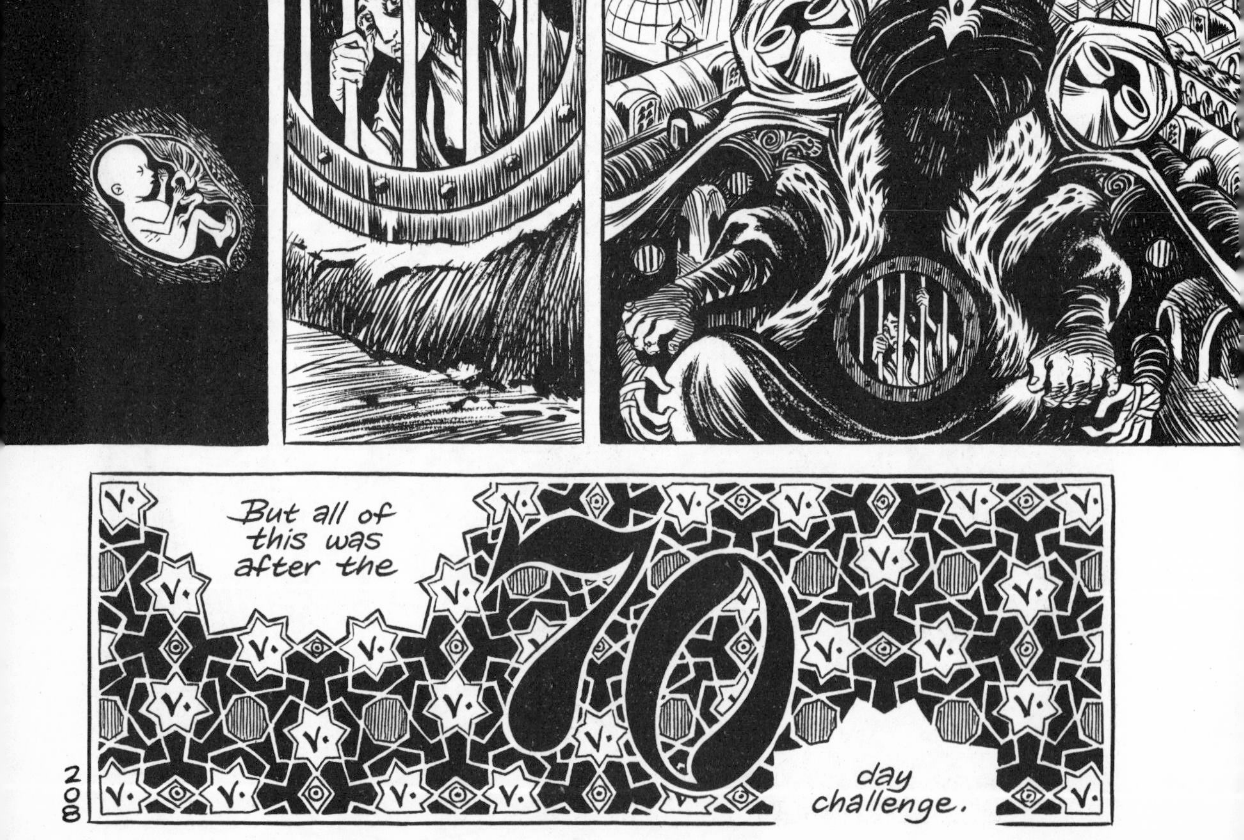
But all of this was after the
70
day challenge.

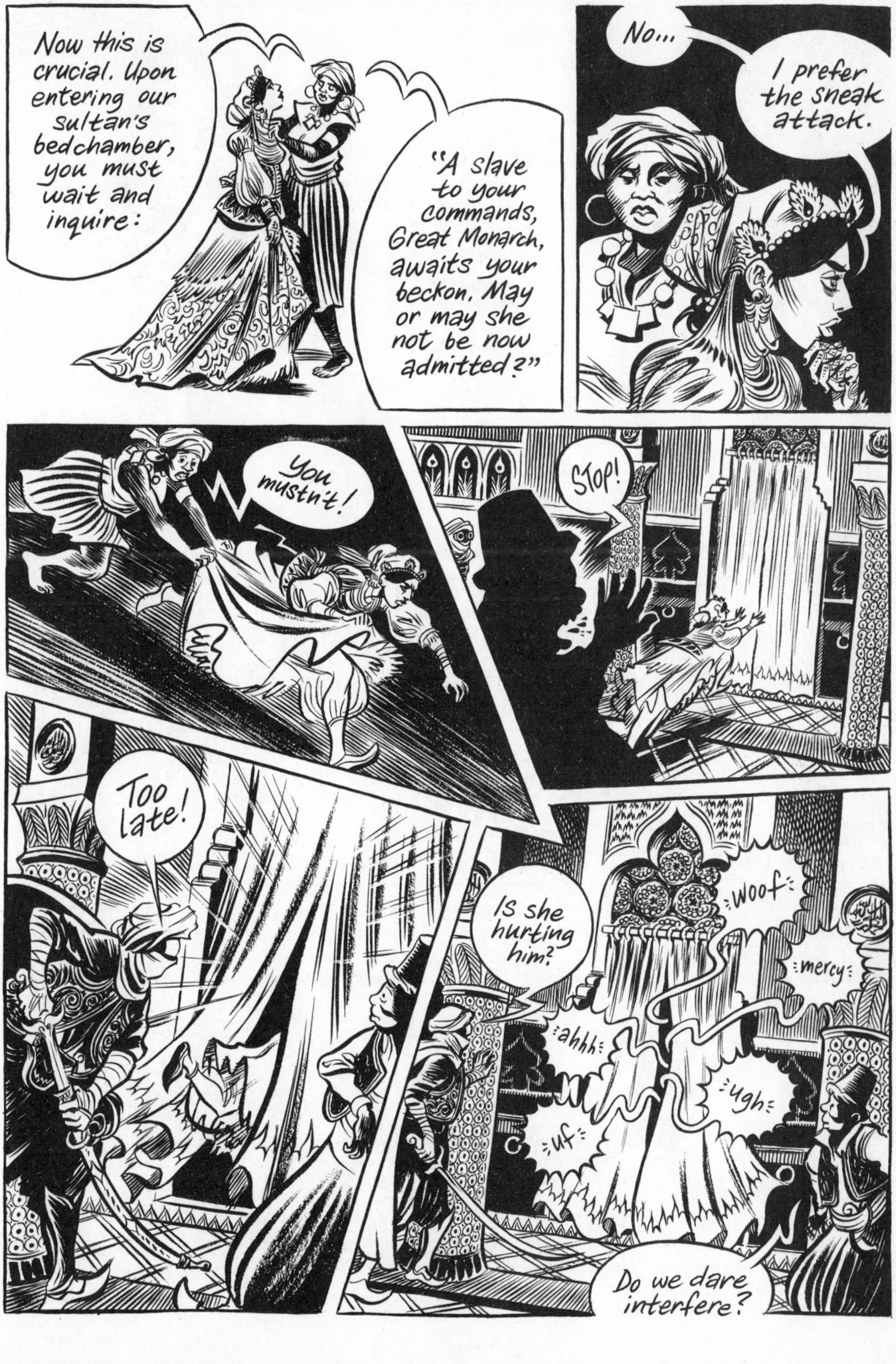
Now this is crucial. Upon entering our sultan's bedchamber, you must wait and inquire:
"A slave to your commands, Great Monarch, awaits your beckon. May or may she not be now admitted?"
No...
I prefer the sneak attack.
You mustn't!
STOP!
Too late!
Is she hurting him?
woof
mercy
ahhh
ugh
uf
Do we dare interfere?

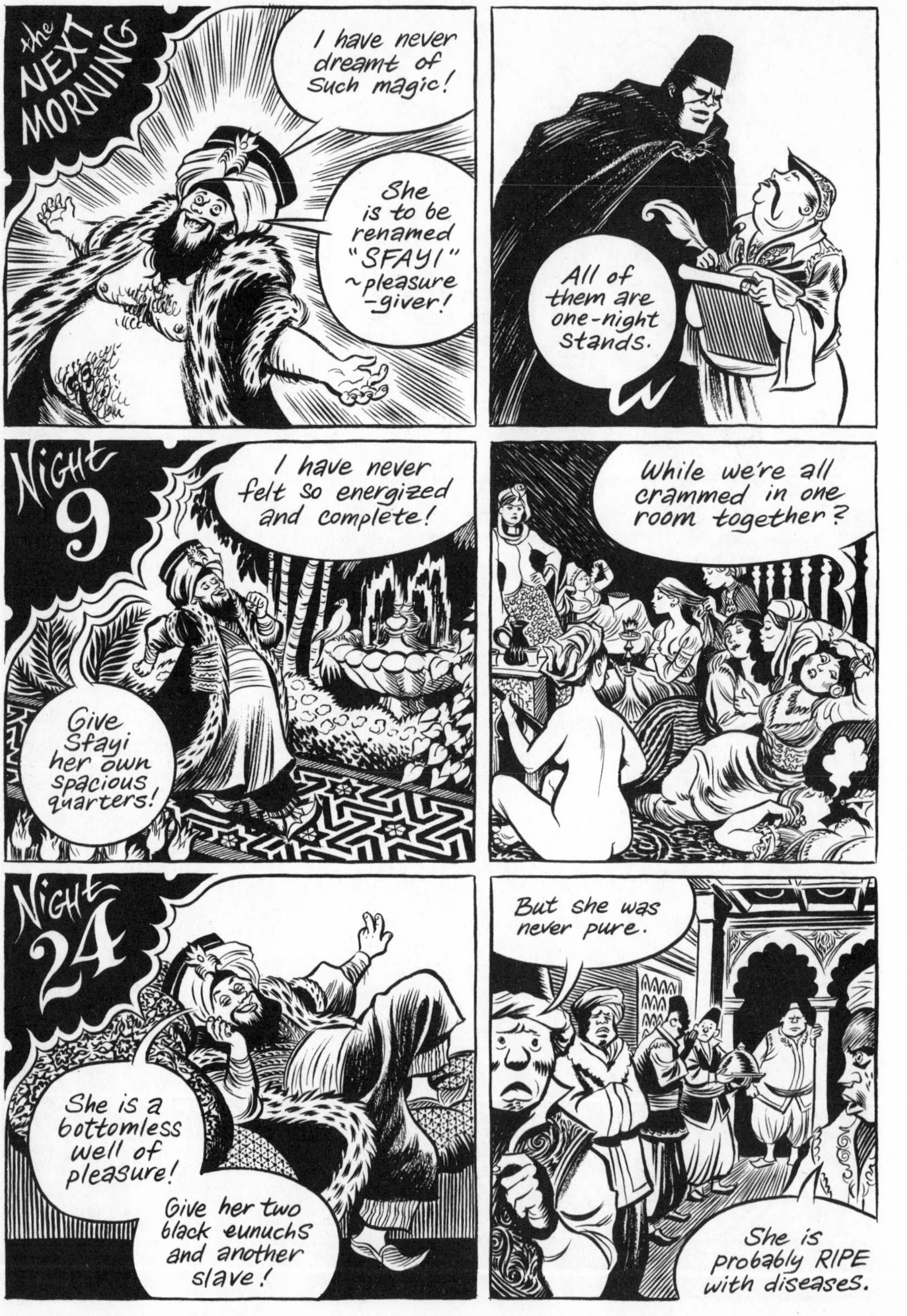
the NEXT MORNING
I have never dreamt of such magic!
She is to be renamed "SFAYI" ~pleasure-giver!
All of them are one-night stands.
NIGHT 9
I have never felt so energized and complete!
Give Sfayi her own spacious quarters!
While we're all crammed in one room together?
NIGHT 24
She is a bottomless well of pleasure!
Give her two black eunuchs and another slave!
But she was never pure.
She is probably RIPE with diseases.

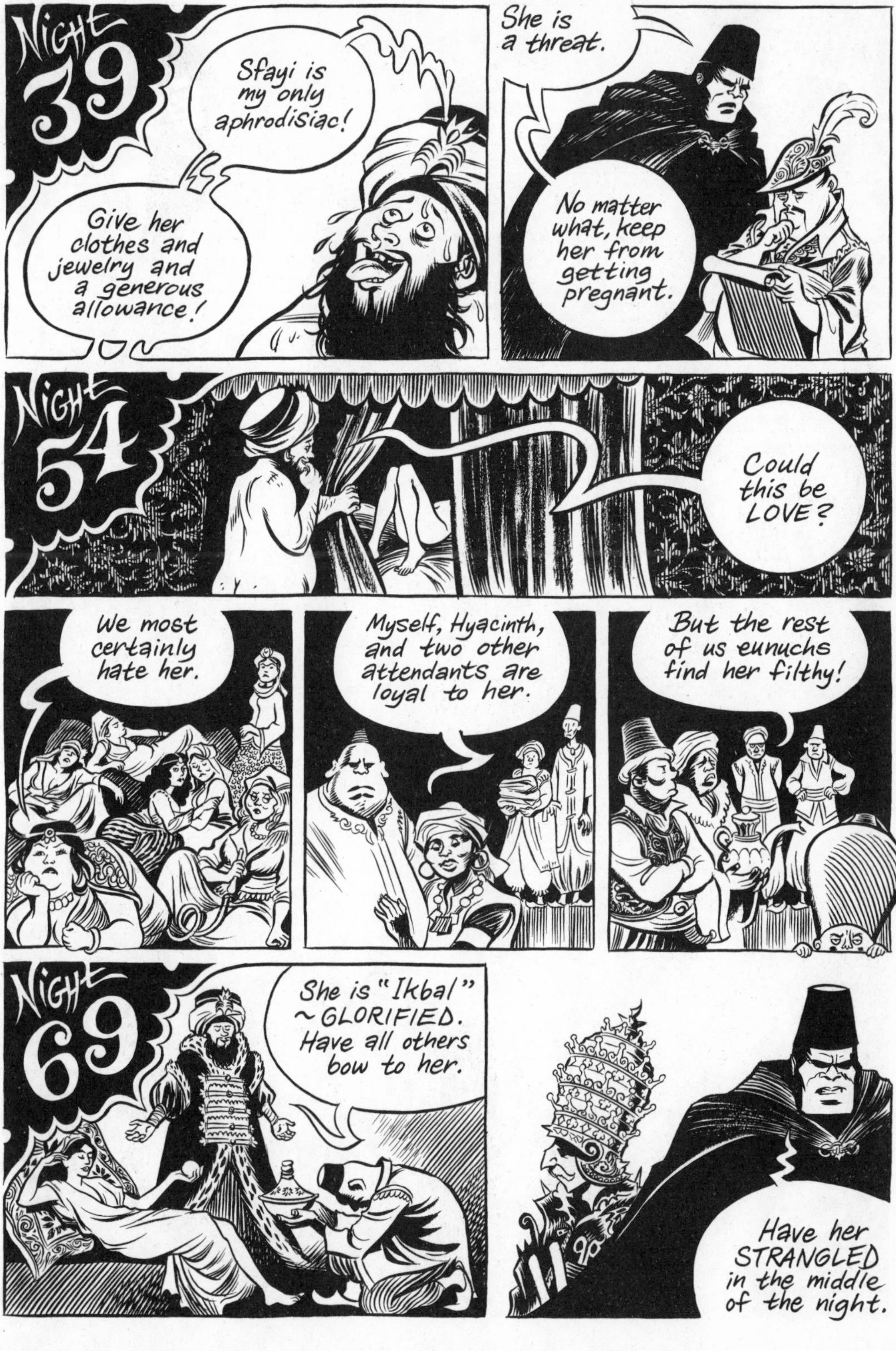
NIGHT 39
Sfayi is my only aphrodisiac!
Give her clothes and jewelry and a generous allowance!
She is a threat.
No matter what, keep her from getting pregnant.
NIGHT 54
Could this be LOVE?
We most certainly hate her.
Myself, Hyacinth, and two other attendants are loyal to her.
But the rest of us eunuchs find her filthy!
NIGHT 69
She is "Ikbal" ~GLORIFIED. Have all others bow to her.
Have her STRANGLED in the middle of the night.

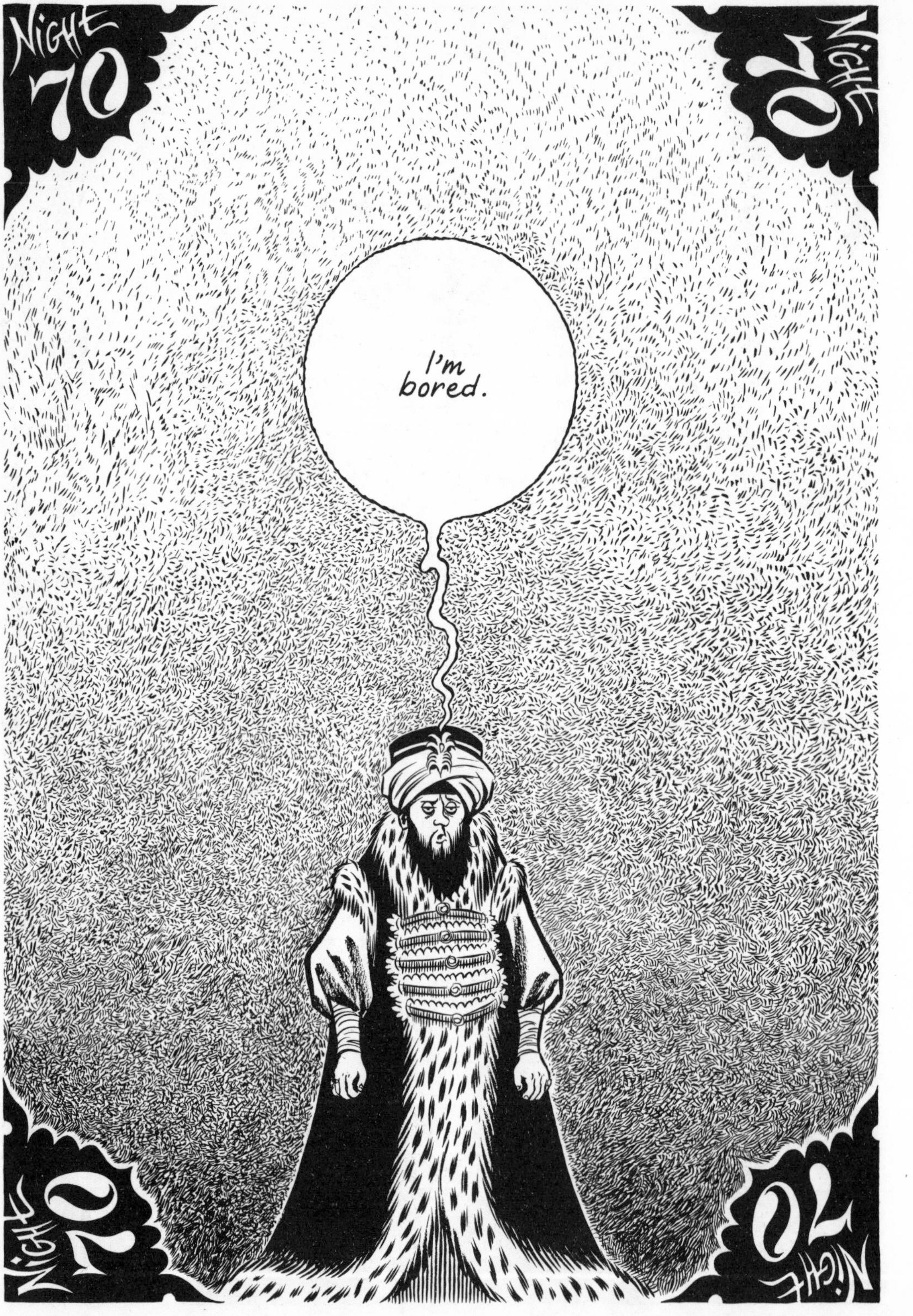
NIGHT 70
NIGHT 70
I'm bored.
NIGHT 70
NIGHT 70

She is to be executed.
Not so fast.
She lost my bargain, but I'd still like to keep her around for the occasional fling.
You promised me freedom!
And you let me down.
You should be grateful I spared your head from the chopping block.
Settle down ...
RRK!

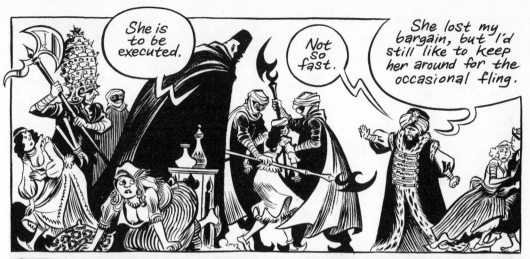

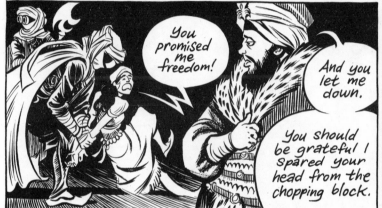

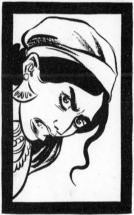

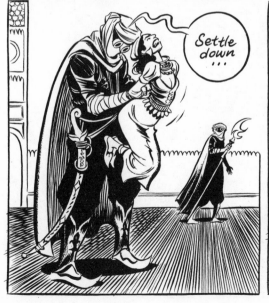

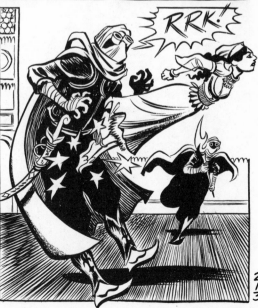

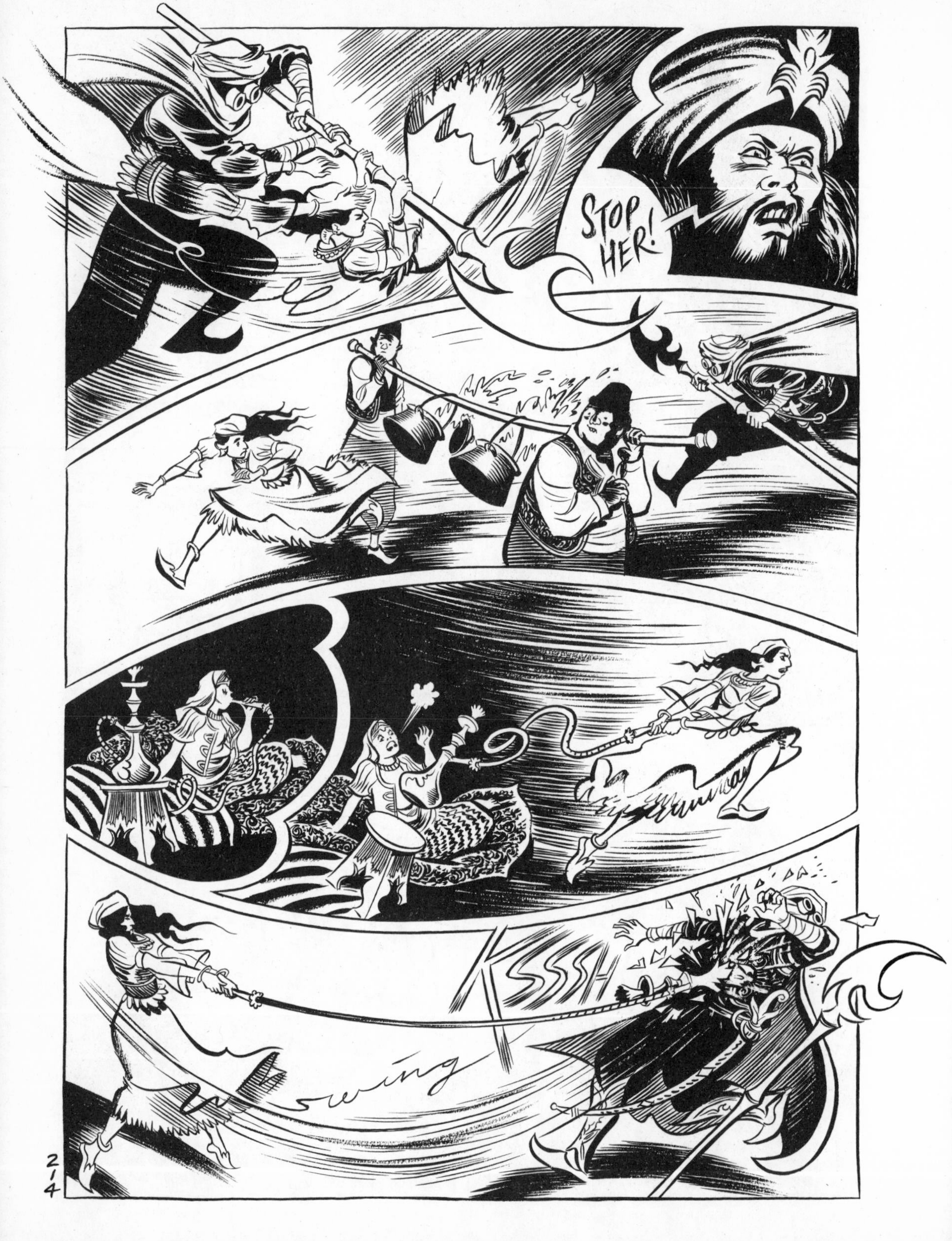
STOP HER!
KSSSH
swing

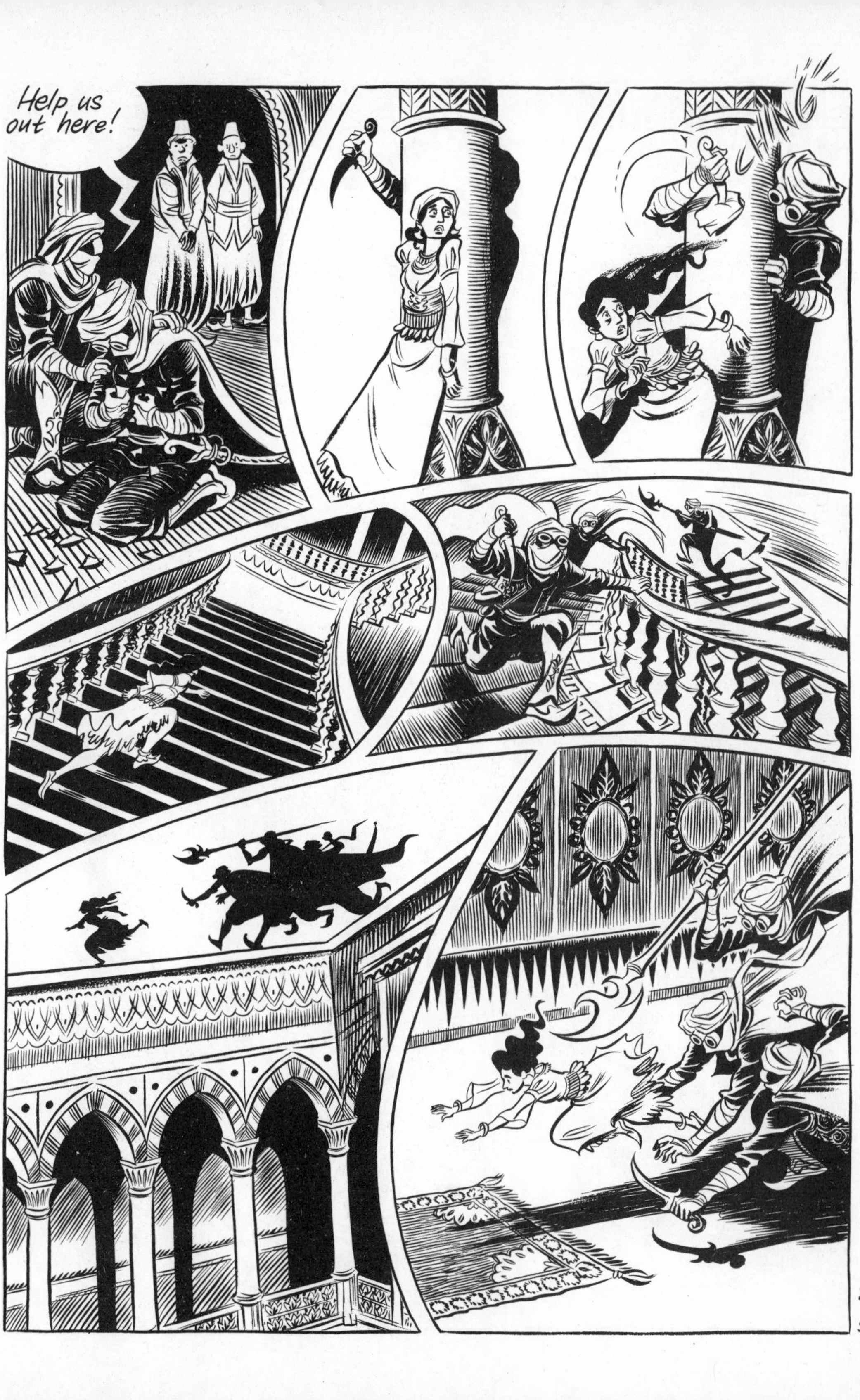
Help us out here!
CHING

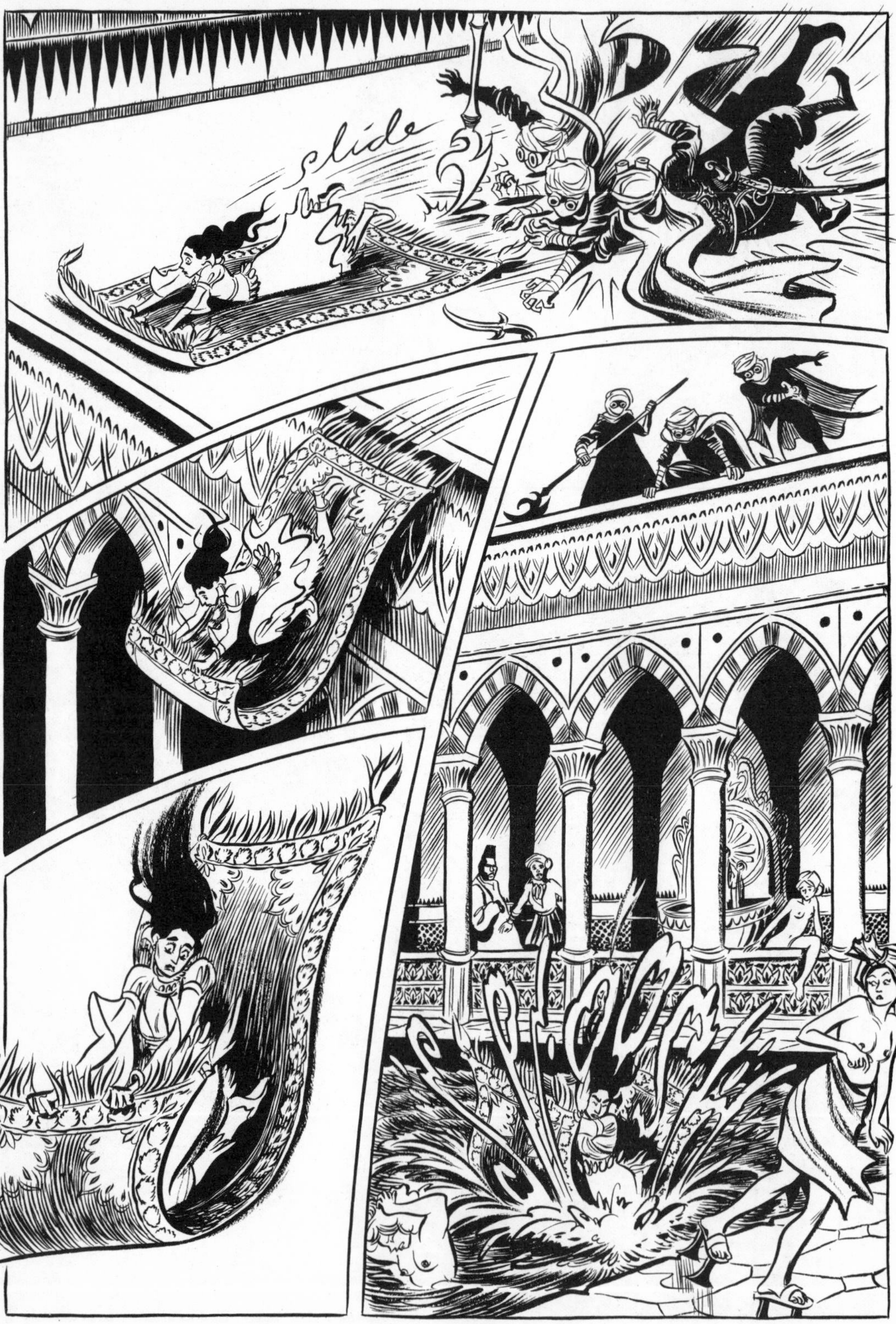
slide
sploosh

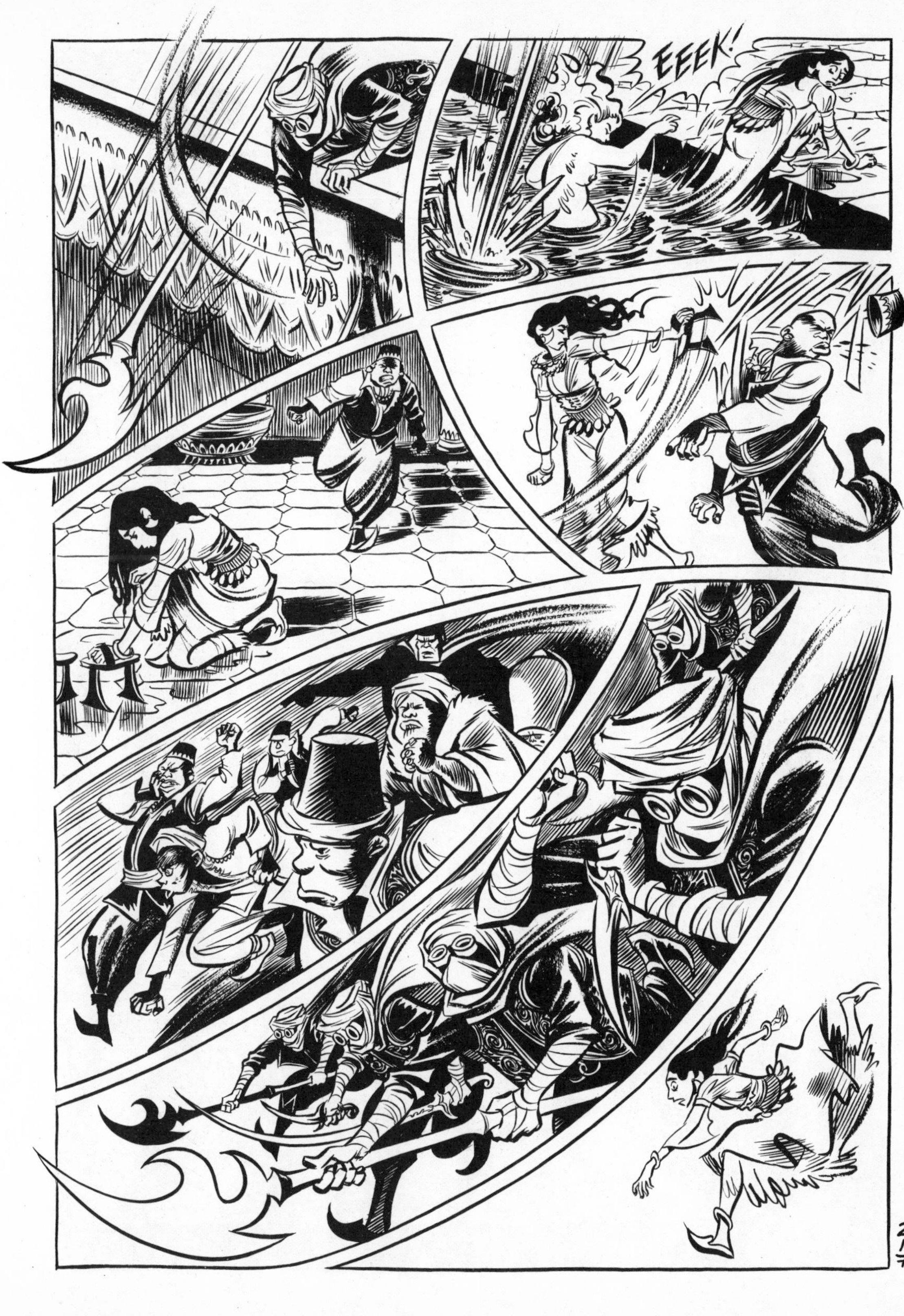
EEEK!

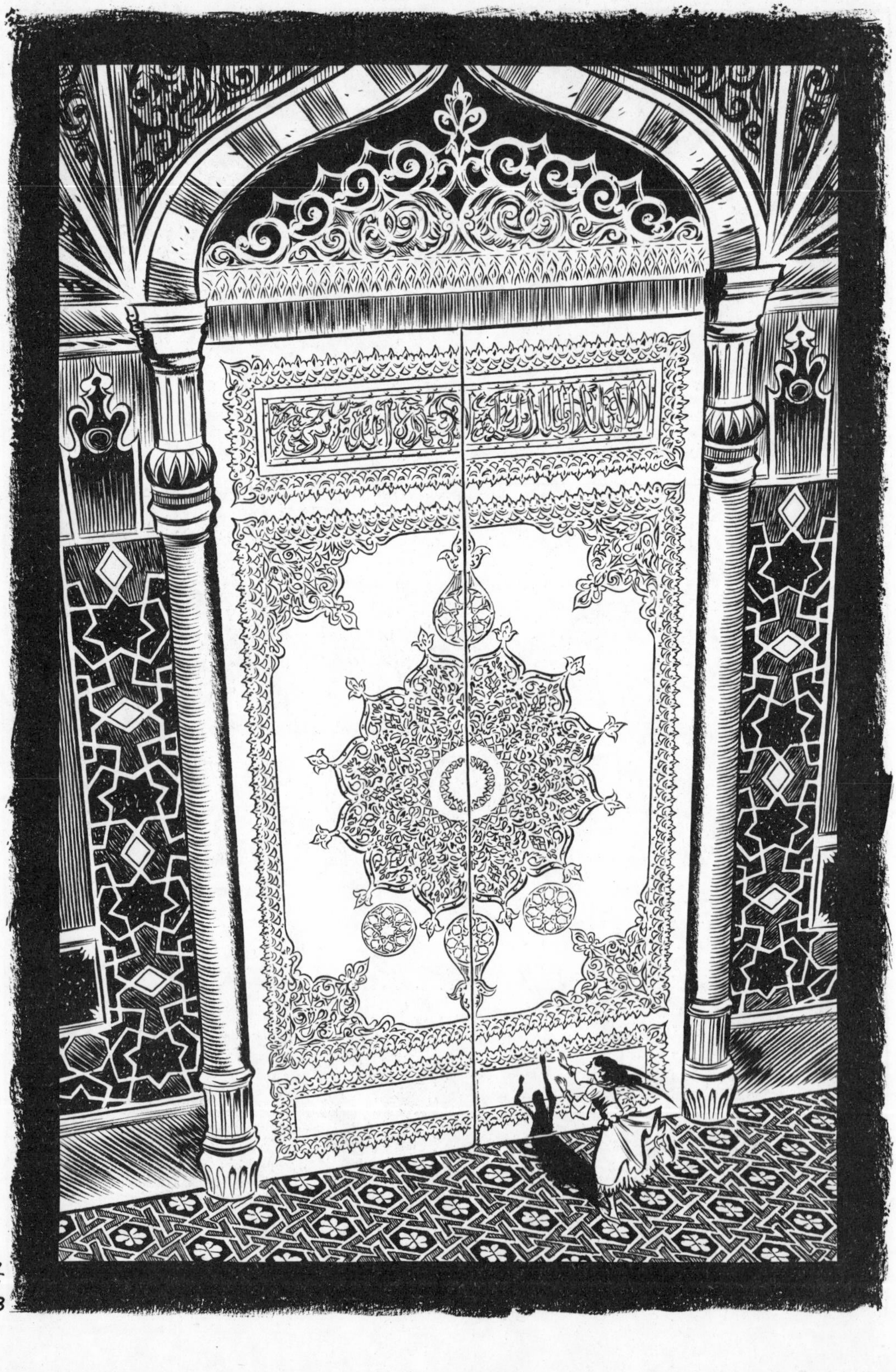

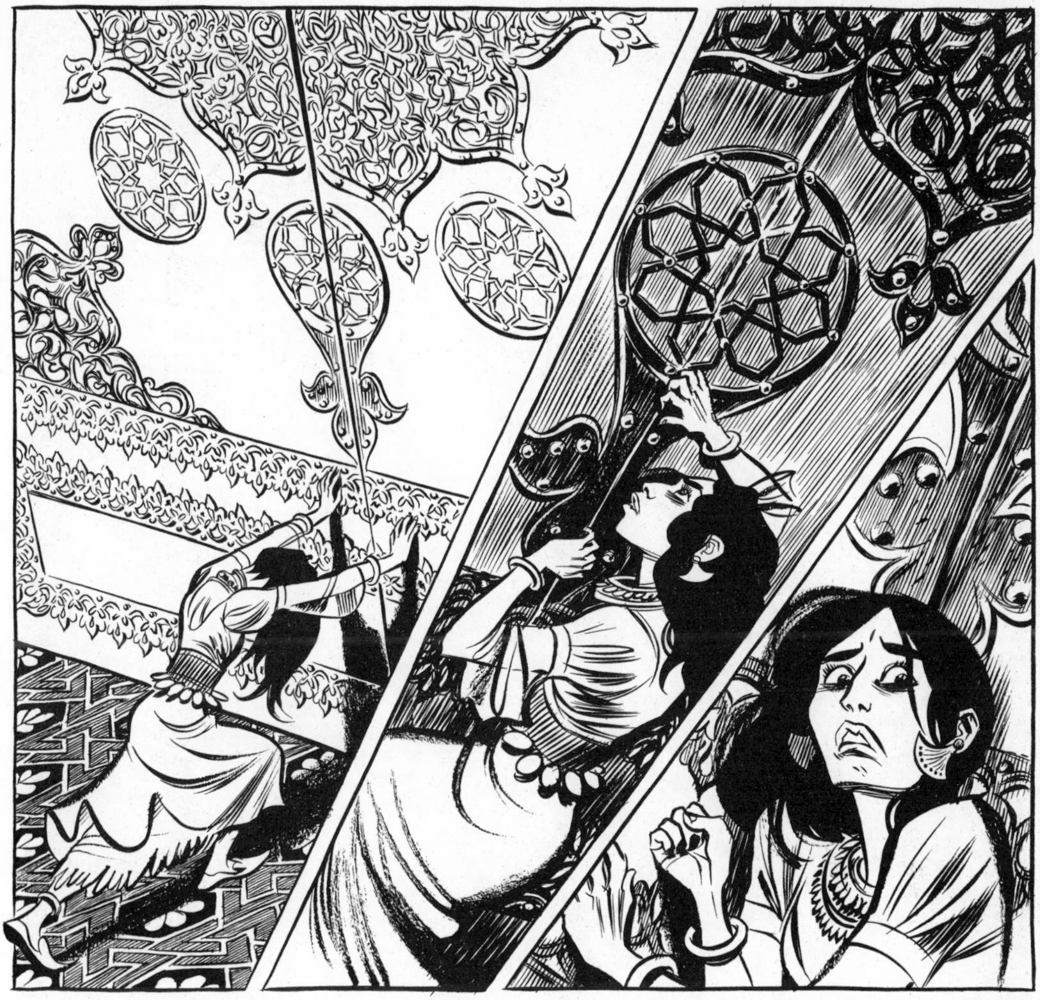

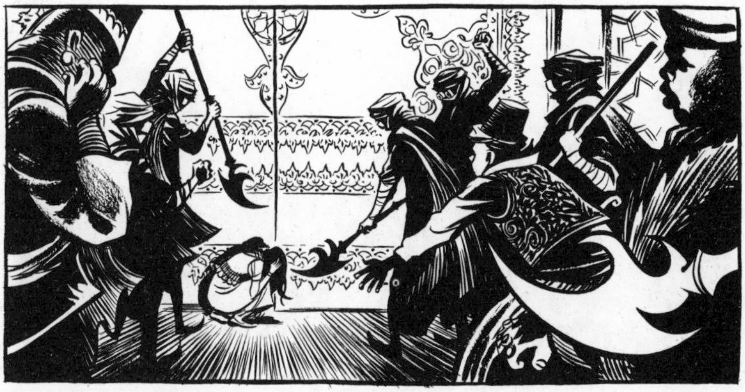

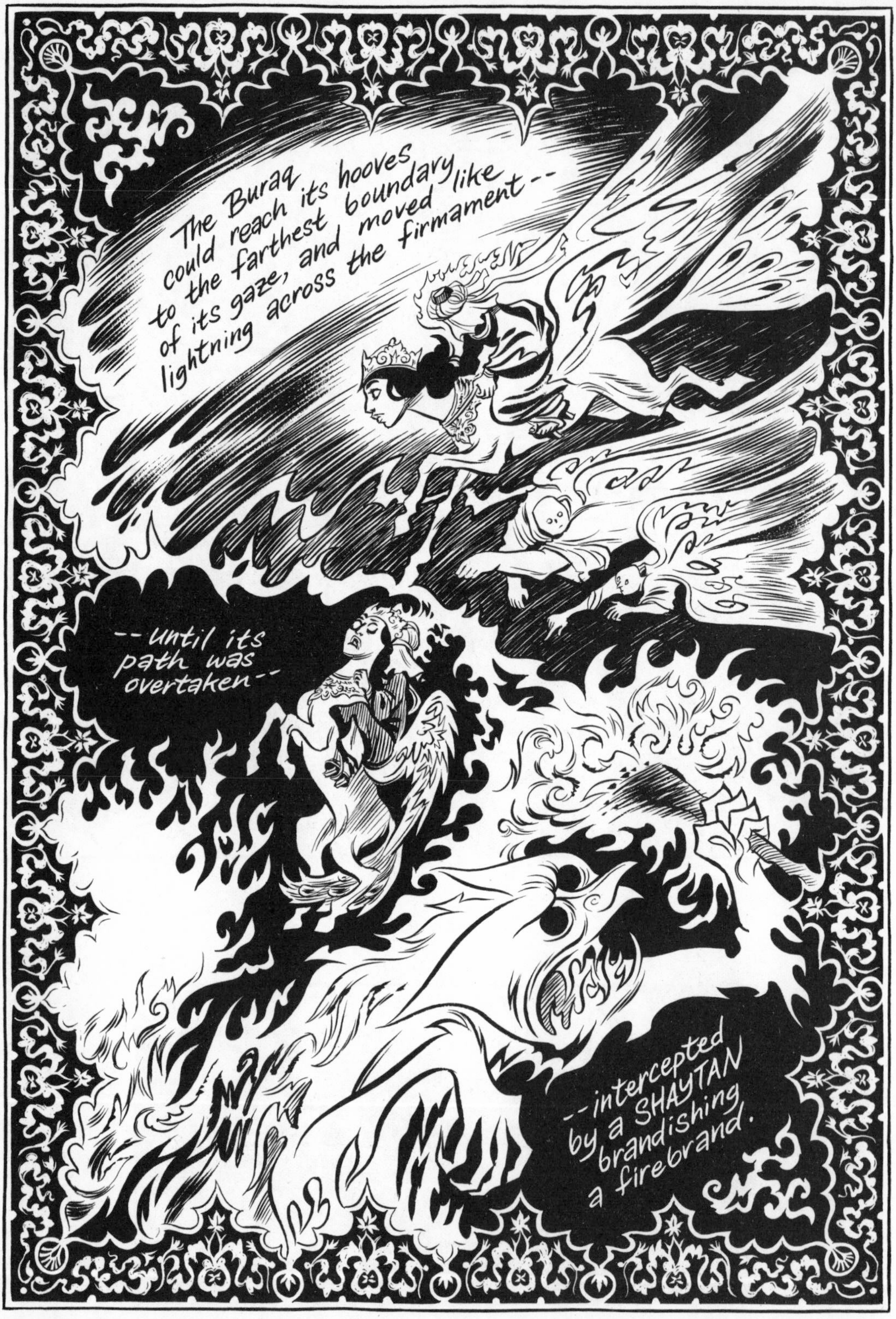
The Buraq could reach its hooves to the farthest boundary of its gaze, and moved like lightning across the firmament--
--until its path was overtaken--
--intercepted by a SHAYTAN brandishing a firebrand.

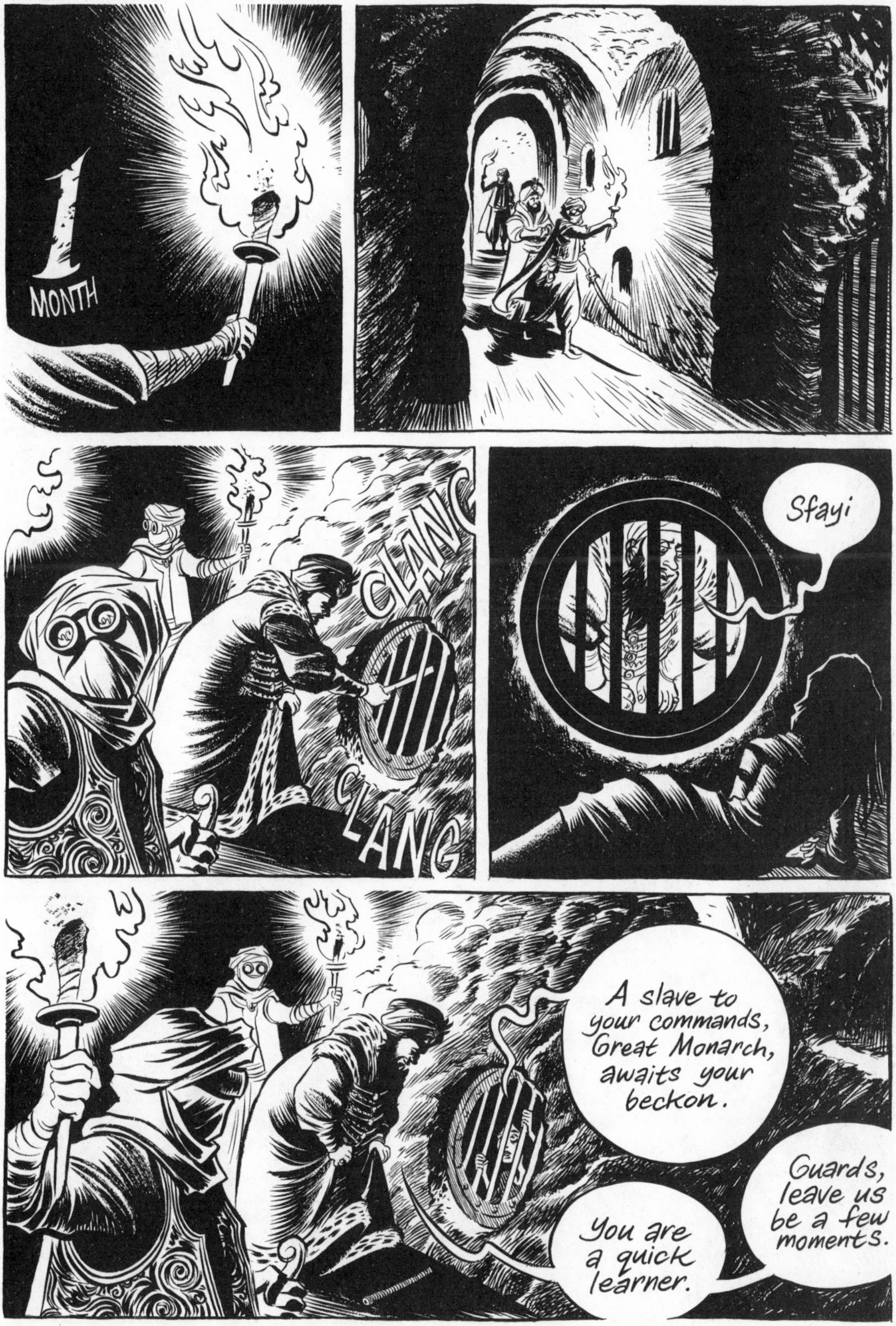
1 MONTH
CLANG
CLANG
Sfayi
A slave to your commands, Great Monarch, awaits your beckon.
You are a quick learner.
Guards, leave us be a few moments.

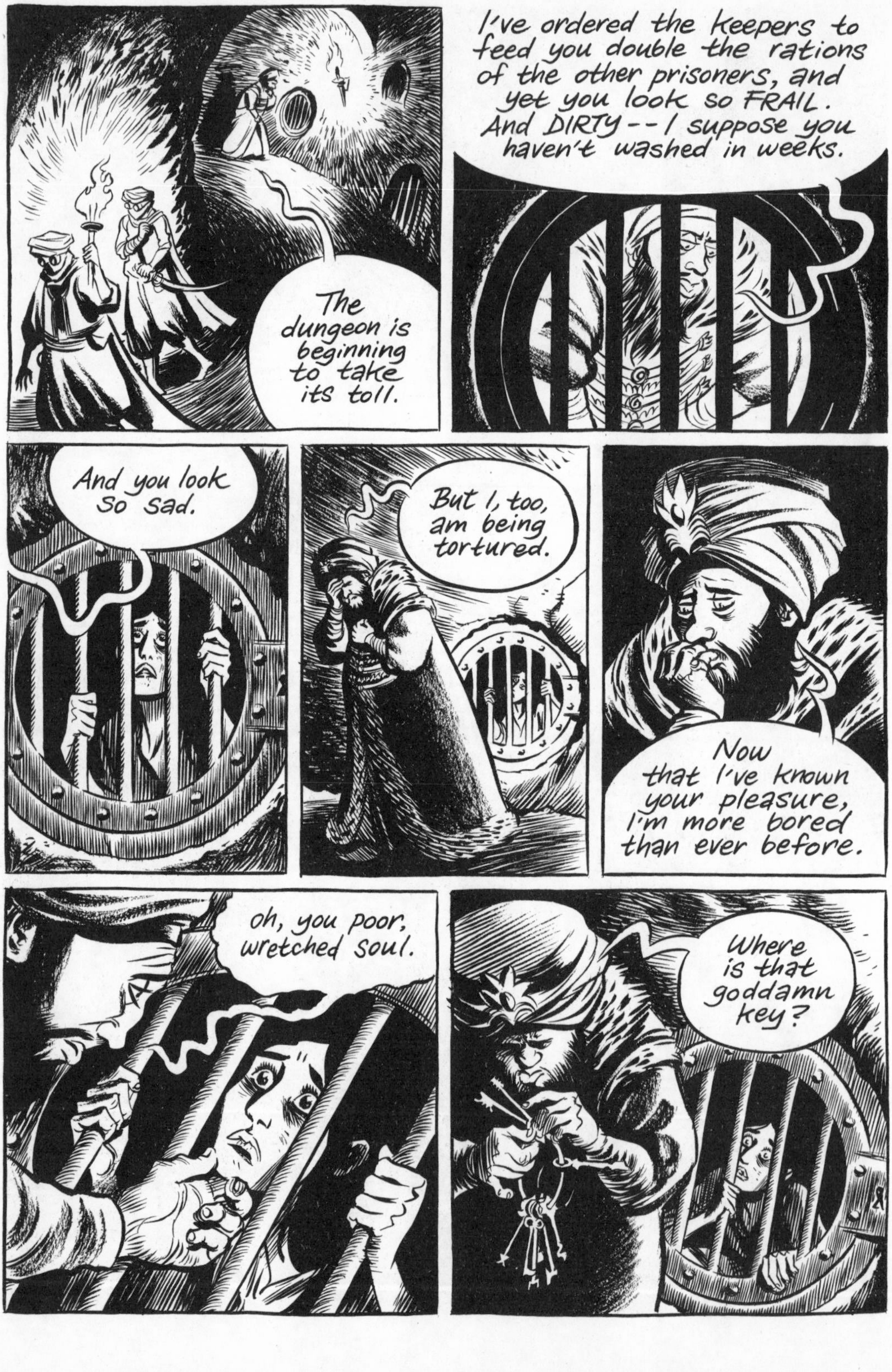
The dungeon is beginning to take its toll.
I've ordered the keepers to feed you double the rations of the other prisoners, and yet you look so FRAIL. And DIRTY-- I suppose you haven't washed in weeks.
And you look so sad.
But I, too, am being tortured.
Now that I've known your pleasure, I'm more bored than ever before.
oh, you poor, wretched soul.
Where is that goddamn key?

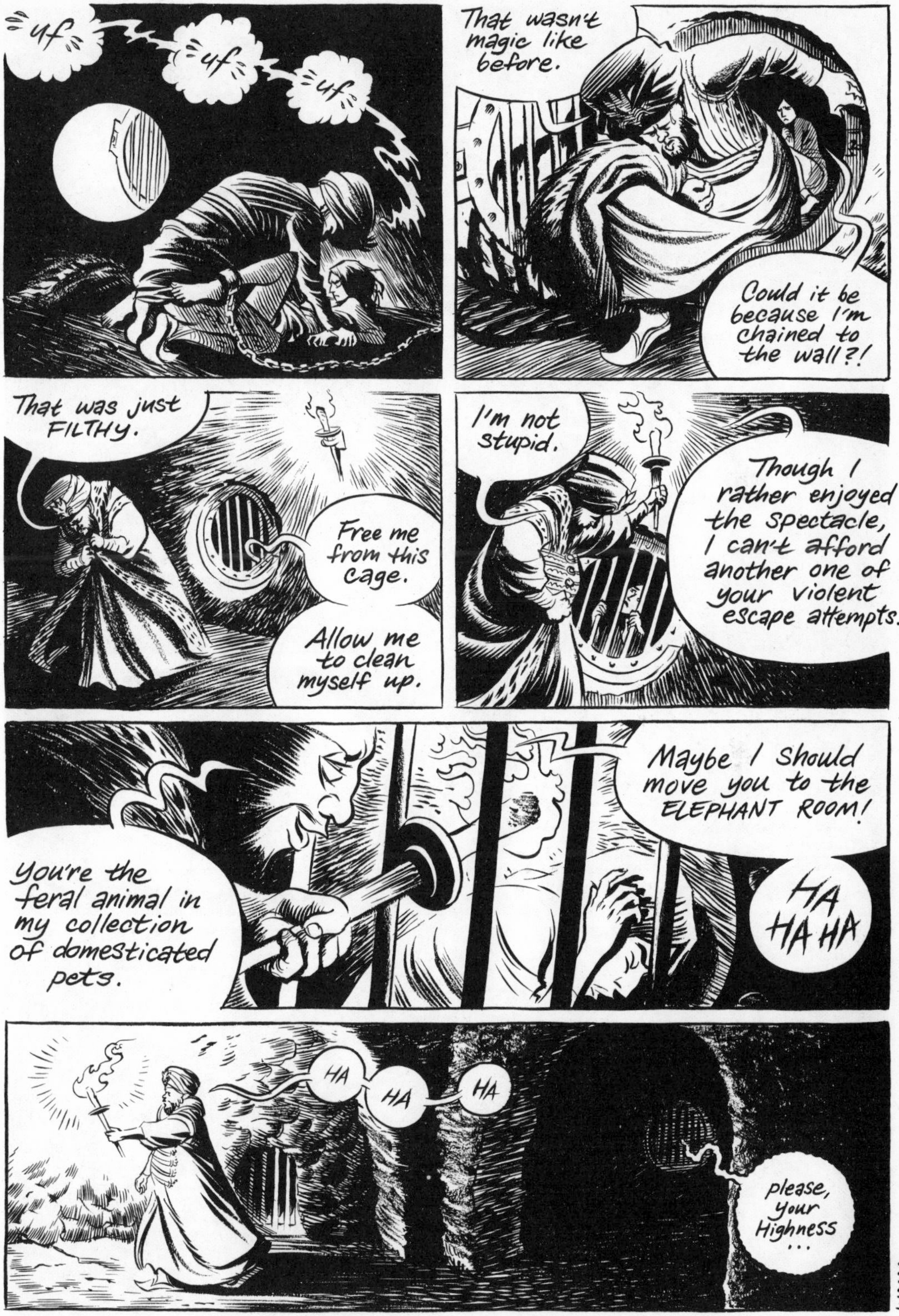
uf
uf
uf
That wasn't magic like before.
Could it be because I'm chained to the wall?!
That was just FILTHY.
Free me from this cage.
Allow me to clean myself up.
I'm not stupid.
Though I rather enjoyed the spectacle, I can't afford another one of your violent escape attempts.
You're the feral animal in my collection of domesticated pets.
Maybe I should move you to the ELEPHANT ROOM!
HA HA HA
HA
HA
HA
please, your Highness . . .

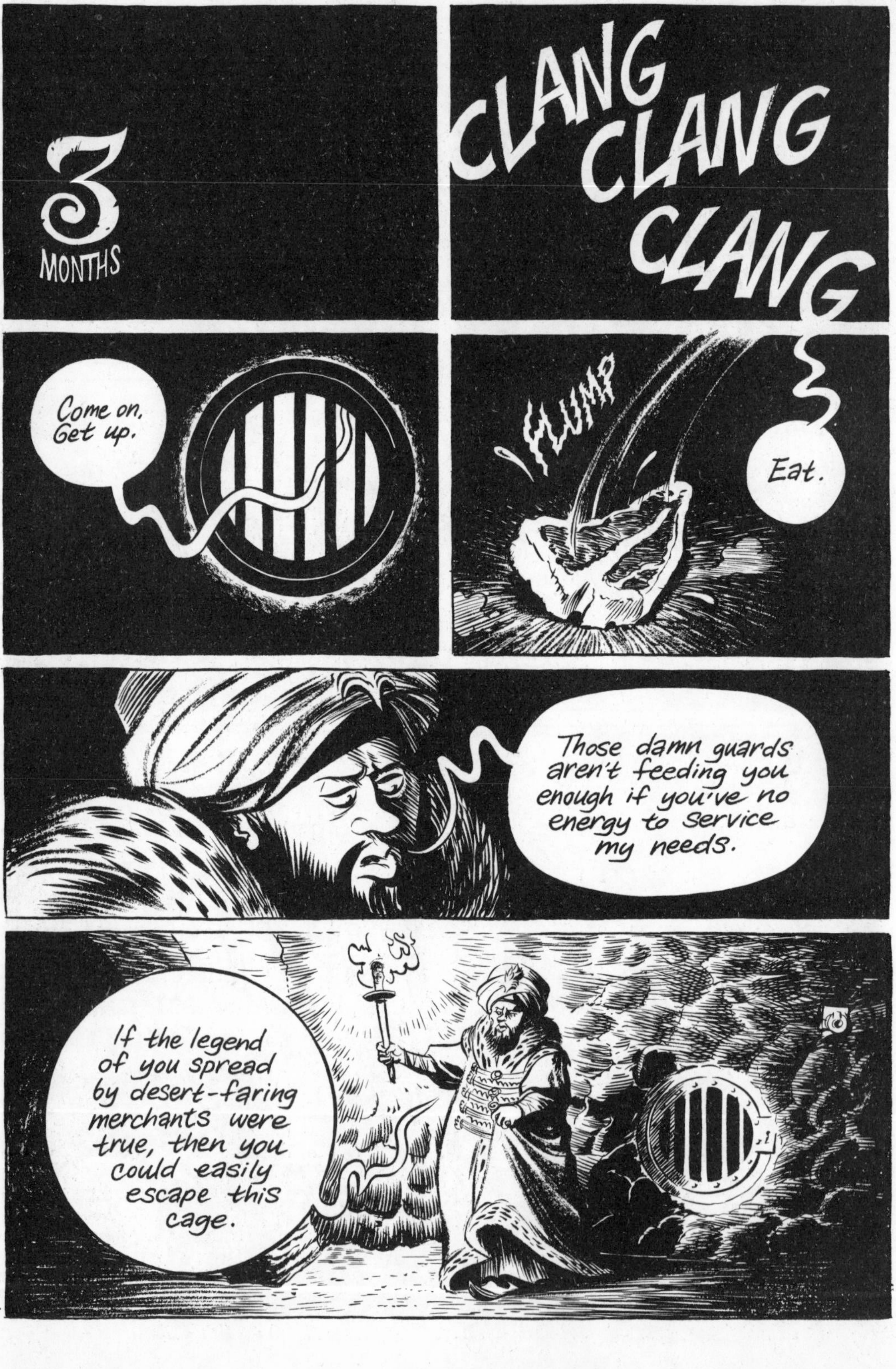
3
MONTHS
CLANG
CLANG
CLANG
CLANG
Come on. Get up.
FLUMP
Eat.
Those damn guards aren't feeding you enough if you've no energy to service my needs.
If the legend of you spread by desert-faring merchants were true, then you could easily escape this cage.

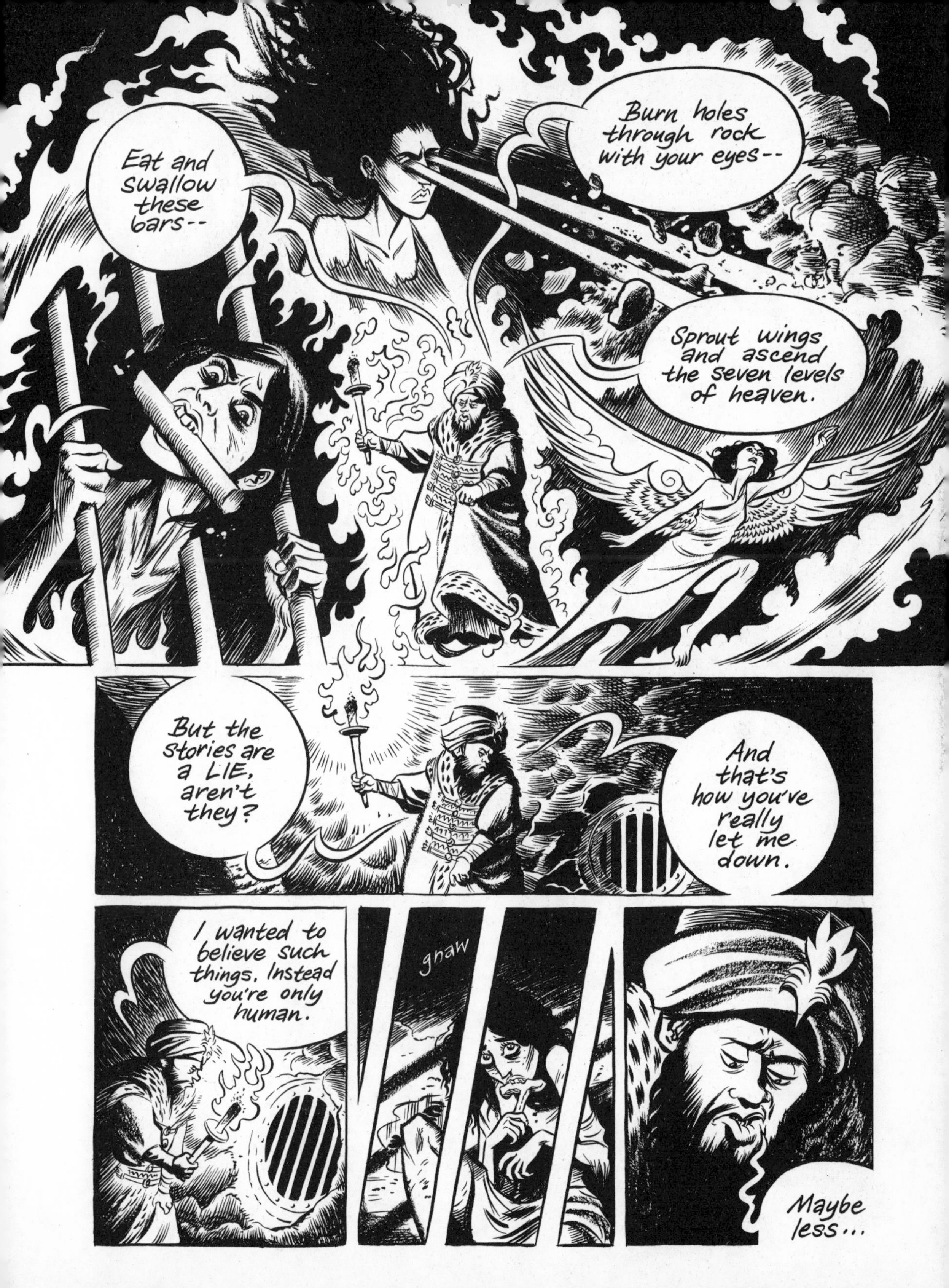
Eat and swallow these bars--
Burn holes through rock with your eyes--
Sprout wings and ascend the seven levels of heaven.
But the stories are a LIE, aren't they?
And that's how you've really let me down.
I wanted to believe such things. Instead you're only human.
ghaw
Maybe less...

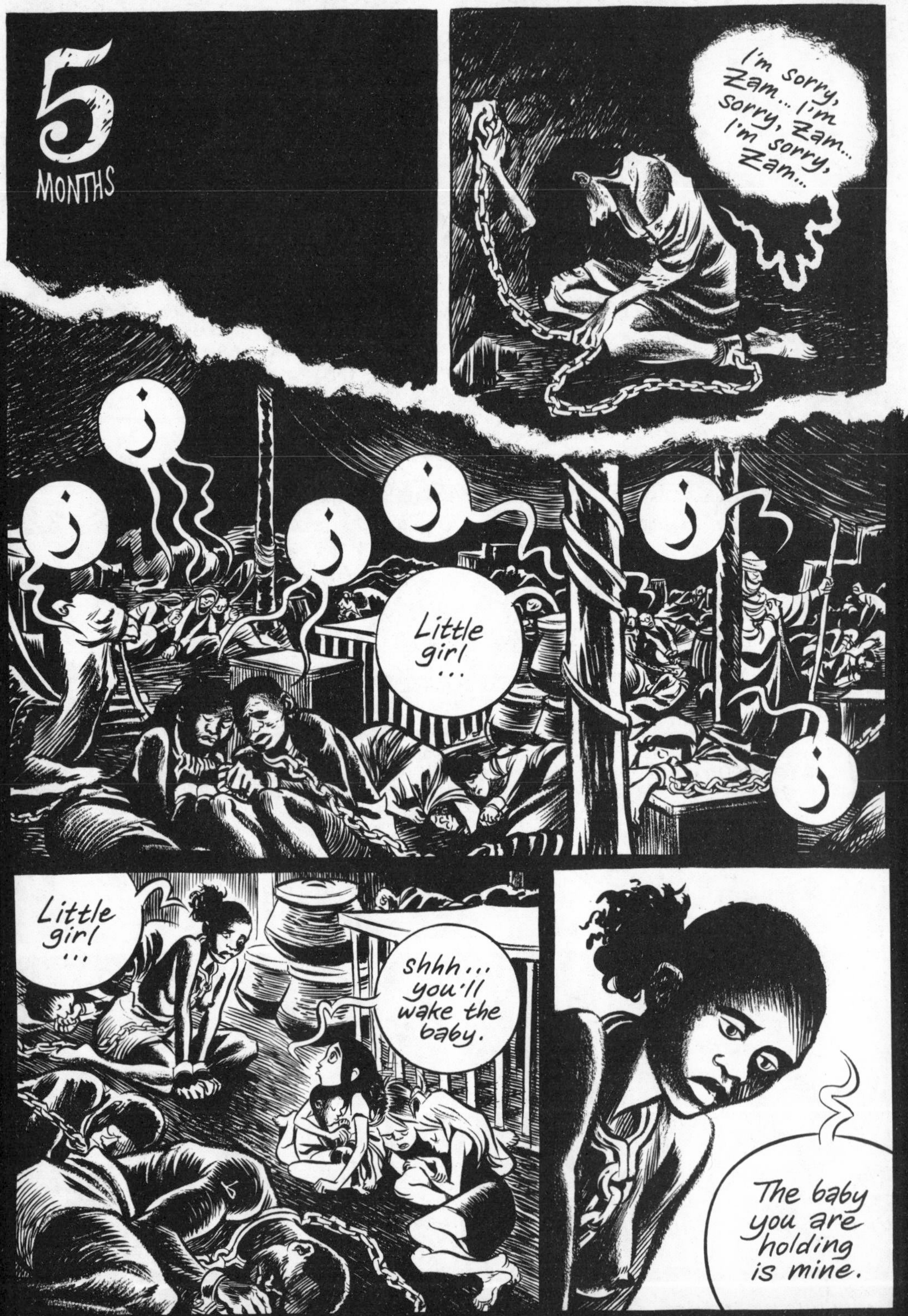
5
MONTHS
I'm sorry, Zam... I'm sorry, Zam... I'm sorry, Zam...
ز
ز
ز
ز
ز
Little girl ...
ز
Little girl ...
shhh... you'll wake the baby.
The baby you are holding is mine.

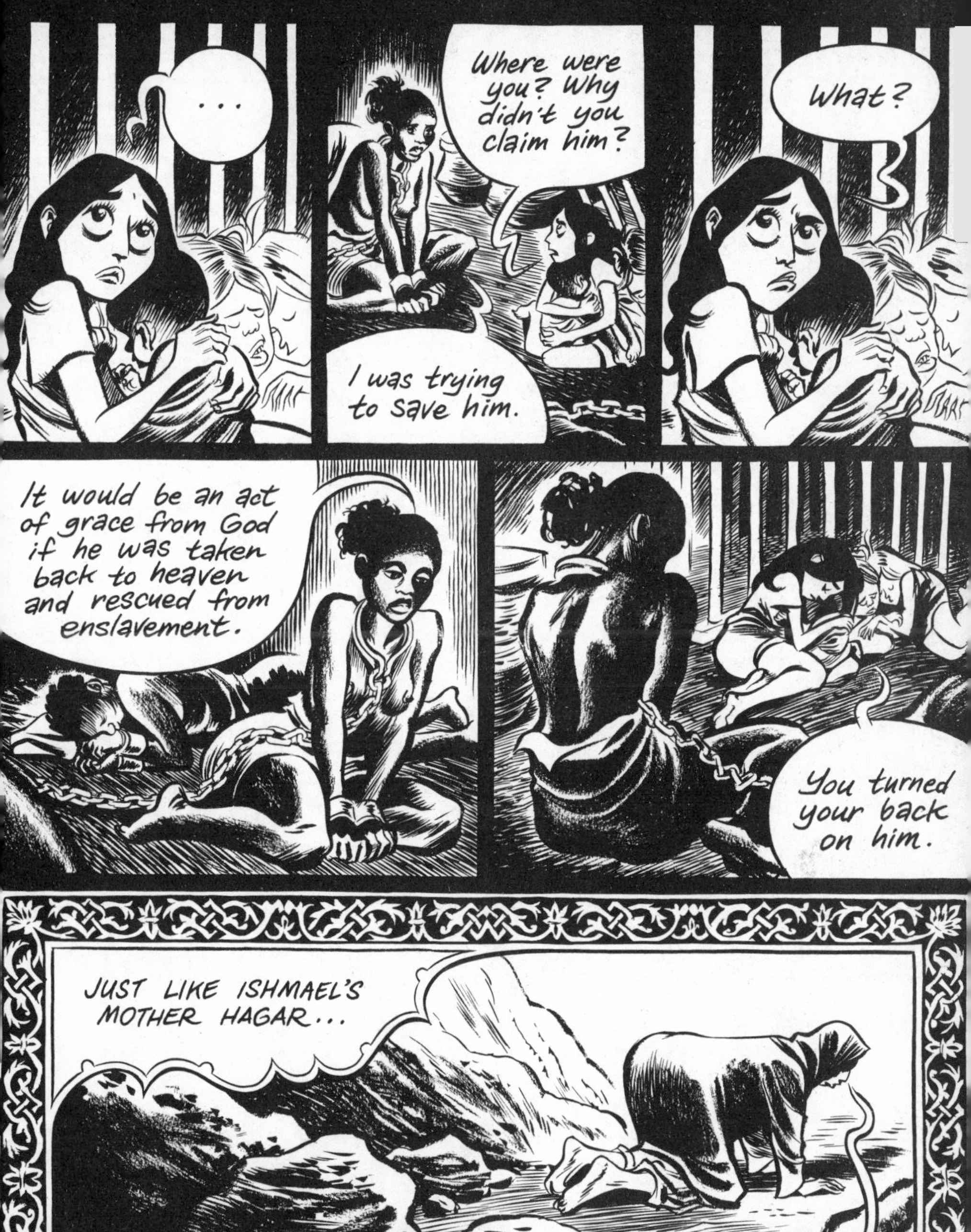
...
Where were you? Why didn't you claim him?
I was trying to save him.
What?
It would be an act of grace from God if he was taken back to heaven and rescued from enslavement.
You turned your back on him.
JUST LIKE ISHMAEL'S MOTHER HAGAR...
Please, God, let me turn my face. I don't want to see him die.

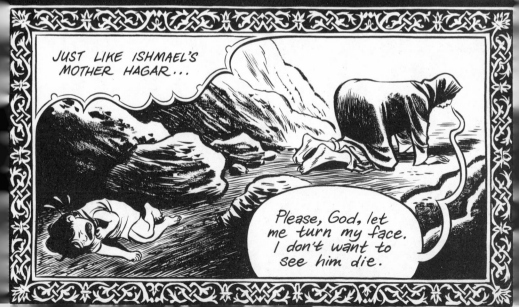

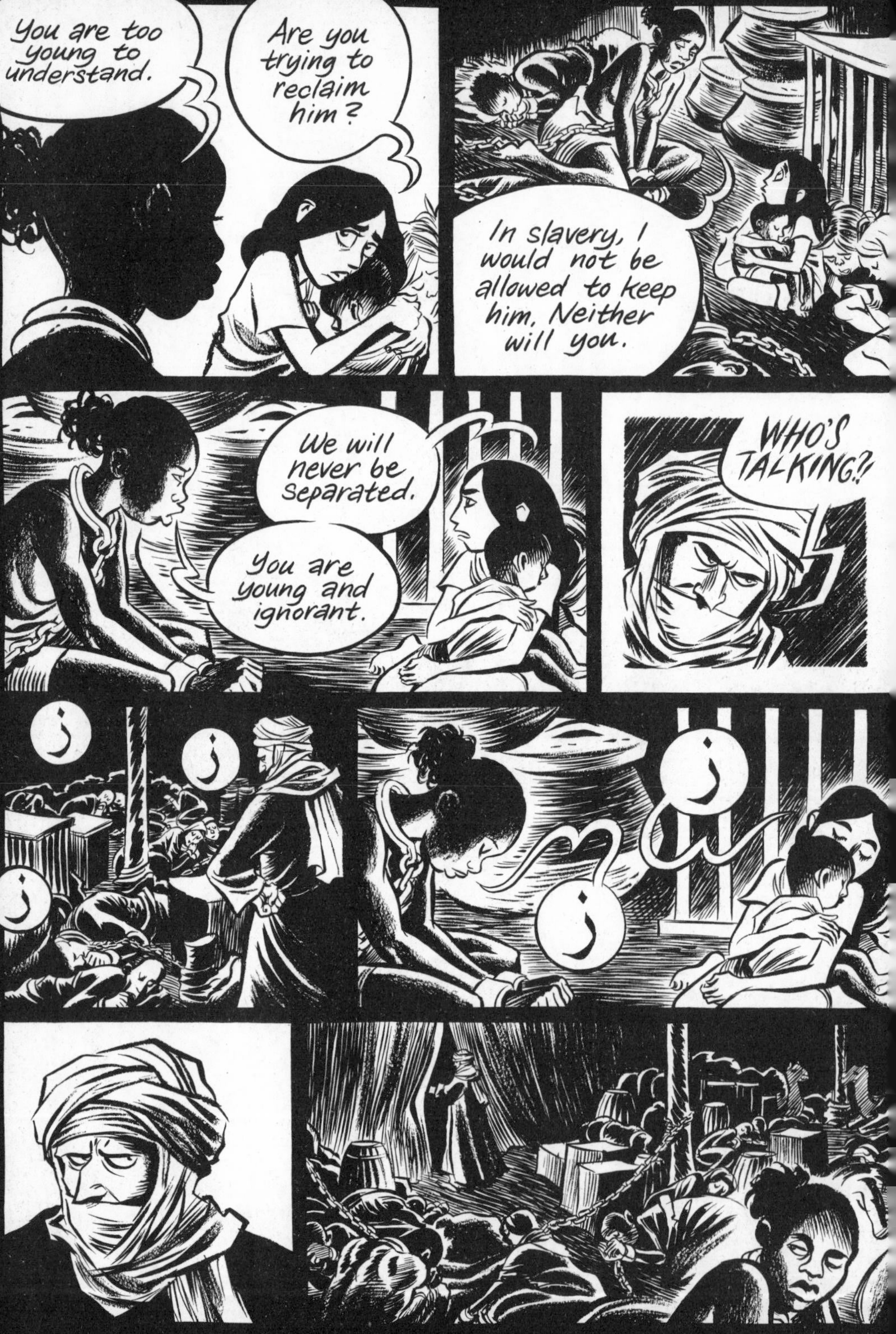
You are too young to understand.
Are you trying to reclaim him?
In slavery, I would not be allowed to keep him. Neither will you.
We will never be separated.
You are young and ignorant.
WHO'S TALKING?!
ز
ز
ز
ز
ز

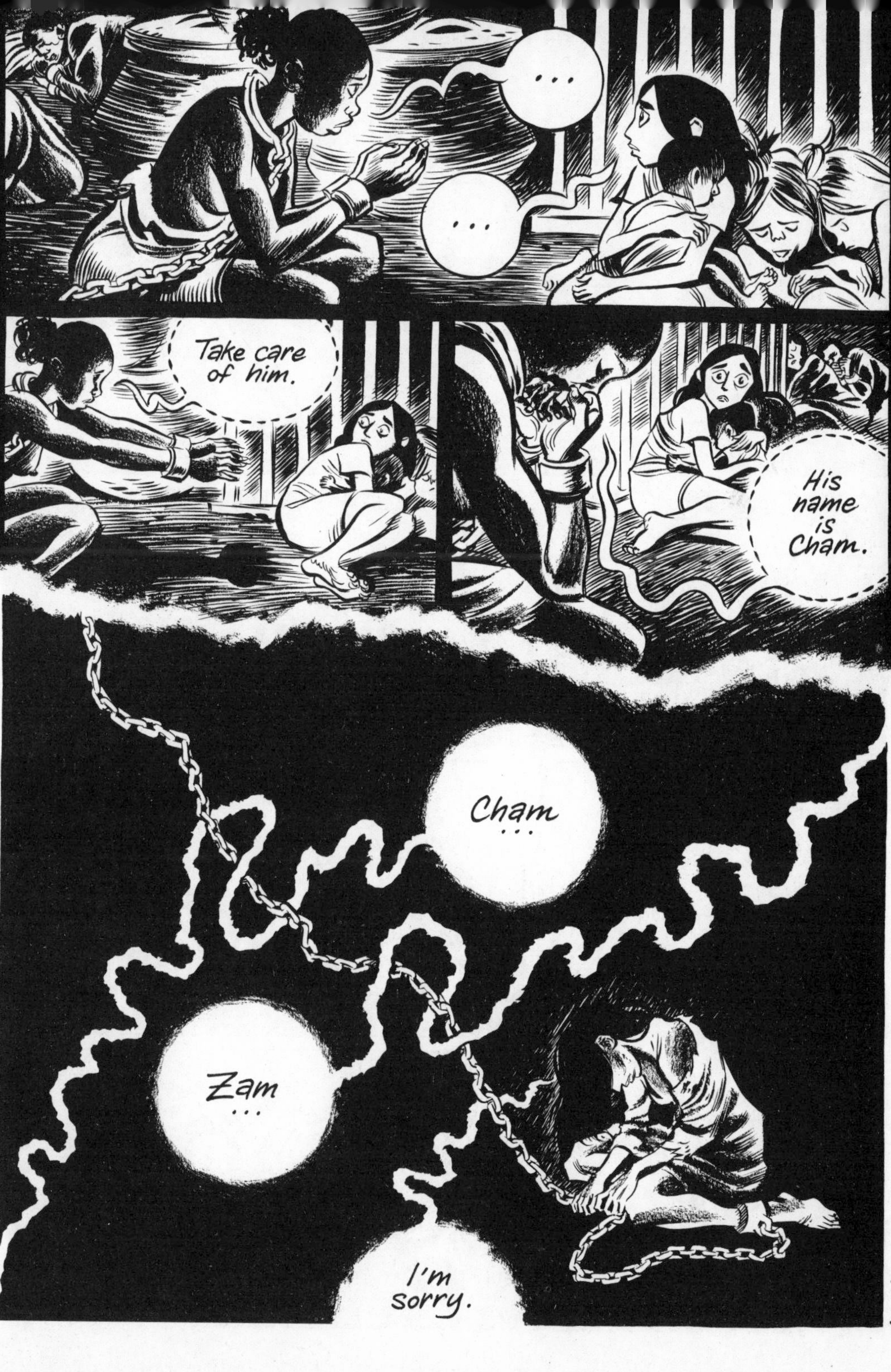
...
...
Take care of him.
His name is Cham.
Cham ...
Zam ...
I'm sorry.

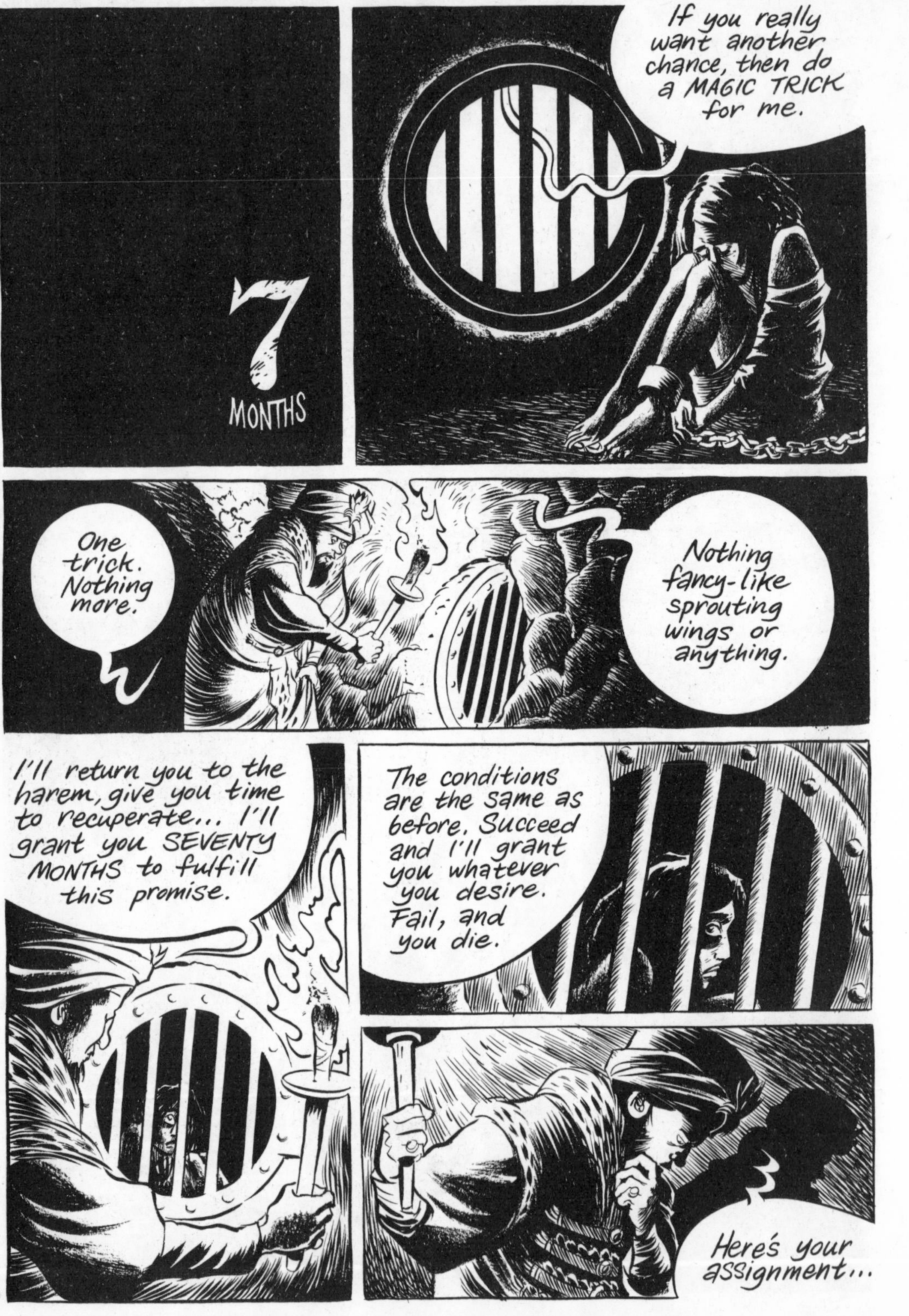
7
MONTHS
If you really want another chance, then do a MAGIC TRICK for me.
One trick. Nothing more.
Nothing fancy-like sprouting wings or anything.
I'll return you to the harem, give you time to recuperate... I'll grant you SEVENTY MONTHS to fulfill this promise.
The conditions are the same as before. Succeed and I'll grant you whatever you desire. Fail, and you die.
Here's your assignment...

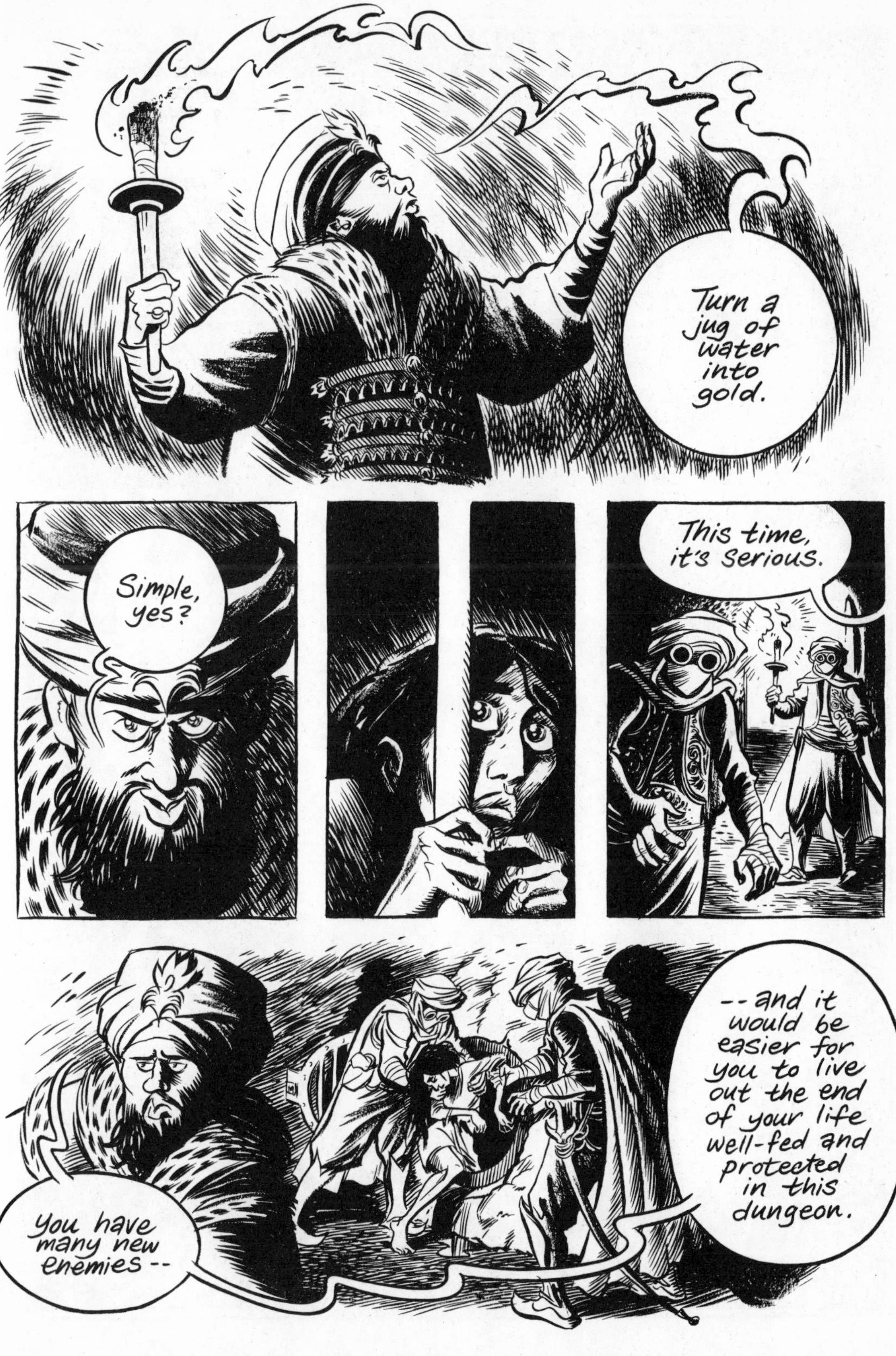
Turn a jug of water into gold.
Simple, yes?
This time, it's serious.
You have many new enemies --
-- and it would be easier for you to live out the end of your life well-fed and protected in this dungeon.

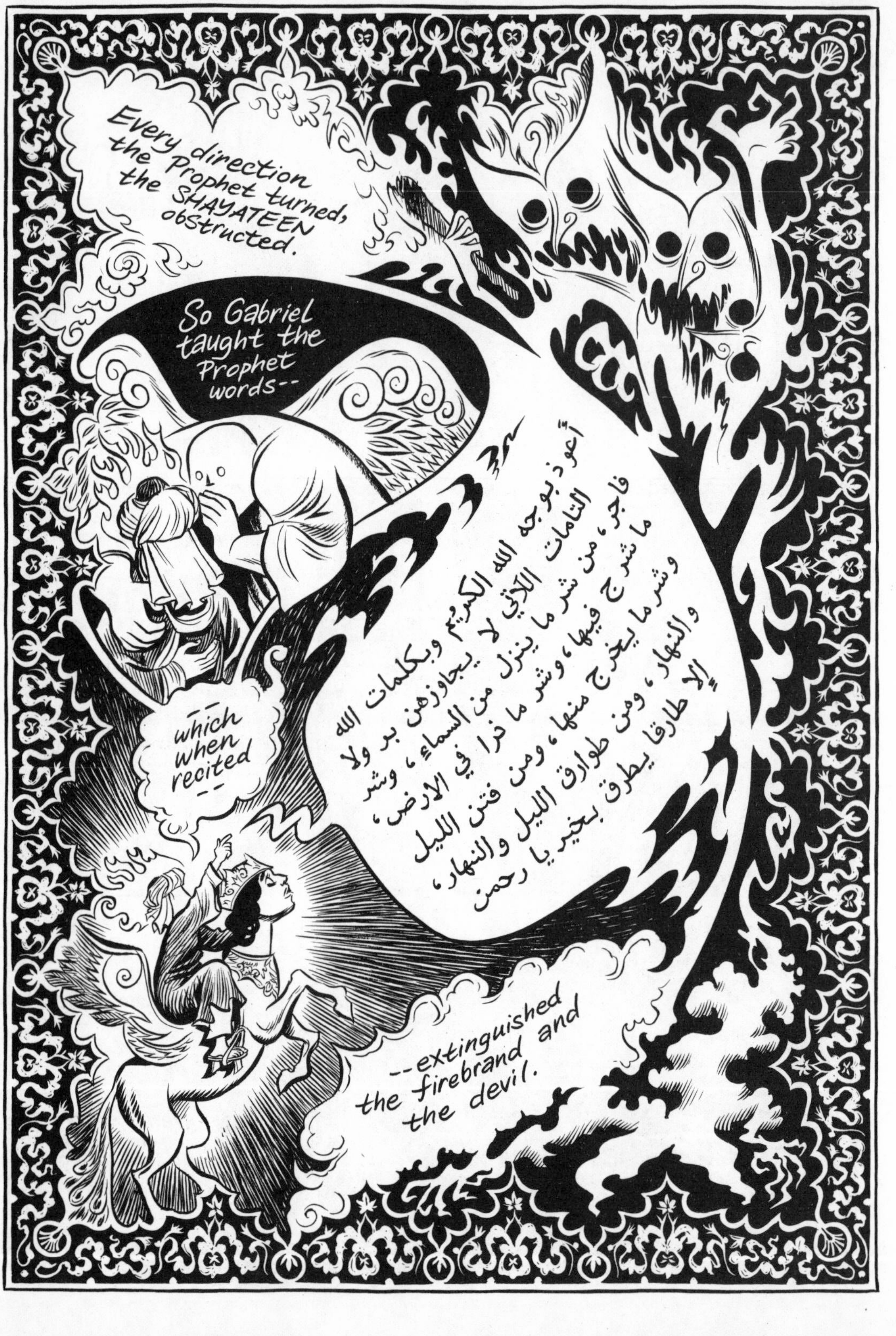
Every direction the Prophet turned, the SHAYATEEN obstructed.
So Gabriel taught the Prophet words--
أعوذ بوجه الله الكريم وبكلمات الله
التامات اللاتي لا يجاوزهن بر ولا
فاجر، من شر ما ينزل من السماء، وشر
ما شرج فيها، وشر ما ذرا في الارض،
وشر ما يخرج منها، ومن فتن الليل
والنهار، ومن طوارق الليل والنهار،
إلا طارقا يطرق بخير يا رحمن
which when recited--
--extinguished the firebrand and the devil.

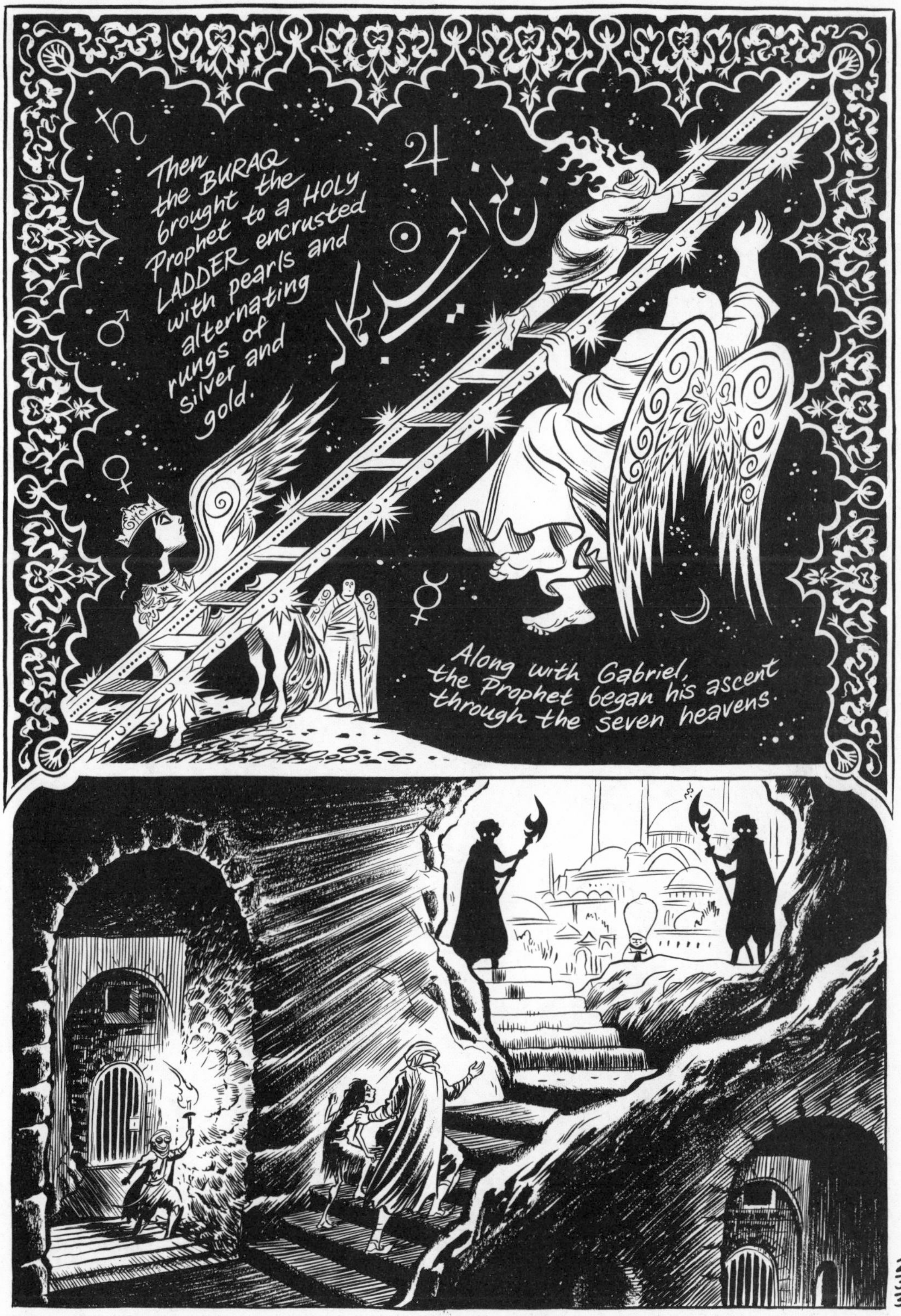
Then the BURAQ brought the Prophet to a HOLY LADDER encrusted with pearls and alternating rungs of silver and gold.
Along with Gabriel, the Prophet began his ascent through the seven heavens.

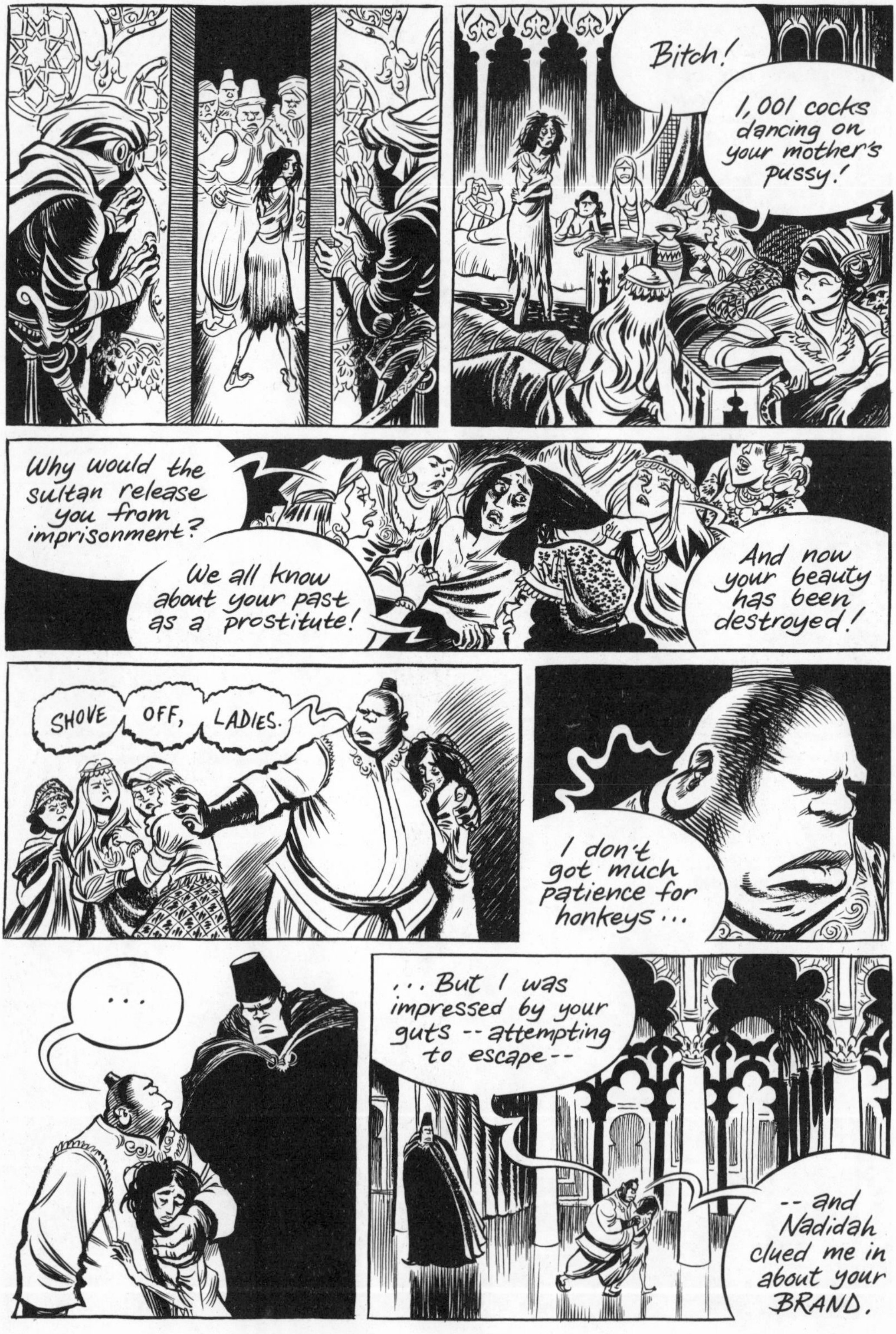
Bitch!
1,001 cocks dancing on your mother's pussy!
Why would the sultan release you from imprisonment?
We all know about your past as a prostitute!
And now your beauty has been destroyed!
SHOVE OFF, LADIES.
I don't got much patience for honkeys...
...
...But I was impressed by your guts -- attempting to escape--
-- and Nadidah clued me in about your BRAND.

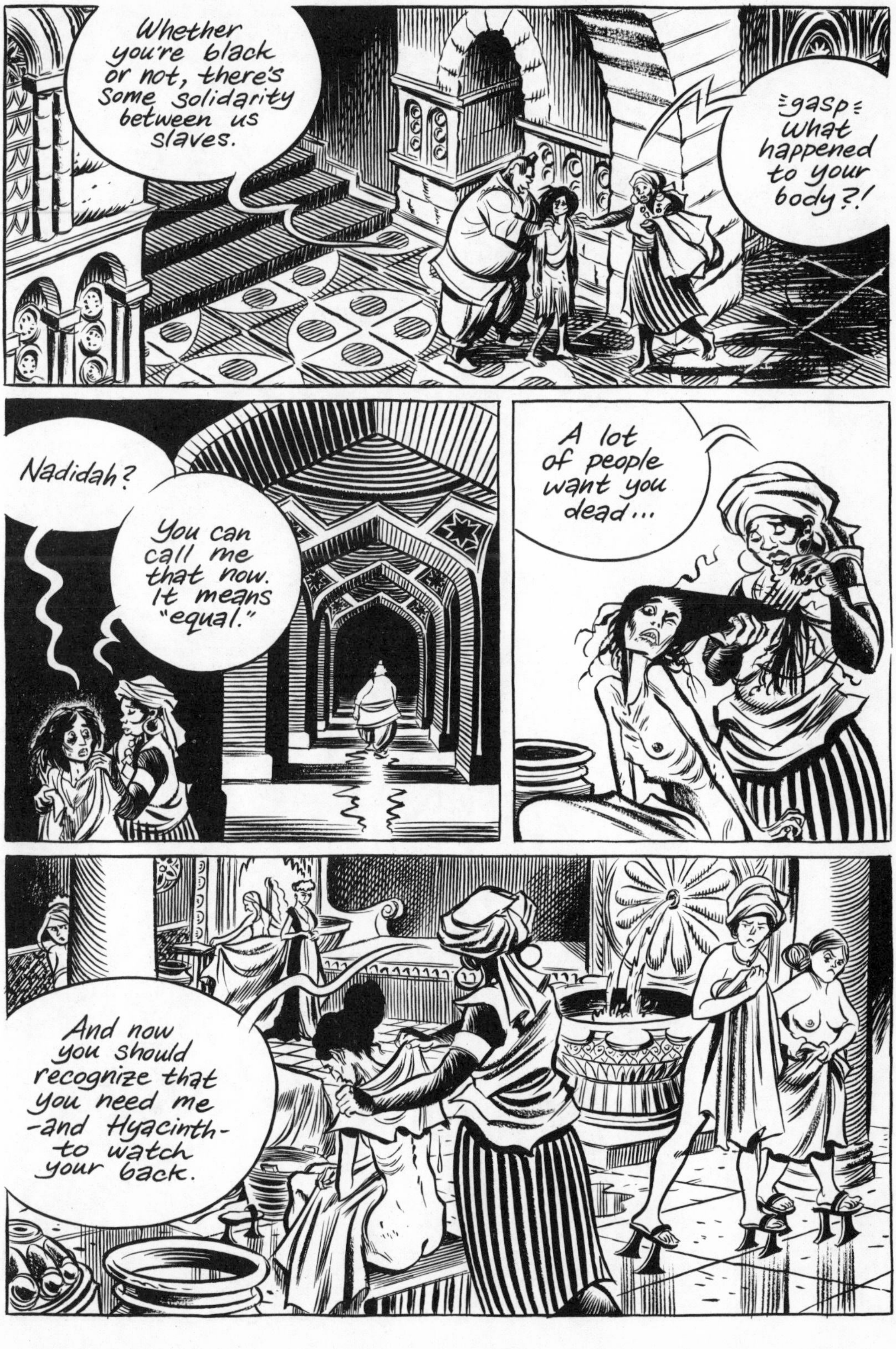
Whether you're black or not, there's some solidarity between us slaves.
gasp what happened to your body?!
Nadidah?
You can call me that now. It means "equal."
A lot of people want you dead...
And now you should recognize that you need me -and Hyacinth- to watch your back.

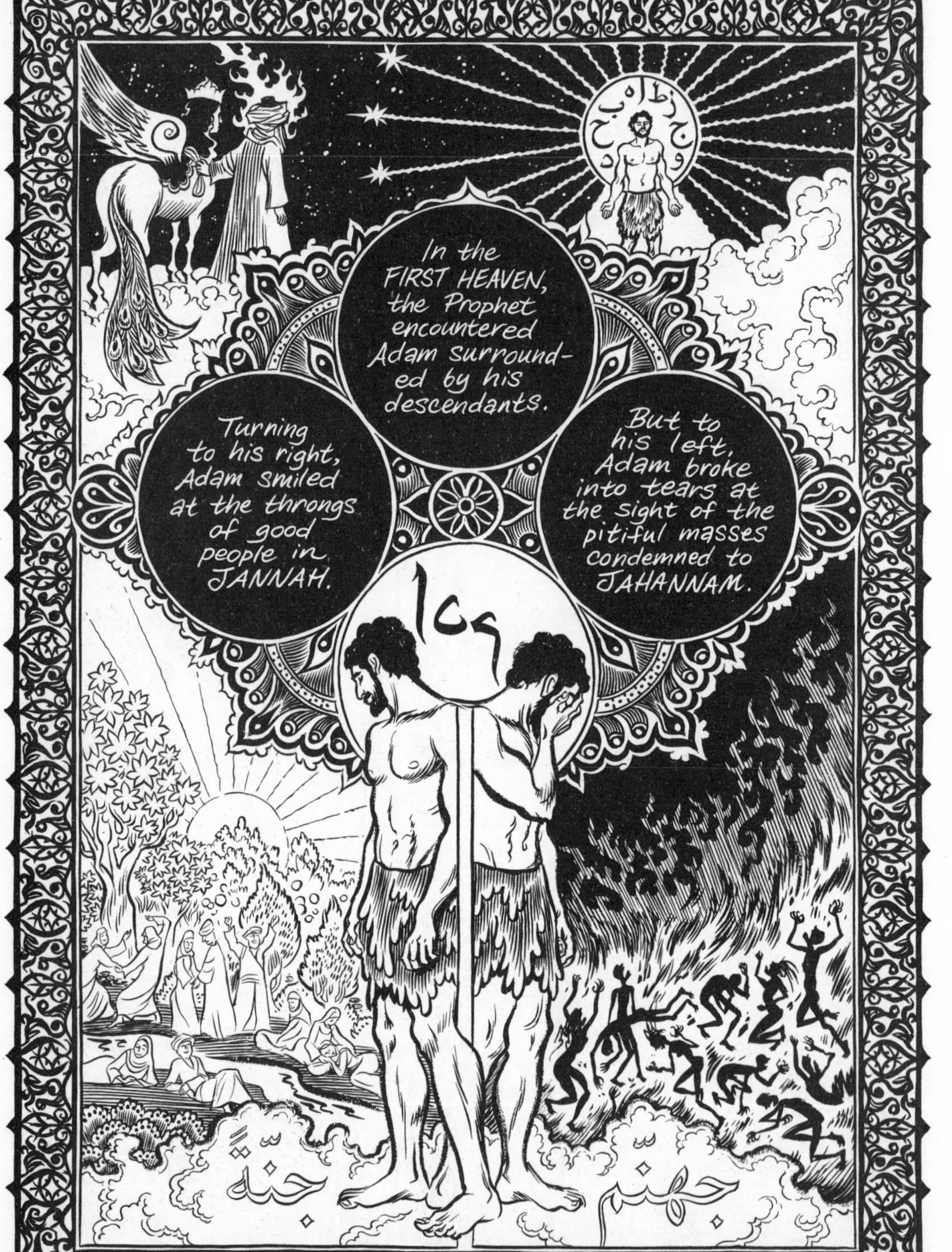
In the FIRST HEAVEN, the Prophet encountered Adam surrounded by his descendants.
Turning to his right, Adam smiled at the throngs of good people in JANNAH.
But to his left, Adam broke into tears at the sight of the pitiful masses condemned to JAHANNAM.
جنة
جهنم

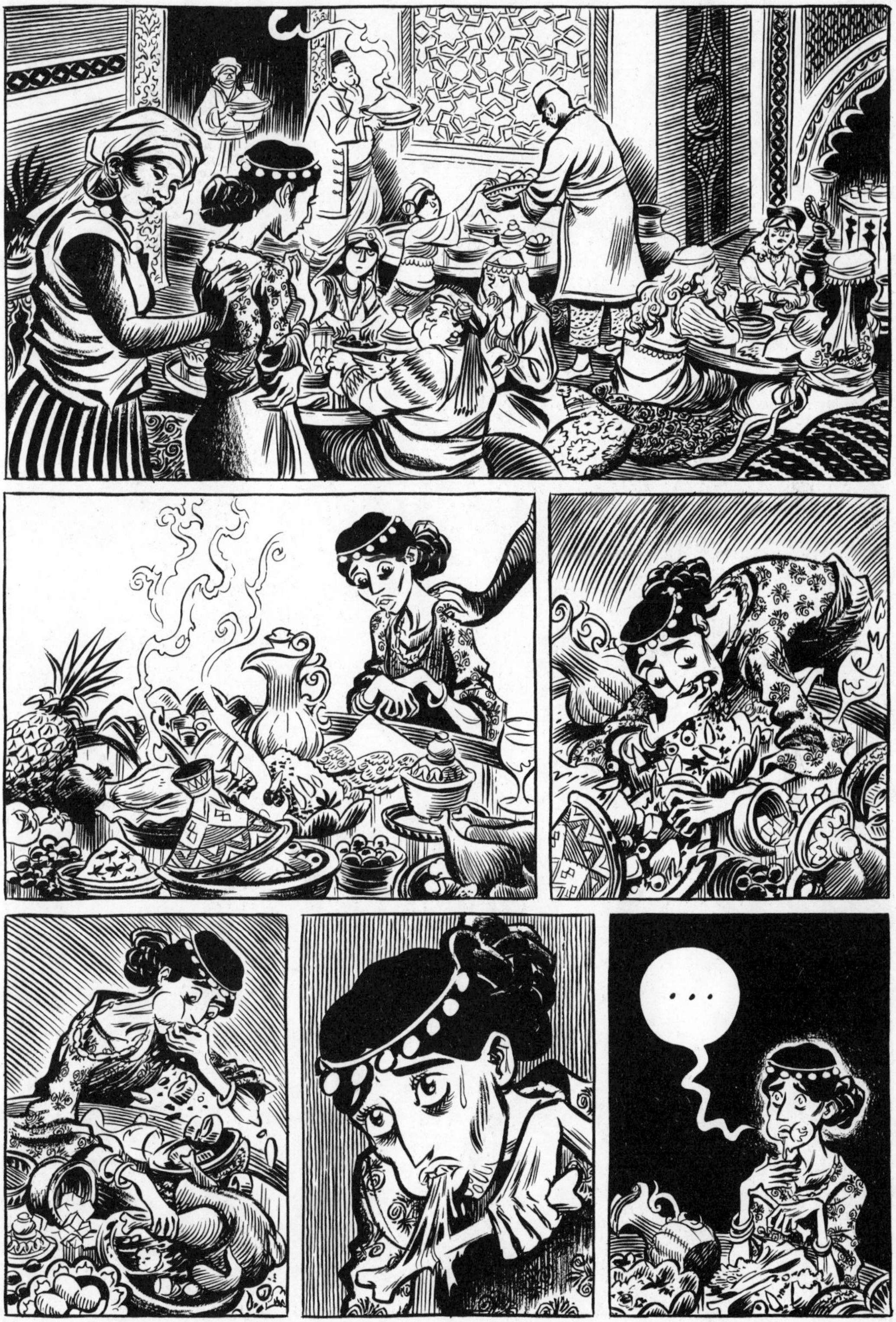
...

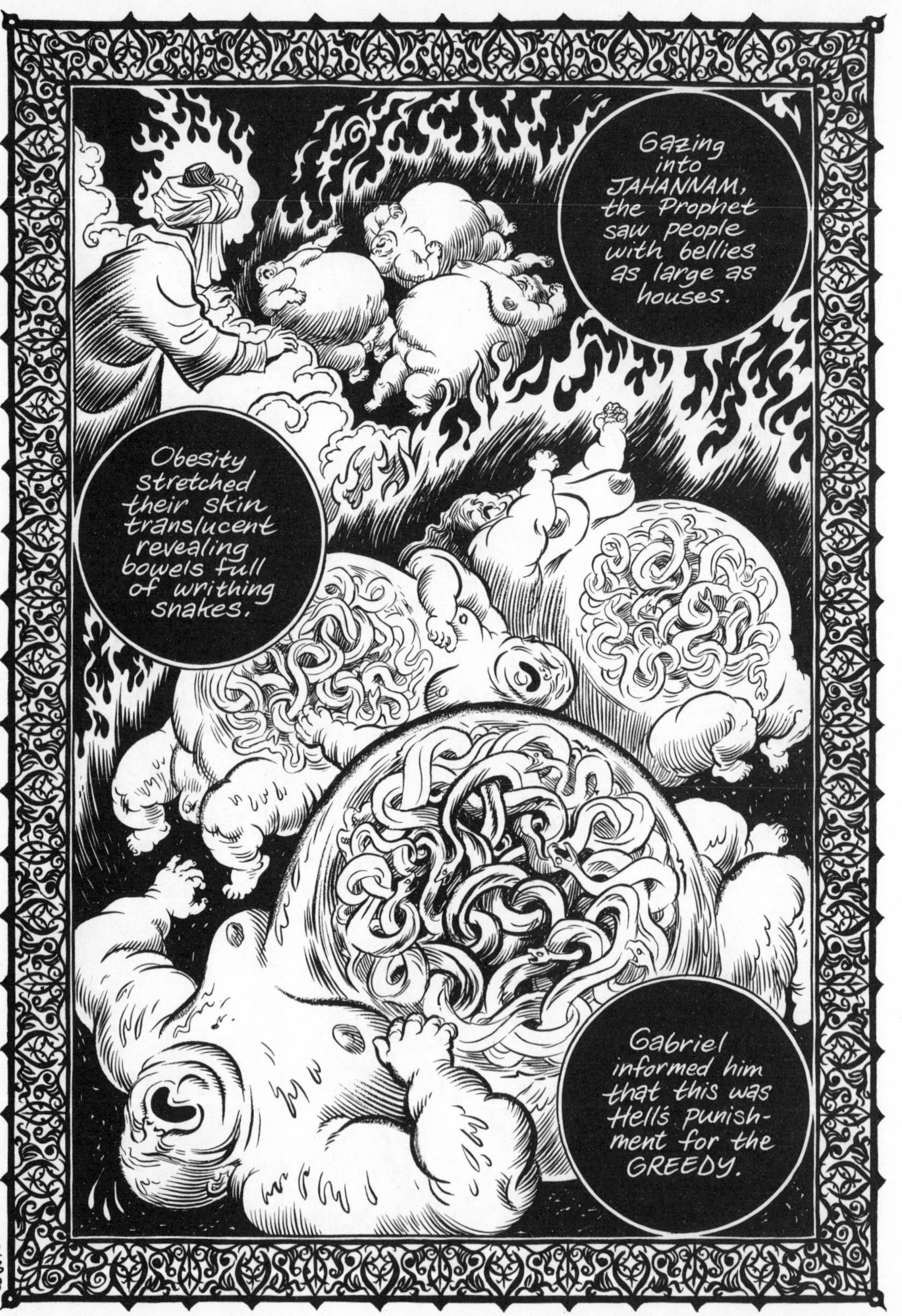
Gazing into JAHANNAM, the Prophet saw people with bellies as large as houses.
Obesity stretched their skin translucent revealing bowels full of writhing snakes.
Gabriel informed him that this was Hell's punishment for the GREEDY.

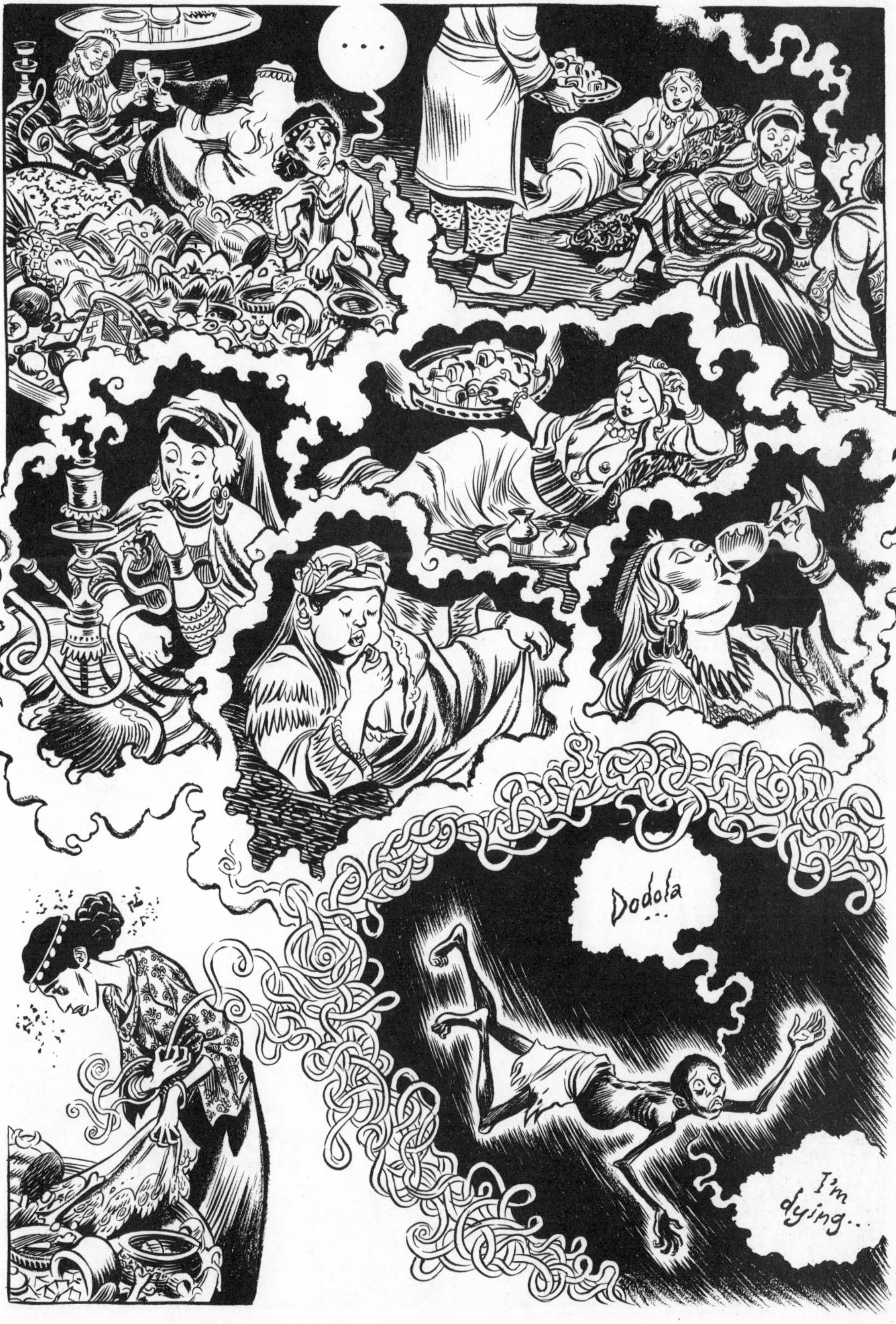
...
Dodola...
I'm dying...

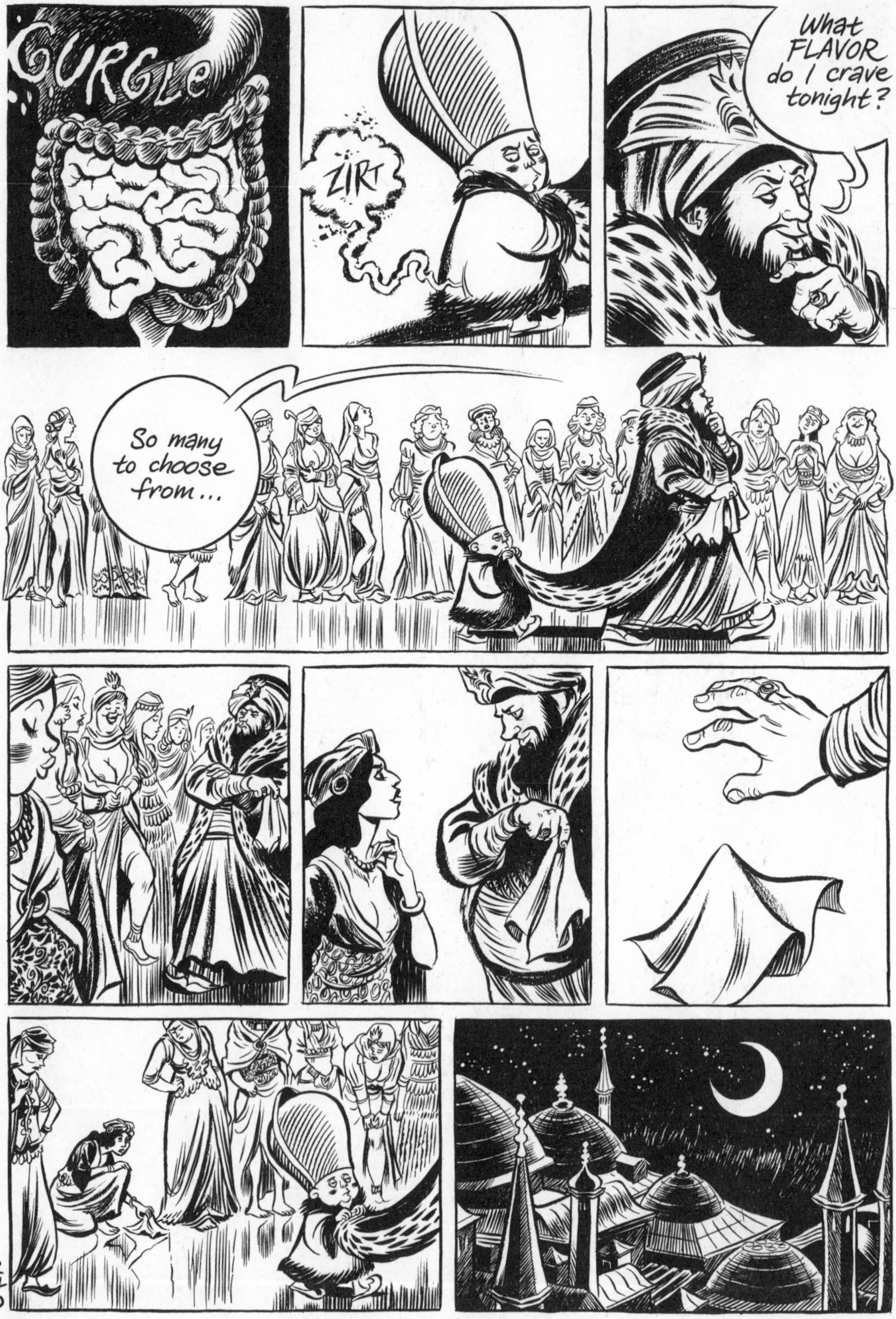
GURGLE
ZIRT
What FLAVOR do I crave tonight?
So many to choose from...

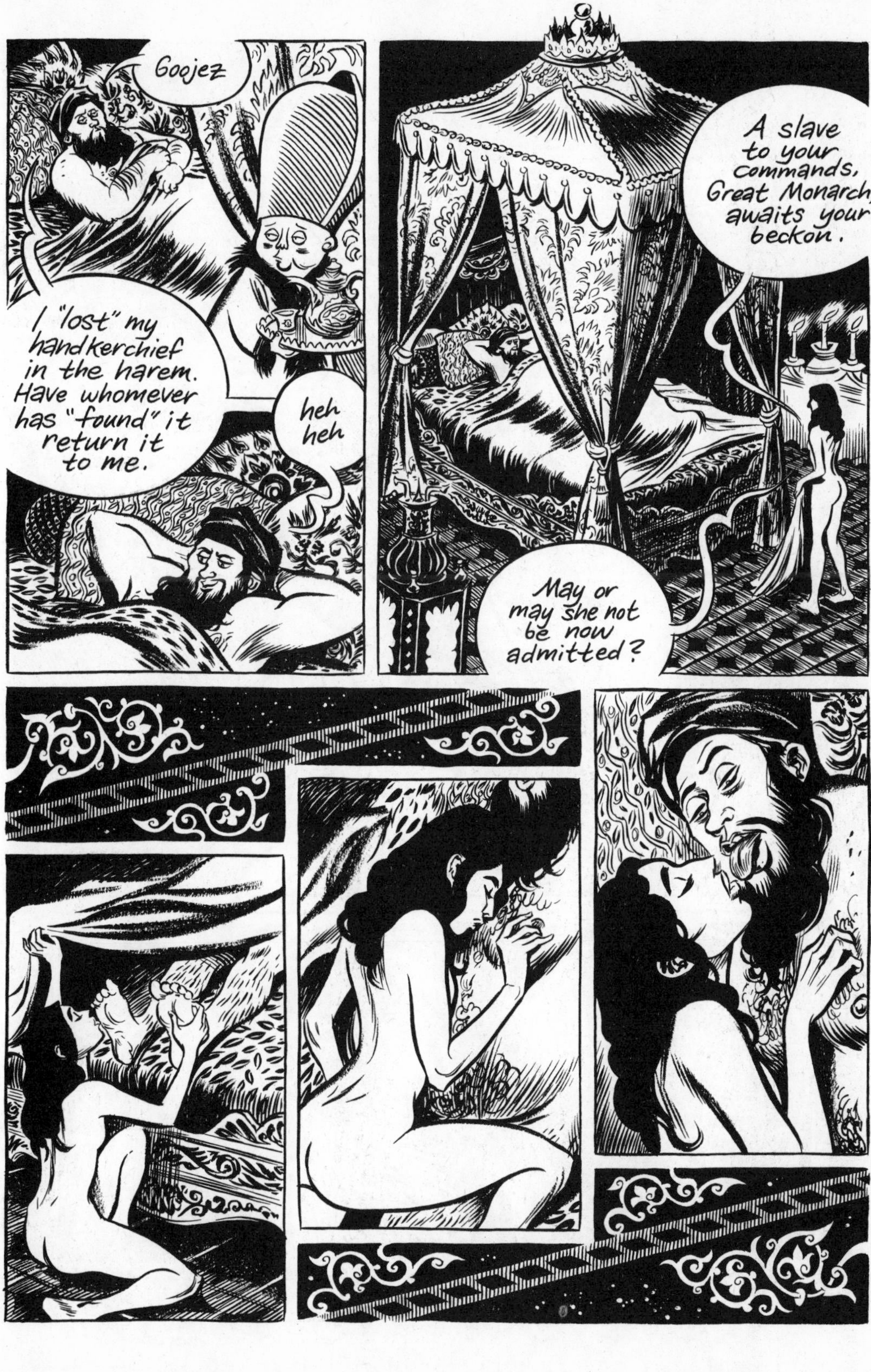
Goojez
I "lost" my handkerchief in the harem. Have whomever has "found" it return it to me.
heh heh
A slave to your commands, Great Monarch, awaits your beckon.
May or may she not be now admitted?

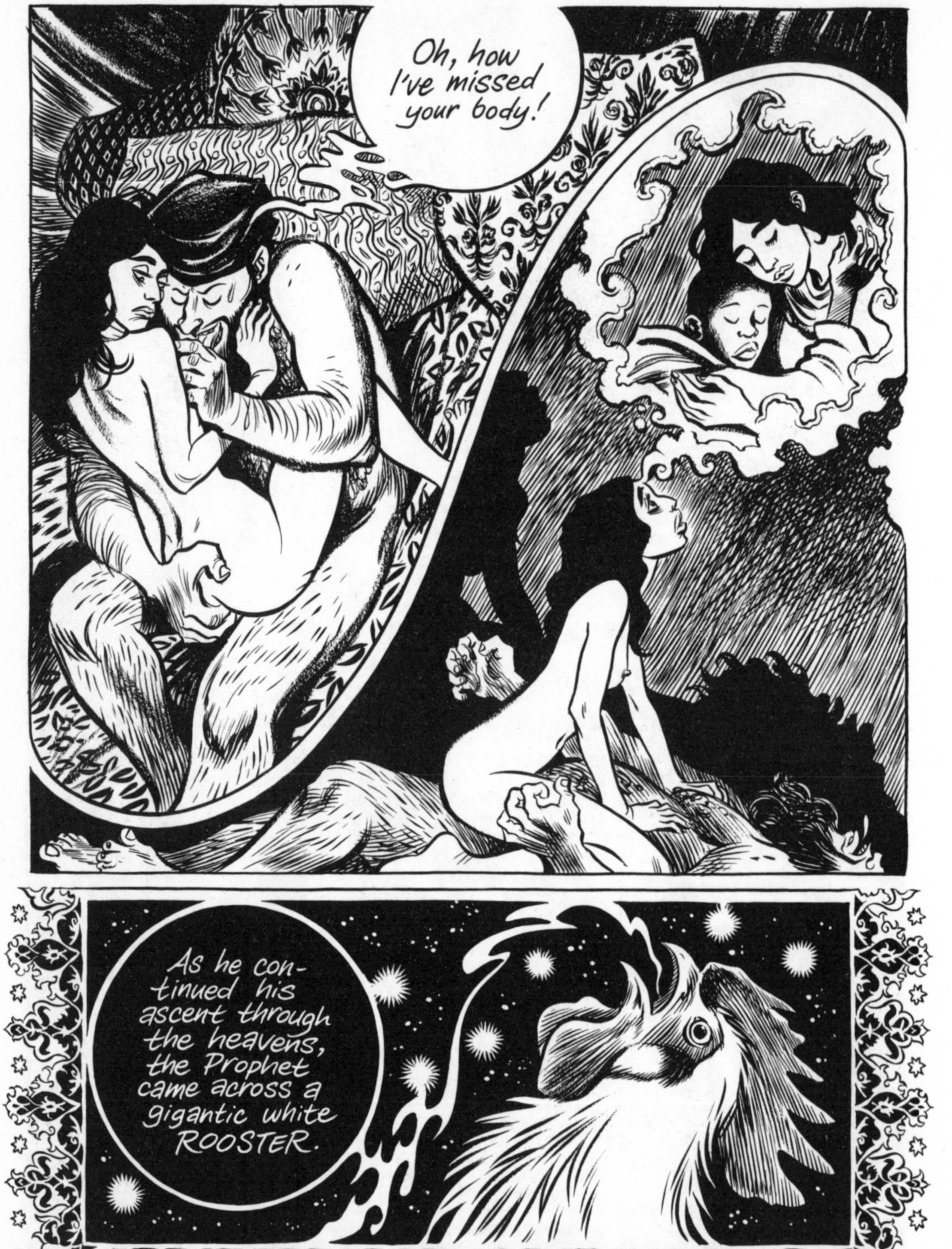
Oh, how I've missed your body!
As he continued his ascent through the heavens, the Prophet came across a gigantic white ROOSTER.

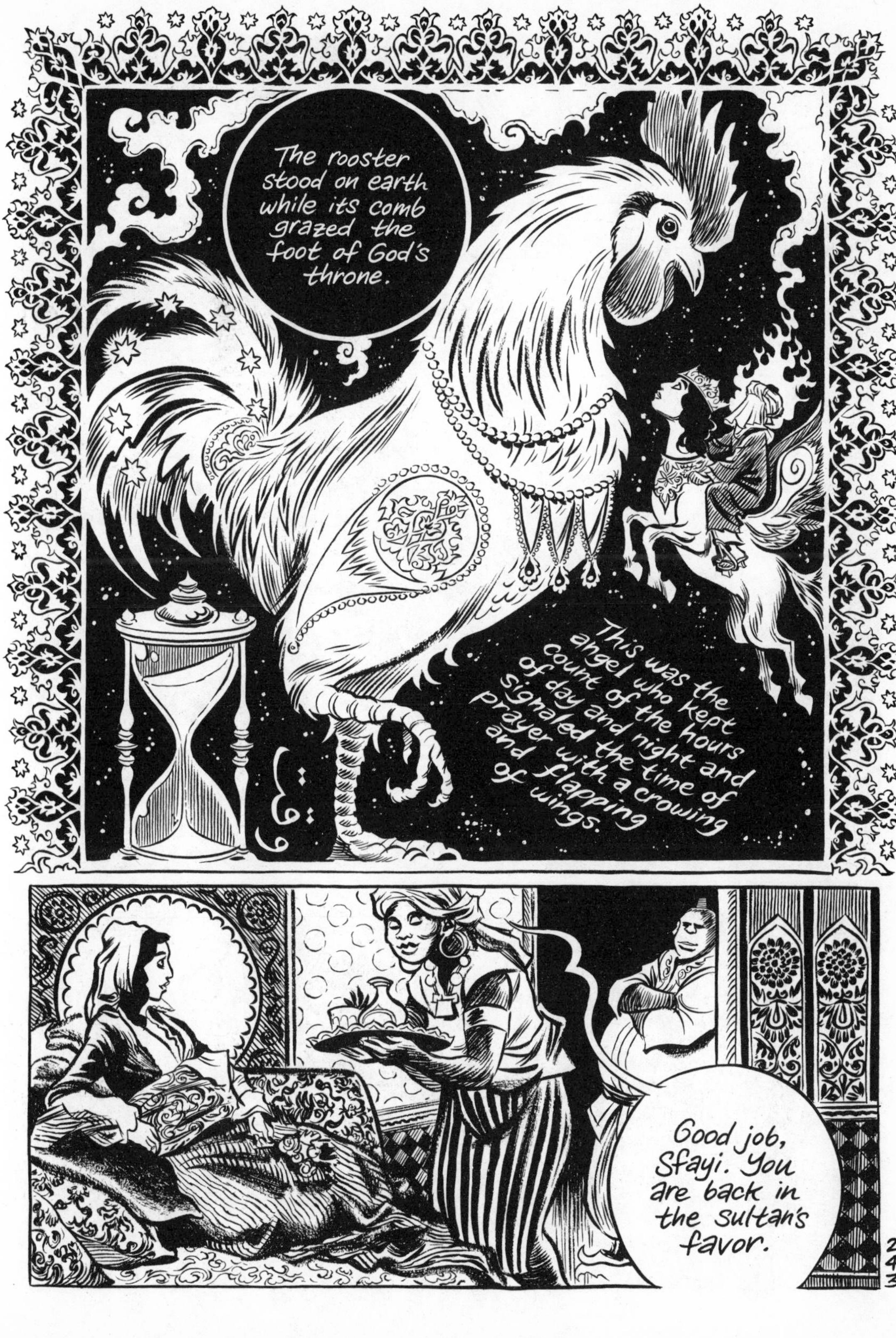
The rooster stood on earth while its comb grazed the foot of God's throne.
This was the angel who kept count of the hours of day and night and signaled the time of prayer with a crowing and flapping of wings.
Good job, Sfayi. You are back in the sultan's favor.

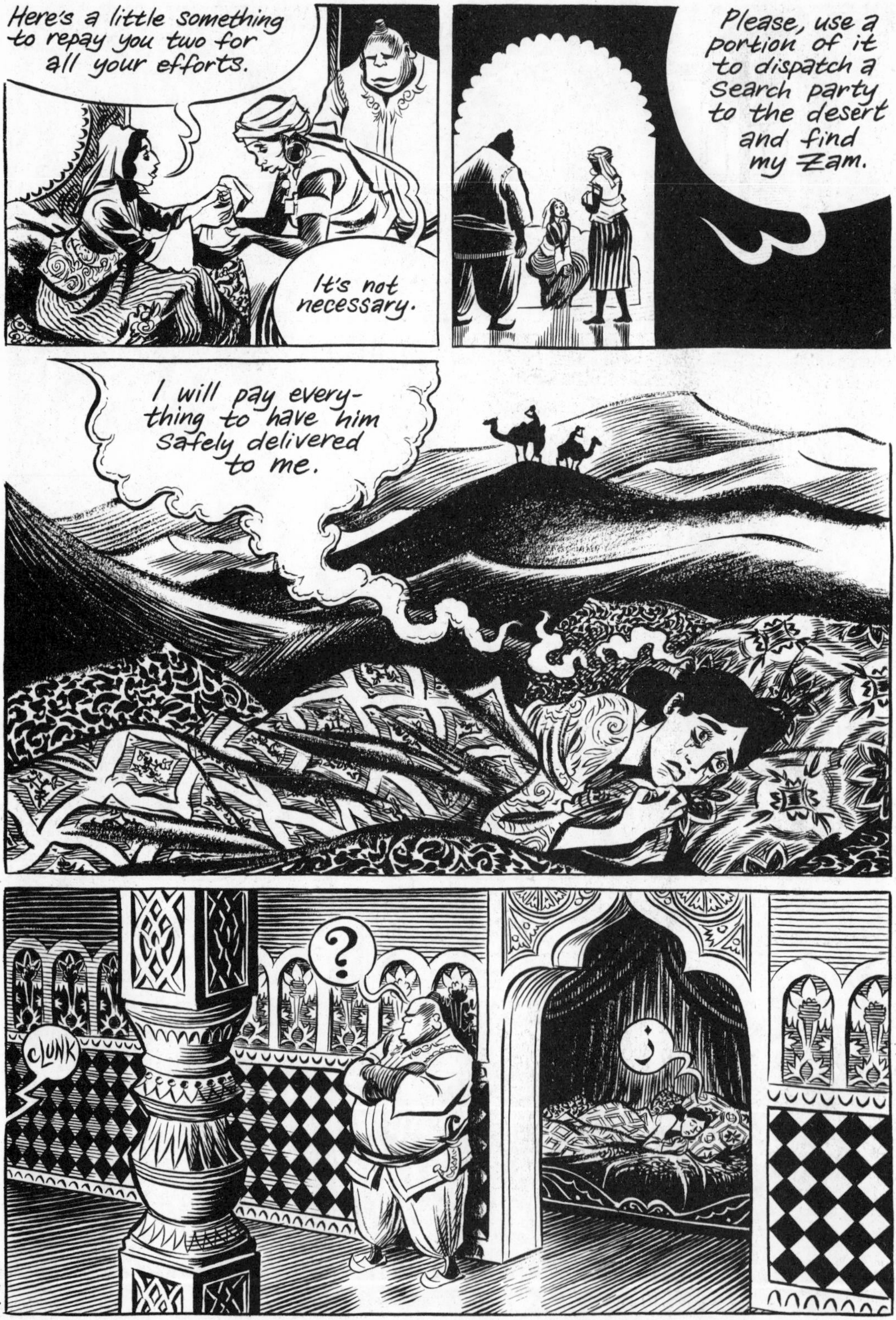
Here's a little something to repay you two for all your efforts.
It's not necessary.
Please, use a portion of it to dispatch a search party to the desert and find my Zam.
I will pay every-thing to have him safely delivered to me.
?
CLUNK

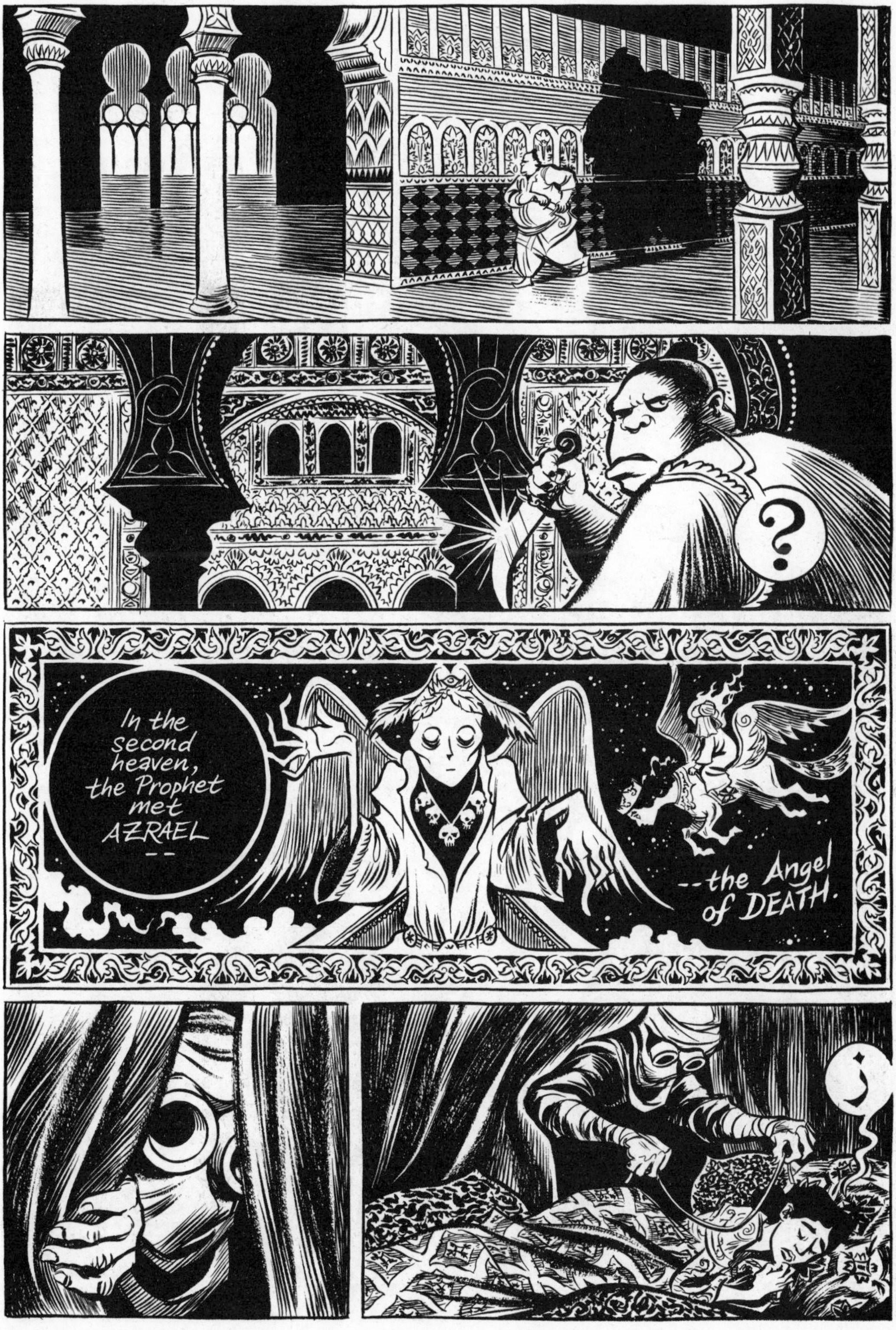
?
In the second heaven, the Prophet met AZRAEL --
-- the Angel of DEATH.

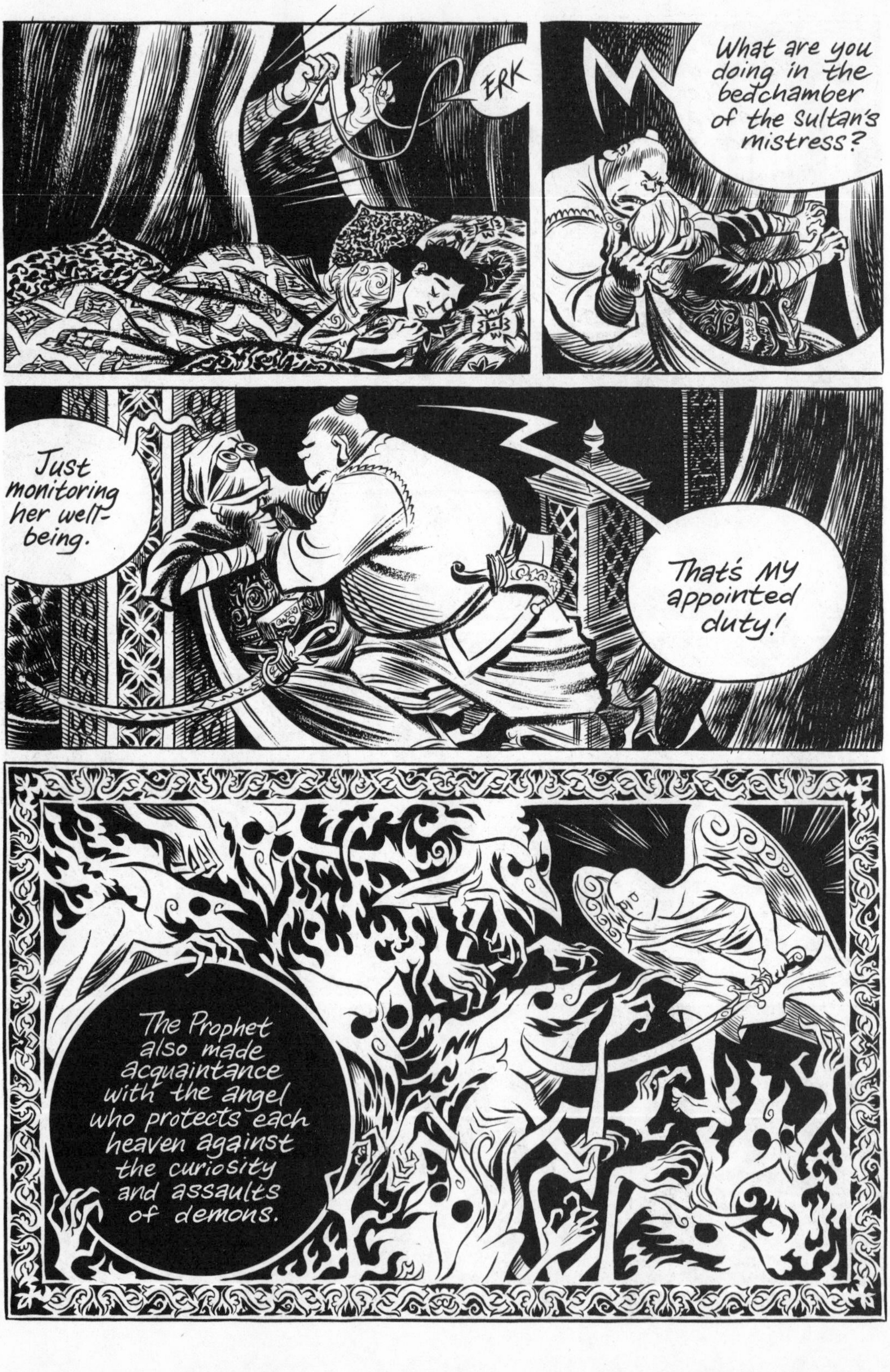
ERK
What are you doing in the bedchamber of the sultan's mistress?
Just monitoring her well-being.
That's MY appointed duty!
The Prophet also made acquaintance with the angel who protects each heaven against the curiosity and assaults of demons.

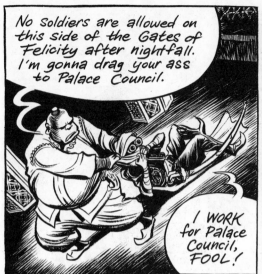

No soldiers are allowed on this side of the Gates of Felicity after nightfall. I'm gonna drag your ass to Palace Council.

I WORK for Palace Council, FOOL!

That WHORE is a threat to the integrity of our harem.

She's the Sultan's CHOSEN. Now get out of my sight or I'll rain a SEA of FIRE on you.

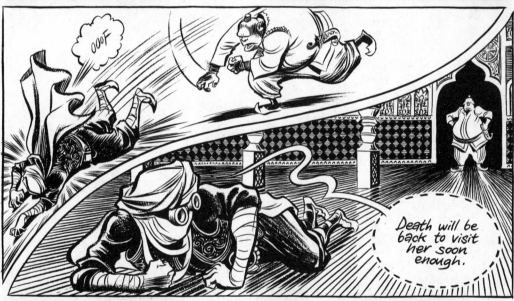

OOOF

Death will be back to visit her soon enough.

...sleeping peacefully...

70 MONTHS...

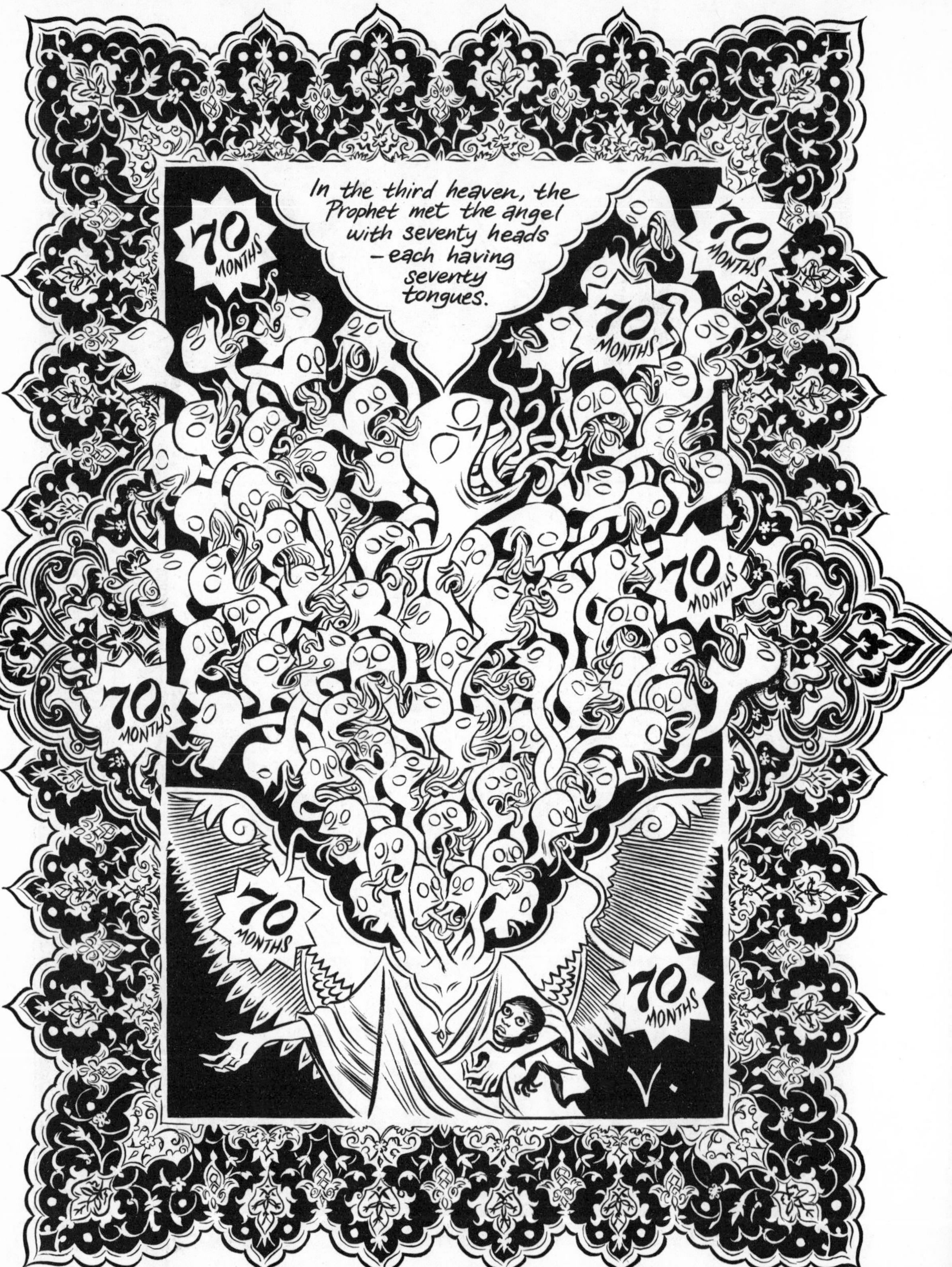
In the third heaven, the Prophet met the angel with seventy heads —each having seventy tongues.
70 MONTHS
70 MONTHS
70 MONTHS
70 MONTHS
70 MONTHS
70 MONTHS
70 MONTHS

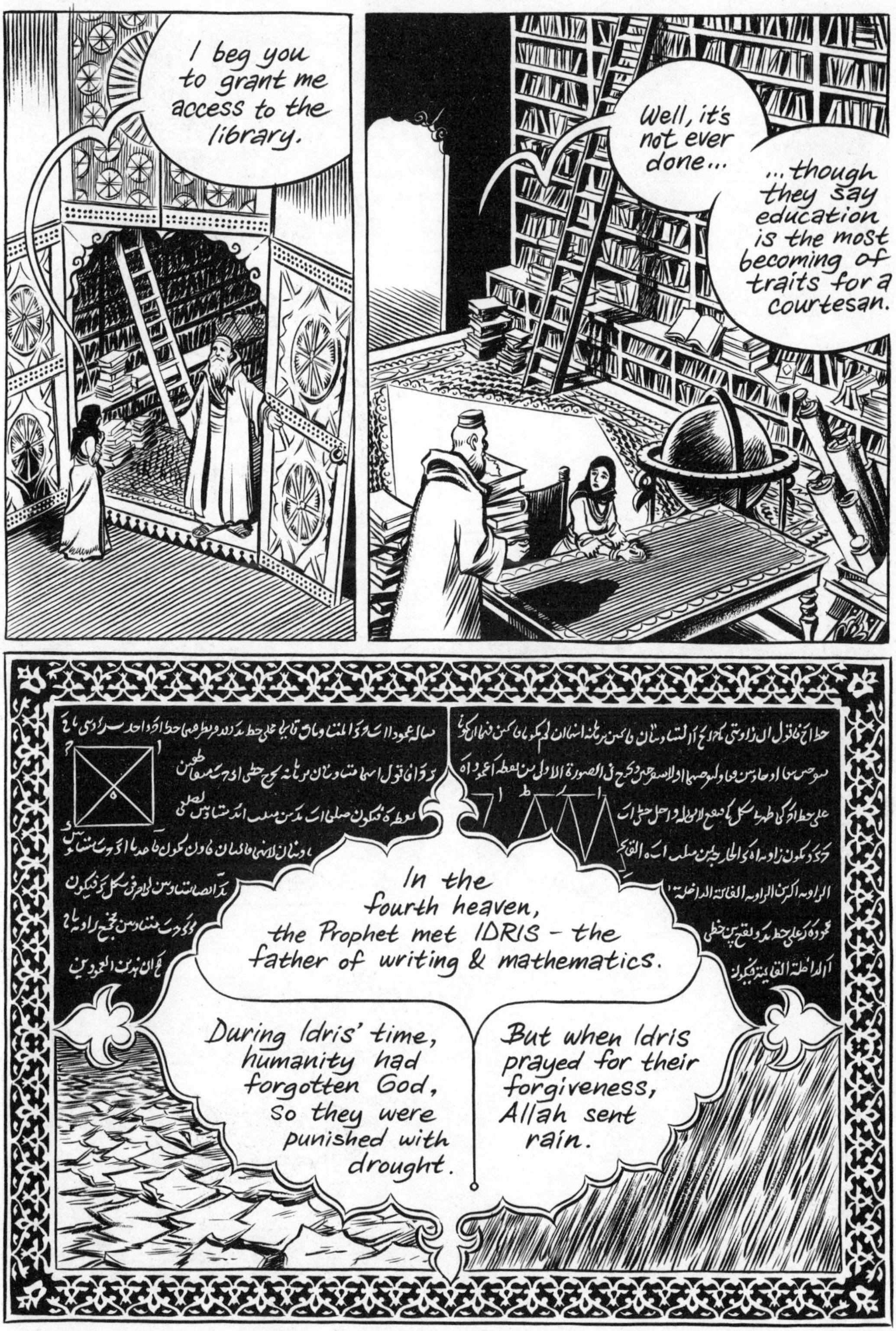
I beg you to grant me access to the library.
Well, it's not ever done...
...though they say education is the most becoming of traits for a courtesan.
In the fourth heaven, the Prophet met IDRIS - the father of writing & mathematics.
During Idris' time, humanity had forgotten God, so they were punished with drought.
But when Idris prayed for their forgiveness, Allah sent rain.

ARISTOTLE
~ the father of biology ~

PROPOSED THAT ALL MATTER IS COMPOSED OF FOUR ELEMENTS:

 EARTH

 WATER

AIR

 FIRE

THESE ELEMENTS ARE DIFFERENTIATED BY FOUR QUALITIES:

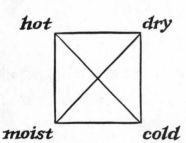

hot   *dry*

moist   *cold*

AND EACH ELEMENT IS BORN OF TWO QUALITIES IN OPPOSITION:

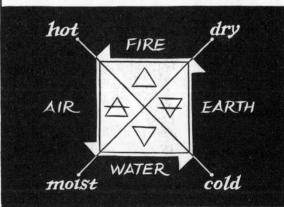

hot   FIRE   *dry*

AIR   EARTH

WATER

moist   *cold*

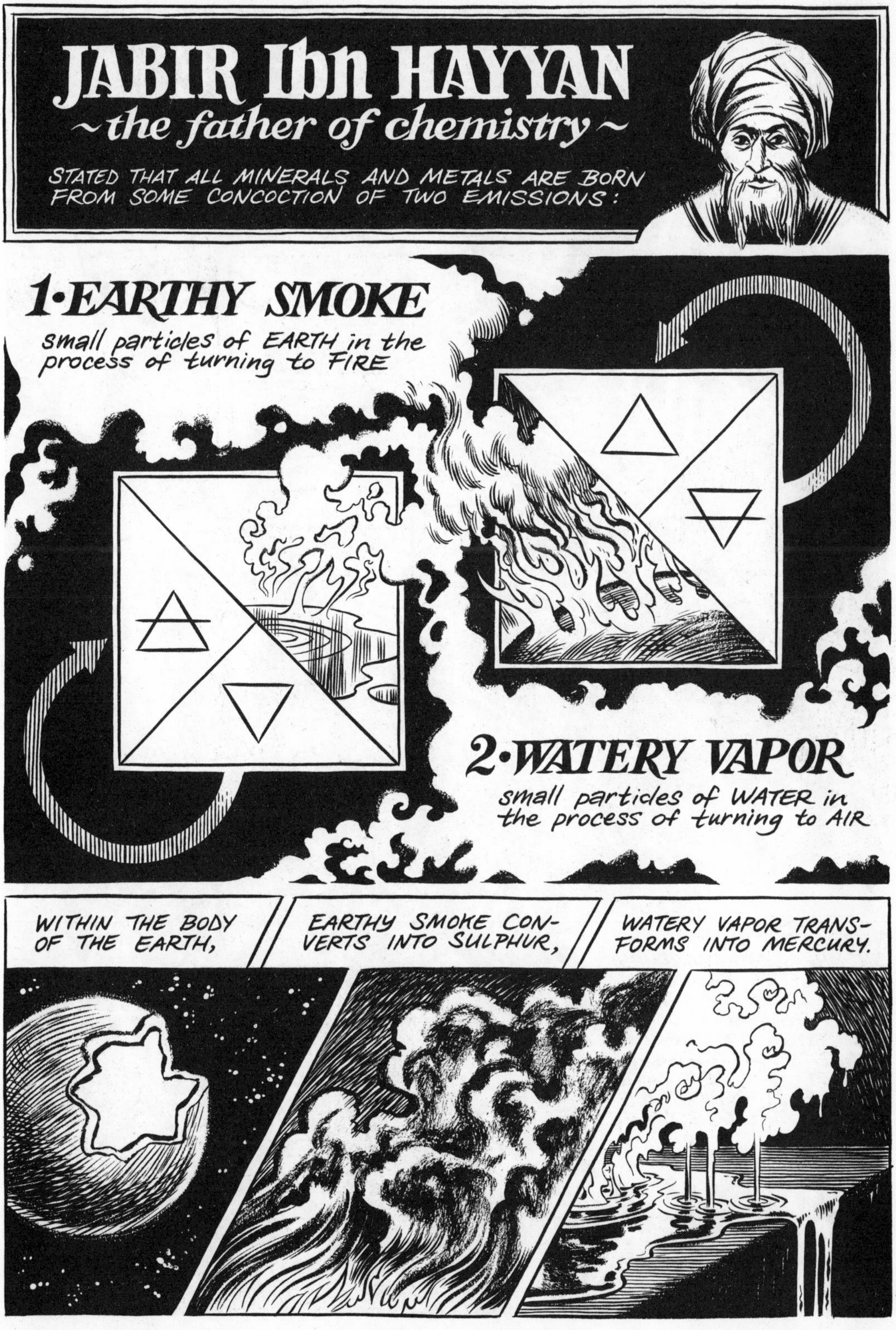
JABIR Ibn HAYYAN
~the father of chemistry~
STATED THAT ALL MINERALS AND METALS ARE BORN FROM SOME CONCOCTION OF TWO EMISSIONS:
1·EARTHY SMOKE
small particles of EARTH in the process of turning to FIRE
2·WATERY VAPOR
small particles of WATER in the process of turning to AIR
WITHIN THE BODY OF THE EARTH,
EARTHY SMOKE CONVERTS INTO SULPHUR,
WATERY VAPOR TRANSFORMS INTO MERCURY.

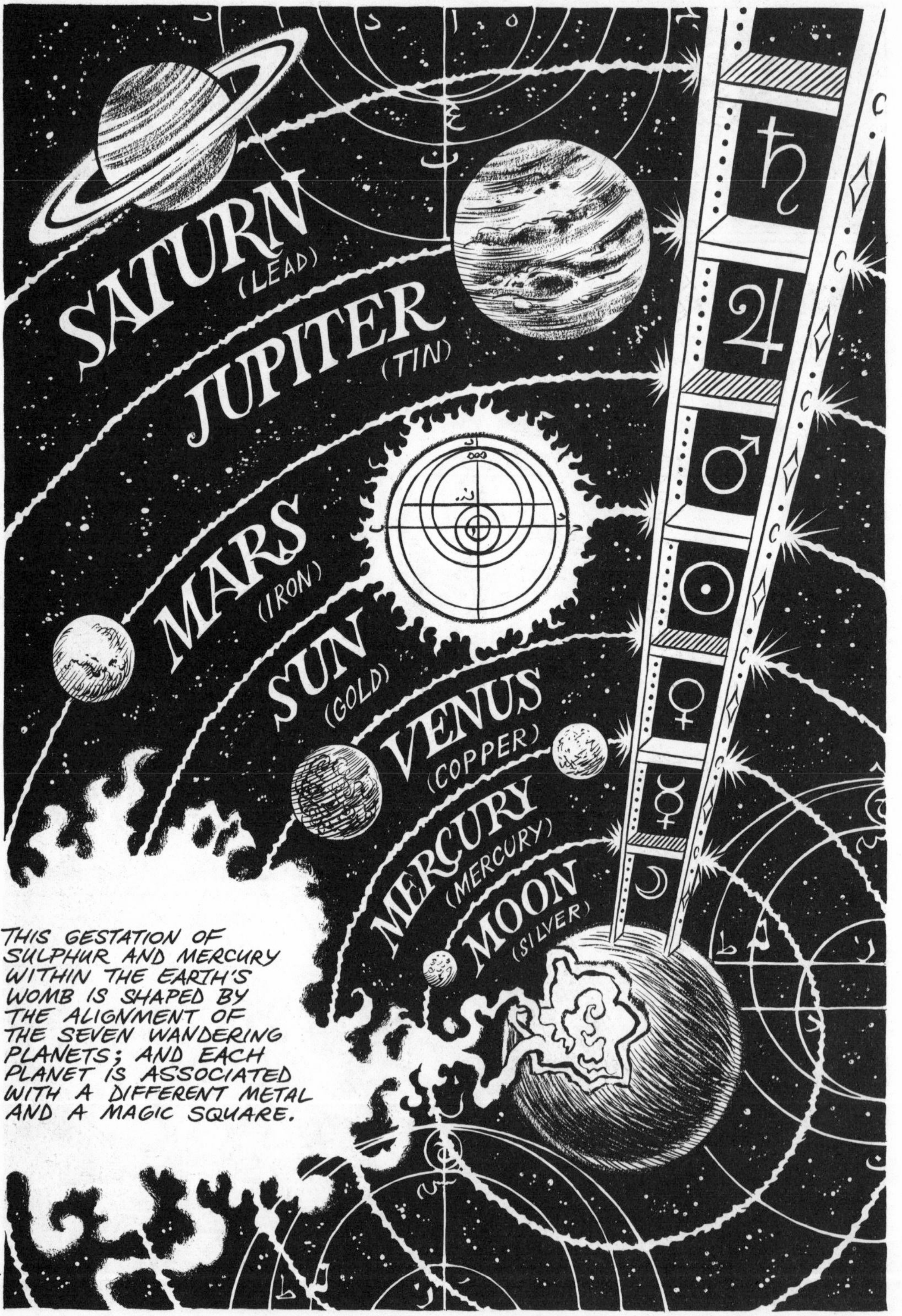
SATURN (LEAD)
JUPITER (TIN)
MARS (IRON)
SUN (GOLD)
VENUS (COPPER)
MERCURY (MERCURY)
MOON (SILVER)
THIS GESTATION OF SULPHUR AND MERCURY WITHIN THE EARTH'S WOMB IS SHAPED BY THE ALIGNMENT OF THE SEVEN WANDERING PLANETS; AND EACH PLANET IS ASSOCIATED WITH A DIFFERENT METAL AND A MAGIC SQUARE.

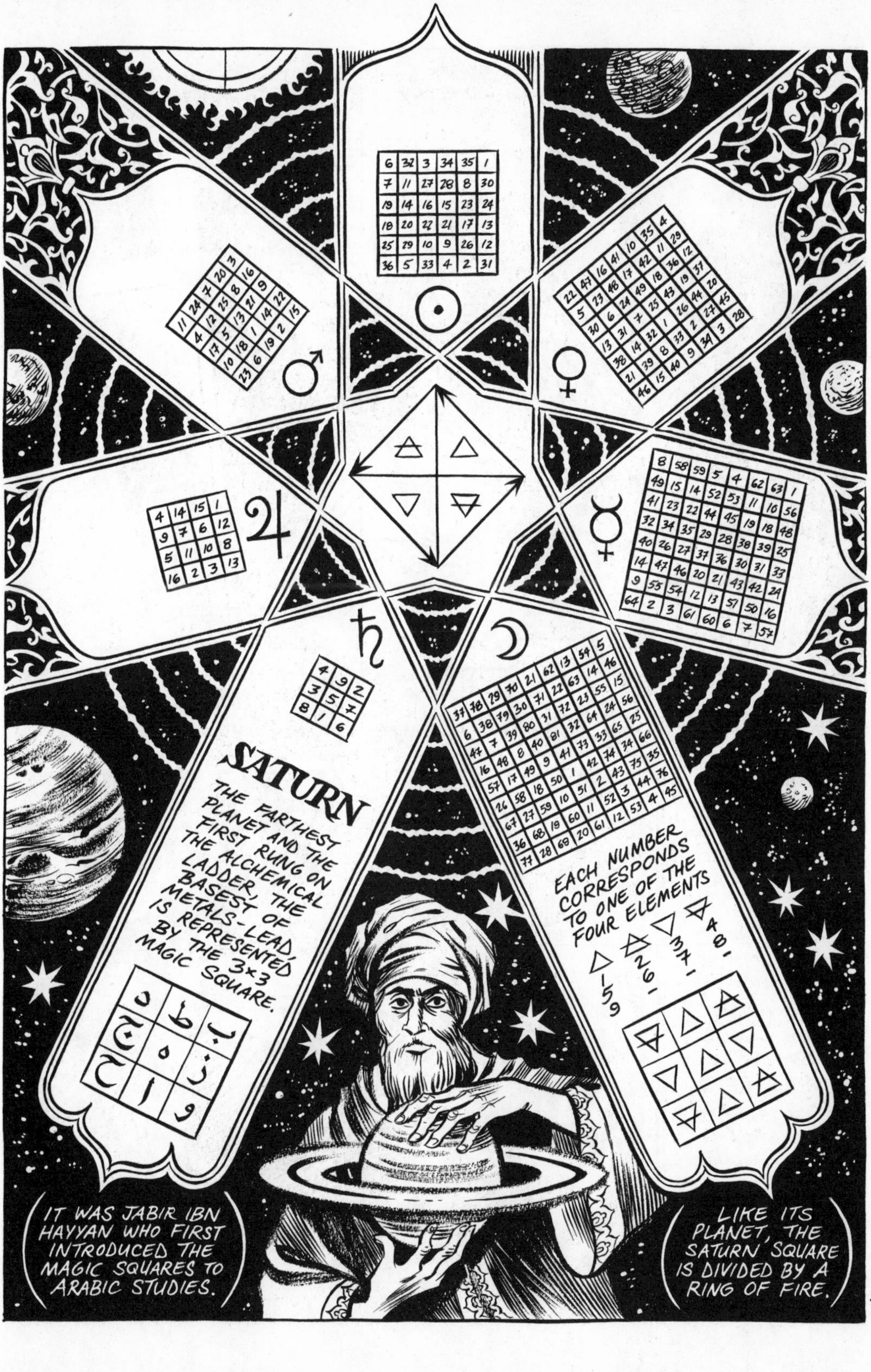

SATURN
THE FARTHEST PLANET AND THE FIRST RUNG ON THE ALCHEMICAL LADDER, THE BASEST OF METALS-LEAD, IS REPRESENTED BY THE 3×3 MAGIC SQUARE.
EACH NUMBER CORRESPONDS TO ONE OF THE FOUR ELEMENTS
IT WAS JABIR IBN HAYYAN WHO FIRST INTRODUCED THE MAGIC SQUARES TO ARABIC STUDIES.
LIKE ITS PLANET, THE SATURN SQUARE IS DIVIDED BY A RING OF FIRE.

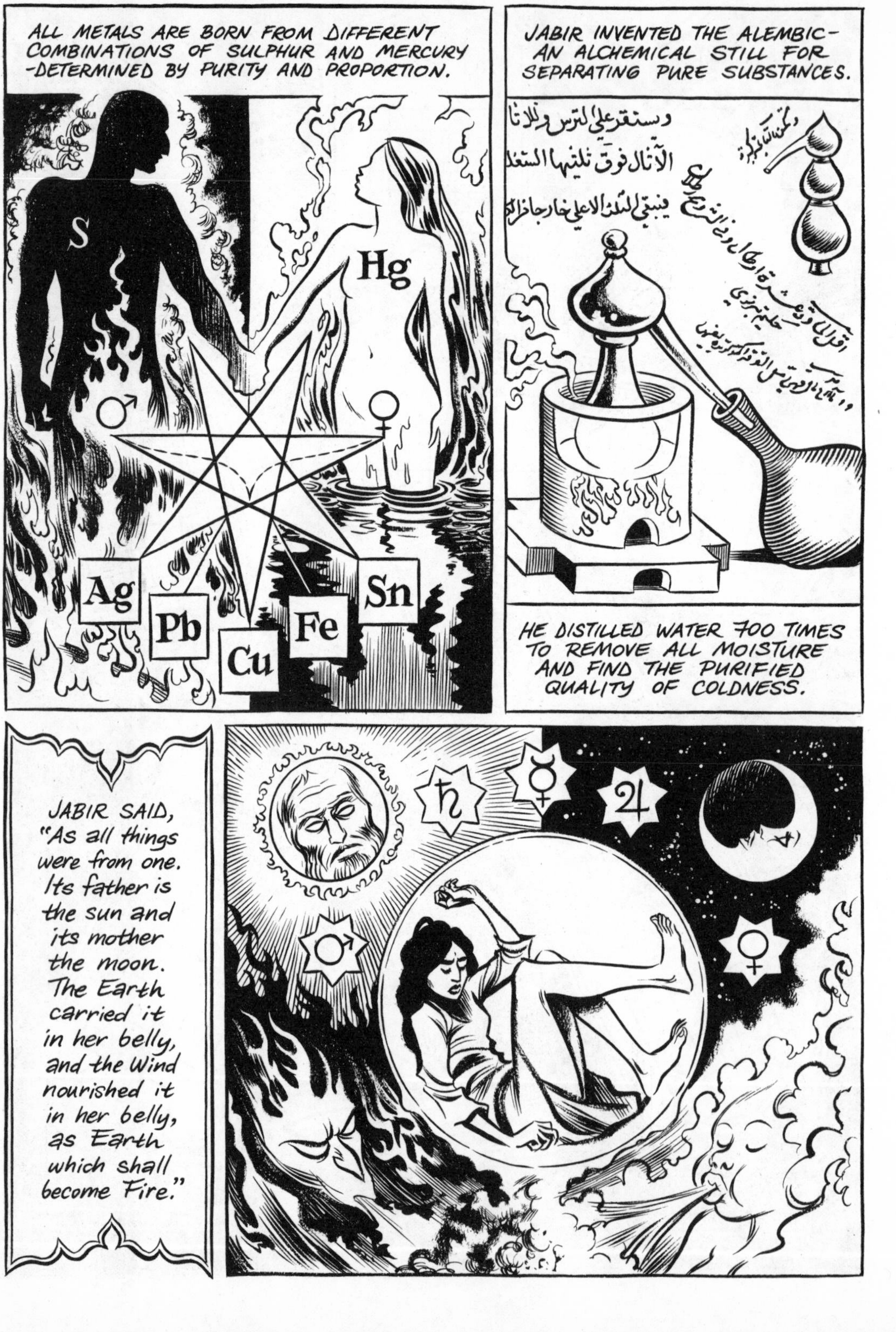
ALL METALS ARE BORN FROM DIFFERENT COMBINATIONS OF SULPHUR AND MERCURY -DETERMINED BY PURITY AND PROPORTION.
S
Hg
Ag
Pb
Cu
Fe
Sn
JABIR INVENTED THE ALEMBIC- AN ALCHEMICAL STILL FOR SEPARATING PURE SUBSTANCES.
HE DISTILLED WATER 700 TIMES TO REMOVE ALL MOISTURE AND FIND THE PURIFIED QUALITY OF COLDNESS.
JABIR SAID, "As all things were from one. Its father is the sun and its mother the moon. The Earth carried it in her belly, and the Wind nourished it in her belly, as Earth which shall become Fire."

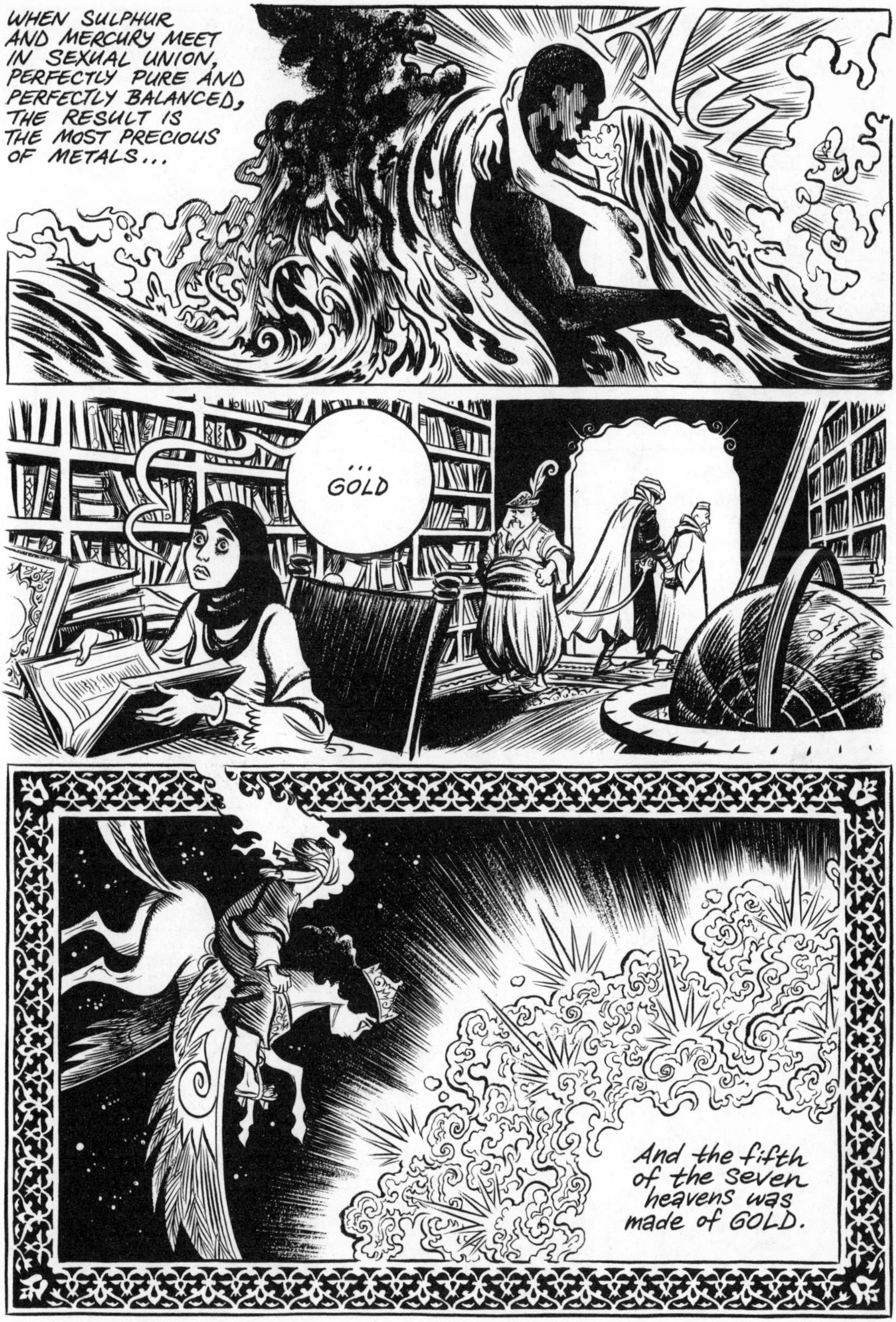
WHEN SULPHUR AND MERCURY MEET IN SEXUAL UNION, PERFECTLY PURE AND PERFECTLY BALANCED, THE RESULT IS THE MOST PRECIOUS OF METALS...
... GOLD
And the fifth of the seven heavens was made of GOLD.

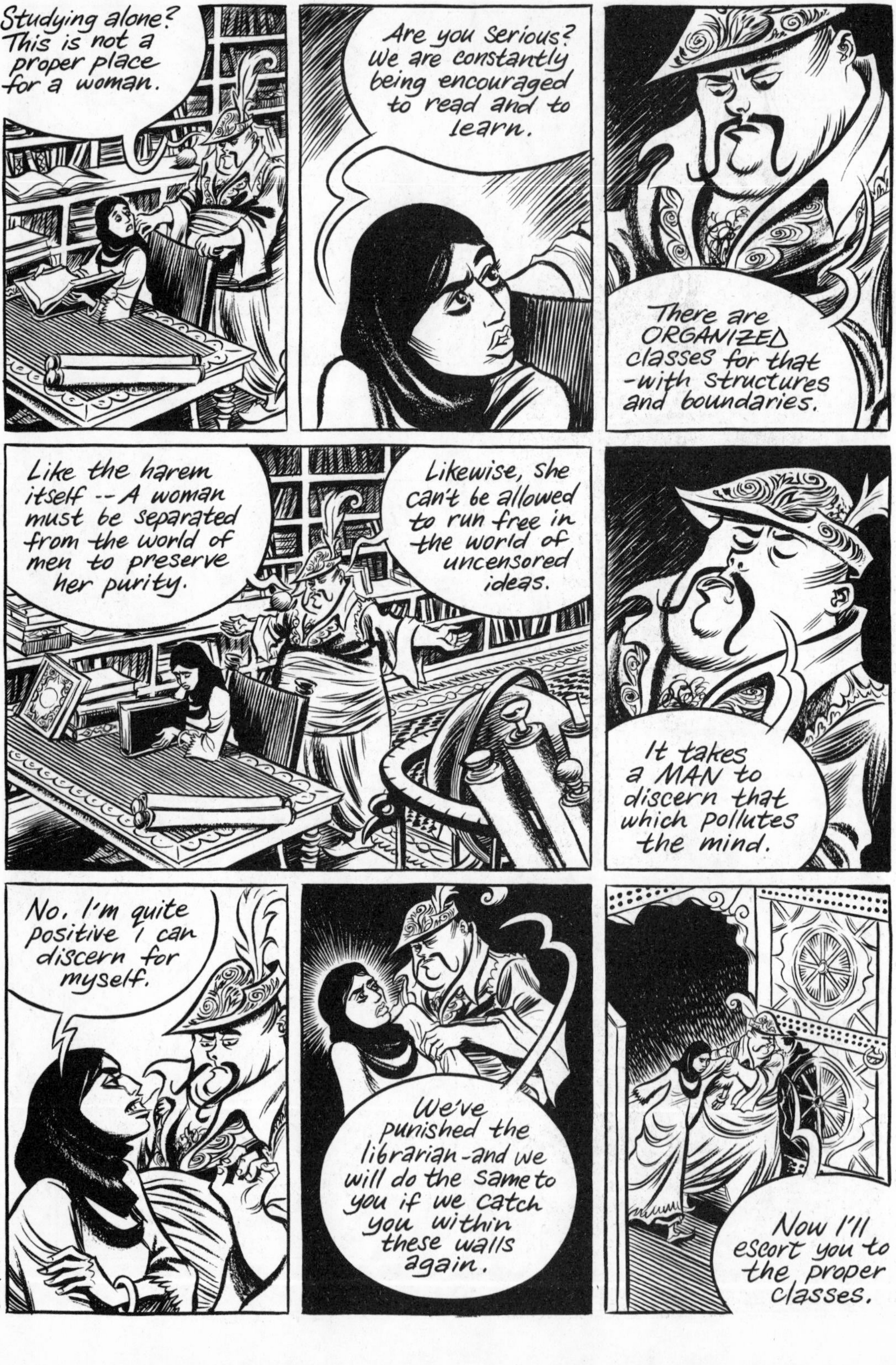

Studying alone? This is not a proper place for a woman.
Are you serious? We are constantly being encouraged to read and to learn.
There are ORGANIZED classes for that -with structures and boundaries.
Like the harem itself --A woman must be separated from the world of men to preserve her purity.
Likewise, she can't be allowed to run free in the world of uncensored ideas.
It takes a MAN to discern that which pollutes the mind.
No. I'm quite positive I can discern for myself.
We've punished the librarian-and we will do the same to you if we catch you within these walls again.
Now I'll escort you to the proper classes.

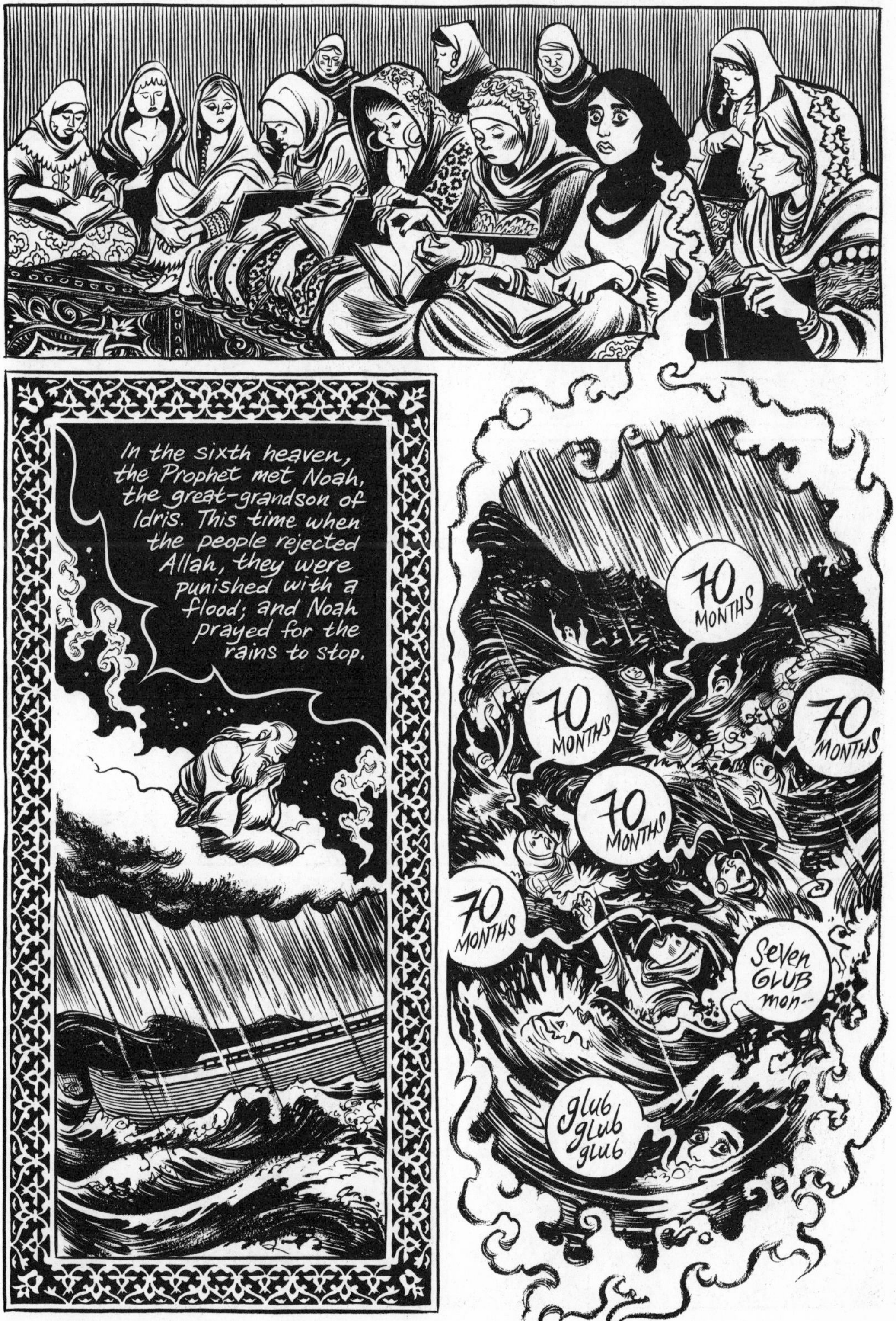
In the sixth heaven, the Prophet met Noah, the great-grandson of Idris. This time when the people rejected Allah, they were punished with a flood; and Noah prayed for the rains to stop.
70 MONTHS
70 MONTHS
70 MONTHS
70 MONTHS
70 MONTHS
Seven GLUB mon--
glub glub glub

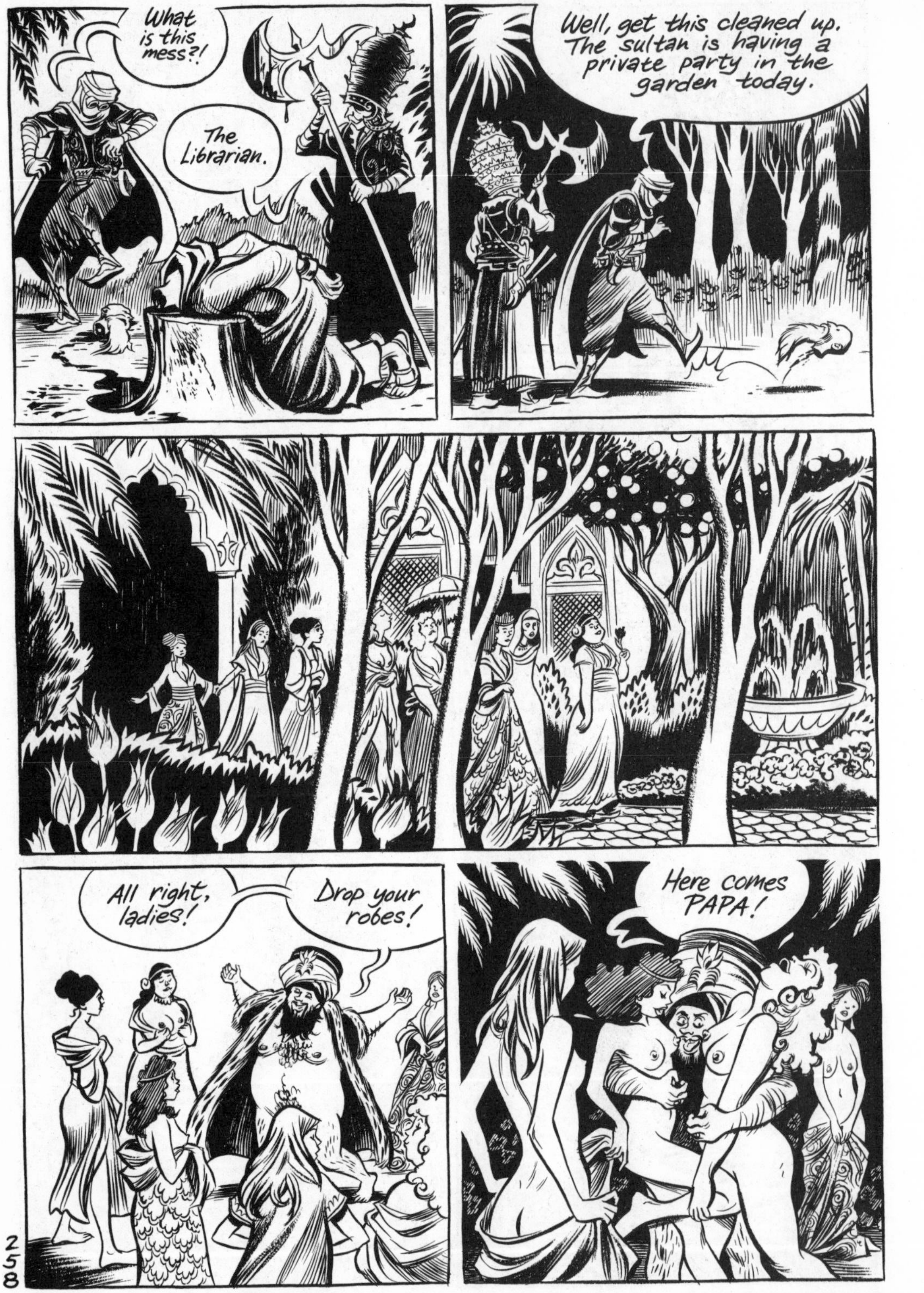
What is this mess?!
The Librarian.
Well, get this cleaned up. The sultan is having a private party in the garden today.
All right, ladies!
Drop your robes!
Here comes PAPA!

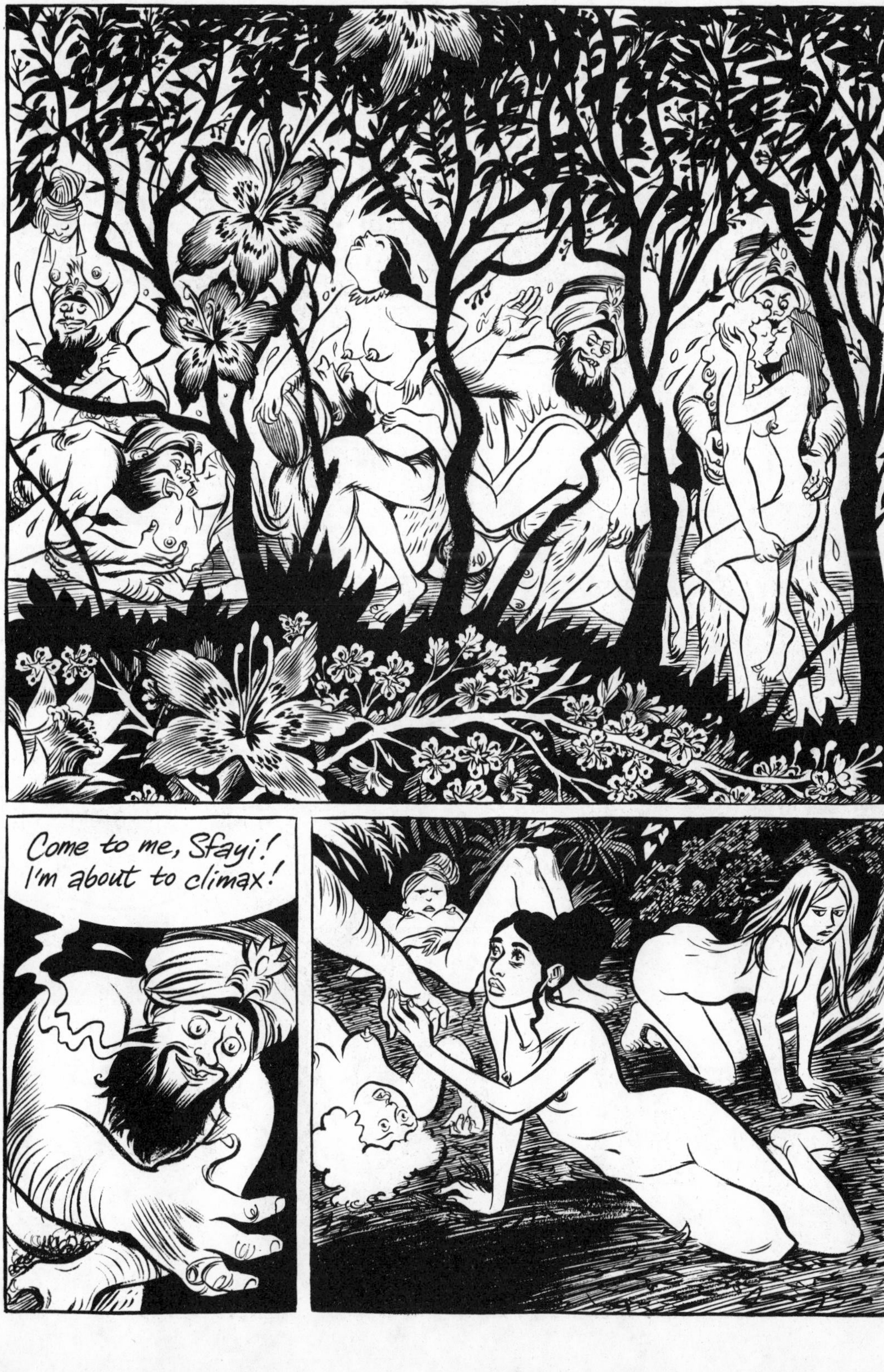
Come to me, Sfayi! I'm about to climax!

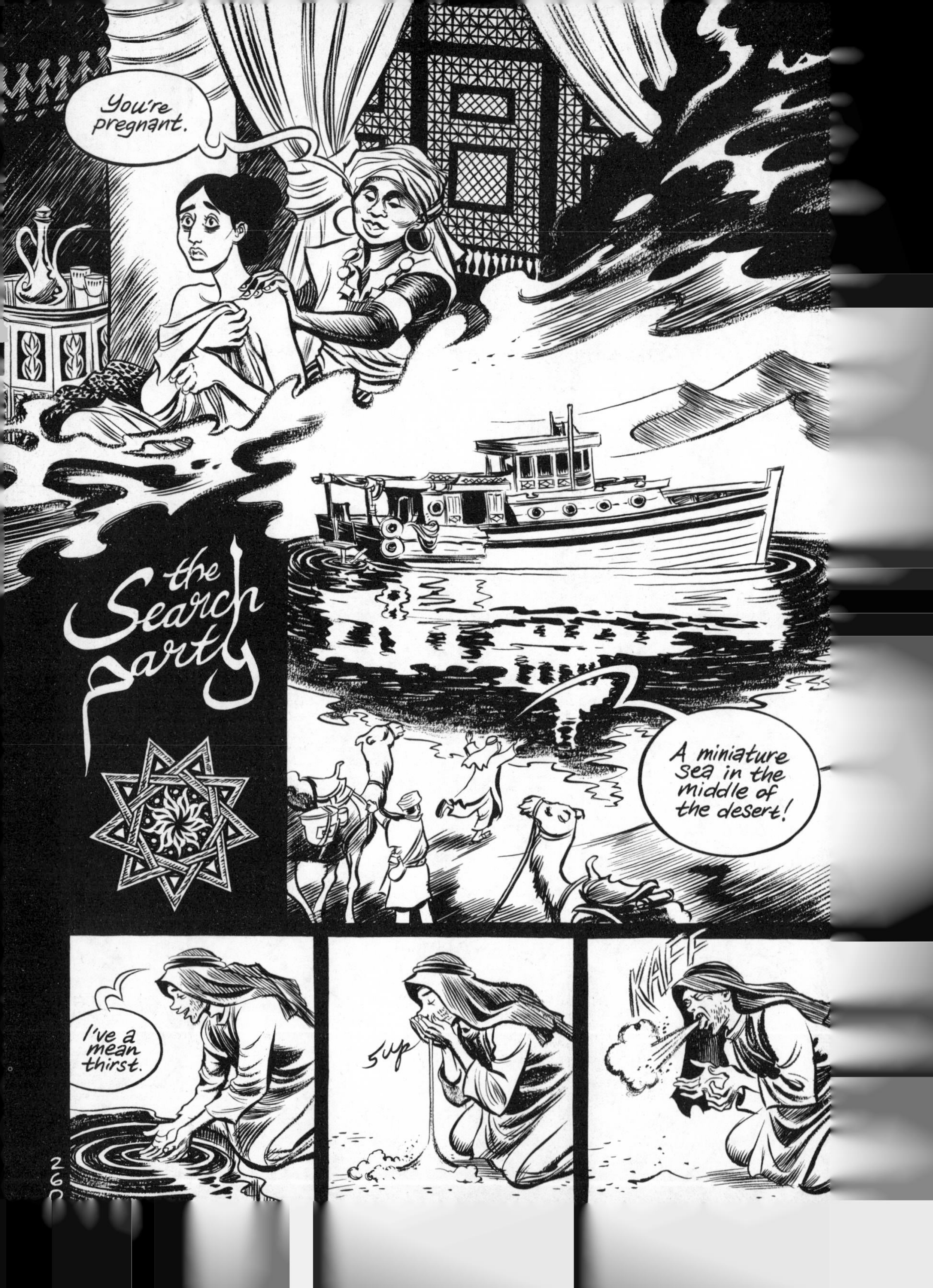
You're pregnant.
the Search party
A miniature sea in the middle of the desert!
I've a mean thirst.
SUP
KAFF

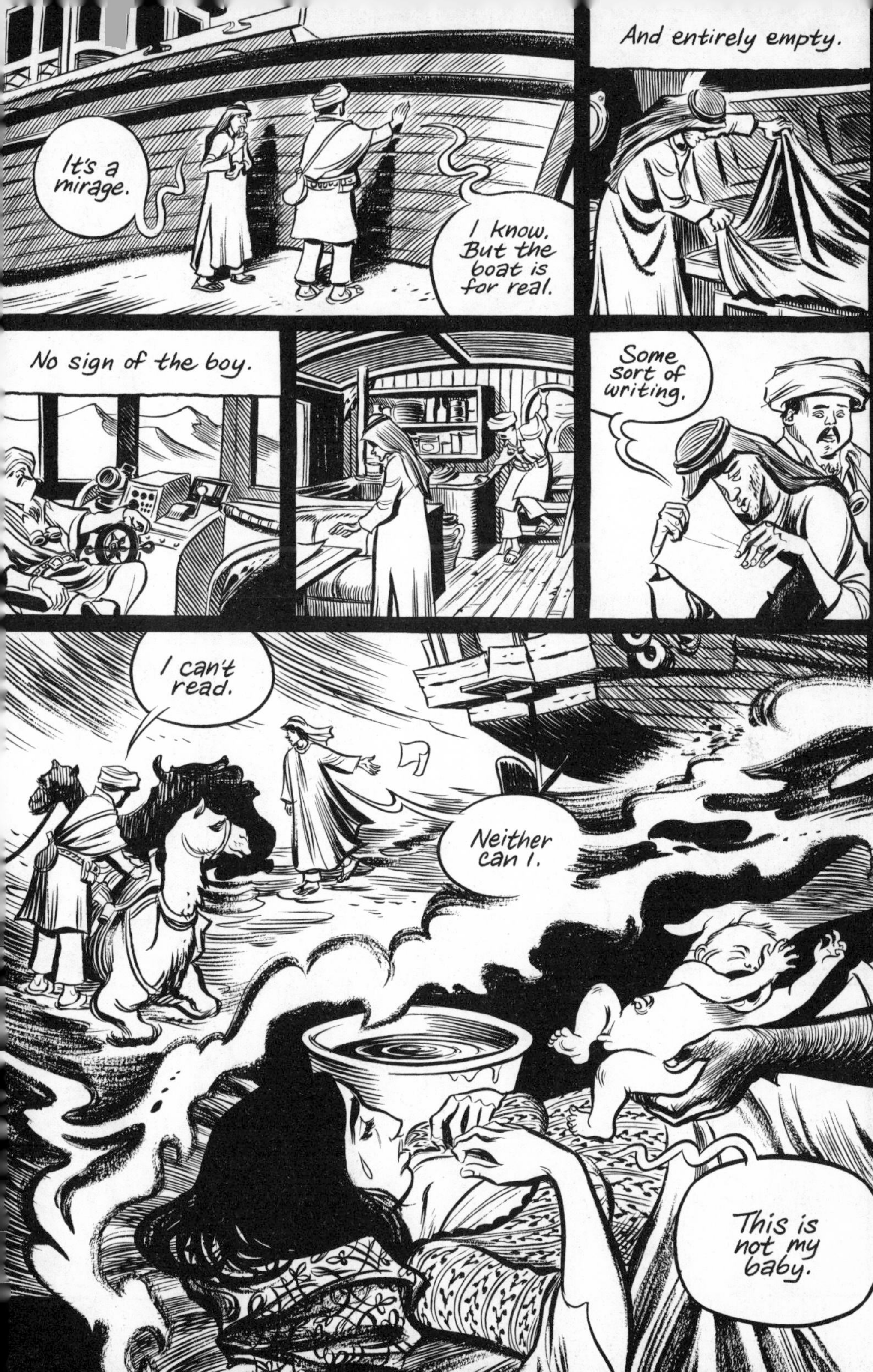
It's a mirage.
I know. But the boat is for real.
And entirely empty.
No sign of the boy.
Some sort of writing.
I can't read.
Neither can I.
This is not my baby.

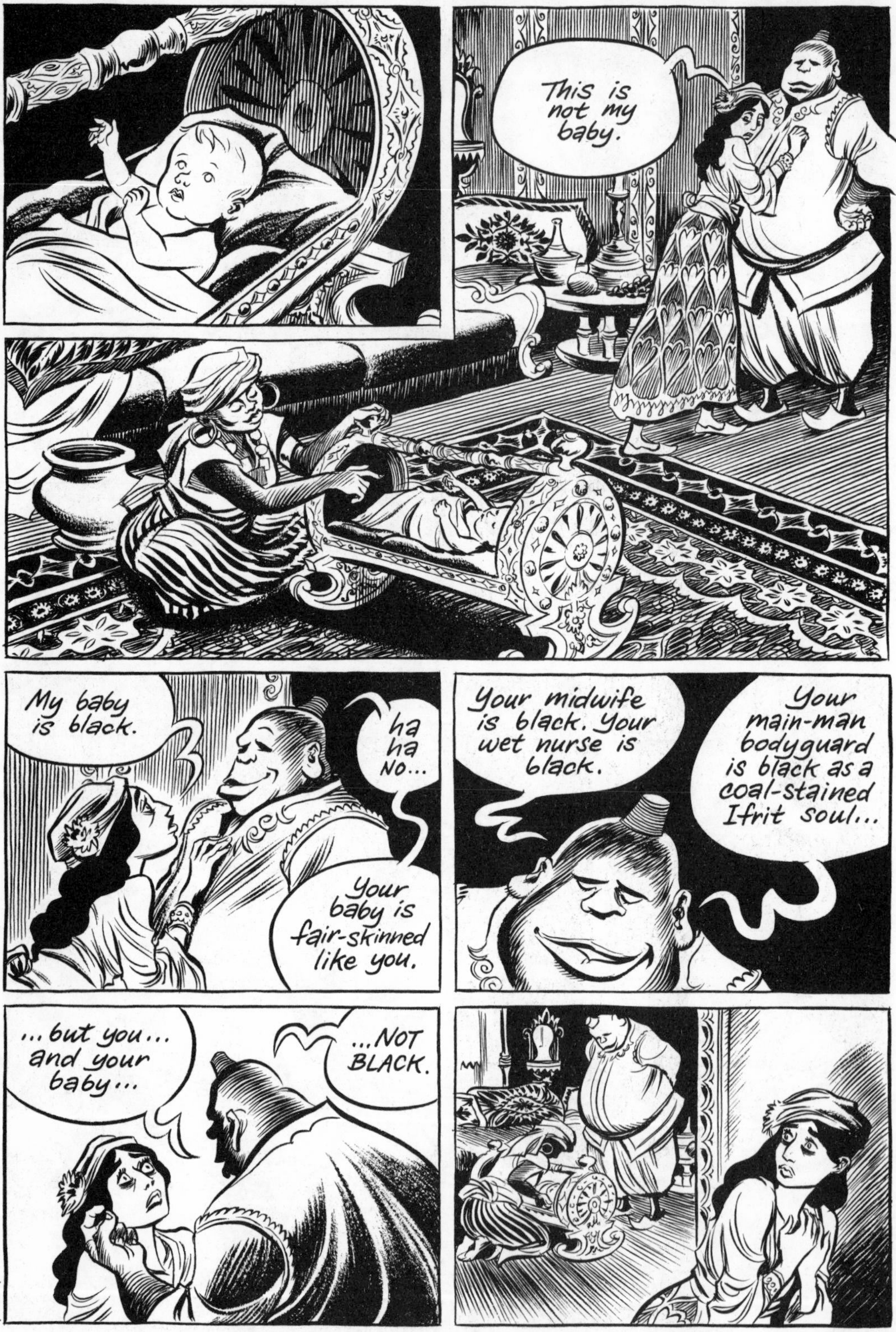
This is not my baby.
My baby is black.
ha ha No...
Your baby is fair-skinned like you.
Your midwife is black. Your wet nurse is black.
Your main-man bodyguard is black as a coal-stained Ifrit soul...
...but you... and your baby...
...NOT BLACK.

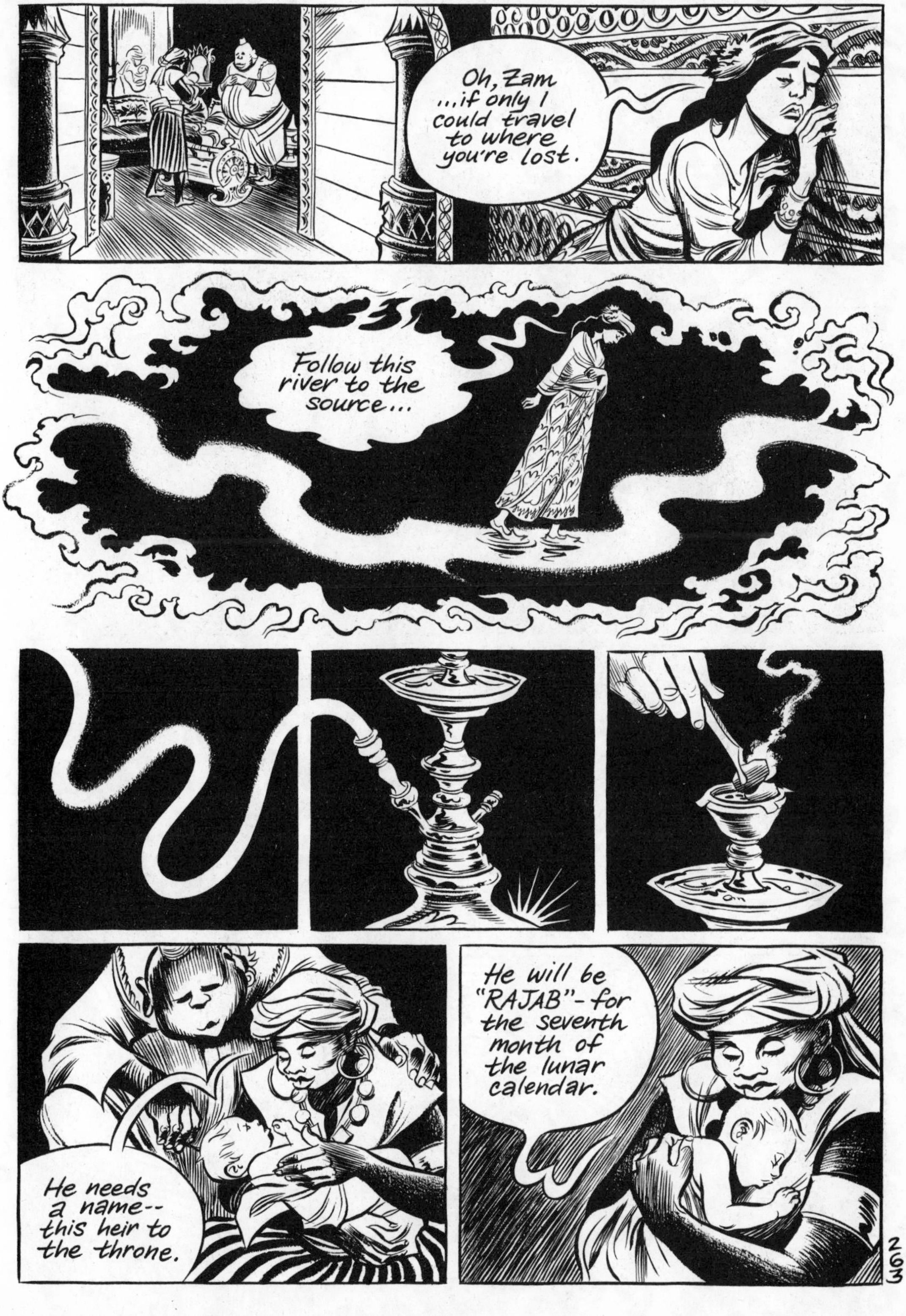
Oh, Zam ...if only I could travel to where you're lost.
Follow this river to the source...
He needs a name-- this heir to the throne.
He will be "RAJAB"- for the seventh month of the lunar calendar.

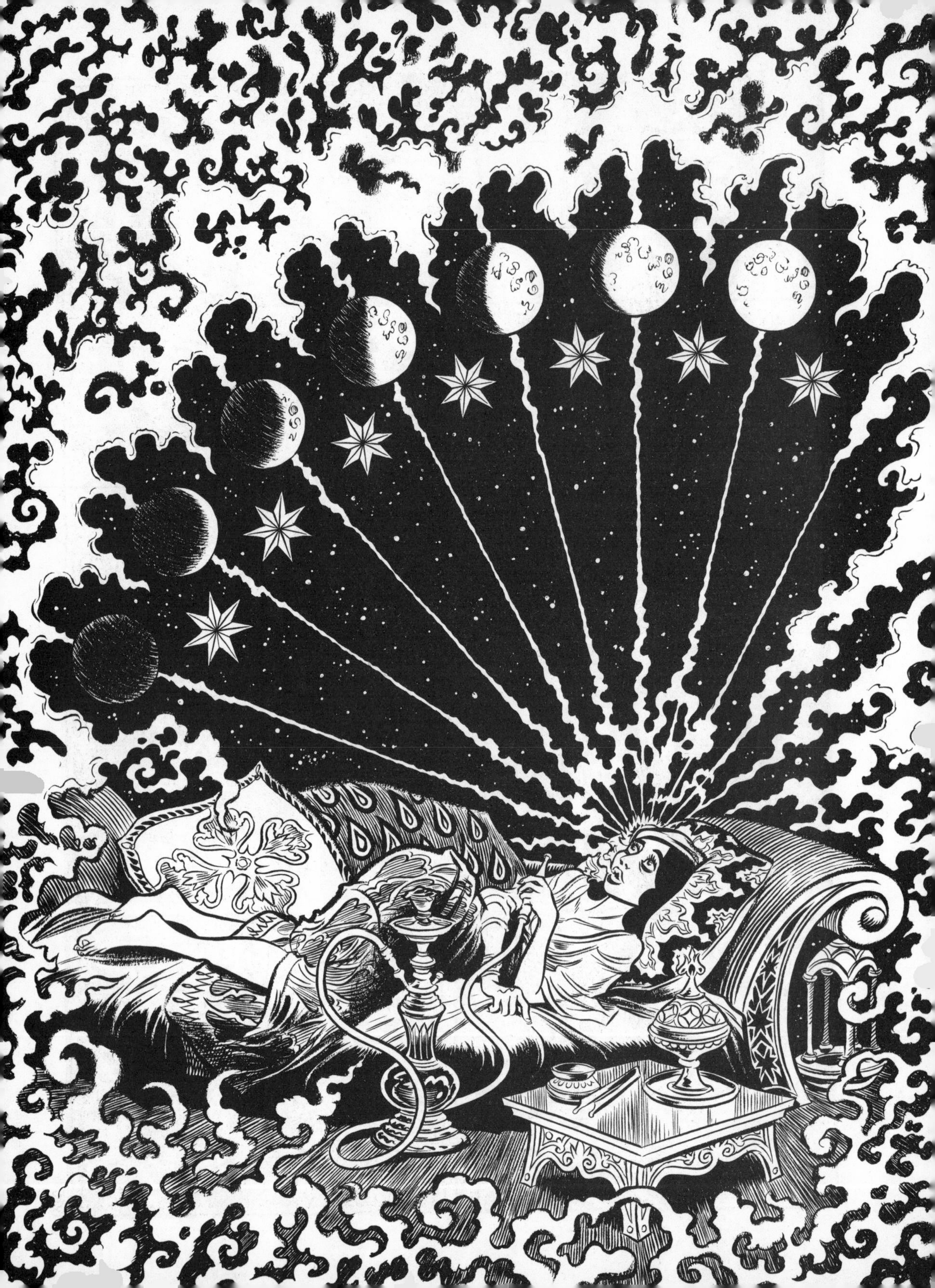

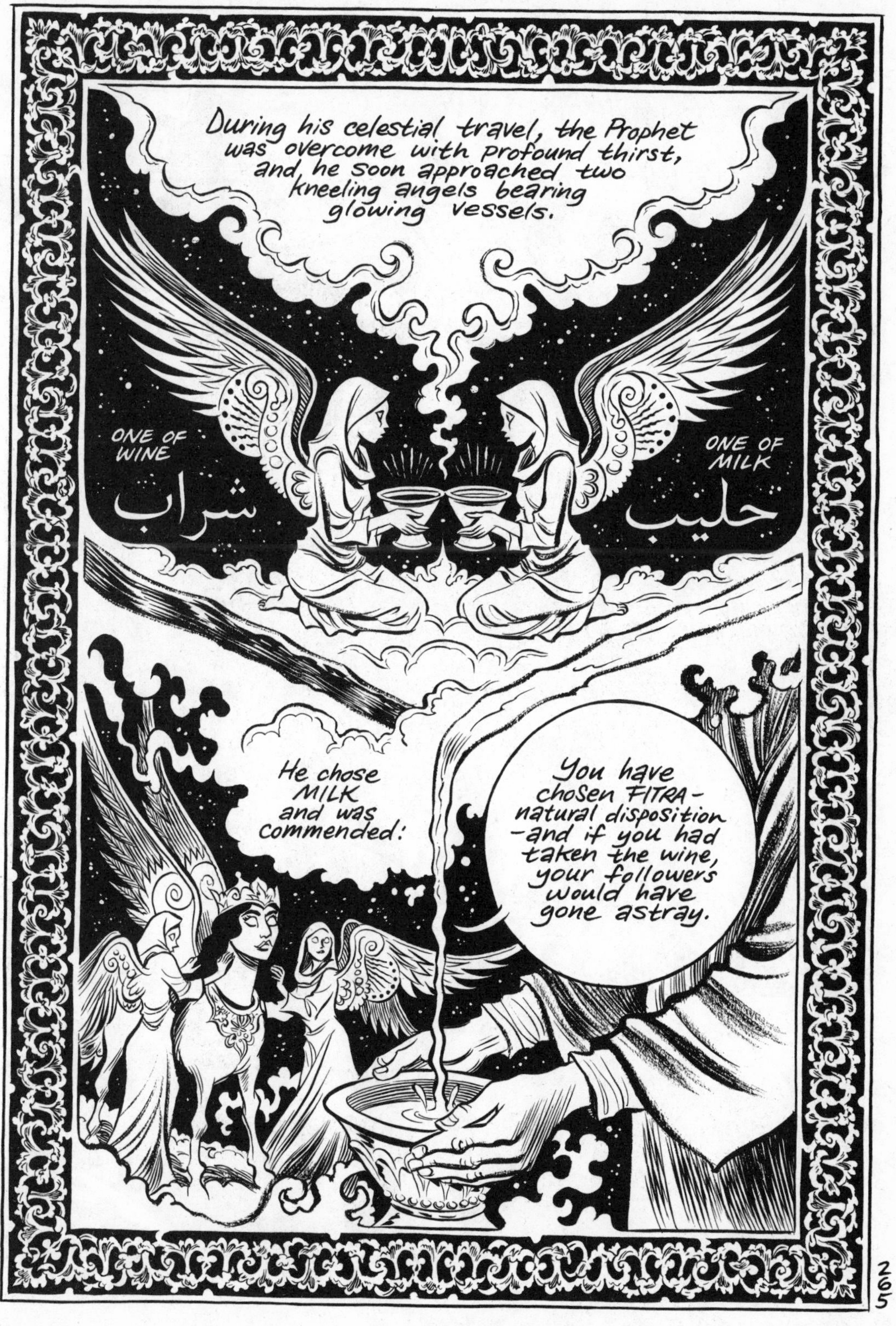

During his celestial travel, the Prophet was overcome with profound thirst, and he soon approached two kneeling angels bearing glowing vessels.
ONE OF WINE
شراب
ONE OF MILK
حليب
He chose MILK and was commended:
You have chosen FITRA - natural disposition - and if you had taken the wine, your followers would have gone astray.

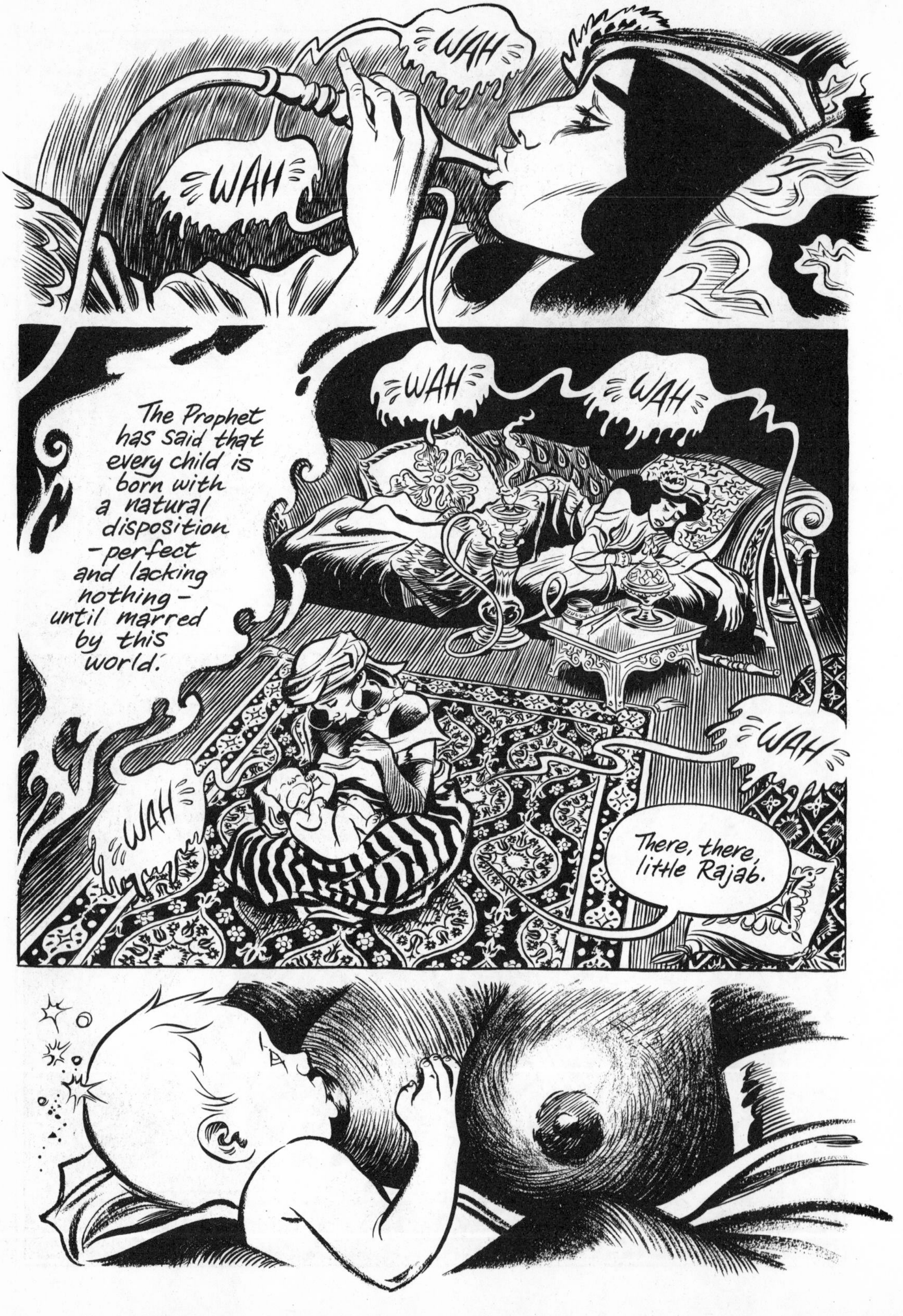
WAH
WAH
The Prophet has said that every child is born with a natural disposition - perfect and lacking nothing - until marred by this world.
WAH
WAH
WAH
WAH
There, there, little Rajab.

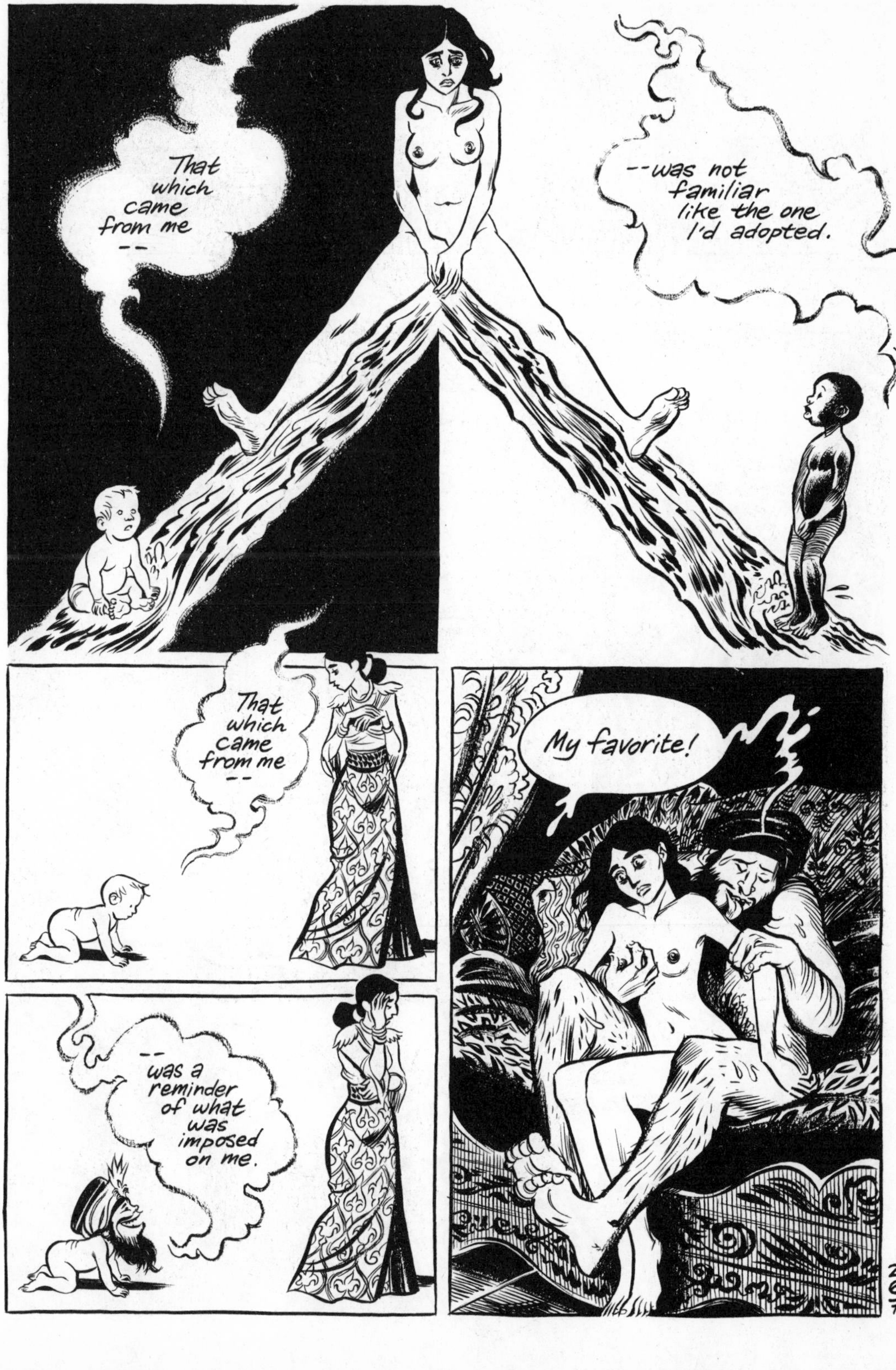
That which came from me --
--was not familiar like the one I'd adopted.
That which came from me --
-- was a reminder of what was imposed on me.
My favorite!

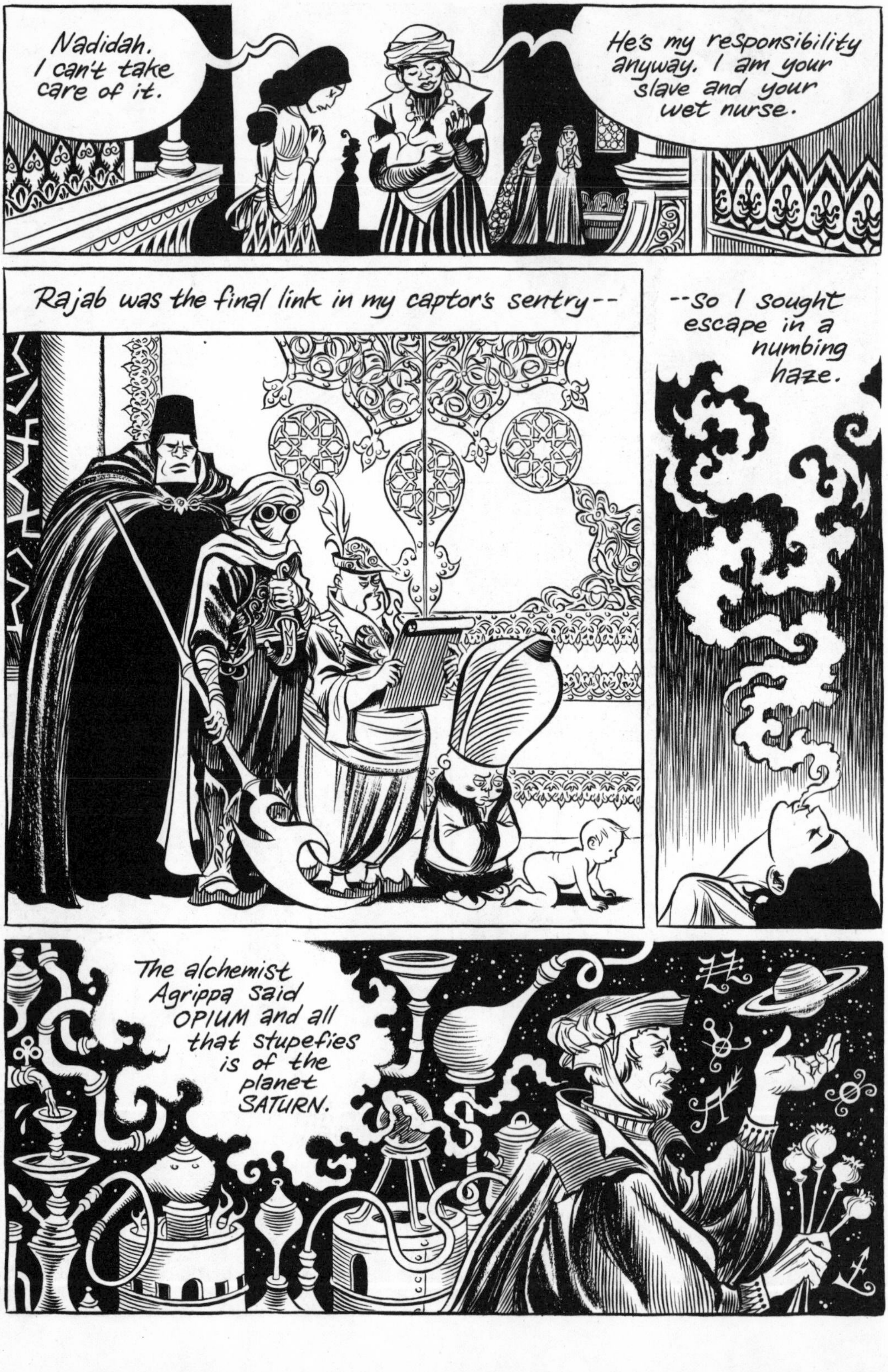
Nadidah. I can't take care of it.
He's my responsibility anyway. I am your slave and your wet nurse.
Rajab was the final link in my captor's sentry--
--so I sought escape in a numbing haze.
The alchemist Agrippa said OPIUM and all that stupefies is of the planet SATURN.

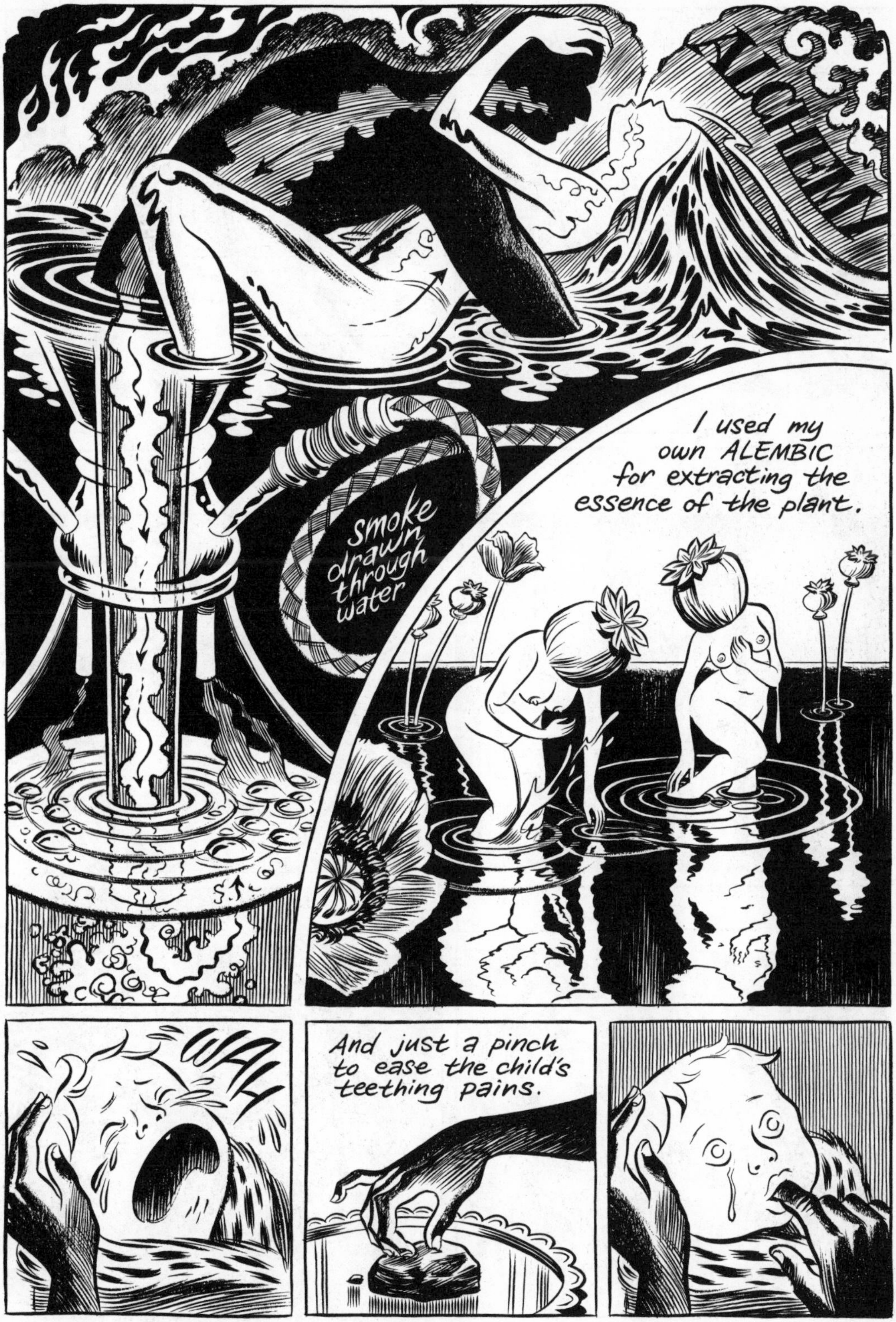
ALCHEM
I used my own ALEMBIC for extracting the essence of the plant.
Smoke drawn through water
WAH
And just a pinch to ease the child's teething pains.

Rajab learned to walk;

I learned to fly --

--to detach.

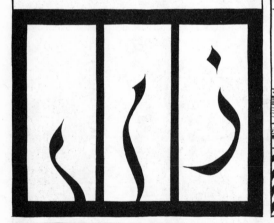

He learned to talk;

I learned to listen --

--to colors.

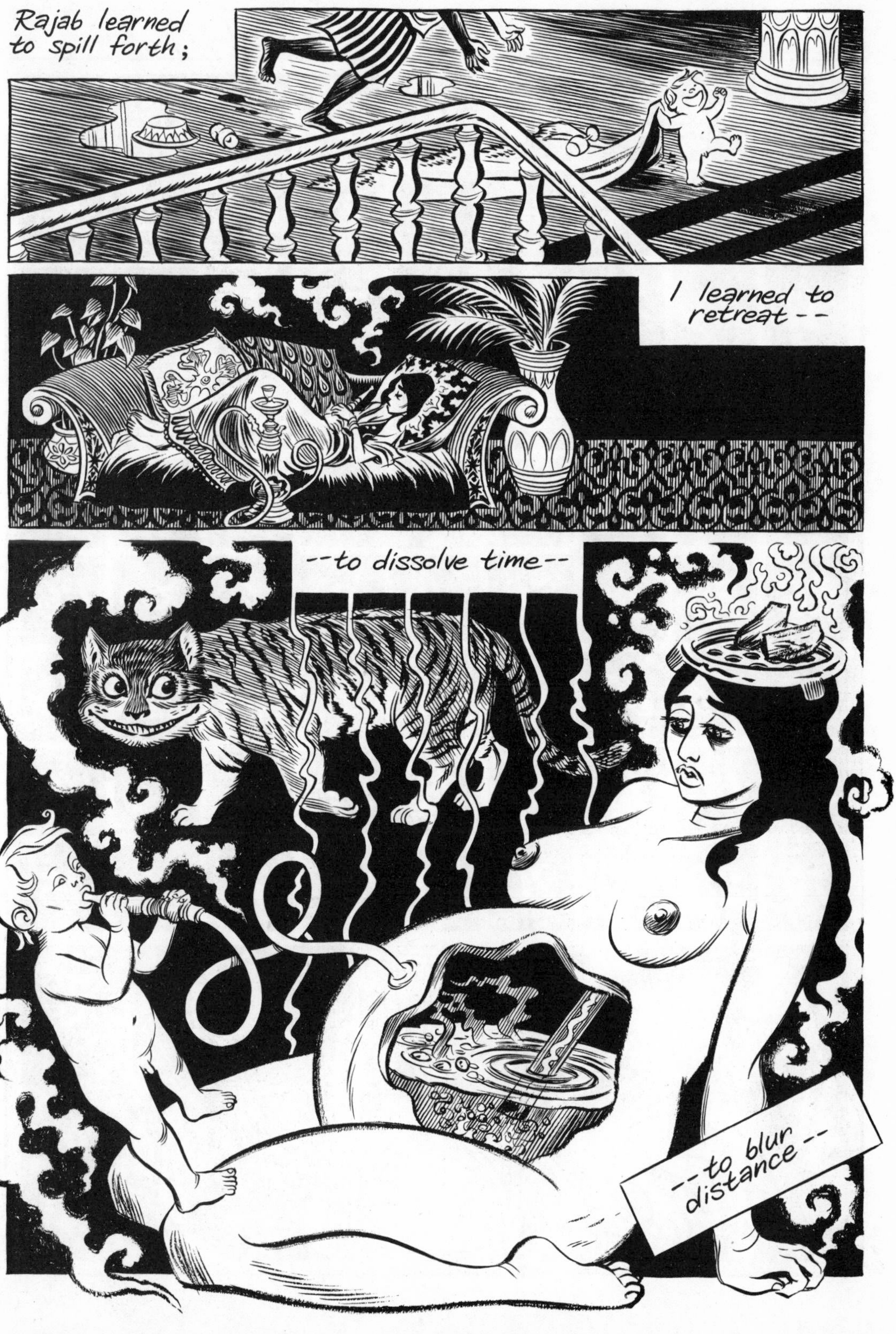
Rajab learned to spill forth;
I learned to retreat--
--to dissolve time--
--to blur distance--

--to swallow days--

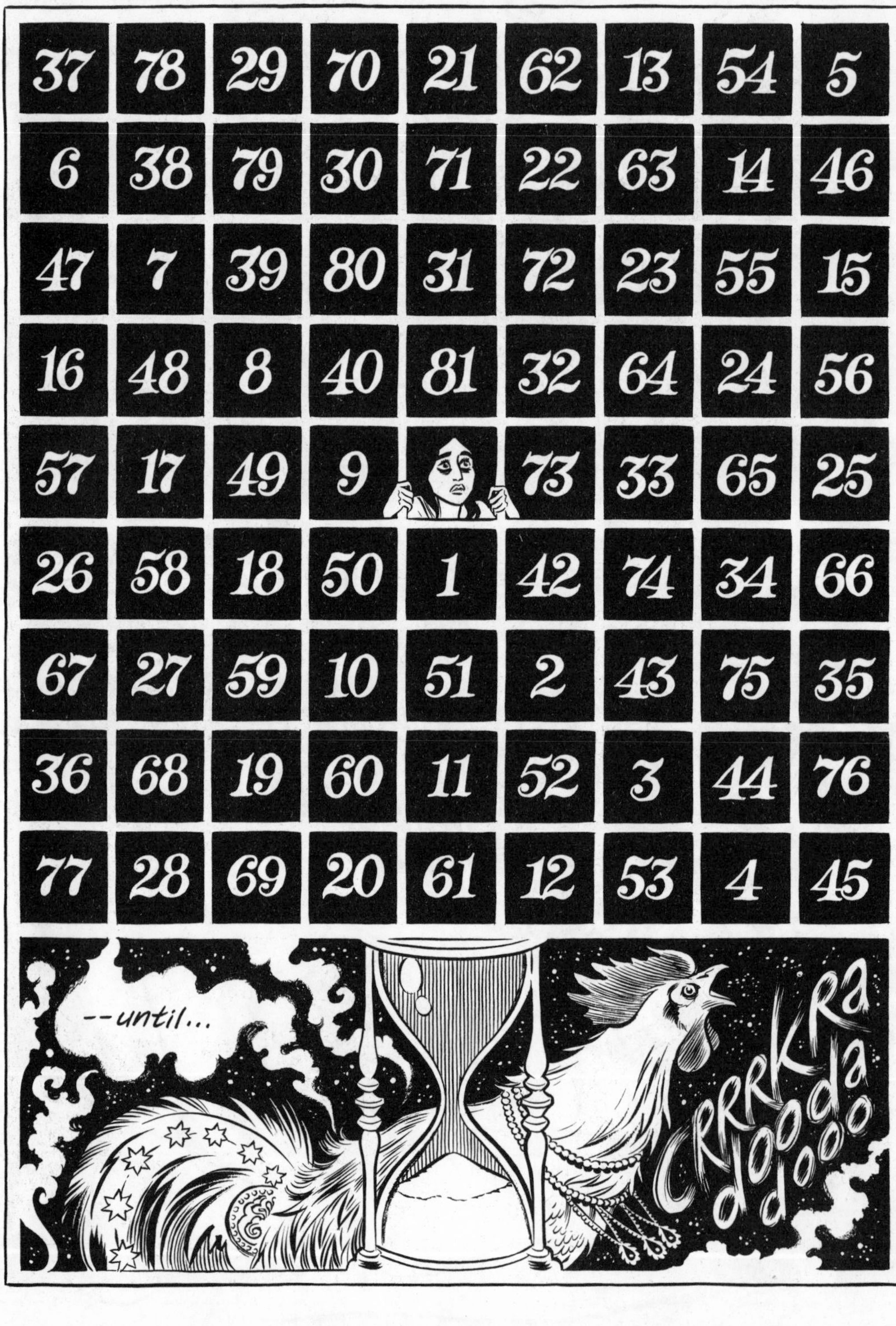

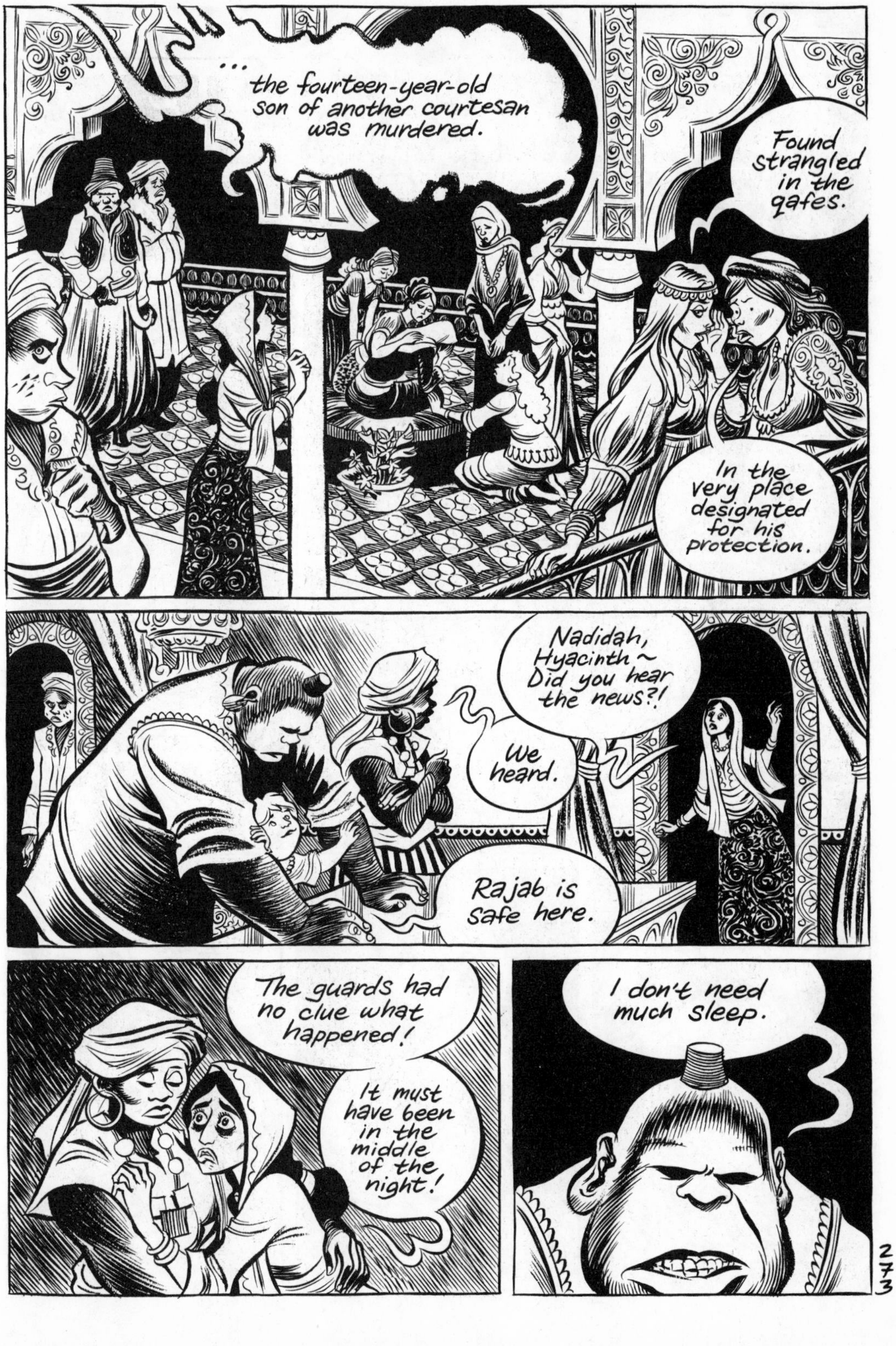
... the fourteen-year-old son of another courtesan was murdered.
Found strangled in the qafes.
In the very place designated for his protection.
Nadidah, Hyacinth ~ Did you hear the news?!
We heard.
Rajab is safe here.
The guards had no clue what happened!
It must have been in the middle of the night!
I don't need much sleep.

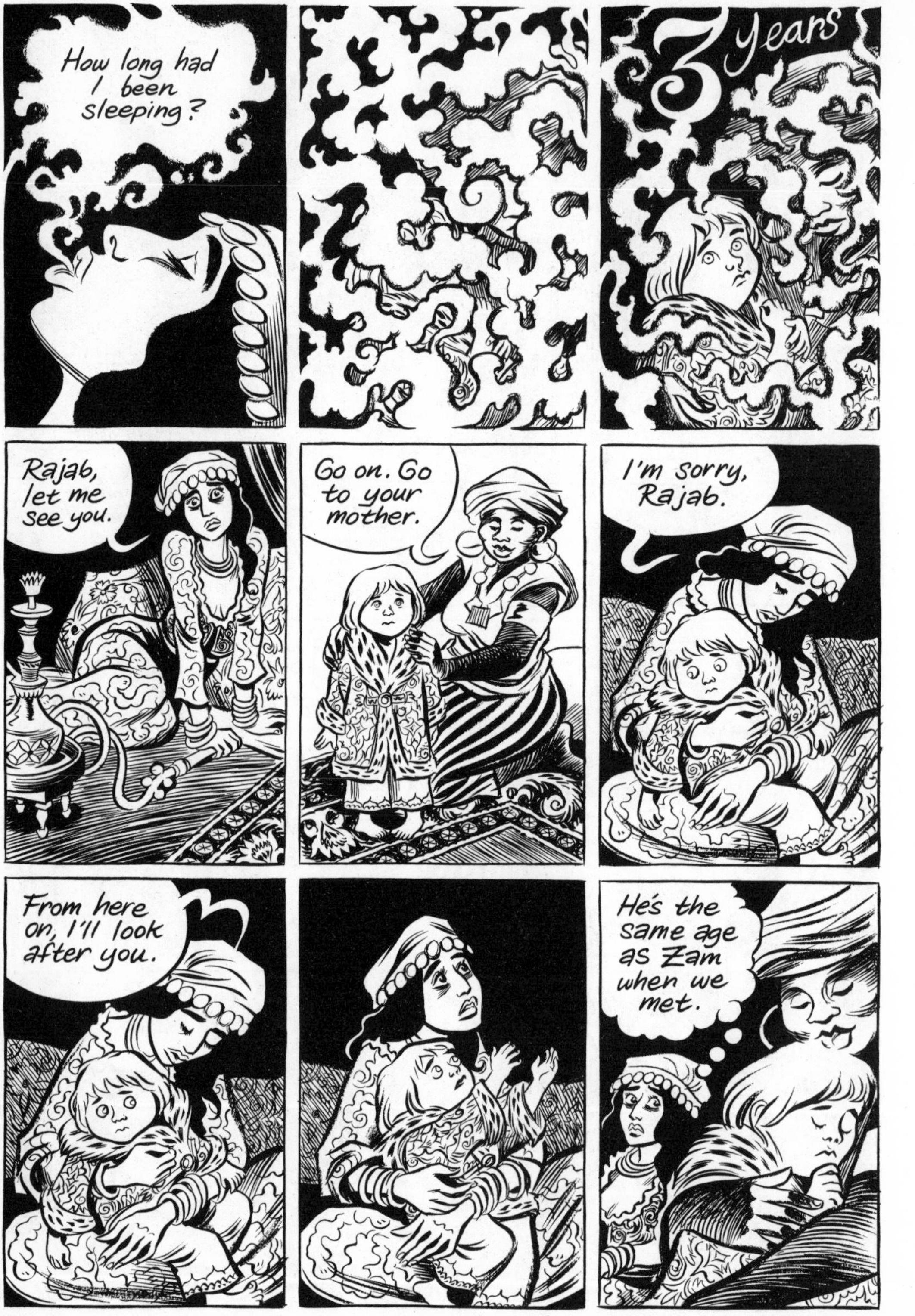
How long had I been sleeping?
7 years
Rajab, let me see you.
Go on. Go to your mother.
I'm sorry, Rajab.
From here on, I'll look after you.
He's the same age as Zam when we met.

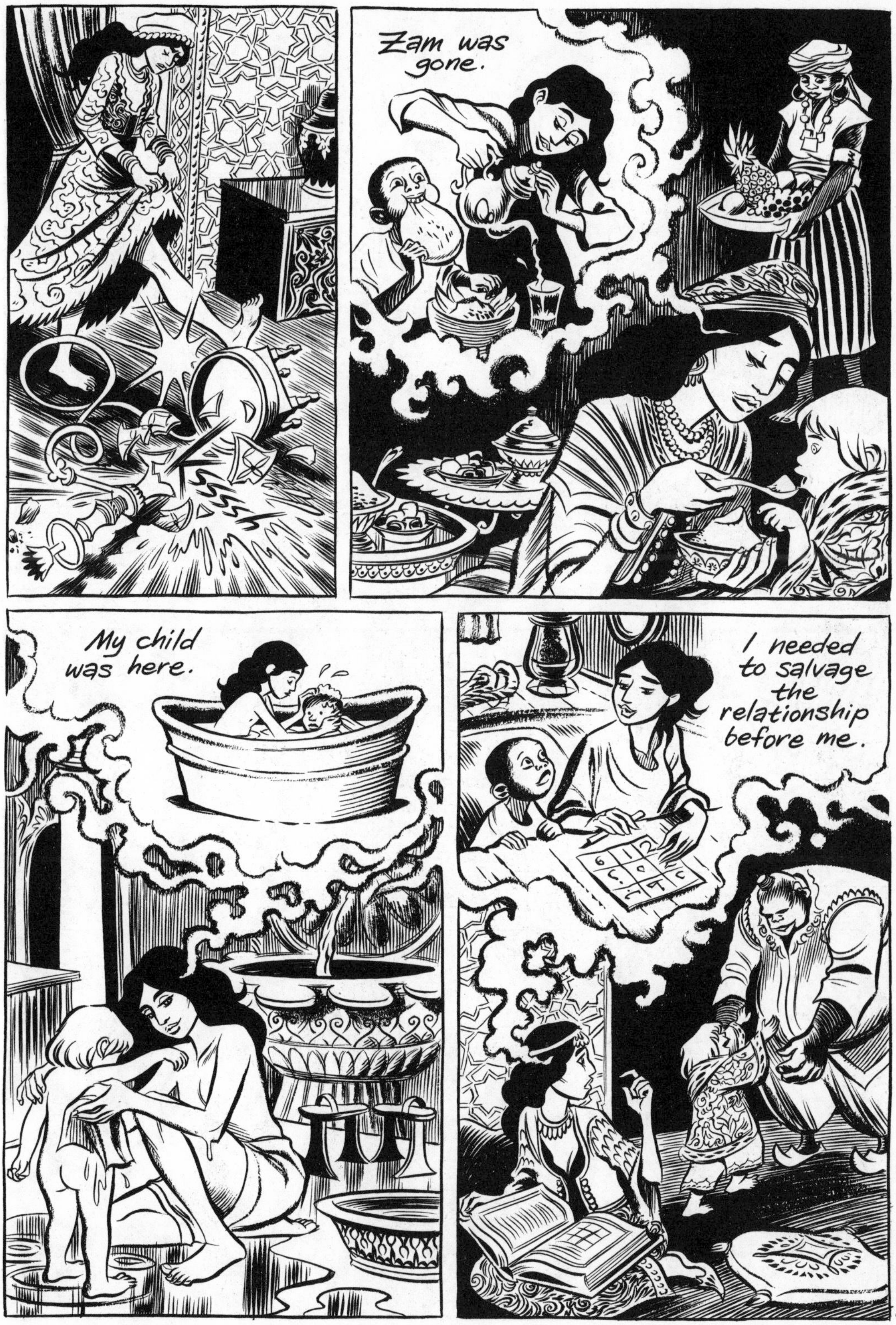
SSSSH
Zam was gone.
My child was here.
I needed to salvage the relationship before me.

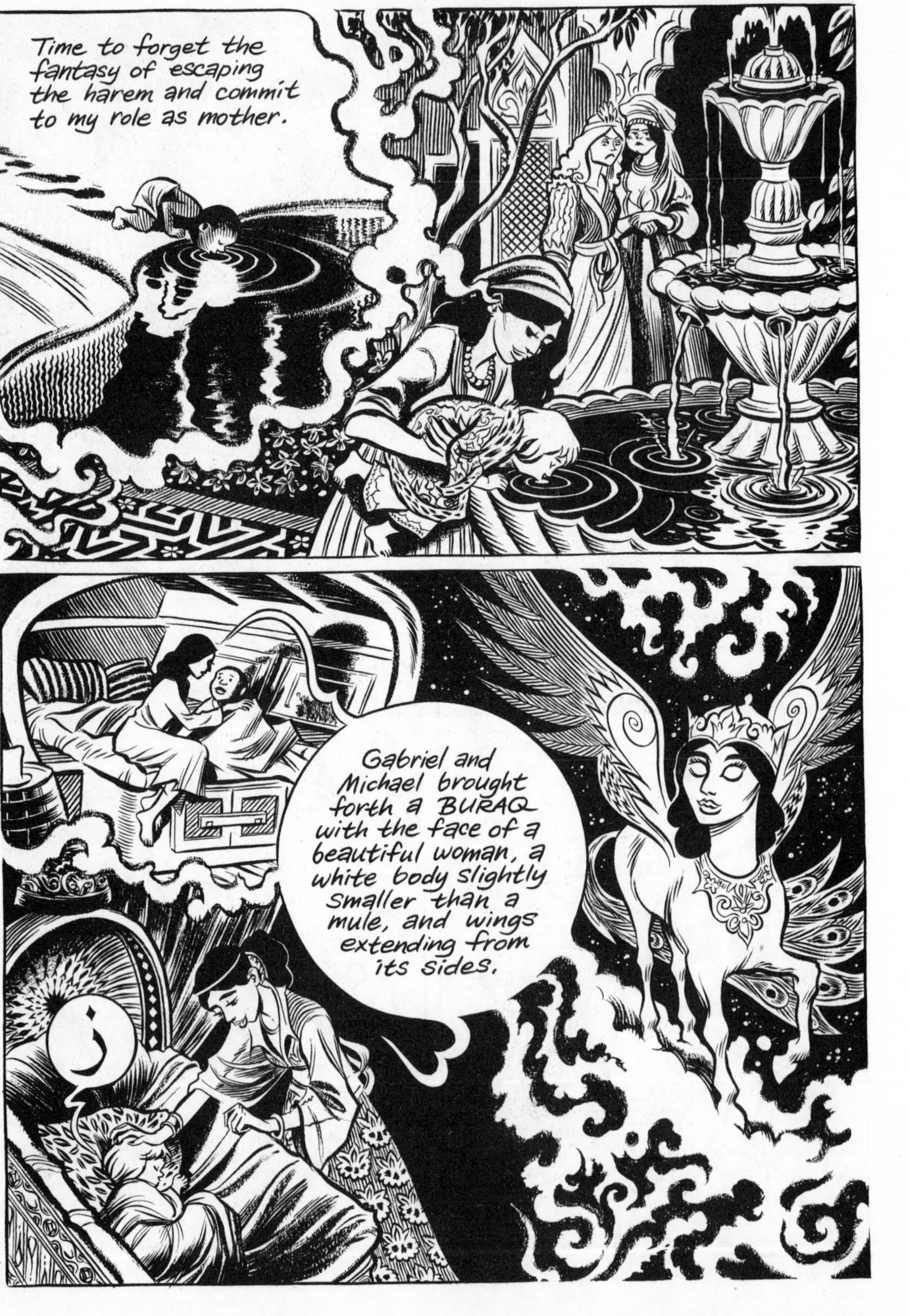
Time to forget the fantasy of escaping the harem and commit to my role as mother.
ز
Gabriel and Michael brought forth a BURAQ with the face of a beautiful woman, a white body slightly smaller than a mule, and wings extending from its sides.

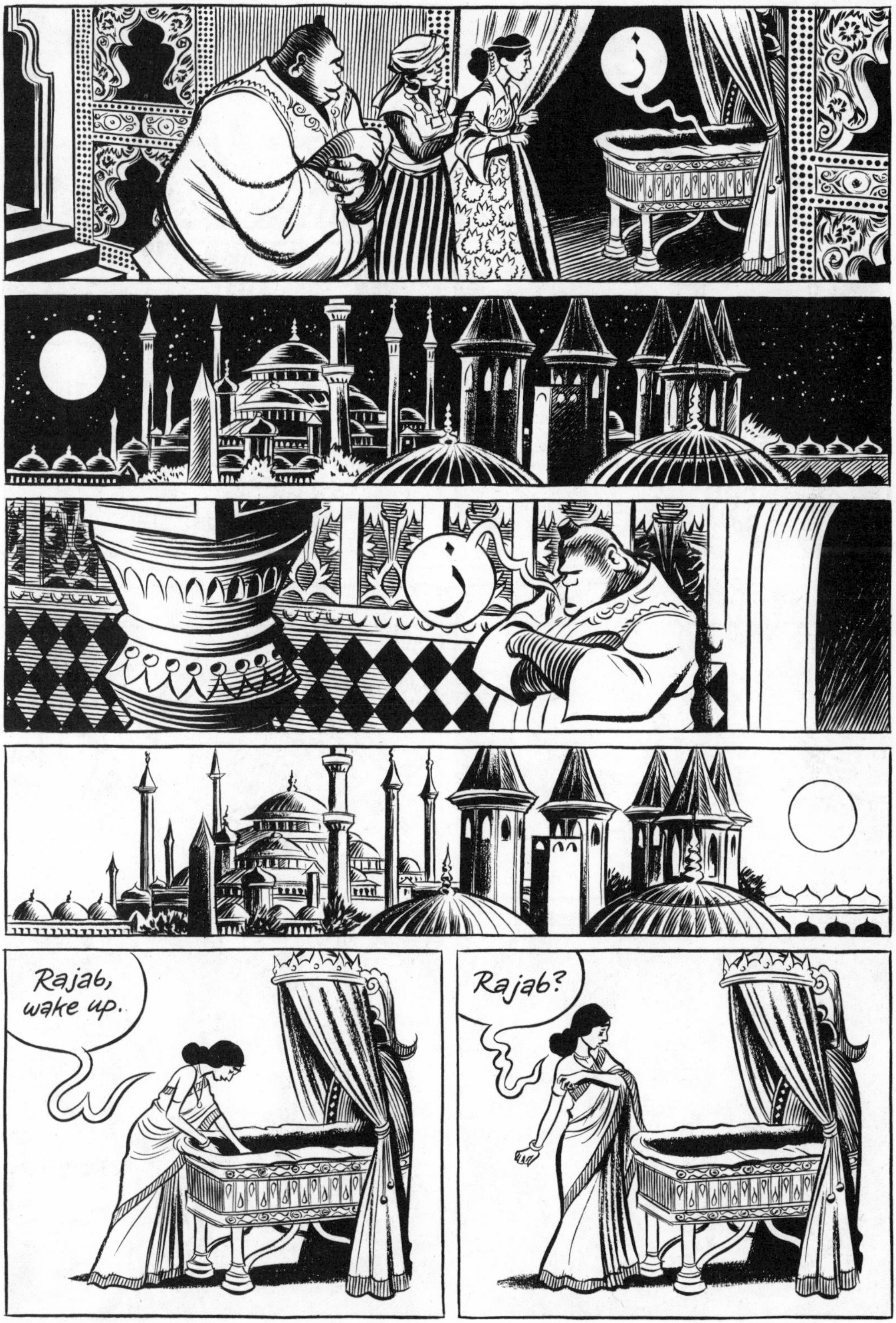
Rajab, wake up..
Rajab?

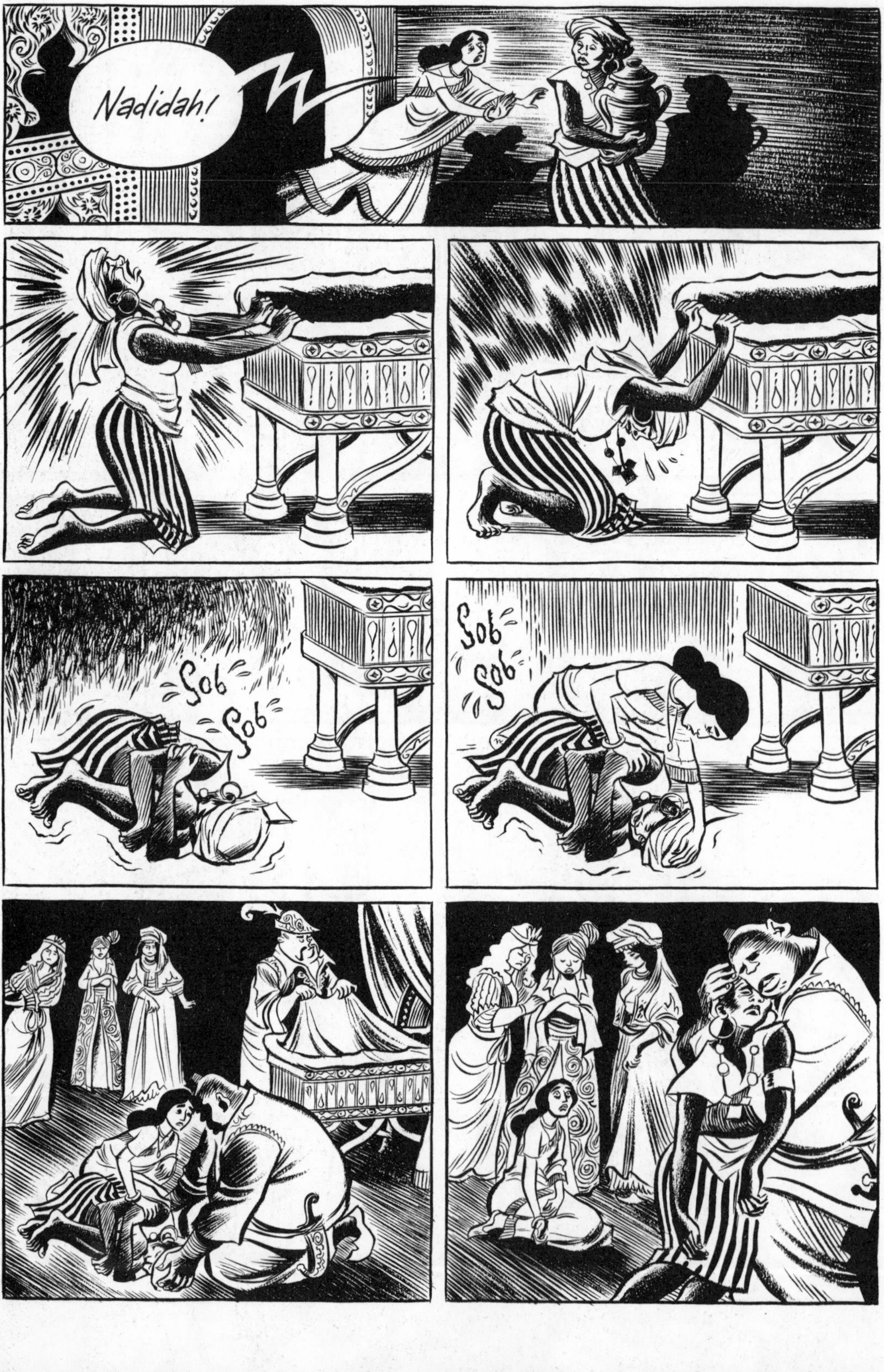

Nadidah!
Sob Sob
Sob Sob

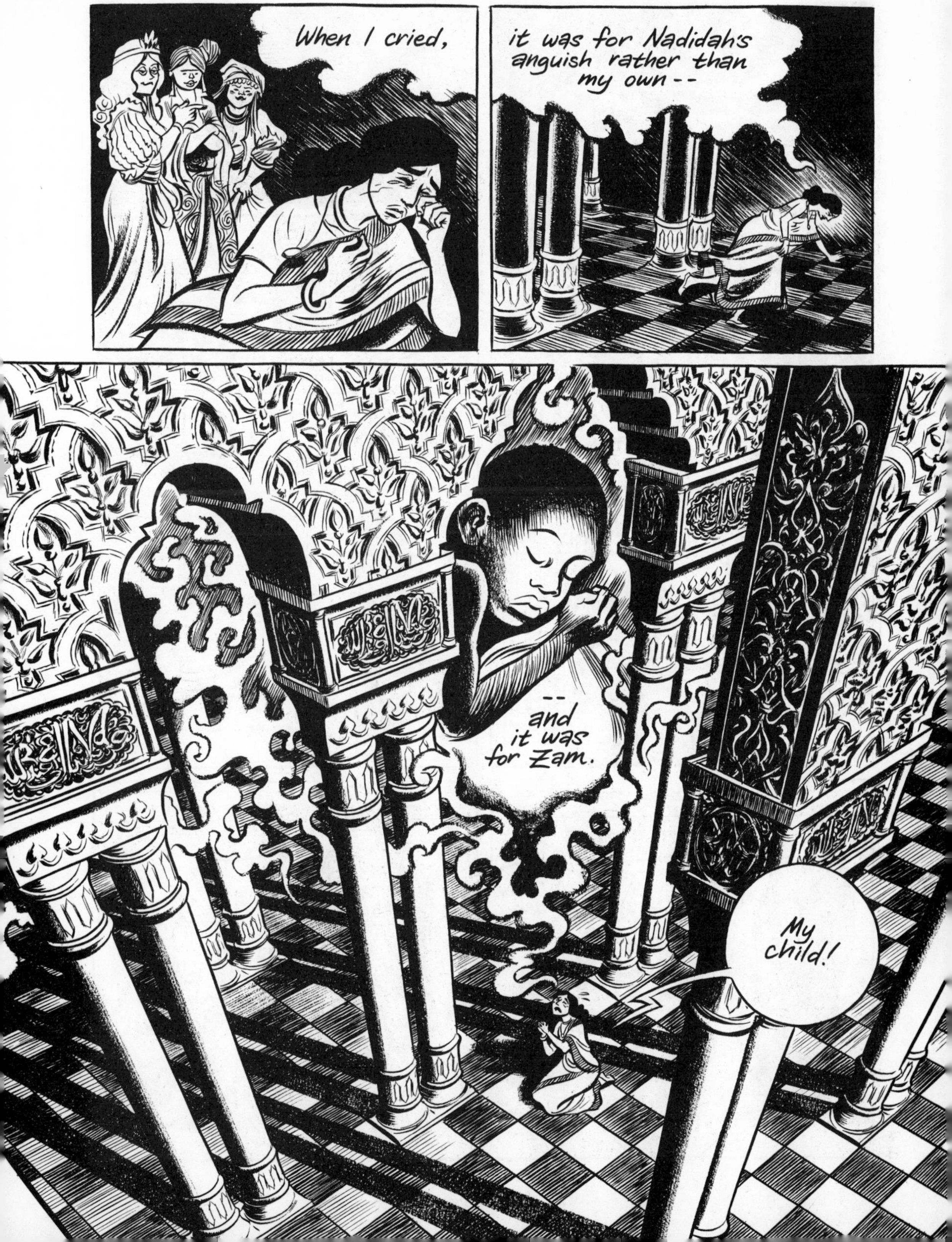
When I cried,
it was for Nadidah's anguish rather than my own --
-- and it was for Zam.
My child!

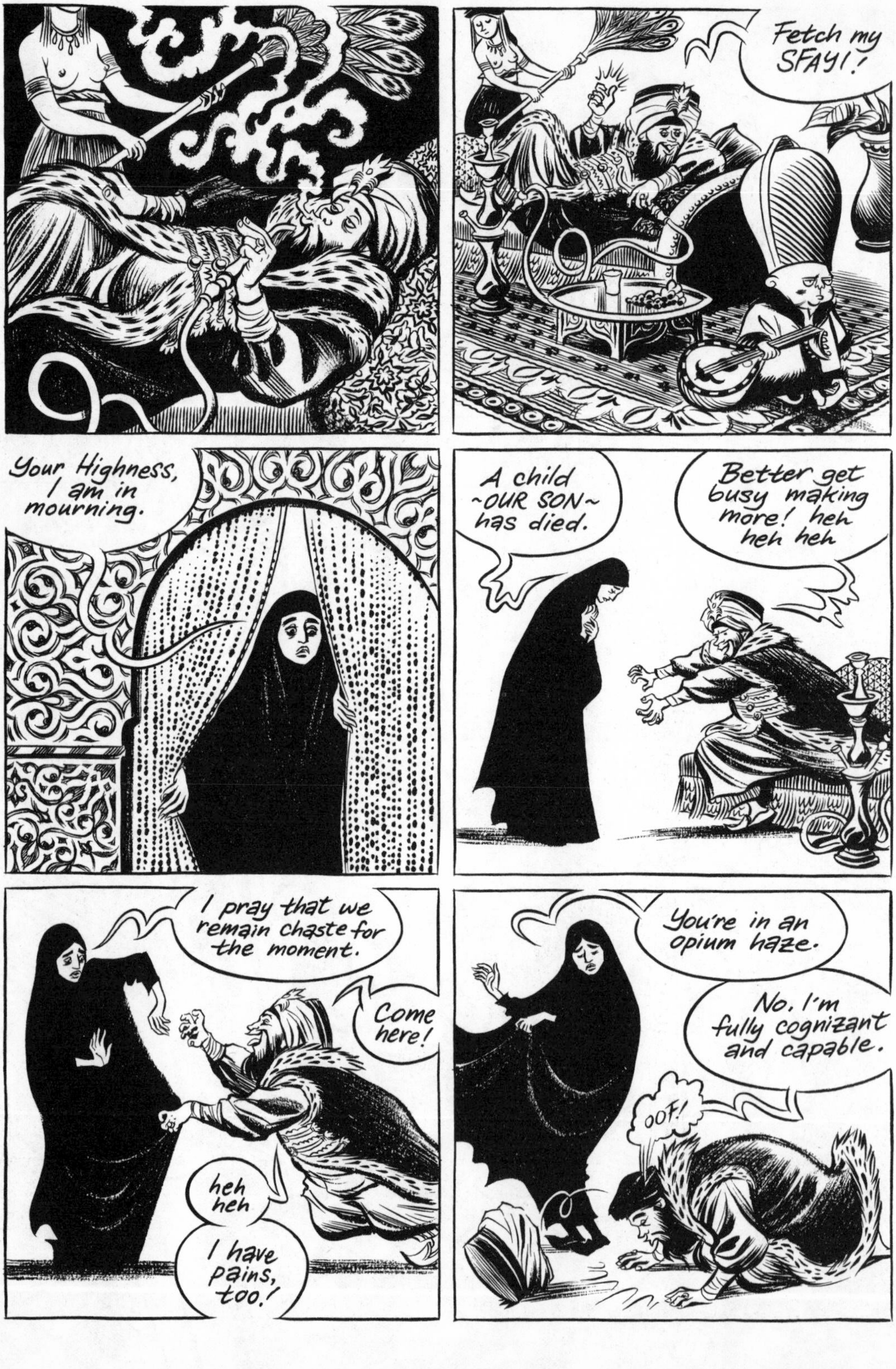

Fetch my SFAYI!
Your Highness, I am in mourning.
A child ~OUR SON~ has died.
Better get busy making more! heh heh heh
I pray that we remain chaste for the moment.
Come here!
heh heh
I have pains, too!
You're in an opium haze.
No. I'm fully cognizant and capable.
OOF!

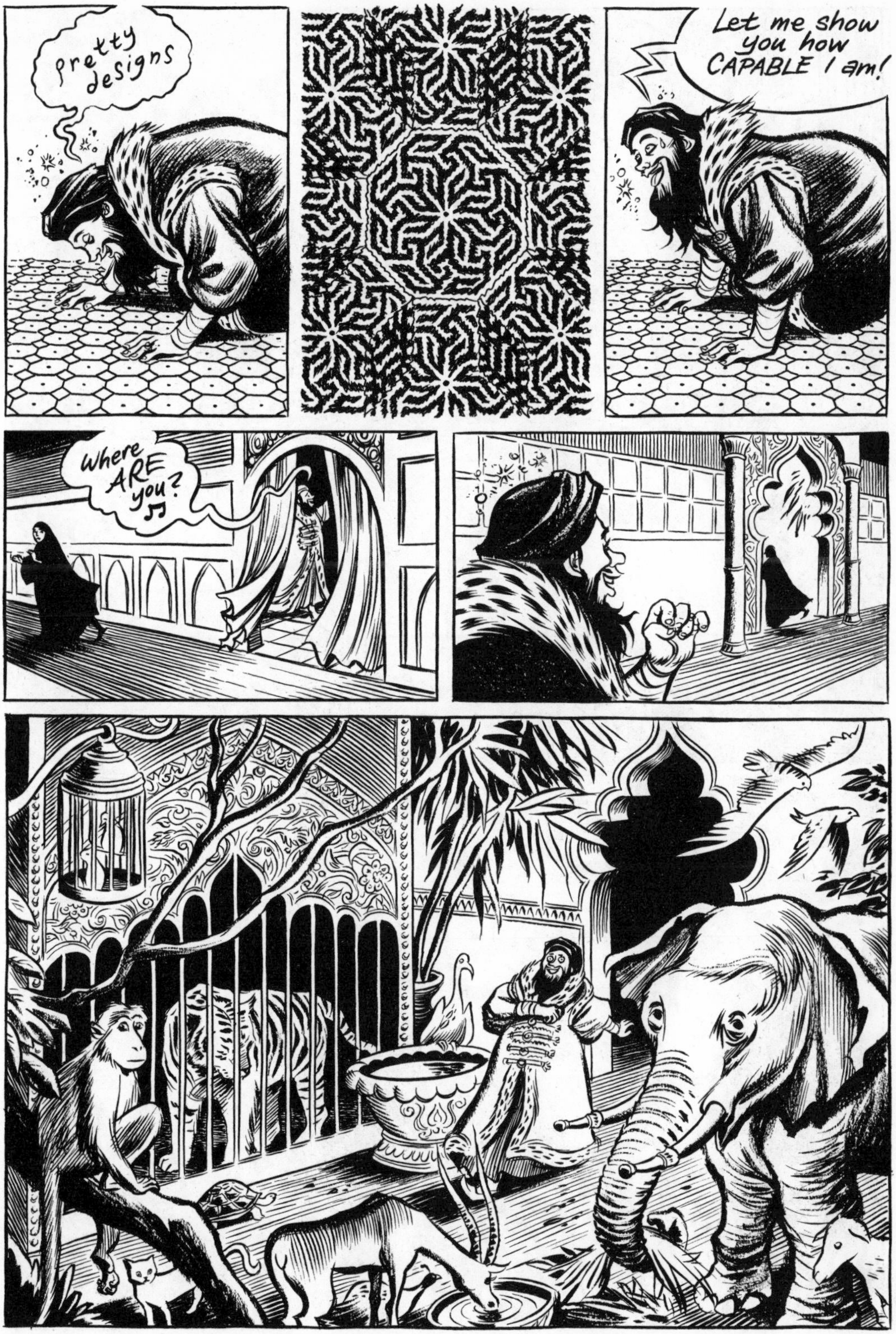
pretty designs
Let me show you how CAPABLE I am!
Where ARE you?

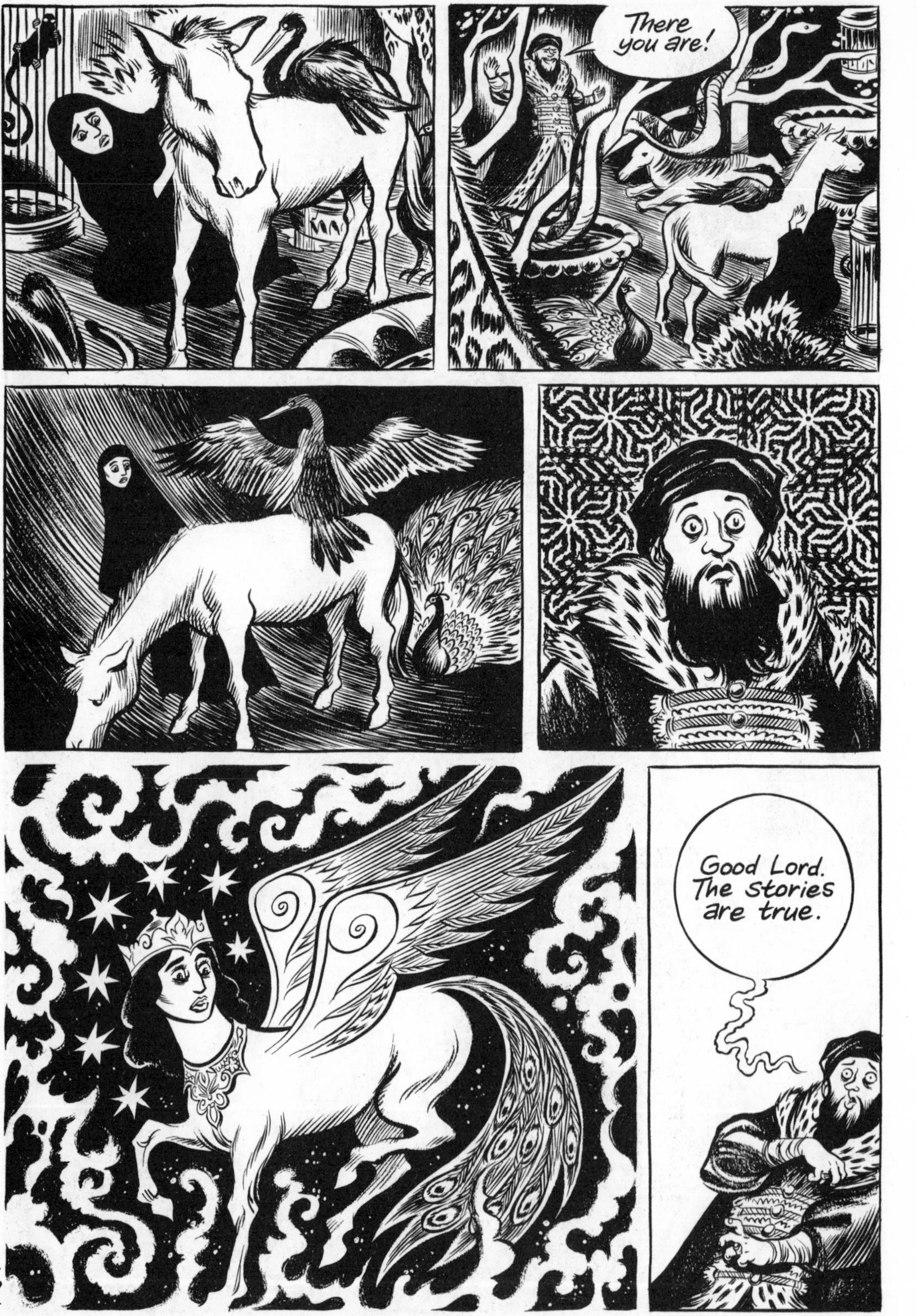
There you are!
Good Lord. The stories are true.

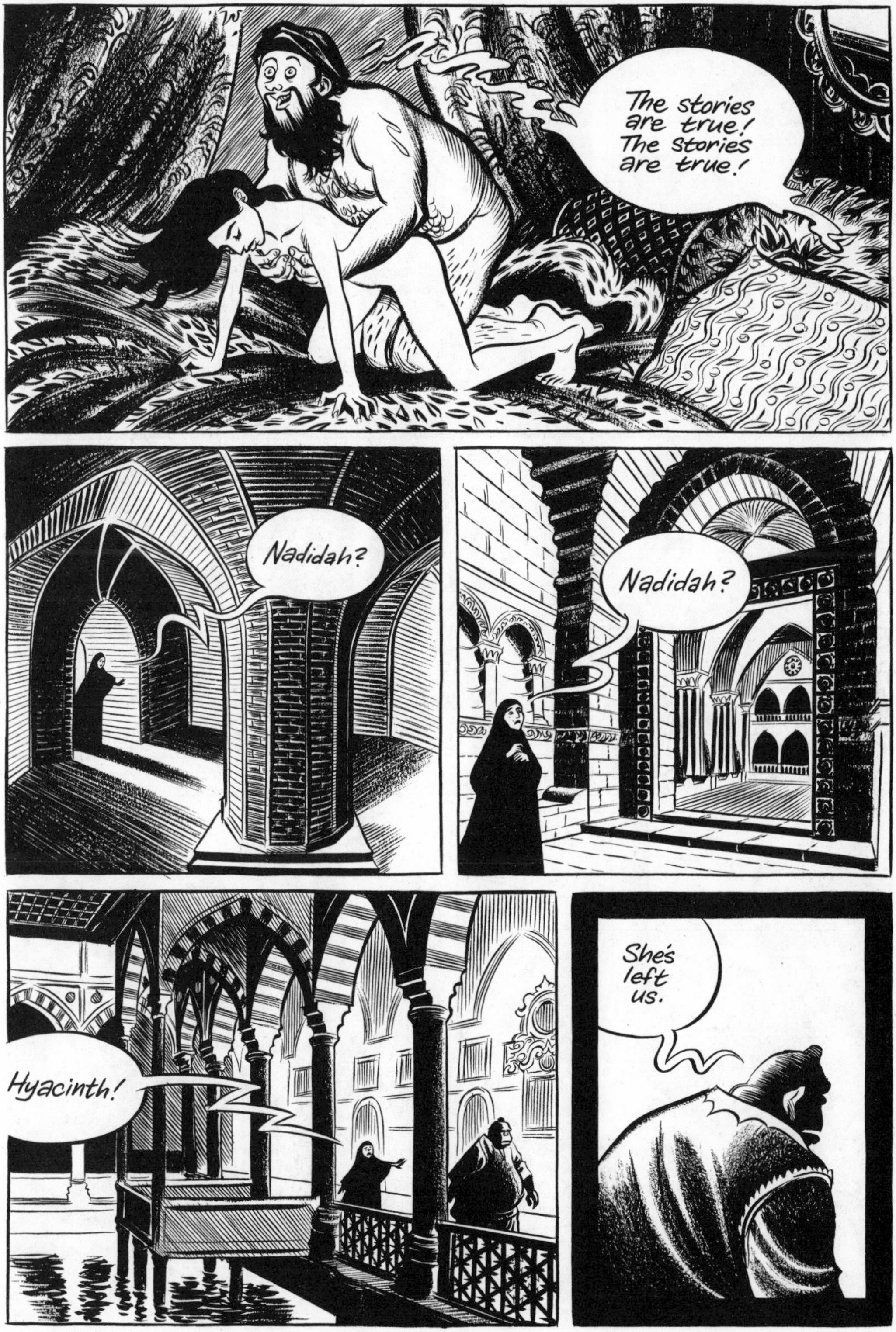
The stories are true! The stories are true!
Nadidah?
Nadidah?
Hyacinth!
She's left us.

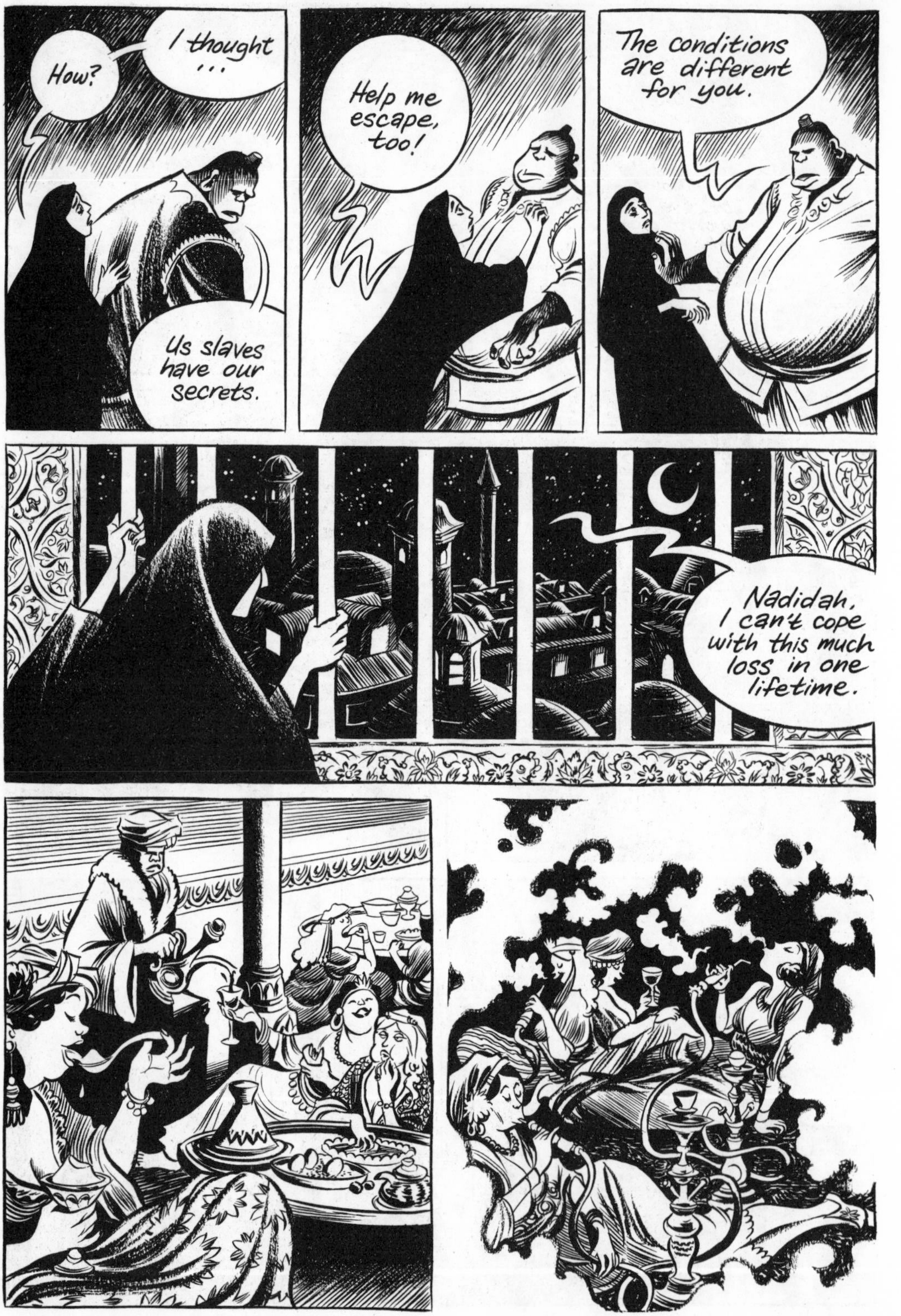
How?
I thought . . .
Us slaves have our secrets.
Help me escape, too!
The conditions are different for you.
Nadidah, I can't cope with this much loss in one lifetime.

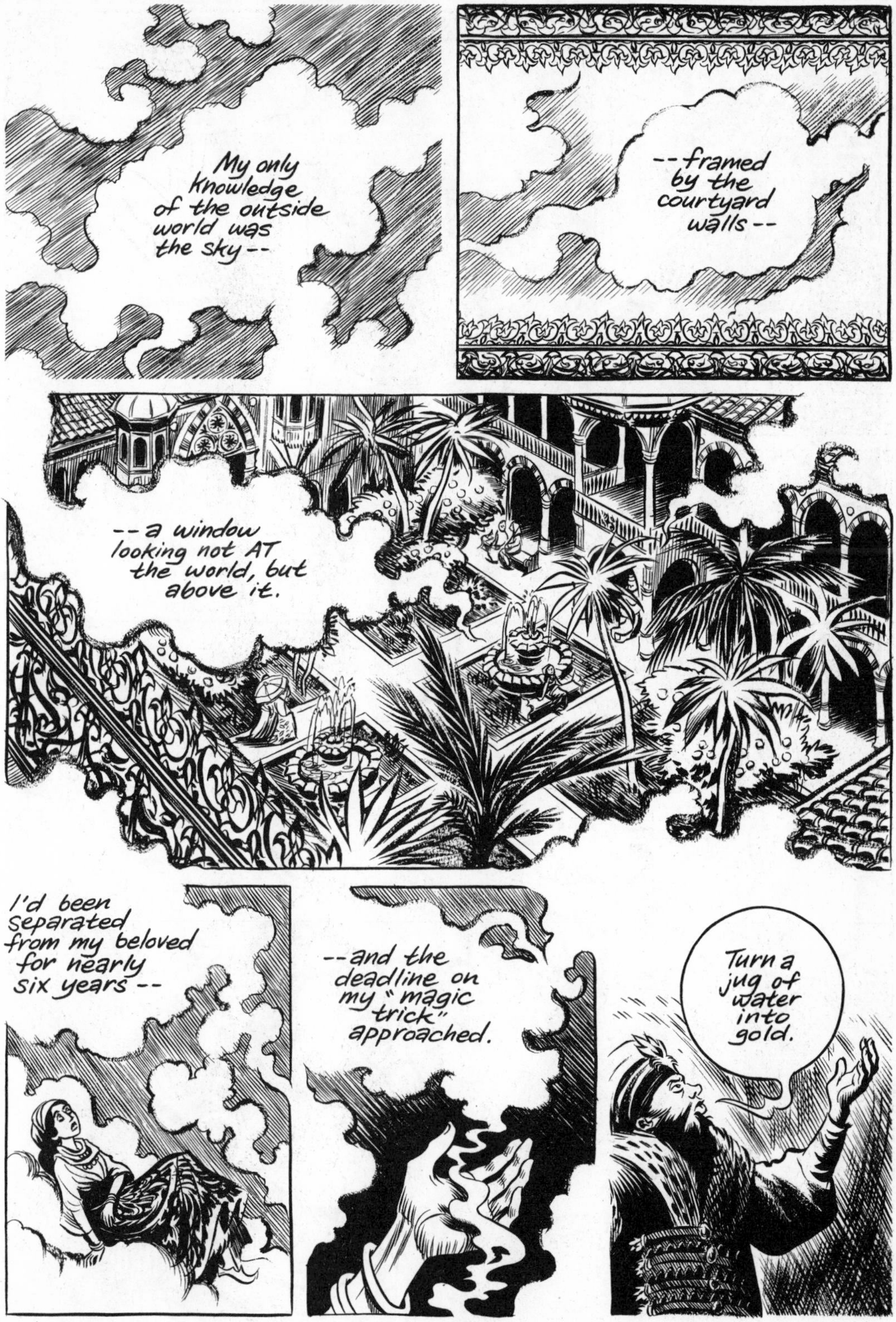
My only knowledge of the outside world was the sky--
--framed by the courtyard walls--
--a window looking not AT the world, but above it.
I'd been separated from my beloved for nearly six years--
--and the deadline on my "magic trick" approached.
Turn a jug of water into gold.

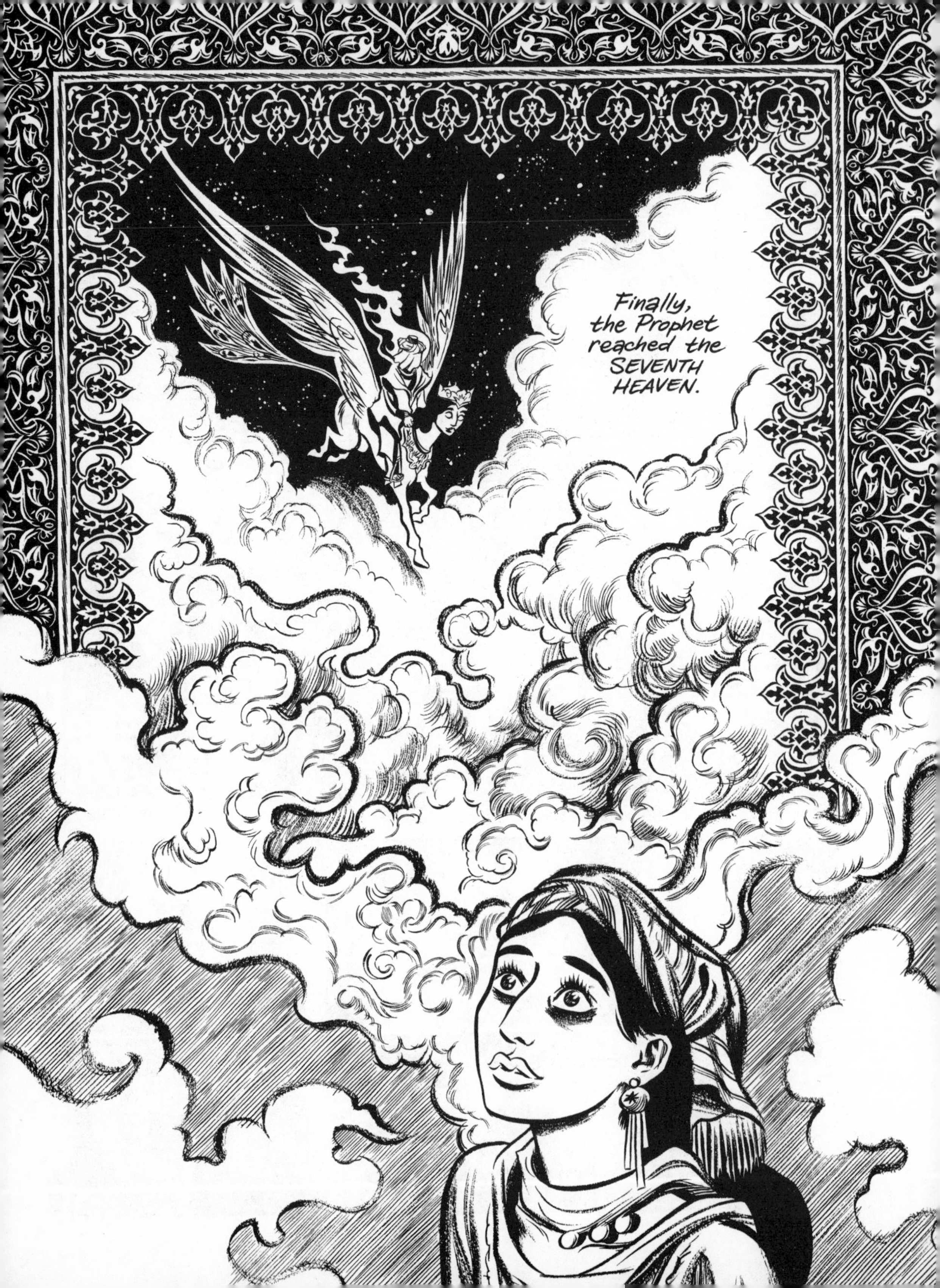
Finally, the Prophet reached the SEVENTH HEAVEN.

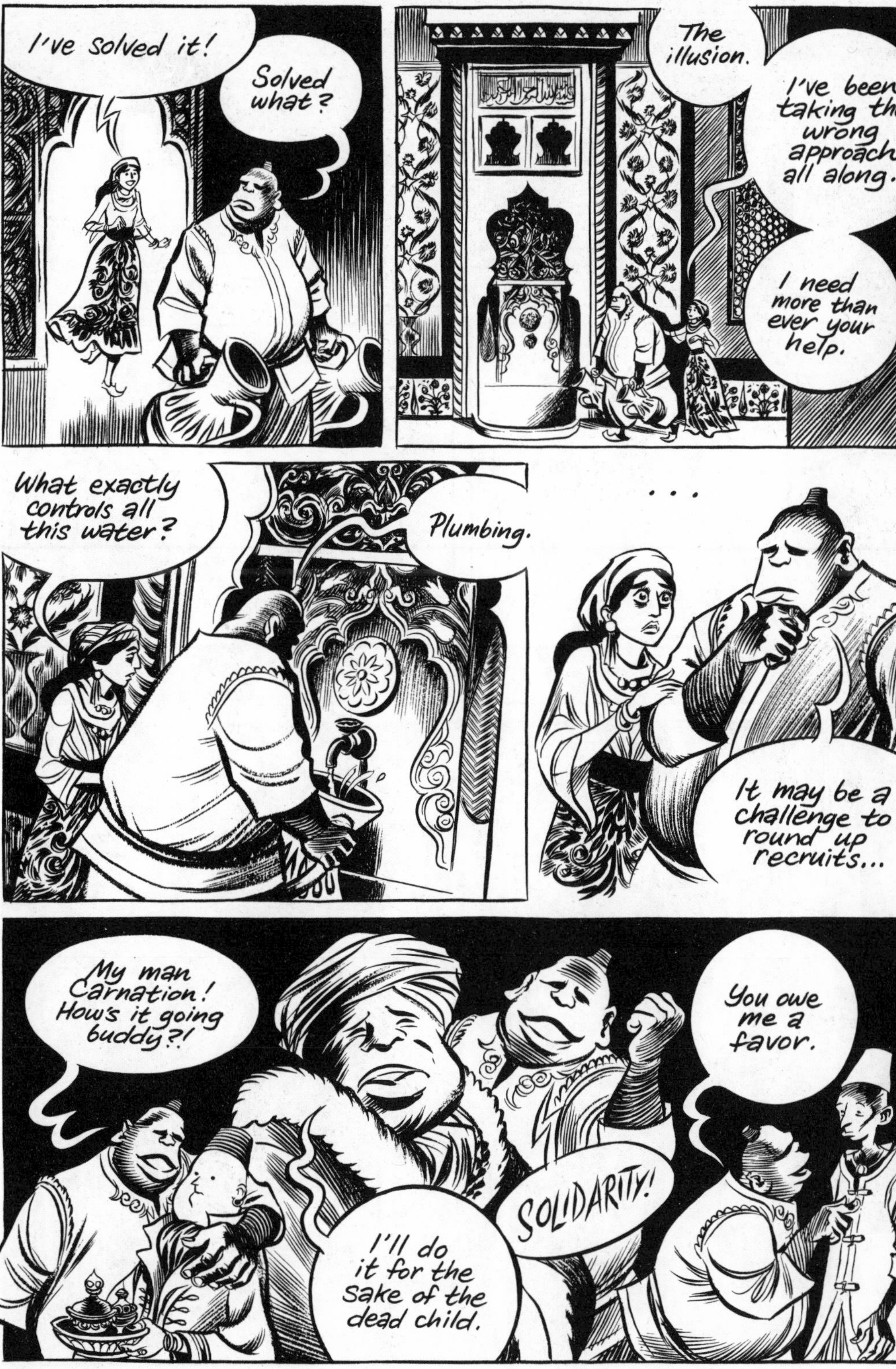
I've solved it!
Solved what?
The illusion.
I've been taking the wrong approach all along.
I need more than ever your help.
What exactly controls all this water?
Plumbing.
...
It may be a challenge to round up recruits...
My man Carnation! How's it going buddy?!
You owe me a favor.
SOLIDARITY!
I'll do it for the sake of the dead child.

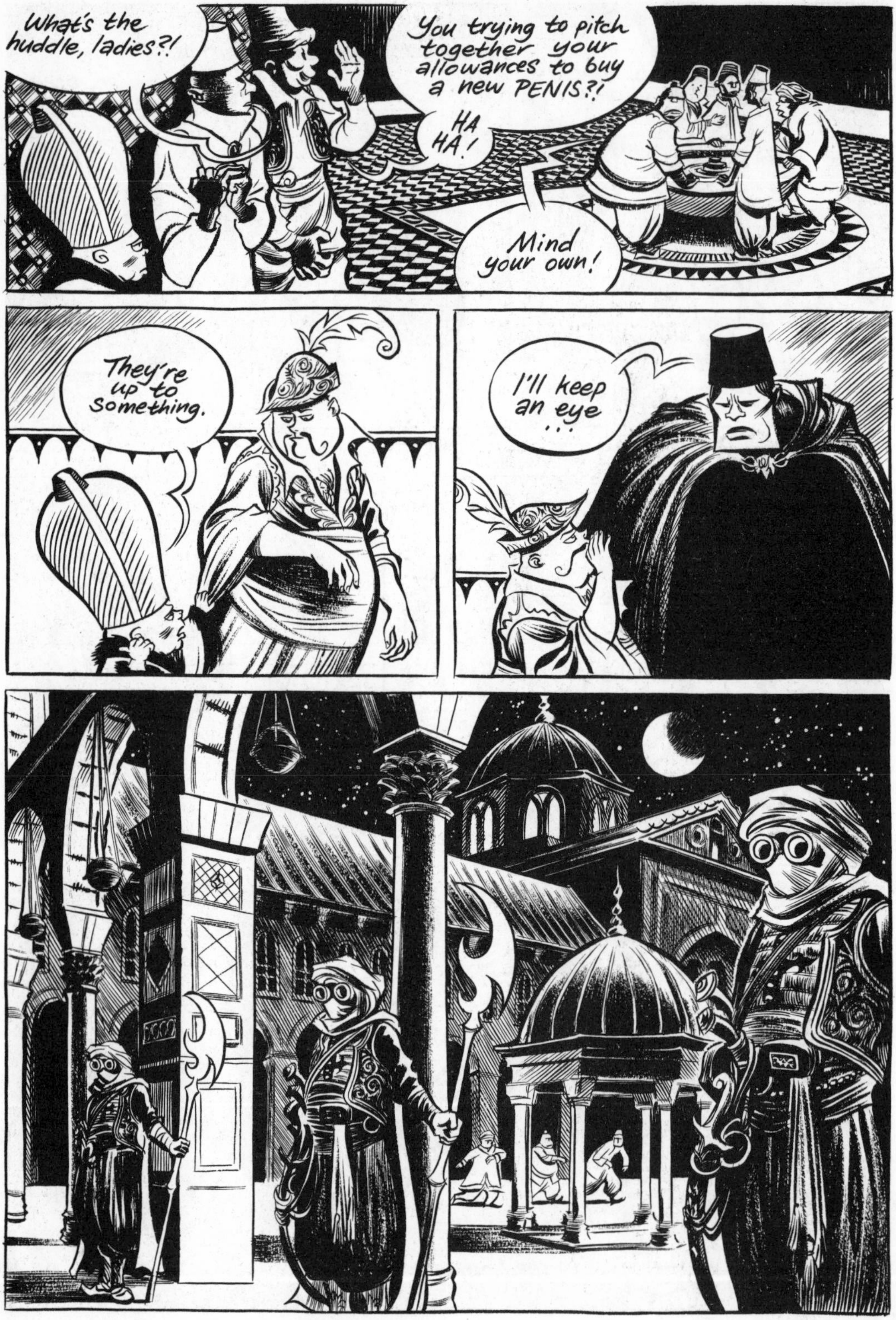
What's the huddle, ladies?!
You trying to pitch together your allowances to buy a new PENIS?!
HA HA!
Mind your own!
They're up to something.
I'll keep an eye ...

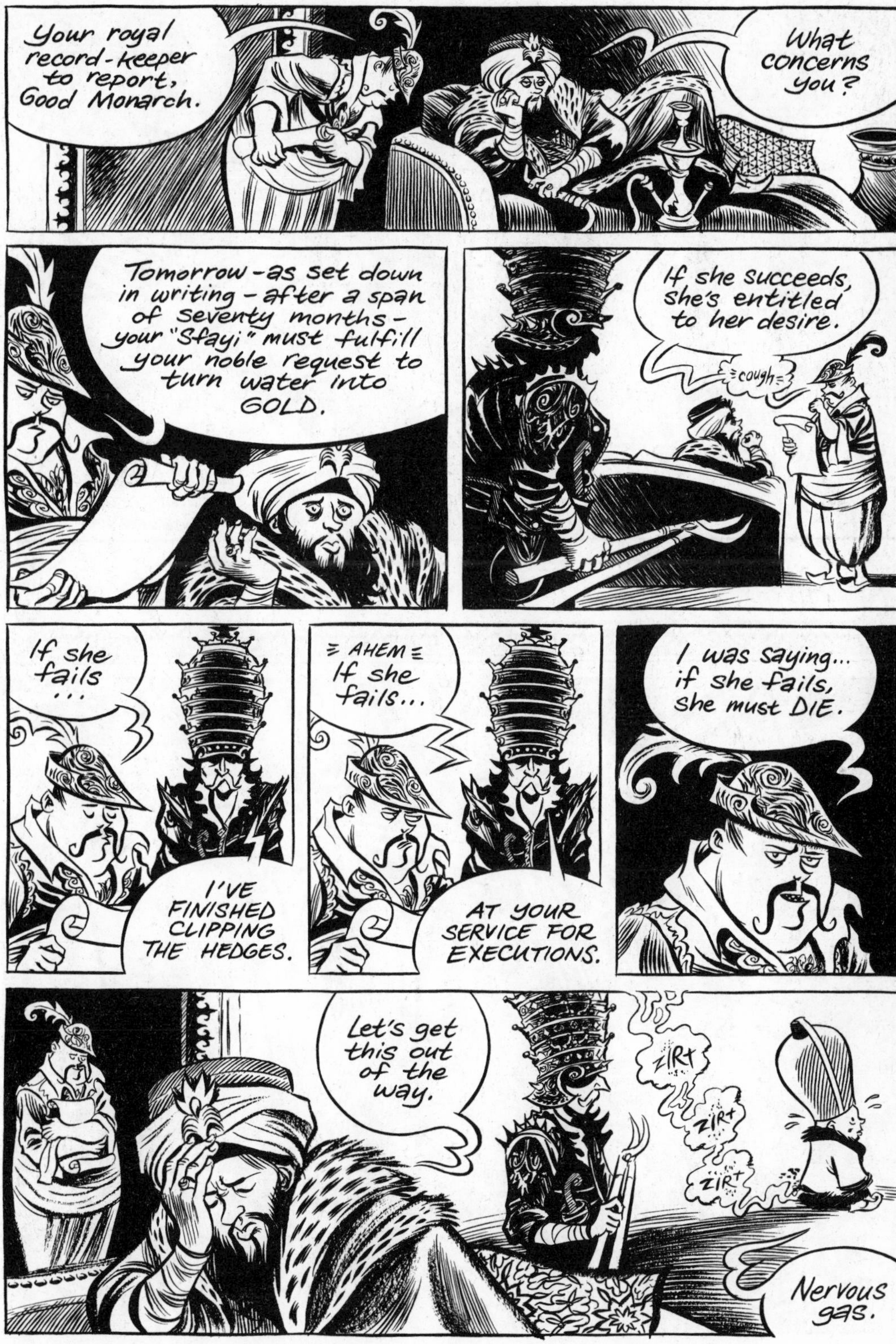
Your royal record-keeper to report, Good Monarch.
What concerns you?
Tomorrow - as set down in writing - after a span of seventy months - your "Sfayi" must fulfill your noble request to turn water into GOLD.
If she succeeds, she's entitled to her desire.
cough
If she fails . . .
I'VE FINISHED CLIPPING THE HEDGES.
AHEM
If she fails...
AT YOUR SERVICE FOR EXECUTIONS.
I was saying... if she fails, she must DIE.
Let's get this out of the way.
ZIRT
ZIRT
ZIRT
Nervous gas.

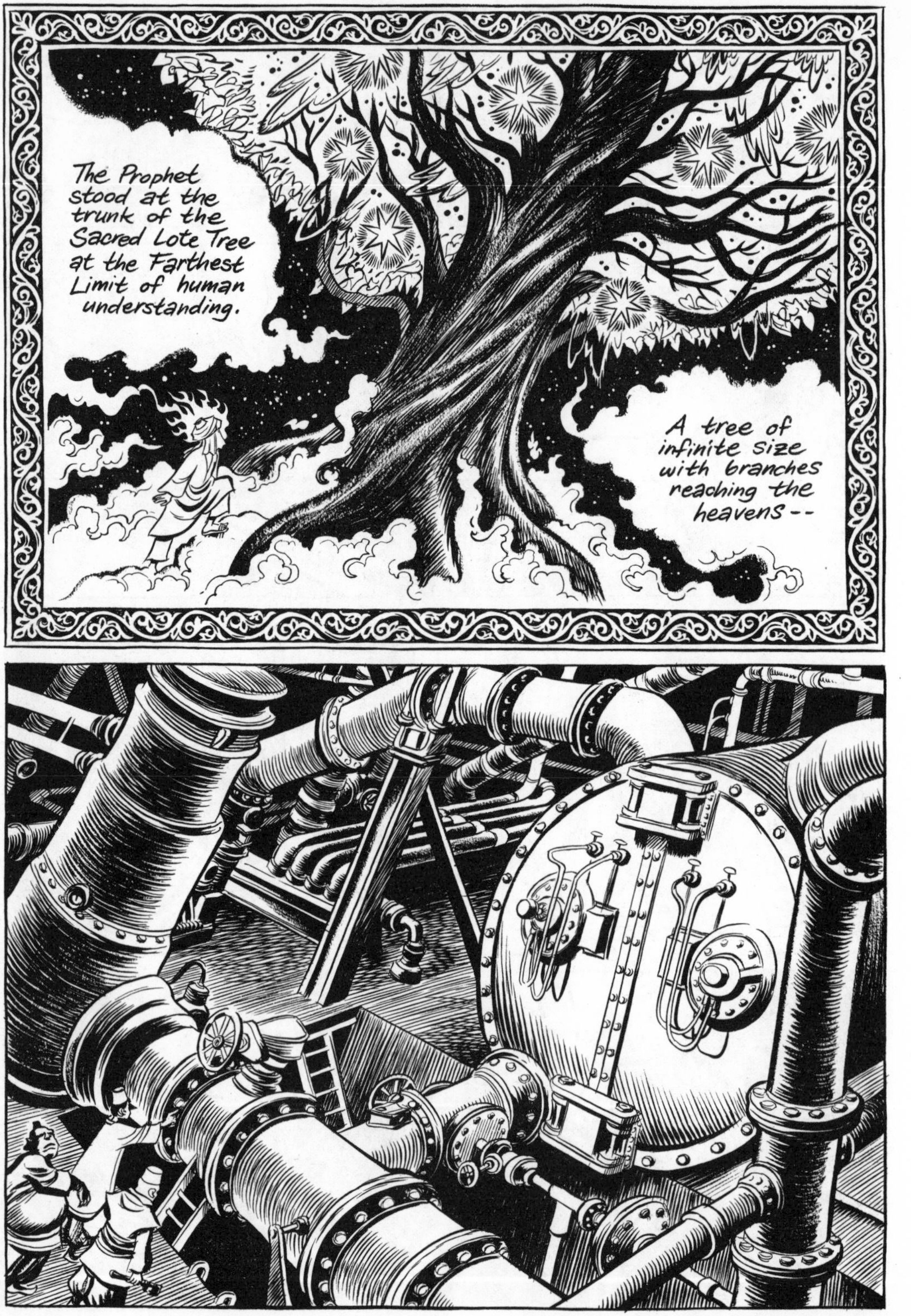
The Prophet stood at the trunk of the Sacred Lote Tree at the Farthest Limit of human understanding.
A tree of infinite size with branches reaching the heavens--

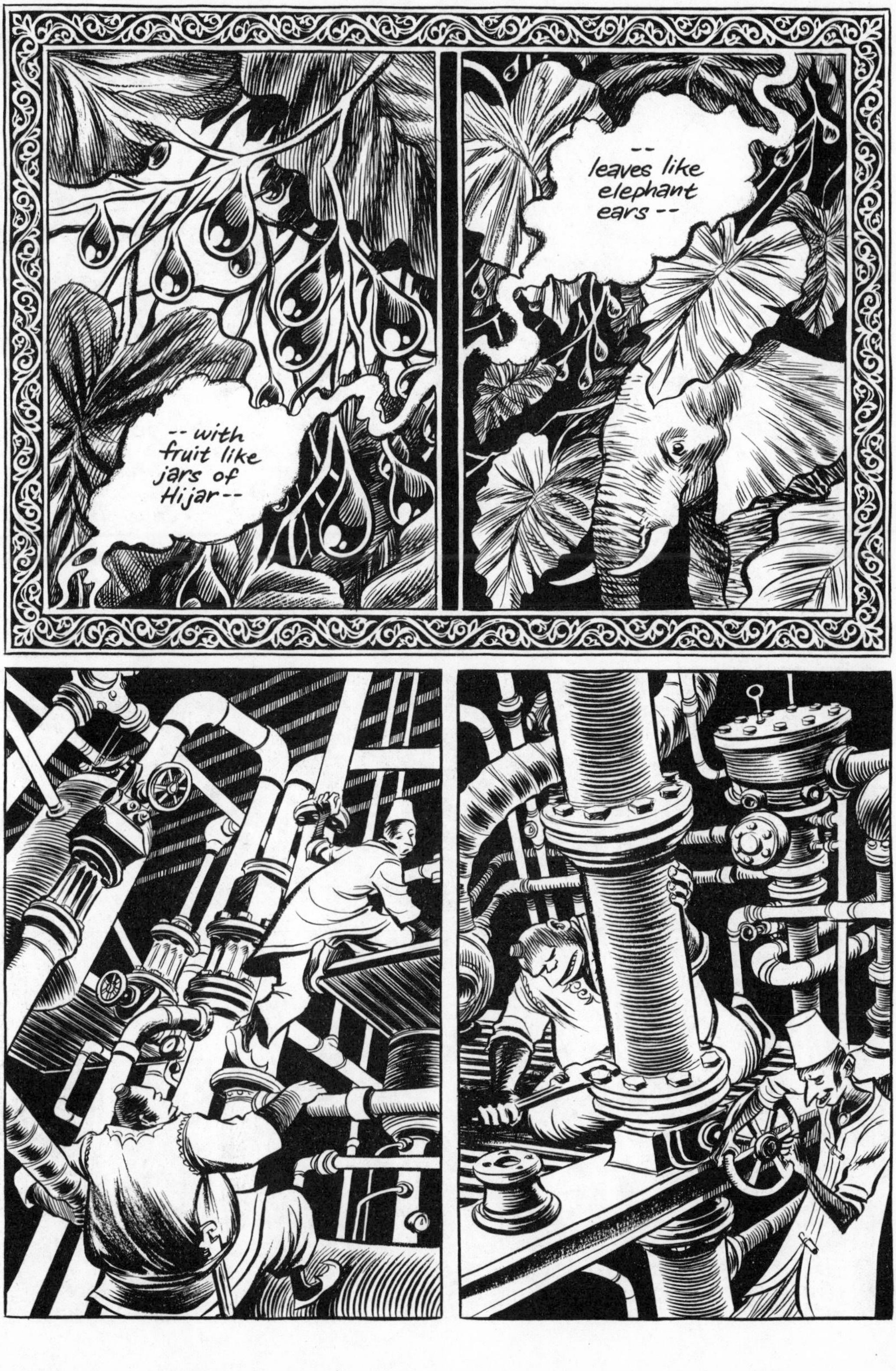
-- with fruit like jars of Hijar --
-- leaves like elephant ears --

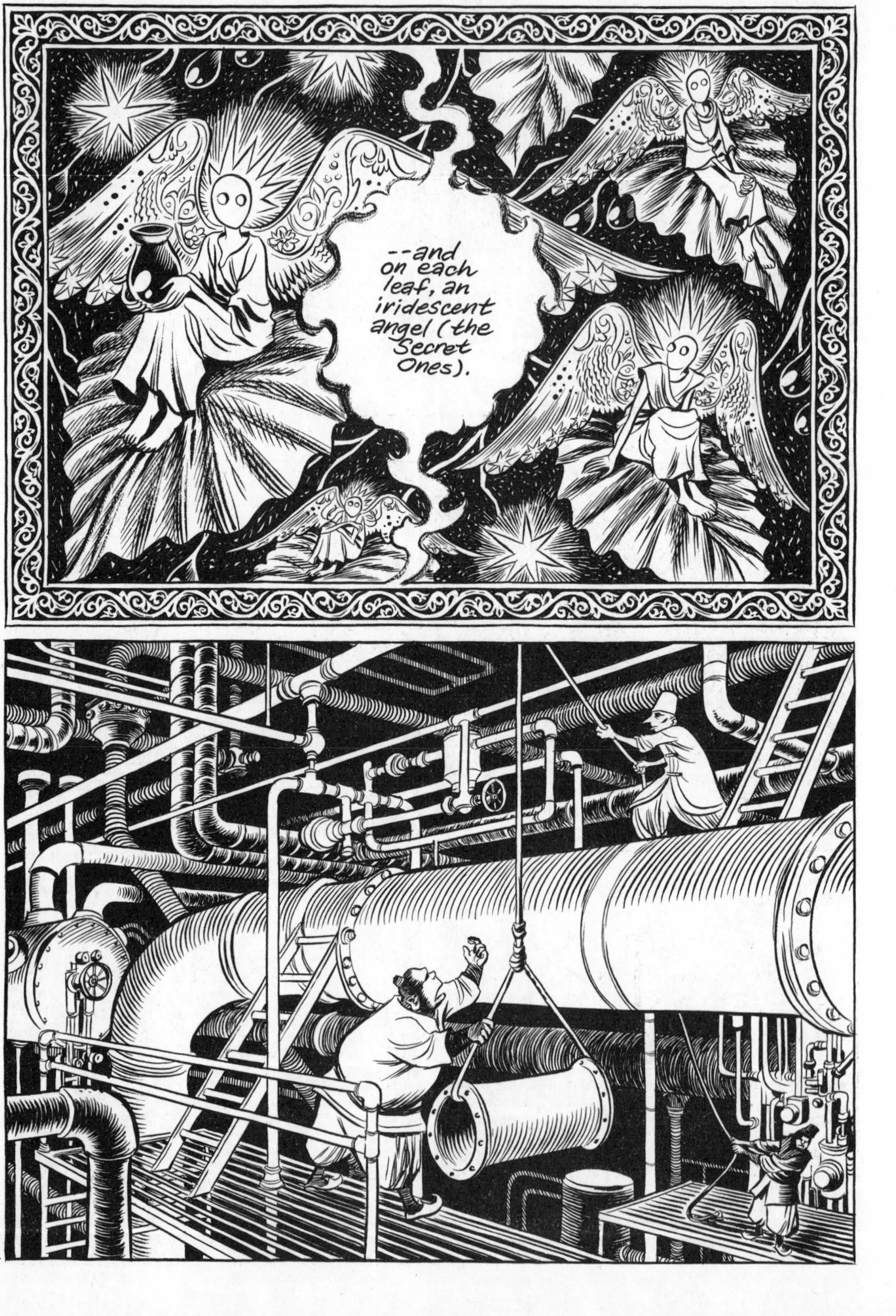
--and on each leaf, an iridescent angel (the Secret Ones).

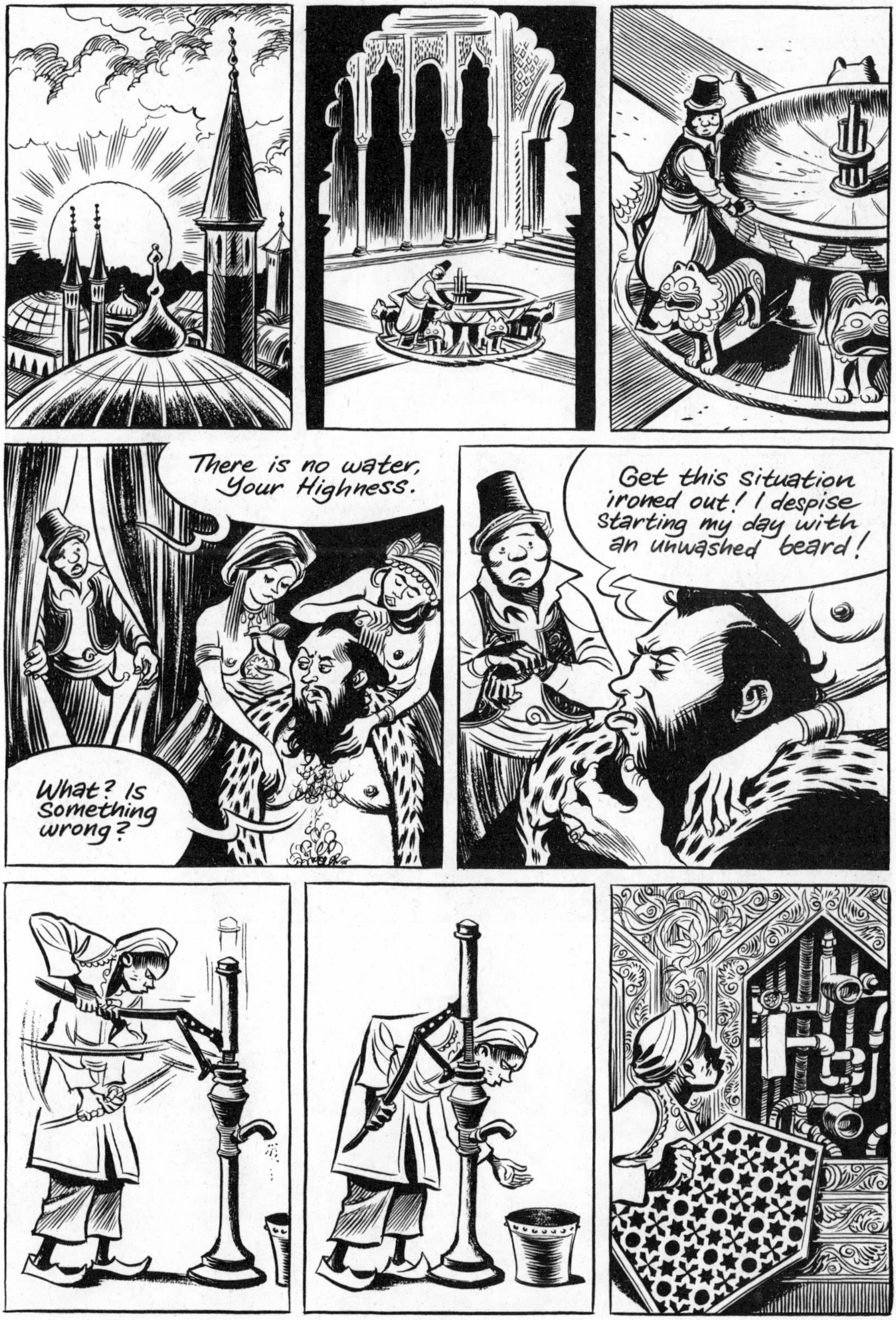
There is no water, Your Highness.
What? Is Something wrong?
Get this situation ironed out! I despise starting my day with an unwashed beard!

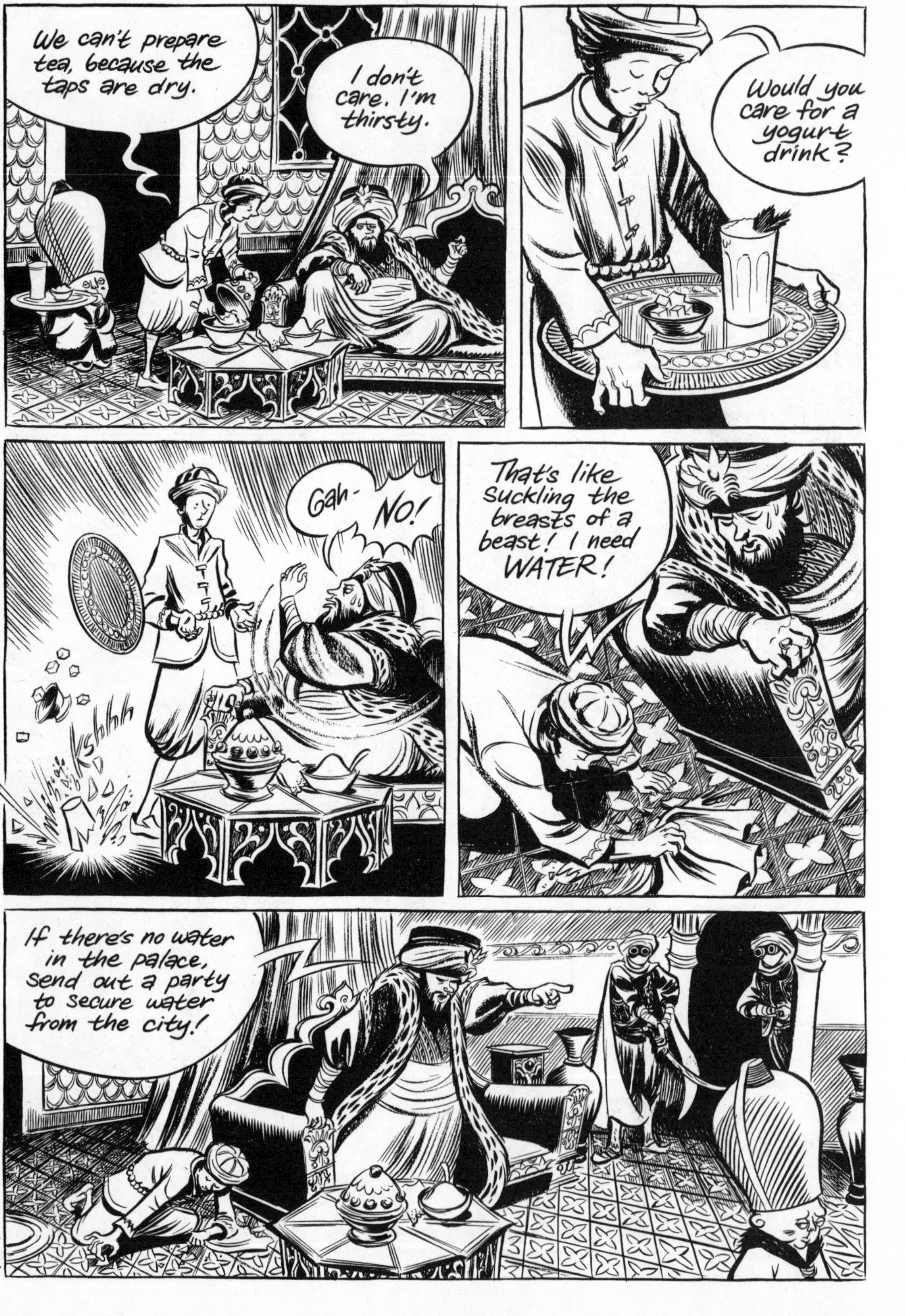
We can't prepare tea, because the taps are dry.
I don't care. I'm thirsty.
Would you care for a yogurt drink?
Gah-
NO!
Kshhh
That's like suckling the breasts of a beast! I need WATER!
If there's no water in the palace, send out a party to secure water from the city!

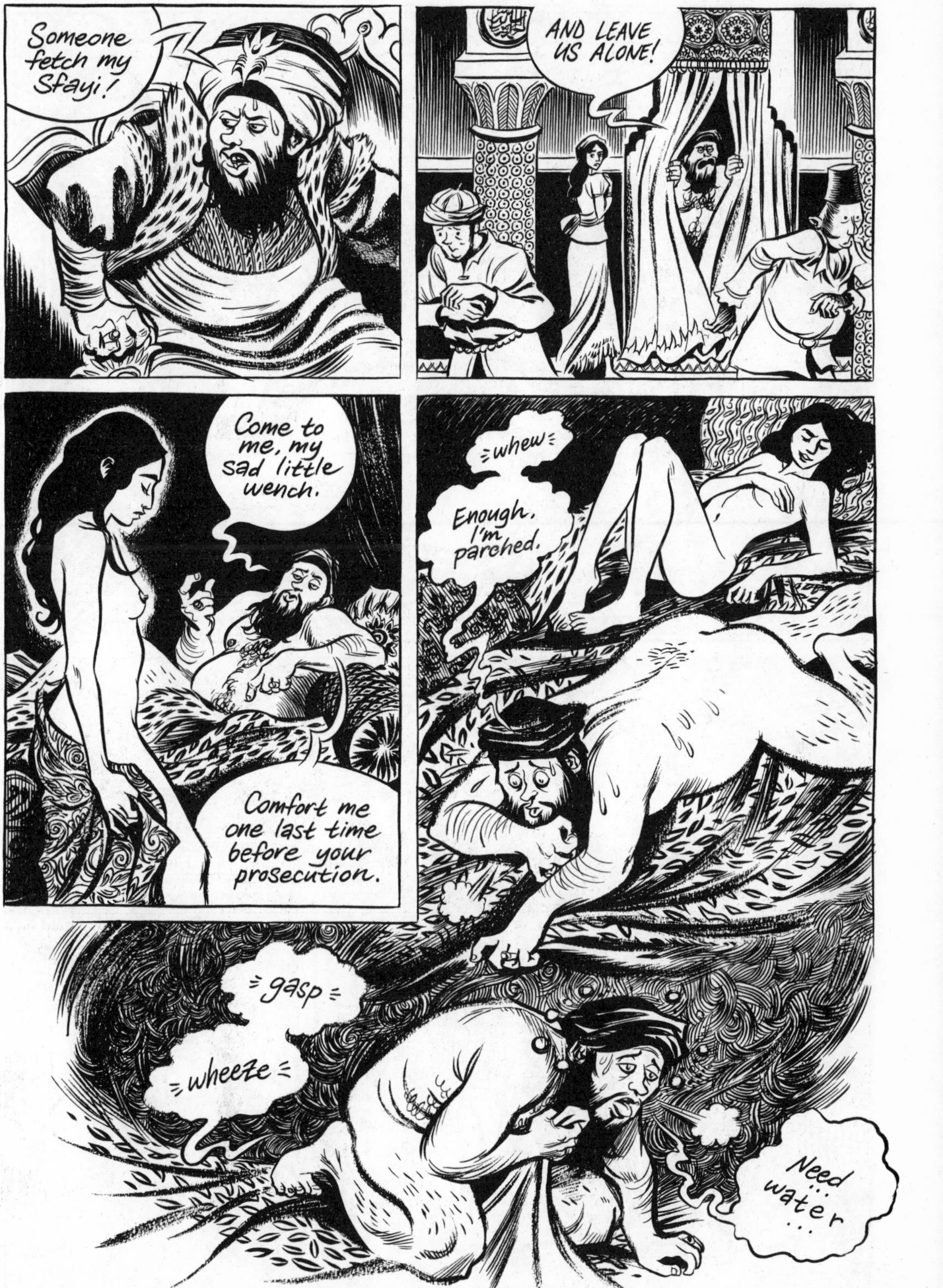
Someone fetch my Sfayi!
AND LEAVE US ALONE!
Come to me, my sad little wench.
Comfort me one last time before your prosecution.
whew
Enough, I'm parched.
gasp
wheeze
Need... water...

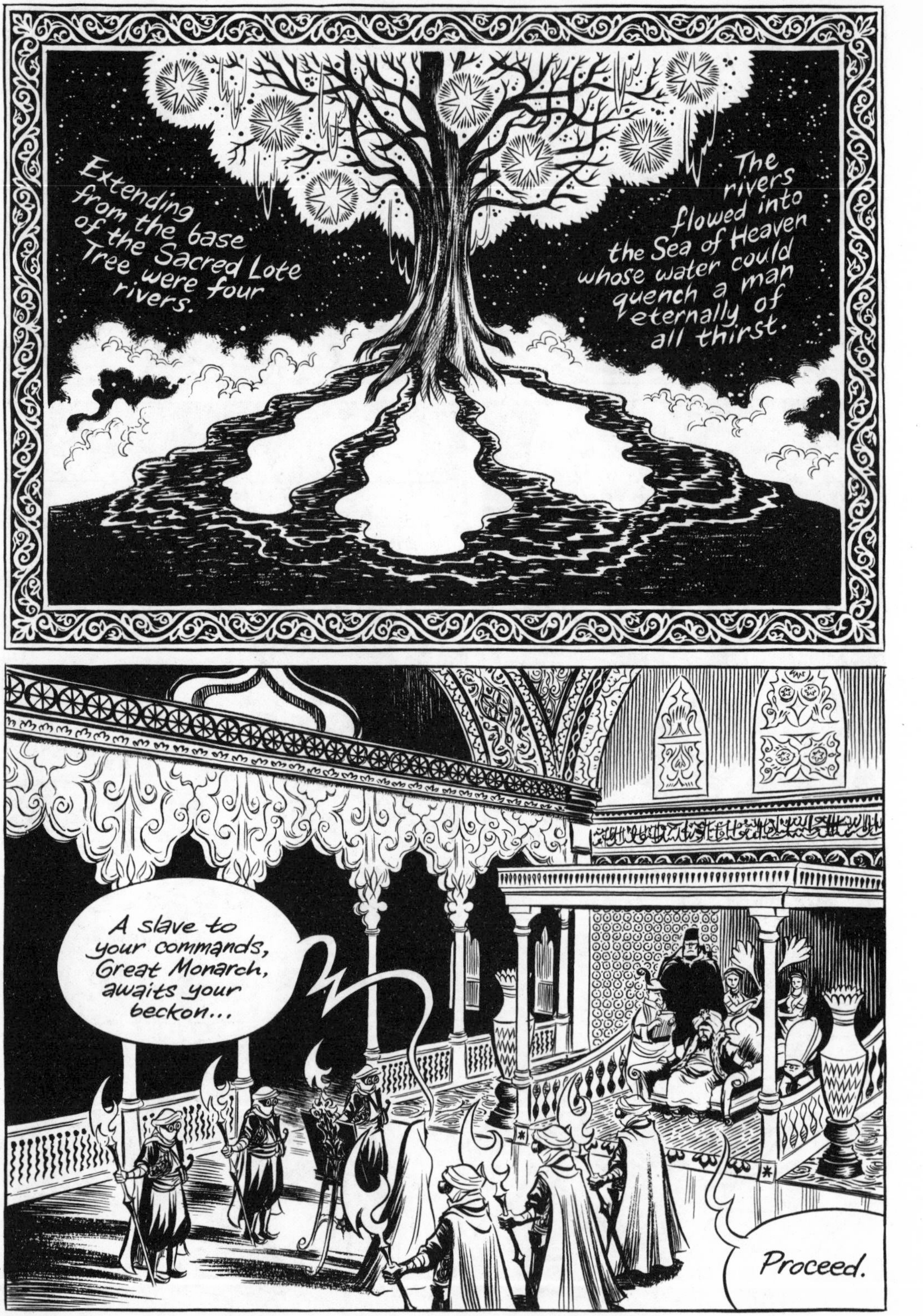
Extending from the base of the Sacred Lote Tree were four rivers.
The rivers flowed into the Sea of Heaven whose water could quench a man eternally of all thirst.
A slave to your commands, Great Monarch, awaits your beckon...
Proceed.

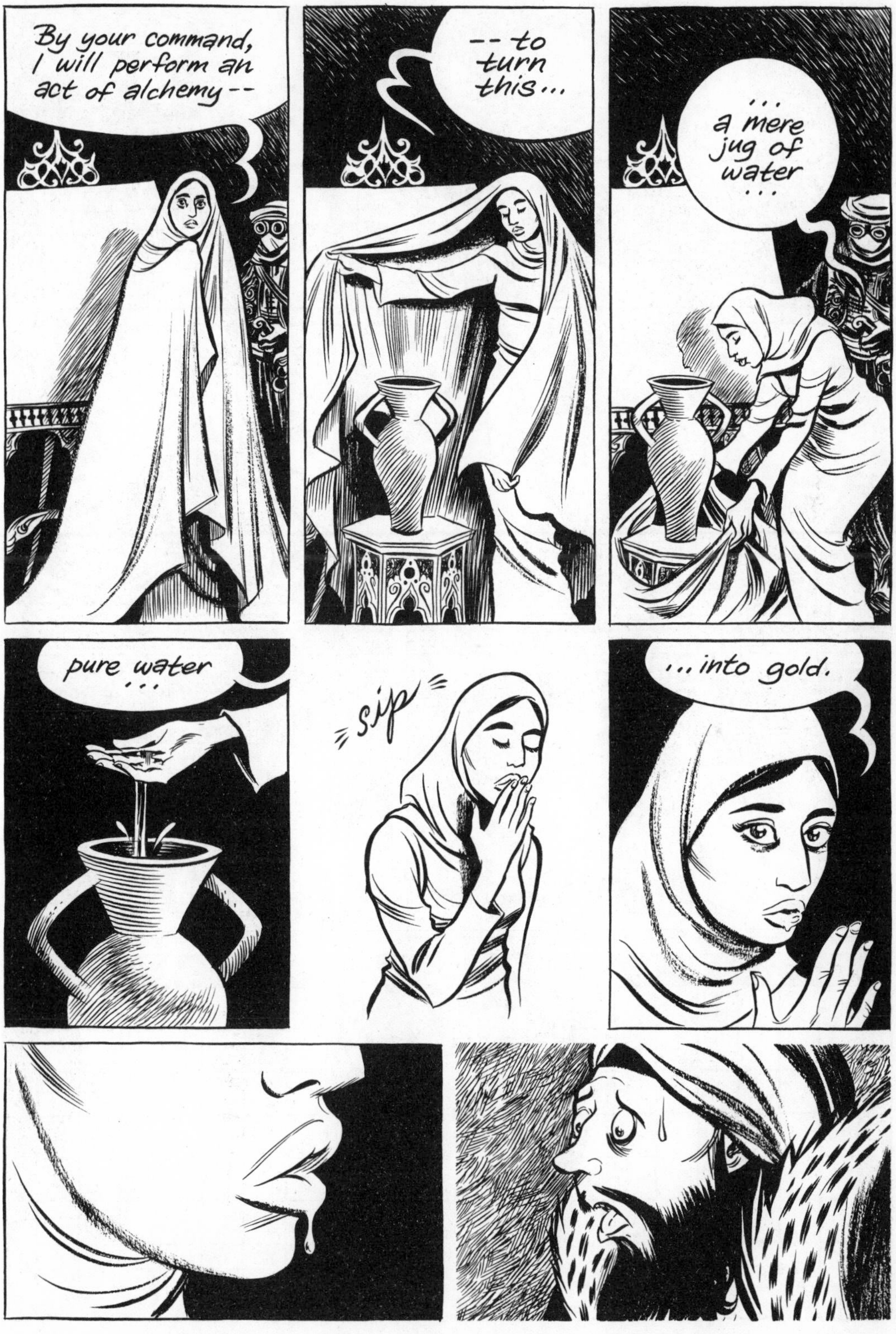

By your command, I will perform an act of alchemy--
--to turn this...
... a mere jug of water ...
pure water ...
sip
... into gold.

That makes it the only one in the palace!

...

Where did she get it?!

A charm must be drawn...

...a 7×7 magic square...

...with ALIF in the center of the top row,

And then ascending from the bottom, a stairway of letters-

-in numerical order:

baa'

haa'

jiim

waaw

daal

zaay

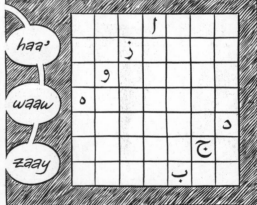

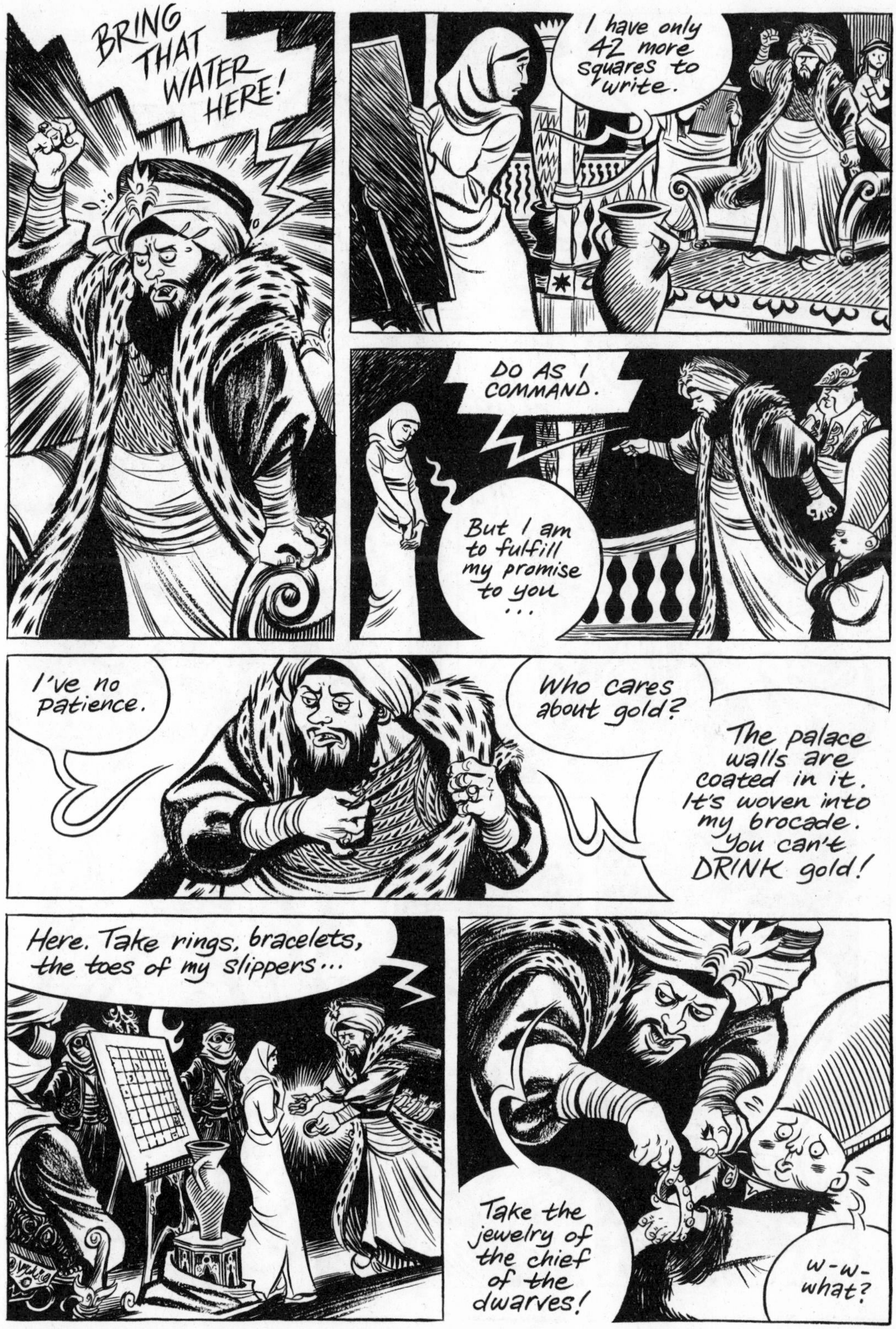
BRING THAT WATER HERE!
I have only 42 more squares to write.
DO AS I COMMAND.
But I am to fulfill my promise to you ...
I've no patience.
Who cares about gold?
The palace walls are coated in it. It's woven into my brocade. You can't DRINK gold!
Here. Take rings, bracelets, the toes of my slippers...
Take the jewelry of the chief of the dwarves!
w-w-what?

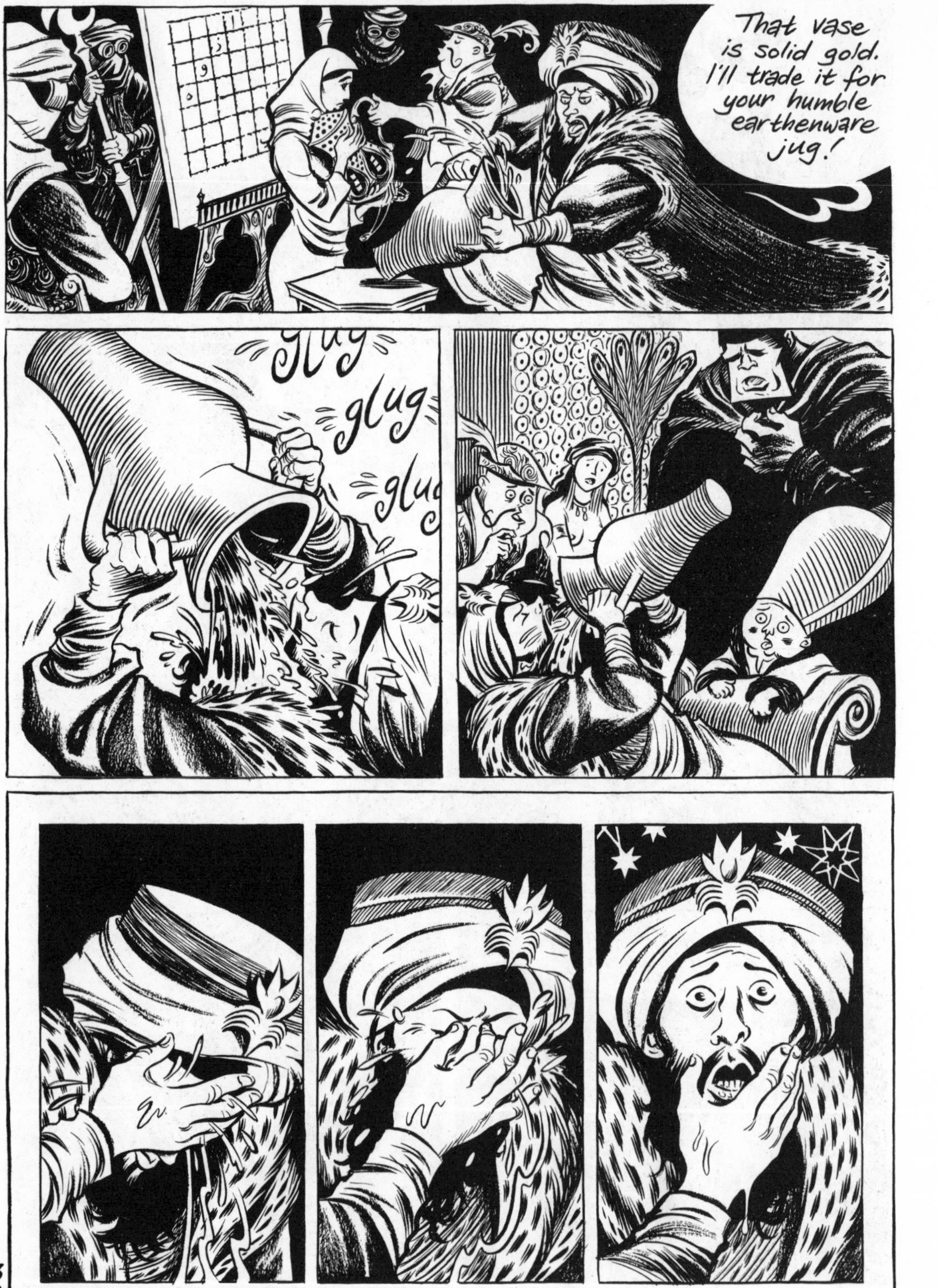
That vase is solid gold. I'll trade it for your humble earthenware jug!
glug

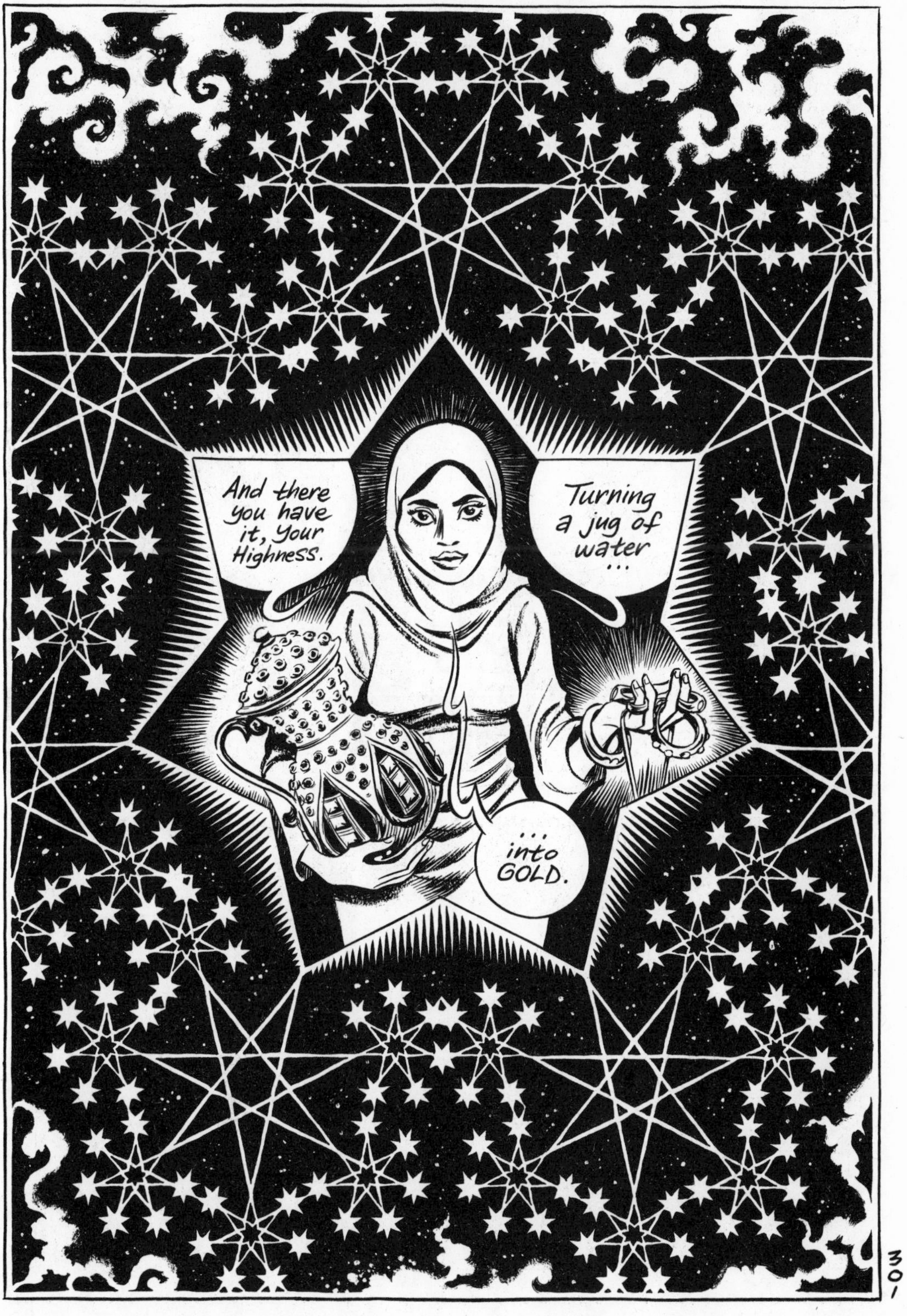
And there you have it, Your Highness.
Turning a jug of water ...
... into GOLD.

د	ط	ب
ج	ه	ز
ح	ا	و

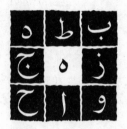

يد
فاطمة

HAND of
FATIMAH

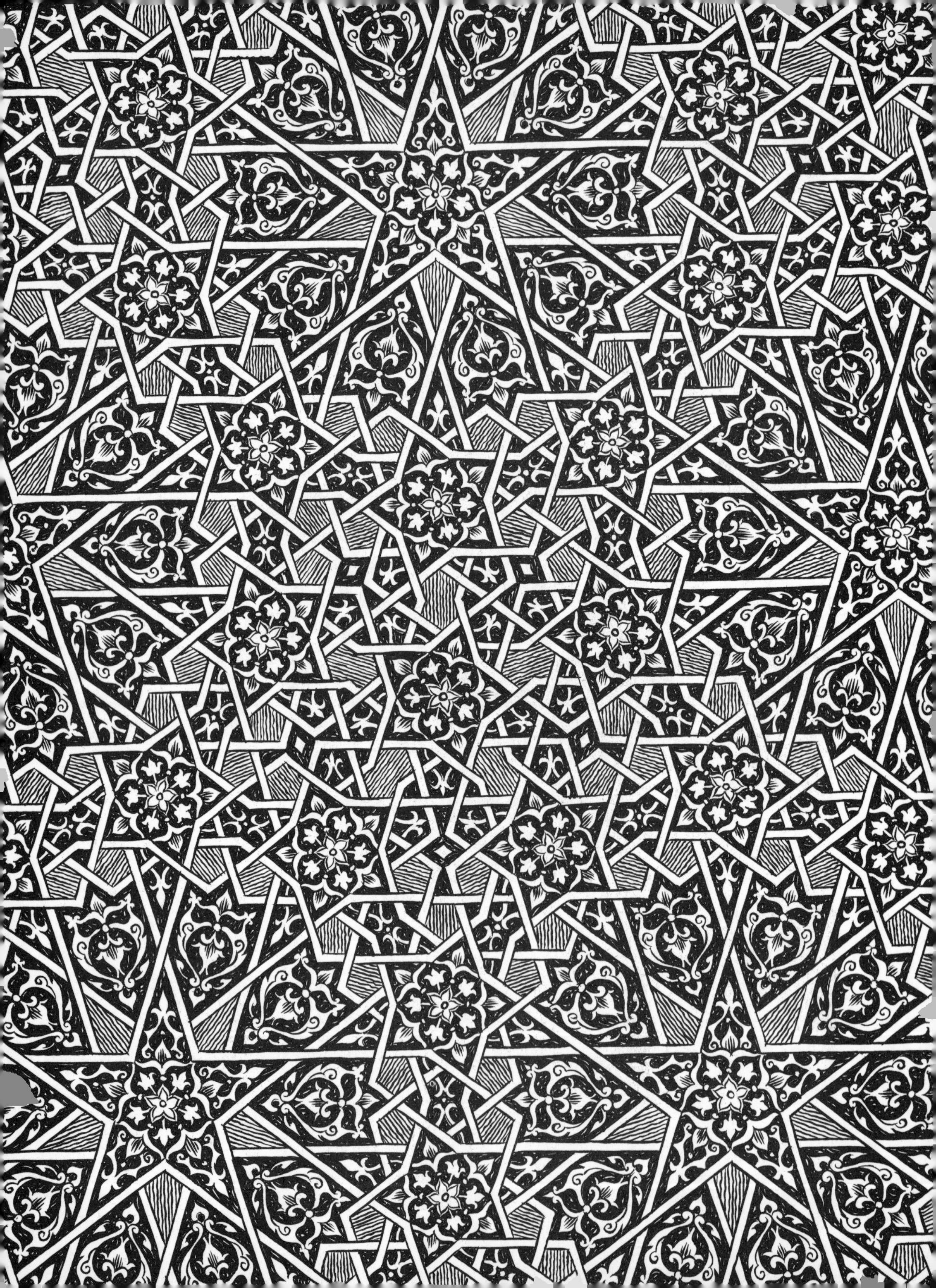

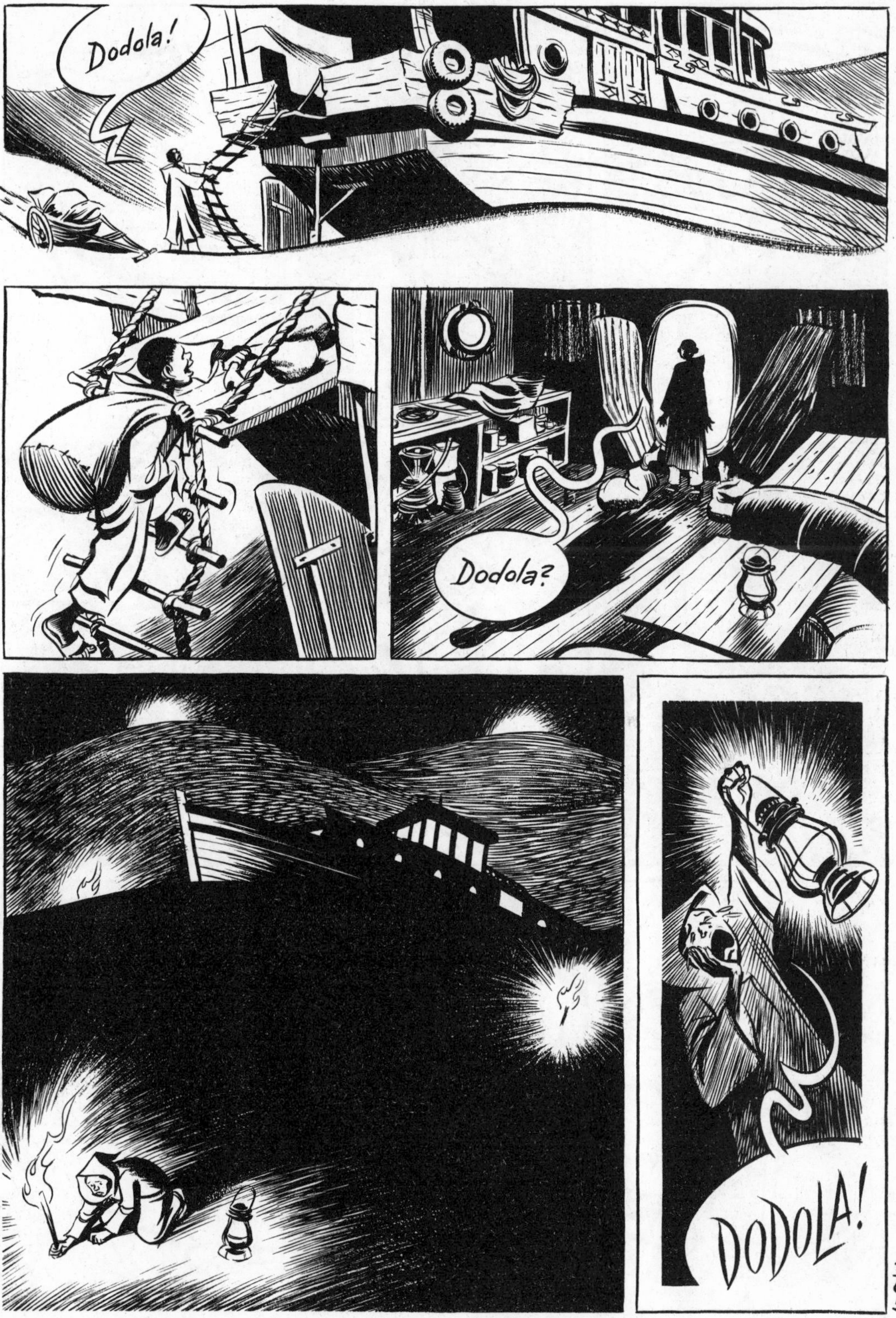
Dodola!
Dodola?
DODOLA!

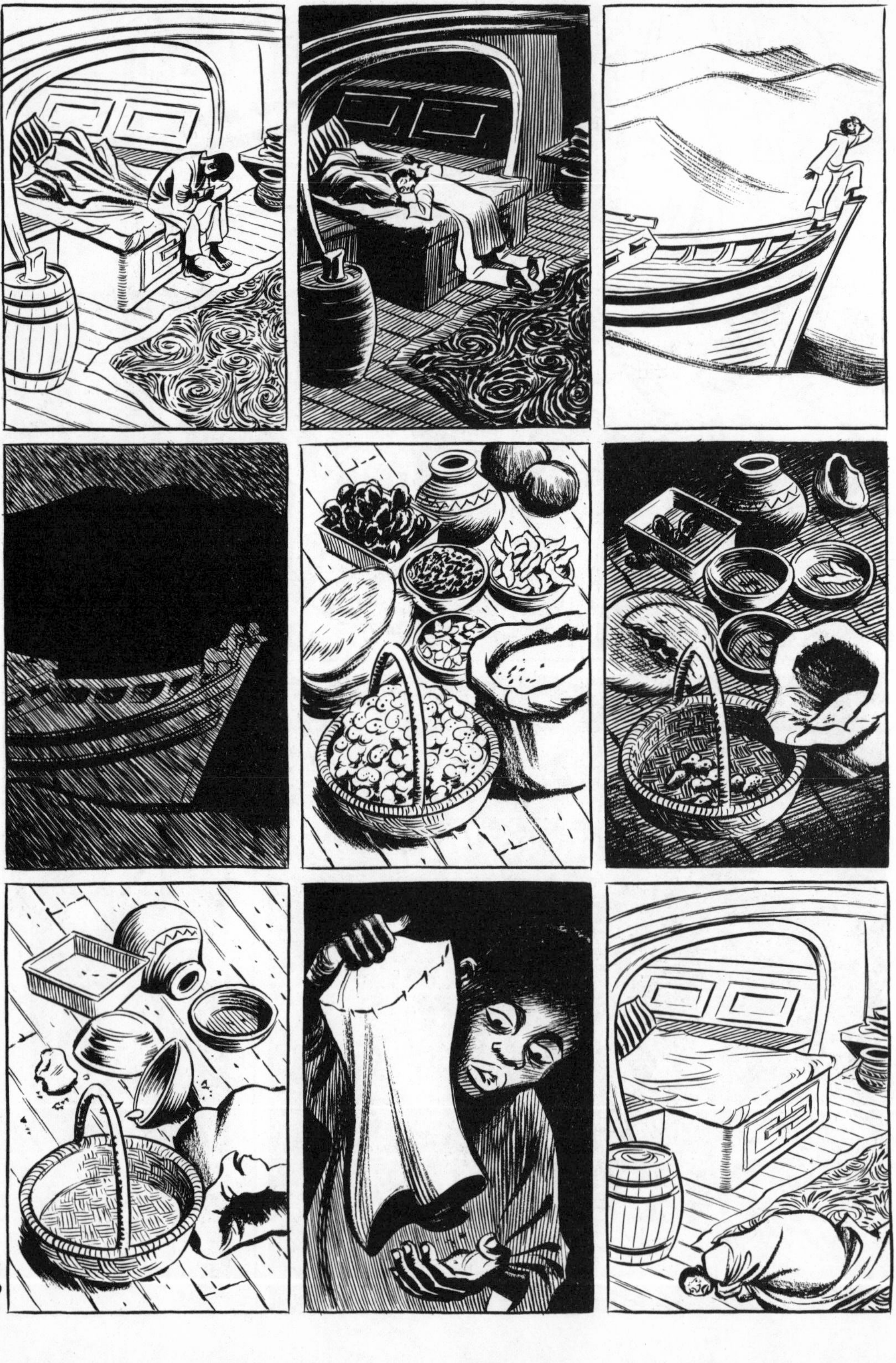

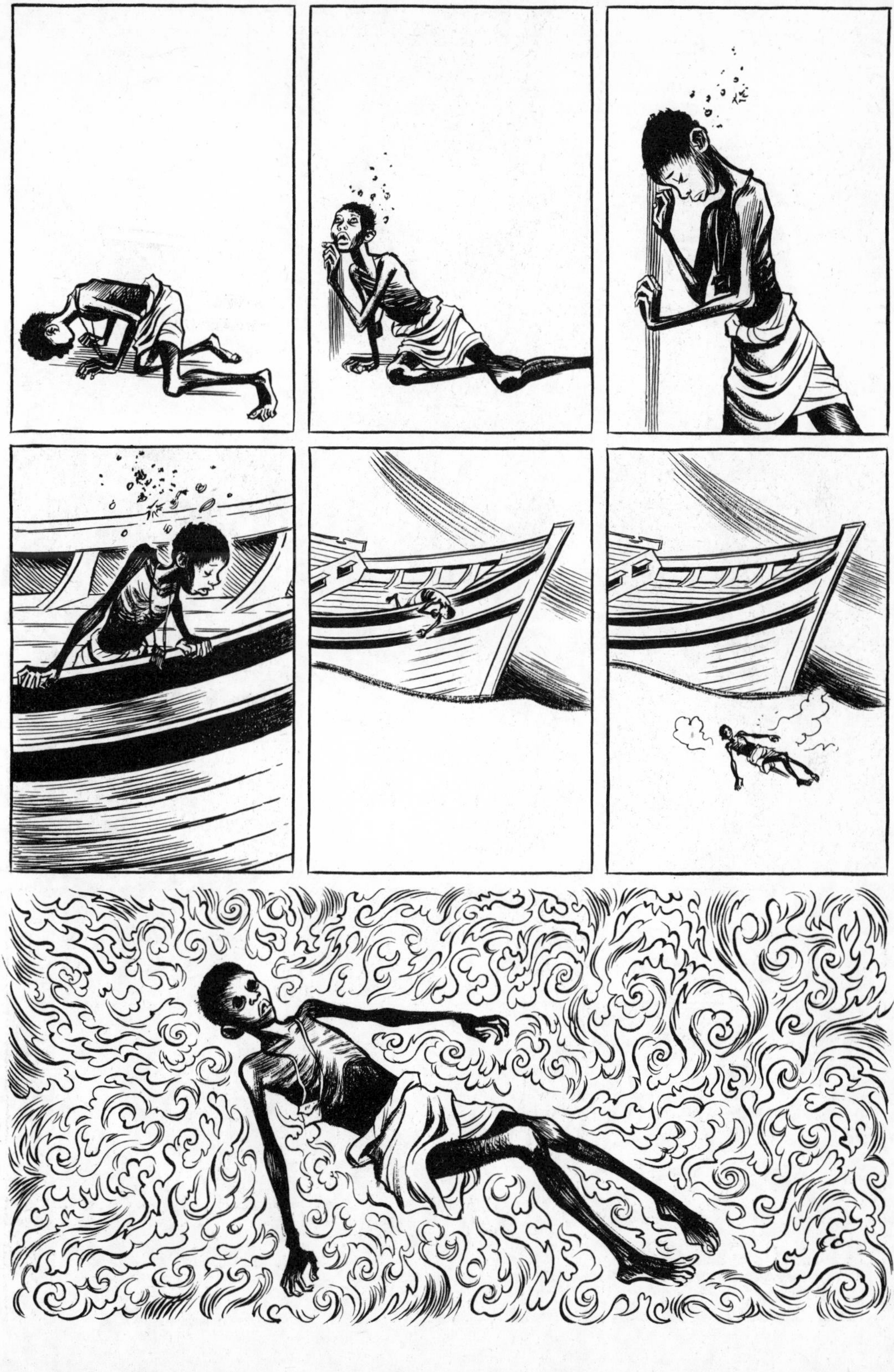

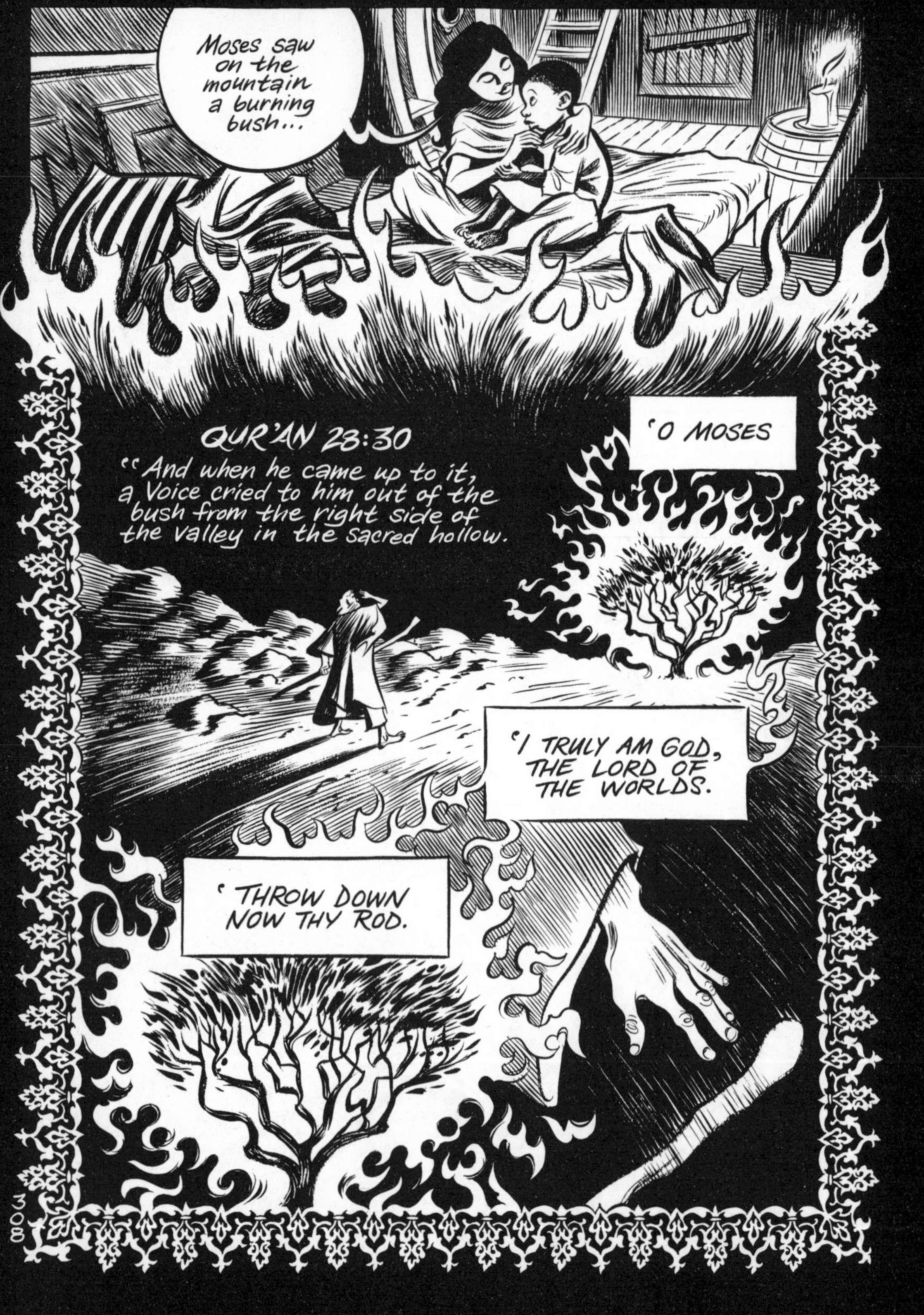
Moses saw on the mountain a burning bush...
QUR'AN 28:30
"And when he came up to it, a Voice cried to him out of the bush from the right side of the valley in the sacred hollow.
'O MOSES
'I TRULY AM GOD, THE LORD OF THE WORLDS.
'THROW DOWN NOW THY ROD.

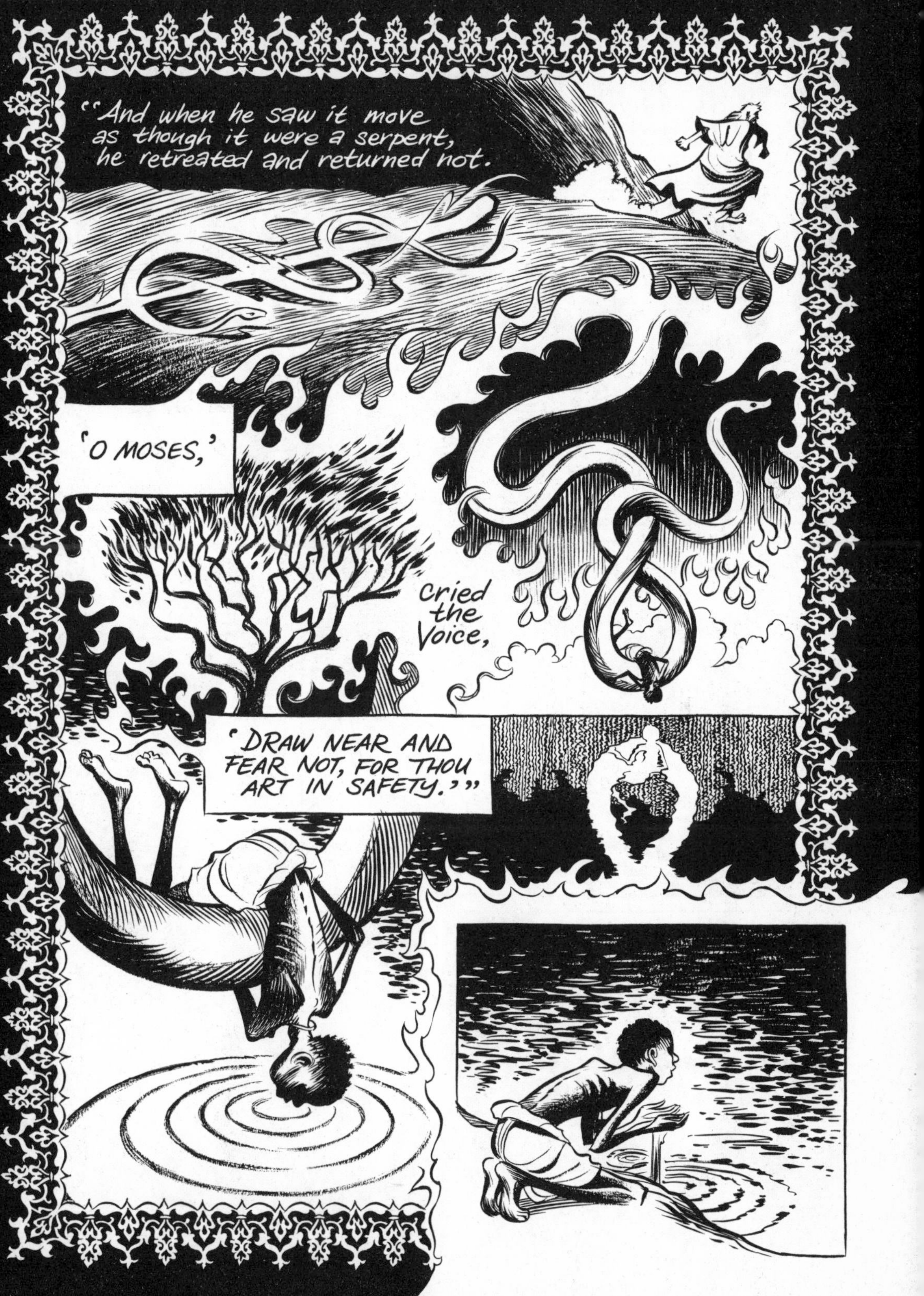
"And when he saw it move as though it were a serpent, he retreated and returned not.
'O MOSES,'
cried the Voice,
"DRAW NEAR AND FEAR NOT, FOR THOU ART IN SAFETY.'"

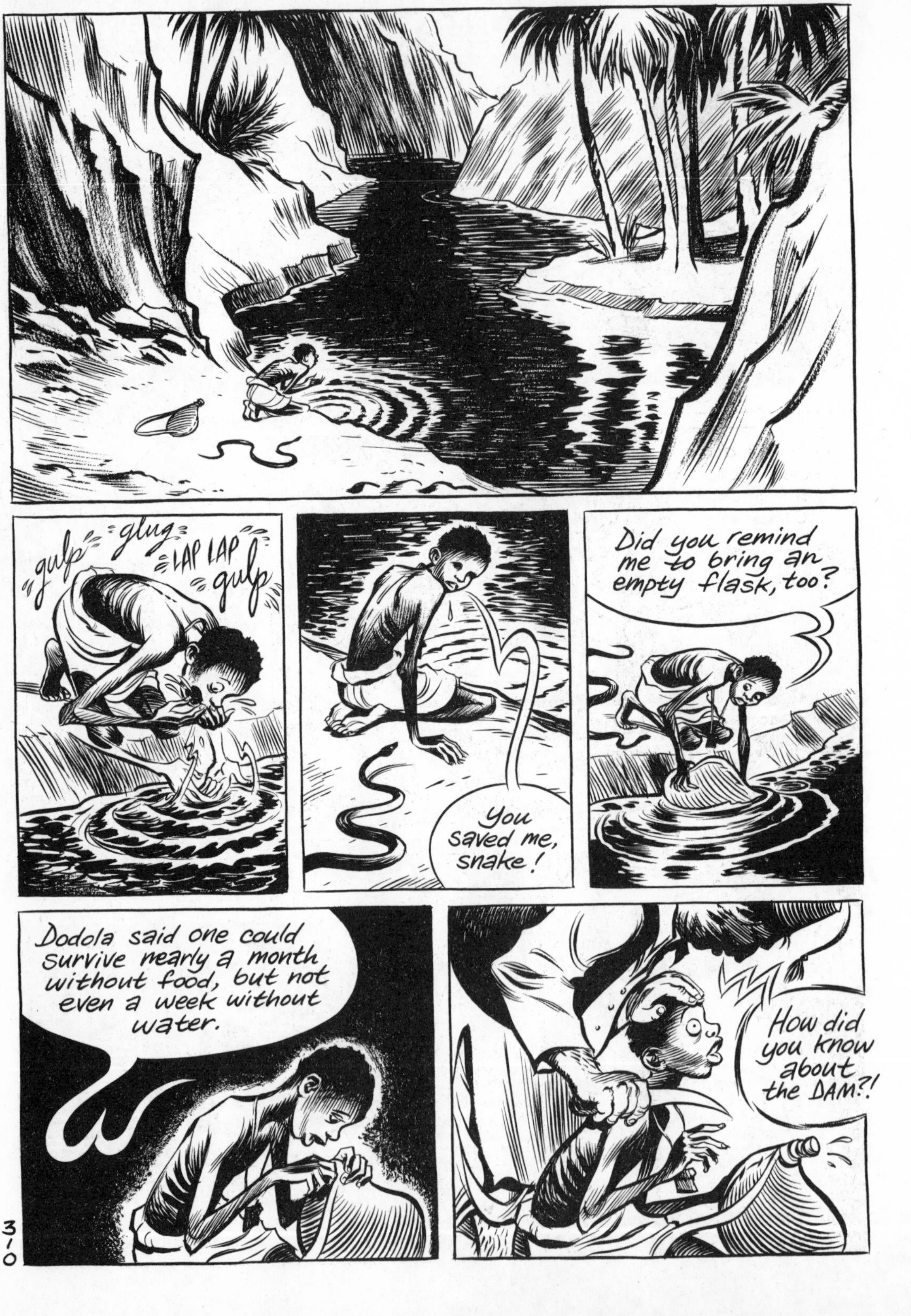
gulp glug LAP LAP gulp
You saved me, snake!
Did you remind me to bring an empty flask, too?
Dodola said one could survive nearly a month without food, but not even a week without water.
How did you know about the DAM?!

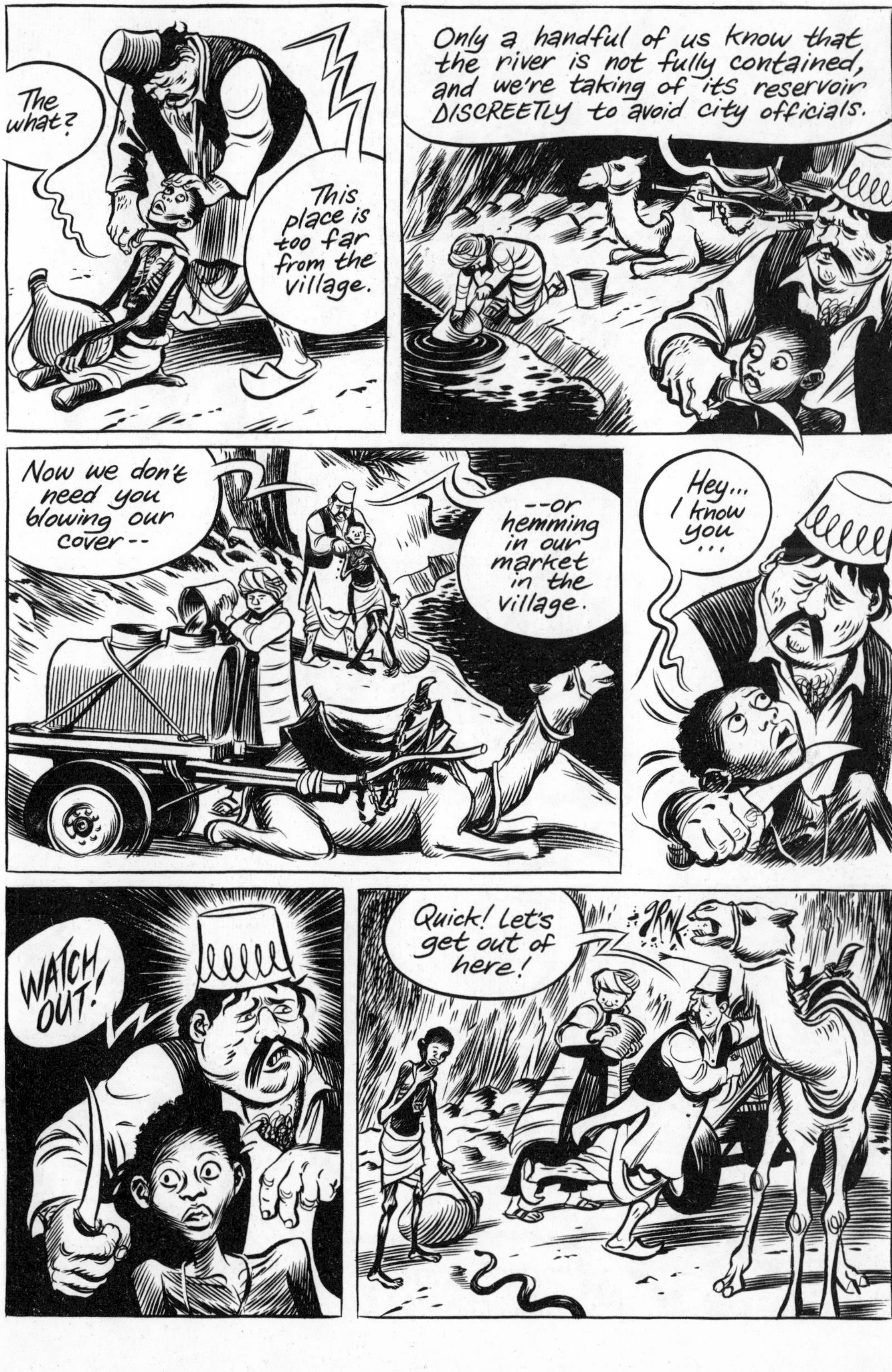

The what?
This place is too far from the village.
Only a handful of us know that the river is not fully contained, and we're taking of its reservoir DISCREETLY to avoid city officials.
Now we don't need you blowing our cover--
--or hemming in our market in the village.
Hey... I know you...
WATCH OUT!
Quick! Let's get out of here!
GRNK!

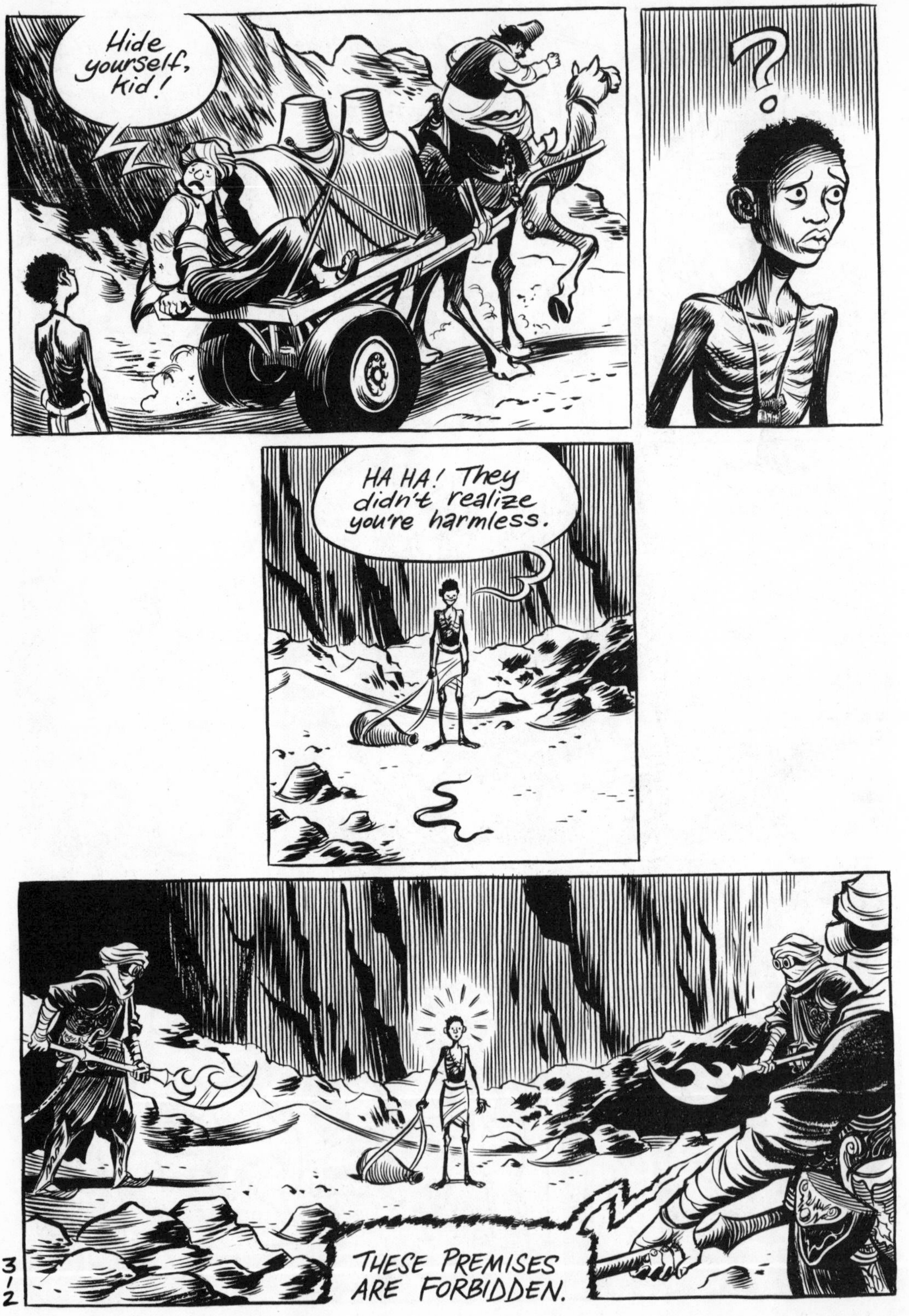
Hide yourself, kid!
?
HA HA! They didn't realize you're harmless.
THESE PREMISES ARE FORBIDDEN.

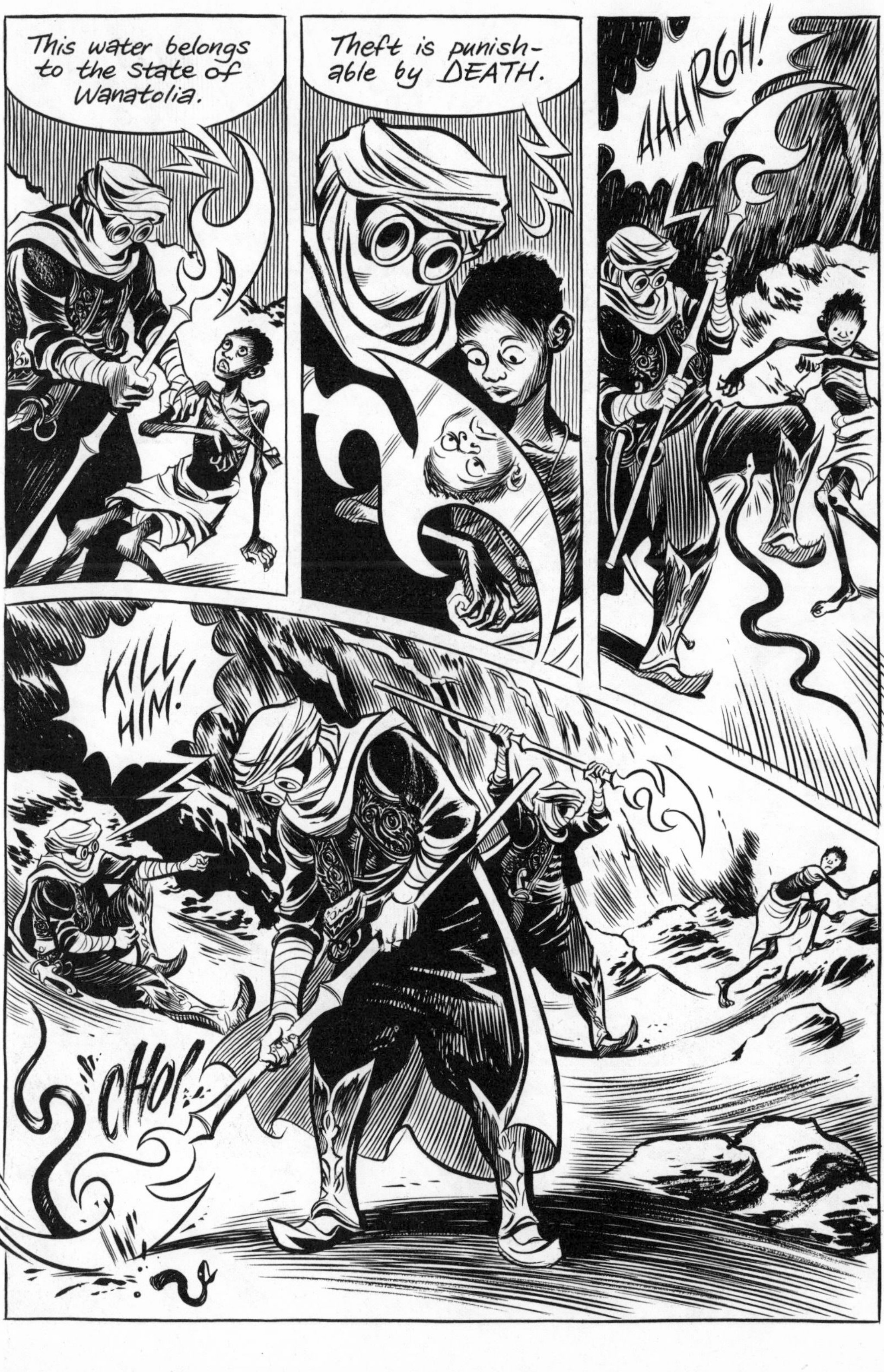
This water belongs to the State of Wanatolia.
Theft is punishable by DEATH.
AAARGH!
KILL HIM!
CHOP!

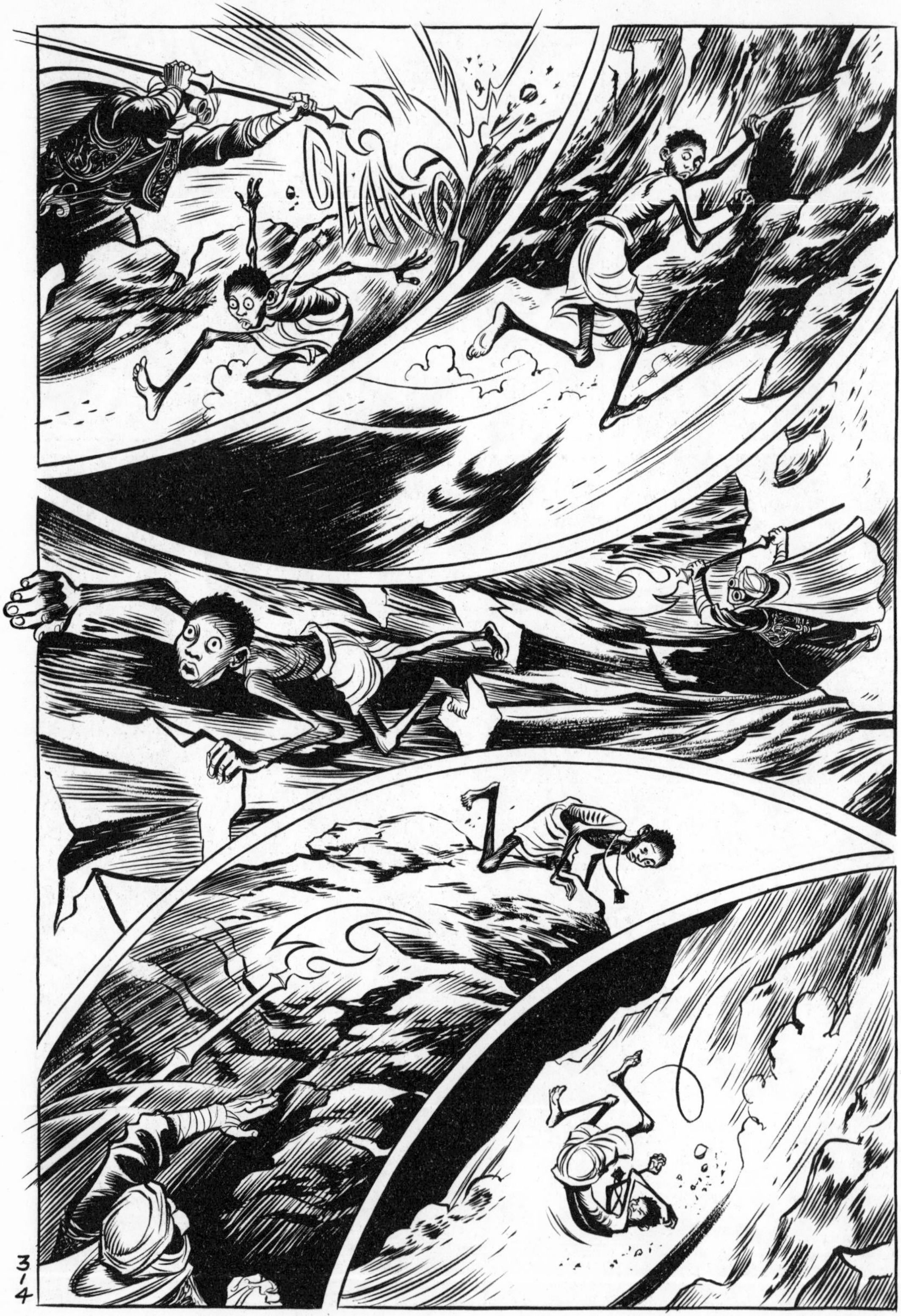
CLANG

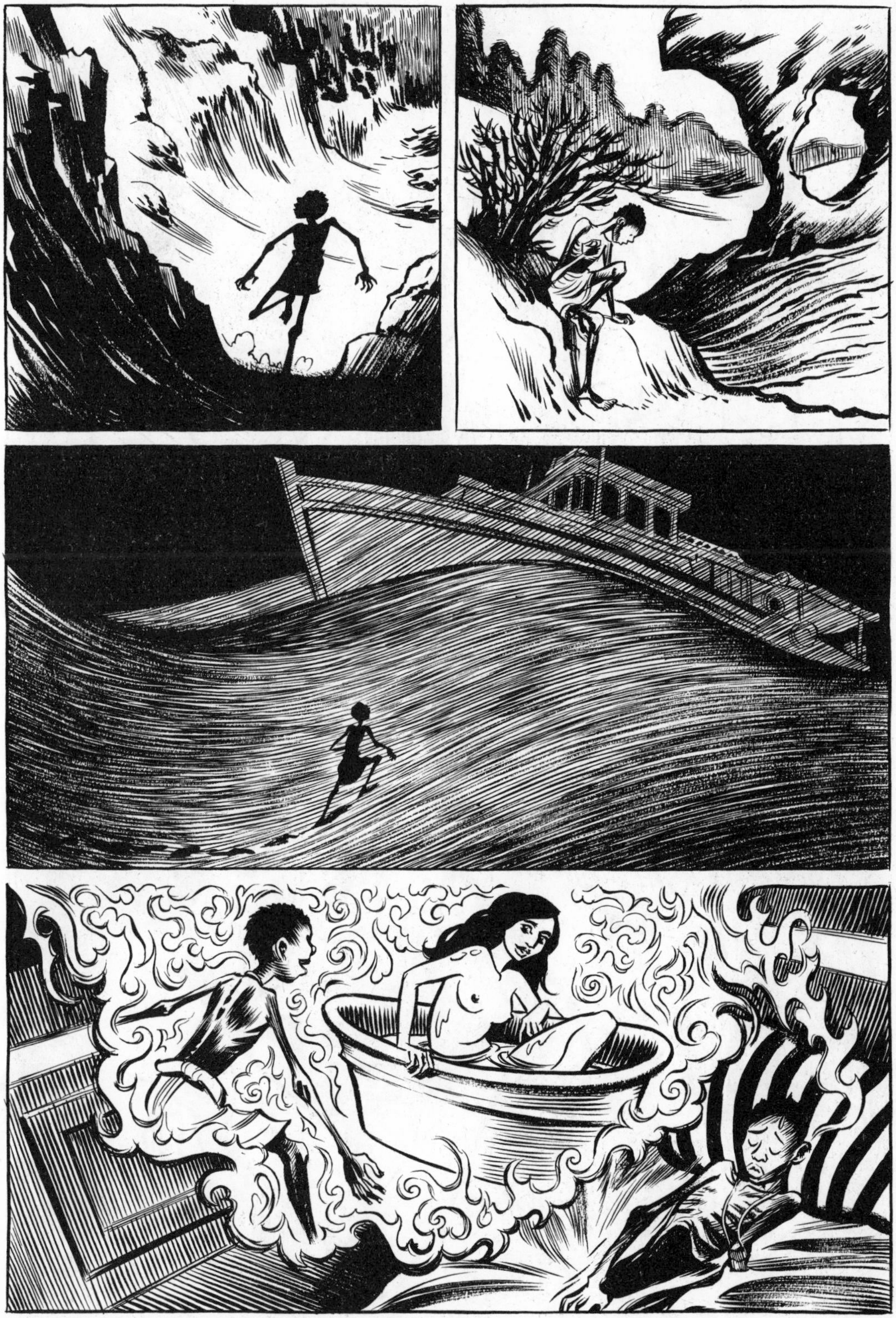

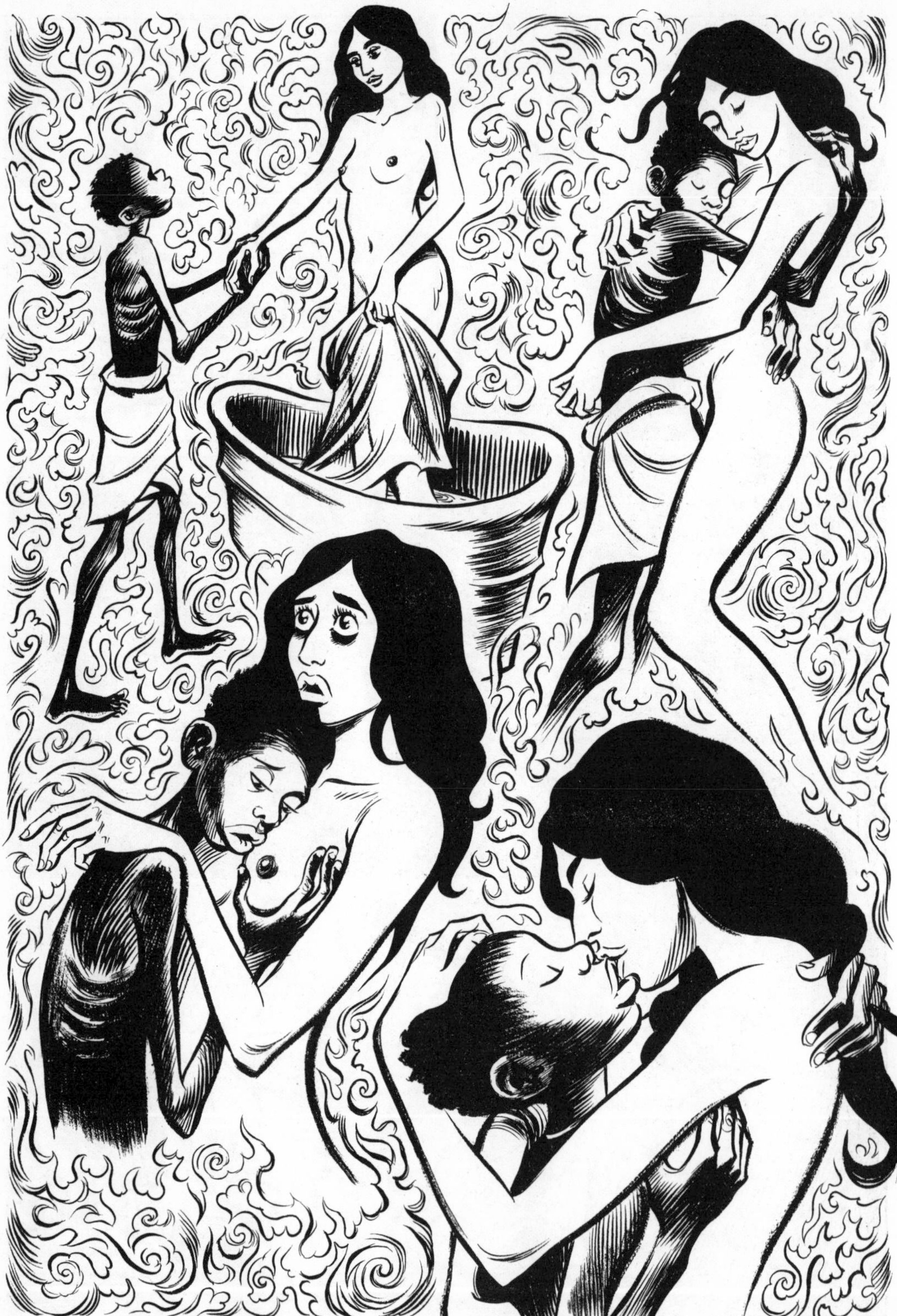

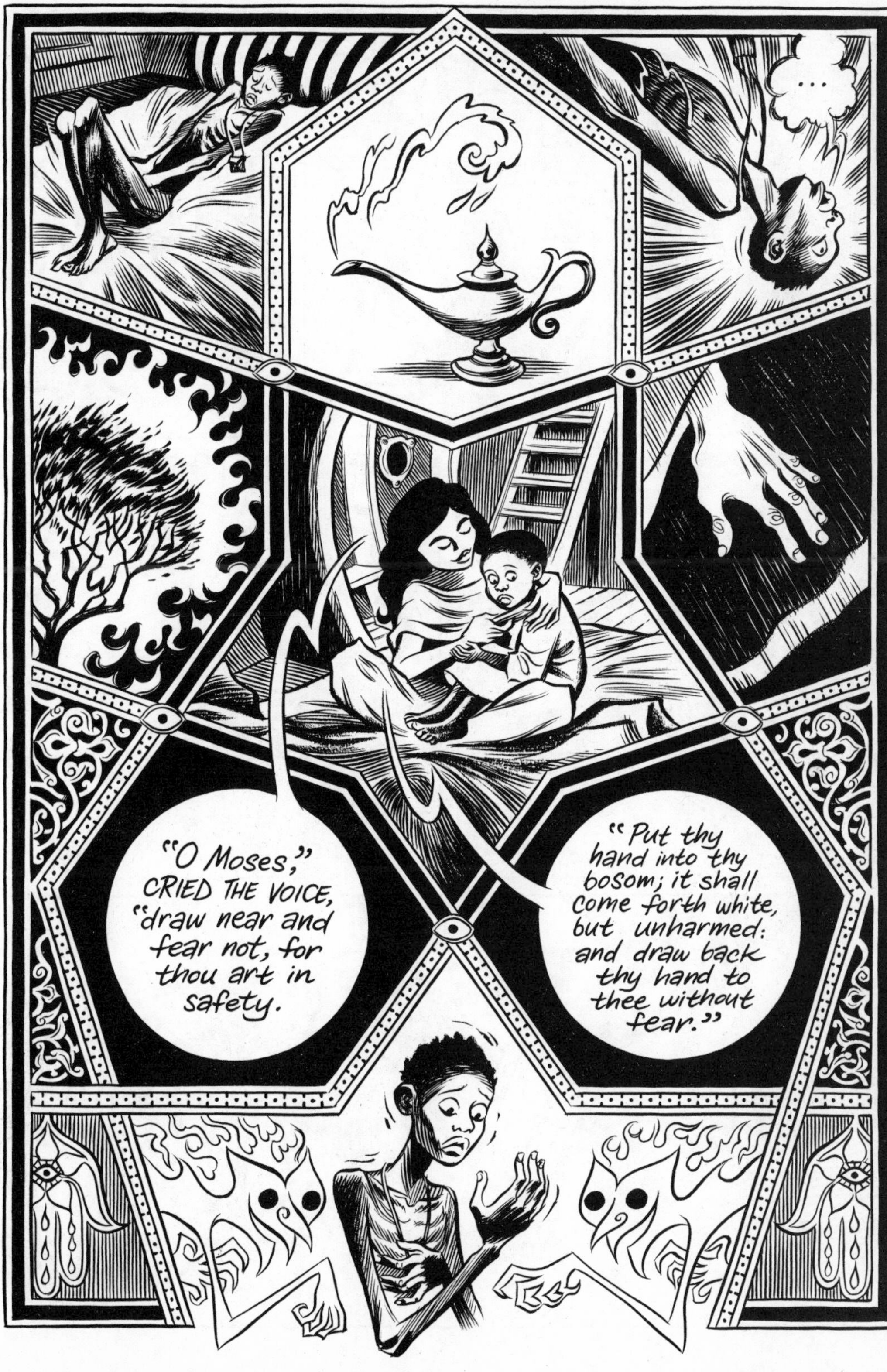
...
"O Moses," CRIED THE VOICE, "draw near and fear not, for thou art in safety.
"Put thy hand into thy bosom; it shall come forth white, but unharmed: and draw back thy hand to thee without fear."

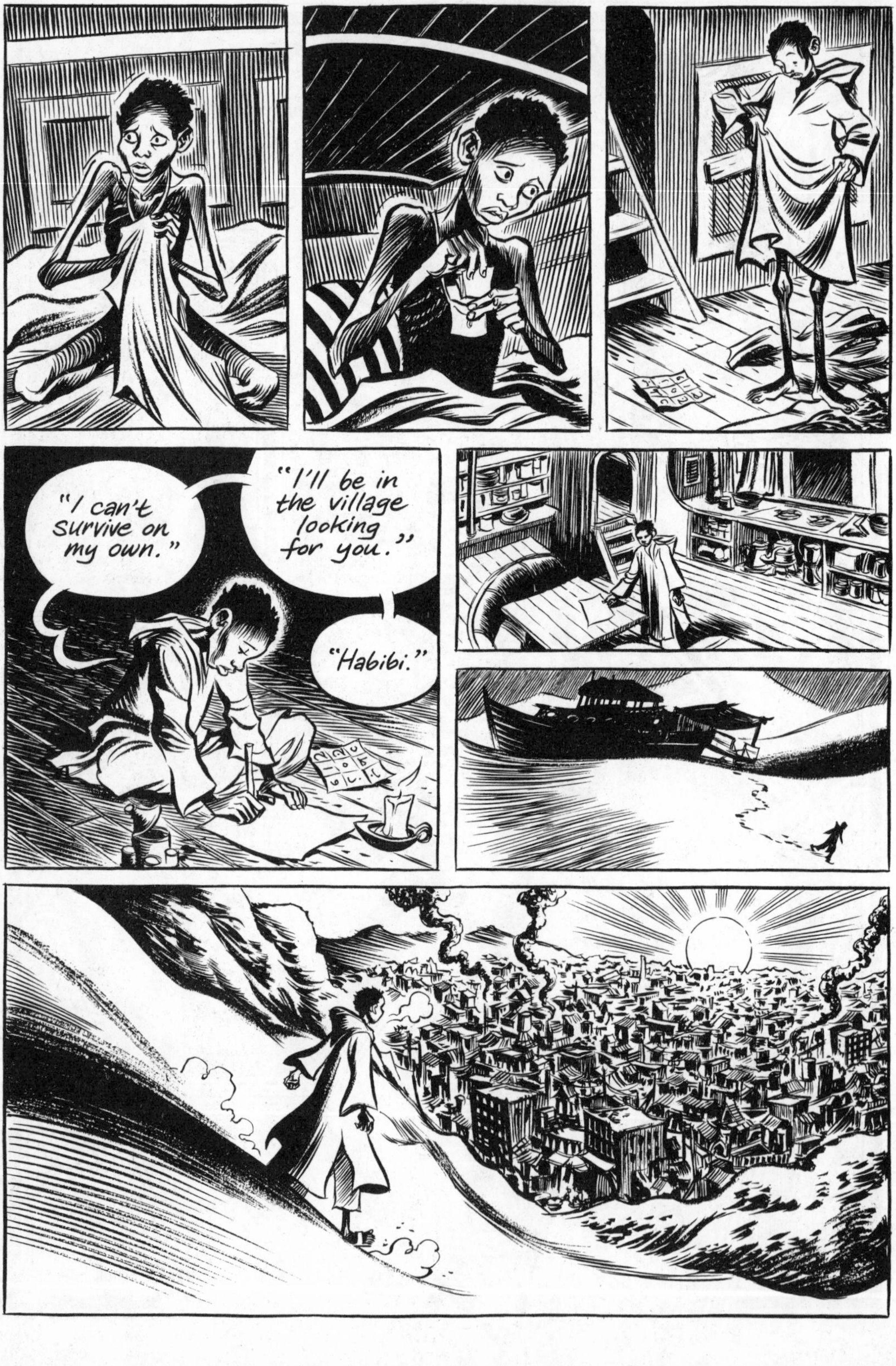
"I can't survive on my own."
"I'll be in the village looking for you."
"Habibi."

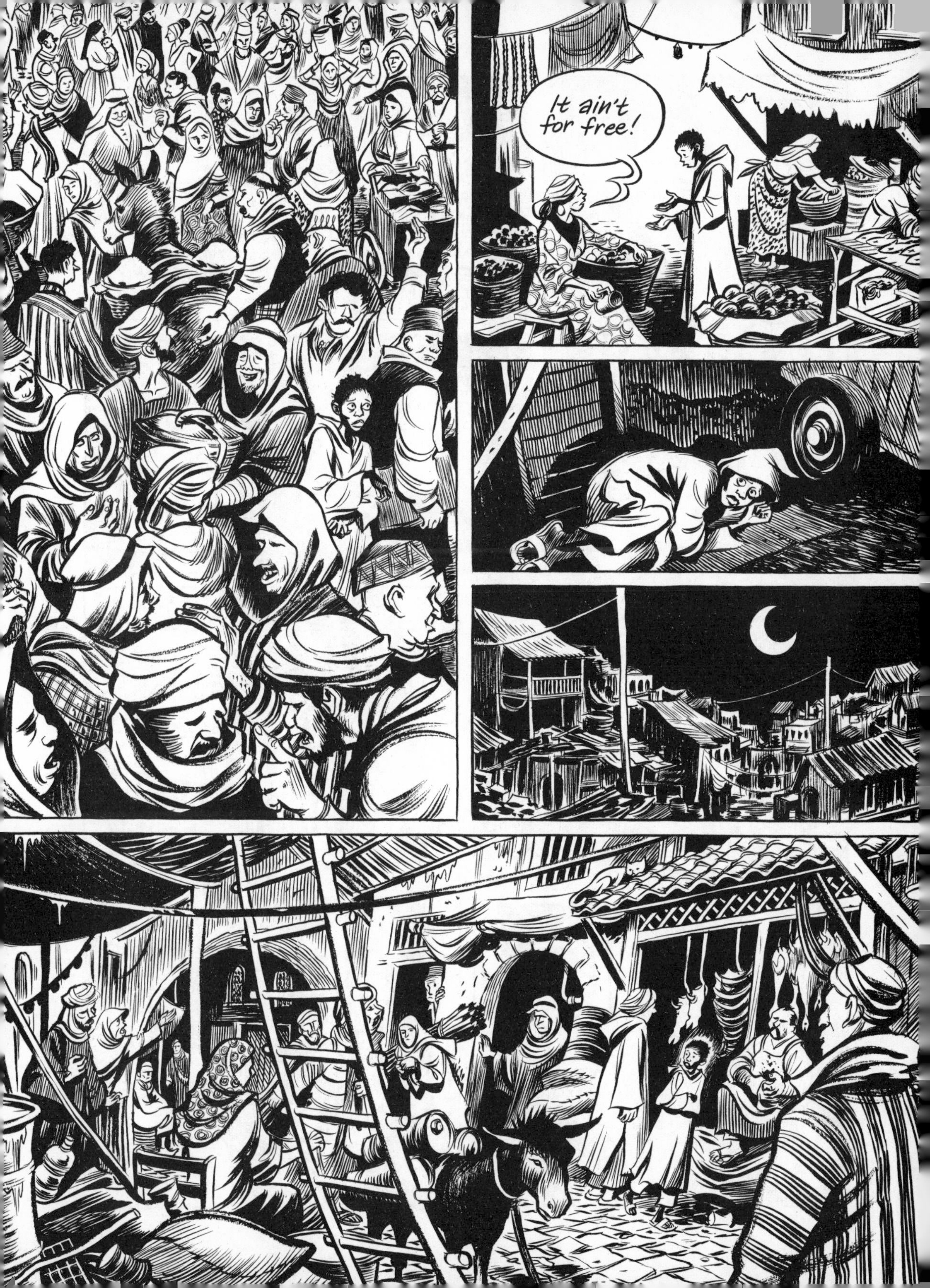
It ain't for free!

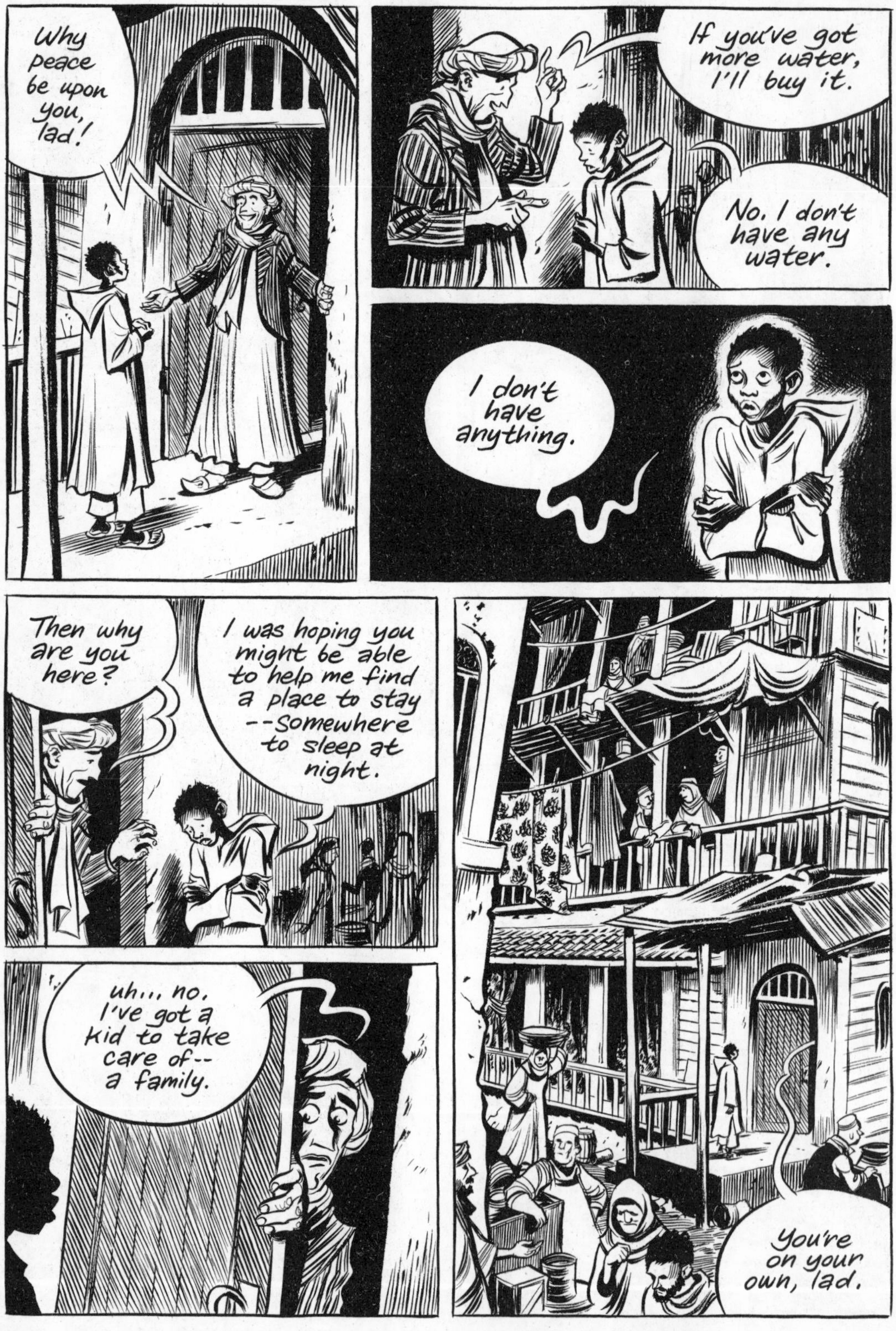
Why peace be upon you, lad!
If you've got more water, I'll buy it.
No. I don't have any water.
I don't have anything.
Then why are you here?
I was hoping you might be able to help me find a place to stay --somewhere to sleep at night.
uh... no. I've got a kid to take care of-- a family.
You're on your own, lad.

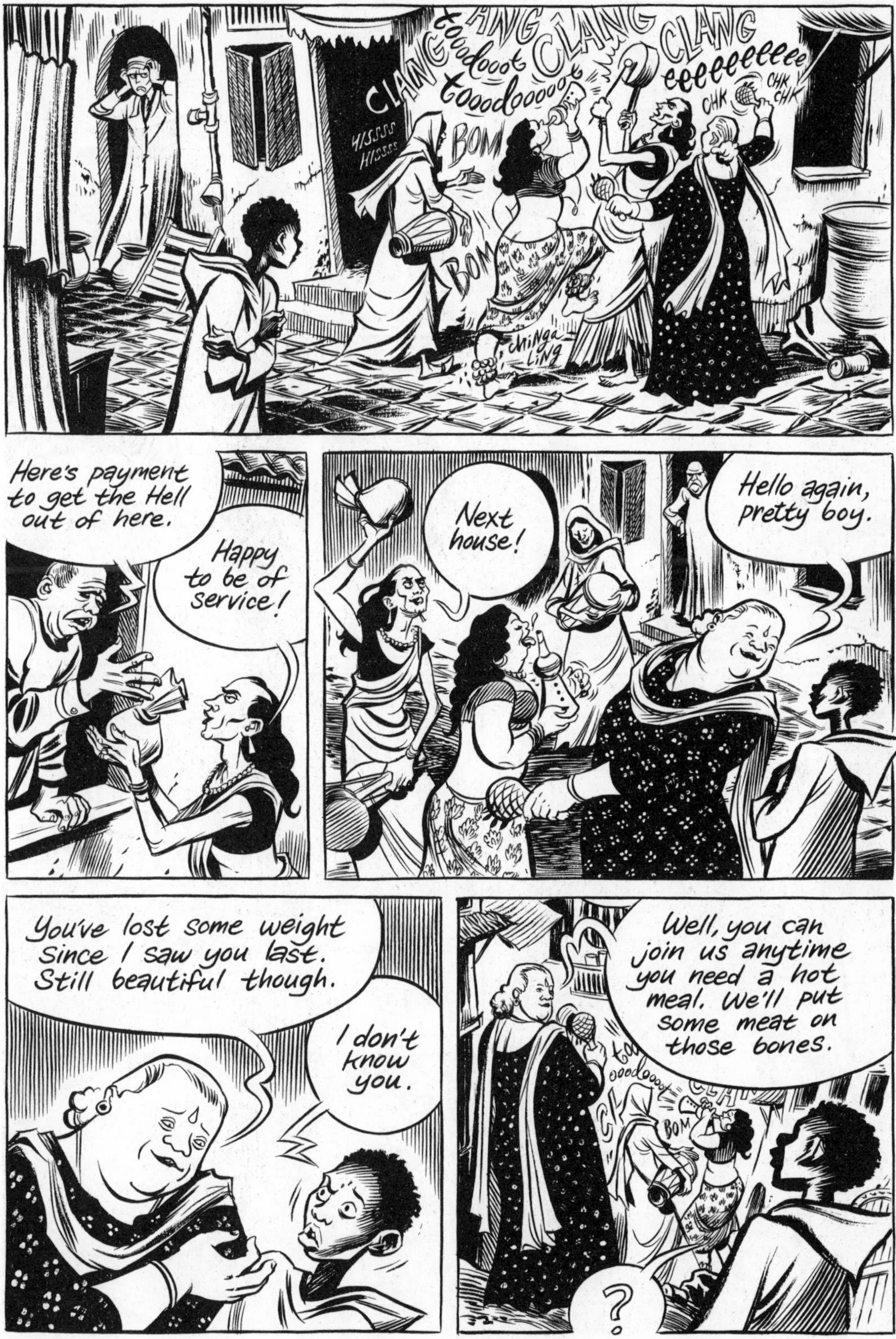
CLANG
ANG
tooodooot
CLANG
CLANG
tooodooooot
eeeeeeeee
CHK
CHK
CHK
CLANG
HISSSS
HISSSS
BOM
BOM
chinga ling
Here's payment to get the Hell out of here.
Happy to be of service!
Next house!
Hello again, pretty boy.
You've lost some weight since I saw you last. Still beautiful though.
I don't know you.
Well, you can join us anytime you need a hot meal. We'll put some meat on those bones.
?

If you help cart this produce across town, I'll gift you a couple spoiled persimmons.

If you clear the sewage off my mother's property, you'll have permanent room and bedding in my dogpen.

If you can tan this mound of hides, I'll set you up with some porridge or whatnot.

CLANG
BOM
BOM
BOM
B

What are you doing, darling?

Go away.

Geeeee
BOM
BOM
BOM
CLANG
BOM
eeee

Shoveling shit? And starving yourself for it!

It's a shame to see a pretty face go to waste.

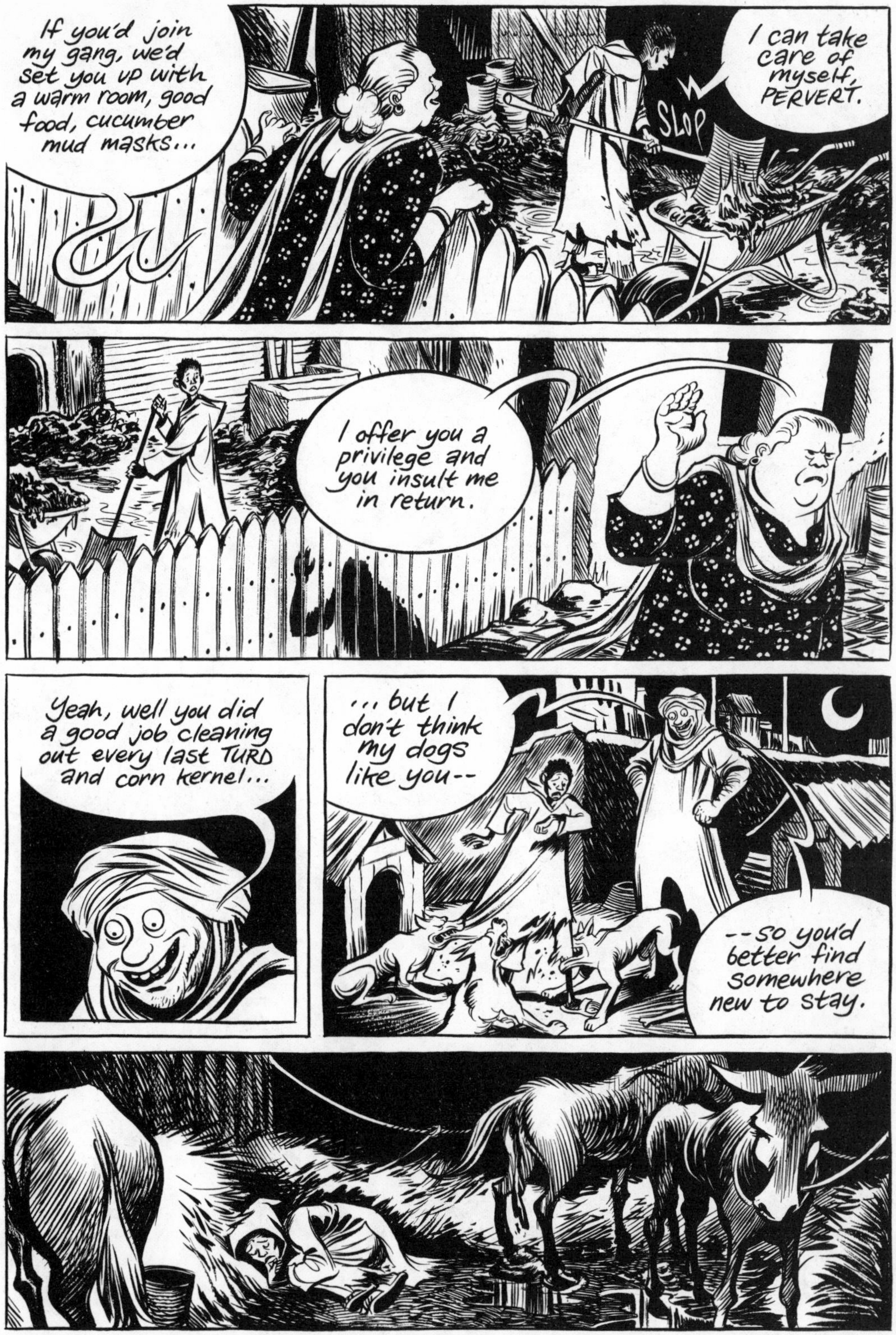
If you'd join my gang, we'd set you up with a warm room, good food, cucumber mud masks...
SLOP
I can take care of myself, PERVERT.
I offer you a privilege and you insult me in return.
Yeah, well you did a good job cleaning out every last TURD and corn kernel...
...but I don't think my dogs like you--
--so you'd better find somewhere new to stay.

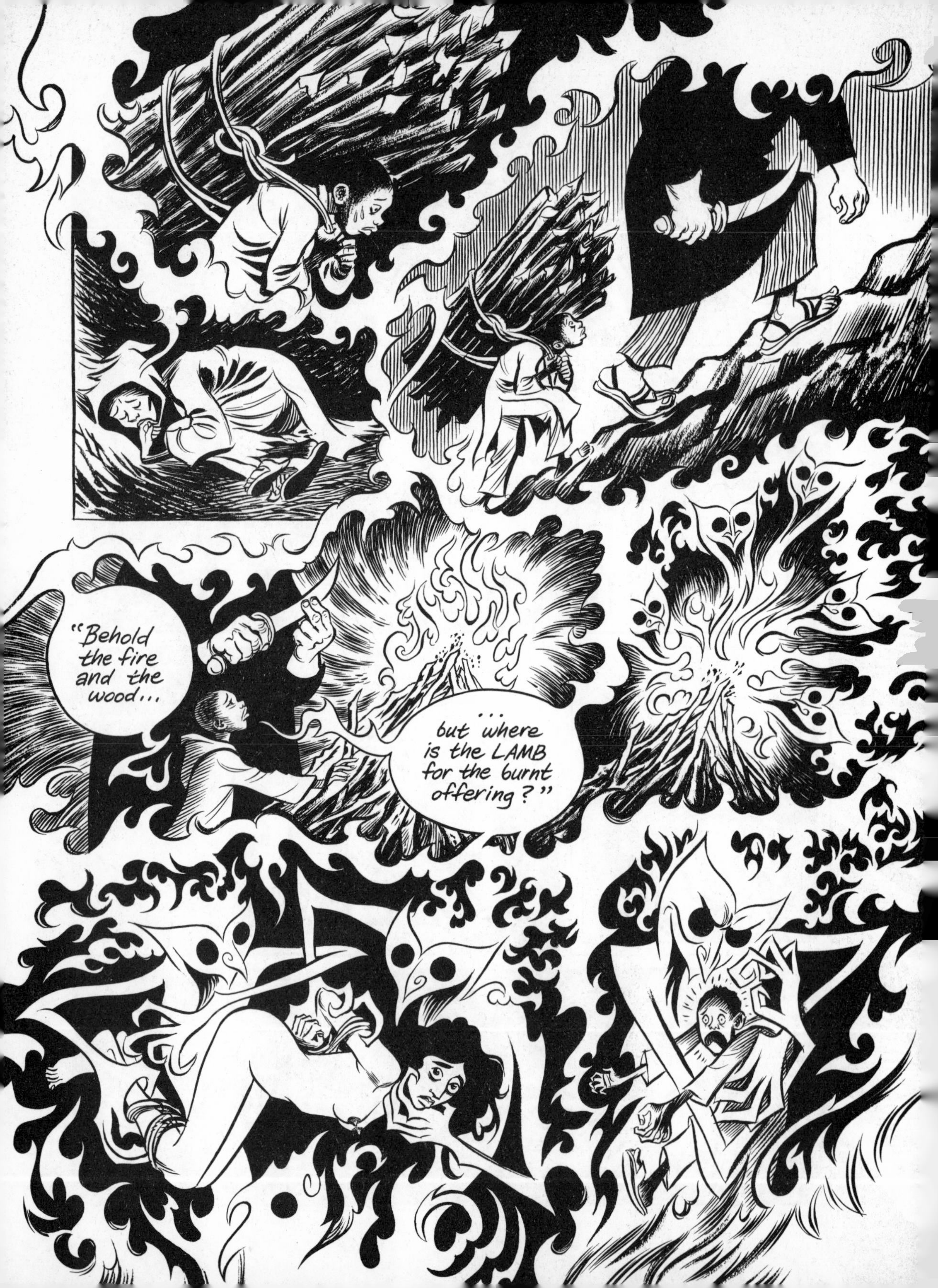
"Behold the fire and the wood...
... but where is the LAMB for the burnt offering?"

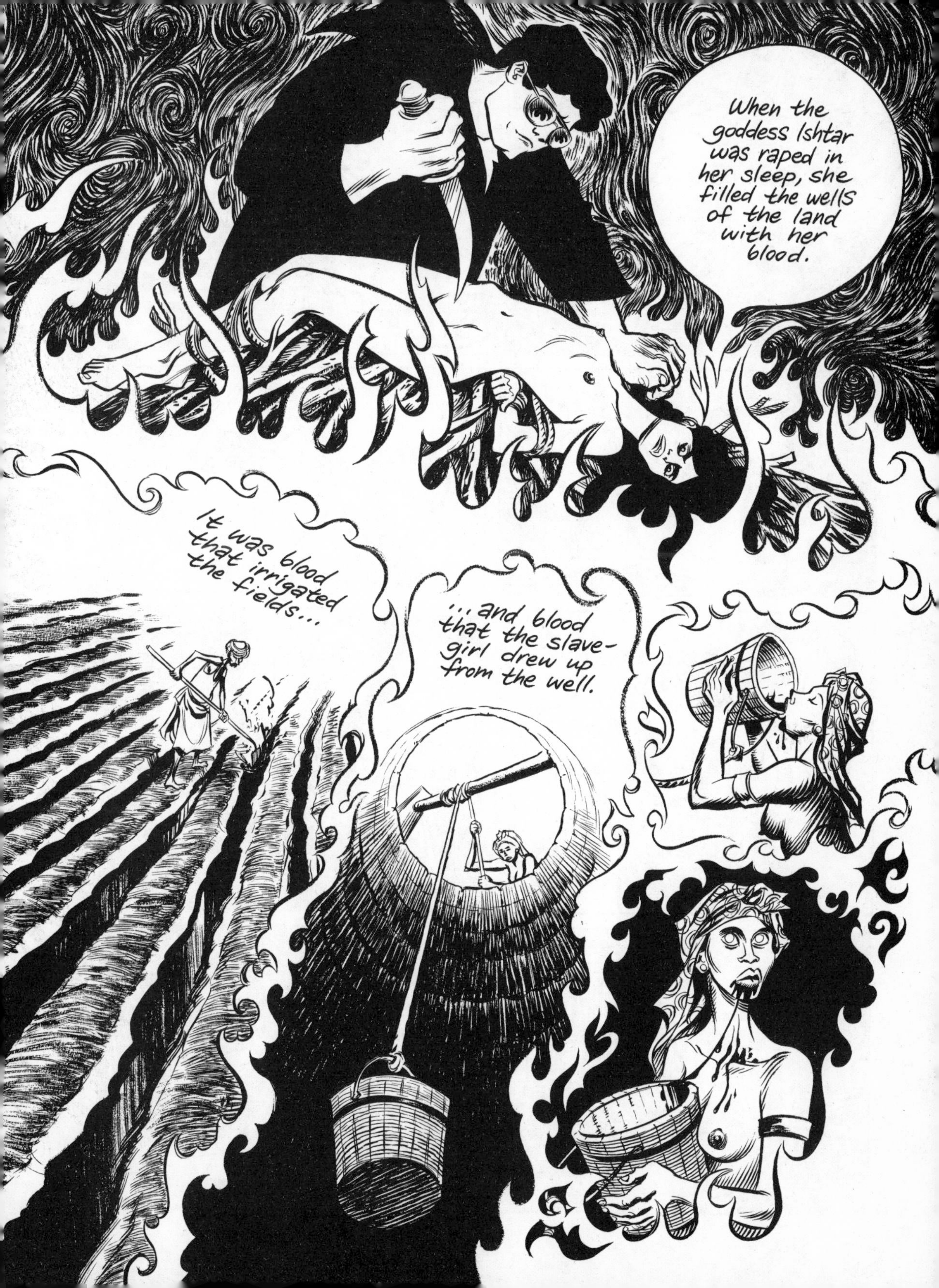
When the goddess Ishtar was raped in her sleep, she filled the wells of the land with her blood.
It was blood that irrigated the fields...
...and blood that the slave-girl drew up from the well.

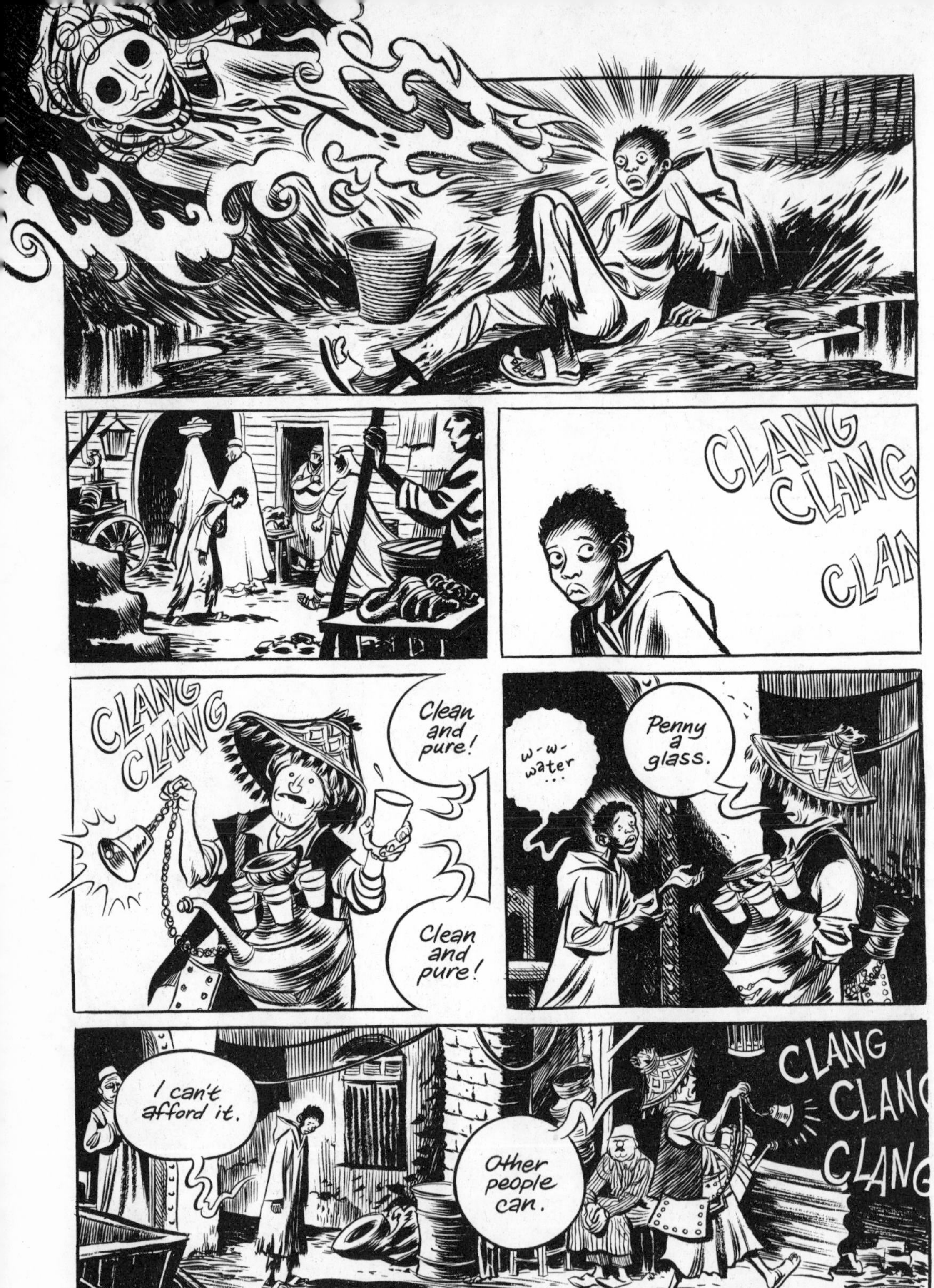
CLANG
CLANG
CLAN
CLANG
CLANG
Clean and pure!
Clean and pure!
w-w-water...
Penny a glass.
I can't afford it.
Other people can.
CLANG
CLANG
CLANG

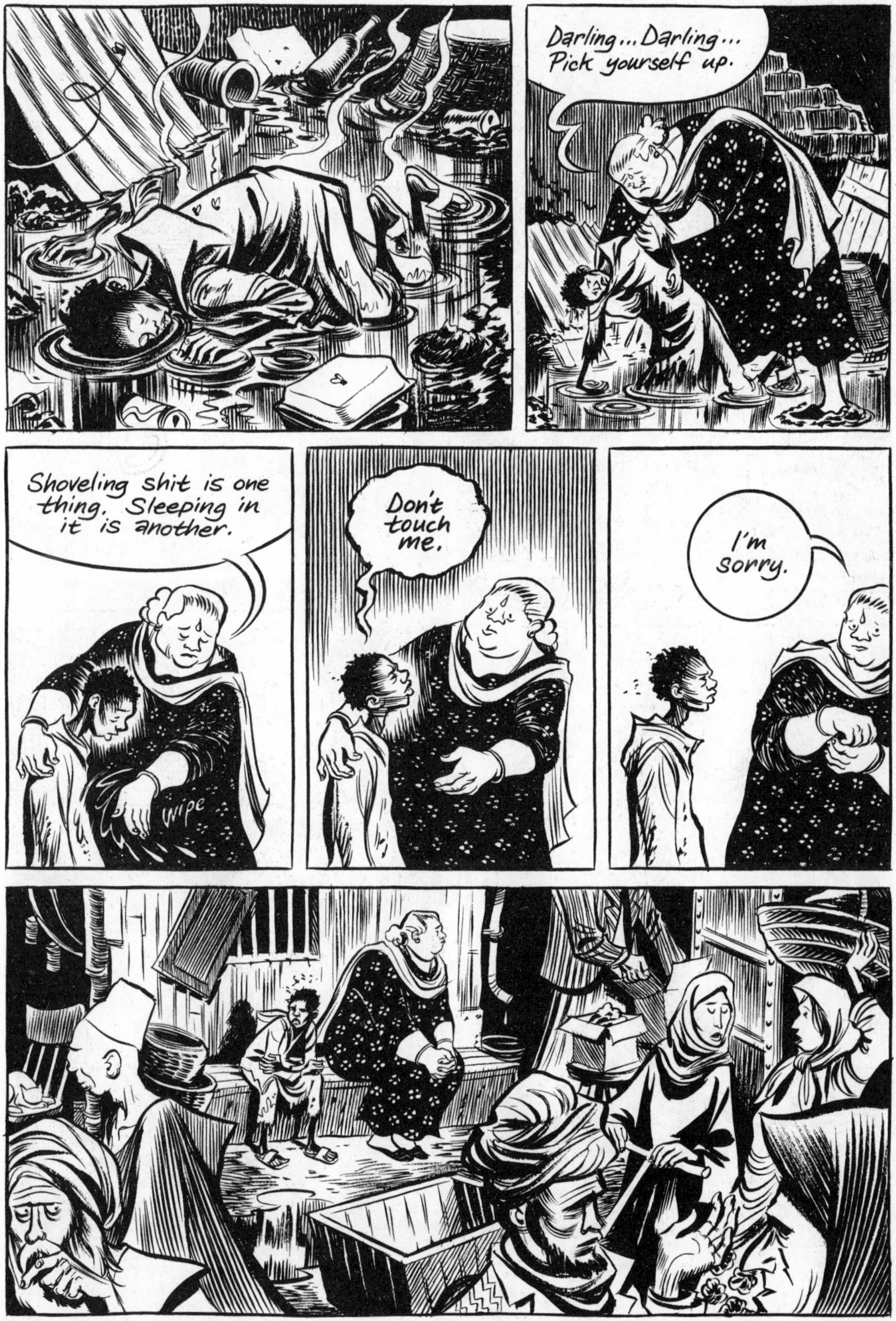
Darling... Darling... Pick yourself up.
Shoveling shit is one thing. Sleeping in it is another.
wipe
Don't touch me.
I'm sorry.

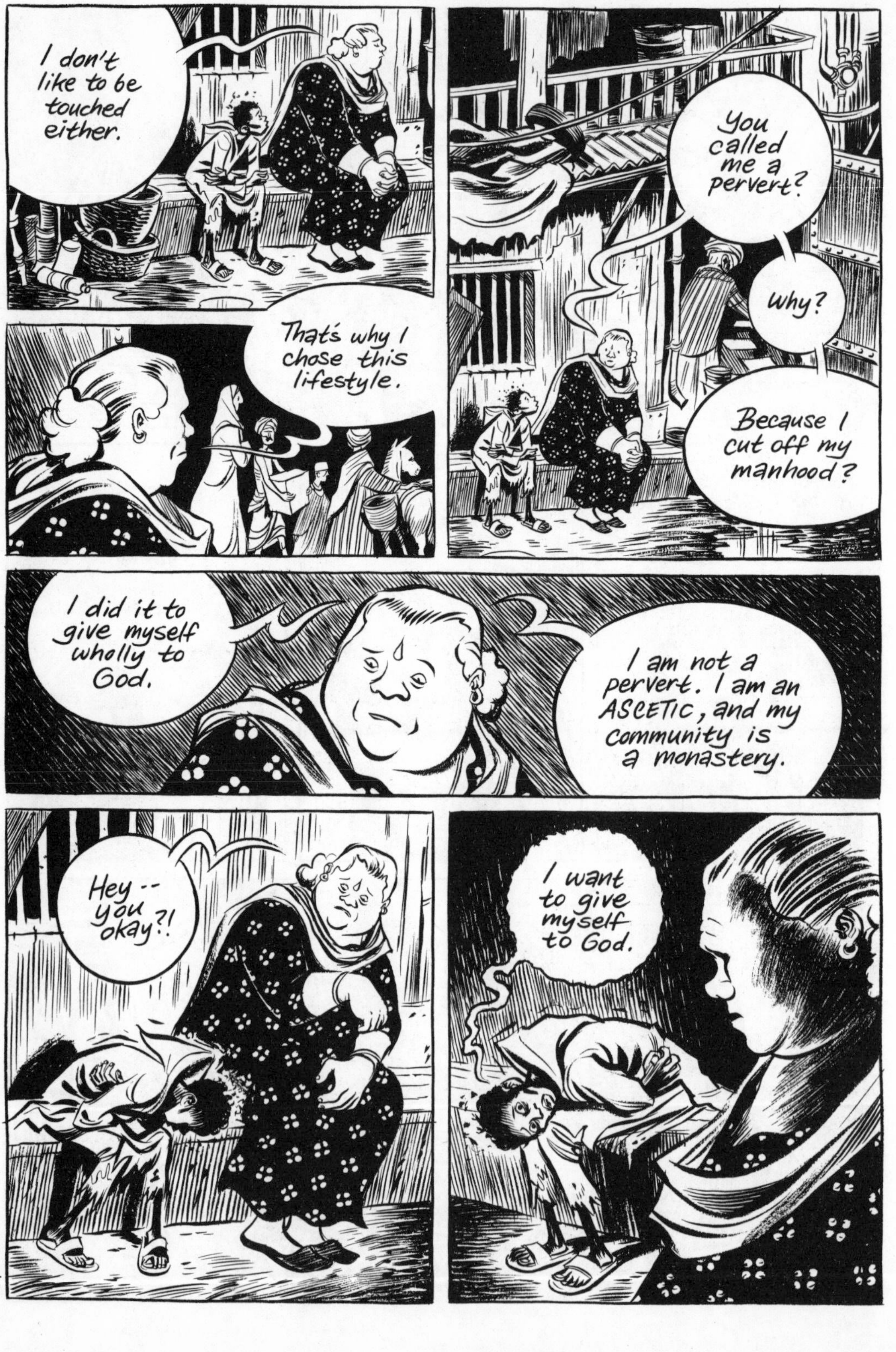
I don't like to be touched either.
You called me a pervert?
Why?
Because I cut off my manhood?
That's why I chose this lifestyle.
I did it to give myself wholly to God.
I am not a pervert. I am an ASCETIC, and my community is a monastery.
Hey -- you okay?!
I want to give myself to God.

What?
Like you...
You're talking crazy. It's 'cuz you're dying of starvation.
Let's get you some food and rest, and then see if you're able to think clearly for yourself.
ز
ز
ز
ز
No...
ز
No...
Jinn...
ز
No...

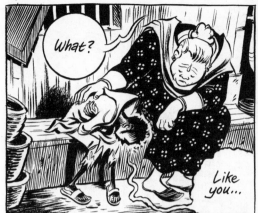

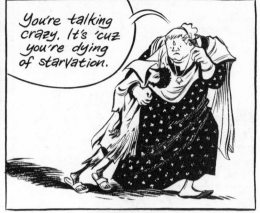

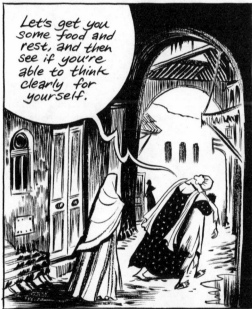

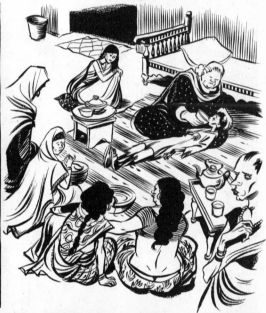

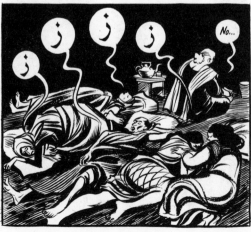

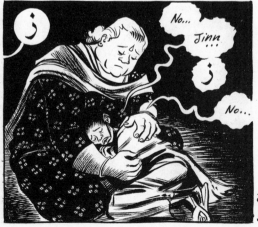

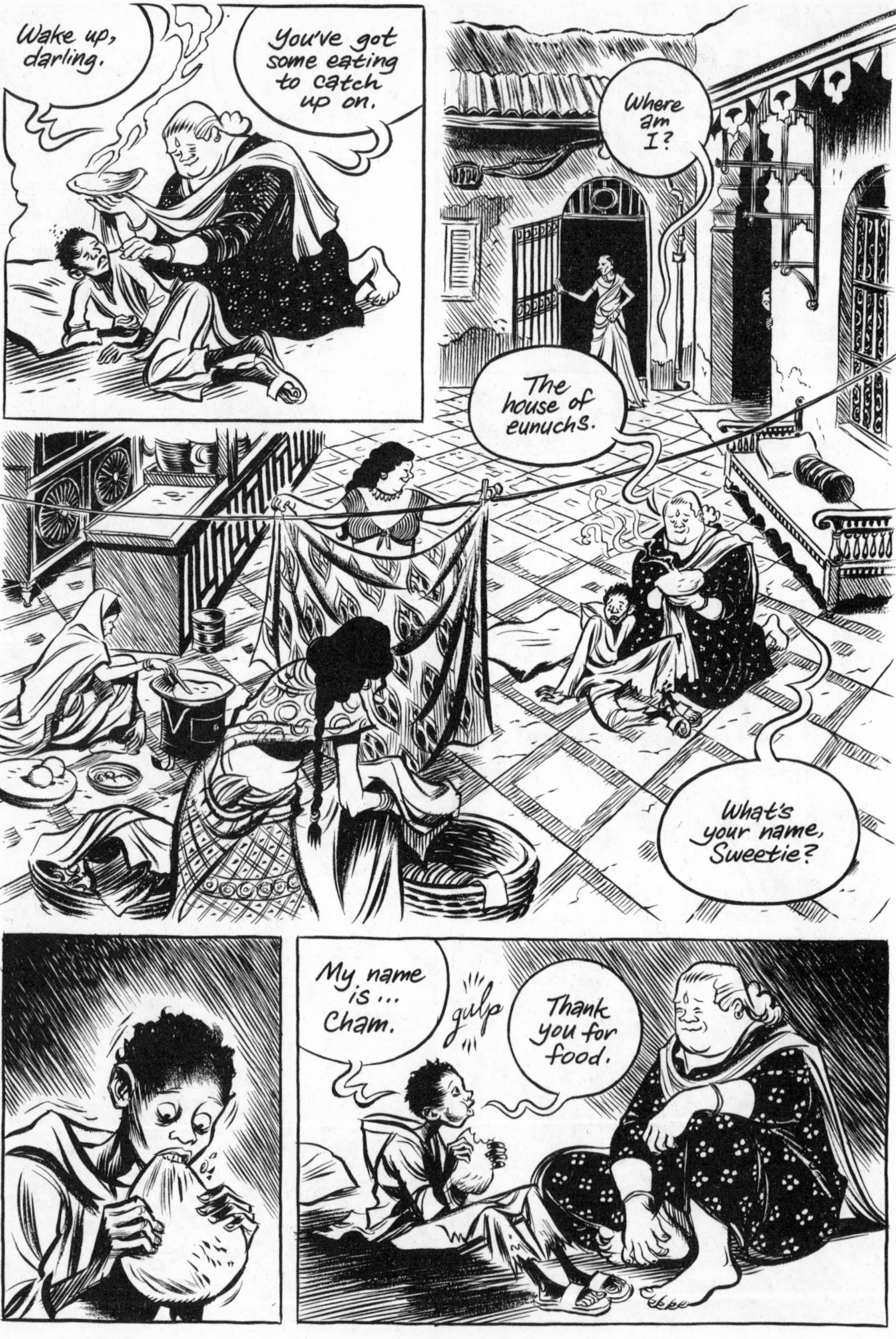
Wake up, darling.
You've got some eating to catch up on.
Where am I?
The house of eunuchs.
What's your name, Sweetie?
My name is... Cham.
gulp
Thank you for food.

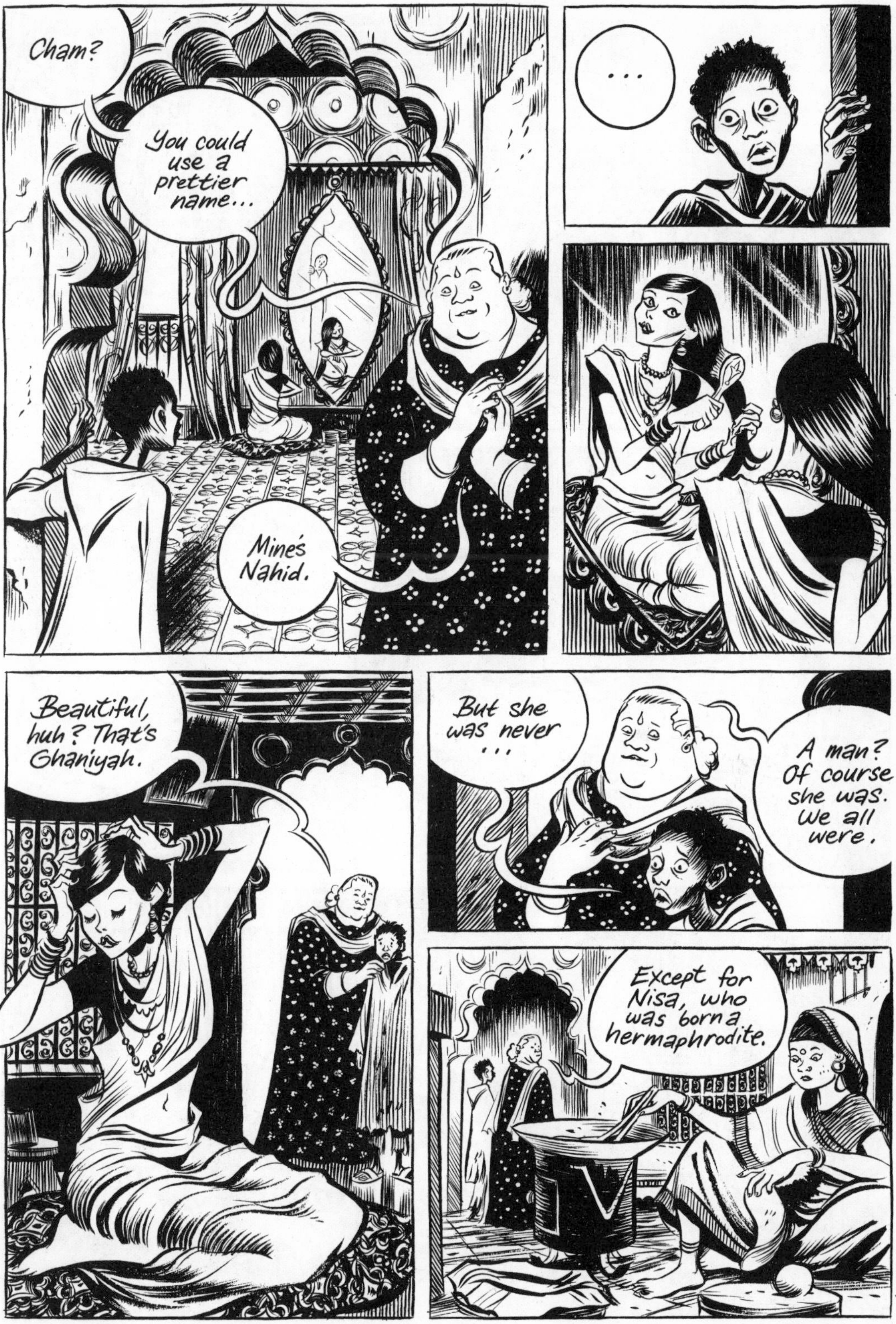
Cham?
You could use a prettier name...
Mine's Nahid.
...
Beautiful, huh? That's Ghaniyah.
But she was never ...
A man? Of course she was. We all were.
Except for Nisa, who was born a hermaphrodite.

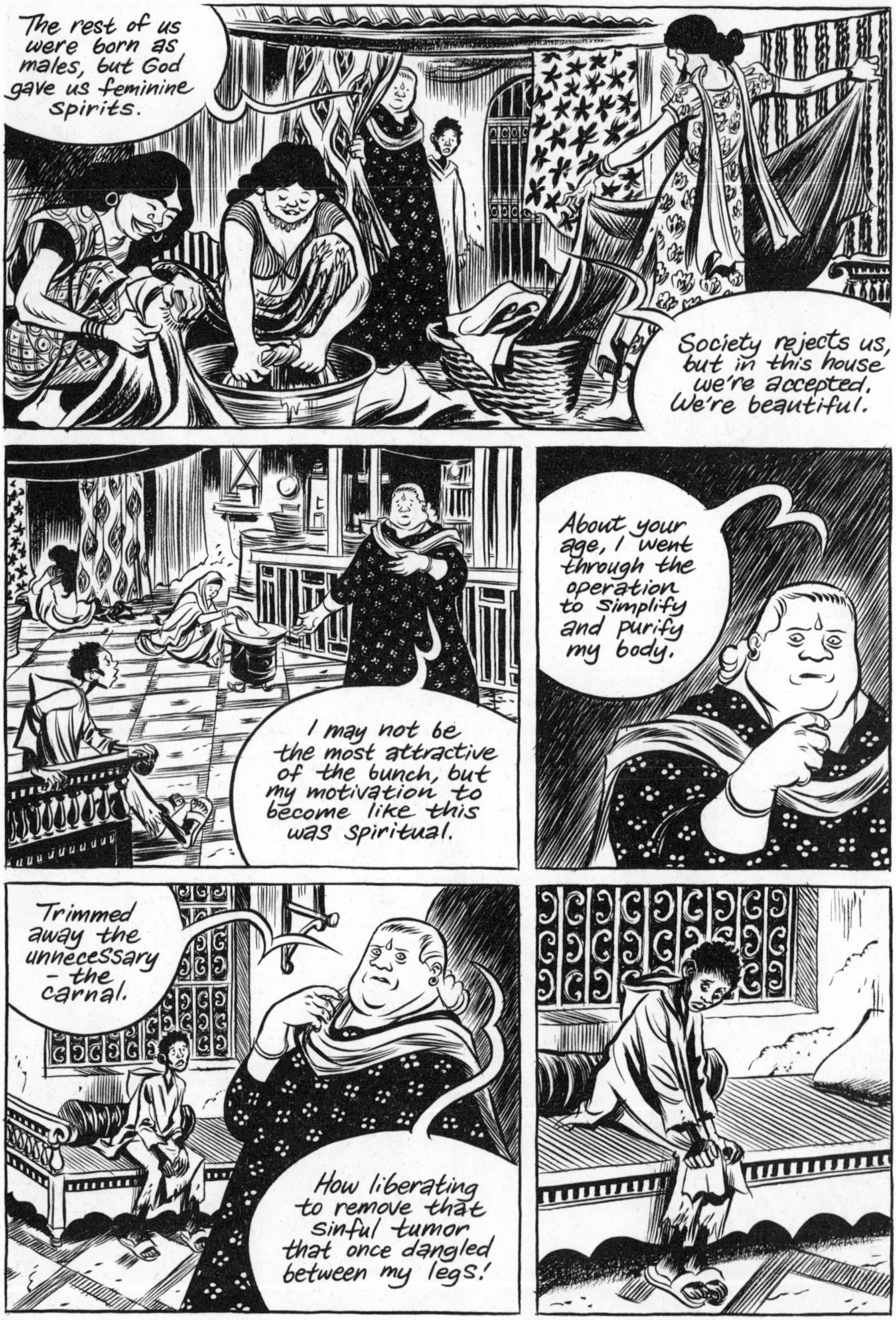
The rest of us were born as males, but God gave us feminine spirits.
Society rejects us, but in this house we're accepted. We're beautiful.
I may not be the most attractive of the bunch, but my motivation to become like this was spiritual.
About your age, I went through the operation to simplify and purify my body.
Trimmed away the unnecessary - the carnal.
How liberating to remove that sinful tumor that once dangled between my legs!

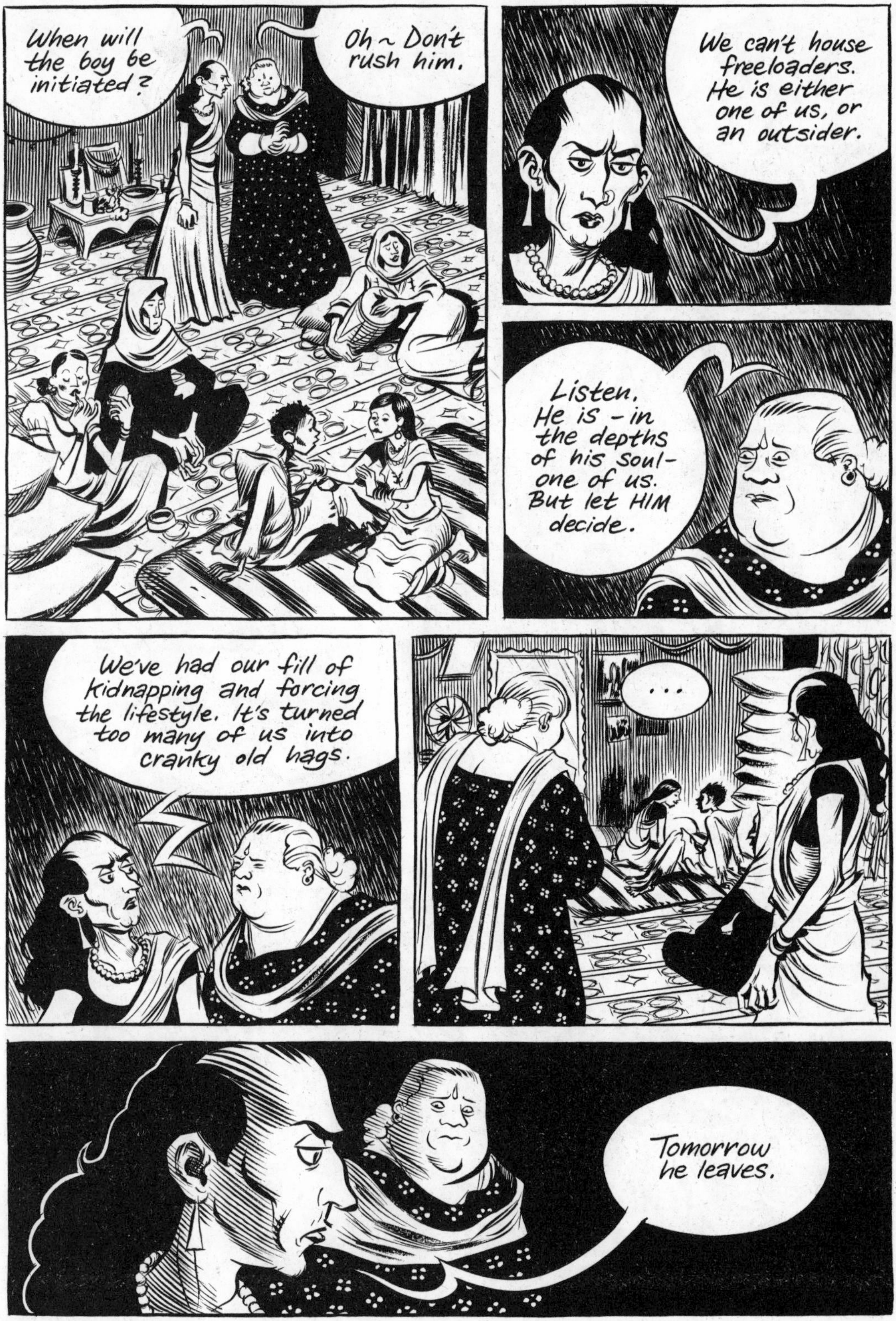
When will the boy be initiated?
Oh ~ Don't rush him.
We can't house freeloaders. He is either one of us, or an outsider.
Listen. He is - in the depths of his soul - one of us. But let HIM decide.
We've had our fill of kidnapping and forcing the lifestyle. It's turned too many of us into cranky old hags.
...
Tomorrow he leaves.

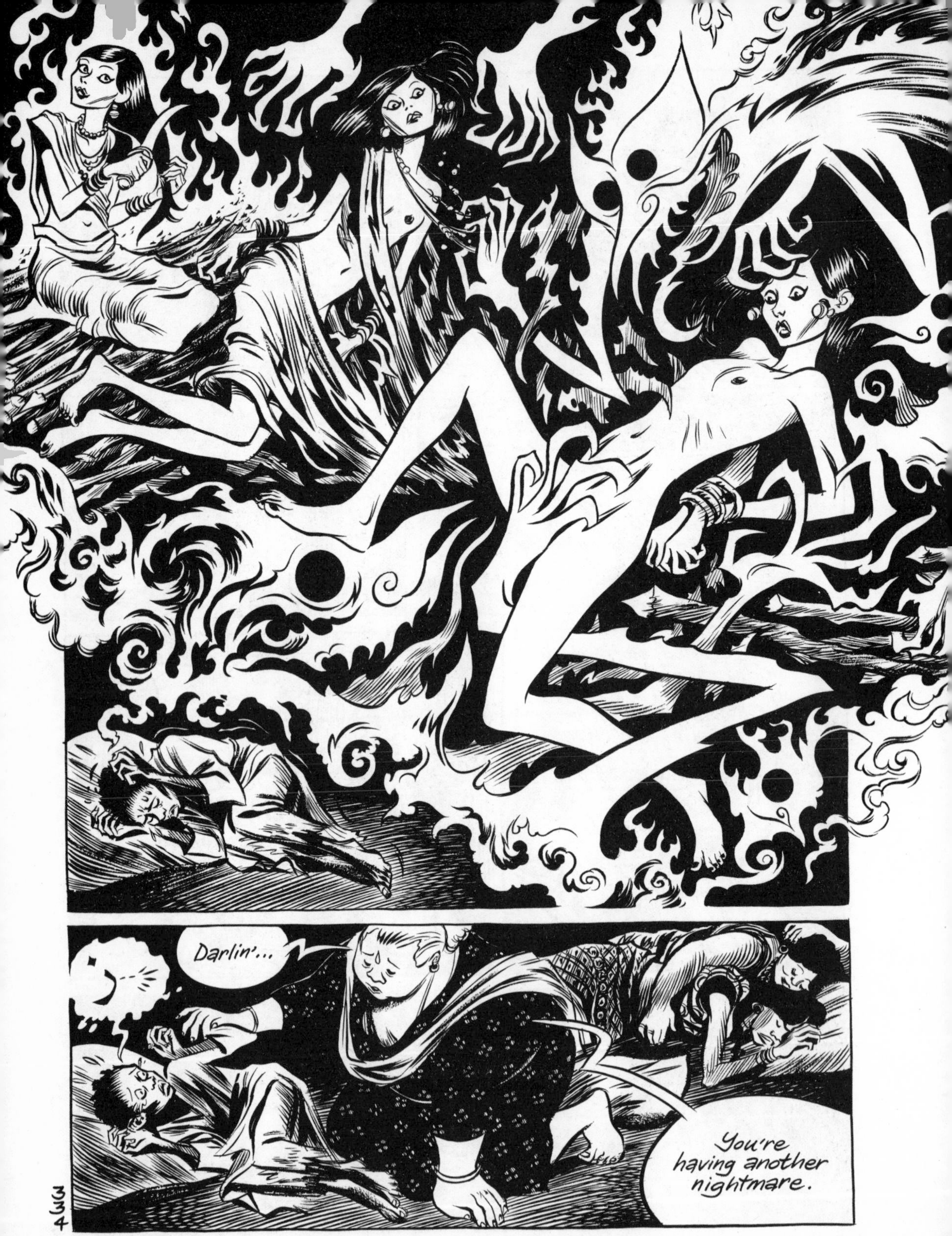
Darlin'...
You're having another nightmare.

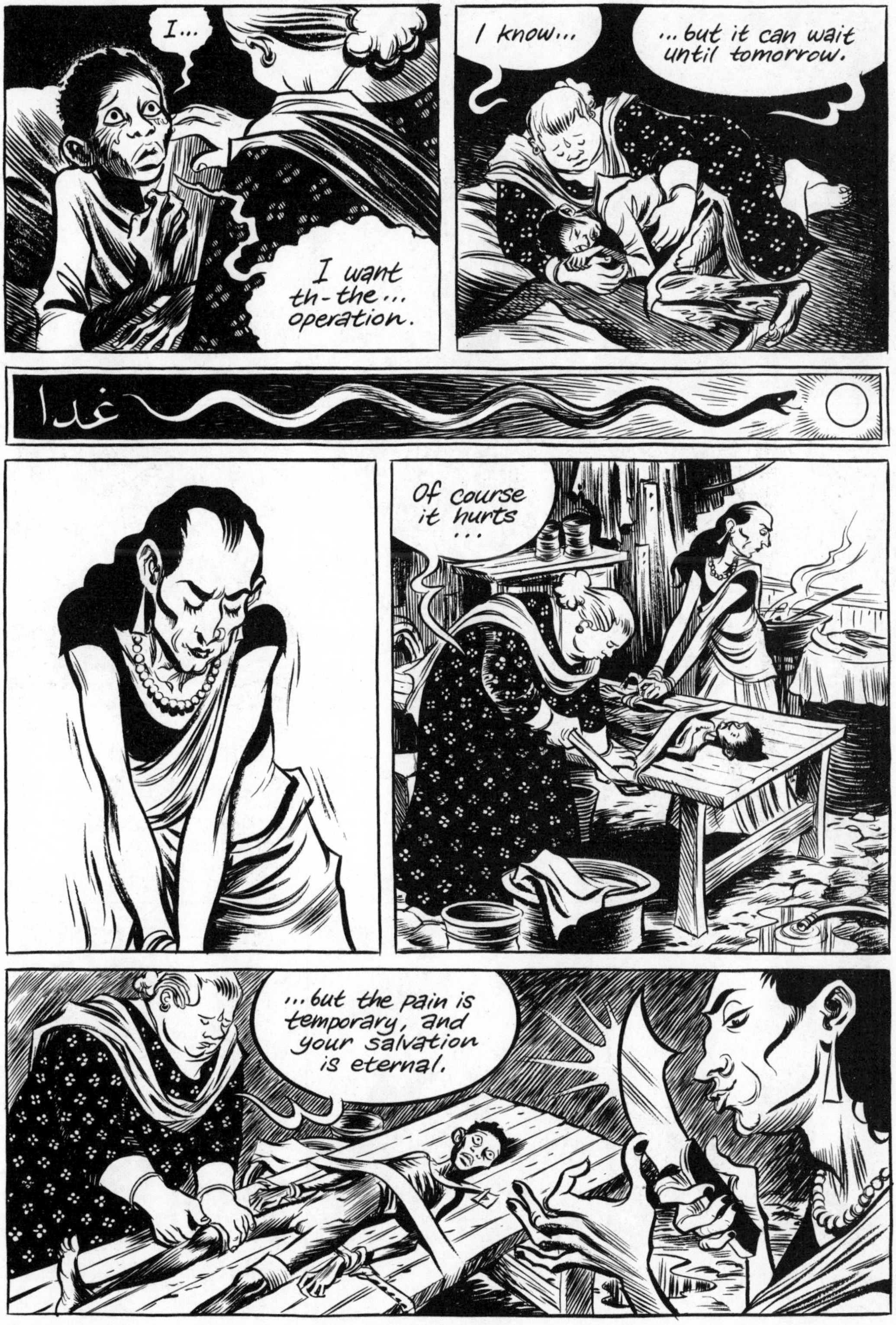
I...
I want th-the... operation.
I know...
...but it can wait until tomorrow.
غدا
Of course it hurts ...
...but the pain is temporary, and your salvation is eternal.

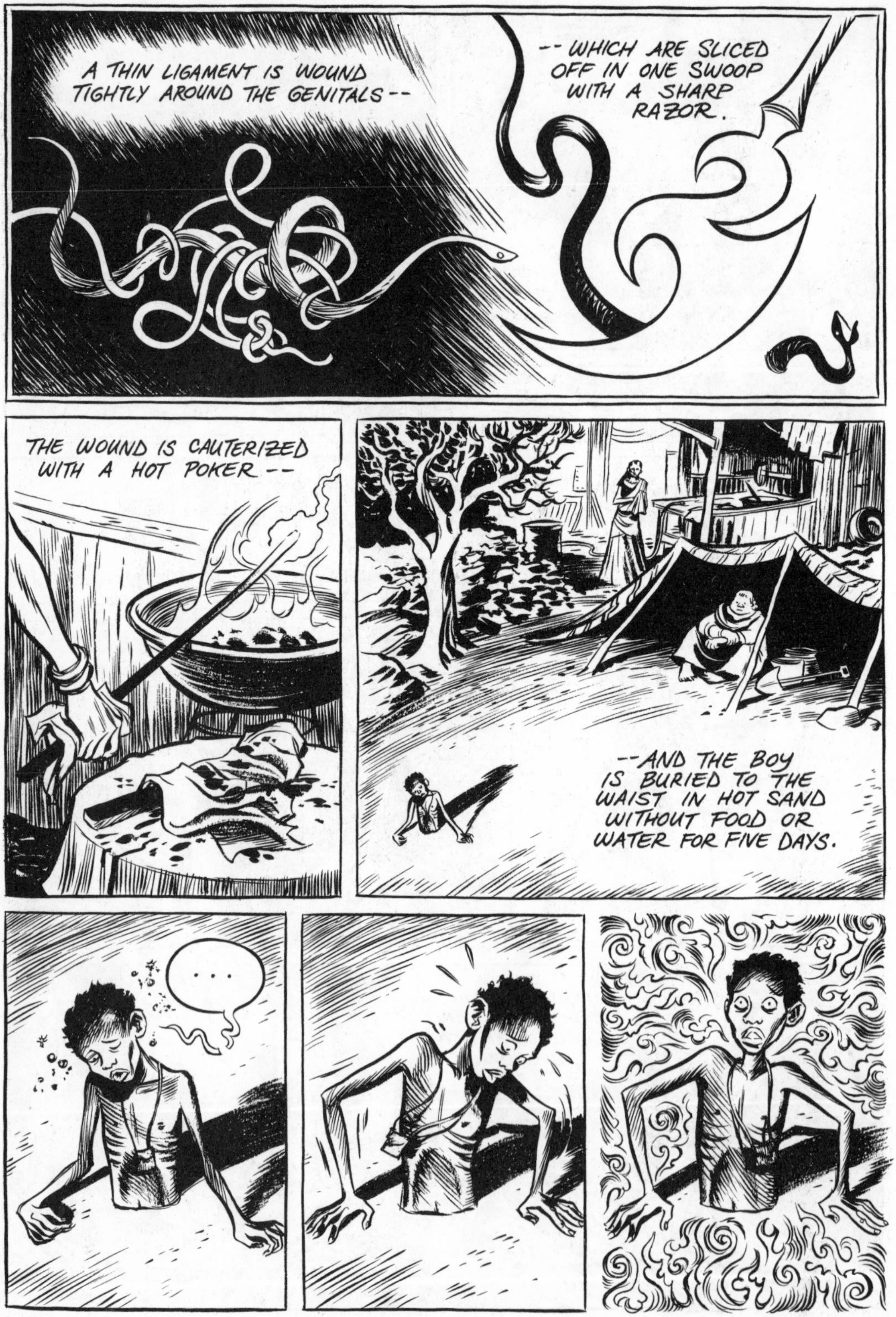
A THIN LIGAMENT IS WOUND TIGHTLY AROUND THE GENITALS--
--WHICH ARE SLICED OFF IN ONE SWOOP WITH A SHARP RAZOR.
THE WOUND IS CAUTERIZED WITH A HOT POKER--
--AND THE BOY IS BURIED TO THE WAIST IN HOT SAND WITHOUT FOOD OR WATER FOR FIVE DAYS.
. . .

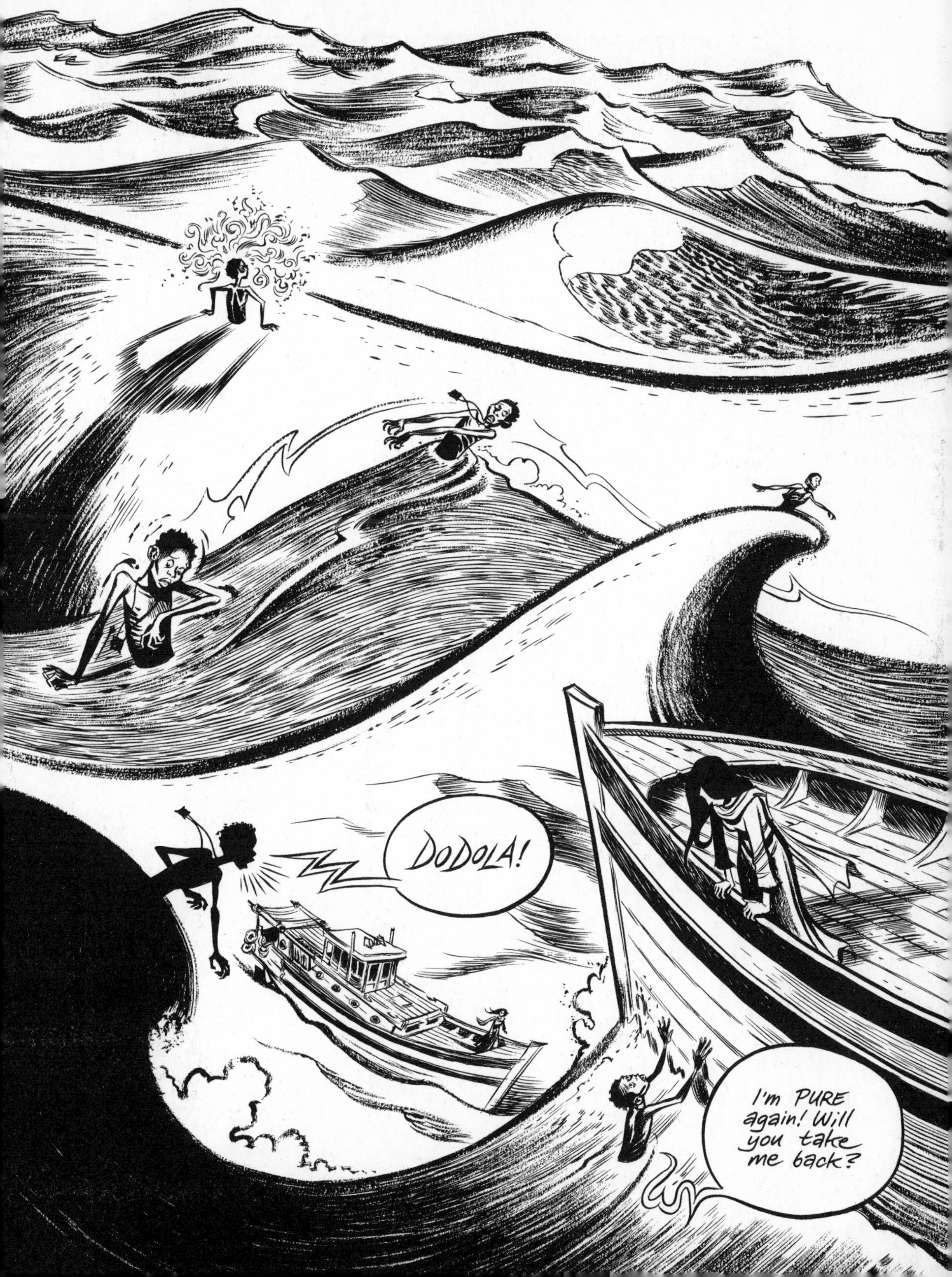
DODOLA!
I'm PURE again! Will you take me back?

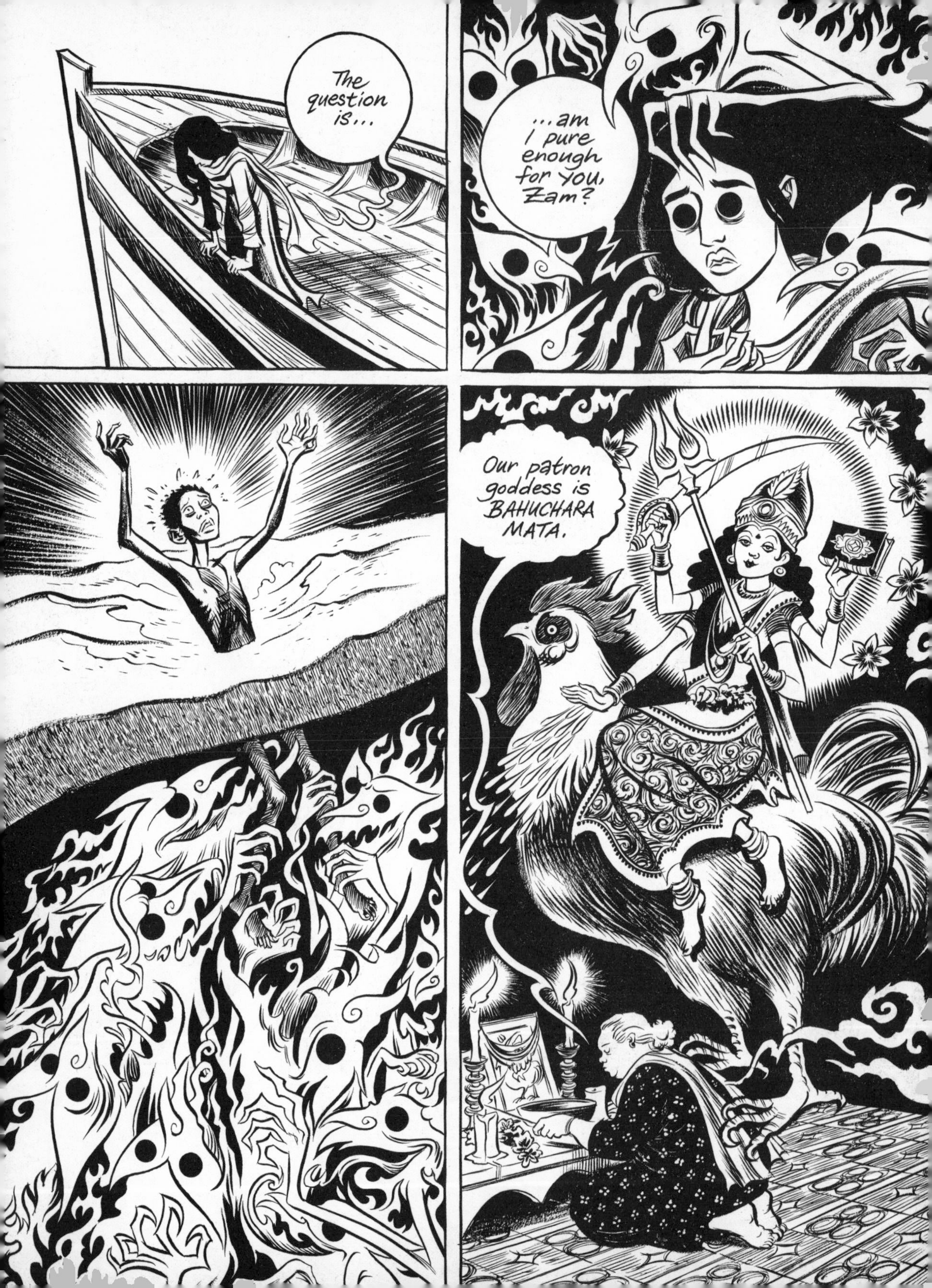

The question is...
...am I pure enough for you, Zam?
Our patron goddess is BAHUCHARA MATA.

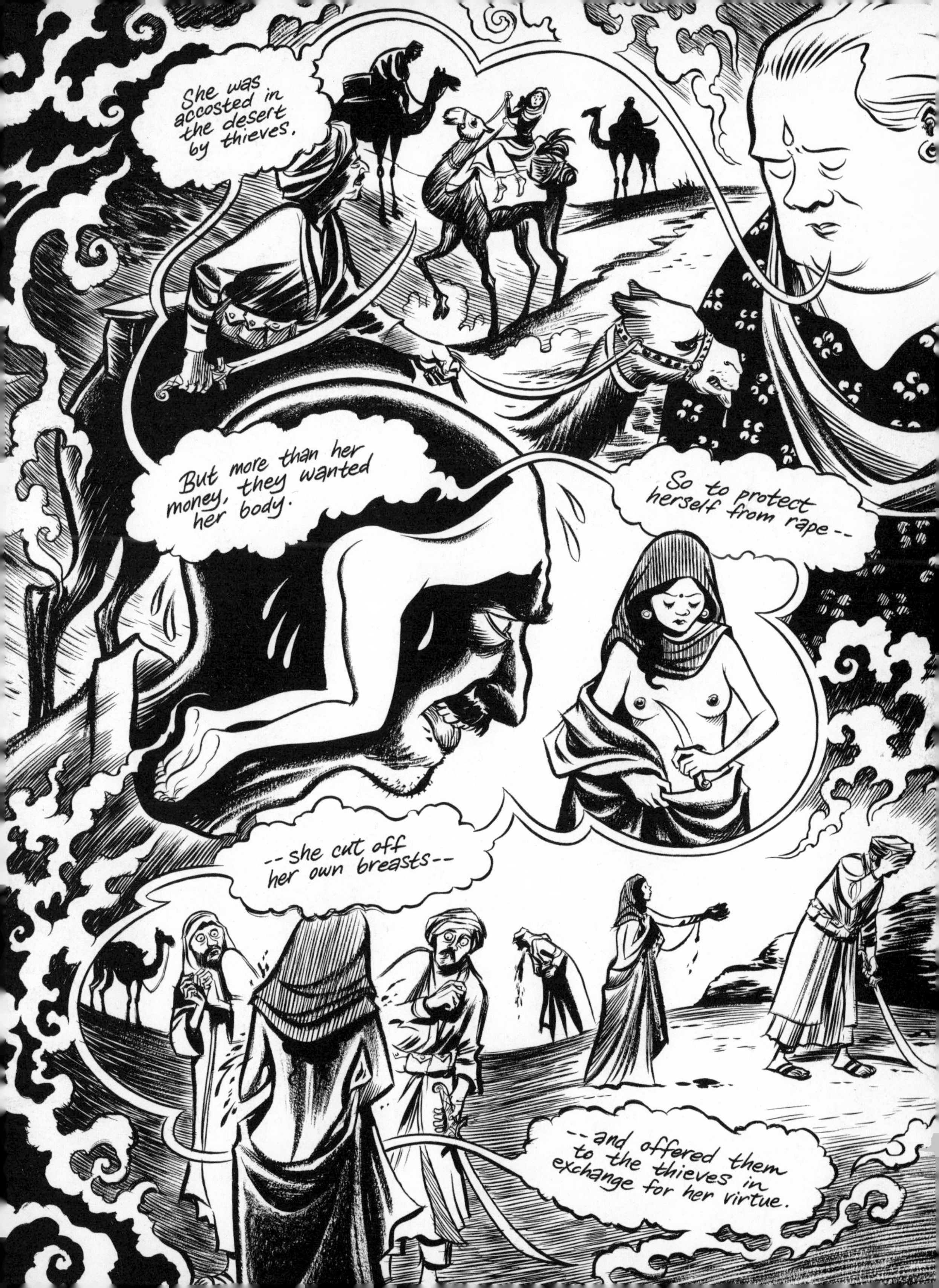
She was accosted in the desert by thieves.
But more than her money, they wanted her body.
So to protect herself from rape--
--she cut off her own breasts--
--and offered them to the thieves in exchange for her virtue.

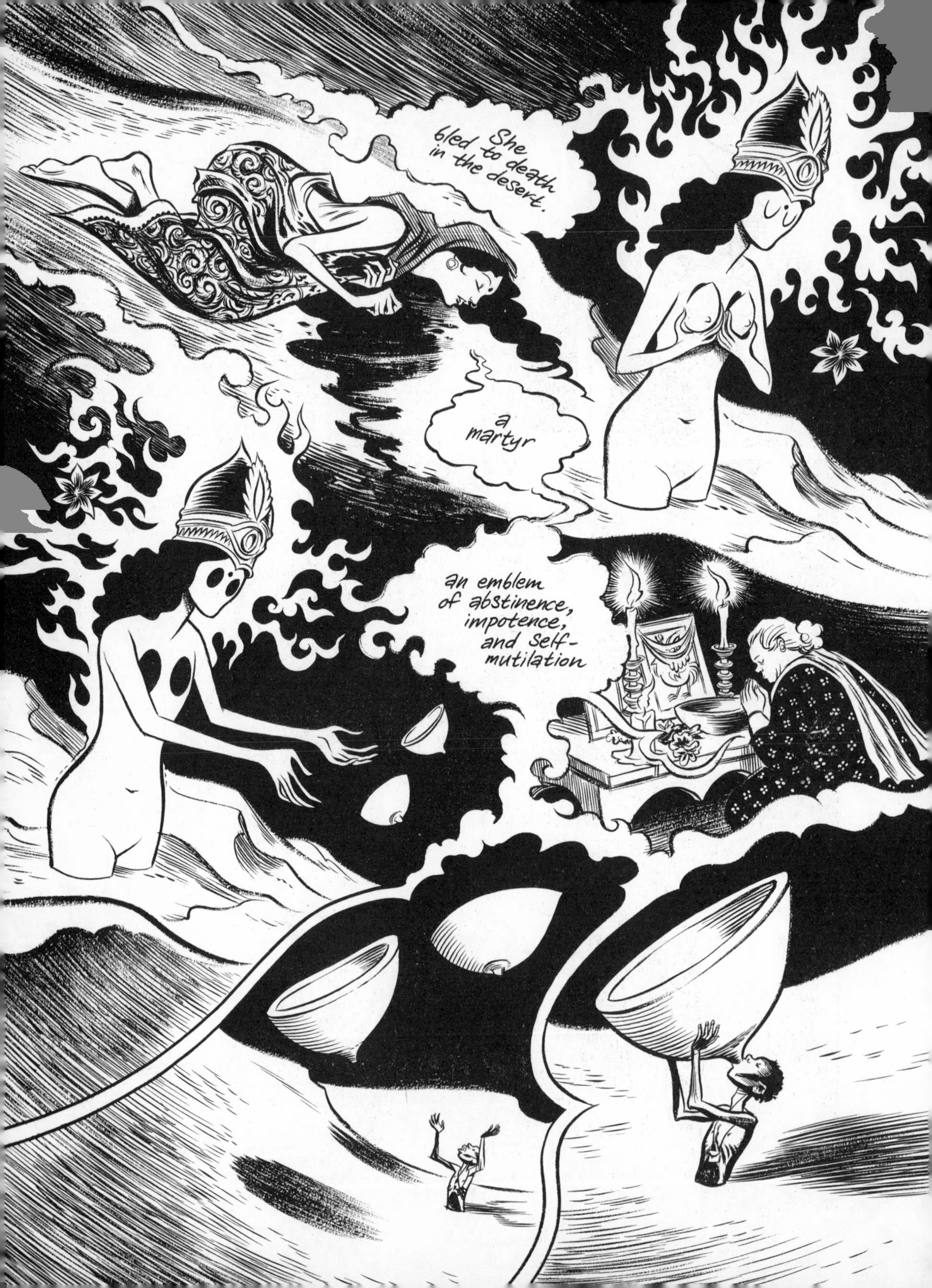
She bled to death in the desert.
a martyr
an emblem of abstinence, impotence, and self-mutilation

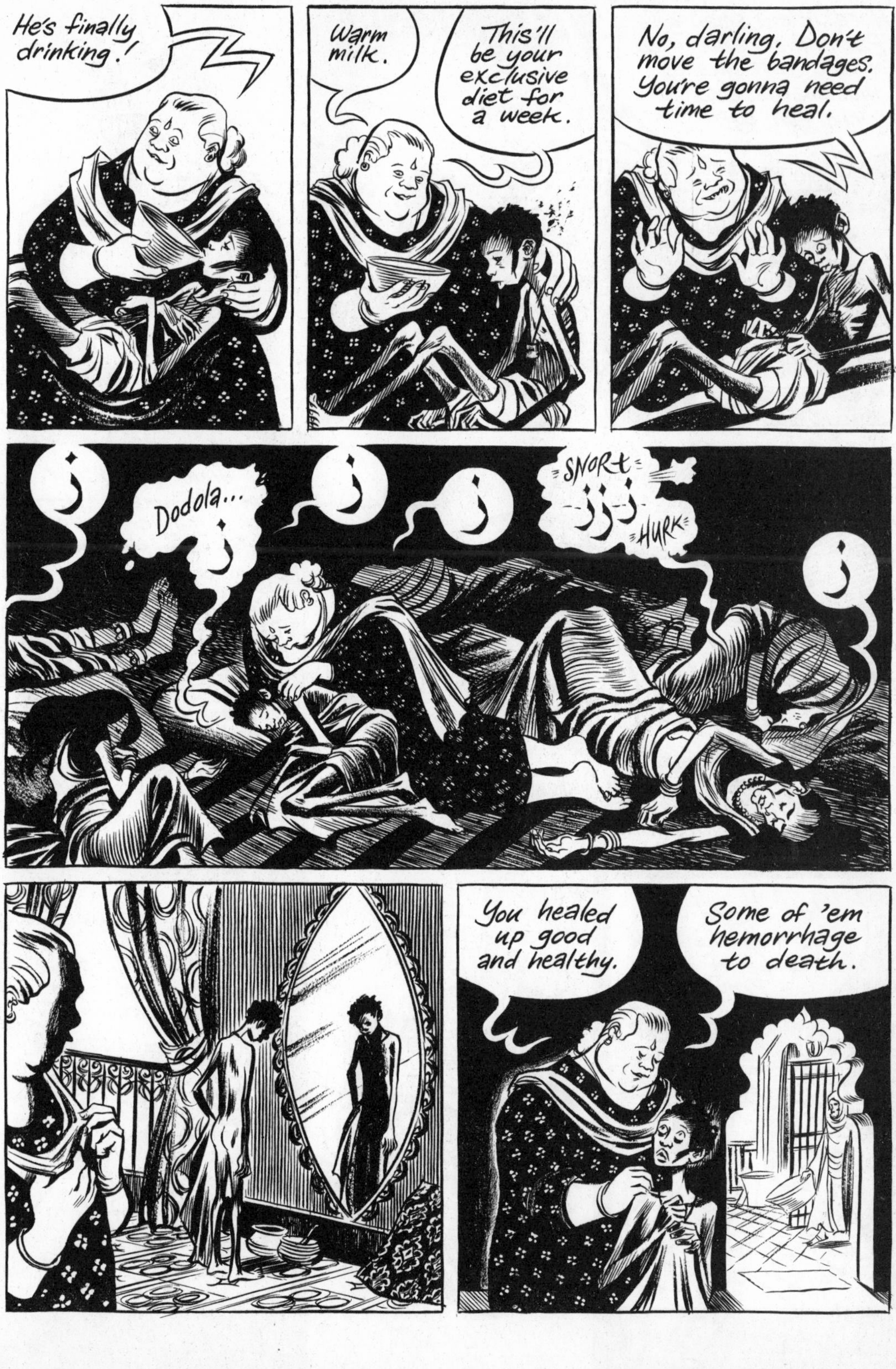
He's finally drinking!
Warm milk.
This'll be your exclusive diet for a week.
No, darling. Don't move the bandages. You're gonna need time to heal.
Dodola...
SNORT
HURK
You healed up good and healthy.
Some of 'em hemorrhage to death.

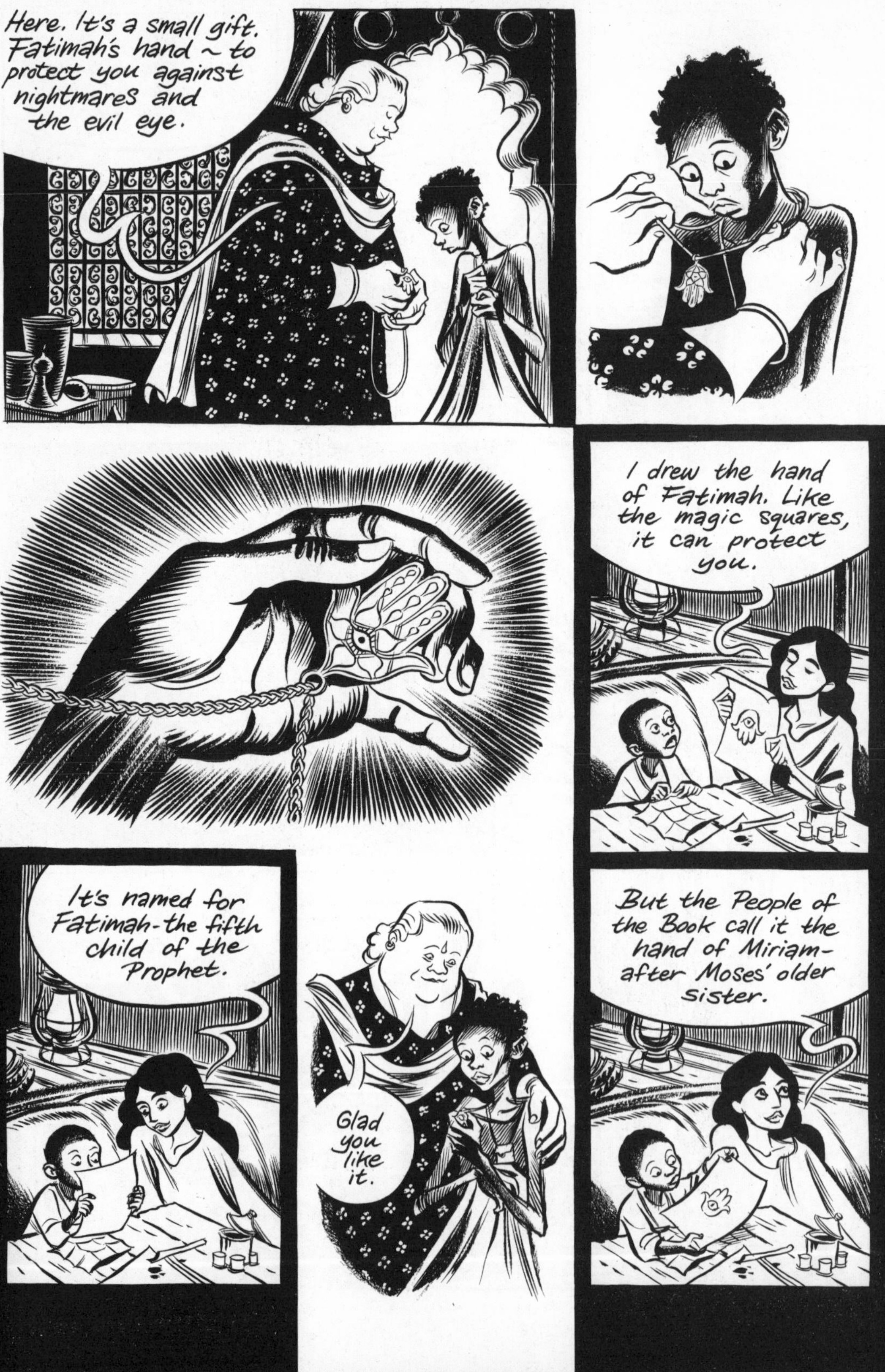
Here. It's a small gift. Fatimah's hand ~ to protect you against nightmares and the evil eye.
I drew the hand of Fatimah. Like the magic squares, it can protect you.
It's named for Fatimah-the fifth child of the Prophet.
Glad you like it.
But the People of the Book call it the hand of Miriam-after Moses' older sister.

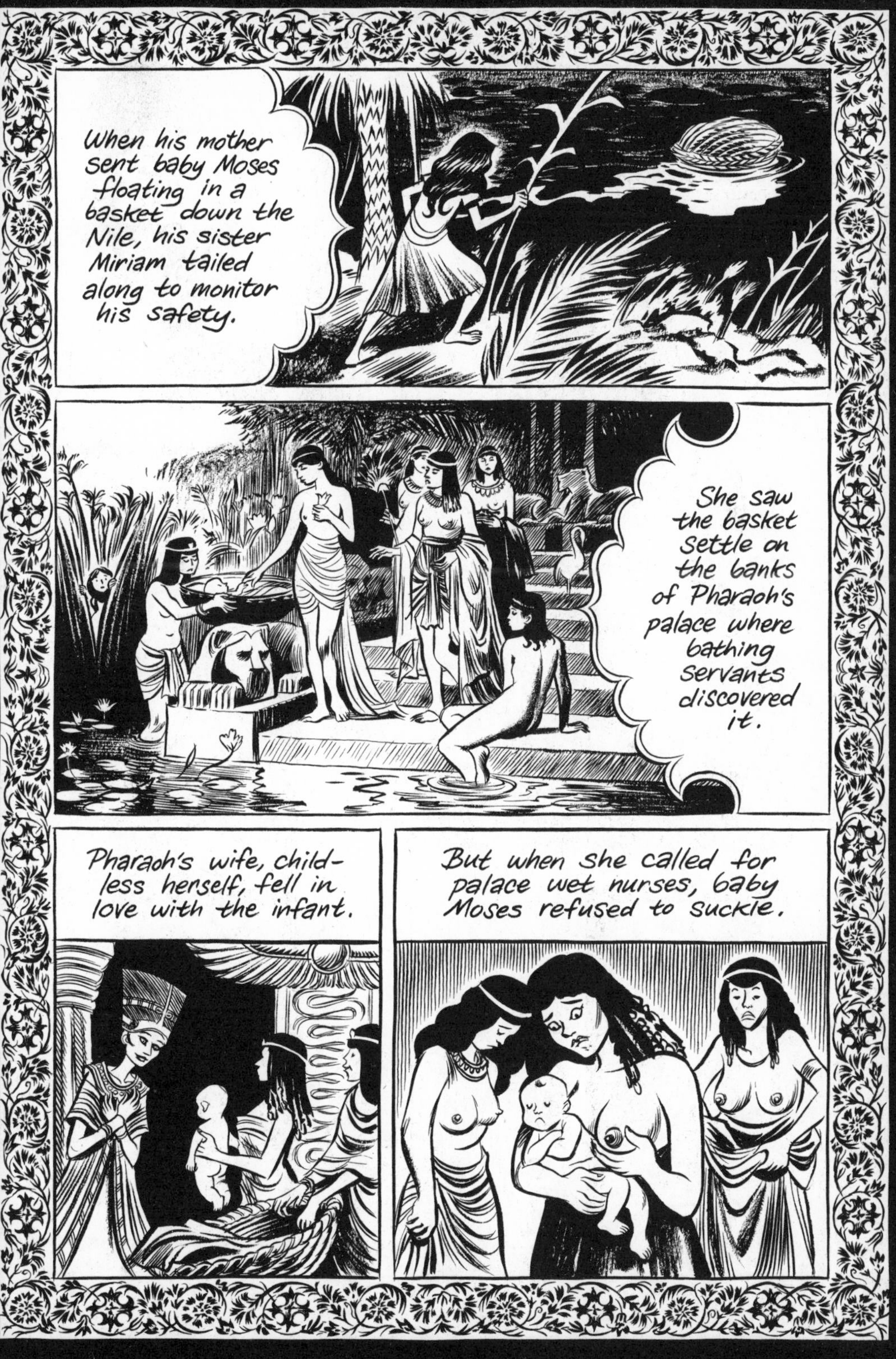
When his mother sent baby Moses floating in a basket down the Nile, his sister Miriam tailed along to monitor his safety.
She saw the basket settle on the banks of Pharaoh's palace where bathing servants discovered it.
Pharaoh's wife, child-less herself, fell in love with the infant.
But when she called for palace wet nurses, baby Moses refused to suckle.

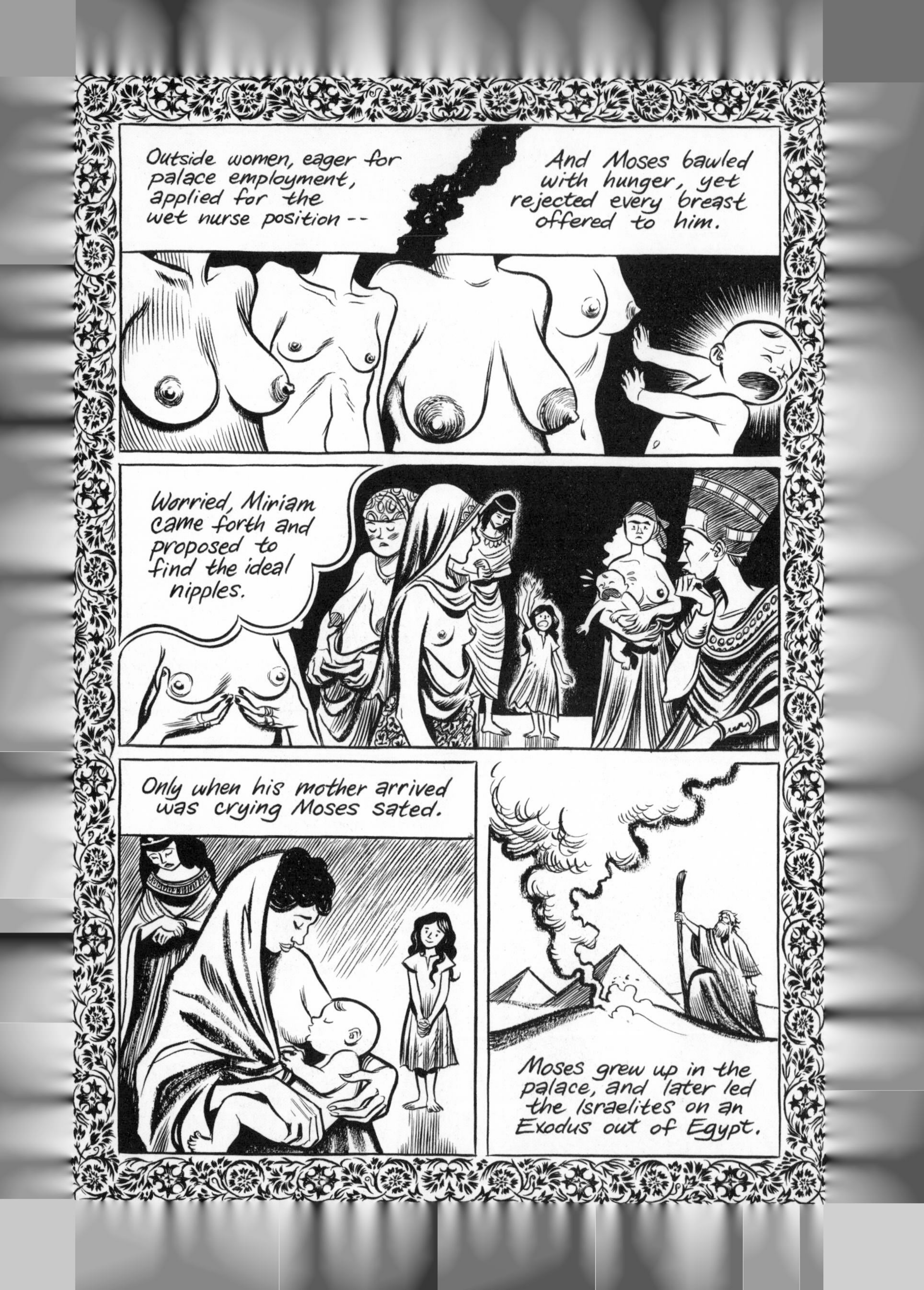
Outside women, eager for palace employment, applied for the wet nurse position --
And Moses bawled with hunger, yet rejected every breast offered to him.
Worried, Miriam came forth and proposed to find the ideal nipples.
Only when his mother arrived was crying Moses sated.
Moses grew up in the palace, and later led the Israelites on an Exodus out of Egypt.

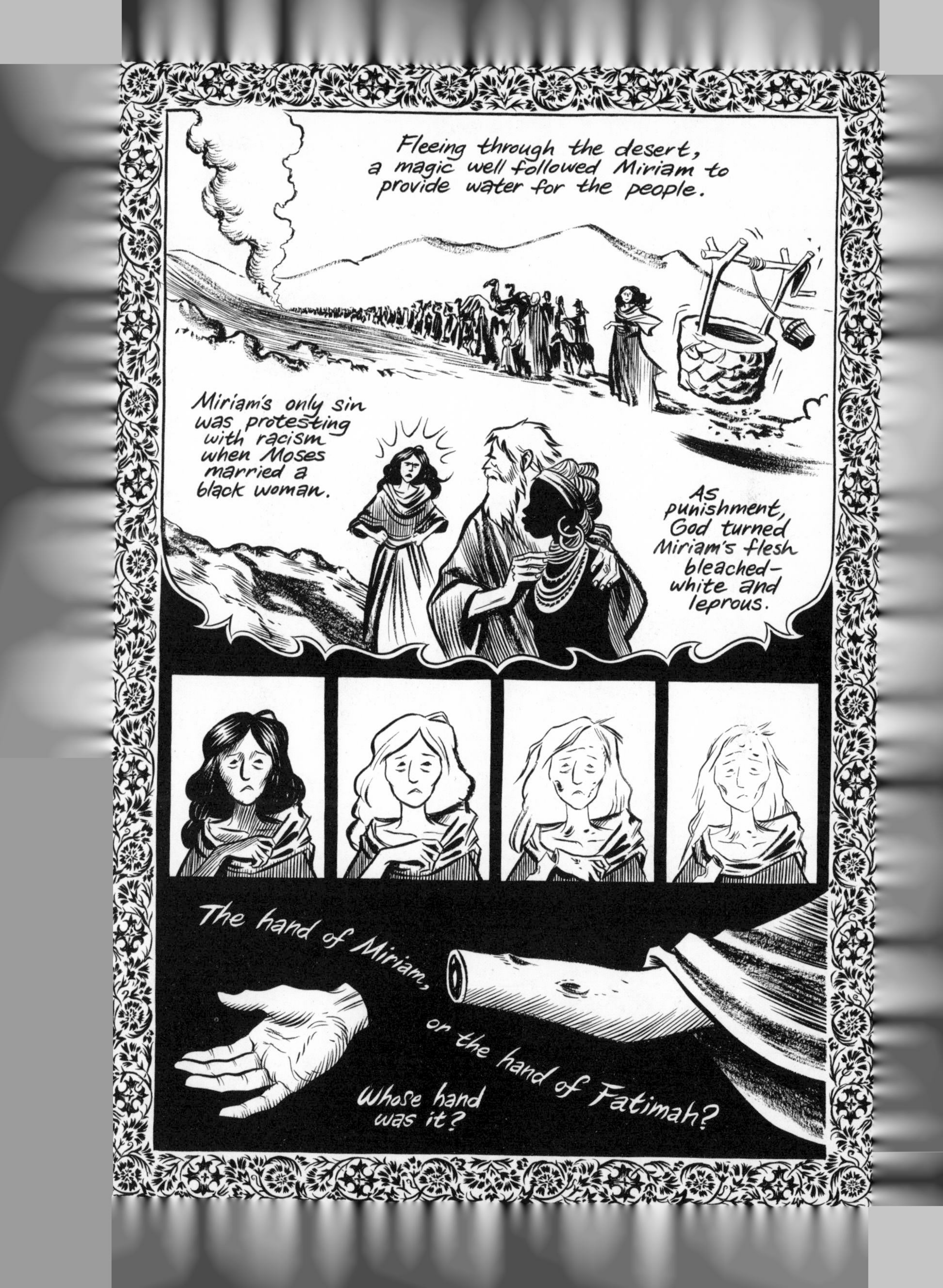
Fleeing through the desert, a magic well followed Miriam to provide water for the people.
Miriam's only sin was protesting with racism when Moses married a black woman.
As punishment, God turned Miriam's flesh bleached-white and leprous.
The hand of Miriam,
or the hand of Fatimah?
Whose hand was it?

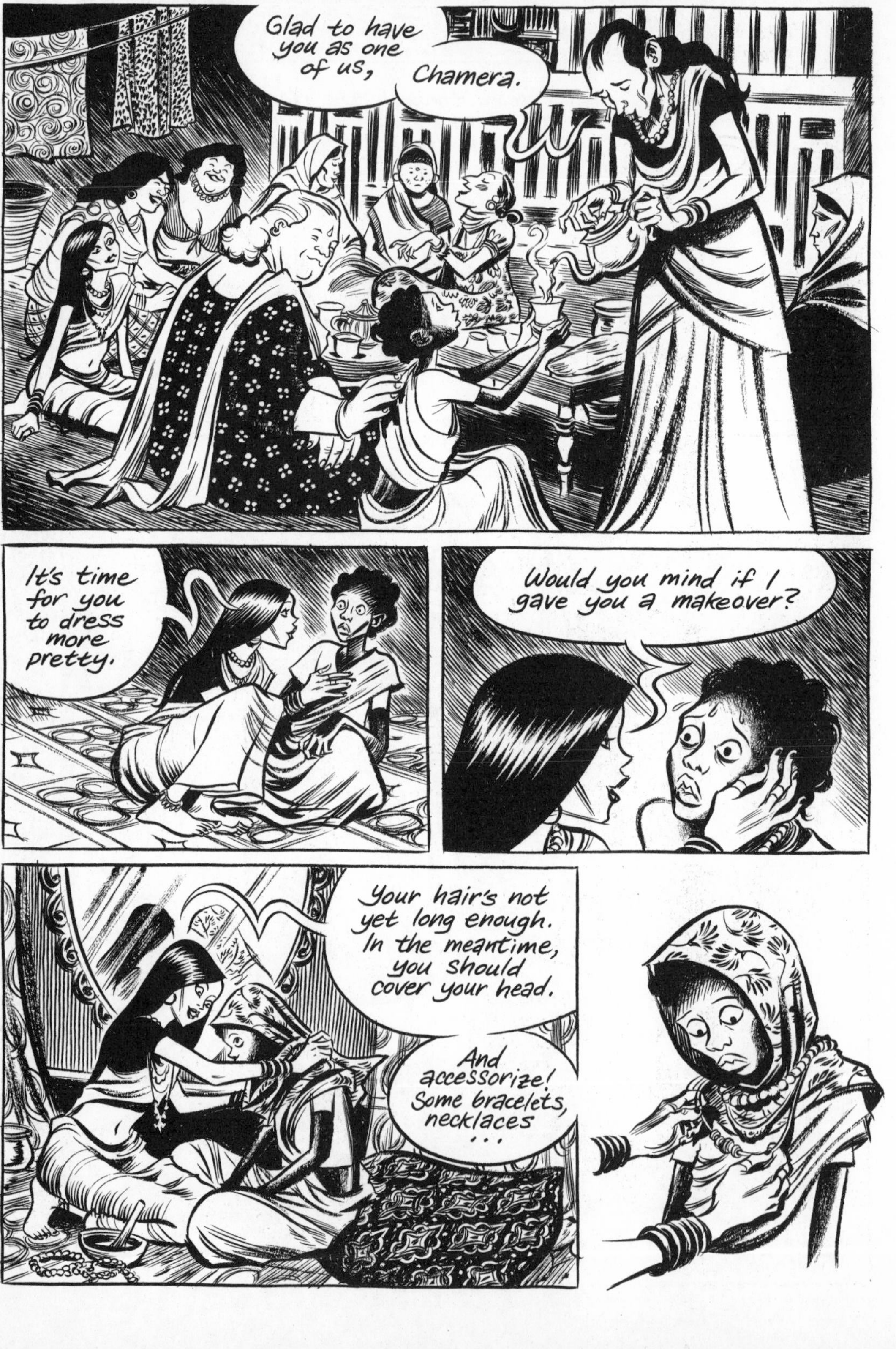
Glad to have you as one of us,
Chamera.
It's time for you to dress more pretty.
Would you mind if I gave you a makeover?
Your hair's not yet long enough. In the meantime, you should cover your head.
And accessorize! Some bracelets, necklaces . . .

346

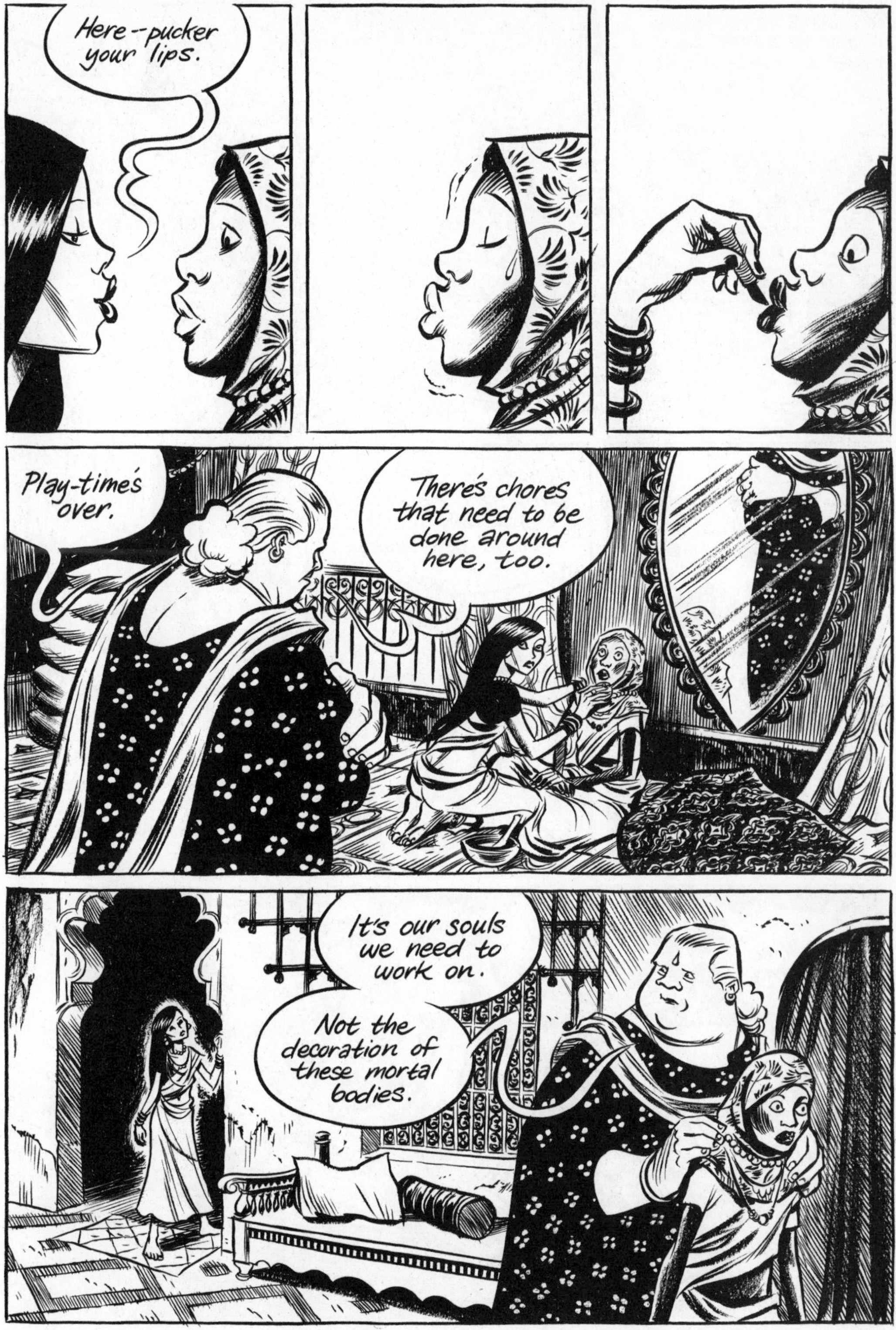

Here--pucker your lips.
Play-time's over.
There's chores that need to be done around here, too.
It's our souls we need to work on.
Not the decoration of these mortal bodies.

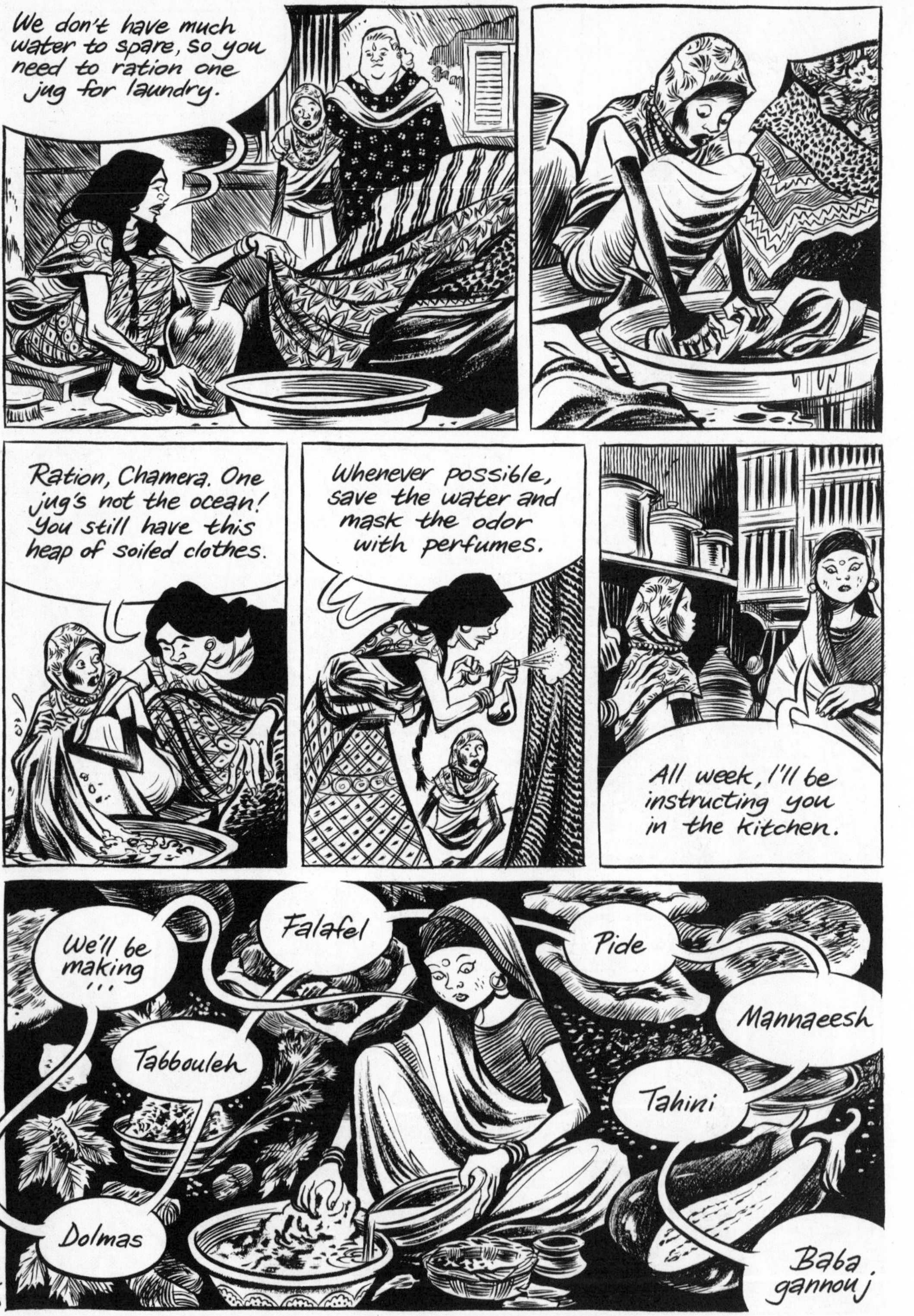
We don't have much water to spare, so you need to ration one jug for laundry.
Ration, Chamera. One jug's not the ocean! You still have this heap of soiled clothes.
Whenever possible, save the water and mask the odor with perfumes.
All week, I'll be instructing you in the kitchen.
We'll be making ...
Falafel
Pide
Tabbouleh
Mannaeesh
Tahini
Dolmas
Baba gannouj

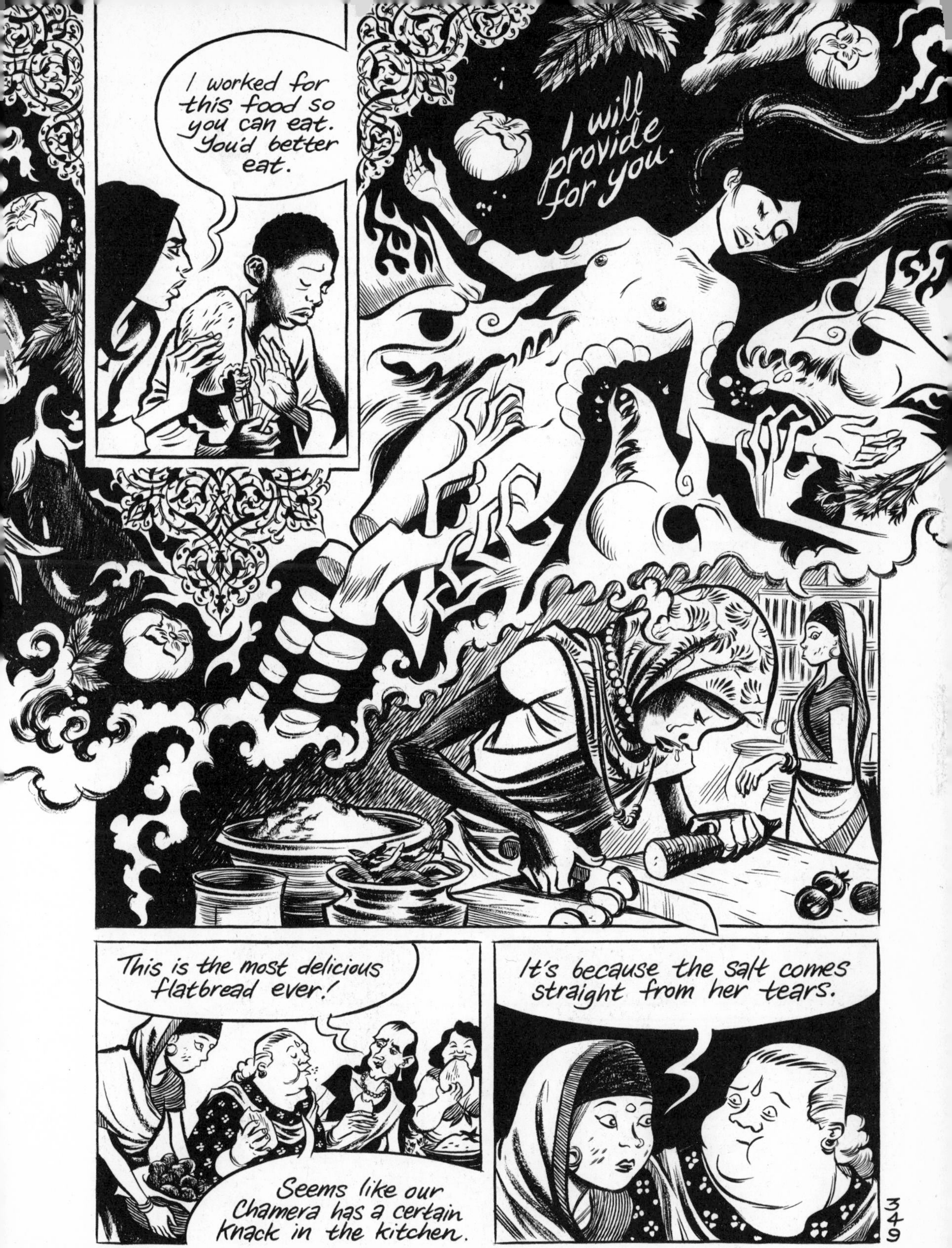
I worked for this food so you can eat. You'd better eat.
I will provide for you.
This is the most delicious flatbread ever!
Seems like our Chamera has a certain knack in the kitchen.
It's because the salt comes straight from her tears.

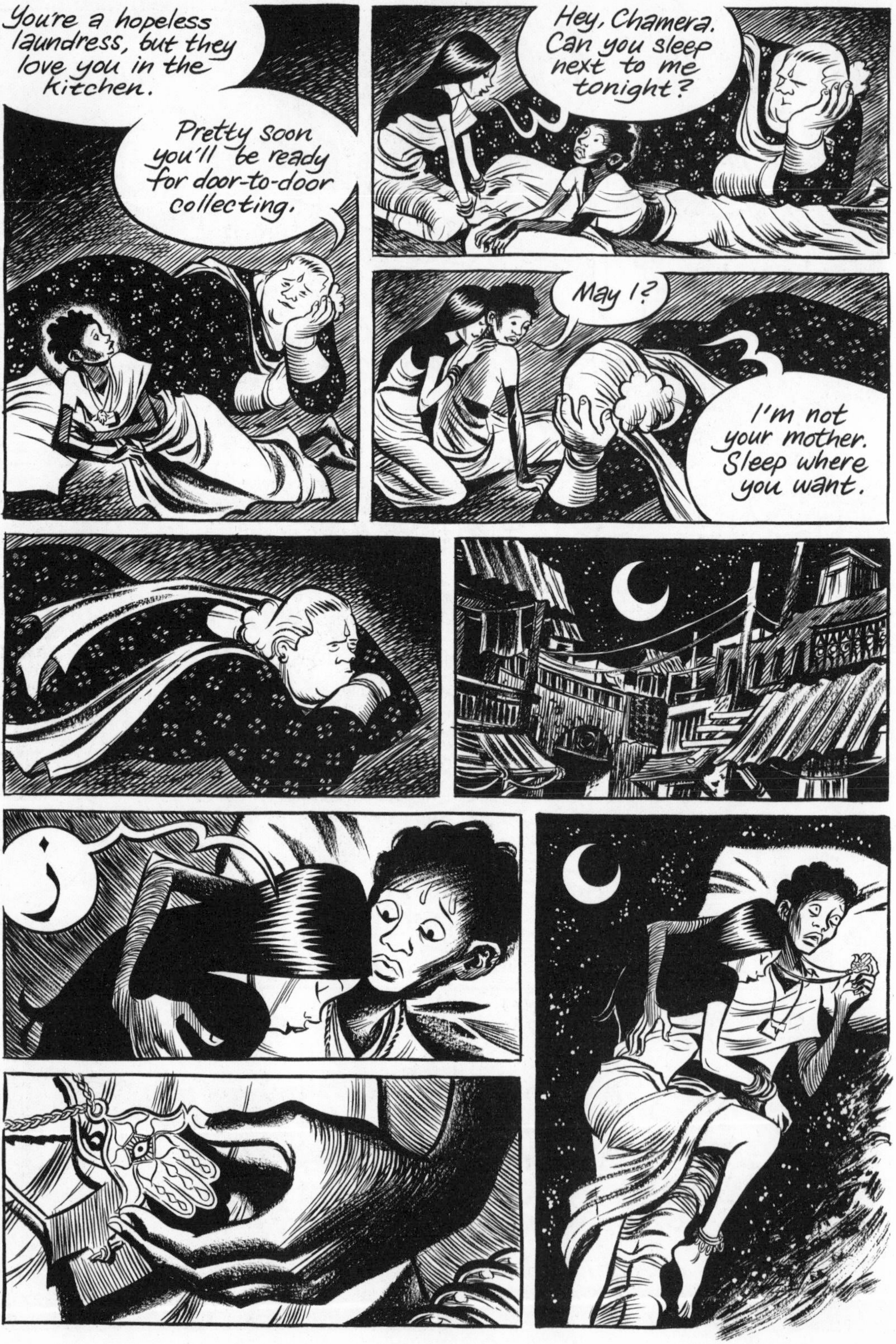
You're a hopeless laundress, but they love you in the kitchen.
Pretty soon you'll be ready for door-to-door collecting.
Hey, Chamera. Can you sleep next to me tonight?
May I?
I'm not your mother. Sleep where you want.

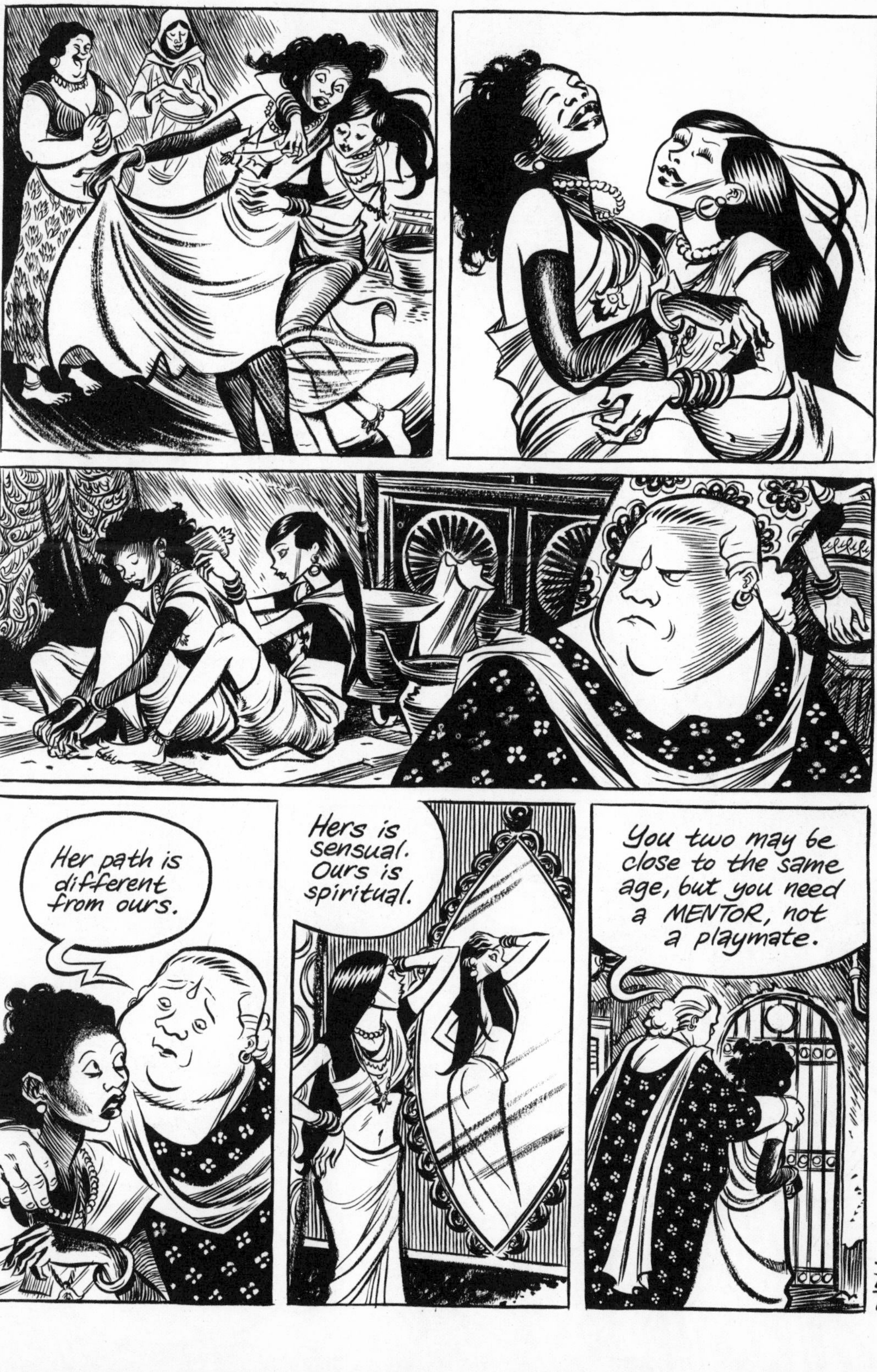
Her path is different from ours.
Hers is sensual. Ours is spiritual.
You two may be close to the same age, but you need a MENTOR, not a playmate.

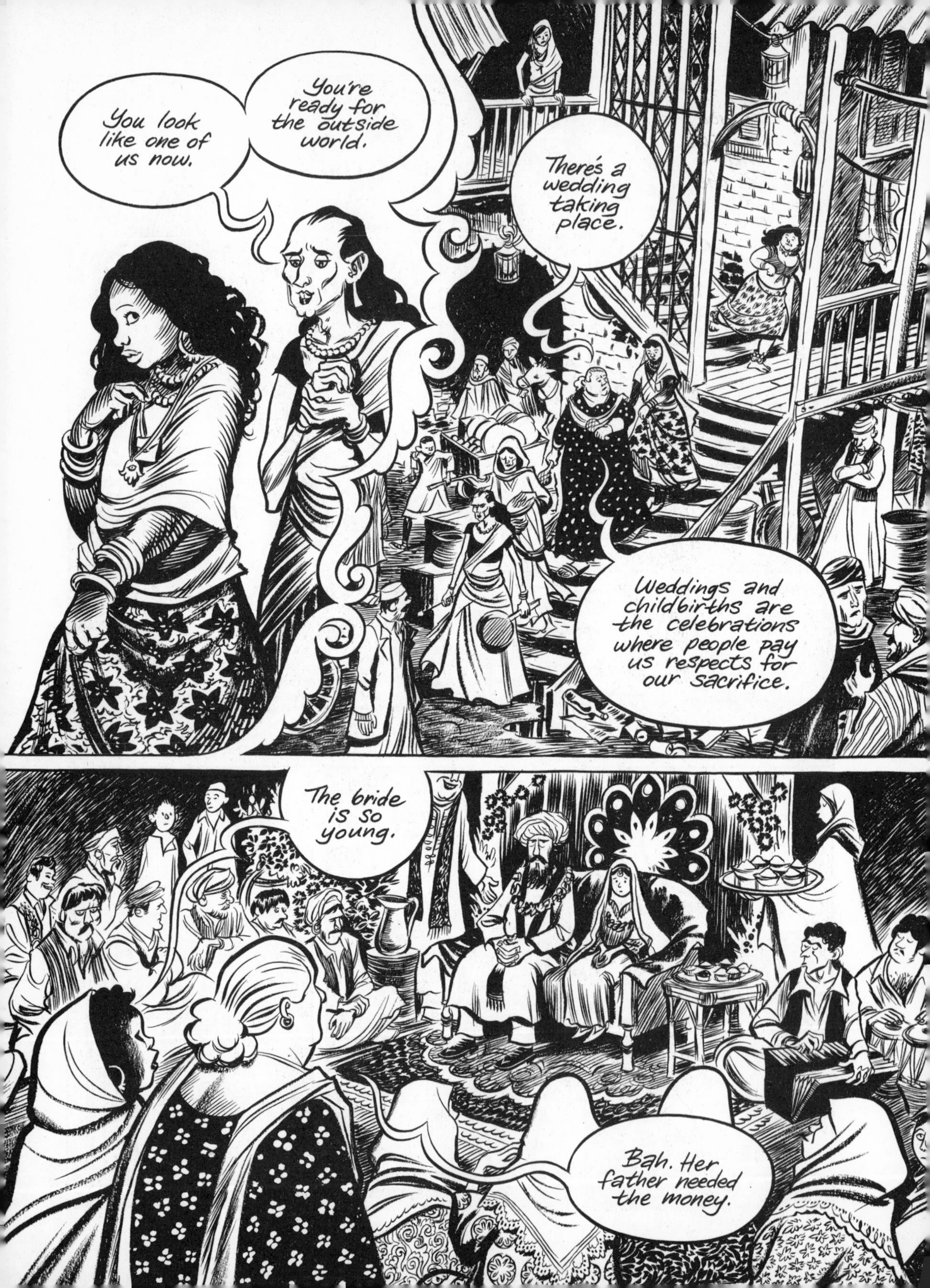
You look like one of us now.
You're ready for the outside world.
There's a wedding taking place.
Weddings and childbirths are the celebrations where people pay us respects for our sacrifice.
The bride is so young.
Bah. Her father needed the money.

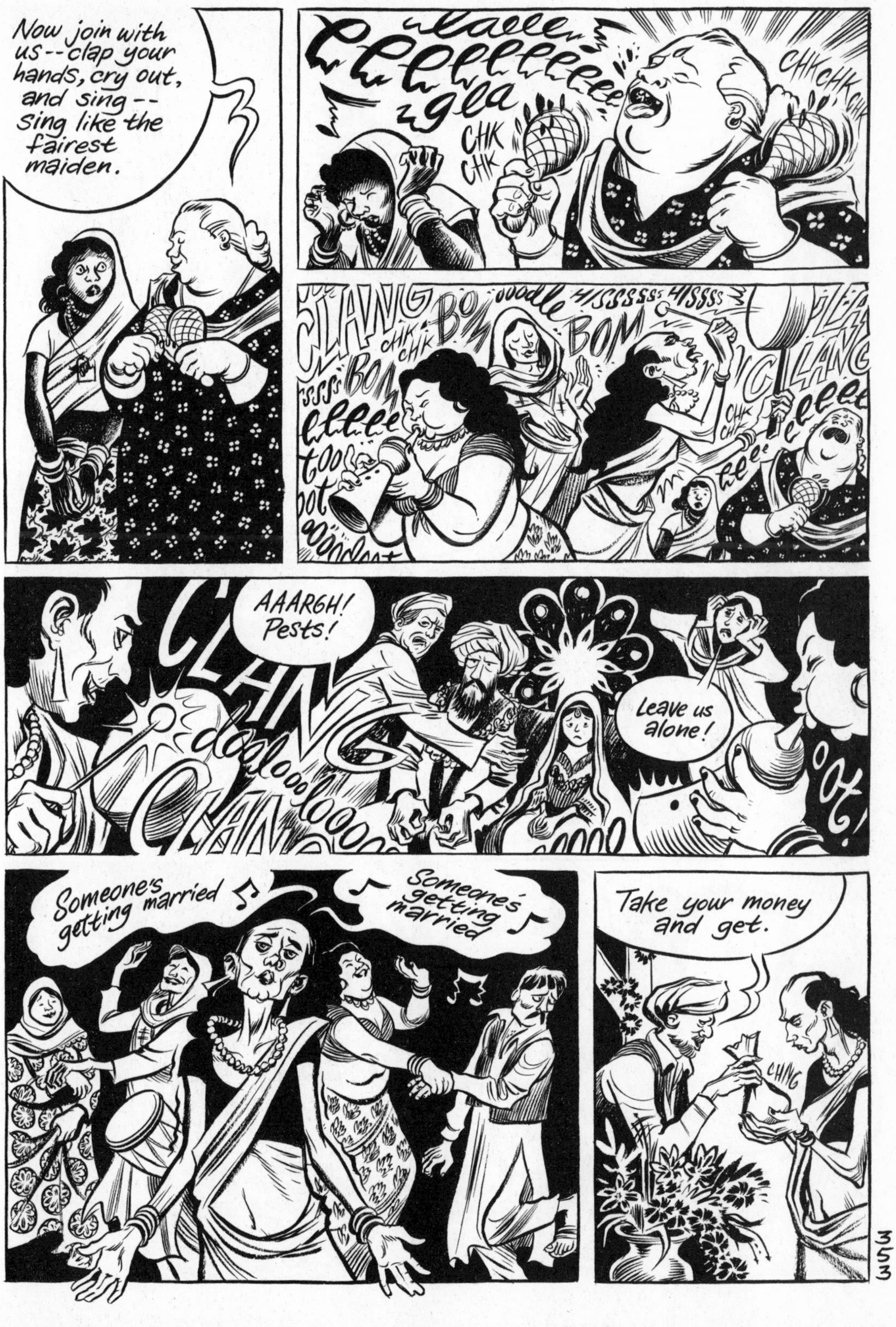
Now join with us--clap your hands, cry out, and sing--sing like the fairest maiden.
CHK CHK
CHK CHK CHK
AAARGH! Pests!
Leave us alone!
Someone's getting married
Someone's getting married
Take your money and get.
CHNG

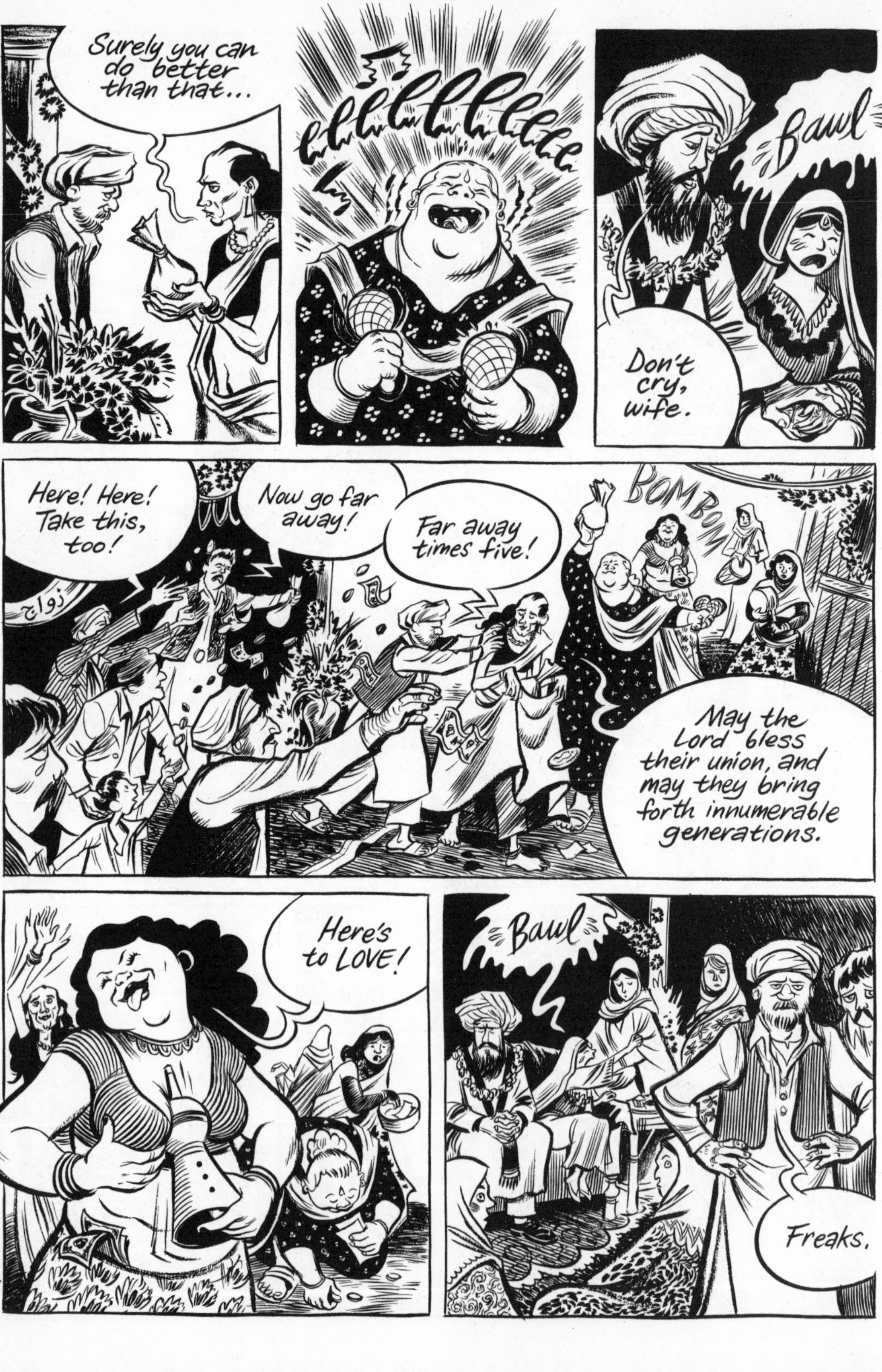
Surely you can do better than that...
Bawl
Don't cry, wife.
Here! Here! Take this, too!
Now go far away!
Far away times five!
زواج
BOMBOM
May the Lord bless their union, and may they bring forth innumerable generations.
Here's to LOVE!
Bawl
Freaks.

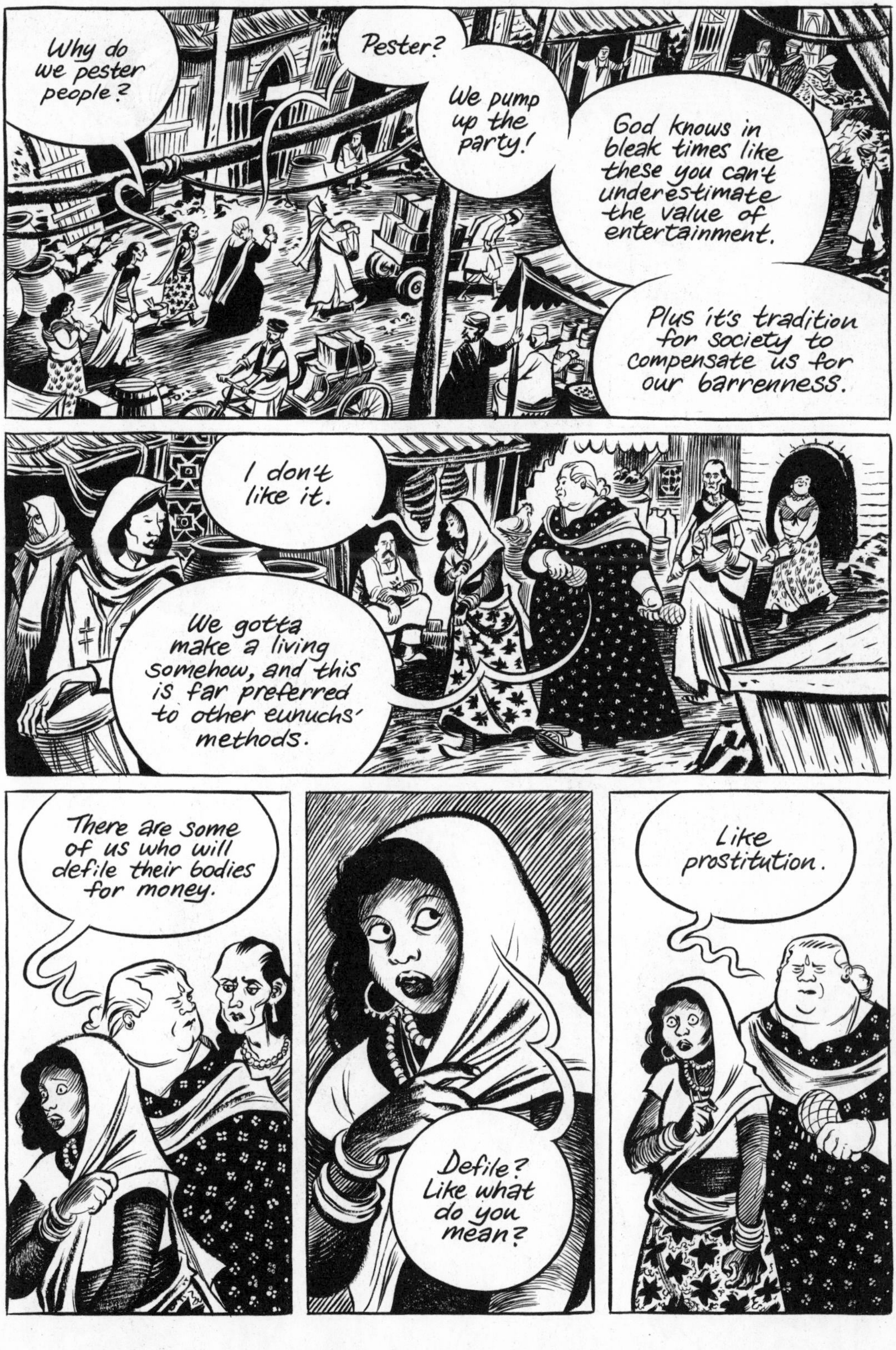
Why do we pester people?
Pester?
We pump up the party!
God knows in bleak times like these you can't underestimate the value of entertainment.
Plus it's tradition for society to compensate us for our barrenness.
I don't like it.
We gotta make a living somehow, and this is far preferred to other eunuchs' methods.
There are some of us who will defile their bodies for money.
Defile? Like what do you mean?
Like prostitution.

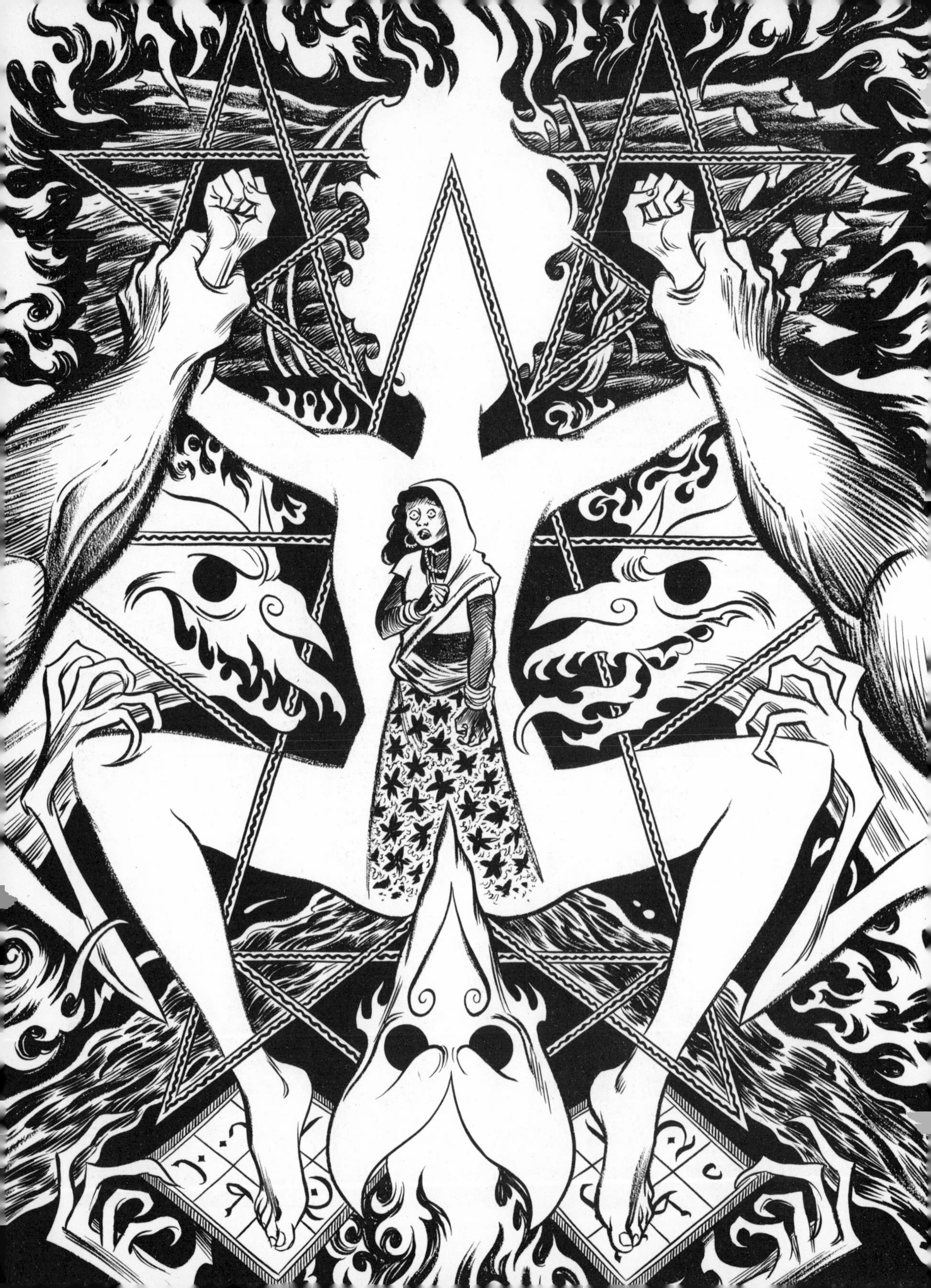

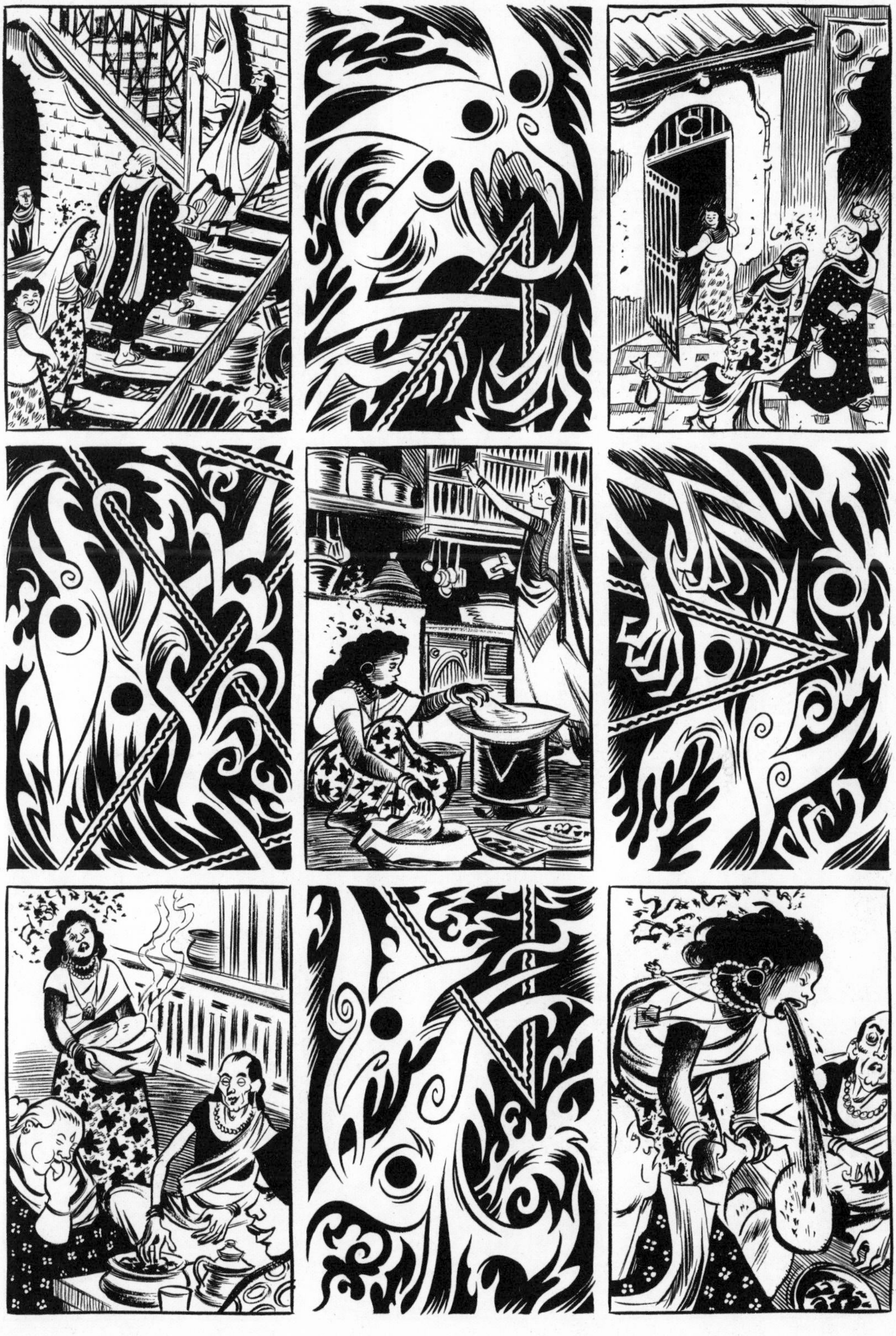

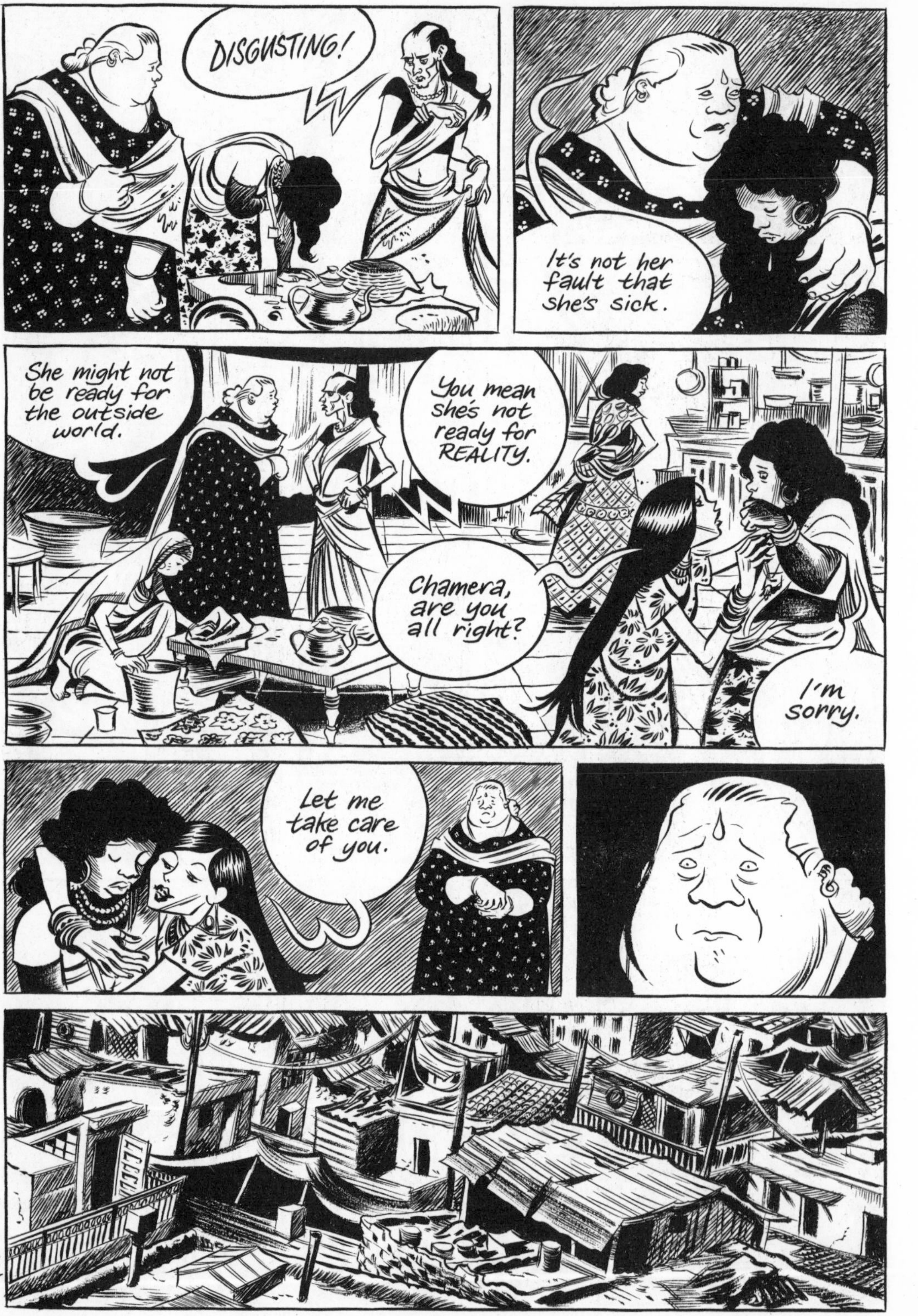

DISGUSTING!
It's not her fault that she's sick.
She might not be ready for the outside world.
You mean she's not ready for REALITY.
Chamera, are you all right?
I'm sorry.
Let me take care of you.

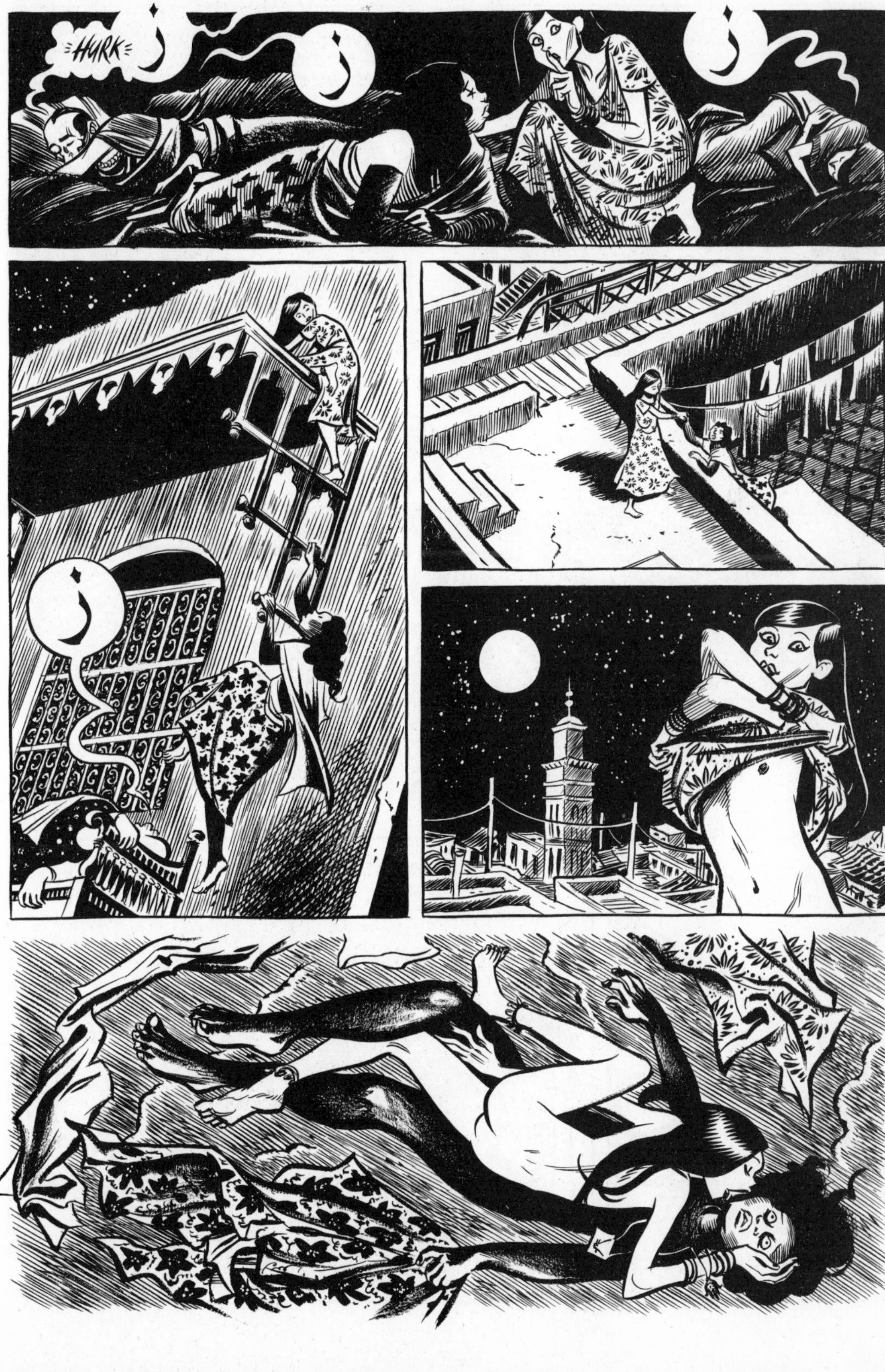

ز
HURK
ز
ز
ز

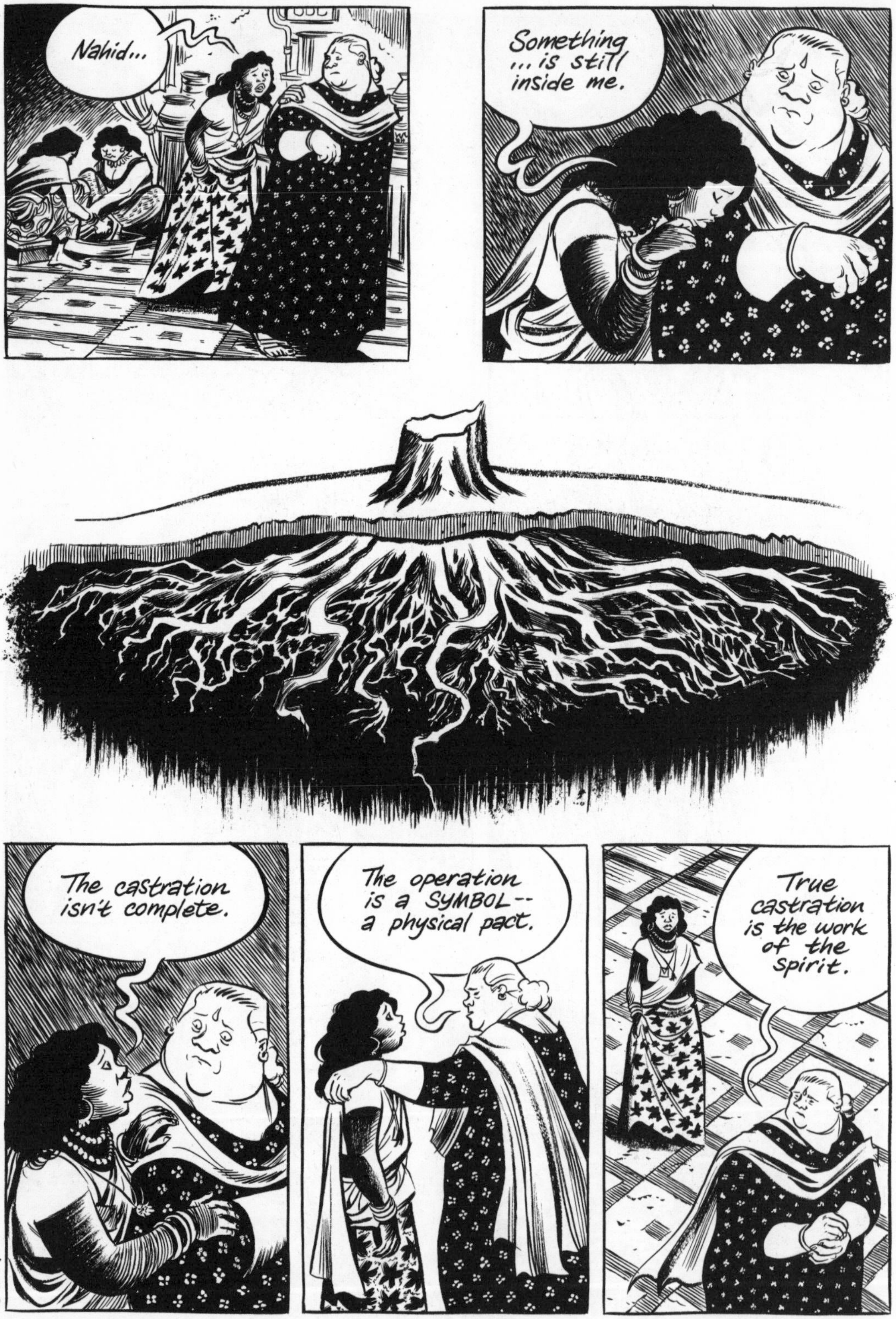
Nahid...
Something ...is still inside me.
The castration isn't complete.
The operation is a SYMBOL-- a physical pact.
True castration is the work of the spirit.

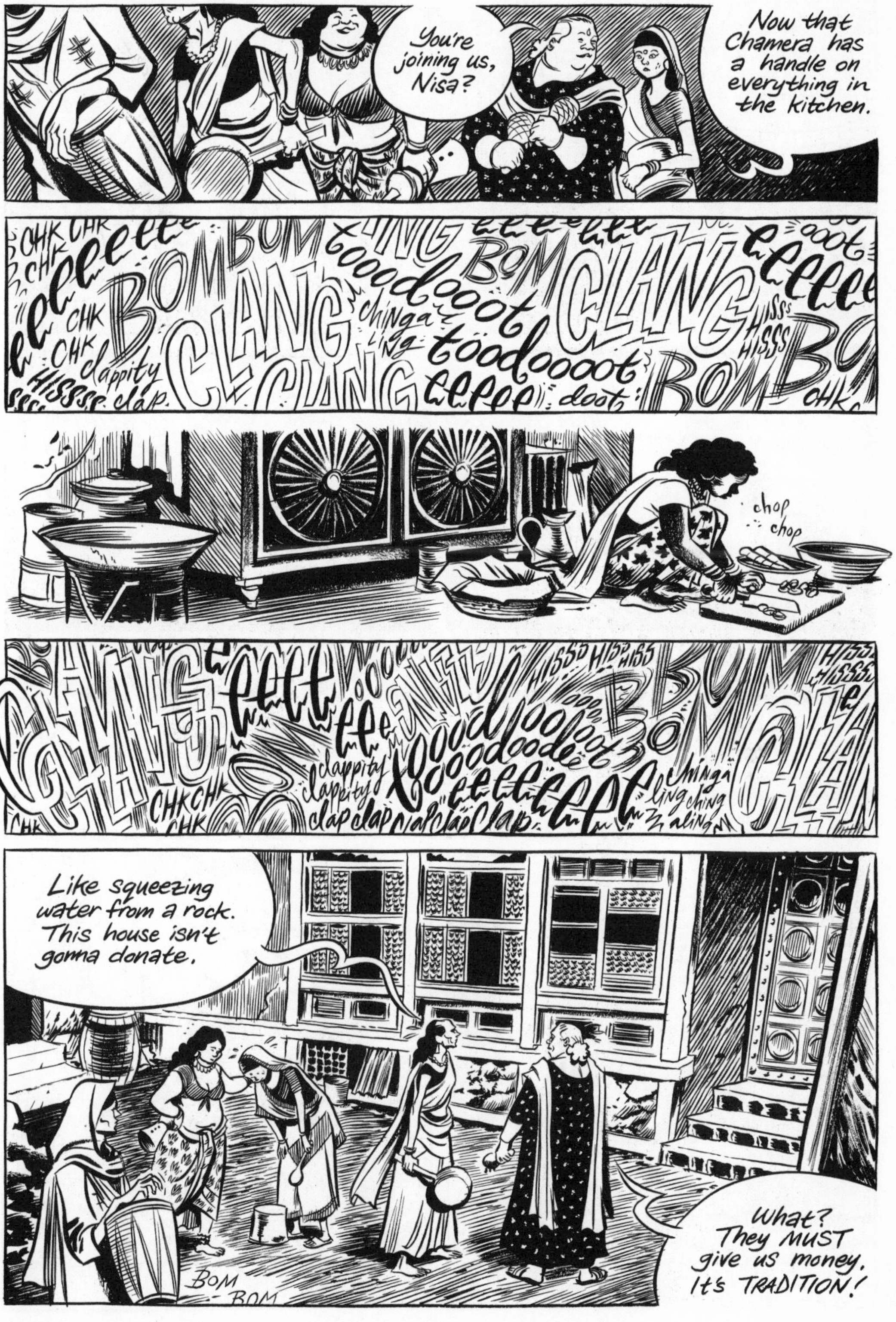
You're joining us, Nisa?
Now that Chamera has a handle on everything in the kitchen.
CLANG
BOM
toooodoooot
chop chop
Like squeezing water from a rock. This house isn't gonna donate.
What? They MUST give us money. It's TRADITION!
BOM BOM

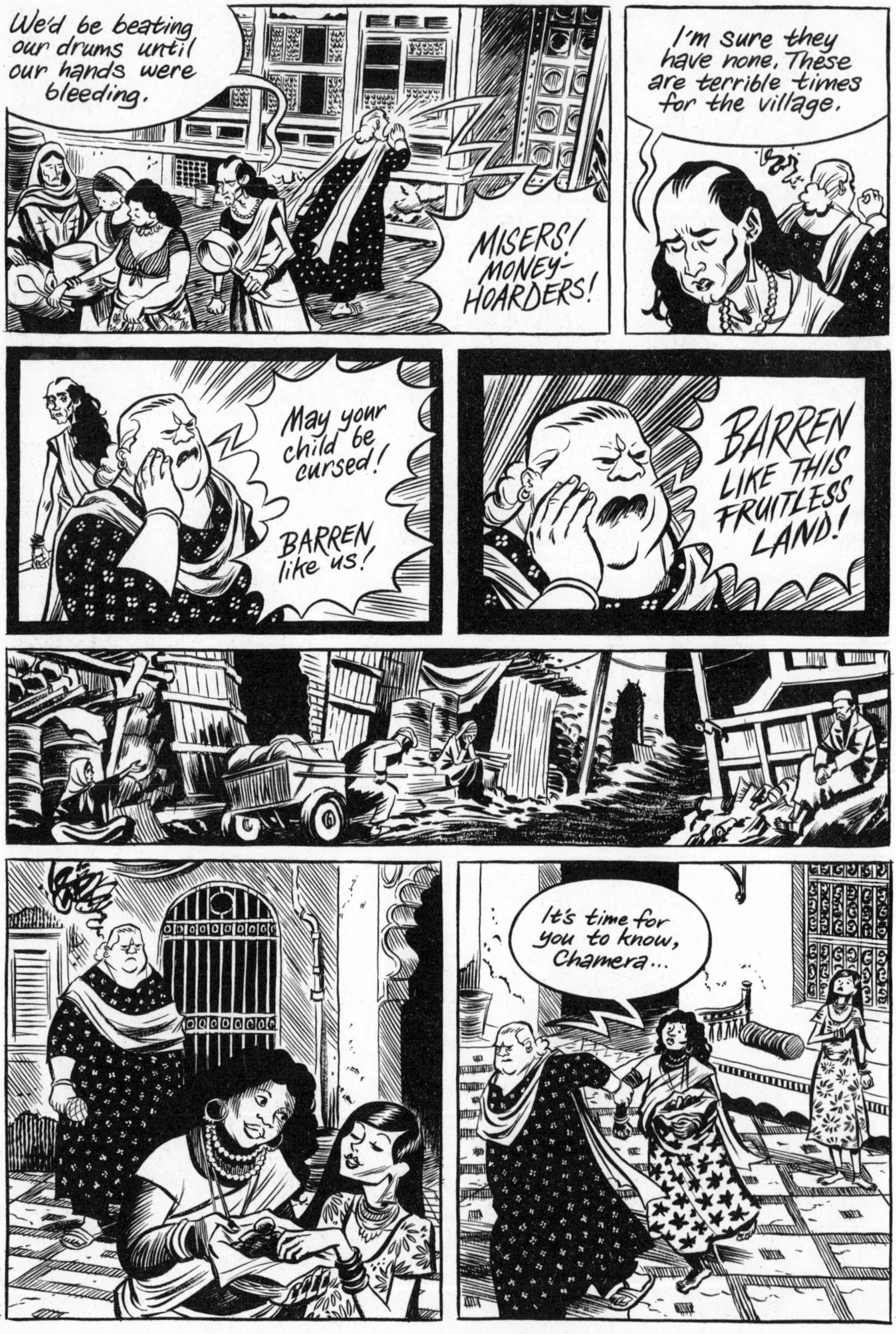
We'd be beating our drums until our hands were bleeding.
MISERS! MONEY-HOARDERS!
I'm sure they have none. These are terrible times for the village.
May your child be cursed!
BARREN like us!
BARREN LIKE THIS FRUITLESS LAND!
It's time for you to know, Chamera...

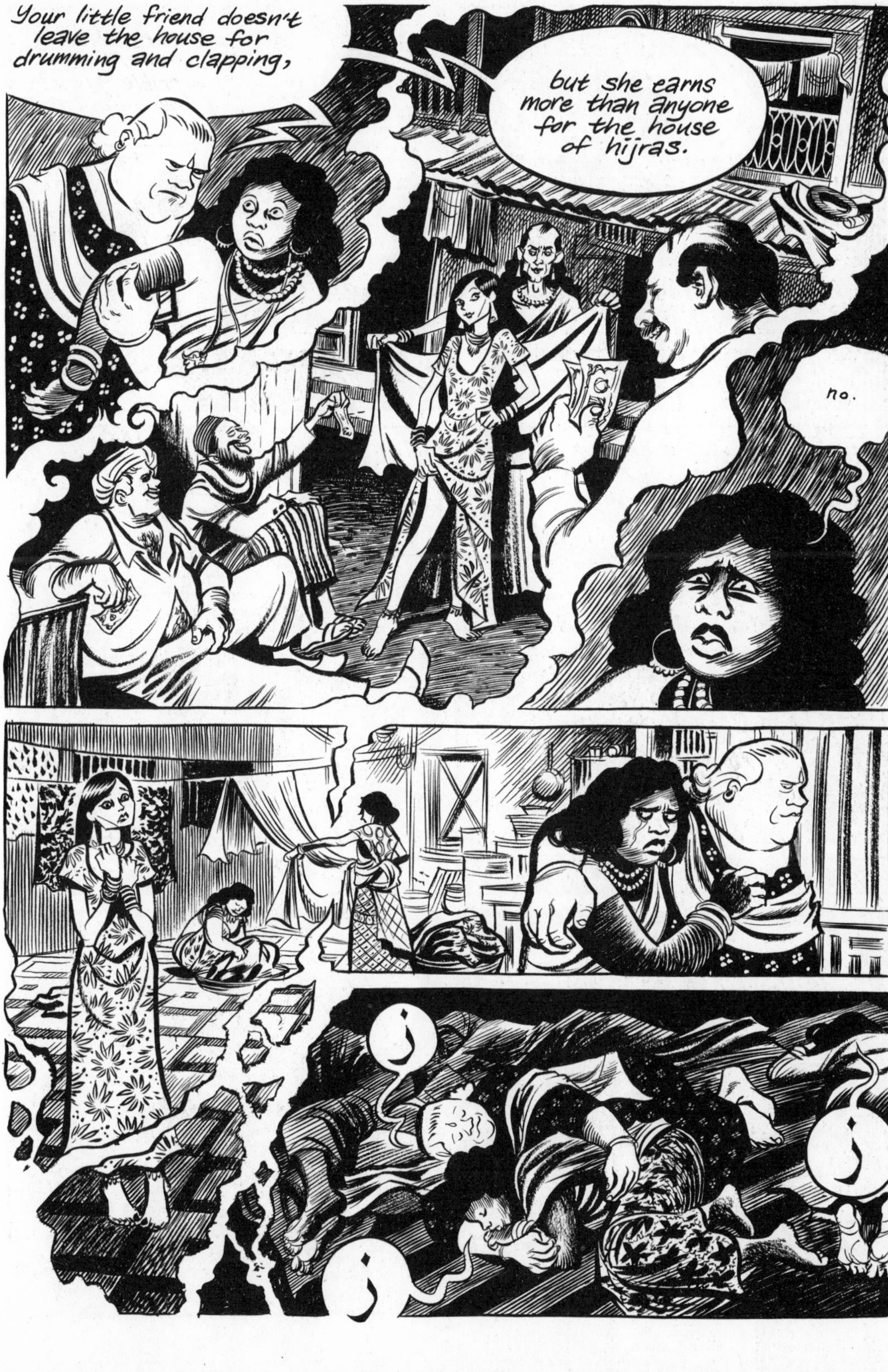
Your little friend doesn't leave the house for drumming and clapping,
but she earns more than anyone for the house of hijras.
no.
ز
ز
ز
ز

You've grown so much.
You see? Our deprivations can feed us.
It is said that God will bless the eunuchs and "give them an everlasting name that will not be cut off".
I can tell you've finally let go of your desires --freeing room for God to fill you.
It's true. All desire is gone.
The world means nothing now.
I need no one.

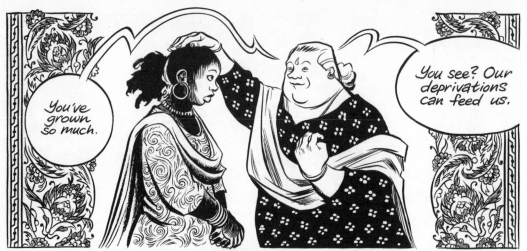

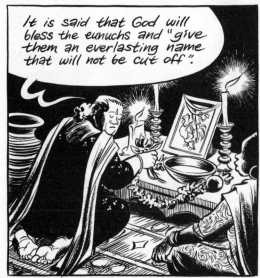

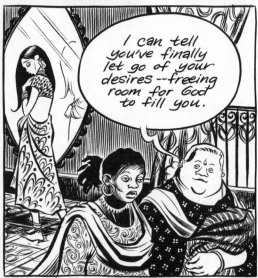

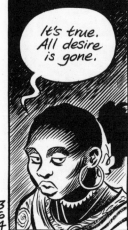

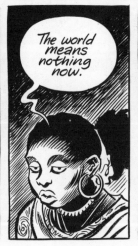

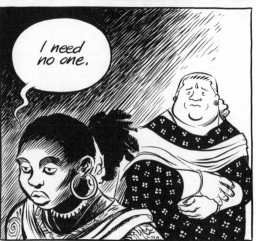

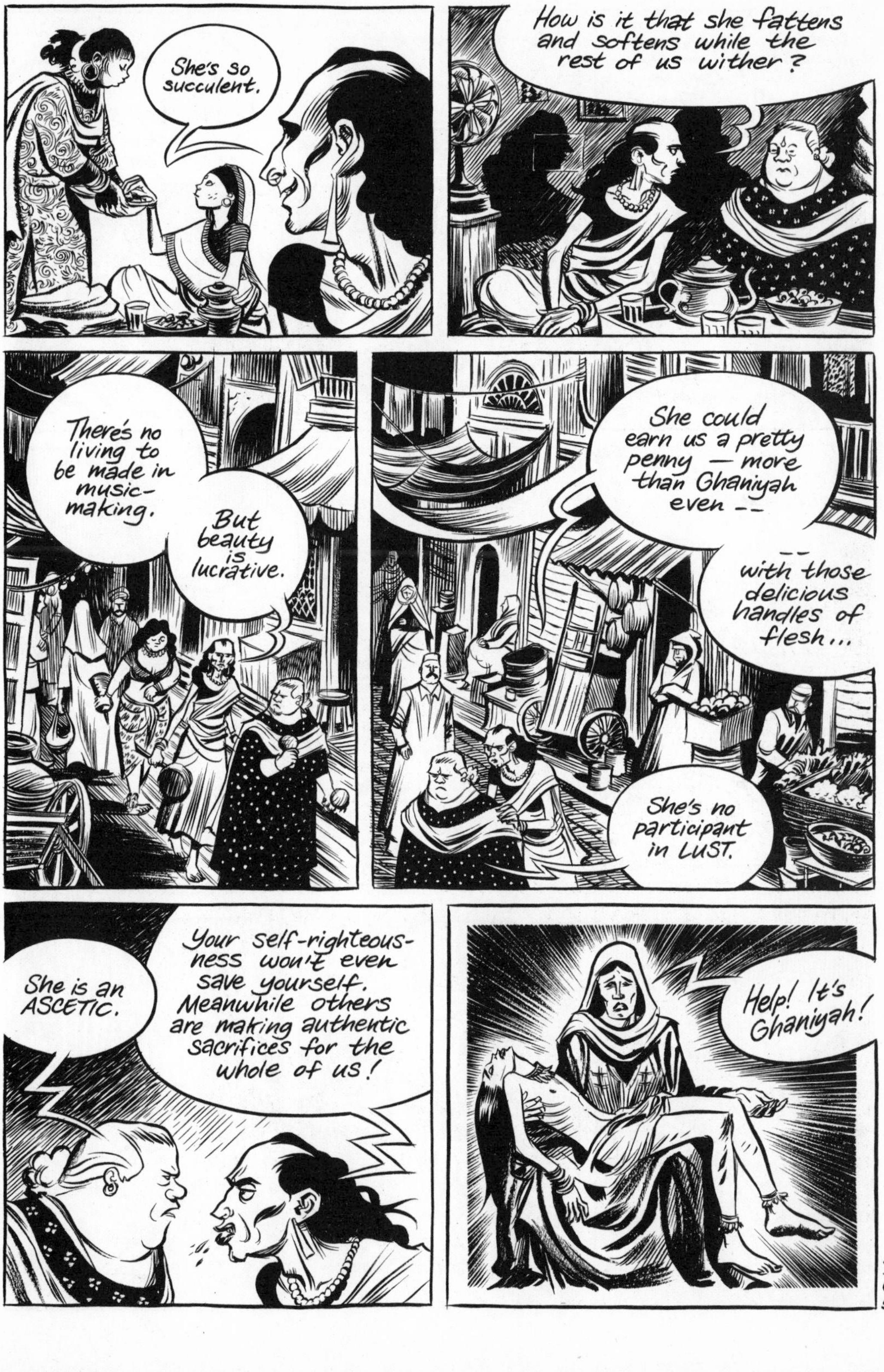
She's so succulent.
How is it that she fattens and softens while the rest of us wither?
There's no living to be made in music-making.
But beauty is lucrative.
She could earn us a pretty penny — more than Ghaniyah even --
-- with those delicious handles of flesh...
She's no participant in LUST.
She is an ASCETIC.
Your self-righteousness won't even save yourself. Meanwhile others are making authentic sacrifices for the whole of us!
Help! It's Ghaniyah!

What happened?

The men on the streets. They abused her.

Don't move her so much! Some bones are broken.

Over here, slowly.

We need to stop the bleeding.

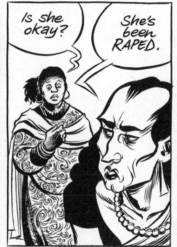

Is she okay?

She's been RAPED.

Ghaniyah...

...

I'm sorry for judging you.

366

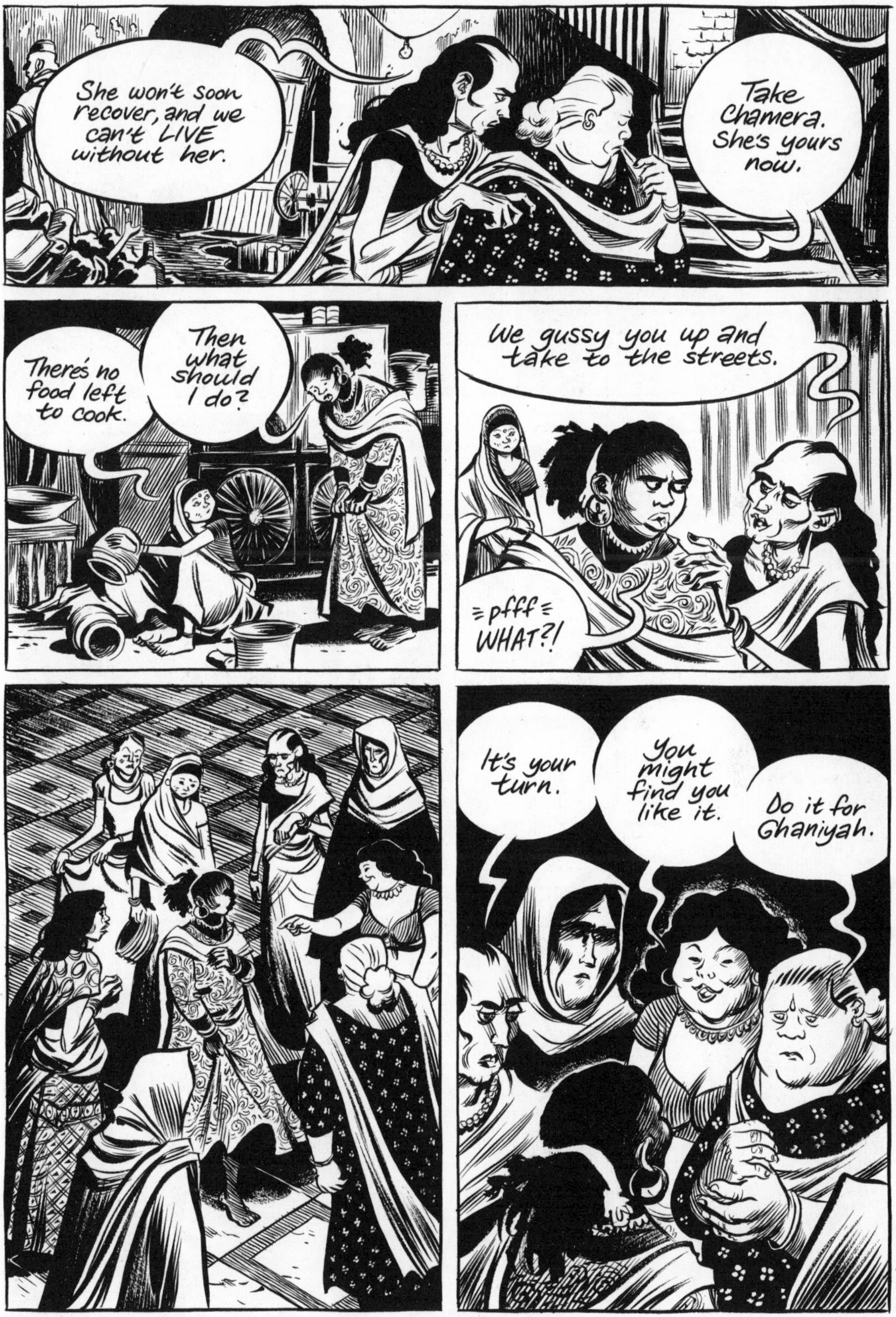
She won't soon recover, and we can't LIVE without her.
Take Chamera. She's yours now.
There's no food left to cook.
Then what should I do?
We gussy you up and take to the streets.
pfff WHAT?!
It's your turn.
You might find you like it.
Do it for Ghaniyah.

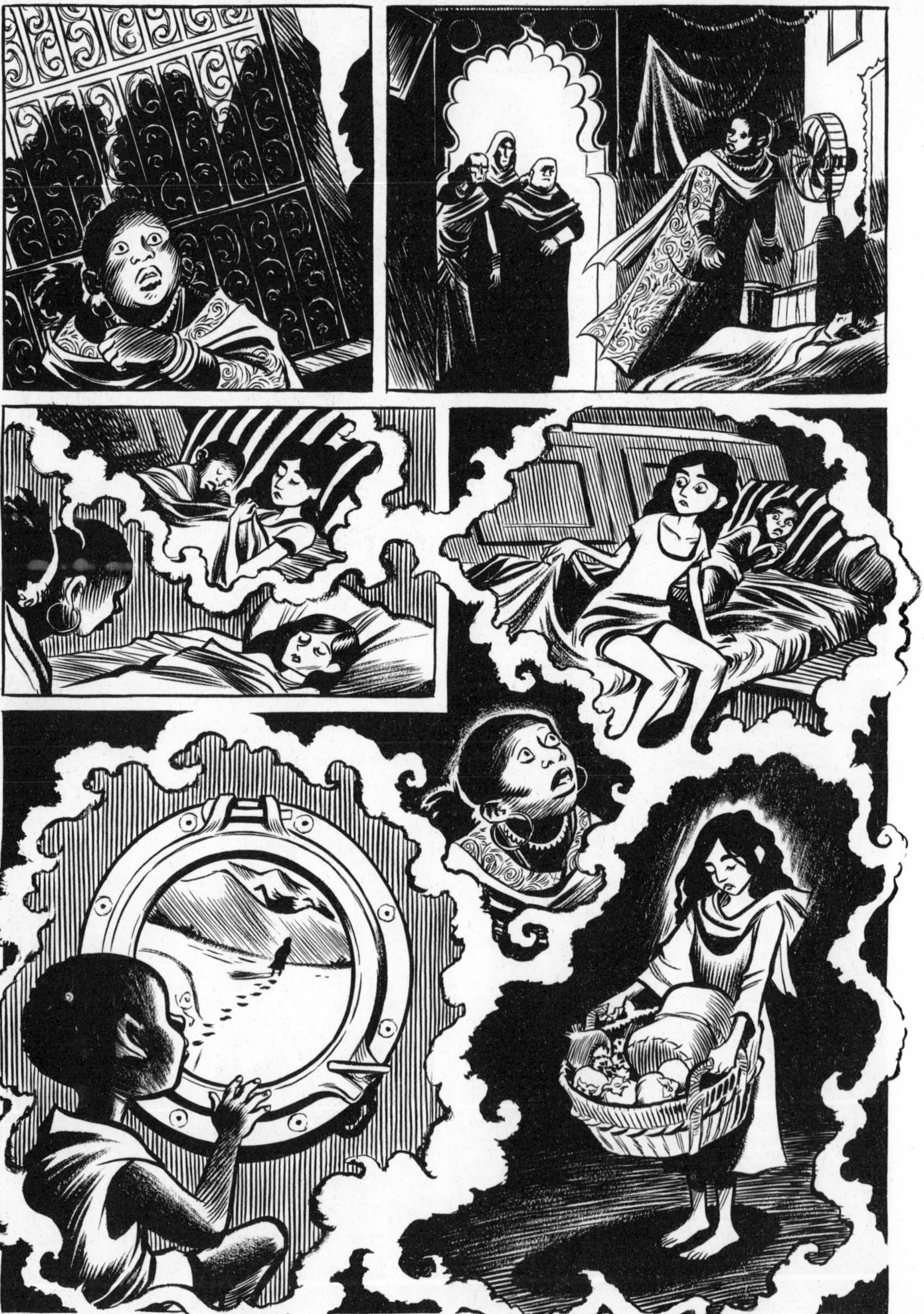

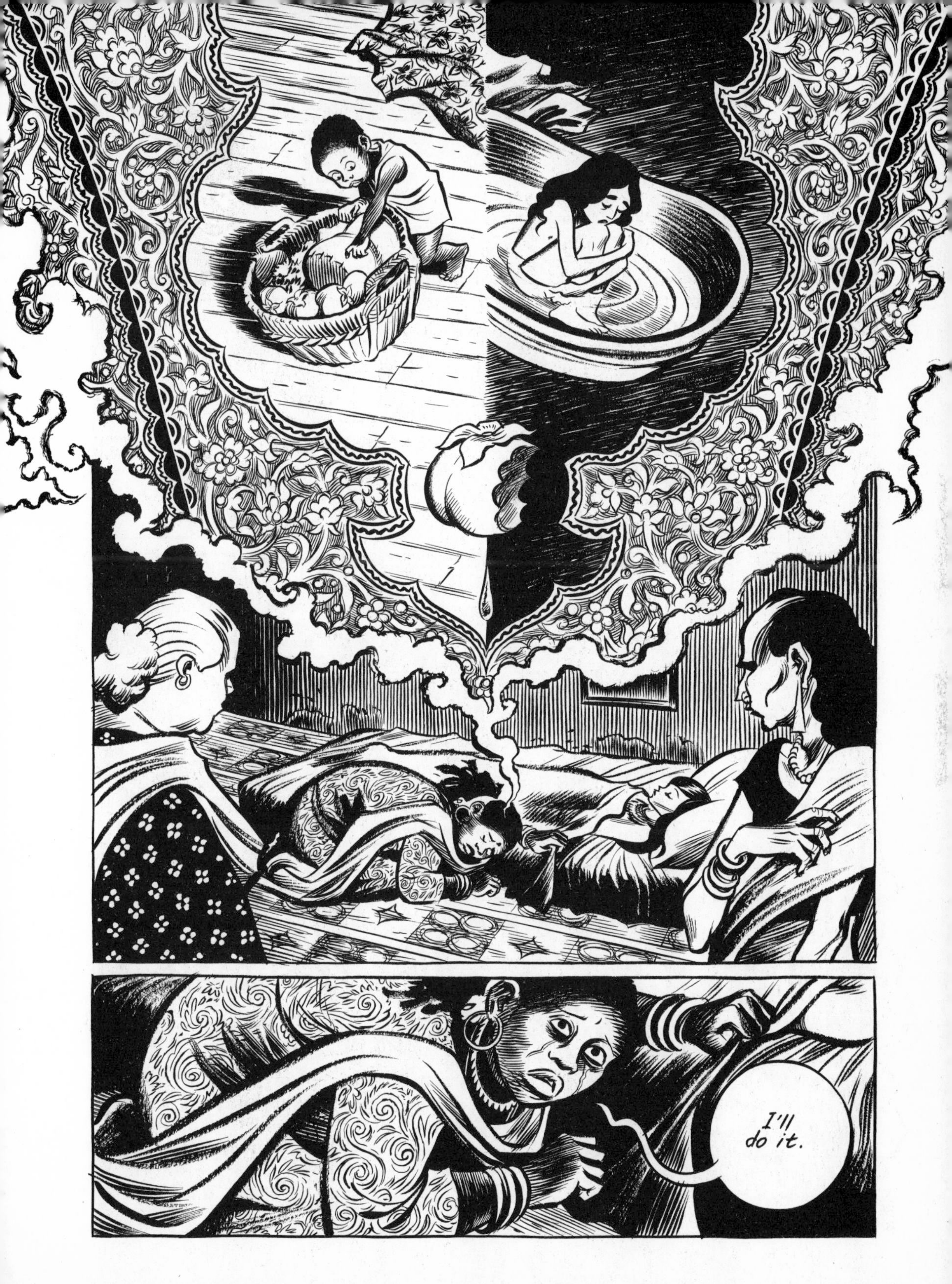
I'll do it.

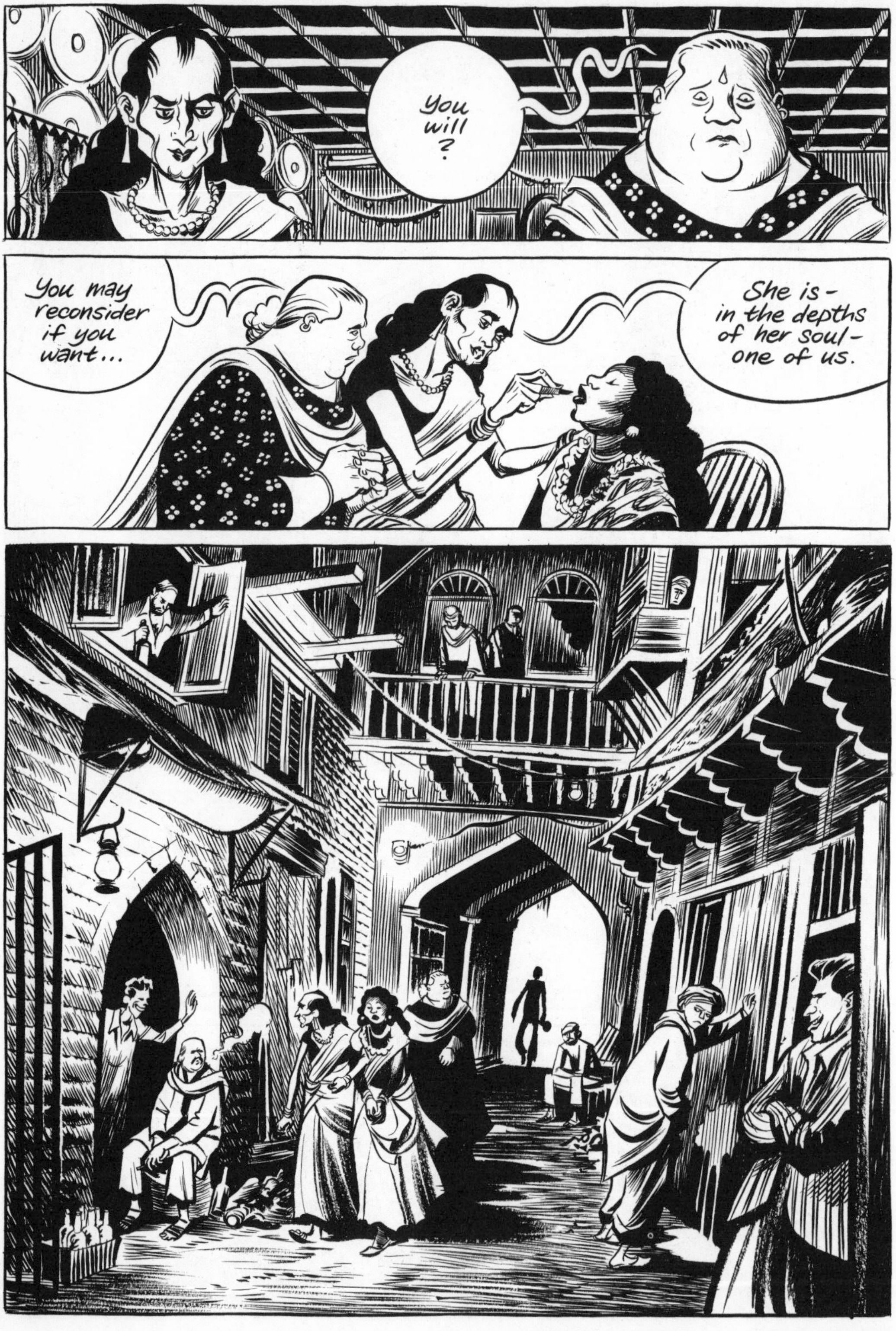
You will?
You may reconsider if you want...
She is - in the depths of her soul - one of us.

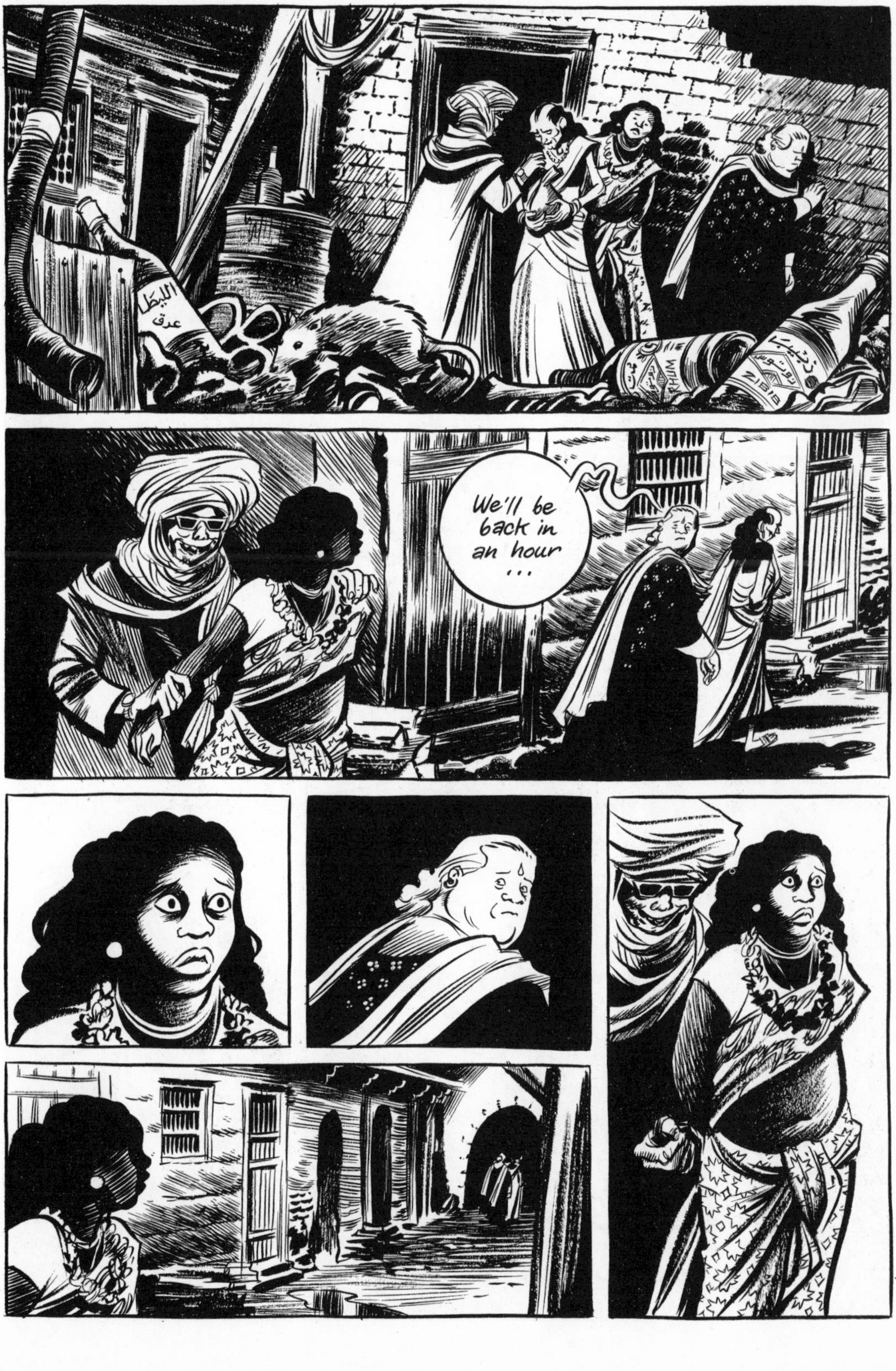
RHUM
We'll be back in an hour ...

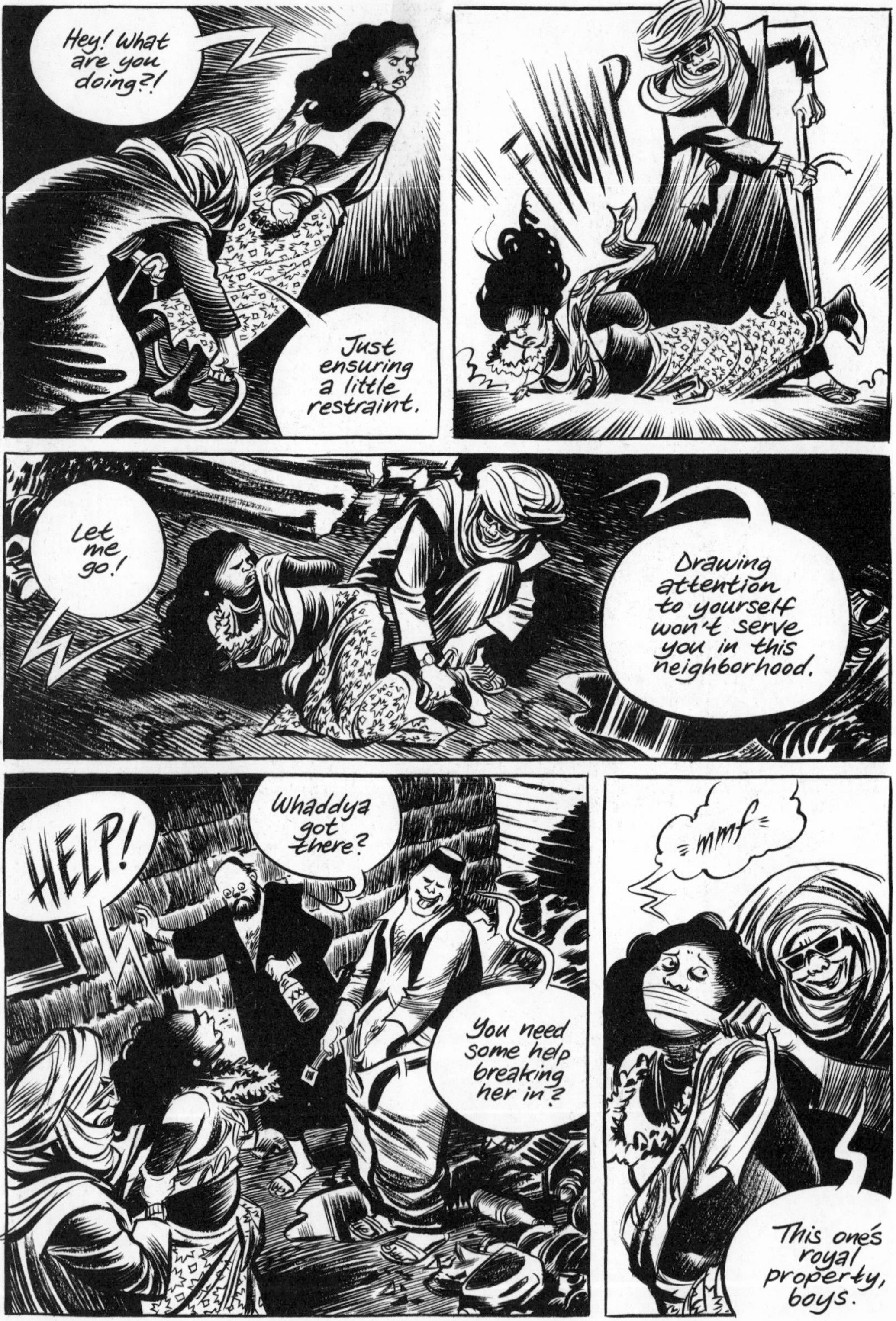

Hey! What are you doing?!
Just ensuring a little restraint.
FWUMP
Let me go!
Drawing attention to yourself won't serve you in this neighborhood.
HELP!
Whaddya got there?
You need some help breaking her in?
mmf
This one's royal property, boys.

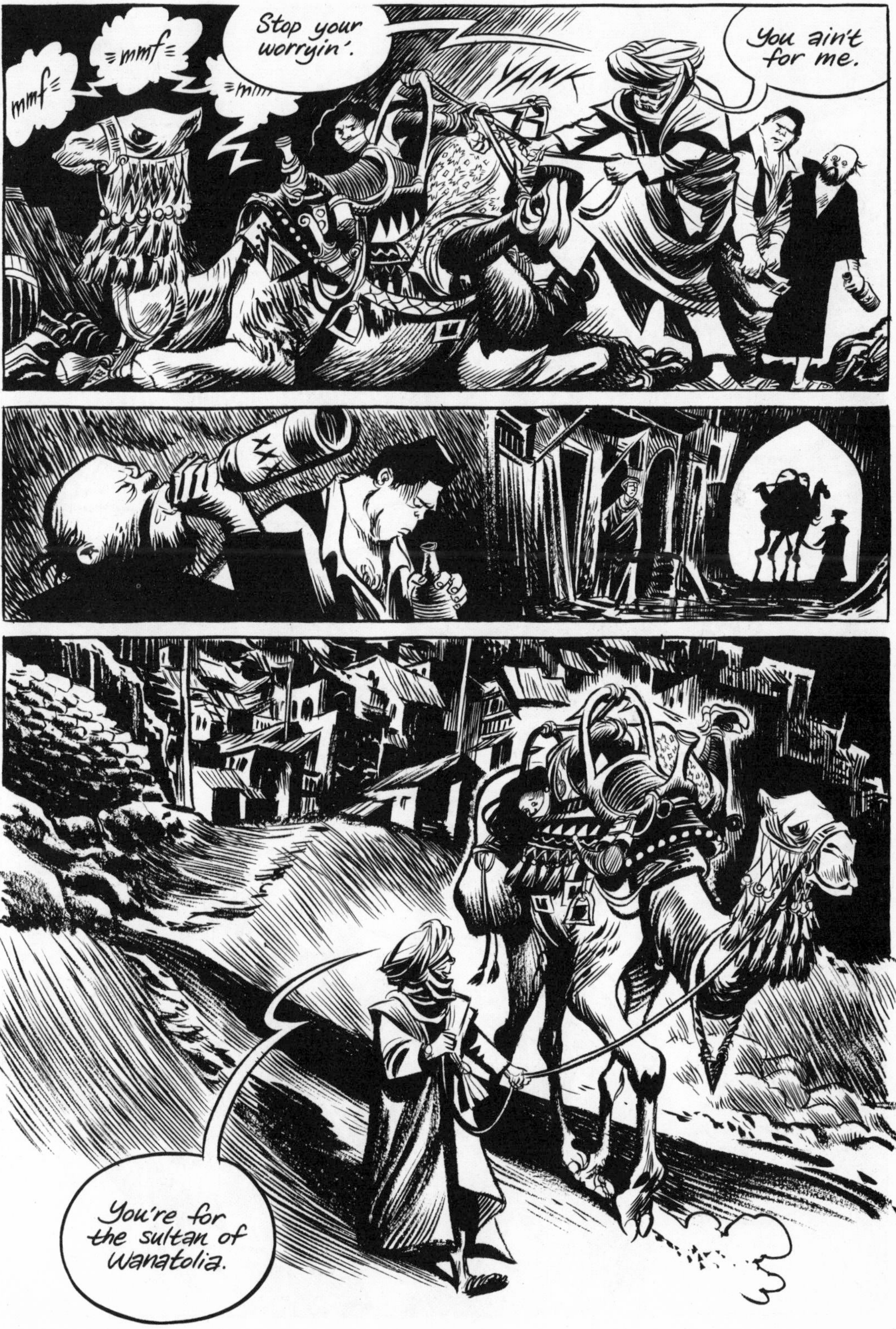
mmf
mmf
mm
Stop your worryin'.
YANK
You ain't for me.
You're for the sultan of Wanatolia.

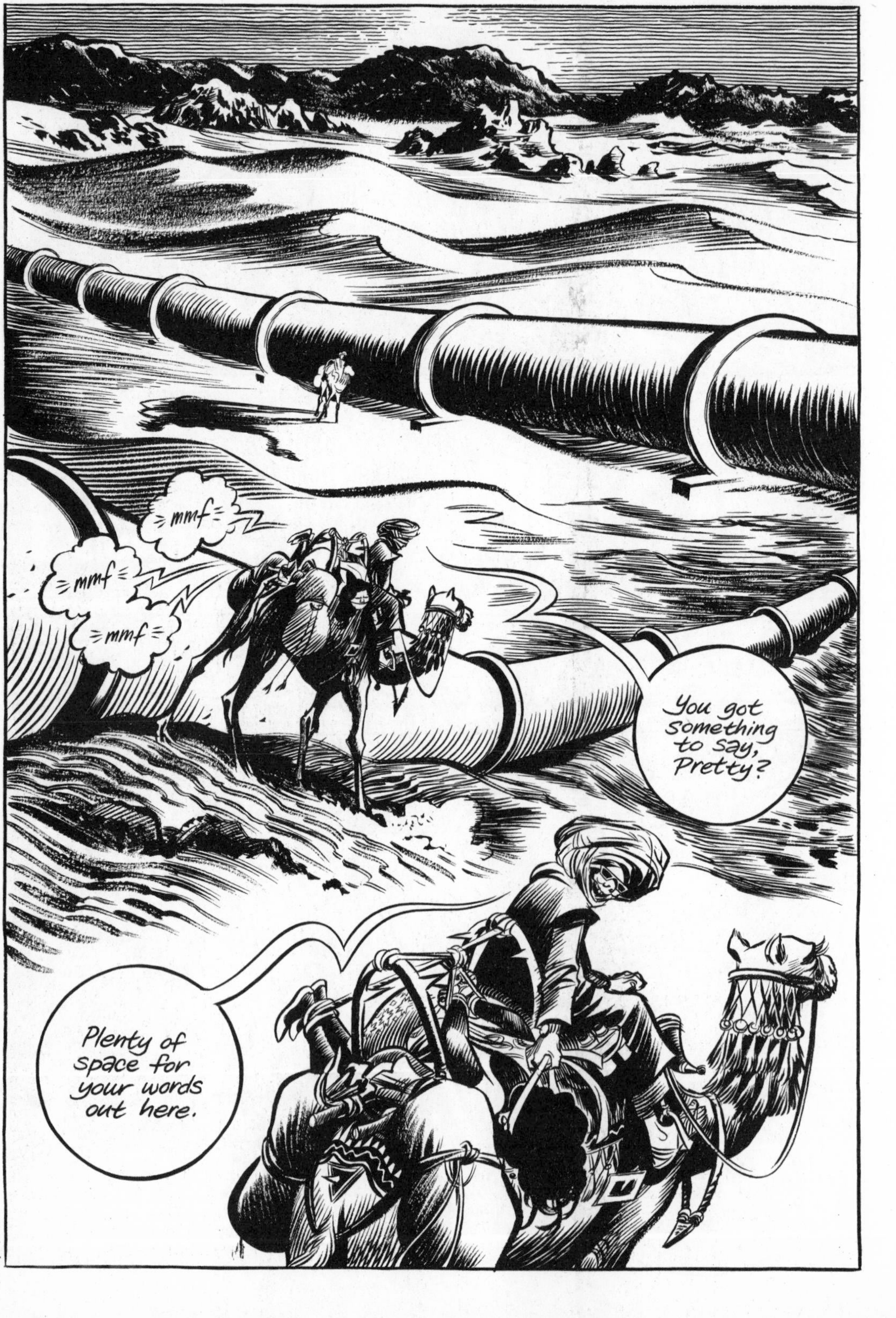
mmf
mmf
mmf
You got something to say, Pretty?
Plenty of space for your words out here.

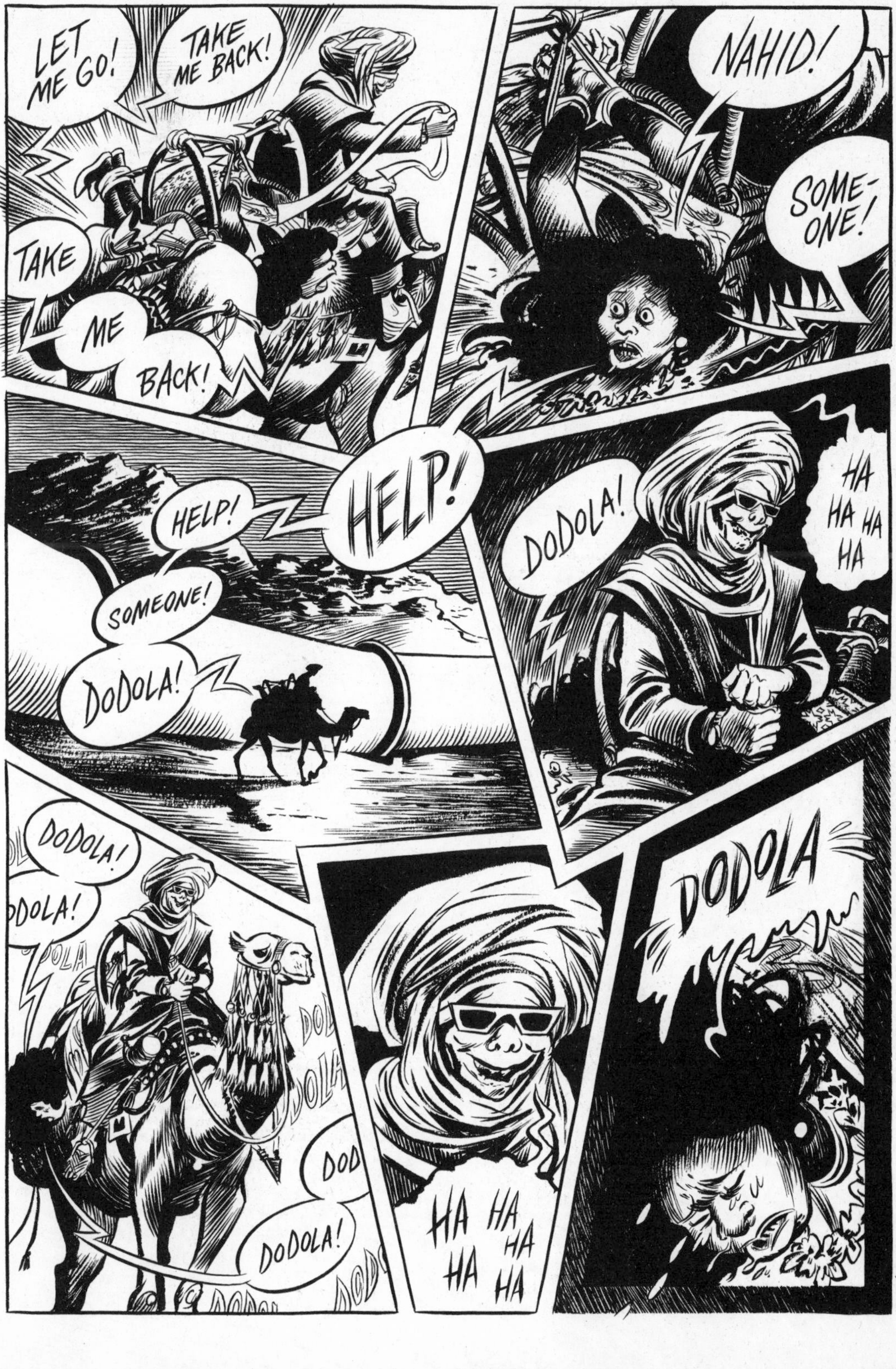
LET ME GO!
TAKE ME BACK!
TAKE
ME
BACK!
NAHID!
SOME-ONE!
HELP!
HELP!
SOMEONE!
DODOLA!
DODOLA!
HA HA HA HA
DODOLA!
DODOLA!
DODOLA!
HA HA HA HA HA HA
DODOLA

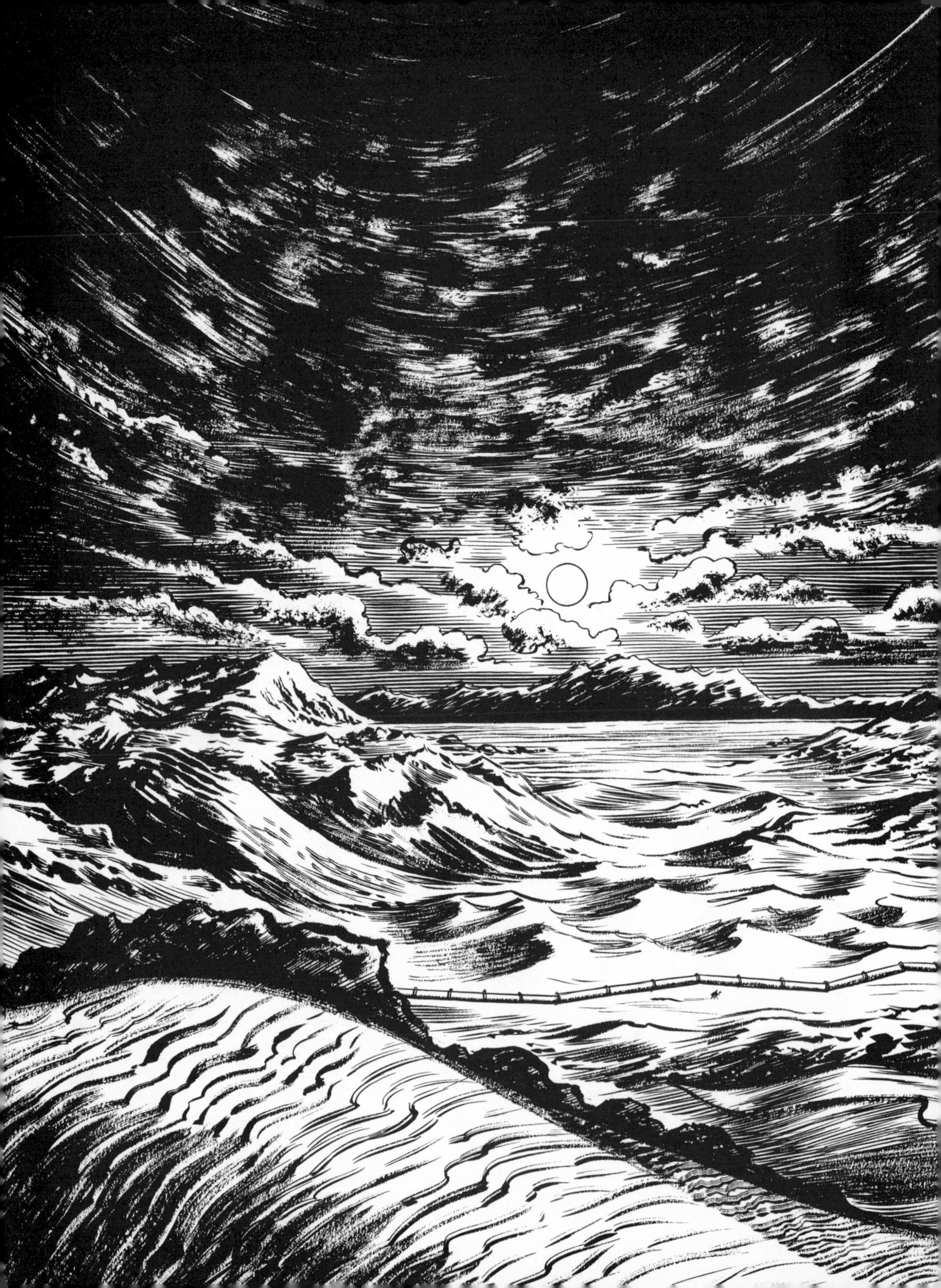

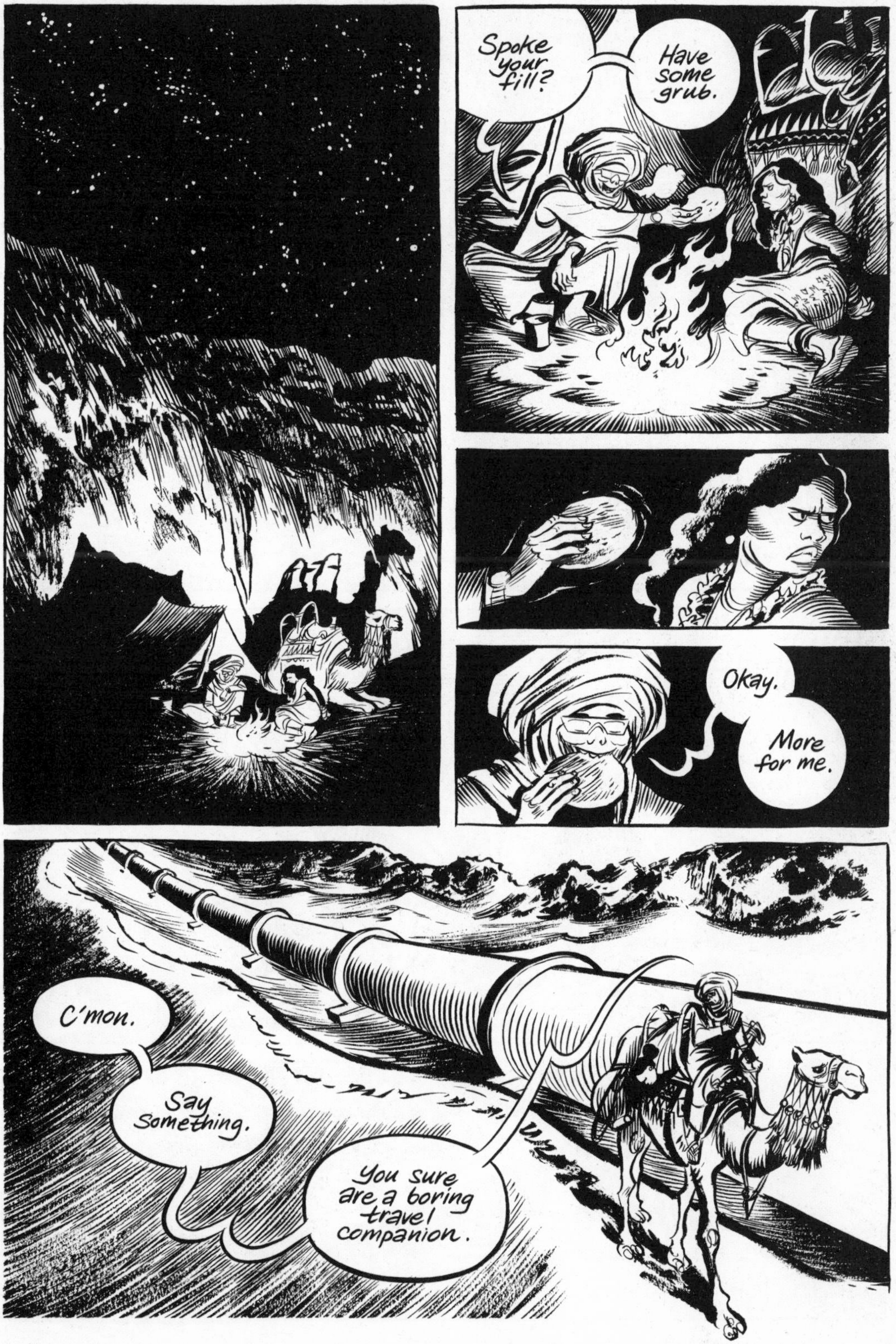
Spoke your fill?
Have some grub.
Okay.
More for me.
C'mon.
Say something.
You sure are a boring travel companion.

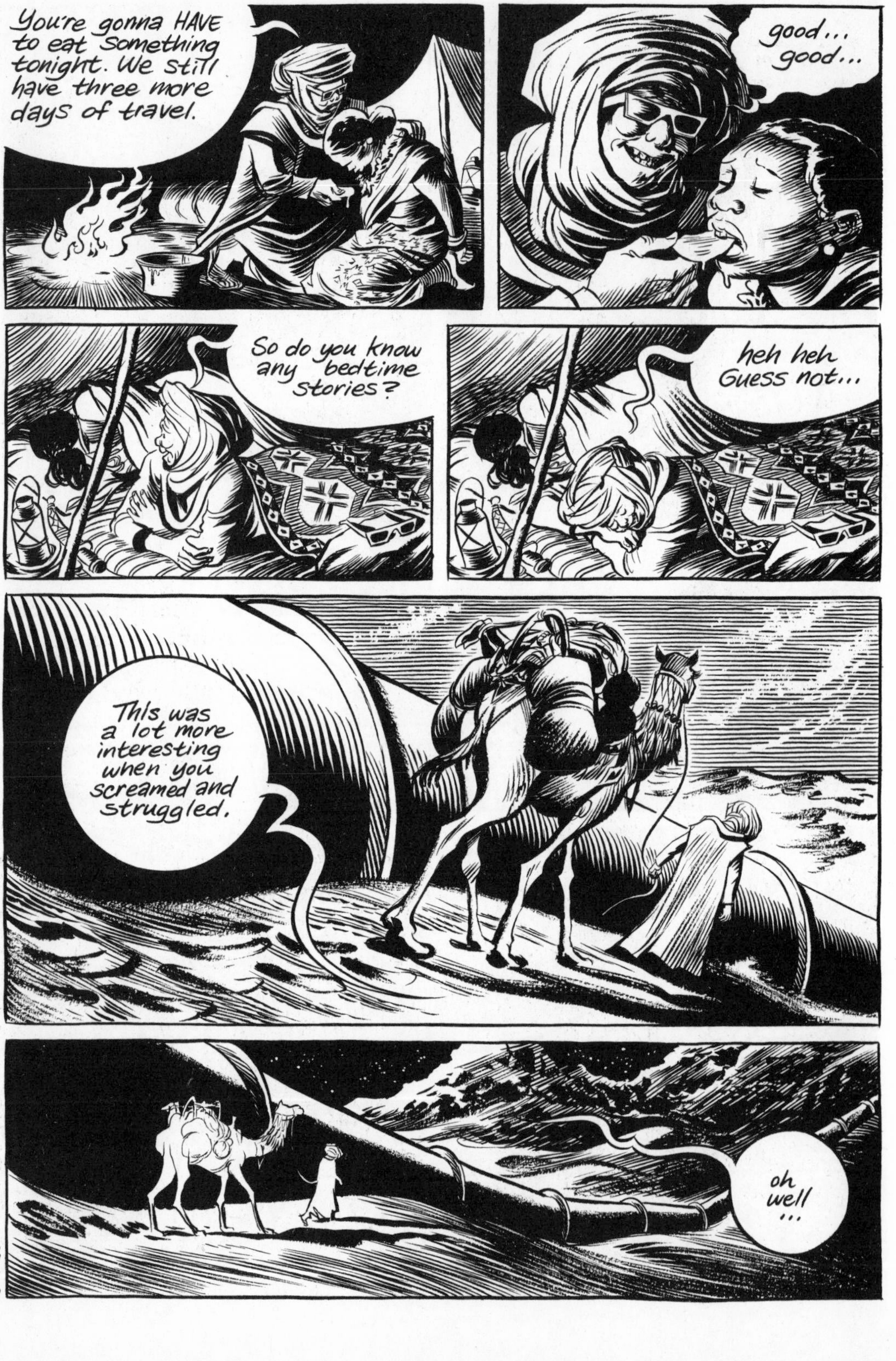
You're gonna HAVE to eat something tonight. We still have three more days of travel.
good... good...
So do you know any bedtime stories?
heh heh Guess not...
This was a lot more interesting when you screamed and struggled.
oh well ...

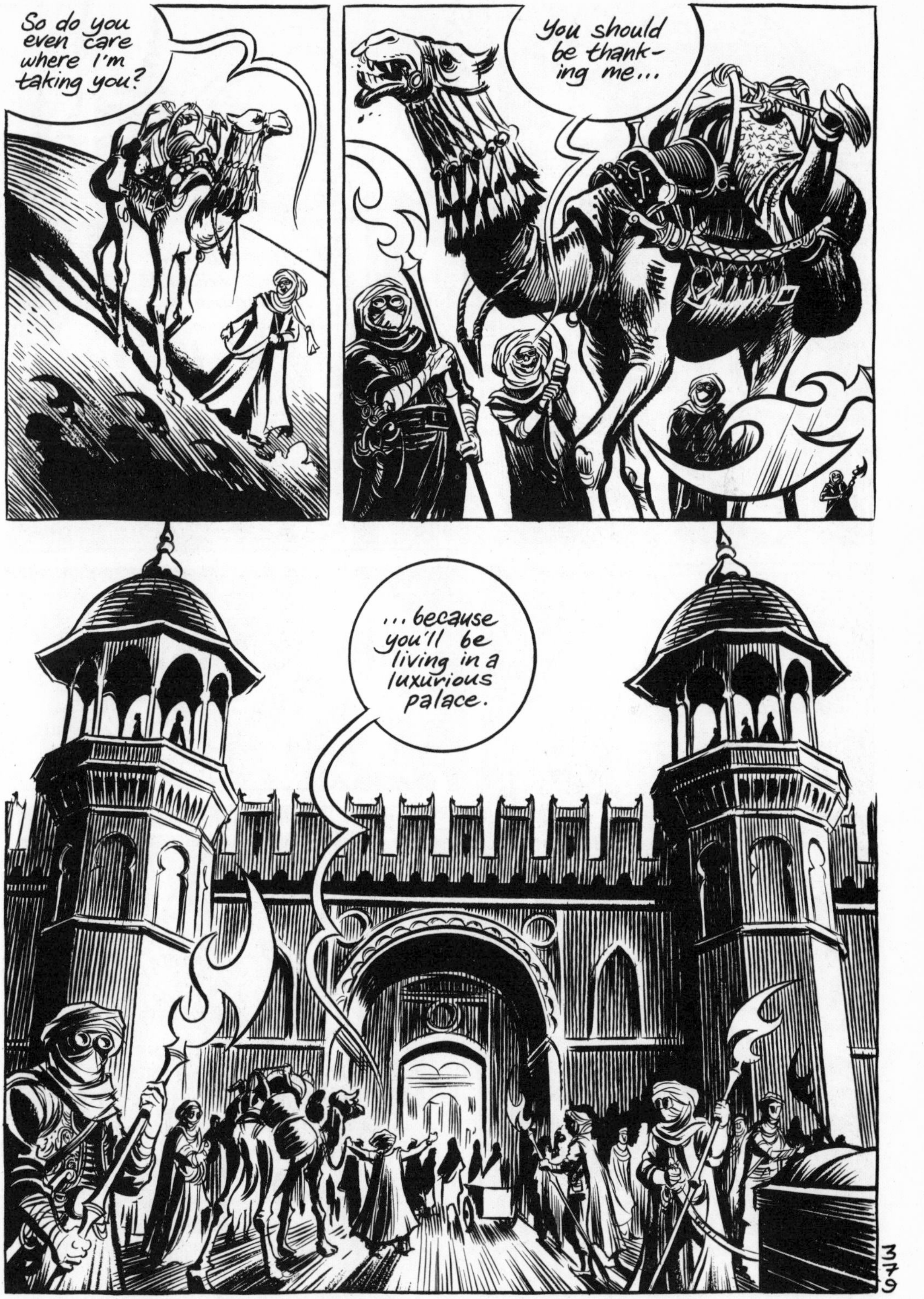
So do you even care where I'm taking you?
You should be thank-ing me...
...because you'll be living in a luxurious palace.

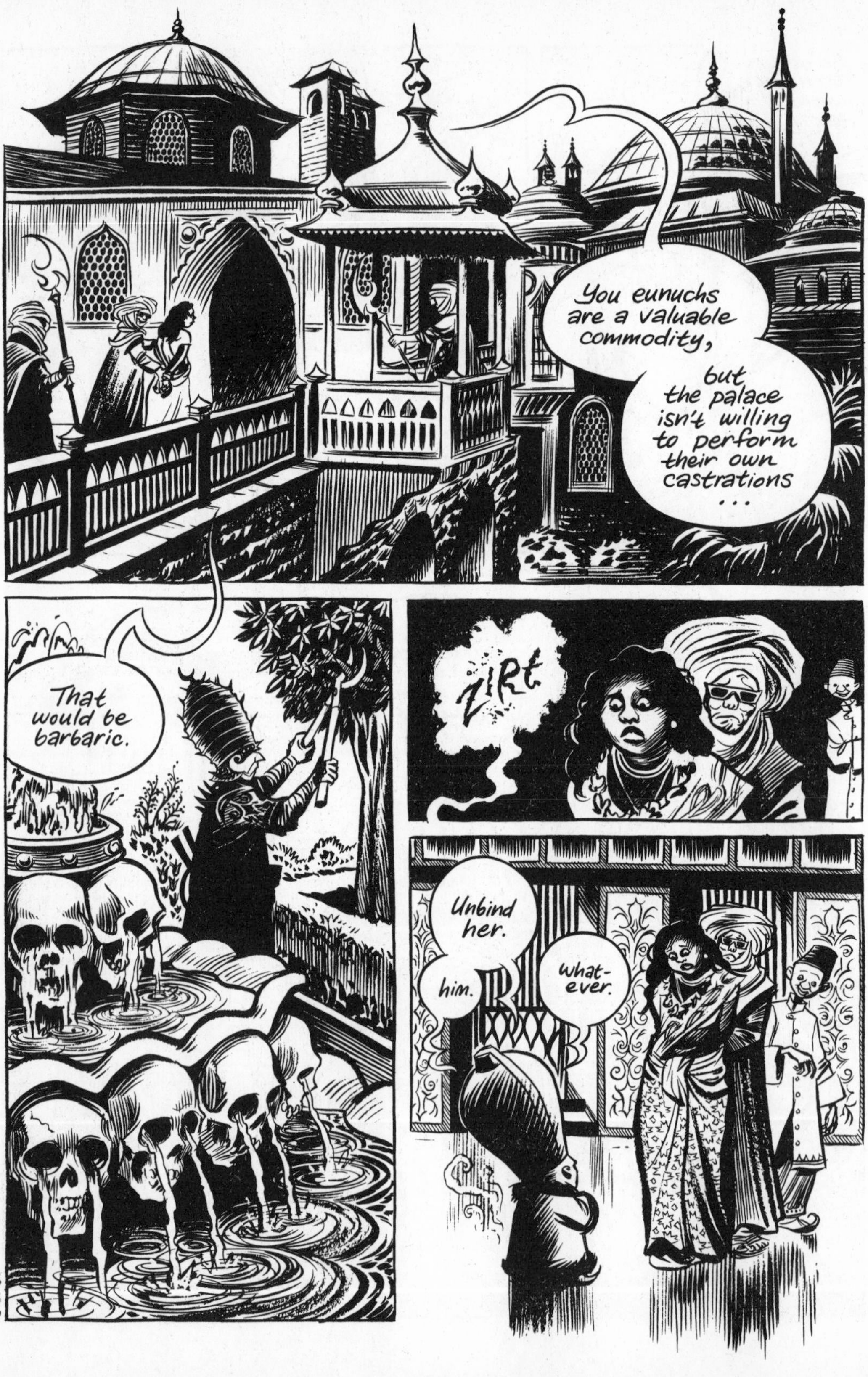
You eunuchs are a valuable commodity,
but the palace isn't willing to perform their own castrations . . .
That would be barbaric.
ZiRt
Unbind her.
him.
what-ever.

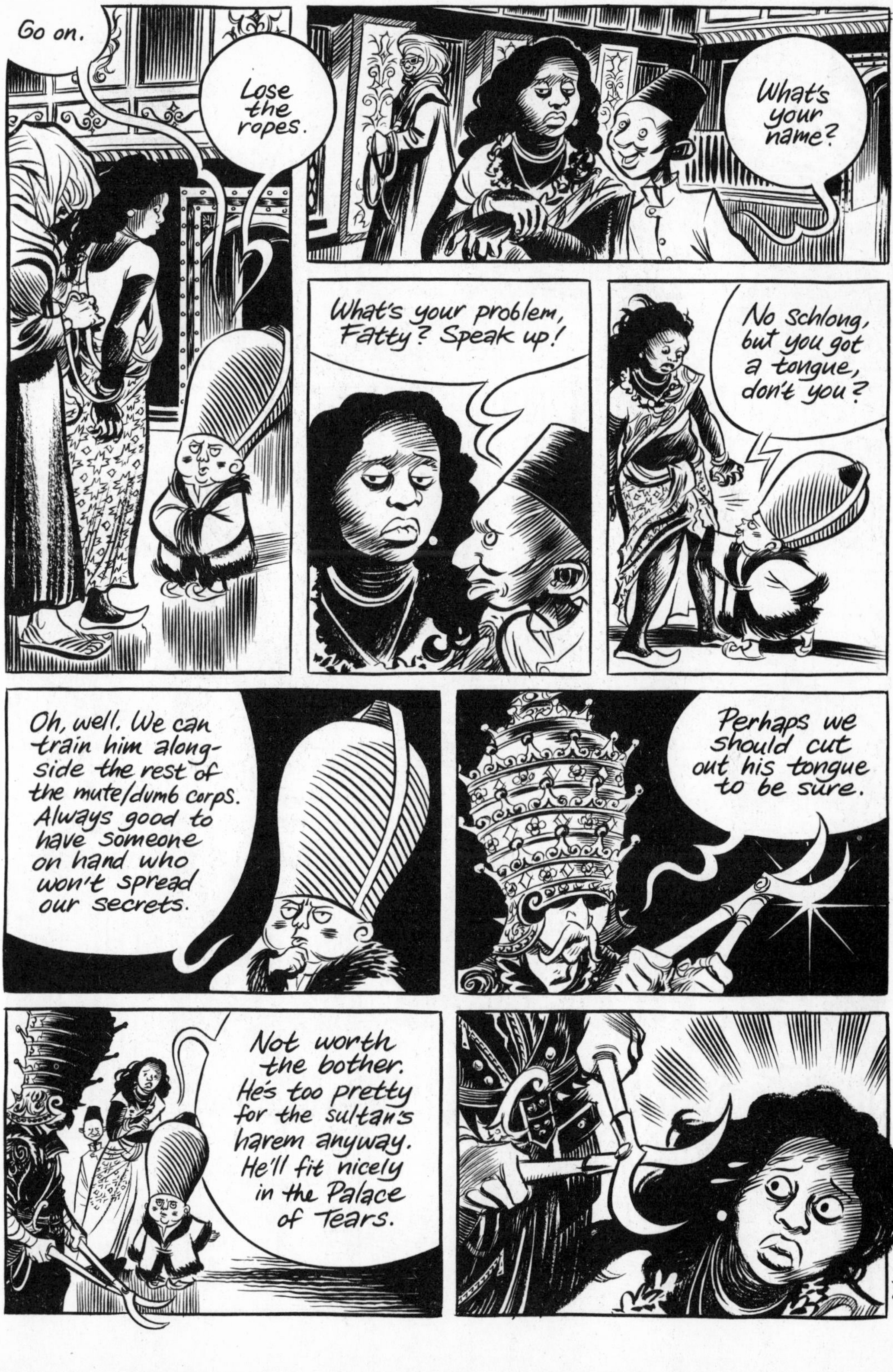

Go on.
Lose the ropes.
What's your name?
What's your problem, Fatty? Speak up!
No schlong, but you got a tongue, don't you?
Oh, well. We can train him alongside the rest of the mute/dumb corps. Always good to have someone on hand who won't spread our secrets.
Perhaps we should cut out his tongue to be sure.
Not worth the bother. He's too pretty for the sultan's harem anyway. He'll fit nicely in the Palace of Tears.

CLIP CLIP CLIP

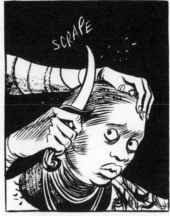

SCRAPE

CLANG

ooops

himmm... His ears still work.

Should we PERFORATE his eardrums?

No, It's easier if we don't need to train him in sign language.

And if he can hear, he can take orders.

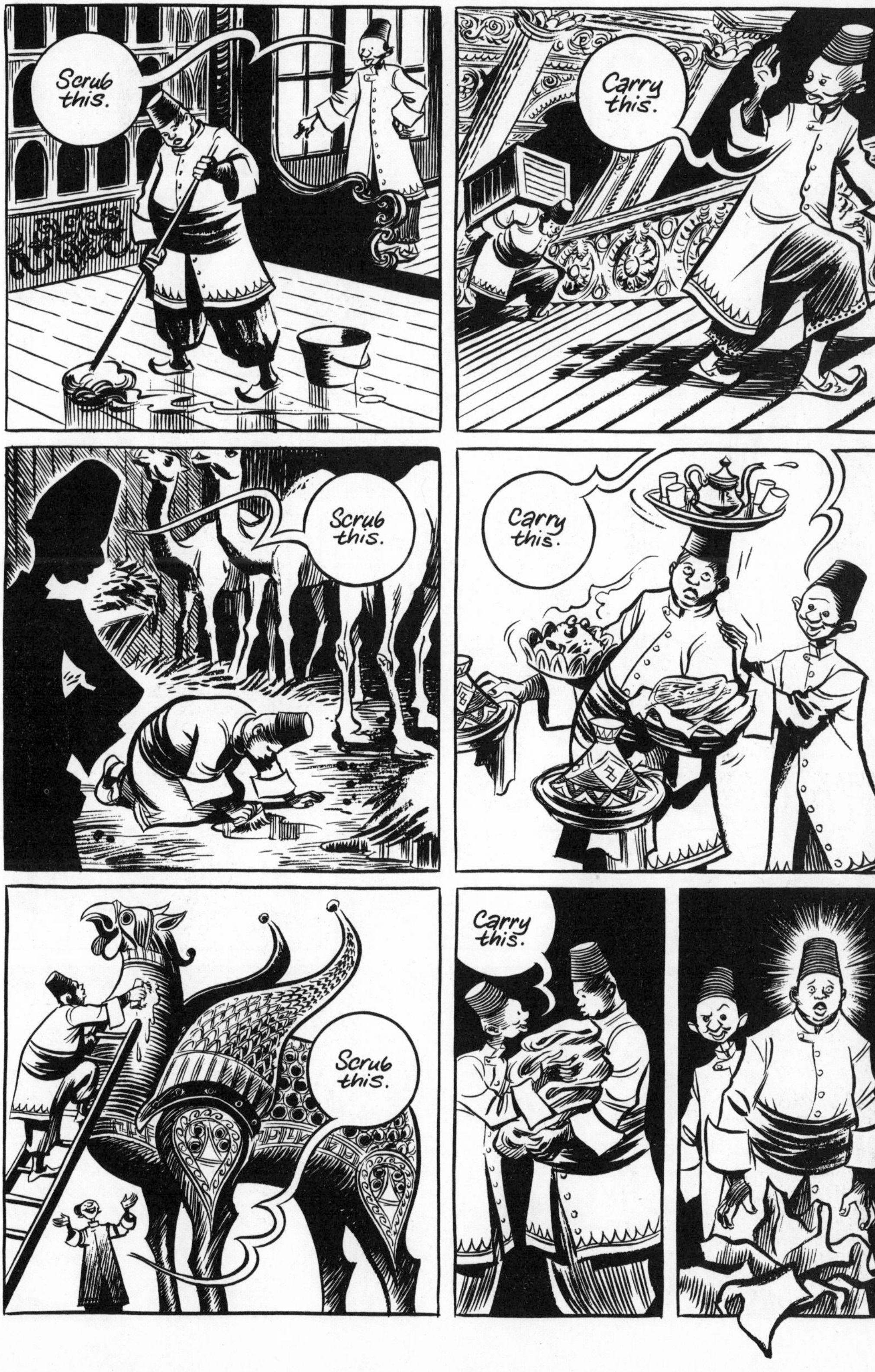

Scrub this.
Carry this.
Scrub this.
Carry this.
Scrub this.
Carry this.

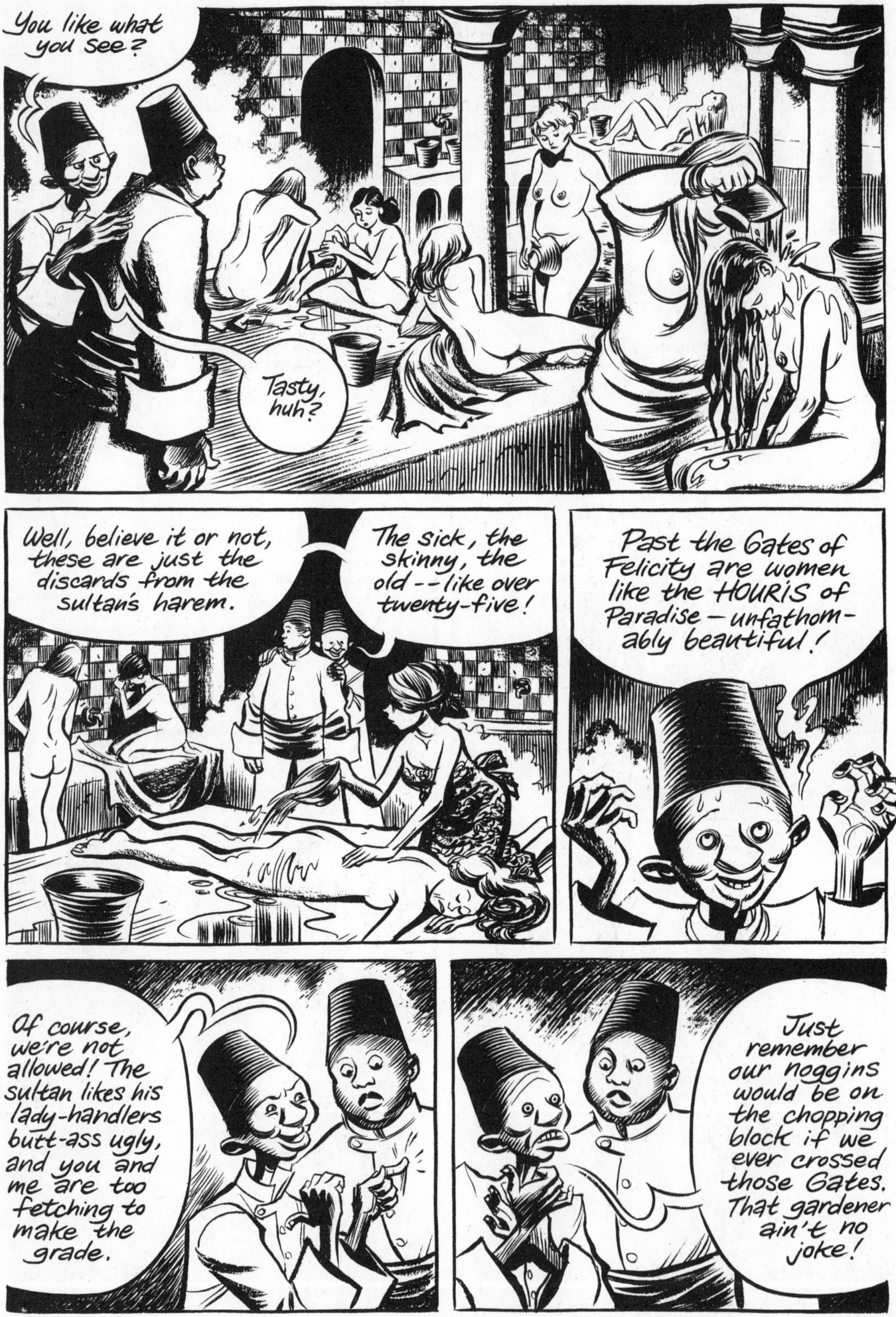
You like what you see?
Tasty, huh?
Well, believe it or not, these are just the discards from the sultan's harem.
The sick, the skinny, the old -- like over twenty-five!
Past the Gates of Felicity are women like the HOURIS of Paradise — unfathom-ably beautiful!
Of course, we're not allowed! The sultan likes his lady-handlers butt-ass ugly, and you and me are too fetching to make the grade.
Just remember our noggins would be on the chopping block if we ever crossed those Gates. That gardener ain't no joke!

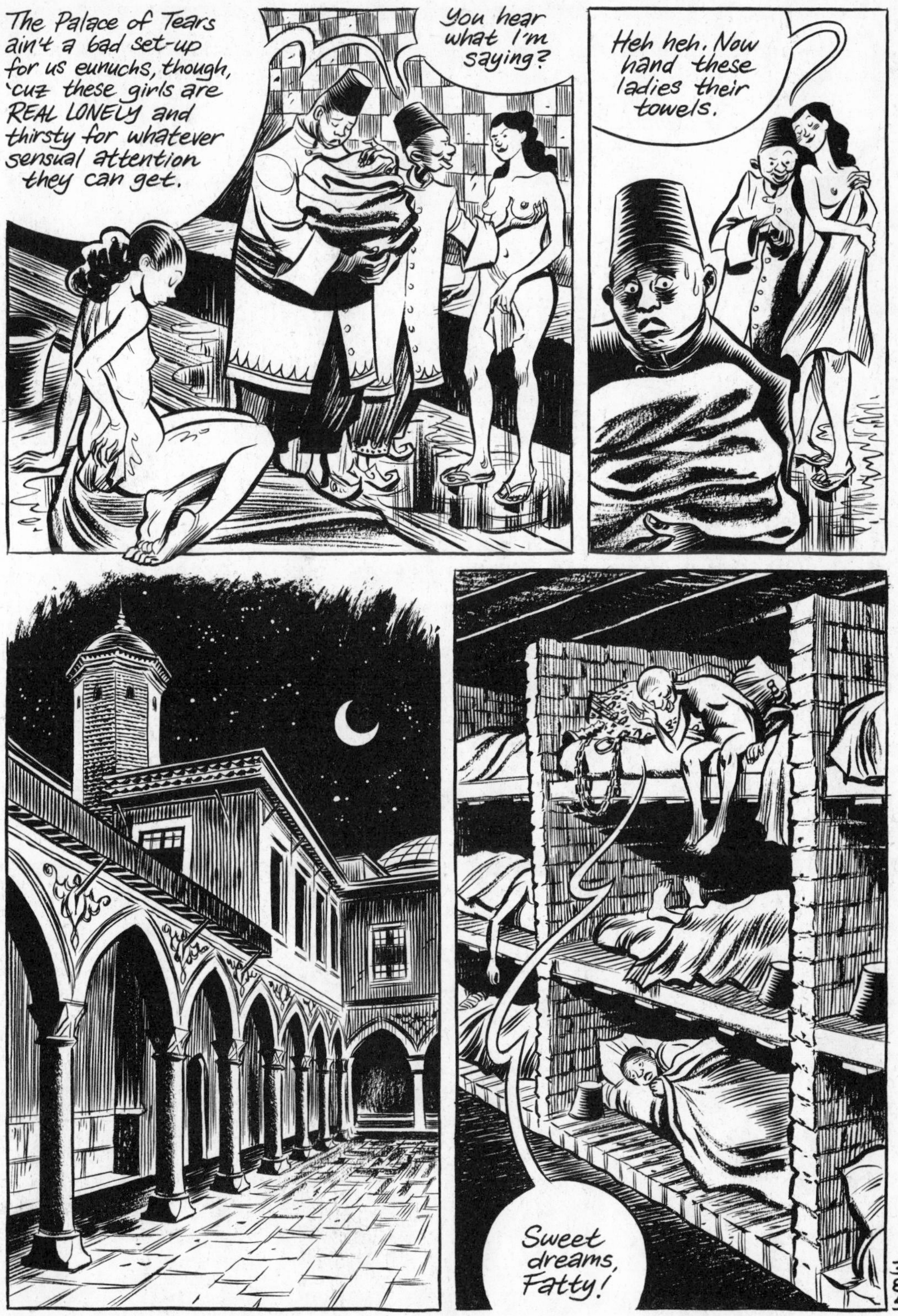
The Palace of Tears ain't a bad set-up for us eunuchs, though, 'cuz these girls are REAL LONELY and thirsty for whatever sensual attention they can get.
You hear what I'm saying?
Heh heh. Now hand these ladies their towels.
Sweet dreams, Fatty!

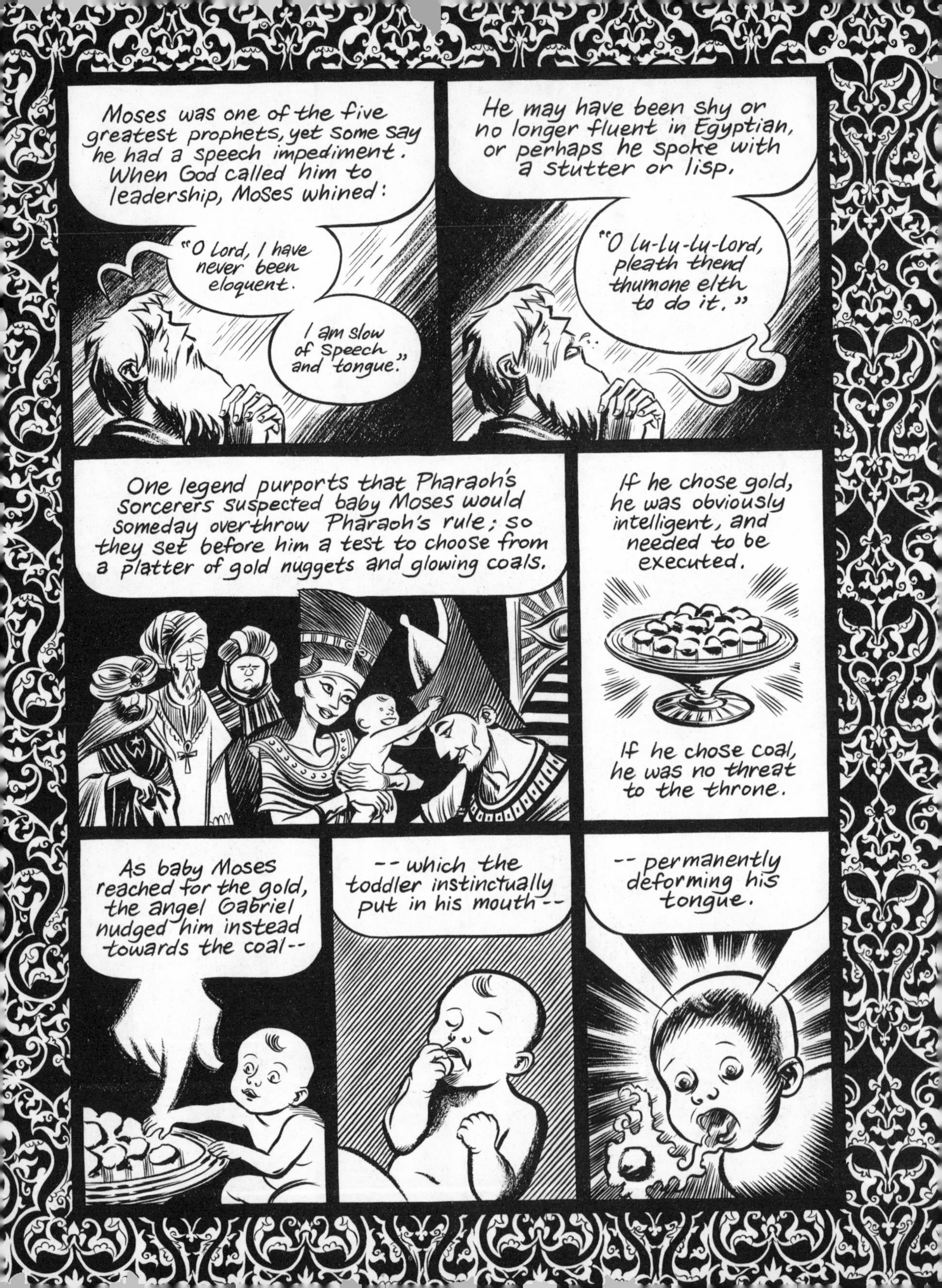
Moses was one of the five greatest prophets, yet some say he had a speech impediment. When God called him to leadership, Moses whined:
"O Lord, I have never been eloquent.
I am slow of speech and tongue."
He may have been shy or no longer fluent in Egyptian, or perhaps he spoke with a stutter or lisp.
"O lu-lu-lu-lord, pleath thend thumone elth to do it."
One legend purports that Pharaoh's sorcerers suspected baby Moses would someday overthrow Pharaoh's rule; so they set before him a test to choose from a platter of gold nuggets and glowing coals.
If he chose gold, he was obviously intelligent, and needed to be executed.
If he chose coal, he was no threat to the throne.
As baby Moses reached for the gold, the angel Gabriel nudged him instead towards the coal--
--which the toddler instinctually put in his mouth--
--permanently deforming his tongue.

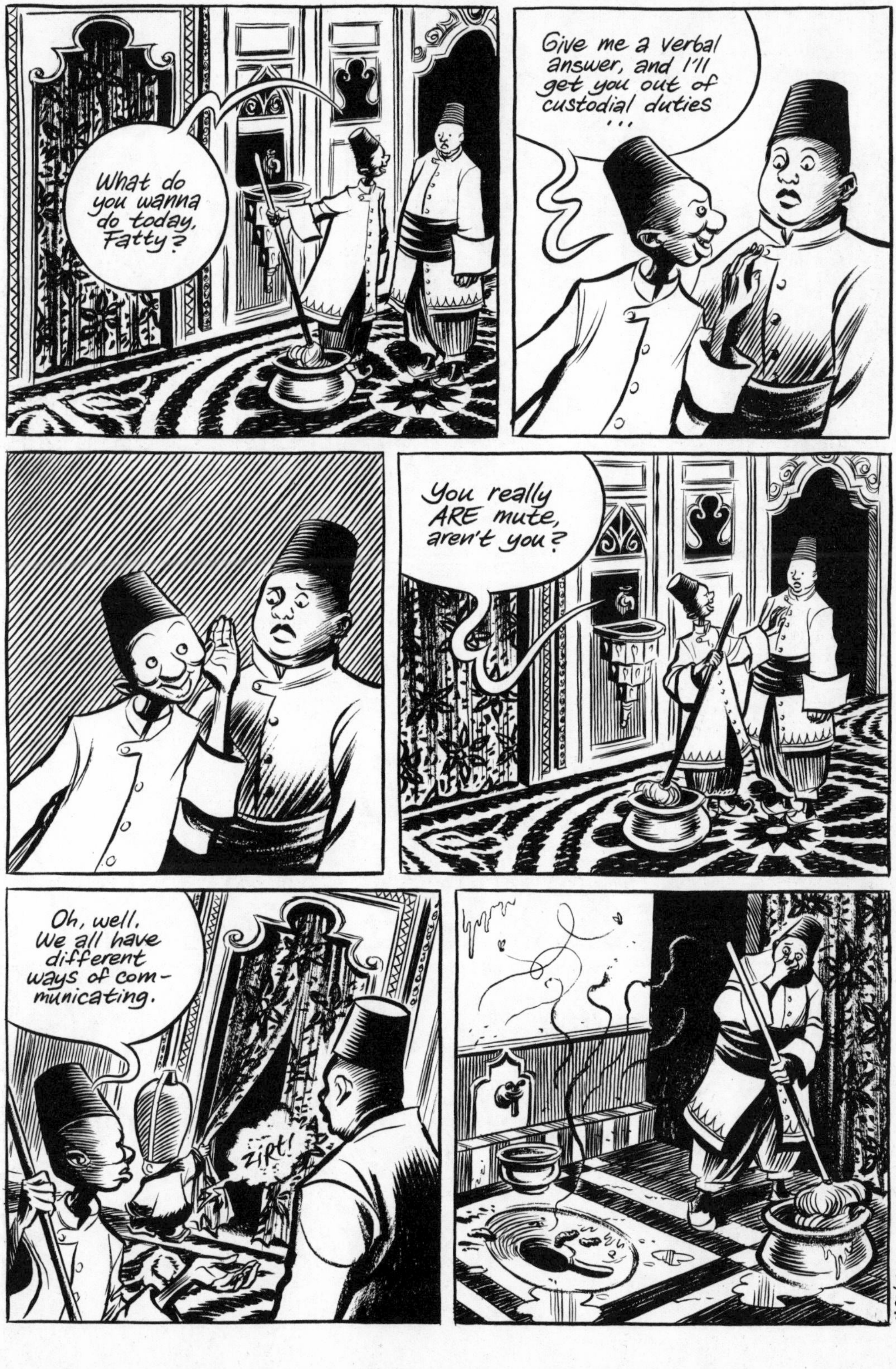
What do you wanna do today, Fatty?
Give me a verbal answer, and I'll get you out of custodial duties . . .
You really ARE mute, aren't you?
Oh, well. We all have different ways of com-municating.
ZIRT!

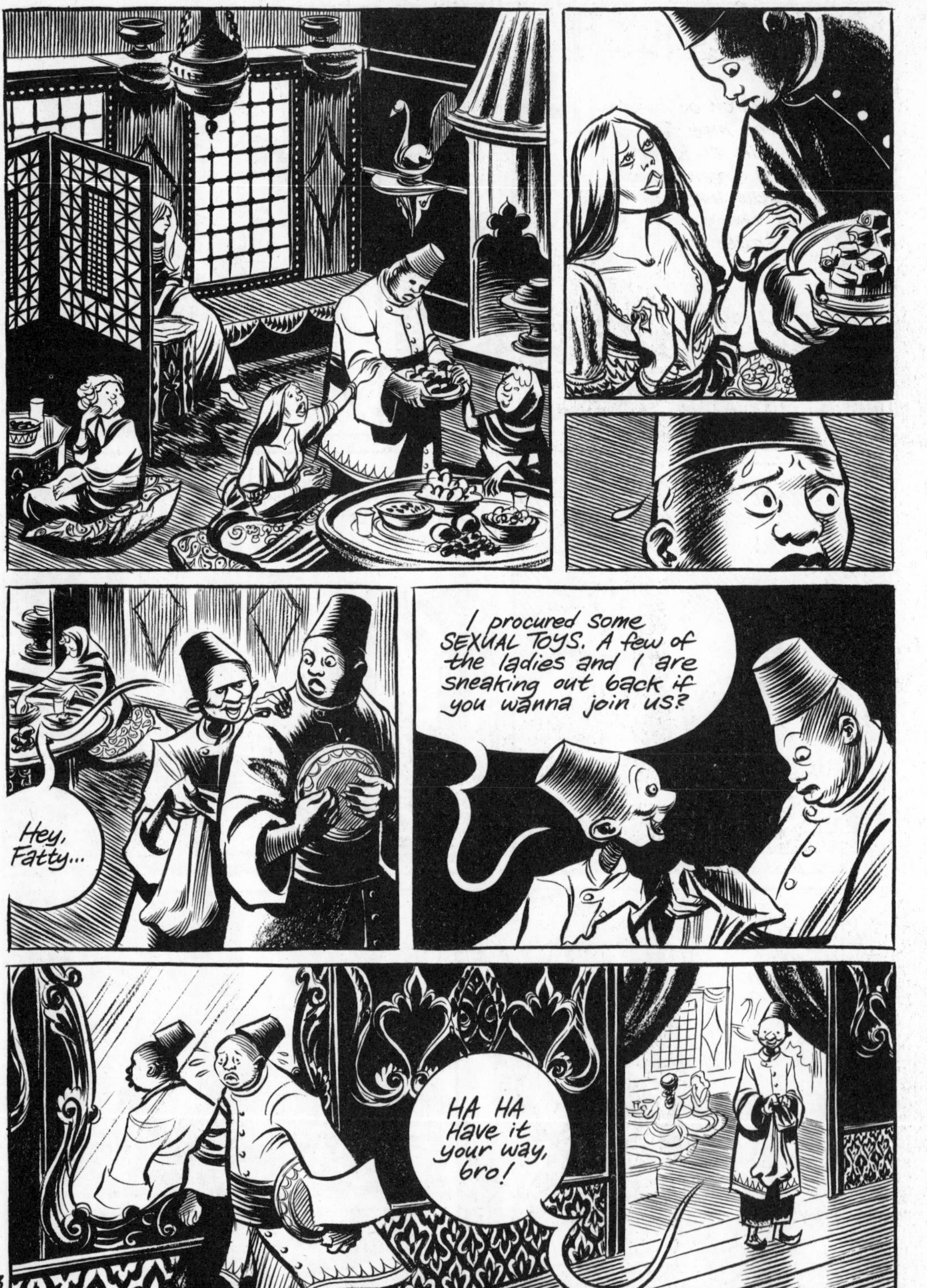
Hey, Fatty...
I procured some SEXUAL TOYS. A few of the ladies and I are sneaking out back if you wanna join us?
HA HA Have it your way, bro!
WOOD

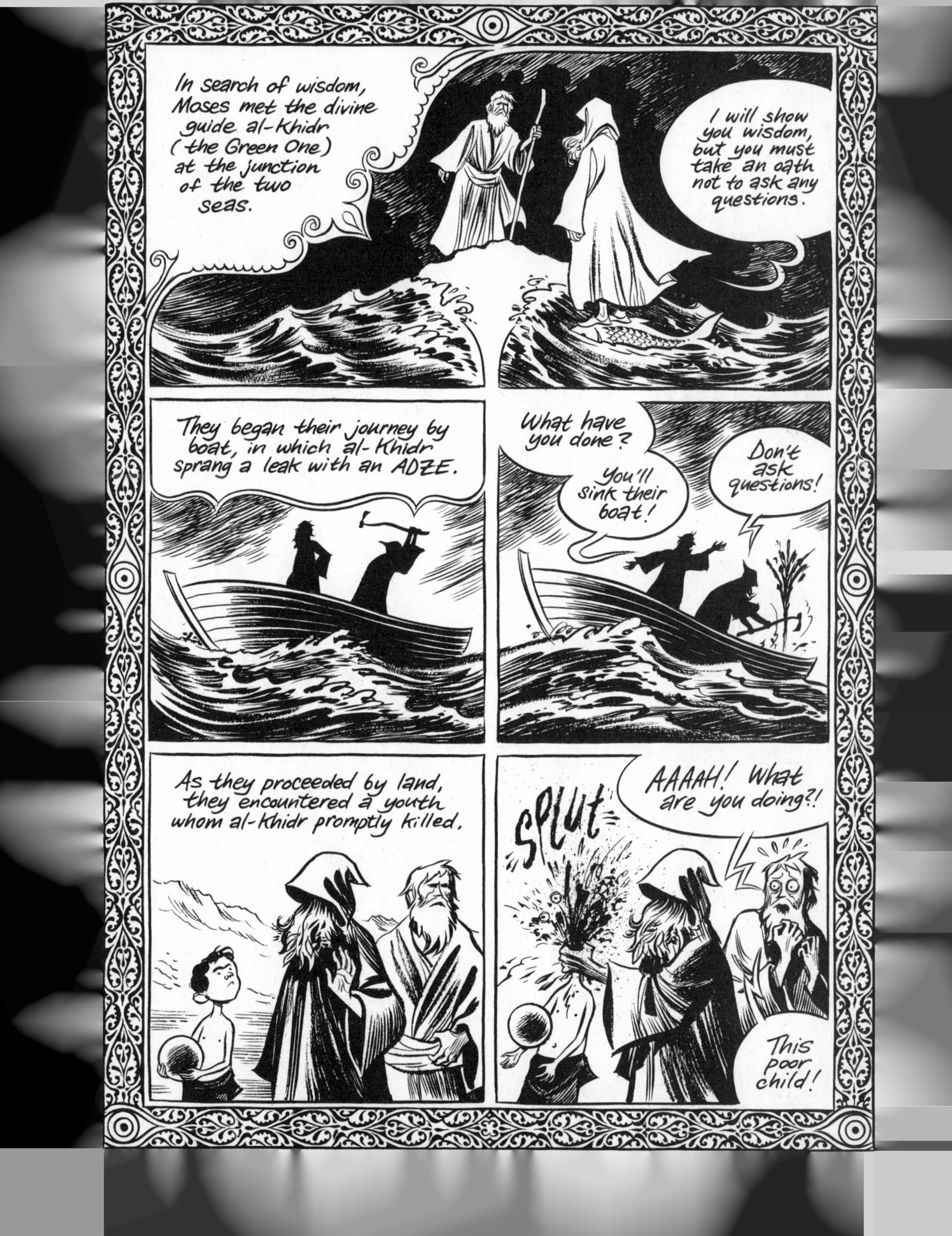
In search of wisdom, Moses met the divine guide al-Khidr (the Green One) at the junction of the two seas.
I will show you wisdom, but you must take an oath not to ask any questions.
They began their journey by boat, in which al-Khidr sprang a leak with an ADZE.
What have you done?
You'll sink their boat!
Don't ask questions!
As they proceeded by land, they encountered a youth whom al-Khidr promptly killed.
SPLUT
AAAAH! What are you doing?!
This poor child!

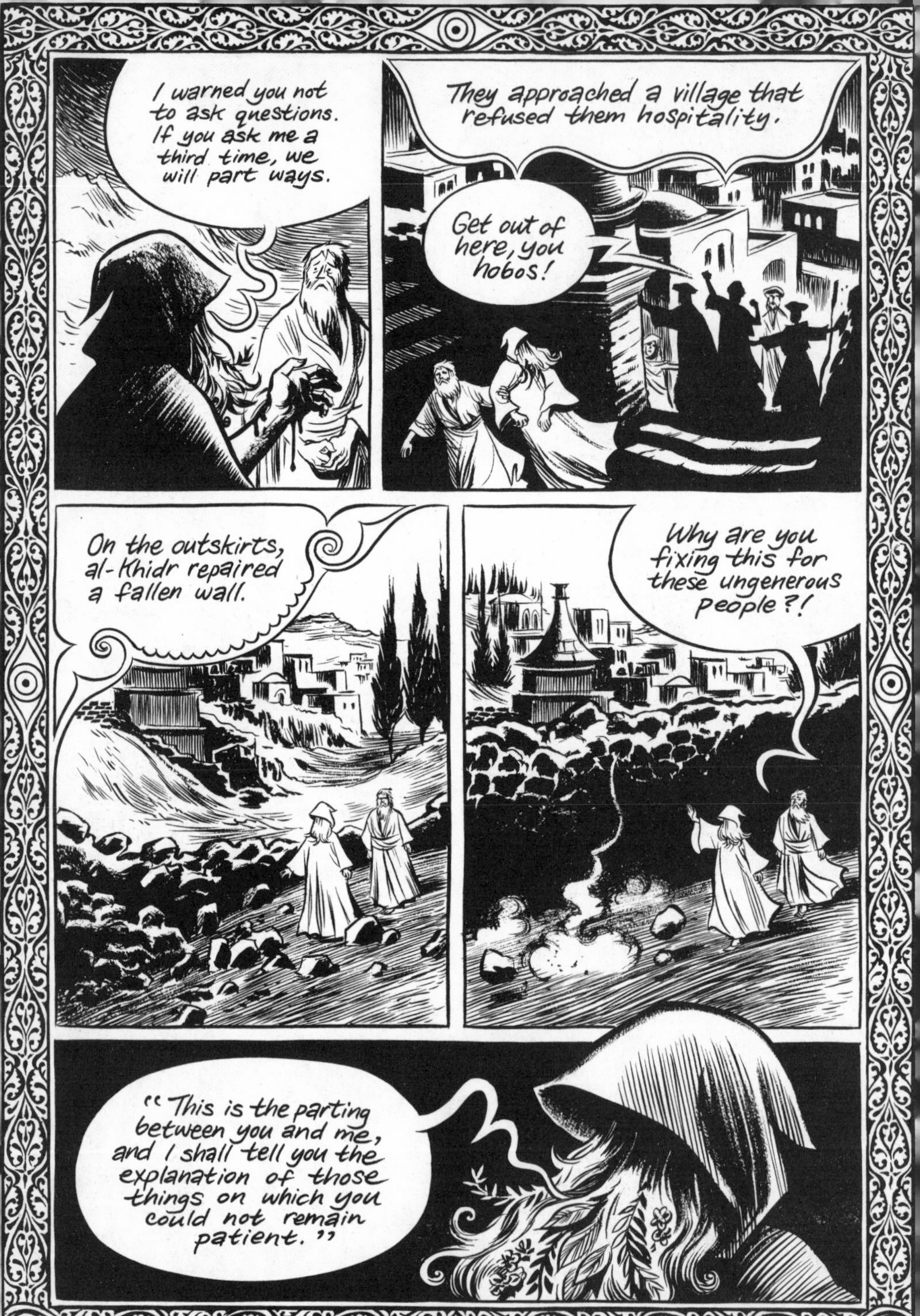
I warned you not to ask questions. If you ask me a third time, we will part ways.
They approached a village that refused them hospitality.
Get out of here, you hobos!
On the outskirts, al-Khidr repaired a fallen wall.
Why are you fixing this for these ungenerous people?!
"This is the parting between you and me, and I shall tell you the explanation of those things on which you could not remain patient."

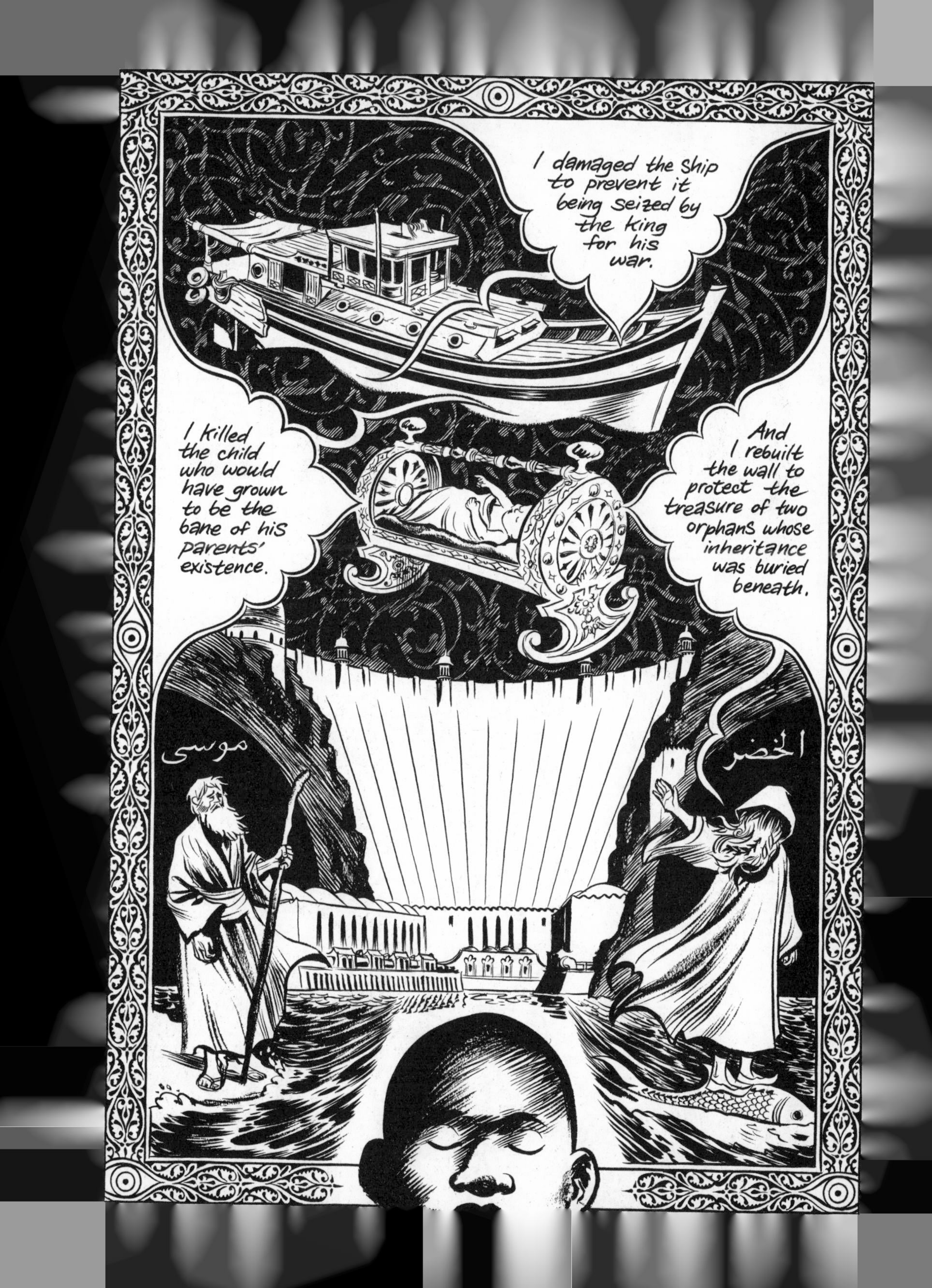
I damaged the ship to prevent it being seized by the king for his war.
I killed the child who would have grown to be the bane of his parents' existence.
And I rebuilt the wall to protect the treasure of two orphans whose inheritance was buried beneath.
موسى
الخضر

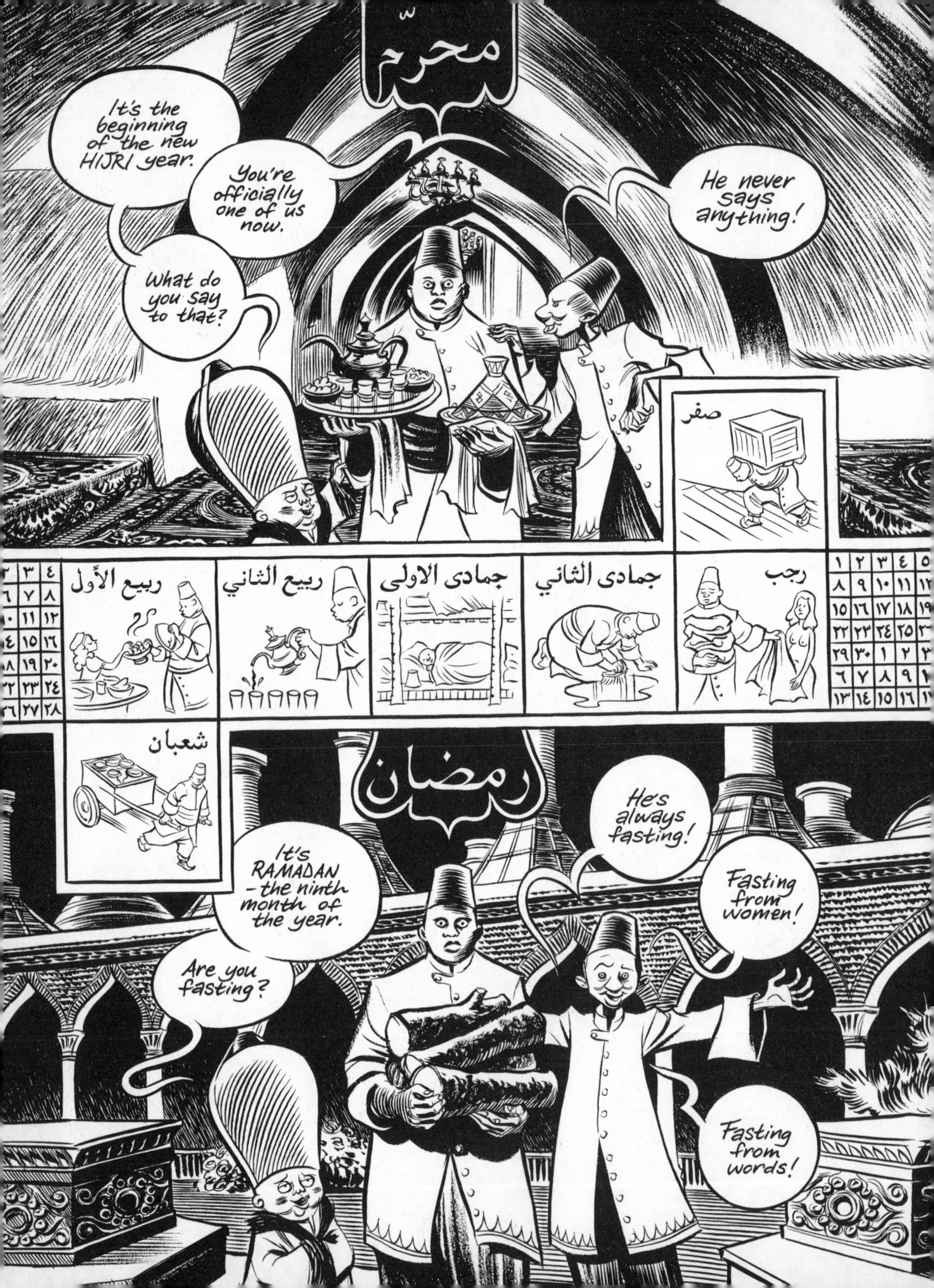

محرّم
It's the beginning of the new HIJRI year.
You're officially one of us now.
What do you say to that?
He never says anything!
صفر
ربيع الأول
ربيع الثاني
جمادى الاولى
جمادى الثاني
رجب
شعبان
رمضان
It's RAMADAN – the ninth month of the year.
Are you fasting?
He's always fasting!
Fasting from women!
Fasting from words!

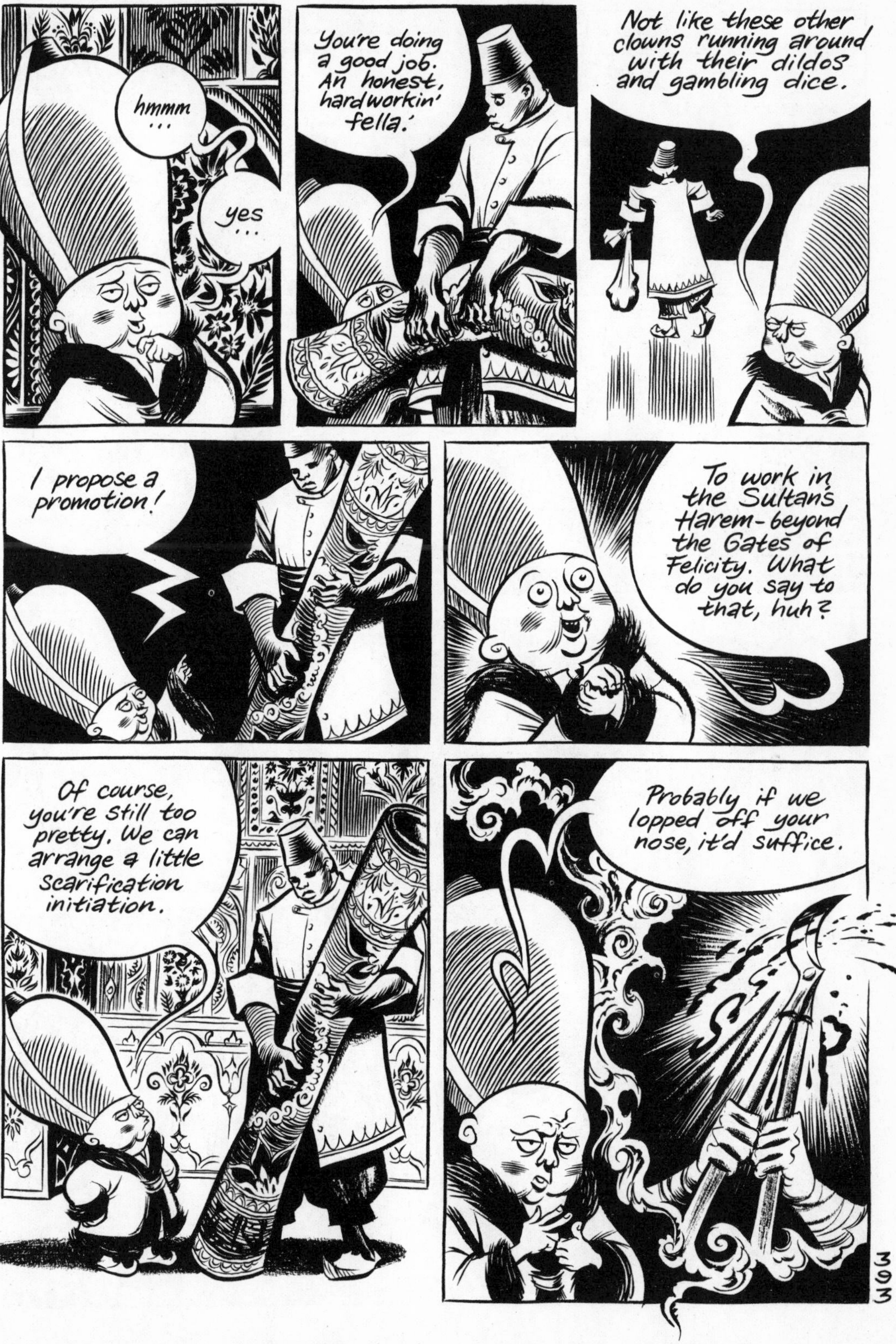
hmmm ...
yes ...
You're doing a good job. An honest, hardworkin' fella.
Not like these other clowns running around with their dildos and gambling dice.
I propose a promotion!
To work in the Sultan's Harem-beyond the Gates of Felicity. What do you say to that, huh?
Of course, you're still too pretty. We can arrange a little scarification initiation.
Probably if we lopped off your nose, it'd suffice.

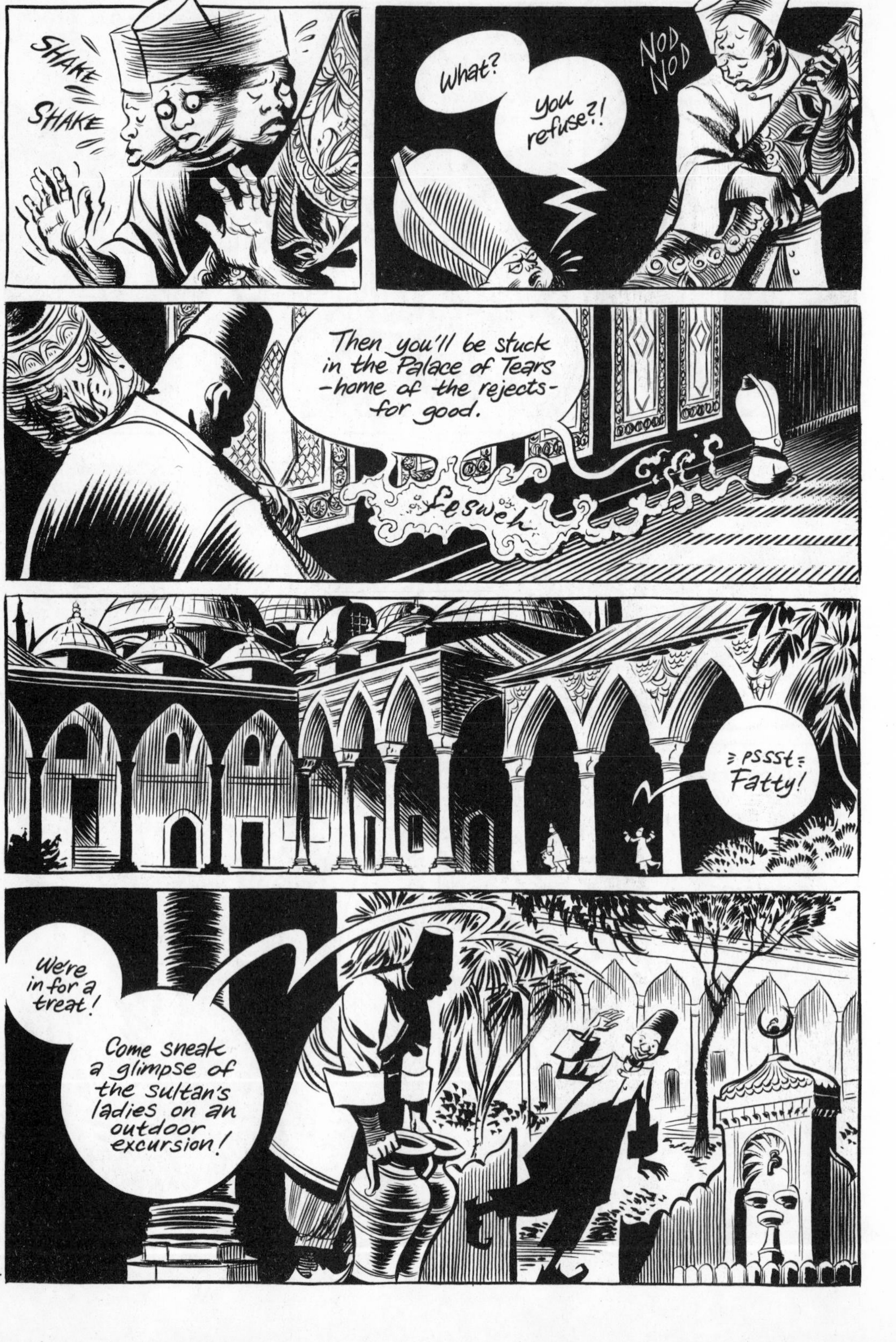
SHAKE
SHAKE
What?
You refuse?!
NOD NOD
Then you'll be stuck in the Palace of Tears -home of the rejects- for good.
fesweh
psssst Fatty!
We're in for a treat!
Come sneak a glimpse of the sultan's ladies on an outdoor excursion!

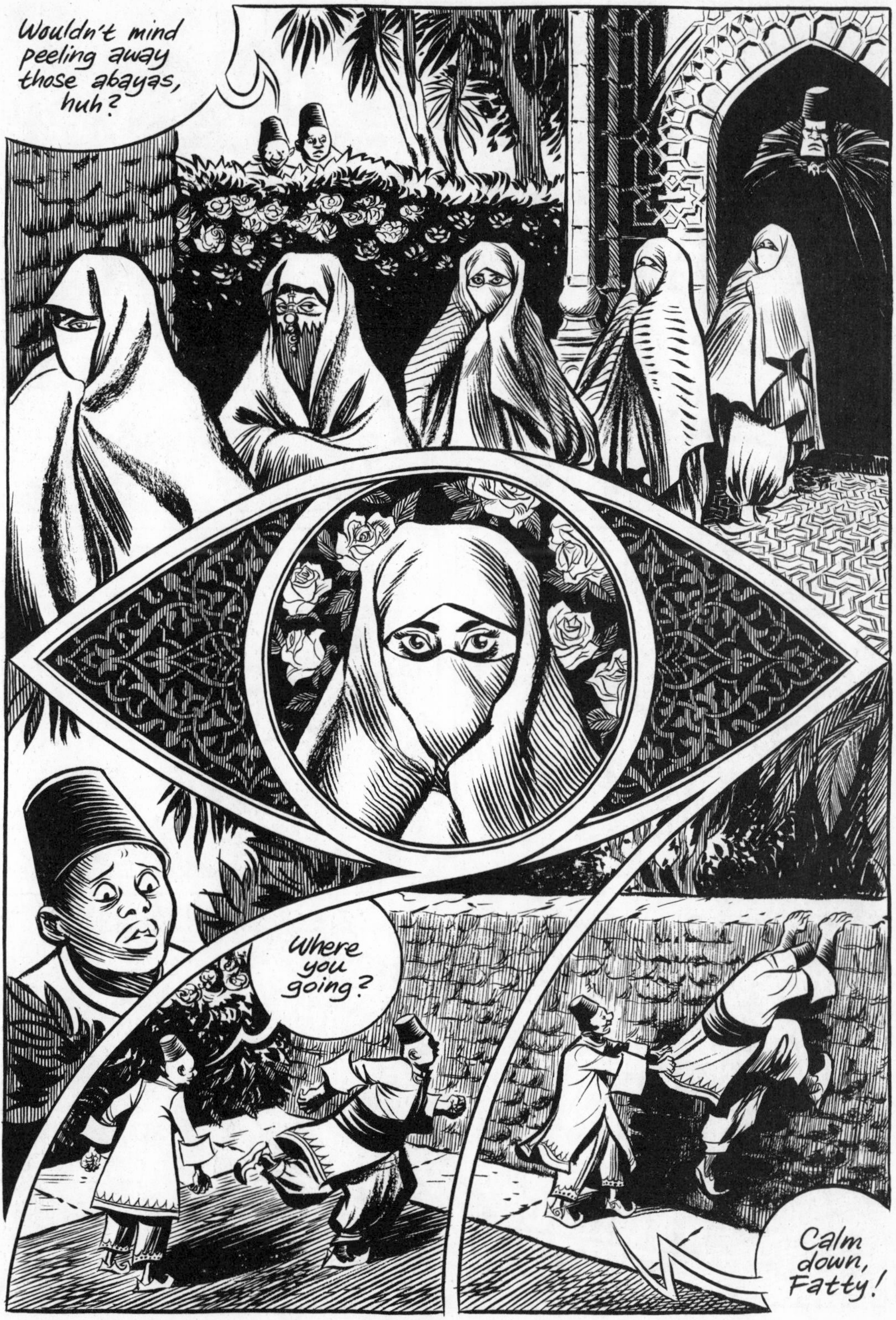
Wouldn't mind peeling away those abayas, huh?
Where you going?
Calm down, Fatty!

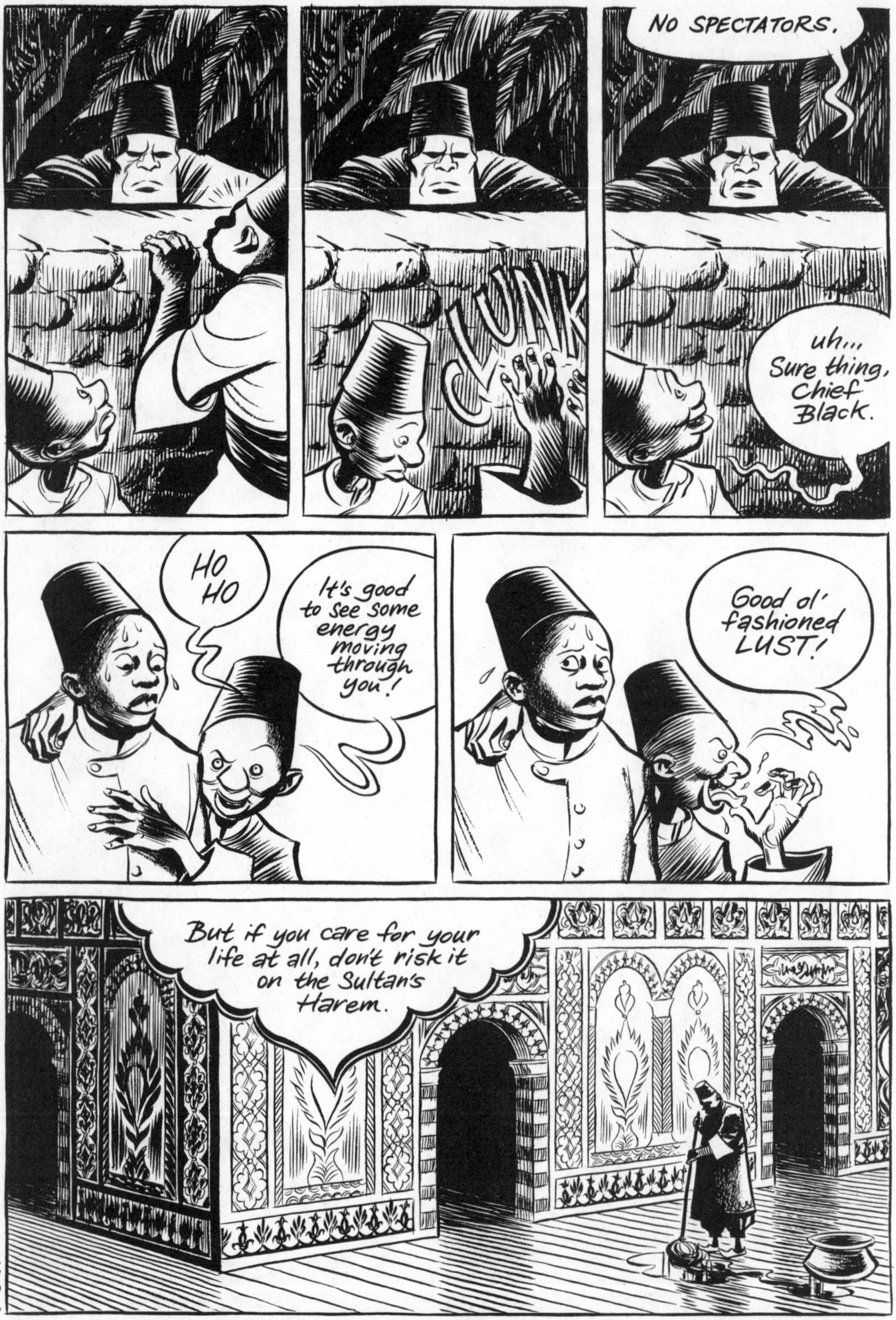
NO SPECTATORS.
CLUNK
uh... Sure thing, Chief Black.
HO HO
It's good to see some energy moving through you!
Good ol' fashioned LUST!
But if you care for your life at all, don't risk it on the Sultan's Harem.

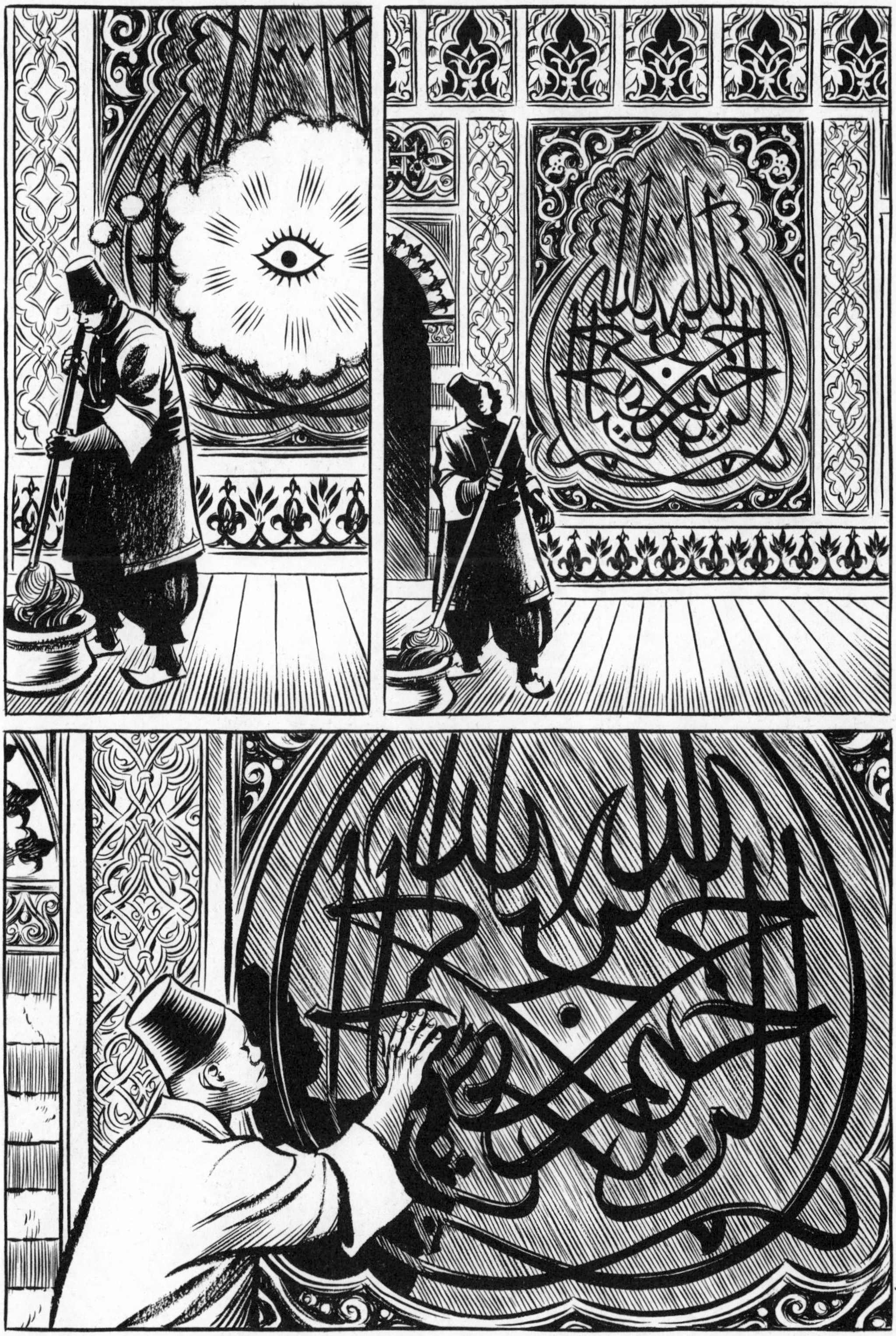

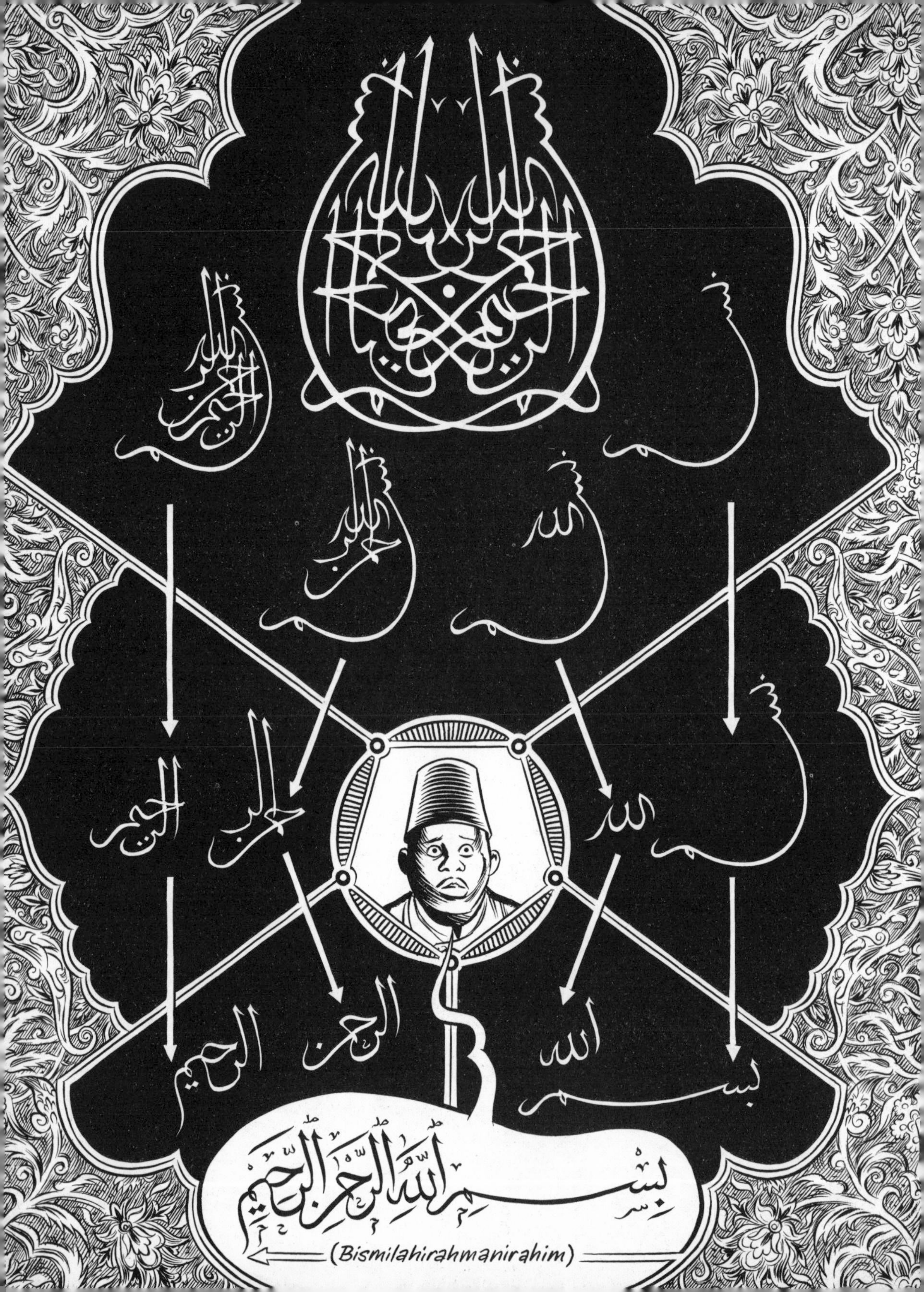

الرحيم
الرحمن
الله
بسم
بسم الله الرحمن الرحيم
(Bismilahirahmanirahim)

Remember those words...

Remember these letters...

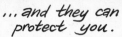

...and they can protect you.

tap tap tap tap tap

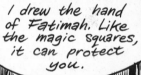

I drew the hand of Fatimah. Like the magic squares, it can protect you.

It's named for Fatimah-the fifth child of the Prophet.

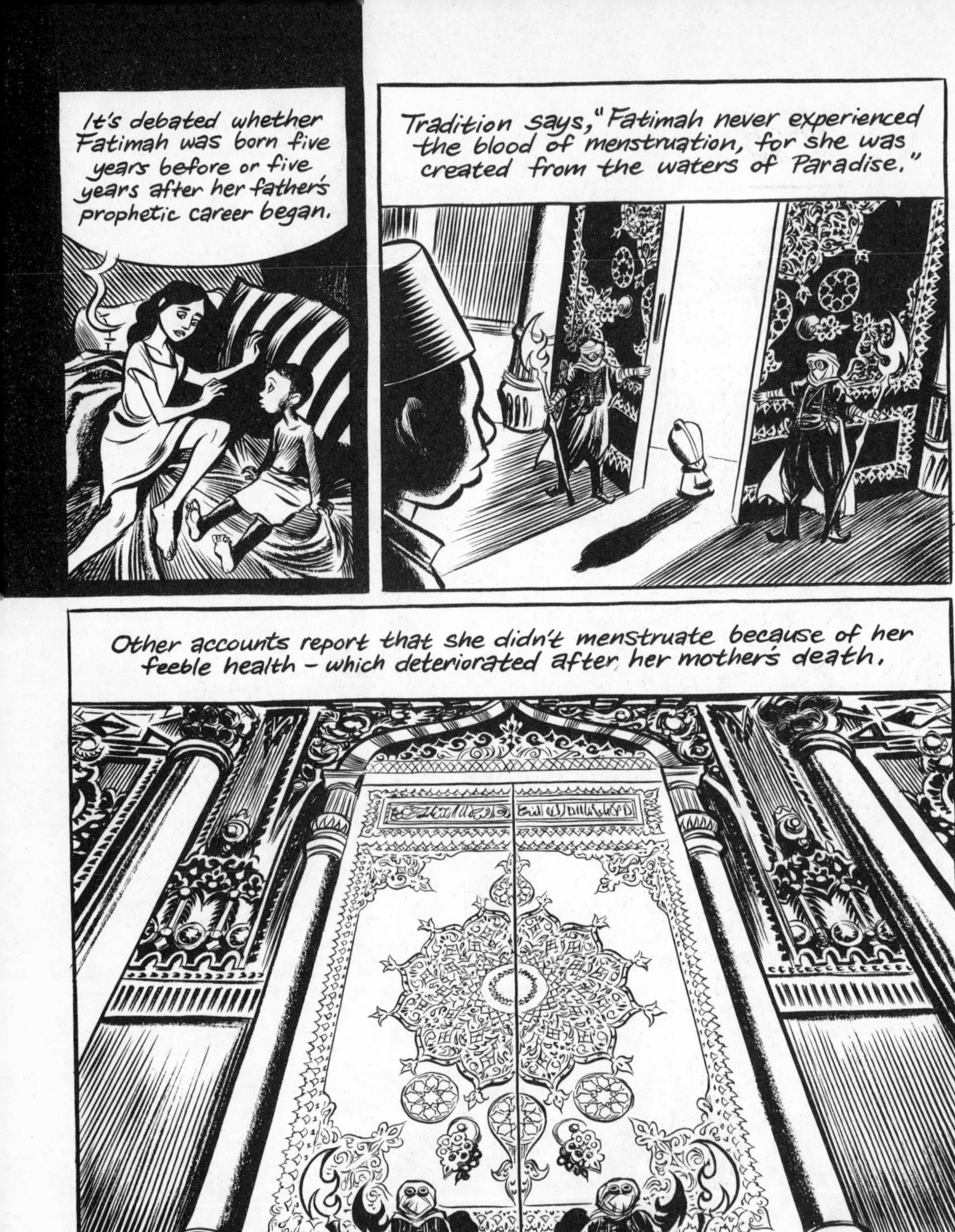
It's debated whether Fatimah was born five years before or five years after her father's prophetic career began.
Tradition says, "Fatimah never experienced the blood of menstruation, for she was created from the waters of Paradise."
Other accounts report that she didn't menstruate because of her feeble health - which deteriorated after her mother's death.

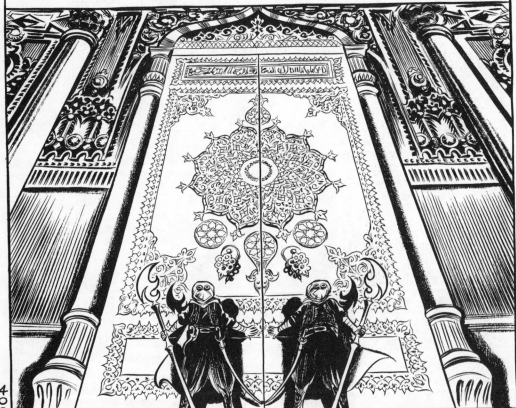

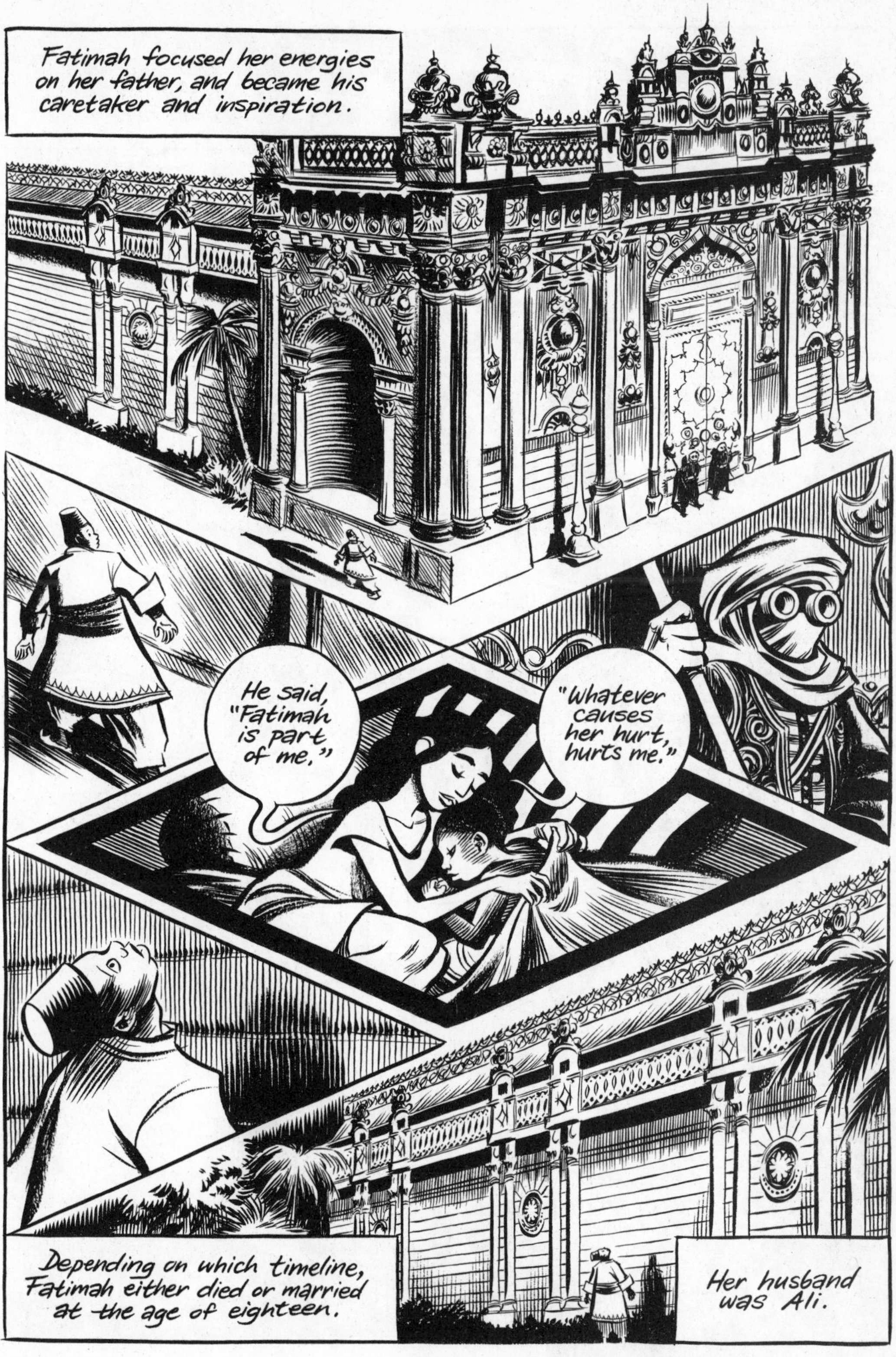
Fatimah focused her energies on her father, and became his caretaker and inspiration.
He said, "Fatimah is part of me."
"Whatever causes her hurt, hurts me."
Depending on which timeline, Fatimah either died or married at the age of eighteen.
Her husband was Ali.

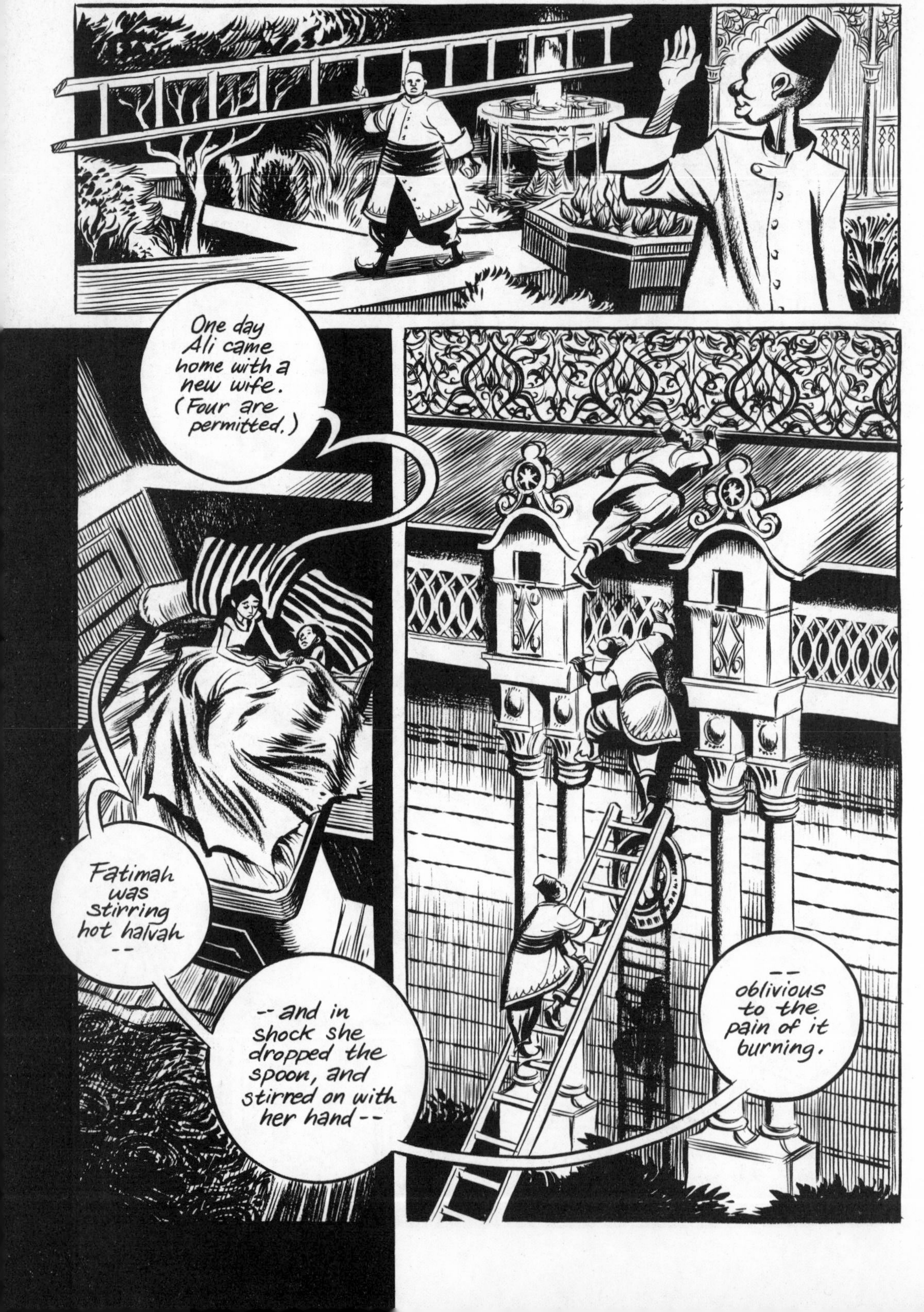

One day Ali came home with a new wife. (Four are permitted.)
Fatimah was stirring hot halvah --
-- and in shock she dropped the spoon, and stirred on with her hand --
-- oblivious to the pain of it burning.

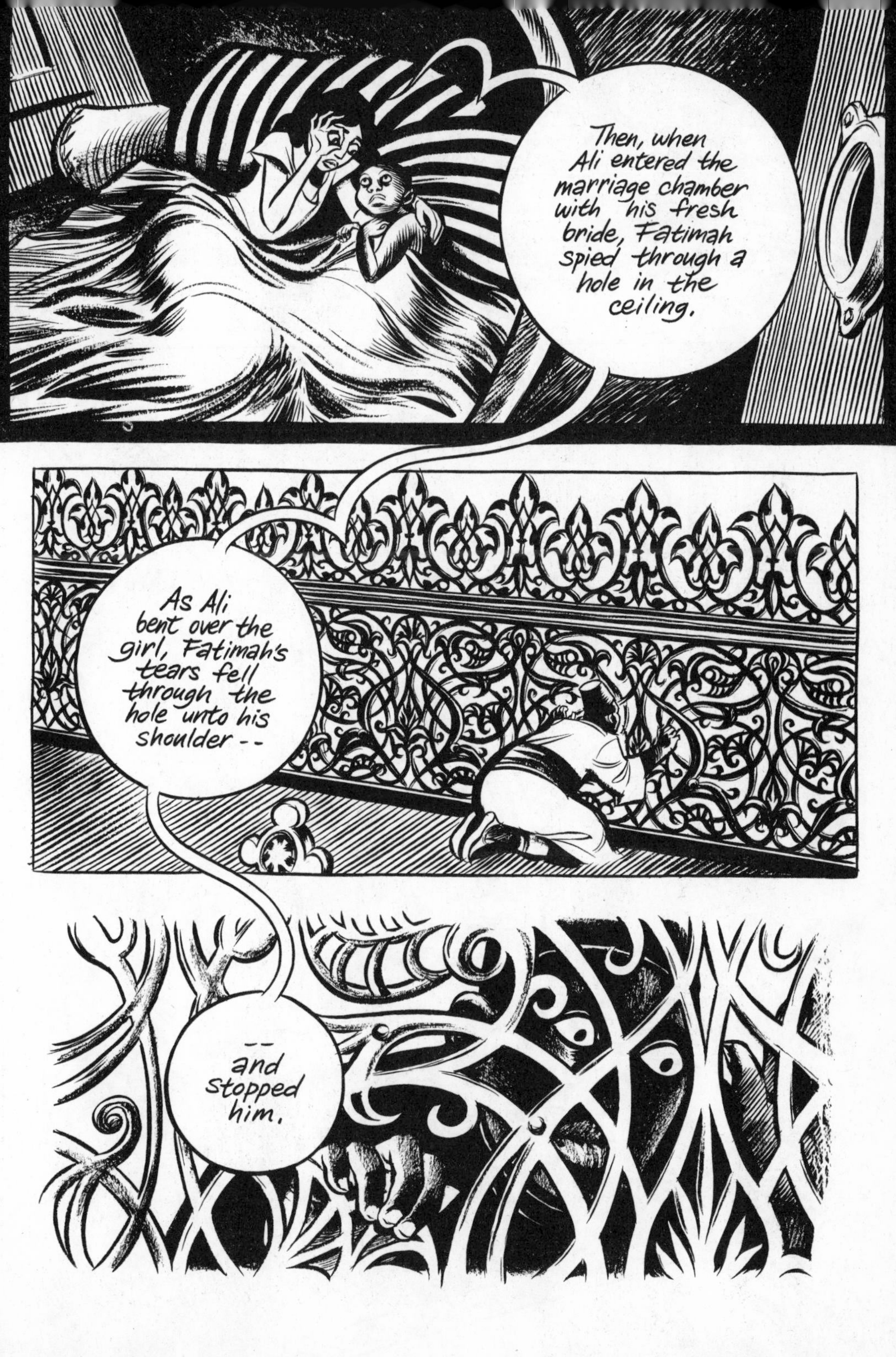
Then, when Ali entered the marriage chamber with his fresh bride, Fatimah spied through a hole in the ceiling.
As Ali bent over the girl, Fatimah's tears fell through the hole unto his shoulder --
-- and stopped him.

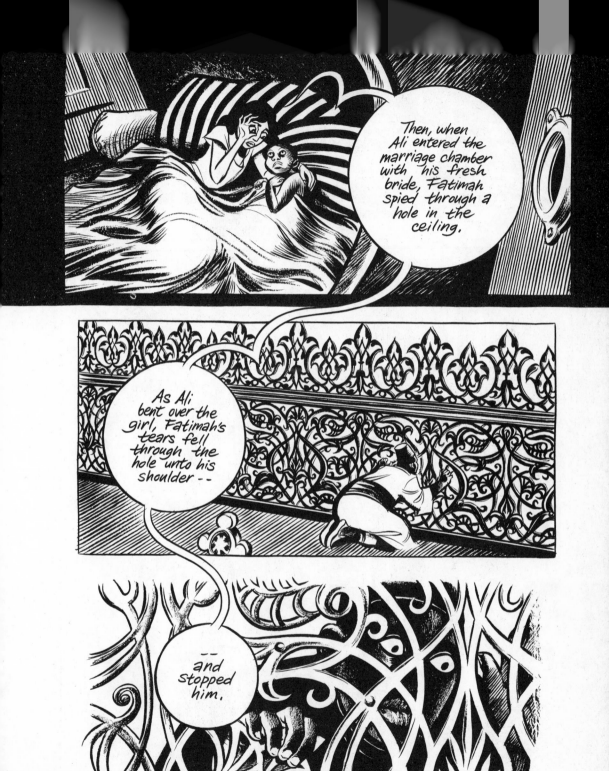

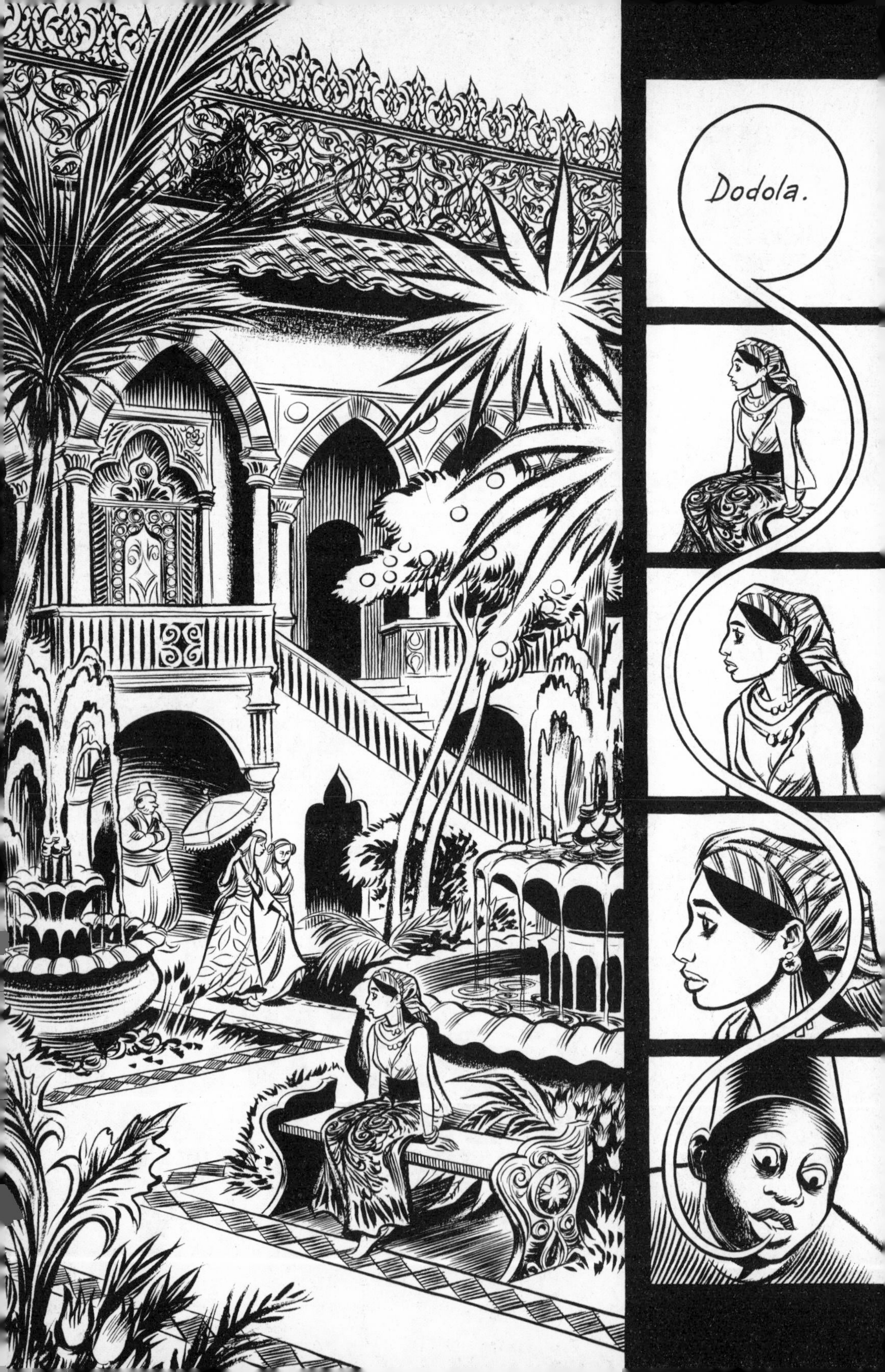
Dodola.

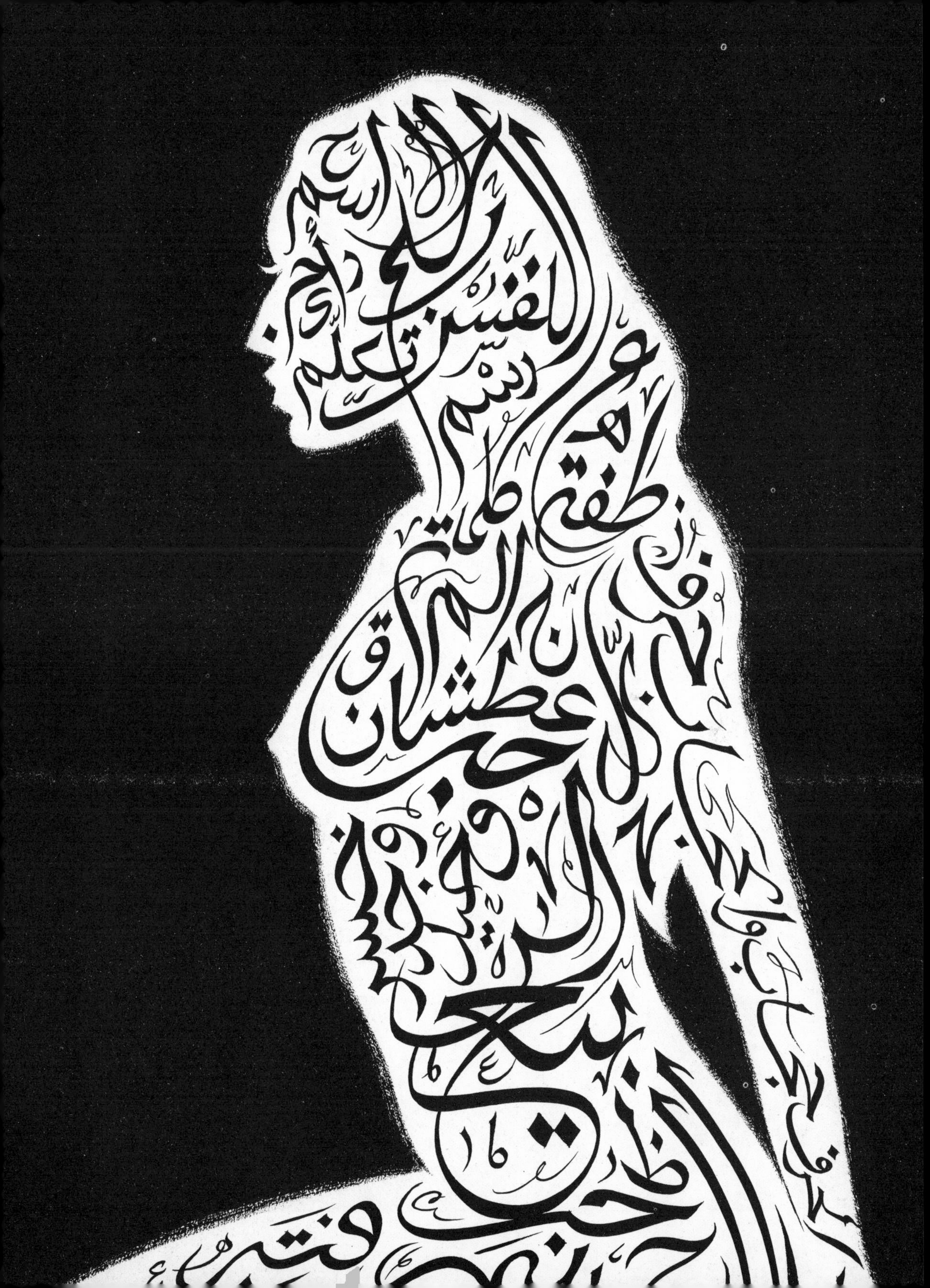

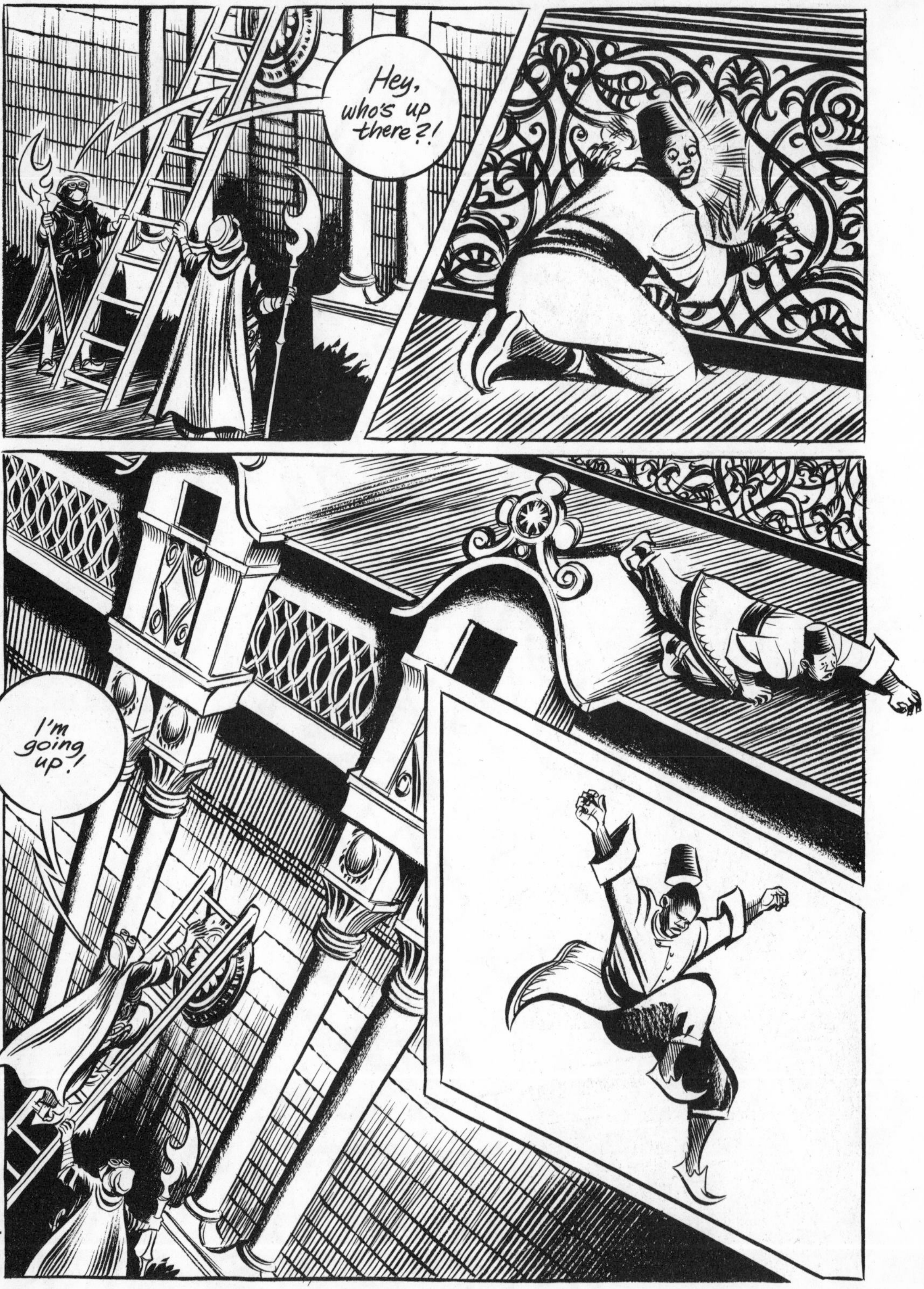
Hey, who's up there?!
I'm going up!

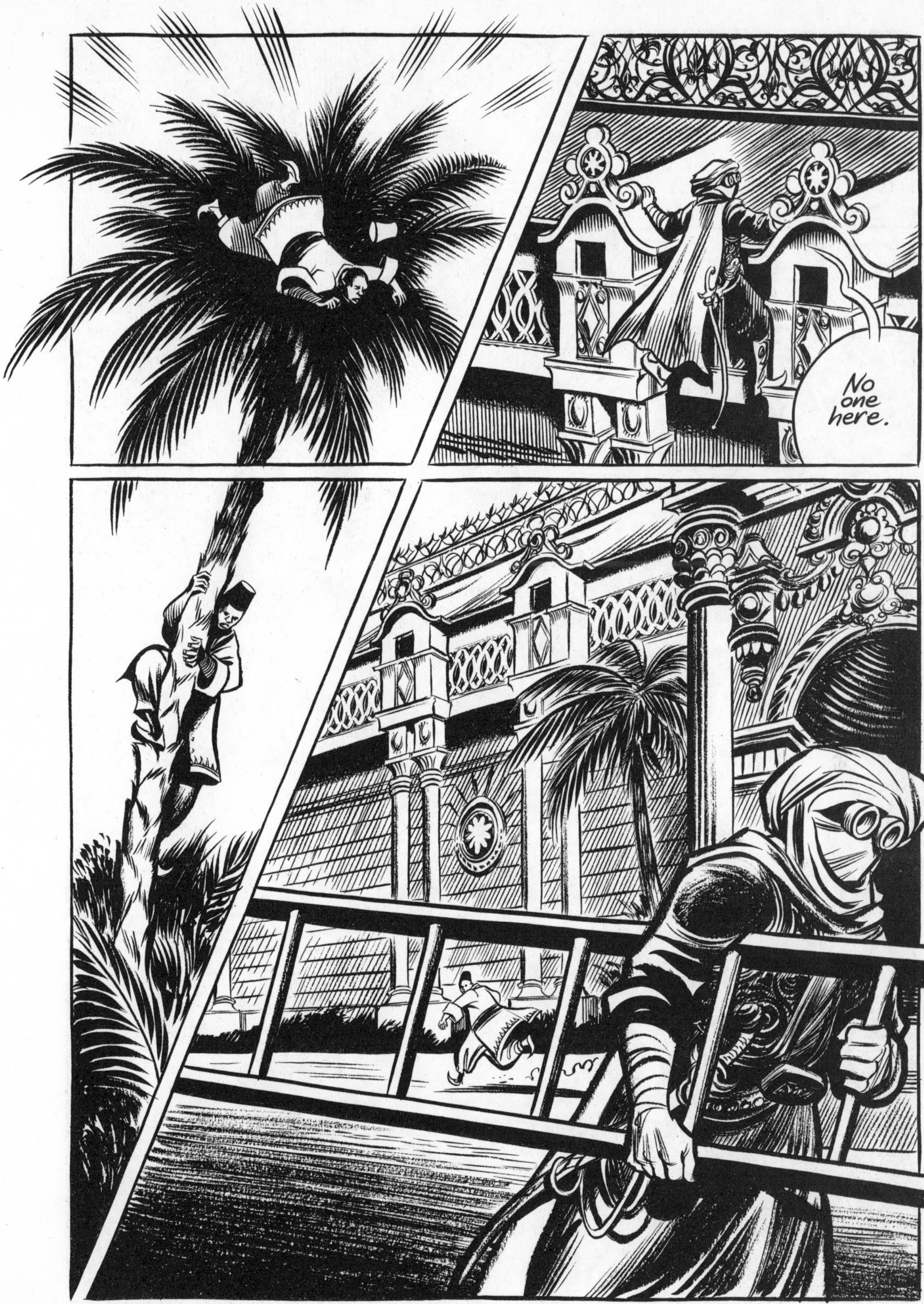
No one here.

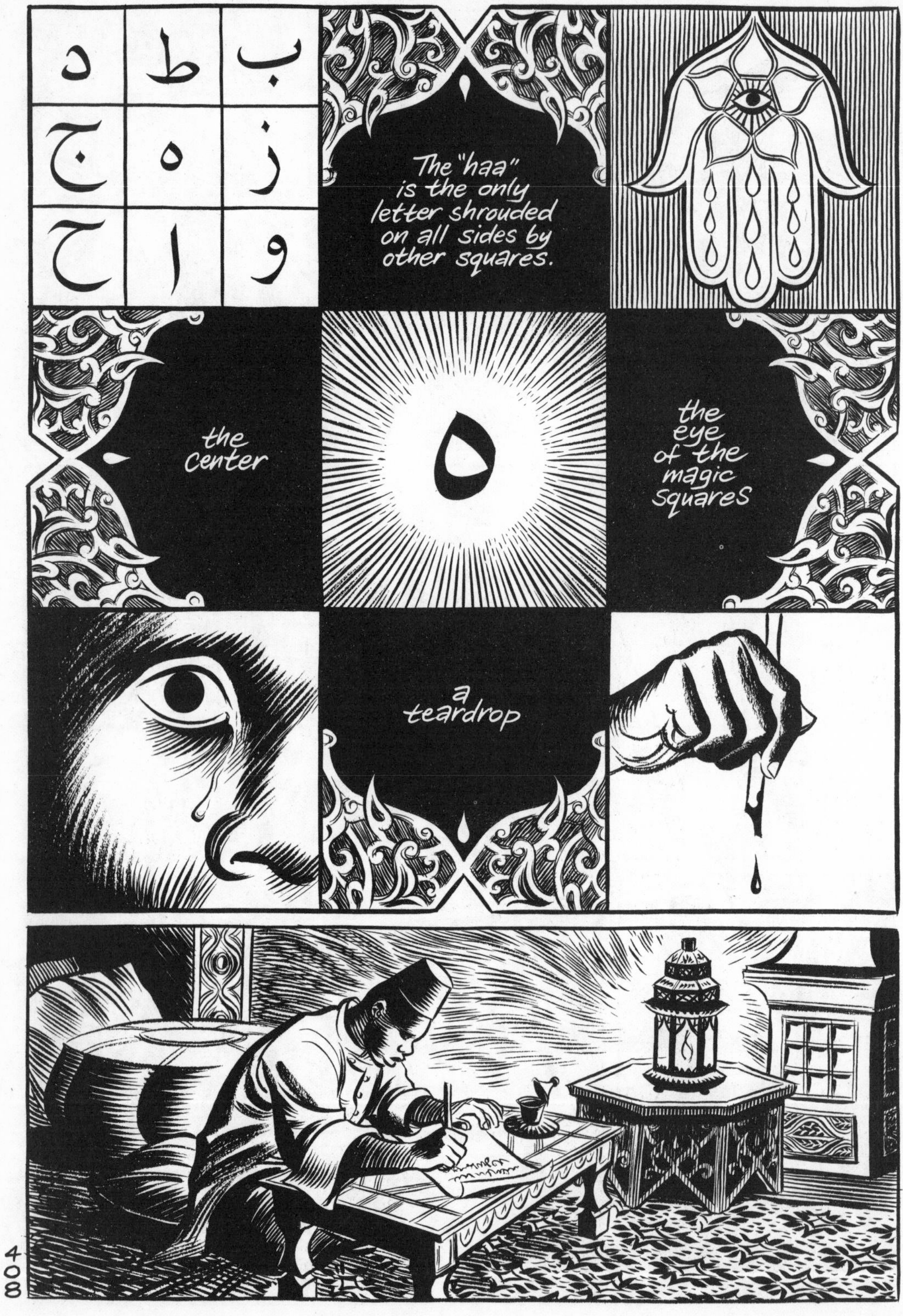
ب ط د
ز ه ج
و ا ح
The "haa" is the only letter shrouded on all sides by other squares.
the center
ه
the eye of the magic squares
a teardrop

What's this?
a letter?
for me?
YOU wrote this?
...
Oh, so NOW you want to be promoted to the Sultan's Harem?
NOD NOD
Too late. You missed your chance.
CRUMPLE
That was a once-in-a-lifetime opportunity.
You displayed to me that you didn't have the BALLS- so to speak - to work outside the Palace of Tears.
boo.
hoo.
hoo.

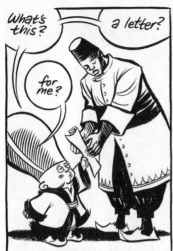

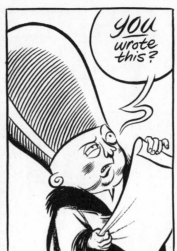

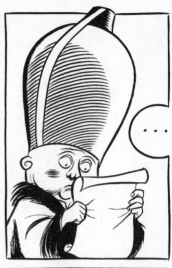

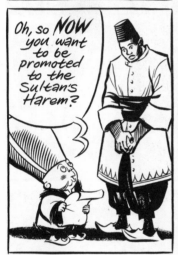

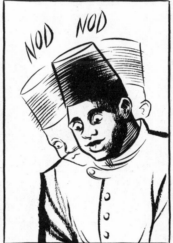

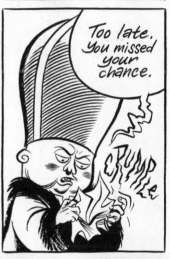

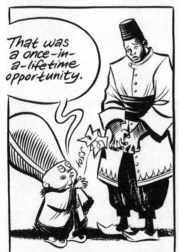

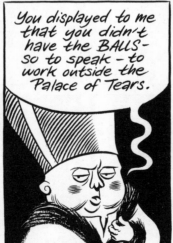

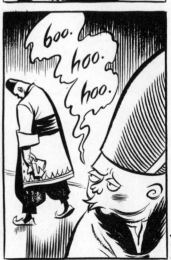

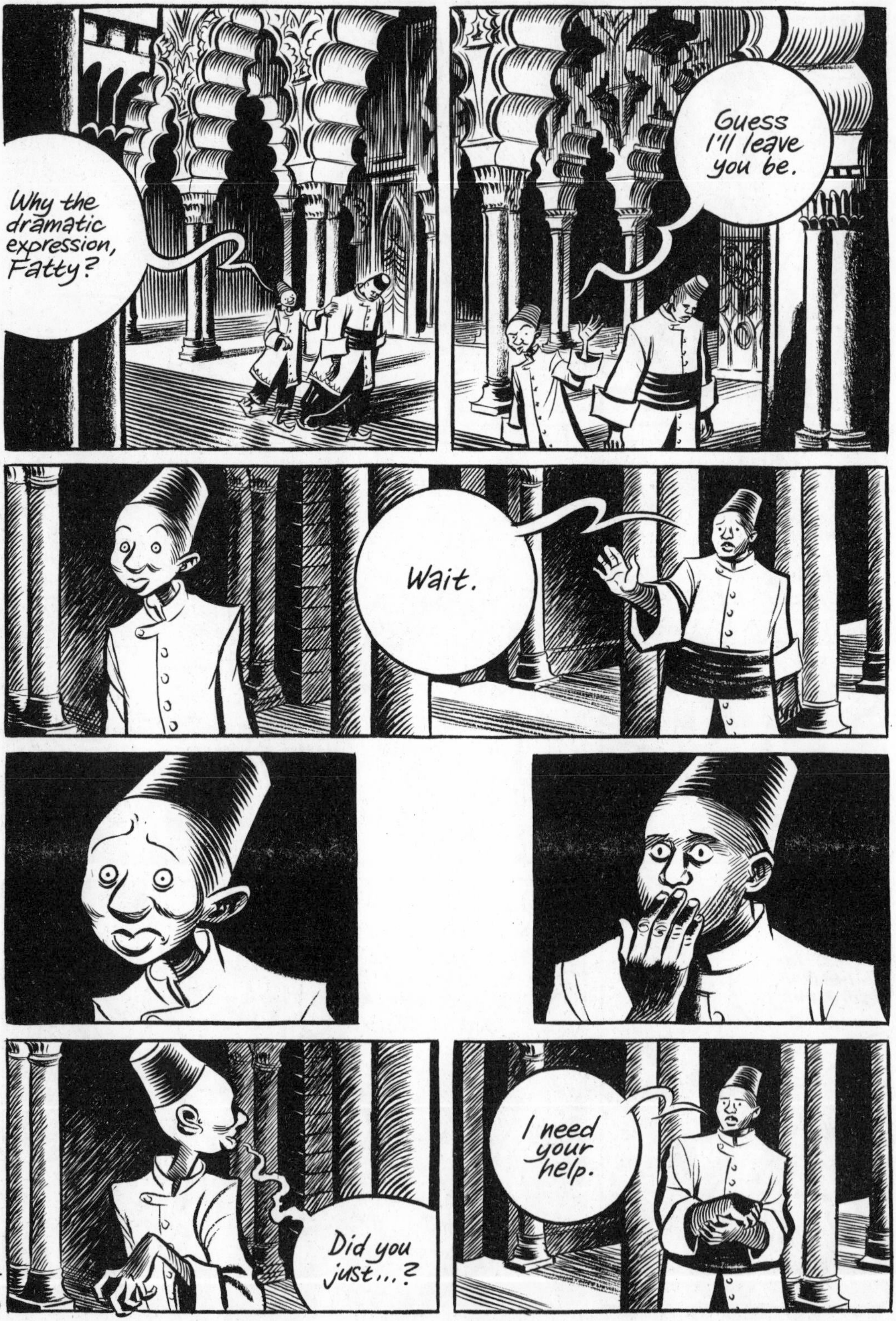
Why the dramatic expression, Fatty?
Guess I'll leave you be.
Wait.
Did you just...?
I need your help.

HO HO HO!
I knew it!
I KNEW you could speak!
You used to talk all sorts of gibberish in your sleep.
?
I damaged the ship...
"Snrrk" I killed the child...
killed?
I rebuilt the wall...
What wall? Tell me more.
Dodola...
Is that a LADY?

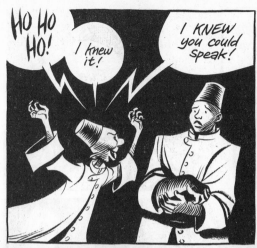

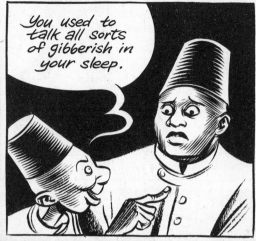

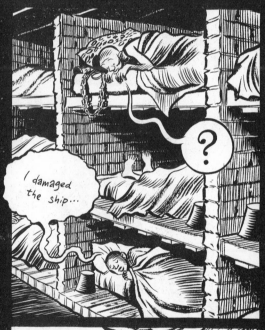

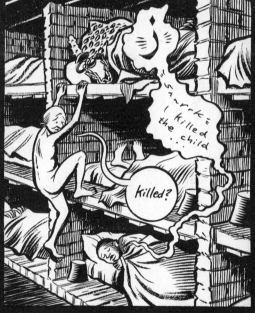

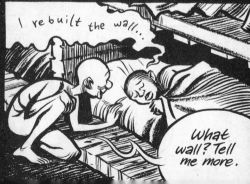

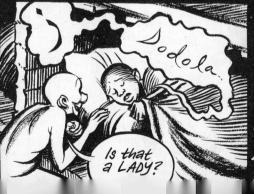

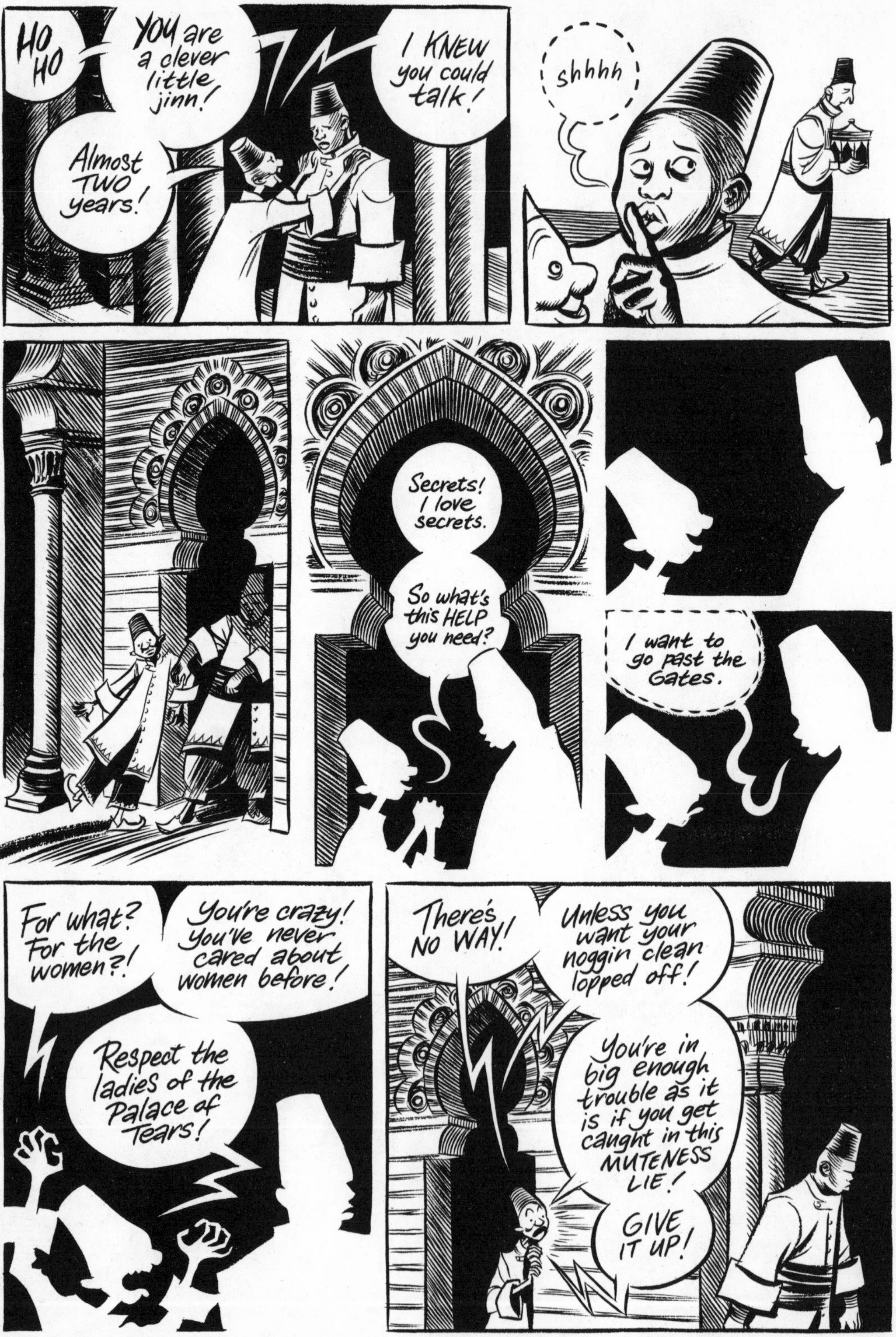
HO HO
YOU are a clever little jinn!
I KNEW you could talk!
Almost TWO years!
shhhh
Secrets! I love secrets.
So what's this HELP you need?
I want to go past the Gates.
For what? For the women?!
You're crazy! You've never cared about women before!
Respect the ladies of the Palace of Tears!
There's NO WAY!
Unless you want your noggin clean lopped off!
You're in big enough trouble as it is if you get caught in this MUTENESS LIE!
GIVE IT UP!

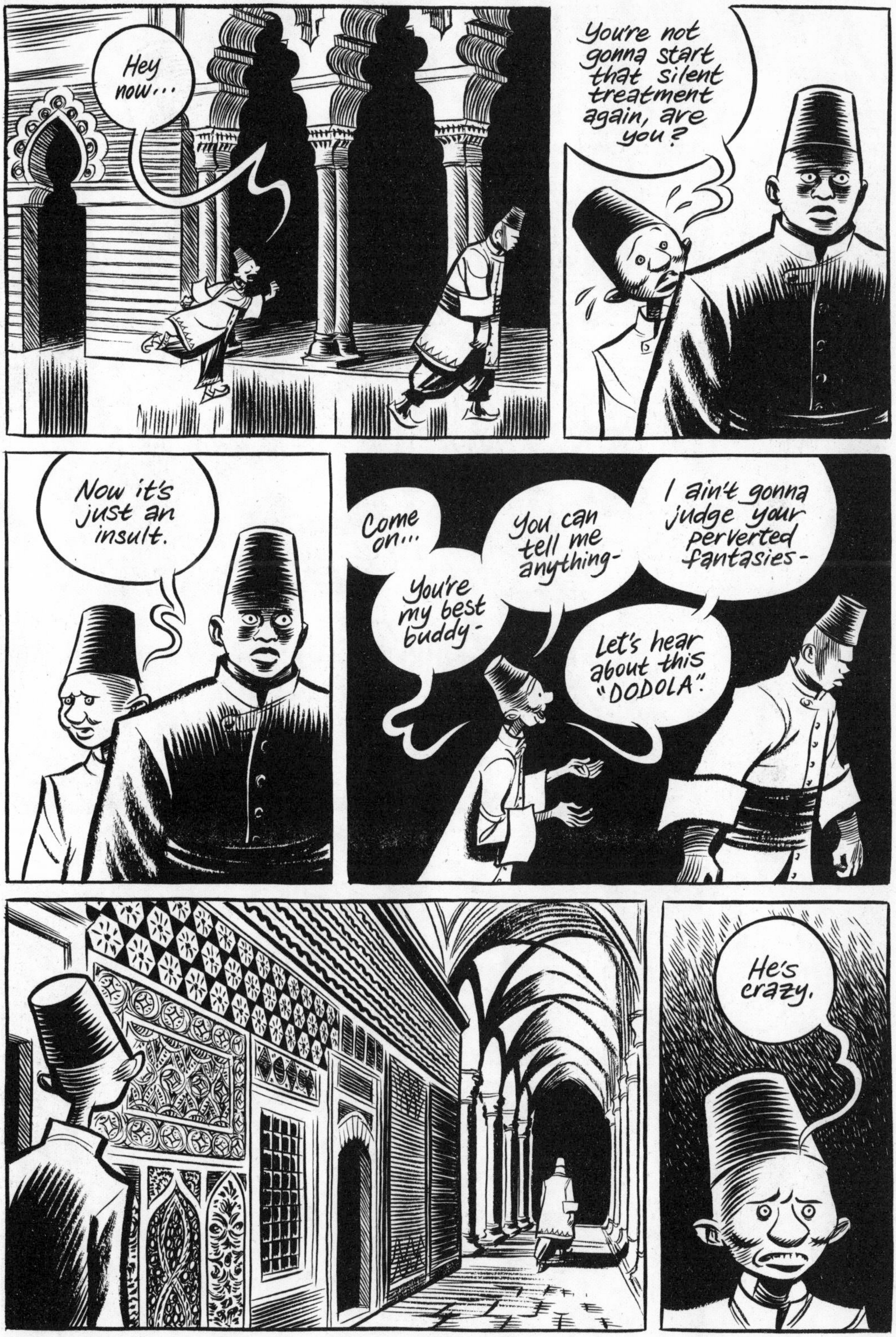
Hey now...
You're not gonna start that silent treatment again, are you?
Now it's just an insult.
Come on...
You're my best buddy-
You can tell me anything-
I ain't gonna judge your perverted fantasies-
Let's hear about this "DODOLA".
He's crazy.

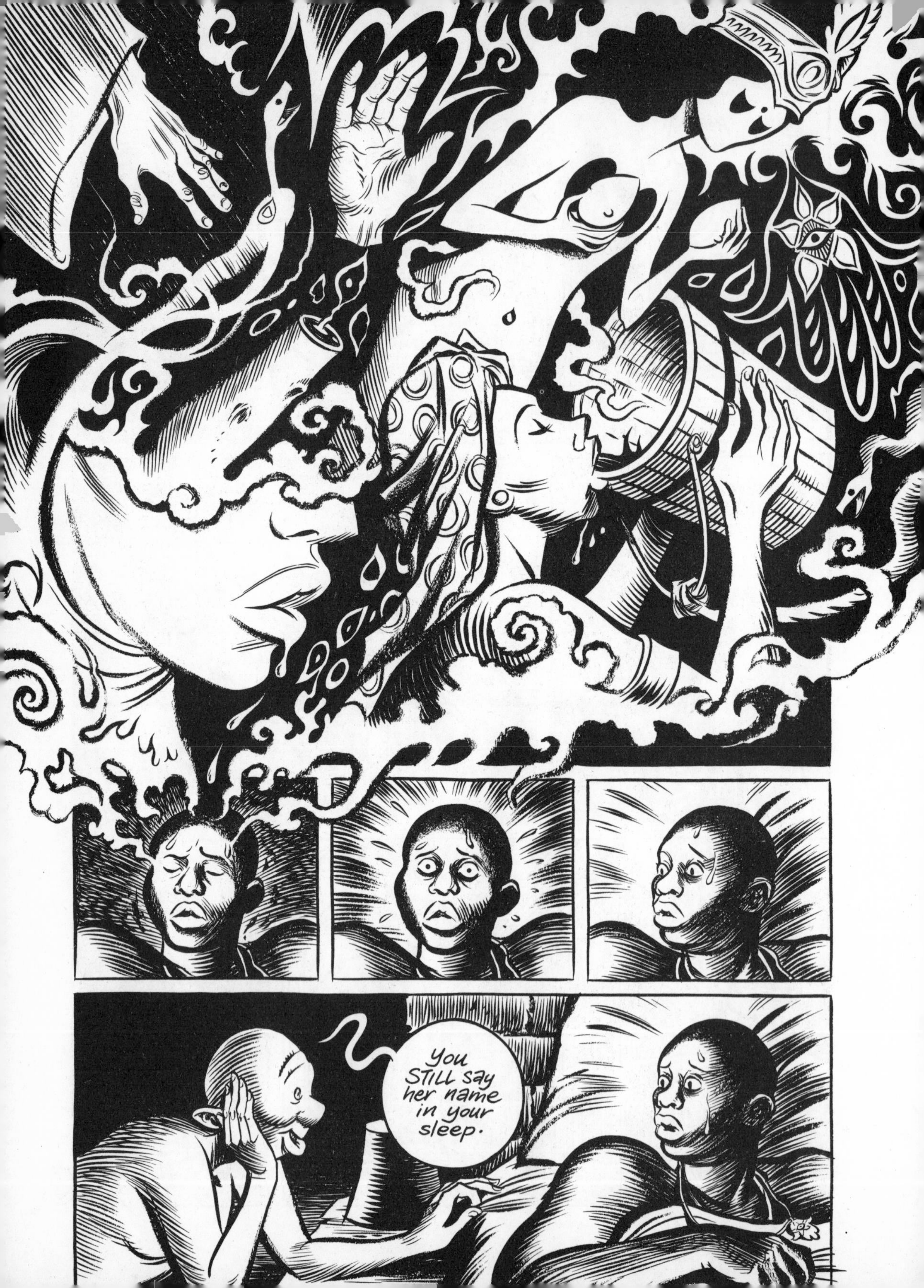
You STILL say her name in your sleep.

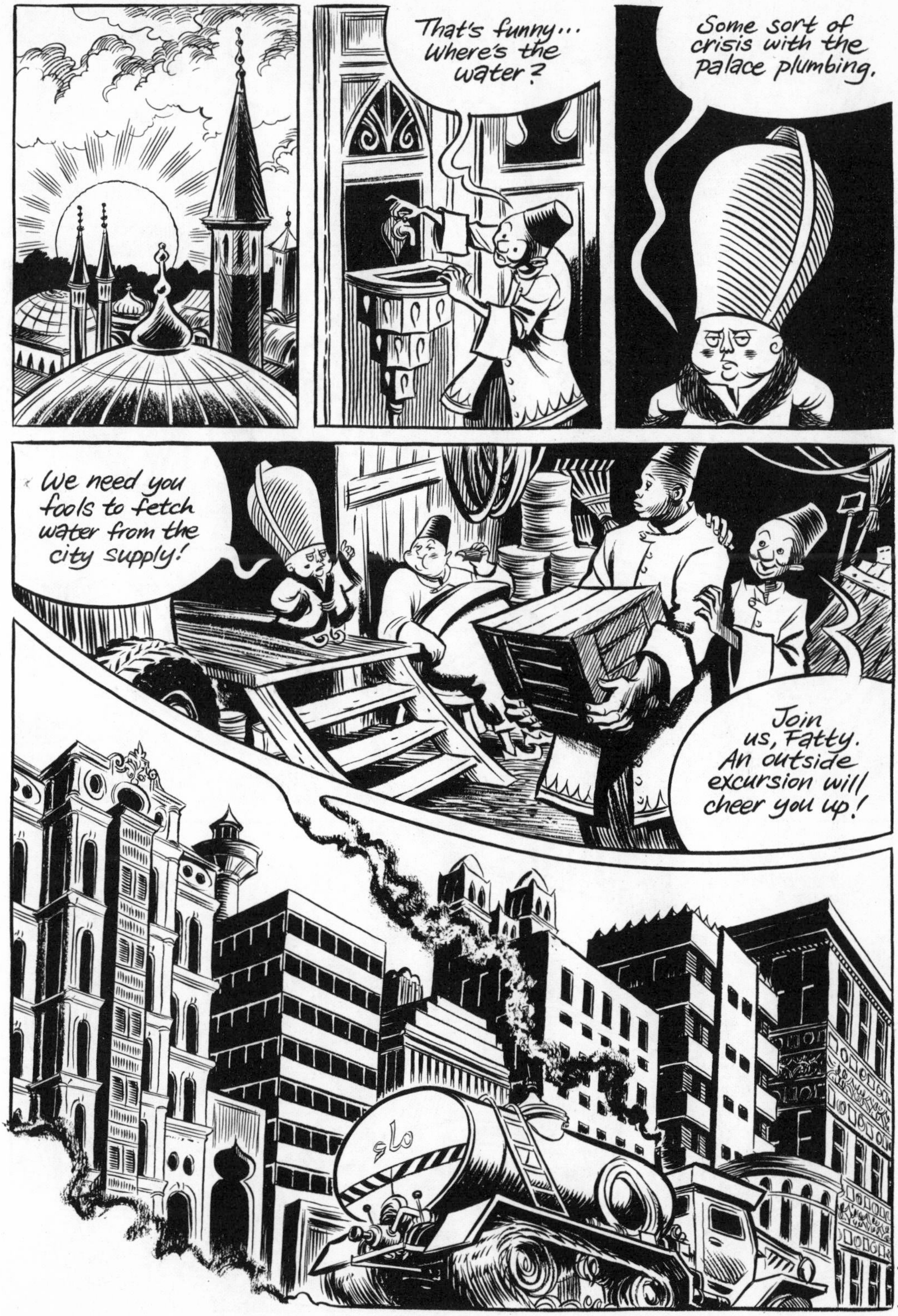
That's funny... Where's the water?
Some sort of crisis with the palace plumbing.
We need you fools to fetch water from the city supply!
Join us, Fatty. An outside excursion will cheer you up!

CHUGGA
CHUG
CHUGGA
CHUGGA
SLURP
That's one more fountain SUCKED DRY!
And the tanker's full.
Let's haul home the bounty!

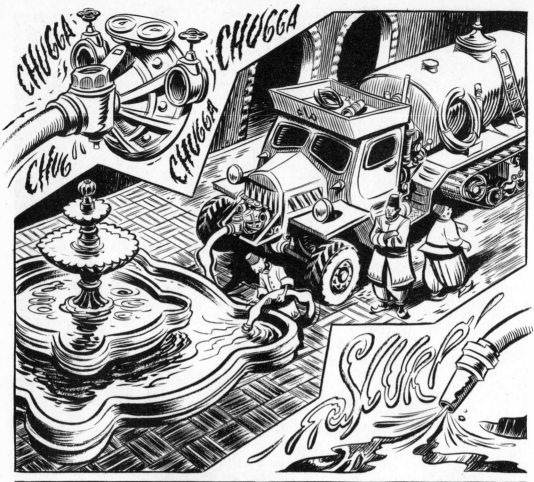

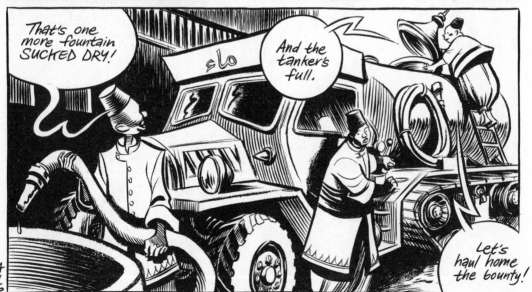

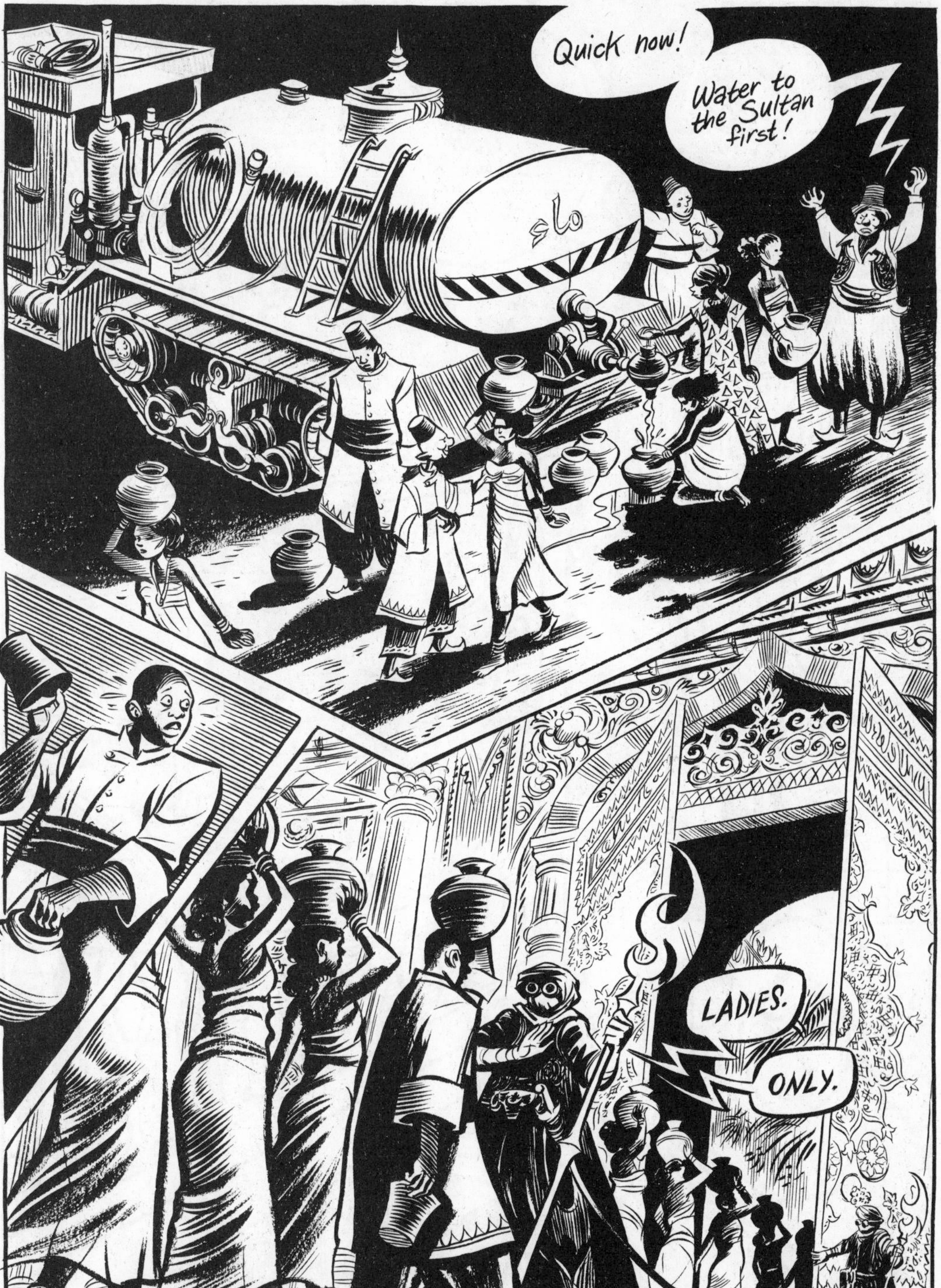
Quick now!
Water to the Sultan first!
LADIES.
ONLY.

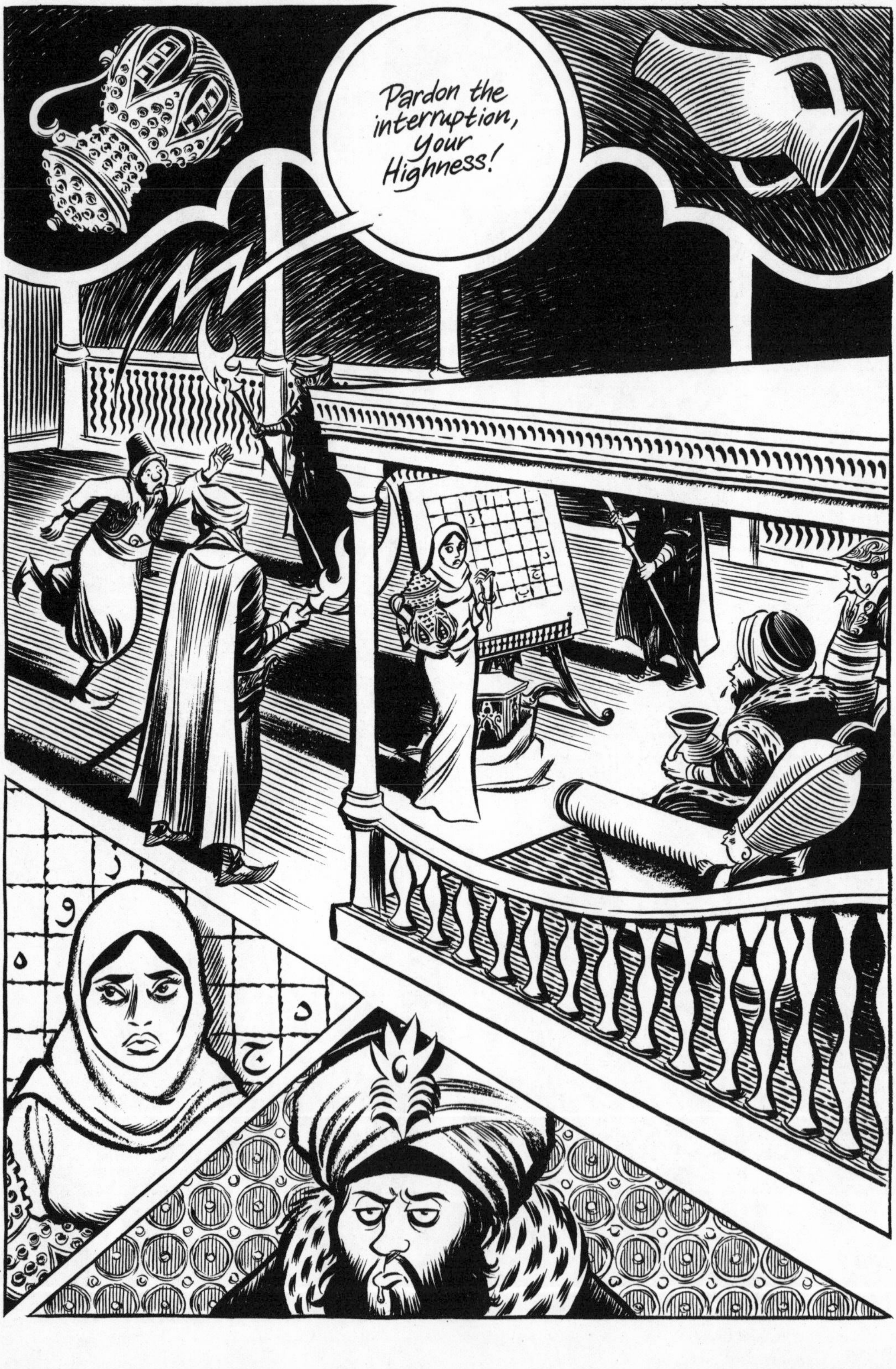
Pardon the interruption, your Highness!

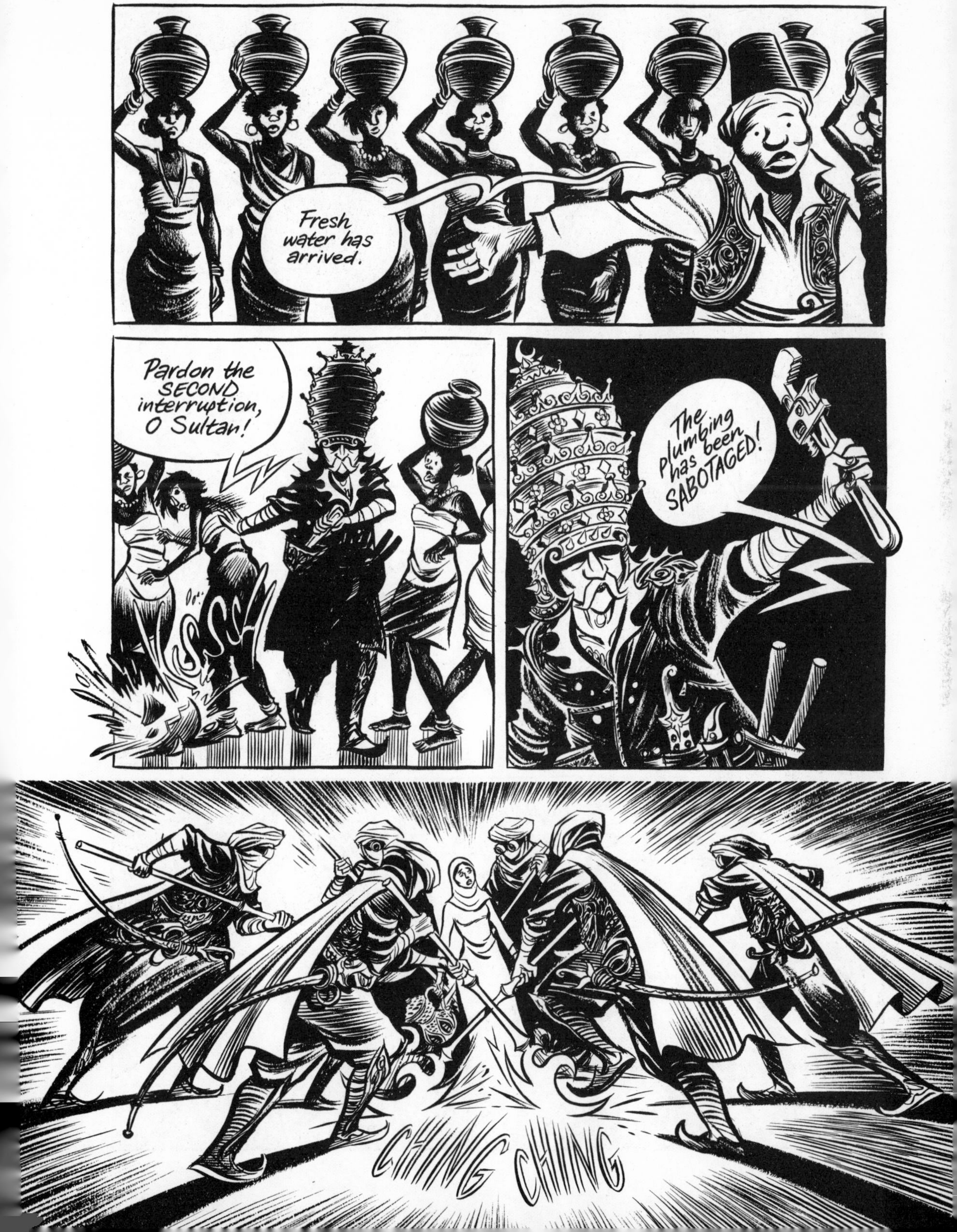
Fresh water has arrived.
Pardon the SECOND interruption, O Sultan!
The plumbing has been SABOTAGED!
CHING CHING

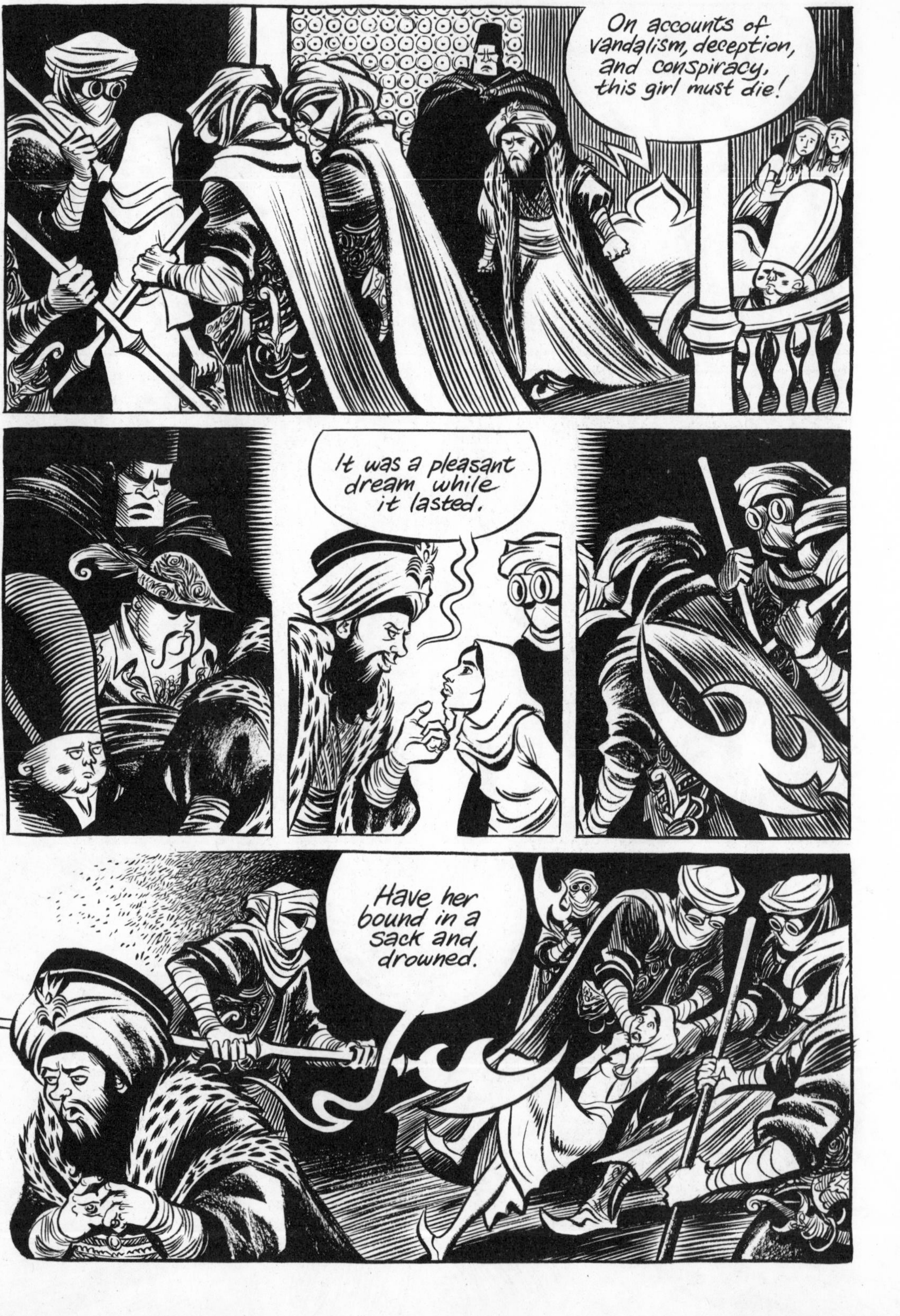
On accounts of vandalism, deception, and conspiracy, this girl must die!
It was a pleasant dream while it lasted.
Have her bound in a sack and drowned.

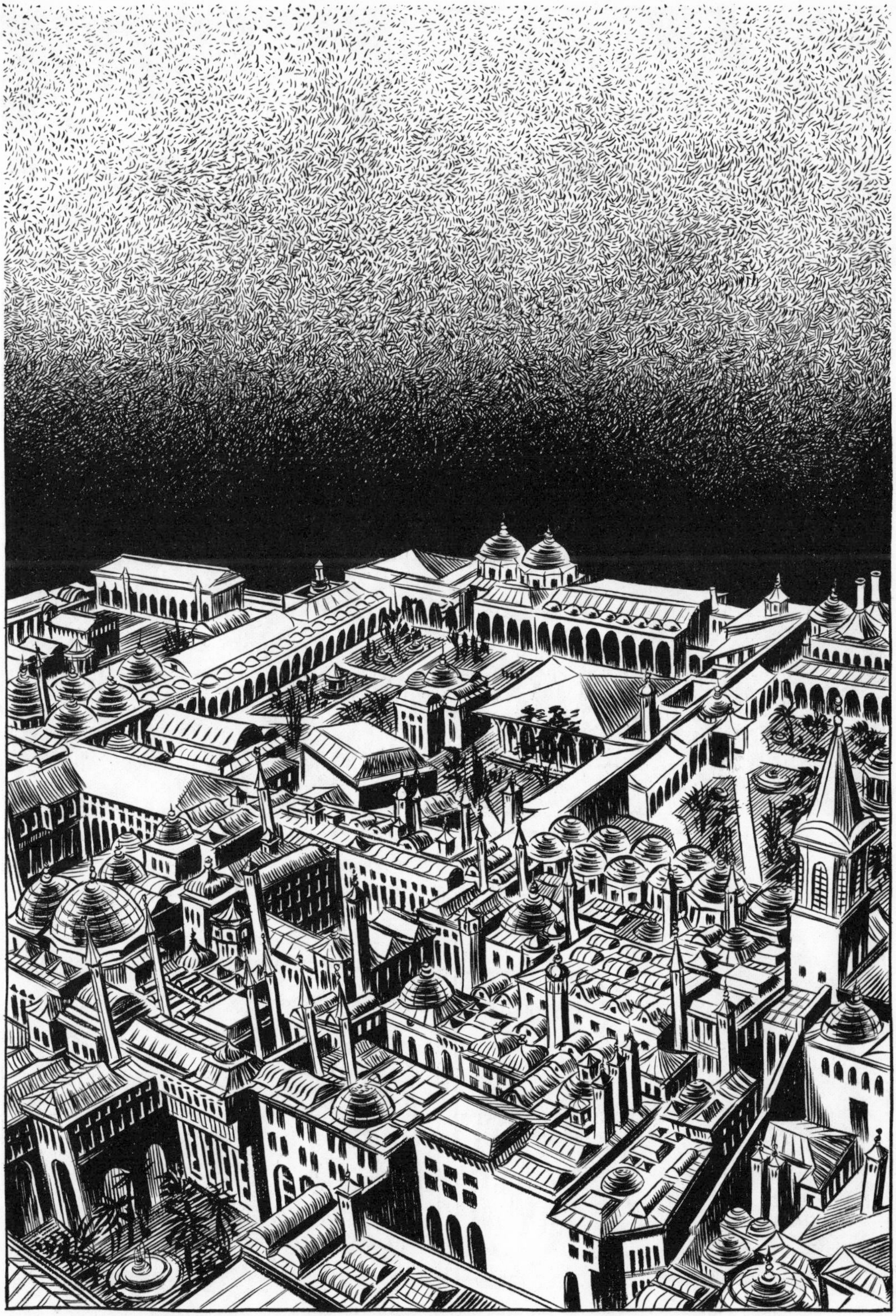

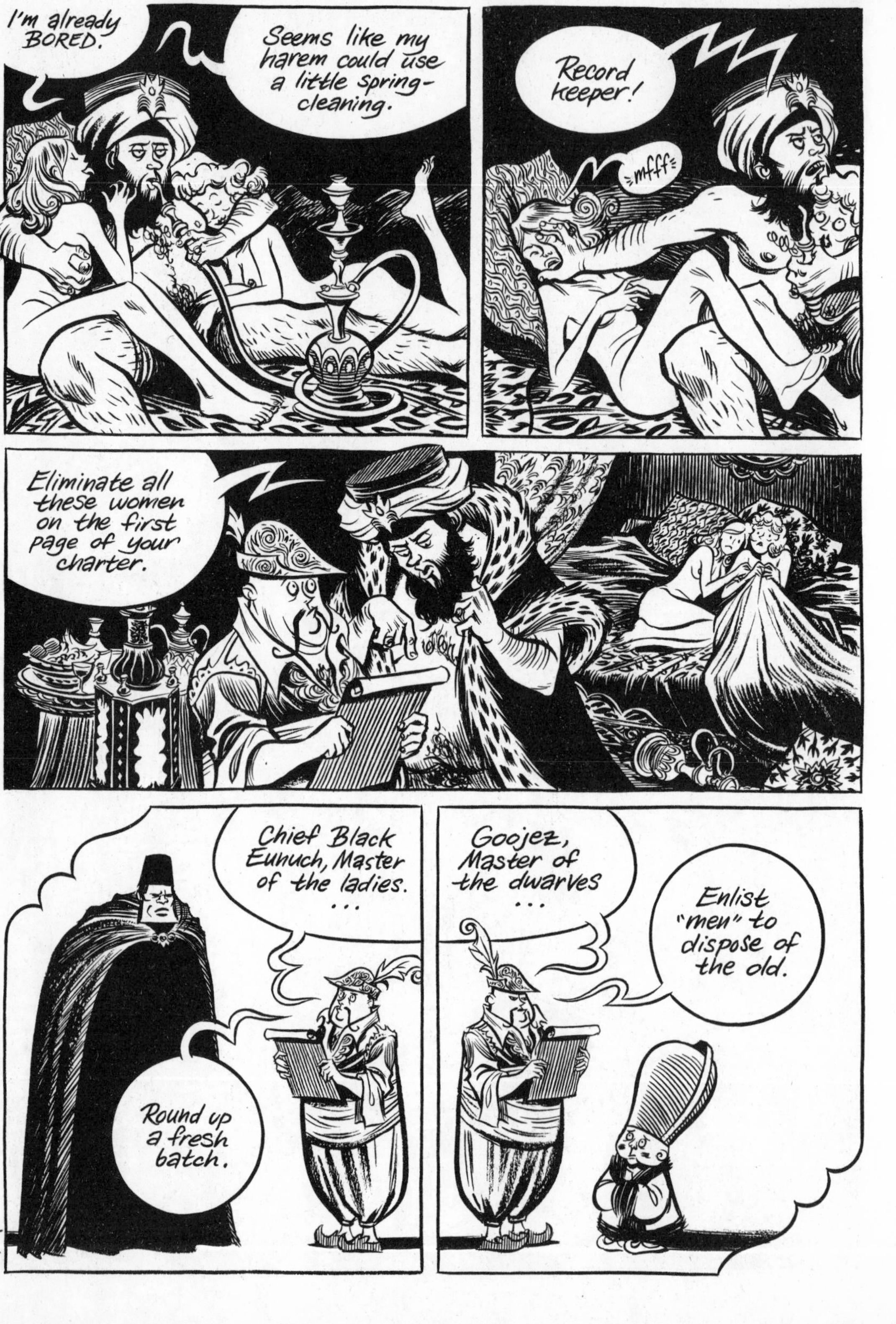
I'm already BORED.
Seems like my harem could use a little spring-cleaning.
Record keeper!
mfff
Eliminate all these women on the first page of your charter.
Chief Black Eunuch, Master of the ladies. ...
Round up a fresh batch.
Goojez, Master of the dwarves ...
Enlist "men" to dispose of the old.

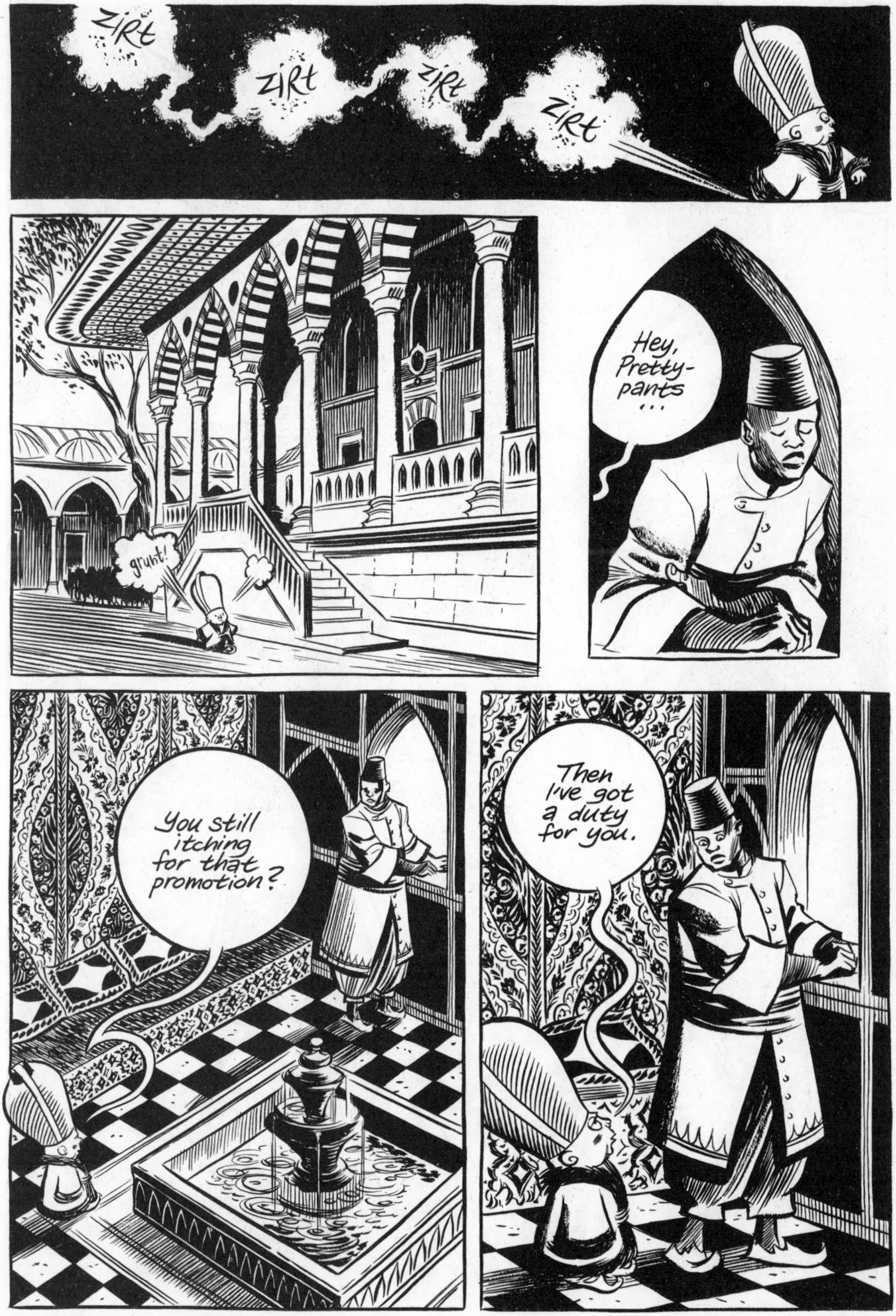
ziRt
ziRt
ziRt
ziRt
grunt!
Hey, Pretty-pants...
You still itching for that promotion?
Then I've got a duty for you.

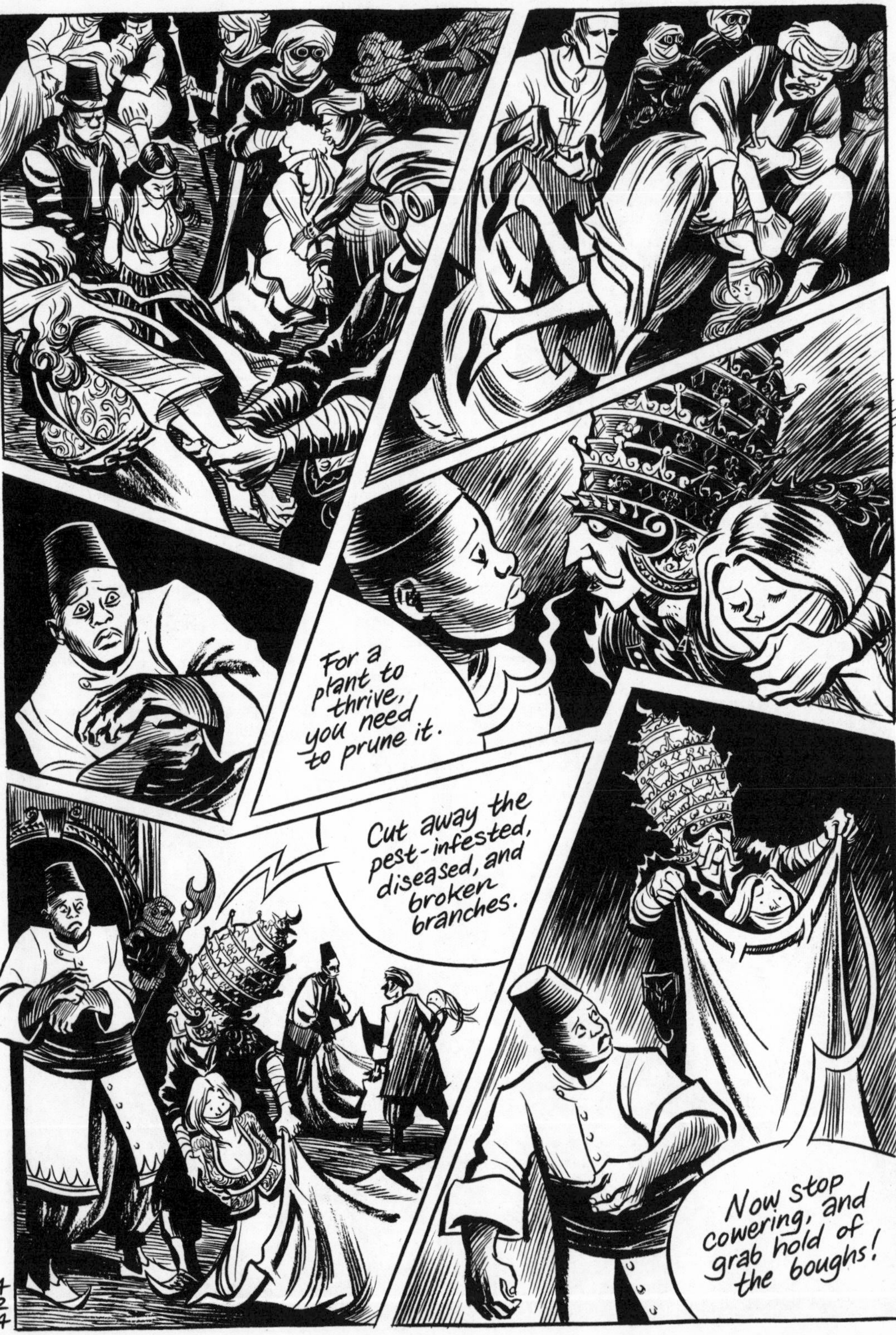
For a plant to thrive, you need to prune it.
Cut away the pest-infested, diseased, and broken branches.
Now stop cowering, and grab hold of the boughs!

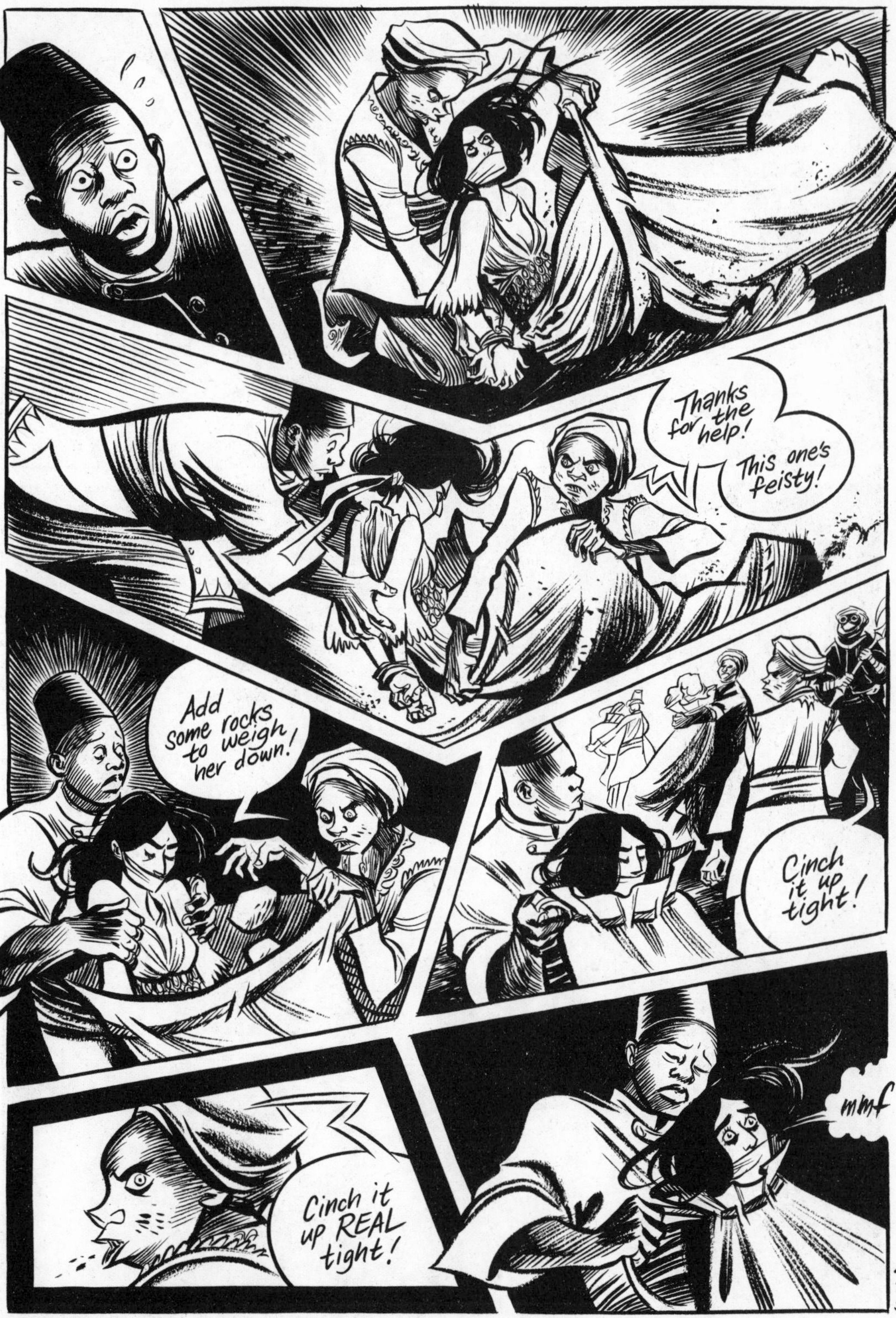

Thanks for the help!
This one's feisty!
Add some rocks to weigh her down!
Cinch it up tight!
Cinch it up REAL tight!
mmf

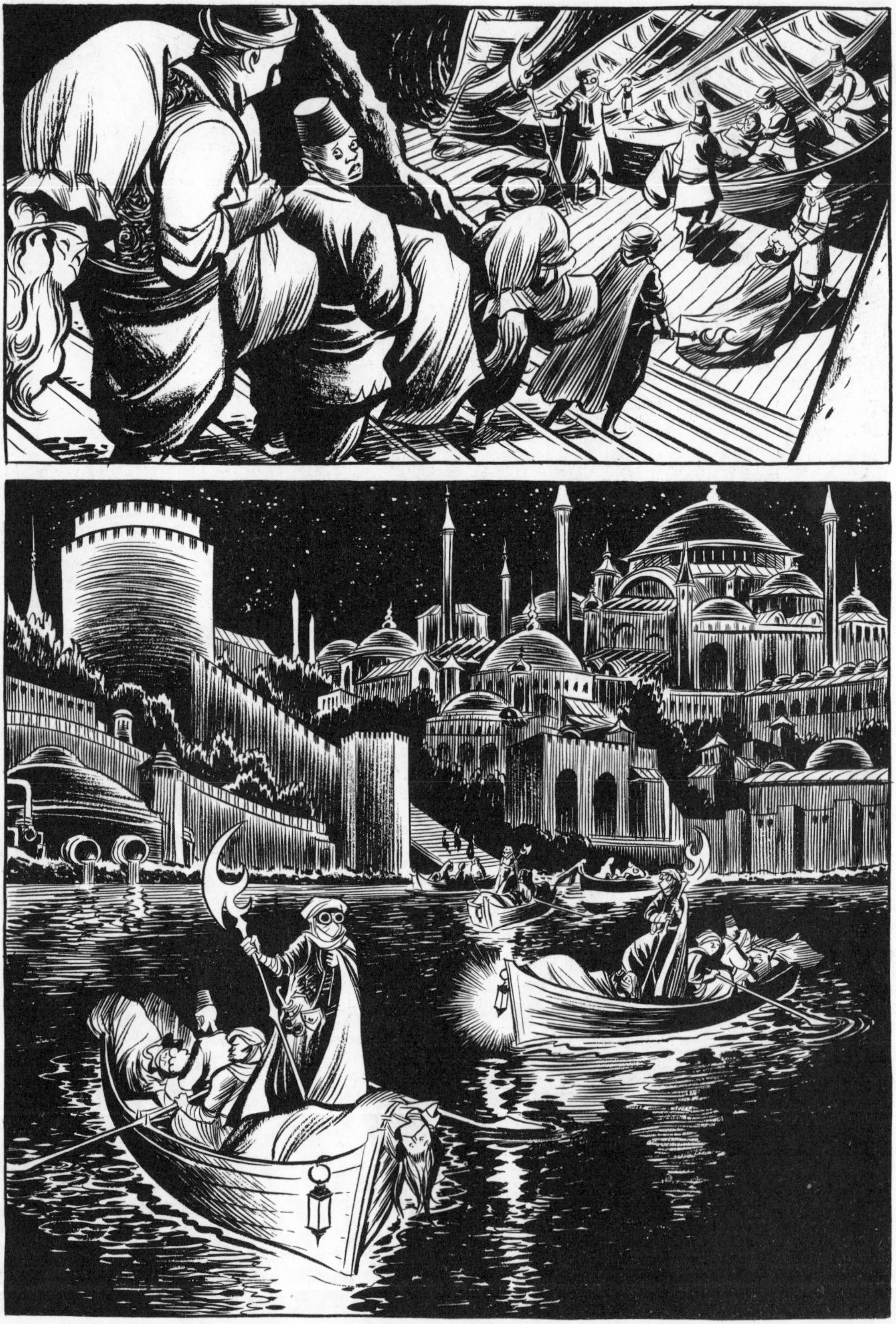

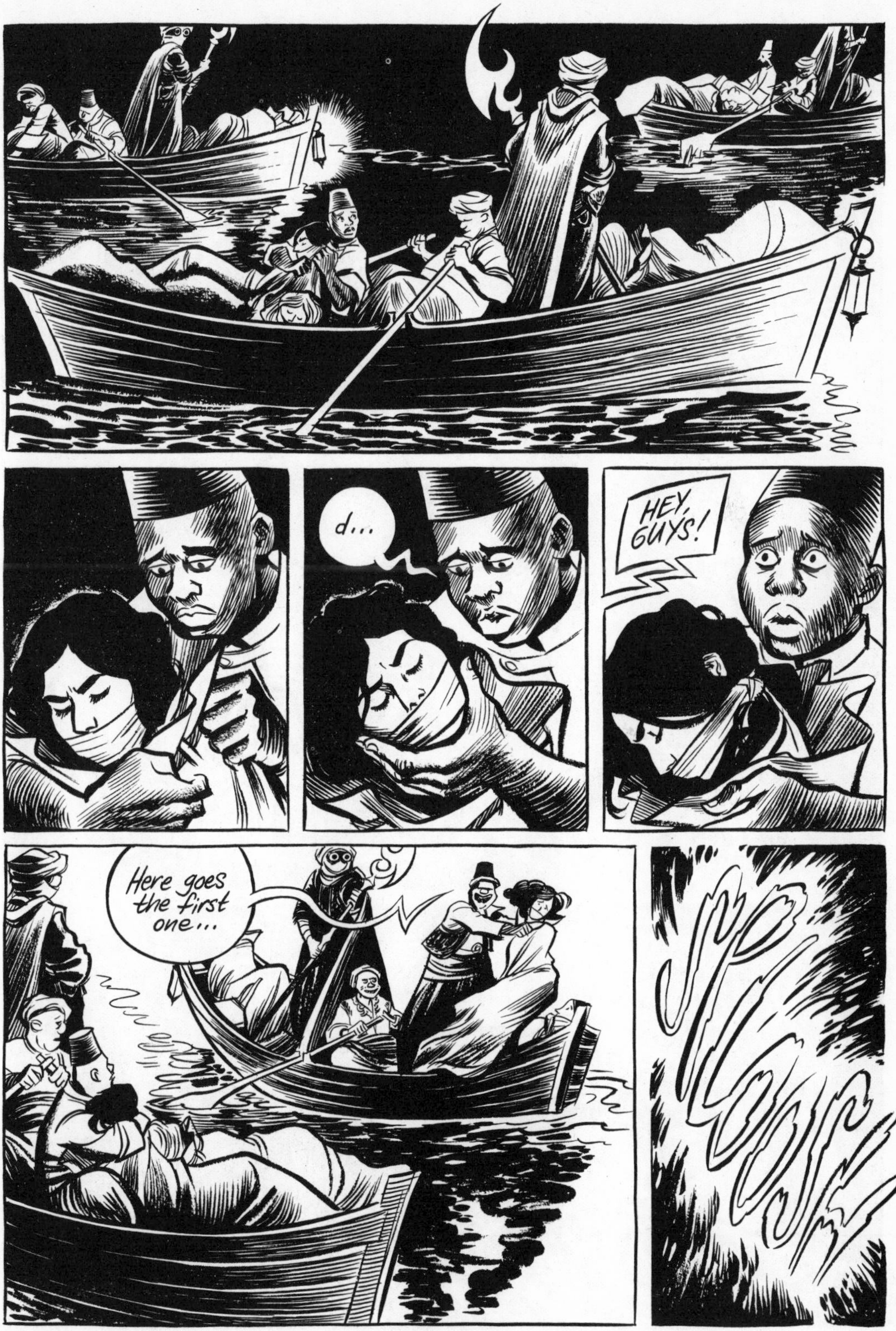
d...
HEY, GUYS!
Here goes the first one...

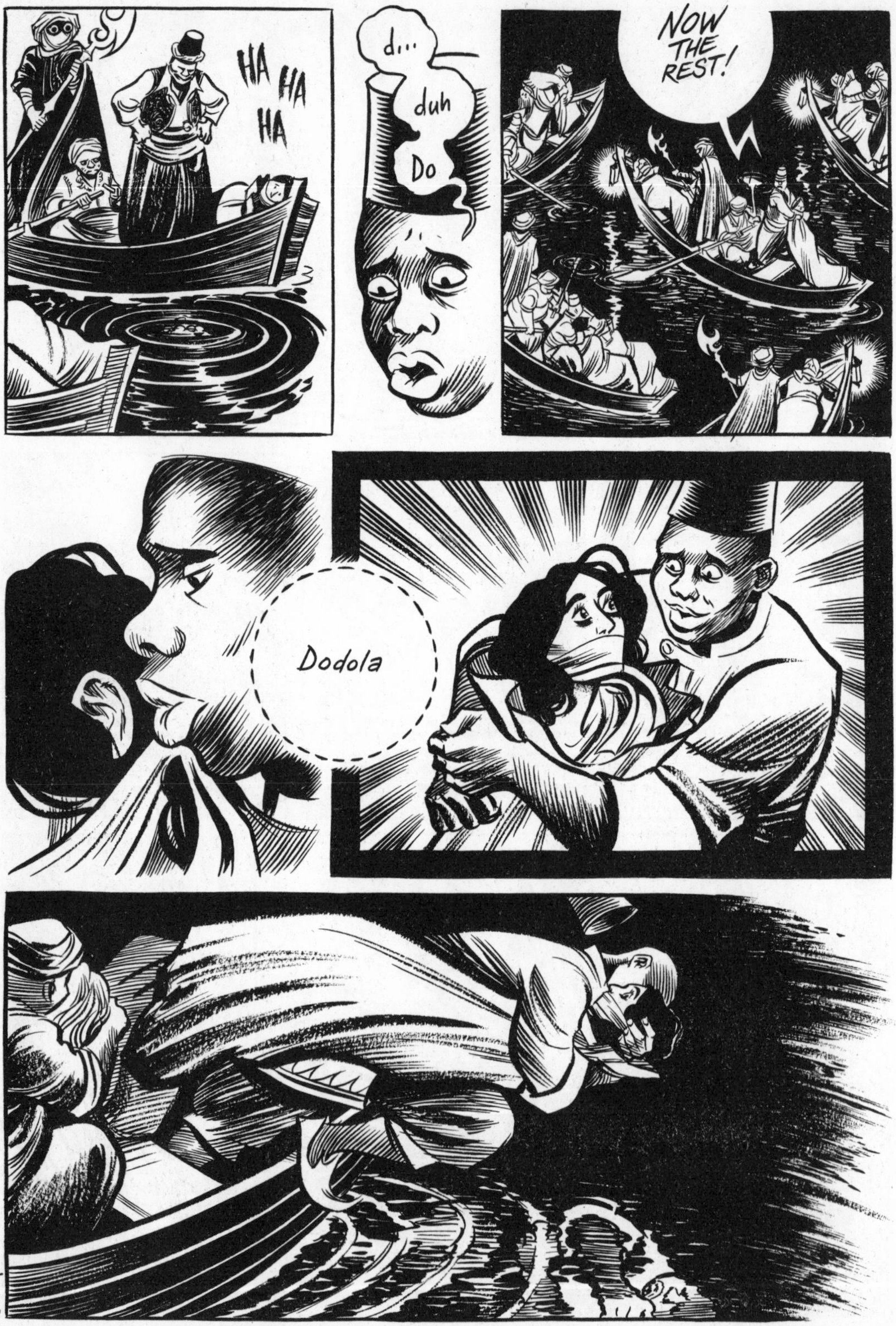
HA HA HA
d...
duh
Do
NOW THE REST!
Dodola

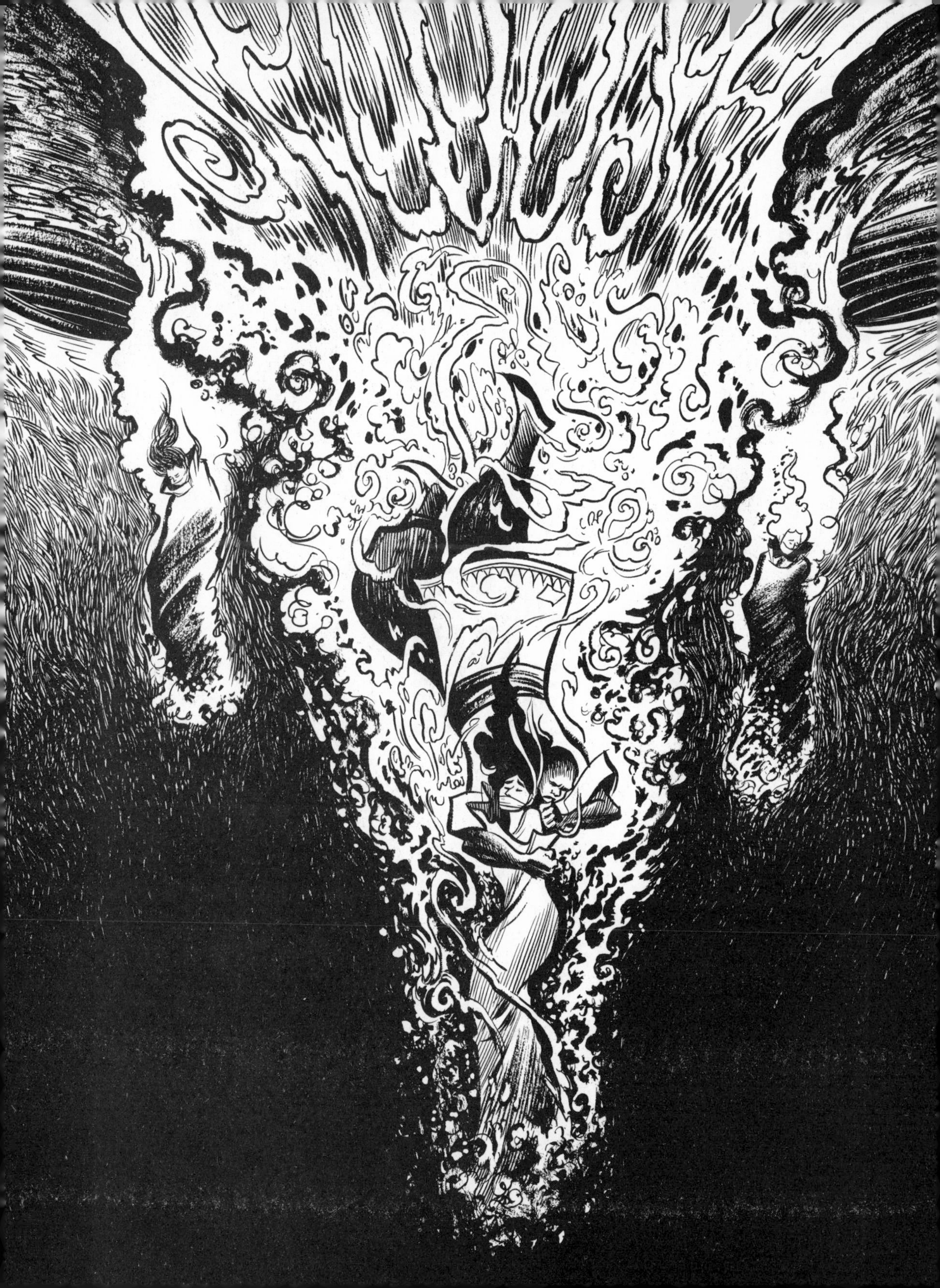

د	ط	ب
ج	ه	ز
ح	ا	و

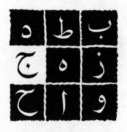

DROWNING

غرق

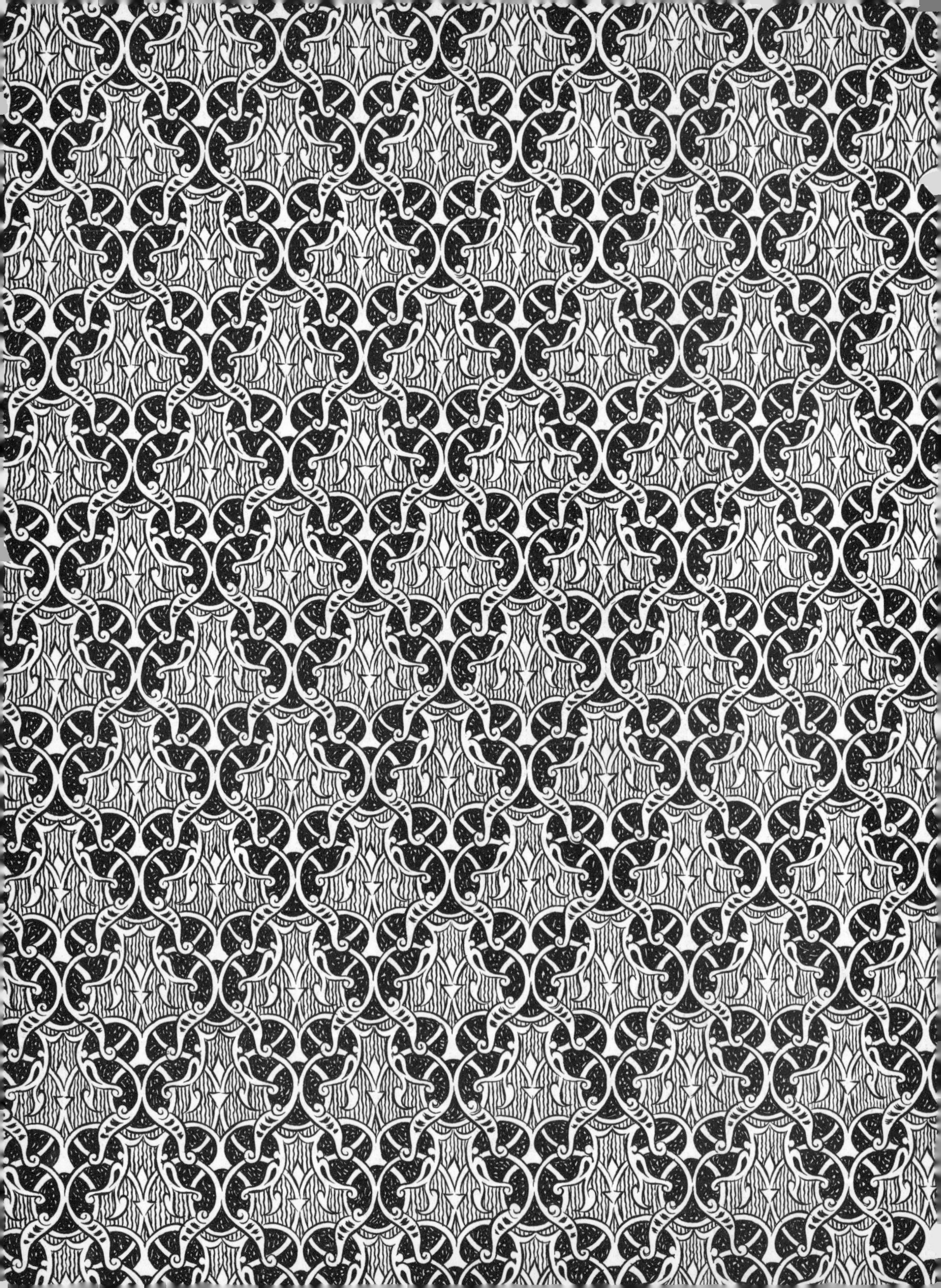

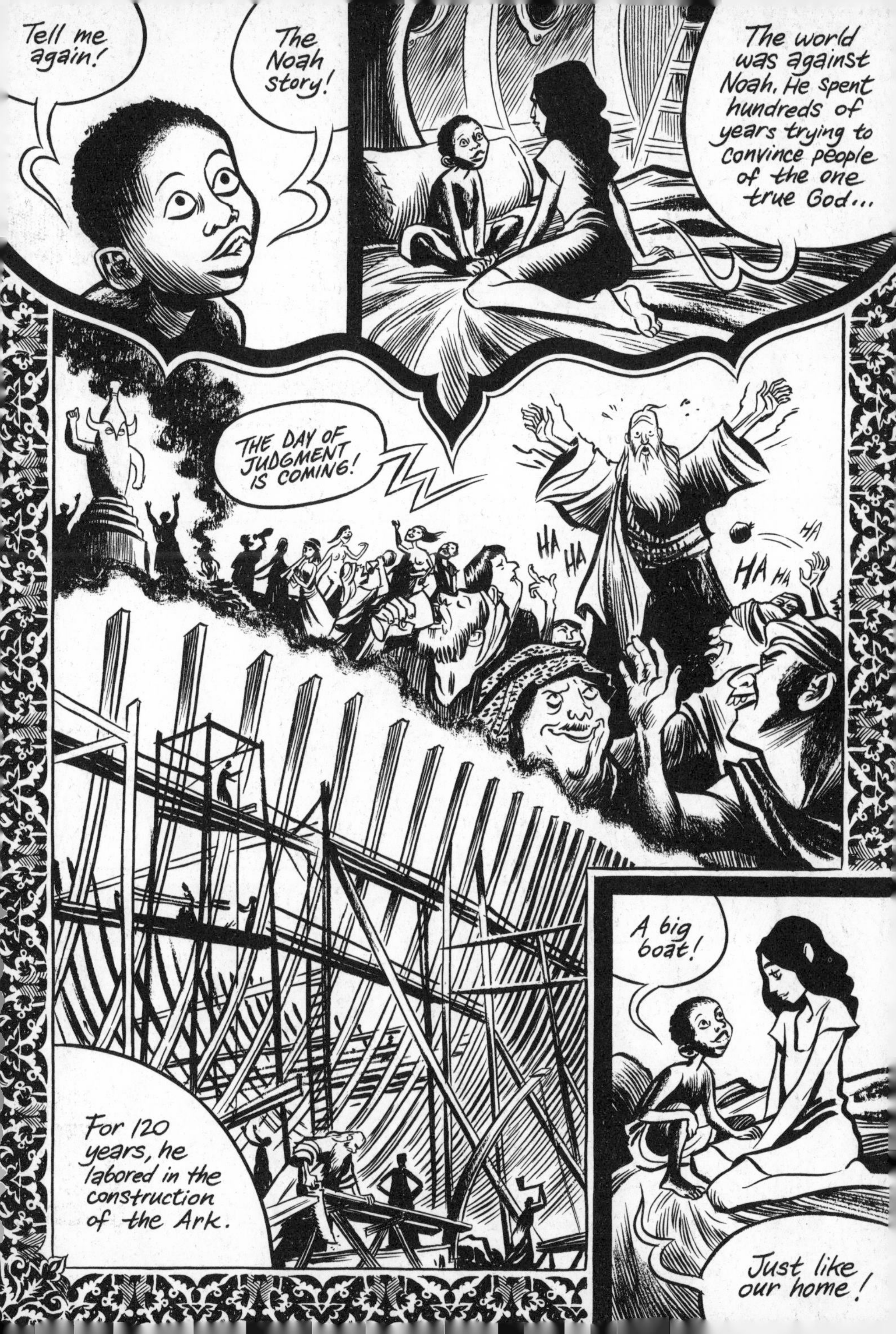
Tell me again!
The Noah story!
The world was against Noah. He spent hundreds of years trying to convince people of the one true God...
THE DAY OF JUDGMENT IS COMING!
HA HA
HA
HA HA
For 120 years, he labored in the construction of the Ark.
A big boat!
Just like our home!

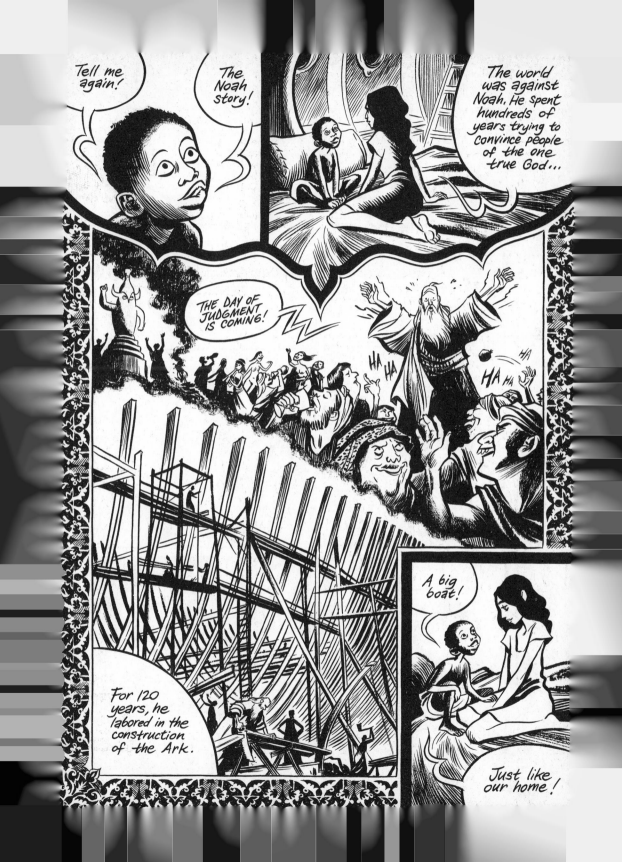

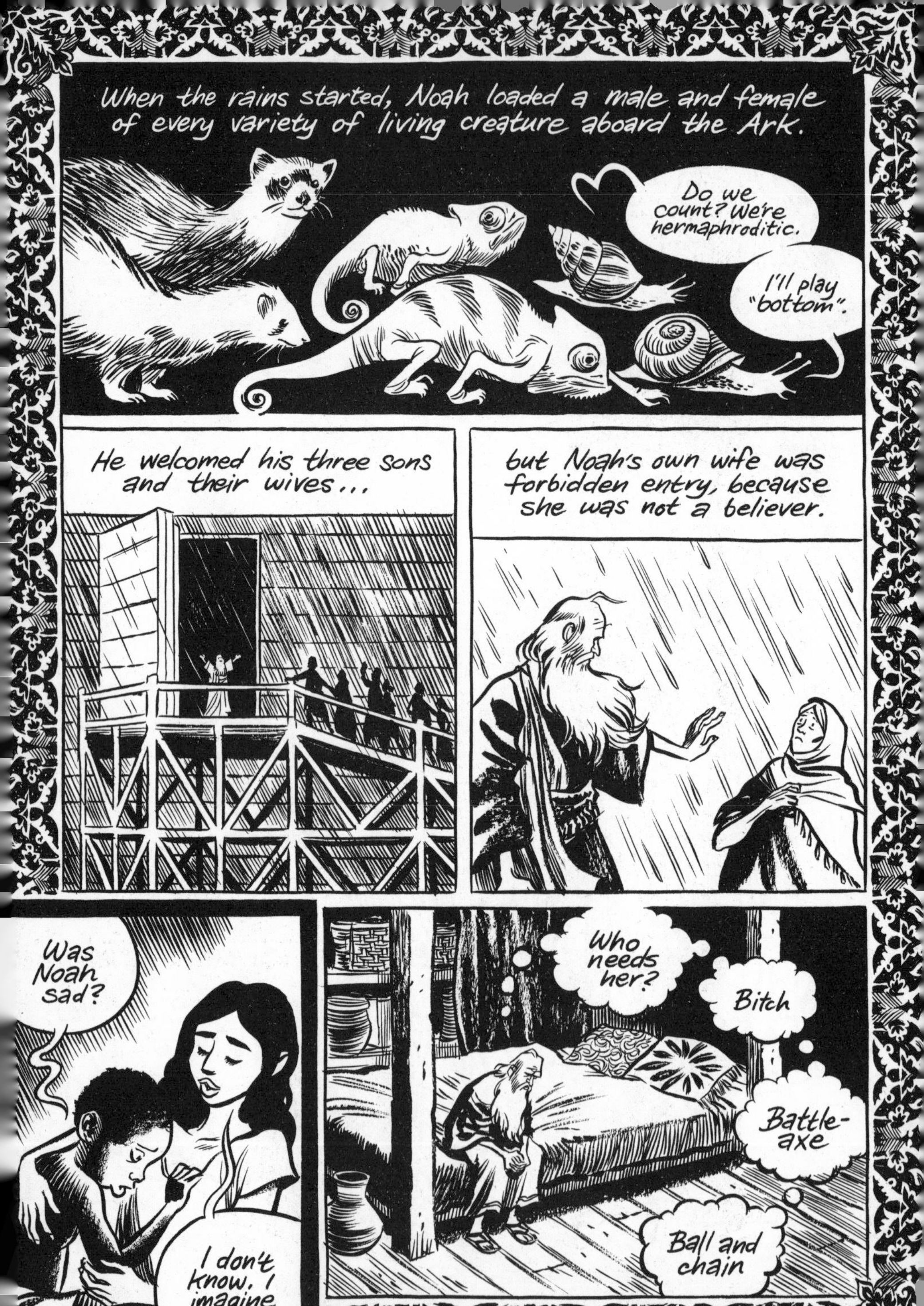
When the rains started, Noah loaded a male and female of every variety of living creature aboard the Ark.
Do we count? We're hermaphroditic.
I'll play "bottom".
He welcomed his three sons and their wives...
but Noah's own wife was forbidden entry, because she was not a believer.
Was Noah sad?
I don't know. I imagine so...
Who needs her?
Bitch
Battle-axe
Ball and chain

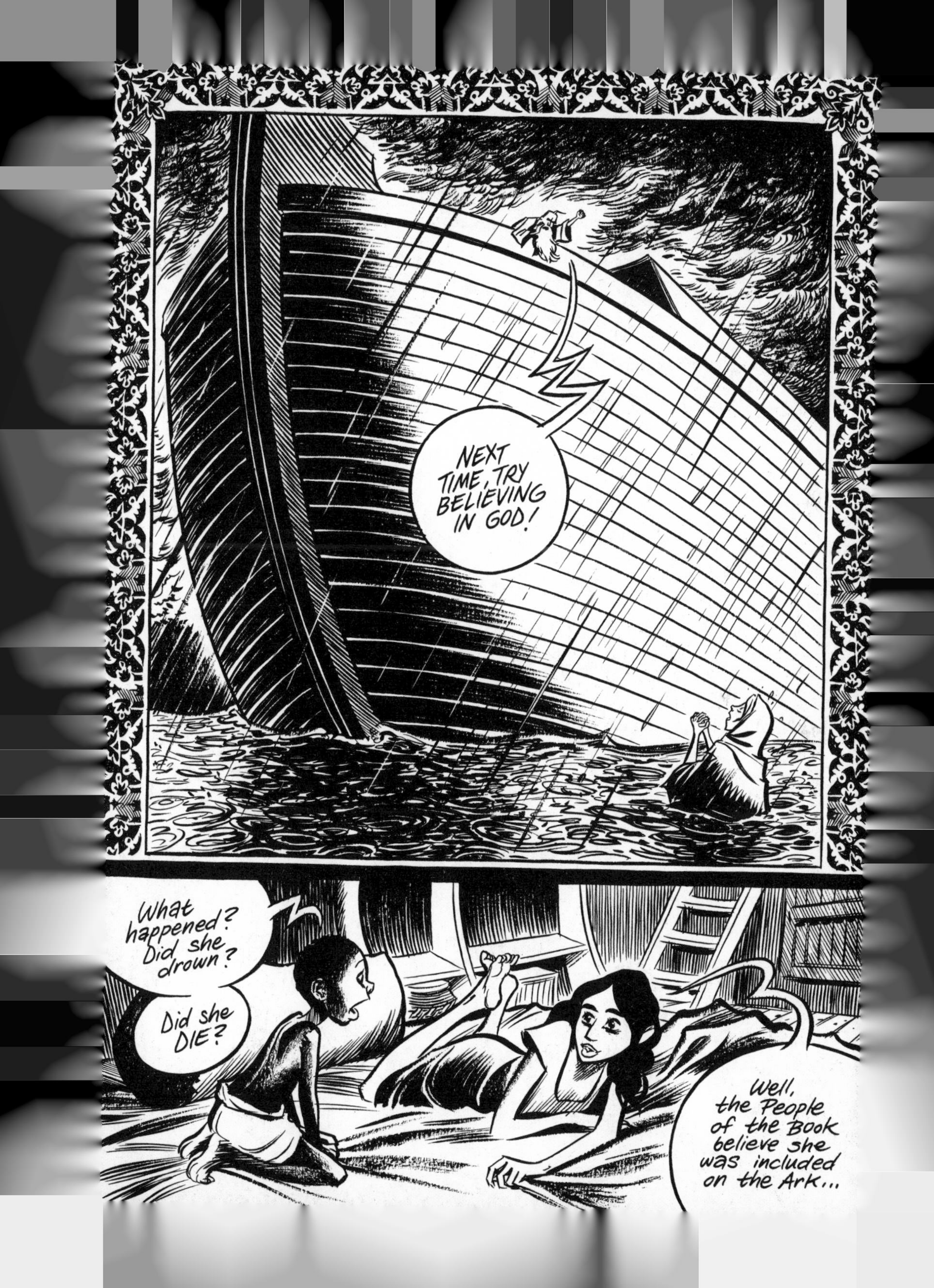
NEXT TIME, TRY BELIEVING IN GOD!
What happened? Did she drown?
Did she DIE?
Well, the People of the Book believe she was included on the Ark...

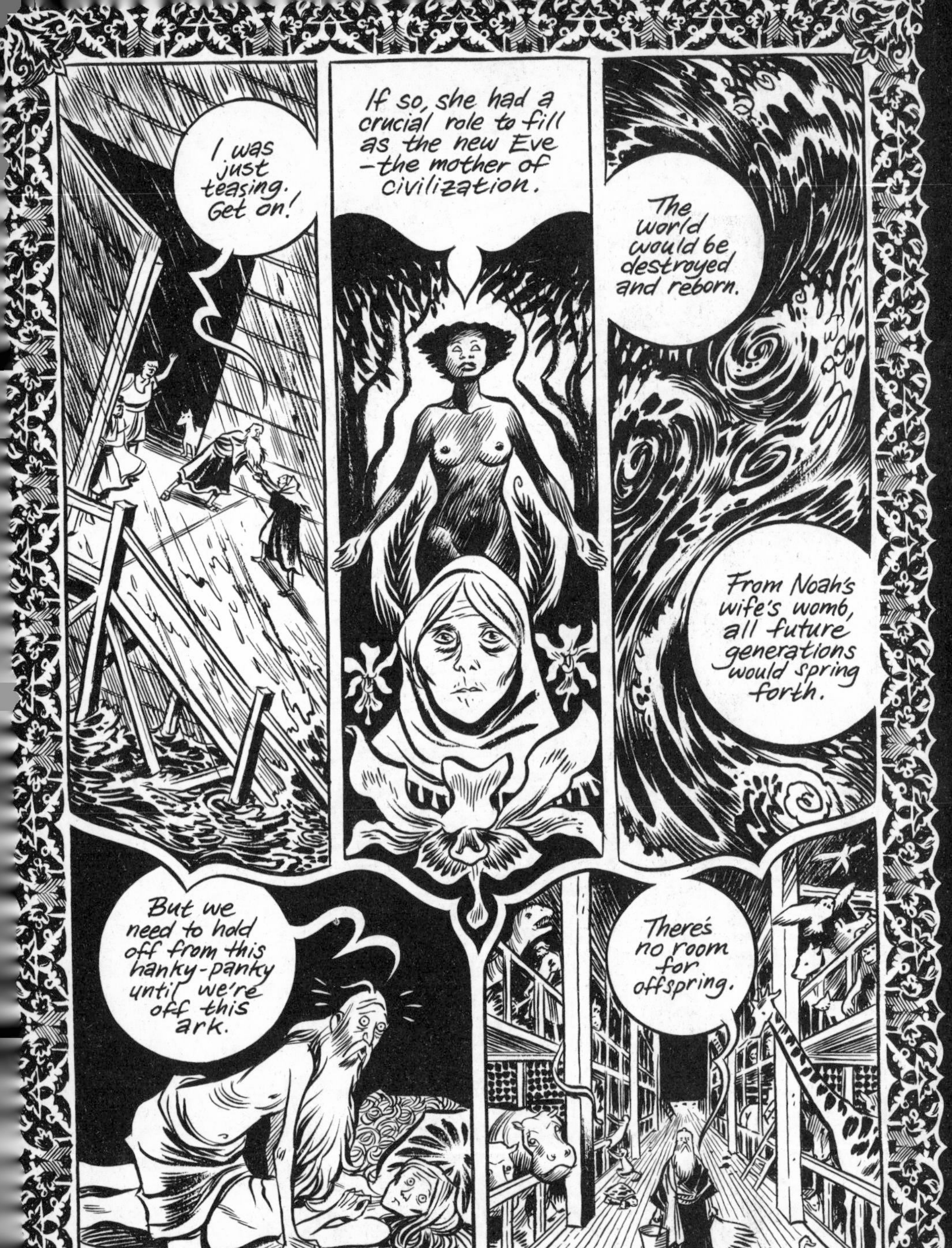
I was just teasing. Get on!
If so, she had a crucial role to fill as the new Eve —the mother of civilization.
The world would be destroyed and reborn.
From Noah's wife's womb, all future generations would spring forth.
But we need to hold off from this hanky-panky until we're off this ark.
There's no room for offspring.

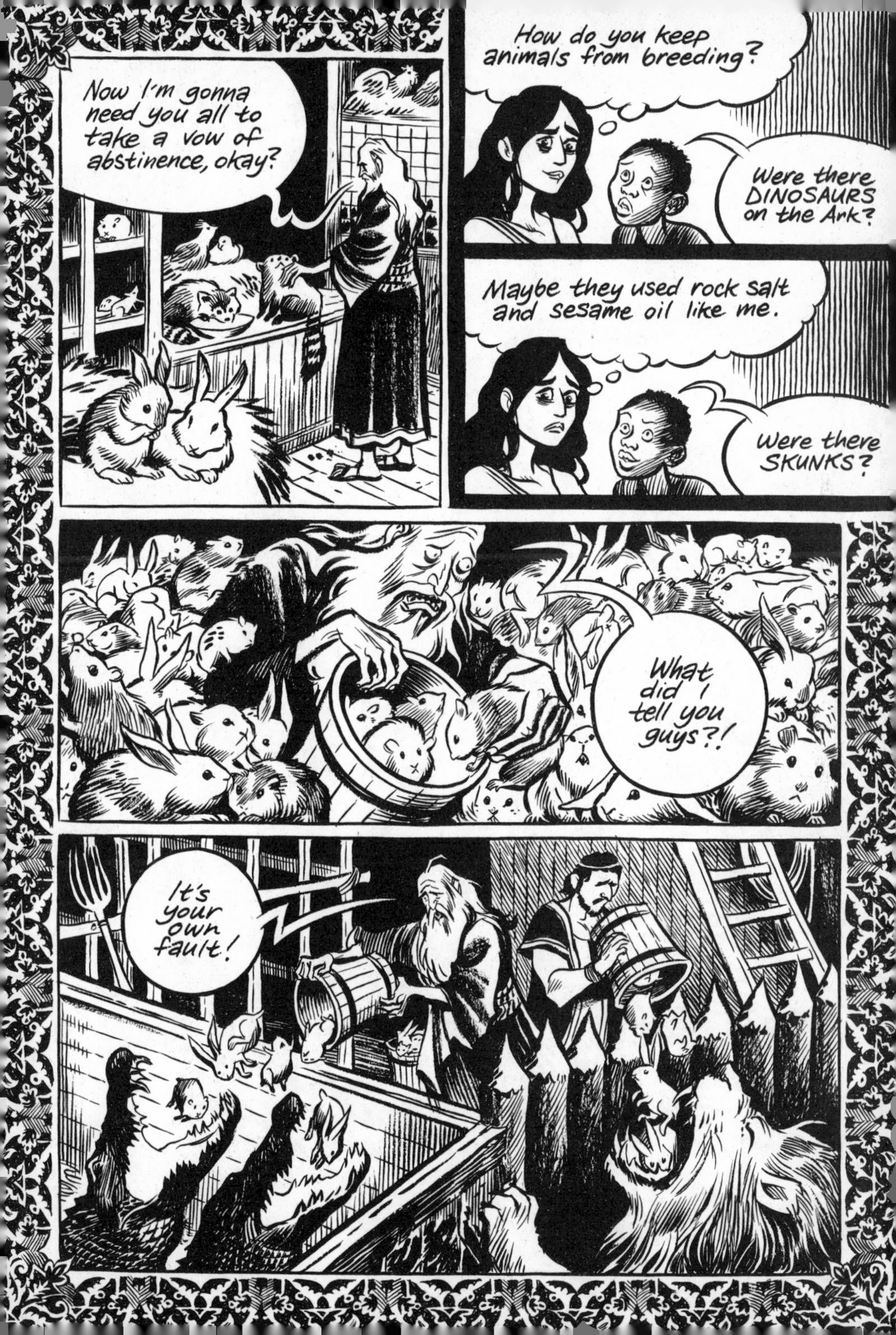

Now I'm gonna need you all to take a vow of abstinence, okay?
How do you keep animals from breeding?
Were there DINOSAURS on the Ark?
Maybe they used rock salt and sesame oil like me.
Were there SKUNKS?
What did I tell you guys?!
It's your own fault!

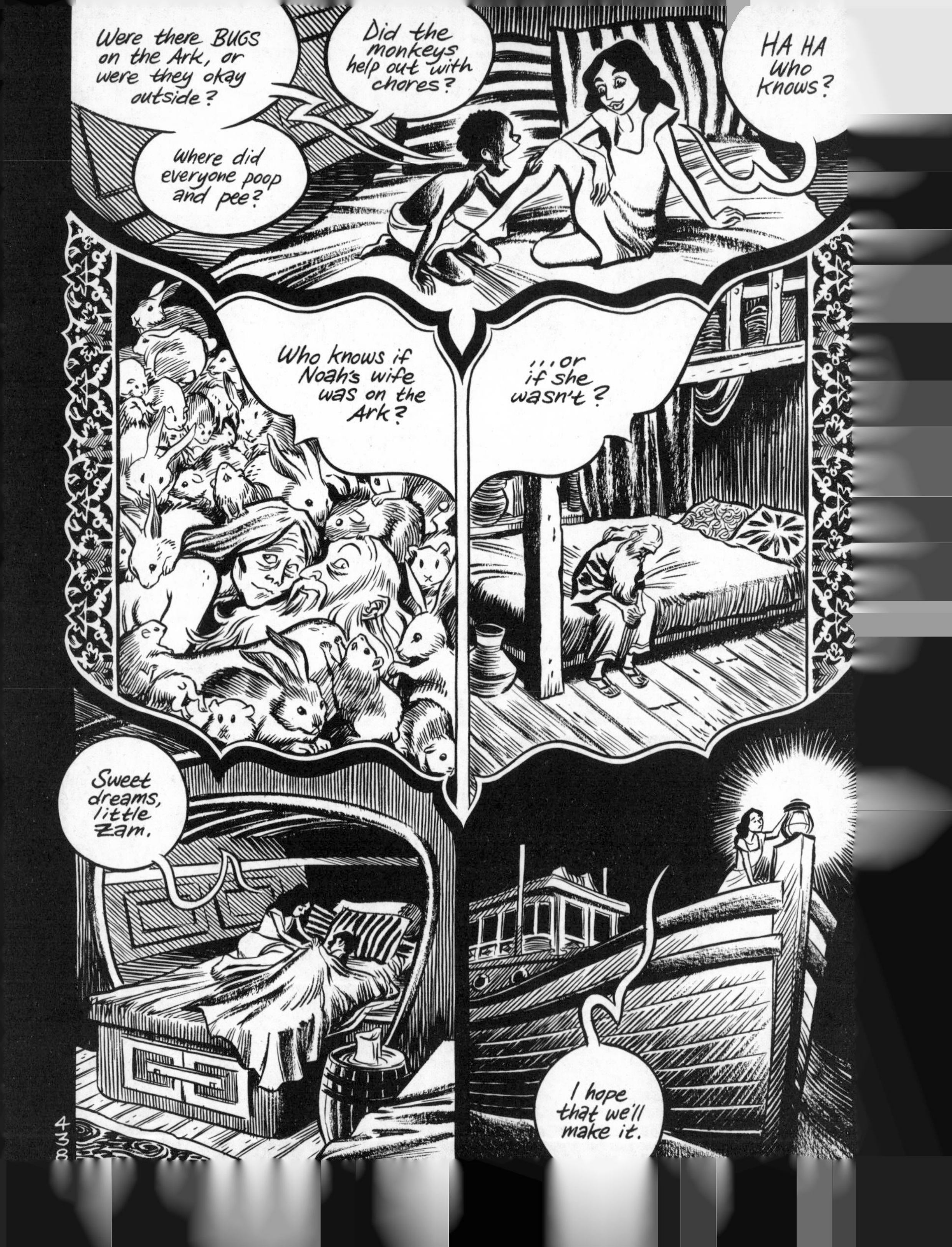
Were there BUGS on the Ark, or were they okay outside?
Did the monkeys help out with chores?
Where did everyone poop and pee?
HA HA Who knows?
Who knows if Noah's wife was on the Ark?
...or if she wasn't?
Sweet dreams, little Zam.
I hope that we'll make it.

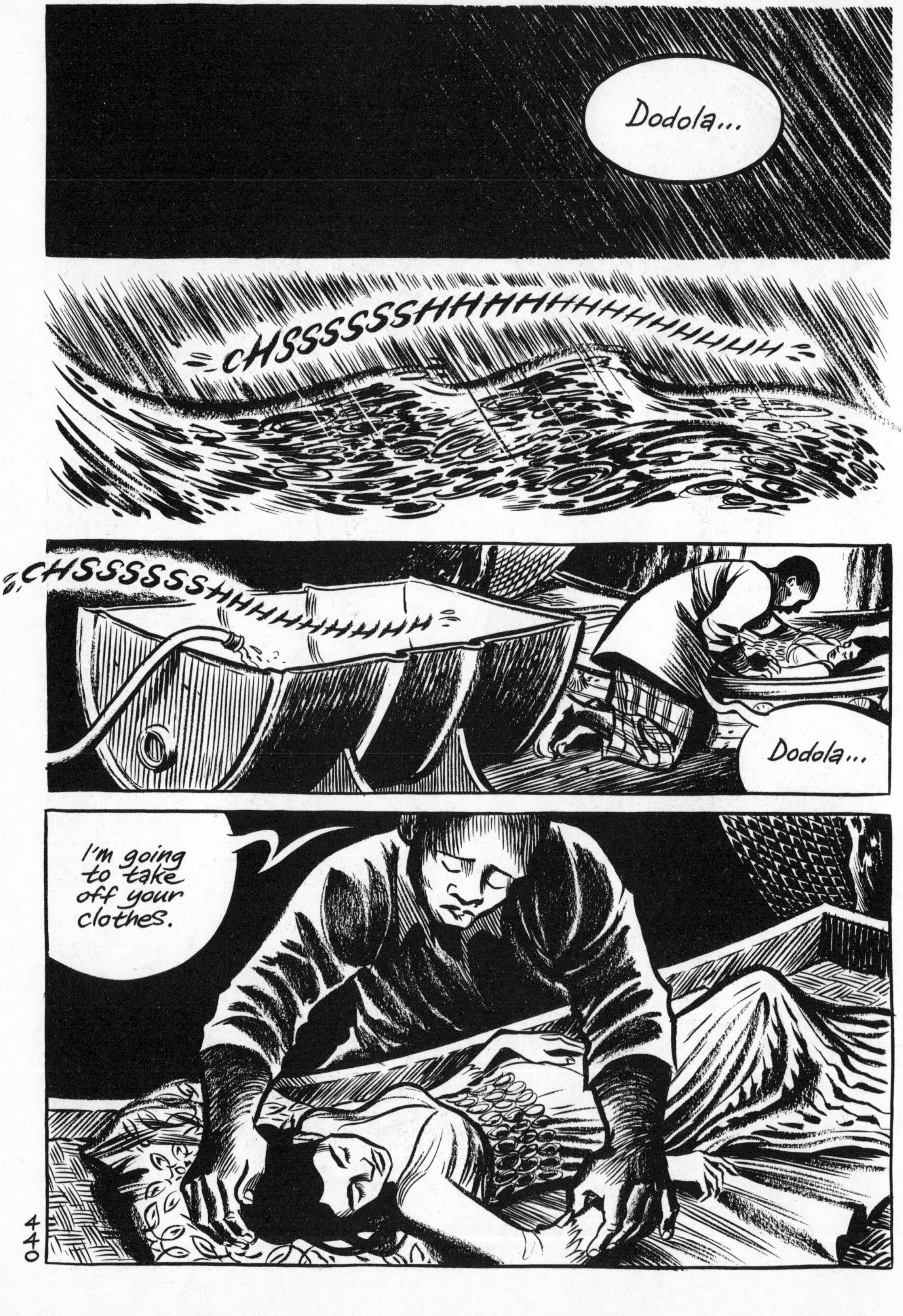
Dodola...
CHSSSSSSHHHHHHHHHHHHHHH
CHSSSSSSSHHHHHHHHHHHH
Dodola...
I'm going to take off your clothes.

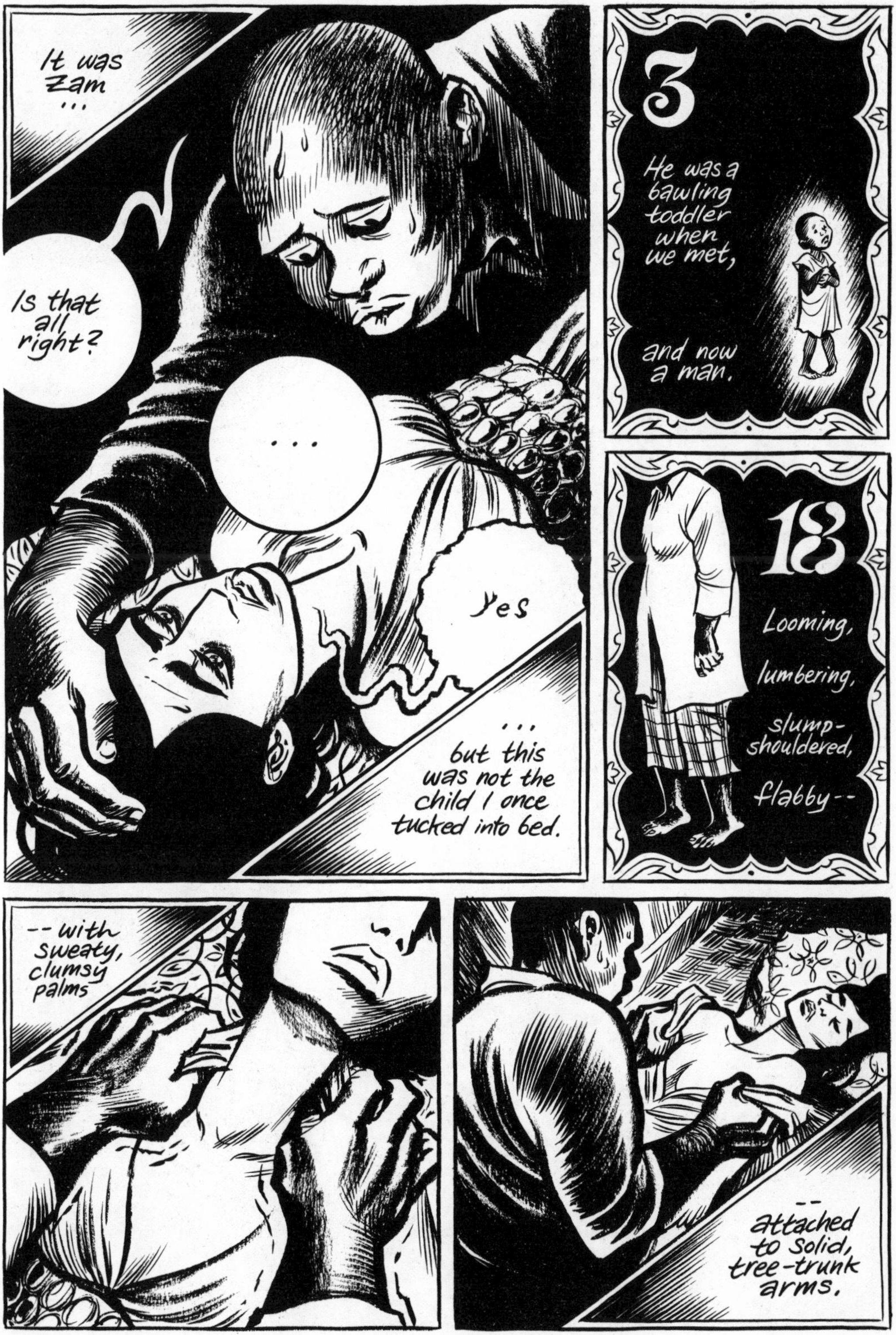
It was Zam ...
Is that all right?
...
Yes
3
He was a bawling toddler when we met,
and now a man.
... but this was not the child I once tucked into bed.
18
Looming,
lumbering,
slump-shouldered,
flabby--
--with sweaty, clumsy palms
--attached to solid, tree-trunk arms.

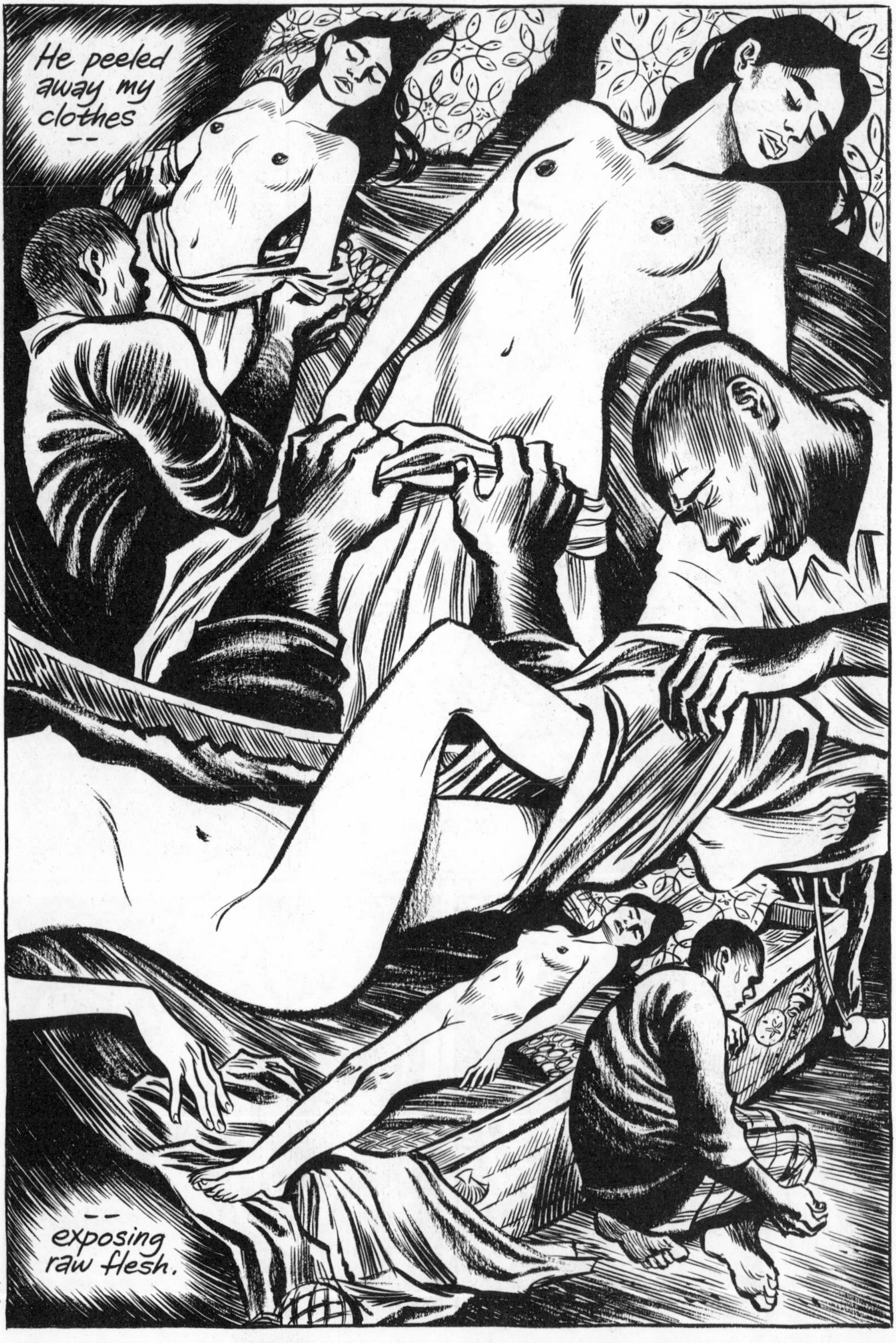
He peeled away my clothes --
-- exposing raw flesh.

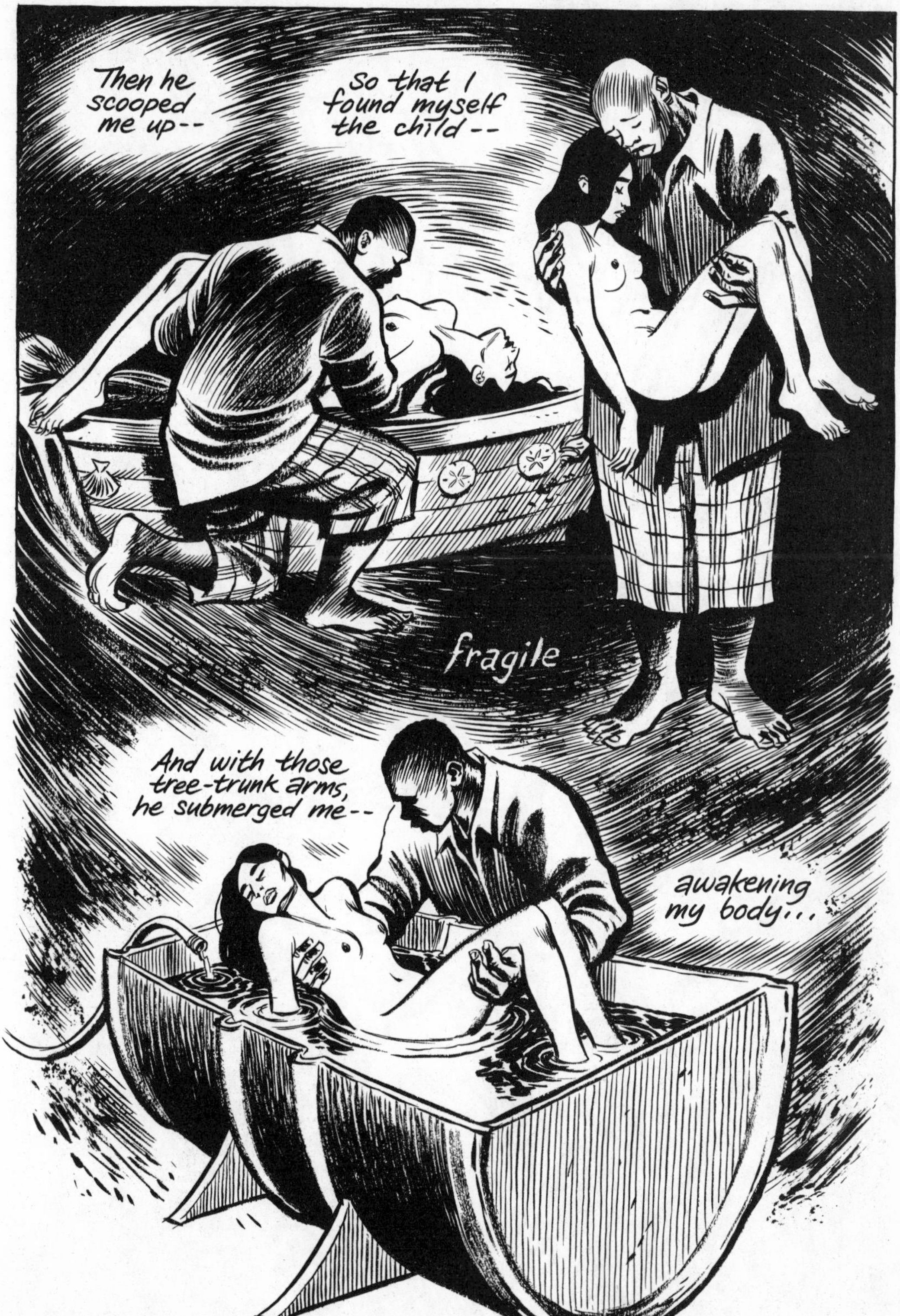
Then he scooped me up--
So that I found myself the child--
fragile
And with those tree-trunk arms, he submerged me--
awakening my body...

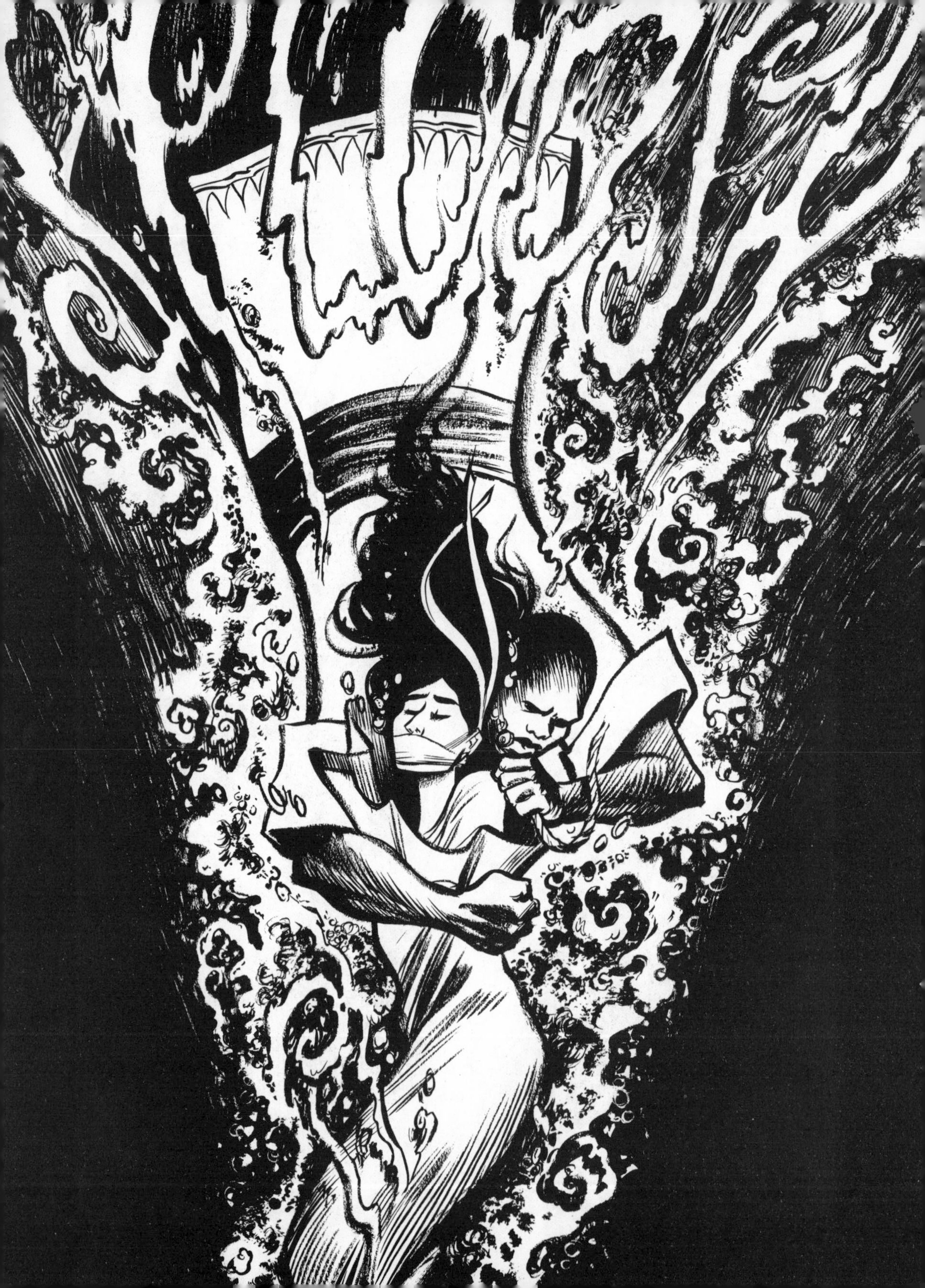

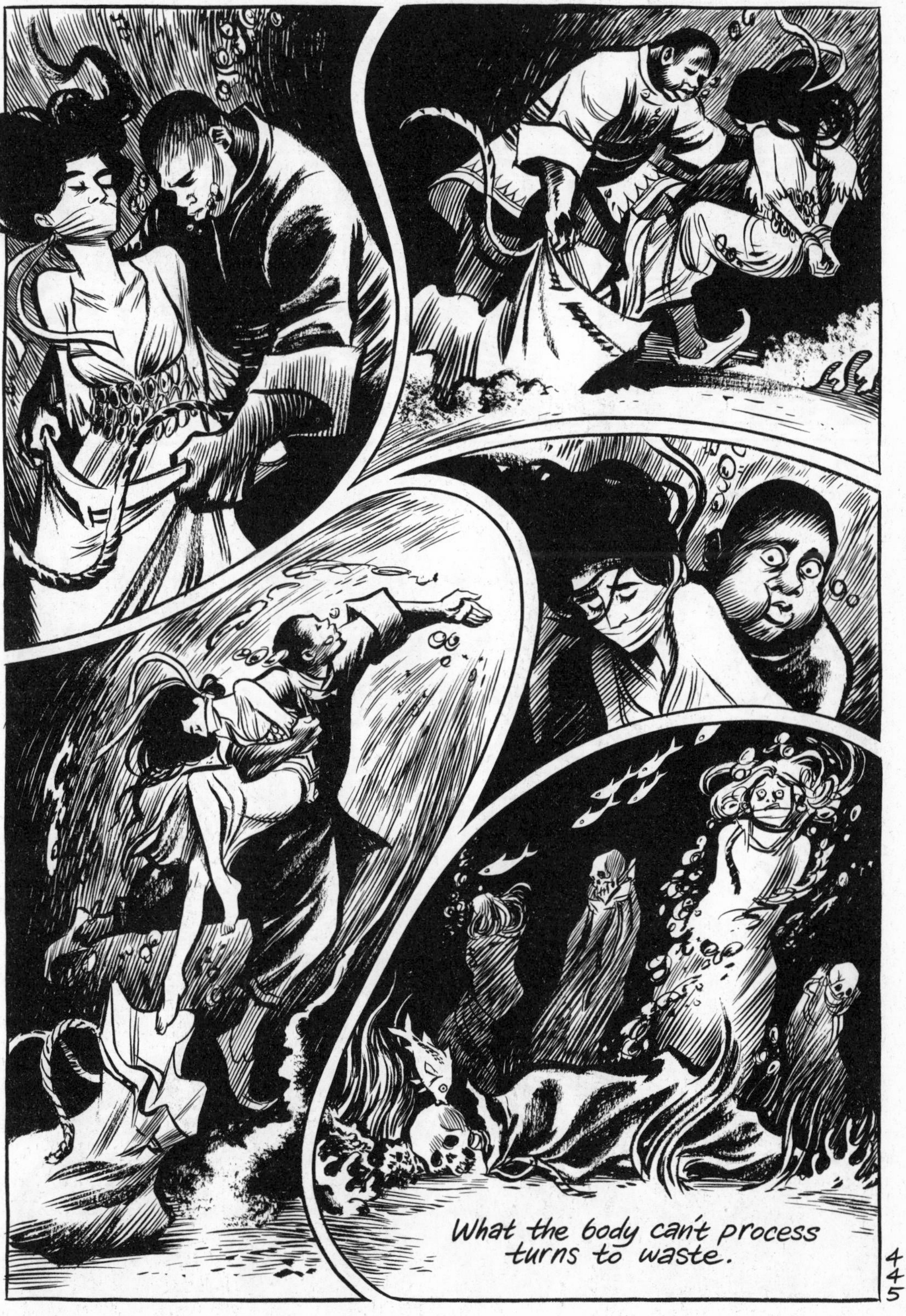
What the body can't process
turns to waste.

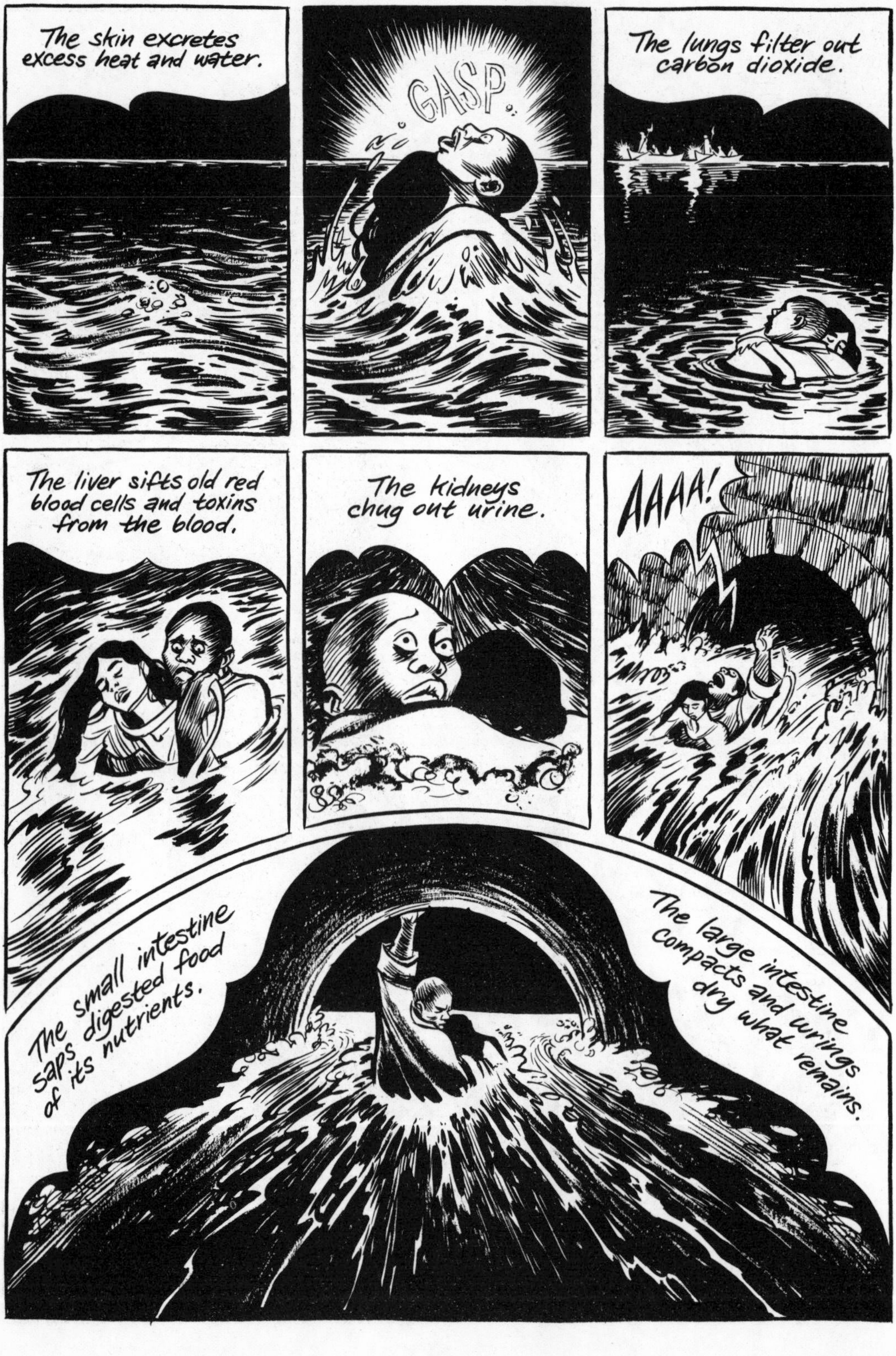
The skin excretes excess heat and water.
GASP.
The lungs filter out carbon dioxide.
The liver sifts old red blood cells and toxins from the blood.
The kidneys chug out urine.
AAAA!
The small intestine saps digested food of its nutrients.
The large intestine compacts and wrings dry what remains.

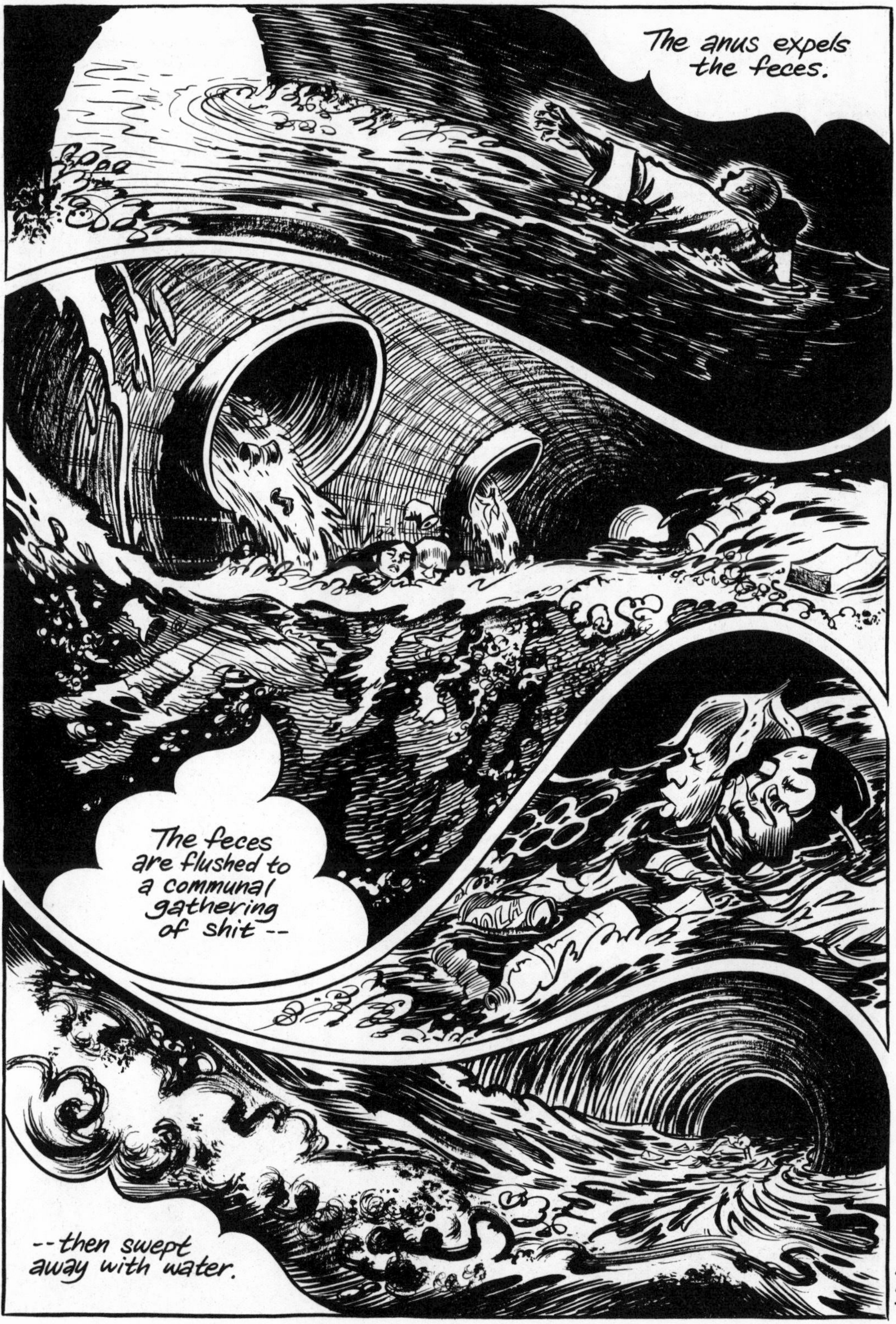
The anus expels the feces.
The feces are flushed to a communal gathering of shit --
-- then swept away with water.

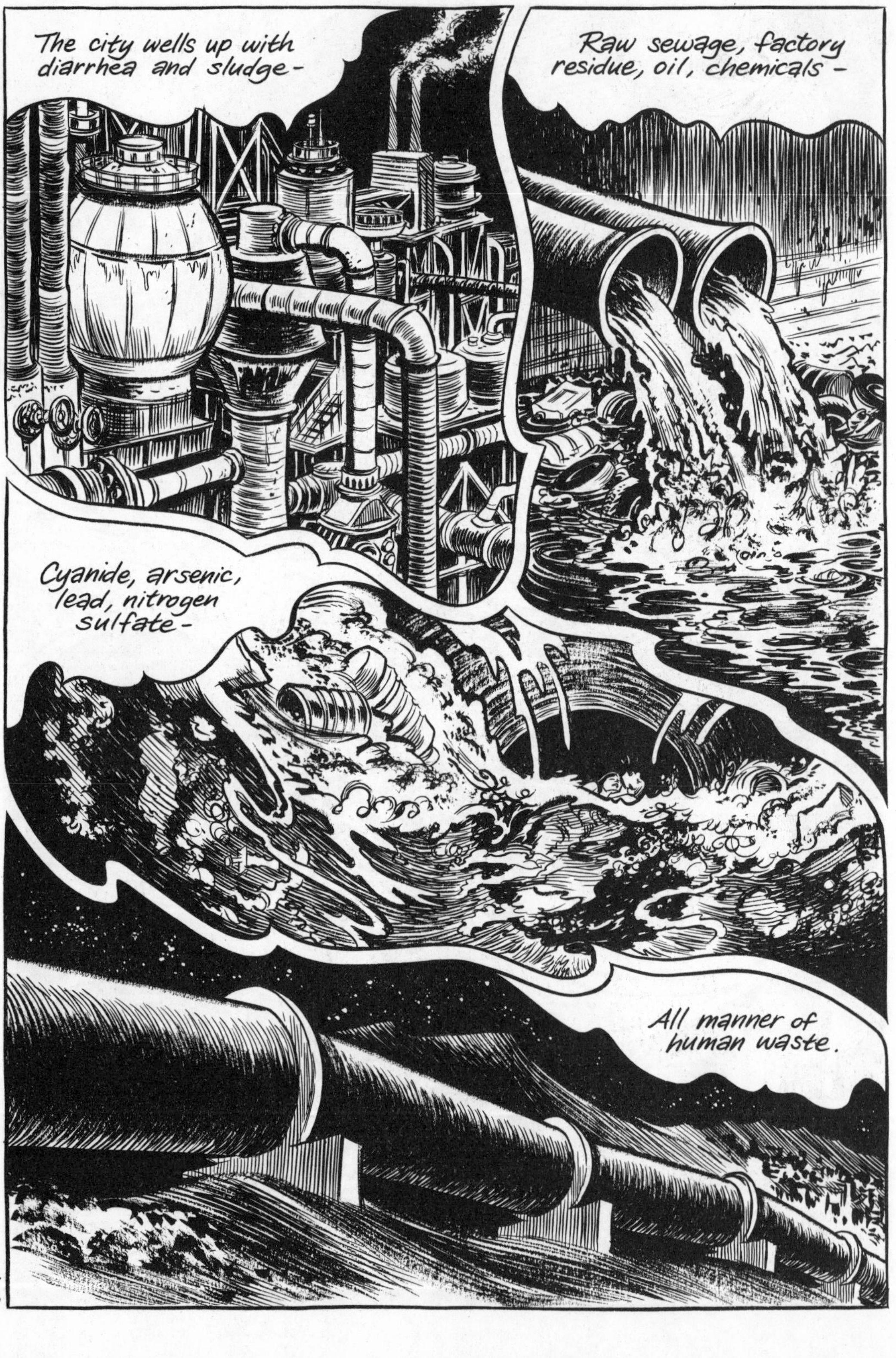
The city wells up with diarrhea and sludge-
Raw sewage, factory residue, oil, chemicals -
Cyanide, arsenic, lead, nitrogen sulfate-
All manner of human waste.

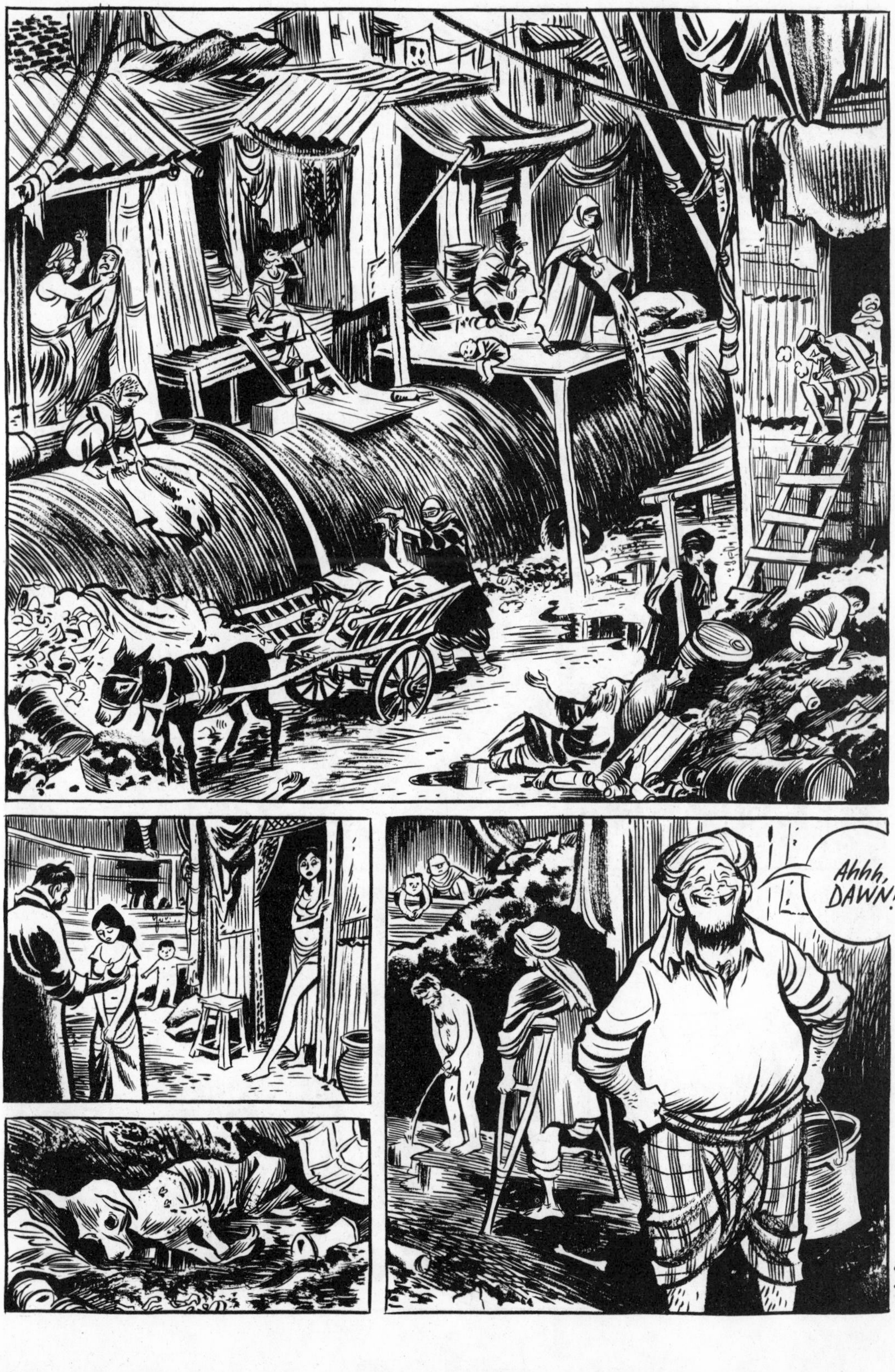
Ahhh, DAWN!

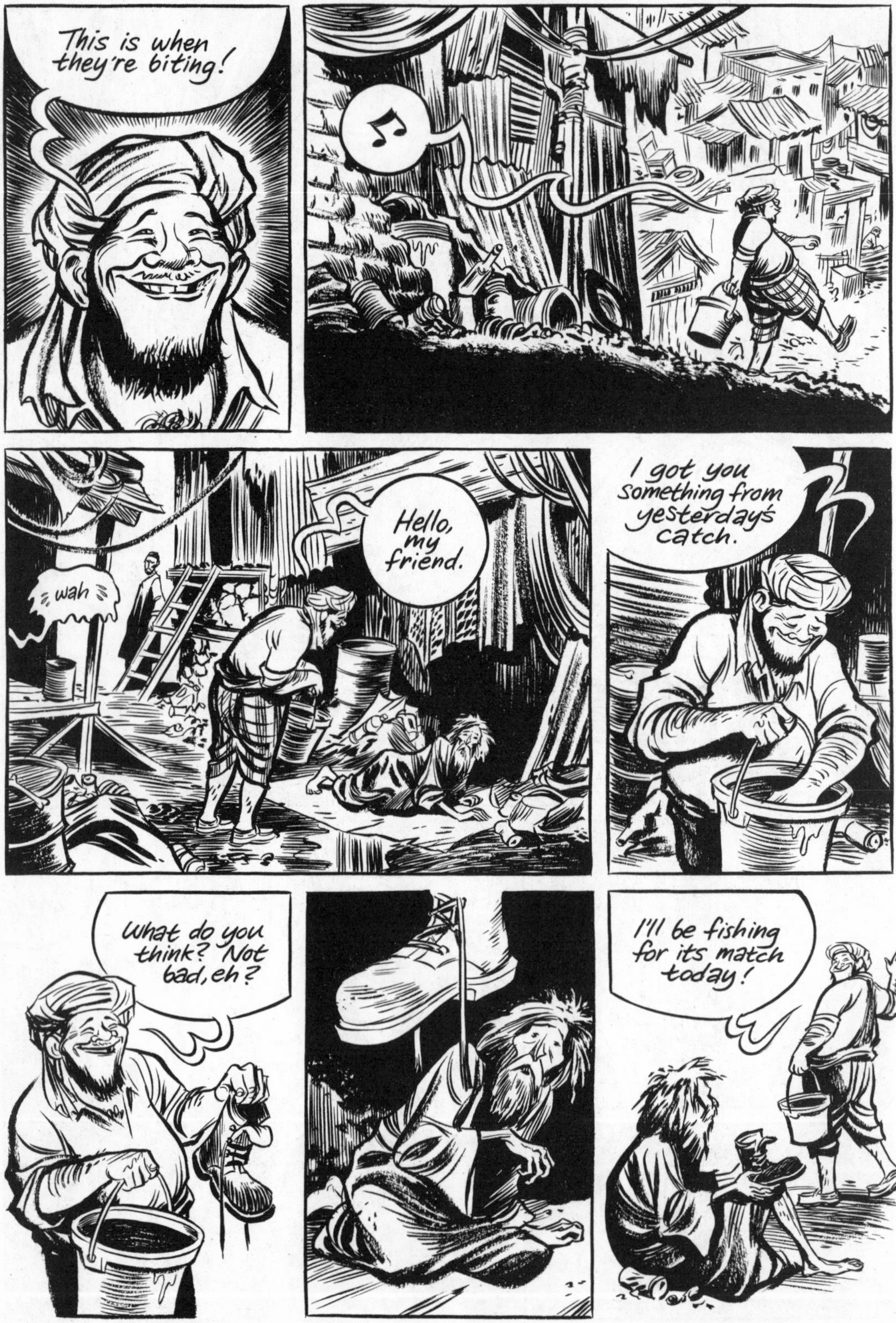
This is when they're biting!
♫
wah
Hello, my friend.
I got you something from yesterday's catch.
What do you think? Not bad, eh?
I'll be fishing for its match today!

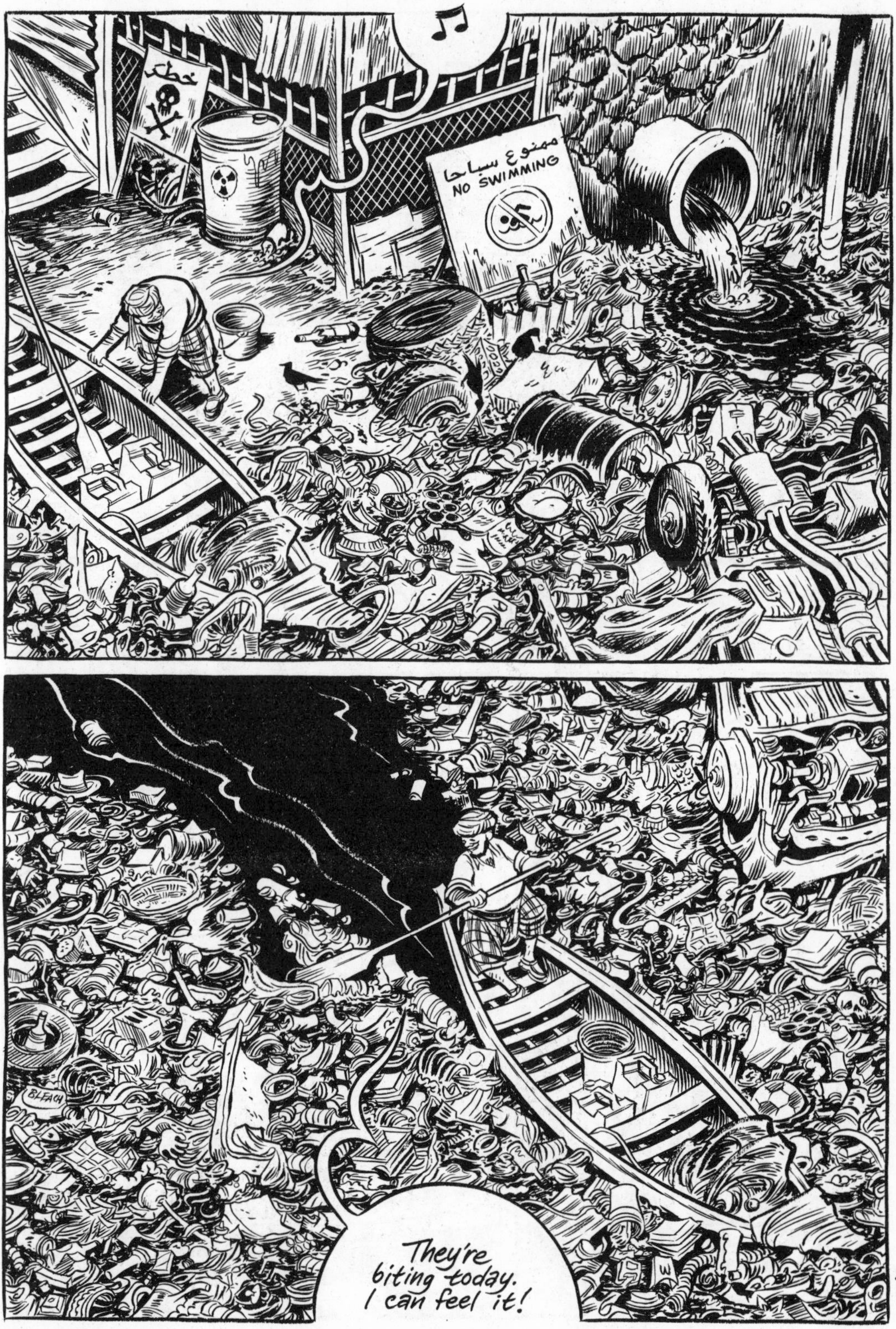
خطر
ممنوع سباحا
NO SWIMMING
BLEACH
They're biting today. I can feel it!

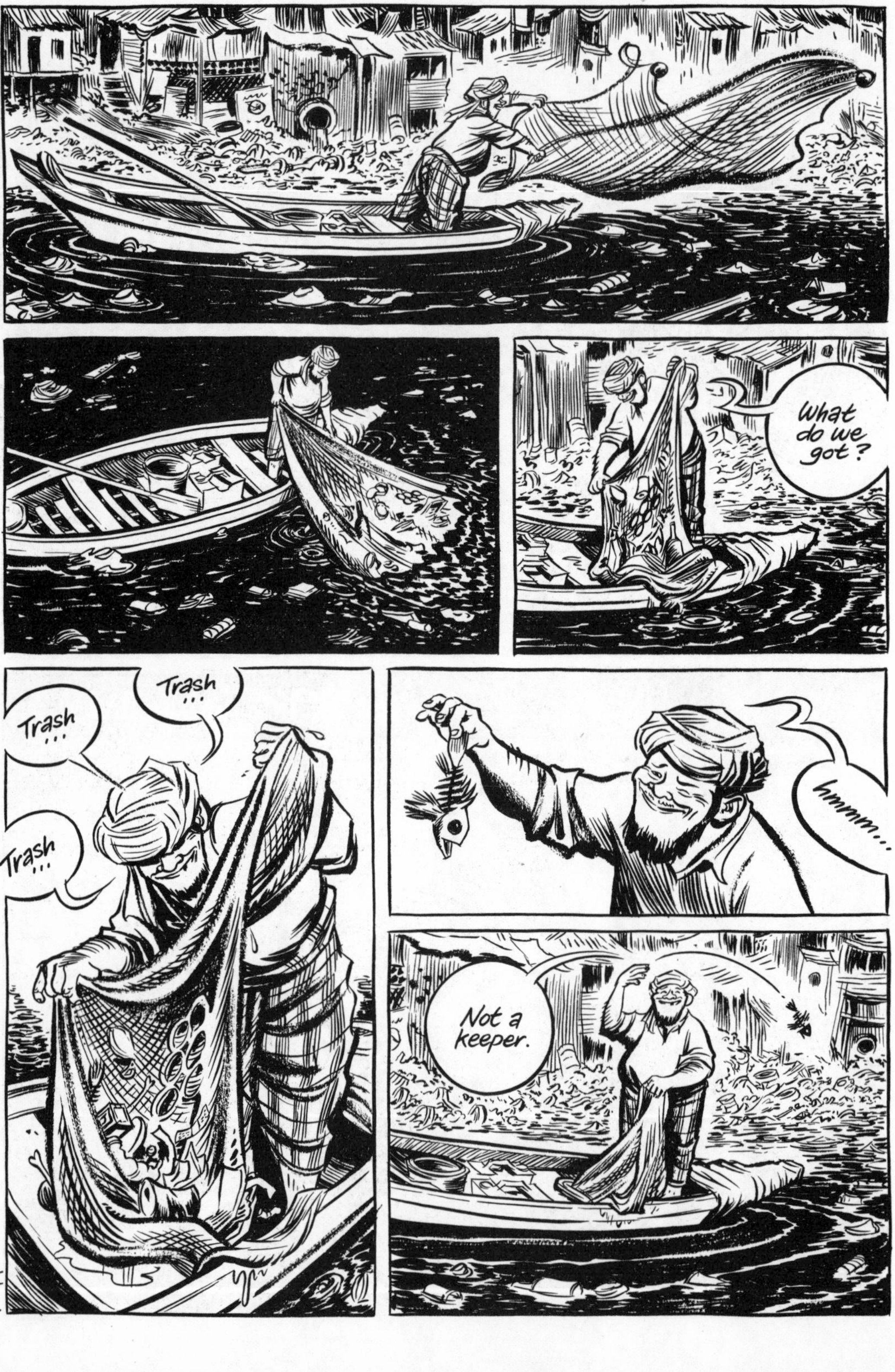

What do we got?
Trash...
Trash...
Trash...
hmmm...
Not a keeper.

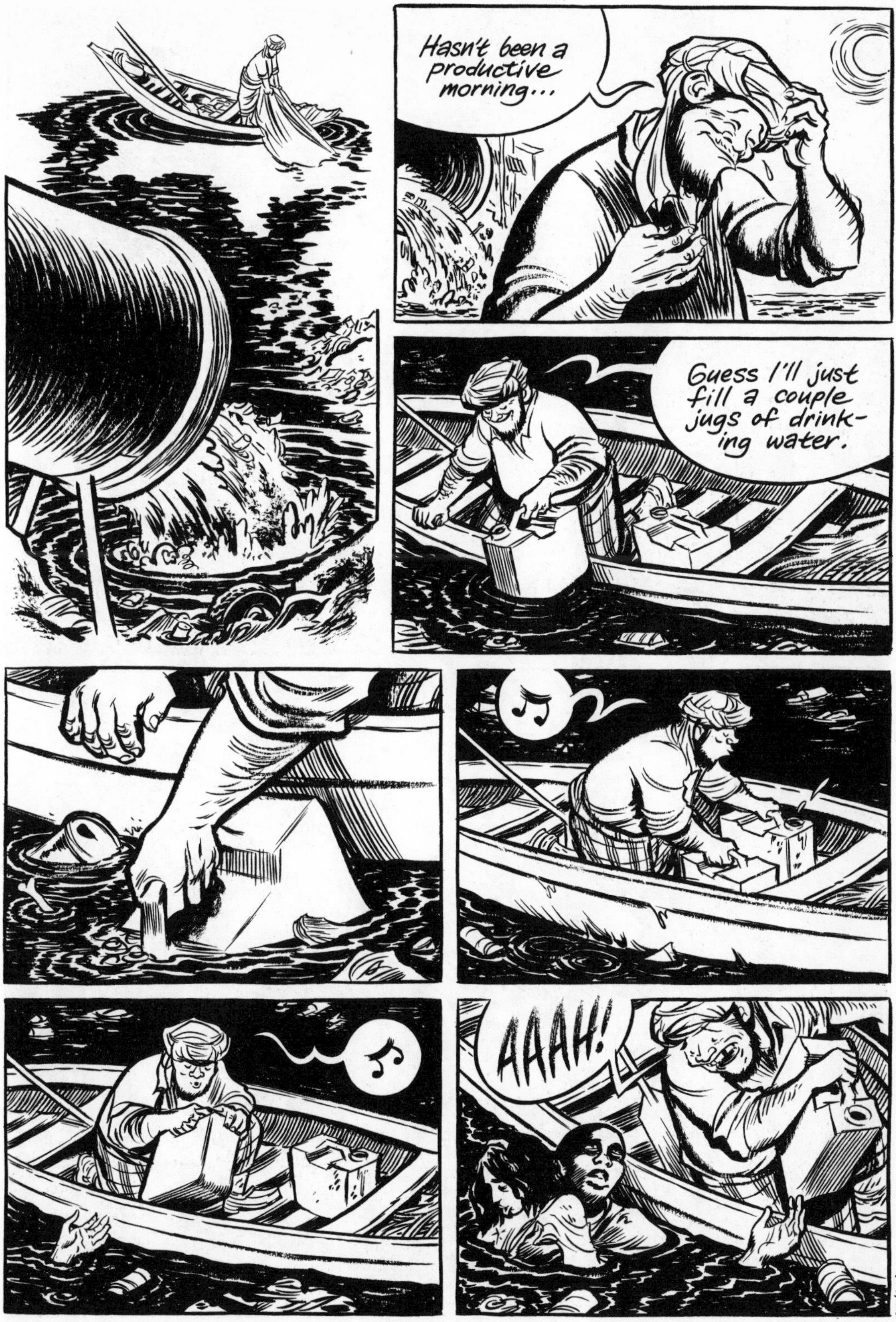

Hasn't been a productive morning...
Guess I'll just fill a couple jugs of drink-ing water.
♫
♫
AAAH!

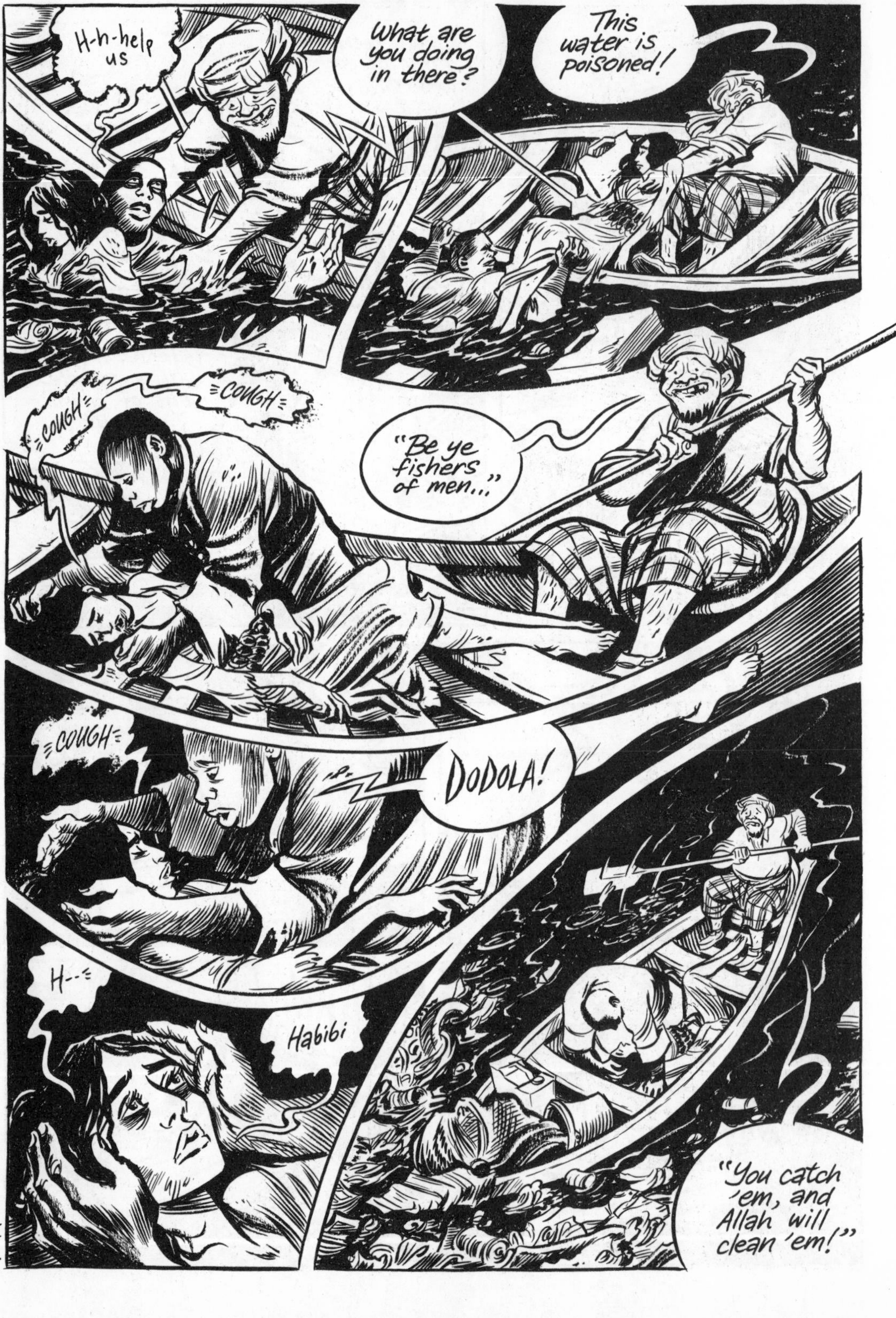
H-h-help us
What are you doing in there?
This water is poisoned!
COUGH
COUGH
"Be ye fishers of men..."
COUGH
DODOLA!
H--
Habibi
"You catch 'em, and Allah will clean 'em!"

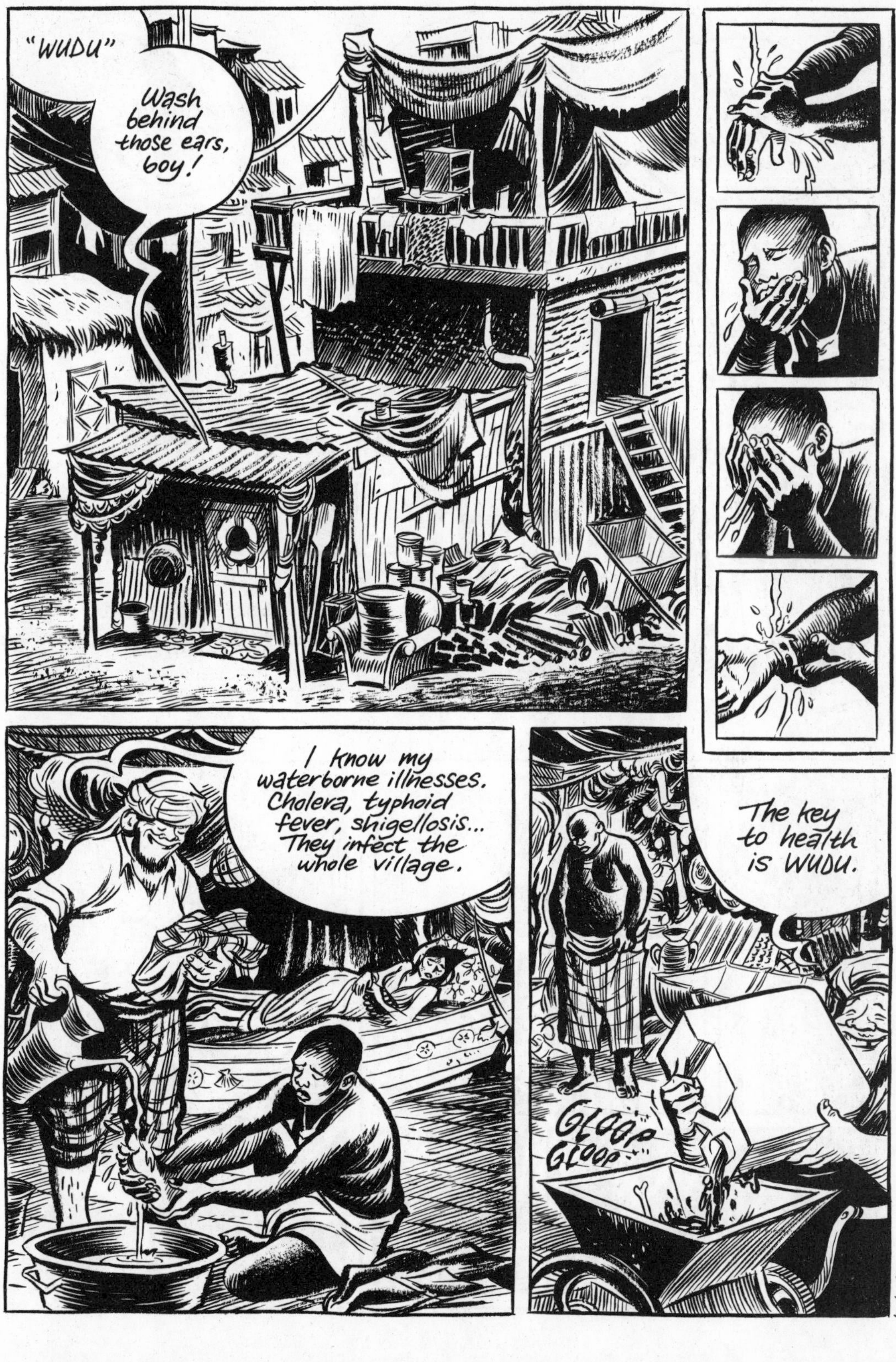
"WUDU"
Wash behind those ears, boy!
I know my waterborne illnesses. Cholera, typhoid fever, shigellosis... They infect the whole village.
The key to health is WUDU.
GLOOP GLOOP

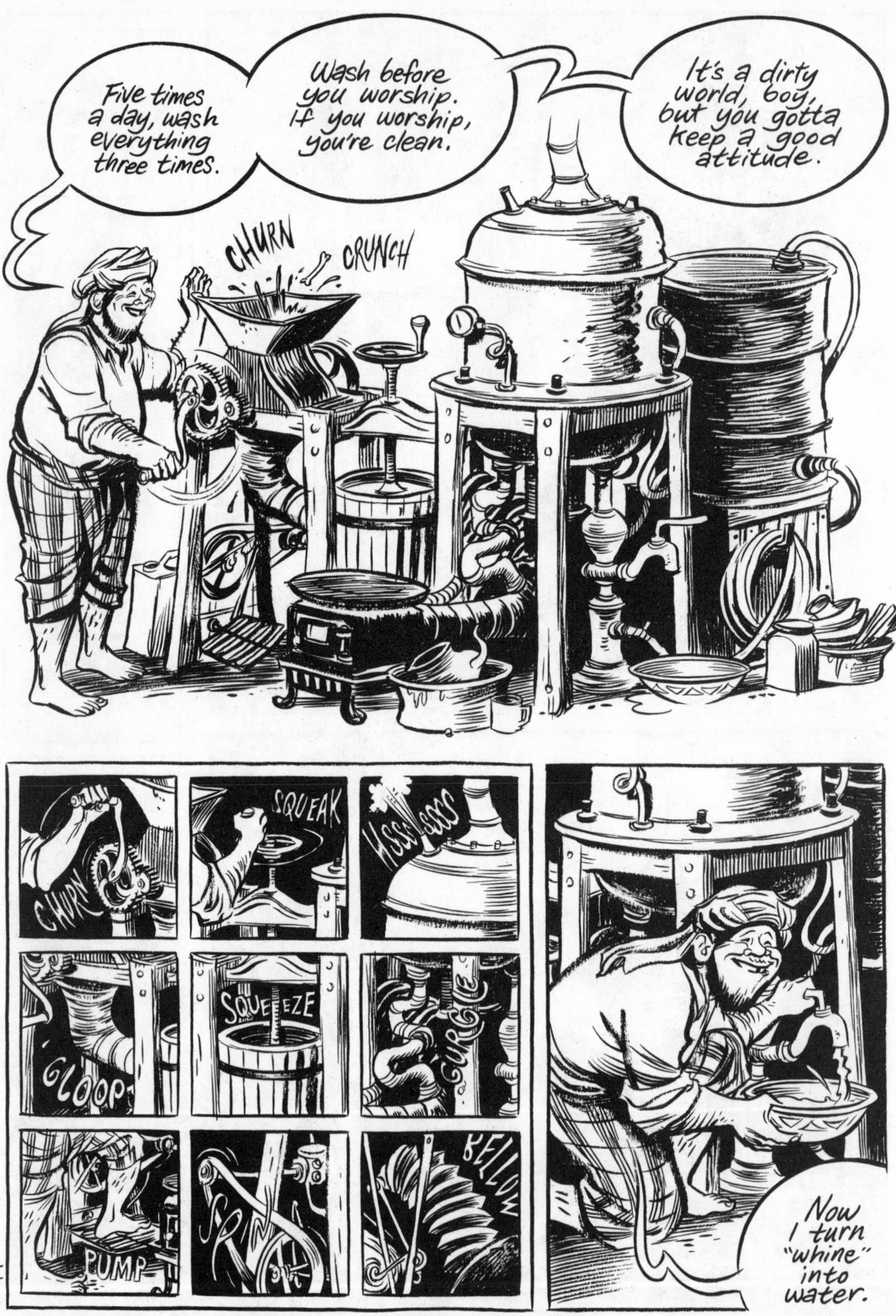
Five times a day, wash everything three times.
Wash before you worship. If you worship, you're clean.
It's a dirty world, boy, but you gotta keep a good attitude.
CHURN
CRUNCH
CHURN
SQUEAK
HSSSSSSS
GLOOP
SQUEEZE
GURGLE
PUMP
SPIN
BELLOW
Now I turn "whine" into water.

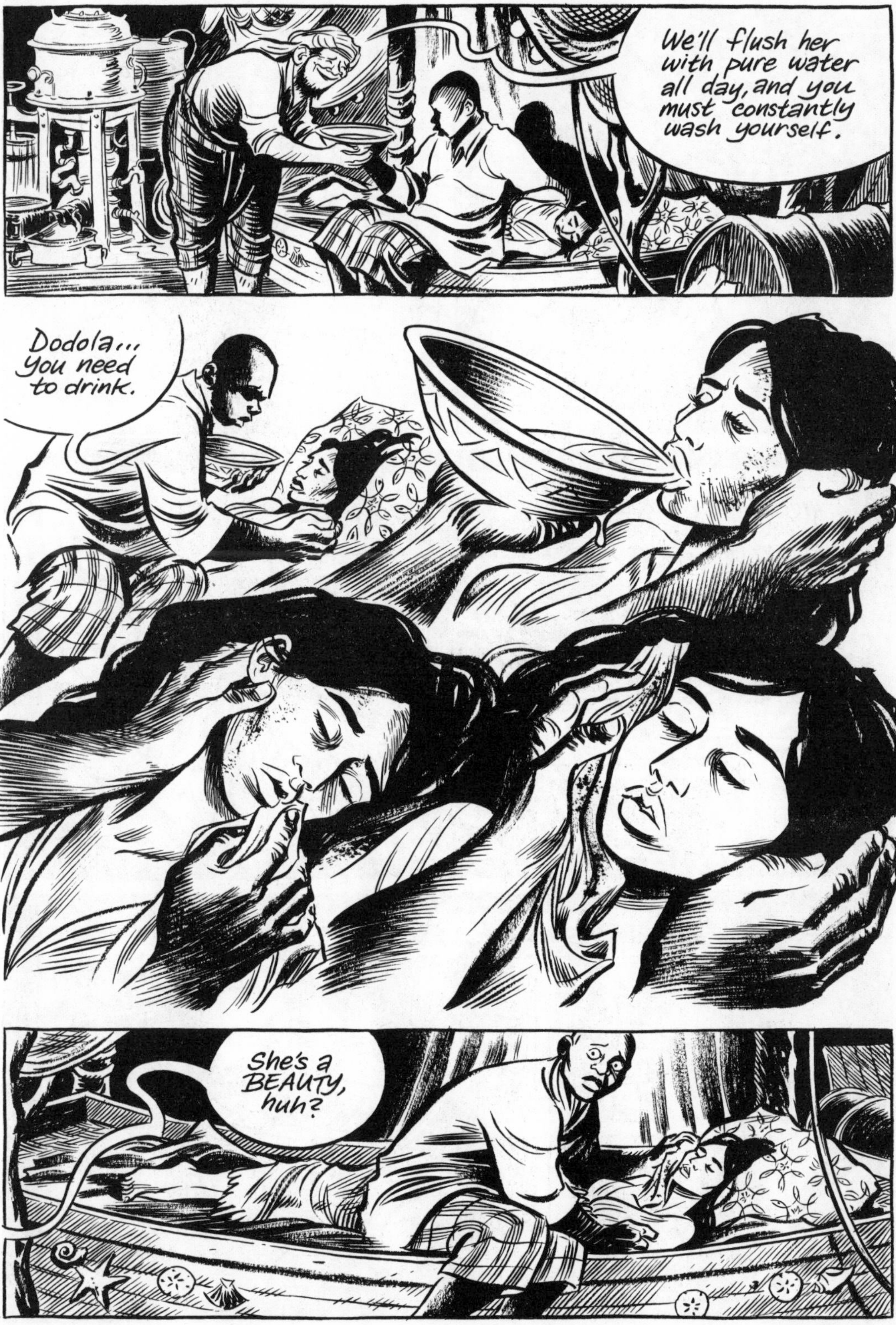
We'll flush her with pure water all day, and you must constantly wash yourself.
Dodola... You need to drink.
She's a BEAUTY, huh?

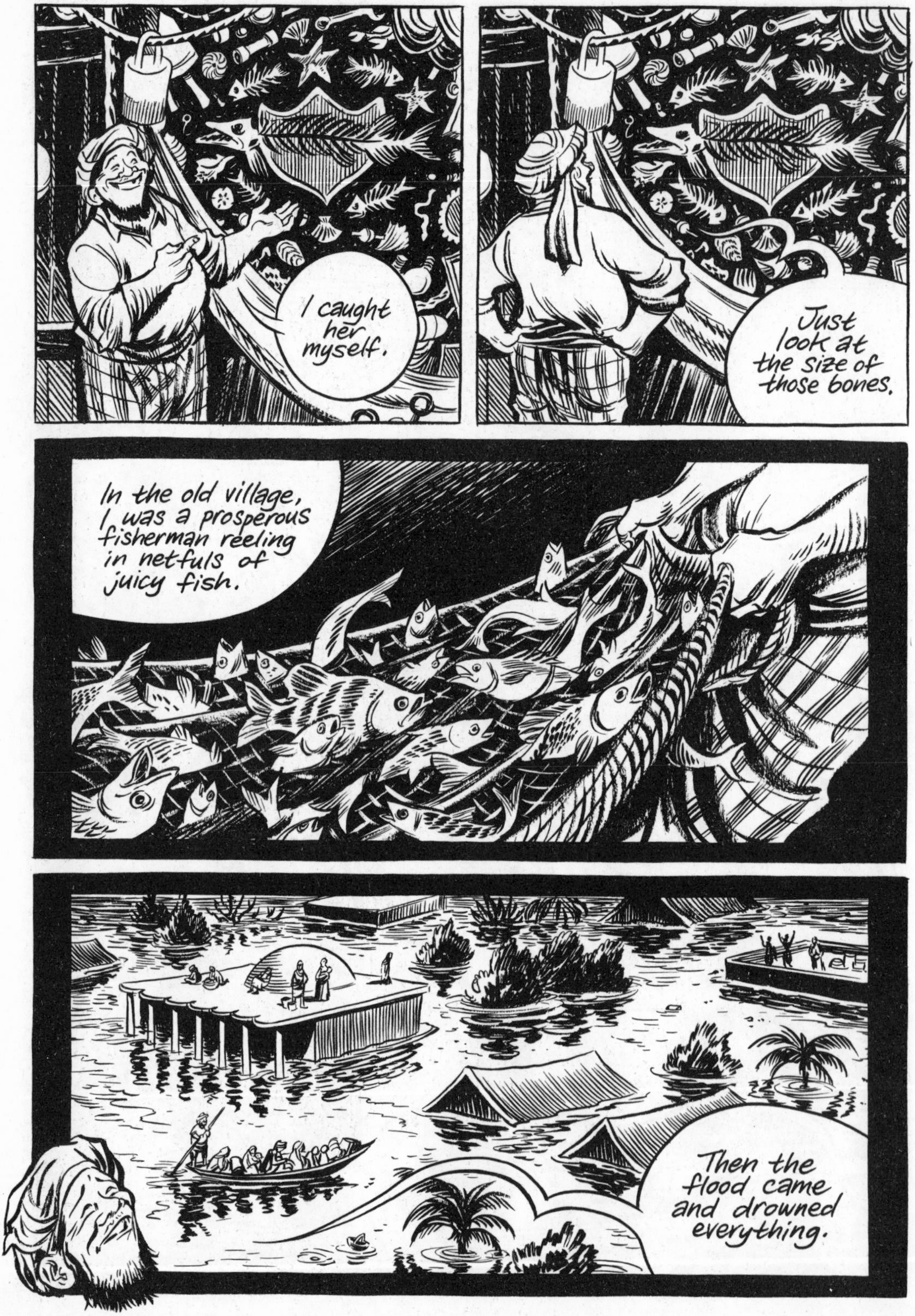
I caught her myself.
Just look at the size of those bones.
In the old village, I was a prosperous fisherman reeling in netfuls of juicy fish.
Then the flood came and drowned everything.

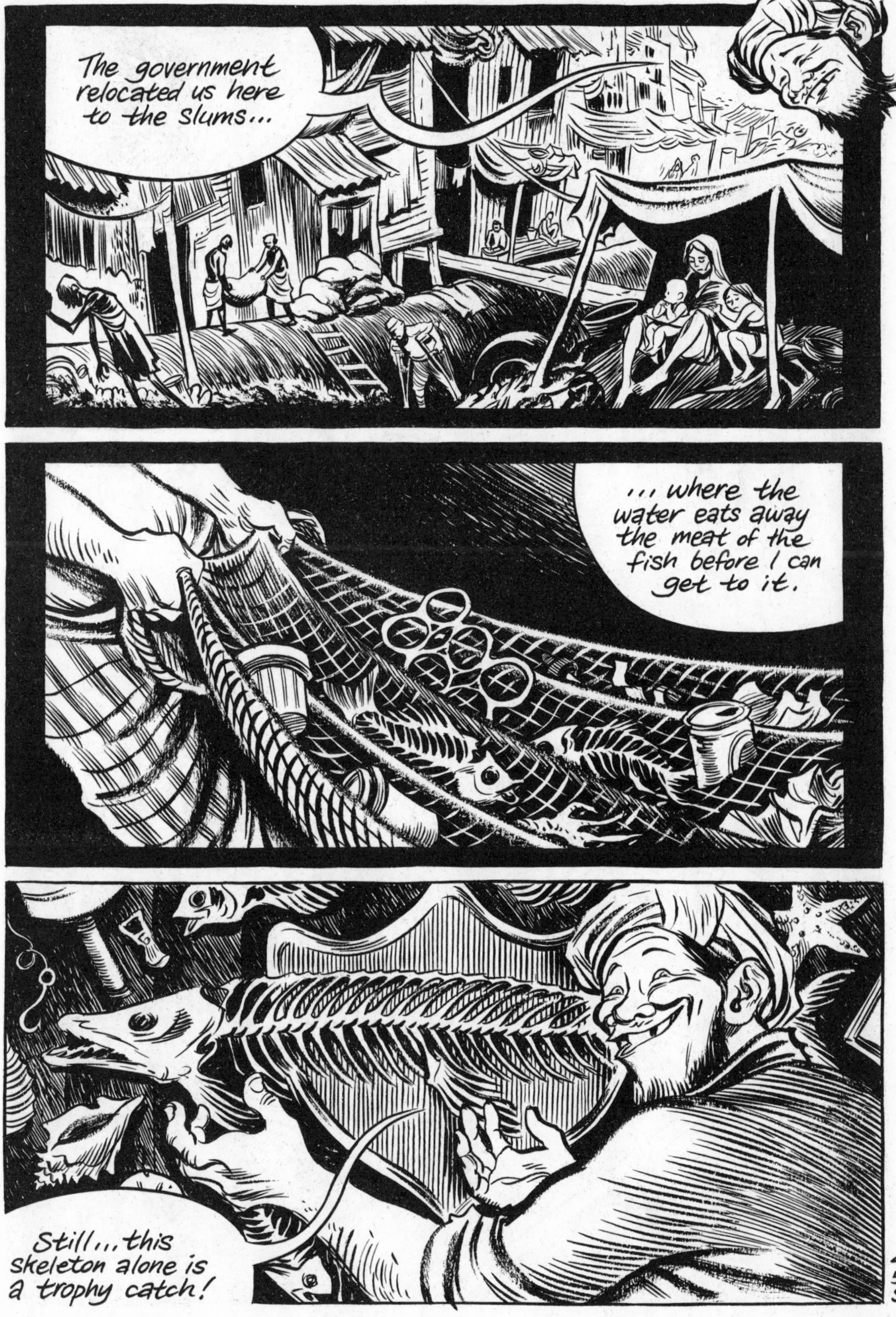
The government relocated us here to the slums...
... where the water eats away the meat of the fish before I can get to it.
Still... this skeleton alone is a trophy catch!

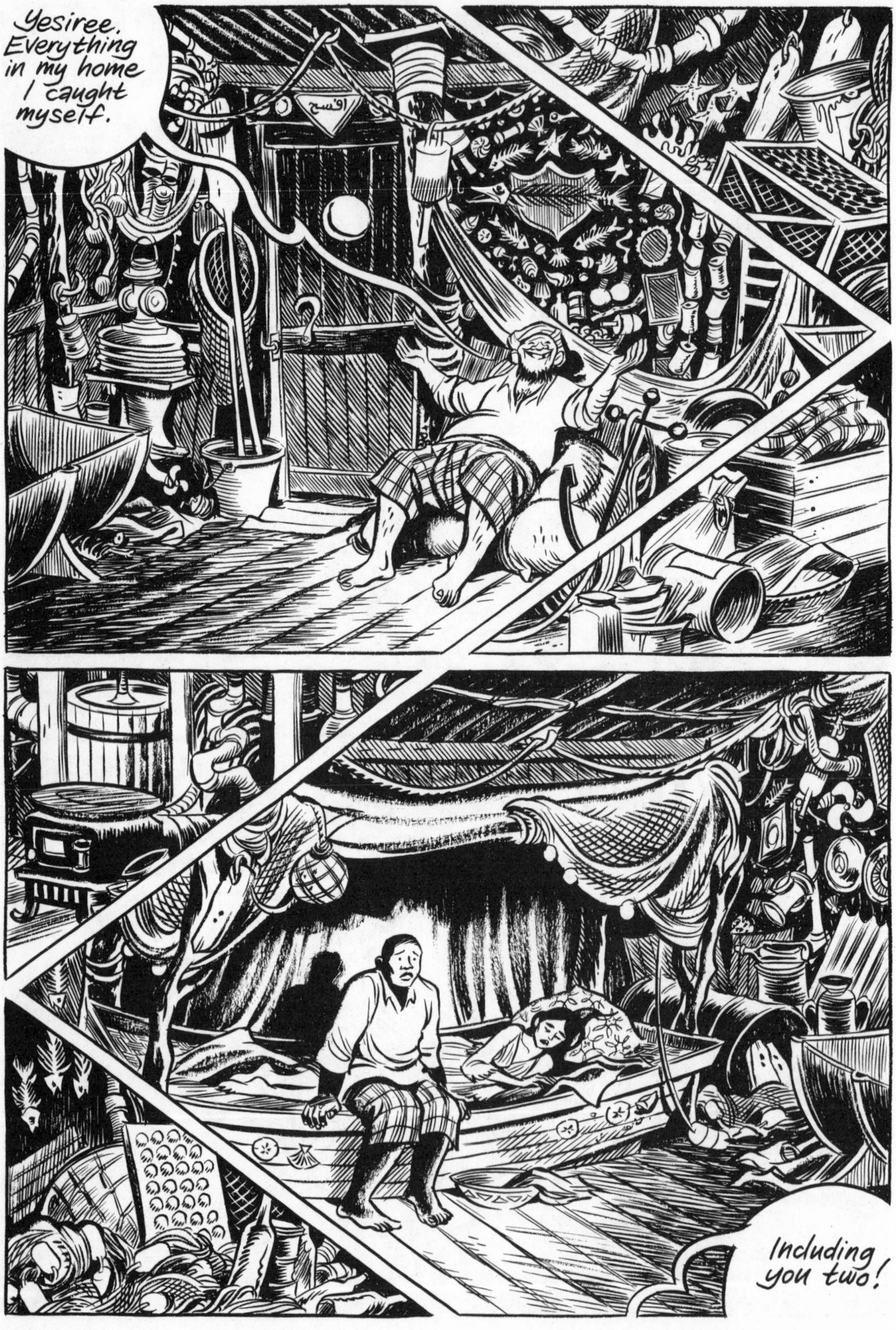
Yesiree. Everything in my home I caught myself.
Including you two!

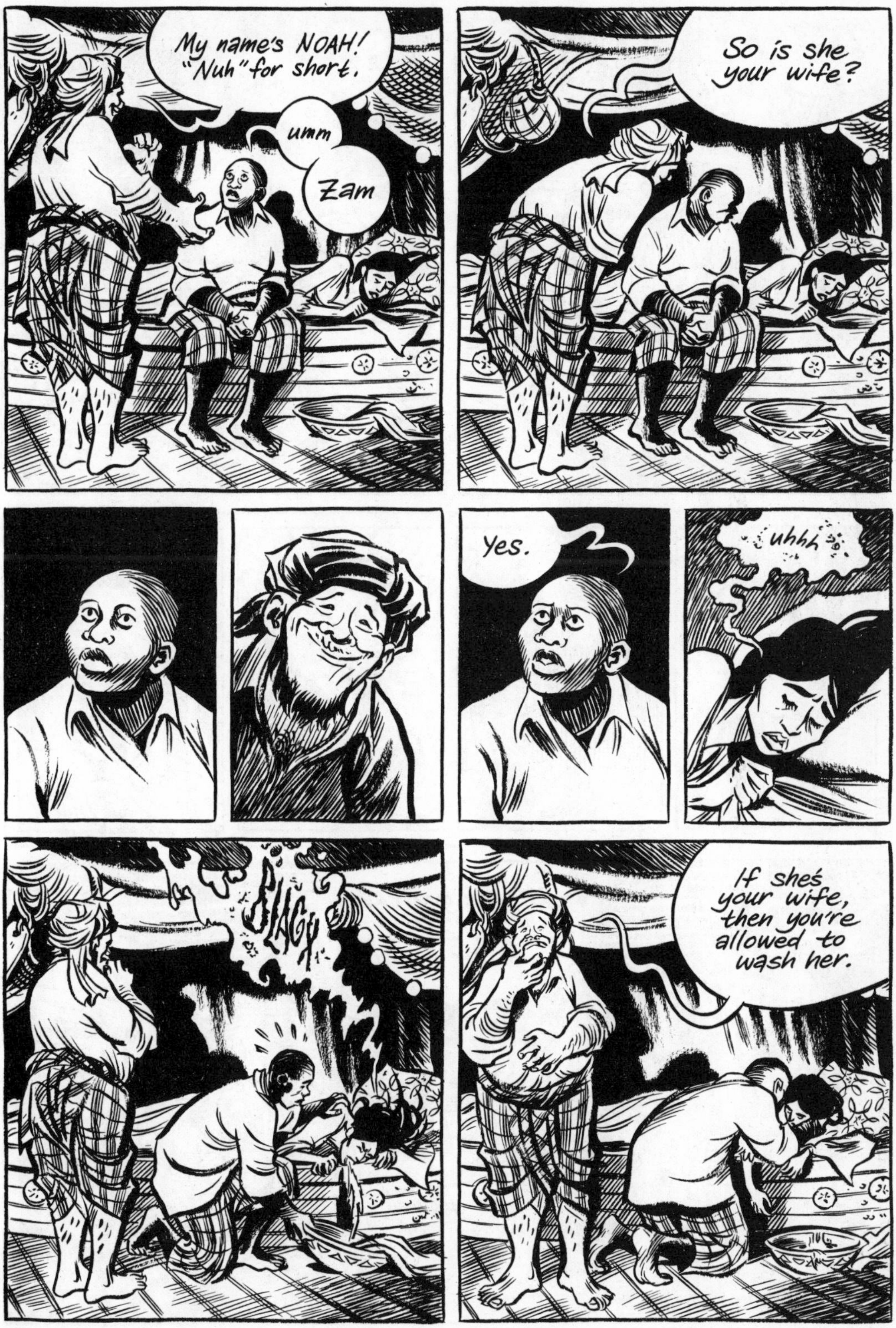
My name's NOAH! "Nuh" for short.
umm
Zam
So is she your wife?
Yes.
uhhh
BLAGH
If she's your wife, then you're allowed to wash her.

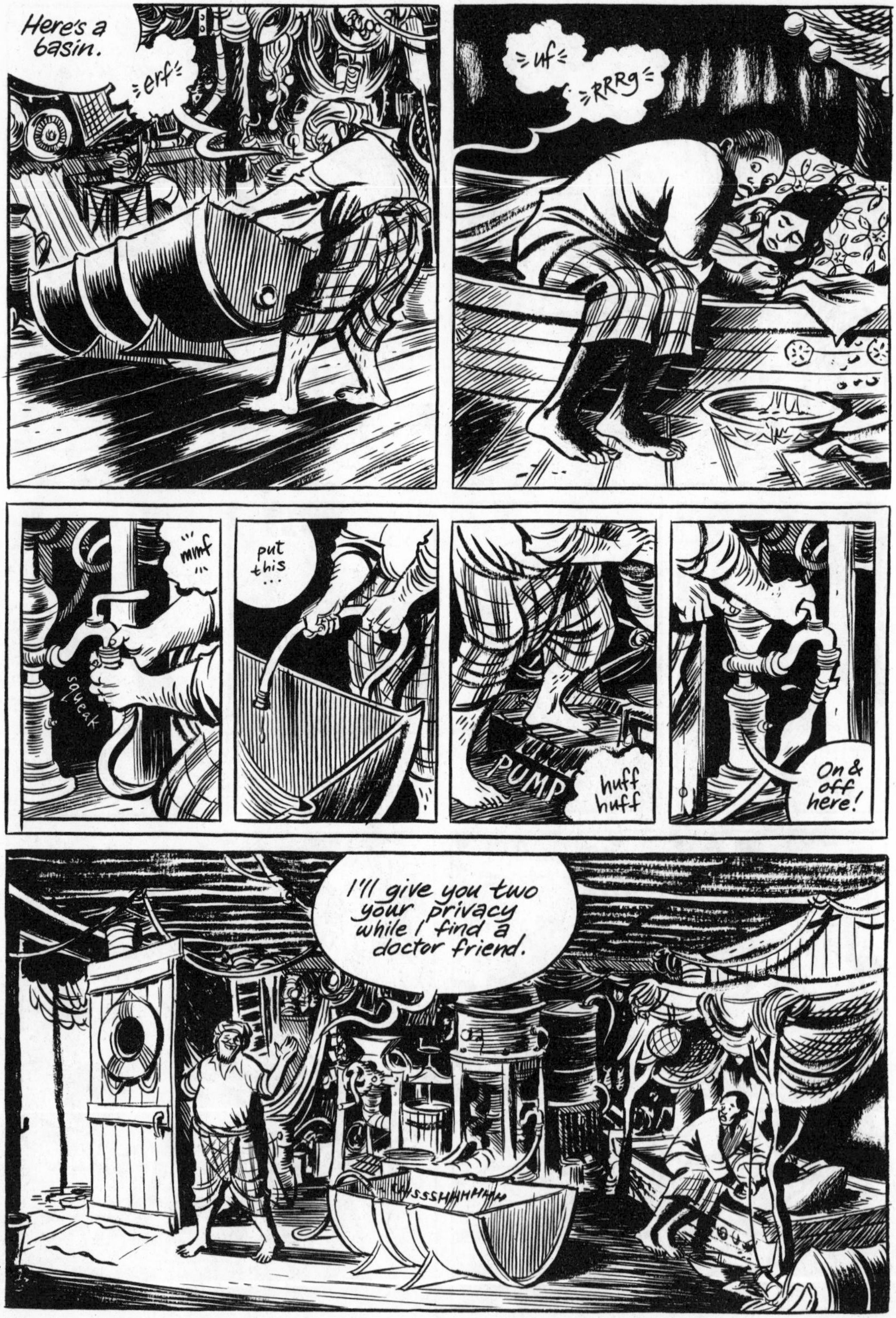
Here's a basin.
erf
uf
RRRg
mmf
squeak
put this...
PUMP
huff huff
On & off here!
I'll give you two your privacy while I find a doctor friend.

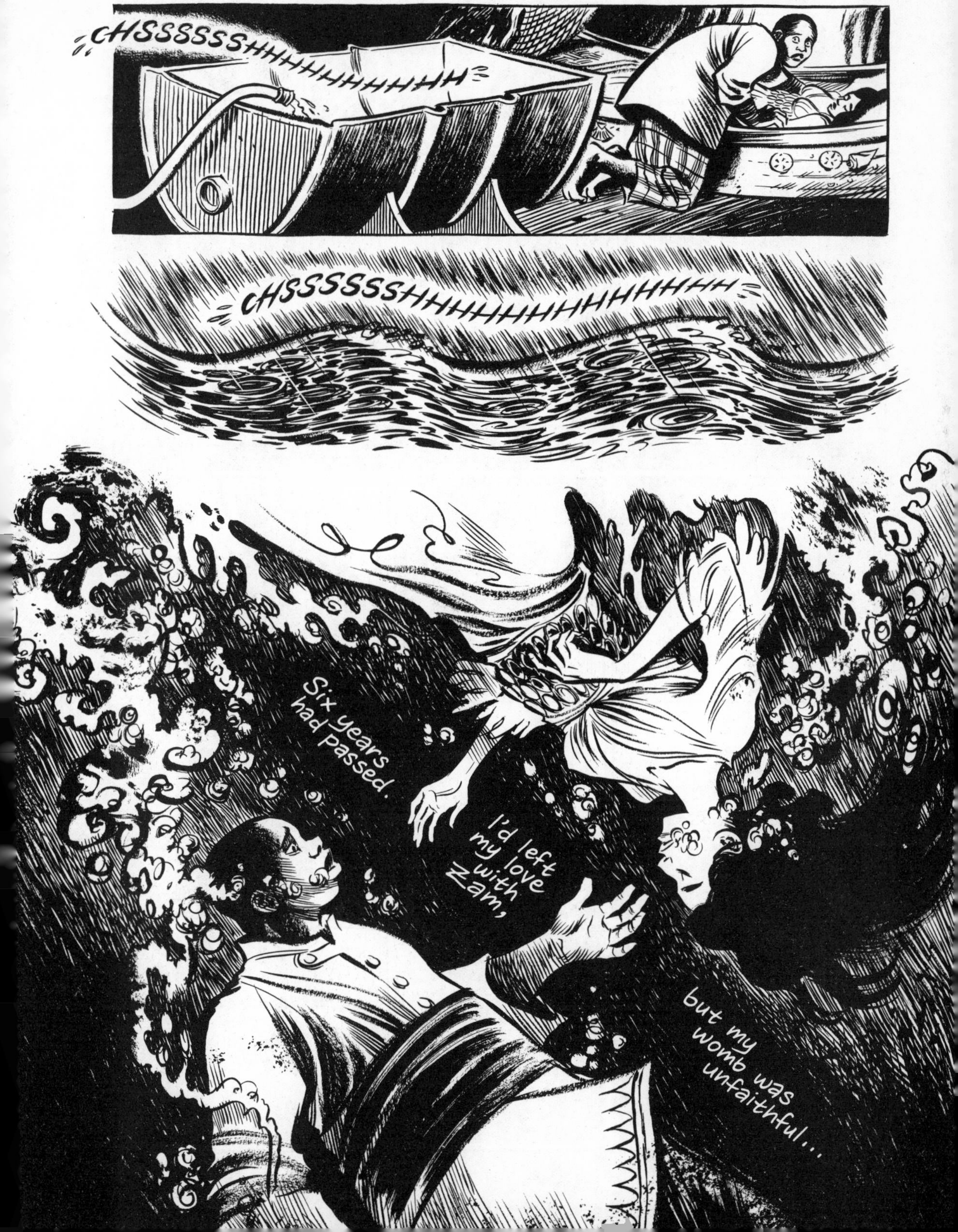
CHSSSSSSHHHHHHHHHHHH
CHSSSSSSHHHHHHHHHHHHHHHHH
Six years had passed.
I'd left my love with Zam,
but my womb was unfaithful...

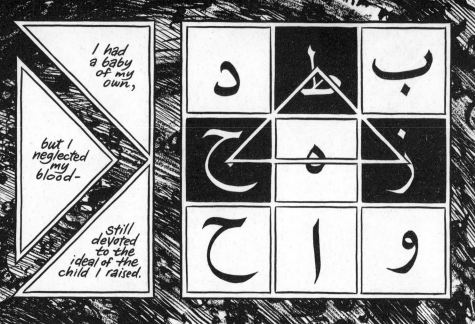

I had a baby of my own,

but I neglected my blood—

still devoted to the ideal of the child I raised.

Now my baby was dead,

and my child was, too—

disappeared into the body of a man.

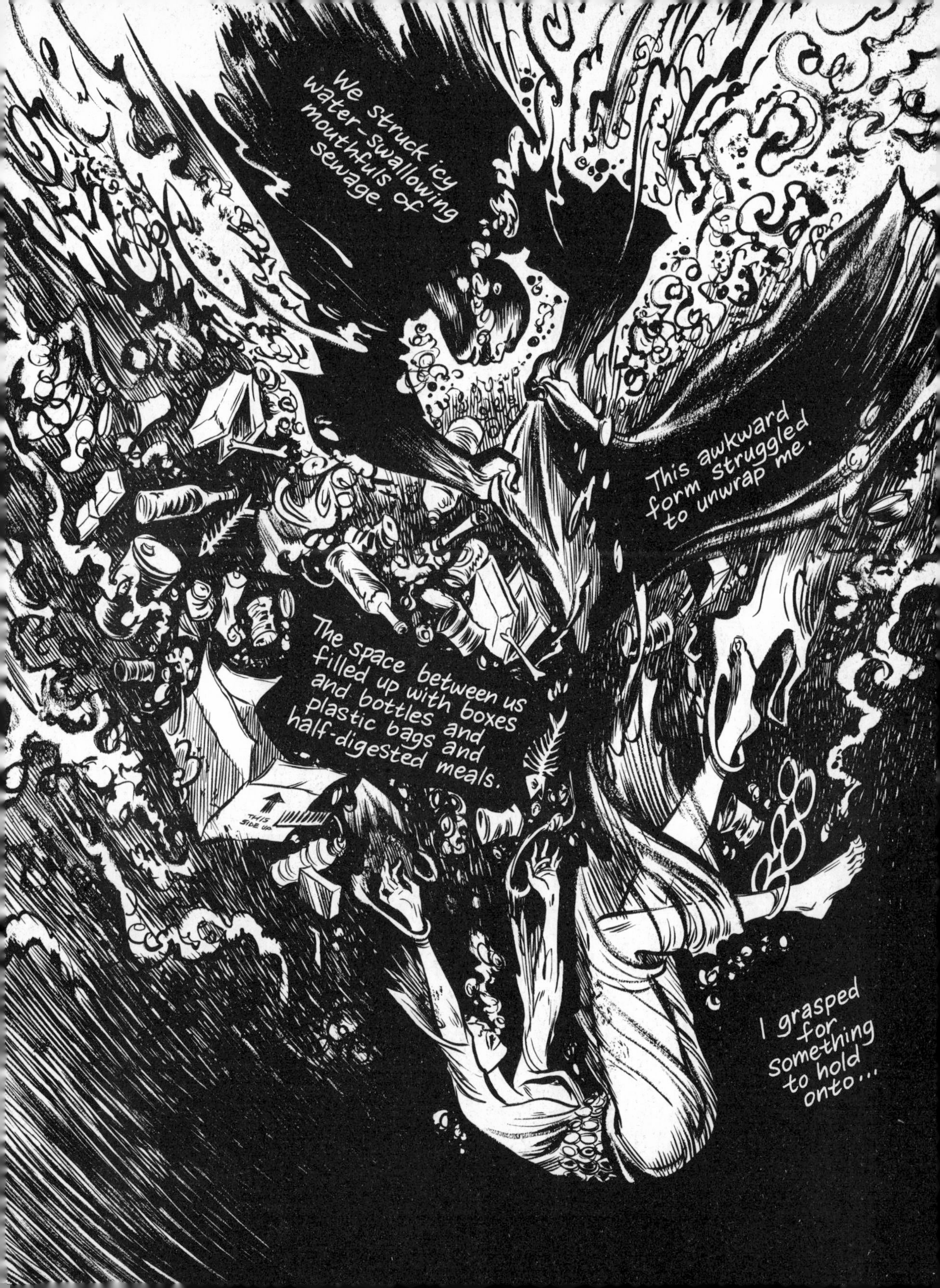
We struck icy water-swallowing mouthfuls of sewage.
This awkward form struggled to unwrap me.
The space between us filled up with boxes and bottles and plastic bags and half-digested meals.
THIS SIDE UP
I grasped for something to hold onto...

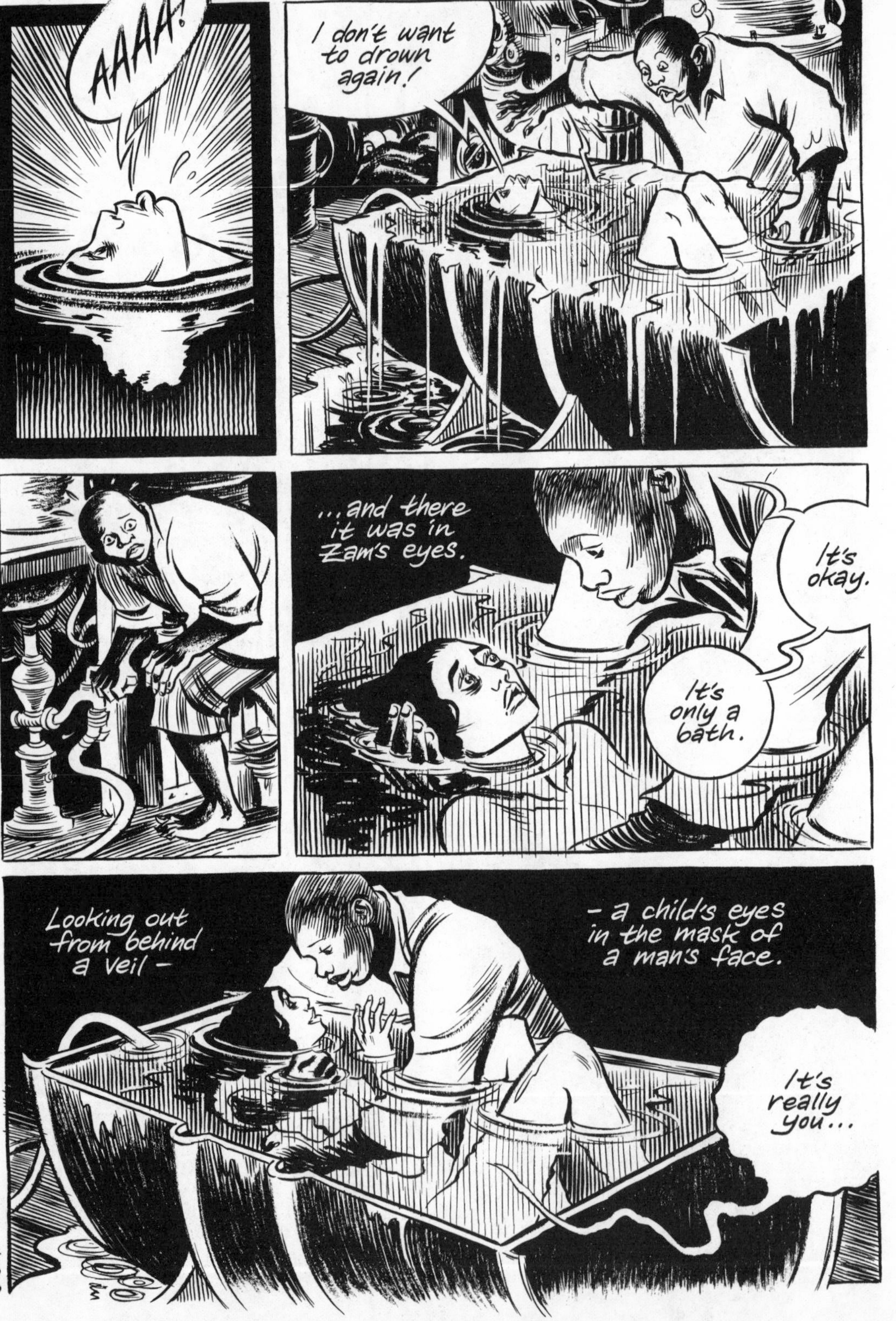
AAAA!
I don't want to drown again!
...and there it was in Zam's eyes.
It's okay.
It's only a bath.
Looking out from behind a veil -
- a child's eyes in the mask of a man's face.
It's really you...

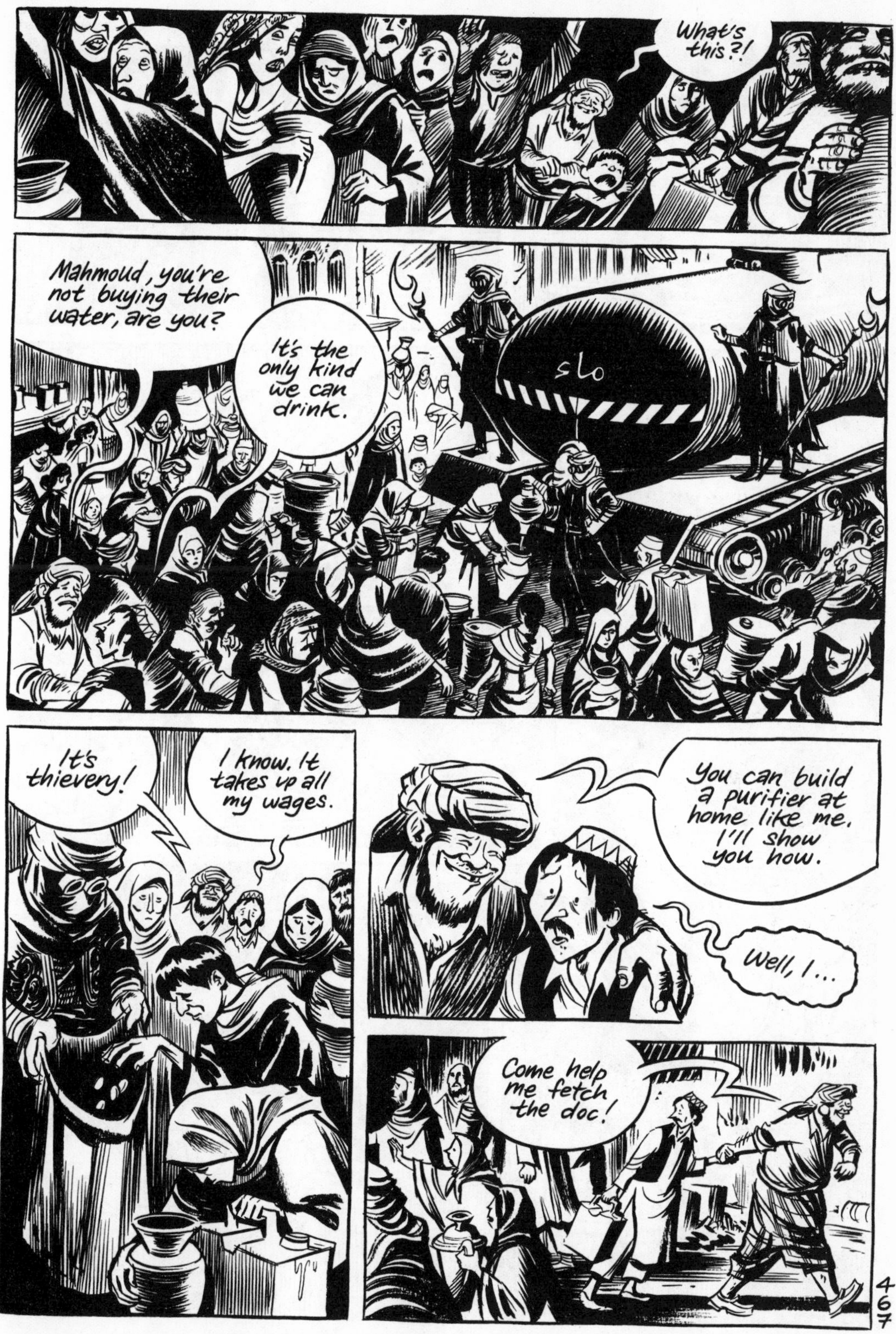
What's this?!
Mahmoud, you're not buying their water, are you?
It's the only kind we can drink.
slo
It's thievery!
I know. It takes up all my wages.
You can build a purifier at home like me. I'll show you how.
Well, I...
Come help me fetch the doc!

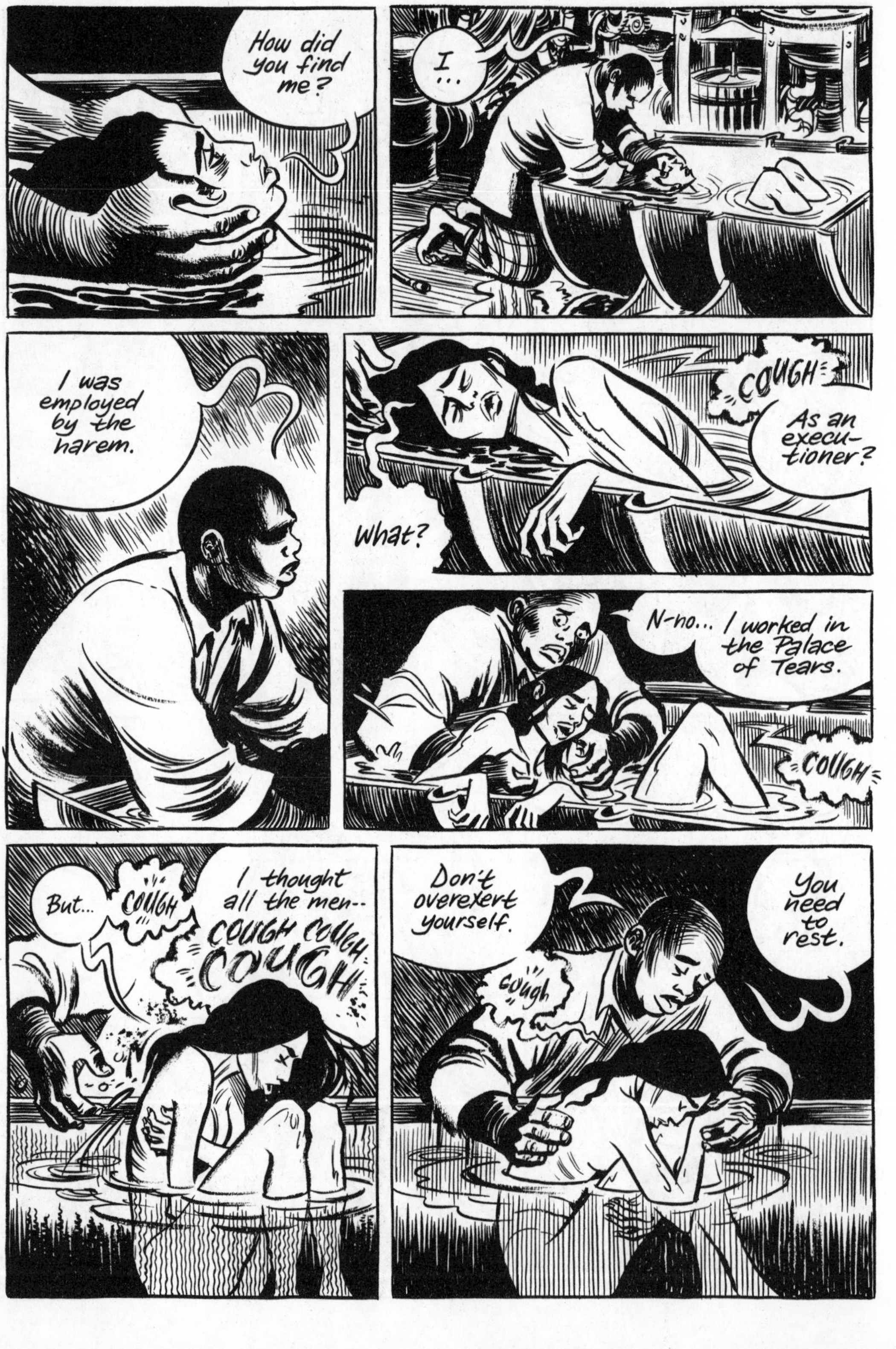
How did you find me?
I ...
I was employed by the harem.
COUGH
As an executioner?
What?
N-no... I worked in the Palace of Tears.
COUGH
But...
COUGH
I thought all the men--
COUGH COUGH COUGH
Don't overexert yourself.
You need to rest.
cough

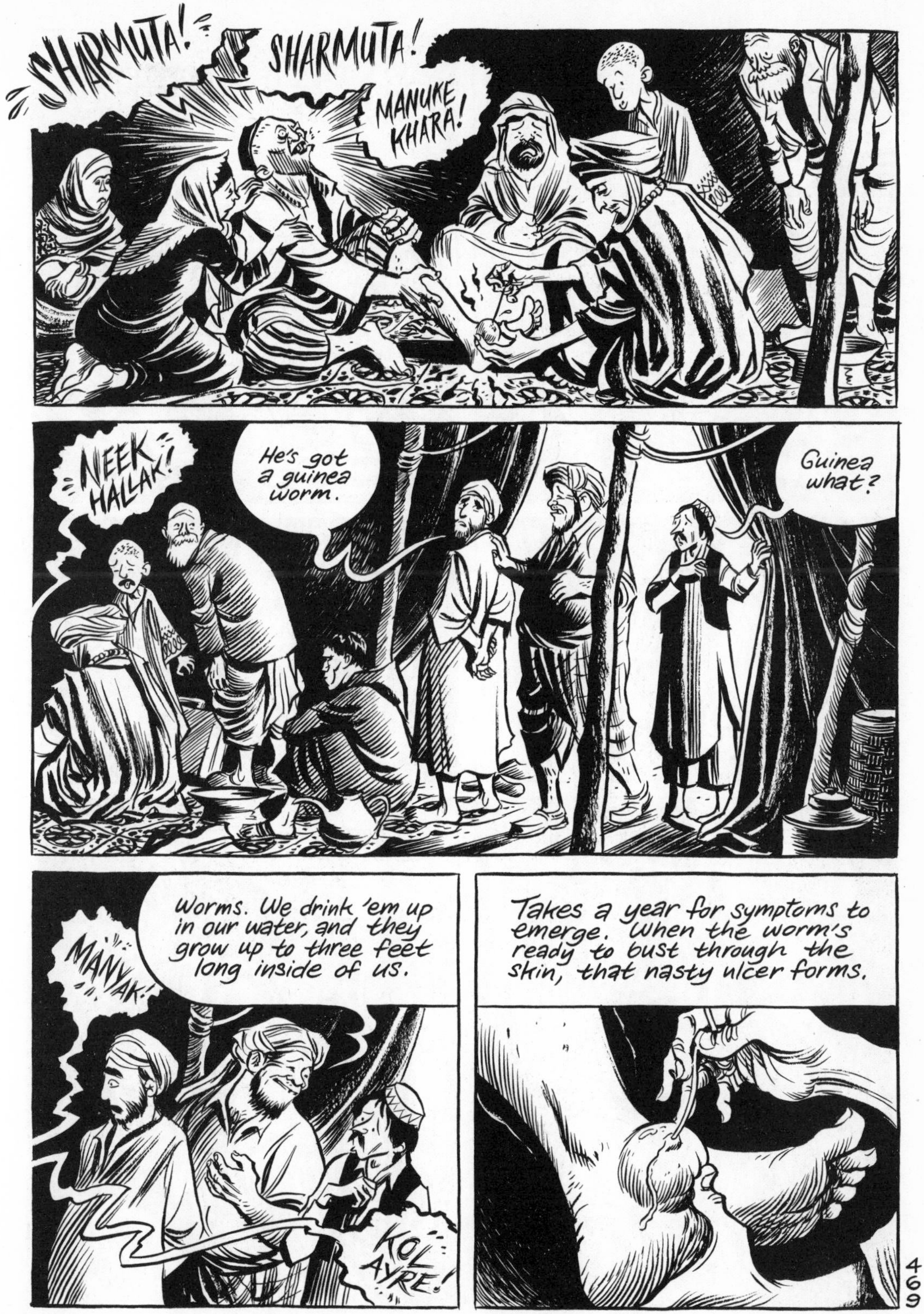
SHARMUTA!
SHARMUTA!
MANUKE KHARA!
NEEK HALLAK!
He's got a guinea worm.
Guinea what?
Worms. We drink 'em up in our water, and they grow up to three feet long inside of us.
MANYAK!
KOL AYRE!
Takes a year for symptoms to emerge. When the worm's ready to bust through the skin, that nasty ulcer forms.

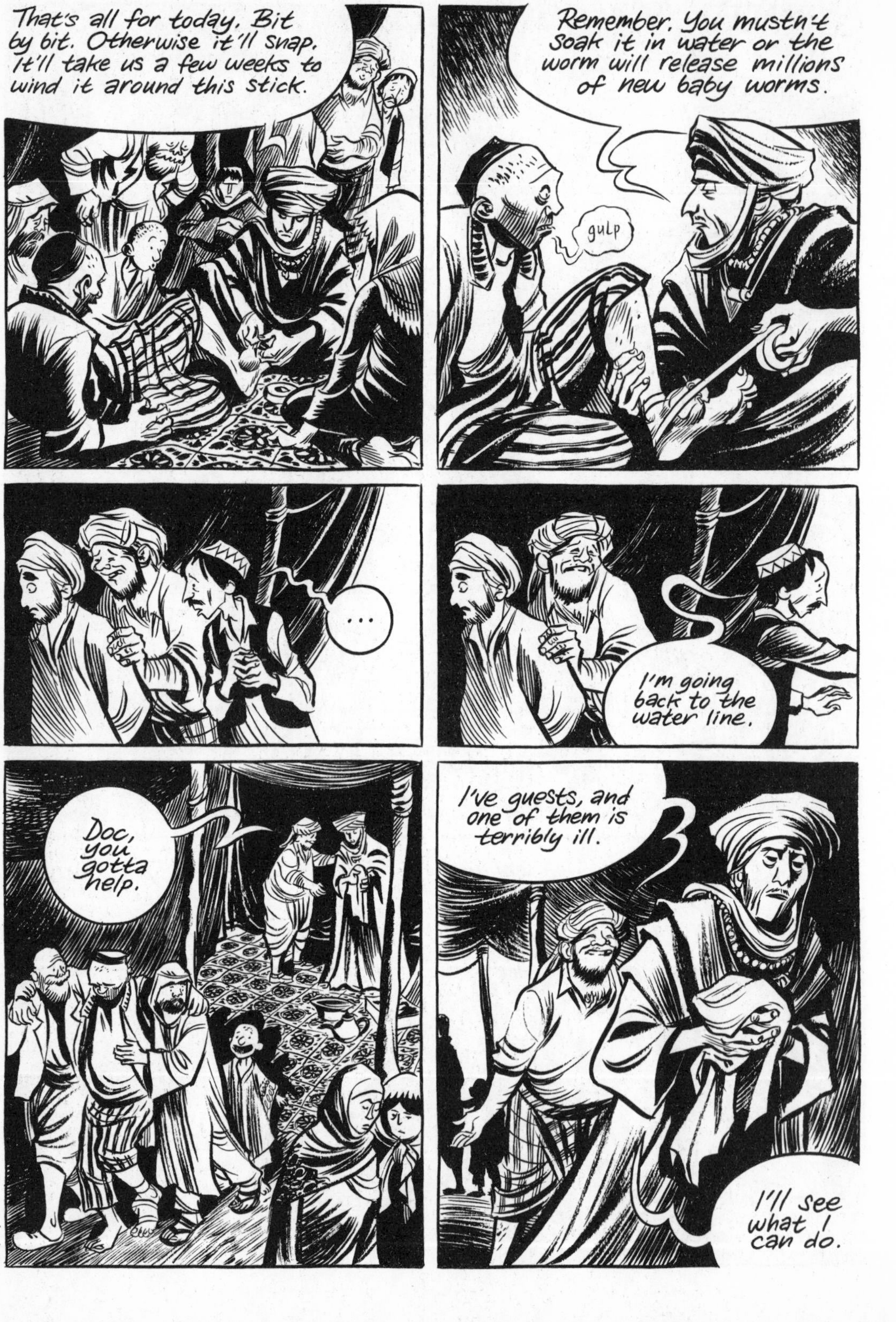
That's all for today. Bit by bit. Otherwise it'll snap. It'll take us a few weeks to wind it around this stick.
Remember. You mustn't soak it in water or the worm will release millions of new baby worms.
gulp
...
I'm going back to the water line.
Doc, you gotta help.
I've guests, and one of them is terribly ill.
I'll see what I can do.

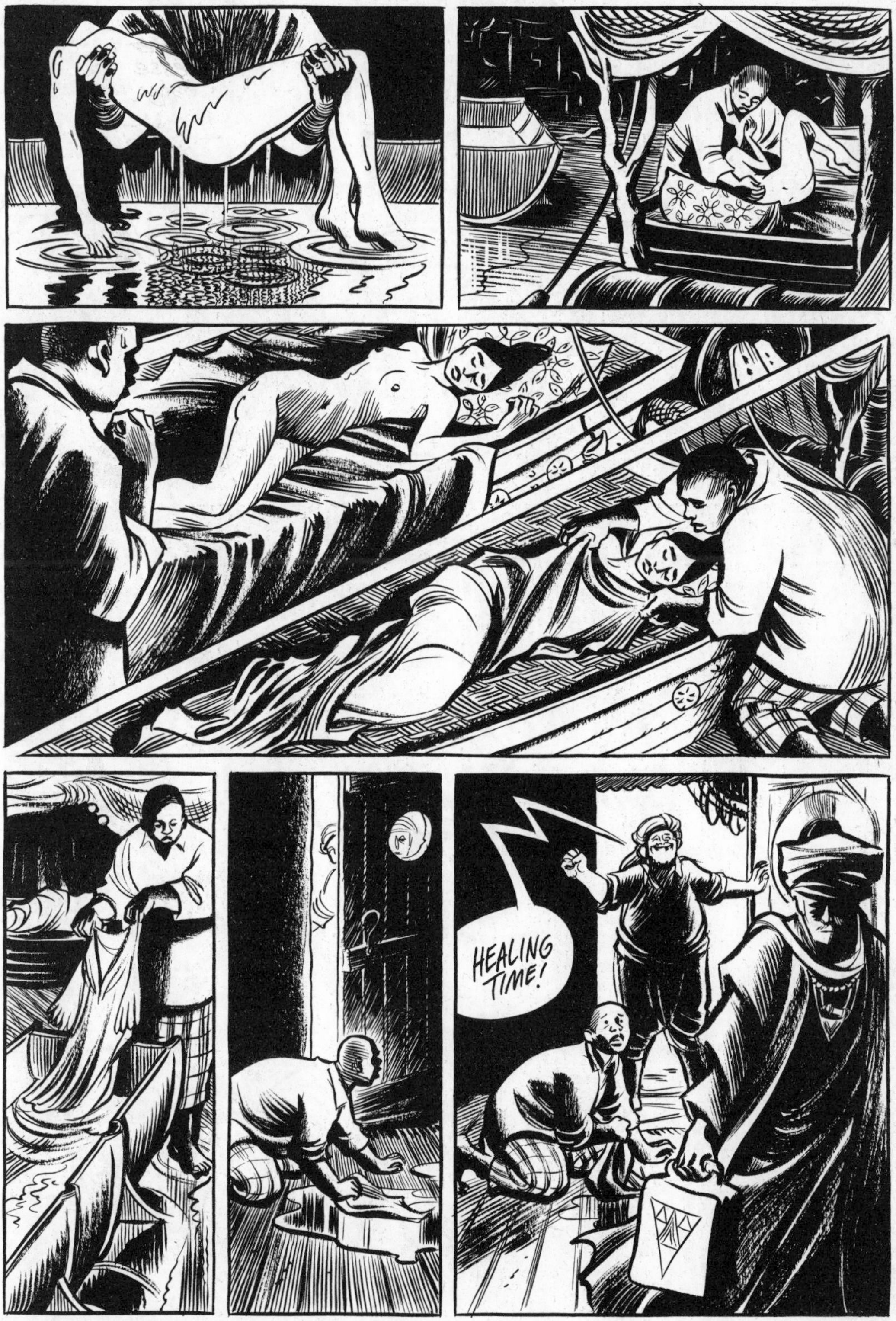
HEALING TIME!

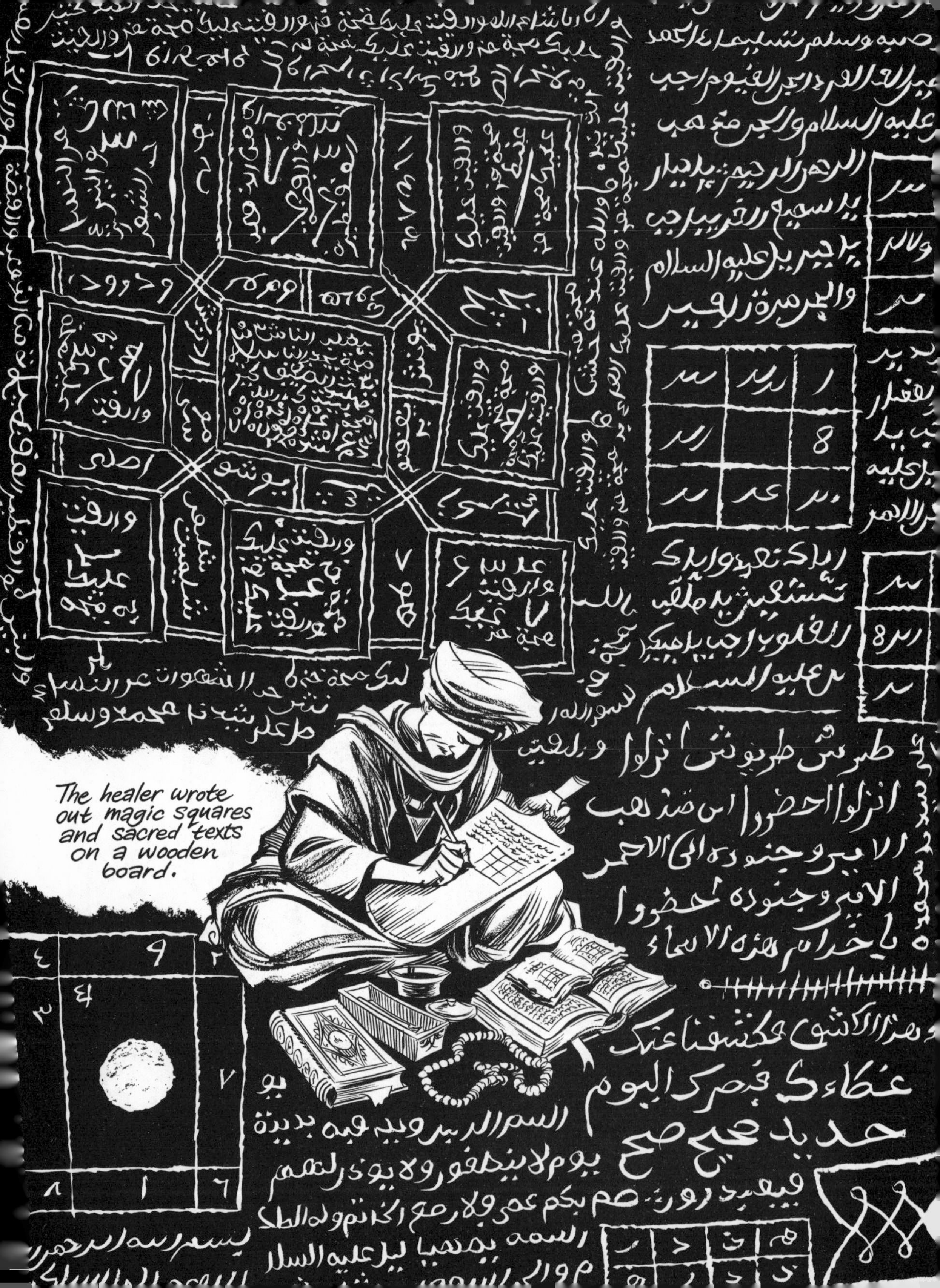
The healer wrote out magic squares and sacred texts on a wooden board.

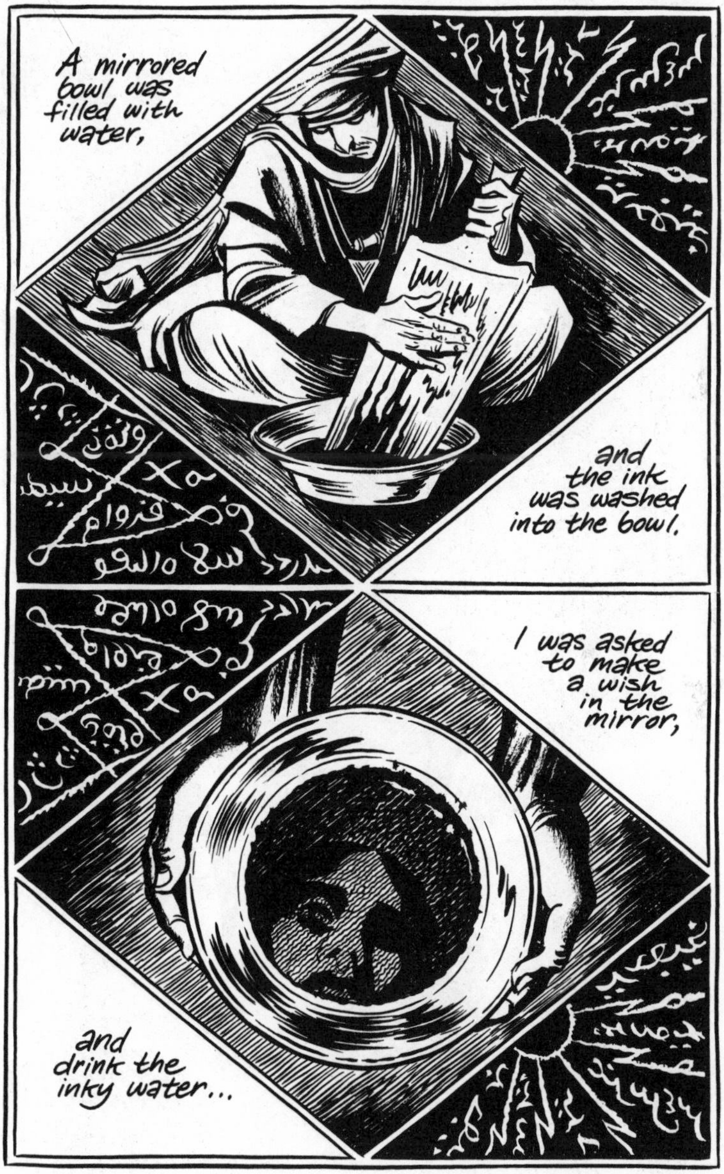
A mirrored bowl was filled with water,
and the ink was washed into the bowl.
I was asked to make a wish in the mirror,
and drink the inky water...

Drink each of the letters
The closest one can get to the text
The body absorbs the message
The word becomes flesh

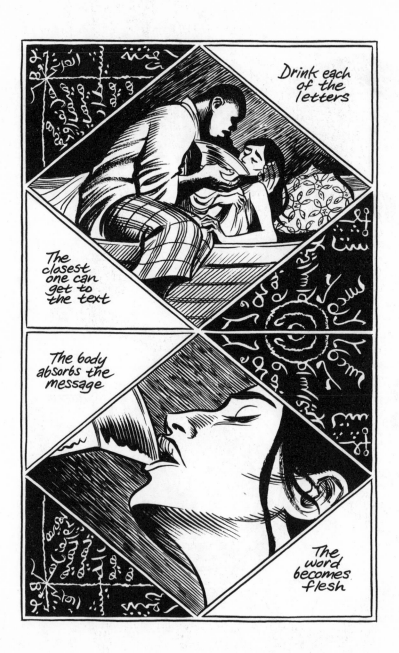

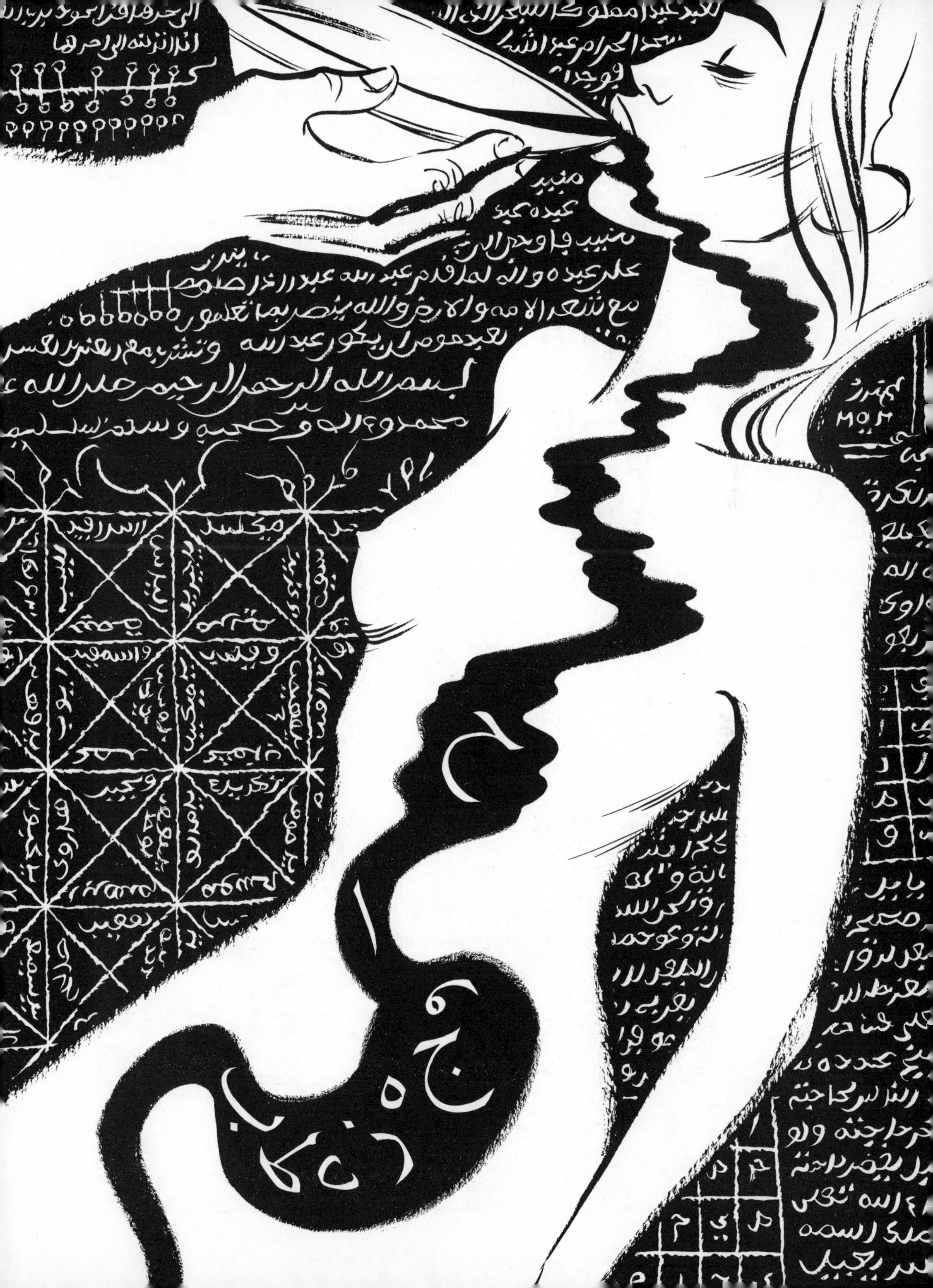

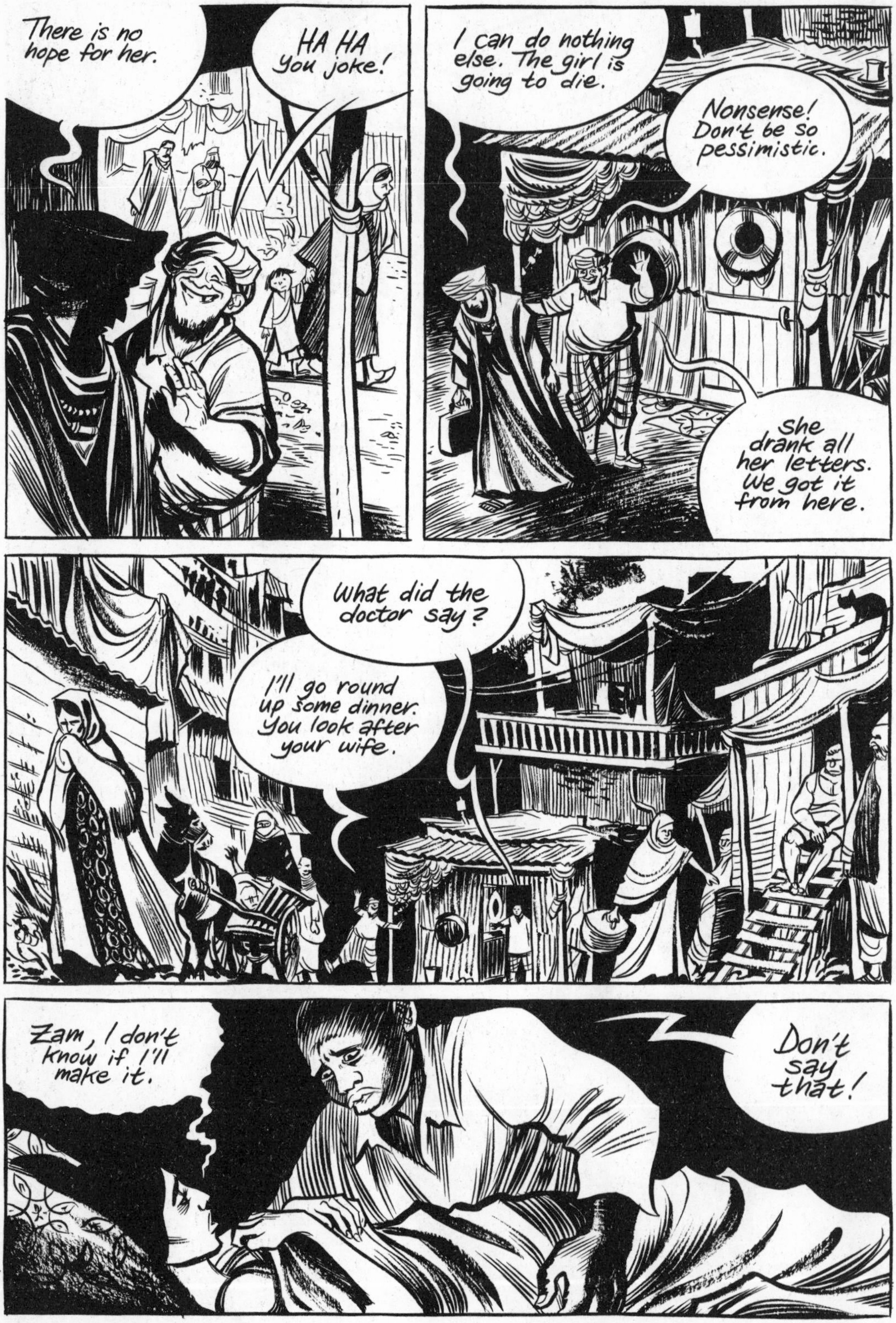

There is no hope for her.
HA HA You joke!
I can do nothing else. The girl is going to die.
Nonsense! Don't be so pessimistic.
She drank all her letters. We got it from here.
What did the doctor say?
I'll go round up some dinner. You look after your wife.
Zam, I don't know if I'll make it.
Don't say that!

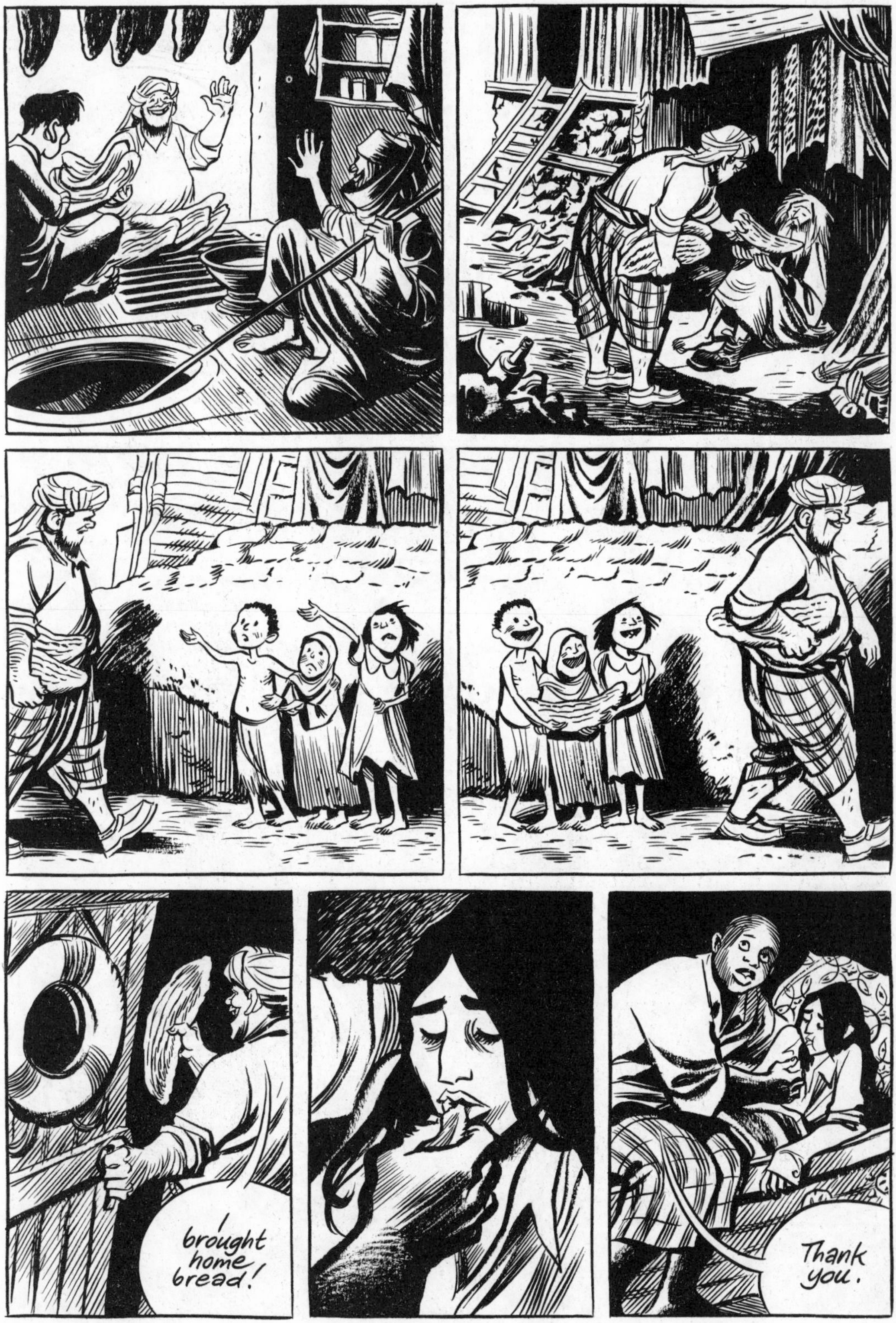
I brought home bread!
Thank you.

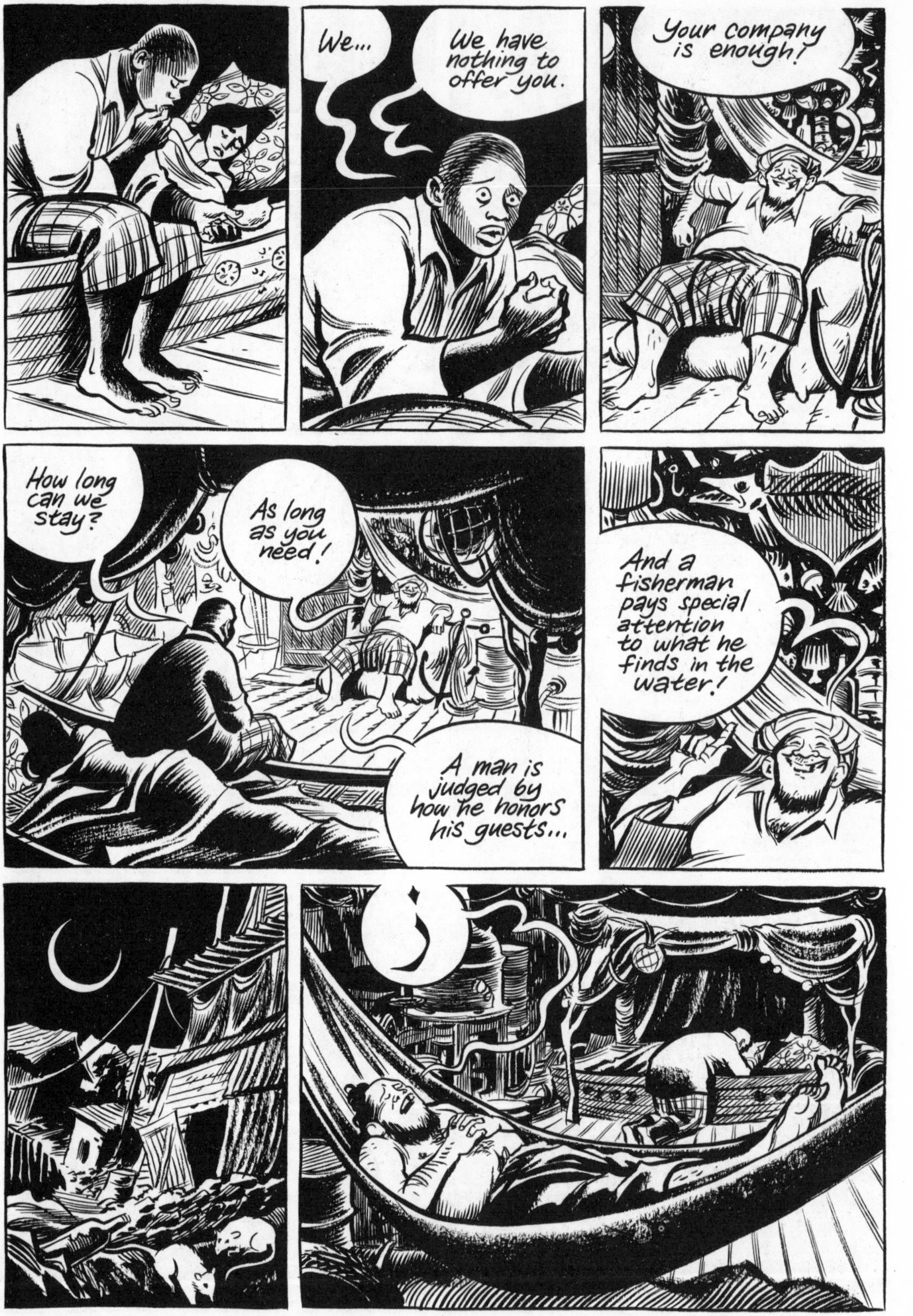

We...
We have nothing to offer you.
Your company is enough!
How long can we stay?
As long as you need!
A man is judged by how he honors his guests...
And a fisherman pays special attention to what he finds in the water!

Dodola... you're feverish...

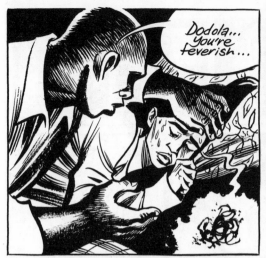

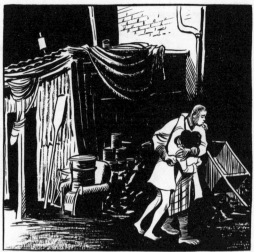

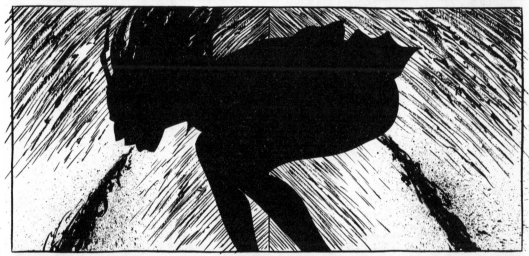

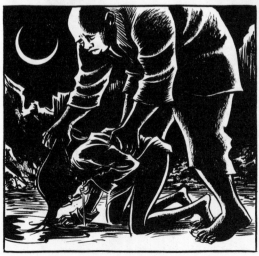

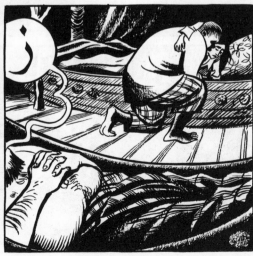

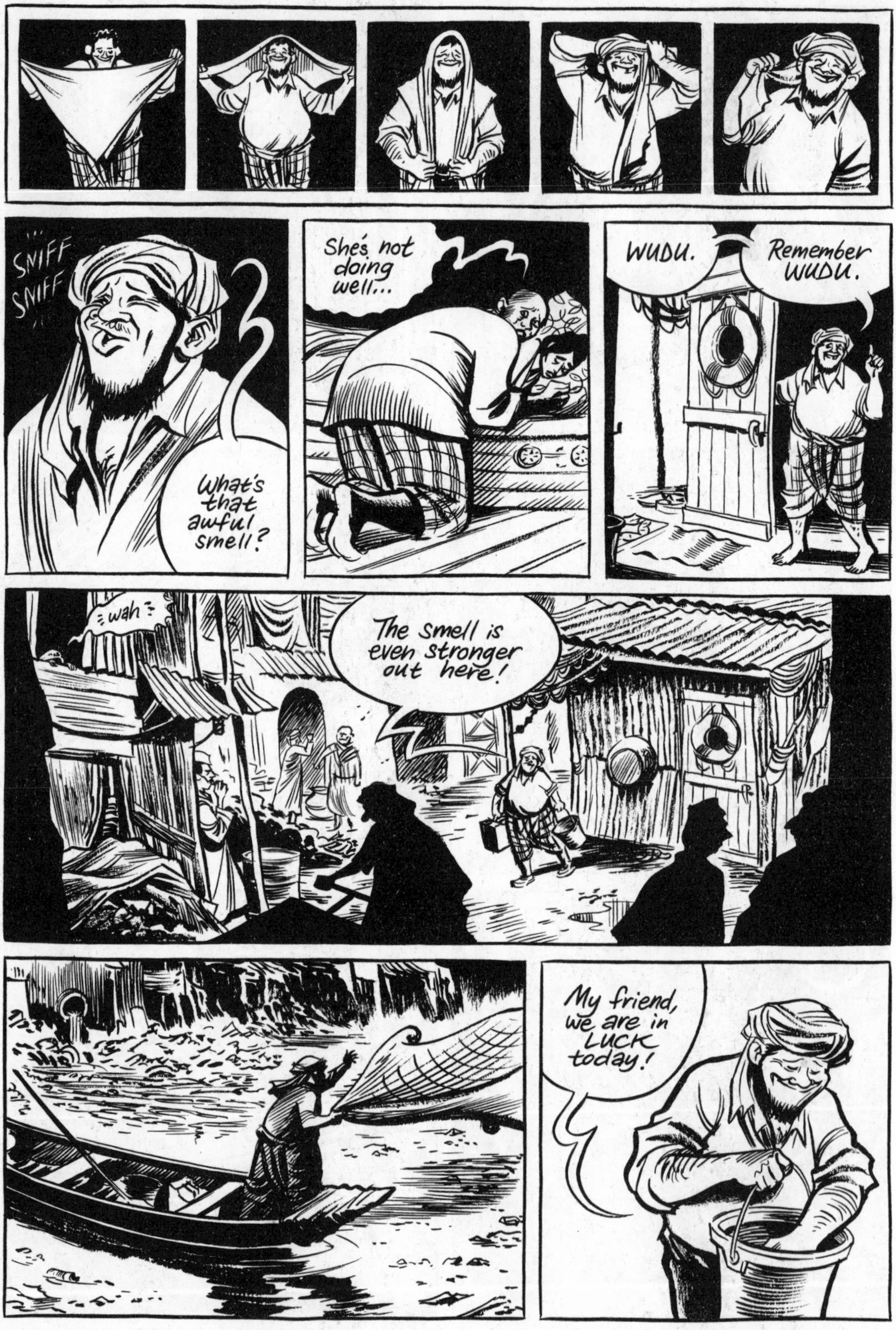
SNIFF SNIFF
What's that awful smell?
She's not doing well...
Remember WUDU.
WUDU.
wah
The smell is even stronger out here!
My friend, we are in LUCK today!

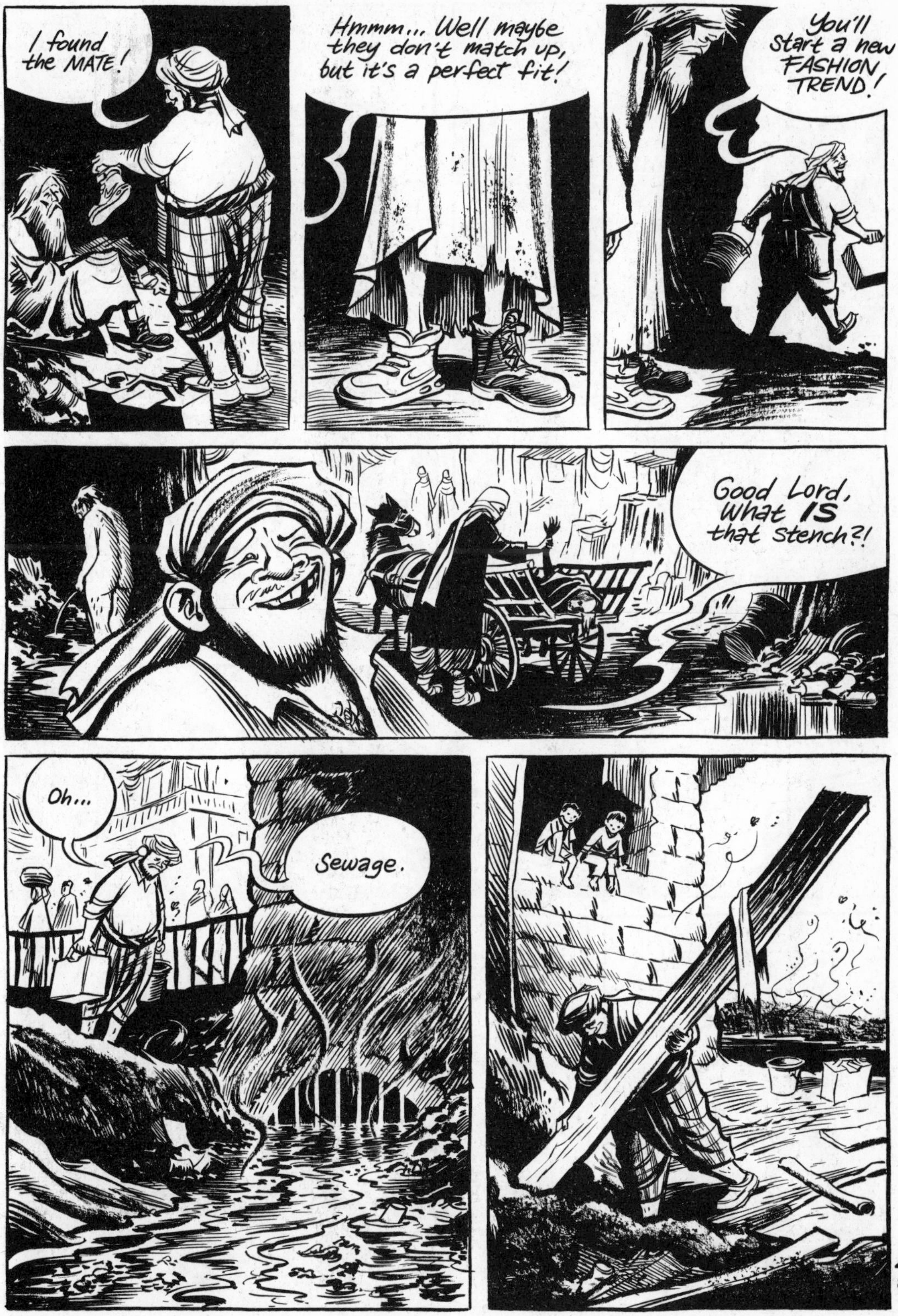
I found the MATE!
Hmmm... Well maybe they don't match up, but it's a perfect fit!
You'll start a new FASHION TREND!
Good Lord, What IS that stench?!
Oh...
Sewage.

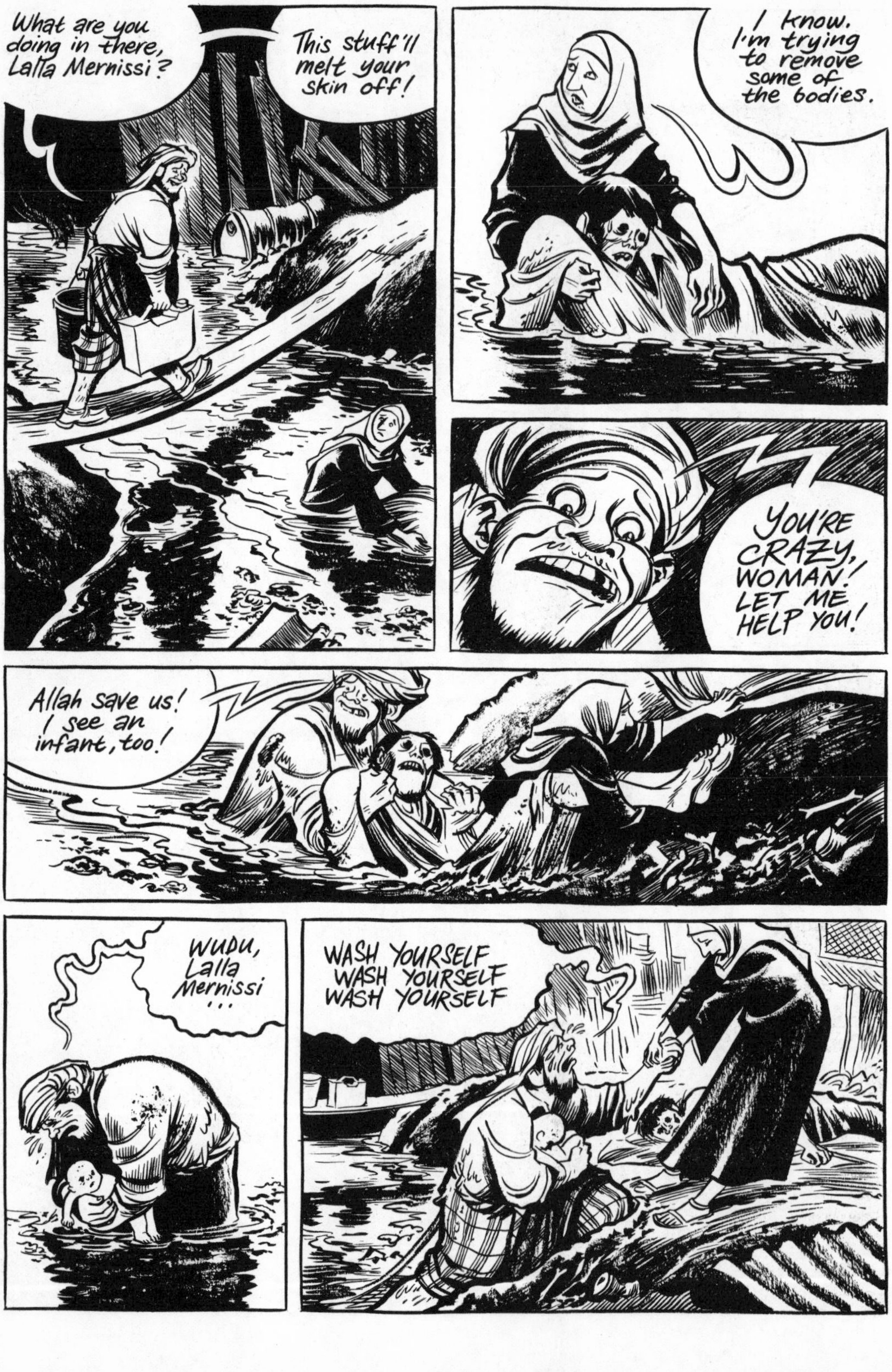
What are you doing in there, Lalla Mernissi?
This stuff'll melt your skin off!
I know. I'm trying to remove some of the bodies.
YOU'RE CRAZY, WOMAN! LET ME HELP YOU!
Allah save us! I see an infant, too!
WUDU, Lalla Mernissi . . .
WASH YOURSELF
WASH YOURSELF
WASH YOURSELF

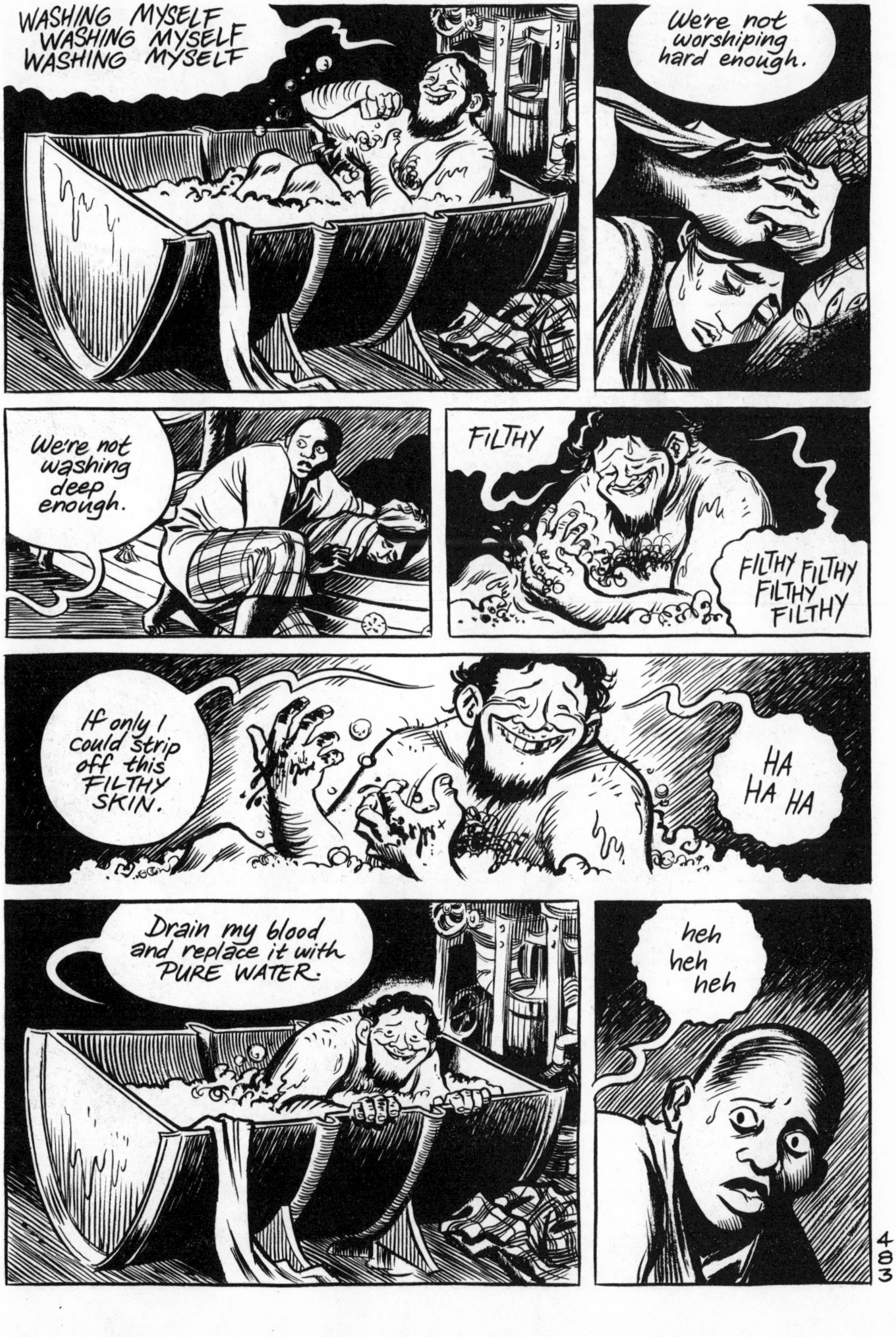
WASHING MYSELF
WASHING MYSELF
WASHING MYSELF
We're not worshiping hard enough.
We're not washing deep enough.
FILTHY
FILTHY FILTHY FILTHY FILTHY
If only I could strip off this FILTHY SKIN.
HA HA HA
Drain my blood and replace it with PURE WATER.
heh heh heh

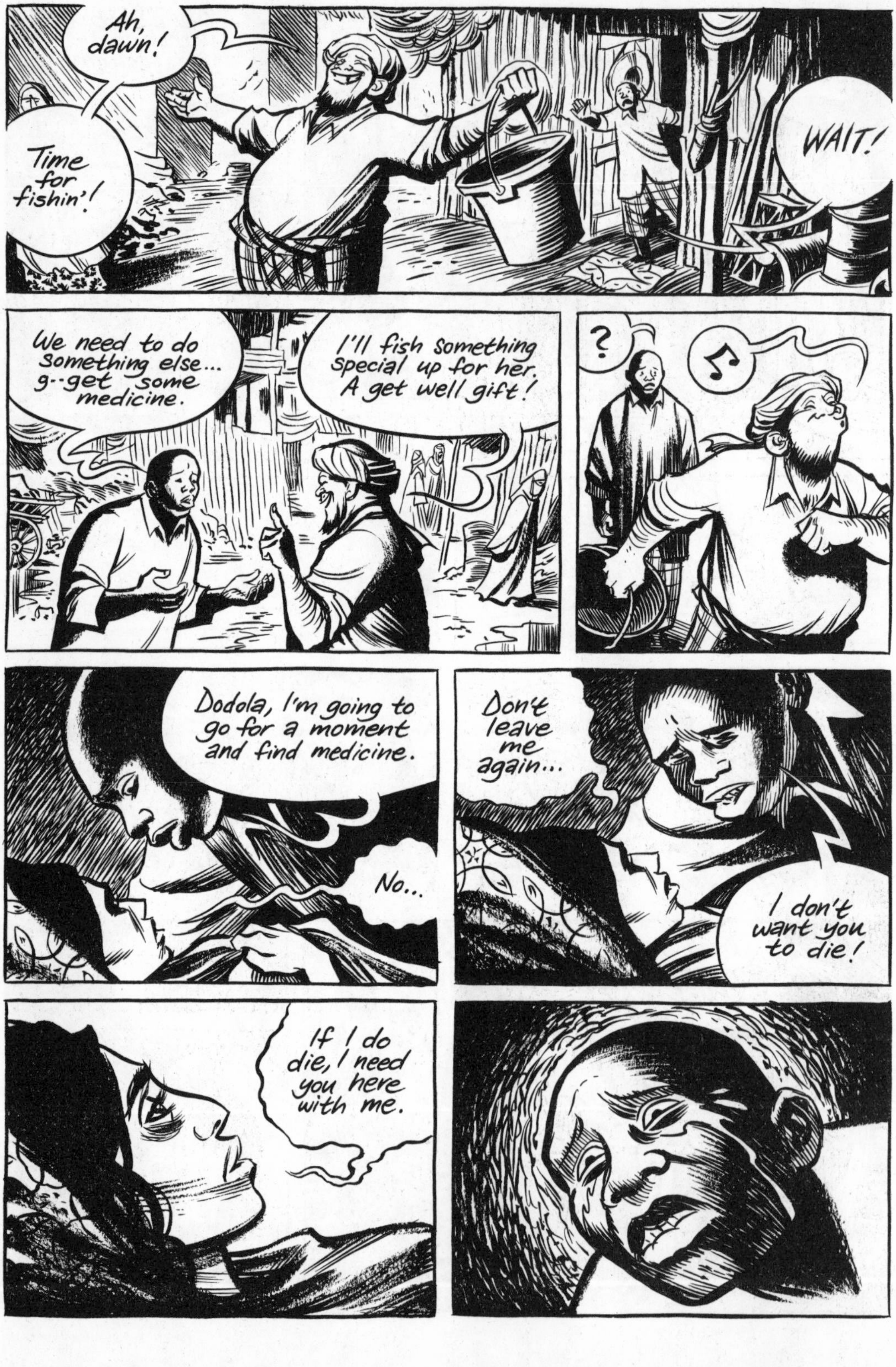
Ah, dawn!
Time for fishin'!
WAIT!
We need to do something else... g--get some medicine.
I'll fish something special up for her. A get well gift!
?
♫
Dodola, I'm going to go for a moment and find medicine.
No...
Don't leave me again...
I don't want you to die!
If I do die, I need you here with me.

SOMEONE HELP!
help?
CLAN
CLANG
CLANG
CLANG
BOM
WAH
WAH
STOP MAKING BABIES!
STOP MAKING BABIES!
CHK
CHK
CHK
CHK
CHK
BOM
BOM
CLANG
CLANG
CLANG
CHK
CHK
NG
BOM
LANG
R
NG
ANG
G

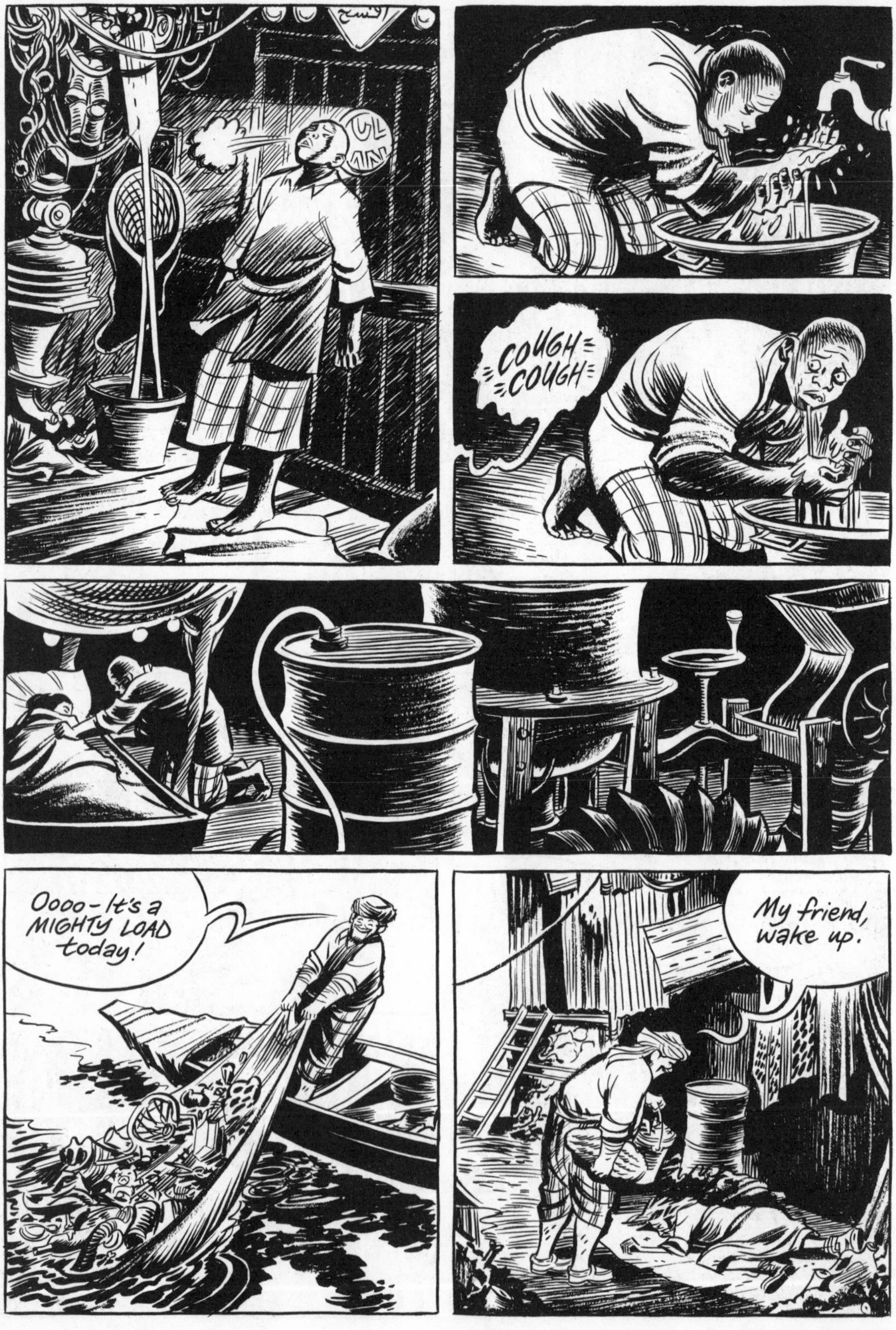
COUGH COUGH
Oooo- It's a MIGHTY LOAD today!
My friend, wake up.

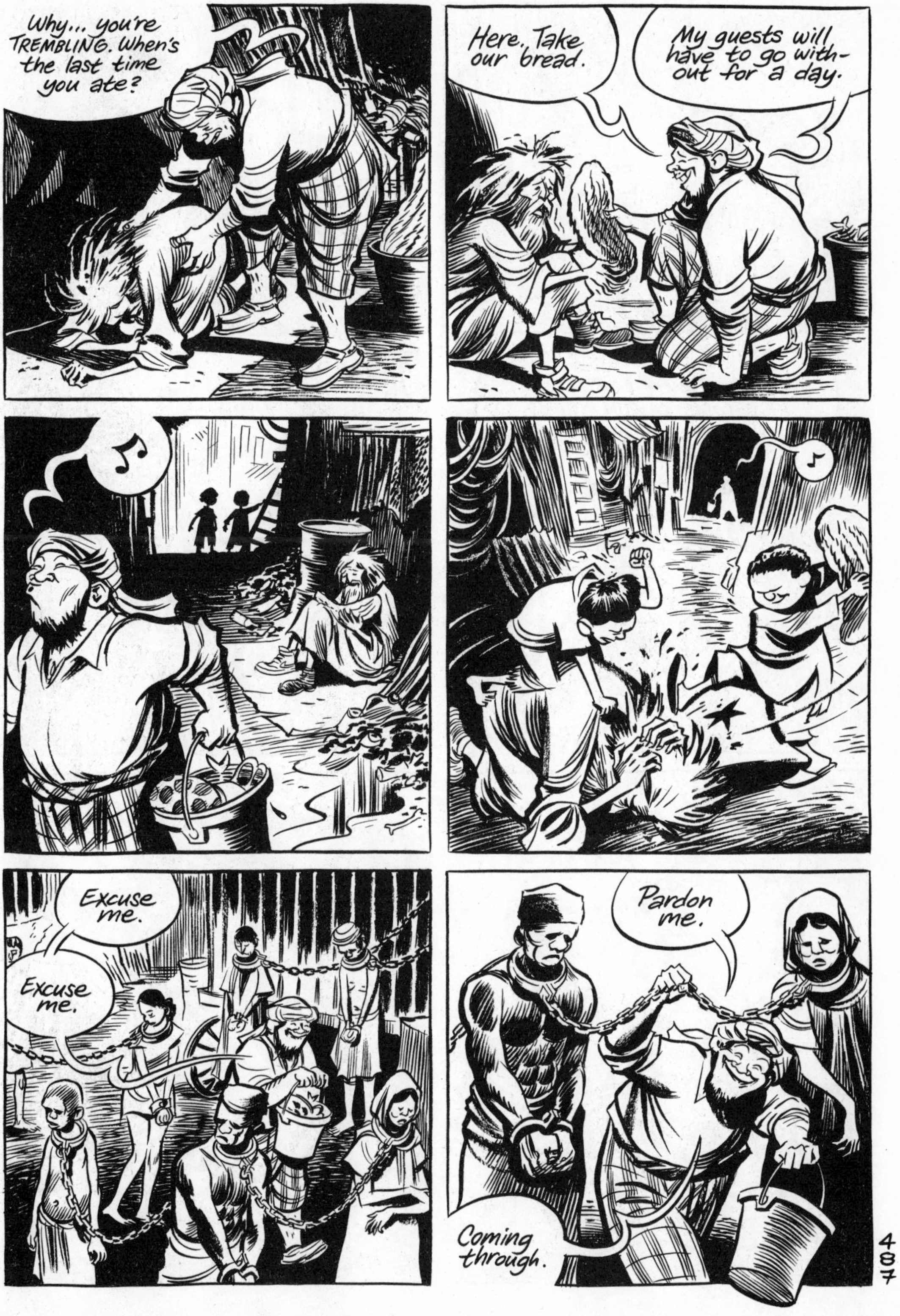
Why... you're TREMBLING. When's the last time you ate?
Here. Take our bread.
My guests will have to go without for a day.
Excuse me.
Excuse me.
Pardon me.
Coming through.

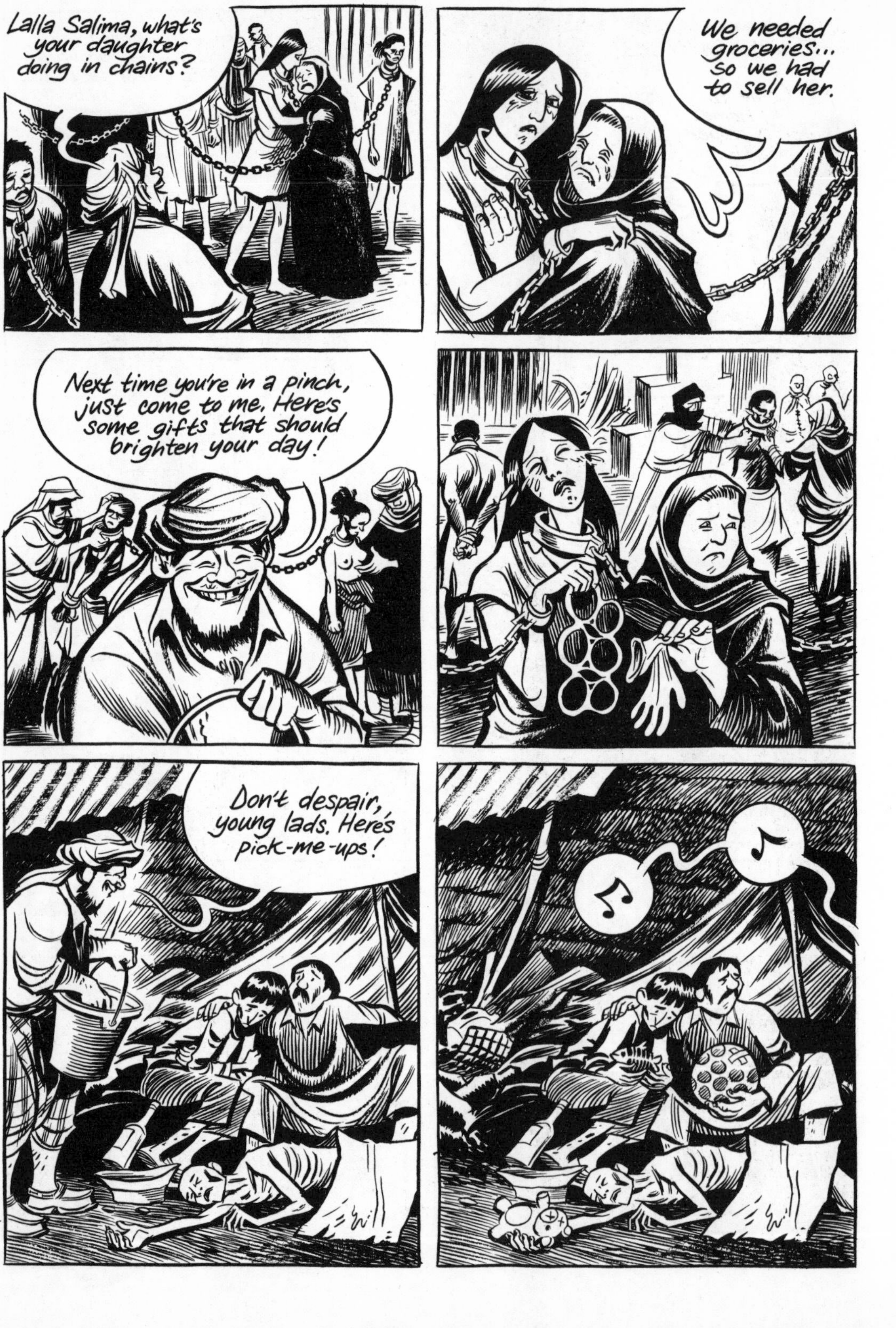
Lalla Salima, what's your daughter doing in chains?
We needed groceries... so we had to sell her.
Next time you're in a pinch, just come to me. Here's some gifts that should brighten your day!
Don't despair, young lads. Here's pick-me-ups!

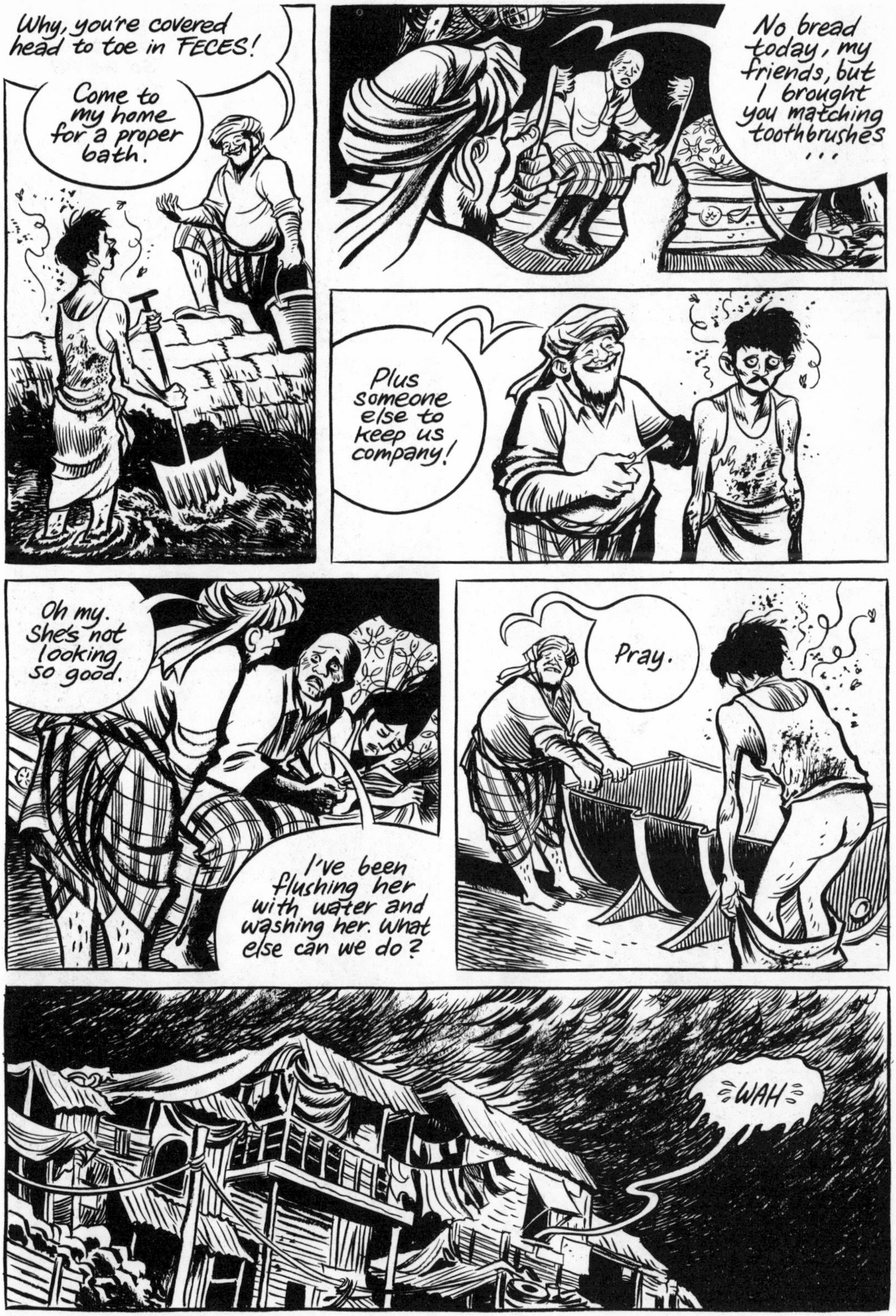

Why, you're covered head to toe in FECES!
Come to my home for a proper bath.
No bread today, my friends, but I brought you matching toothbrushes . . .
Plus someone else to keep us company!
Oh my. She's not looking so good.
I've been flushing her with water and washing her. What else can we do?
Pray.
WAH

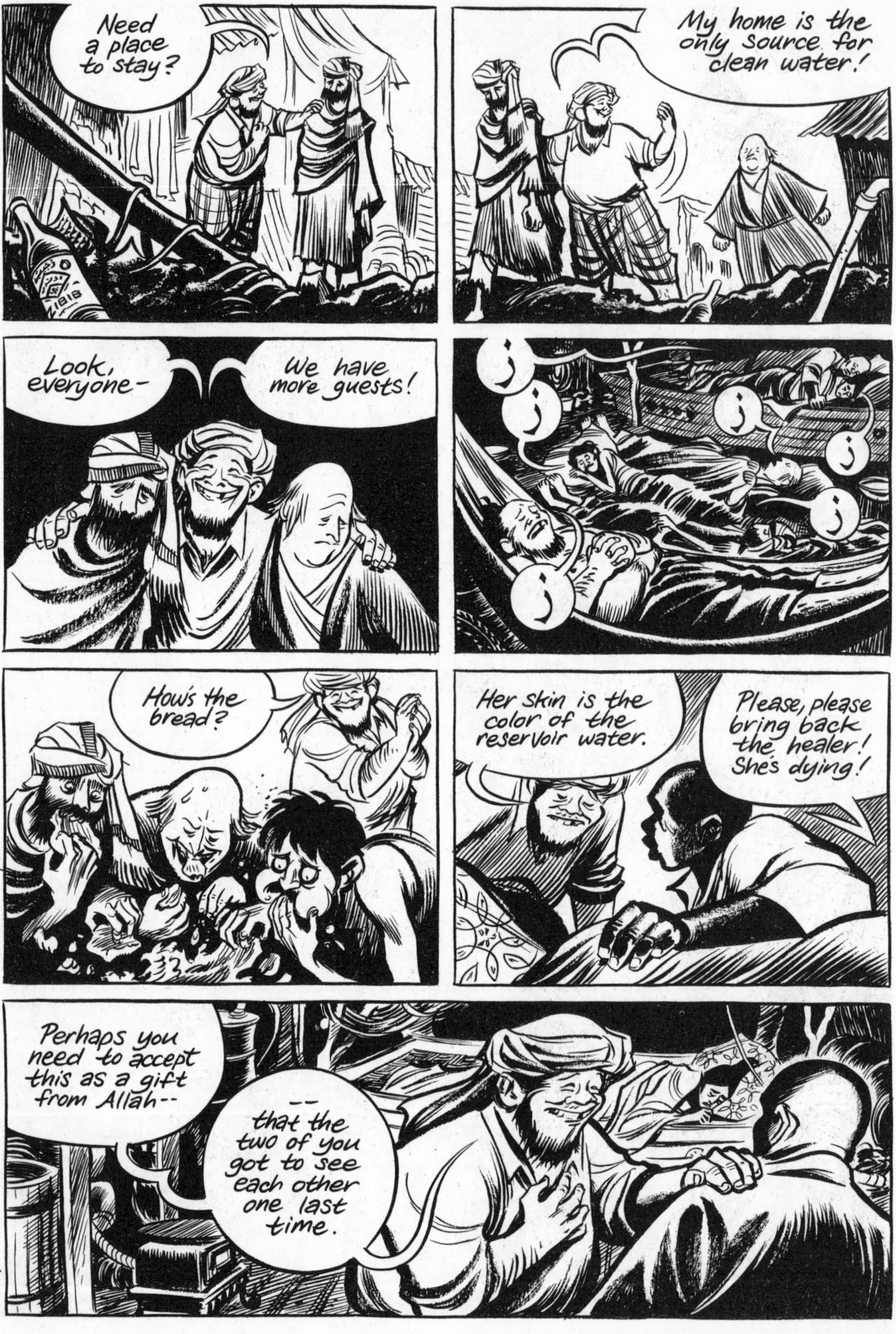
Need a place to stay?
My home is the only source for clean water!
Look, everyone-
We have more guests!
ز
ز
ز
ز
ز
ز
How's the bread?
Her skin is the color of the reservoir water.
Please, please bring back the healer! She's dying!
Perhaps you need to accept this as a gift from Allah--
--that the two of you got to see each other one last time.

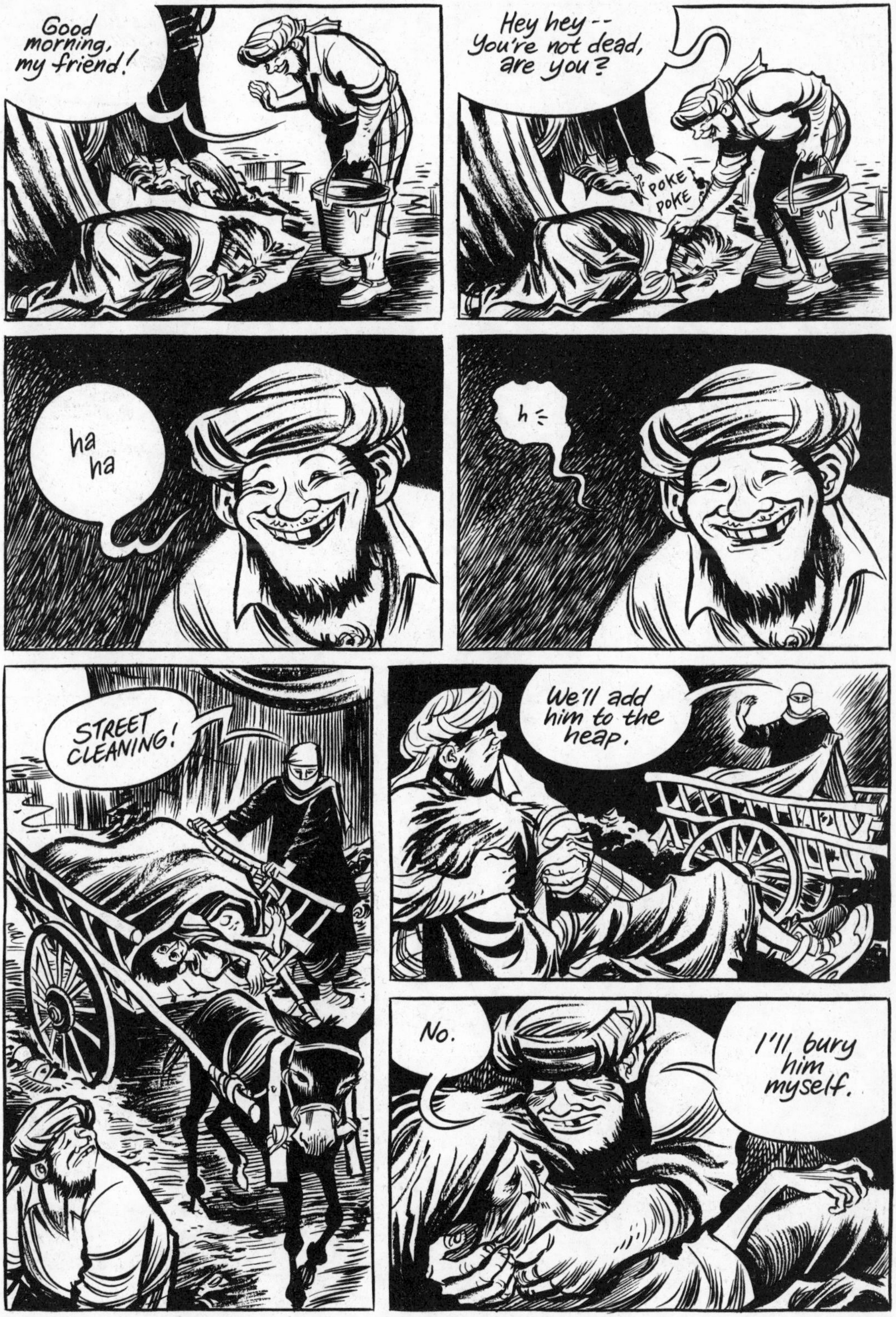
Good morning, my friend!
Hey hey -- You're not dead, are you?
POKE POKE
ha ha
h
STREET CLEANING!
We'll add him to the heap.
No.
I'll bury him myself.

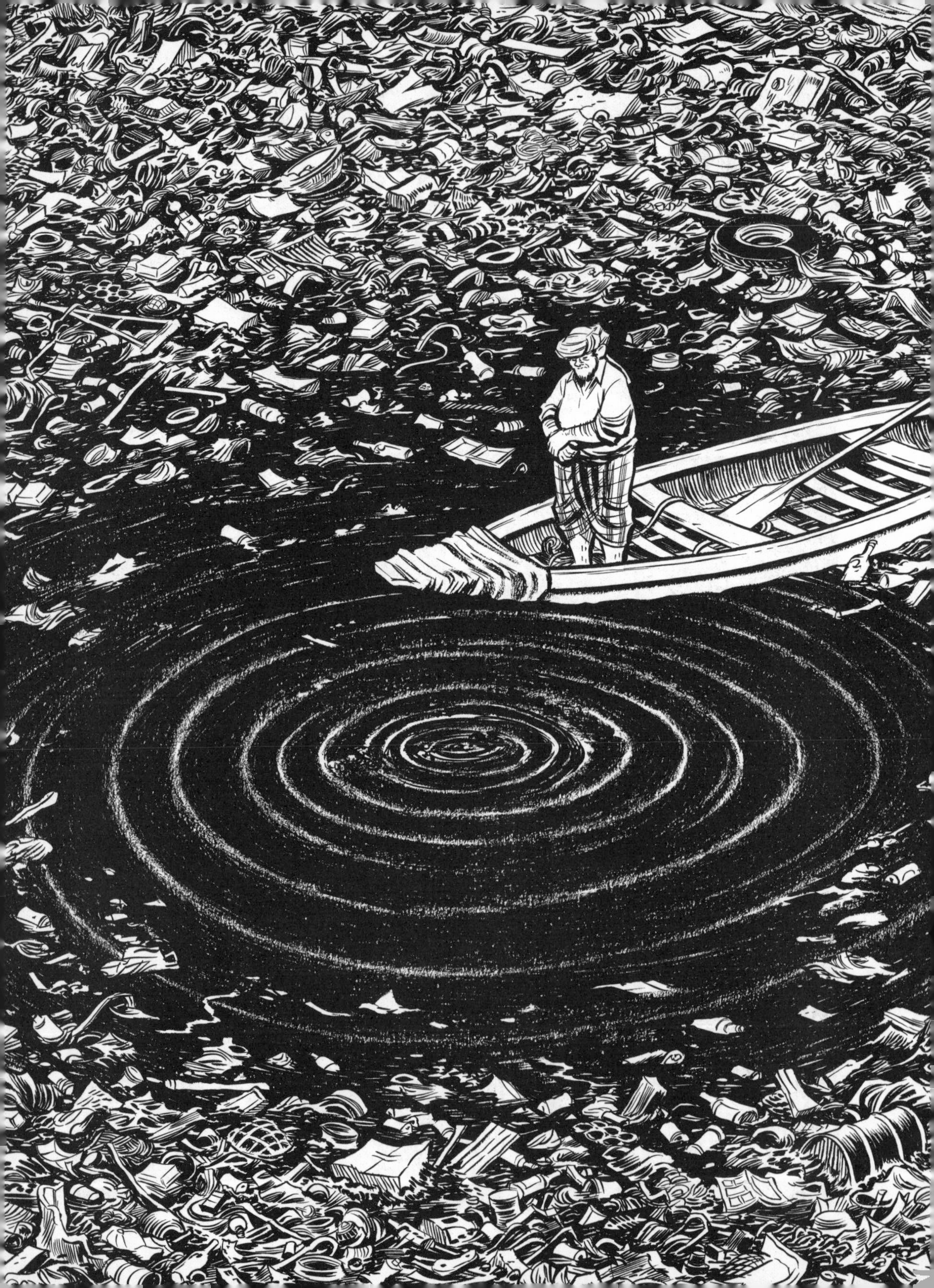

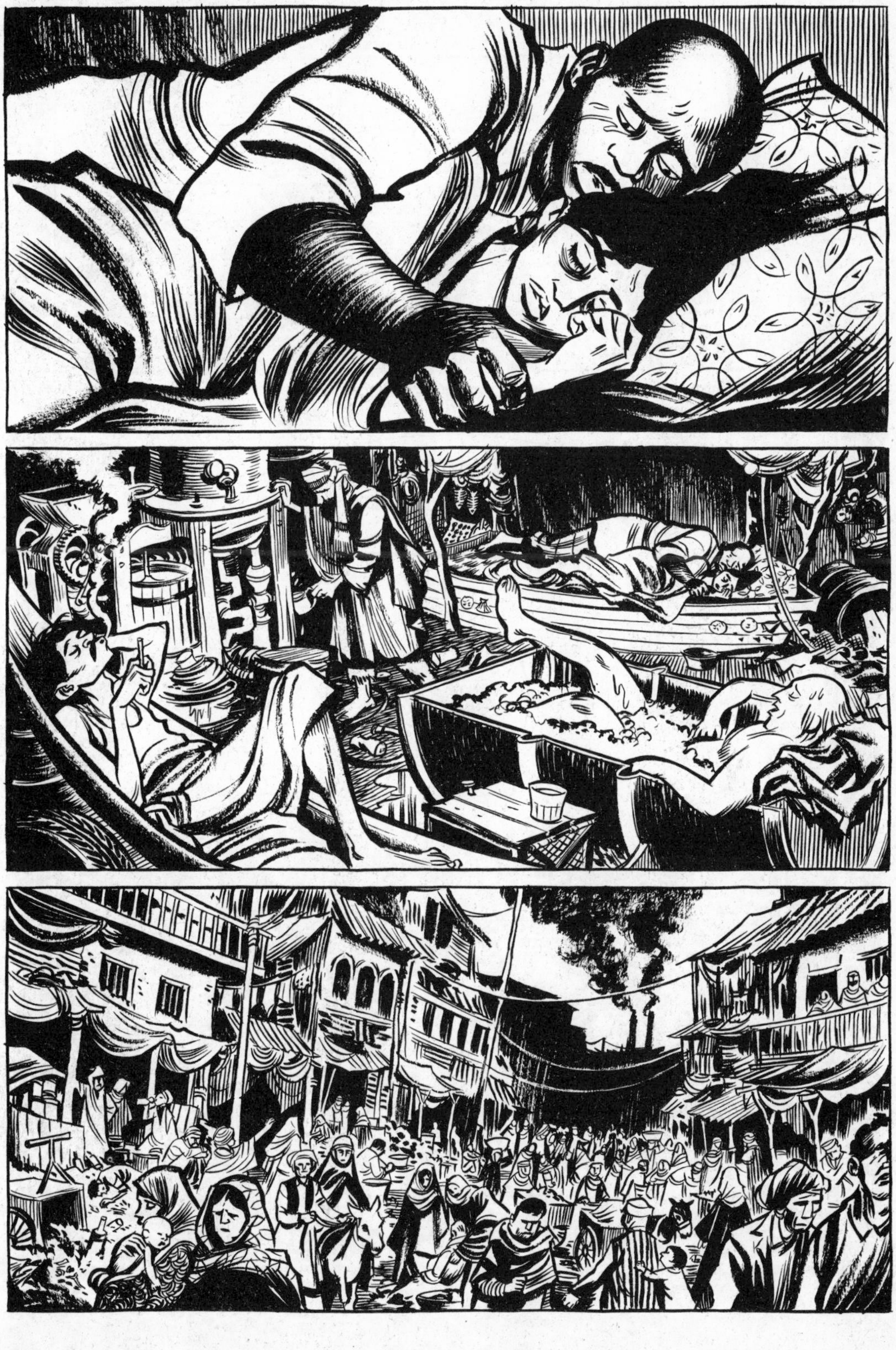

Faced with the destruction of his world, Noah had to find hope to regenerate life.

So God sent a symbol of reassurance that He would never again destroy the Earth by flooding.

Did this exclude other forms of deluge?

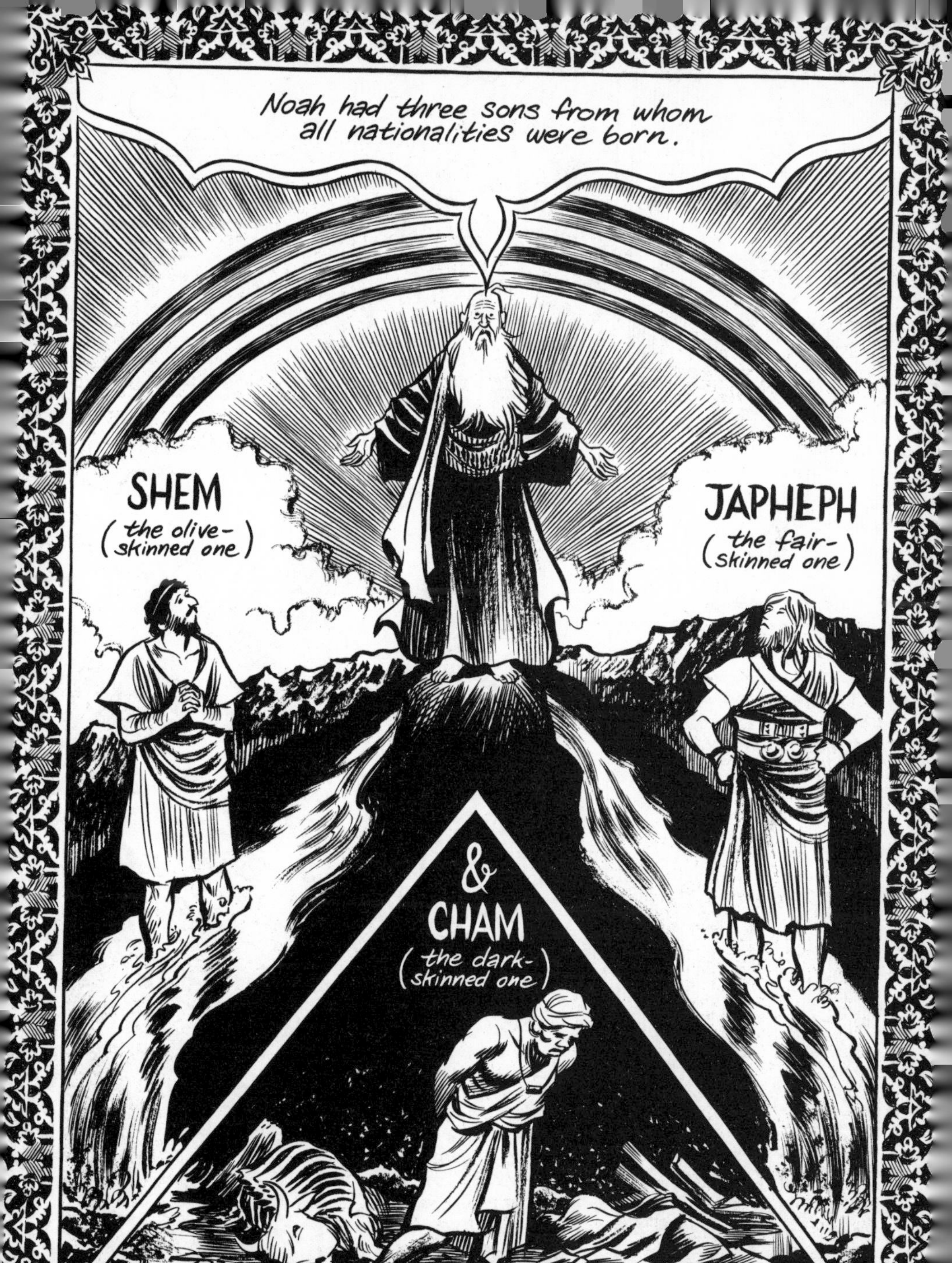
Noah had three sons from whom all nationalities were born.
SHEM
(the olive-skinned one)
JAPHEPH
(the fair-skinned one)
& CHAM
(the dark-skinned one)

But Noah cursed the offspring of Cham to forever be "a servant of servants" to his brethren.

Why such a harsh judgment?

Some say it was for deriding his father's nakedness. Others say Cham used magic to hex Noah with impotency.

Shem was his father's favorite, remaining closest in heart and geography. He was also the most spiritually attuned, from whom all prophets have descended.

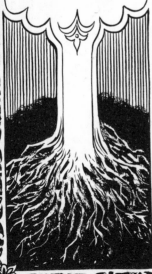

Japheph was the craftiest. Blessed by Noah to expand beyond all others, his children multiplied in number and power.

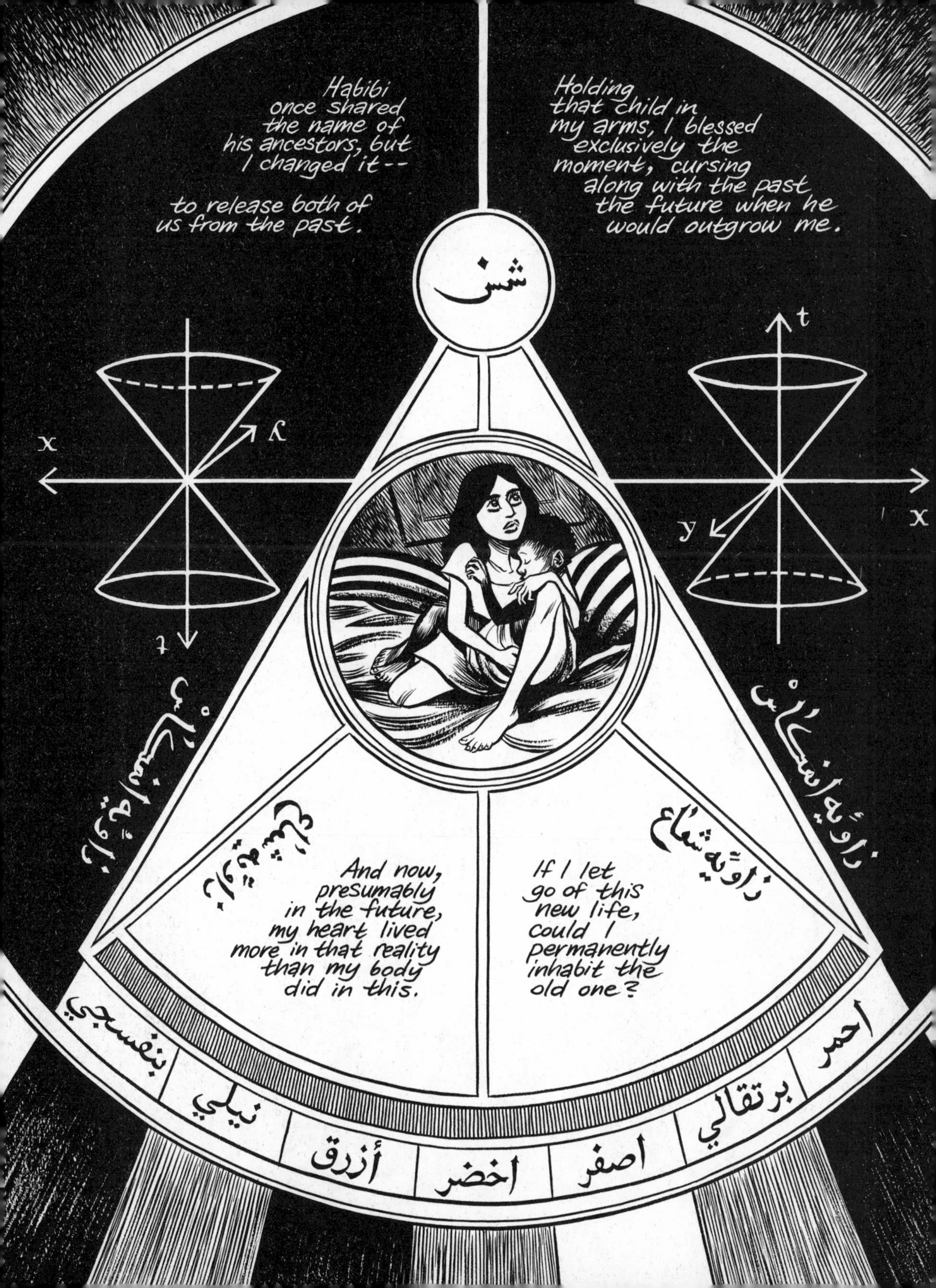

Habibi once shared the name of his ancestors, but I changed it --
to release both of us from the past.
Holding that child in my arms, I blessed exclusively the moment, cursing along with the past the future when he would outgrow me.
شن
زاوية شعاع
And now, presumably in the future, my heart lived more in that reality than my body did in this.
If I let go of this new life, could I permanently inhabit the old one?
أحمر
برتقالي
اصفر
اخضر
أزرق
نيلي
بنفسجي

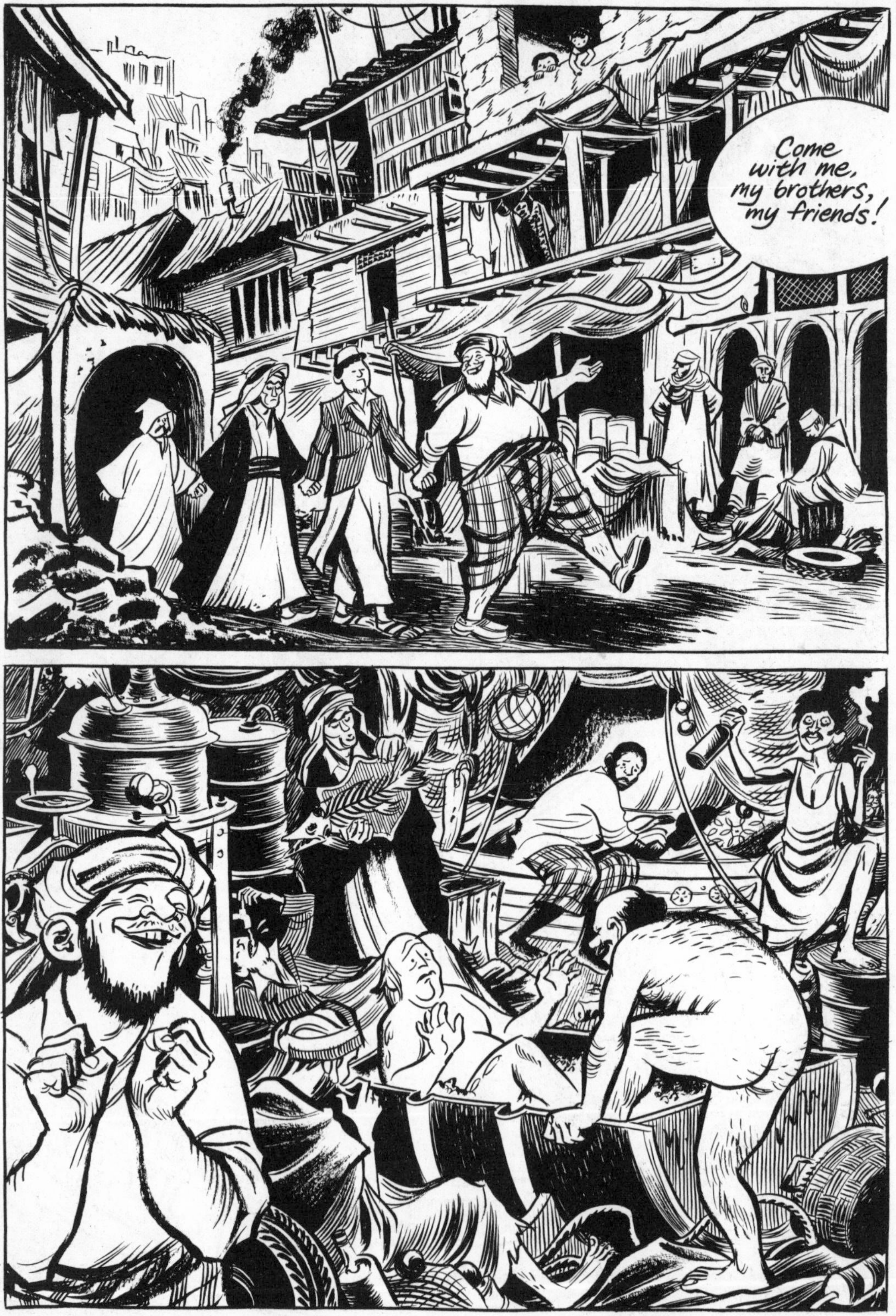
Come with me, my brothers, my friends!

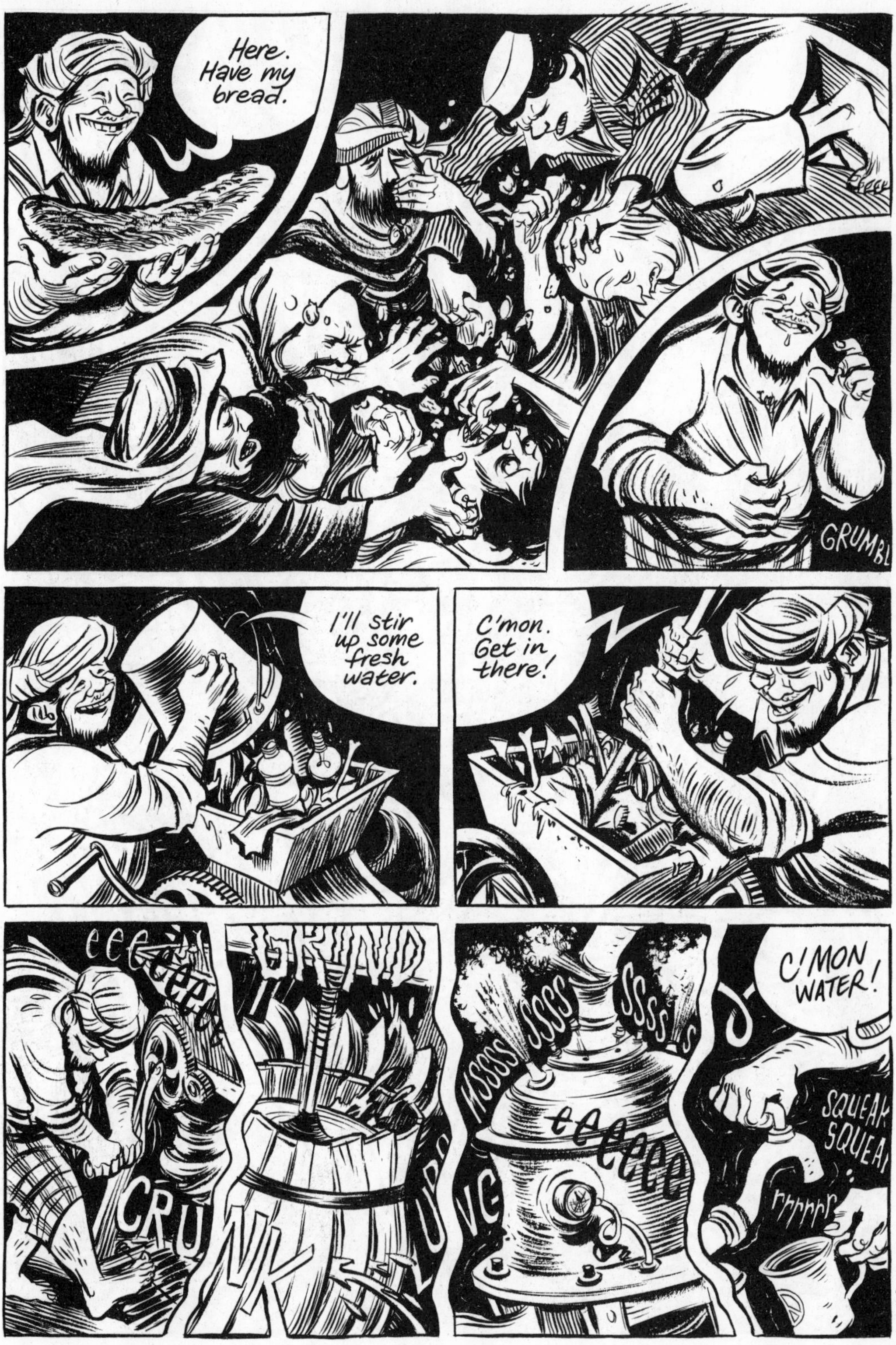
Here. Have my bread.
GRUMBL
I'll stir up some fresh water.
C'mon. Get in there!
GRIND
CRUNK
HSSSS SSSS SSSS S
eeeeee
C'MON WATER!
SQUEAK SQUEA

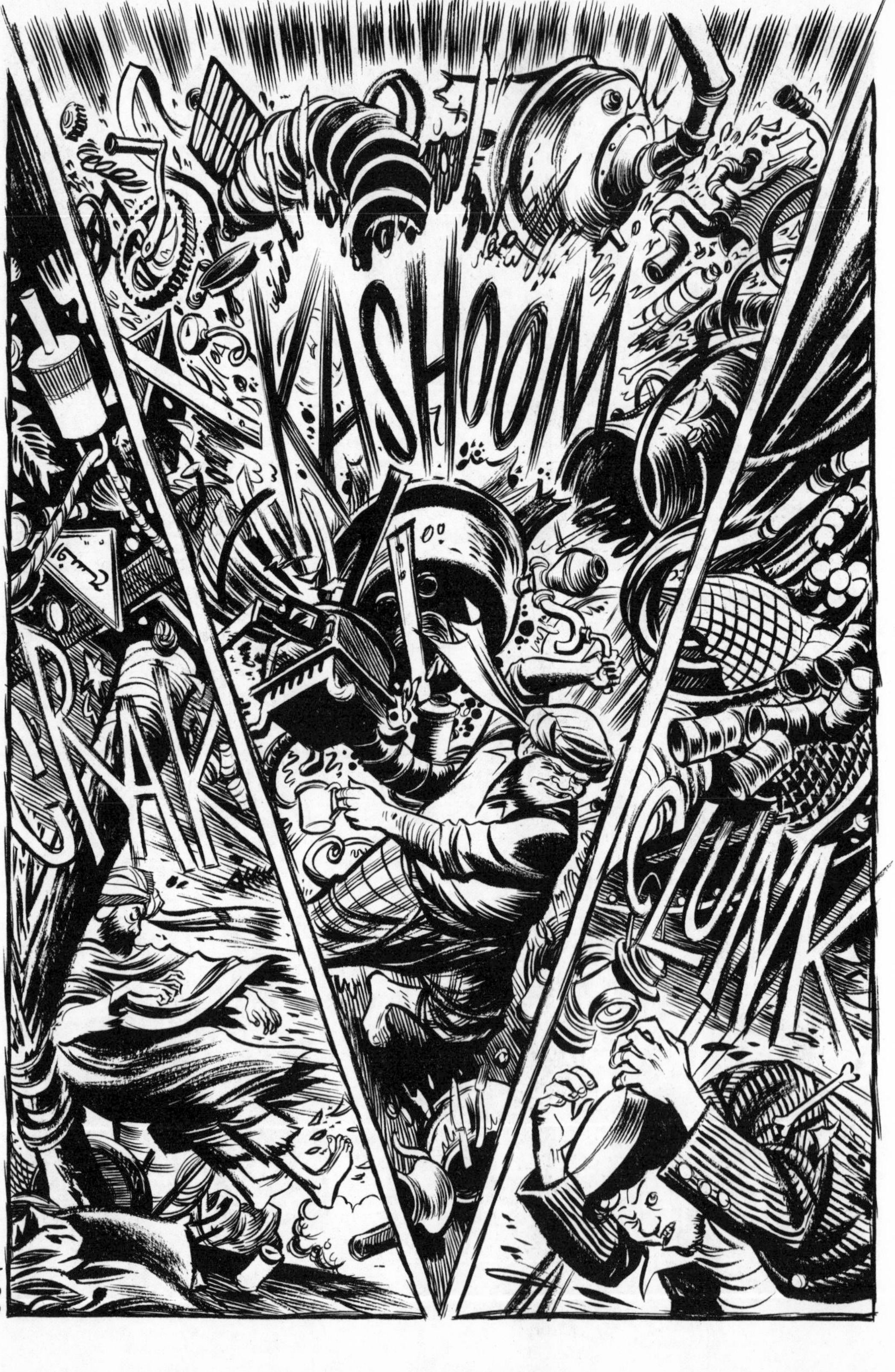
CRAK
KASHOOM
CLUNK

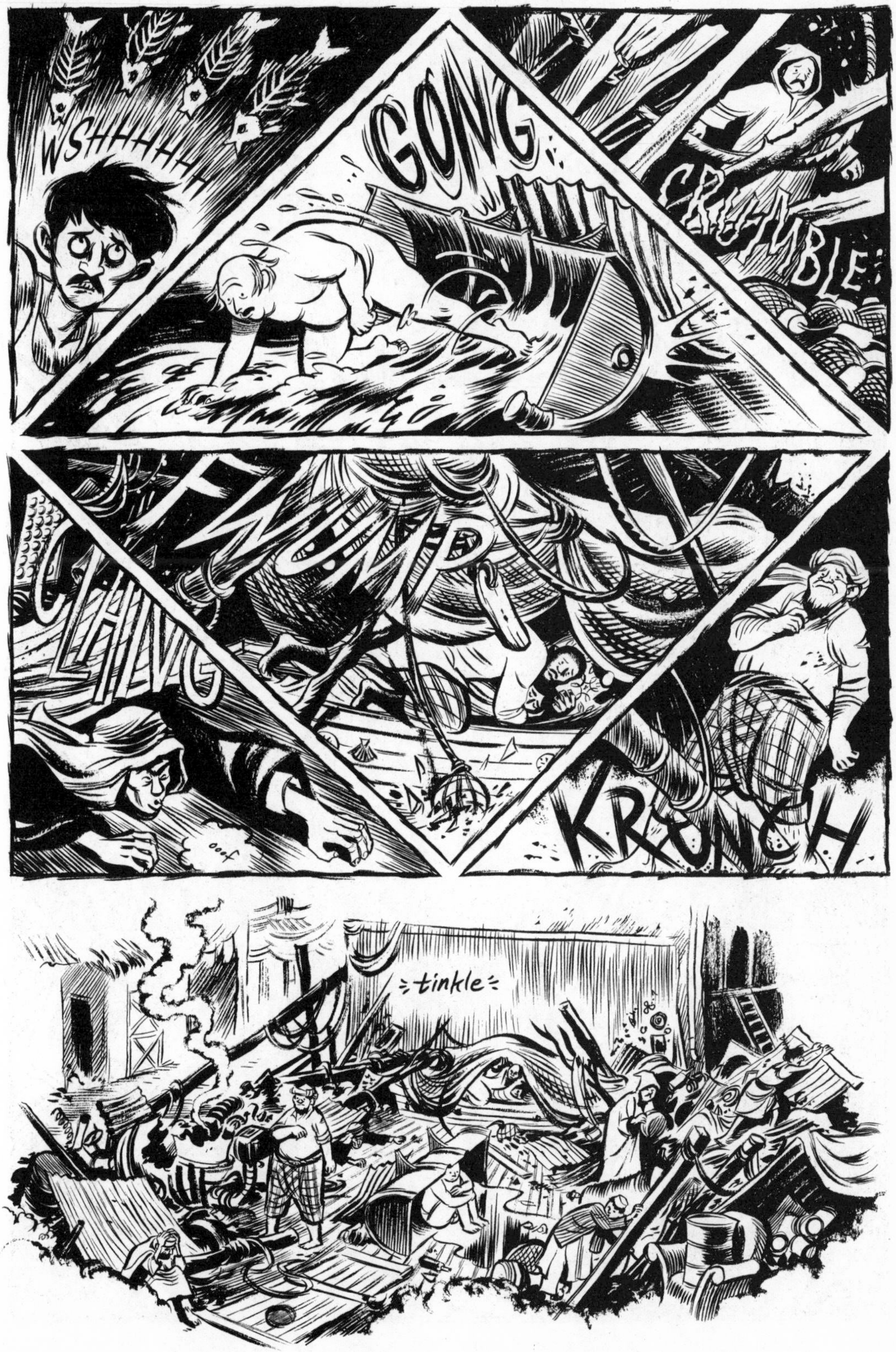
WSHHHHHH
GONG
CRUMBLE
FWUMP
CHING
oof
KRUNCH
tinkle

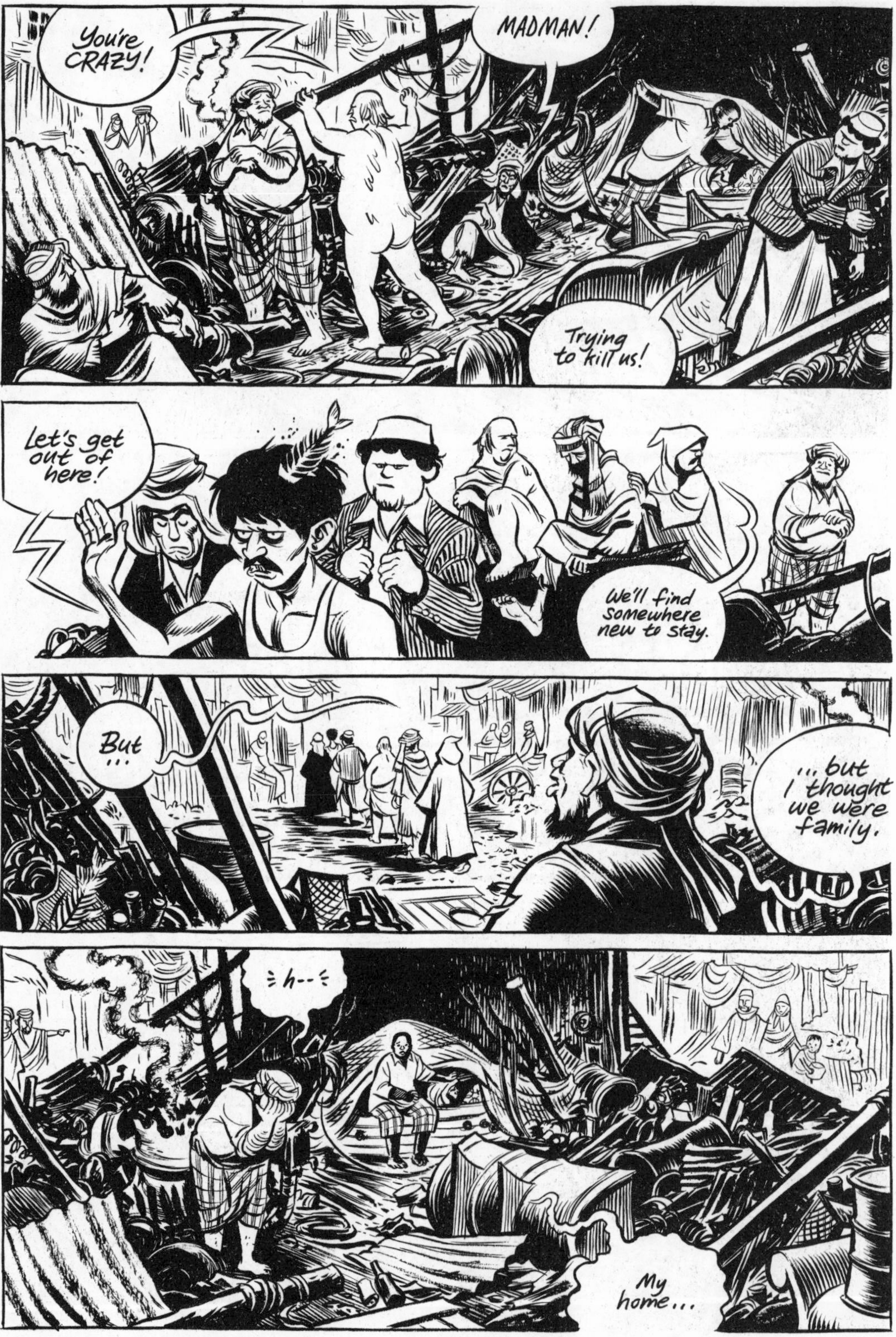

You're CRAZY!
MADMAN!
Trying to kill us!
Let's get out of here!
We'll find somewhere new to stay.
But ...
... but I thought we were family.
h--
My home...

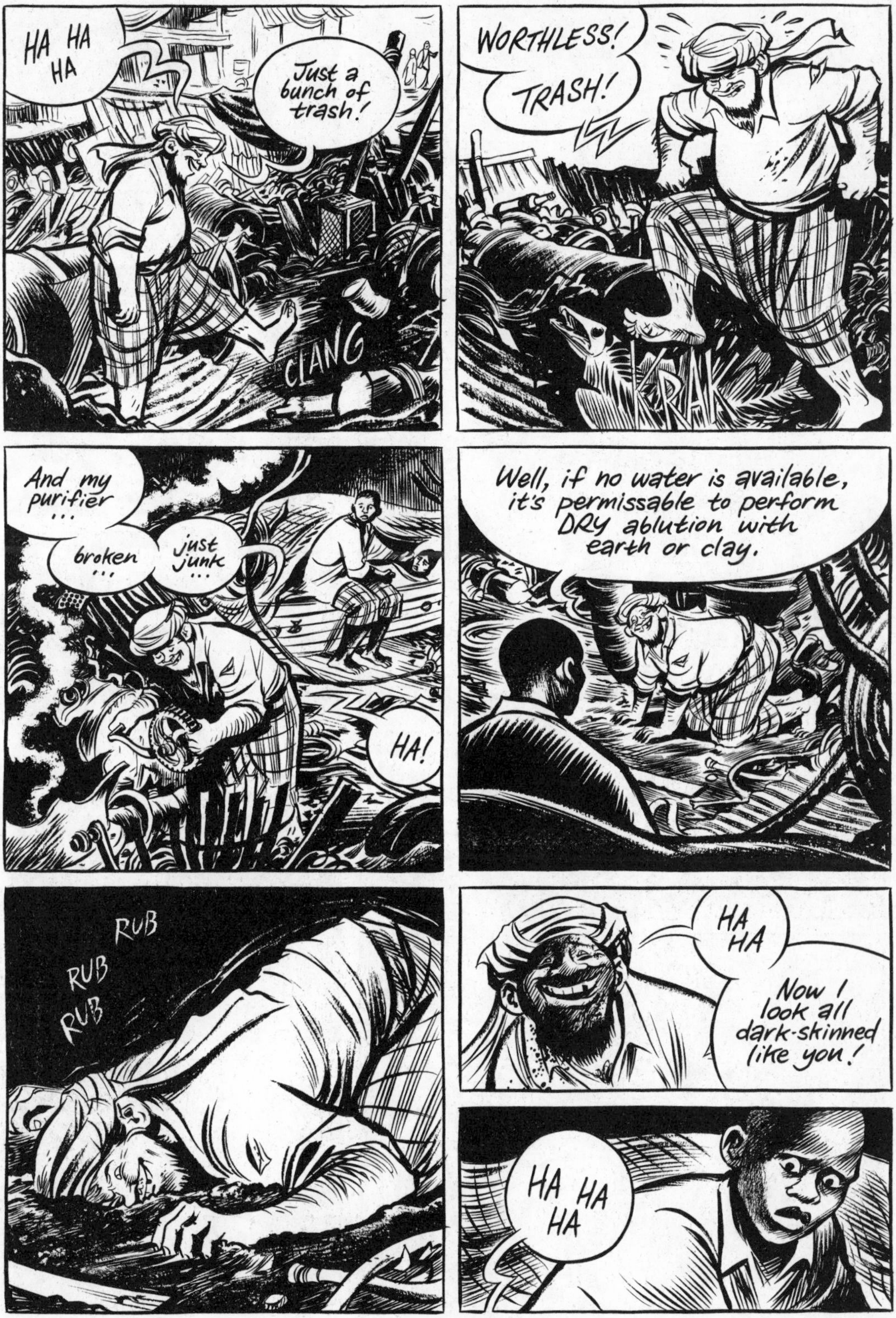
HA HA HA
Just a bunch of trash!
CLANG
WORTHLESS!
TRASH!
KRAK
And my purifier ...
broken ...
just junk ...
HA!
Well, if no water is available, it's permissable to perform DRY ablution with earth or clay.
RUB
RUB
RUB
HA HA
Now I look all dark-skinned like you!
HA HA HA

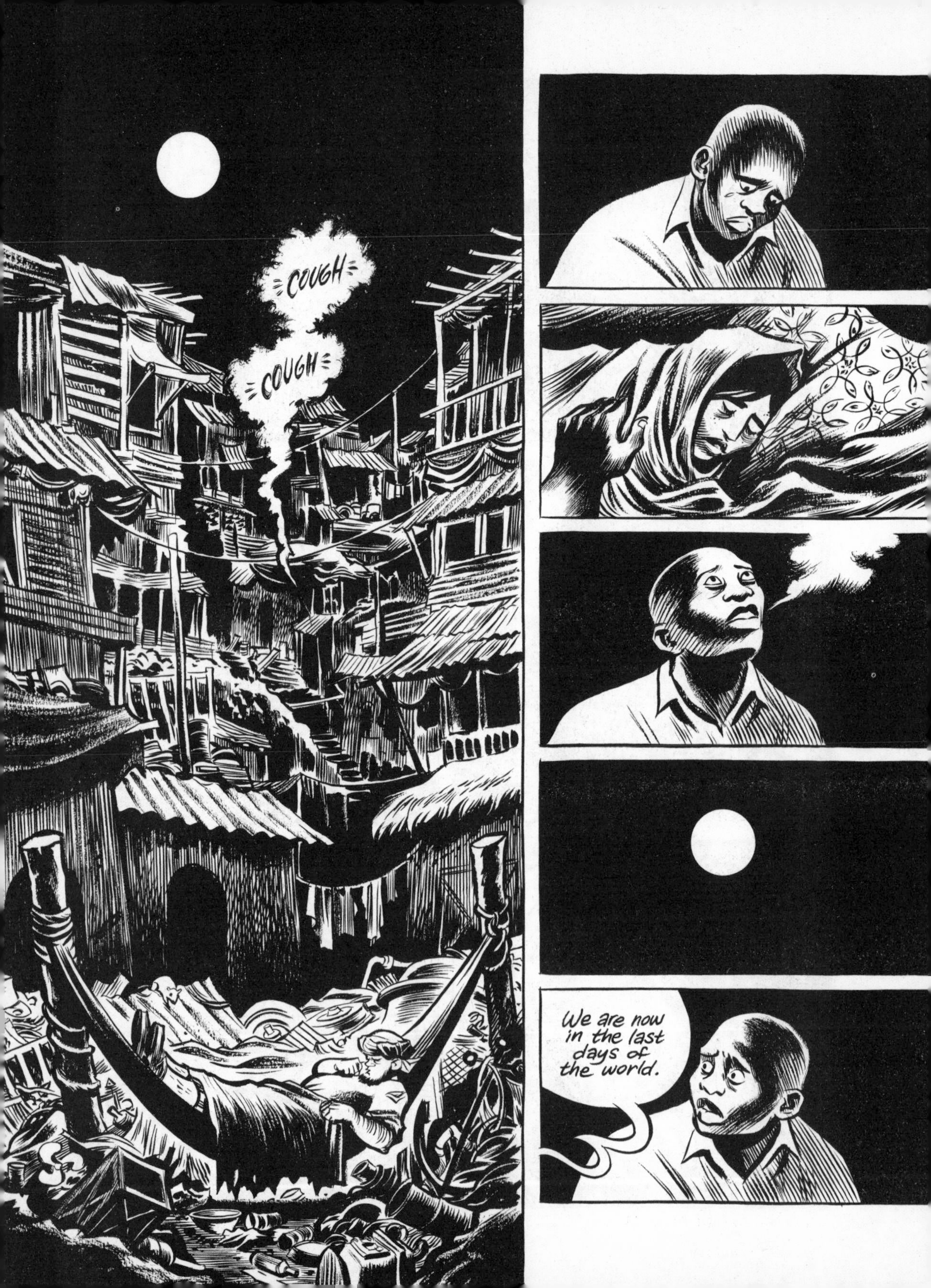
COUGH
COUGH
We are now in the last days of the world.

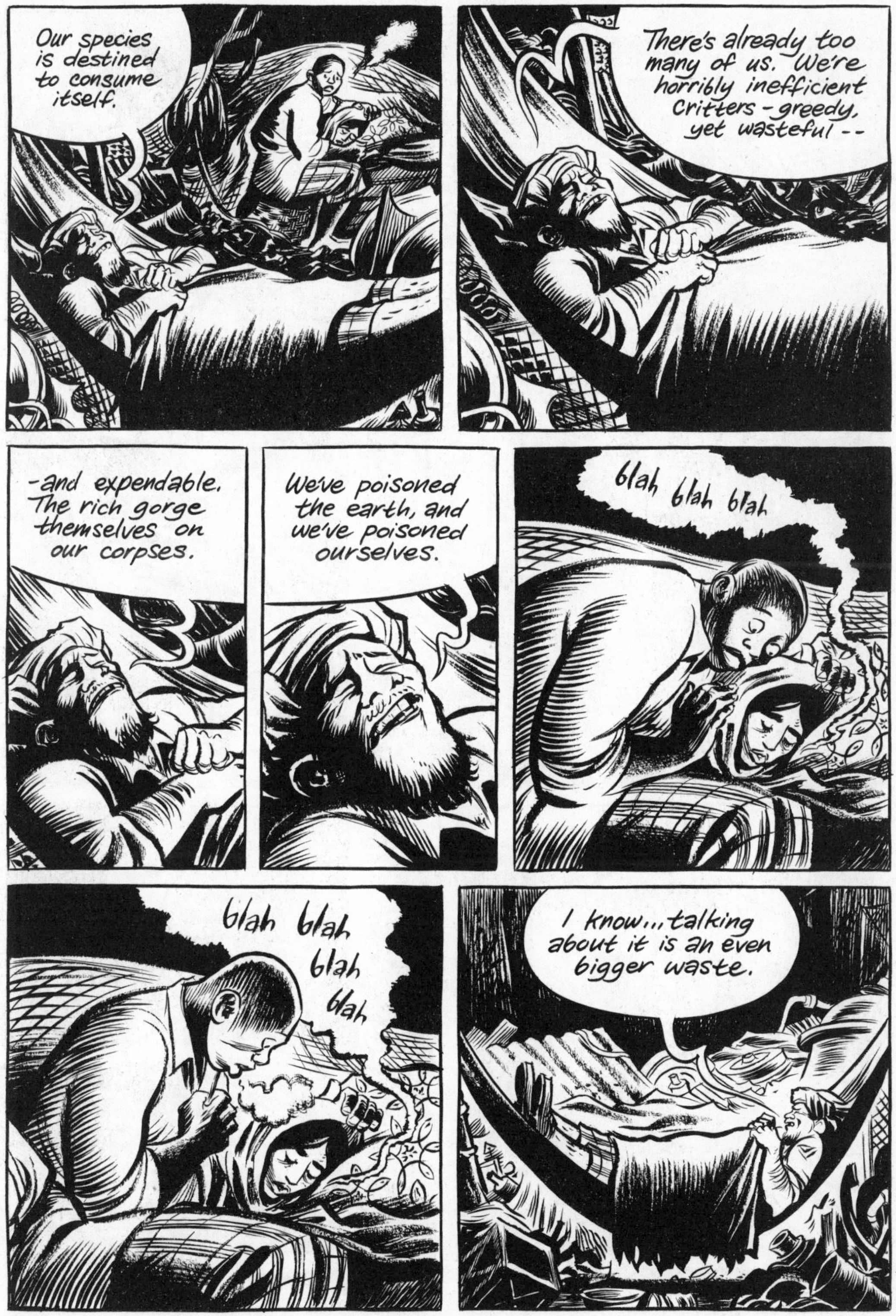

Our species is destined to consume itself.
There's already too many of us. We're horribly inefficient critters - greedy, yet wasteful --
-and expendable. The rich gorge themselves on our corpses.
We've poisoned the earth, and we've poisoned ourselves.
blah blah blah
blah blah blah blah
I know... talking about it is an even bigger waste.

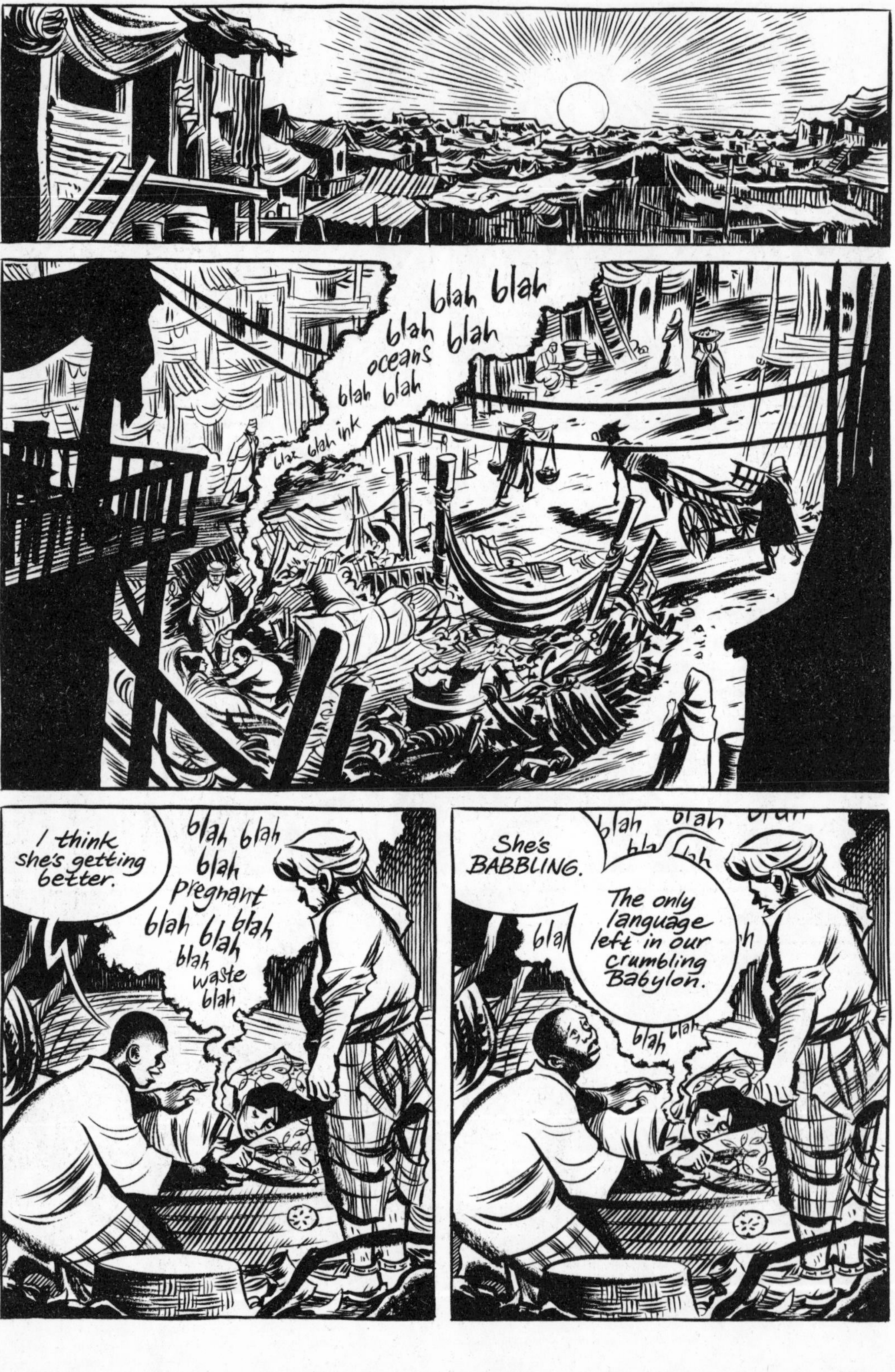
blah blah
blah oceans blah
blah blah
blaz blah ink
I think she's getting better.
blah blah blah pregnant blah blah blah blah waste blah
She's BABBLING.
The only language left in our crumbling Babylon.
blah blah

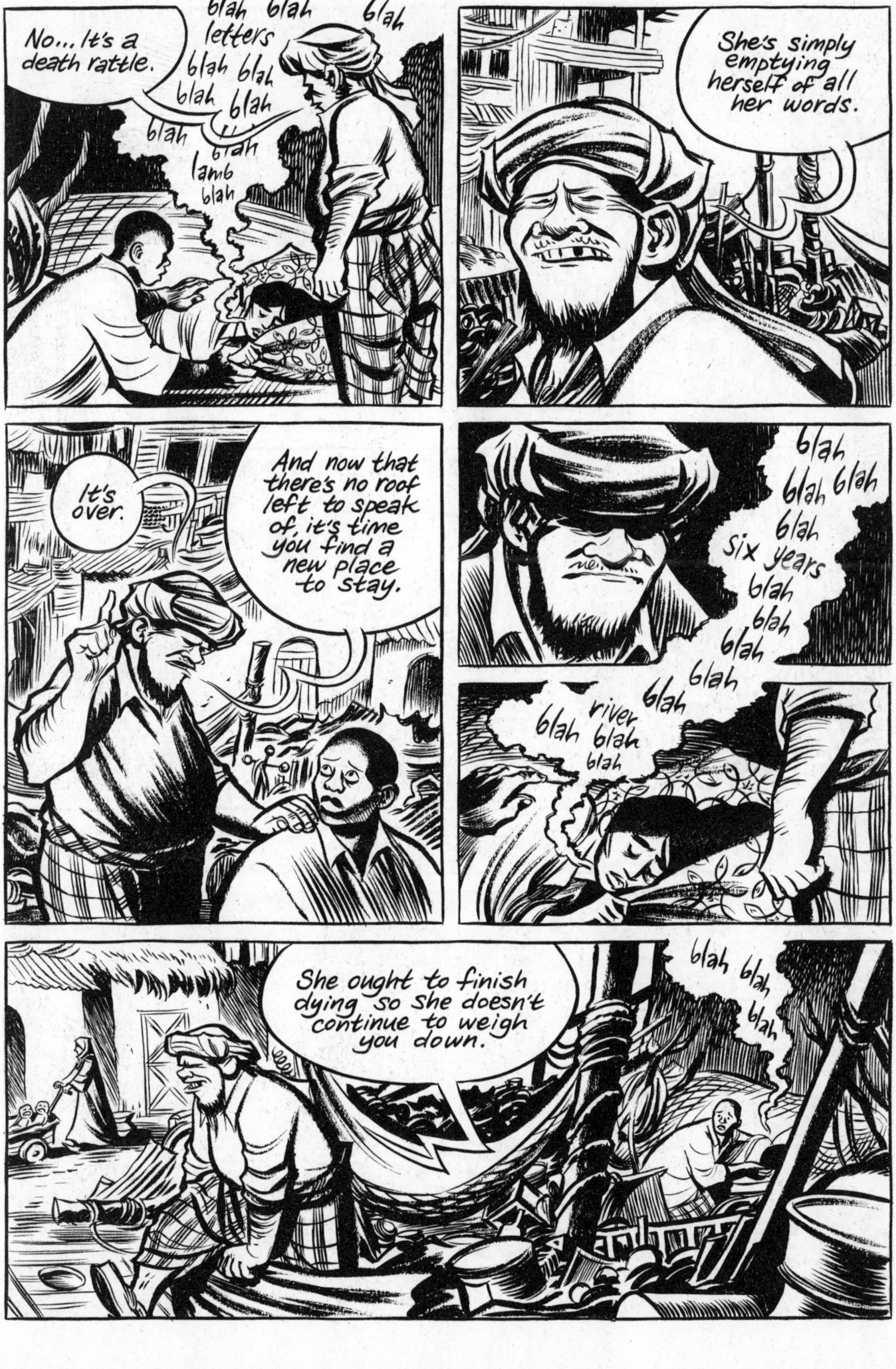
No... It's a death rattle.
blah blah blah letters blah blah blah blah blah blah lamb blah
She's simply emptying herself of all her words.
It's over.
And now that there's no roof left to speak of, it's time you find a new place to stay.
blah blah blah blah Six years blah blah blah
blah blah river blah blah blah
She ought to finish dying so she doesn't continue to weigh you down.
blah blah blah

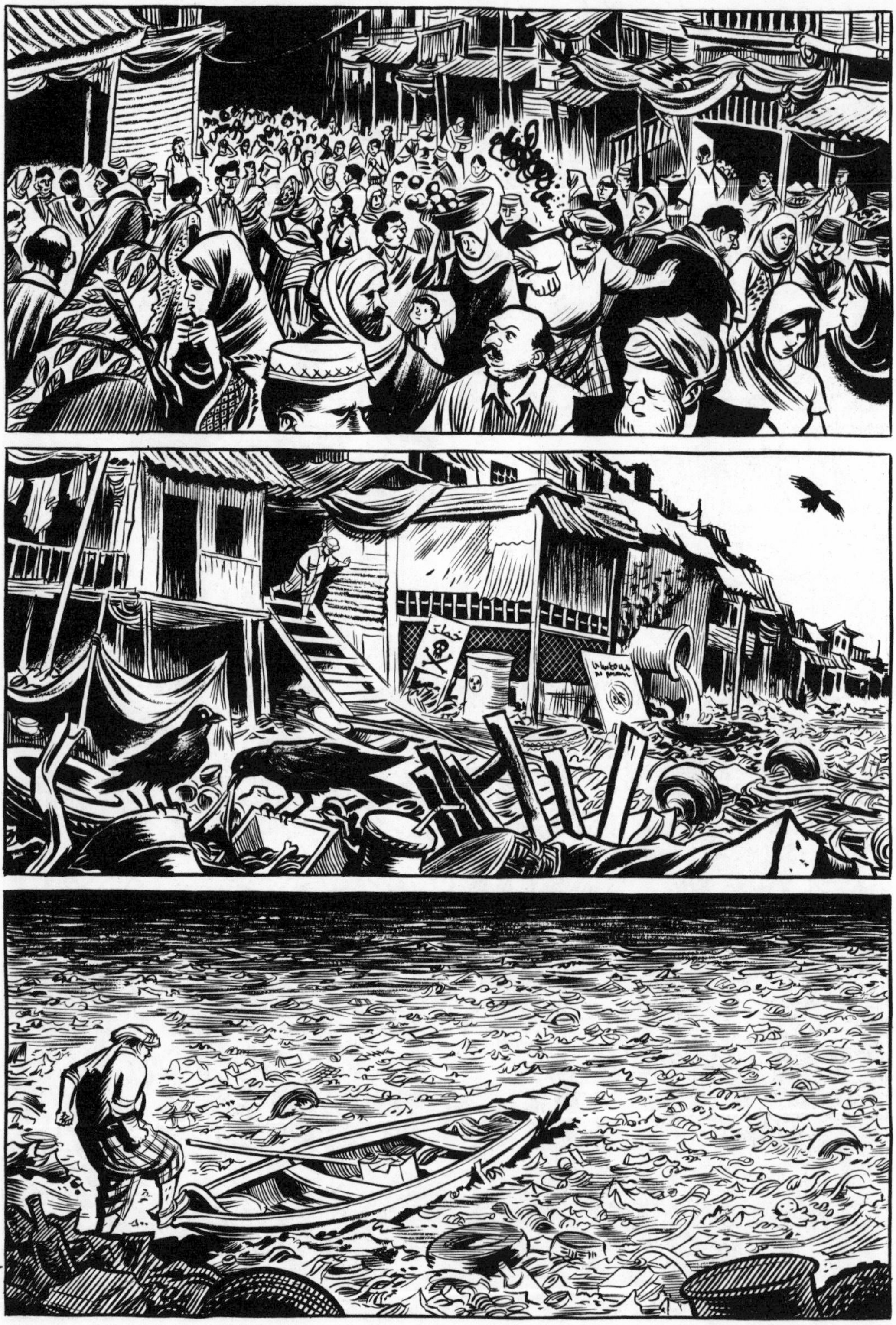

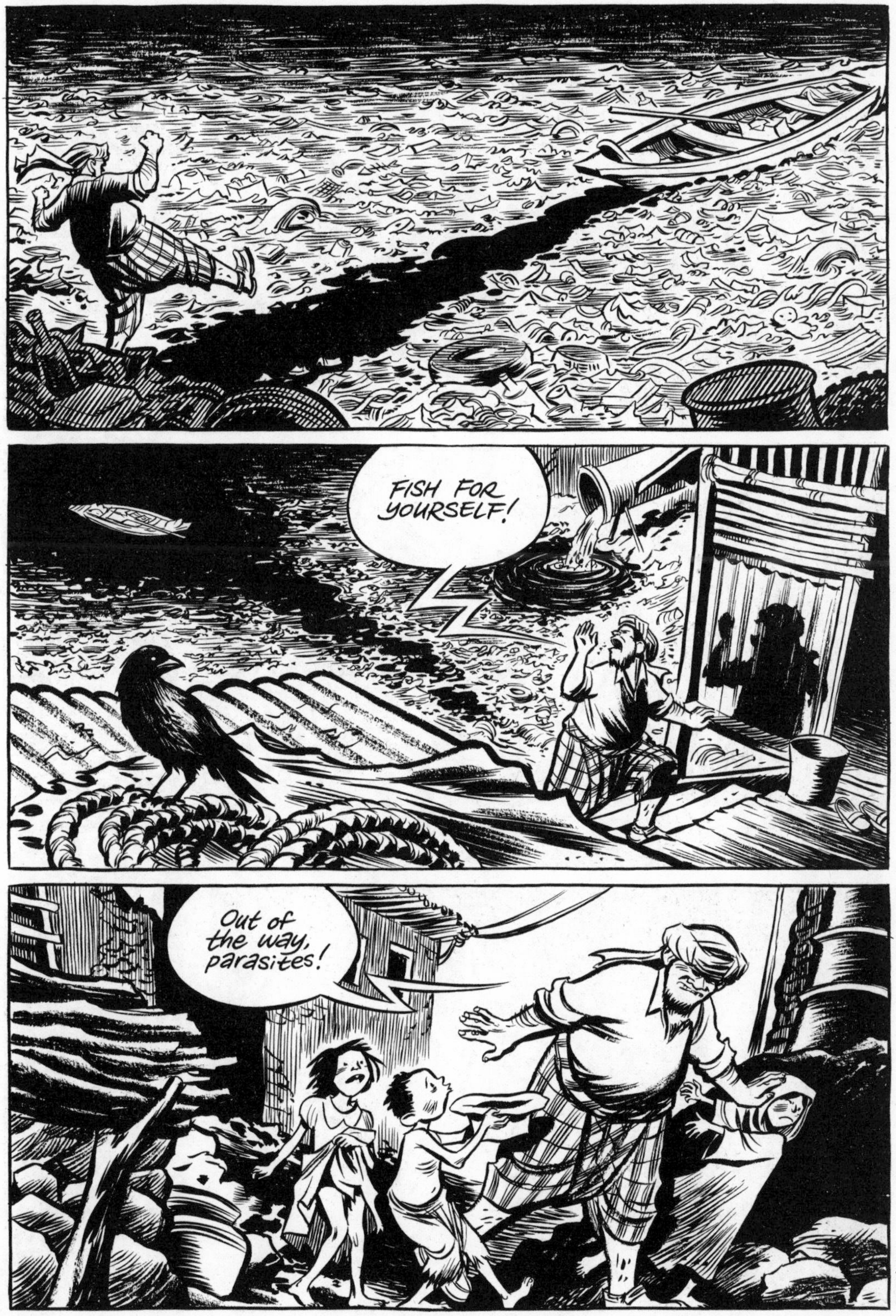
FISH FOR YOURSELF!
Out of the way, parasites!

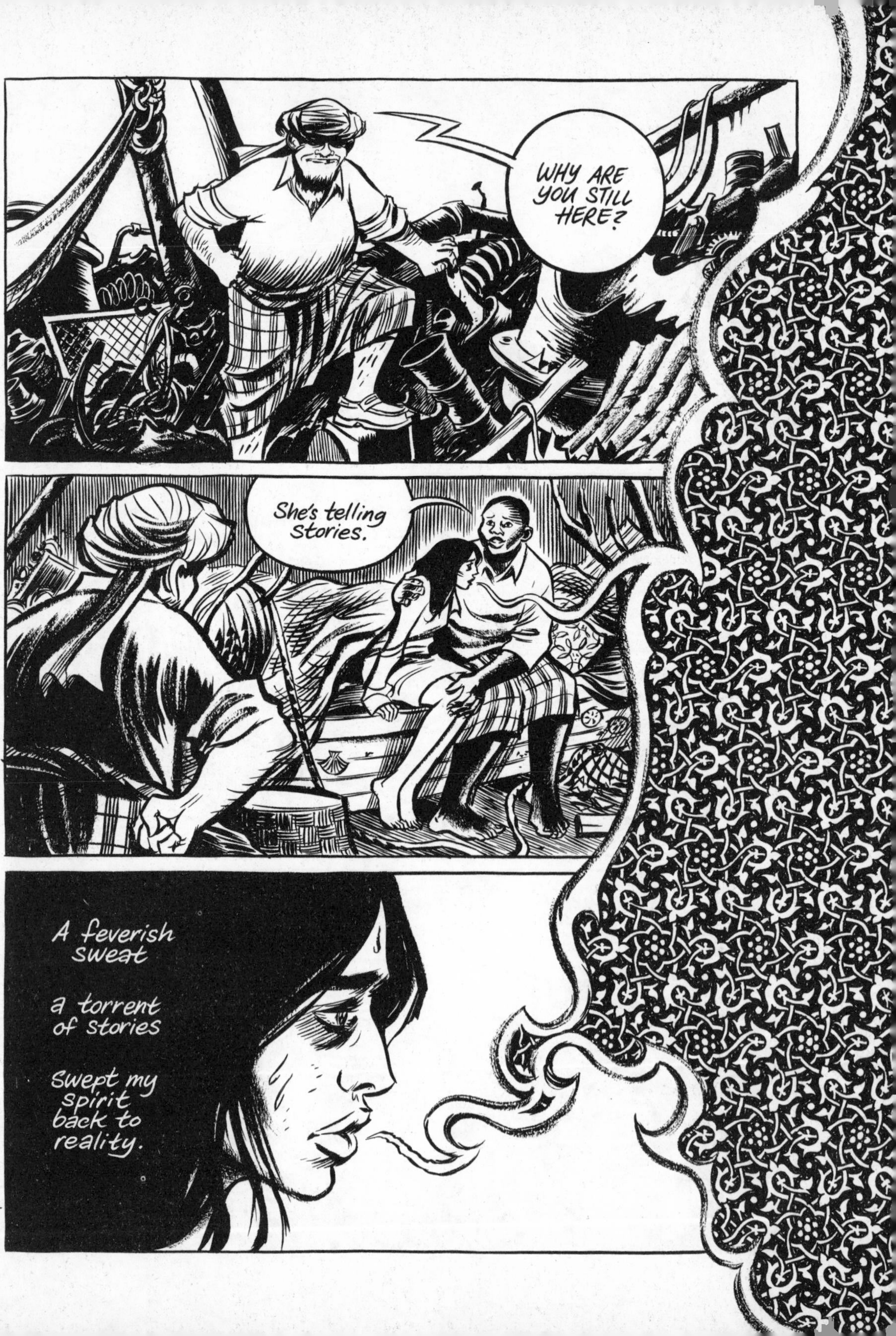
WHY ARE YOU STILL HERE?
She's telling stories.
A feverish sweat
a torrent of stories
Swept my spirit back to reality.

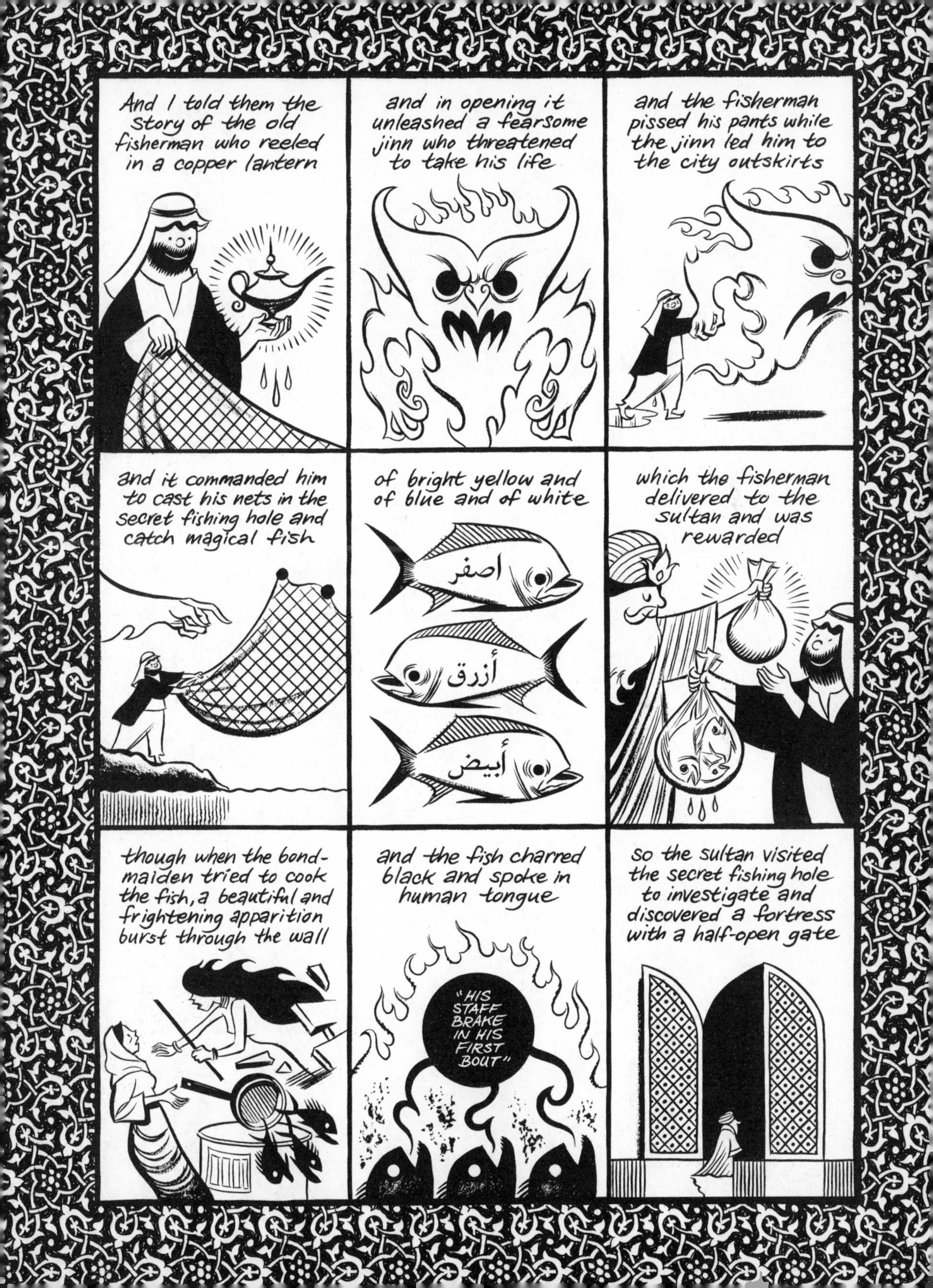
And I told them the story of the old fisherman who reeled in a copper lantern
and in opening it unleashed a fearsome jinn who threatened to take his life
and the fisherman pissed his pants while the jinn led him to the city outskirts
and it commanded him to cast his nets in the secret fishing hole and catch magical fish
of bright yellow and of blue and of white
اصفر
أزرق
أبيض
which the fisherman delivered to the sultan and was rewarded
though when the bond-maiden tried to cook the fish, a beautiful and frightening apparition burst through the wall
and the fish charred black and spoke in human tongue
"HIS STAFF BRAKE IN HIS FIRST BOUT"
so the sultan visited the secret fishing hole to investigate and discovered a fortress with a half-open gate

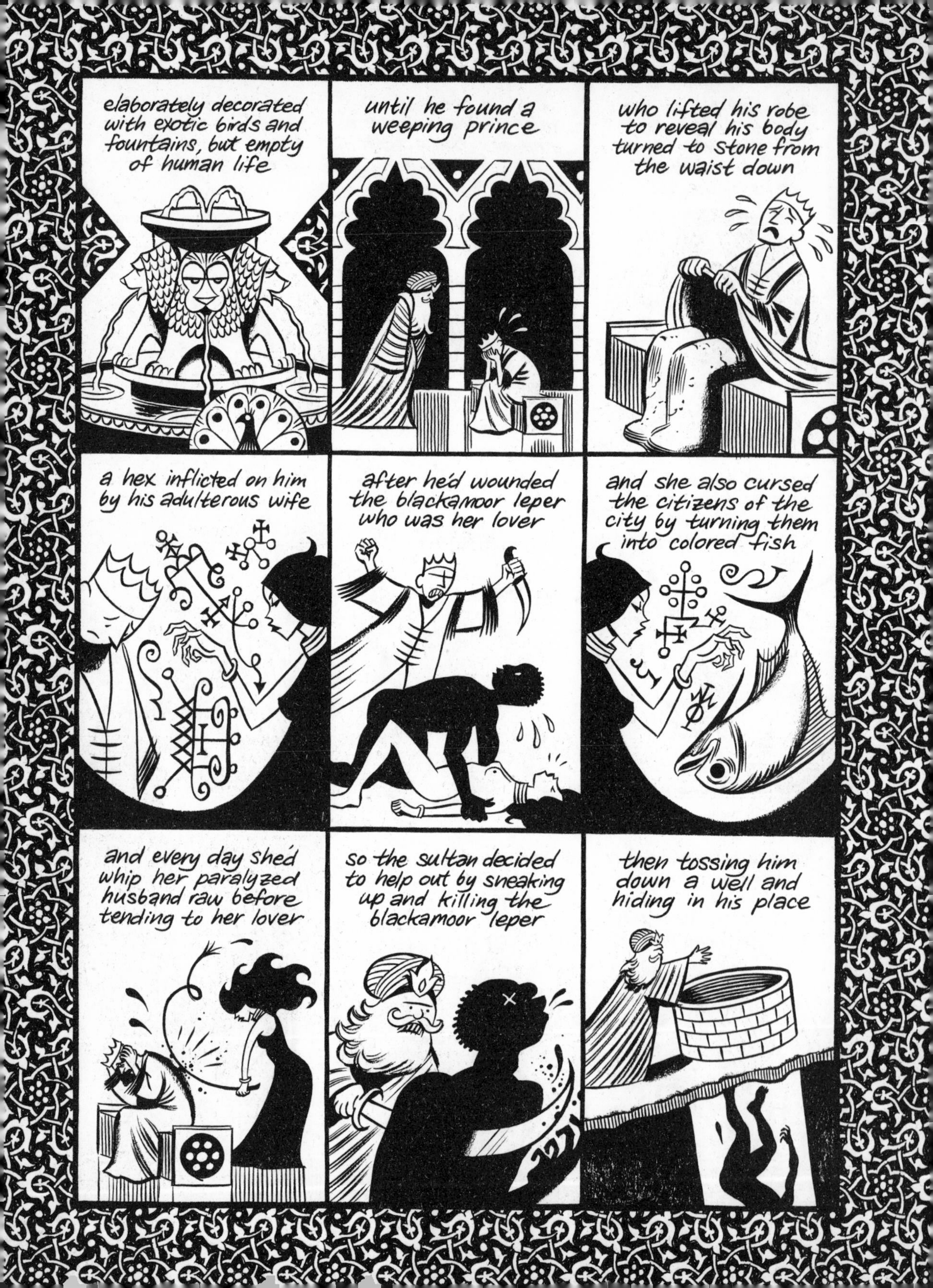
elaborately decorated with exotic birds and fountains, but empty of human life
until he found a weeping prince
who lifted his robe to reveal his body turned to stone from the waist down
a hex inflicted on him by his adulterous wife
after he'd wounded the blackamoor leper who was her lover
and she also cursed the citizens of the city by turning them into colored fish
and every day she'd whip her paralyzed husband raw before tending to her lover
so the sultan decided to help out by sneaking up and killing the blackamoor leper
then tossing him down a well and hiding in his place

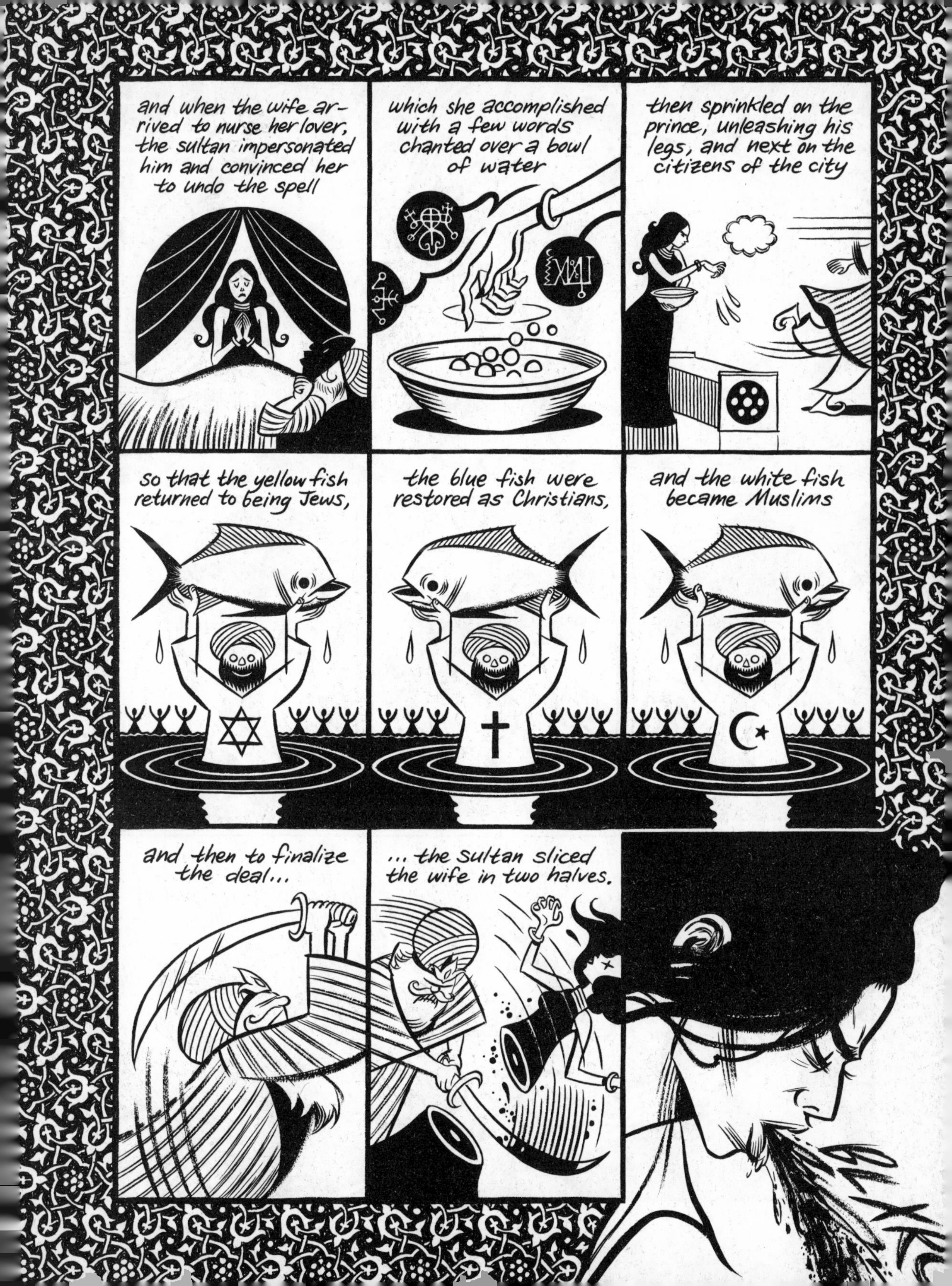
and when the wife arrived to nurse her lover, the sultan impersonated him and convinced her to undo the spell
which she accomplished with a few words chanted over a bowl of water
then sprinkled on the prince, unleashing his legs, and next on the citizens of the city
so that the yellow fish returned to being Jews,
the blue fish were restored as Christians,
and the white fish became Muslims
and then to finalize the deal...
... the sultan sliced the wife in two halves.

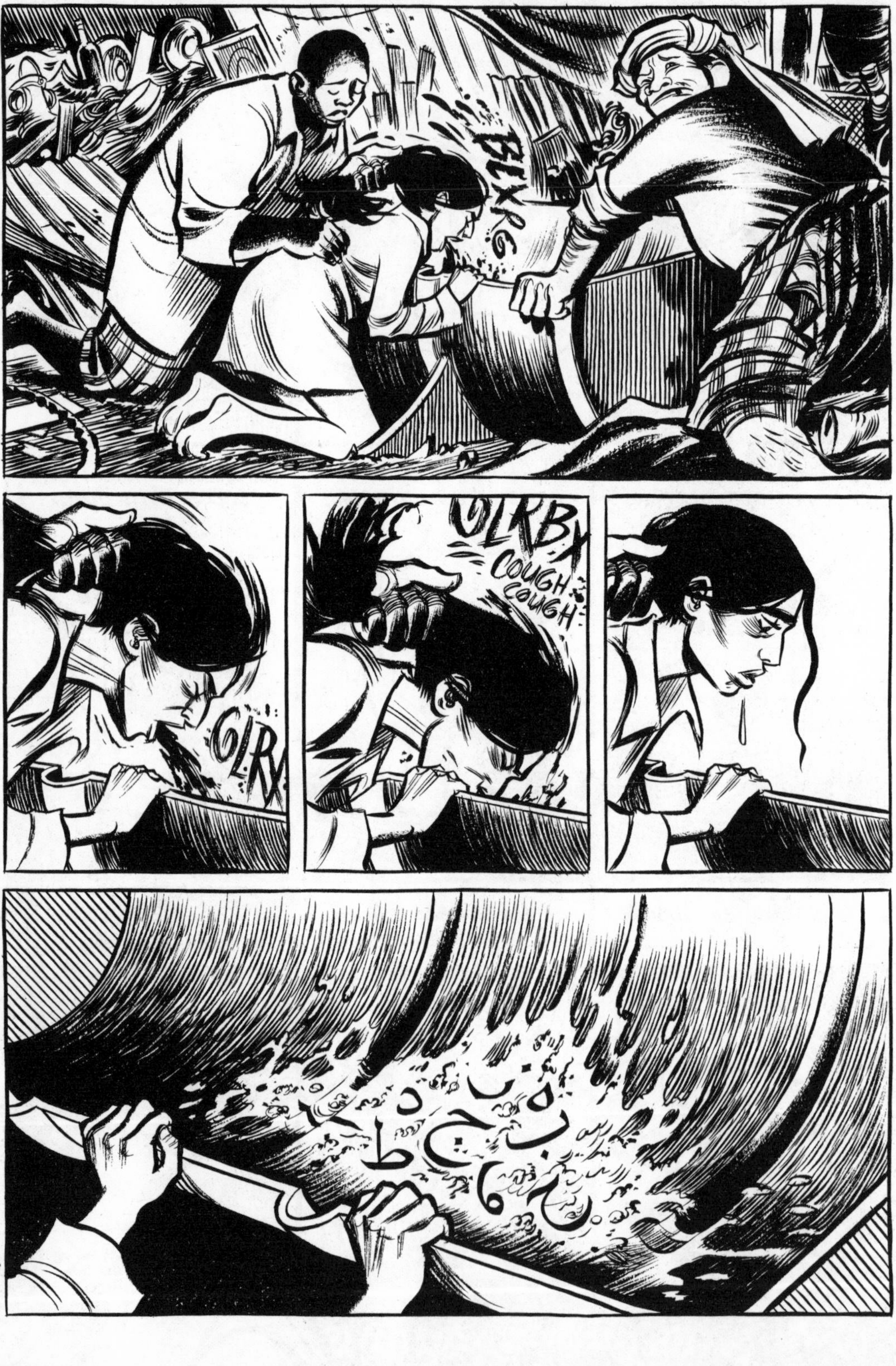
COUGH
COUGH

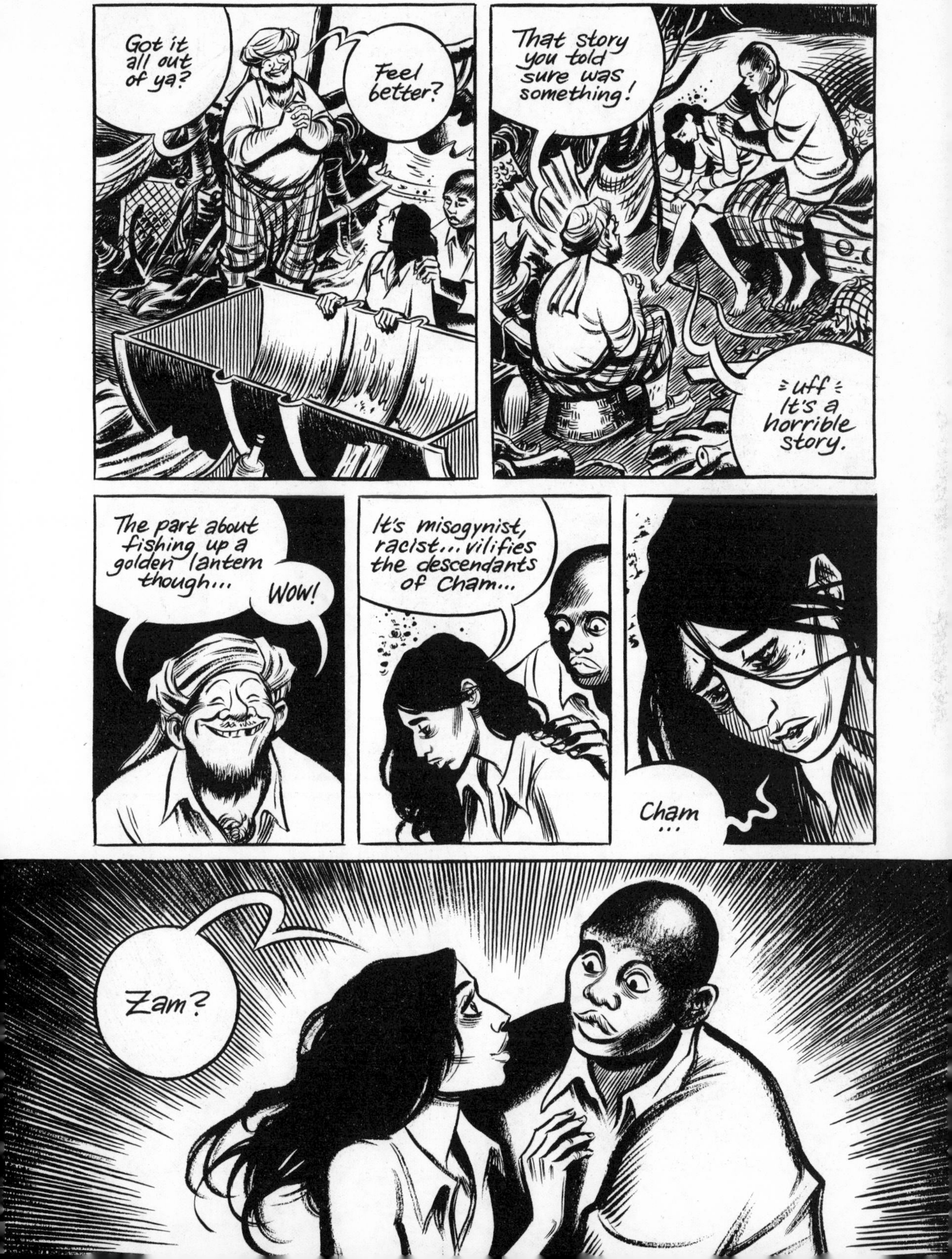

Got it all out of ya?
Feel better?
That story you told sure was something!
uff It's a horrible story.
The part about fishing up a golden lantern though...
WOW!
It's misogynist, racist... vilifies the descendants of Cham...
Cham ...
Zam?

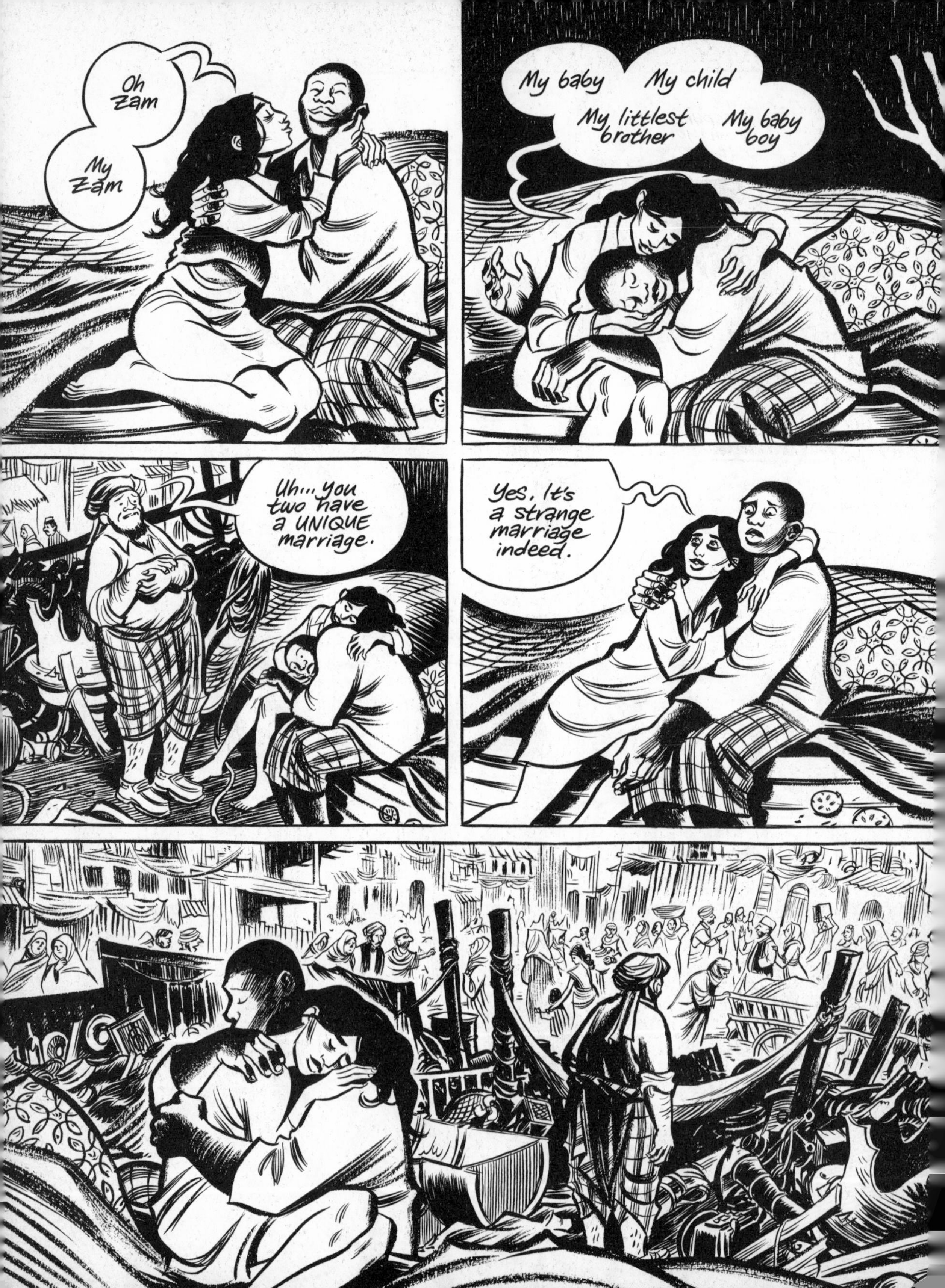

Oh Zam
My Zam
My baby
My child
My littlest brother
My baby boy
Uh... you two have a UNIQUE marriage.
Yes. It's a strange marriage indeed.

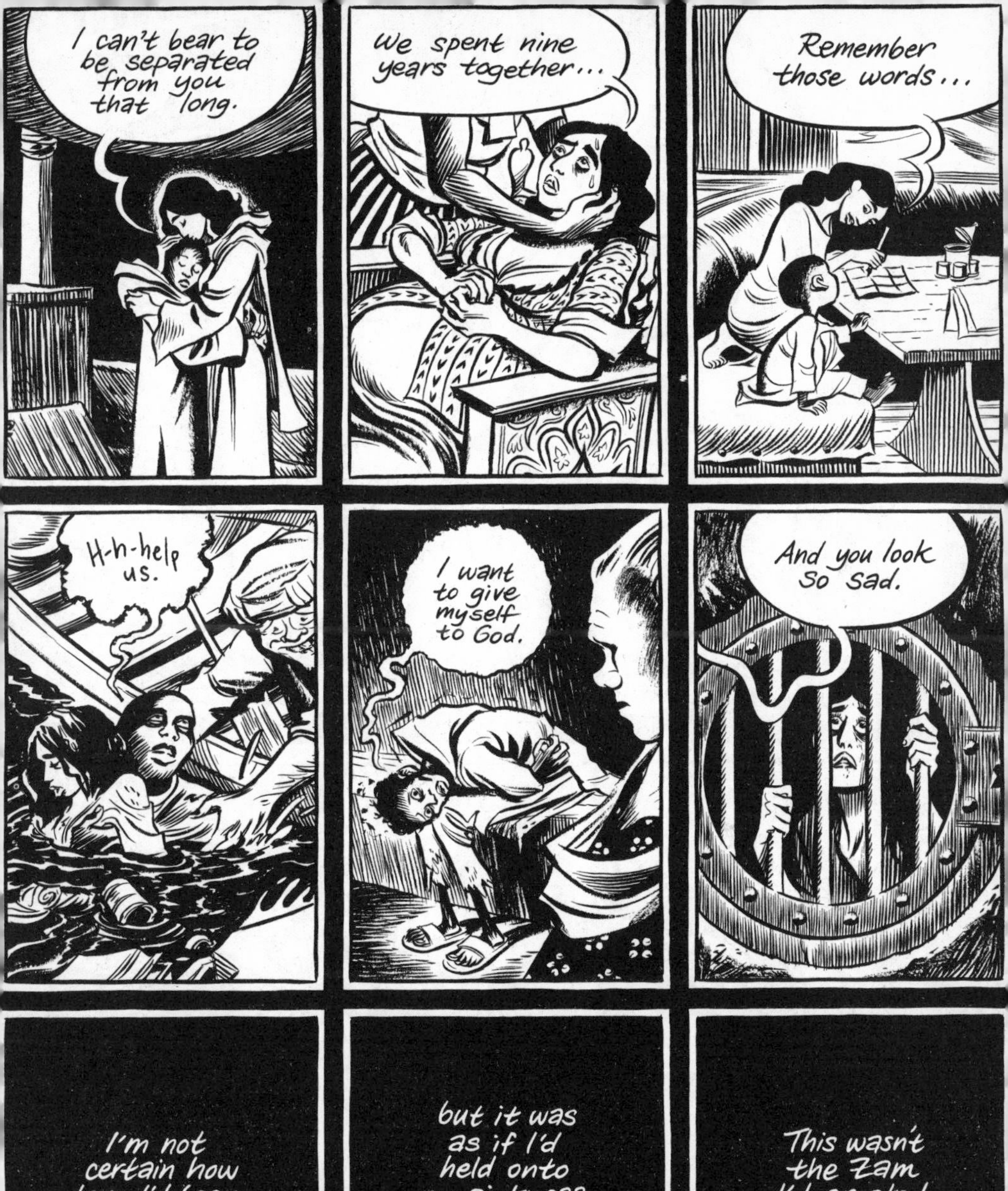
I can't bear to be separated from you that long.
We spent nine years together...
Remember those words...
H-h-help us.
I want to give myself to God.
And you look so sad.
I'm not certain how long I'd been sick, as the suffering rearranged any linear sense of time,
but it was as if I'd held onto my sickness, taking my time to accept the loss of my ideal and the curiousness of this stranger.
This wasn't the Zam I'd created, but the Zam who'd created himself in the last six years...

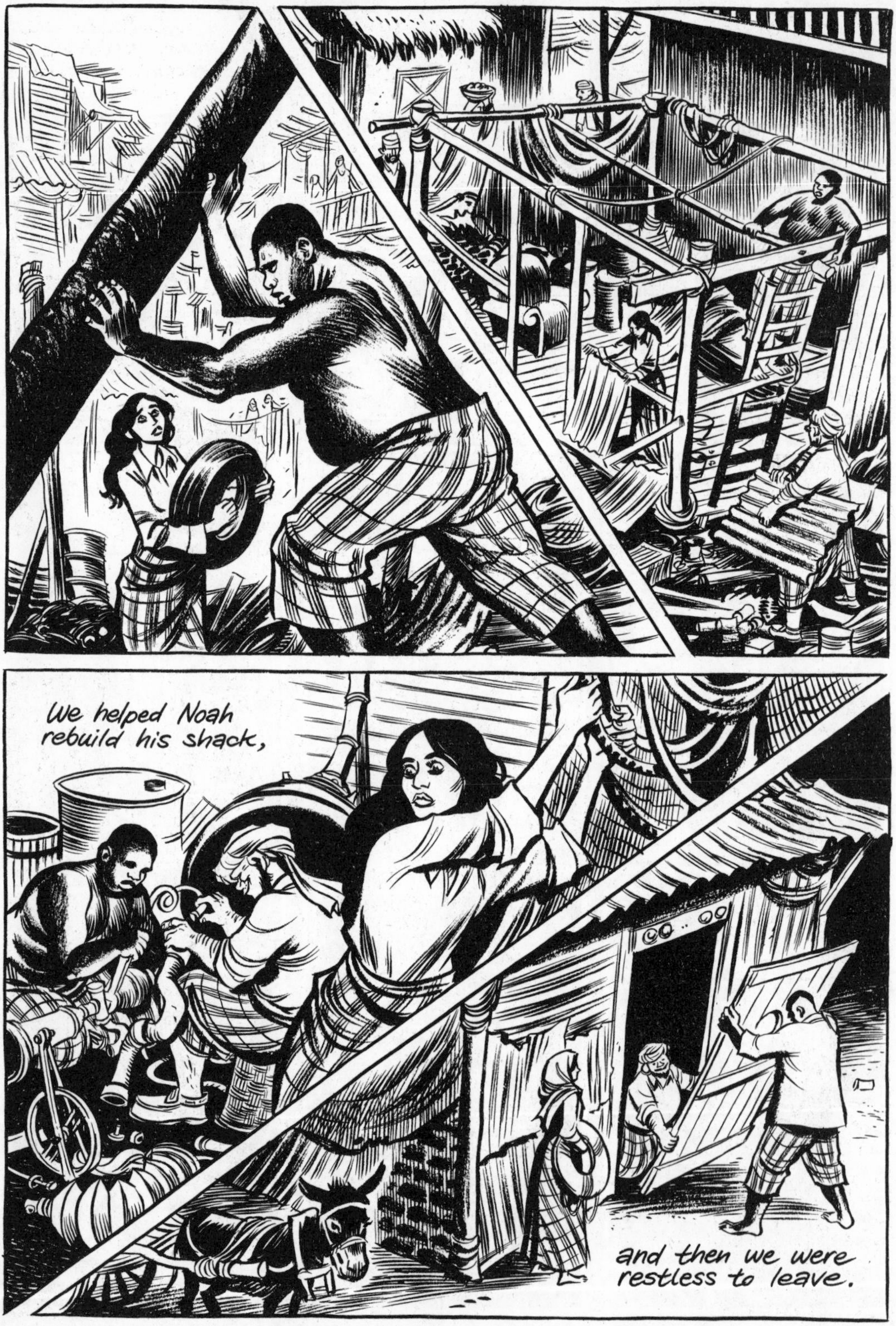
We helped Noah rebuild his shack,
and then we were restless to leave.

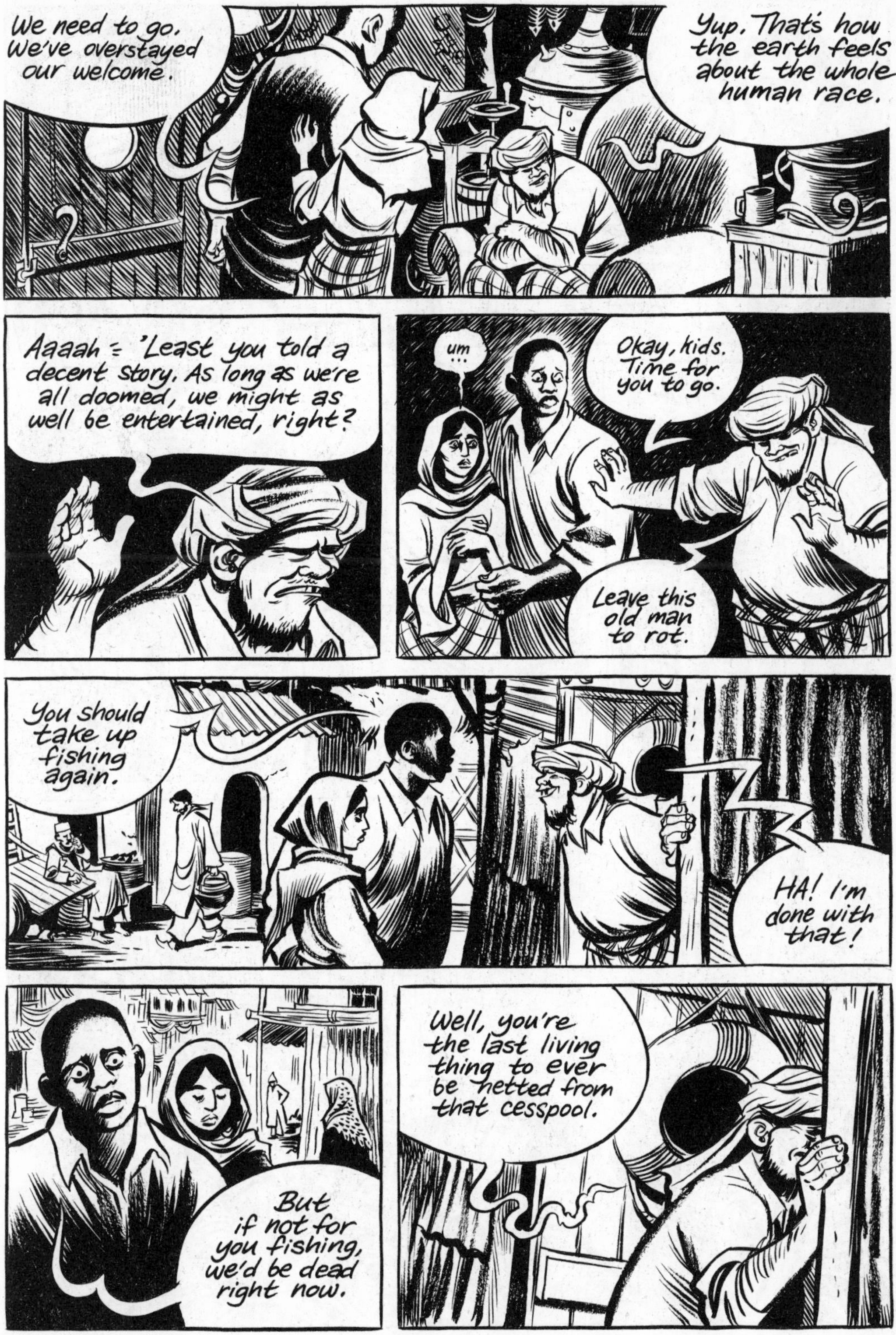
We need to go. We've overstayed our welcome.
Yup. That's how the earth feels about the whole human race.
Aaaah = 'Least you told a decent story. As long as we're all doomed, we might as well be entertained, right?
um ...
Okay, kids. Time for you to go.
Leave this old man to rot.
You should take up fishing again.
HA! I'm done with that!
But if not for you fishing, we'd be dead right now.
Well, you're the last living thing to ever be netted from that cesspool.

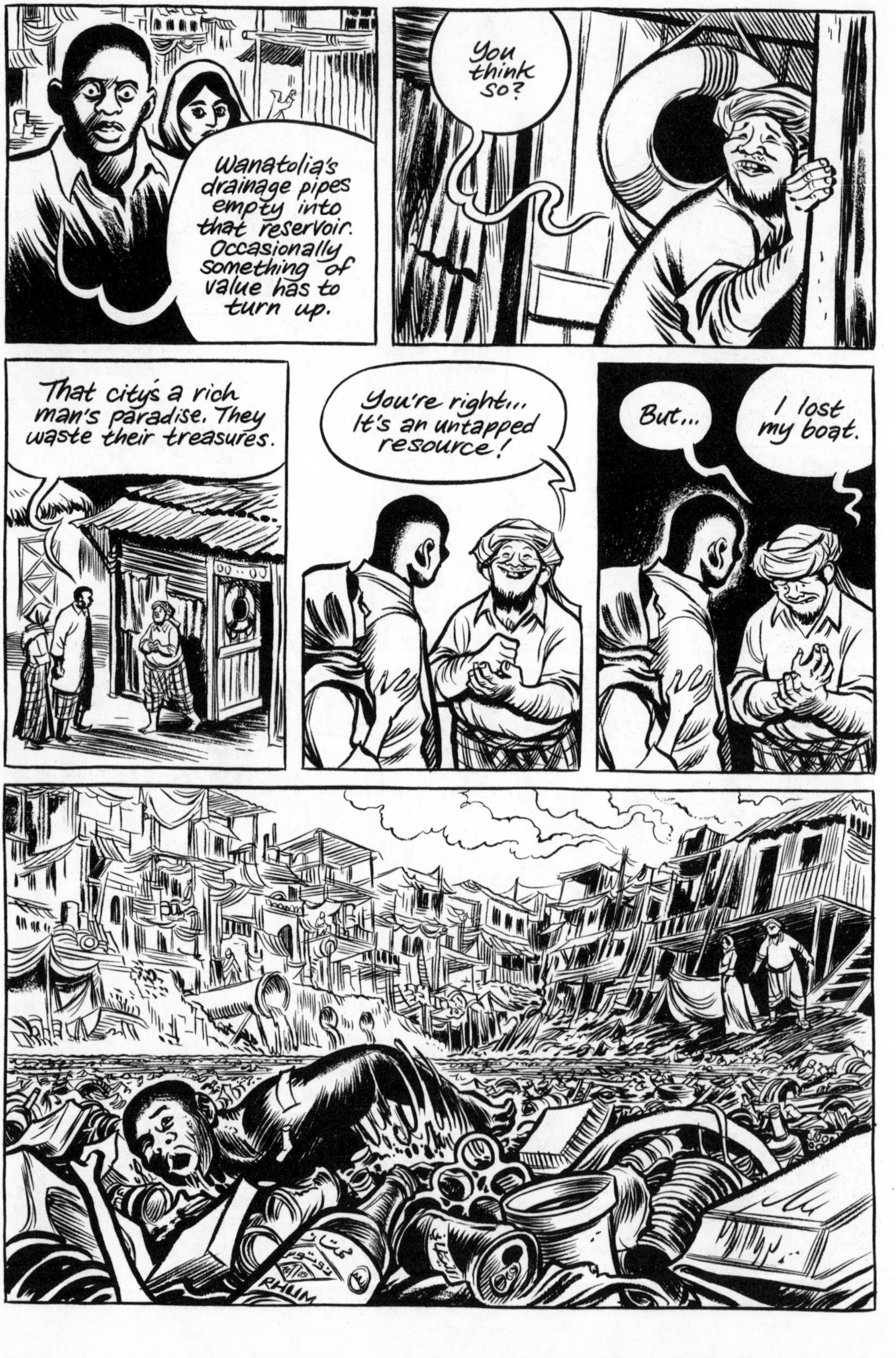

Wanatolia's drainage pipes empty into that reservoir. Occasionally something of value has to turn up.
You think so?
That city's a rich man's paradise. They waste their treasures.
You're right... It's an untapped resource!
But...
I lost my boat.
RHUM

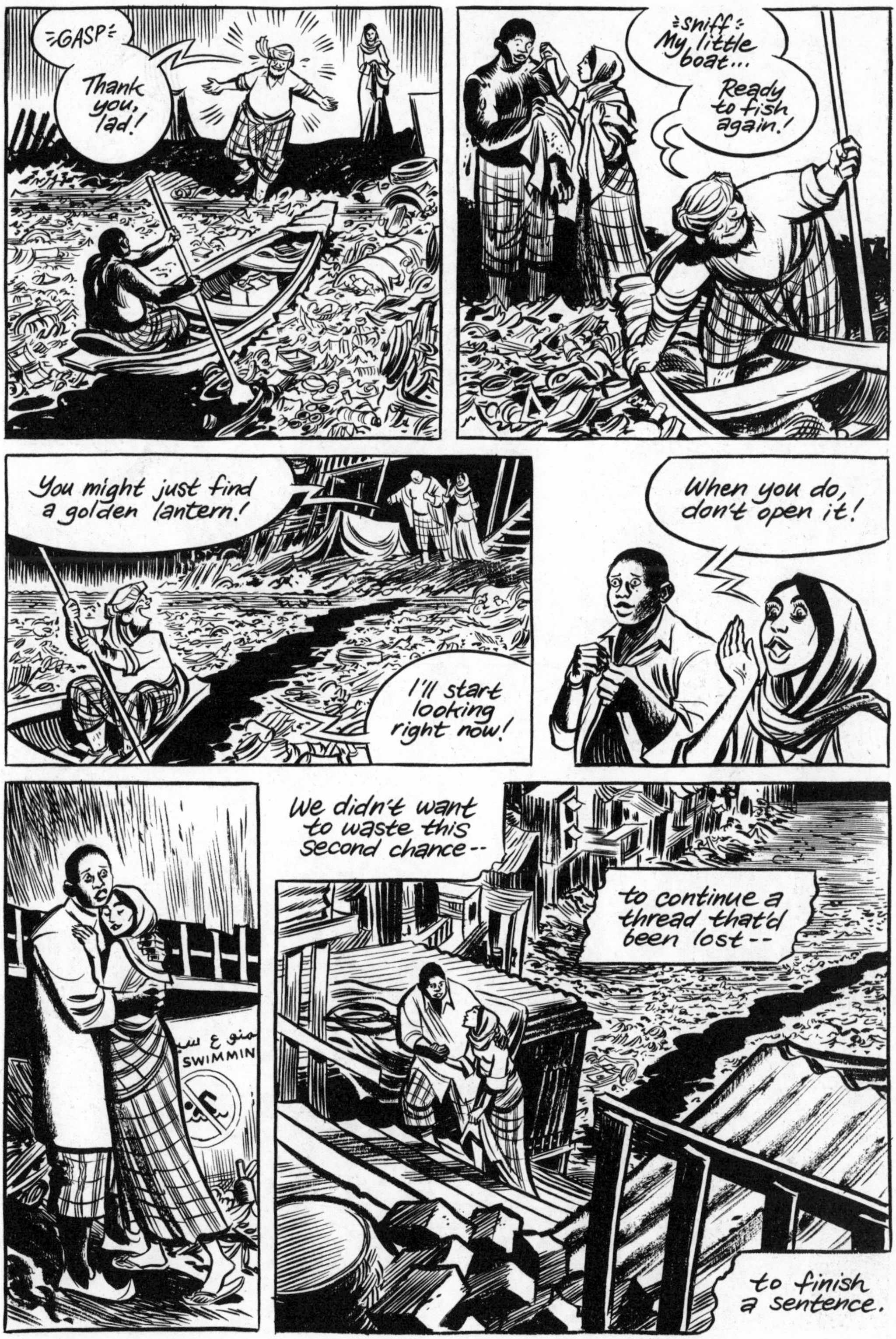
GASP
Thank you, lad!
sniff My little boat...
Ready to fish again!
You might just find a golden lantern!
I'll start looking right now!
When you do, don't open it!
SWIMMIN
We didn't want to waste this second chance--
to continue a thread that'd been lost--
to finish a sentence.

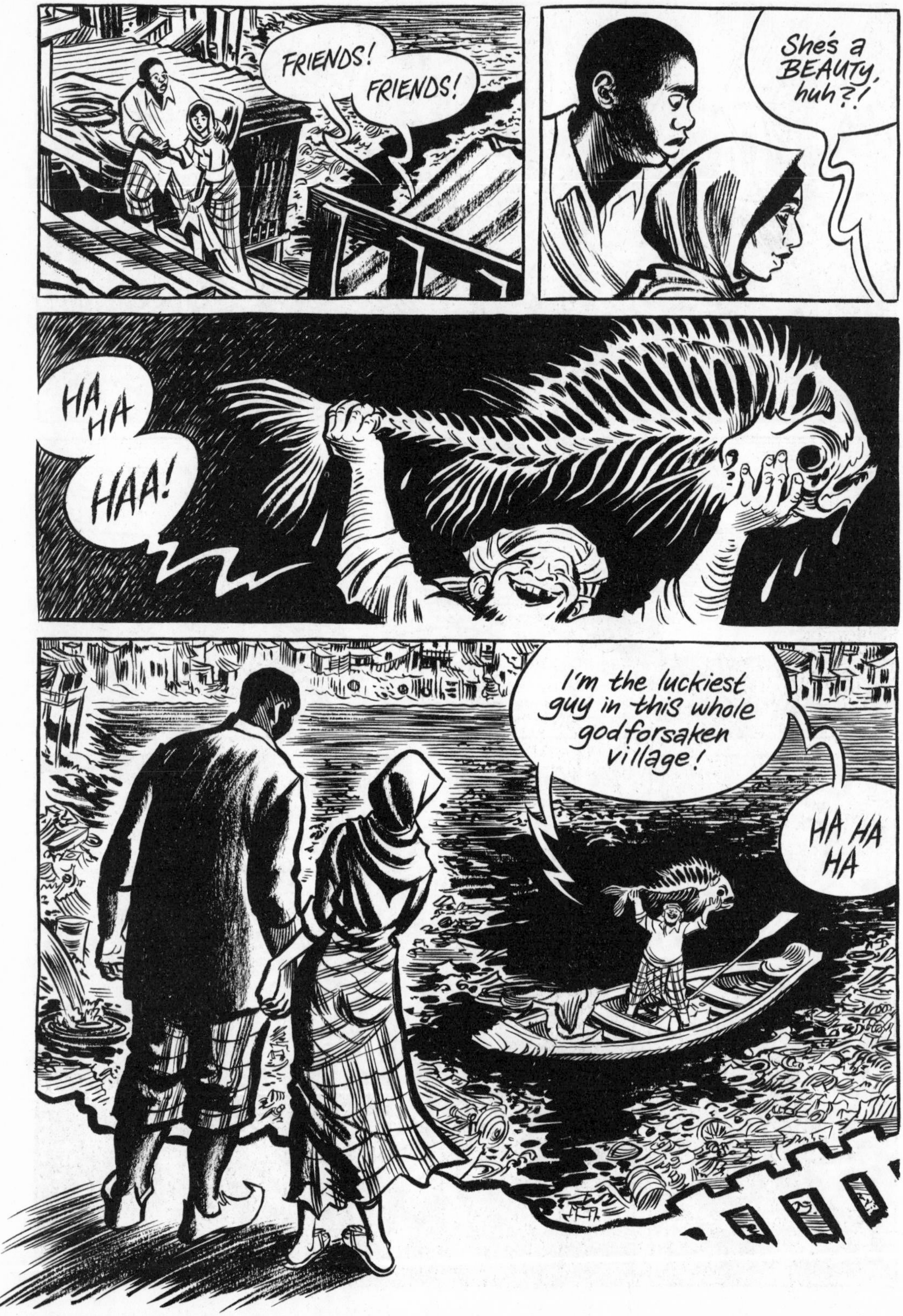
FRIENDS! FRIENDS!
She's a BEAUTY, huh?!
HA HA HAA!
I'm the luckiest guy in this whole godforsaken village!
HA HA HA

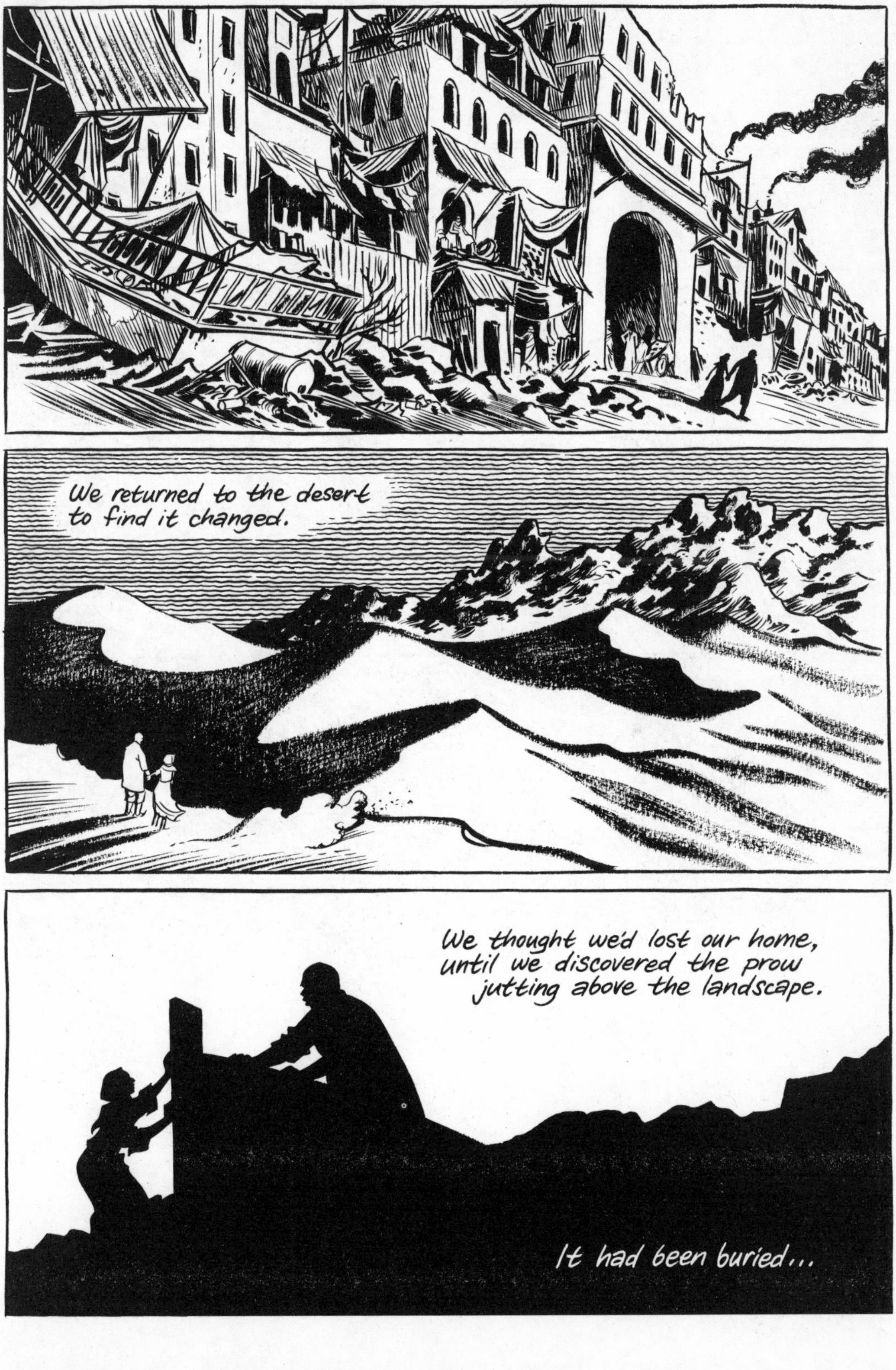
We returned to the desert to find it changed.
We thought we'd lost our home, until we discovered the prow jutting above the landscape.
It had been buried...

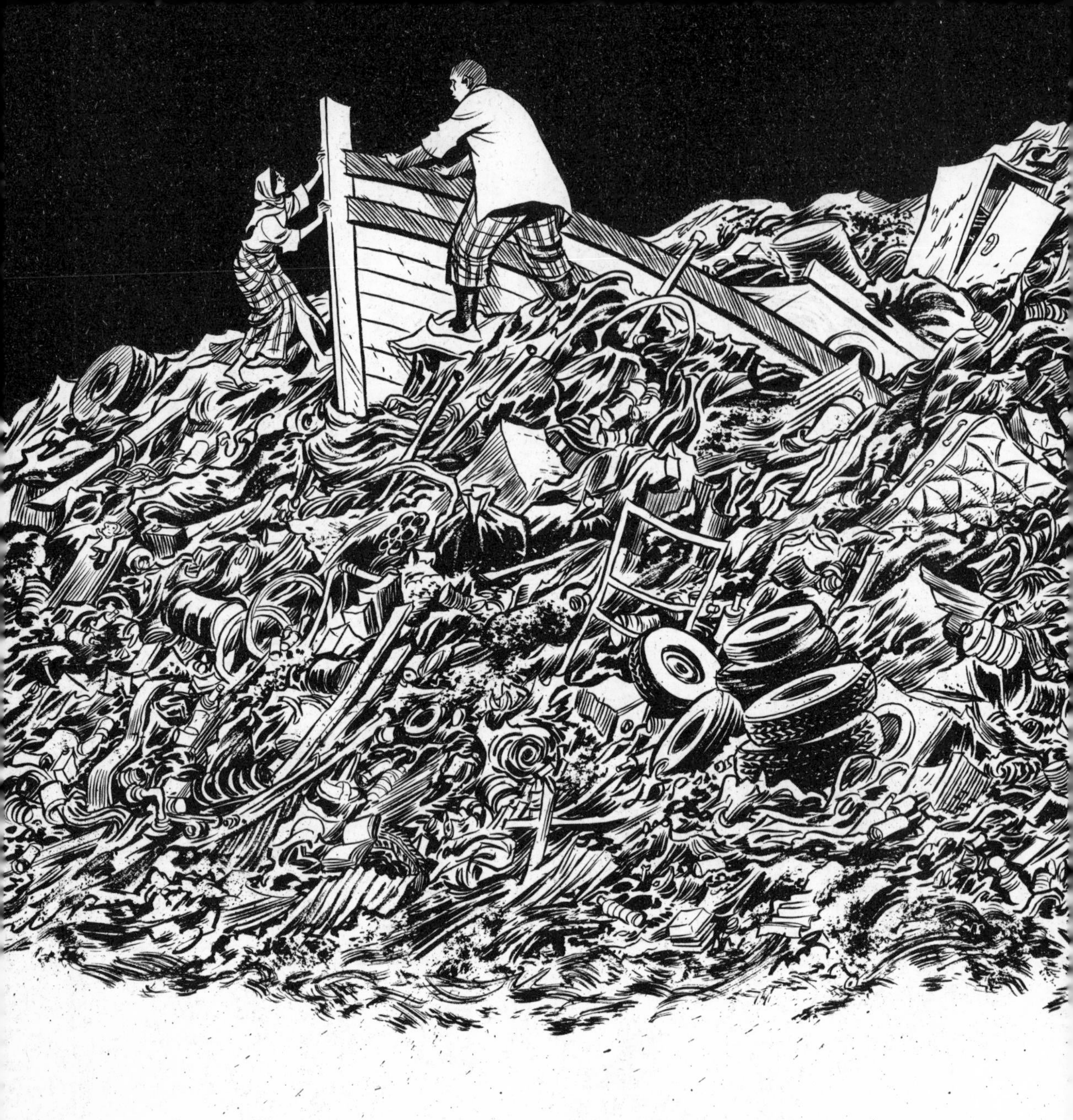

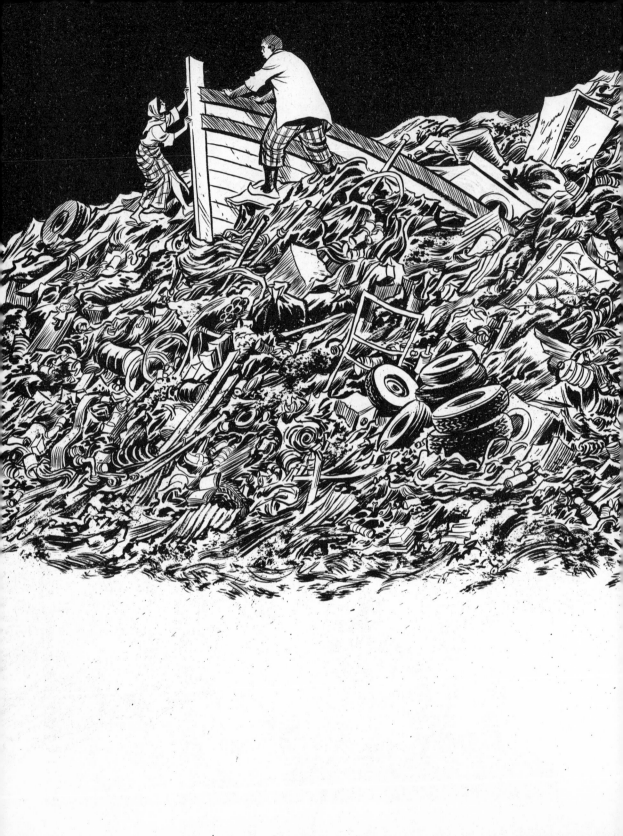

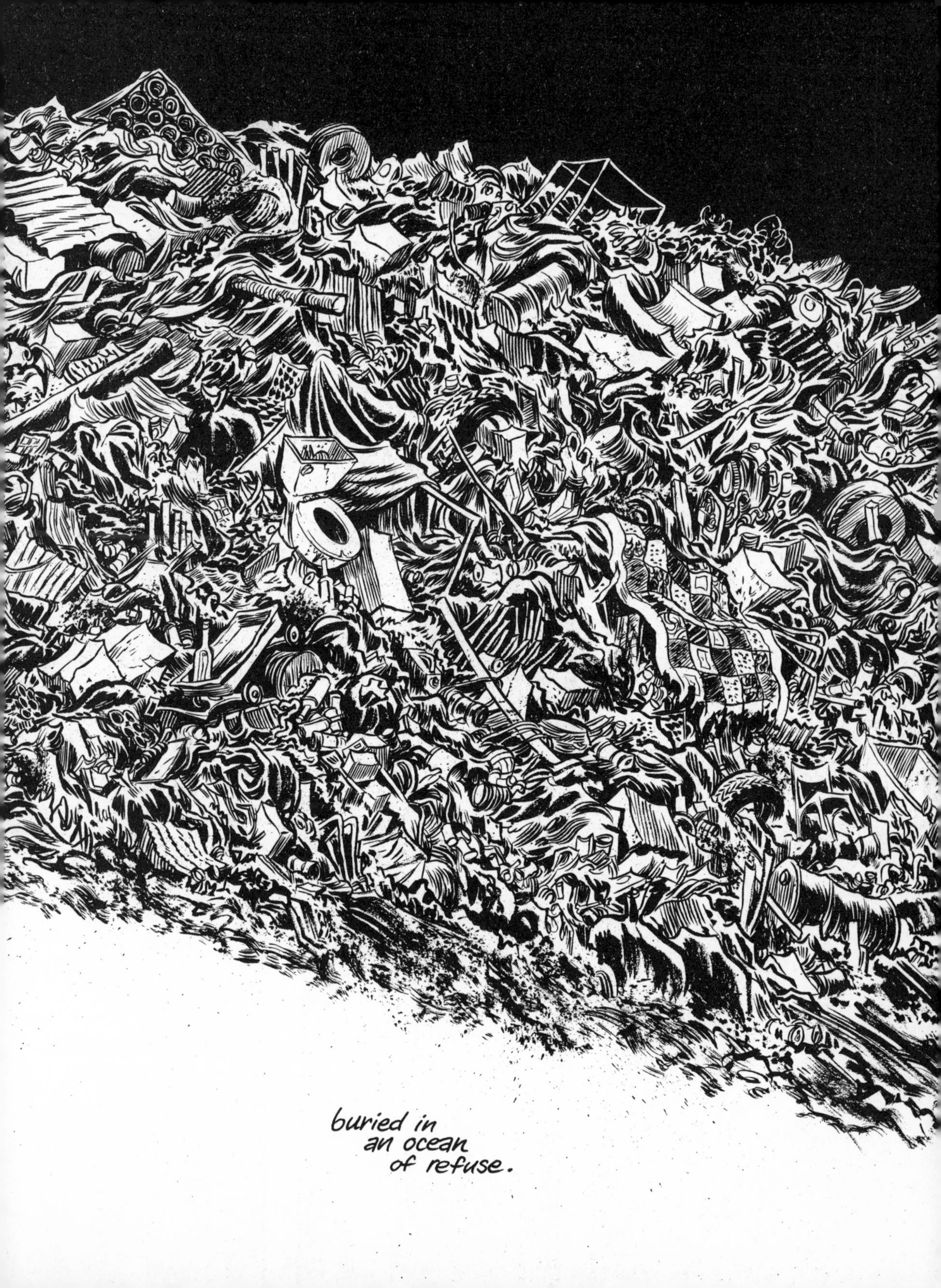
buried in
an ocean
of refuse.

د	ط	ب
ج	ه	ز
ح	ا	و

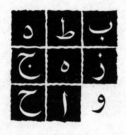

خاتم سليمان

RiNG of
SOLOMON

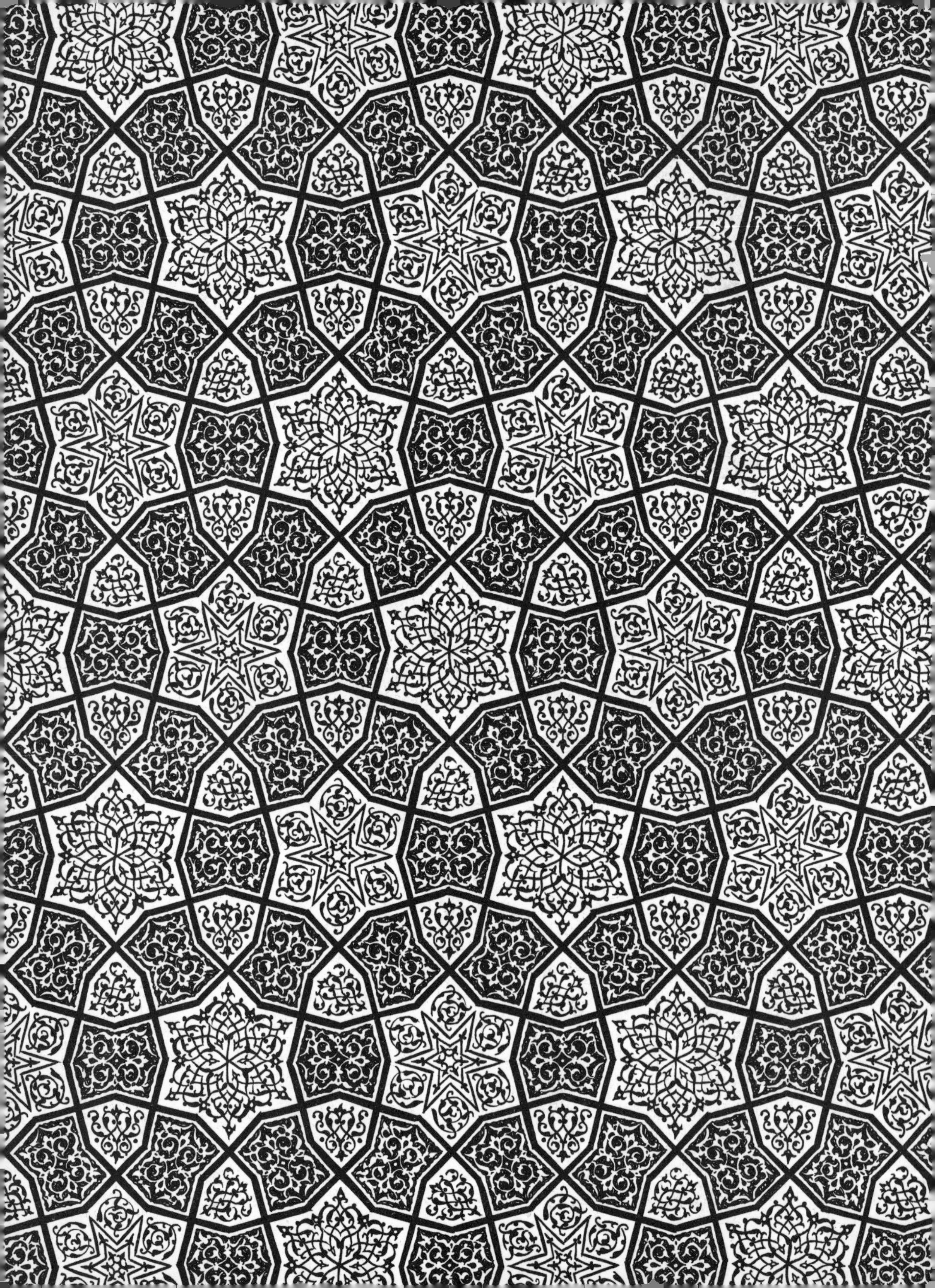

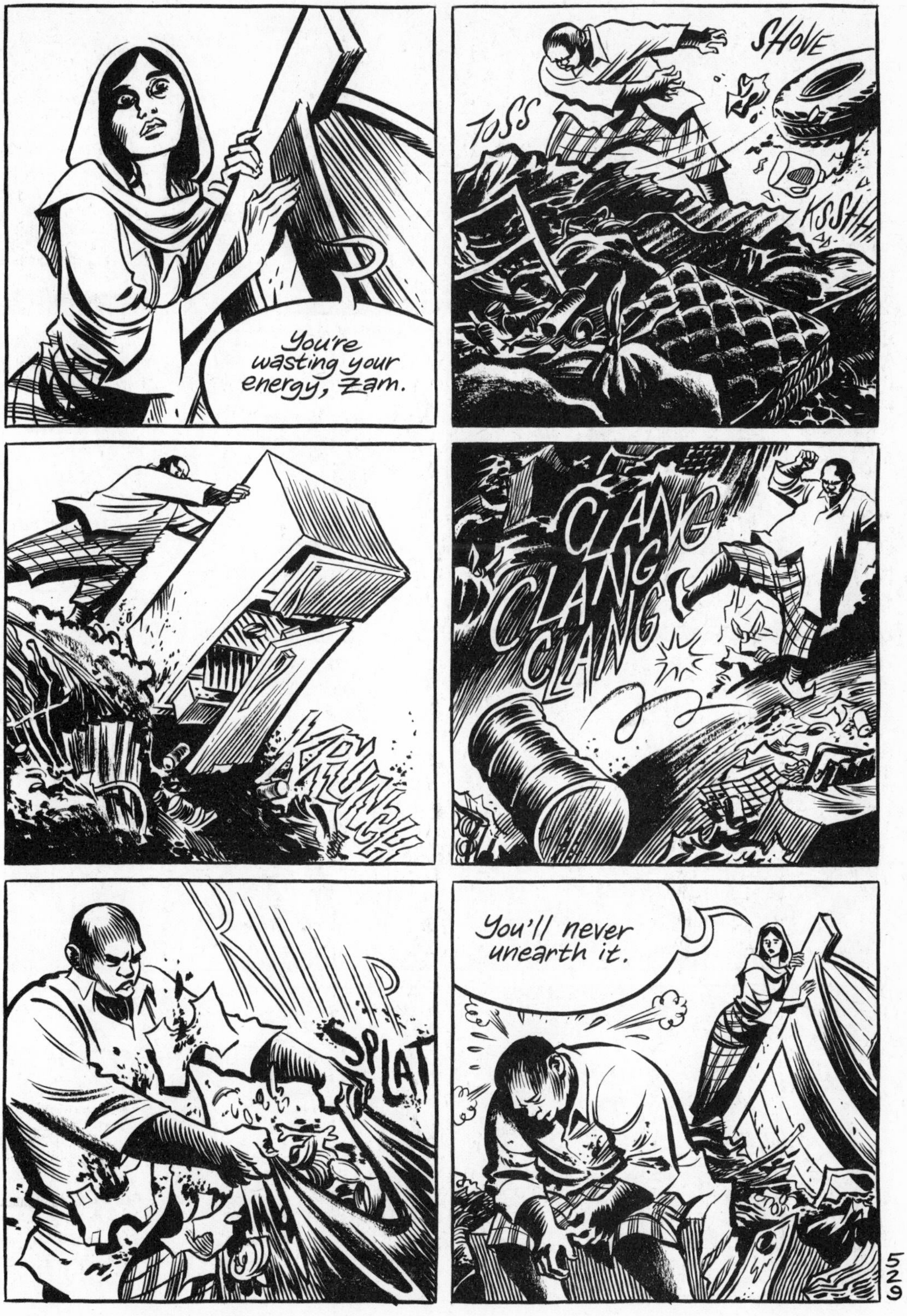
You're wasting your energy, Zam.
TOSS
SHOVE
CLANG
CLANG
CLANG
SPLAT
You'll never unearth it.

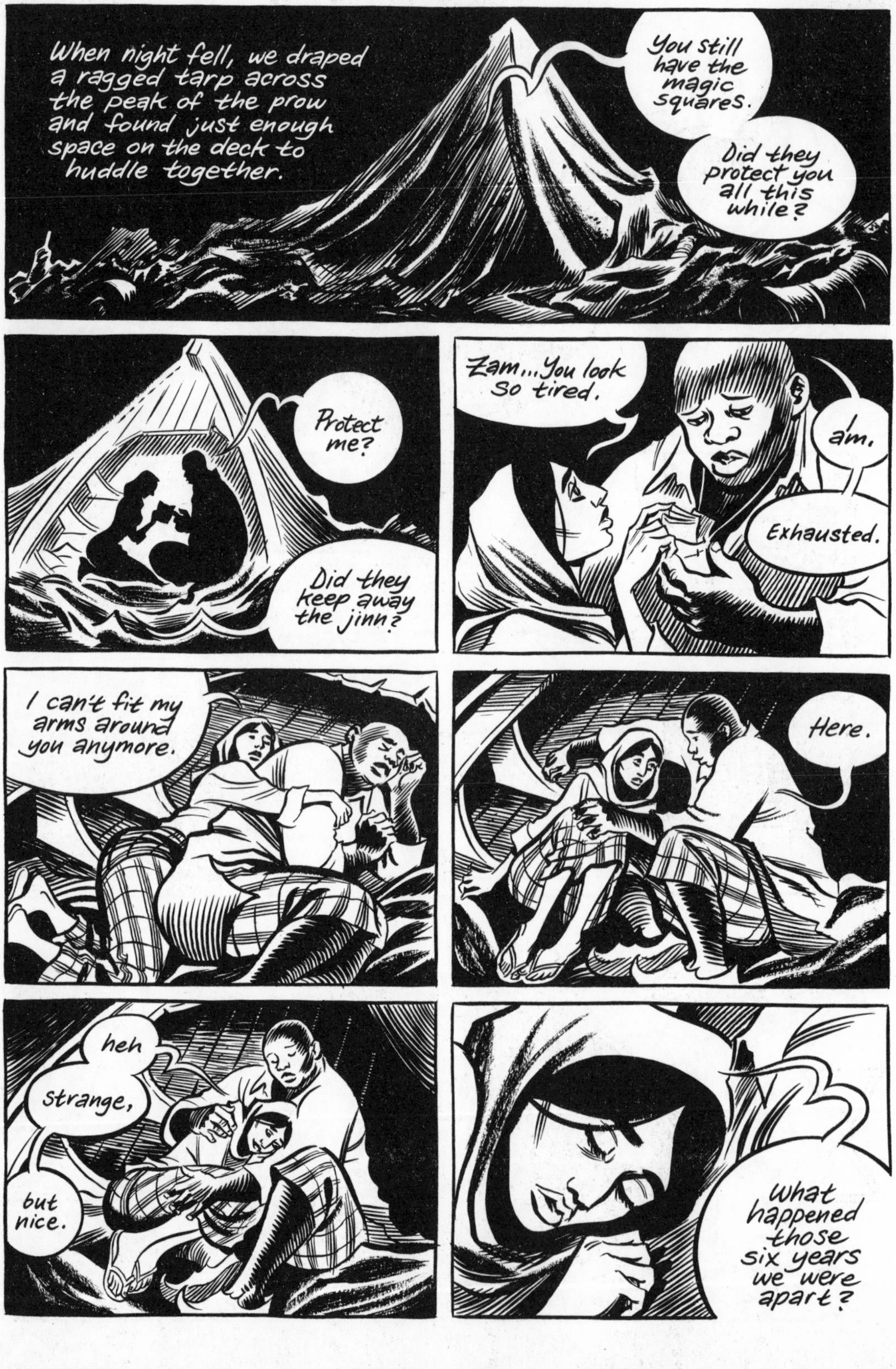
When night fell, we draped a ragged tarp across the peak of the prow and found just enough space on the deck to huddle together.
You still have the magic squares.
Did they protect you all this while?
Protect me?
Did they keep away the jinn?
Zam... You look so tired.
I am.
Exhausted.
I can't fit my arms around you anymore.
Here.
heh
strange,
but nice.
What happened those six years we were apart?

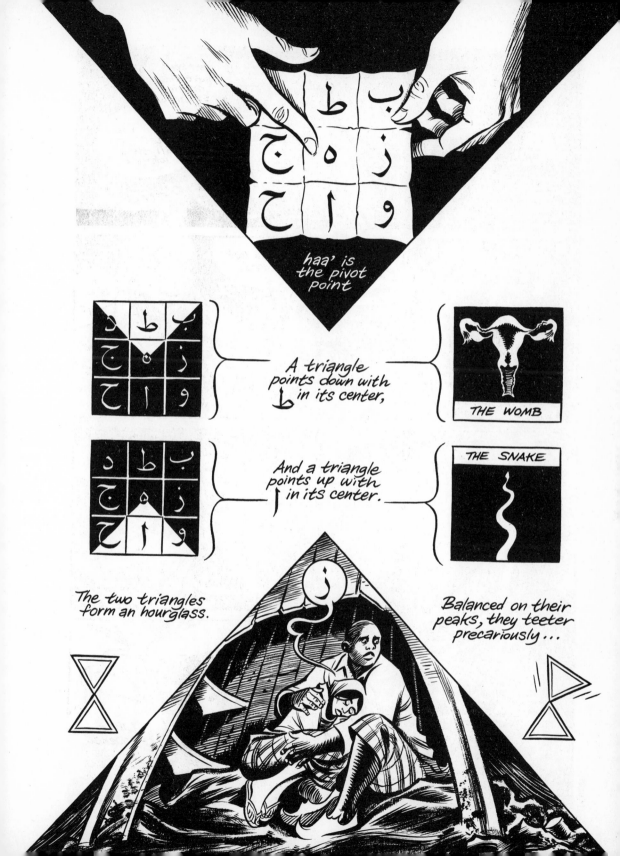

haa' is the pivot point

A triangle points down with ط in its center,

THE WOMB

And a triangle points up with ط in its center.

THE SNAKE

The two triangles form an hourglass.

Balanced on their peaks, they teeter precariously...

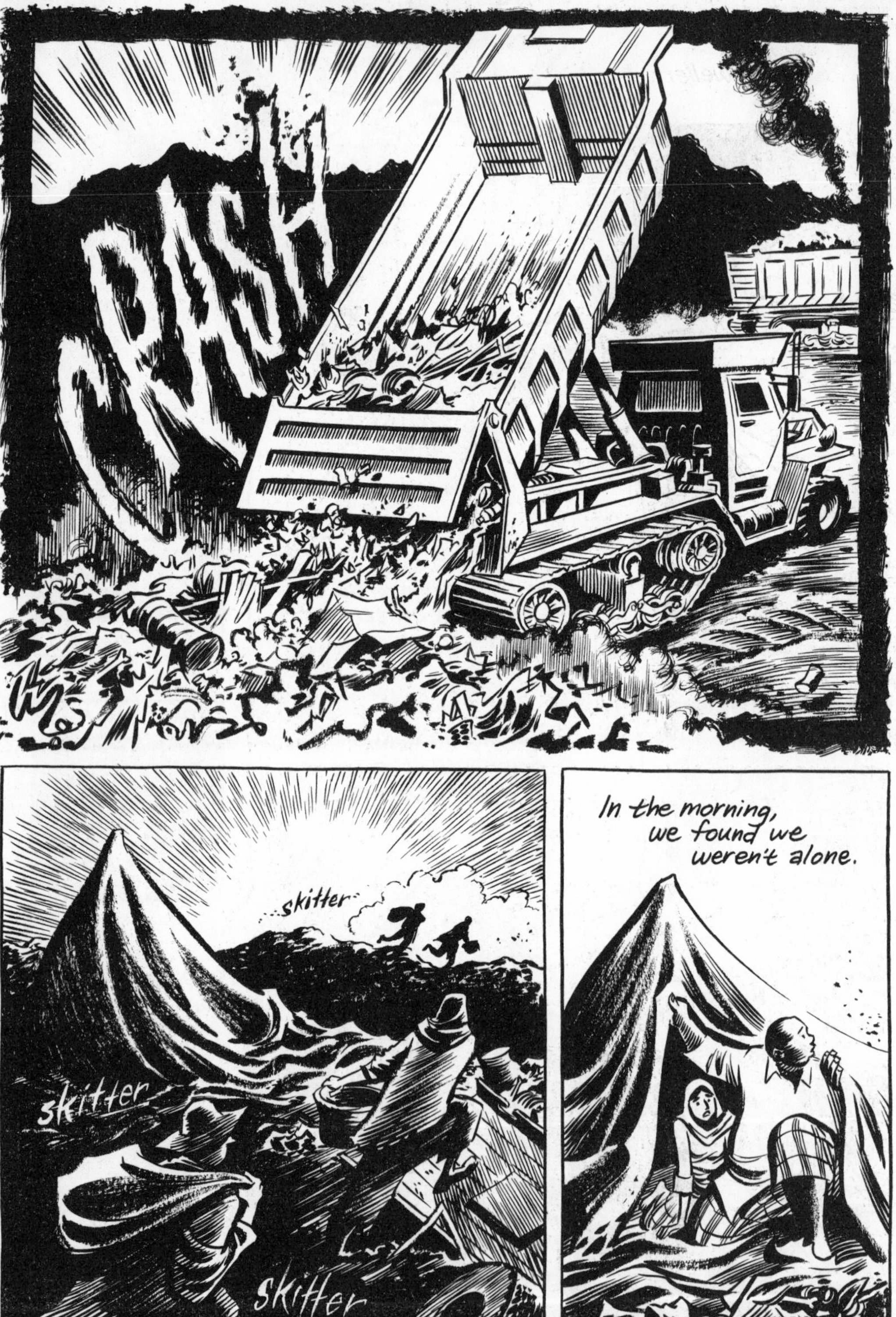
CRASH
skitter
skitter
skitter
In the morning, we found we weren't alone.

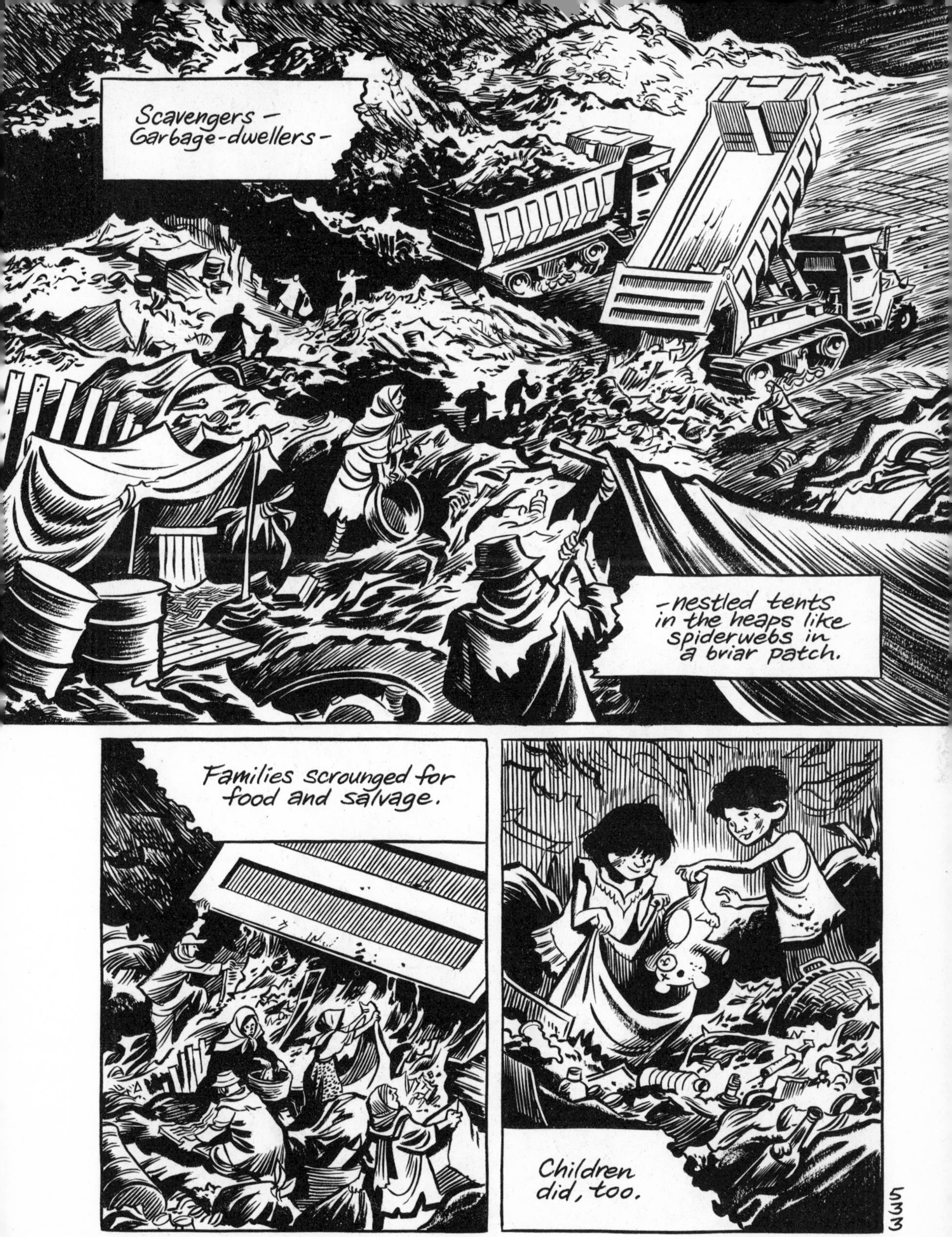
Scavengers –
Garbage-dwellers –
– nestled tents in the heaps like spiderwebs in a briar patch.
Families scrounged for food and salvage.
Children did, too.

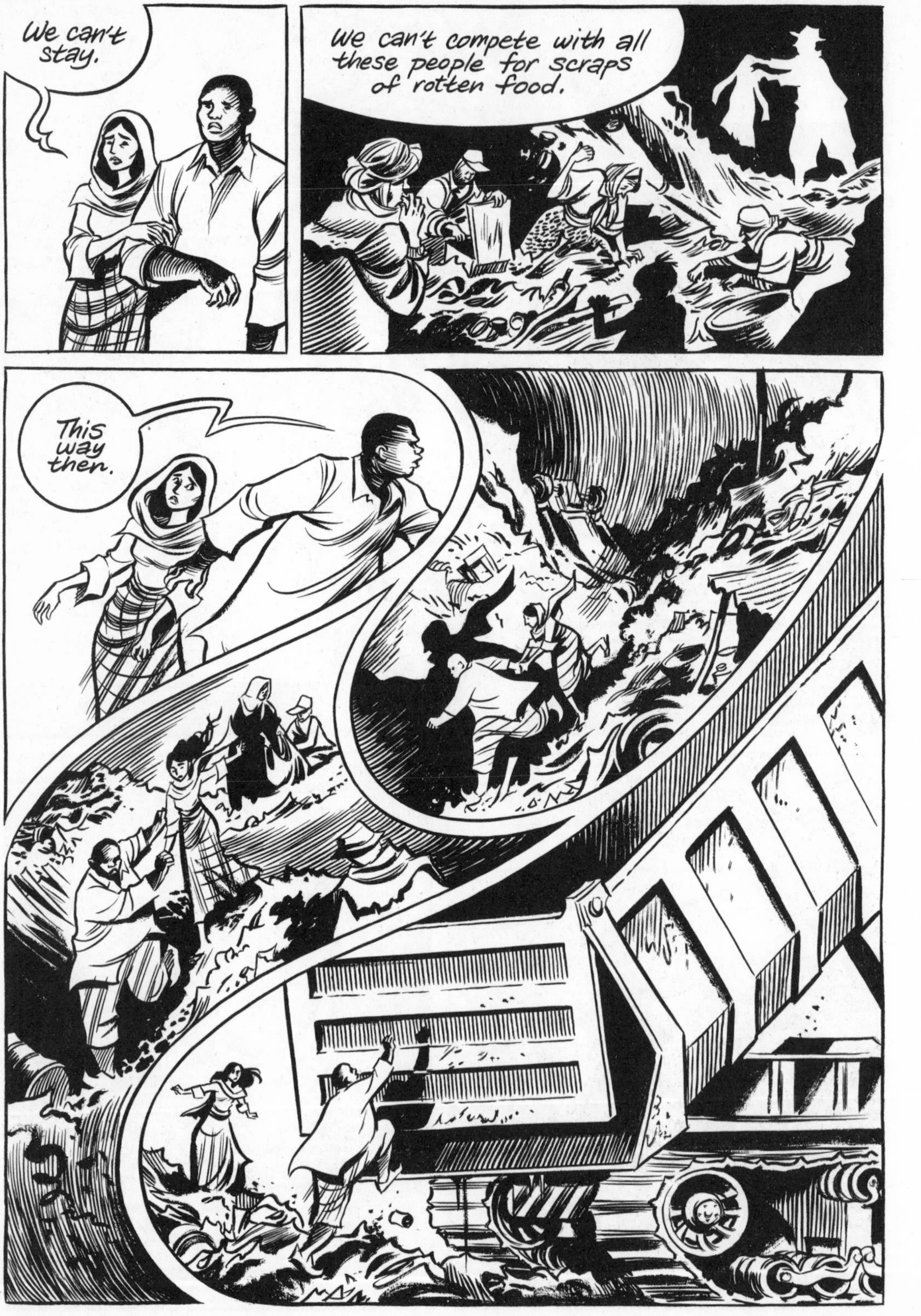
We can't stay.
We can't compete with all these people for scraps of rotten food.
This way then.

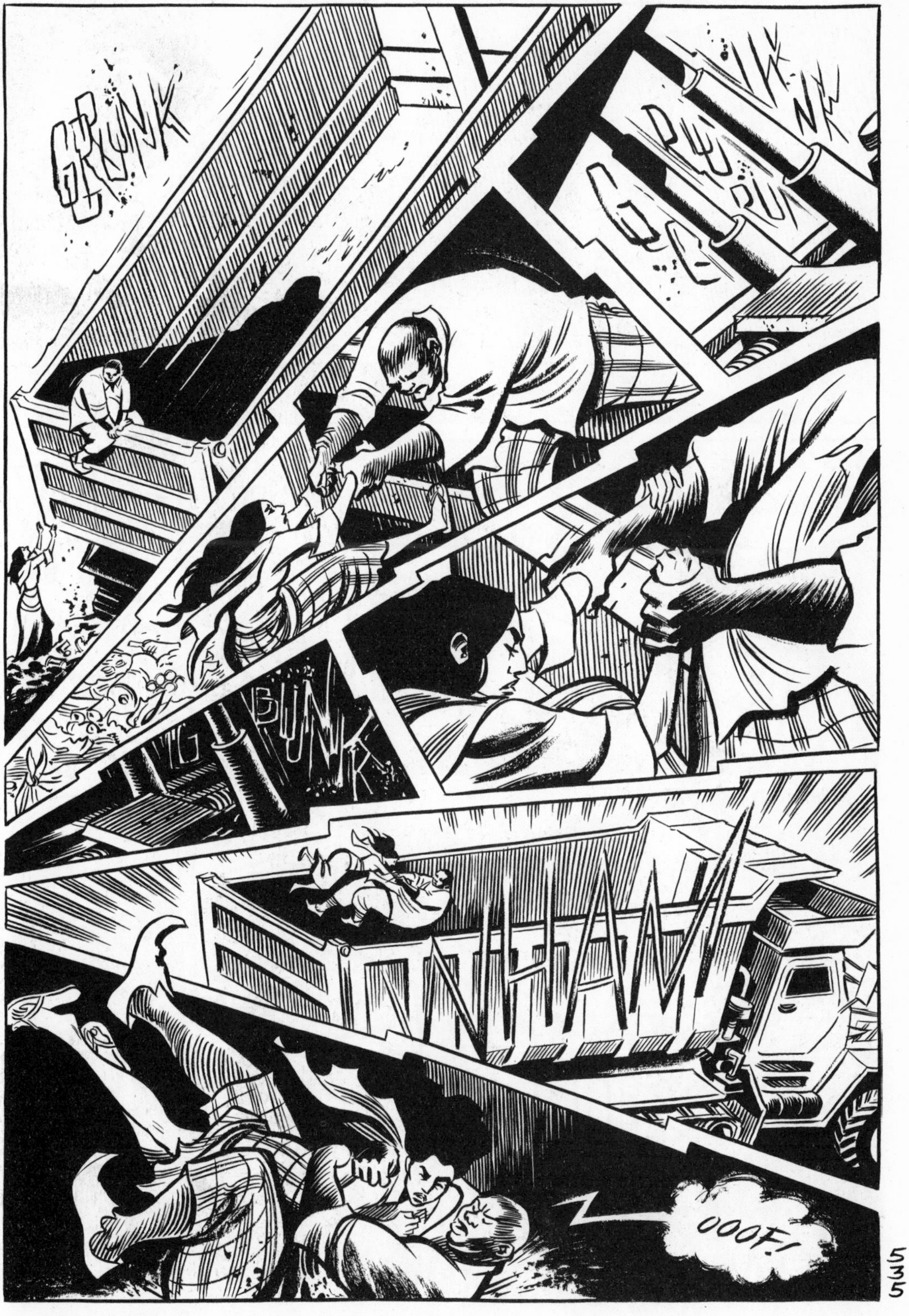
GRUNK
WHAM
OOOF!

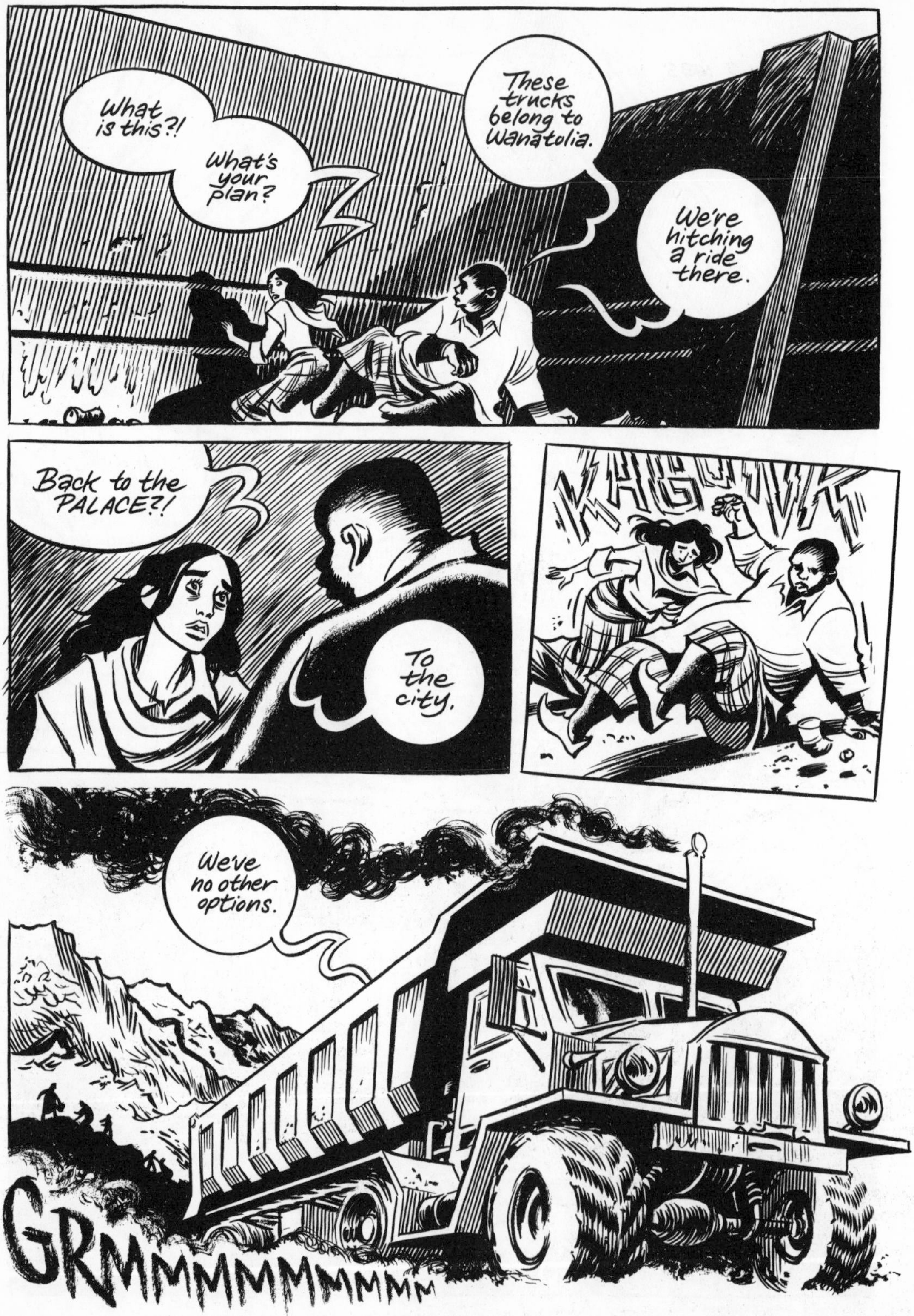
What is this?!
What's your plan?
These trucks belong to Wanatolia.
We're hitching a ride there.
Back to the PALACE?!
To the city.
We've no other options.
GRMMMMMMMMMM

Wanatolia was only a WADI.

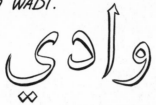

A sudden and heavy rainfall carved a valley in the desert.

Water collected in underground aquifers.

Migrating birds spread plant seeds.

Vegetation sprouted, sheltered by towering palms.

Humans gathered around the oasis, sank wells, manipulated irrigation...

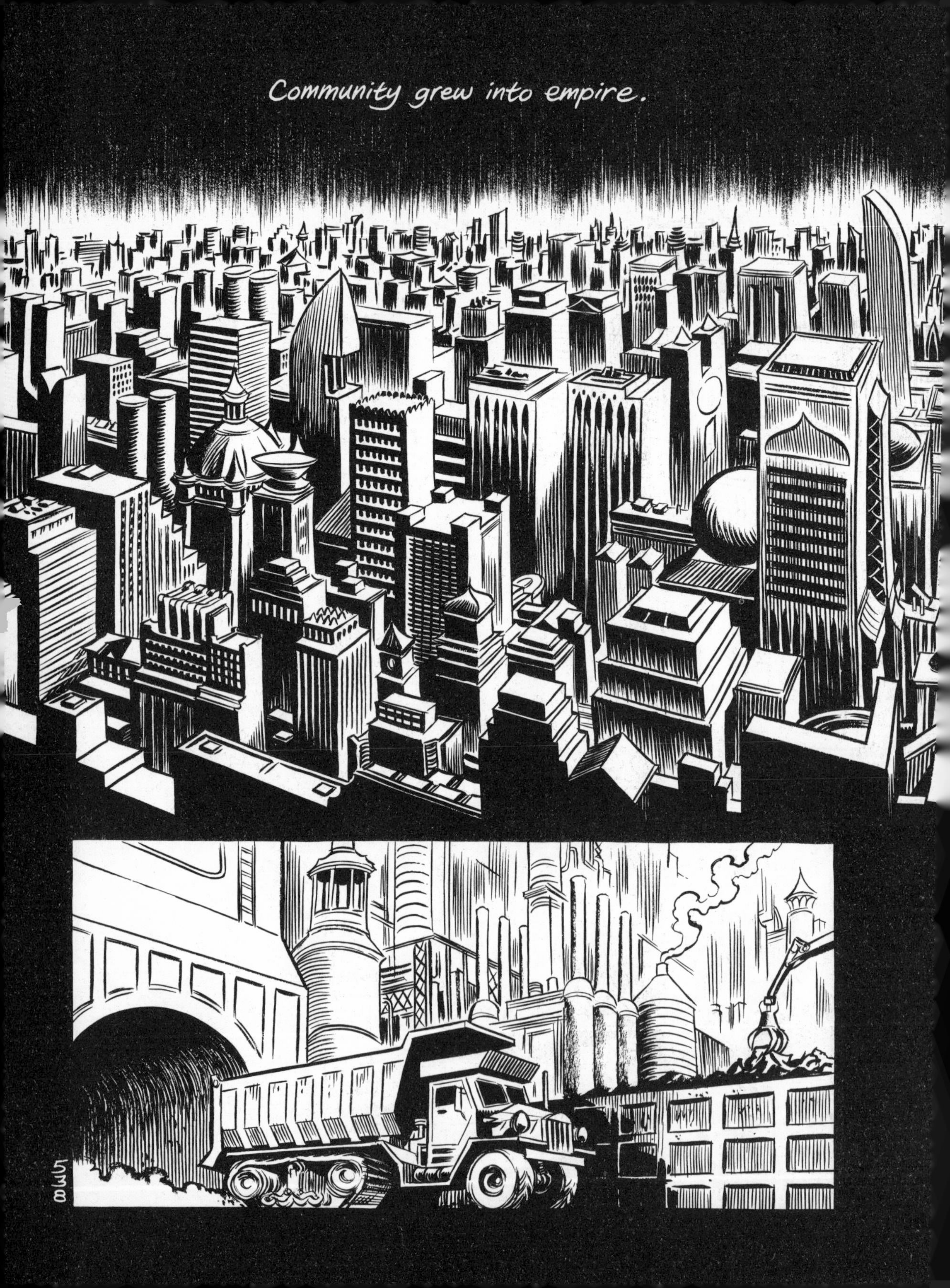
Community grew into empire.

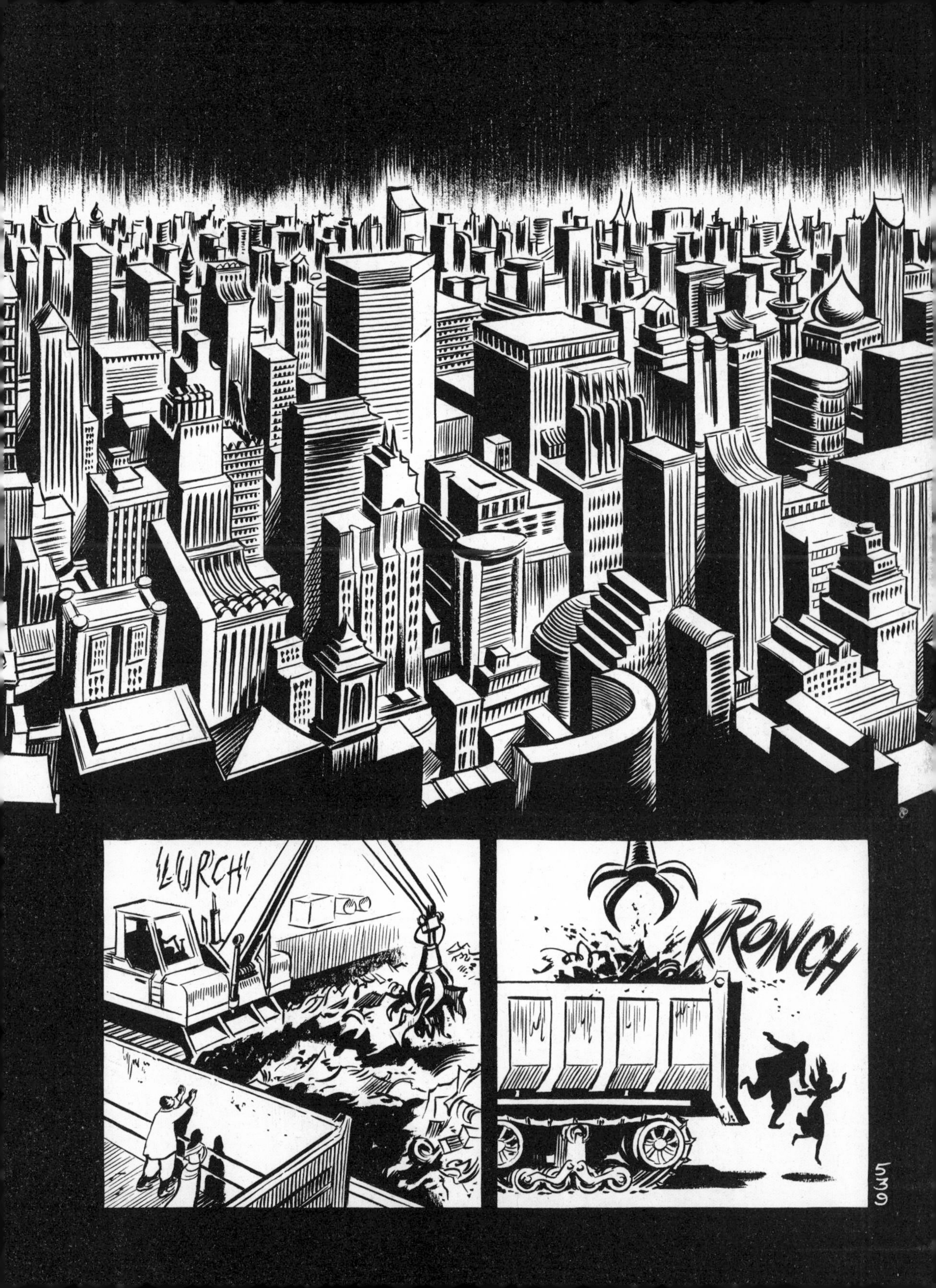
LURCH
KRONCH

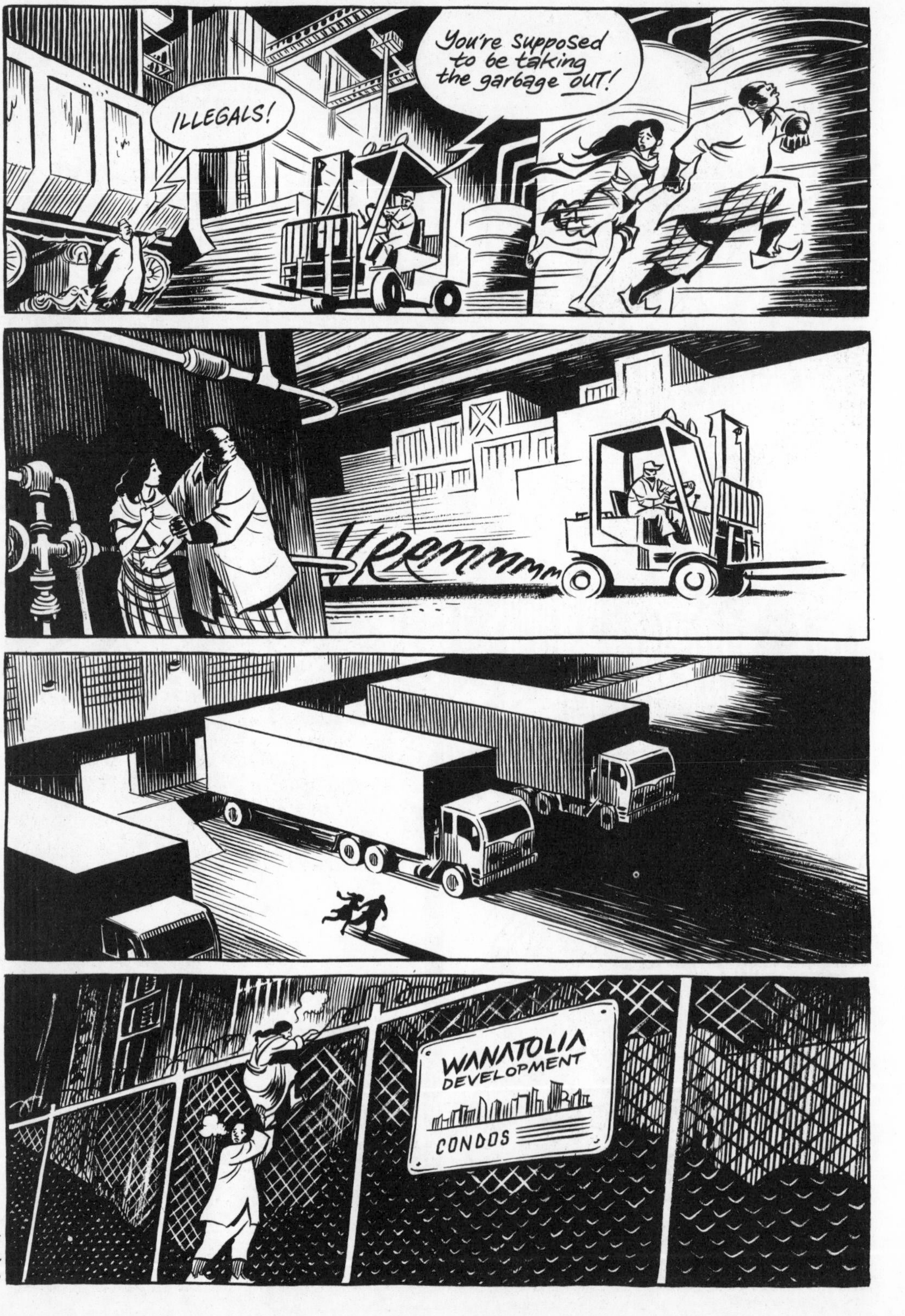
ILLEGALS!
You're supposed to be taking the garbage OUT!
VREMMMMM
WANATOLIA DEVELOPMENT
CONDOS

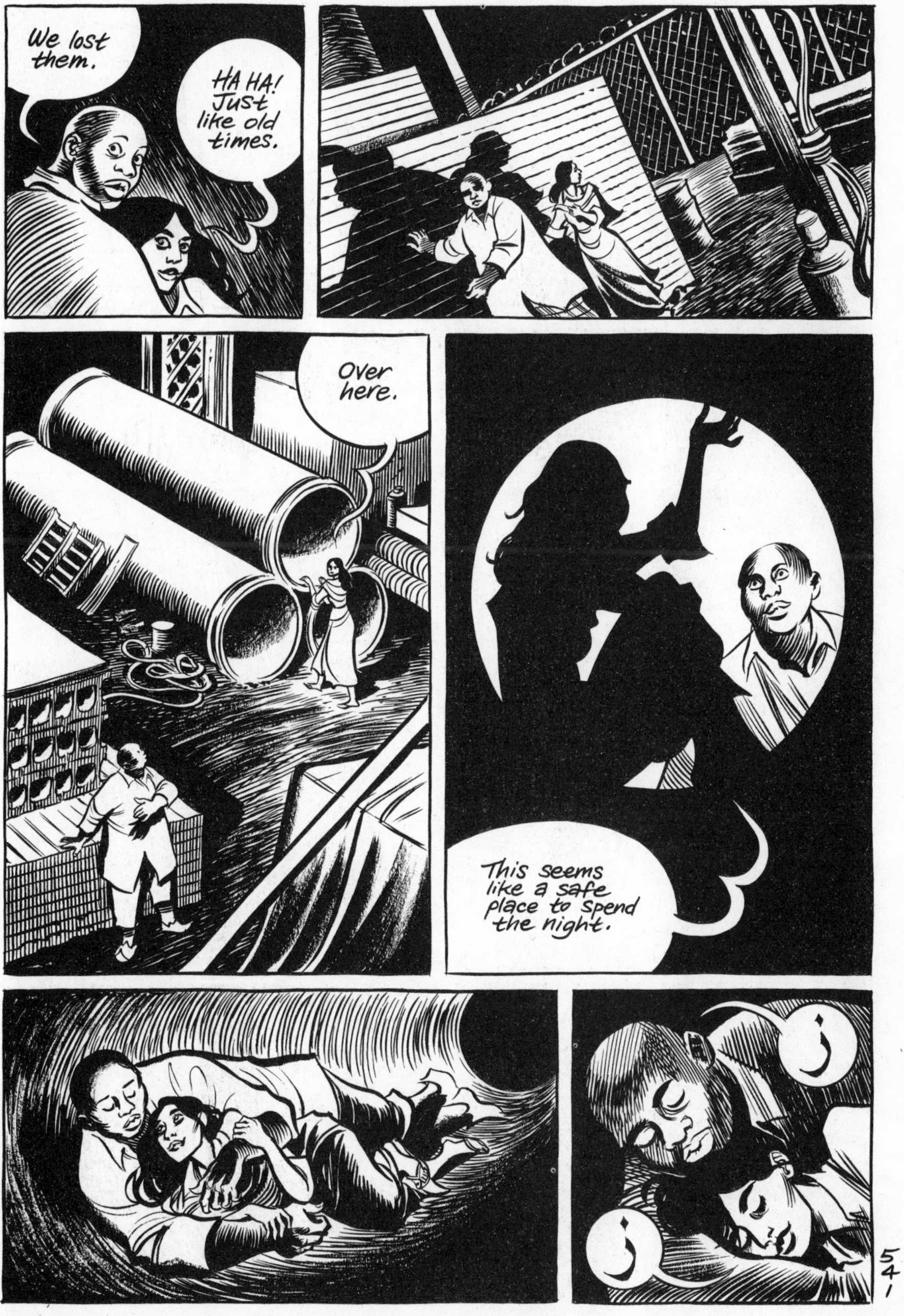
We lost them.
HA HA! Just like old times.
Over here.
This seems like a safe place to spend the night.
ز
ز

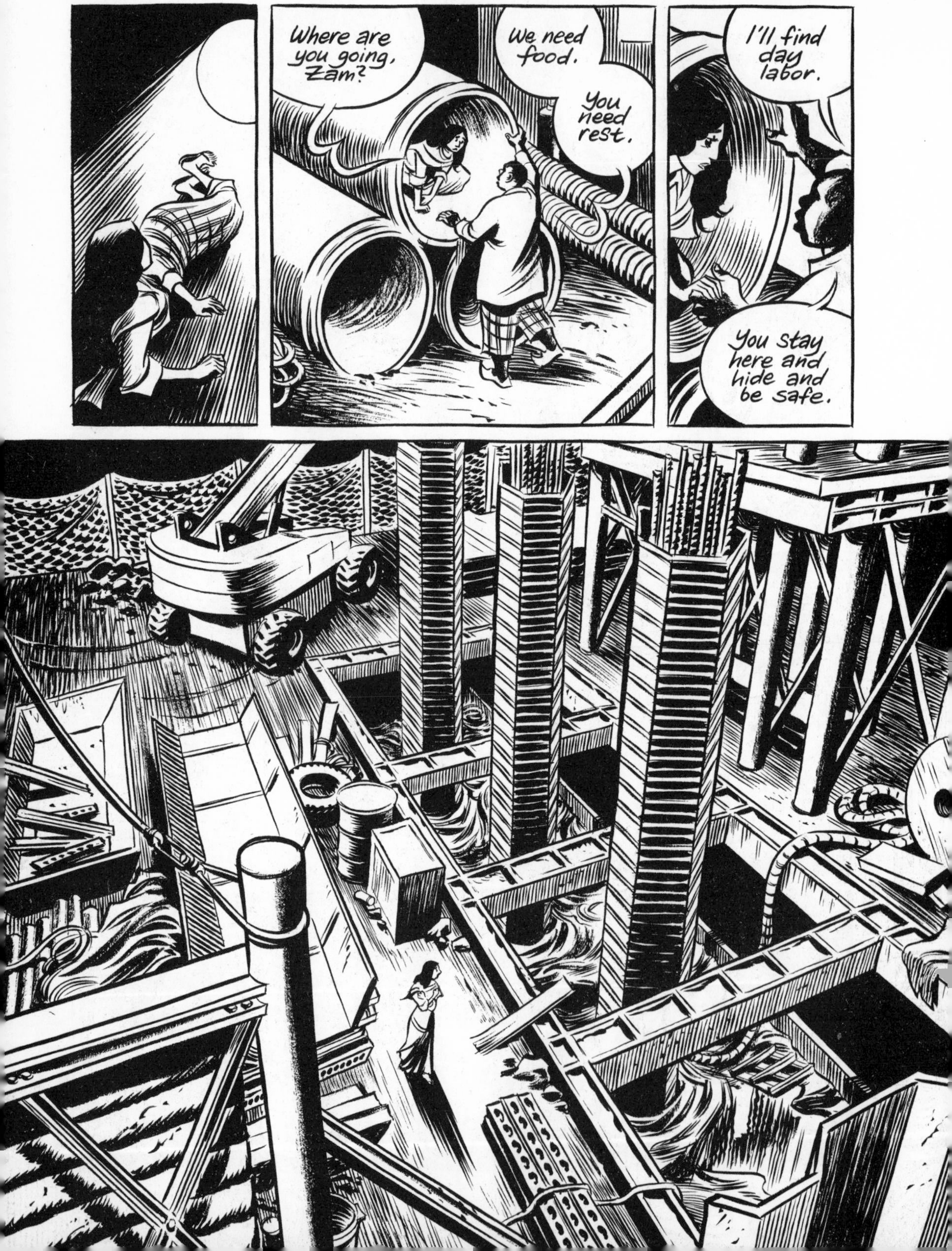
Where are you going, Zam?
We need food.
You need rest.
I'll find day labor.
You stay here and hide and be safe.

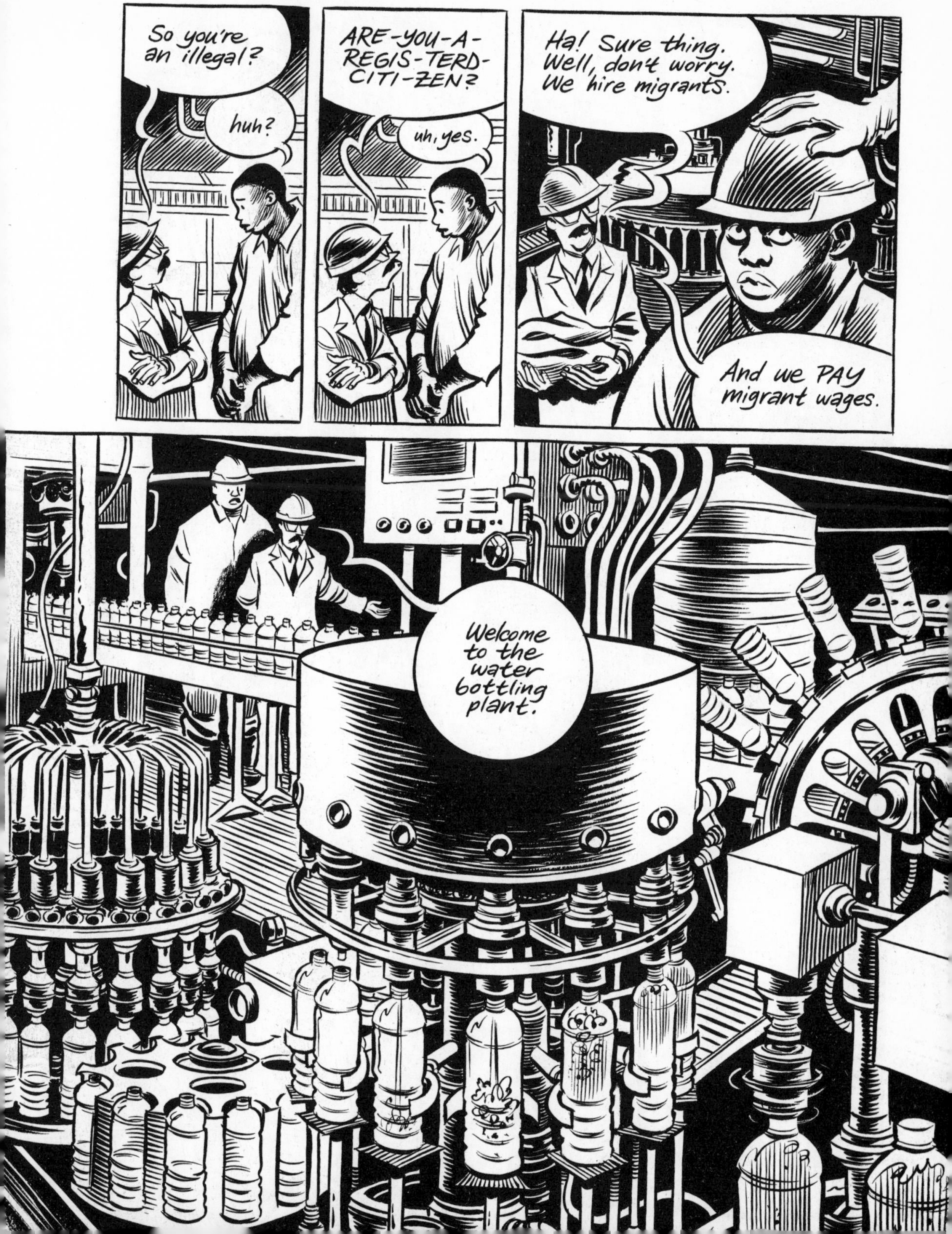
So you're an illegal?
huh?
ARE-YOU-A-REGIS-TERD-CITI-ZEN?
uh, yes.
Ha! Sure thing. Well, don't worry. We hire migrants.
And we PAY migrant wages.
Welcome to the water bottling plant.

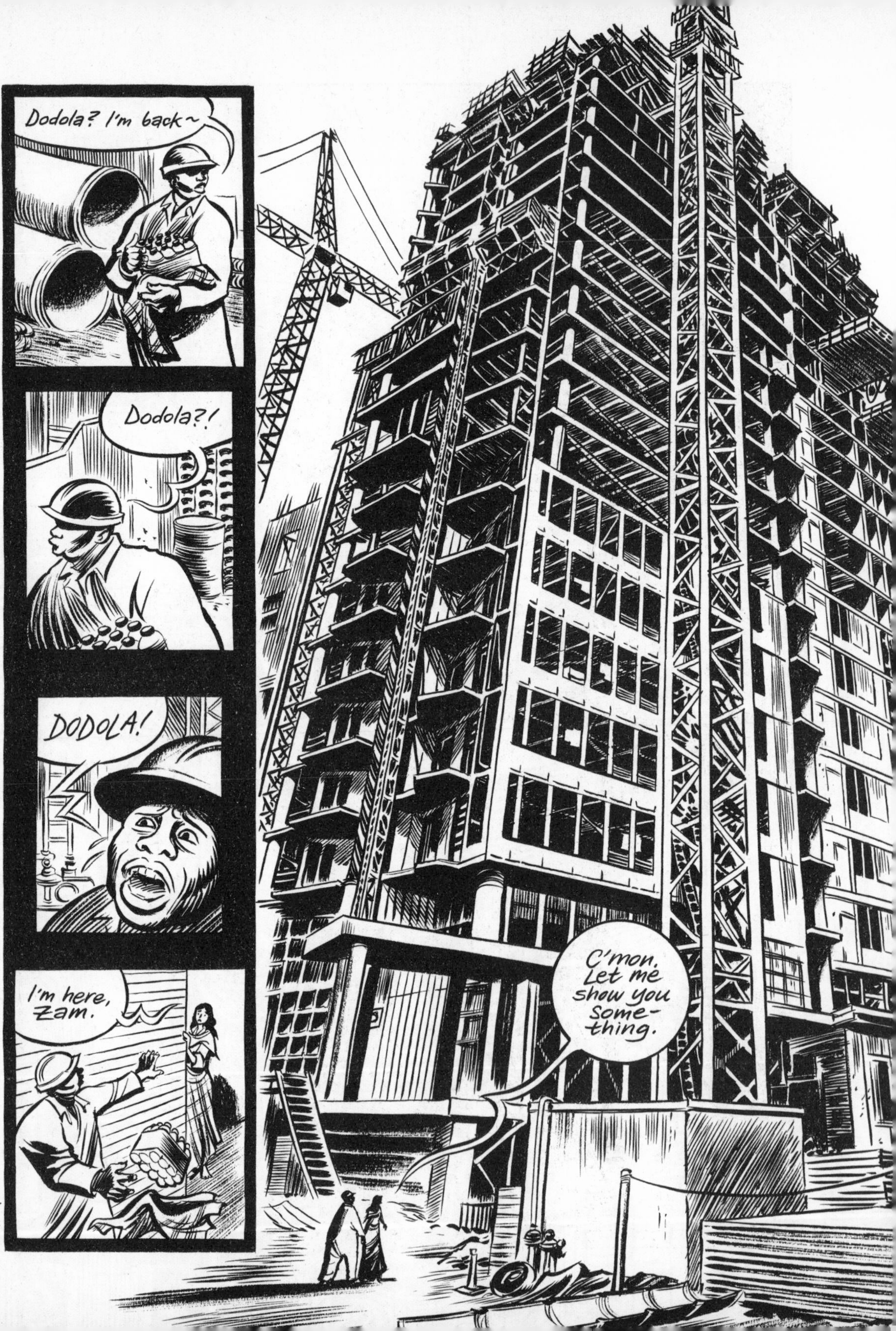

Dodola? I'm back~
Dodola?!
DODOLA!
I'm here, Zam.
C'mon, let me show you some-thing.

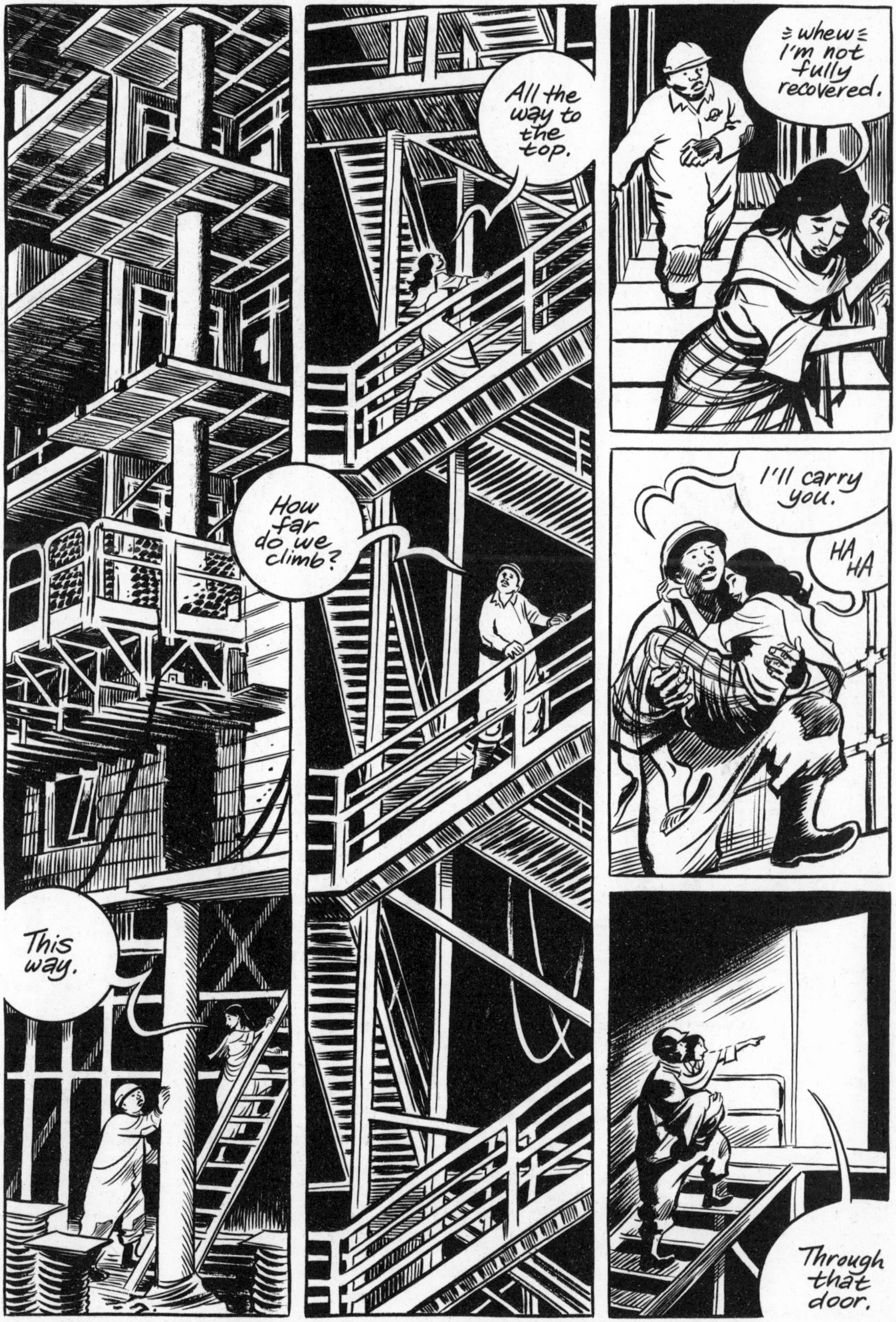
How far do we climb?
All the way to the top.
This way.
whew I'm not fully recovered.
I'll carry you.
HA HA
Through that door.

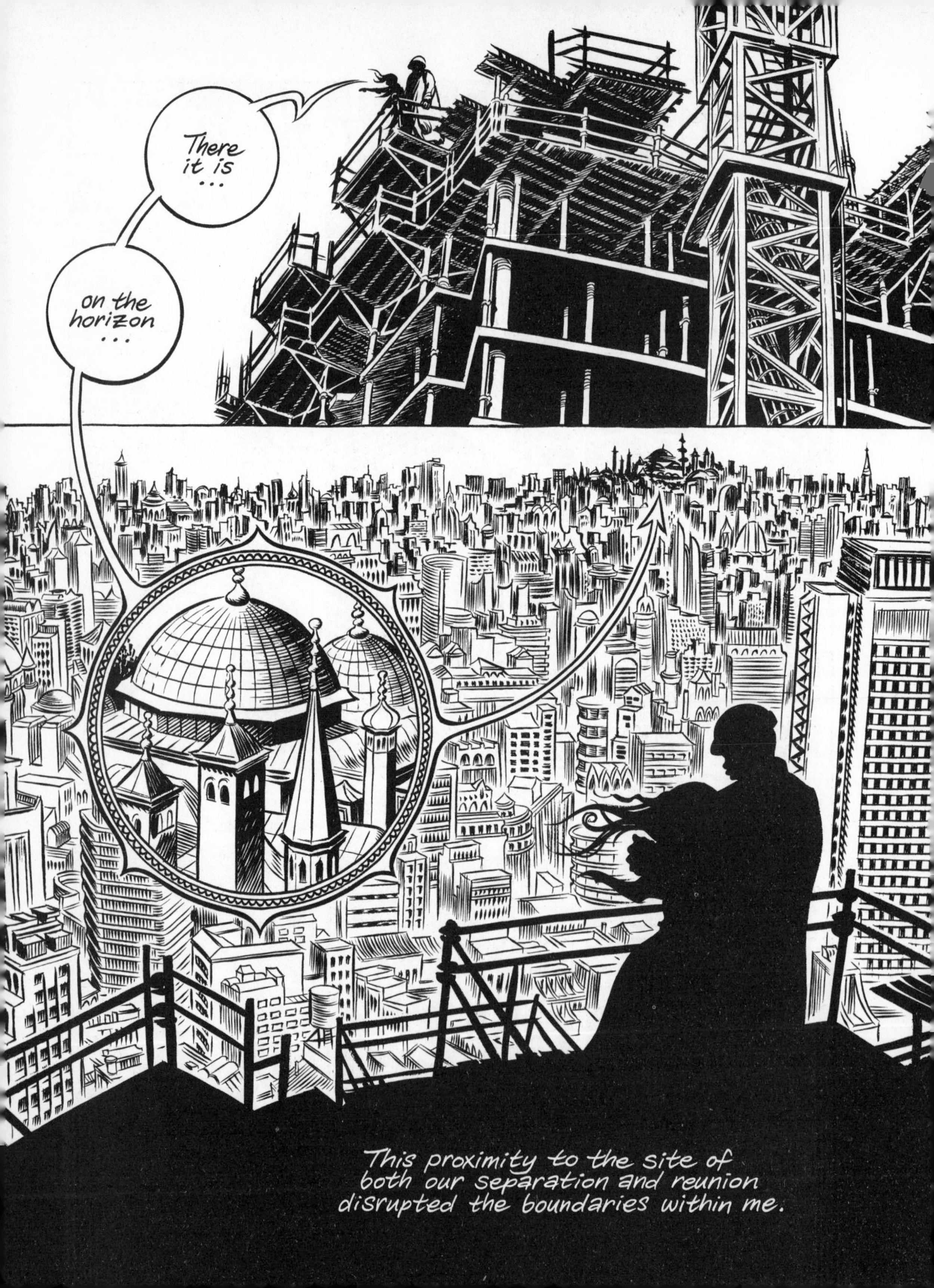
There it is ...
on the horizon ...
This proximity to the site of both our separation and reunion disrupted the boundaries within me.

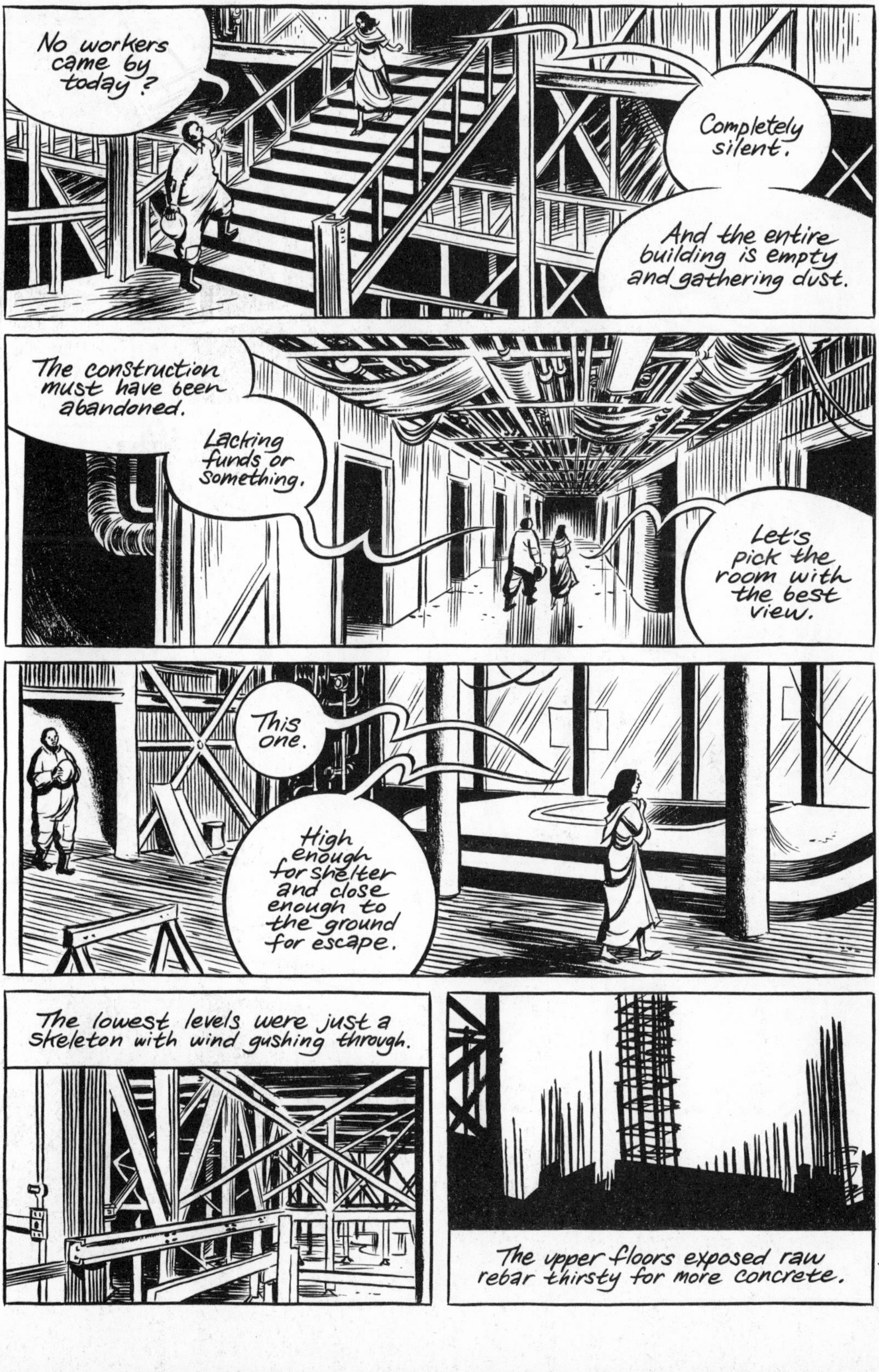
No workers came by today?
Completely silent.
And the entire building is empty and gathering dust.
The construction must have been abandoned.
Lacking funds or something.
Let's pick the room with the best view.
This one.
High enough for shelter and close enough to the ground for escape.
The lowest levels were just a skeleton with wind gushing through.
The upper floors exposed raw rebar thirsty for more concrete.

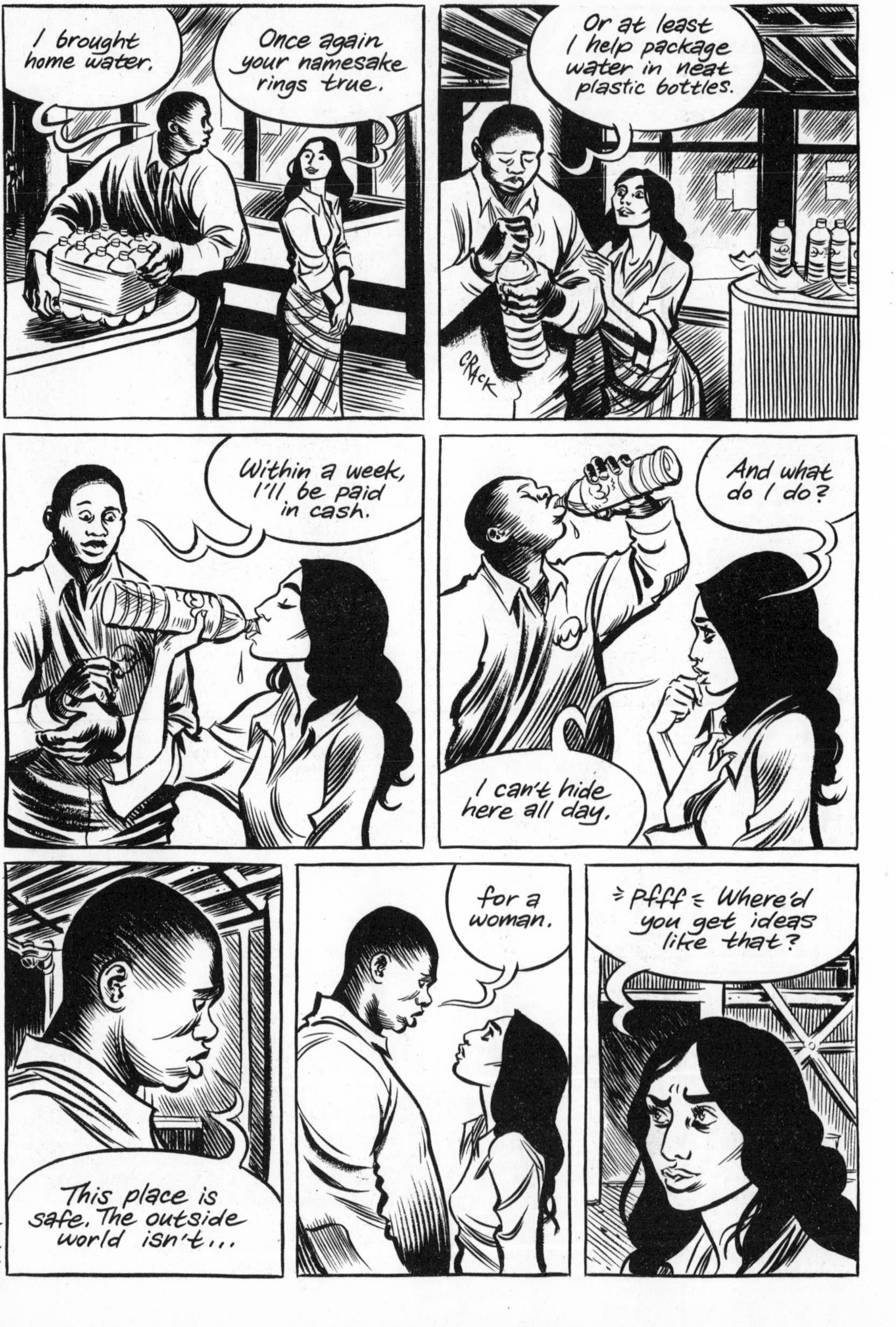
I brought home water.
Once again your namesake rings true.
Or at least I help package water in neat plastic bottles.
CRACK
Within a week, I'll be paid in cash.
And what do I do?
I can't hide here all day.
This place is safe. The outside world isn't...
for a woman.
≡Pfff≡ Where'd you get ideas like that?

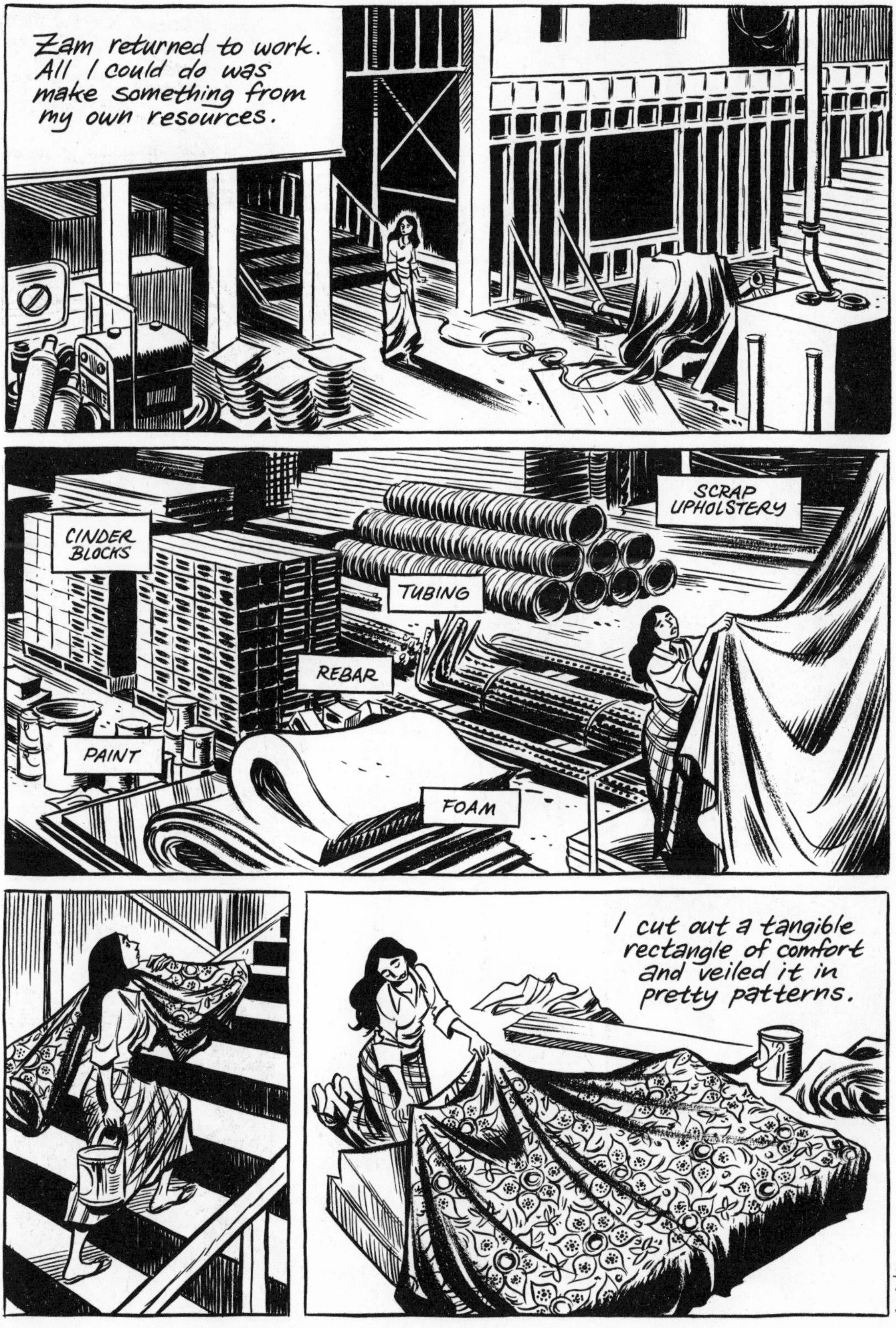
Zam returned to work. All I could do was make something from my own resources.
CINDER BLOCKS
TUBING
SCRAP UPHOLSTERY
REBAR
PAINT
FOAM
I cut out a tangible rectangle of comfort and veiled it in pretty patterns.

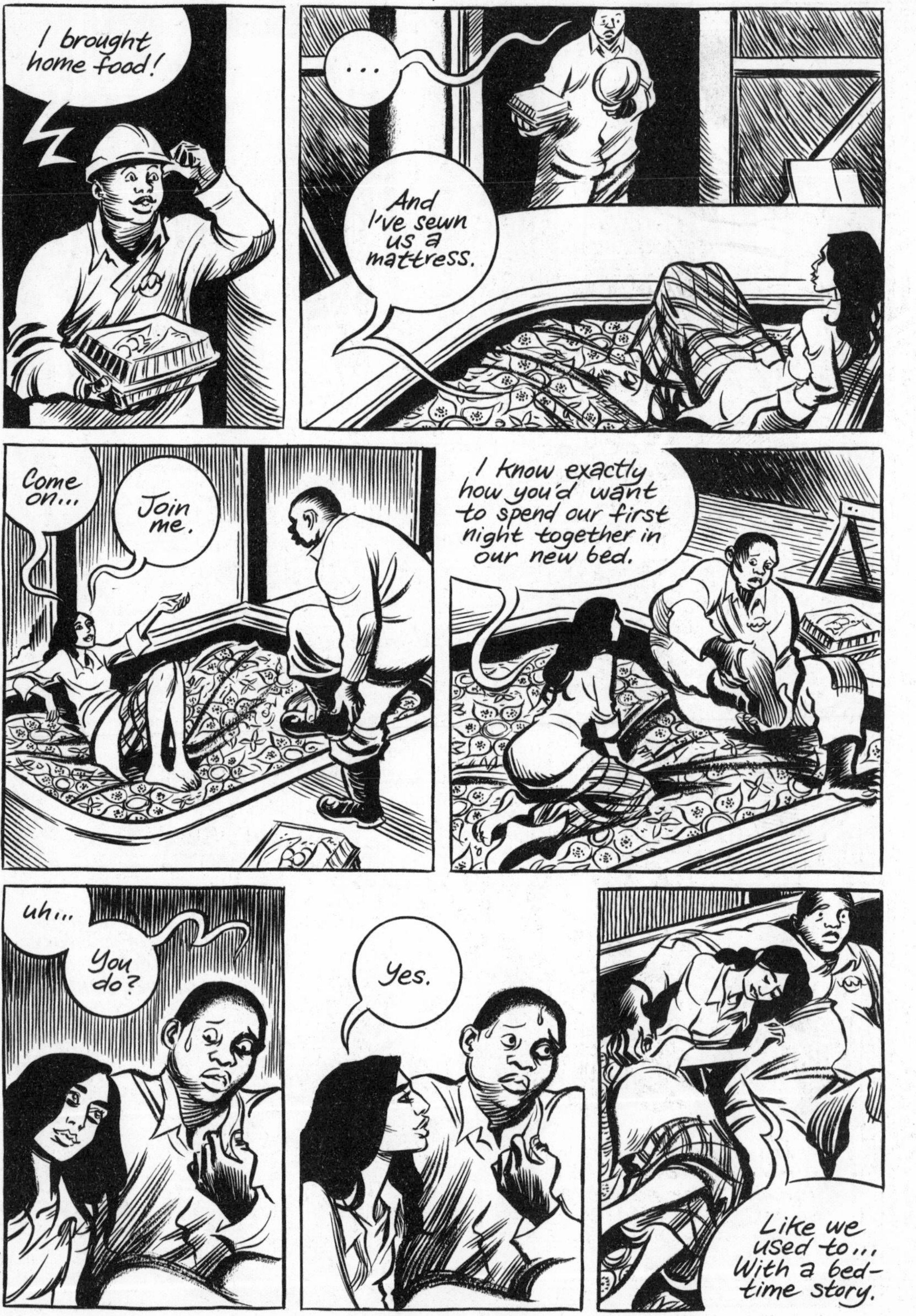
I brought home food!
...
And I've sewn us a mattress.
Come on...
Join me.
I know exactly how you'd want to spend our first night together in our new bed.
uh...
You do?
Yes.
Like we used to... With a bed-time story.

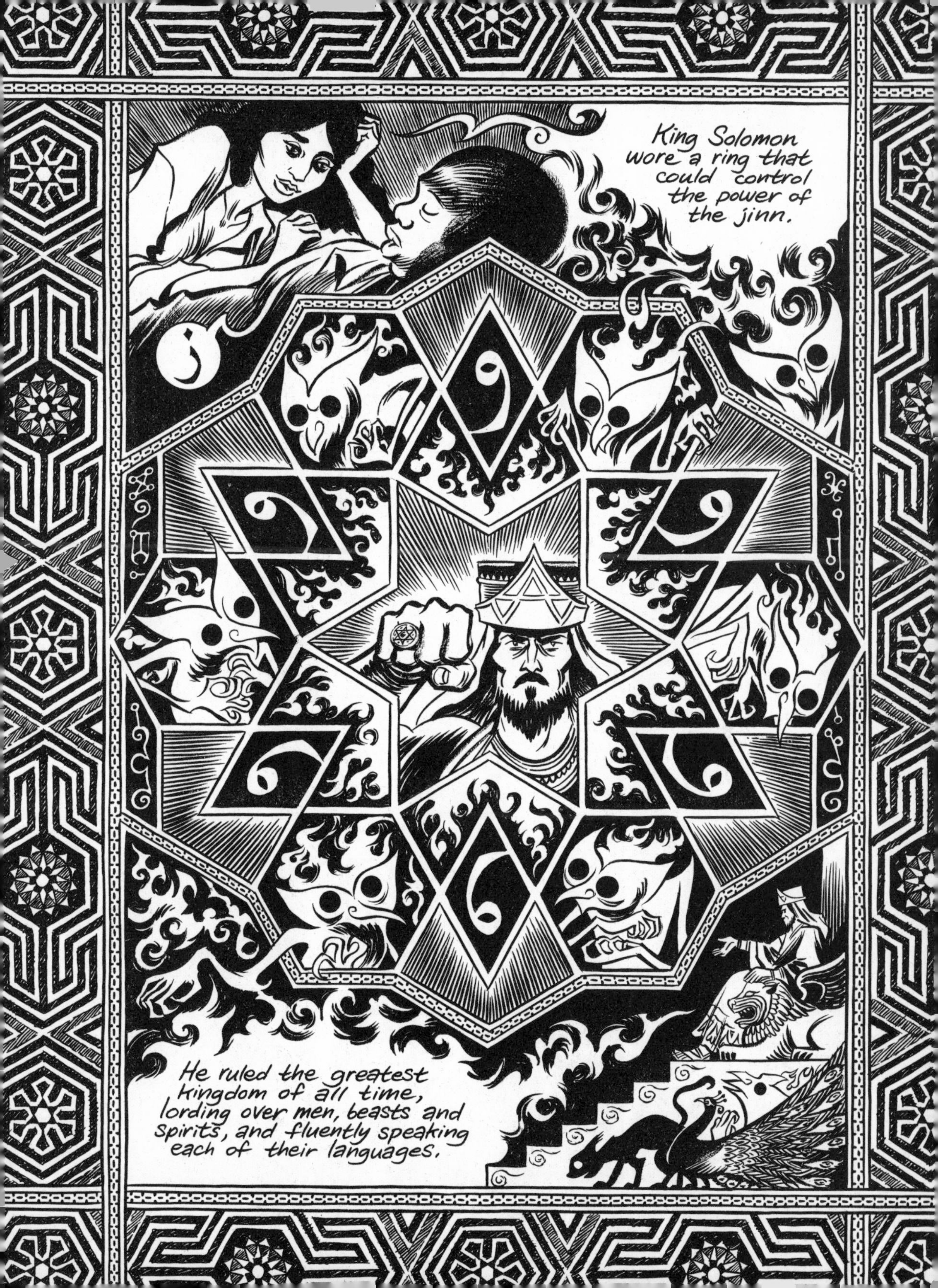
King Solomon wore a ring that could control the power of the jinn.
He ruled the greatest kingdom of all time, lording over men, beasts and spirits, and fluently speaking each of their languages.

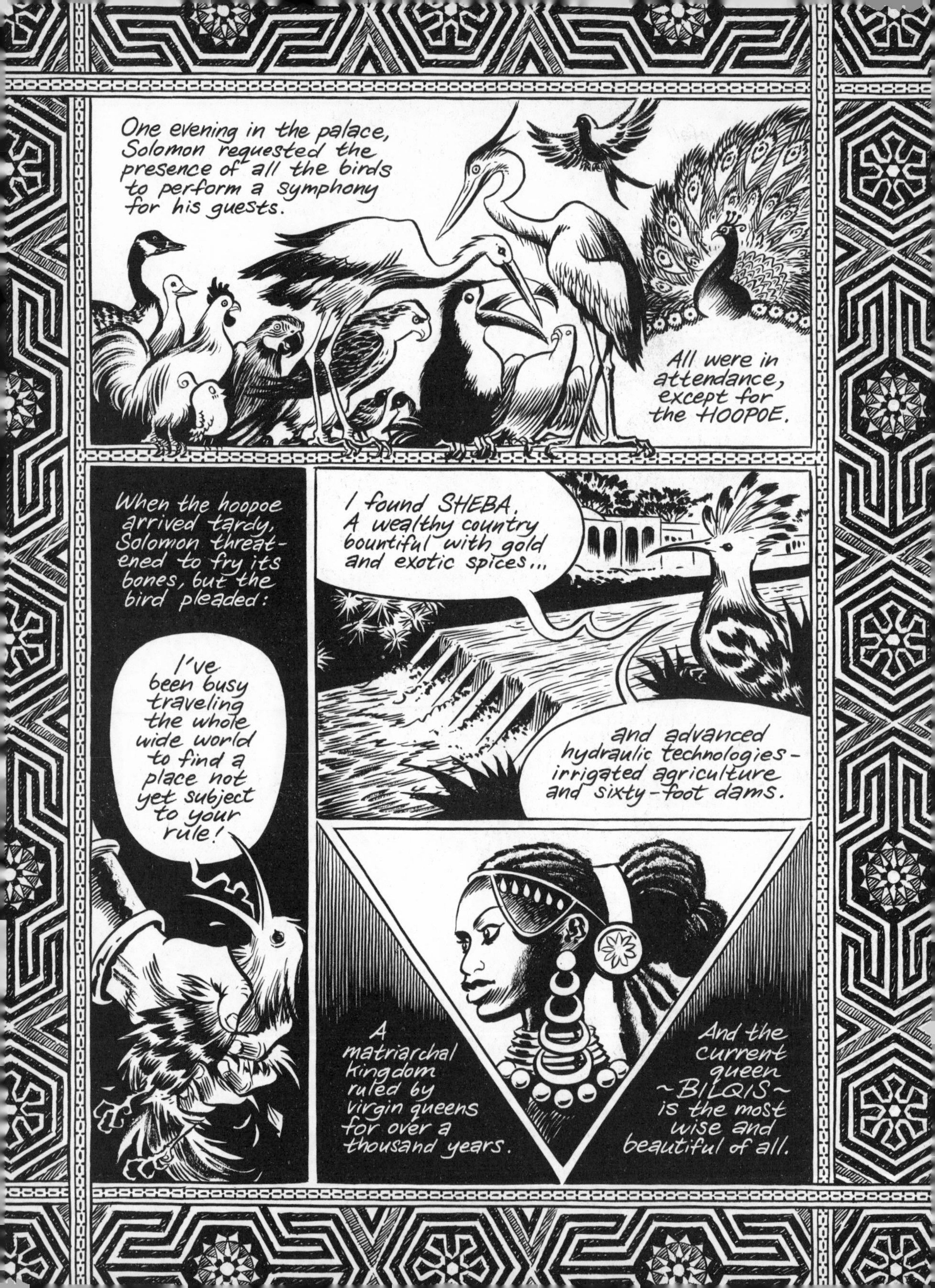

One evening in the palace, Solomon requested the presence of all the birds to perform a symphony for his guests.
All were in attendance, except for the HOOPOE.
When the hoopoe arrived tardy, Solomon threat-ened to fry its bones, but the bird pleaded:
I've been busy traveling the whole wide world to find a place not yet subject to your rule!
I found SHEBA. A wealthy country bountiful with gold and exotic spices...
and advanced hydraulic technologies - irrigated agriculture and sixty-foot dams.
A matriarchal kingdom ruled by virgin queens for over a thousand years.
And the current queen ~BILQIS~ is the most wise and beautiful of all.

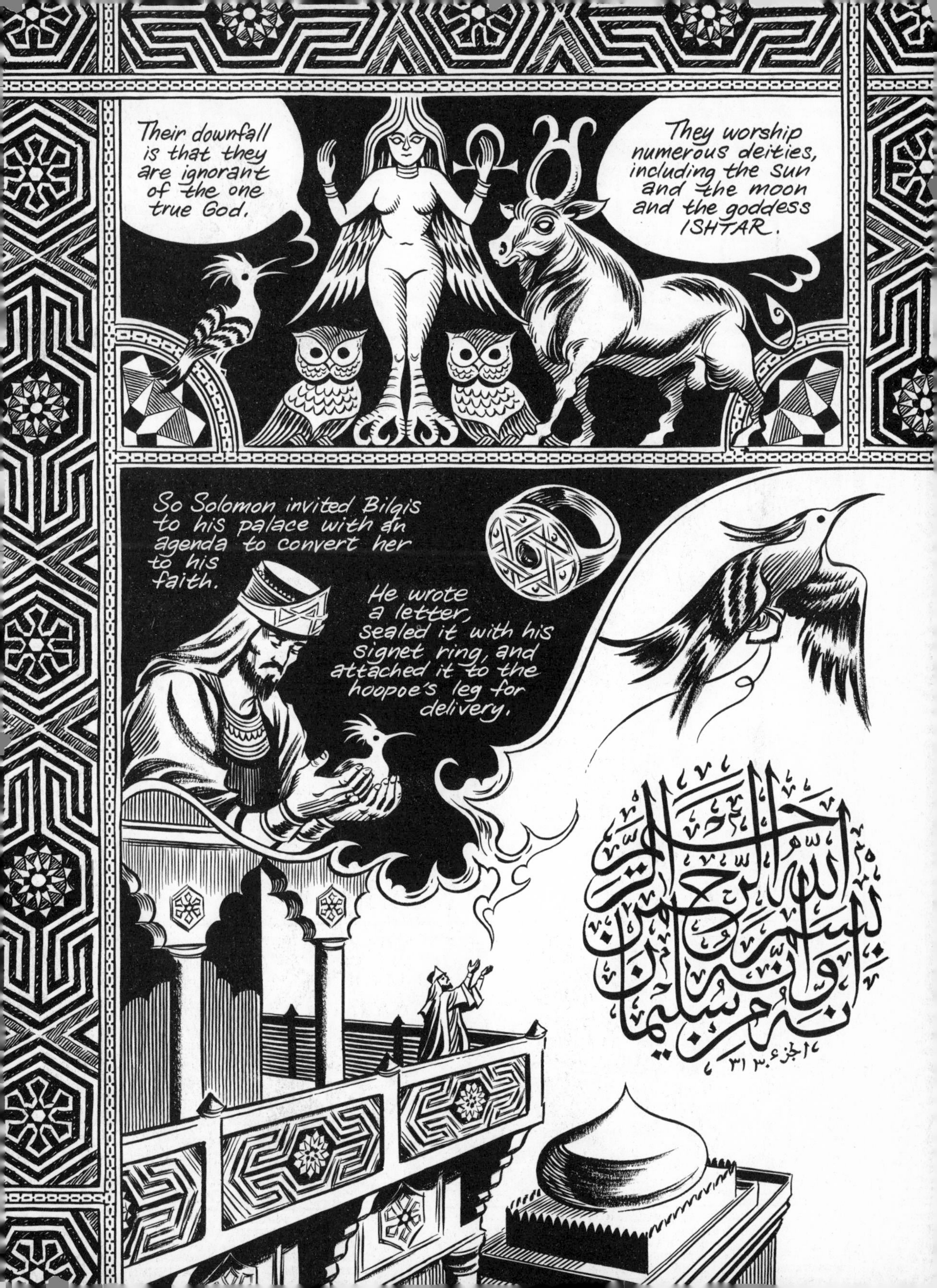

Their downfall is that they are ignorant of the one true God.
They worship numerous deities, including the sun and the moon and the goddess ISHTAR.
So Solomon invited Bilqis to his palace with an agenda to convert her to his faith.
He wrote a letter, sealed it with his signet ring, and attached it to the hoopoe's leg for delivery.
انه من سليمان وانه بسم الله الرحمن الرحيم

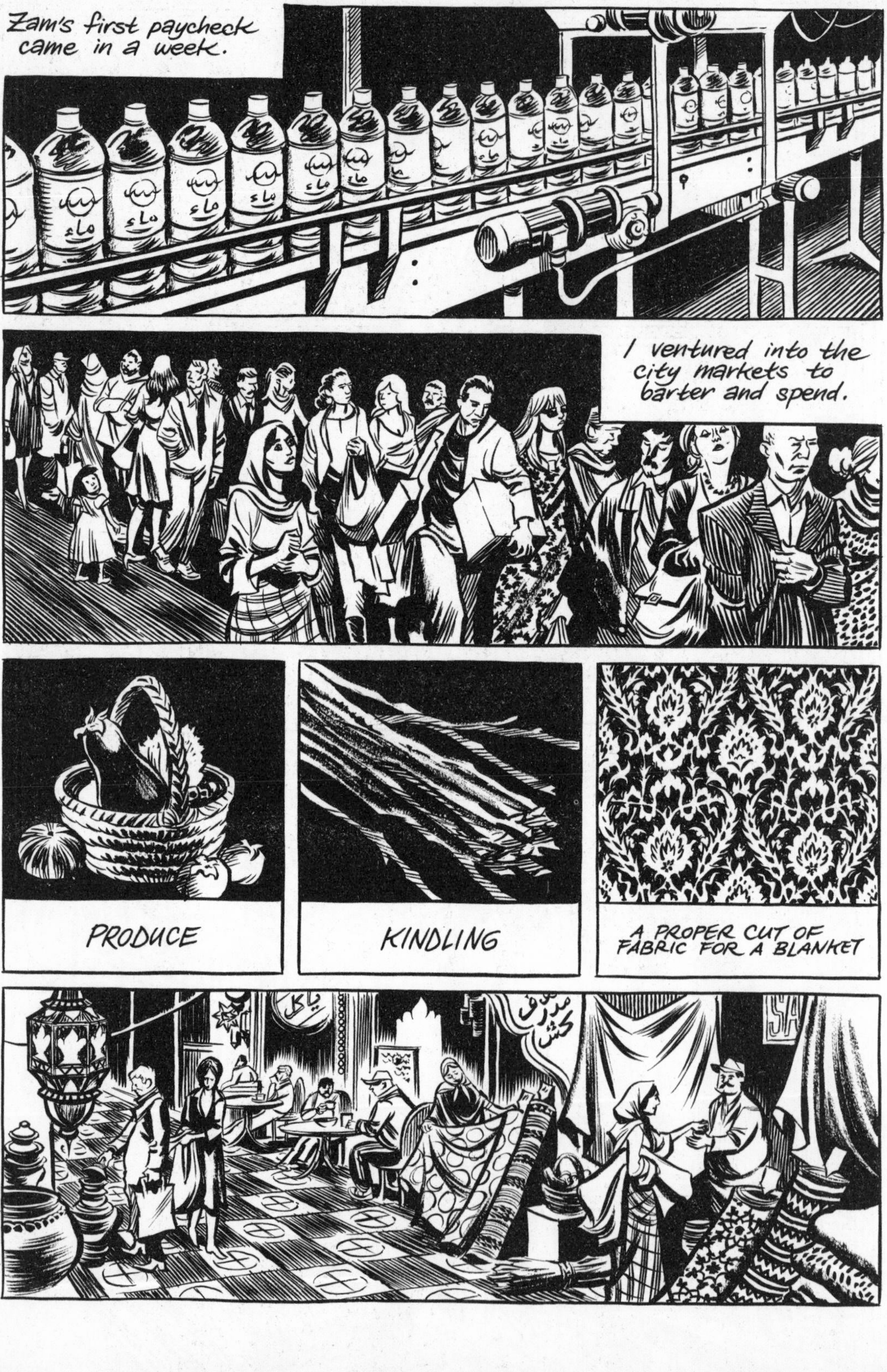

Zam's first paycheck came in a week.
I ventured into the city markets to barter and spend.
PRODUCE
KINDLING
A PROPER CUT OF FABRIC FOR A BLANKET

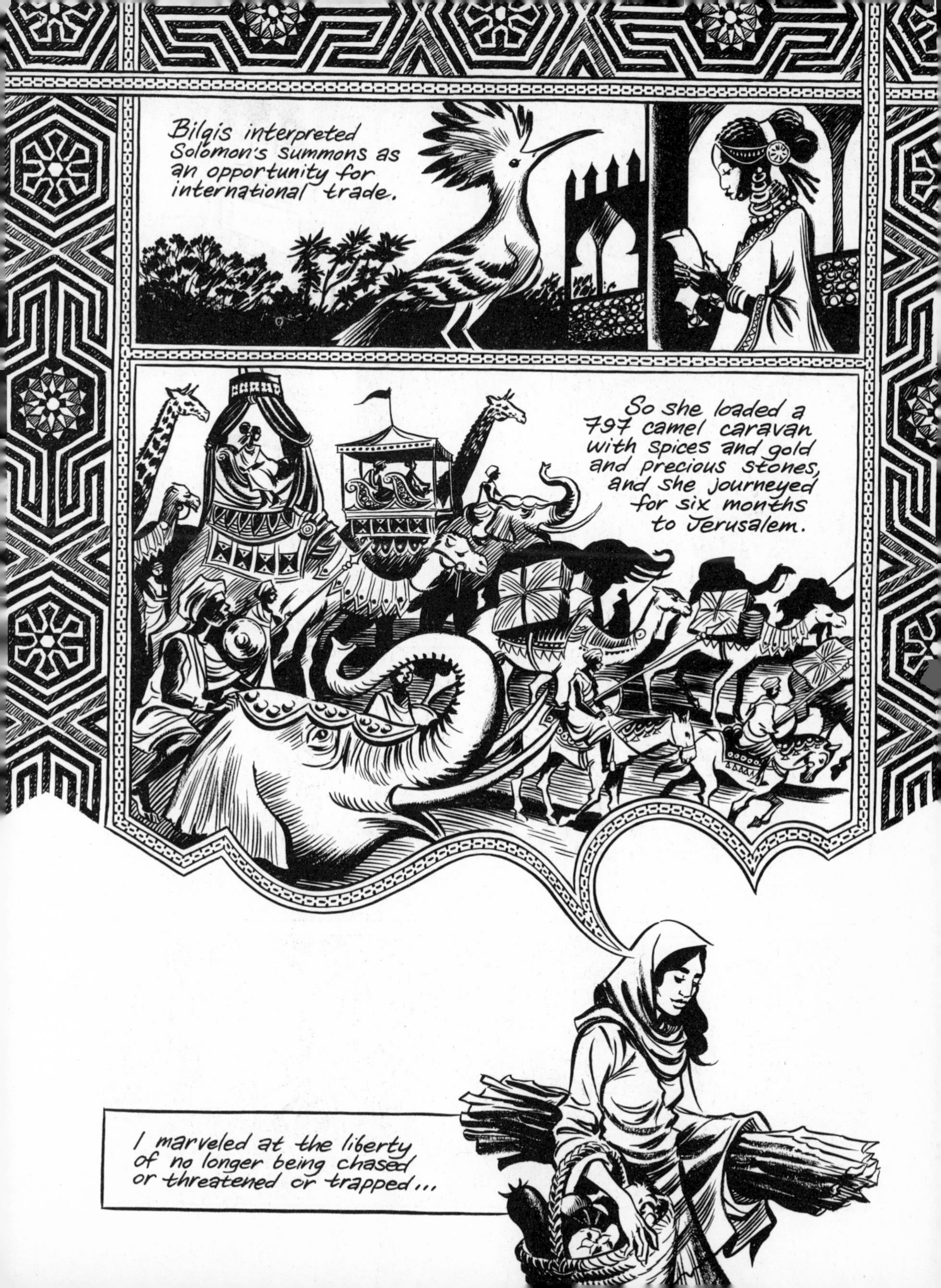

Bilqis interpreted Solomon's summons as an opportunity for international trade.
So she loaded a 797 camel caravan with spices and gold and precious stones, and she journeyed for six months to Jerusalem.
I marveled at the liberty of no longer being chased or threatened or trapped...

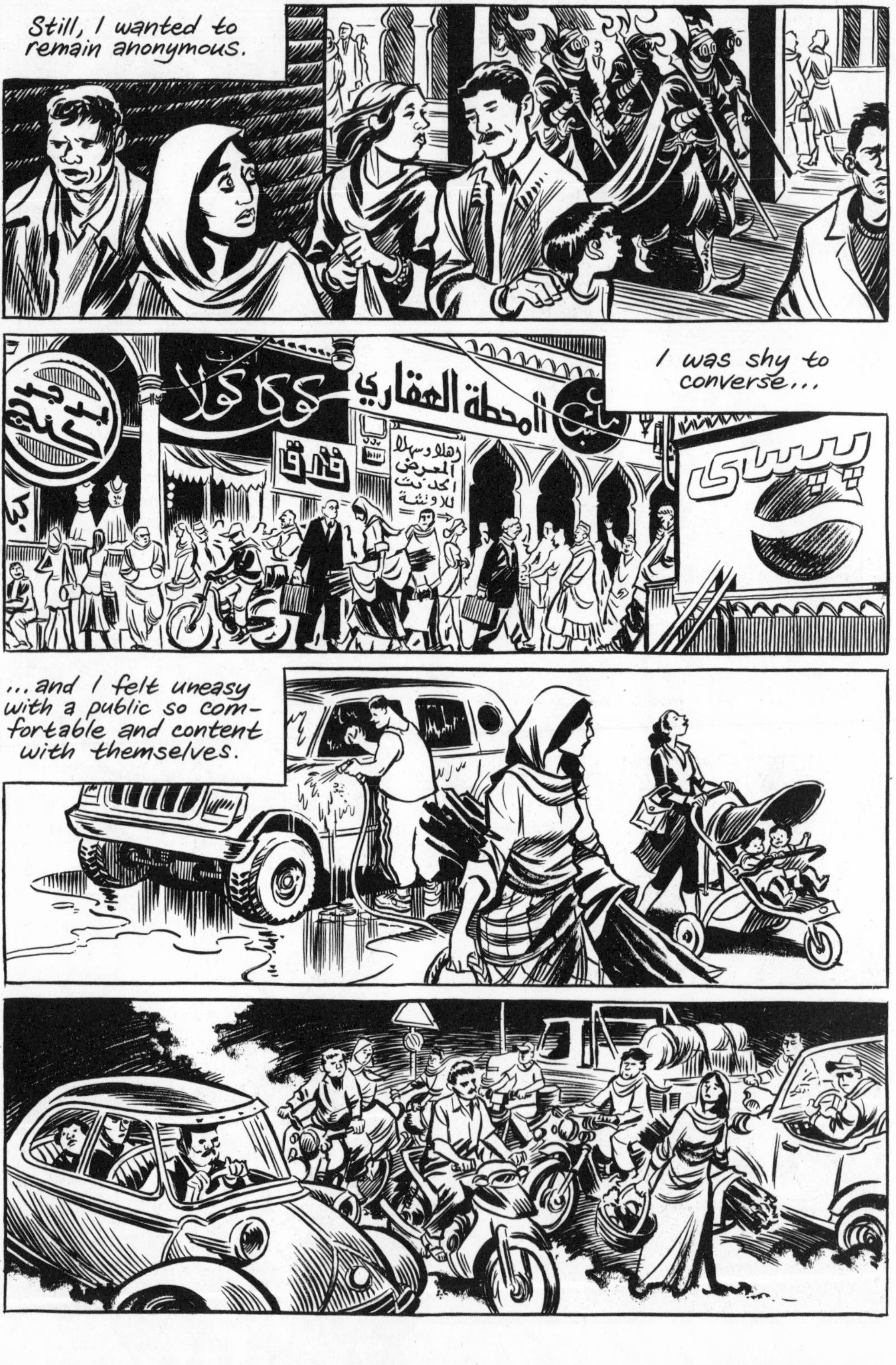
Still, I wanted to remain anonymous.
I was shy to converse...
كوكا كولا
المحطة العقاري
فندق
...and I felt uneasy with a public so comfortable and content with themselves.

Home was safe.

Zam rigged a stove on the balcony...

and we amassed quite a water supply.

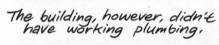

The building, however, didn't have working plumbing.

You need a bath.

But I used a whole bottle.

You need SUBMERSION.

I know just the place.

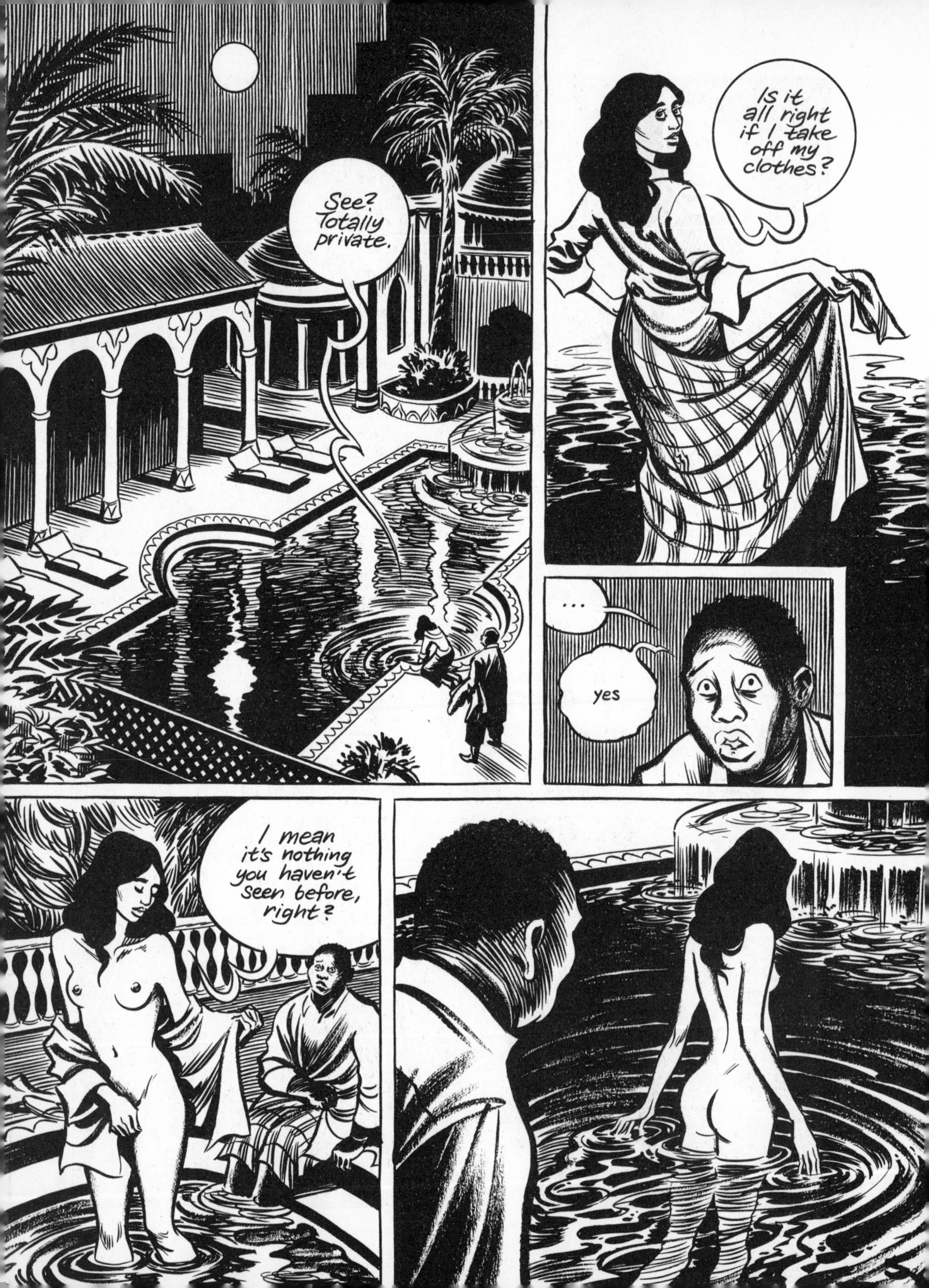
See? Totally private.
Is it all right if I take off my clothes?
...
yes
I mean it's nothing you haven't seen before, right?

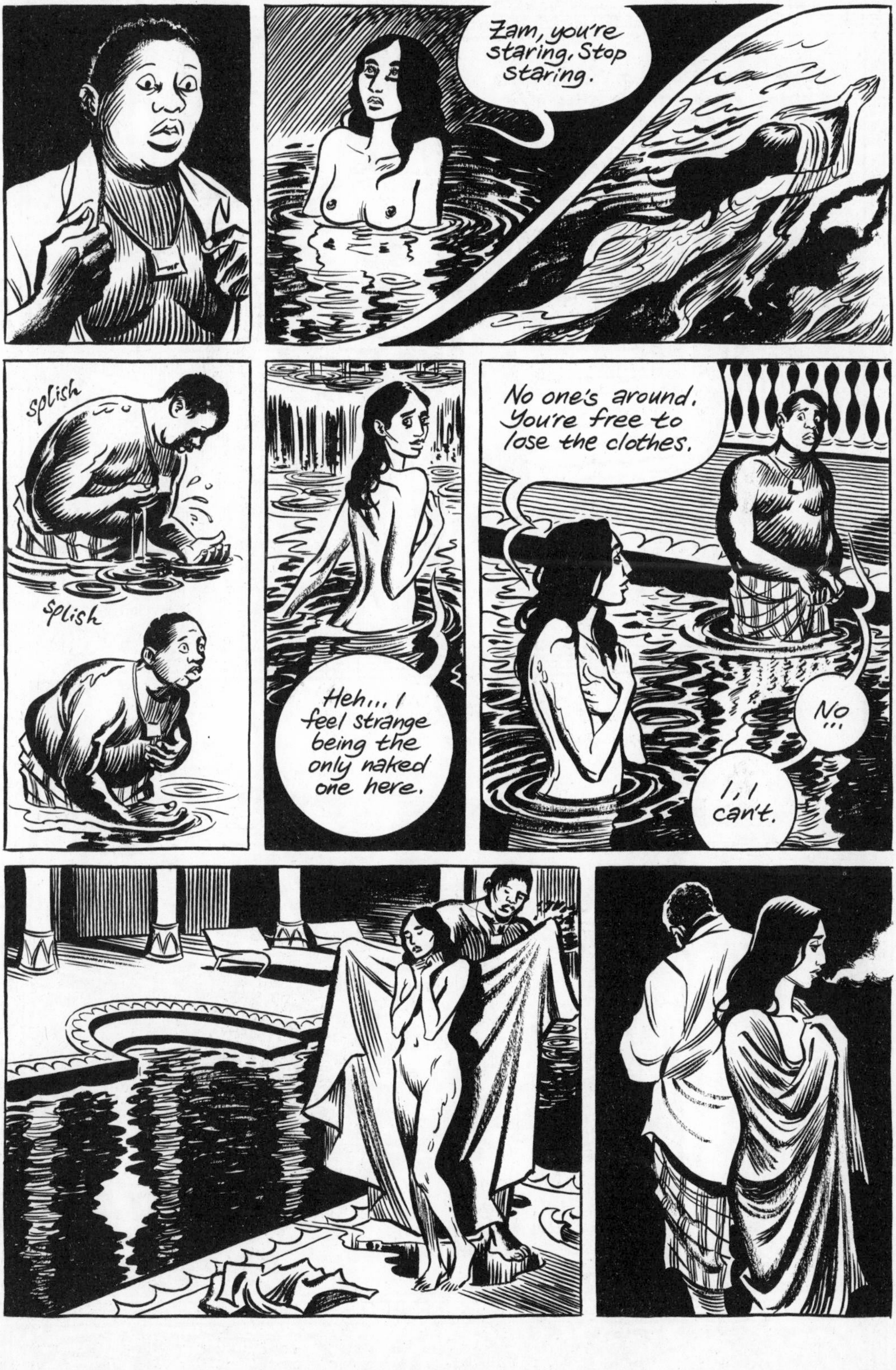

Zam, you're staring. Stop staring.
splish
splish
No one's around. You're free to lose the clothes.
Heh... I feel strange being the only naked one here.
No...
I, I can't.

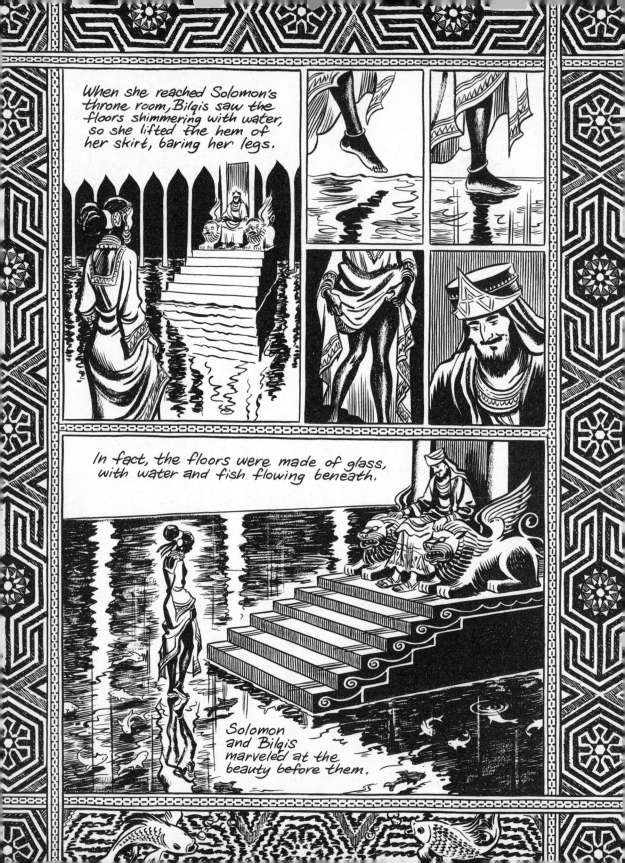

When she reached Solomon's throne room, Bilqis saw the floors shimmering with water, so she lifted the hem of her skirt, baring her legs.

In fact, the floors were made of glass, with water and fish flowing beneath.

Solomon and Bilqis marveled at the beauty before them.

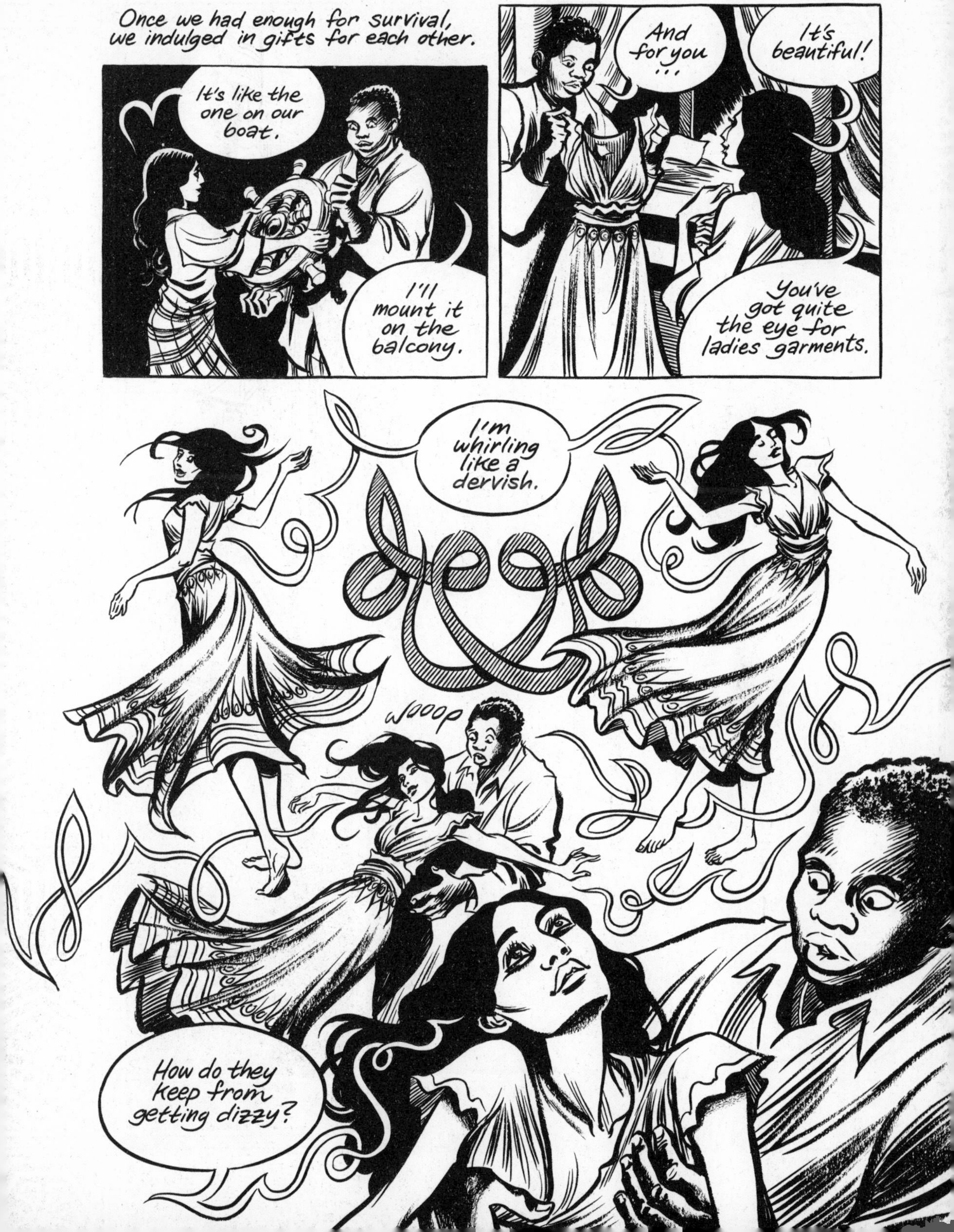
Once we had enough for survival, we indulged in gifts for each other.
It's like the one on our boat.
I'll mount it on the balcony.
And for you . . .
It's beautiful!
You've got quite the eye for ladies garments.
I'm whirling like a dervish.
wooop
How do they keep from getting dizzy?

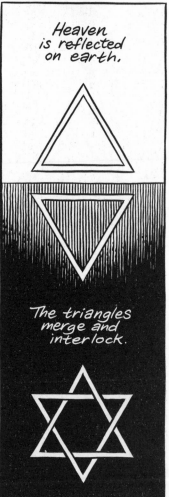

Heaven is reflected on earth.

The triangles merge and interlock.

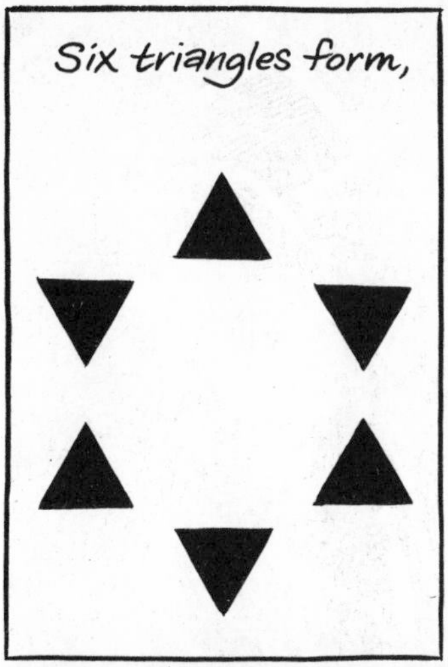
Six triangles form,

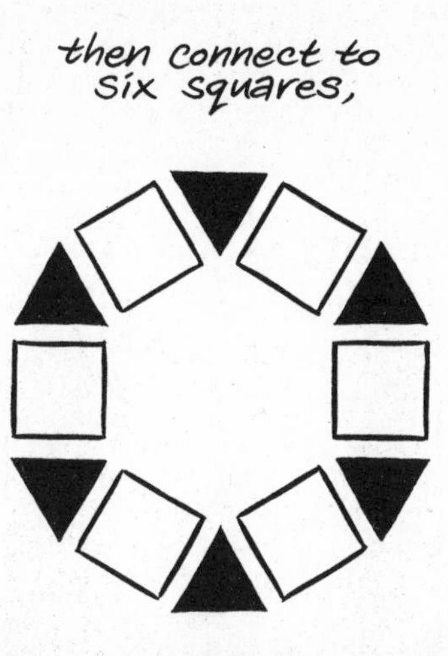
then connect to six squares,

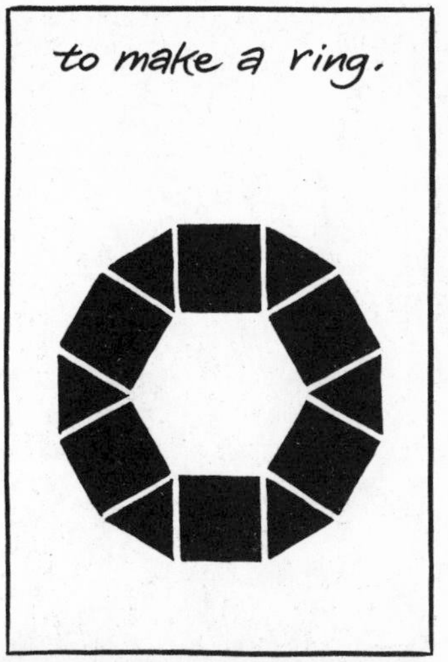
to make a ring.

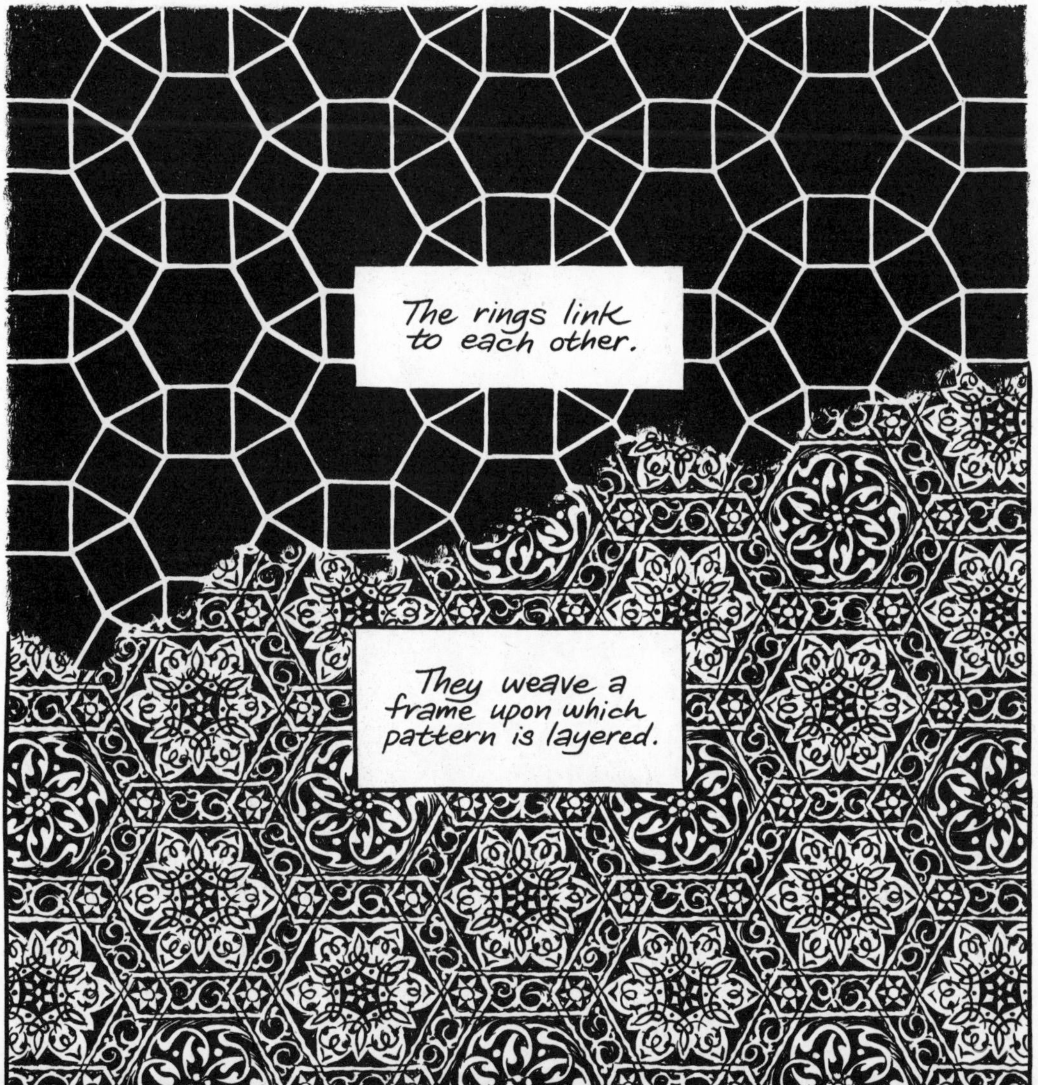
The rings link to each other.
They weave a frame upon which pattern is layered.

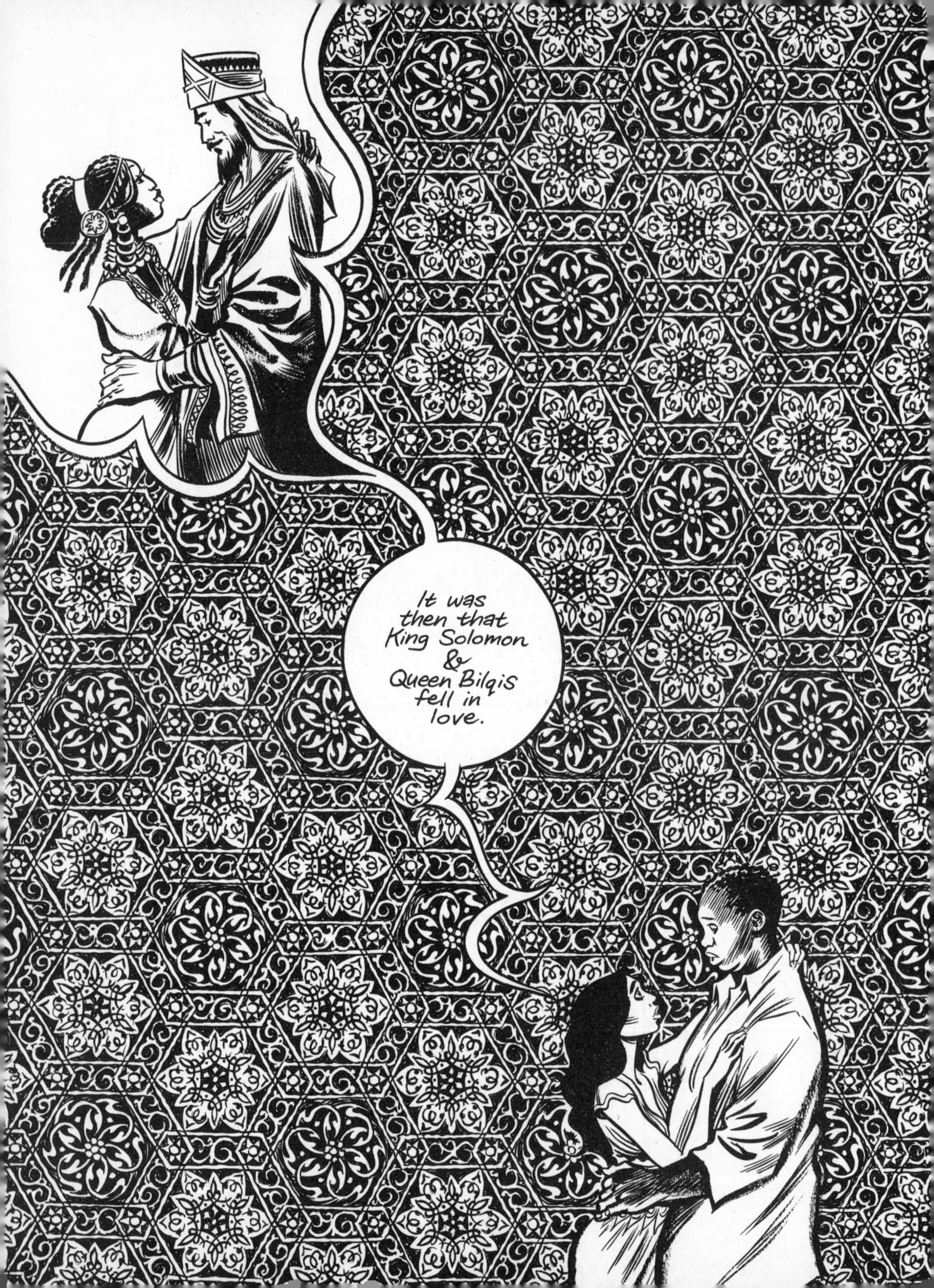
It was then that King Solomon & Queen Bilqis fell in love.

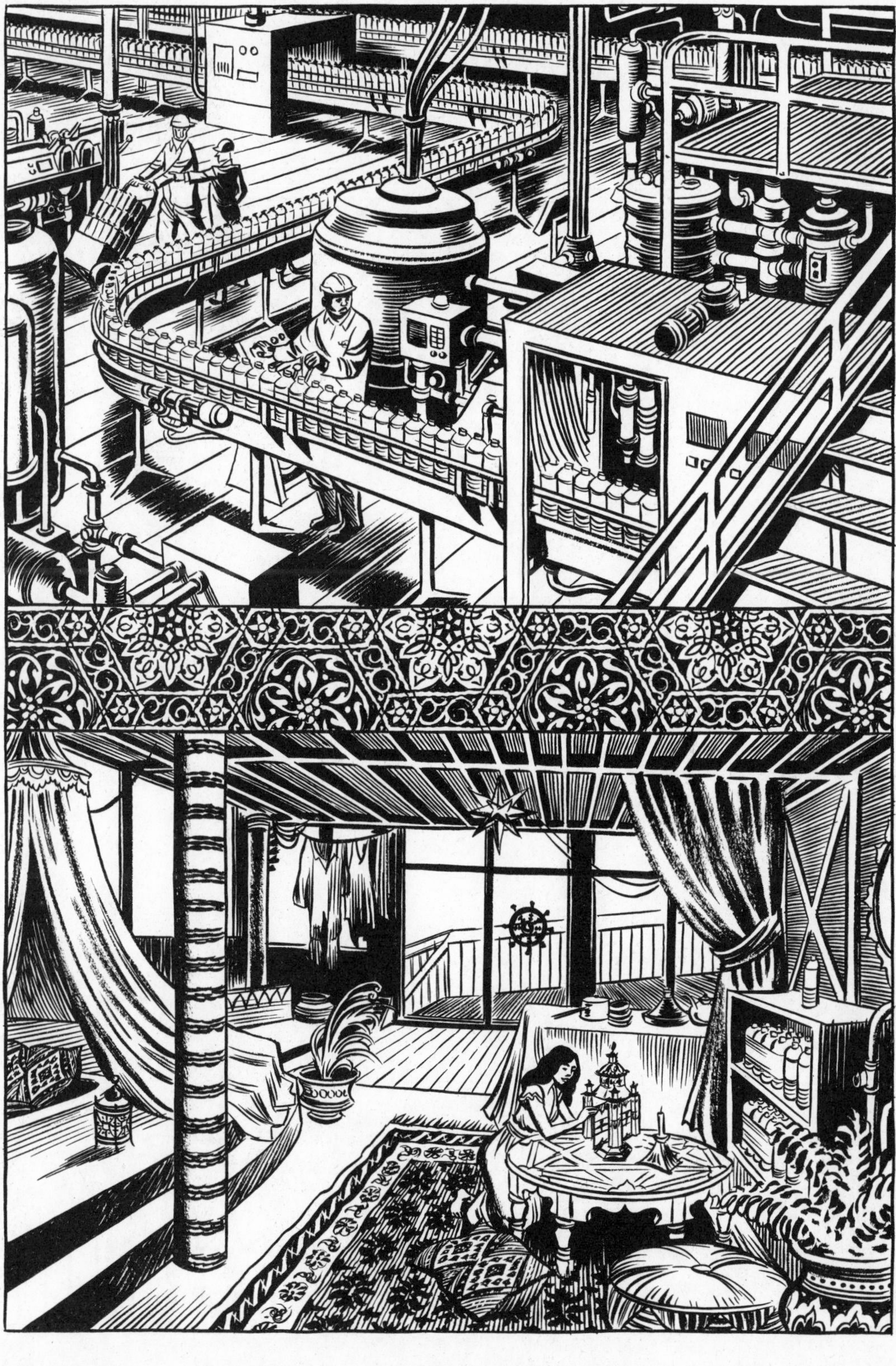

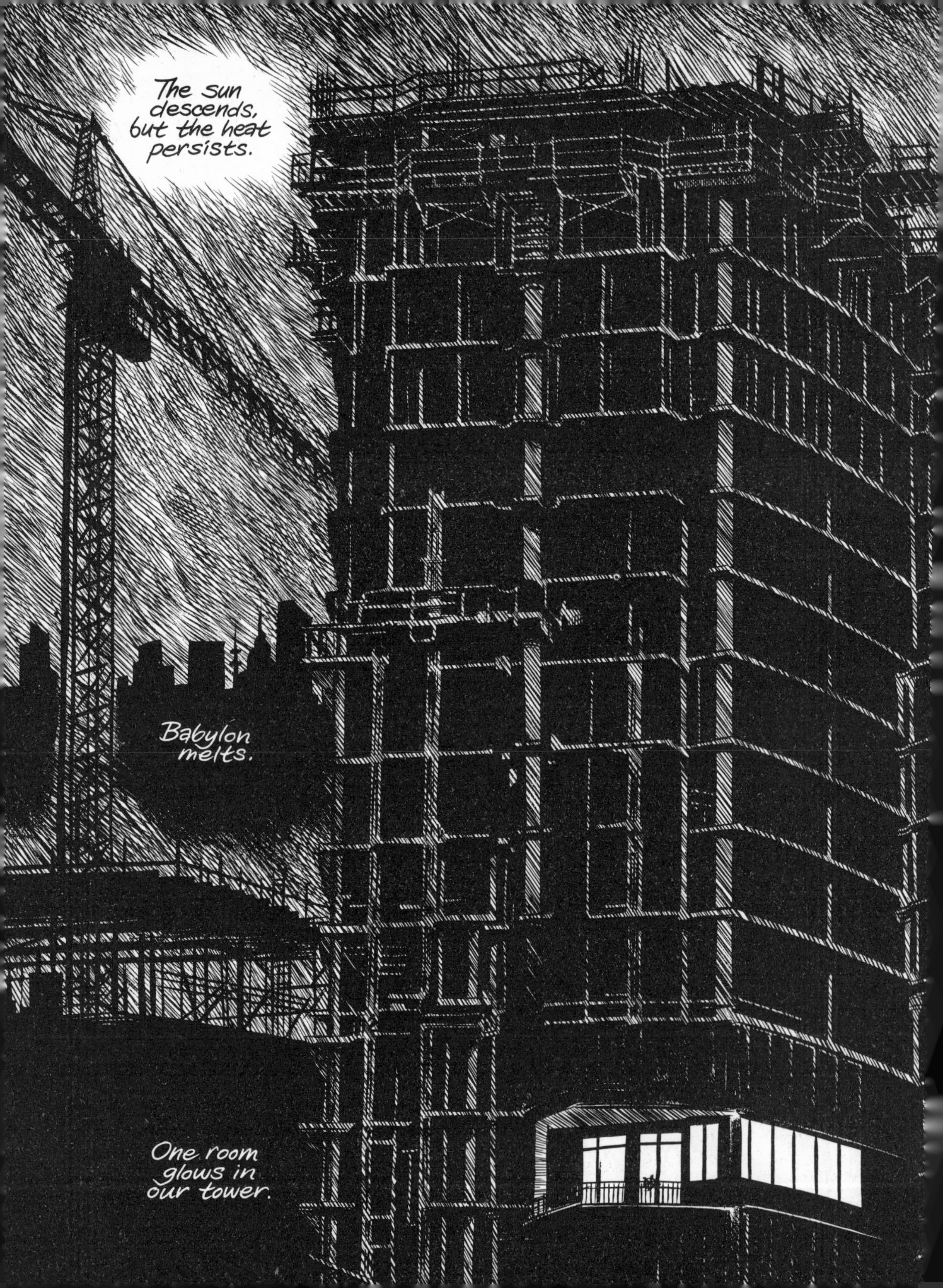
The sun descends, but the heat persists.
Babylon melts.
One room glows in our tower.

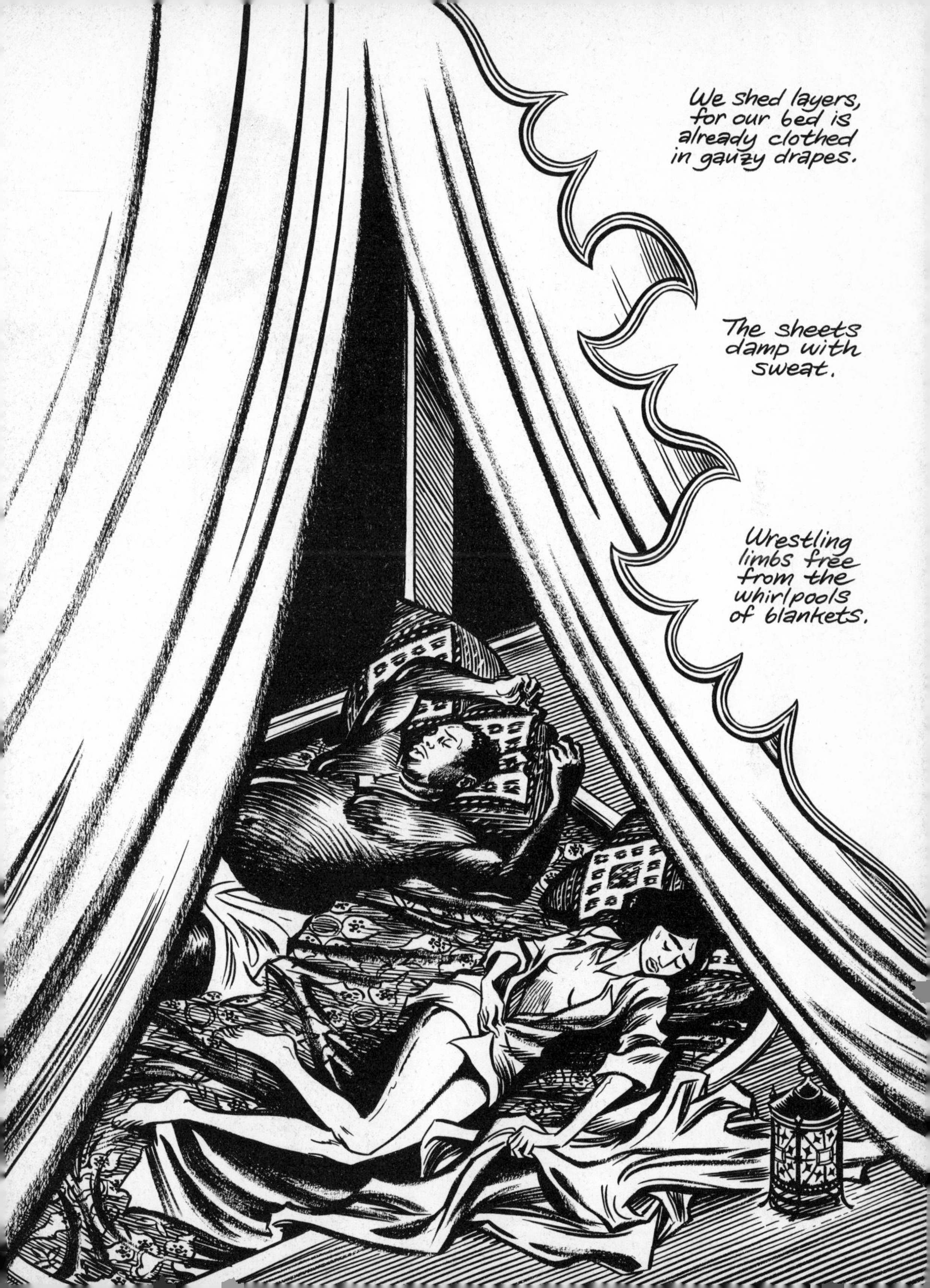
We shed layers, for our bed is already clothed in gauzy drapes.
The sheets damp with sweat.
Wrestling limbs free from the whirlpools of blankets.

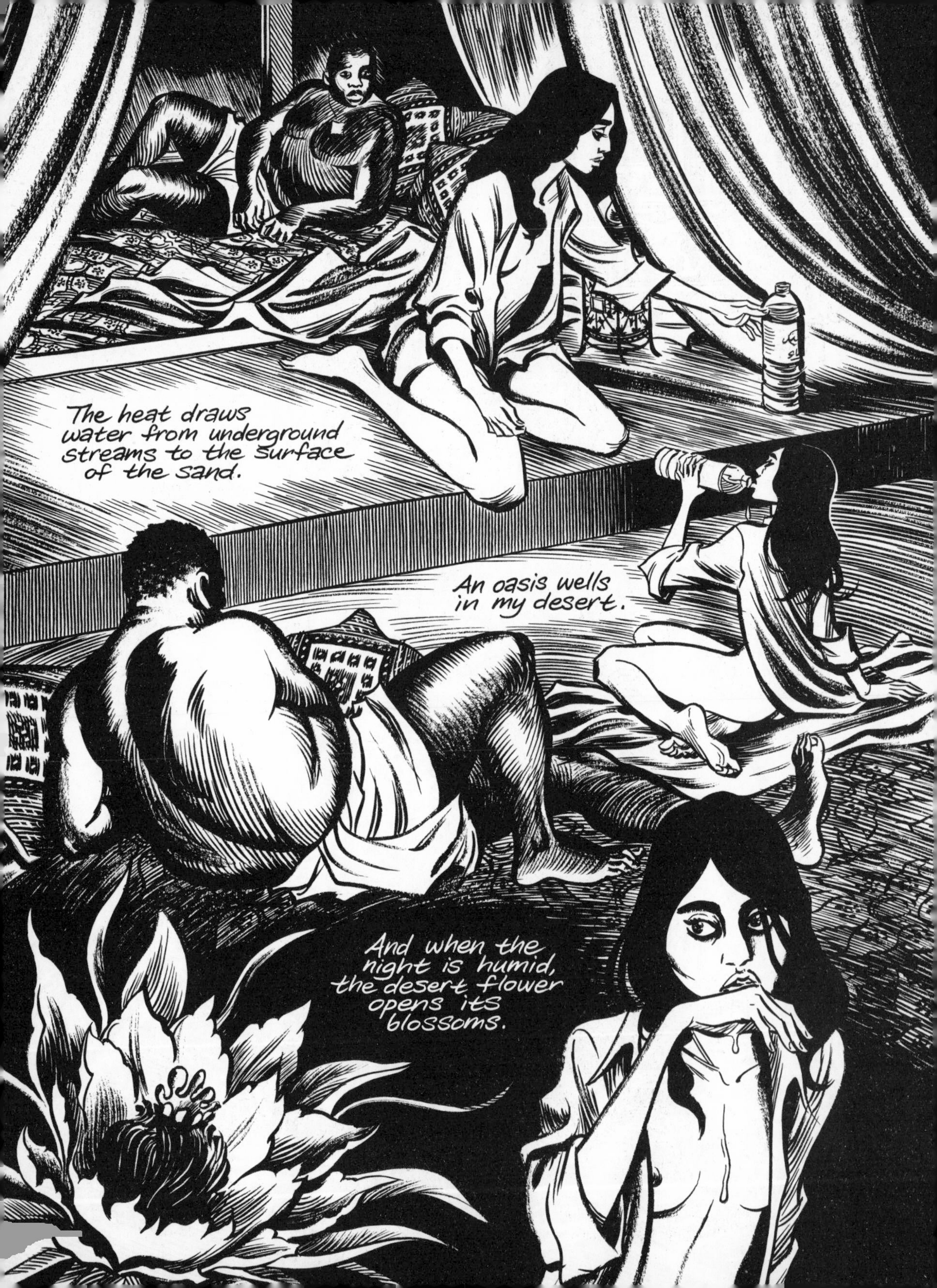
The heat draws water from underground streams to the surface of the sand.
An oasis wells in my desert.
And when the night is humid, the desert flower opens its blossoms.

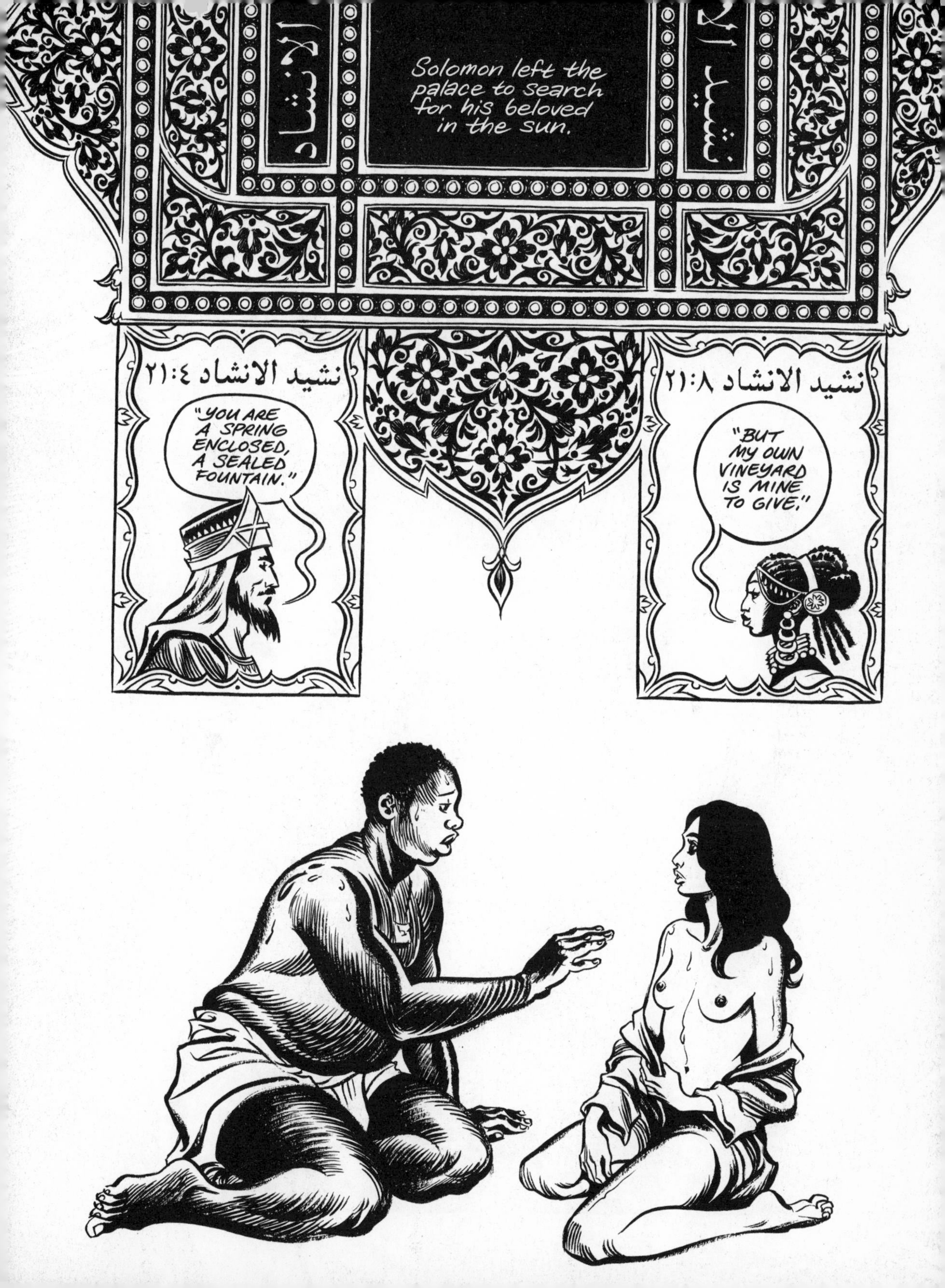
نشيد الانشاد
نشيد الانشاد
Solomon left the palace to search for his beloved in the sun.
نشيد الانشاد ٤:٢١
"YOU ARE A SPRING ENCLOSED, A SEALED FOUNTAIN."
نشيد الانشاد ٨:٢١
"BUT MY OWN VINEYARD IS MINE TO GIVE."

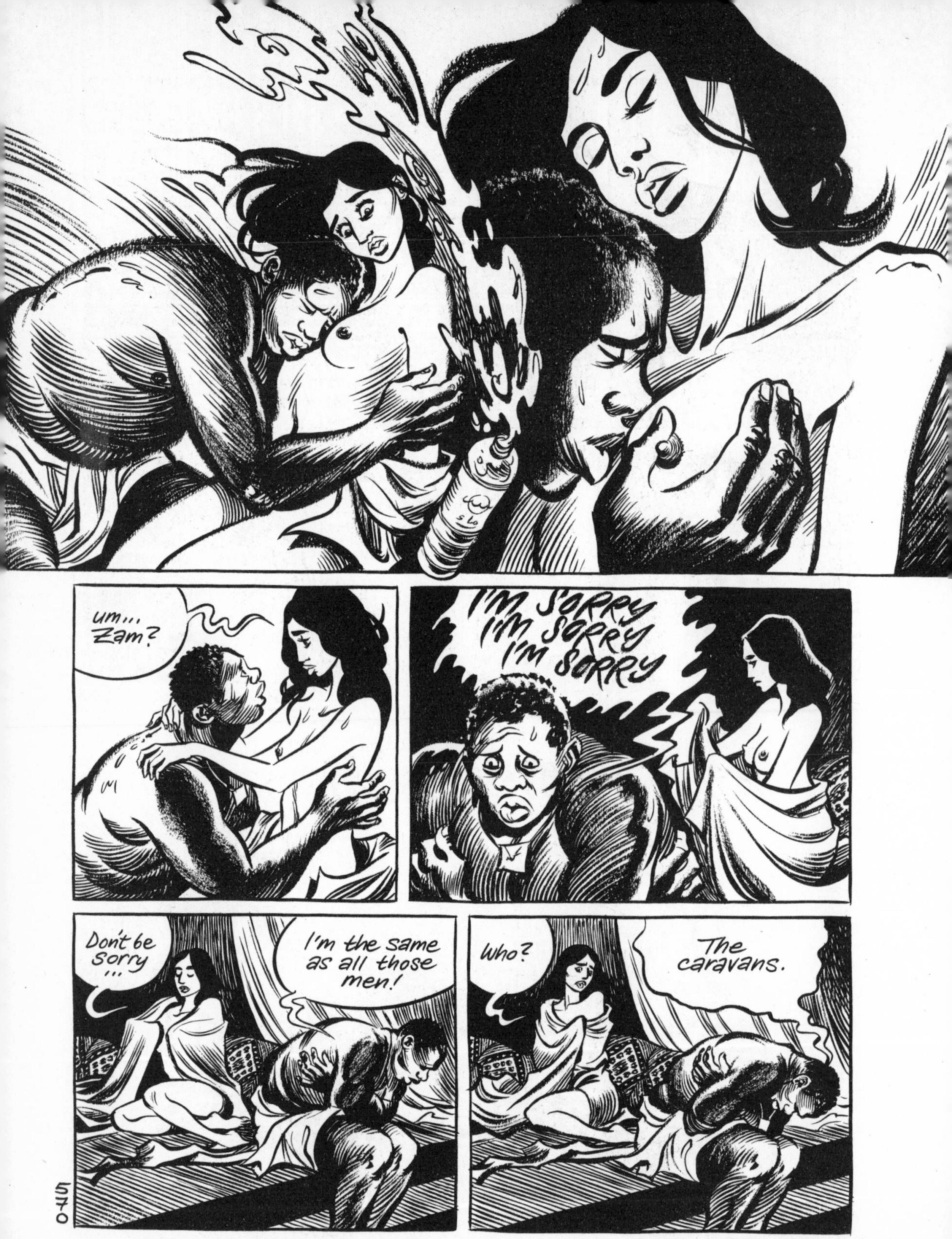
um... Zam?
I'M SORRY I'M SORRY I'M SORRY
Don't be sorry ...
I'm the same as all those men!
Who?
The caravans.

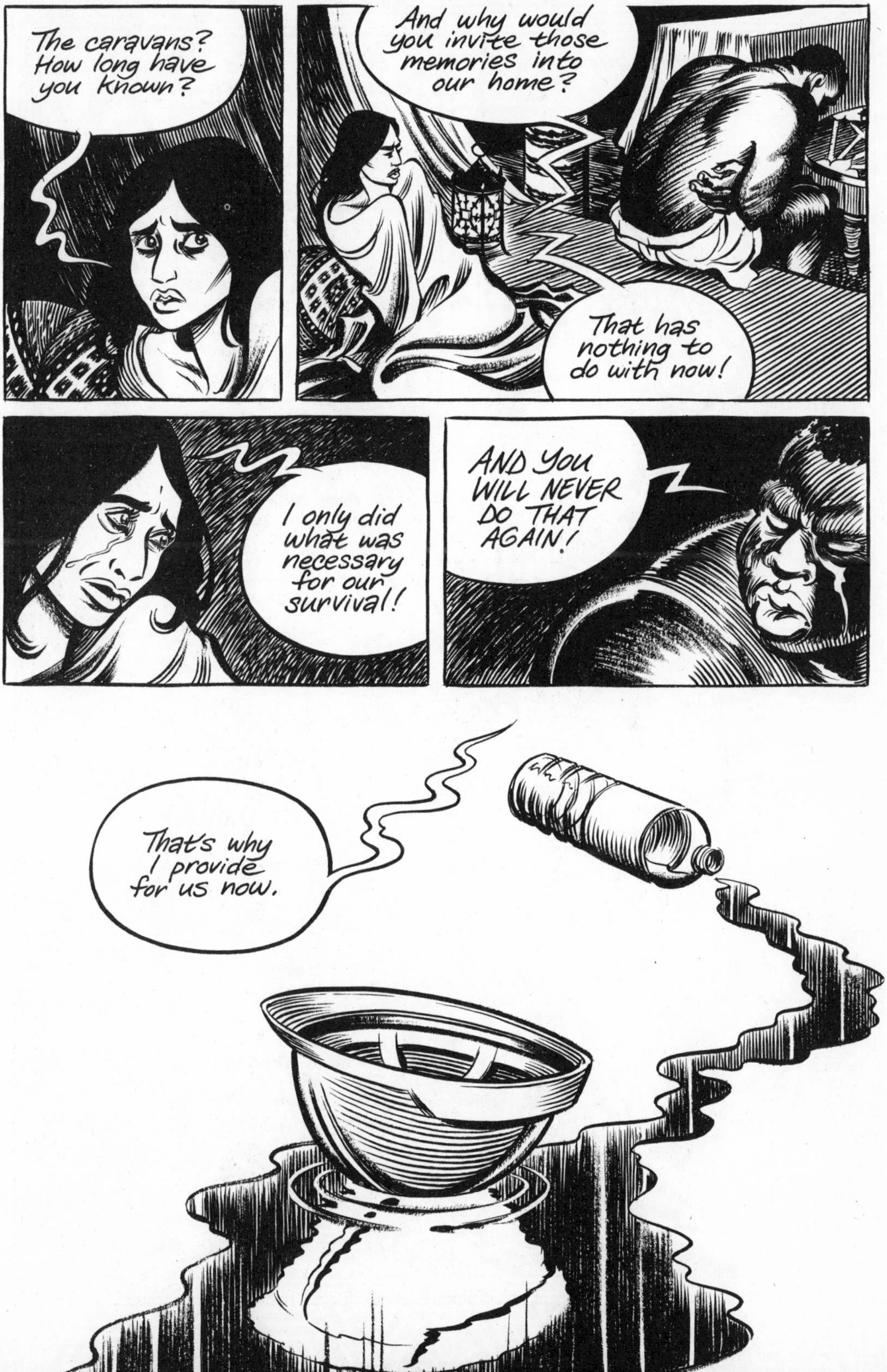
The caravans? How long have you known?
And why would you invite those memories into our home?
That has nothing to do with now!
I only did what was necessary for our survival!
AND YOU WILL NEVER DO THAT AGAIN!
That's why I provide for us now.

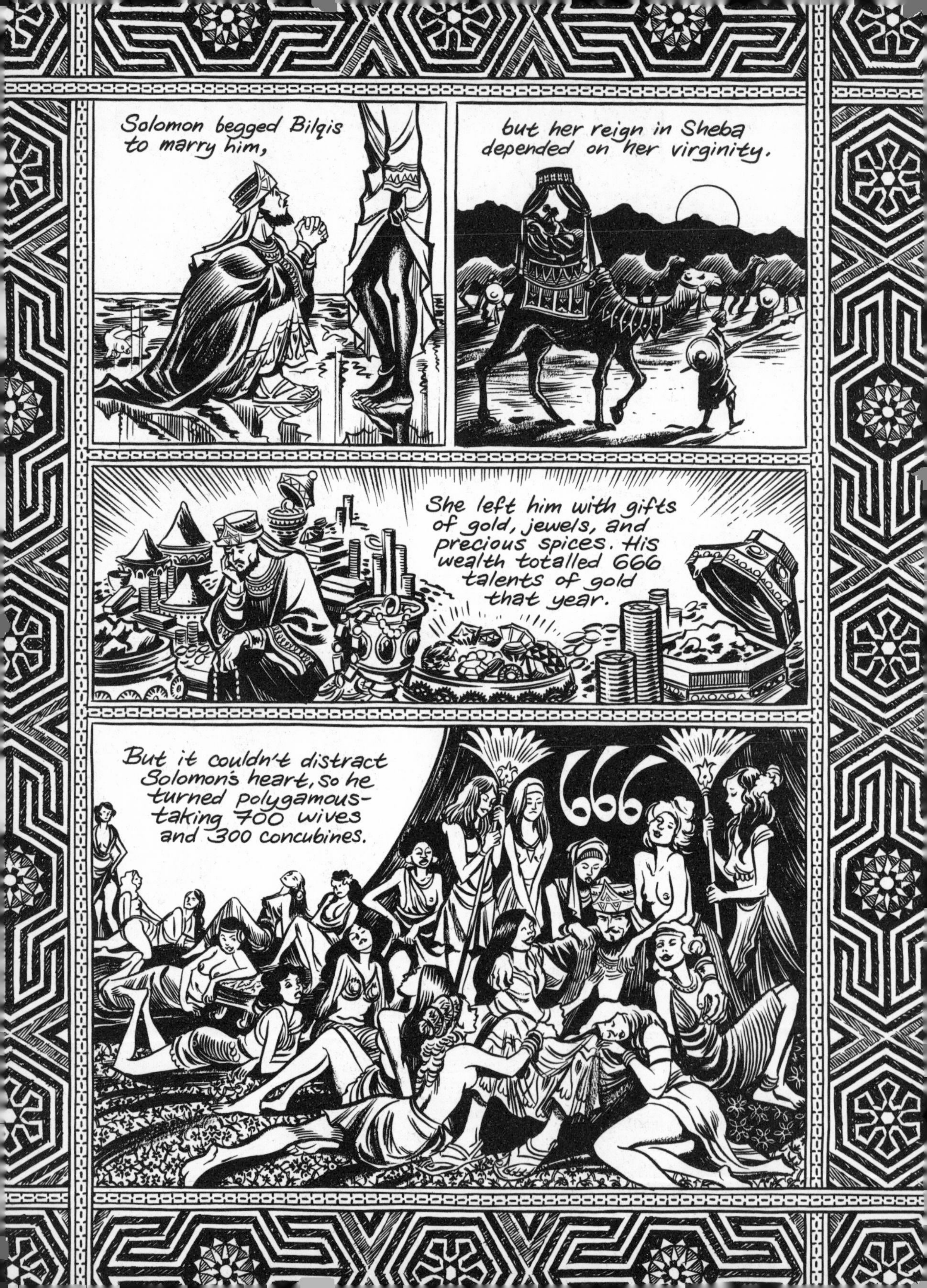
Solomon begged Bilqis to marry him,
but her reign in Sheba depended on her virginity.
She left him with gifts of gold, jewels, and precious spices. His wealth totalled 666 talents of gold that year.
But it couldn't distract Solomon's heart, so he turned polygamous-taking 700 wives and 300 concubines.
666

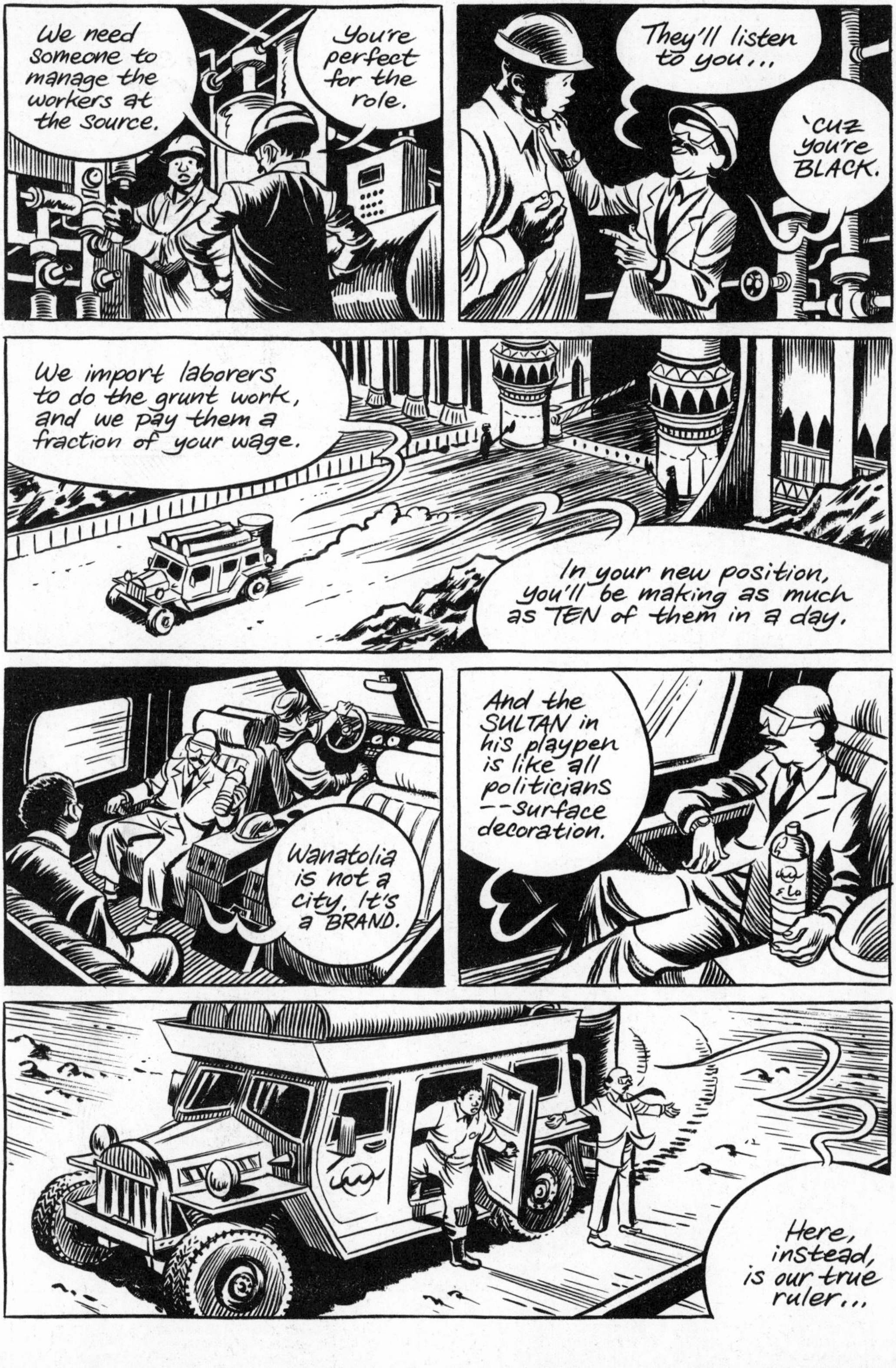
We need someone to manage the workers at the source.
You're perfect for the role.
They'll listen to you...
'CUZ you're BLACK.
We import laborers to do the grunt work, and we pay them a fraction of your wage.
In your new position, you'll be making as much as TEN of them in a day.
Wanatolia is not a city, It's a BRAND.
And the SULTAN in his playpen is like all politicians --surface decoration.
Here, instead, is our true ruler...

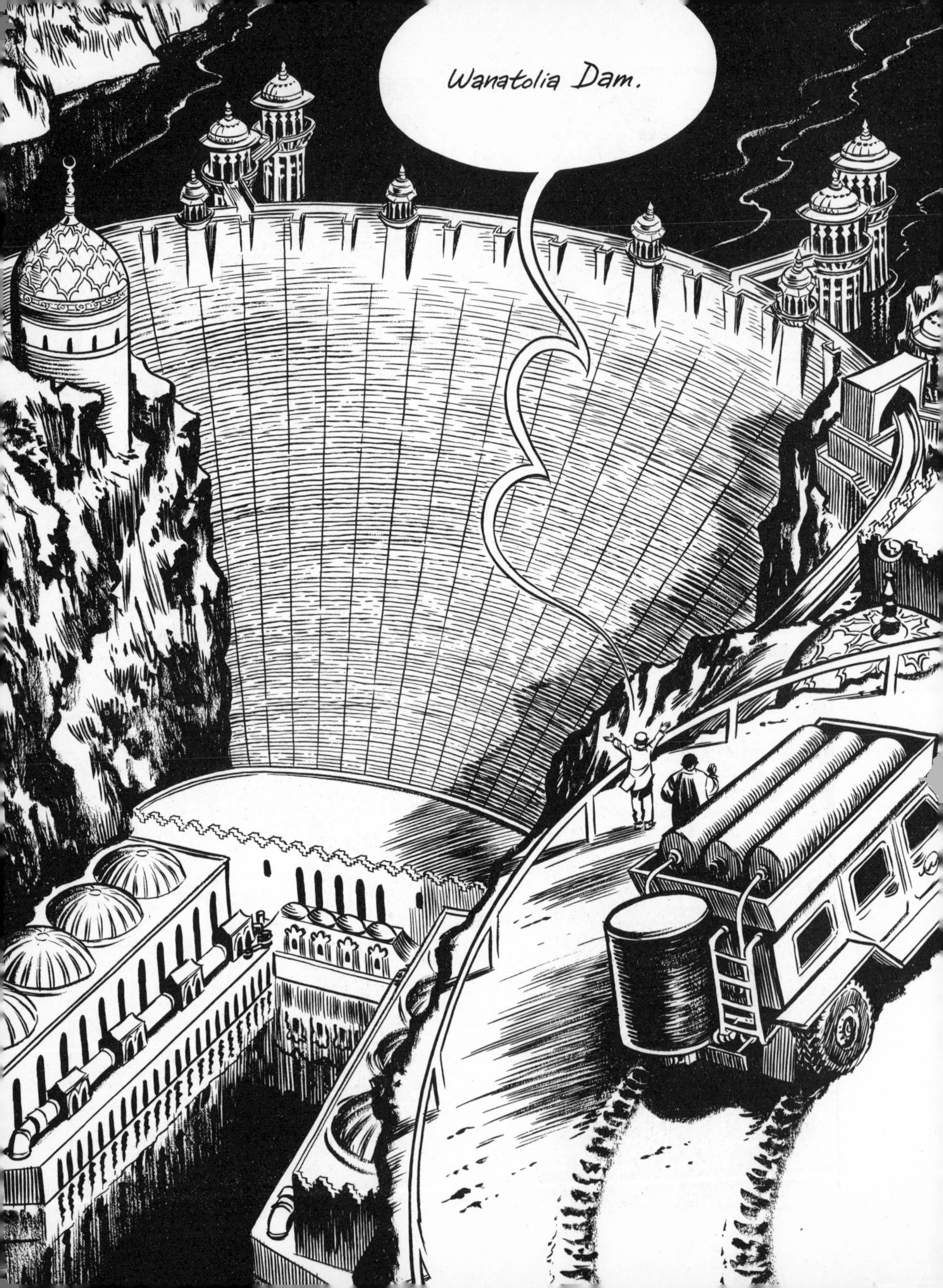
Wanatolia Dam.

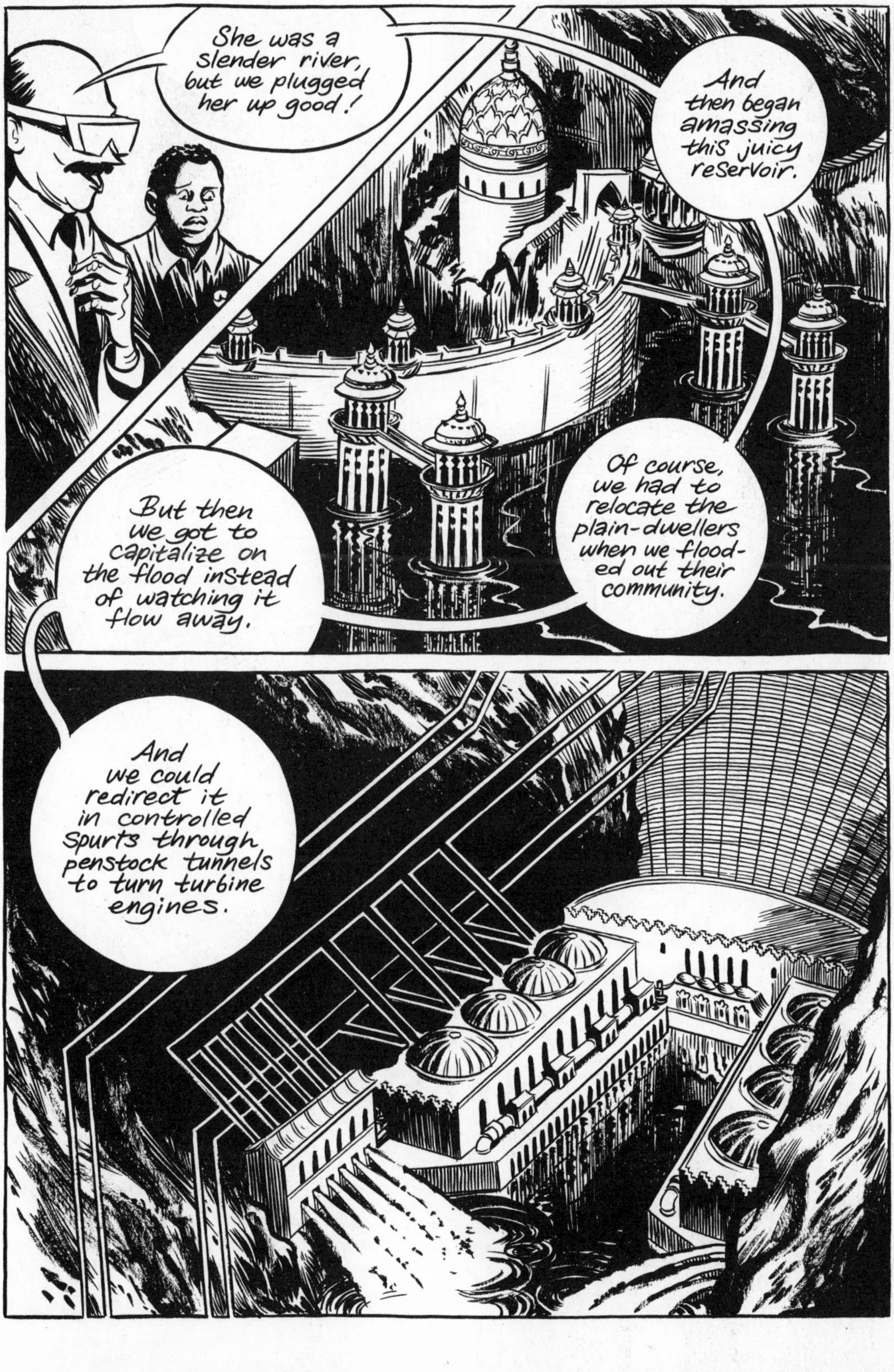
She was a slender river, but we plugged her up good!
And then began amassing this juicy reservoir.
Of course, we had to relocate the plain-dwellers when we flooded out their community.
But then we got to capitalize on the flood instead of watching it flow away.
And we could redirect it in controlled spurts through penstock tunnels to turn turbine engines.

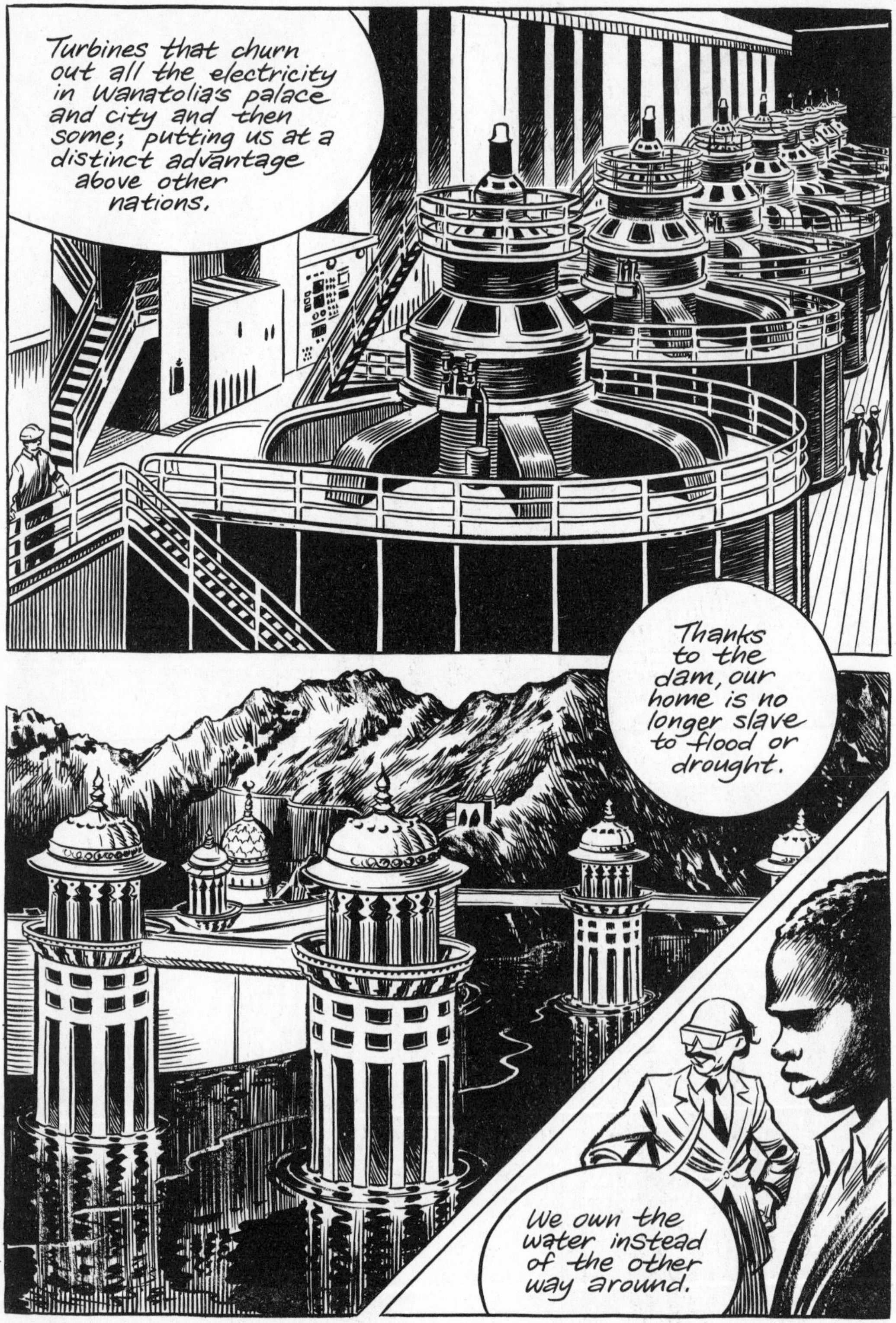
Turbines that churn out all the electricity in Wanatolia's palace and city and then some; putting us at a distinct advantage above other nations.
Thanks to the dam, our home is no longer slave to flood or drought.
We own the water instead of the other way around.

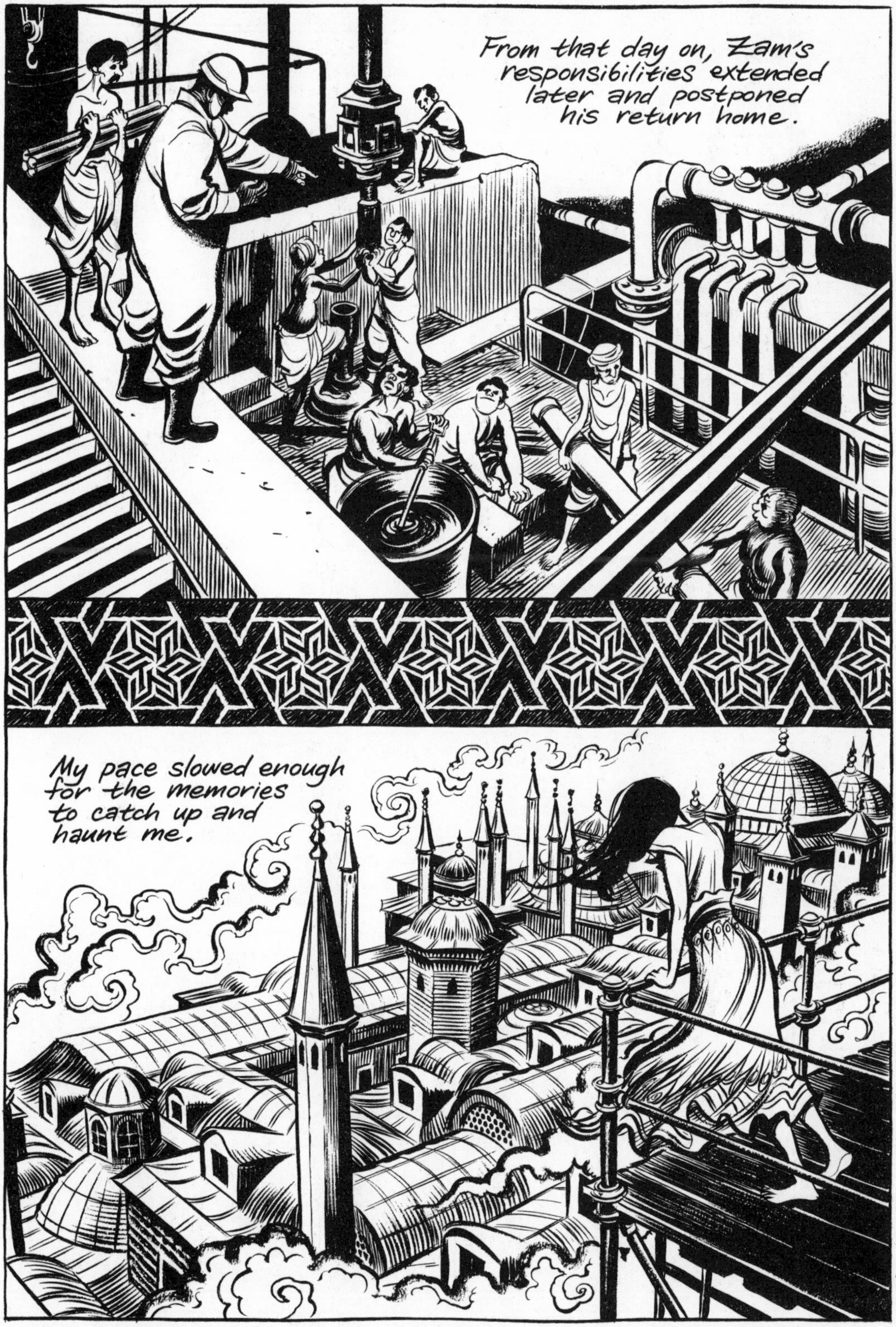
From that day on, Zam's responsibilities extended later and postponed his return home.
My pace slowed enough for the memories to catch up and haunt me.

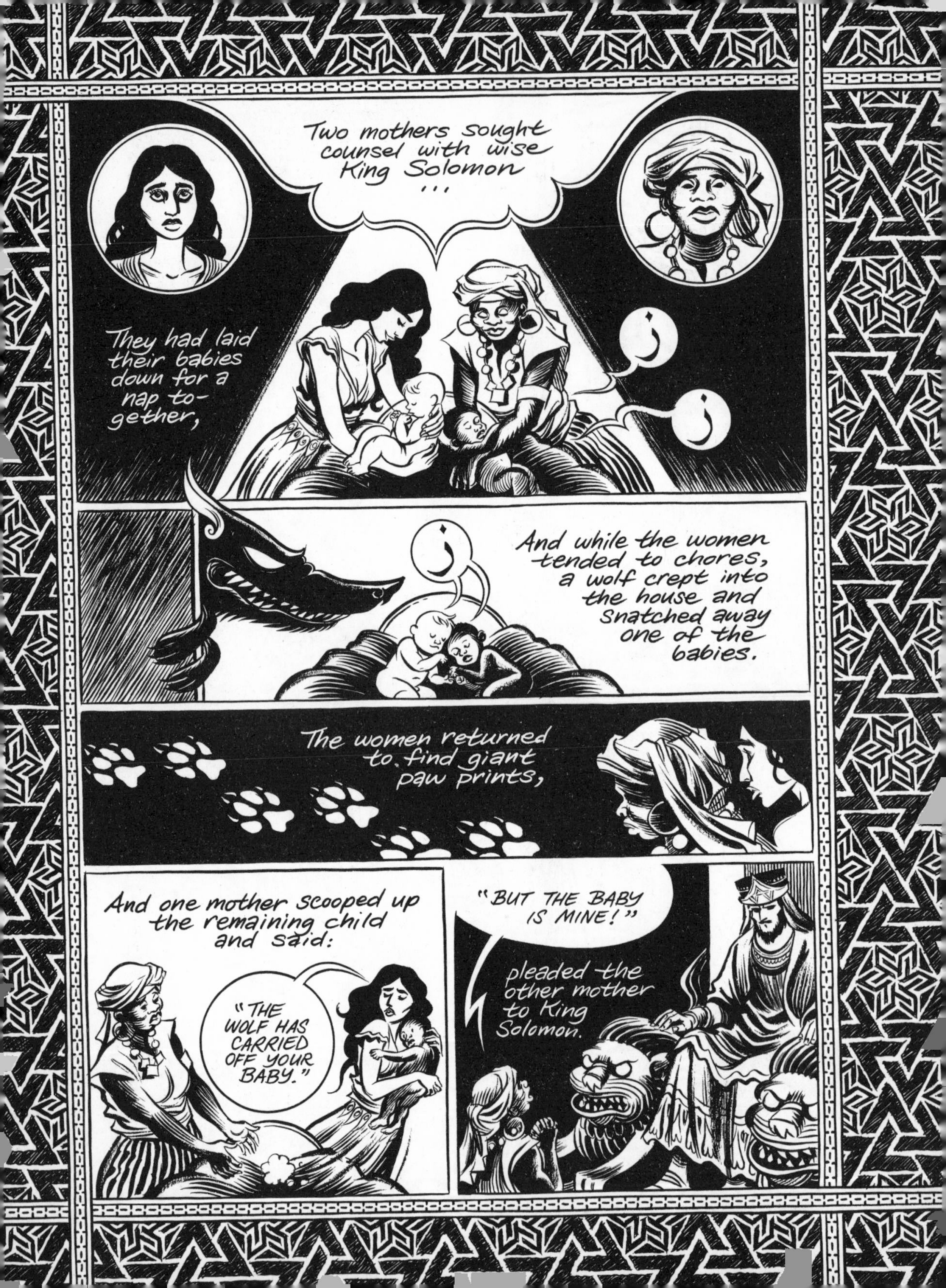
Two mothers sought counsel with wise King Solomon . . .
They had laid their babies down for a nap to-gether,
ز
ز
And while the women tended to chores, a wolf crept into the house and snatched away one of the babies.
ز
The women returned to find giant paw prints,
And one mother scooped up the remaining child and said:
"THE WOLF HAS CARRIED OFF YOUR BABY."
"BUT THE BABY IS MINE!"
pleaded the other mother to King Solomon.

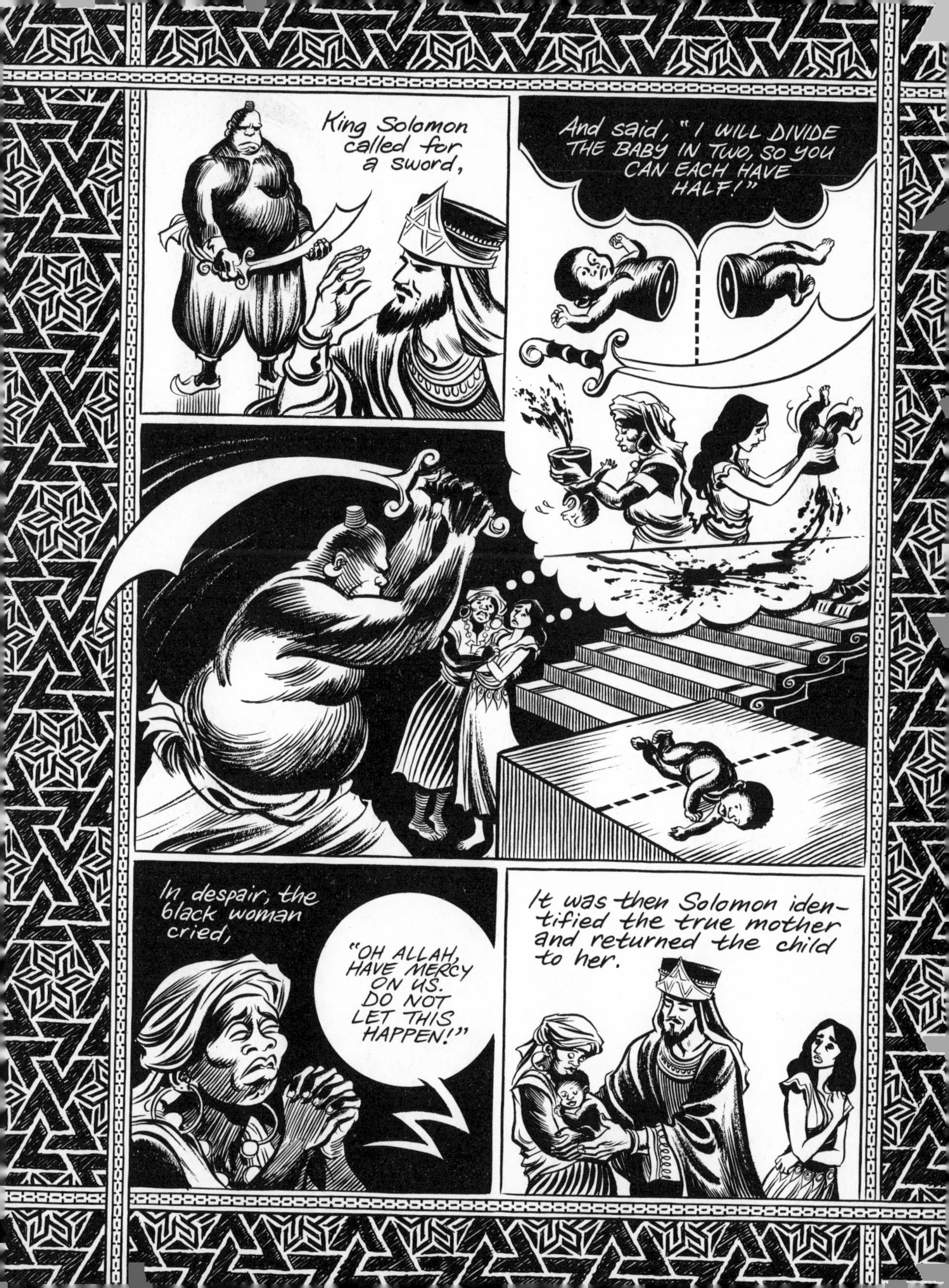

King Solomon called for a sword,
And said, "I WILL DIVIDE THE BABY IN TWO, SO YOU CAN EACH HAVE HALF!"
In despair, the black woman cried,
"OH ALLAH, HAVE MERCY ON US. DO NOT LET THIS HAPPEN!"
It was then Solomon identified the true mother and returned the child to her.

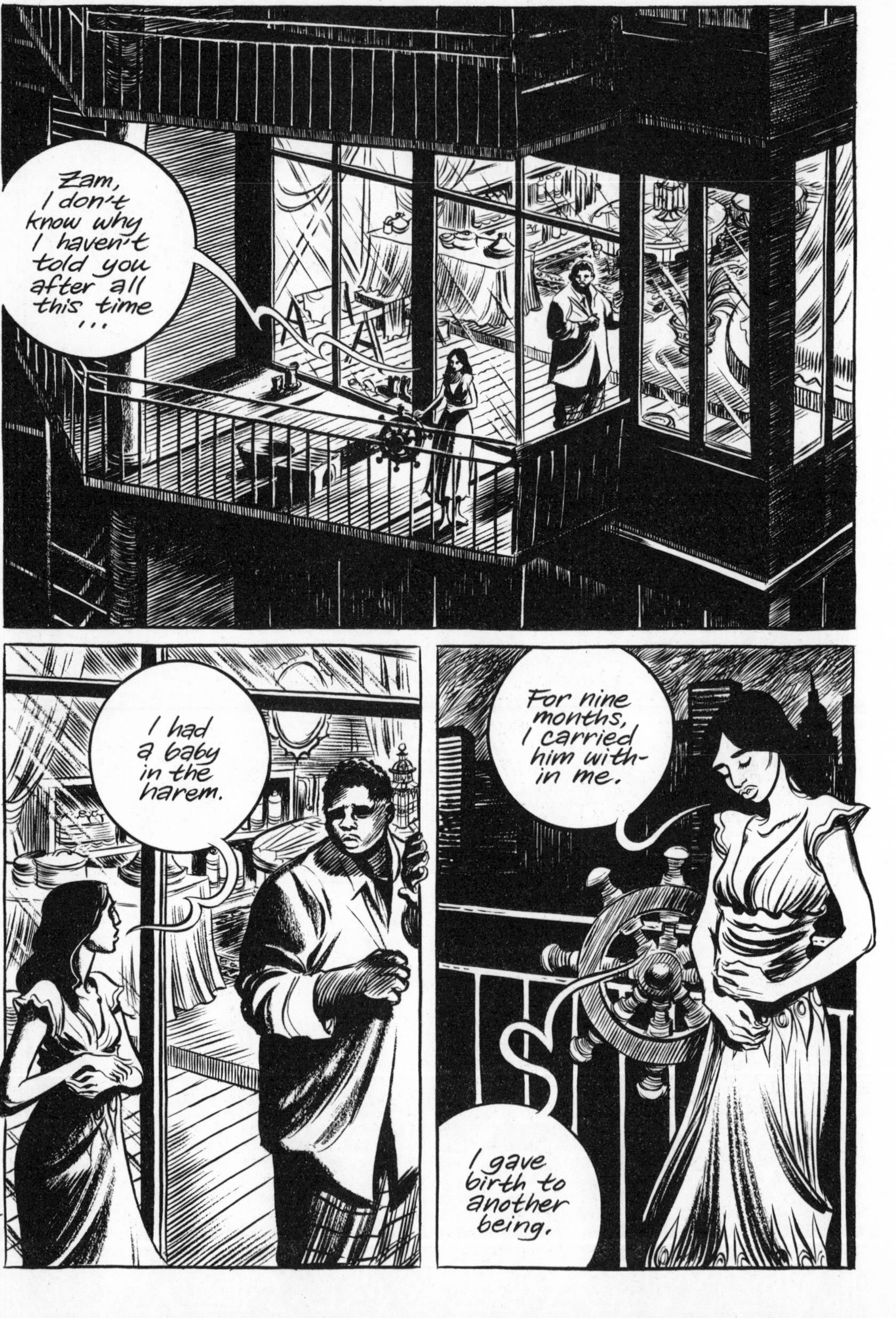

Zam, I don't know why I haven't told you after all this time . . .
I had a baby in the harem.
For nine months, I carried him within me.
I gave birth to another being.

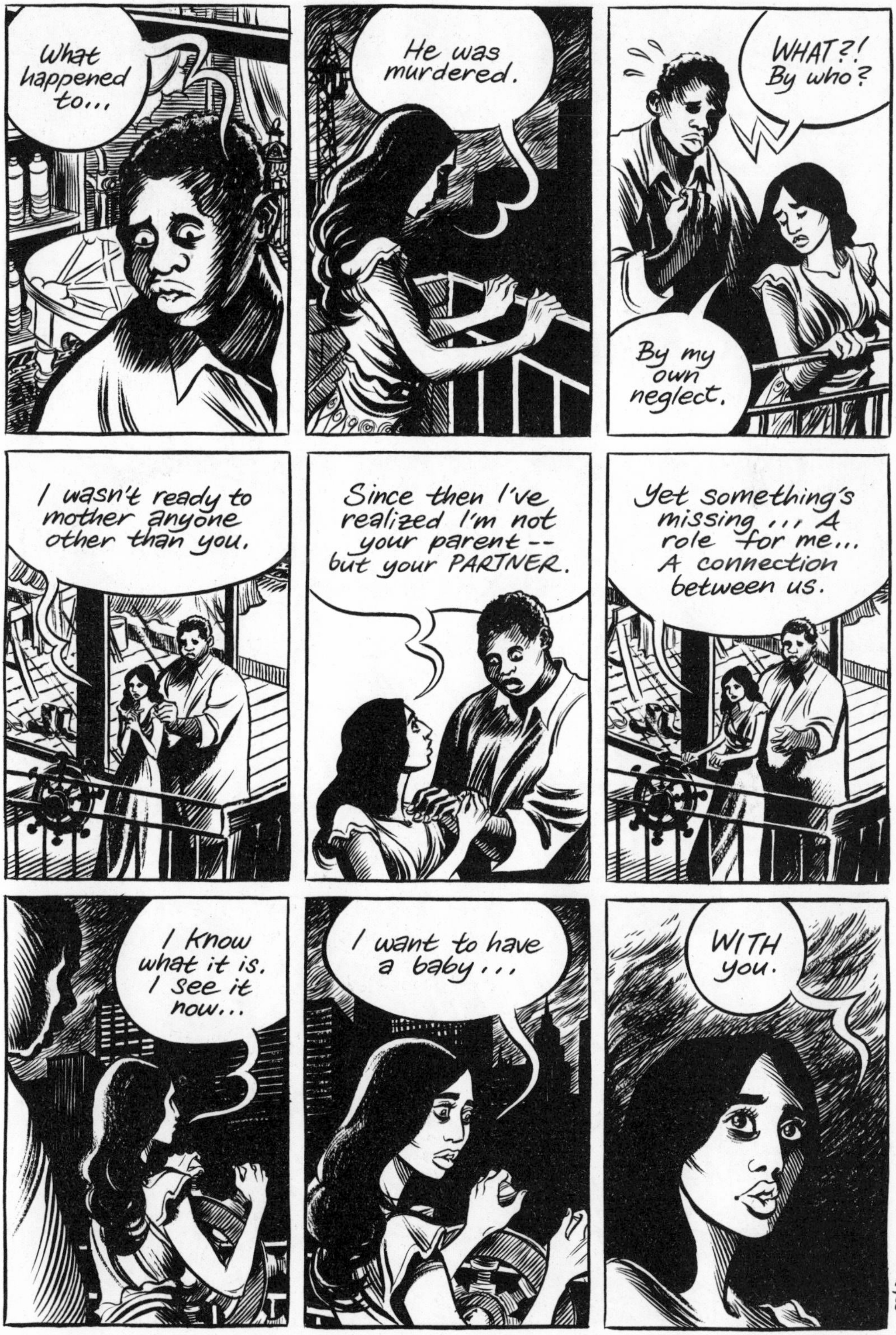
What happened to...
He was murdered.
WHAT?! By who?
By my own neglect.
I wasn't ready to mother anyone other than you.
Since then I've realized I'm not your parent -- but your PARTNER.
Yet something's missing ... A role for me... A connection between us.
I know what it is. I see it now...
I want to have a baby...
WITH you.

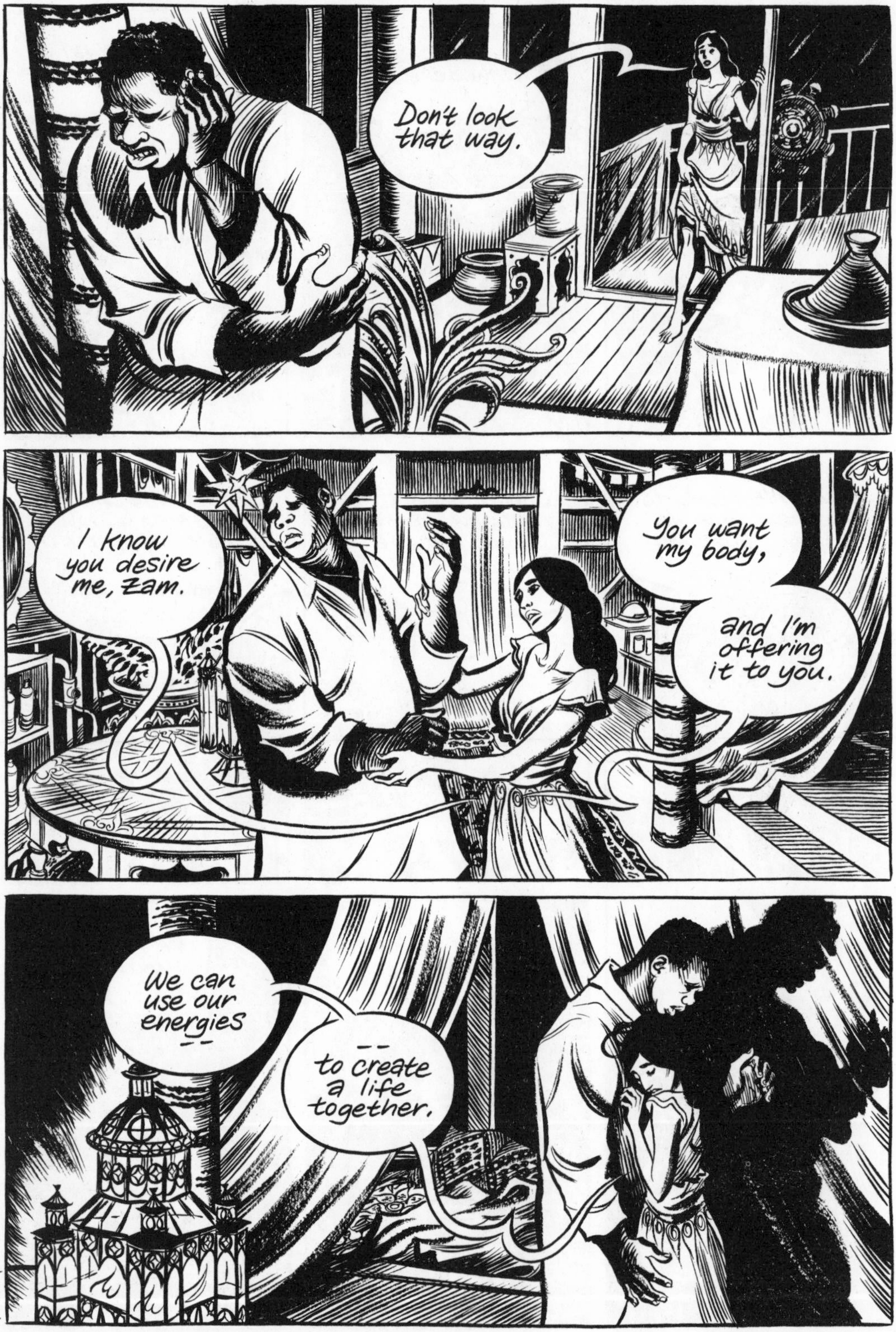
Don't look that way.
I know you desire me, Zam.
You want my body,
and I'm offering it to you.
We can use our energies --
-- to create a life together.

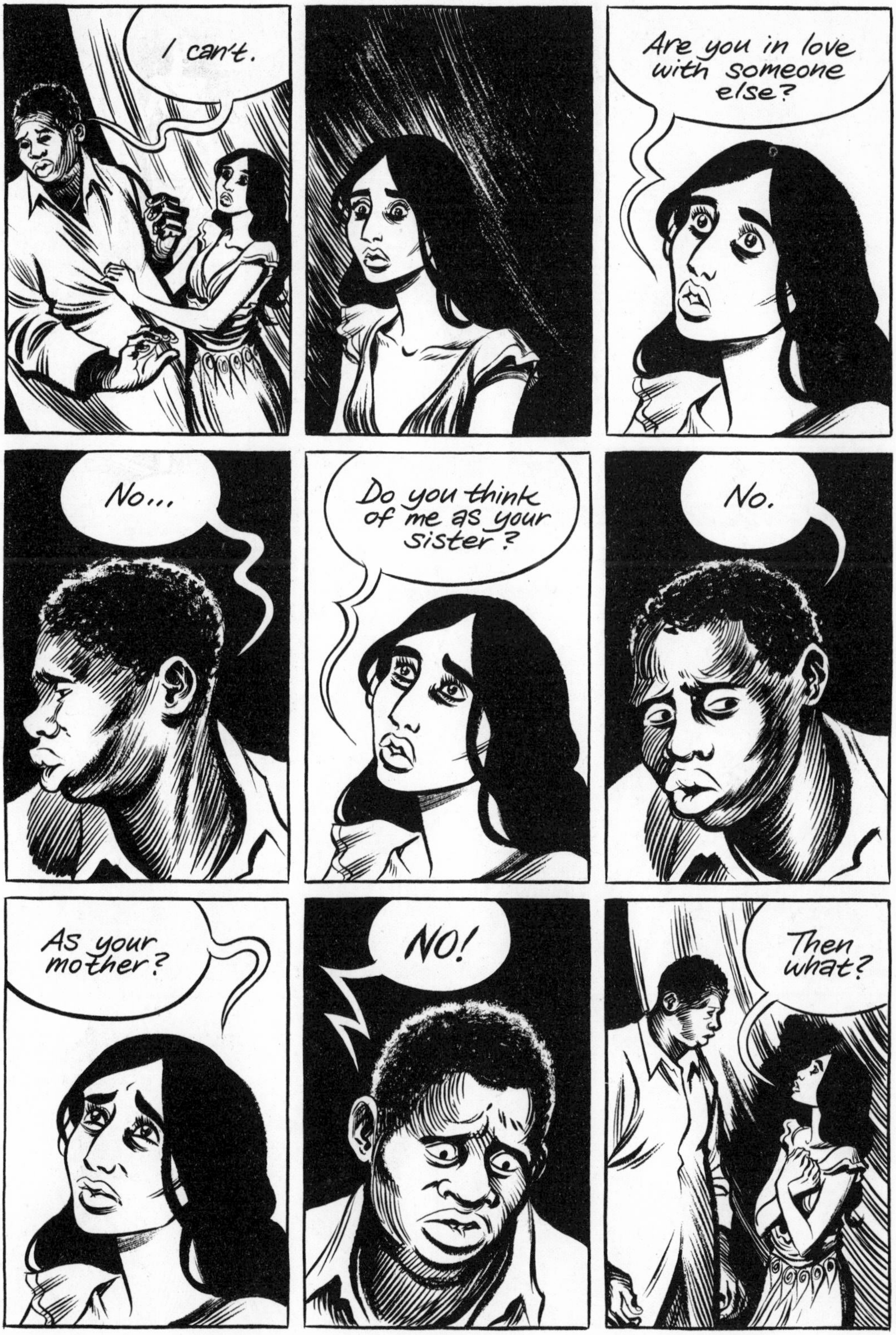
I can't.
Are you in love with someone else?
No...
Do you think of me as your sister?
No.
As your mother?
NO!
Then what?

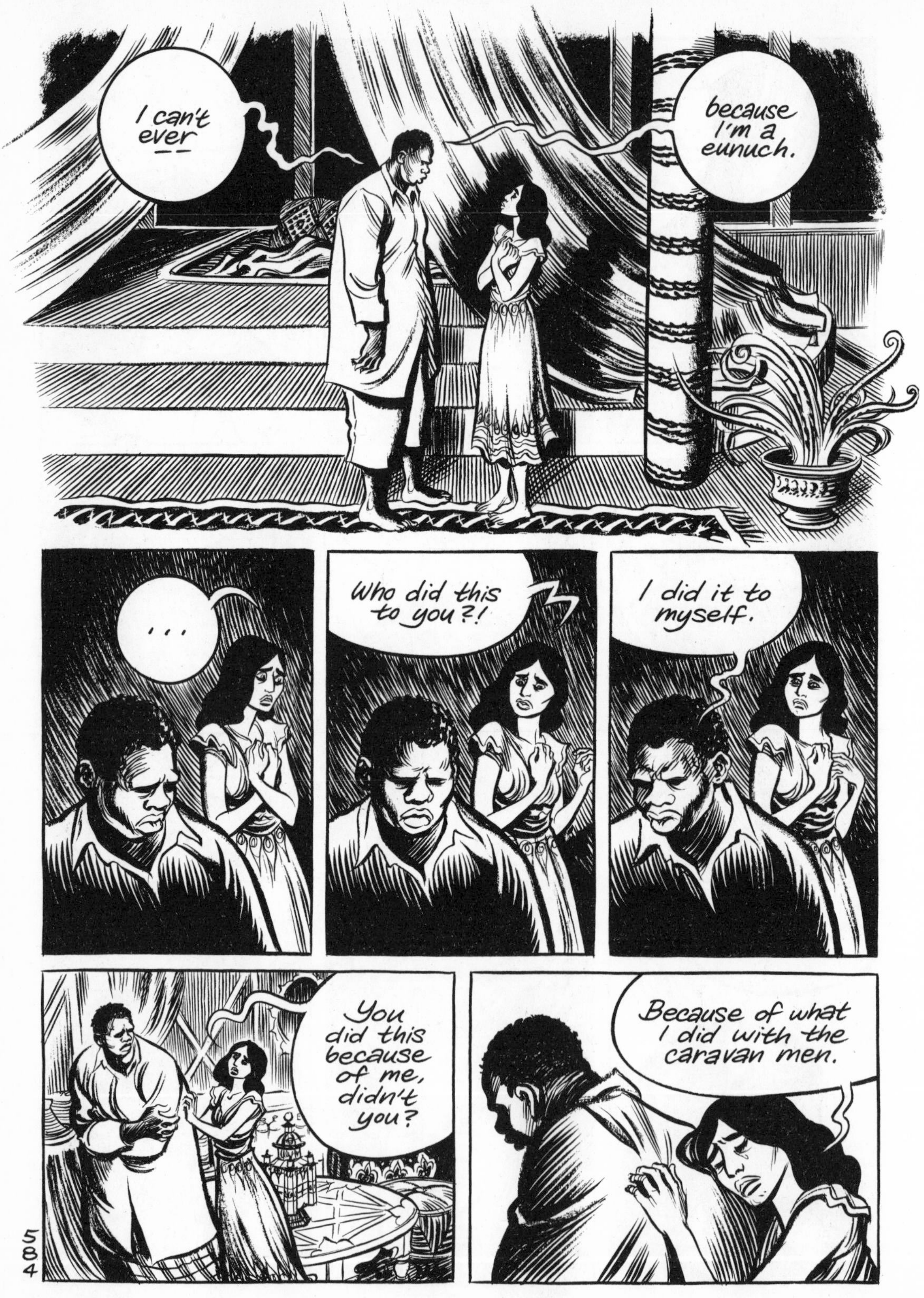
I can't ever --
because I'm a eunuch.
. . .
Who did this to you?!
I did it to myself.
You did this because of me, didn't you?
Because of what I did with the caravan men.

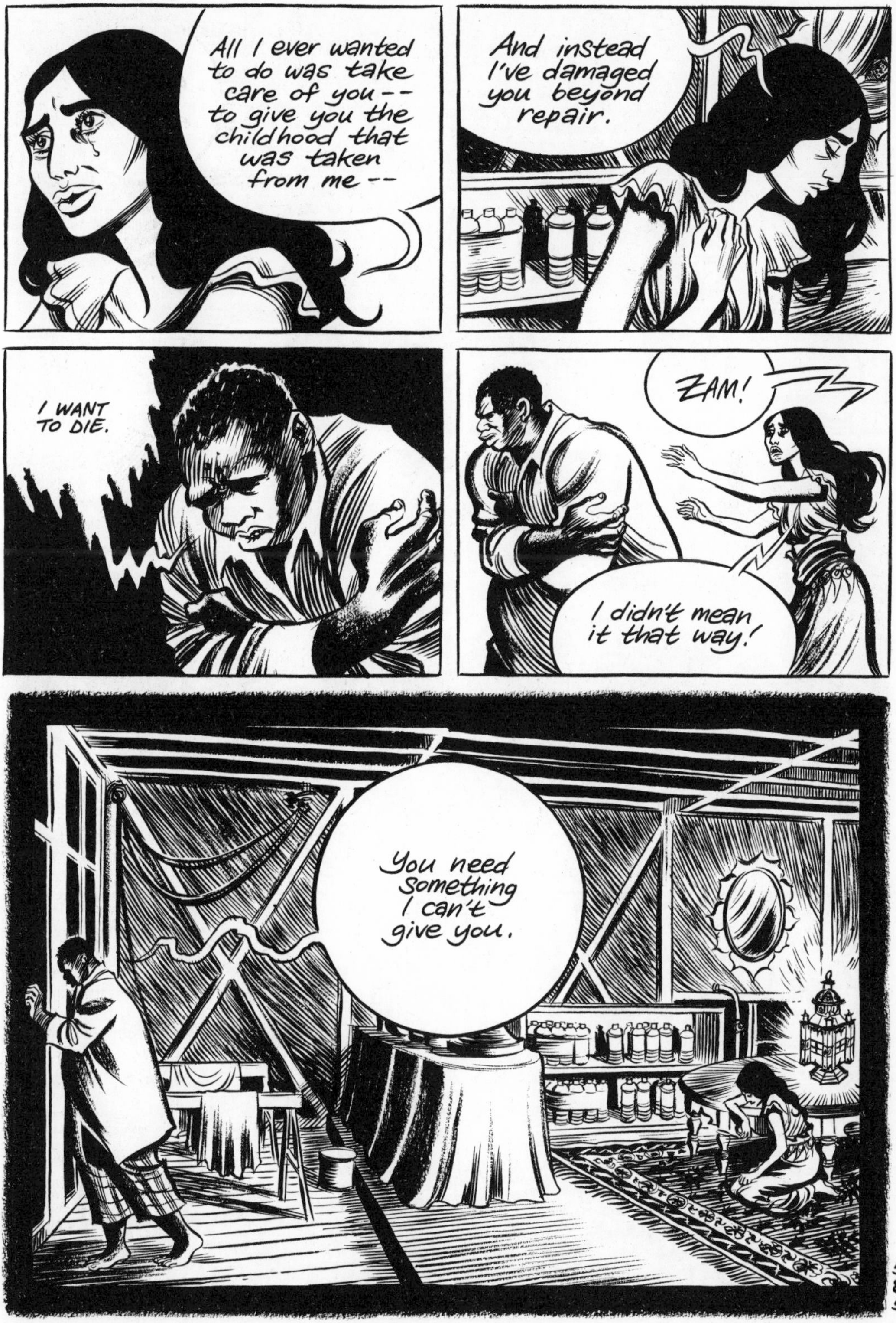
All I ever wanted to do was take care of you -- to give you the childhood that was taken from me --
And instead I've damaged you beyond repair.
I WANT TO DIE.
ZAM!
I didn't mean it that way!
You need something I can't give you.

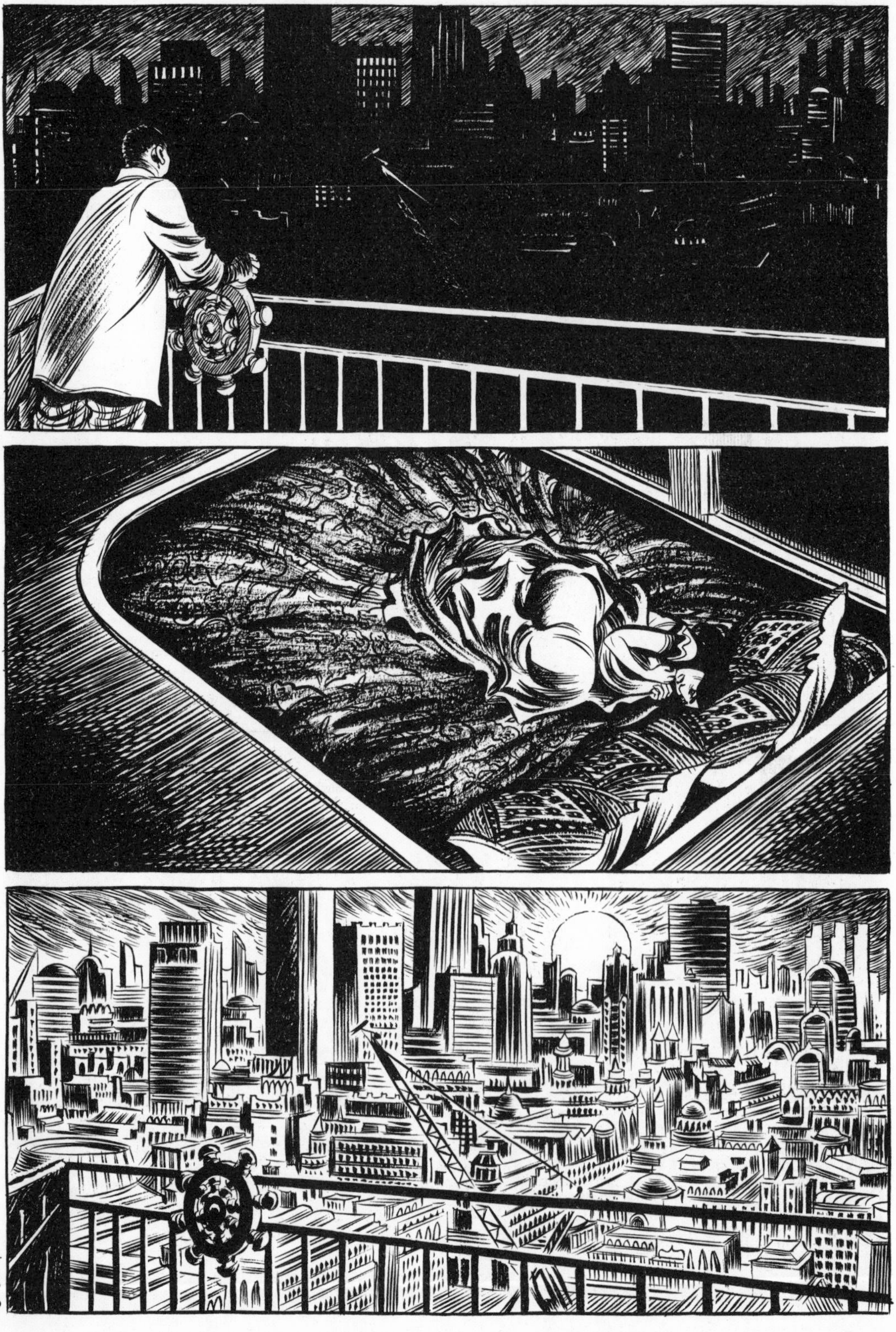

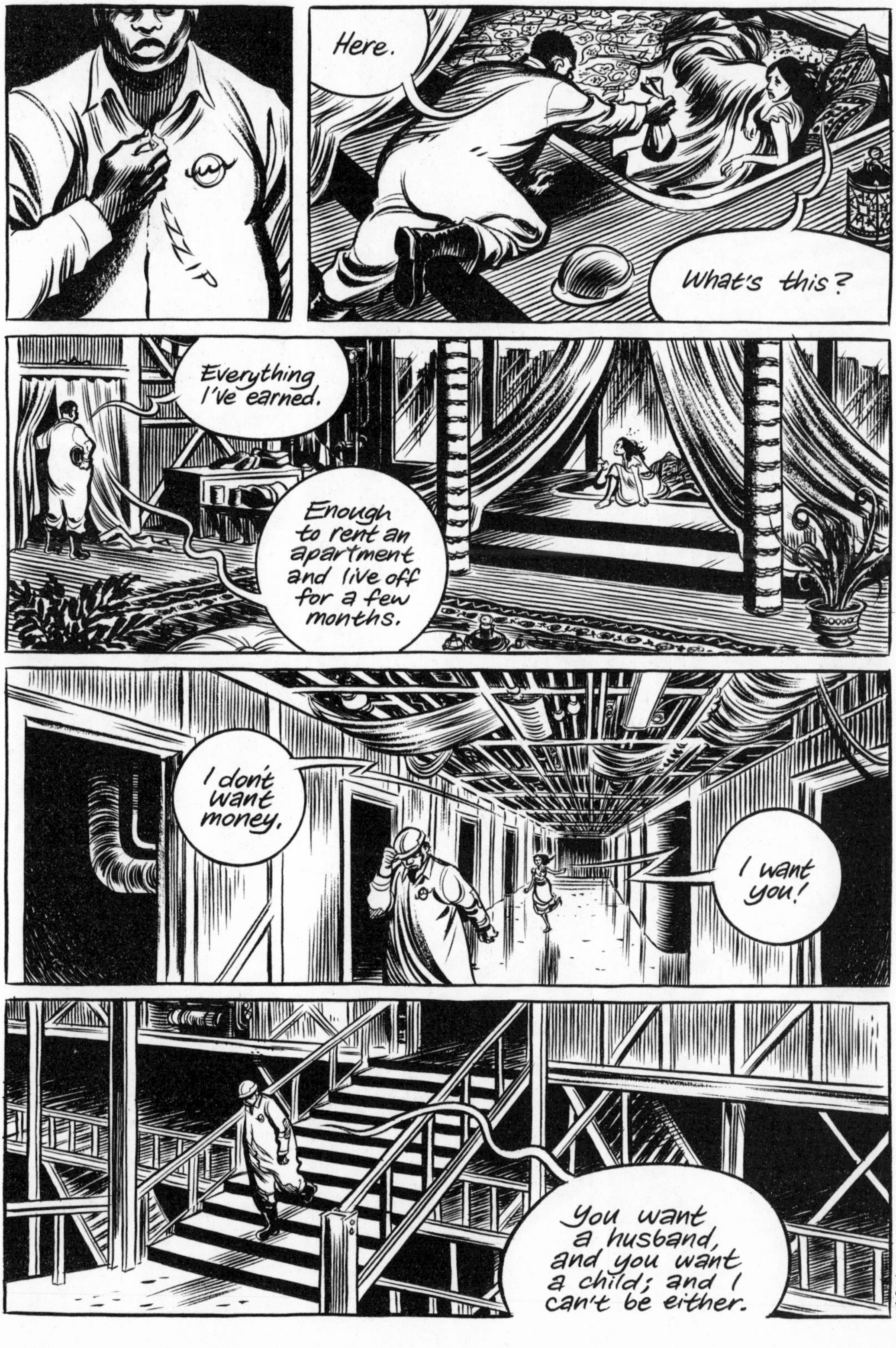
ZZIP
Here.
What's this?
Everything I've earned.
Enough to rent an apartment and live off for a few months.
I don't want money.
I want you!
You want a husband, and you want a child; and I can't be either.

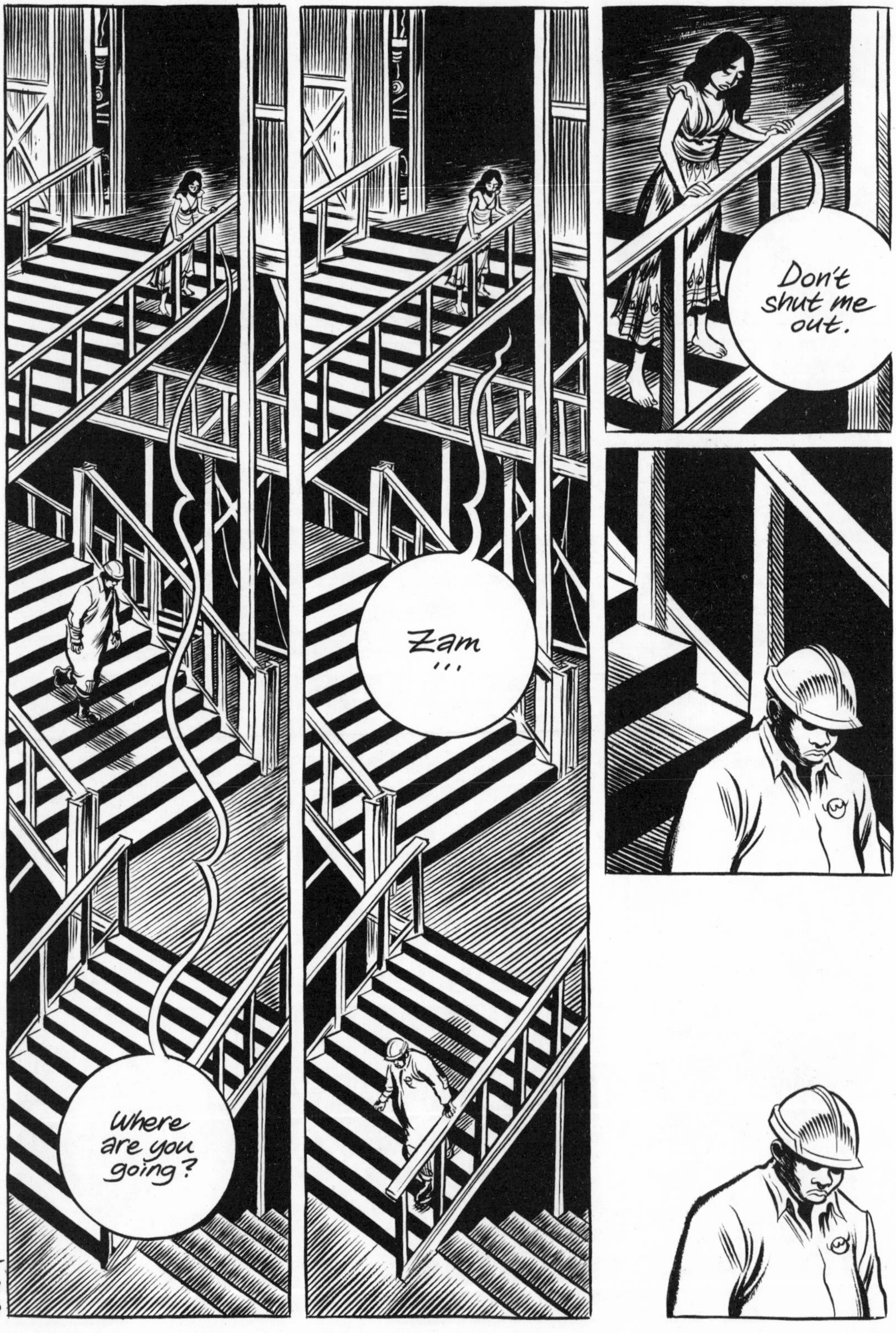
Where are you going?
Zam ...
Don't shut me out.

Most Arabic letters blend together in a cursive flow.

فَأَقْطَعْ لُبَانَةً مَنْ تَعَرَّضَ وَصْلُهُ ۝ وَلِلْخَيْرِ وَاصِلْ خُلَّةٍ صَرَّامُهَا

They shift shape depending on their placement in a word.

ح

INITIAL ح   ح   MEDIAL ح   ح   **FINAL JOINED**

In its initial form, the HAA's tail doesn't swoop down in a sickle, but reaches out to join the next letter.

وحيد

The WAAW, however, never connects to the letter following it.

وحيد

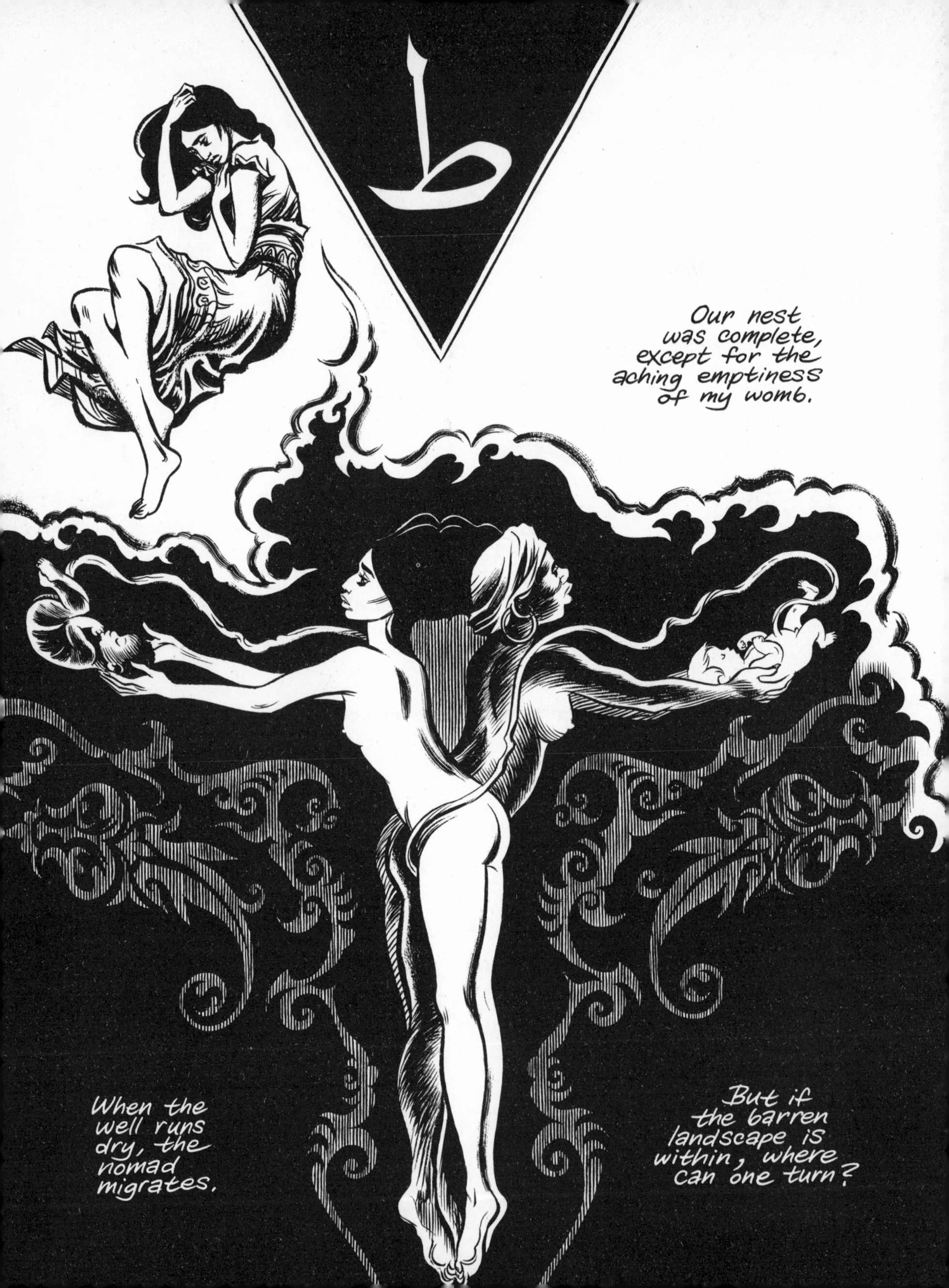
ط
Our nest was complete, except for the aching emptiness of my womb.
When the well runs dry, the nomad migrates.
But if the barren landscape is within, where can one turn?

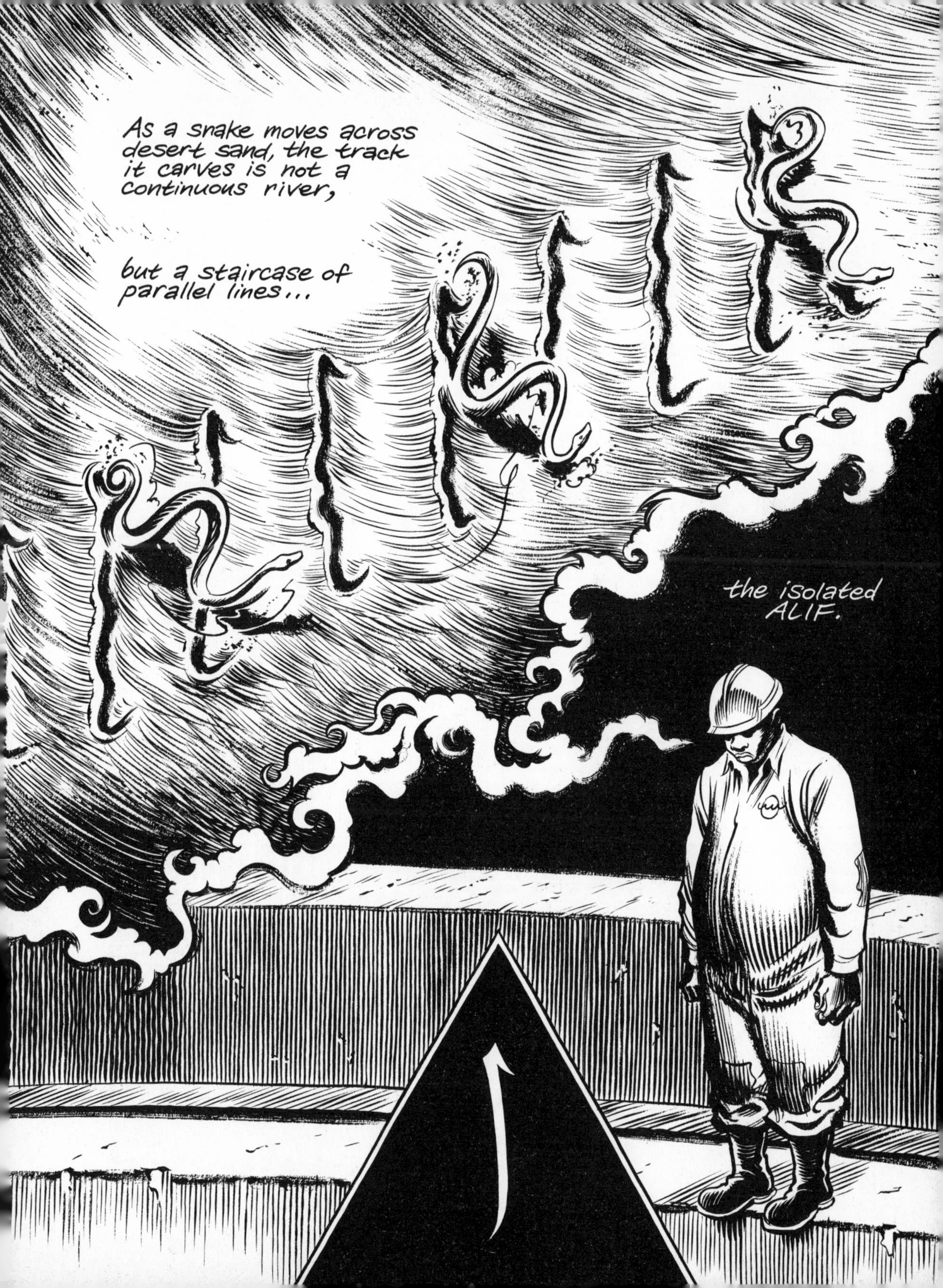
As a snake moves across desert sand, the track it carves is not a continuous river,
but a staircase of parallel lines...
the isolated ALIF.

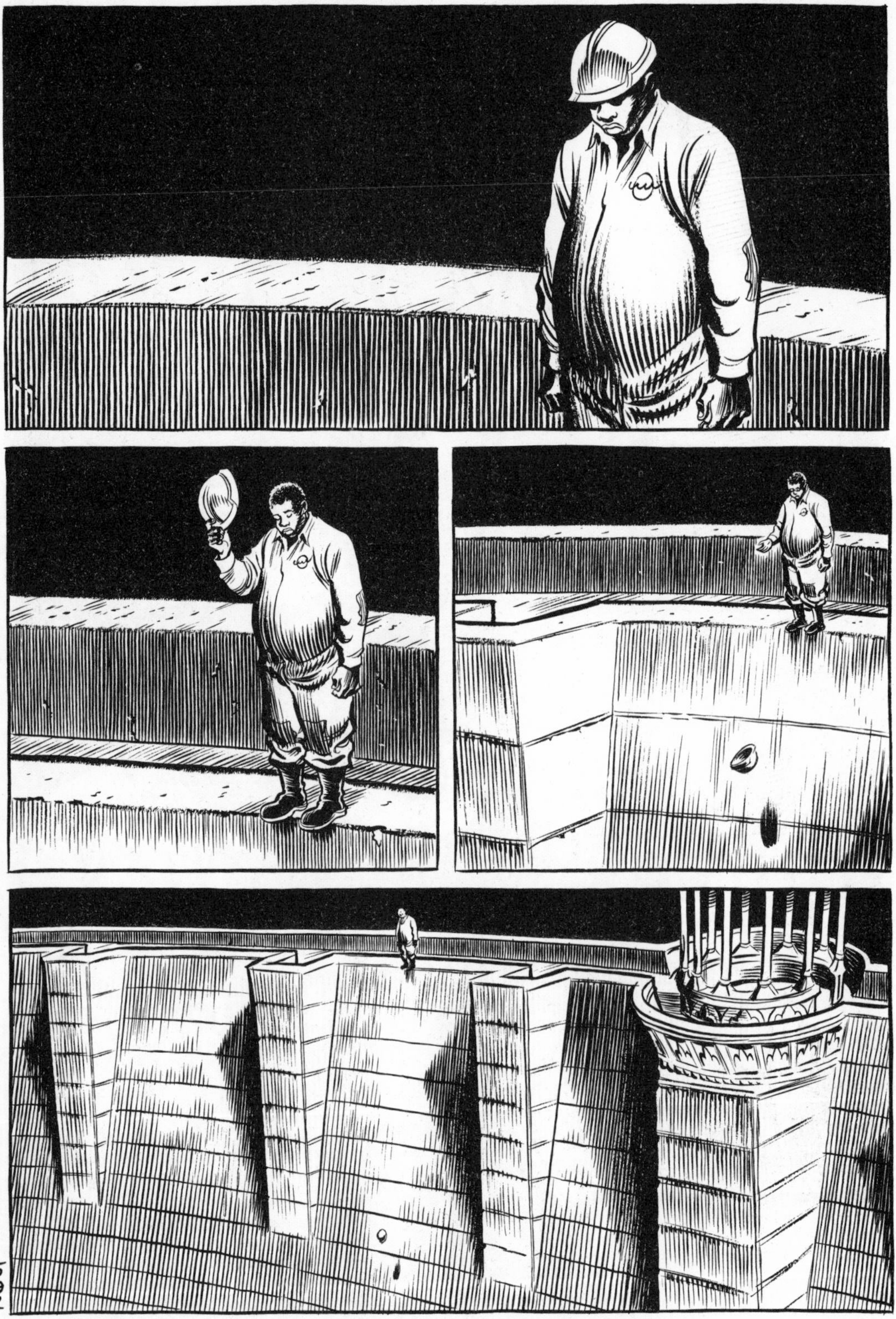

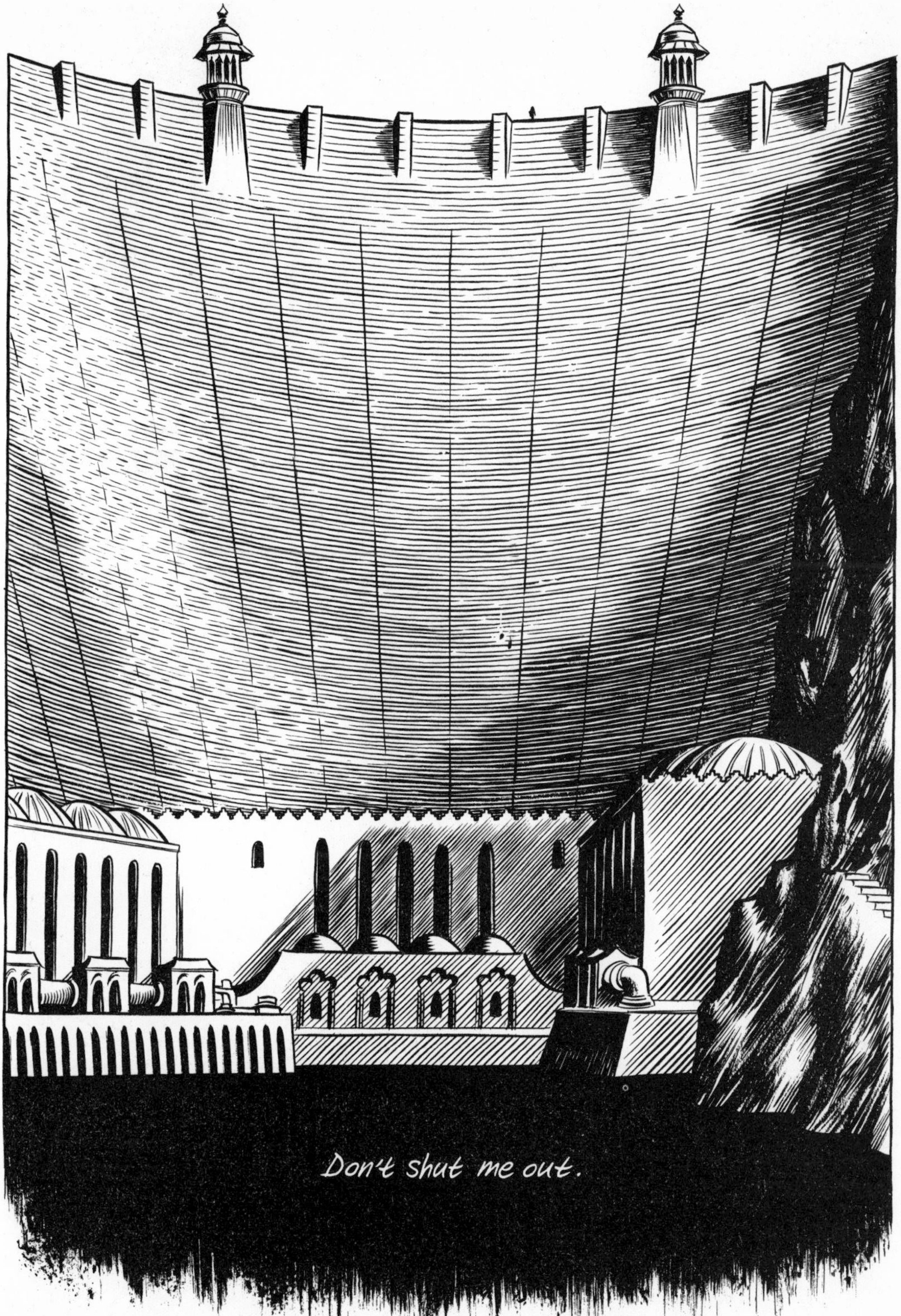
Don't shut me out.

د	ط	ب
ج	ه	ز
ح	ا	و

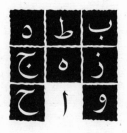

دعاء
يتيم

ORPHAN'S
PRAYER

It was the snake that first led me here.

To this structure.
To water.

The day *Dodola* was raped.

The soldiers killed the snake, chopped it to pieces, but it was my fault. And I'm responsible, too, for what happened to *Dodola*.

A knife was tangled in her cloak.

I could have sunk it in his back.

One thrust for each of his.

I failed. And so turned the blade upon myself.

But my castration isn't complete. Now I can cut off my entire being.

This wall is my altar. I am my own sacrifice. I want to dash this ugly container of dust and bone and shit, and spill out my spirit.

O ALLAH, You had to wipe out the filth of mankind during Noah's time.

I am volunteering myself for elimination now.

Why create man in the first place?

Man forsakes his Creator.

Man desecrates Creation.

Man consumes and excretes.

Lusts and rapes.

I am all these things.

Why give life to a creature so depraved?

A creature so incomplete?

A creature so alone?

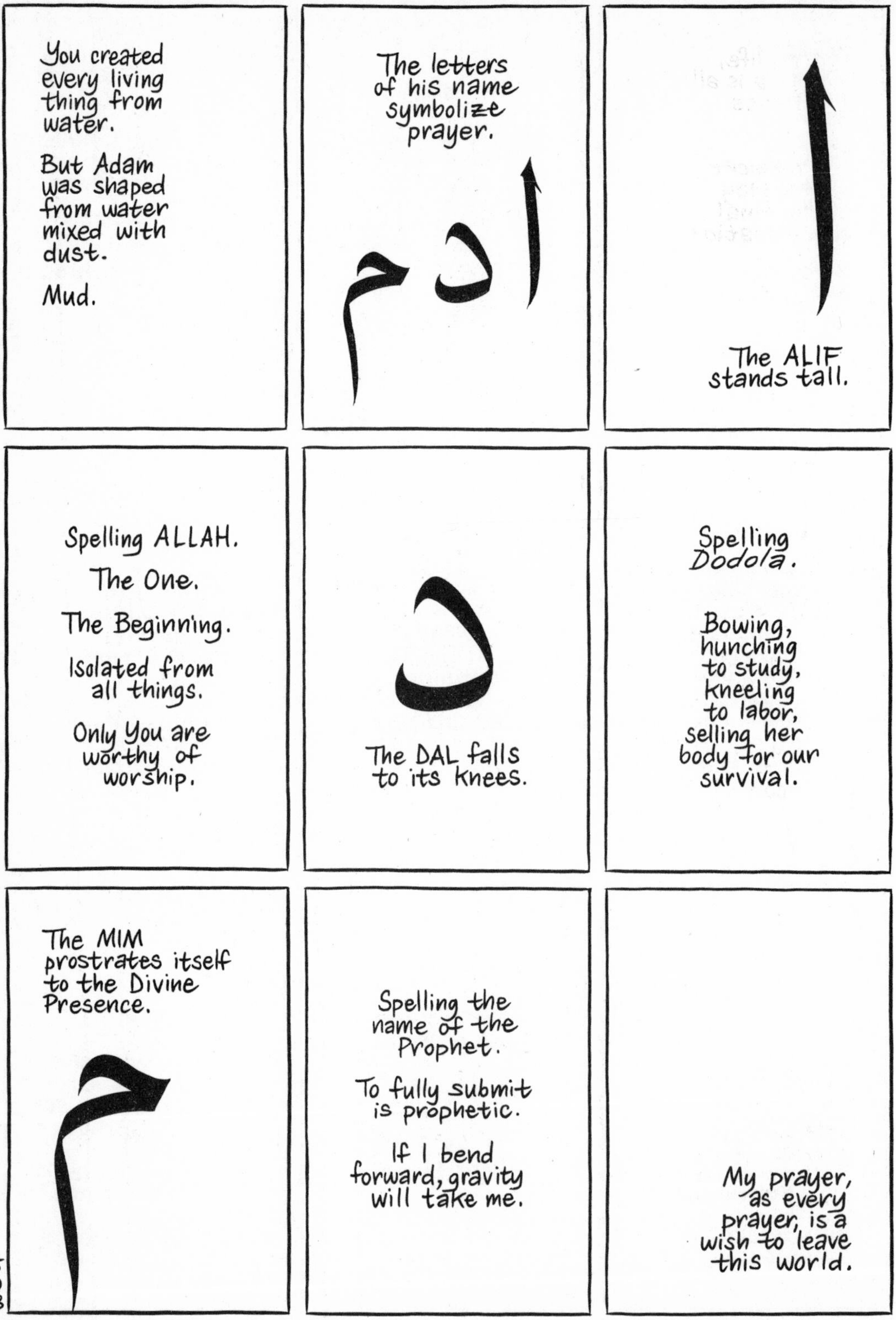
You created every living thing from water.
But Adam was shaped from water mixed with dust.
Mud.
The letters of his name symbolize prayer.
ادم
ا
The ALIF stands tall.
Spelling ALLAH.
The One.
The Beginning.
Isolated from all things.
Only You are worthy of worship.
د
The DAL falls to its knees.
Spelling *Dodola*.
Bowing, hunching to study, kneeling to labor, selling her body for our survival.
The MIM prostrates itself to the Divine Presence.
م
Spelling the name of the Prophet.
To fully submit is prophetic.
If I bend forward, gravity will take me.
My prayer, as every prayer, is a wish to leave this world.

Of this life, *Dodola* is all I will miss.

But my attachment to her may be my final condemnation.

In my distress, it's her name I called upon, even before You, God.

I wanted to pray to *her*.

She is my sister, my mother, my teacher.

Then I turned her into an object of lust.

It seems every curve of her form was carved specially for me.

I needed *Dodola* as Adam needed Eve.

You created us this way. Incomplete.

Halves, desperately searching for our missing counterpart.

What choice do we have but to construct an ideal, an idol, to impose on the beloved?

But image-making violates the most sacred of commandments.

There is none worthy of worship except God.

"He who makes images will suffer the harshest punishment on the day of resurrection."

"Every painter will go to Hell, and for every portrait he has made, there will be appointed one who will chastise him in Hell."

Dodola can't save me from my own darkness.

The opposite; I can only drag her into my mire, drown her.

I searched for *Dodola* in my own femininity.

I claimed I wanted to be closer to God, but — again in my blasphemy — I meant *Dodola*.

I cut off what made us different.

I wanted both halves to meet within me.

Bahuchara Mata, another false god.

I lived as a boy, then a girl, then a eunuch, but never as a man.

Severed my ability to reproduce, to participate in creation.

Now I've no pen to write with.

I've no "other half" to offer *Dodola*.

I'm useless and broken.

I can never be her lover.

And I can never fulfill her deepest wish —

to be a mother.

If Paradise lies beneath the feet of the mothers

— those tender feet of *Dodola* —

then it's Hell that waits beneath mine.

Seven levels of Hell below.

Seven layers of Heaven above.

One level in between where I've tried and failed to exist.

I've believed women to be pure, and men possessed by evil jinn — SHAYATEEN.

But I'm not a man. I bottled the ifrit, cemented a wall.

Now the jinn can only strike internally, and the clearest way to exorcise them is to shatter this container.

But the snake was a good jinn, leading me to water.

Your gift to us.

Hagar and Ishmael's salvation.

Now the snake's been killed, the well's been capped, claimed and contained, and denied to those needing.

Another form of violence inflicted by man.

What's worse, O ALLAH, is I've participated.

I work to maintain this dam that chokes off other nations.

I wanted *Dodola* to never work again.

I was willing to prostitute myself - to participate in her sacrifice.

Instead, I work as an overseer against my own race.

Our skin stained with shadow, closer to Hell, visibly singed by its flames.

Cham was responsible for Noah's impotence. I'm responsible for my own.

I desecrated my body, and I'm disgusted by my disfigurement.

At this ledge, I'm flanked by two towers. But all the other workers have left for the night. No one will see me fall.

The two towers are Safa and Marwa —the hills Hagar dashed frantically between, crying out to you, O ALLAH.

I'm kicking the sand. Stomping my boot on the concrete edge.

But no water is coming.

601

No one is in
those towers.

But then
who is
watching this
tiny figure
perched on
the ledge?

Who is this
frail, pathetic,
insignificant
figure?
Is it me?

Then who is this
consciousness
watching me?

It is ALLAH.

How do I have
access to your
vantage point,
ALLAH?

You are
only ONE.

I am already
broken into
pieces.

When we're
abandoned on
earth, our focus
turns to YOU,
the Divine
Parent.

The
inheritance of
two orphans
is buried
beneath
the wall.

Dodola, too,
is an orphan.

And so was
the Prophet
Muhammad.

The first
prophet
was Adam.

The final
prophet was
Muhammad.

No more
revelation
is available.

But even
Muhammad
considered
suicide when
he began
receiving the
revelation.
He thought
himself crazy,
wanted to
throw himself
from a
mountain.

I know that
I'm crazy,
poisoned
of spirit.

That I'm
sickly, inferior,
wanting to
drop myself
from this
mountain.

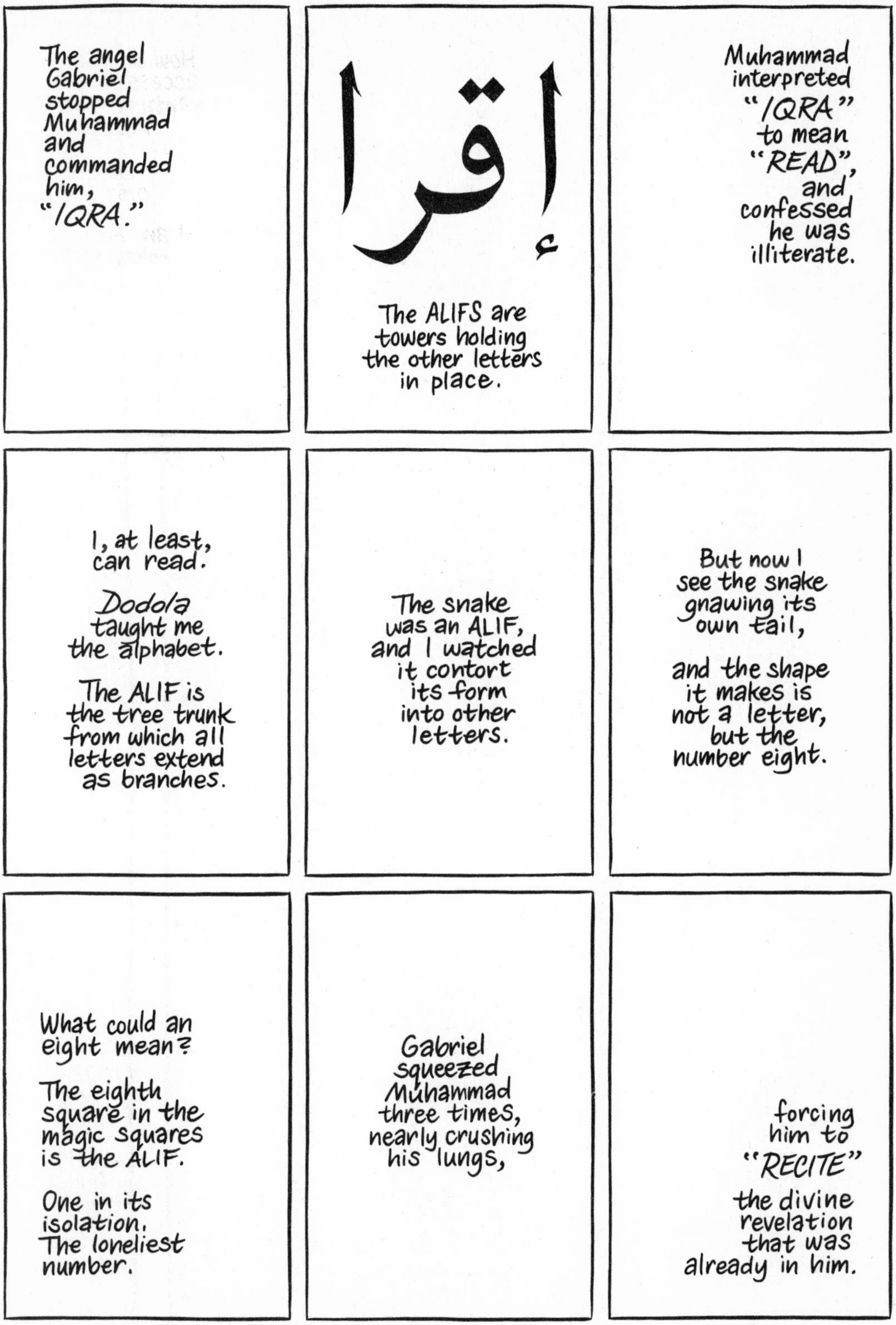
The angel Gabriel stopped Muhammad and commanded him, "IQRA."
إقرا
The ALIFS are towers holding the other letters in place.
Muhammad interpreted "IQRA" to mean "READ", and confessed he was illiterate.
I, at least, can read.
Dodola taught me the alphabet.
The ALIF is the tree trunk from which all letters extend as branches.
The snake was an ALIF, and I watched it contort its form into other letters.
But now I see the snake gnawing its own tail,
and the shape it makes is not a letter, but the number eight.
What could an eight mean?
The eighth square in the magic squares is the ALIF.
One in its isolation. The loneliest number.
Gabriel squeezed Muhammad three times, nearly crushing his lungs,
forcing him to "RECITE" the divine revelation that was already in him.

Those arms are squeezing everybody. They're squeezing me, too.

Only I'm no prophet, and I've nothing to recite.

To pray is to recite, but then what kind of prayer is this?

I'm kicking the sand and no water is coming.

I have nothing to give, not to *Dodola*.

I removed my own potential for creation.

It seems my calling is to destroy rather than create. To finish removing my body. To erase my presence from this world.

If only my heart would explode and crumble this dam. Tear down this wall, release this river, drain this empire, and nourish the slums below.

If I could tear it down with me, I might have value.

Let me atone for all the sins of men.

Let me release the DELUGE pent up in me.

Let me die.

The head of the sacrificed animal is aligned with the direction of prayer.

The direction of prayer was changed by the Prophet.

If I change direction from this drop, I face the reservoir.

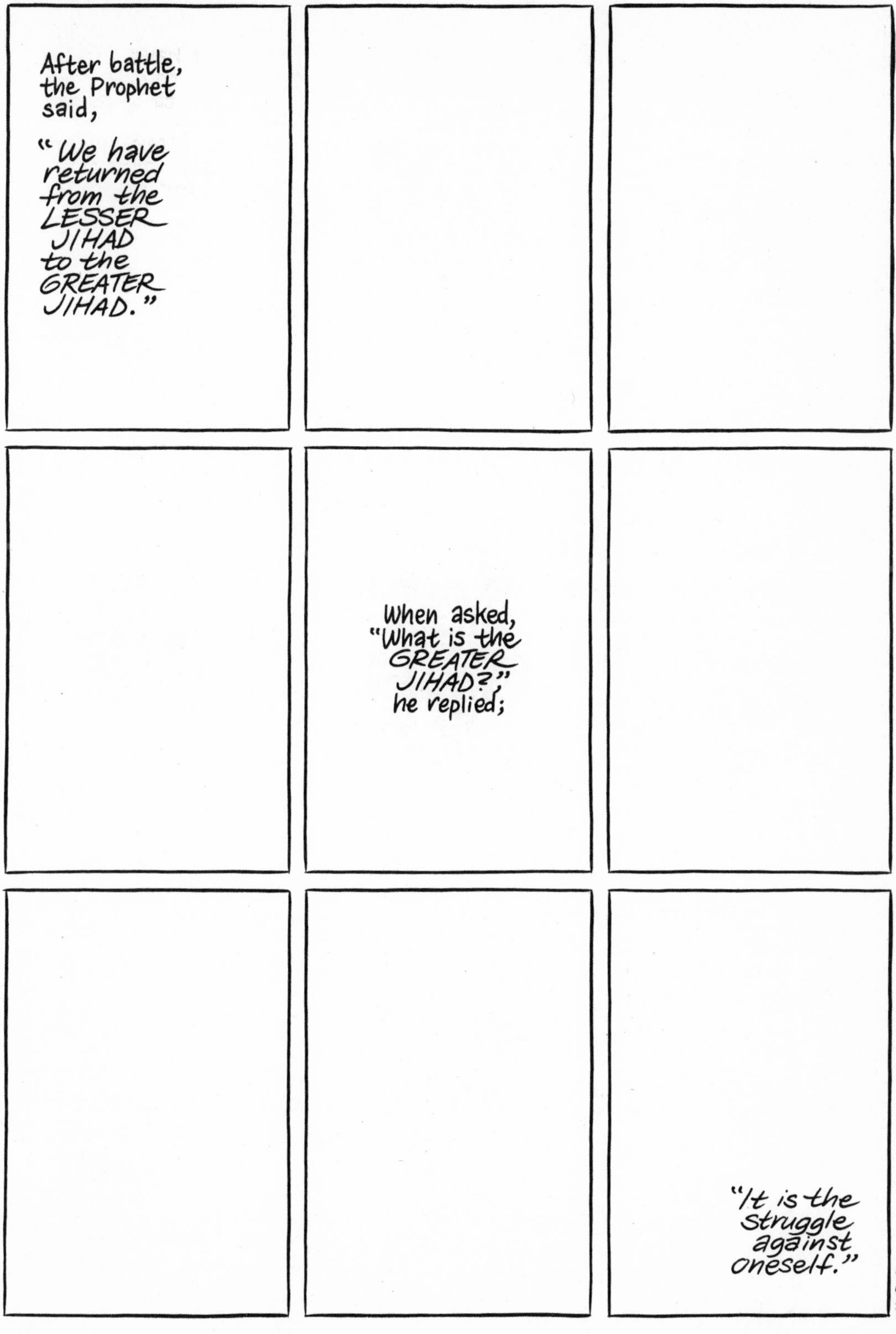
After battle, the Prophet said,
"We have returned from the LESSER JIHAD to the GREATER JIHAD."
When asked, "What is the GREATER JIHAD?," he replied;
"It is the struggle against oneself."

د	ط	ب
ج	ه	ز
ح	ا	و

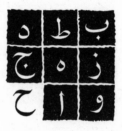

ابدء تتنفس

START BREATHING

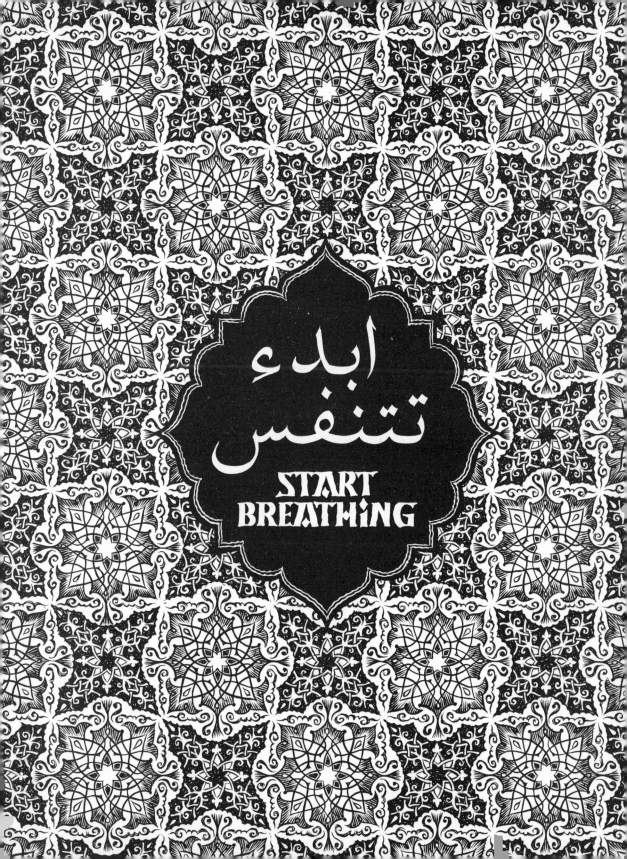

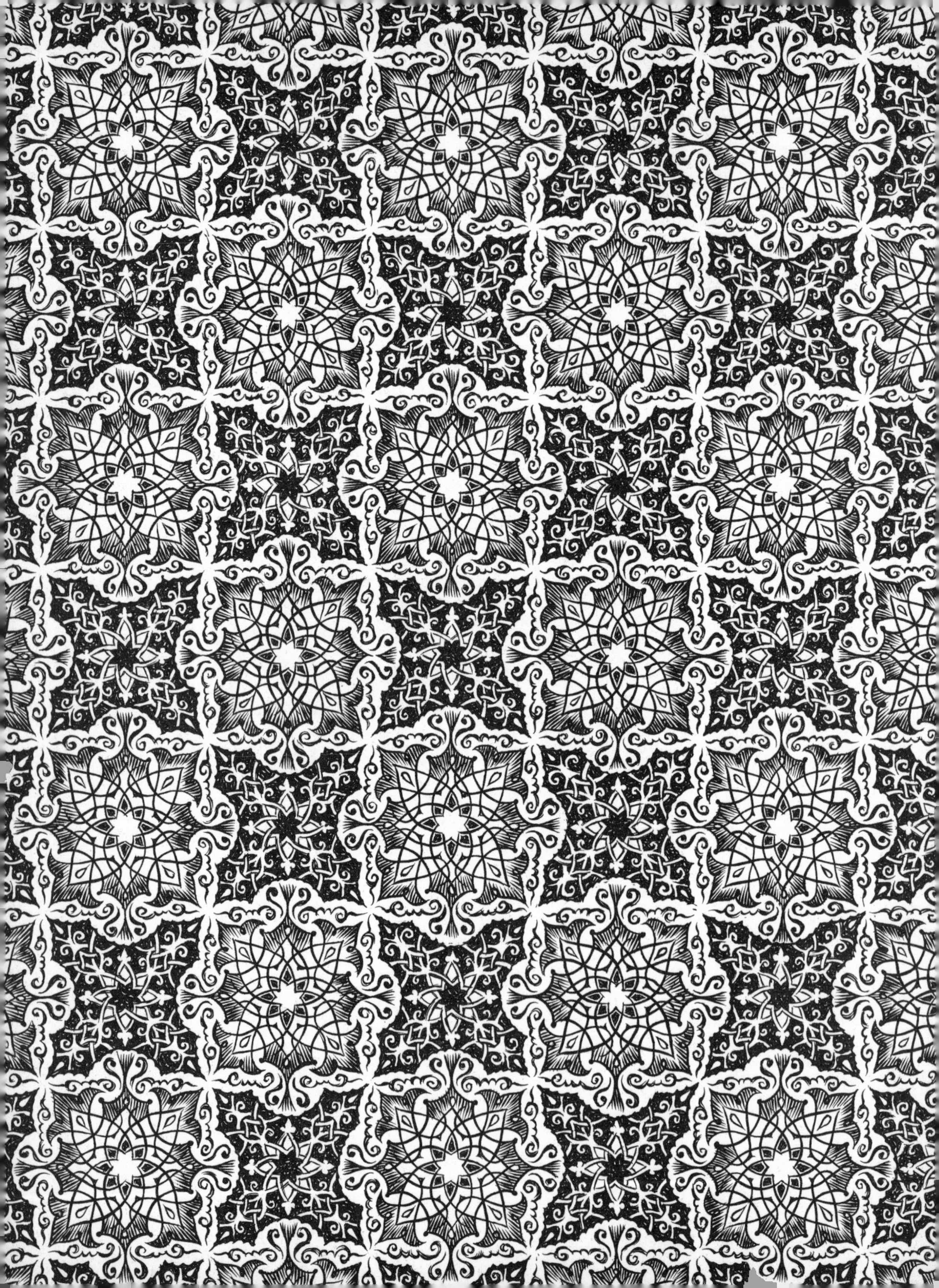

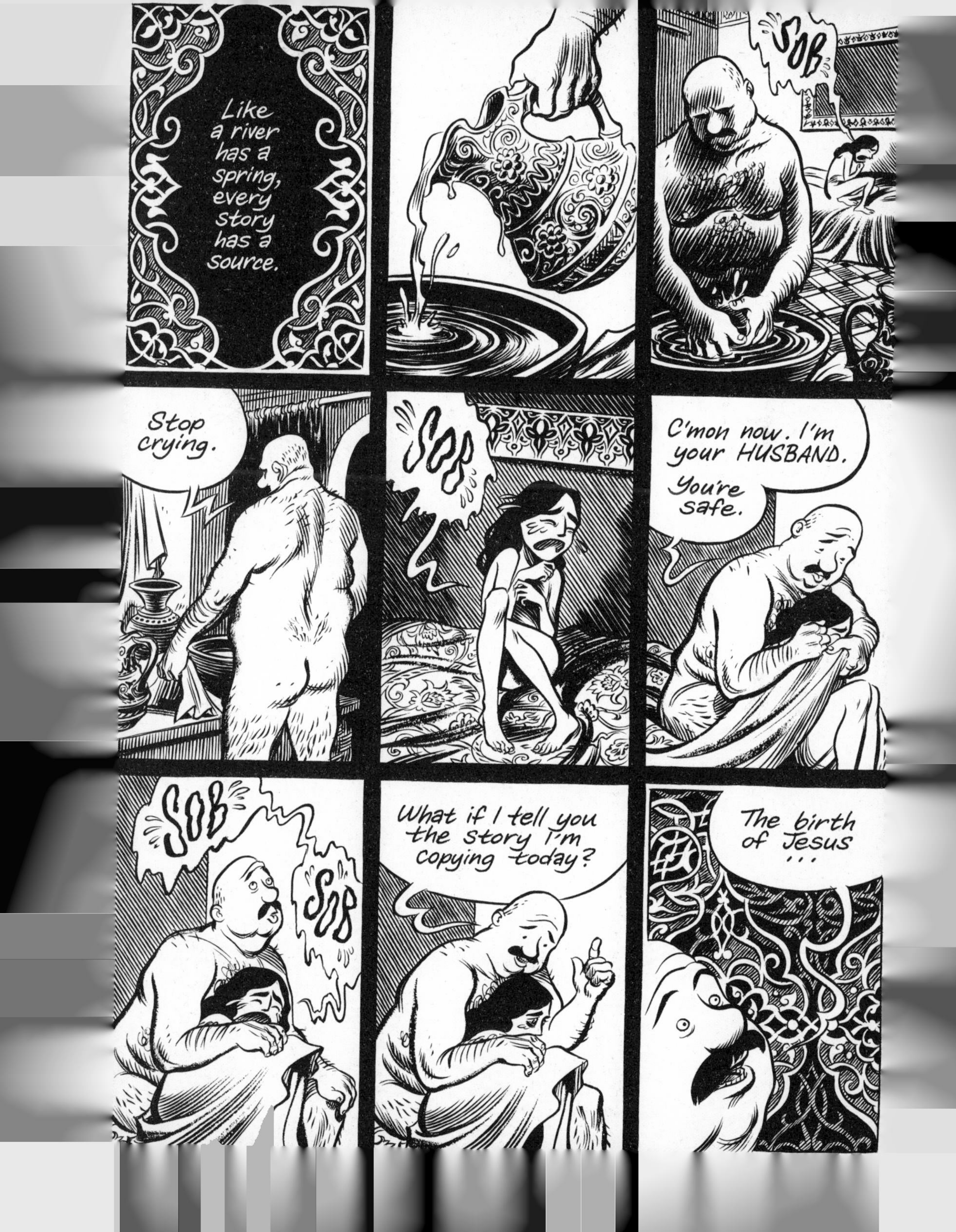
Like a river has a spring, every story has a source.
SOB
Stop crying.
SOB
C'mon now. I'm your HUSBAND.
You're safe.
SOB
SOB
What if I tell you the story I'm copying today?
The birth of Jesus ...

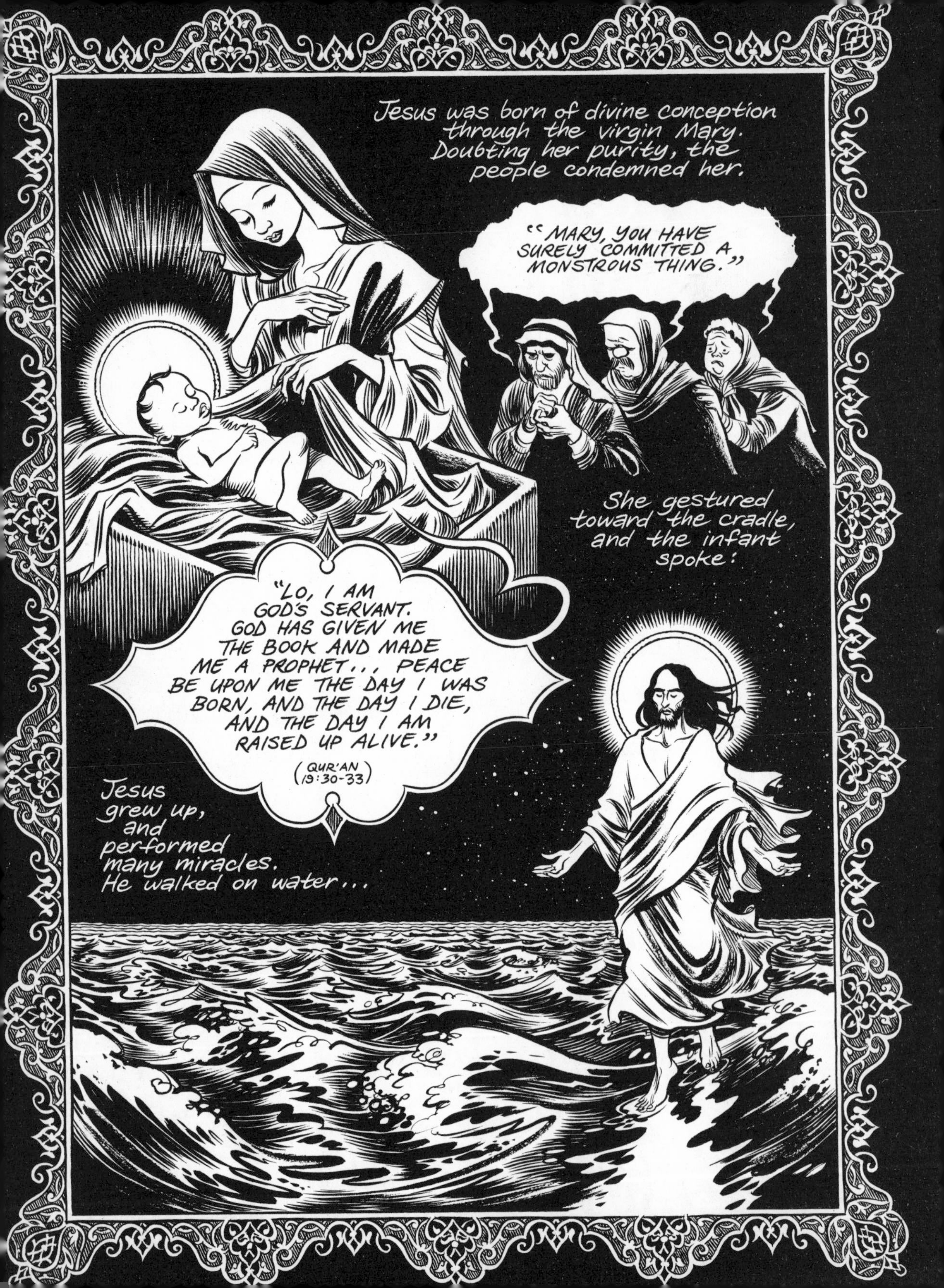
Jesus was born of divine conception through the virgin Mary. Doubting her purity, the people condemned her.
"MARY, YOU HAVE SURELY COMMITTED A MONSTROUS THING."
She gestured toward the cradle, and the infant spoke:
"LO, I AM GOD'S SERVANT. GOD HAS GIVEN ME THE BOOK AND MADE ME A PROPHET... PEACE BE UPON ME THE DAY I WAS BORN, AND THE DAY I DIE, AND THE DAY I AM RAISED UP ALIVE."
(QUR'AN 19:30-33)
Jesus grew up, and performed many miracles. He walked on water...

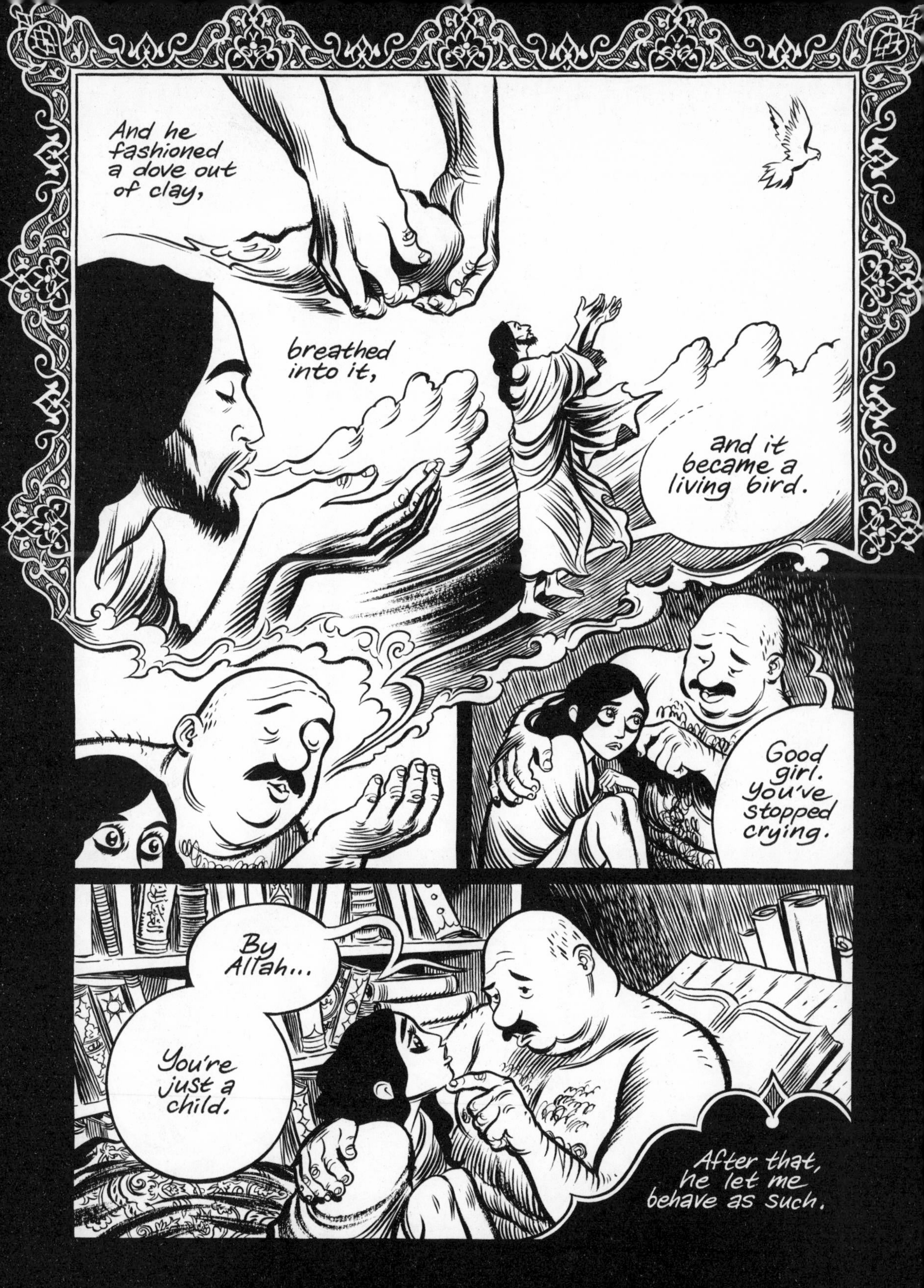

And he fashioned a dove out of clay,
breathed into it,
and it became a living bird.
Good girl. You've stopped crying.
By Allah...
You're just a child.
After that, he let me behave as such.

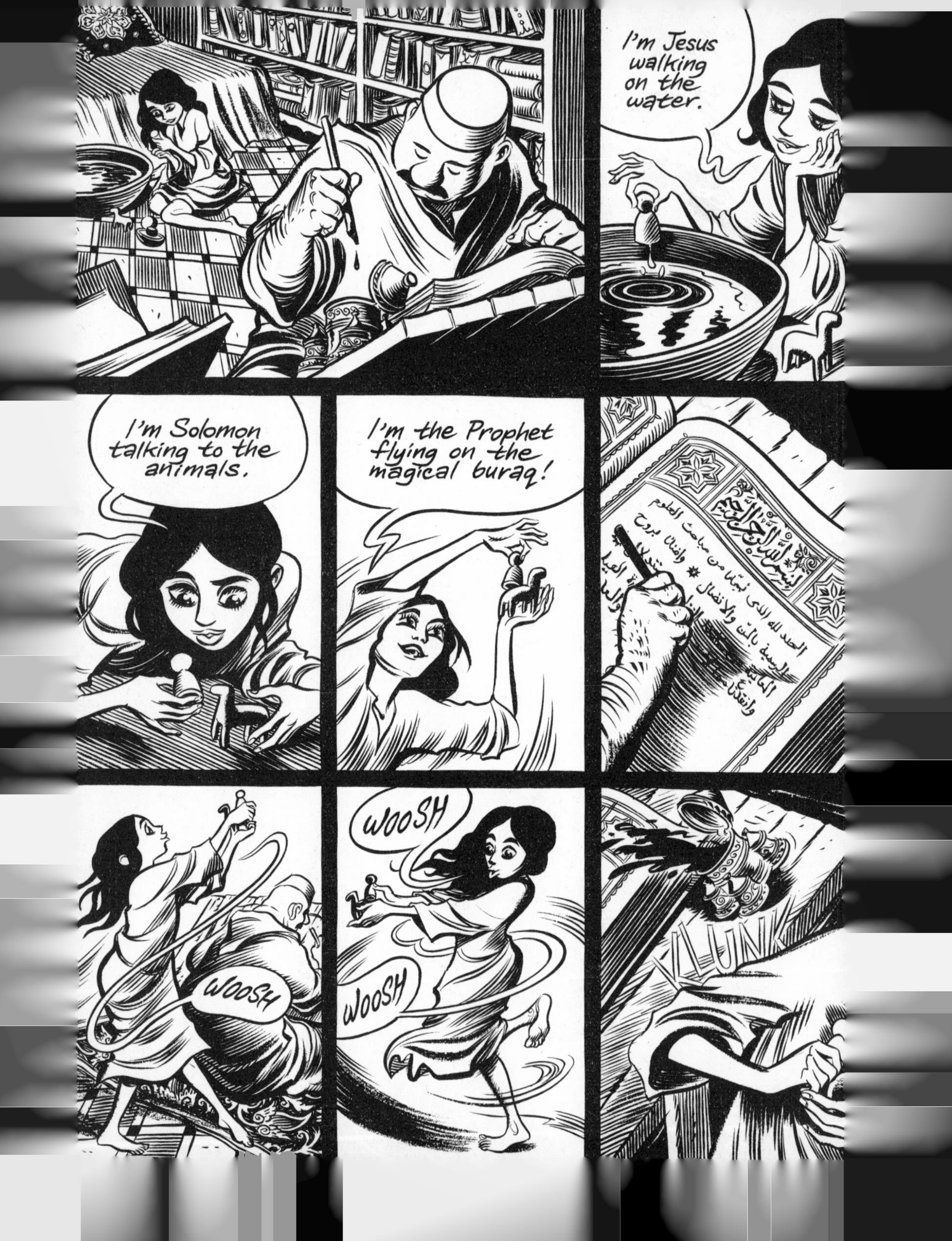
I'm Jesus walking on the water.
I'm Solomon talking to the animals.
I'm the Prophet flying on the magical buraq!
WOOSH
WOOSH
WOOSH
KLUNK

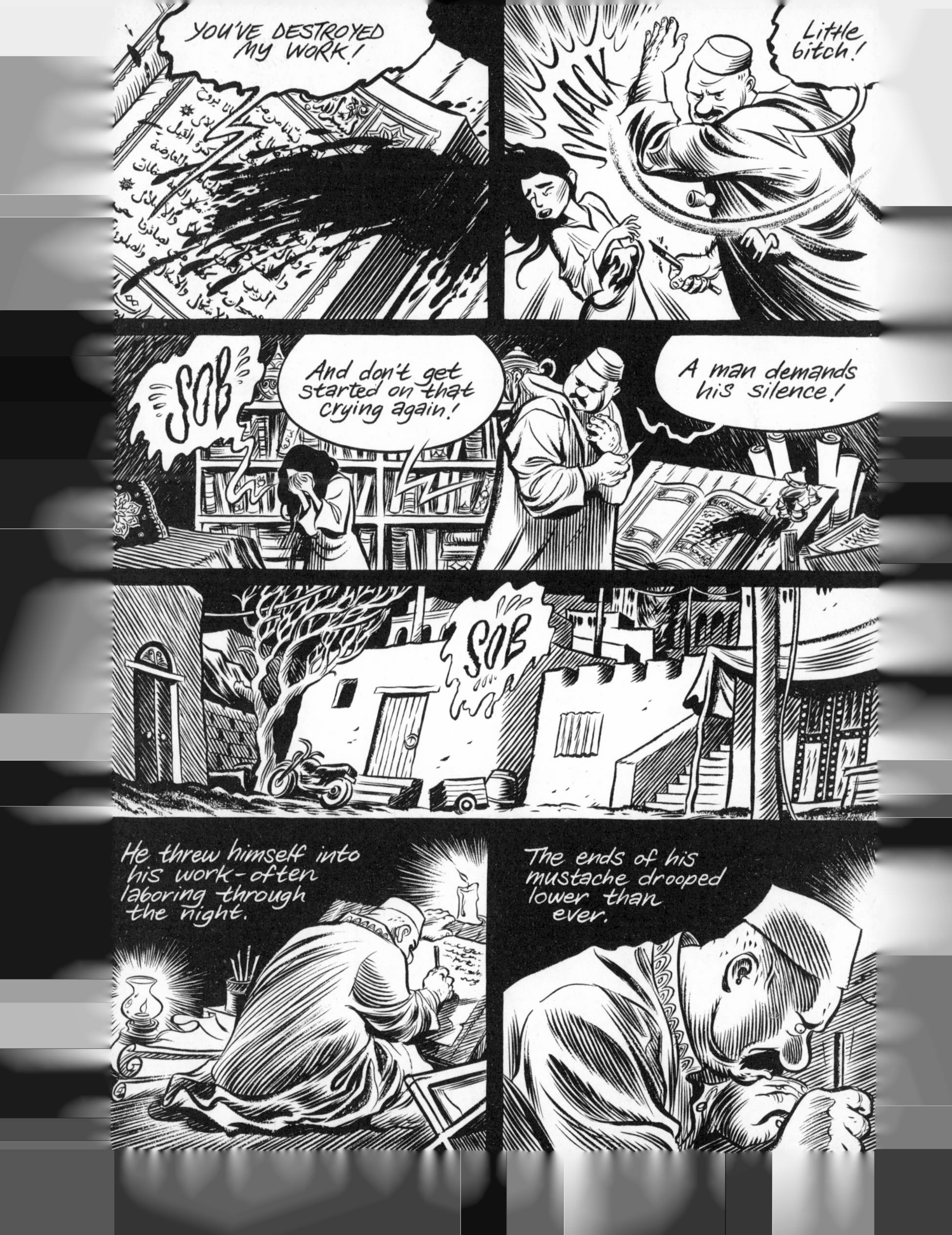
YOU'VE DESTROYED MY WORK!
SMACK
Little bitch!
SOB
And don't get started on that crying again!
A man demands his silence!
SOB
He threw himself into his work-often laboring through the night.
The ends of his mustache drooped lower than ever.

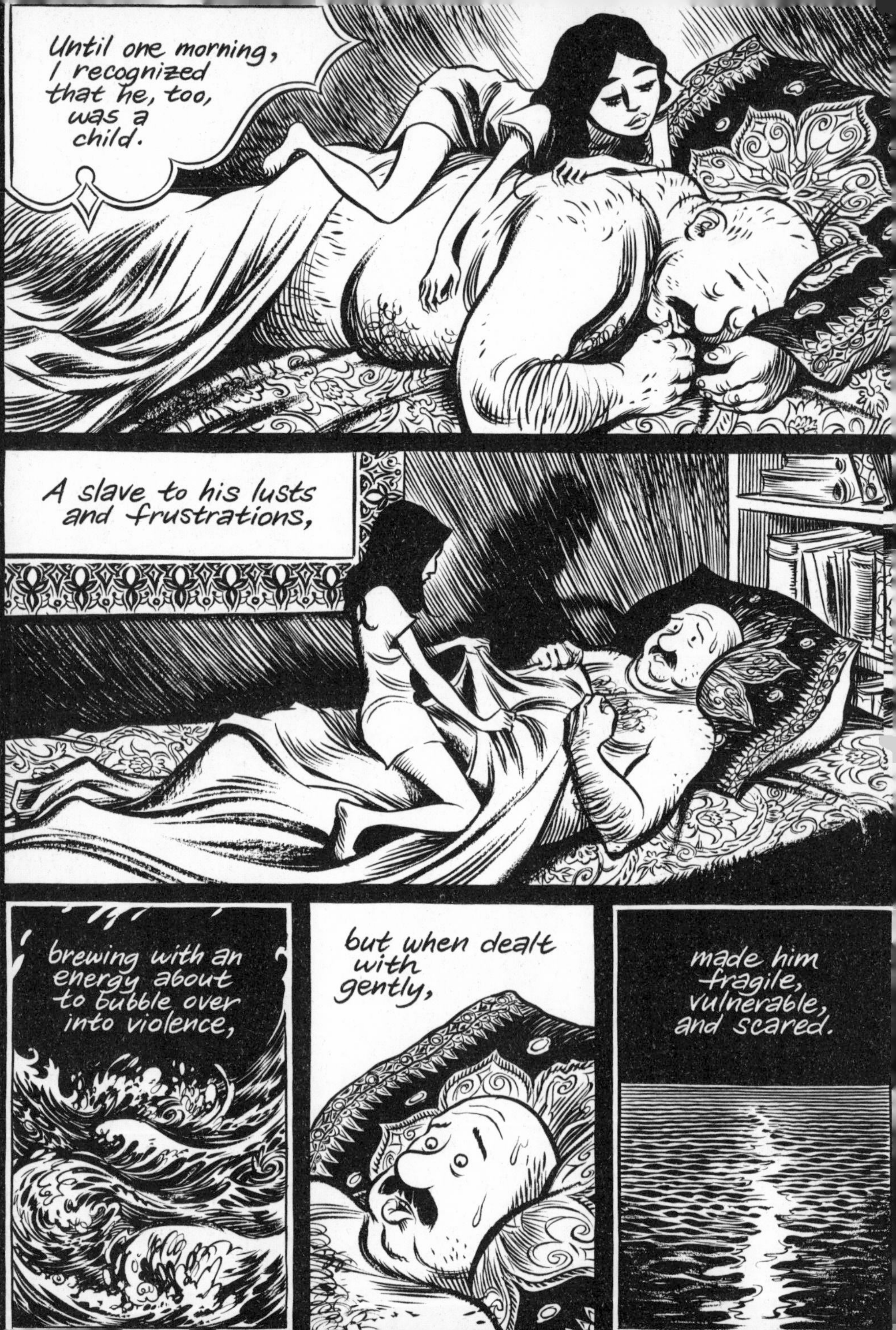
Until one morning, I recognized that he, too, was a child.
A slave to his lusts and frustrations,
brewing with an energy about to bubble over into violence,
but when dealt with gently,
made him fragile, vulnerable, and scared.

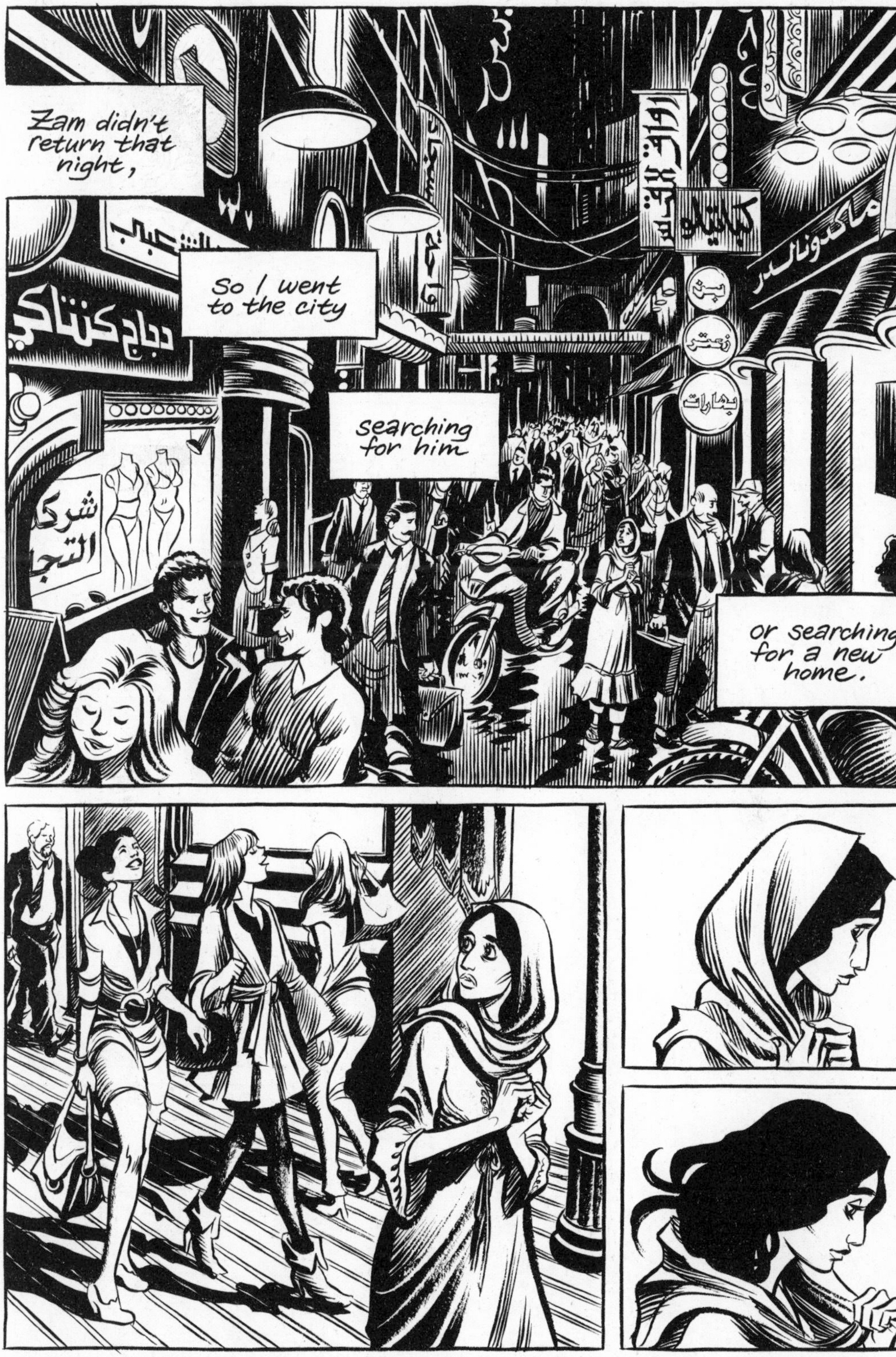
Zam didn't return that night,
So I went to the city
searching for him
or searching for a new home.

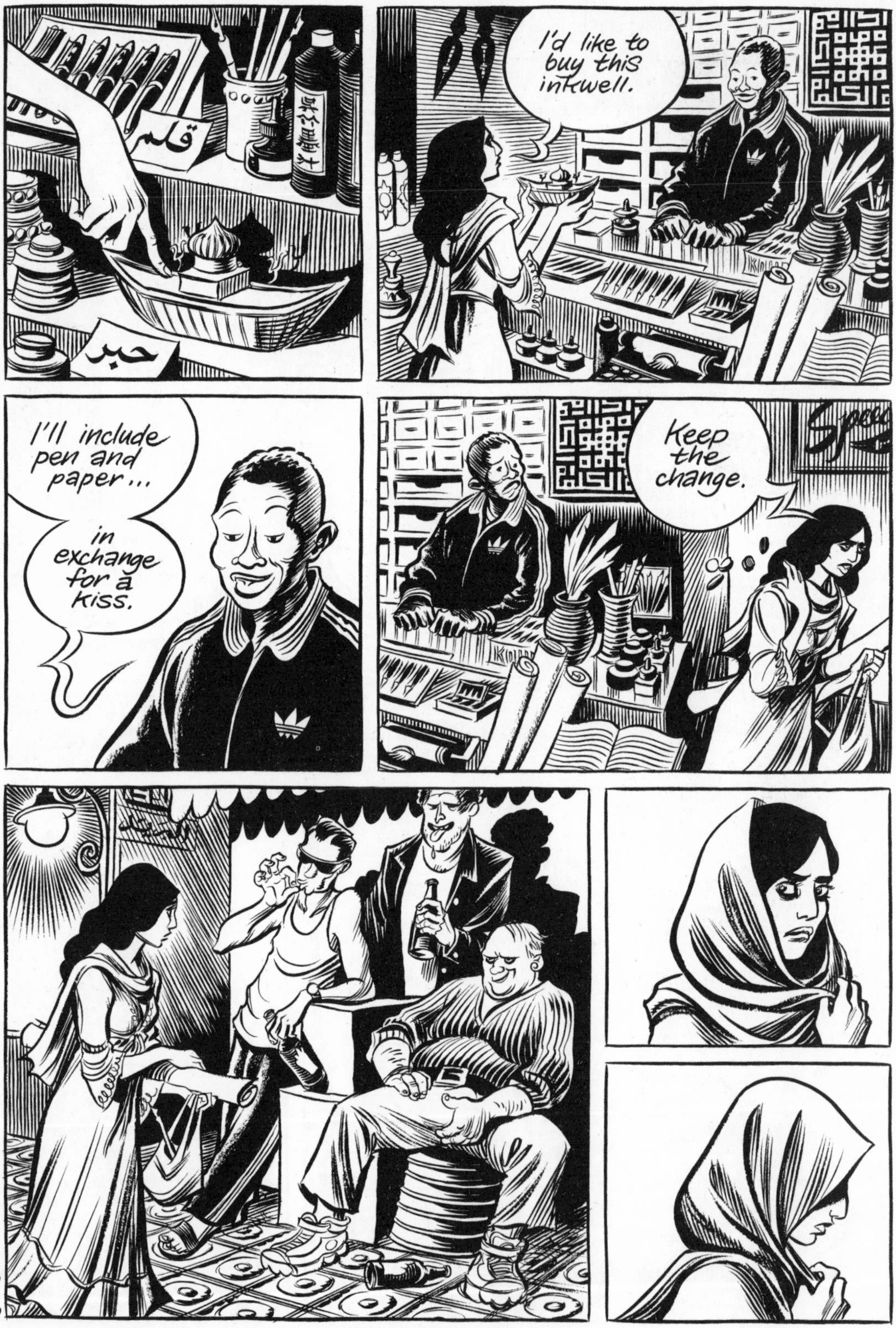
قلم
حبر
I'd like to buy this inkwell.
I'll include pen and paper...
in exchange for a kiss.
Keep the change.

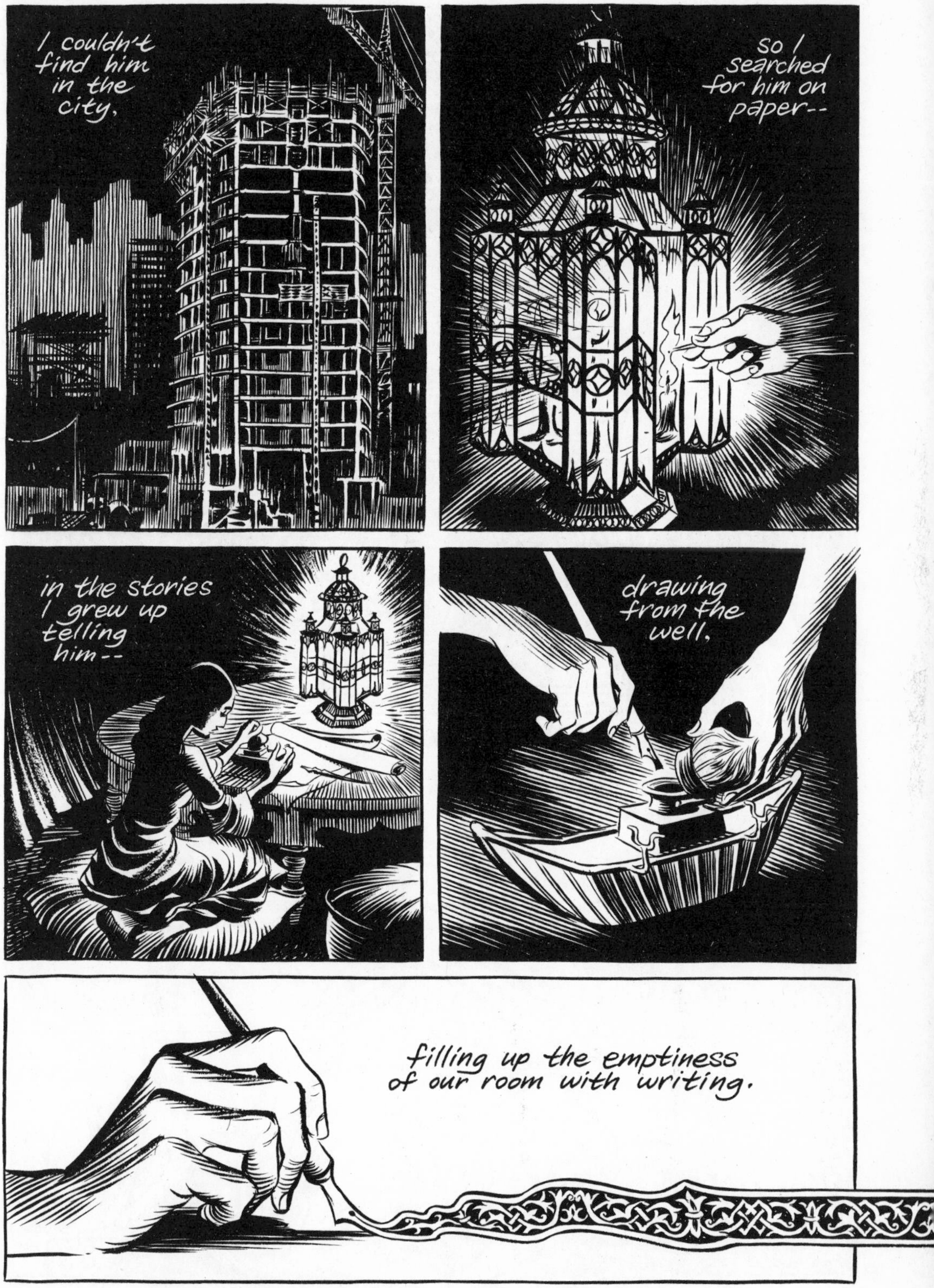
I couldn't find him in the city,
so I searched for him on paper--
in the stories I grew up telling him--
drawing from the well,
filling up the emptiness of our room with writing.

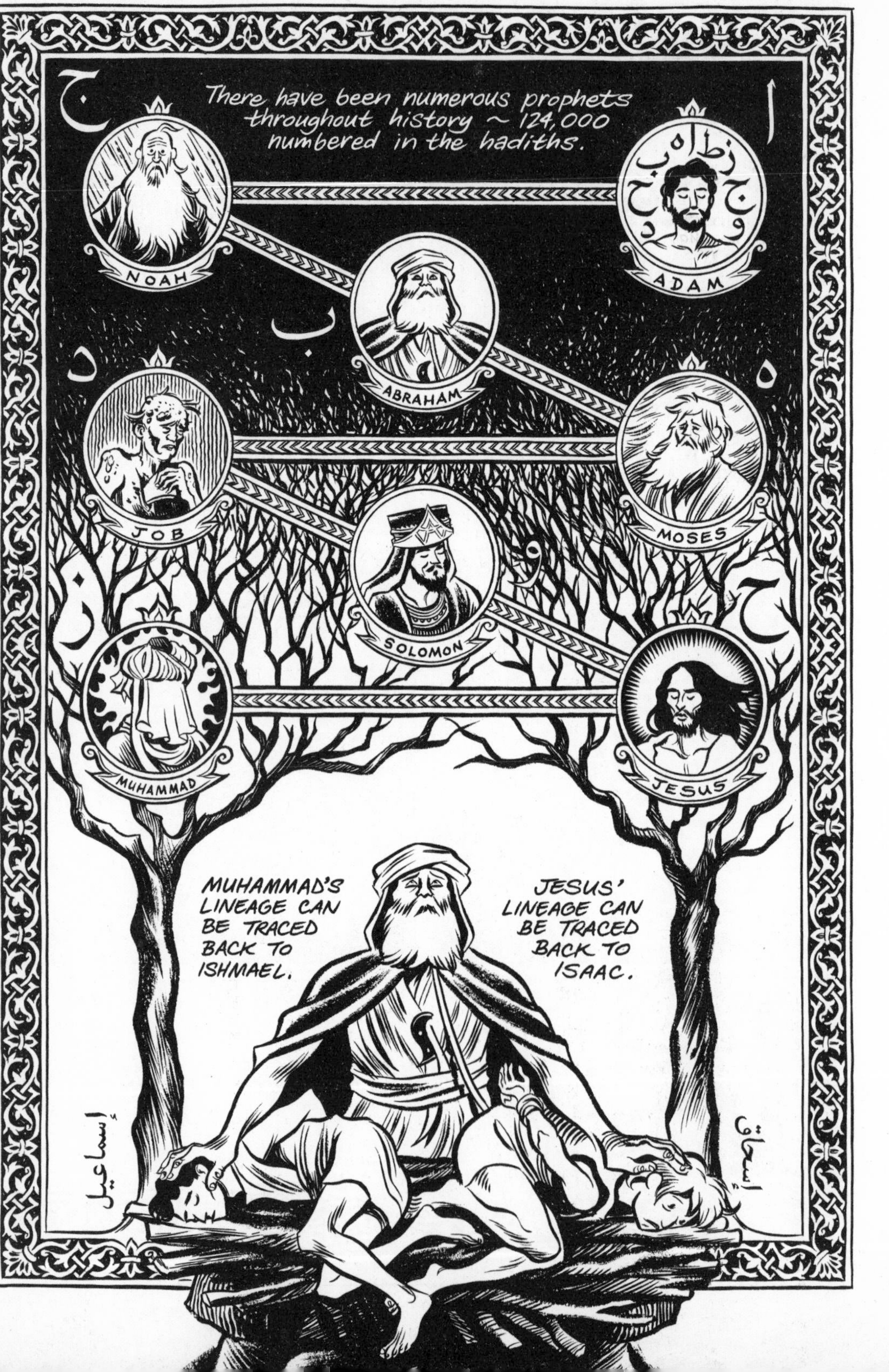

There have been numerous prophets throughout history ~ 124,000 numbered in the hadiths.
NOAH
ADAM
ABRAHAM
JOB
MOSES
SOLOMON
MUHAMMAD
JESUS
MUHAMMAD'S LINEAGE CAN BE TRACED BACK TO ISHMAEL.
JESUS' LINEAGE CAN BE TRACED BACK TO ISAAC.
إسماعيل
إسحاق

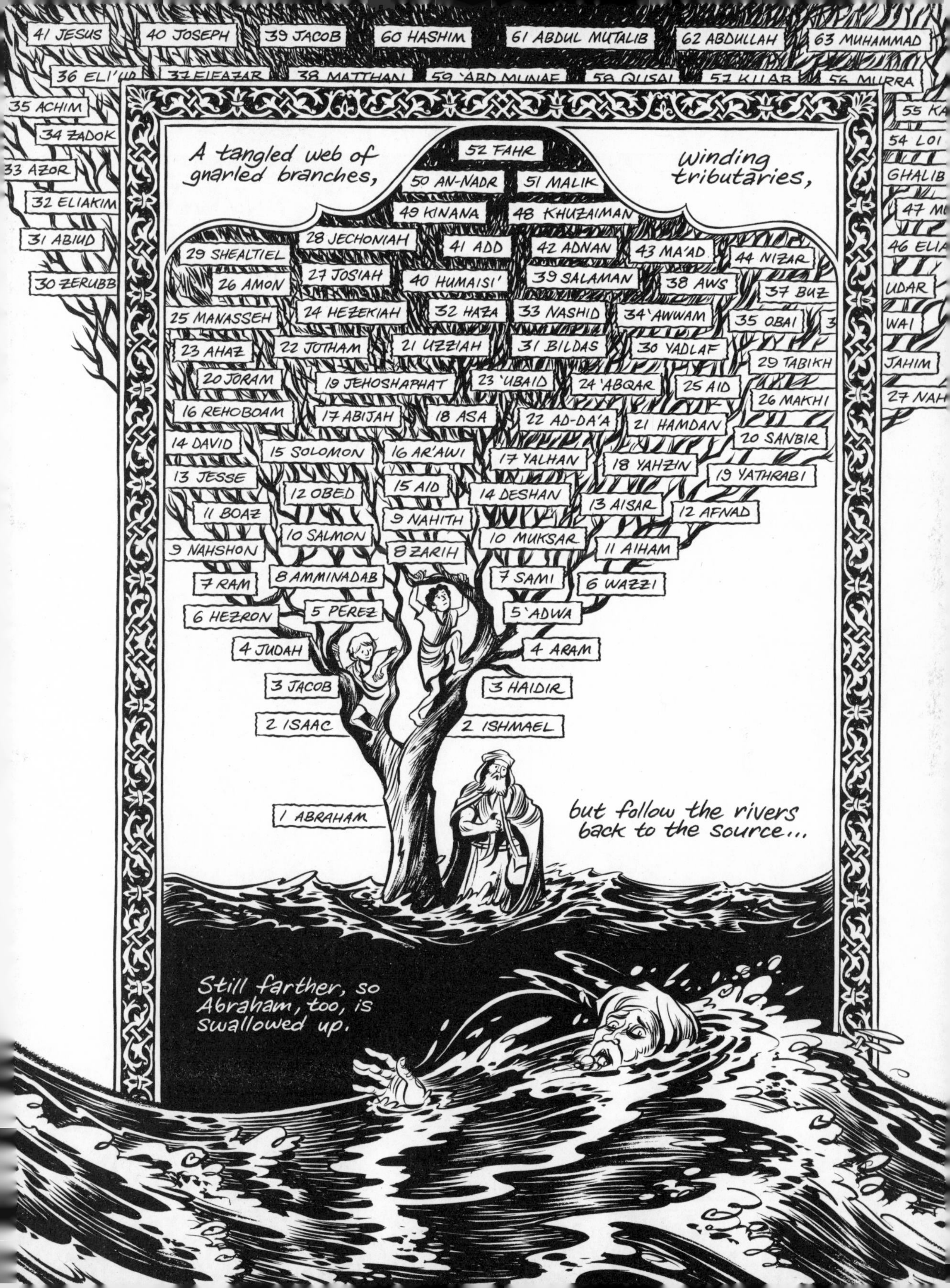

A tangled web of gnarled branches,
winding tributaries,
but follow the rivers back to the source...
Still farther, so Abraham, too, is swallowed up.
41 JESUS
40 JOSEPH
39 JACOB
60 HASHIM
61 ABDUL MUTALIB
62 ABDULLAH
63 MUHAMMAD
35 ACHIM
34 ZADOK
33 AZOR
32 ELIAKIM
31 ABIUD
GHALIB
52 FAHR
50 AN-NADR
51 MALIK
49 KINANA
48 KHUZAIMAN
29 SHEALTIEL
28 JECHONIAH
41 ADD
42 ADNAN
43 MA'AD
44 NIZAR
26 AMON
27 JOSIAH
40 HUMAISI'
39 SALAMAN
38 AWS
37 BUZ
25 MANASSEH
24 HEZEKIAH
32 HAZA
33 NASHID
34 'AWWAM
35 OBAI
23 AHAZ
22 JOTHAM
21 UZZIAH
31 BILDAS
30 YADLAF
29 TABIKH
20 JORAM
19 JEHOSHAPHAT
23 'UBAID
24 'ABQAR
25 AID
26 MAKHI
16 REHOBOAM
17 ABIJAH
18 ASA
22 AD-DA'A
21 HAMDAN
20 SANBIR
14 DAVID
15 SOLOMON
16 AR'AWI
17 YALHAN
18 YAHZIN
19 YATHRABI
13 JESSE
12 OBED
15 AID
14 DESHAN
13 AISAR
12 AFNAD
11 BOAZ
9 NAHITH
10 SALMON
10 MUKSAR
9 NAHSHON
8 ZARIH
11 AIHAM
7 RAM
8 AMMINADAB
7 SAMI
6 WAZZI
6 HEZRON
5 PEREZ
5 'ADWA
4 JUDAH
4 ARAM
3 JACOB
3 HAIDIR
2 ISAAC
2 ISHMAEL
1 ABRAHAM

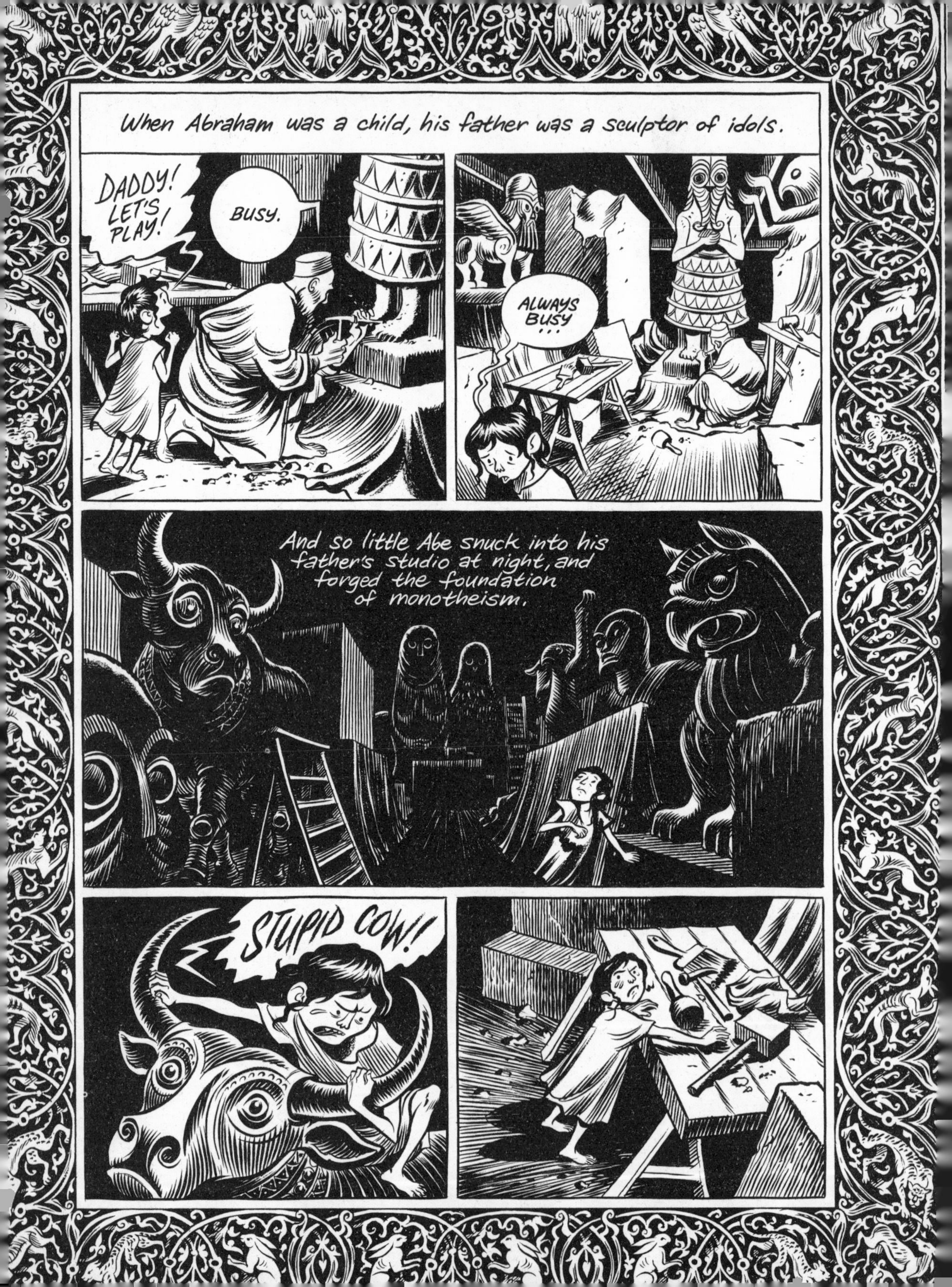
When Abraham was a child, his father was a sculptor of idols.
DADDY! LET'S PLAY!
BUSY.
ALWAYS BUSY...
And so little Abe snuck into his father's studio at night, and forged the foundation of monotheism.
STUPID COW!

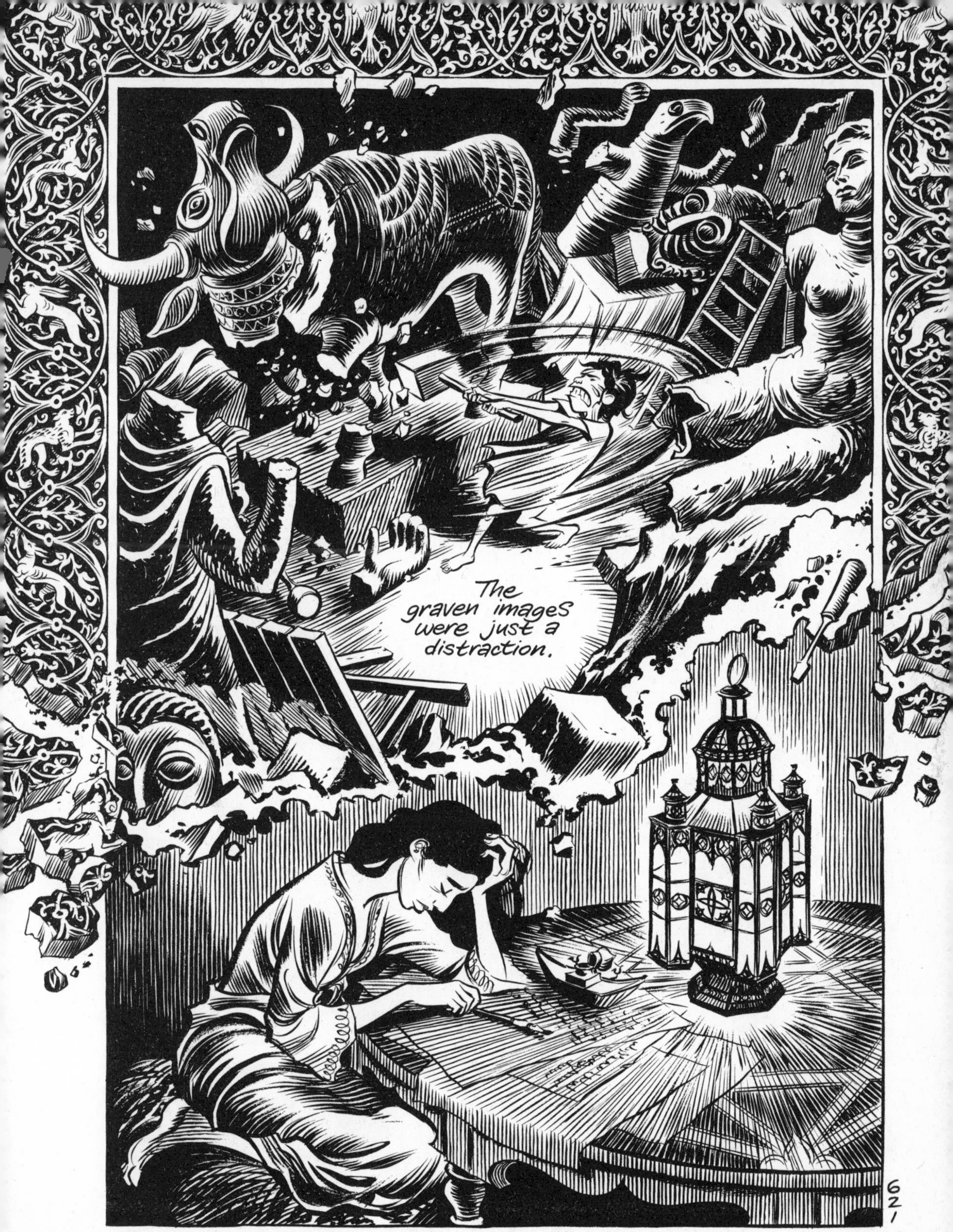
The graven images were just a distraction.

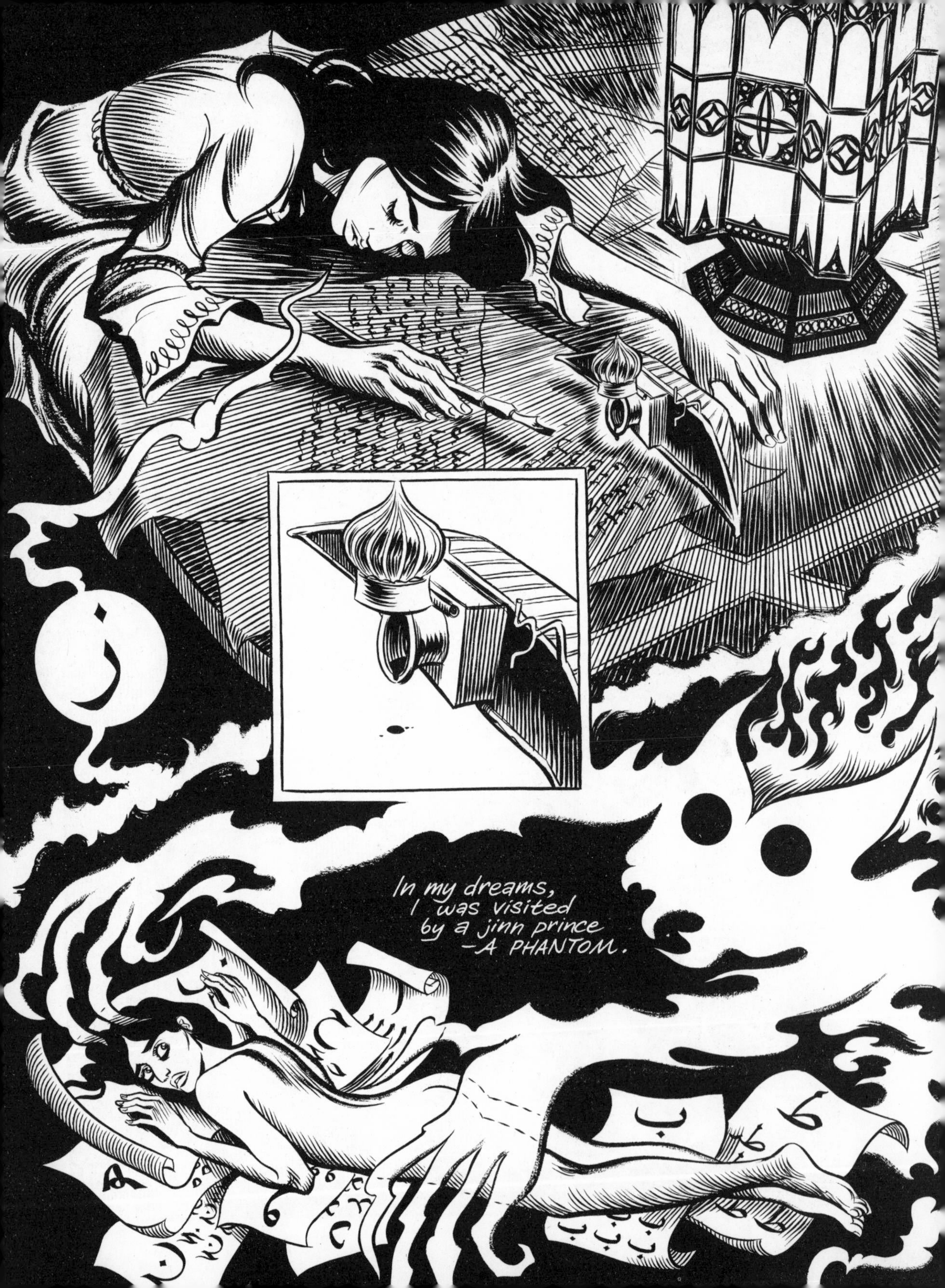
In my dreams, I was visited by a jinn prince —A PHANTOM.

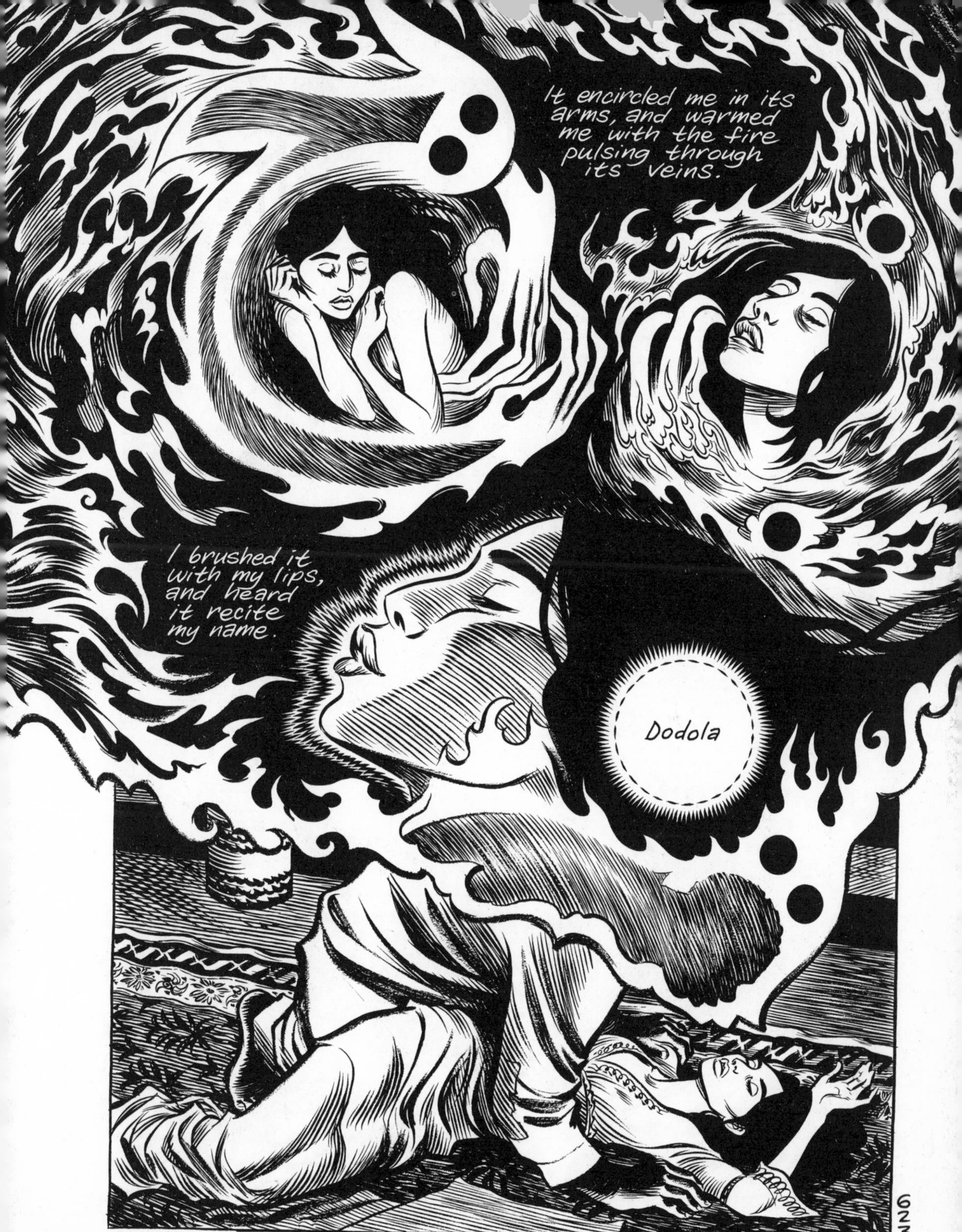
It encircled me in its arms, and warmed me with the fire pulsing through its veins.
I brushed it with my lips, and heard it recite my name.
Dodola

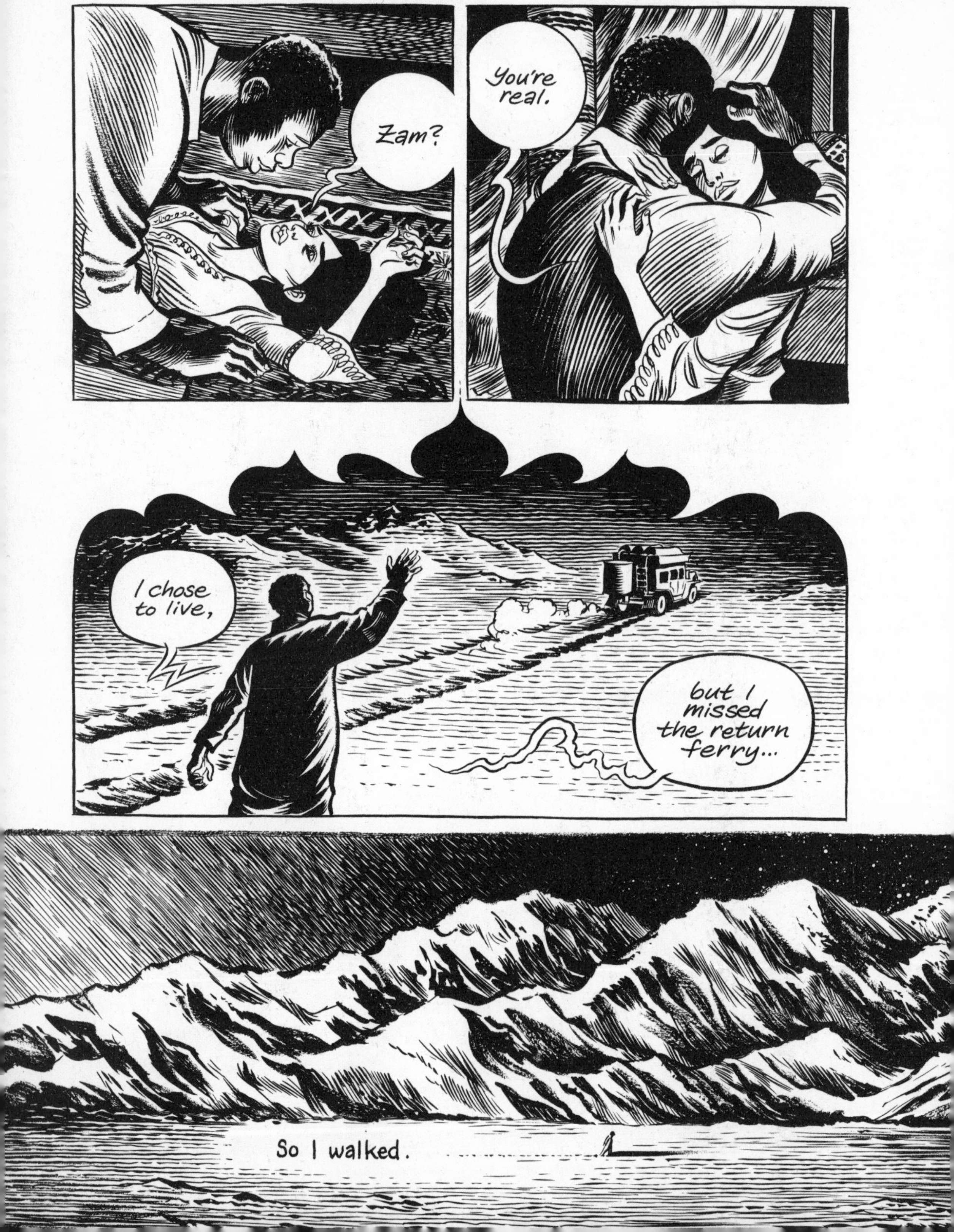
Zam?
You're real.
I chose to live,
but I missed the return ferry...
So I walked.

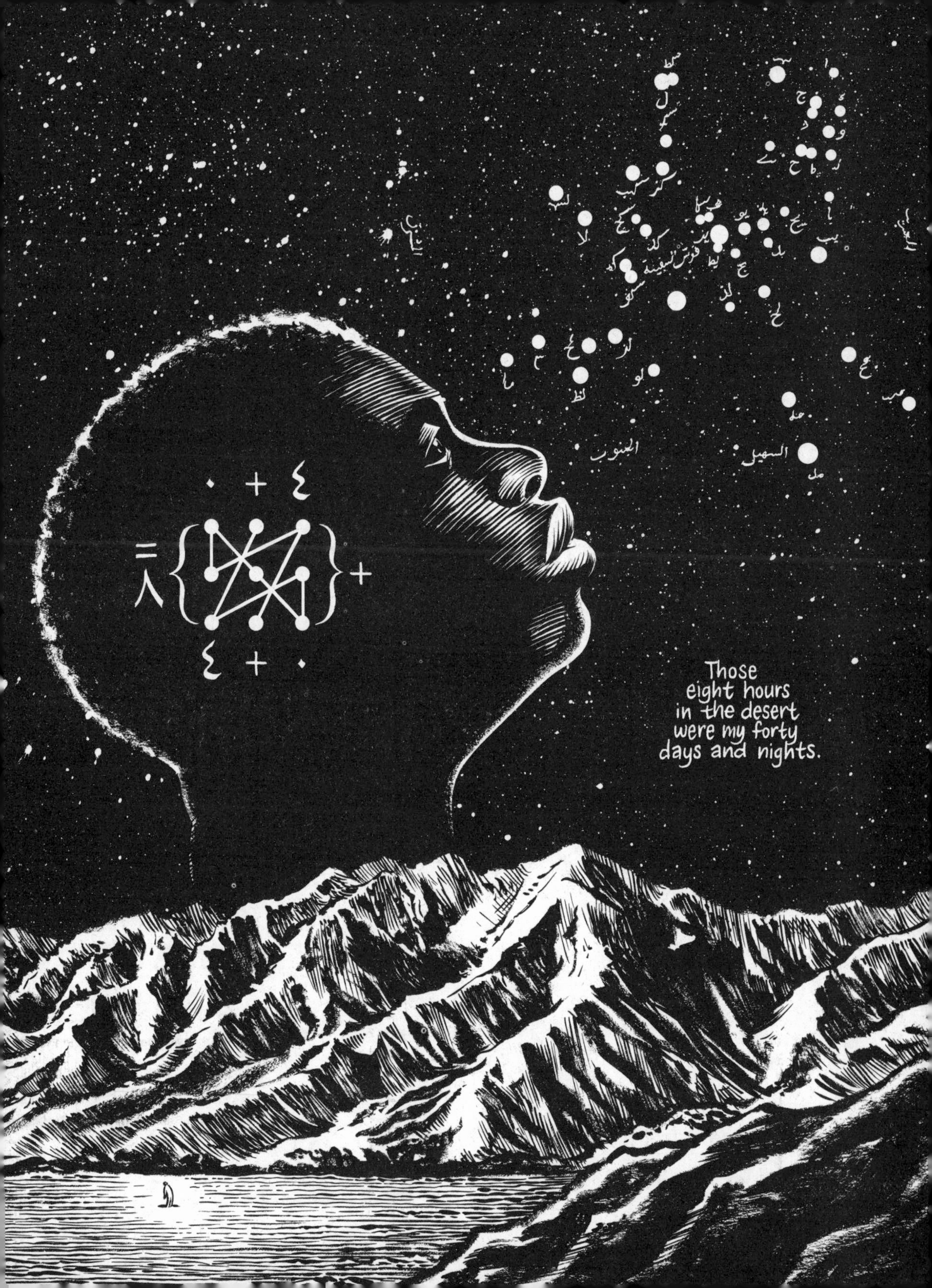
Those eight hours in the desert were my forty days and nights.

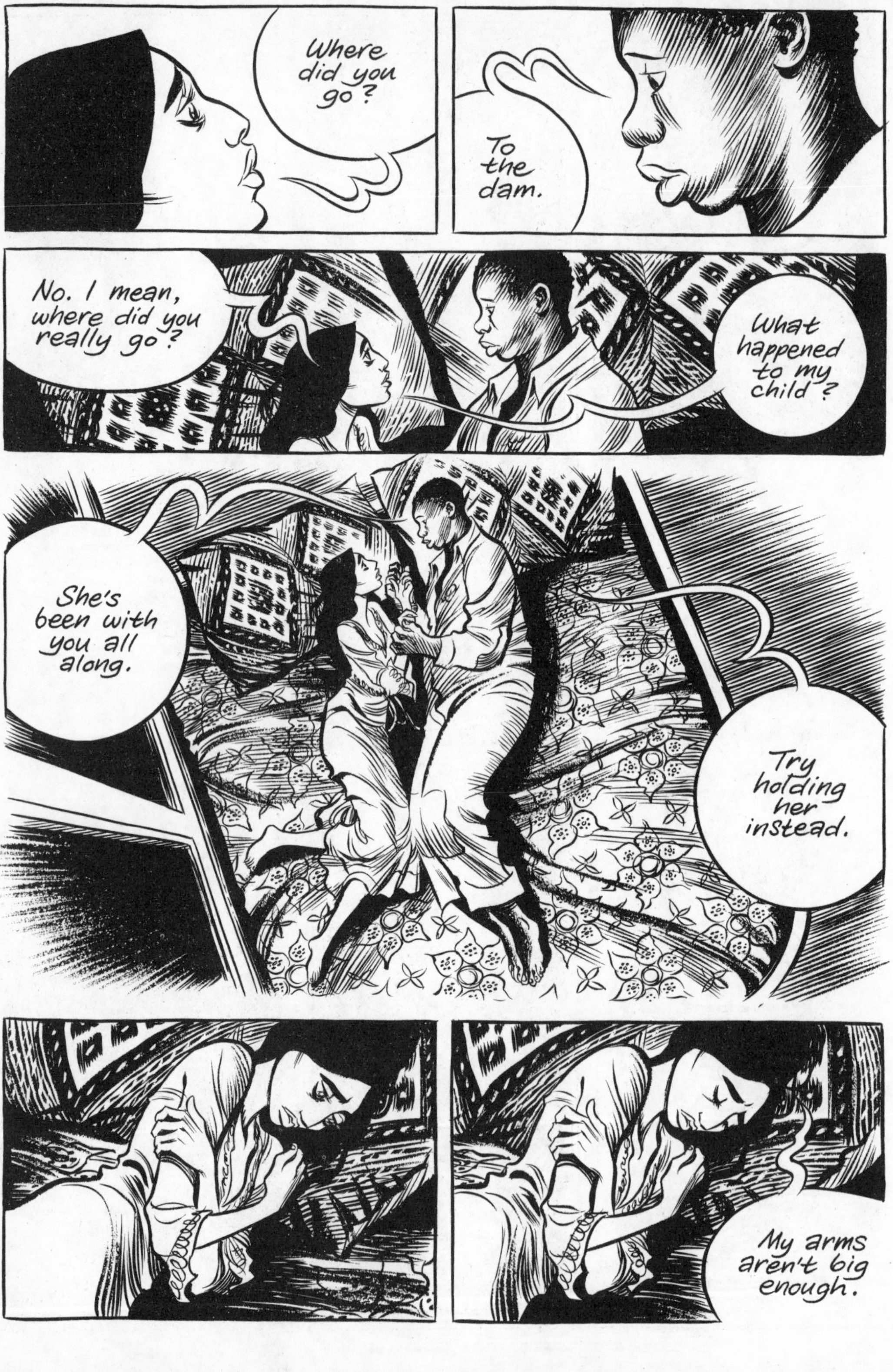

Where did you go?
To the dam.
No. I mean, where did you really go?
What happened to my child?
She's been with you all along.
Try holding her instead.
My arms aren't big enough.

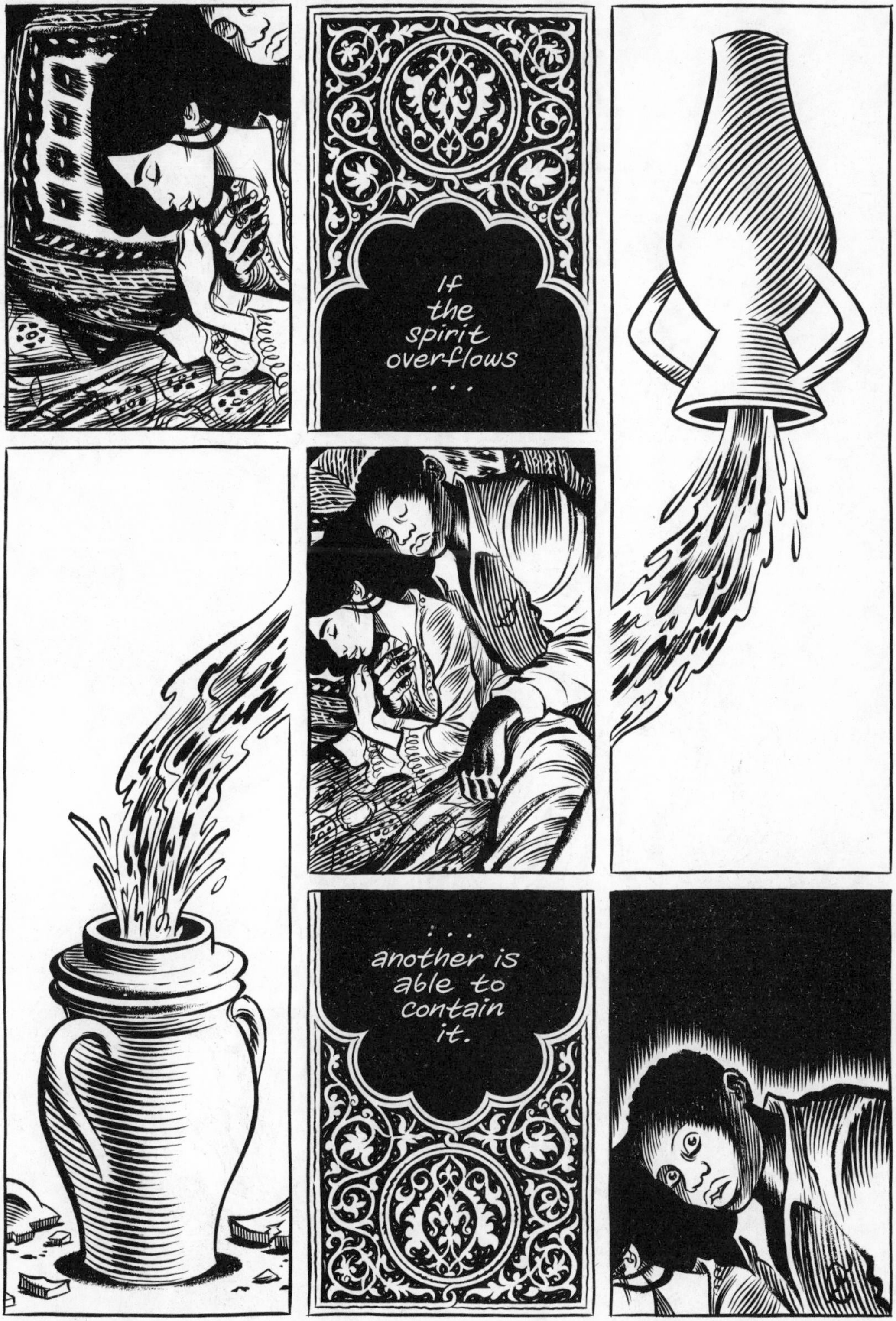
If the spirit overflows . . .
. . . another is able to contain it.

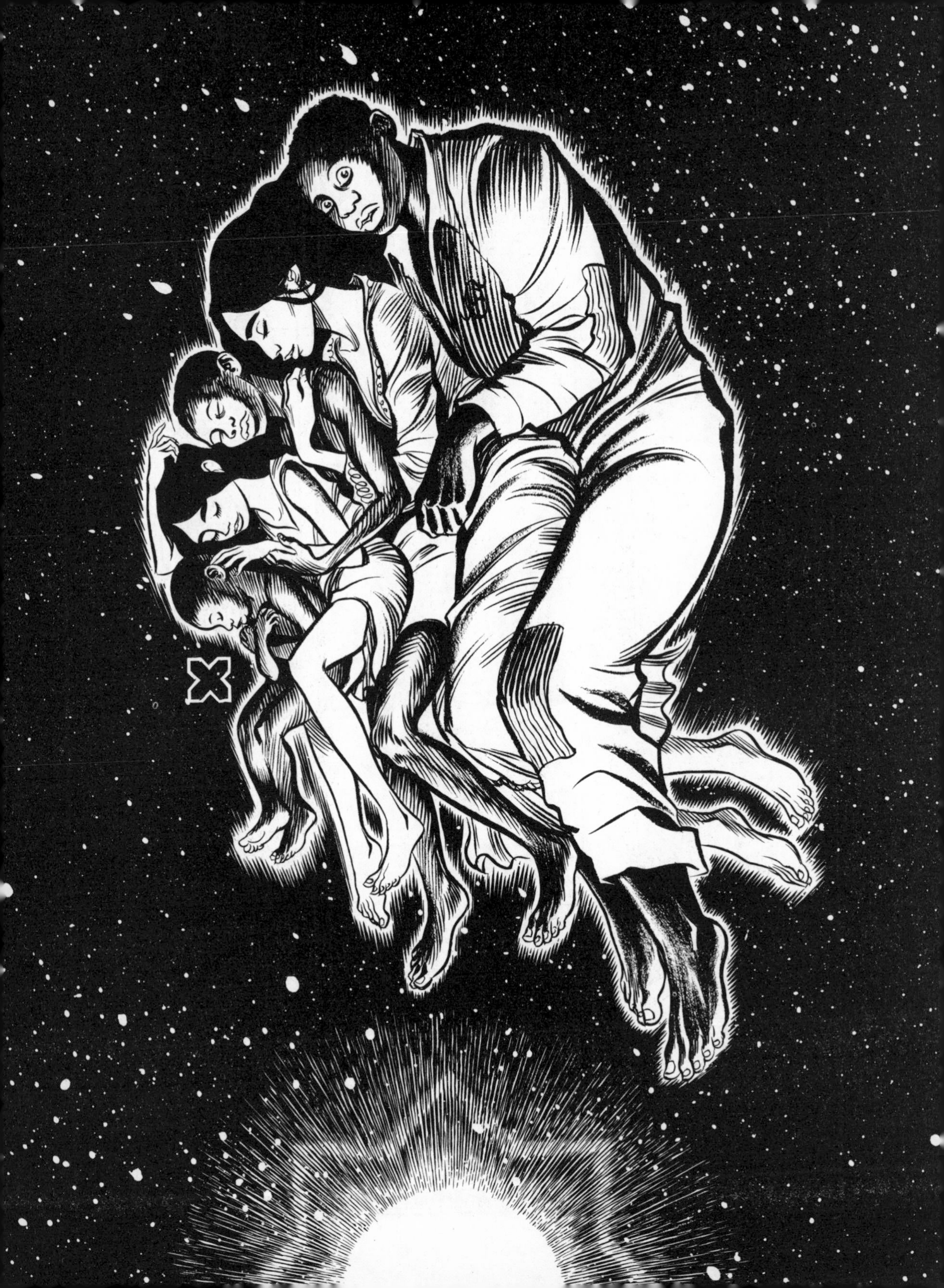

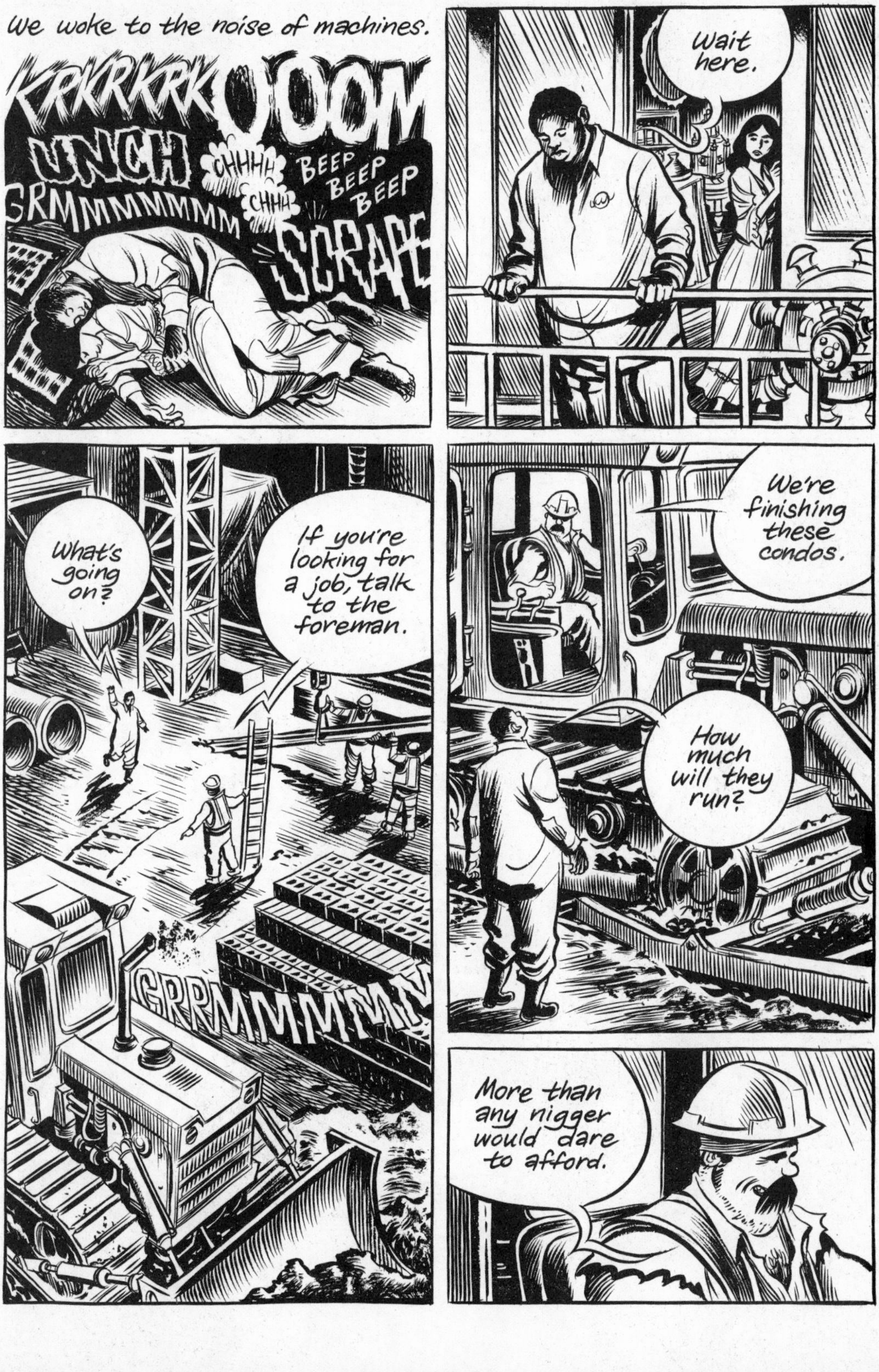
We woke to the noise of machines.
KRKRKRKRK VOOOM
UNCH
CHHHH
BEEP BEEP BEEP
CHHH
GRMMMMMMMM
SCRAPE
Wait here.
What's going on?
If you're looking for a job, talk to the foreman.
GRRMMMM
We're finishing these condos.
How much will they run?
More than any nigger would dare to afford.

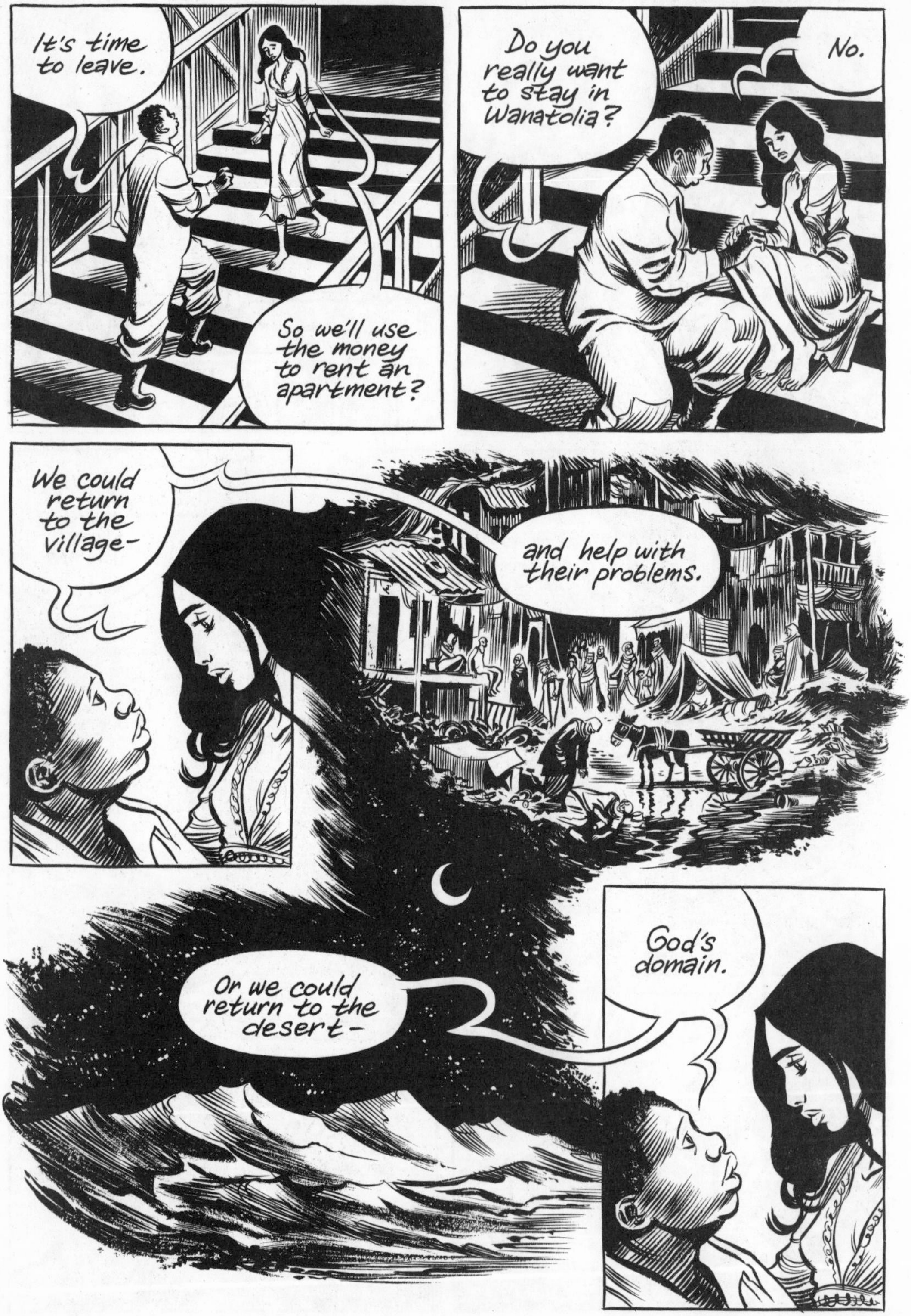
It's time to leave.
So we'll use the money to rent an apartment?
Do you really want to stay in Wanatolia?
No.
We could return to the village-
and help with their problems.
Or we could return to the desert-
God's domain.

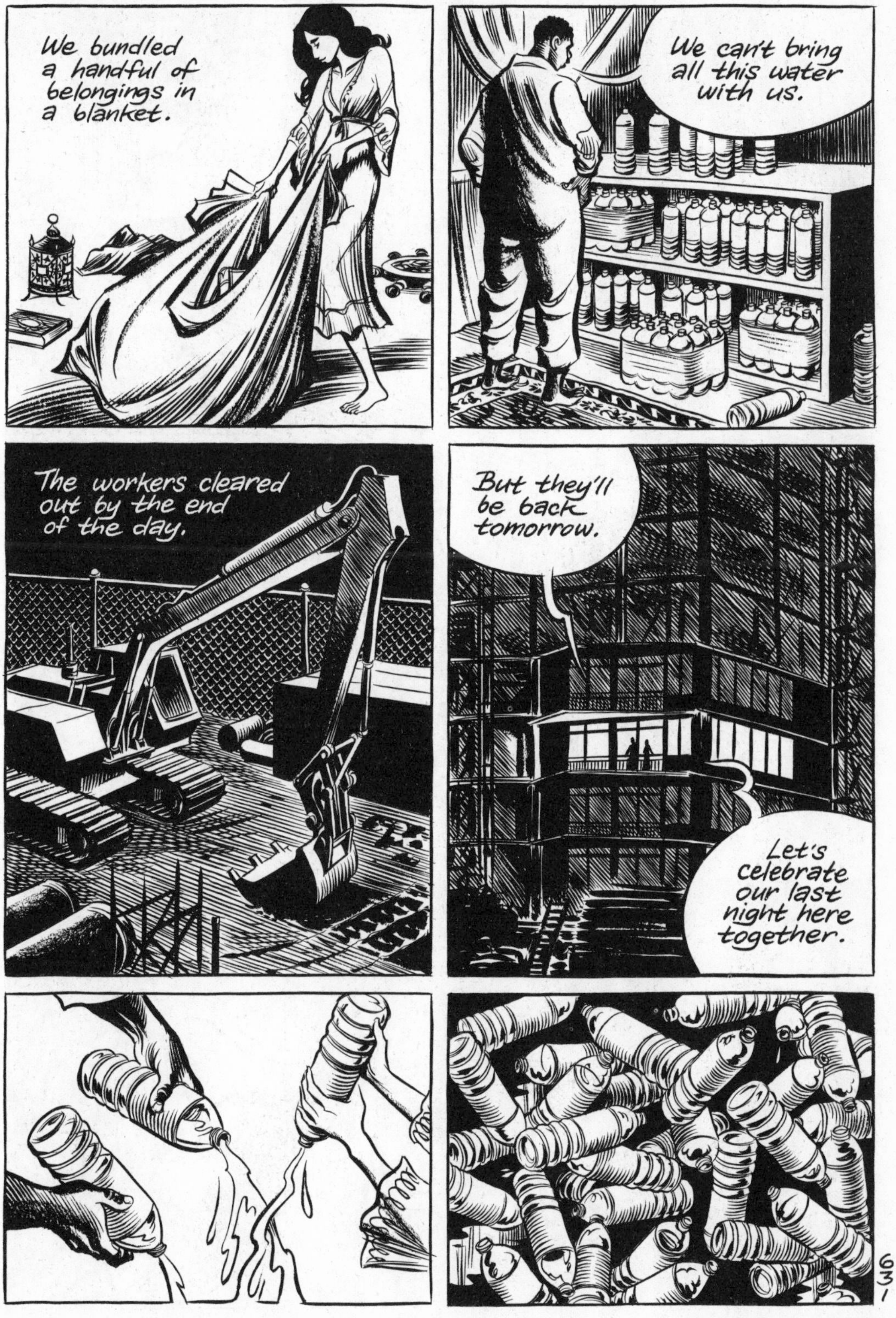
We bundled a handful of belongings in a blanket.
We can't bring all this water with us.
The workers cleared out by the end of the day.
But they'll be back tomorrow.
Let's celebrate our last night here together.

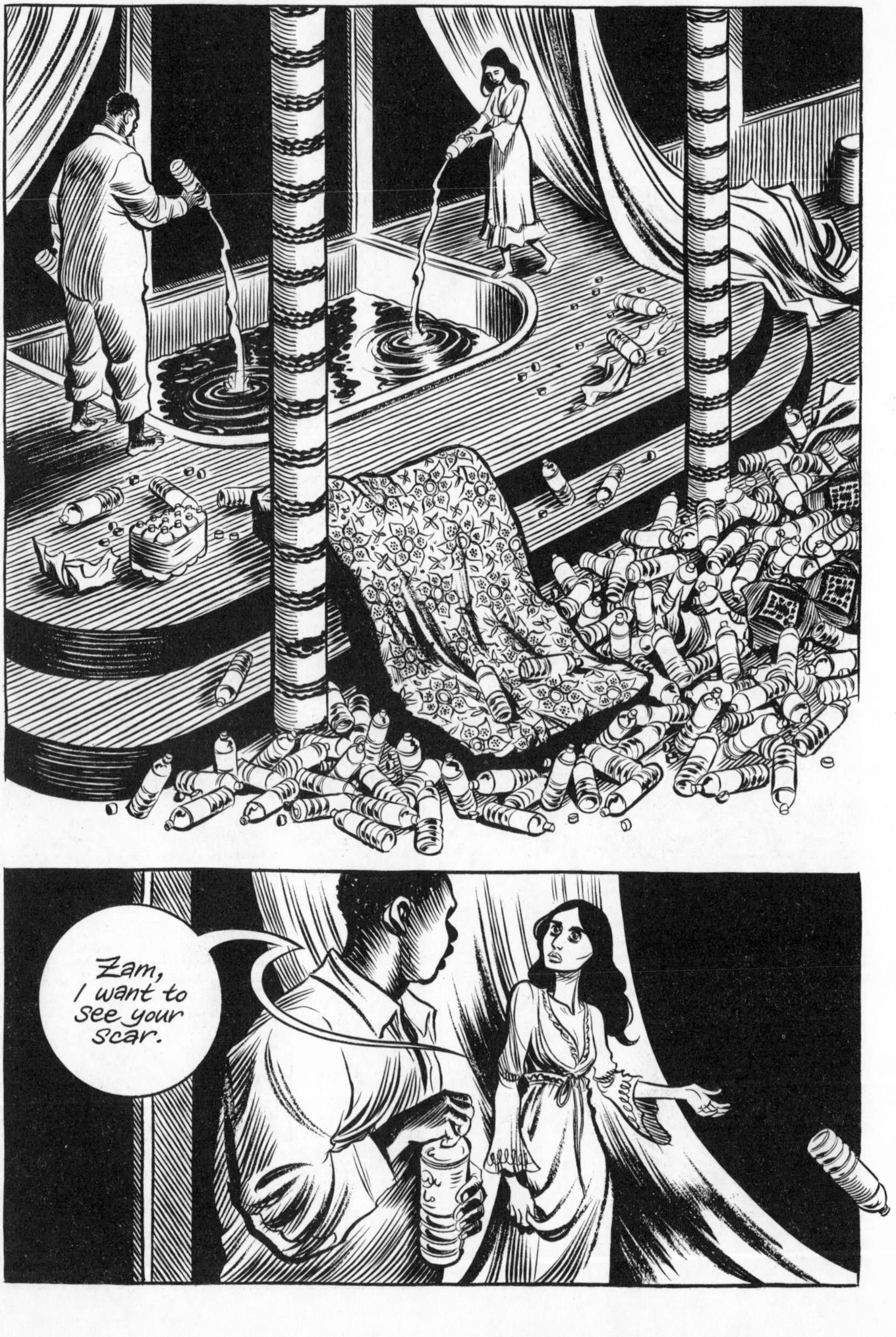
Zam, I want to see your scar.

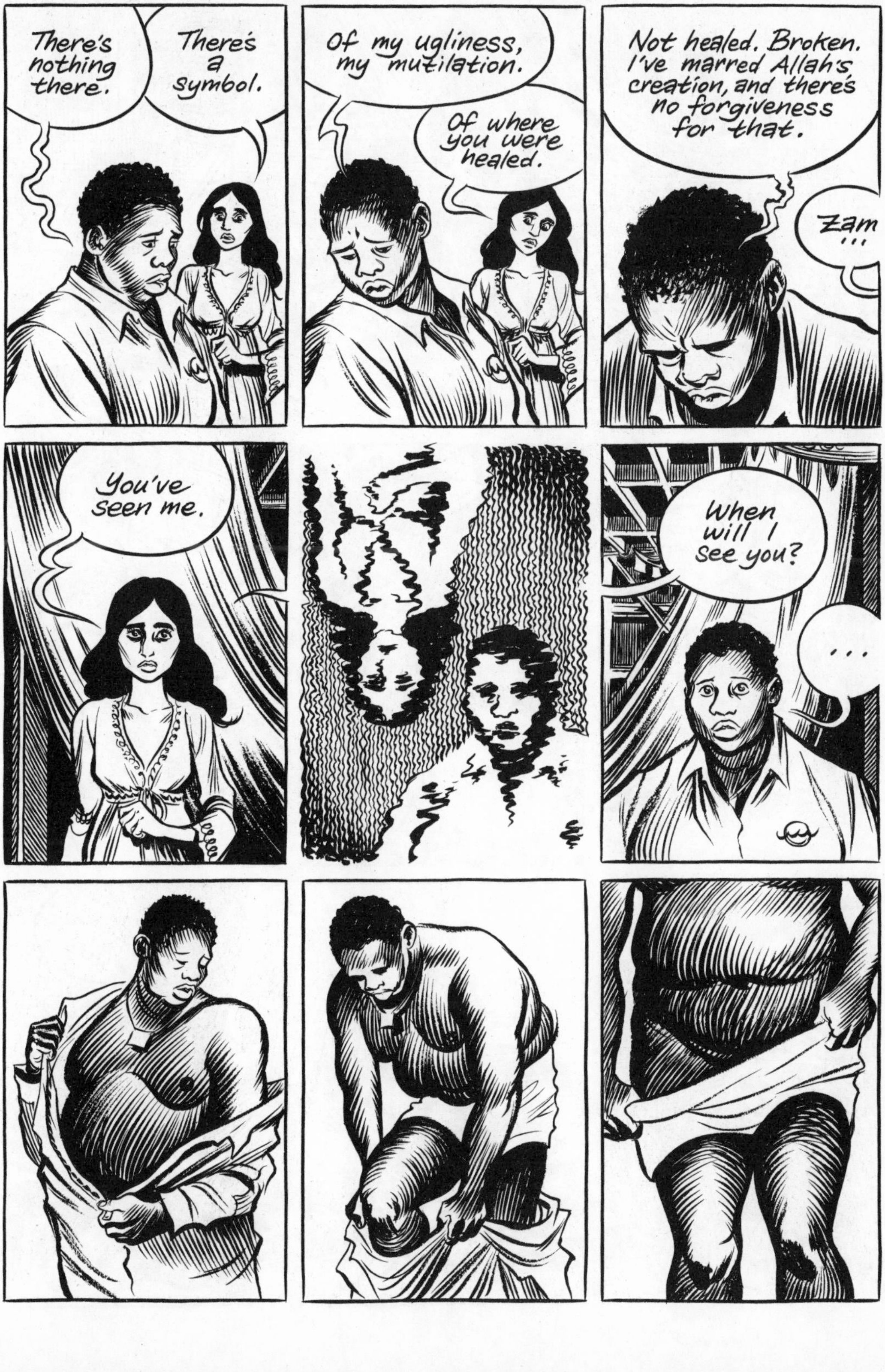
There's nothing there.
There's a symbol.
Of my ugliness, my mutilation.
Of where you were healed.
Not healed. Broken. I've marred Allah's creation, and there's no forgiveness for that.
Zam ...
You've seen me.
When will I see you?
...

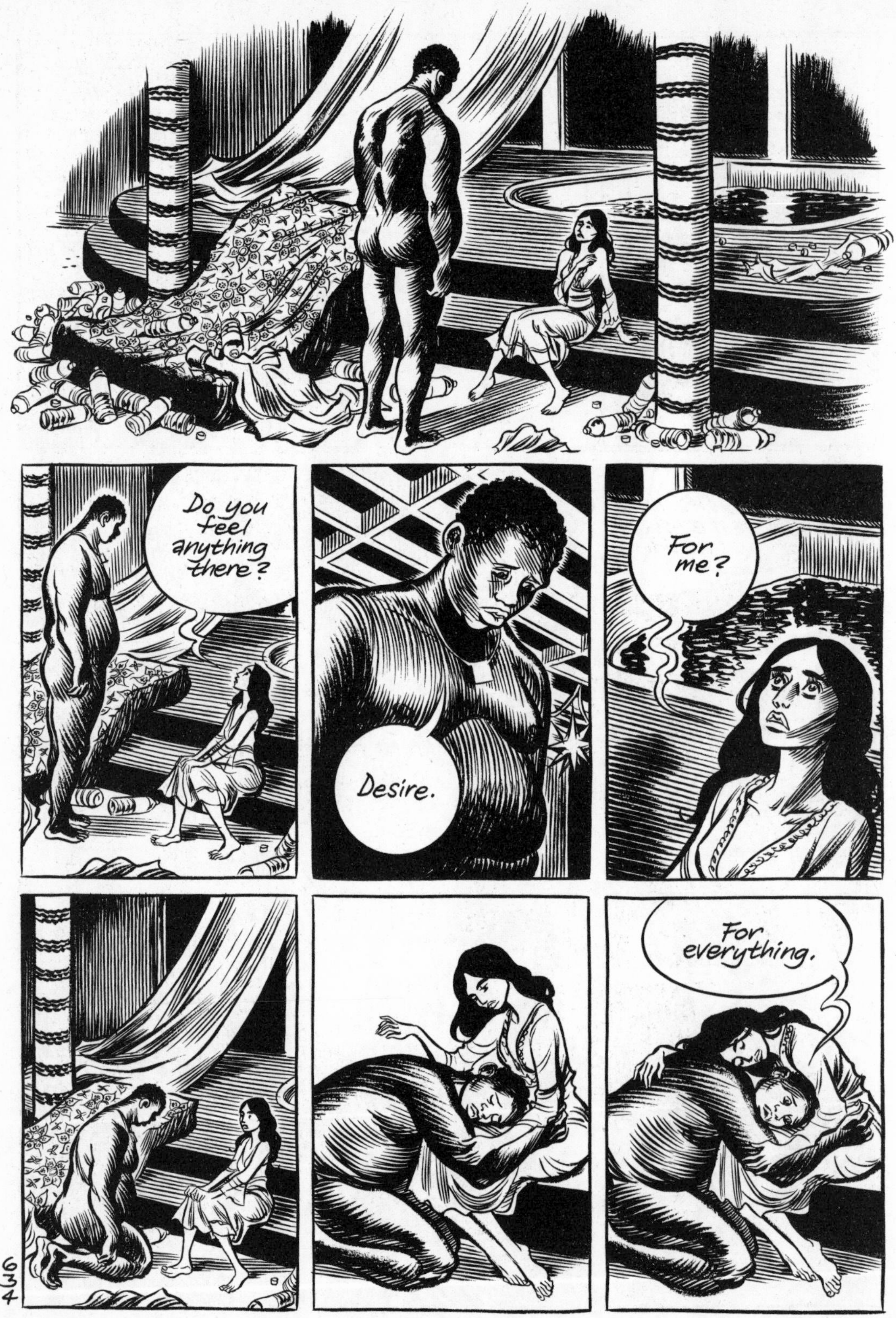

Do you feel anything there?
Desire.
For me?
For everything.

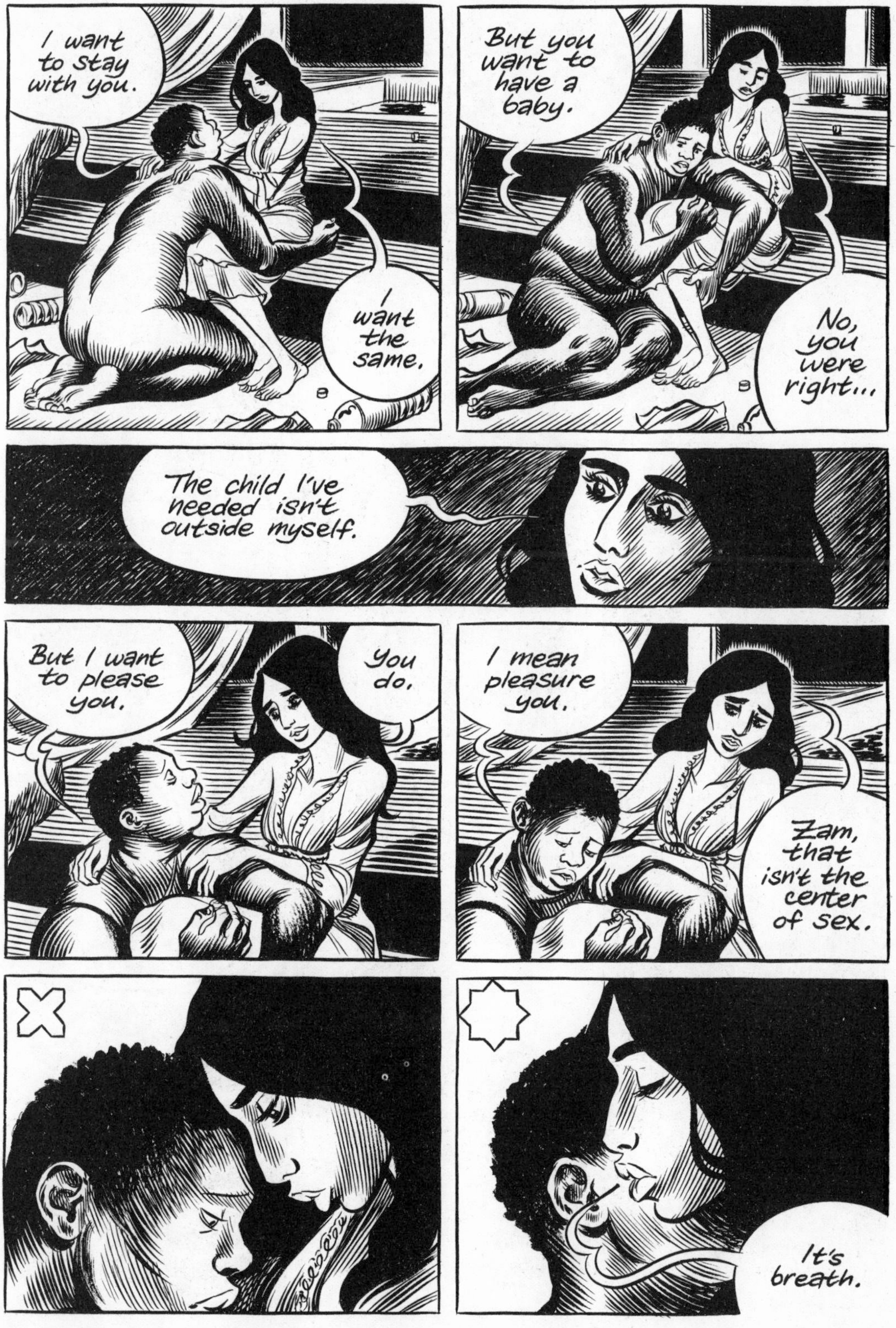
I want to stay with you.
I want the same.
But you want to have a baby.
No, you were right...
The child I've needed isn't outside myself.
But I want to please you.
You do.
I mean pleasure you.
Zam, that isn't the center of sex.
It's breath.

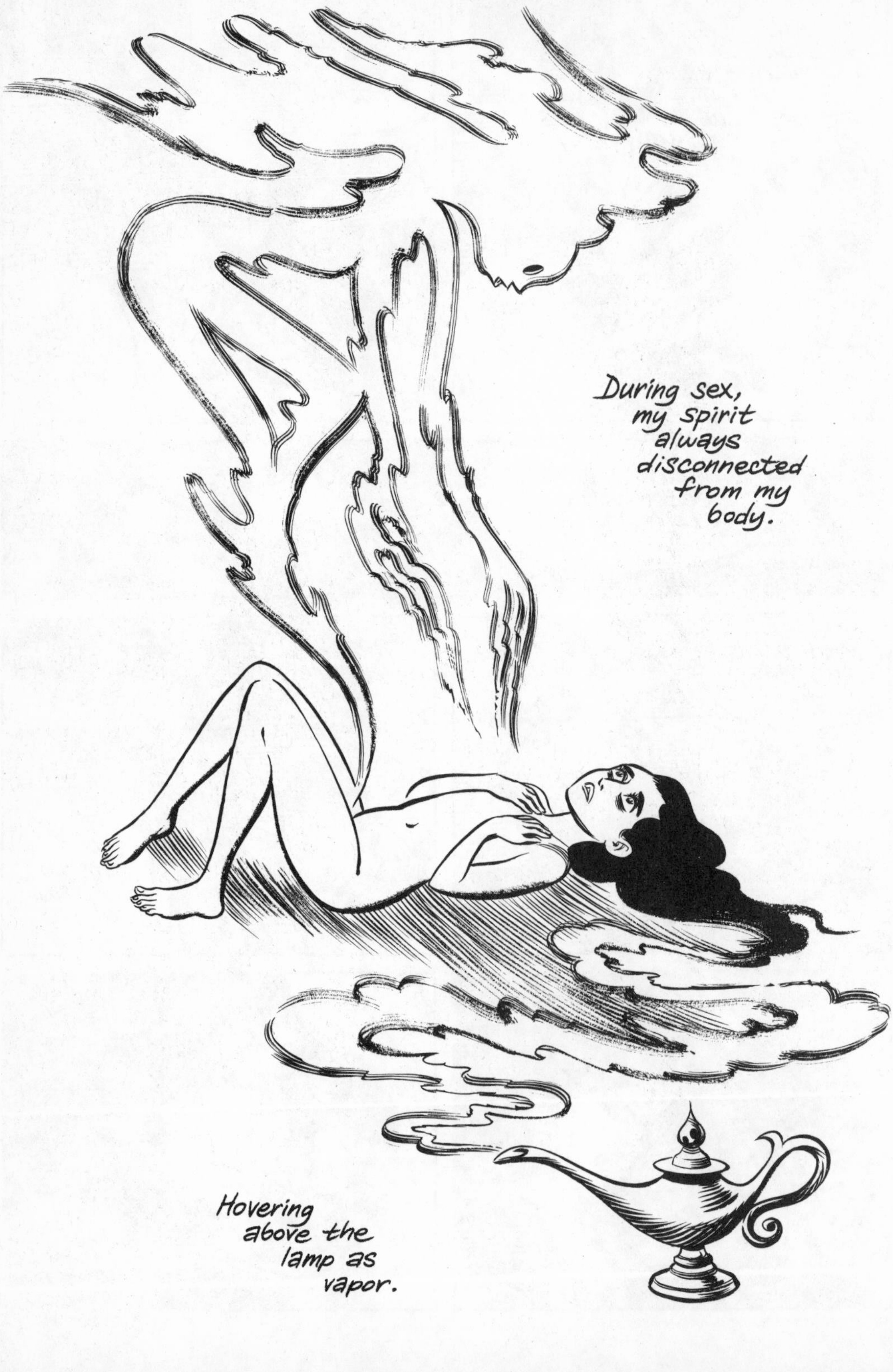
During sex, my spirit always disconnected from my body.
Hovering above the lamp as vapor.

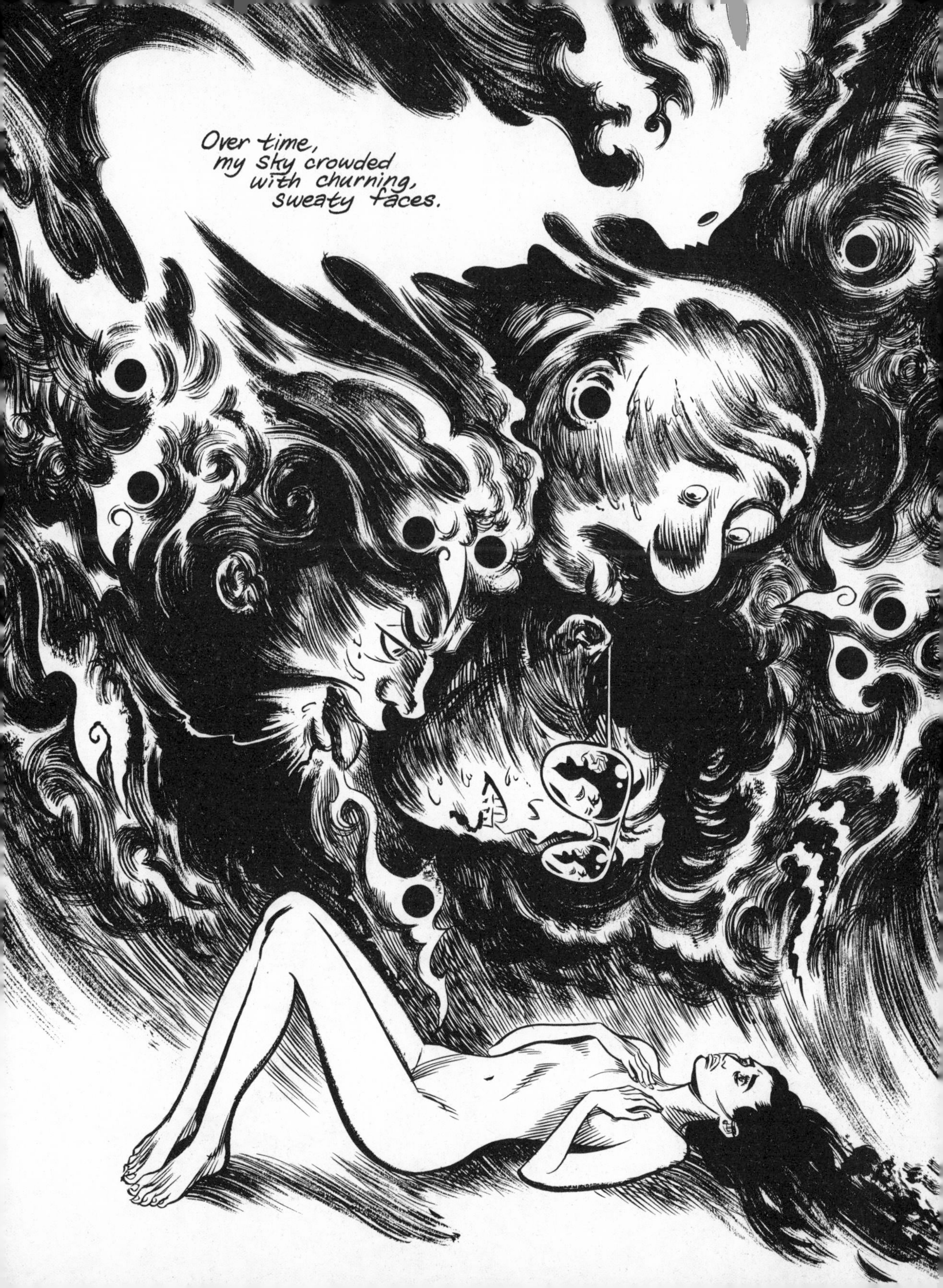
Over time, my sky crowded with churning, sweaty faces.

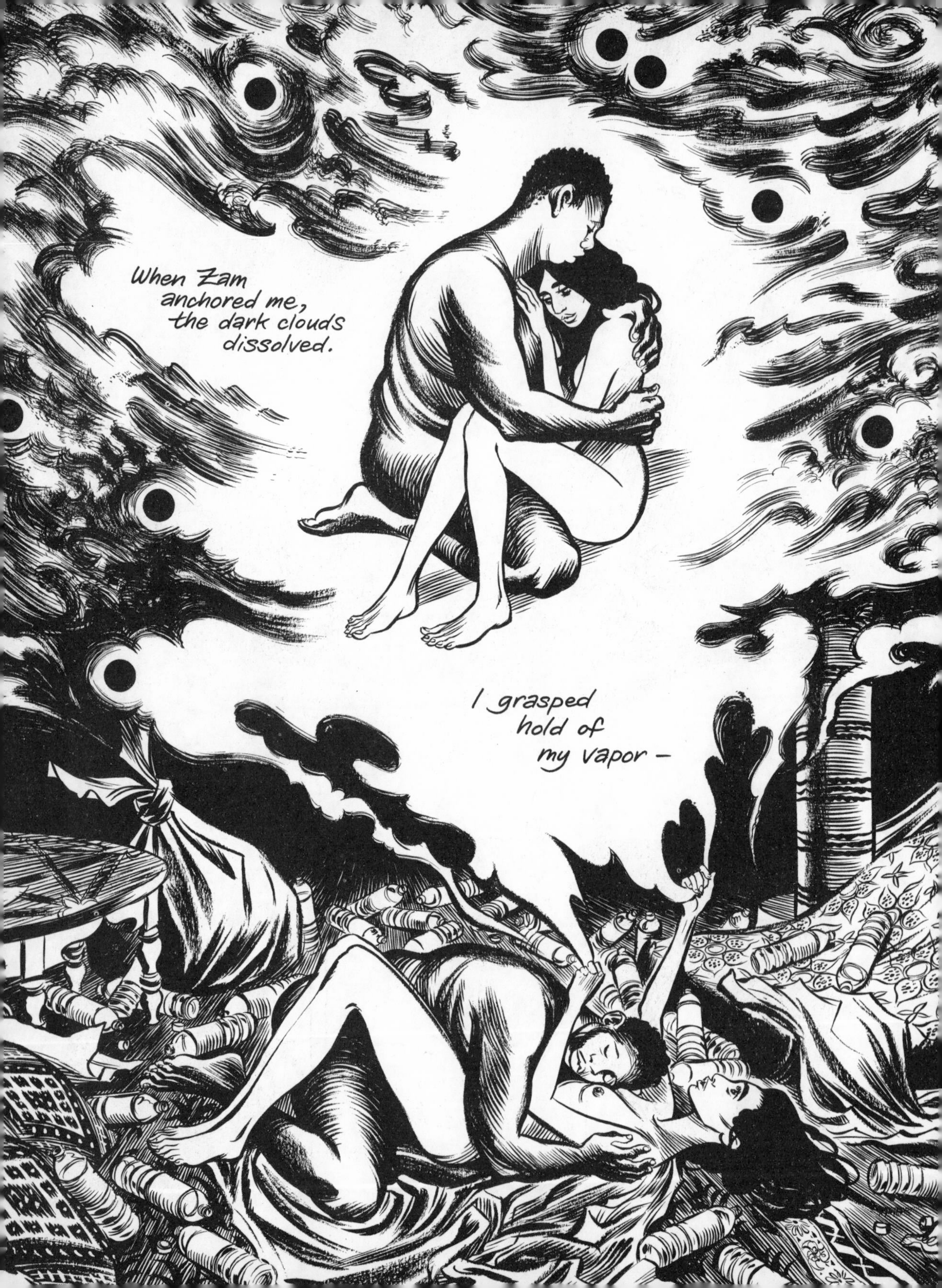
When Zam anchored me, the dark clouds dissolved.
I grasped hold of my vapor –

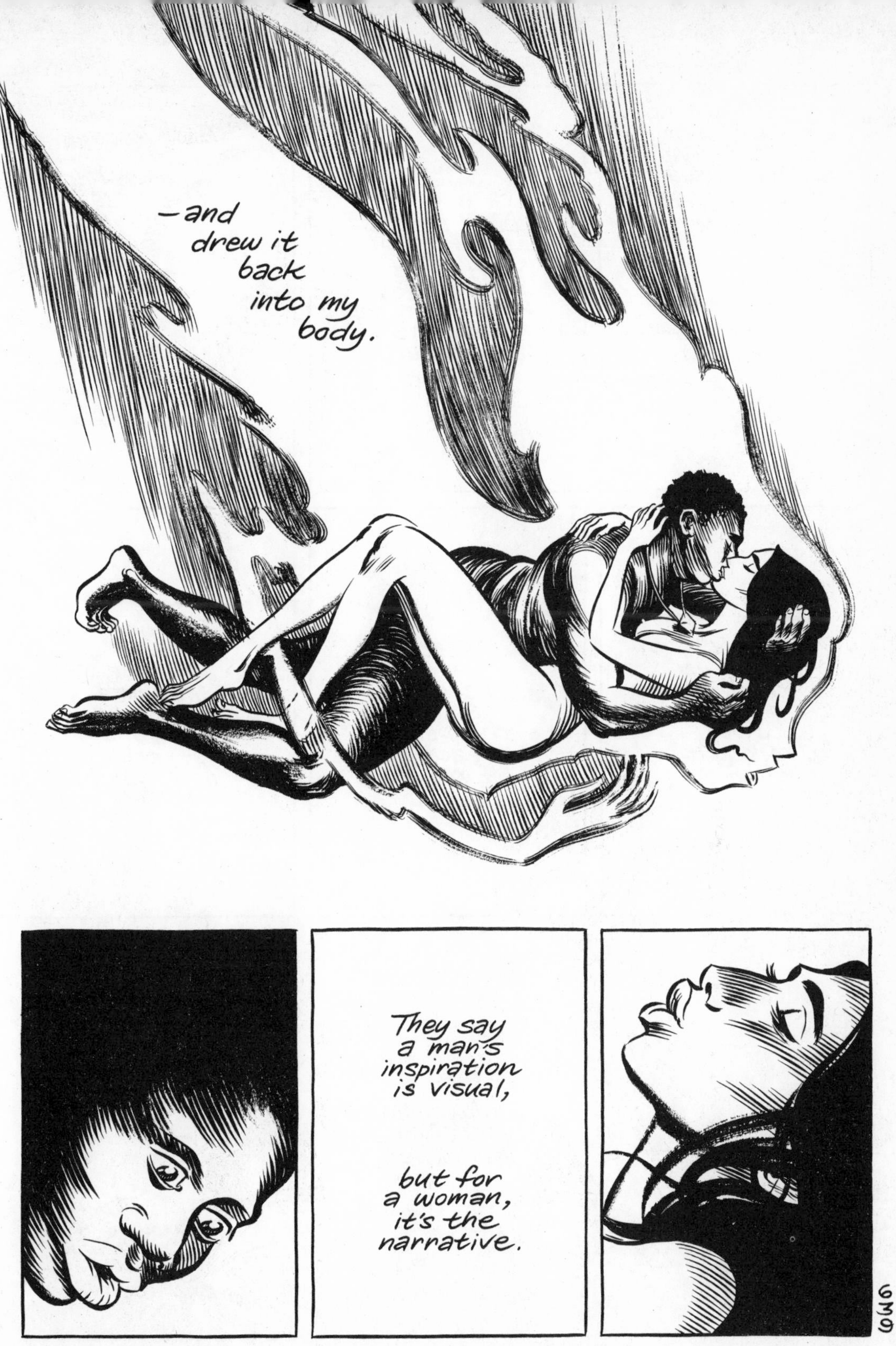
–and drew it back into my body.
They say a man's inspiration is visual,
but for a woman, it's the narrative.

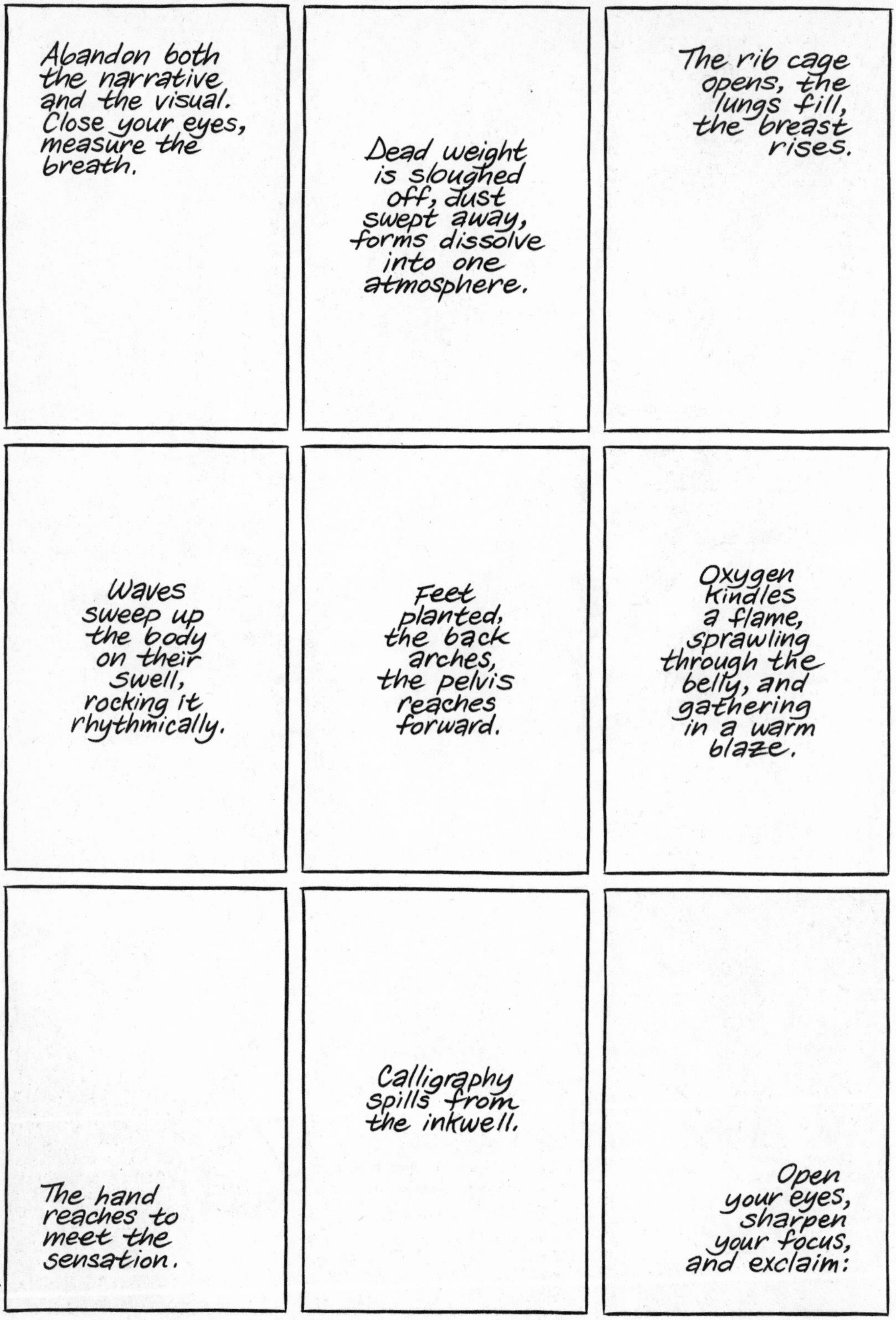
Abandon both the narrative and the visual. Close your eyes, measure the breath.
Dead weight is sloughed off, dust swept away, forms dissolve into one atmosphere.
The rib cage opens, the lungs fill, the breast rises.
Waves sweep up the body on their swell, rocking it rhythmically.
Feet planted, the back arches, the pelvis reaches forward.
Oxygen kindles a flame, sprawling through the belly, and gathering in a warm blaze.
The hand reaches to meet the sensation.
Calligraphy spills from the inkwell.
Open your eyes, sharpen your focus, and exclaim:

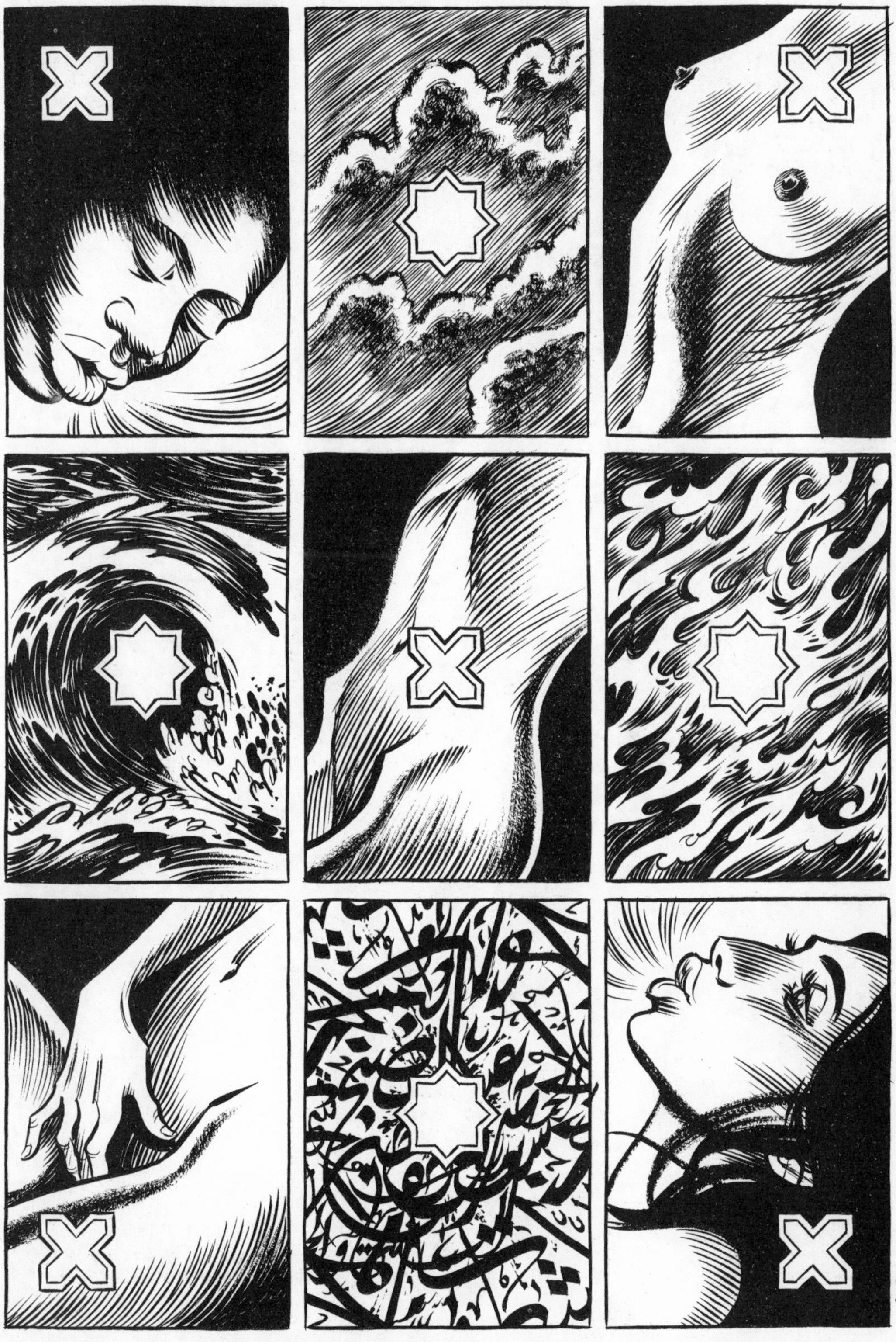

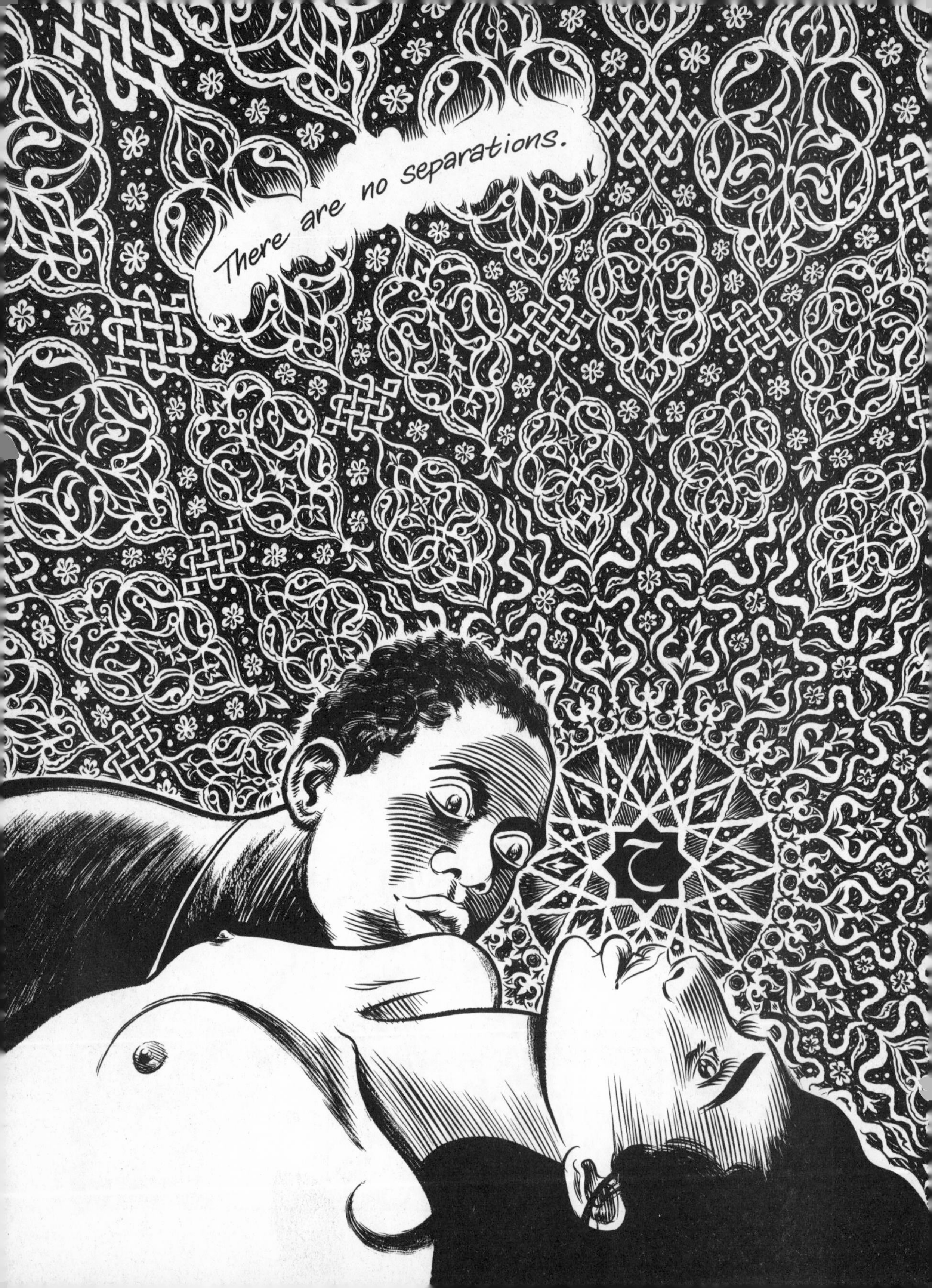
There are no separations.

In the magic squares, the letters are not arranged in numerical order.
ب ط د
ز ه ج
و ا ح
Yet each square encompasses a point,
and when they are connected in increasing value,
a design of perfect rotational symmetry emerges.
LABOR
AGES
NAME
DROWNING
in the middle of
SLEEPING
LOVE
ONE
SHELTER

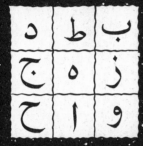

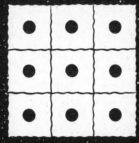

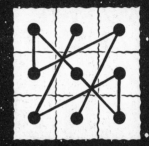

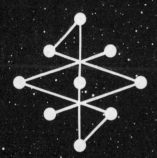

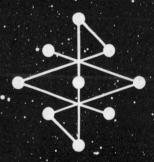

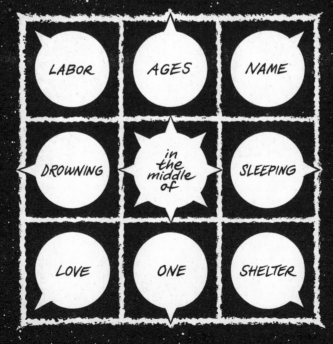

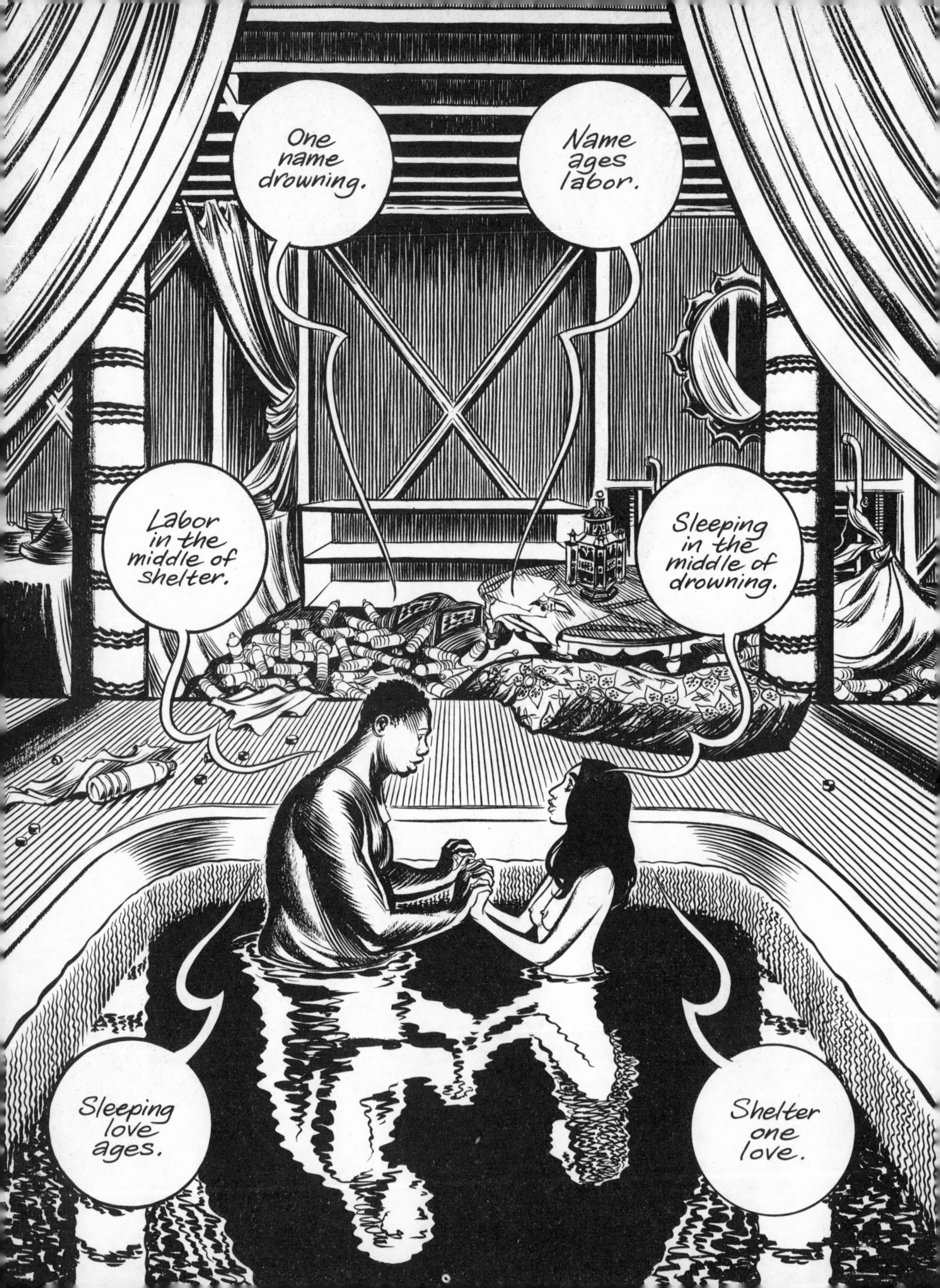
One name drowning.
Name ages labor.
Labor in the middle of shelter.
Sleeping in the middle of drowning.
Sleeping love ages.
Shelter one love.

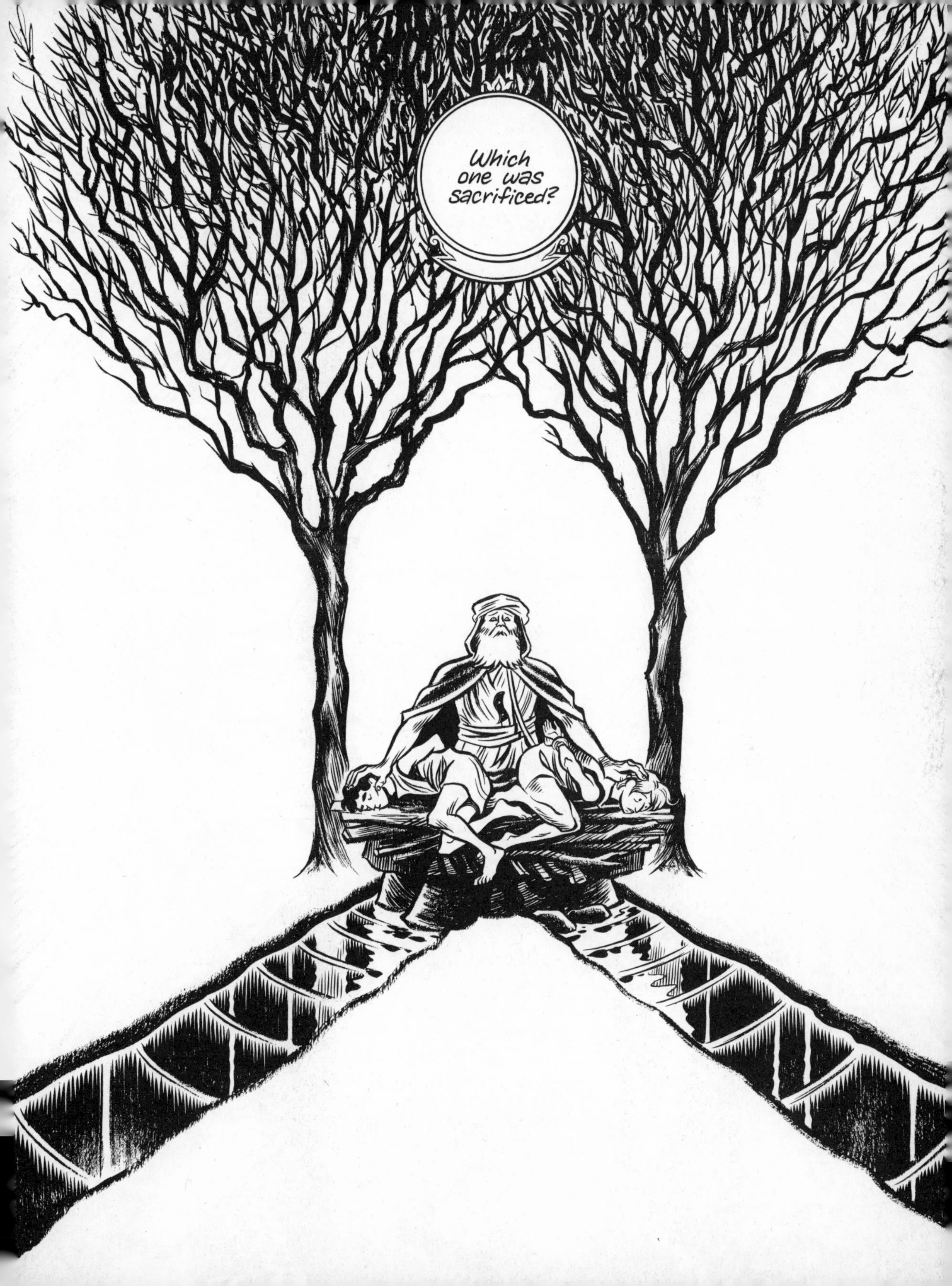
Which one was sacrificed?

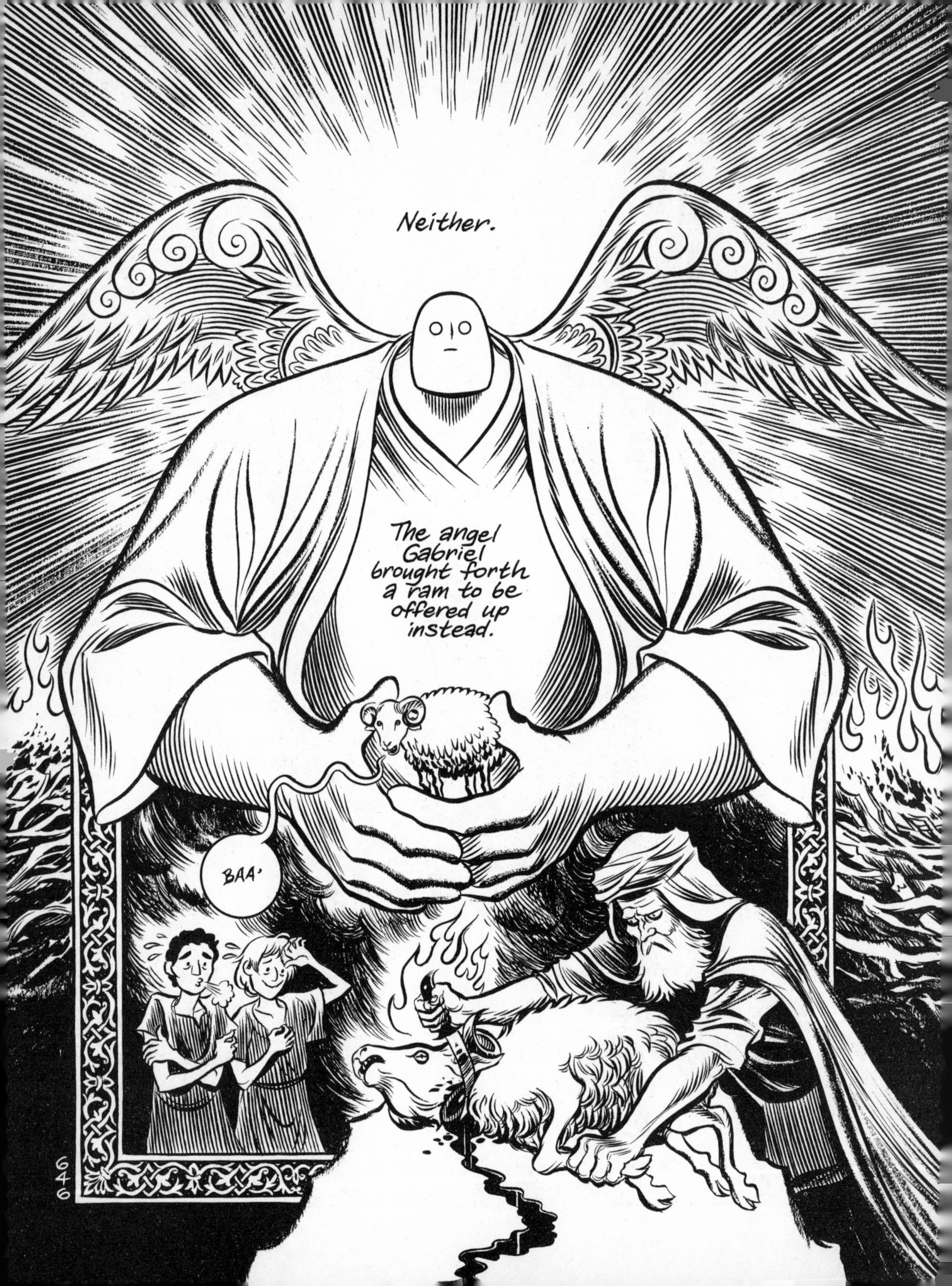
Neither.
The angel Gabriel brought forth a ram to be offered up instead.
BAA.
646

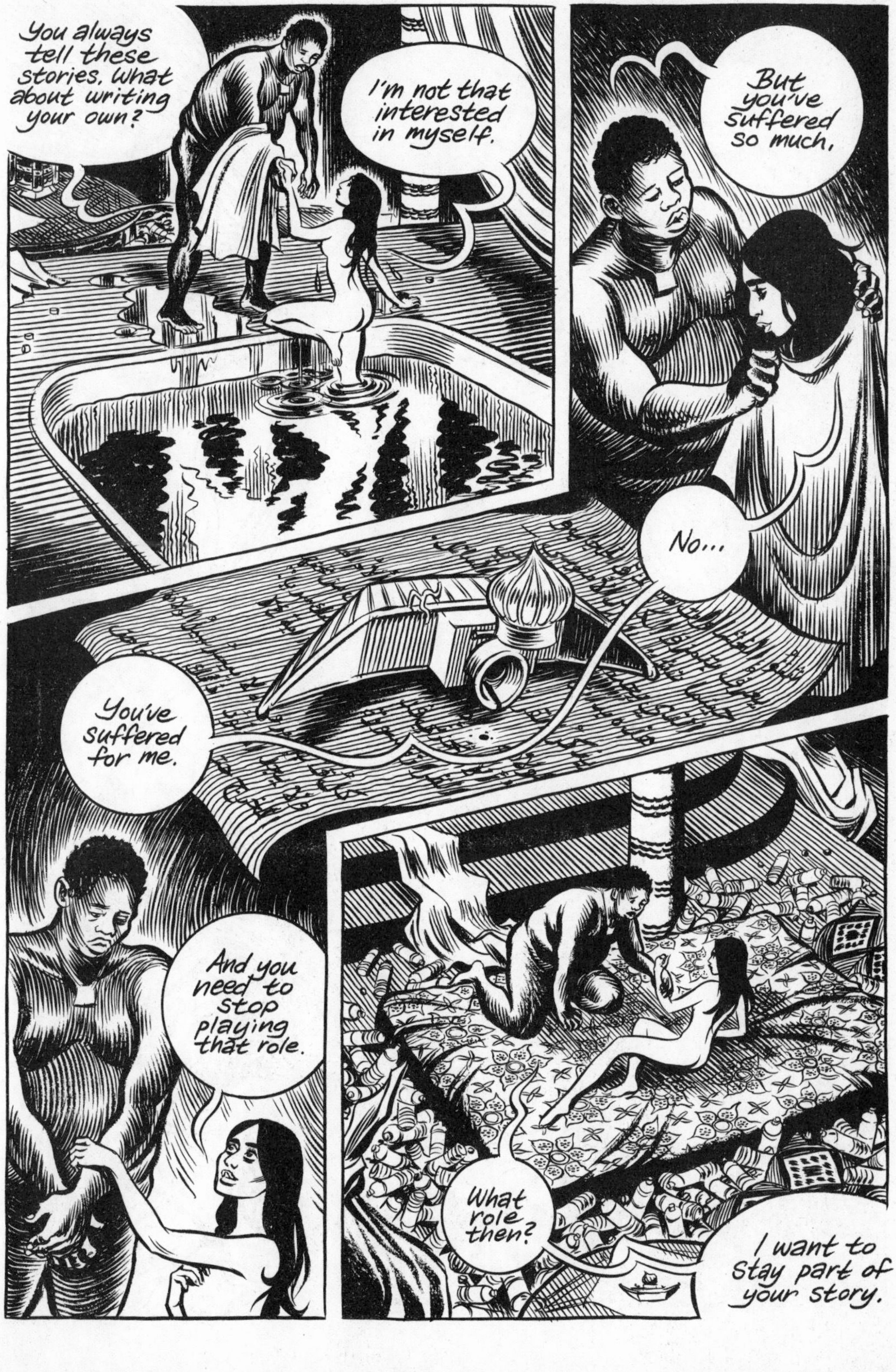
You always tell these stories. What about writing your own?
I'm not that interested in myself.
But you've suffered so much.
No...
You've suffered for me.
And you need to stop playing that role.
What role then?
I want to stay part of your story.

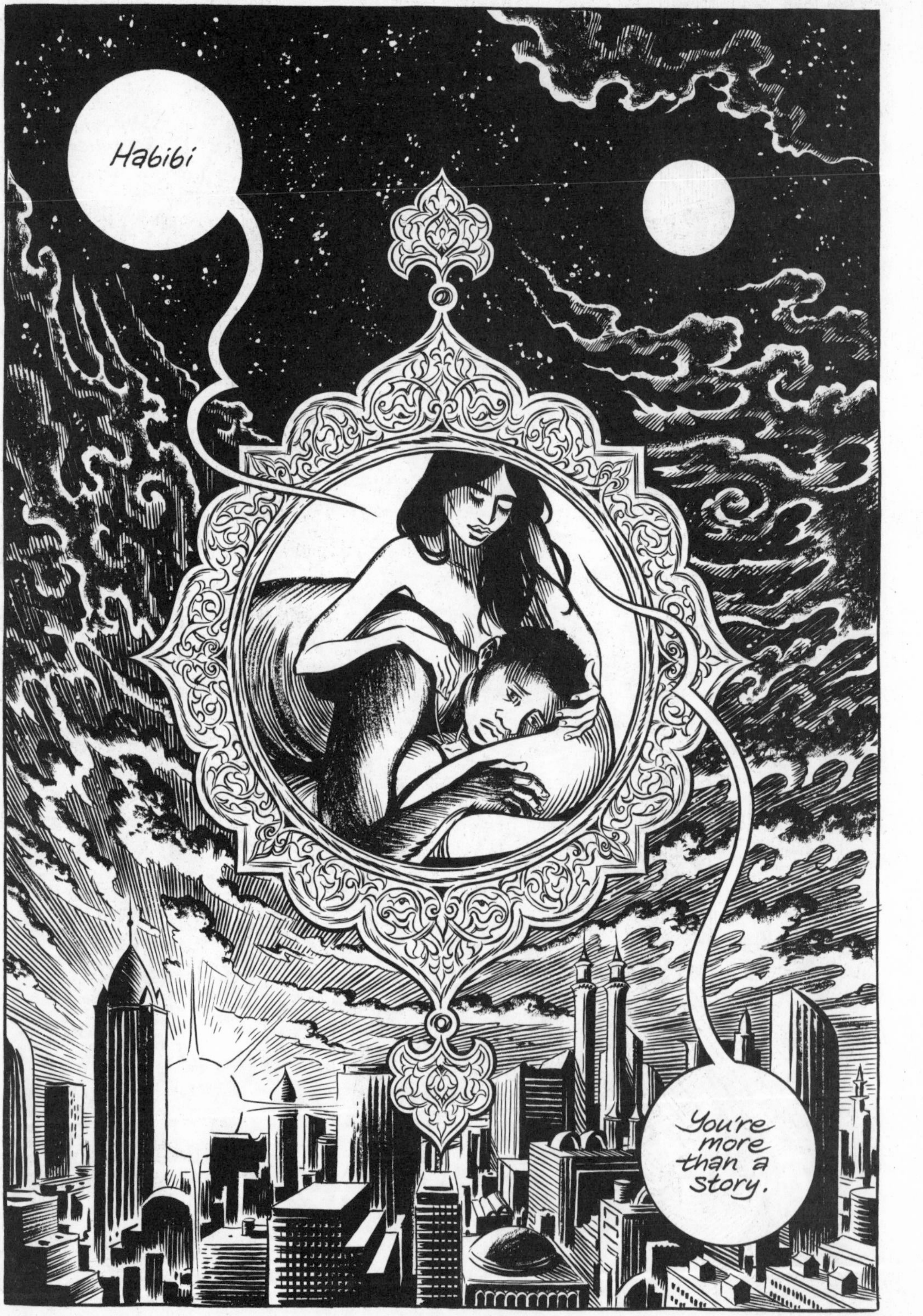
Habibi
You're more than a story.

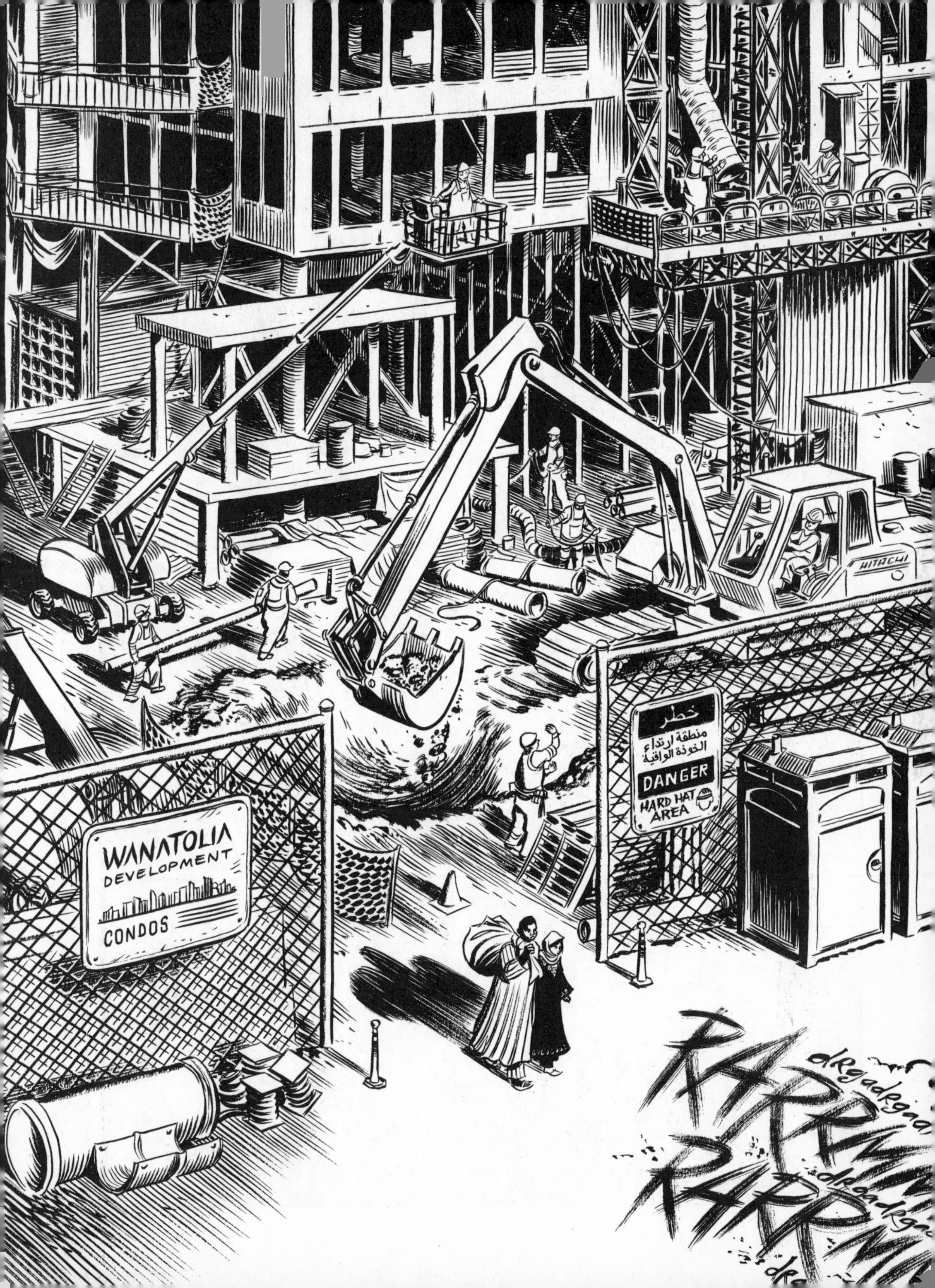
HITACHI
خطر
منطقة ارتداء
الخوذة الواقية
DANGER
HARD HAT AREA
WANATOLIA
DEVELOPMENT
CONDOS

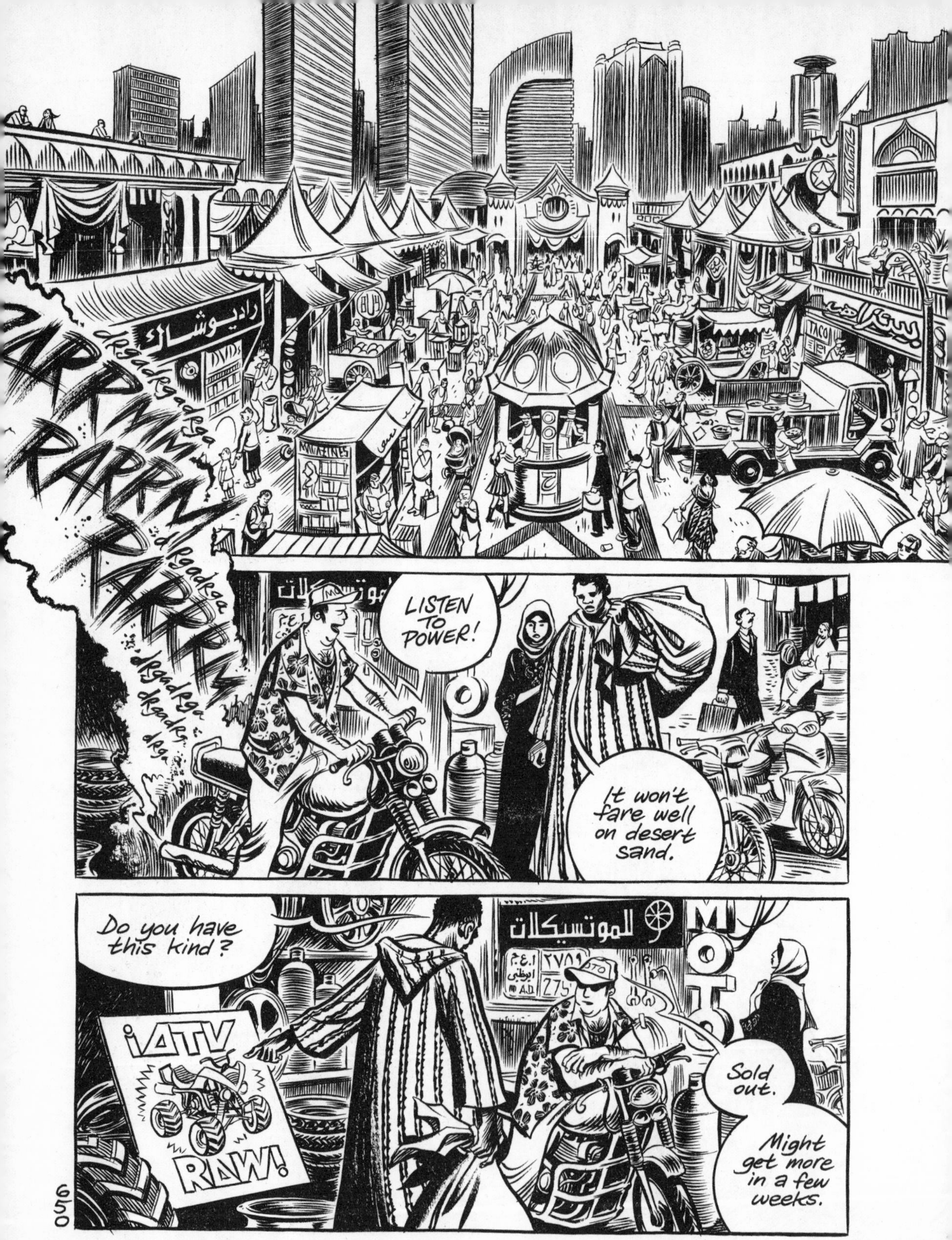
LISTEN TO POWER!
It won't fare well on desert sand.
Do you have this kind?
ATV RAW!
Sold out.
Might get more in a few weeks.

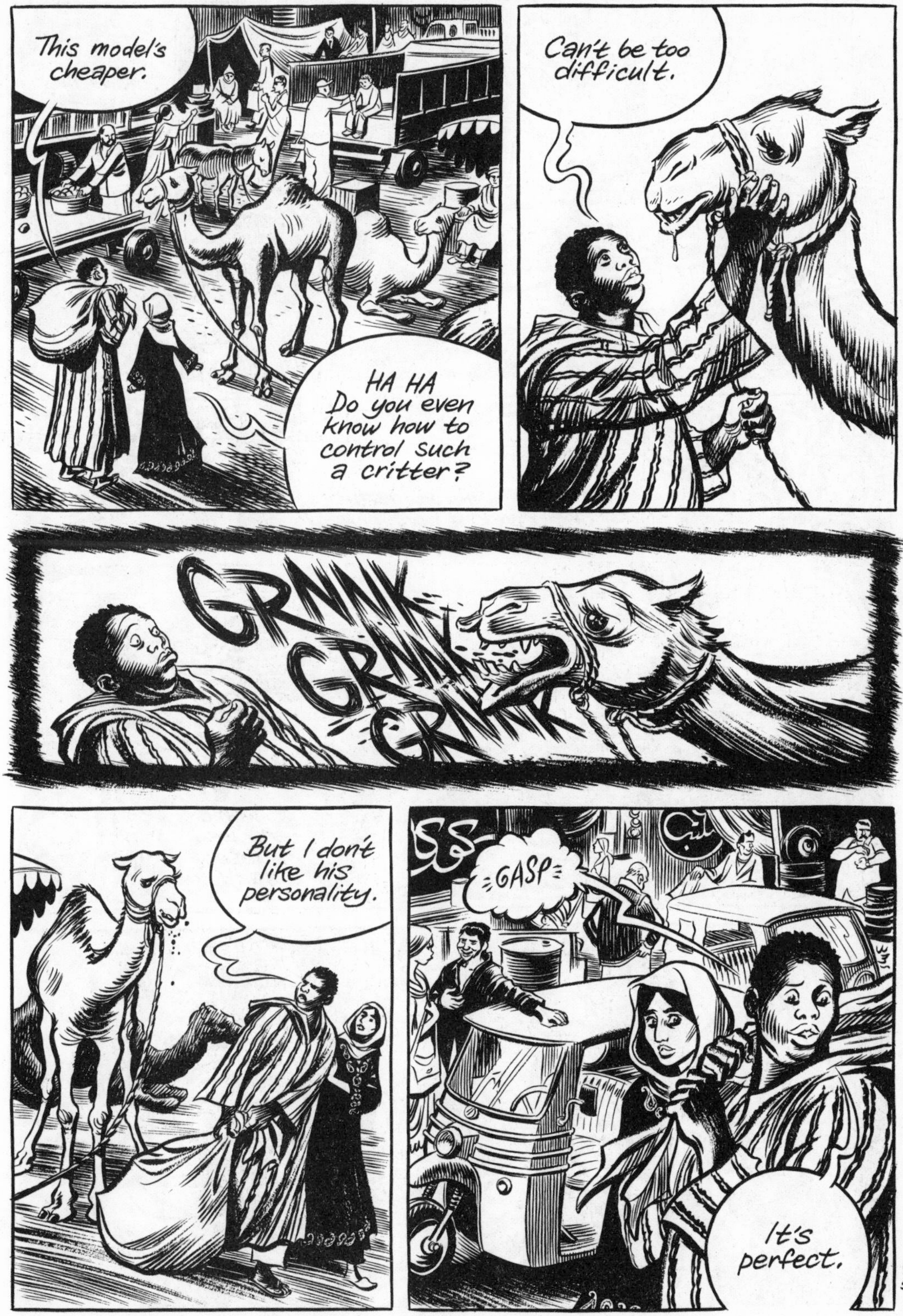
This model's cheaper.
HA HA Do you even know how to control such a critter?
Can't be too difficult.
GRNNK
GRNNK
GRNNK
But I don't like his personality.
GASP
It's perfect.

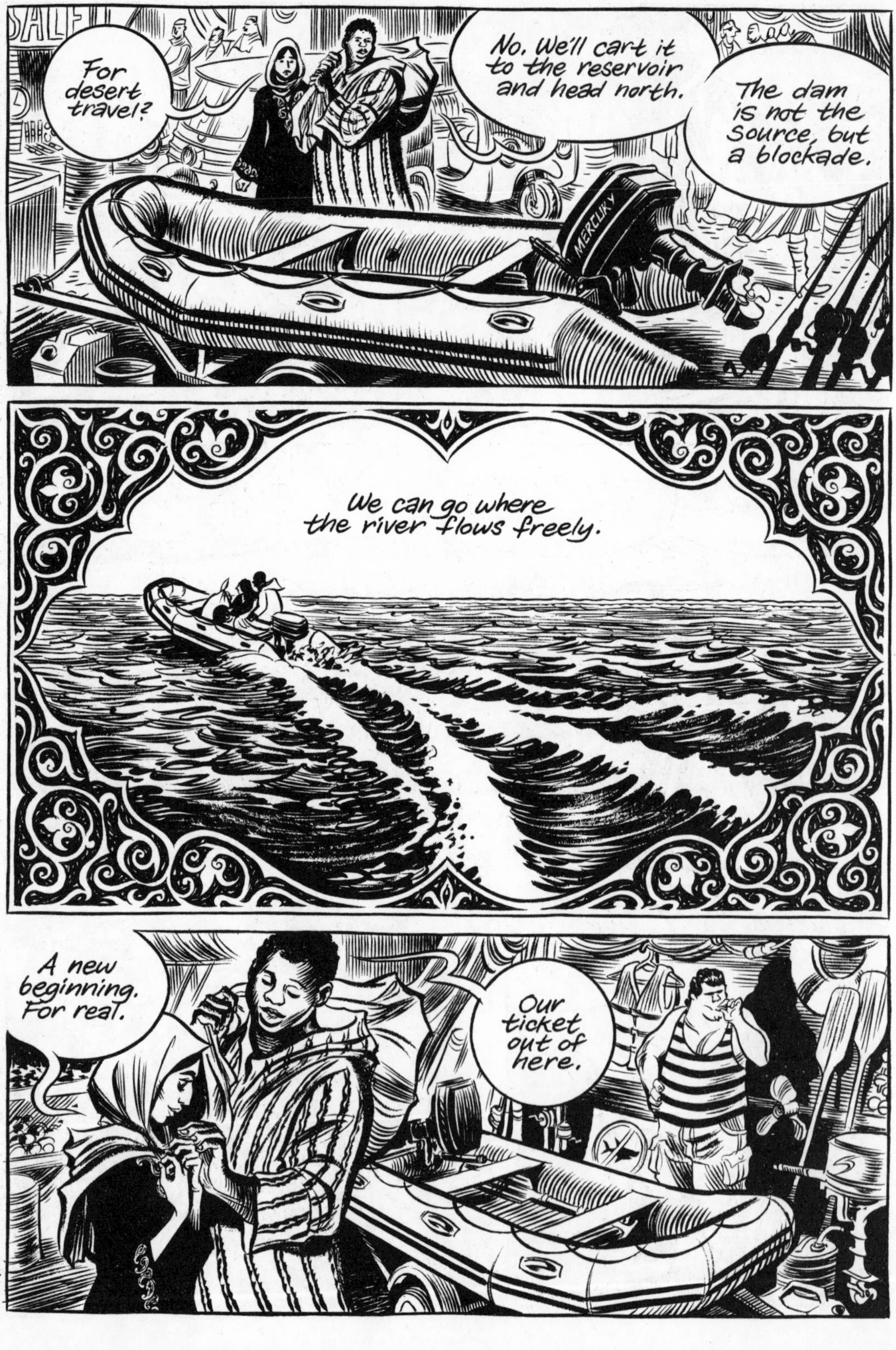
For desert travel?
No. We'll cart it to the reservoir and head north.
The dam is not the source, but a blockade.
MERCURY
We can go where the river flows freely.
A new beginning. For real.
Our ticket out of here.

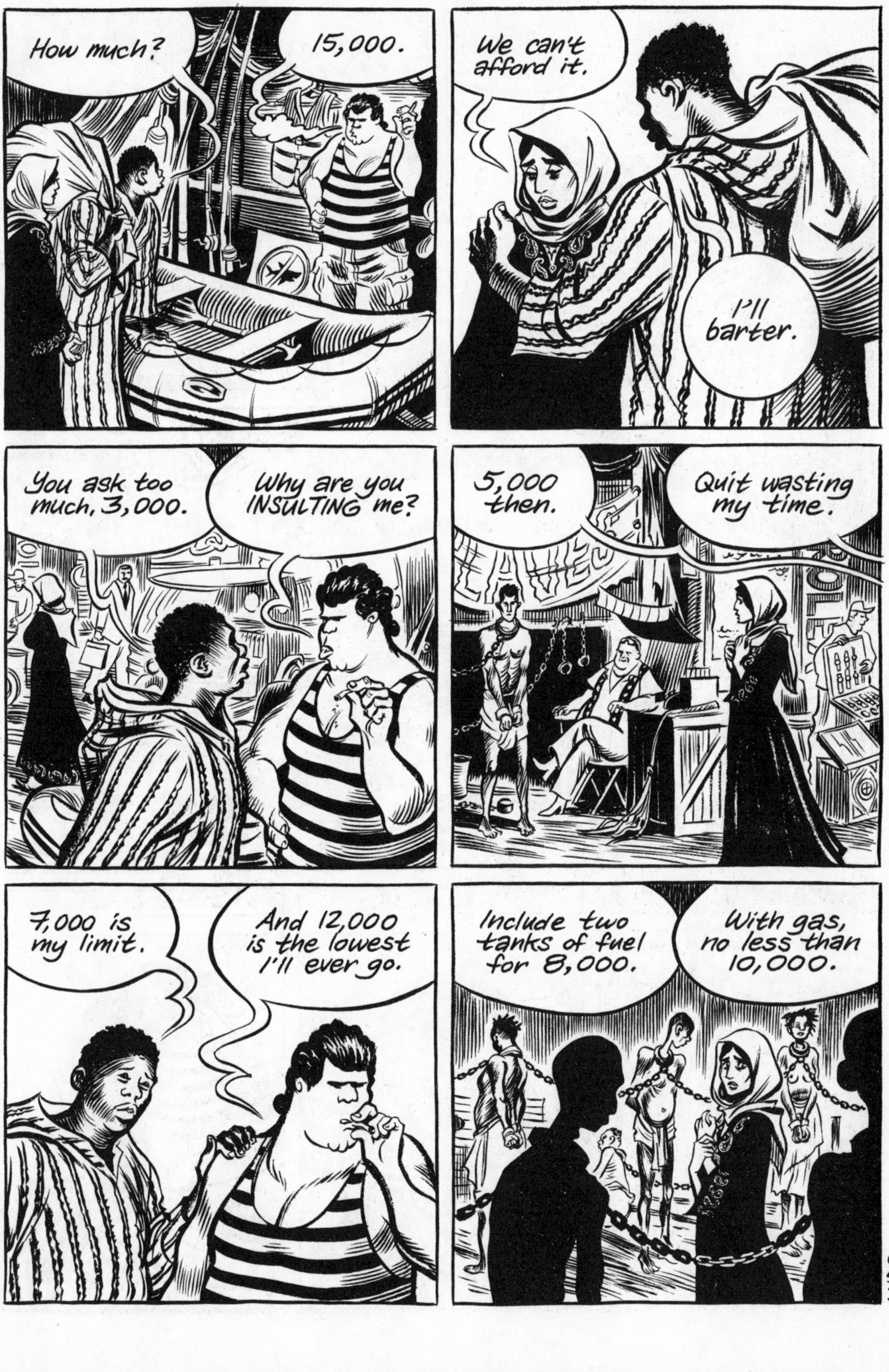
How much?
15,000.
We can't afford it.
I'll barter.
You ask too much, 3,000.
Why are you INSULTING me?
5,000 then.
Quit wasting my time.
7,000 is my limit.
And 12,000 is the lowest I'll ever go.
Include two tanks of fuel for 8,000.
With gas, no less than 10,000.

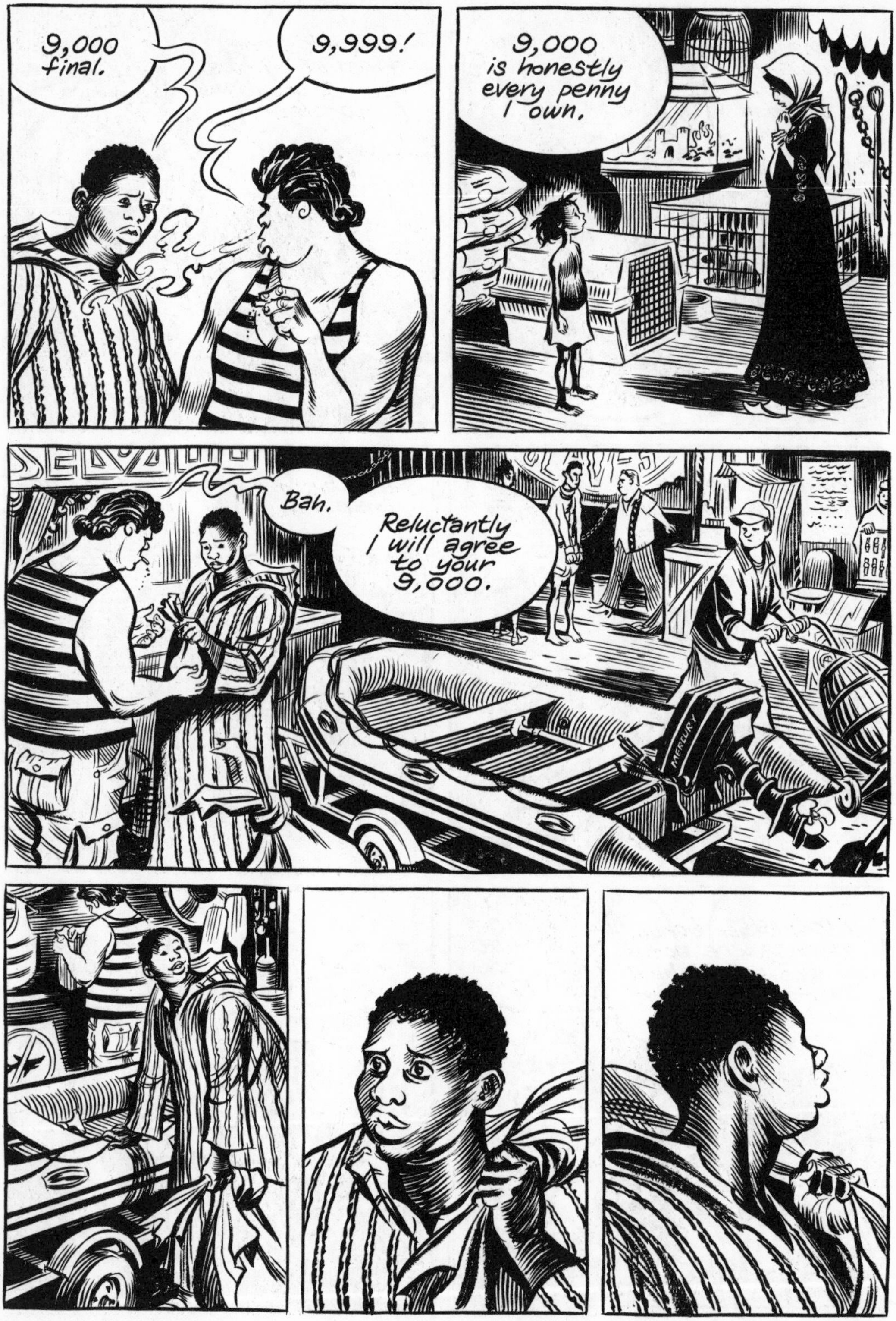

9,000 final.
9,999!
9,000 is honestly every penny I own.
Bah.
Reluctantly I will agree to your 9,000.
MERCURY

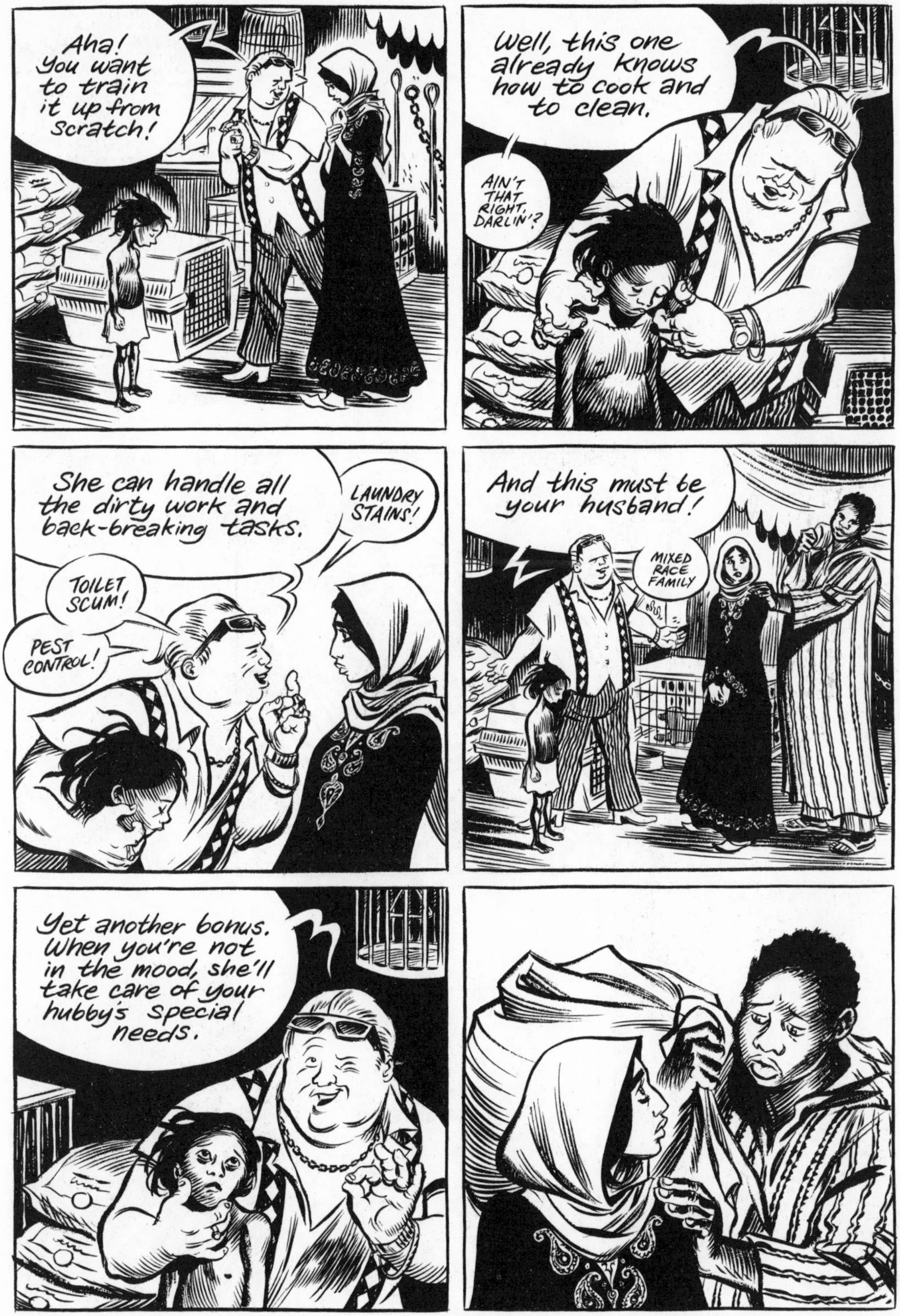
Aha! You want to train it up from scratch!
Well, this one already knows how to cook and to clean.
AIN'T THAT RIGHT, DARLIN'?
She can handle all the dirty work and back-breaking tasks.
LAUNDRY STAINS!
TOILET SCUM!
PEST CONTROL!
And this must be your husband!
MIXED RACE FAMILY
Yet another bonus. When you're not in the mood, she'll take care of your hubby's special needs.

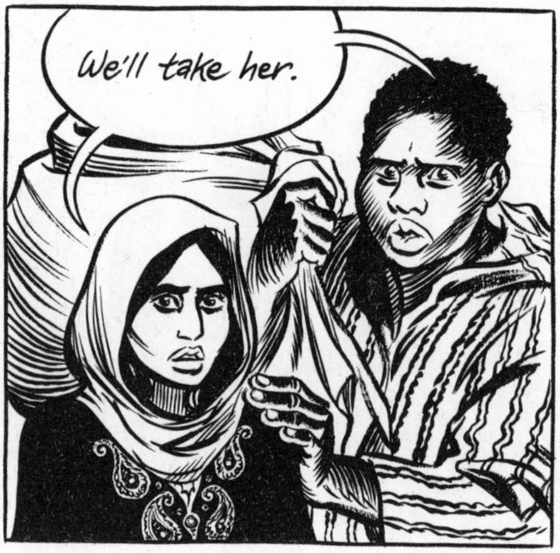
We'll take her.

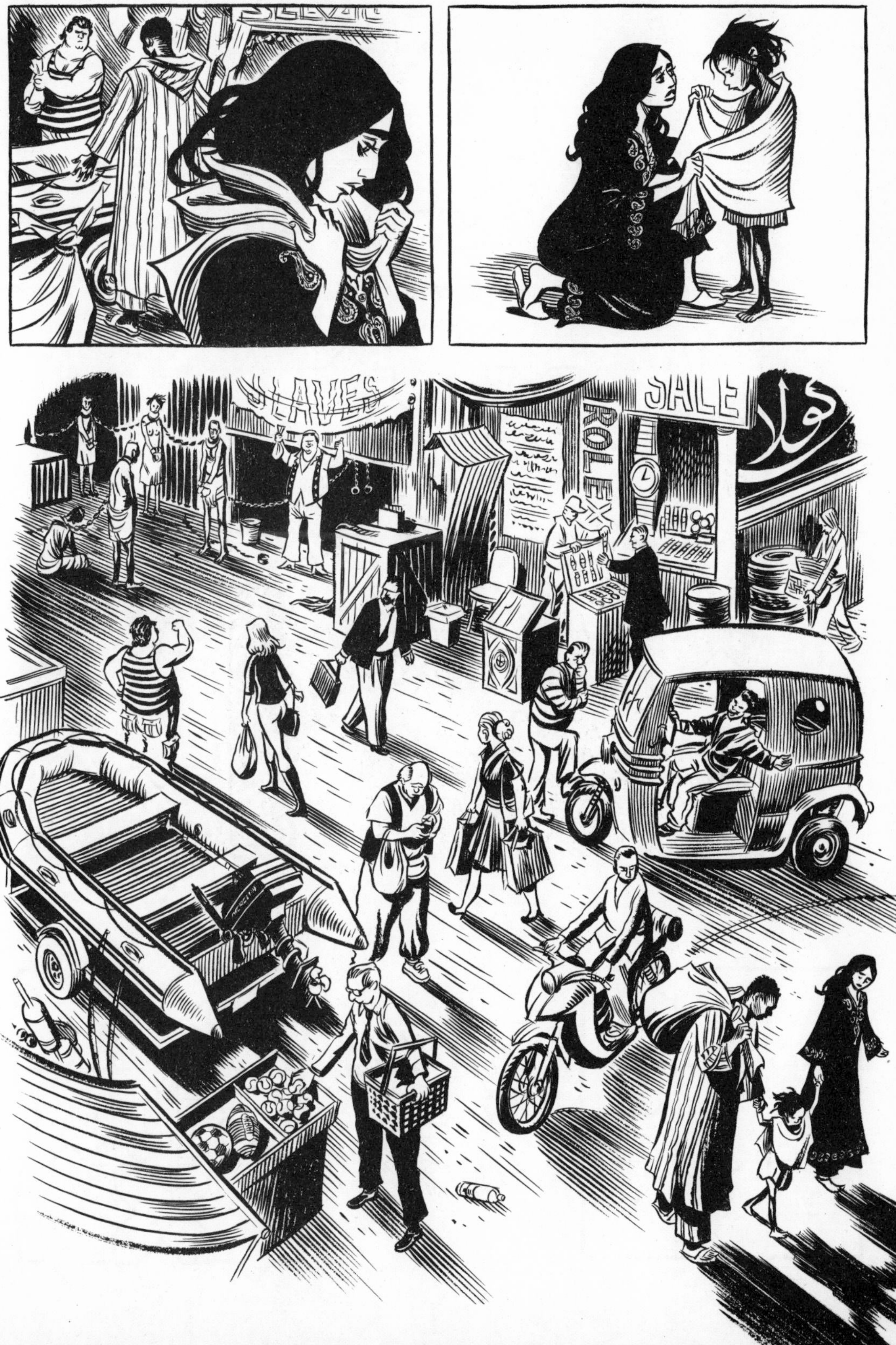
SLAVES
SALE
ROLEX

The square is 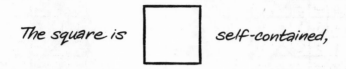 self-contained,

but it breathes like lungs.

INHALING EXHALING

 The four-pointed
star contracts
into introspection.
The CRUCIFORM
symbolizes sacrifice.

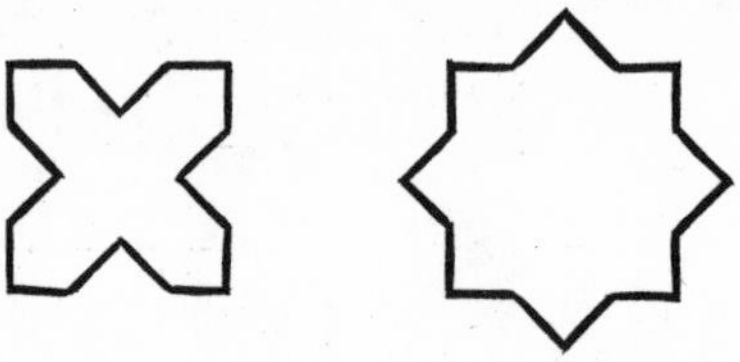

The eight-pointed star
expands. It's called THE
BREATH OF THE COMPASSIONATE
for the moment Allah breathes
the spirit into our bodies.

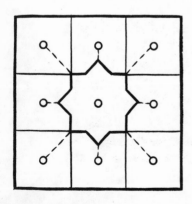

When the
square reaches
out in every
direction,
eight more
squares are
formed.

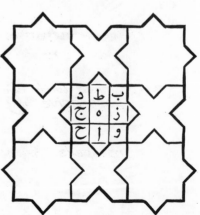

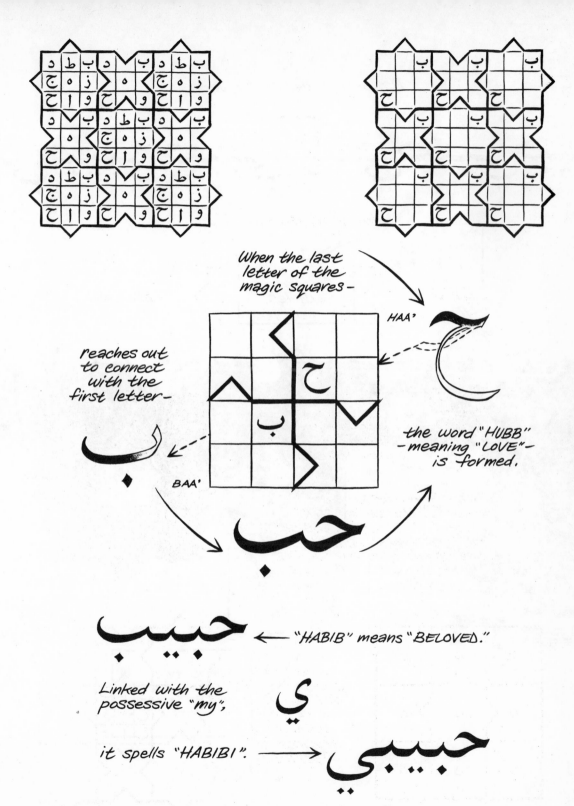

When the last letter of the magic squares—

HAA'

reaches out to connect with the first letter—

BAA'

the word "HUBB" —meaning "LOVE"— is formed.

← "HABIB" means "BELOVED."

Linked with the possessive "my",

it spells "HABIBI". →

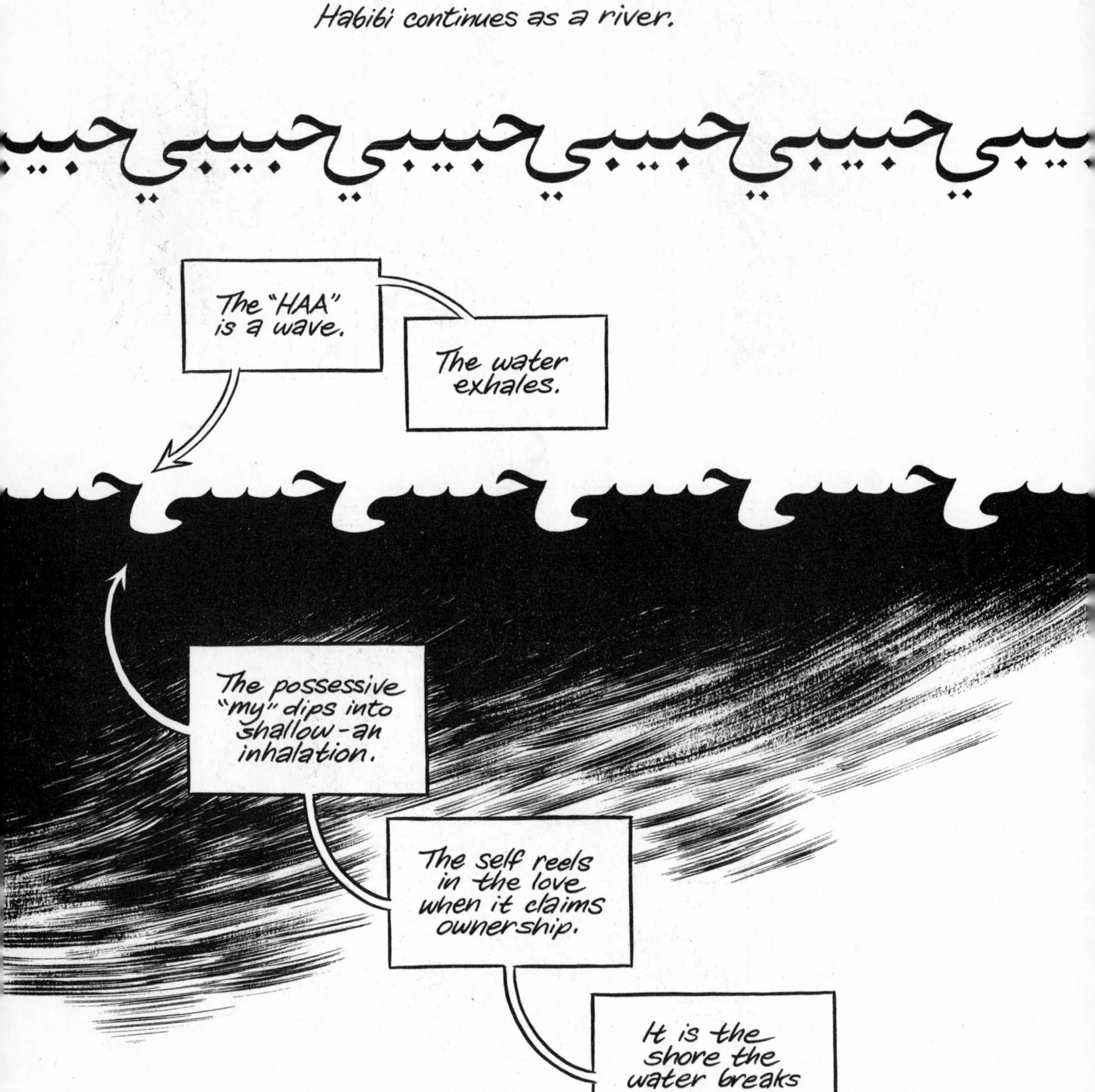
Habibi continues as a river.
حبيبي حبيبي حبيبي
The "HAA" is a wave.
The water exhales.
The possessive "my" dips into shallow-an inhalation.
The self reels in the love when it claims ownership.
It is the shore the water breaks upon.

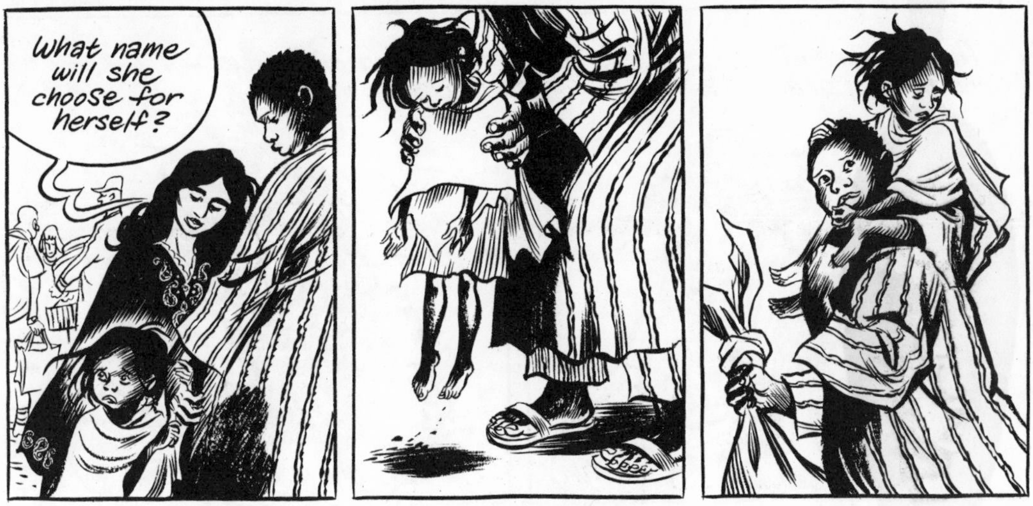
What name will she choose for herself?

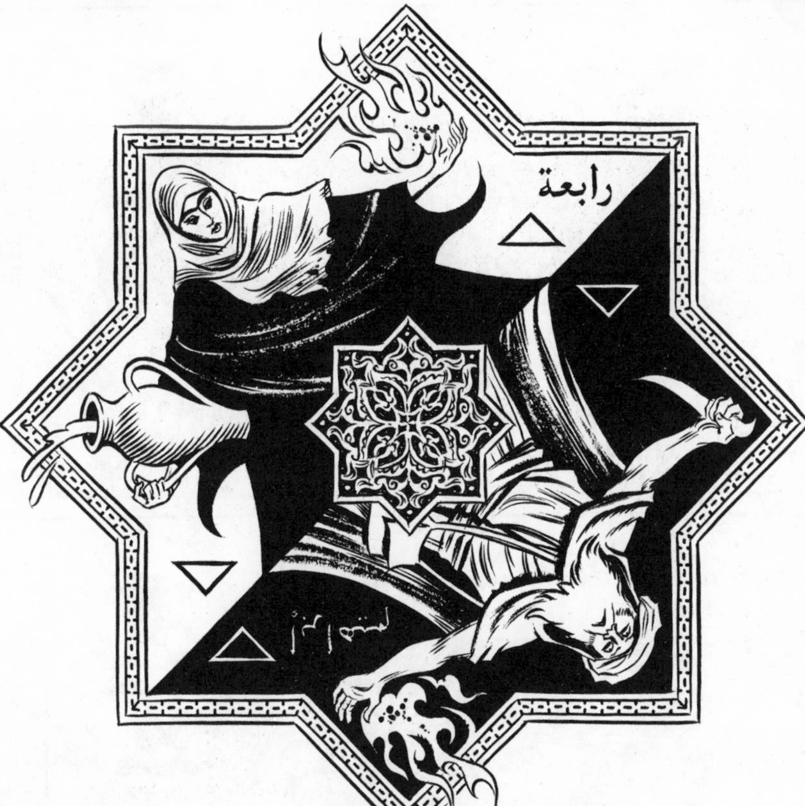
رابعة

The Sufi saint
RABI'A AL-ADAWIYYA
was seen carrying a firebrand
and a jug of water.

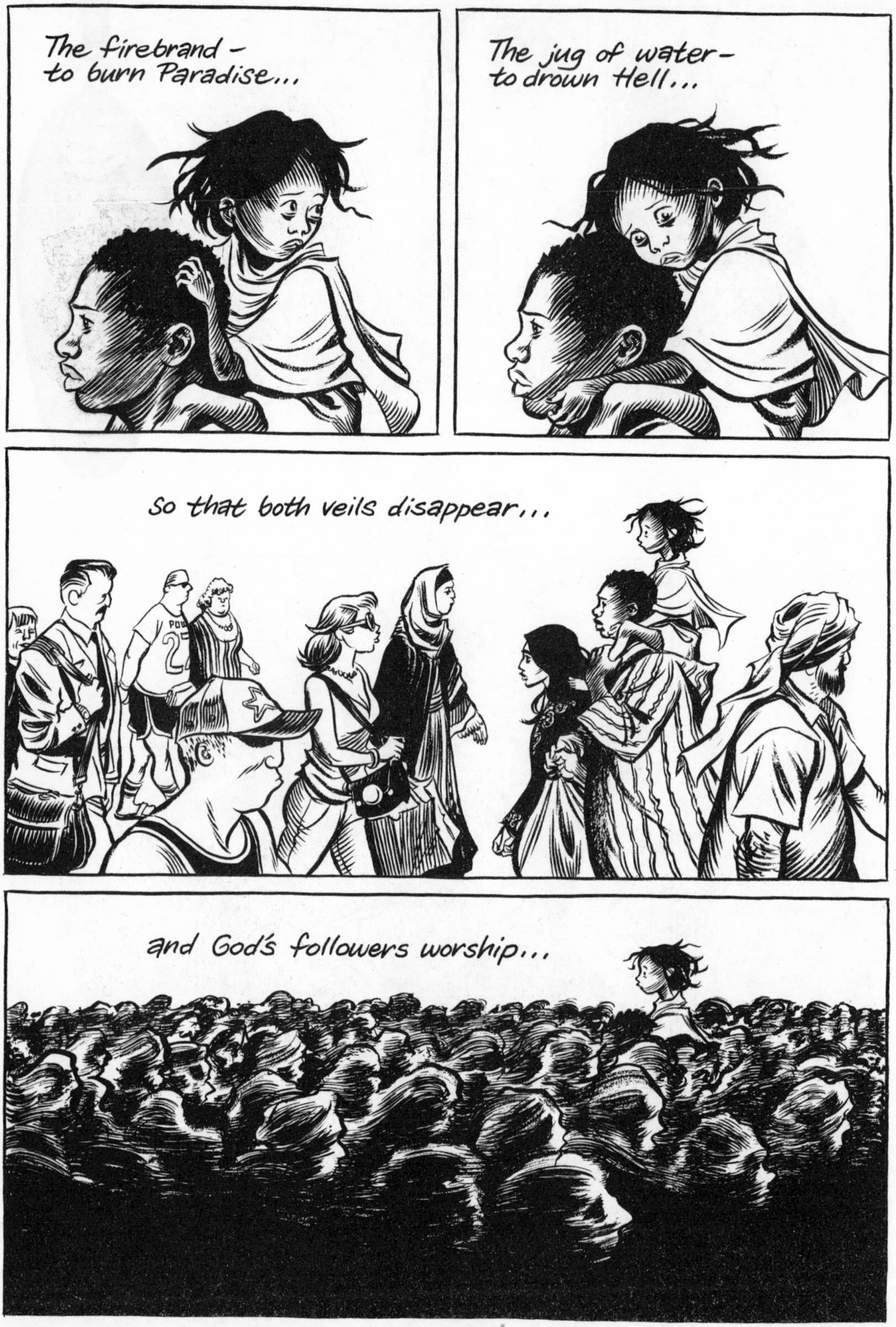
The firebrand - to burn Paradise...
The jug of water- to drown Hell...
So that both veils disappear...
and God's followers worship...

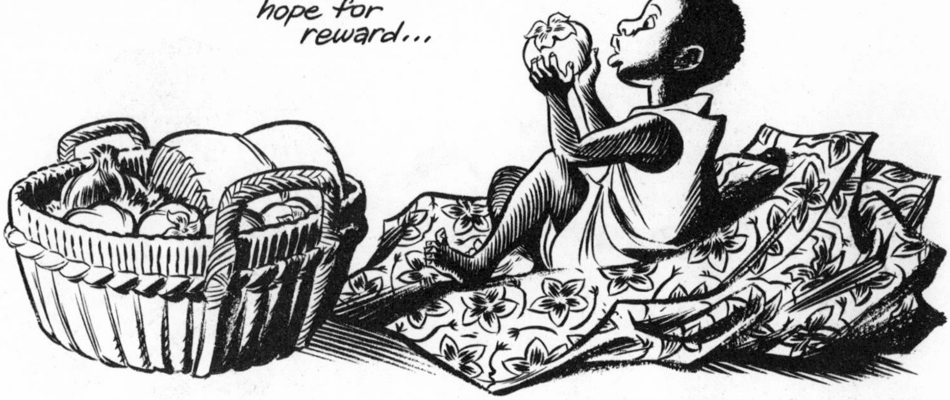
not out of hope for reward...

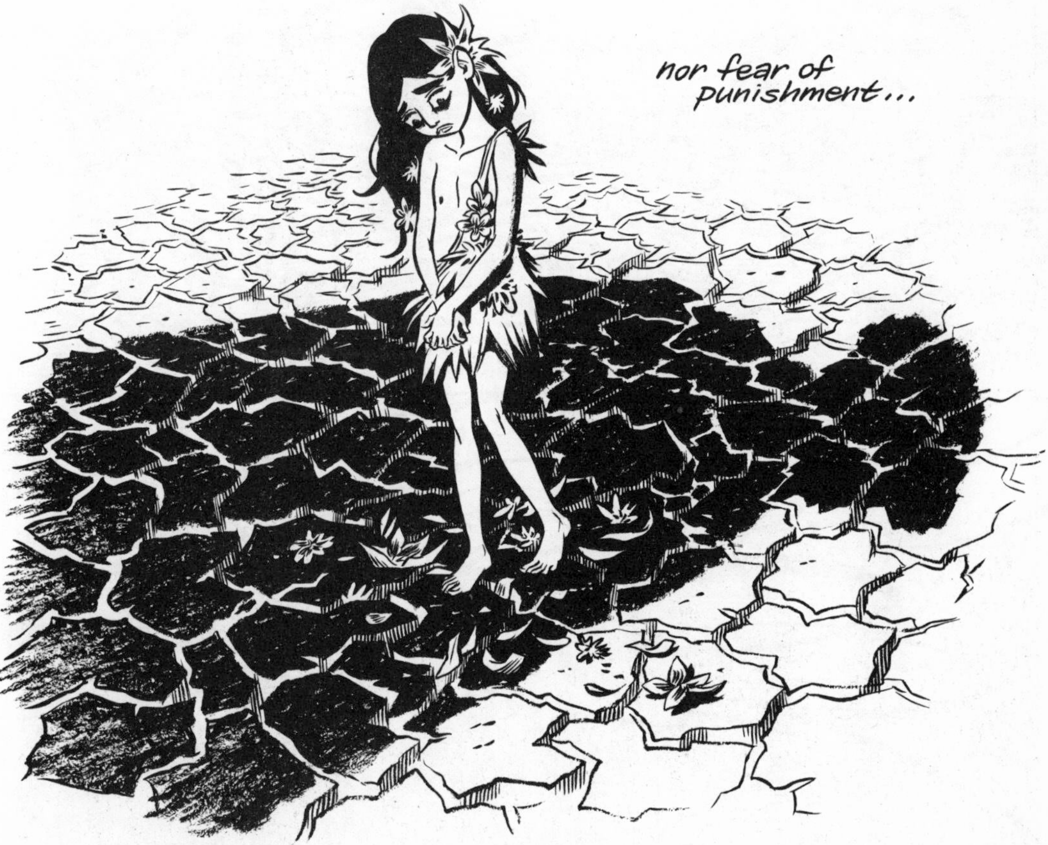
nor fear of punishment...

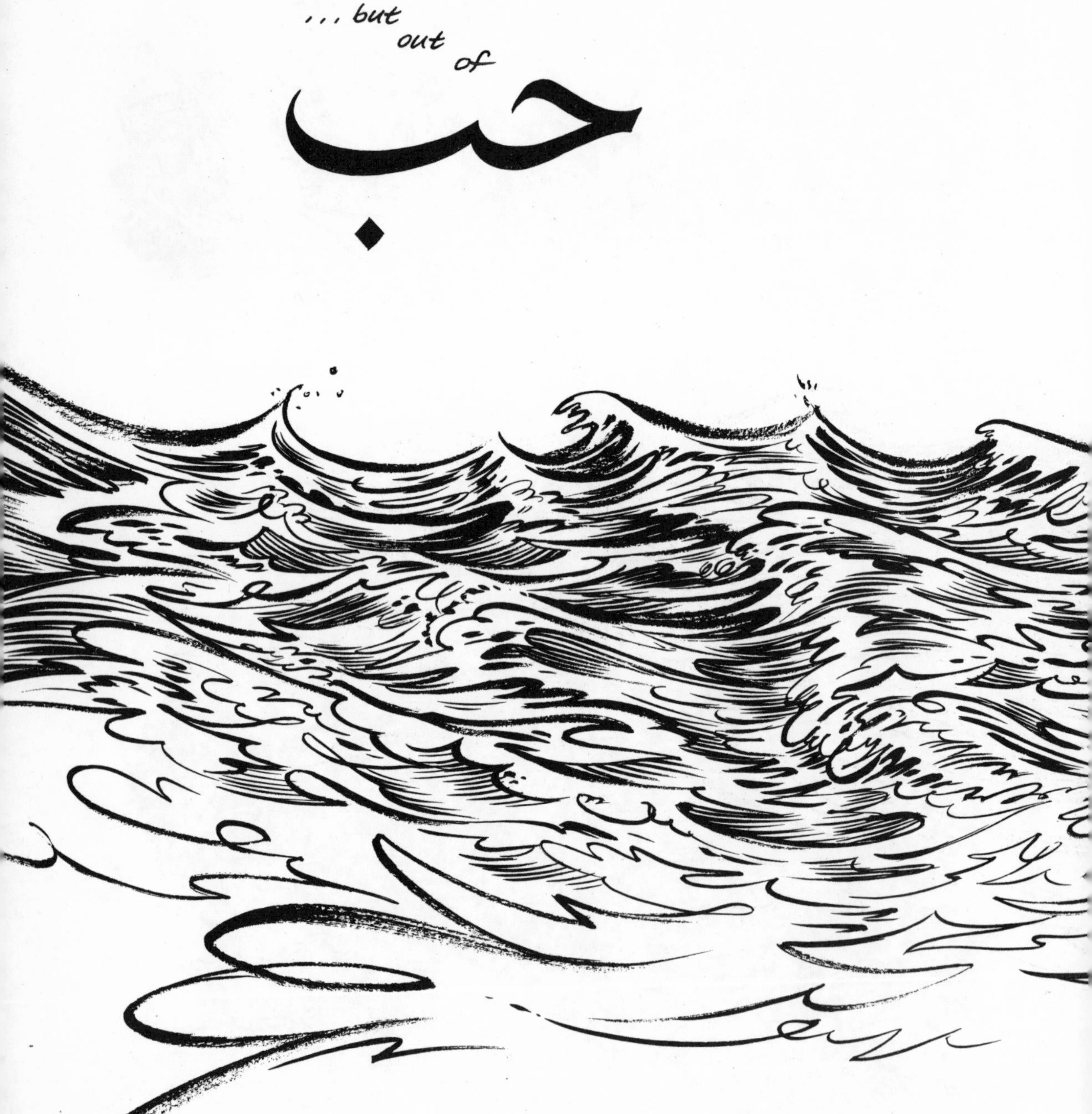
... but out of
حب

Dedicated
to
Sierra Hahn
& PJ Mark
for enduring
with me.

AND TO THE
FOLLOWING
PEOPLE WHO
GUIDED THIS
BOOK TO
COMPLETION:

Esther Ahn
Kazim Ali
Dan & Azure ATTOE
Lucie Bonvalet
Evan Cass
Pegi Christiansen
Miriam Elman
Theo Ellsworth
Alessandro Ferrari
Dan Frank
Aaron Gorski
Justin Harris
Hatem
Hudhud
Georgia Hussey
Bahar Jaberi
David Naimon
Aaron Renier
Joe Sacco
Anjali Singh
Shannon Stewart
Jon & Ami
THOMPSON
Julie Thi Underhill
Laëtitia &
Frédéric VIVIEN
Mark Wald

THANKS, ALSO,
TO MY FAMILY
AND FRIENDS,
AND YOU READERS.

NOTES

PAGE 15
"Unwary person thinks that the things I collect [are] mine forever. He is not aware of his meaningless struggle." Based on calligraphy by Abdülhadi Erol Dönmez.

PAGE 16
Obscured text reads, " Calligraphy is hidden in the teachings of the master..." Attributed to 'Ali ibn Abi Talib, from Mustafa Ja'far's book ARABIC CALLIGRAPHY (British Museum Press, 2002).

PAGE 31
Based on calligraphy from THE GOLDEN ODE by Labid Ibn Rabiah (University of Chicago Press, 1974). English translation by William R. Polk.

"And the flash floods uncover the traces just as though they were Writing whose text has been renewed by pens.

" Living on moist food, their abstinence from water had been long."

PAGE 42
From the Rumi poem "Bismillah." (See PAGE 671 for the full version.)

PAGE 110
English text written by author. "The rupture of the membranes is the tearing of the veil. It's known as 'water breaking'- the amniotic sac surrounding the baby breaks and the fluid is discharged. This is the beginning of labor. In the QUR'AN, when Mary was in the throes of birth pangs, a voice called from beneath her: ' Do not grieve; Verily your Lord has made a river flow right below you' (19:24)." ARABIC TRANSLATION COURTESY HUDHUD.

PAGE 141
Shikesté script is based on calligraphy transcribed by Mahmud Khan from THE SPLENDOR OF ISLAMIC CALLIGRAPHY by Abdelkebir Khatibi and Mohammed Sijelmassi (Thames & Hudson, 1976). Central text is the verse: " Now let man but think from what he is created" (QUR'AN 86:5) based on calligraphy by Mohamed Zakariya-- after Mehmed Esad Yesari.

PAGE 163
JOB 7:5 ; JOB 10:1

PAGE 179
Arabic text is an excerpt from the poem "RAIN SONG" by Iraqi poet Badr Shakir al-Sayyab. (See PAGE 670 for English translation.)

PAGE 182
Inner calligraphy is from QUR'AN verse 14:34: " But if ye count the favors of Allah, never will you be able to number them." Outer calligraphy is a calligraphic exercise by Mahmut Celaleddin Dagistani from Gabriel Mandel Khan's ARABIC SCRIPT (Abbeville Press, 2000).

PAGE 232
Arabic text reads: "I seek refuge in the Face of Allah the Munificent and in Allah's perfect words which neither the righteous nor the disobedient overstep from the evil of what descends from

(continued...)

heaven and the evil of what ascends to it and the evil of what is created in the earth and the trials of the night and the day and the visitors of the night and the day except the visitor that comes with goodness, O Beneficent One!" (From THE COLLATED HADITH OF ISRA' AND MI'RAJ.)

✳ PAGE 233
Arabic approximately translates to: "He reached heights by his perfection." (From a poem by Saadi Shirazi.)

✿ PAGE 249
Arabic is from page 186 of THE WORLD OF ISLAM, edited by Bernard Lewis (Thames & Hudson, 1976), showing Nasir ad-Din at-Tusi's examination of Euclid's parallel lines.

✳ PAGE 317
QUR'AN 27:10,12

✿ PAGE 386
Moses's speech from EXODUS 4:10, 13.

✳ PAGE 390
Al-Khidr's speech from QUR'AN 18:78.

✿ PAGES 472-475
Reference taken from PRINCETON UNIVERSITY LIBRARY DIGITAL COLLECTIONS: Islamic Manuscripts Collection: Collection of Prayers and Talismans.

✳ PAGE 497
Principal diagram based on Avicenna's (Ibn Sina's) explanation of the rainbow from THE WORLD OF ISLAM, edited by Bernard Lewis (Thames & Hudson, 1976).

✿ PAGE 553
Calligraphy references QUR'AN 27:30,31: "It is from Solomon, and is (as follows): 'In the name of Allah, Most Gracious, Most Merciful: Be ye not arrogant against me, but come to me in submission (to the true religion).'" (The second mention of "Bismillah" in this sura compensates for the missing "Bismillah" in sura nine -- see PAGE 37.)

✳ PAGE 569
"SONG OF SONGS" in Arabic. References verses 4:12 and 8:12.

✿ PAGE 589
Based on calligraphy from THE GOLDEN ODE by Labid Ibn Rabiah (University of Chicago Press, 1974), English translation by William R. Polk.

"So [poet], make an end to longing for one whose union has been thwarted. Even the best lover of women is one who decisively cuts her off."

✳ PAGE 599
From HADITHS (anecdotes and sayings attributed to the Prophet) collected by Muhammad ibn Ismail al-Bukhari. Chapter 305: 1680, 1681 Prohibition of Drawing Portraits.

✿ PAGE 612
Based on SUFI TERMINOLOGY by Kamal al-Din al-Qashani from page 138 of Gabriel Mandel Khan's ARABIC SCRIPT (Abbeville Press, 2000).

✳ PAGE 647
Repeat of Mary's birth pangs text (See PAGE 110).

✿ Also, thanks to the calligraphy of Lassaâd Metoui (PAGES 16, 405, 641).

THE FALLING RAIN ON PAGE 179 IS BASED ON AN EXCERPT FROM
THE POEM "RAIN SONG" BY IRAQI POET BADR SHAKIR AL-SAYYAB.
BELOW IS AN ENGLISH TRANSLATION OF THE EXCERPT BY
LENA JAYYUSI AND CHRISTOPHER MIDDLETON.

It is as if archways of mist drank the clouds
15 And drop by drop dissolved in the rain...
As if children snickered in the vineyard bowers,
The song of the rain
Rippled the silence of birds in the trees...
Drip, drop, the rain...
20 Drip...
Drop...the rain

Evening yawned, from low clouds
Heavy tears are streaming still.
It is as if a child before sleep were rambling on
25 About his mother (a year ago he went to wake her, did not find her,
Then was told, for he kept on asking,
"After tomorrow, she'll come back again...")

That she must come back again,
Yet his playmates whisper that she is there
30 In the hillside, sleeping her death for ever,
Eating the earth around her, drinking the rain;
As if a forlorn fisherman gathering nets
Cursed the waters and fate
And scattered a song at moonset,
35 Drip, drop, the rain...
Drip, drop, the rain...

Do you know what sorrow the rain can inspire?
Do you know how gutters weep when it pours down?
Do you know how lost a solitary person feels in the rain?
40 Endless, like spilt blood, like hungry people, like love,
Like children, like the dead, endless the rain.

HERE IS THE ENTIRETY OF RUMI'S POEM
"BISMILLAH" REFERENCED ON PAGE 42 —
TRANSLATED TO ENGLISH AND REPRINTED
WITH PERMISSION BY COLEMAN BARKS.

It's a habit of yours to walk slowly.
You hold a grudge for years.
With such heaviness, how can you be modest?
With such attachments, do you expect to arrive anywhere?

Be wide as the air to learn a secret.
Right now you're equal portions clay
and water, thick mud.

Abraham learned how the sun and moon and the stars all set.
He said, *No longer will I try to assign partners for God.*

You are so weak. Give up to grace.
The ocean takes care of each wave
till it gets to shore.
You need more help than you know.
You're trying to live your life in open scaffolding.
Say Bismillah, *In the name of God,*
as the priest does with a knife when he offers an animal.

Bismillah your old self
To find your real name.

CRAIG THOMPSON was born in Traverse City, Michigan, in 1975, and raised in rural Wisconsin. His three previous books — GOOD-BYE, CHUNKY RICE (1999), BLANKETS (2003), and CARNET DE VOYAGE (2004) — have garnered numerous awards and been published in nearly twenty languages. He's lived in Portland, Oregon, for the past fifteen years.

Author photo by ALICIA J. ROSE

Loughborough

[redacted]

from

[redacted]

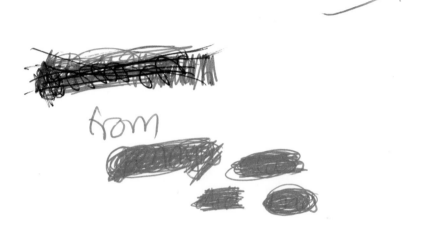

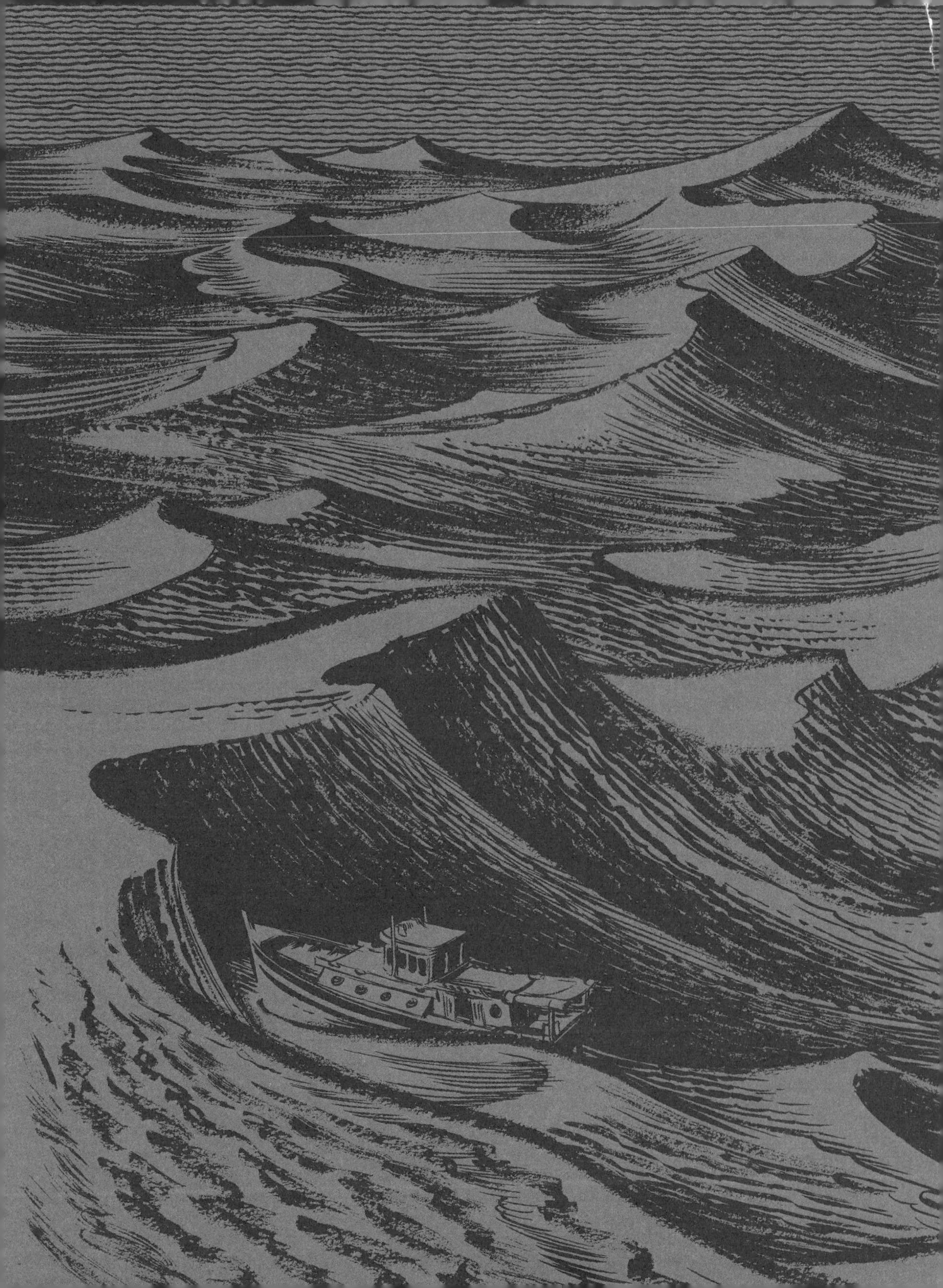

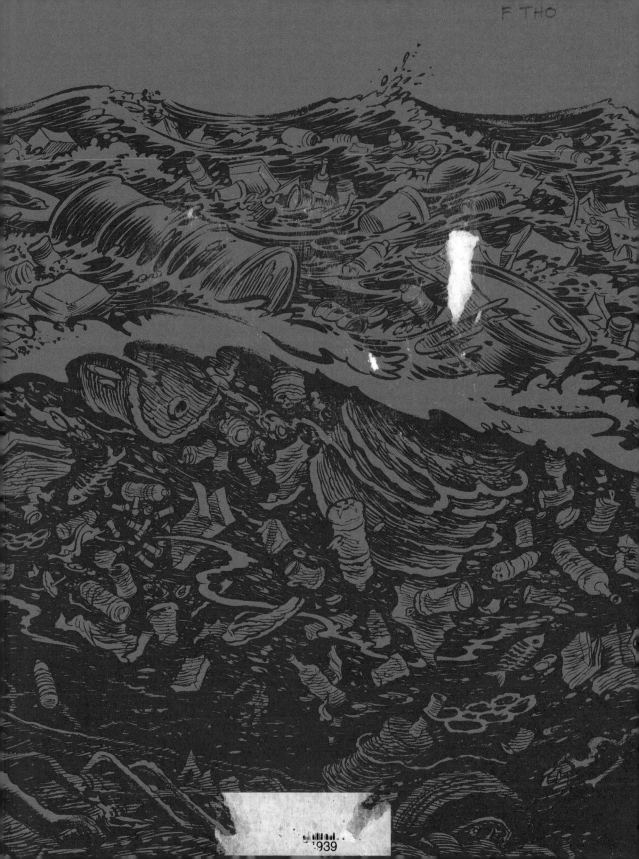

F THO

1939